W9-BKF-206

MARY BAKER EDDY

RADCLIFFE BIOGRAPHY SERIES

RADCLIFFE BIOGRAPHY SERIES

On behalf of Radcliffe College, I am pleased to present this volume in the Radcliffe Biography Series.

The series is an expression of the value we see in documenting and understanding the varied lives of women. Exploring the choices and circumstances of these extraordinary women—both famous and unsung—is not merely of interest to the historian, but is central to anyone grappling with what it means to be a woman. The biographies of these women teach us not only about their lives and their worlds, but about ours as well. When women strive to forge their identities, as they do at many points throughout the lifespan, it is crucial to have models to look toward. These women provide such models. We are inspired through their example and are taught by their words.

Radcliffe College's sponsorship of the Radcliffe Biography Series was sparked by the publication in 1972 of *Notable American Women,* a scholarly encyclopedia sponsored by Radcliffe's Schlesinger Library. We became convinced of the importance of expanding the public's awareness of the many significant contributions made by women to America, continuing the commitment to educating people about the lives and work of women that is reflected in much of Radcliffe's work. In addition to commissioning new biographies, we decided to add reprints of distinguished books already published, with introductions written for this series.

It is with great pride and excitement that I present this latest volume.

LINDA S. WILSON, PRESIDENT
Radcliffe College
Cambridge, Massachusetts

Earliest known picture of Mary Baker Eddy, probably taken when she was a widow in her late twenties. Daguerreotype owned by Abigail Baker Tilton. *Courtesy of Church History Department, The First Church of Christ, Scientist.*

Radcliffe Biography Series

MARY BAKER EDDY

GILLIAN GILL

A MERLOYD LAWRENCE BOOK

PERSEUS BOOKS

Cambridge, Massachusetts

For permission to reprint copyrighted material, grateful acknowledgment is made to the following: The Christian Science Board of Directors for quotations from Mrs. Eddy's published and unpublished works; Trustees of The Christian Science Publishing Society for quotations from works published by them.

Many of the designations used by manufacturers and sellers to distinguish their products are claimed as trademarks. Where those designations appear in this book and Perseus Books was aware of a trademark claim, the designations have been printed in initial capital letters.

Library of Congress Catalog Card Number: 99-64866

ISBN 0-7382-0227-4

Copyright © 1998 by Gillian Gill

All rights reserved.
No part of this publication may be reproduced,
stored in a retrieval system, or transmitted,
in any form or by any means, electronic, mechanical,
photocopying, recording, or otherwise,
without the prior written permission of the publisher.
Printed in the United States of America.

Perseus Books is a member of the Perseus Books Group

Cover design by Suzanne Heiser
Text design by Ruth Kolbert
Set in 10.5-point Garamond Simoncini by Pagesetters, Inc.

2 3 4 5 6 7 8 9-   -02 01 00 99

Find us on the World Wide Web at
http://www.perseusbooks.com

FOR MY FATHER
William Everitt Scobie
1914–1998

who taught me how to head out
and steer a good course
even when the seas are high

CONTENTS

PART THREE

THE NEW MRS. EDDY
1 8 8 3 – 1 9 0 5

PART FOUR

MARY BAKER EDDY FIGHTS ON
1 9 0 6 – 1 9 1 0

PREFACE

When we do not know a person—and also when we do—we have to judge the size and nature of his achievements as compared with the achievements of others in his special line of business—there is no other way. Measured by this standard, it is thirteen hundred years since the world has produced anyone who could reach up to Mrs. Eddy's waistbelt.

In several ways she is the most interesting woman that ever lived, and the most extraordinary.

—MARK TWAIN

THE MOTHER CHURCH OF CHRIST, SCIENTIST NESTLES IN THE flank of its Extension, a proud parent dwarfed by its elegant offspring. Standing under the little tower of the church, I see a stained glass window depicting a woman seated at a table as light pours down on her from above. Surely this is Mrs. Eddy, shown as she was writing the first edition of *Science and Health* under the skylight in the garret in Lynn. Close to the window an inscription reads:

> The First Church of Christ, Scientist, erected Anno Domini, 1894. A testimonial to our beloved teacher, The Rev. Mary Baker Eddy, Discoverer and Founder of Christian Science; author of "Science and Health with Key to the Scriptures"; president of the Massachusetts Metaphysical College, and the first pastor of this denomination.

I turn away from this inscription toward the sharp-edged brilliance of a New England autumn and the cool, discrete spaces of the Christian Science complex, one of the most beautiful parts of the Back Bay in Boston. Behind me to the right soars the gray-domed crown of the 1906 Extension designed to accommodate 5,000 people, completed in under two years at a cost of $2 million, all contributed in advance by loyal Christian Scientists throughout the United States. In the 1970s the internationally famous American architect I. M. Pei, artfully blending new with old, designed the glass and marble main entrance into the Extension, as well as a tower block to house the administrative offices and an attractive building for the Sunday School, and the great Publishing Society. The whole complex is linked and spaced by a wide plaza and the rippling length of the reflecting pool. The only discordant note is a young man wading in the forbidden waters.

I have come to attend my first Christian Science service and am surprised how few people are climbing the church steps or, like myself, standing in the sunshine for a moment of admiration. I learn later that most Christian Scientists use the large parking garage under the plaza and take the reversible escalator to emerge directly into the church lobby, but, be that as it may, there are at most four hundred people gathered in the huge building as I enter. The sparseness of the congregation emphasizes the sense of uncluttered spaciousness. Domes and arches lift the great bulk of Indiana limestone over our heads and permit an uninterrupted view of the two lecterns below the organ.

The decoration inside consists principally of pairs of inscriptions, one from the Bible and one from the writings of Mary Baker Eddy. This pattern is repeated in the hour-long service, more than half of which is composed of pairs of quotations, the first from the Bible, the second from *Science and Health with Key to the Scriptures* by Mary Baker Eddy. Slowly and with crystal clear diction, the Bible passages are read by a silver-haired woman, the passages from *Science and Health* by a silver-haired man. Hymns are sung with Christian Science words set to some of the great old Protestant tunes. A beautiful young African-American woman with an ethereal soprano voice sings a more complex musical setting of words from one of the readings from the Psalms, each sung word as clear as the spoken words of the Readers.

The aesthetic appeal of the service is restrained. The church setting has an abstract grandeur that in no way allows the eye to distract the mind. Here is not the graceful line of Vèzelay or the complex subtlety of Chartres or the polychrome eccentricity of St. Basil's in Red Square; here is not even the simple comeliness of the little Unitarian octagon I know in nearby Lexington. The organ, advertised as one of the ten greatest in the world, is limited mainly to the role of accompanying the singing: Bach and Handel and Messiaen are allowed no place in the service. Even the Bible passages, though taken from the King James Authorized Version, which I have grown to love from childhood, are almost all unfamiliar, selected, it would seem, for their allegorical meaning rather than for their textual beauty or human drama.

Emotion too is restrained. Even the sense of community I had thought offered in every church is missing. Certainly I was welcomed as I entered the church and shown to my pew by a succession of smiling people, but no subsequent attempt is made to confirm or establish any bonds. No one shakes my hand on the church steps as I leave. I am not invited to stay for refreshments and conversation after the service. No announcements are made of upcoming events to be held in the church or its church hall. I wonder if this vast edifice even contains a hall—the kind of place believers and nonbelievers are familiar with in my suburban town, where we deliver a child for nursery school, rehearse with our amateur choir, eat a pancake breakfast, attend a rummage sale. It seems that in Christian Science there are no choral recitals, no organ concerts. No Christmas trees are decorated here, no Easter eggs hidden. No weddings, baptisms, or funerals take place in any Christian Science church, and communion is celebrated twice a year.

After the service, I join a group for one of the half-hourly tours that are conducted in the Mother Church throughout the day on almost every day of the year. After getting the vital statistics of the Extension, we are led into the smaller, older church. It would comfortably have housed all those pres-ent at the service I had just attended, but it is used now for the identical Sunday evening service which, the guide tells us, attracts fewer people than the morning one.

I know from my reading that this is the original 1894 church which Mary Baker Eddy refused to allow her Board of Directors to demolish or enclose when the new building was planned in 1904–1905. Yes, she maddeningly decreed from her New Hampshire retreat, I do want a newer, bigger church, one that will make Augusta Stetson and her New York branch church look small, but the architect must accommodate the old church in his plans. I want both. And, with a sigh and perhaps a raised eyebrow, the Board of Directors did exactly what Mrs. Eddy told them. Mrs. Eddy came three times to the first Mother Church, speaking twice, unannounced, never using the pew still marked for her use today. She glimpsed the Extension on only two occasions, the second with pain-glazed eyes, just before her death in 1910.

As I enter it today, the low, muted, womblike structure of the older church seems to gather me in. The warm brown painted walls have stencilled patterns at the top, pairs of inscribed texts in the center, and mosaic panels at the bottom. The shining pews are made from the most beautiful golden wood I have ever seen, and the velvet upholstery is apricot pink. Light from outside comes through a number of stained glass windows, local New England work of very high quality. Some of the scenes are allegorical; one shows the lion lying down with the lamb and the little child leading; several, predictably, show Christ's healings; four show different New Testament Marys;

one depicts the woman of Revelation, clothed with the sun, her feet on the moon, crowned with twelve stars. I feel at home in what strikes me as a deeply female space.

I ask the guide a question to which I know the answer: why have we not seen the stained glass window of Mary Baker Eddy which is visible from the plaza outside? "Ah yes," says the guide, a charming, cultured woman of patent sincerity, "that window is in what was originally called 'The Mother's Room.' It was set up specifically for Mrs. Eddy's use, and she spent one night there. Now the room is a storage area which no one enters. I should like to see it myself," says the guide, almost wistfully. "However, the window does not represent Mrs. Eddy but truth coming down to the individual soul, depicted as a woman. And now we will finish our tour with a look at the room where children too young to attend Sunday school are cared for during services." With this final, tactful reminder that whatever we may have read in the sensationalist press, Christian Scientists have children and indeed offer them the finest care money can buy, the tour ends.

I had come to The Mother Church of Christ, Scientist on that autumn day in 1992 to clarify my thinking about Mary Baker Eddy, whom I had known hitherto only from books. Certain things were indeed clearer—first, the nature of her material achievement. Everything to be seen at the Christian Science complex is of the finest quality and was produced by America's own designers and craftsmen. The plaster is not allowed to crumble, the walls to stain, the metal to tarnish, the glass to dim. All is immaculate, pristine, obedient to the exacting housekeeping standards Christian Science tells us Mrs. Eddy insisted upon in all her homes. Unlike the British churches I know, there are no collection boxes here, and even by the winter of 1996–1997, when a major refurbishing of parts of the Mother Church was under way and reports were appearing in the *Boston Globe* about important efforts to save money on large-ticket items such as water-cooling the whole Christian Science complex, the small pamphlets outlining the capital improvement plans made only the most subtle and indirect appeal for funds. Mrs. Eddy did not believe in charity, or in debt, and the tradition of economic self-sufficiency she founded is still in evidence to the general observer.

Bostonians tend to see the Christian Science Center as a kind of elegant backdrop, but as soon as one concentrates on the buildings themselves one becomes aware of the power, wealth, and influence that radiate from this quiet place. Perhaps the *Christian Science Monitor* has exemplified that power most prominently, and the story of the founding of the *Monitor* emphasizes how much that power was a personal one, exercised by one woman. On August 8, 1908, in her eighty-seventh year, two years before her death, Mrs. Eddy sent this communication to the Board of Trustees of the Publishing Society:

> *Beloved Students:* It is my request that you start a daily newspaper at once, and call it the <u>Christian Science Monitor</u>. Let there be no delay. The Cause demands that it be issued now.
>
> You may consult with the Board of Directors. I have notified them of my intention.
>
> *Lovingly yours,*
> *Mary Baker G. Eddy*

On November 25, 1908, the first copy of the *Christian Science Monitor* rolled off the presses. Not even the Roman Catholic Church can claim a daily newspaper of such high international reputation.

What other woman in modern times has had this kind of vision and this kind of power to implement it? What other woman has established a religious movement of international stature? In what other religion or religious denomination is a woman's message offered next to that of Jesus Christ? What other woman's writing is written and read side by side with the Bible? What other woman dared to subtitle her own work "Key to the Scriptures"? Simply on the material evidence we find at the Christian Science complex in Boston, it becomes clear that Mrs. Eddy played a unique part not only in the history of American Protestantism but in the movement toward a woman-inclusive theology and church governance.

But there is another side to Christian Science which the quiet power of these buildings conceals. From the beginning, Christian Science has aroused hostility and opposition as strong as the fervor and loyalty of its devotees. From the beginning it has been wracked by schism, riven by internal quarrels which often made their way into courts of law and which were covered with intense interest by the local and national press. Two issues have proven particularly sensitive: first, the right of Christian Science parents to treat their sick children using spiritual healing methods alone, and, second, the church's organization and finances.

Today, as in the nineteenth century, the most painful and sensational issue associated with Christian Science in the public mind is the death of children under the care of Christian Science practitioners. In perhaps the most highly publicized case of recent years, David and Ginger Twitchell of Hyde Park, Massachusetts, were convicted in 1990 of the manslaughter of their little son Robyn. That the Twitchells were loving and devoted parents was not in doubt during the eight-week trial, but the jury finally decided that Robyn would not have died if his parents had sought conventional medical treatment for his bowel blockage. Similarly tragic emotions had been roused in Mrs. Eddy's lifetime when her disciple, Christian Science practitioner Abby

Corner, was tried and acquitted for the manslaughter of her own daughter and grandchild, who died in childbirth under her care. Similar court cases in other states have occurred since 1990, consistently arousing the public indignation, and a fresh discussion, with new examples, of the old issues is aired in the print media or on talk radio. If the average American knows anything about Christian Science, it is that this sect defends the rights of parents to deny conventional medical care to their minor children.

In comparison with the universal resonance of the child-death issue, the disputes over church governance and finances, which began almost as soon as Mrs. Eddy died, have aroused interest mainly in New England and California, where there are significant populations of Christian Scientists. The unelected and self-perpetuating five-member Board of Directors, which has governed the Church since 1910, has often been criticized inside and outside the Church as being closed and autocratic. But in recent years, as increasingly urgent efforts have been made to halt the continuing decline in Church membership, the board's wisdom and trustworthiness have also come under fire. The directors launched the ambitious *Monitor* cable television station on May 1, 1991, which received critical plaudits but proved disastrously expensive. The effect on the Church of what has been publicly estimated as a $473 million dollar mistake was exacerbated when, in 1992, news of intense disagreement within the membership over the Church's commitment to its media venture was leaked to the *Boston Globe,* which also published allegations of large-scale financial mismanagement of pension funds by the board. The truth of these allegations is still much in dispute, but there is no doubt that further damage was done to the already weakened Christian Science movement.

Financial problems were highlighted over the next two years as the Church struggled to find a way to comply with the terms of the will of Bliss Knapp and his heirs so as to inherit some $100 million of the millions it needed. The Knapp will, which was filed under the jurisdiction of the California courts, required that the Christian Science Publishing Society issue and distribute through "substantially all" its reading rooms Mr. Knapp's biography of Mary Baker Eddy. First written in the 1940s, the book presents Mrs. Eddy as more God than woman; it is considered heretical by many Christian Scientists. When the Publishing Society quietly issued the book, purportedly as part of a new Twentieth-Century Biography Series offering divergent views of Mrs. Eddy, they failed to overcome the resistance of individual Christian Science communities and thus secure its presence in "substantially all" of the supposedly independent and autonomous reading rooms. Therefore, Stanford University and Los Angeles County, the residuary legatees to the Knapp estate, sued the Church, charging that the terms of Bliss Knapp's will had not been met, and the money should revert to them. After years of expensive litigation, a settlement was negotiated by 1997 in which the Church received, according to one account I was given, $53 million, and the other legatees $27 million each.

As the quarrel over the Bliss Knapp biography indicates, Mrs. Eddy's life is still an issue of intense concern for Christian Scientists. Given that Mrs. Eddy died in 1910, it is surprising to an outsider that one of the questions often raised in the Christian Science community during the pensions scandal was whether Mrs. Eddy would have embraced television as she had print journalism. Such public controversy and the reopening of old wounds indicate a need to look again at the life and achievements of the woman who all agree created the Church of Christ, Scientist and continues to influence it to an extraordinary degree.

If Christian Science is controversial today as an institution, so also was Mrs. Eddy during her lifetime. Few women have been so bitterly attacked, so insistently torn from the pedestal upon which she climbed and on which her devotees sought to maintain her. The hagiographic zeal of loyal Christian Scientist biographers has been more than matched by the energy her detractors have expended in producing damning facts and damaging documents about her. Shallow, egotistic, incapable of love; painted, bedizened, affected; hysteric, paranoiac, mad; ambitious, mercenary, tyrannical; man-eater, drug addict, mesmerist; illiterate, illogical, uncultured, plagiarist: these are only a few of the accusations that were aimed at Mary Baker Eddy during her life and afterward (see Appendix).

It is because Mrs. Eddy was so unlikely a saint and prophet, so flawed, so unexpected, so achieving, that she is so interesting from a nonecclesiastical, noninstitutional point of view. She transcends the boundaries not only of her historical period but of the religious movement she founded, and in some measure appreciation of her as a historical figure has been severely hampered by the controversies generated by her church.

Truth, in Mrs. Eddy's case, is often stranger than fiction. Conventional in her twenties, weak in her thirties, struggling in her forties, a social outcast in her fifties, indefatigably working in her sixties, famous in her seventies, formidable in her eighties, Mrs. Eddy rewrites the female plot and offers new ways to strive and achieve. Parts of her life seem too unlikely to be true. What are we to make of Mrs. Eddy's one-time loyal disciple Daniel Spofford, accused in 1878, and in Salem court no less, of practicing witchcraft upon another Christian Scientist, Miss Lucretia Brown? Of Asa Gilbert Eddy, Mrs. Eddy's third and last husband, who was arrested with Edward Arens on the charge of hiring the unsavory James Sargent to assassinate Daniel Spofford? What of the twelve Christian Scientists detailed in two hourly shifts to "take up" and use their mental powers to foil those persons who were exerting malicious animal magnetism upon Mrs. Eddy and thereby making her ill, causing unwanted precipitation to fall in Concord, New Hampshire, or introducing errata in the proofs of her book? What of the onetime Christian

Science healer and teacher Josephine Woodbury and her "parthenogeneti-cally conceived" son, baptized Prince of Peace in a rock pool on the Maine coast?

Mrs. Eddy was recognized in her day as the most influential and con-troversial woman in America, and she has continued to attract the attention of historians of religion. There has been no full-scale treatment of her as a historical figure and cultural phenomenon, however, even if Garry Wills's essay on Mrs. Eddy in *Certain Trumpets* (Simon and Schuster, 1994) points in that direction. The general-interest historical biographer has, I think, not been tempted to take on Mrs. Eddy as a subject because she does not fit into traditional categories of female eminence: she did not achieve fame as a young woman, she was not a celebrated beauty and had no famous men as lovers and husbands, she was not born rich and did not have a family or acquaintances of interest to the general public. More surprising, the increas-ingly successful and ambitious discipline of women's history has taken little note of Mrs. Eddy. Even the eminent and pathbreaking feminist historian Gerda Lerner makes no mention of Mrs. Eddy in her survey essay "One Thousand Years of Feminist Bible Criticism" (Oxford University Press, 1993). The only work that considers Mrs. Eddy within the framework of recent scholarship in women's studies and feminist theory has been done mainly by women who were Christian Scientists, such as Jewel Spangler Smaus and Jean A. MacDonald, and has received little general attention or academic reputation.

I see two main reasons for this neglect of Mrs. Eddy and her church by historians of women, the first ideological, the second practical. First, she does not fit the established feminist pattern of female achievement; that is, she did not achieve prominence as a suffragist or an abolitionist or a sup-porter of the temperance movement, though, as I shall show, she was in basic ideological agreement with all these movements. Those areas of Mrs. Eddy's life that make her own church uncomfortable and attract the ire and scorn of her critics are also those that make most American feminist scholars squirm—mesmerism, alternative medicine, and fringe religious sects. For liberal, intellectual, middle-class feminists she is too weird and irrational and commercial. For the more recent New Age style feminists, on the other hand, with their essential oils and crystals and Eastern mysticism and channellings, Mrs. Eddy is too establishment, too abstract and intellectual, too textual.

The second reason that Mrs. Eddy has not been considered by histori-ans of women or feminists working on religion is that she has been impossi-ble to study seriously because the great mass of documentation relating to her has been legendarily inaccessible. The limited access to research materi-als for the purpose of scholarly inquiry is a result of her religious importance. Mrs. Eddy is preeminent among American women because she founded her own religious sect. To Christian Scientists, and particularly to those who direct and administer the Church of Christ, Scientist in Boston, nothing relating to Mrs. Eddy is trivial or routine, and they have strived to collect and control all information about her. The archival records now preserved on the twenty-second floor of the administrative tower of The Mother Church in Boston's Back Bay constitute the great majority of documents that relate to Mrs. Eddy, and over the whole history of the institution only a handful of scholars has been granted permission to read even a small portion of the holdings.

Access to research materials was the central problem that I faced as I embarked upon my study of Mrs. Eddy. As I explain in the "Research Note" toward the end of this book, I spent some two years negotiating in person and through legal counsel with Christian Science officers at The Mother Church for access to their archival holdings. The access I was finally able to win to the Mother Church archives was frustratingly limited, but nonetheless it was sufficient for me to uncover vital new material and therefore to alter significantly the standard accounts of Mrs. Eddy's life. My research was also enriched by materials, published and unpublished, oral and written, offered by several other rich sources, most notably the Longyear Museum in Brookline, Massachusetts.

In terms of its organization and emphasis, this biography differs from previous ones in that it gives much more careful attention to Mrs. Eddy's first sixty years, before Christian Science became a national force. This is where earlier biographies tend to be most inaccurate, and where the record therefore needs to be set straight most carefully. I have managed to consult almost all the archival material on Mrs. Eddy up to 1882 scattered through various collections, and have trolled the evidence with a very fine net.

In the second half of the book, which is devoted to Mrs. Eddy's years of international fame and intradenominational authority, I have chosen to focus more on Mrs. Eddy's private experience, her public image, and her achievement as a thinker and a writer and less on her day-to-day work in building and administering her movement. Much distinguished work has already been done on the founding and discovering of Christian Science, and on the theology of the movement, more is under way. I am convinced that historians and theologians of many stripes will find a treasure trove of material once the doors of the Christian Science archives are opened wider to scholars. Although I am fascinated by the subject of Mrs. Eddy's ecclesiastical politics, I was unable in a single volume to address everything of interest, and my concern has been Mary Baker Eddy, Christian Scientist, rather than Mrs. Eddy, leader of the Church of Christ, Scientist. It is the process whereby Mrs. Eddy became a religious leader and her experience of holding ecclesiastic authority that have interested me, and how that process and that experience are influenced by gender. I believe my book will help readers understand how Mary Baker of Bow, New Hampshire, became the legendary

Mrs. Eddy of Christian Science, and what it was like to be the woman who lived that change. As Mrs. Eddy remarked in an 1891 letter to Augusta Stetson, "Oh, the marvel of my life! What would be thought of it if it was known in a millionth of its detail."

I do not claim to be unprejudiced about Mary Baker Eddy, or to view her with cool objectivity. From the moment I began to read about her she fascinated me, and although she and I appeared to have little or nothing in common, she came to command my respect, my admiration, and even my affection. I wish, with surprising passion, that I could have met her, particularly in her last years.

One of the most salient points about Mrs. Eddy's life is that she was constantly under attack, often in court of law, and as this biography developed I noticed myself increasingly taking the position of her defense attorney, responding to a wide array of substantial charges brought by many, often talented, attorneys who represented a large group of interested parties. The defense counsel is expected to be informed, intelligent, and talented, and to observe due process; his or her job is not to make judgments or suggest sentences but to argue the client's case and represent the client's interests before the court. Correctly defining the legal issues, marshalling the evidence, responding as logically and carefully as possible to the prosecution's case, establishing the network of relationships, events, and interests that led to the charges being filed are all part of the defense counsel's brief, but so too is using rhetoric and sympathetic identification to appeal to the judge and jury on behalf of the client.

In this biography I try to lay out what could be called the prosecution's case as fairly as possible, but then I present a defense counsel's brief which I leave to the reader to judge. I argue strongly that there is no reliable evidence that Mrs. Eddy was an uncontrollable hysteric as a teenager, though this is one of the "facts" about her repeated in all the conventional accounts. I look carefully at her relations with her only son and quarrel with her reputation as a heartless, unloving mother. I consider in detail the vexed question of Mrs. Eddy's debt to Phineas Parkhurst Quimby, examining the highly politicized atmosphere of personal animosity and professional rivalry in which charges of plagiarism and ingratitude were laid against her, and explaining the complex issues of intellectual originality, documentary authenticity, and dating involved in the dispute surrounding the so-called Quimby "manuscripts." I carefully sift all the tantalizing scraps of evidence that have survived about Mrs. Eddy's relations with the enigmatic figures that haunted her movement in its early days—Richard Kennedy, Daniel Spofford, and Edward Arens. I reconsider the evidence submitted to the courts about the supposed plot by Asa Gilbert Eddy and Edward Arens to kill Daniel Spofford, and the way the newspapers covered the event. I reexamine Mrs. Eddy's stormy relations with three women—Clara Choate,

Josephine Woodbury, and Augusta Stetson—and take another look at the issue that dominated early Christian Science history—Malicious Animal Magnetism. Finally, I focus on the extraordinarily vicious barrage of press reporting that darkened Mrs. Eddy's last years, and on the unsuccessful 1907 "Next Friends" suit brought by her son, granddaughter, adopted son, nephew, and second cousin in an attempt to prove her legally incompetent to manage her own affairs, and to divest her of her estate.

My defense of Mary Baker Eddy rests on an assumption of her competence to act, her responsibility for her actions, and hence on her ability to accept credit or blame for those acts. This has not been the dominant assumption among those who have chosen to take her on as a biographical subject. When I came to study Mrs. Eddy's life and career, I was struck by the fact that, though split over the value they place on her public prominence between 1885 and 1910, Mrs. Eddy's biographers of all stripes are implicitly agreed on one essential point—that she deserved no personal credit for anything important she did. Whereas some see her as angel and some as demon, all agree that she was a very ordinary and flawed woman whose achievements—while undeniable and extraordinary—bear no relation to her talents.

Faced with the paradox of Mrs. Eddy's assumed ordinariness and extraordinary success, biographers have adopted two essential models. According to the first model, that adopted by devout Christian Scientists, Mrs. Eddy was the special instrument of God, a prophet with a direct line to the divine word and the divine will. Since God moves in mysterious ways, the extraordinary facts of her life are, *eo ipso,* inexplicable in merely human, materialist terms. A specifically Christological subset of this view would point out that Jesus Christ was a carpenter of humble origins, his disciples simple fishermen; that he consorted with lepers, tax gatherers, prostitutes, and so forth. Thus when the poorly educated Mary Baker Eddy consorts with barely literate people and finds her first followers among the shoe factory workers of Lynn, Massachusetts, these aspects of her story can be interpreted as part of a divine pattern.

According to the second model, adopted by those unsympathetic to Christian Science, Mrs. Eddy, insofar as she achieved anything the biographer considers worthwhile or remarkable, was merely very lucky and very unscrupulous. Born in the right time and the right place, she consistently plagiarized the ideas of other people, notably the Maine mental healer Phineas Parkhurst Quimby, and was smart enough to get other, more competent people to work for her. European critics, such as the Oxford writer H. A. L. Fisher, explain that Mrs. Eddy's brand of mediocrity fitted peculiarly well with what they perceive to be the mediocrity of the American society she lived in. This approach is somewhat schizophrenic since it tends to exaggerate both Mrs. Eddy's ultimate power and hence her potential for evil, and at the same time her personal incapacity. In a strange version of the Cinderella story, a woman whom the critics have presented as so unremarkable, so unattractive, so weak, so poor, so pathetic, so alone, and, finally, so old, is transformed, almost overnight and by some unidentified force (public credulity? modern media manipulation? mesmerism?) into the almighty Mother of Christian Science, who must be pulled down off her pedestal by right-thinking men.

My model in this biography is quite different. I believe Mary Baker Eddy's life starts to make sense only if we accept that she was born with an exceptional combination of abilities, desires, and energies, which circumstances for a long time prevented her from realizing. As I will show and as her later life proves, Mary Baker Eddy's gifts were for inspirational leadership and religious doctrine, organizational planning and structure, law and finance, propaganda and public relations. These were qualities which flourished in the nineteenth century generally, and which the United States in particular prized and encouraged—but mainly in its male citizens. Had Mary Baker been born a man, these same gifts would probably have brought her success and fulfillment early in life. In fact, however, these abilities moldered until she was almost fifty, blossomed in her sixties, and bore fruit only in the last two decades of an unusually long and stressful life.

American women in the nineteenth century were expected to be different from their men. This difference was maintained or exaggerated as American society accelerated away from the old "homespun," domestic industry structures in which women were considered helpmates, playing an essentially similar but subordinate economic role, by the side of their menfolk. In the new industrial-mercantile society, woman was required not to be man's useful assistant but his complement and opposite, weak where man was strong; otherworldly where man was materialistic; soft, self-sacrificing, and modest where man was hard, ambitious, and self-promoting. Even as the home was being drained of value as an income-producing unit, conventional ideology was insisting that the home was woman's specific and exclusive world. A woman literally had no business in the public sphere since her true concerns were private—marital, familial, domestic, and spiritual. The burgeoning of the American women's movement, which runs parallel to the adult life of Mary Baker Eddy, was a reaction to this narrowing and redefining of women's position in society.

Mary Baker Eddy's main problem was that she had an extraordinary talent for life in the public sphere but was barred from entering it. In many ways she resembled her father far more than her mother, and this resemblance caused intense conflict with her family and friends in midlife, with her critics in later years, and within her own psyche throughout her life. Mary Baker Eddy spent more than forty years trying out various conventional feminine roles, and failing. The reasons for this failure are many, but throughout the pre–Christian Science period of her life, there is abundant evidence of her unhappiness, her frustration, her square-peg inability to fit comfortably into the round hole allotted her. The chronic and increasingly debilitating ill health she suffered from until 1866 was, among other things, the most obvious symptom of this intense dissatisfaction.

Particularly during her lifetime, the criteria applied to Mary Baker Eddy have been notably different from those applied to famous men in general, and to religious leaders—who have been male almost by definition—in particular. Interestingly, both Mary Baker Eddy's apologists and her detractors share the view that a woman who is not happy and successful as a wife, mother, and homemaker cannot be admired. Whereas the serious deficiencies of Charles Dickens or Mark Twain or Leo Tolstoy as husbands and fathers are considered to be irrelevant to their achievement or even seen as the sad but inevitable result of their genius, Mary Baker Eddy has consistently been held to a different standard: expected to fulfill all the tasks and roles of a "normal" wife and mother of her period as well as found a new denomination. Thus two of her most important hostile biographers, Georgine Milmine and Edwin Dakin, gleefully offer example after example of her marital, maternal, and domestic inadequacies. Loyal biographers like Sibyl Wilbur and Lyman Powell for their part merely mirror this approach by advancing counter examples of Mrs. Eddy's exquisite neatness, her fond relations with children, and her faithful devotion to three husbands. Given the constant attacks Mary Baker Eddy met with merely because she was a divorcée who married three times, one wonders if she would have been criticized much more violently if she had followed in the steps of Joseph Smith and Brigham Young and advocated polyandry out of religious principle. Found wanting in her femininity, she is also attacked or at best grudgingly admired for giving evidence of qualities traditionally associated with the male: originality, ambition, drive, ruthlessness, self-confidence, business acumen, a willingness to take risks and break new ground, single-minded devotion to a cause, choosing intimates from outside the family circle, and, above all, a prophetic belief that she was the chosen vessel for God's purpose and the exponent of new Revelation.

Mary Baker Eddy deserves to be something more than a name on a wall, a figure depicted in a stained glass window that faces only outward from a locked and abandoned room. My purpose in this book is to move beyond the stereotypes of Mary Baker Eddy as prophet or adventuress and to present her as a real woman with strengths and weaknesses, born in a specific time and place, and facing specific challenges and opportunities. I want to give a sense of Mrs. Eddy's strangeness, her energy, her charisma, her power, to tell the story of her spiritual pilgrimage, and to show what it was about her that evoked both so much love and so much hate. Hers is a story that stands the retelling, hers a voice that asks to be heard.

ACKNOWLEDGMENTS

Merloyd Lawrence, Tom Proctor, Stephen Gottschalk, and Judith Huenneke have been especially important to me in this project.

Merloyd was the first person ever to mention the name of Mary Baker Eddy to me, and without her support this biography would not have been written. Merloyd believed in me, and I count having her as my editor an extraordinary piece of good luck.

When I began this biography, Tom Proctor was the head curator at the Longyear Museum, and he was of enormous assistance in the early years of my research. Not only did he open the resources of the collection to me, but he was willing to spend time discussing Mrs. Eddy, helping me to formulate some of the lines of inquiry I would pursue, and also giving me a sense of Christian Science as a living community.

After Tom Proctor left Longyear, Stephen Gottschalk became the key friend who was as interested in Mrs. Eddy as I was, the person with whom I could gossip and argue and be outrageously speculative. Steve is a major scholar of Christian Science, and I can never repay him for giving me so many hours of his time. While I was writing the body of this book, he was my most dedicated, informed, and challenging reader, sending me pages of valuable comments.

Judith Huenneke was chosen by the Church History Department to be my research liaison with the Mother Church collection, and it is hard to imagine how a better choice could have been made. Judy is a fine archivist as well as a dedicated student of history, and I have always been able to rely on her accuracy, her fairness, her rectitude.

Tom, Steve, and Judy are all Christian Scientists who worked so hard with me in large part because they feel a deep personal devotion to Mrs. Eddy. None of them has ever tried to convert me, however, and this may be a main reason why the book actually got written. I know that they disagree with many of the things I have written about Mrs. Eddy, and I wish here to both thank them and clear them of all responsibility.

I have felt the spirit of my first husband, David Michael Gill, with me as I wrote this biography, although he would have been the first to reprove the very notion of spirits. When he died, Mike left me a legacy—not only the resources to do independent research but the resolution to look for new challenges and the confidence to follow my own way—just as he had always done.

Nadya Aisenberg, Mona Harrington, Judith Nies, and Lynda Laurence read sections of the manuscript and offered good advice and precious support. My son Christopher Gill researched spermatorrhea for me in the medical literature and was of great help with the history of infectious disease in the nineteenth century. Judge Kenneth Laurence gave valuable advice on some of Mrs. Eddy's legal issues. Keith McNeil, who owns an important collection of Eddyana and has done sterling work on Mrs. Eddy's life, was generous with information. Ann Beals, the publisher and editor of The Bookmark of Santa Clarita, California, was unfailingly efficient and allowed me to get copies of some important and rare Christian Science texts. Sue Bridge read sections of the manuscript and offered useful comments. I am indebted to Professor Clarissa Atkinson of the Harvard Divinity School who valiantly read the first draft and offered valuable suggestions and comments.

I owe a deep debt of gratitude to Yvonne Caché von Fettweis and all her staff at the Church History Department, and to Alan Lester and his staff at the Longyear Museum. These people did everything possible to help me get the facts on Mary Baker Eddy right. They bear no responsibility for the opinions and interpretations in this book which are my own.

A very special thank-you to Virginia Harris, the Chair of the Board of Directors of The Mother Church, who made it possible for me to do research in the Church's archives on my terms.

I would like to thank the staff at the following institutions for their help: the New Hampshire Historical Society, the Mugar Memorial Library at Boston University, the Houghton Library at Harvard University, the Lynn Historical Society, the Radcliffe College Alumnae Society.

It is hard to imagine a team more able, efficient, and dedicated than the one I found at Perseus Books. My thanks to Beth Burleigh Fuller, Maggie Carr, Sharon Rice, Michelle Hansen, Elizabeth Carduff, and the rest of the team.

Finally, thanks to all the members of my family, so distant in miles but close in spirit—to Christopher and Noriko and my grandchildren in Portland, to my daughter Catherine in Spain, to my sister Rose and brother Harry, to Martin, Sue, Vera, Stewart, Tom, Joan, Margot, Ady in Great Britain. Most of all, thanks to my husband and partner, Stuart Esten, whose computer expertise keeps me on line and whose love gives me the energy to keep writing.

The author and publisher are grateful to the following organizations for permission to quote from the unpublished and copyrighted material in their collections: the Board of Directors of The First Church of Christ, Scientist in Boston; the Longyear Museum; the Mugar Memorial Library at Boston University; the New Hampshire Historical Society.

The author and publisher are also grateful to the Board of Directors of The First Church of Christ, Scientist for permission to reproduce copyrighted photographic material and for all the help provided by staff members of the Church History Department in preparing the illustrations for this book.

In addition we would like to thank the Longyear Museum for permission to reproduce the portraits of Mrs. Eddy's father, Mark Baker, and of her first husband, George Glover.

CHRONOLOGY

1821 *July 16* Mary Morse Baker born Bow, New Hampshire, last of the six children of Mark Baker and Abigail Ambrose Baker.

1836 *January* Bakers move to new farm near Sanbornton Bridge (now Tilton), New Hampshire.

1841 Albert Baker, aged thirty-one, dies of kidney disease.

1843 *December 10* Mary Baker marries George Washington Glover, a building contractor.

December 25 Glovers sail for Charleston, South Carolina.

1844 *Early February* Move to Wilmington, North Carolina. George Glover plans to build a cathedral in Haiti and invests all his capital.

June 27 George Glover dies, probably of yellow fever, leaving his pregnant widow penniless.

September 12 Mary Glover returns to her parents' home and has her first and only child, George Washington Glover II. She falls ill.

1849 *November 21* Abigail Ambrose Baker dies.

1850 *December* Mark Baker marries Elizabeth Patterson Duncan. Abigail Baker Tilton offers Mary Glover a home, but not George.

1851 *May* George sent to live in North Groton, New Hampshire, with Mahala and Russell Cheney. Mary Glover's health declines.

1853 *June 21* Marries Daniel Patterson, dentist and homeopathist.

1855   Bakers set Patterson up in North Groton, near where George lives. Patterson falls rapidly into debt and refuses to let George into the house. Mrs. Mary Patterson's health declines further. Studies homeopathy.

1856   *April*   Cheneys move to Minnesota with young George Glover.

1860   *March 19*   Bankrupt, Pattersons are forced out of North Groton.

1861   George Glover, abused and kept illiterate by Cheney, joins the Union army, Eighteenth Wisconsin regiment.

1862   *March*   Patterson captured while sightseeing on battlefield at Bull Run.

   October 10   Mrs. Mary Patterson consults Phineas Parkhurst Quimby in Portland, Maine. Health improves dramatically. Becomes absorbed in Quimby's ideas on mental healing.

   December–January   Patterson escapes from Confederate prison.

1863   *July*   Mrs. Mary Patterson studies with Quimby on and off for the next nine months.

1864   *June*   Rejoins Patterson, who is practicing in Lynn, Massachusetts.

1865   Patterson, increasingly unfaithful, neglects his practice. Mary becomes active in the Lynn temperance movement.

   October 6   Mark Baker dies.

1866   *January 16*   Death of P. P. Quimby in Belfast, Maine.

   February 1   Mrs. Mary Patterson falls on the ice in downtown Lynn, awakens unable to move, and seems close to death.

   February 3   To the astonishment of friends, she gets up unaided and resumes normal life. Dates discovery of Christian Science to this event.

   March   Patterson goes off with a married woman. Forced to rely on the charity of friends, Mrs. Mary Patterson moves numerous times. Begins Genesis manuscript in the fall.

1867   *April*   Teaches her first student, Hiram Crafts, a shoe worker.

   Summer   Heals her niece Ellen Pilsbury. Takes shelter in Amesbury, Massachusetts, with Mrs. Webster, an active Spiritualist. Wins support of Sarah Bagley and Richard Kennedy.

   November 21   Brother George Sullivan Baker dies.

1868   *c. June*   Reverts to the name of Glover. Is forced out by the Websters and moves into the Bagley home.

   September   Mrs. Mary Glover finds a home with the Wentworths in Stoughton, Massachusetts.

1869   Completes Genesis manuscript and a teaching document, "The Science of Man."

1870 *June* Sets up partnership in healing practice and teaching with Richard Kennedy in Lynn.

August Holds her first class and copyrights "The Science of Man."

1872 *January–February* Falls out with Kennedy over issue of "manipulation." Letters in Lynn press accuse her of being an avaricious mesmerist.

May 11 Partnership with Kennedy ends. Mrs. Mary Glover ceases her classes and devotes herself to writing a book.

1873 *November 4* Wins divorce from Daniel Patterson on charge of desertion.

1875 *March 31* Purchases her first home at 8 Broad Street, Lynn. Adds a new section to her book and renames it *Science and Health*.

June 1 Leads first Sunday services at Good Templars Hall in Lynn.

October 30 Publishes first edition of *Science and Health*.

1876 *February 14* Publishes *The Science of Man*.

July 4 Formation of the Christian Scientist Association.

1877 *January 1* Marries Asa Gilbert Eddy, a recent student, some ten years younger than herself.

May 30 Daniel Spofford breaks with her.

1878 Mrs. Eddy engages in a series of disastrous lawsuits at the instigation of a new student, Edward Arens.

October The second (Ark) edition of *Science and Health* is so mishandled by the printer that only volume 2 can be distributed.

October 29 Edward Arens and Asa Eddy are arrested and charged with conspiring to assassinate Daniel Spofford.

November 24 Mrs. Eddy starts delivering Sunday afternoon sermons at the Baptist Tabernacle in Boston.

1879 *January* Conspiracy case dismissed when key witness admits to perjury.

April 12 The Association votes to form a church.

November Her son, George Glover, last seen in 1856, arrives from Lead, South Dakota, seeking capital for mining ventures.

1881 *January 31* Charter obtained for the Massachusetts Metaphysical College, which becomes the formal setting for Mrs. Eddy's classes.

August 17 Third edition of *Science and Health*, which includes the chapter "Demonology," published by University Press of Cambridge.

October 26 Eight of the original students from Lynn make a public break.

November 9 Mary Baker Eddy is ordained Pastor of the Church.

1882 *May 12* Massachusetts Metaphysical College reopens in Boston.

June 3   Asa Gilbert Eddy dies.

August 14   Calvin Frye joins the household as chief aide.

1883   *February 8*   Julius Dresser begins campaign to establish P. P. Quimby as father of Christian Science with a letter to the Boston *Post*.

April   Mary Baker Eddy enters a bill of complaint against Edward Arens, now a Dresser ally, for plagiarism.

April 14   Starts bimonthly (later monthly) journal, first called the *Journal of Christian Science,* renamed in 1885 *The Christian Science Journal*.

June 2   First publishes "The People's God" in *The Christian Science Journal*. (Renamed *The People's Idea of God* as a pamphlet.)

September 21   Publishes the sixth edition of *Science and Health*, which for the first time includes *Key to the Scriptures* in text and title.

October 4   Injunction issued against Edward Arens. His pamphlets are destroyed.

1885   *February*   Publishes *Historical Sketch of Metaphysical Healing*.

March   Publishes "Defence of Christian Science" in the *Christian Science Journal*.

March 16   Gives a brief defense of Christian Science before a hostile audience in Tremont Temple in Boston.

July 30   Hires J. H. Wiggin as literary advisor.

1886   *February*   National Christian Scientist Association (NCSA) formed.

1887   *August*   Publishes *Christian Science: No and Yes*.

October 19   Rival metaphysical healers challenge Mary Baker Eddy by staging a convention at the Parker Memorial Hall in Boston.

November   George Glover's family arrives from South Dakota, uninvited. Stays six months. Mrs. Eddy publishes *Rudiments and Rules of Divine Science*.

1888   *March*   Publishes *Unity of Good and Unreality of Evil*.

c. April   Abby H. Corner is indicted for the deaths, during labor, of her daughter and grandchild. She is later acquitted.

June   Mrs. Eddy and her closest advisors attend Christian Science Convention in Chicago.

June 12   In her absence thirty-six Boston students manage to get possession of the Association records and defect.

June 14   Mary Baker Eddy scores her greatest public triumph in an unrehearsed speech at the Chicago Central Music Hall.

November 5   Legally adopts Ebenezer J. Foster.

1889 *May*   Leaves Boston and disengages from the day-to-day running of her church. Resigns pastorate of Boston church.

September 23   Dissolves Christian Scientist Association.

October 29   Closes Massachusetts Metaphysical College.

December 2   Formally disorganizes the Church.

1890 Focuses on completing a major new edition of *Science and Health.*

July 4   Josephine Woodbury, Christian Science teacher, baptizes "Prince of Peace," the son she claims she bore parthenogenetically.

1891 *January*   Mrs. Eddy publishes landmark fiftieth edition of *Science and Health.*

November   Publishes *Retrospection and Introspection.*

1892 *June 20*   Moves into Pleasant View on outskirts of Concord.

September 1   Mary Baker Eddy gives a four-man Board of Directors land on which to construct a building for the Mother Church in Boston.

September 23   The Mother Church, the First Church of Christ, Scientist, is formally reorganized with the election of twelve First Members.

1893 *September 20*   Christian Science achieves new recognition at the World's Parliament of Religions in Chicago.

October   Building of the Mother Church begins.

December 2   Mary Baker Eddy publishes *Christ and Christmas.*

1894 *May 21*   Cornerstone of the church building laid.

December 30   First service held in the Mother Church.

1895 *January 6*   Dedication of the Mother Church.

April   Ordains Bible and *Science and Health* as Pastor throughout the whole of the Church of Christ, Scientist. Publishes *Pulpit and Press.* Accepts title of Pastor Emeritus.

April 1   Mary Baker Eddy visits the Boston church for the first time.

May 26   Gives first address in the Mother Church.

September 10   Publishes *Manual of The Mother Church.*

1896 *January 5*   Gives second address in the Mother Church.

April 4   Josephine Woodbury is excommunicated.

1897 *February*   Mrs. Eddy publishes *Miscellaneous Writings.*

March   Suspends all Christian Science teaching for one year.

July 21   Breaks with Ebenezer Foster Eddy.

1898 *January*   Board of Lectureship founded.

January 25   Mary Baker Eddy makes deed of trust establishing The

Christian Science Publishing Society in its present form.

September 1   First issue of the *Christian Science Weekly* published, soon renamed the *Christian Science Sentinel.*

November 20–21   Teaches her last class in Concord.

December 13   Three-man Publication Committee authorized.

1899   *May*   Horatio W. Dresser and Josephine Curtis Woodbury publish a two-part piece in the *Arena* called "Eddyism Exposed."

June 4   Mary Baker Eddy's annual Communion Message includes a denunciation of the "Babylonish woman" of Revelation.

June 6   Comes to Boston to address three thousand members at the Annual Meeting, held at Tremont Temple.

July 31   Frederick Peabody files suit against Mrs. Eddy and Church officials, charging the Communion Message libeled his client, Josephine Woodbury.

October   Mark Twain publishes his first piece on Christian Science in *Cosmopolitan.*

1901   *June 5*   Mrs. Woodbury's libel suit collapses in court.

1902   *January 30*   Mary Baker Eddy publishes revised and essentially definitive (226th) edition of *Science and Health with Key to the Scriptures.*

June 18   Christian Scientists pledge $2 million to build the Extension to the Mother Church.

December   First of four articles on Christian Science by Mark Twain appears in the *North American Review.*

1903   *March*   Deeply in debt, George Glover comes to Concord to ask his mother for money. Given only $5,000, George impugns the honesty of Calvin Frye. Mary Baker Eddy breaks off communications with George.

July 1   Ten thousand Christian Scientists gather and listen to the address Mary Baker Eddy gives from Pleasant View balcony.

1904   *July 10*   Long, anonymous article in *New York Times*, probably by Peabody, claims Mary Baker Eddy plagiarized Quimby's work.

1906   *June 10*   Dedication of Extension to the Mother Church.

October 28   Sensational article in Joseph Pulitzer's New York *World* claims that Mary Baker Eddy is sick, senile, and incapacitated.

October 30   Reporters come to Pleasant View to verify her health.

November   *World* reporter persuades George Glover to join the paper in a suit being prepared by former Senator William Chandler to establish his mother's incapacity.

1907   *January*   *McClure's Magazine* begins series on Mary Baker Eddy.

January 2   George and Mary Glover interview Mary Baker Eddy.

February 18   Ralph Pulitzer withdraws the *World* from the suit.

March 1   Suit on behalf of Mary Baker Eddy, alleging misuse of her property and abuse of her person, is filed against ten church members by her "next friends," George W. Glover, Mary B. Glover, and George W. Baker (her nephew).

March 6   Mary Baker Eddy places her entire estate in trust.

March 11   Foster Eddy and Fred W. Baker (a cousin) join the suit.

Summer   Highly sympathetic and laudatory interviews with Mary Baker Eddy appear in major newspapers.

August 14   Court-appointed masters come to Pleasant View to determine whether Mrs. Eddy is competent.

August 21   Chandler withdraws the petition of the next friends.

August 25   Famous alienist Allen McLane Hamilton publishes account of an interview with Mrs. Eddy and pronounces her not only sane but remarkably intelligent and in full control.

1908   *January 26*   For more privacy and security, Mrs. Eddy moves to 384 (now 400) Beacon Street, Chestnut Hill, Boston.

August 8   Writes to the Trustees of the Publishing Society requesting that they begin a daily newspaper.

November 25   First issue of the *Christian Science Monitor.*

1909   *November 17*   Augusta Stetson is excommunicated.

1910   *November*   Mary Baker Eddy publishes *Poems.*

December 1   Last written words: "God is my life."

December 3   Mary Baker Eddy dies peacefully at the age of eighty-nine.

PART ONE

MARY BAKER GLOVER PATTERSON

1821 – 1862

1

Early Influences, Later Memories

O N   A   H O T ,   S U N N Y   J U L Y   D A Y   I N   1 8 2 1 ,   M A R Y   M O R S E
Baker was born in Bow, New Hampshire, in the little farmhouse
where her father and her own brothers and sisters had been born before her.[1]
The last of six children, Mary was born when her father, Mark Baker, was
thirty-five, and her mother, Abigail Ambrose Baker, thirty-six. Cheerful,
serene, self-sacrificing, and domestic, a pattern of womanhood, as her kins-
men and friends all agreed,[2] Mrs. Mark Baker was nowhere more exemplary
than in her regular, balanced, and healthy childbearing. She presented her
husband with three strong sons in neat succession, Samuel Dow in 1808,
Albert in 1810, and George Sullivan in 1812, and then went on to complete
the family with three daughters, Abigail Barnard in 1816, Martha Smith in
1819, and finally, in 1821, Mary Morse.[3] Rooted in their Anglo-American
heritage, the Bakers used traditional, unfanciful Christian names for their
children,[4] usually adding the family name of some close friend or relative as
a middle name to distinguish their George or Martha or Abigail from others.[5] Mary was a very common girl's name in the Bakers' social circle, yet the
choice of this name with its unique resonance in the Gospels was to have its
own significance to the woman whom we know as Mary Baker Eddy.[6]

By the standards of the day, Abigail and Mark Baker did not have a particularly large family. Mark himself was one of nine children, Abigail one of
seven, and by the time that Mary was born, Bakers, Ambroses, Moors,
McNeils, Dows, Smiths, Huntoons, Lovejoys, Whittemores, and other kin
were scattered over a good part of New England. Both Ambroses and Bakers

were sturdy stock, the Bow property was far from endemic centers of infection, and Mrs. Abigail Baker seems to have been an especially healthy and fortunate woman since she did not suffer the multiple miscarriages common among women of her time, and there is no record that she ever lost a child in infancy. Mark Baker seemed assured of the continuation of his family when, in due time, five of his children produced children of their own. In fact, however, only Mary, ironically long considered the frailest of the Baker offspring, produced a bloodline that continues to the present day.[7]

The farm where Mary Baker spent her first fourteen years was part of the original Lovewell or Lovell land grant in what are now the townships of Pembroke and Bow, New Hampshire. Captain John Lovewell was a military man, a great Indian fighter, after whom the 1722–1725 phase in the New England Indian wars was named. When he fell at the battle of Pigwacket, Maine, in 1725, his two sons and his daughter, Hannah, inherited equal shares in the land grant made to him,[8] and when Hannah Lovewell married Captain Joseph Baker, she made him the most important taxpayer in the district. Baker himself was the third of his line in New England, grandson of one Thomas Baker who had come in the 1630s from Lyminge in Kent to escape religious intolerance.[9] Hannah Lovewell Baker inherited no little of her father's fighting spirit as well as his property. In a story narrated in the *History of Pembroke,* Hannah was doing her washing in the stream when men came up to warn her that there was a threat of imminent Indian attack. Unflurried, she refused to stop her work, the men went back to the stockade, and Hannah finally walked to safety on her own, carrying her clean, wet wash.[10]

Hannah's eldest son, also named Joseph Baker, married Mary Ann McNeil Moore, a woman of Scottish ancestry and Covenanter tradition, who presented him with nine children, seven of whom lived to adulthood. One picturesque family story concerned a Scottish ancestress, Christian Kenney McNeil.

> His [Capt. Joseph Baker, Jr.'s] wife was Mary Ann or Marion Moore, daughter of Marion McNeil Moore and William Moore. Marion McNeil was daughter of Christian Kenney McNeil and John McNeil who came from Hillsborough, Scotland. John McNeil was a stalwart man of Herculean strength and his wife was almost his equal. It is related that upon one occasion a stranger came to the door and inquired for McNeil. Christian told him that her 'gude mon' was not at home, upon which the stranger expressed much regret. Christian inquired as to the business upon which he came, and the stranger told her he had heard a good deal of the strength of McNeil and his skill in wrestling, and he had come some considerable distance to throw him. "An troth, mon," said Christian McNeil, "Johnny is gone, but I'm not the woman to see ya disappointed, an' I think if ye'll try, mon, I'll throw ye mee-

self." The stranger, not liking to be thus bantered by a woman, accepted the challenge and sure enough, Christian tripped his heels and threw him upon the ground. The stranger, upon getting up, thought he would not wait for "Johnny" but left without deigning to leave his name.[11]

Even though Mary Baker was the youngest child of a youngest child, she shared thirteen years of her life with her paternal grandmother, living in the house to which that grandmother had come as a bride, and forming a close relationship to her. The rocking chair is a motif that will recur throughout the story of Mary Baker Eddy's life, and later in life Mrs. Eddy was to remember herself as a tiny girl sitting in her little rocking chair next to her grannie.[12] To little Mary, Mrs. Mary Ann Baker was a living link with the pioneer world of Hannah Lovewell, Mary Ann's mother-in-law, with the time when New Hampshire was the frontier, and men and women worked together and faced such dangers as marauding Indians. Mary Ann Baker was also a source of precious secular reading matter for a granddaughter who loved reading more than her father thought was good for her, and who lived in a home where books were prized but scarce and mainly of a religious and educational nature.[13] As Mrs. Eddy tells it in the first pages of her 1891 autobiographical essay, *Retrospection and Introspection,* in her grandmother's trunk there was an ancient rusty sword but also tales of the Covenanters, famous for their brave and doomed passion for religious autonomy. There were scriptural sonnets and enigmas written by Mary Ann's foremother, who, Mary Ann insisted, was related to the famous English authoress Hannah More. There were yellowing newspapers from the Revolutionary War era, one of which narrated the death of George Washington.[14]

In the passage of her autobiographical essay where Mrs. Eddy recalls the contents of her grandmother's trunk and the stories she associates with that old lady, she points to themes that threaded through her whole life. There is the theme of women who were strong in their religious faith, in their fruitful bodies, in their property rights, in their talents—women who were helpmates rather than dependents. Mary Baker Eddy was to struggle all her life to find out how to live up to the traditions of her female ancestors in a nineteenth-century world where women were increasingly valued for frailty not strength. Then there is the Covenanter theme of strong religious faith, intransigent will, and a determination to trace one's own religious path, whatever opposition and criticism one might meet. In the old Revolutionary War newspapers there is the theme of American patriotism and of commitment to the public arena. Finally, there is the theme of authorship, of text as the crucial repository of wisdom, an instrument to link people separated by time and space. Mary Baker Eddy would succeed in large part through her brilliant and innovative use of books and magazines.

The important collection of early Baker family papers contained in the

Longyear Museum[15] shows that Mary Ann Moore Baker remained a vital family member in the Bow farmhouse where Mary Baker grew up not just because of her energetic character and venerable life but because, under the provisions of her husband's will, she retained a major economic stake in the family property. Widowhood often leaves a woman uncomfortably dependent on the goodwill of her family, and elderly women with failing strength can be as much resented for their current demands on the family resources as revered for their earlier contributions.[16] The legal documents at Longyear which relate to Mary Ann Moore Baker offer a fascinating glimpse into the difficult social and economic issues faced by women in their later years even when families were loving and solvent. Her grandmother's long years of widowhood offered Mary a lesson in survival that she would live to heed.

Joseph Baker had been a loving and provident husband to Mary Ann since he had used the full resources of the law to endow his widow, rather than simply leaving her care to the dutiful attention of their children. Well before his death, old Joseph divided up his lands among his sons and then leased some of them back. At the same time, he gave his wife a life interest in much of the family land. Joseph's will of 1815 thus refers to the disposition of only his remaining property—his house, his stock, agricultural equipment, furniture and personal belongings such as a desk and the pew at the Bow meetinghouse. The will is mainly concerned with establishing guarantees of his widow's personal comfort and care. Joseph bequeaths "unto my beloved wife Mary Ann Baker the use and occupancy of such part of the House as I now occupy and the use of all the furniture I now own—also the use of two cows and two sheep during her natural life, and also the use of a horse when she wants. Also the entire use and diposal of such other part of the personal estate as is not hereinafter disposed of."[17] Mark Baker, the youngest child of Joseph Baker, was to inherit a large part of the family farm after his mother's death, the rest would go to his nephew Aaron, but he was also charged with chief responsibility for her care in return for his larger inherited portion.

An agreement signed on January 7, 1829, between Mark Baker and Aaron Baker makes it clear that Mark and Aaron were in dispute over the care of Mary Ann, and that the commitments enjoined under Joseph's will needed to be spelled out further. Thus Mark agrees,

> that he will take good care of his Mother during her natural life except when she is sick so as to need nursing and then the said Mark is to give the said Aaron Information of her situation and the said Aaron is to do one half of the nursing and to pay one half of the Dr's bills by the said Mark's being at the expense of Boarding one person that is taking care of her more then what he requires the said Aaron to do, and if by old age she grows ever so feble the said Aaron is to do nothing more then

he hereafter agrees to do. (the true meaning of this Instrument is that the said Marke is to take all of the care and cloth his Mother while she remains except when she is raly sick) In case watchers are necessary the said Aaron is to be at one half of their expence.

For his part, Aaron agrees

to find one half of the wood that is necessary for her use at the door of her house choped up fit for the fire and to give the said Mark at his House one sixth part of the Cider and Apples that grows on land that ever was his fathers, one Dollars worth of wheat flour four Bushel of Rye Ten Bushel of Corn that is good and fit for table, Ten Bushel of Ears of Corn that is of the second quality for Hogs etc. Ten Bushel of Oats Ten Bushel of potatoes, six Cabbage Heads and one peck of onions.

Mary Ann Moore Baker lived to be ninety-one, and the legal battles with Aaron Baker over his contributions to her upkeep were no doubt one of the hottest subjects of discussion in the Mark Baker household in Bow. From the life of their paternal grandmother, Mary's brothers, especially George, were learning that the care of dependent women could be a heavy duty. Mary and her sisters, on the other hand, were learning that they too might need the law on their side, especially if they remained single or were later widowed.

In 1835 Mary Ann Baker finally died, and all the property in which she had a life interest reverted at last to her sons. Both Mark and his brother Phillip decided to sell their land at Bow and purchase new farms in Sanbornton Bridge, a small but prosperous town with a growing textile industry.[18] The old Lovewell property was later reunited in part by the much despised Aaron Baker, who, it seems, cared about family property and, unlike his male relatives, actually enjoyed farming the land he had inherited as a relatively young man.[19]

Mary Baker was only in her mid-teens when her family left Bow, but she seems to have retained fonder memories and stronger connections to the family acres than her siblings did. Certainly, when, in the 1880s, she decided to leave Boston and retire from the everyday management of her church, inclination led Mary Baker Eddy back to the area around Concord, New Hampshire, only a few miles from her birthplace, and she eventually settled on an estate she would name Pleasant View. She would spend fifteen years of her life in this commodious but unpretentious house, not isolated, but set close to the high road, and with a distant view of the Bow hills. Mrs. Eddy's Christian Science followers worked the land and tilled the garden as well as serving her in the house, and it is clear that she took great pleasure in managing her acreage as carefully but more lovingly than her father had his in Bow. In her home on the outskirts of Concord, Mrs. Eddy certainly sought seclusion, but seclusion within the beloved and sustaining setting of field and forest and hill. The framework of cousinage was also there, and she was able, when and if she wished, to pick up some of the threads of the thick and complex fabric of extended family life she had known in her youth.

Public records, family letters, account books, and town chronicles offer a skeleton of Mary Baker's childhood years in Bow, but we have little to put flesh on the bones. Mary Baker Eddy was in her sixties before she became a subject of public interest, and by then most of her parental generation had passed on. When, toward the end of the nineteenth century, people aggressively started to collect information about Mrs. Eddy's life, all her siblings were dead, and only a handful of close relatives remained. None of her own generation of family members wrote memoirs about their lives in the 1820s and 1830s. Mrs. Eddy's own son George Washington Glover II had been separated from her when he was a boy and had little contact with her or her family thereafter; thus he was not an important repository of family information about his mother's youth.

Thus, for first-person testimony to the Bow years, we have only what Mrs. Eddy herself left us—a few pages in her memoir and some odd anecdotes she confided in her last years. Like most memoirs written by public figures in mid-career, *Retrospection and Introspection* was framed by debate and public scrutiny at the time of its appearance. It was motivated less by the author's nostalgia and desire for self-expression than by the need to promote the nascent and vulnerable Christian Science movement and to define her own highly contested role as a religious leader. Even Mrs. Eddy's private memories cannot be set outside the context of her religious mission, since they were recorded by men and women who had been chosen to serve in her household because of their exceptional faith in Christian Science and reverence for its founder and leader. Unblessed with literary talent and unconcerned with aesthetic values or reportorial objectivity, they recorded in their own diaries the things their beloved leader said which seemed significant to them.

Unsurprisingly, then, Mary Baker Eddy's own memories as an old woman of these first years of her life in Bow, as recorded by her own pen or entrusted to others, are of a largely religious nature.[20] She reported that once, as a small child, she had overheard her mother confiding in her friend Sarah Gault that when she was pregnant with Mary, she had had an intuition that this child was destined for great and spiritual things. Given little Mary Baker's later career, these words were obviously influential.[21] In keeping with this saintly promise, Mrs. Eddy remembered herself as an earnestly religious child—earning a reproof from her parents when she gave her clothes away to children less fortunate than herself, running down to try to sing the squealing pigs to sleep, giving up to her father all the precious chestnuts she had gathered, trying to outdo the prophet Daniel by praying to God not three times a day, but seven. More picturesquely, she told of how she had stood up to another, bigger girl in school, a bully who was forcing the littler children to drink from a cucumber hollowed out and filled with mud, but then that child became her friend.[22]

Four of Mrs. Eddy's childhood memories are of especial importance, both in themselves and for the critical reactions they have occasioned. The first is an incident that Mrs. Eddy confided soon before her death to one of her secretaries at Chestnut Hill, William Rathvon. Her father, Mark Baker, was a deeply religious man who led his family in prayer every morning. The family would kneel as Mark, who had a very loud voice, engaged in lengthy and extemporaneous praying. One day the child Mary, unable to kneel quietly any longer,

> took a long shawl pin from the pincushion on the table, crawled along the floor until she got behind the chair where he was kneeling and vehemently exhorting, applied the pin at a point where it brought immediate results, and in the confusion that followed made her escape.[23]

To stab your father in the behind with a long pin while he is leading the family in prayer is not an example of the early natural piety expected of a future religious leader. Yet this story strikes me as epigrammatic for a woman who, as we shall see in this book, will take the members of the male religious establishment on at their own game, putting together a religion that, like the pin from her mother's pincushion, would shock, pain, and confuse them. Mrs. Eddy's decision in her years of authority to allow no extempore preaching in her church and her commitment to silent prayer bear some relation to her rebellion against her father's loud and wordy form of worship.

The second two important stories can be found in *Retrospection and Introspection*. They are much more devotional and are clearly influenced by Mrs. Eddy's reading of the Bible and by her search for authority as a religious leader. The first story, entitled "Voices Not Our Own," tells of how in her eighth year Mary repeatedly heard a voice "calling me distinctly, by name, three times in an ascending scale." Interestingly, Mary takes the voice to be her mother (not her father) calling her, but Mrs. Abigail Baker insists she has not called out. At last Mary's cousin Mehitable Huntoon also hears the voice, asks Mary why she makes no response, and then goes to tell Mrs. Baker. Now convinced by this impartial witness that the voice is real, Mrs. Baker reads to Mary the story of the child Samuel and urges her to reply as Samuel had done, "Speak, Lord, for thy servant heareth." When finally Mary gains the courage to do as her mother has bidden and says Samuel's words of commitment to the divine will, the voice is still. "Never again to the material senses was that mysterious call repeated" Mary Baker Eddy later wrote (*Ret.*, p. 9).[24]

Mrs. Eddy then goes on, in the chapter "Theological Reminiscence," to narrate an event from her twelfth year that clearly parallels Christ's meeting with the elders in the Temple.

> At the age of twelve I was admitted to the Congregational (Trinitarian) Church, my parents having been members of that body for a half-century. In connection with this event, some circumstances are noteworthy. Before this step was taken, the doctrine of unconditional election, or predestination, greatly troubled me; for I was unwilling to be saved, if my brothers and sisters were to be numbered among those who were doomed to perpetual banishment from God. So perturbed was I by the thoughts aroused by this erroneous doctrine, that the family doctor was summoned, and pronounced me stricken with fever. (*Ret.*, p. 13)

According to her account, nursed by her mother who urges her to turn to God, Mary prays, and at once the fever leaves her, she dresses and emerges fully cured, much to the amazement of her attending physician.

These two stories have become foundational myths in Christian Science, but they have been received with deep skepticism by those outside the faith. To the religious, it is clearly acceptable, even doctrinally enjoined, to believe that God has at different times spoken directly to men and women. Such individuals may, like Joan of Arc, have suffered death for claiming to have heard the voice of God, but, in the end, those claims have been believed. Mary Baker Eddy, unfortunately, does not fit the usual mold of female sainthood; she was neither an ascetic virgin, starving her way into holiness like Catherine of Siena, nor the revered head of a religious order, dictating mystic visions to her confessor like Teresa of Ávila. When she recorded this revelation in her memoir, she was instead known to be an elderly New Hampshire woman, twice widowed and once divorced, who preferred to forget the twenty-some years she lived on the fringes of respectable society. That such a woman should claim experiences comparable to those of the maid of Orleans or the great Hebrew prophet has proved unacceptable to many religious people and has provoked the cruel invective of many.

The critiques of Mrs. Eddy's childhood memories have taken various tacks. Some have wondered why, if little Mary discovered the secret of healing her fevers through prayer at the age of twelve, she had to rediscover it again in 1866, after her famous fall in Lynn. Milmine and her collaborators were able to cite the records of the Sanbornton church to show that Mary became a church member at the age of seventeen, not twelve, and they portray the whole story of her struggle with the elders and their doctrines as a ridiculous, self-aggrandizing, sacrilegious fabrication.

In fact, more recent documentary research has shown that as far as church membership goes, the gap in years between Mrs. Eddy's recollection and the contemporary records is much less than Milmine and Cather claimed. A letter Albert Baker wrote to Mary in March 1837—that is, four months before her sixteenth birthday—proves that she had had a conversion experience during a revival meeting that winter and had already decided to apply for church membership. The Baker family papers prove definitively that none of Mary's elder brothers and sisters had experienced a conversion and applied for membership in the church, so within the doctrinal context she was educated in Mary would have had reason to fear for their salvation. In his 1837 letter Albert Baker commented on how important Mary's decision to seek church membership was felt to be by the family, and he reassured her that he was in no way angry with her for taking the step at such a young age, and before her older siblings. Apart from the revival of 1836 or 1837, the Congregational church records show that a very important and emotional revival meeting occurred near Bow when Mary was about twelve, and it is possible that she may have "come forward" to declare her faith in public at that point, as was not uncommon for children of her age. This moment may have been the spiritual turning point in her life when she committed herself to the church, even though she was unable to gain membership officially until she was seventeen.[25]

The available evidence also strongly supports Mrs. Eddy when she claims in *Retrospection and Introspection* that theological debates of a fervent nature were part of her everyday experience as a child, and that she listened to them with passionate interest and understanding. Interest in doctrine was characteristic of New Englanders of this period, and, ill-educated and unsophisticated as they perhaps were, the Bakers and their kin were vigorously engaged in the great theological issues of their time, notably the discussion of free will and the new doctrines of Unitarianism. Cousin Joseph Baker, writing to George in 1833, remarks bitterly on the family's treatment of him when he converted to Universalism and became a preacher in that sect. Asked once by one of her household many years later if she had not been wearied by these lengthy theological debates, Mrs. Eddy replied in substance:

> Never—I always wanted to know who won. It was always my joy to listen to a sermon or to hear a discussion upon a Bible subject. After hearing it, I would go over it again and again and pray over it far into the night. Even in my childhood days, I would much rather study the Bible or listen to a discussion of it than to go out to play with the children. After school I would seat myself in the rocker, and while I rocked read the Psalms of David or the life of the Master.[26]

The incidental reference Mrs. Eddy makes here to her rocker, and her habit of *reading her Bible while rocking* is an important one I think. In her seventies and eighties, every day, Mrs. Eddy would go out onto the closed veranda at Pleasant View and spend time reading, thinking, talking, looking out into the distance, in her porch swing. Rocking chairs or swings, as we shall see, will feature in every room Mrs. Eddy called her own, and they form a small but significant part of Christian Science iconography. One of the many injustices of the Milmine biography is that the writers seek to give Mrs. Eddy's love of swings and rockers some kind of sinister, even pathological, significance. It seems clear to me that Mary Baker Eddy found in rocking a source of comfort—a reminder of home, of her mother and her grand-mother—and also an aid to meditation and prayer.

To return, however, to Mrs. Eddy's childhood, and her exposure to the-ology, it is wholly likely, given the history of Protestant doctrine in the first half of the nineteenth century, that the traditional Calvinist doctrine of pre-destination was discussed constantly in the Baker home and was a source of conflict between the generations and possibly between the sexes. Mrs. Eddy's father, Mark Baker, spent hours of the night arguing with his nephew Aaron over doctrine because he was convinced that Aaron would go to hell if he adopted the new Universalist ideas. What has been called the femi-nization of American religion in the nineteenth century is strongly associated with the abandonment of strict Calvinist concepts of grace and the redemp-tion of the elect.[27]

In my view, Mary Baker Eddy is acute when she dates her disputes with her father and her subsequent relapse into illness to her twelfth year, the age when girls were assumed to be leaving childhood behind. Her story is sup-ported by all that we know about the Baker family's life and about Mrs. Eddy's later career. Even at the age of twelve, Mary was the admitted book-worm of the family, and she was treated, as all sources agree, with unusual favor and forbearance by her father. Her lifelong interest in religion has never been disputed, nor has her extraordinary willingness to challenge traditional religious ideas, and there is every reason to assume that these propensities, nourished in a very religious environment, would find expression as early as the twelfth year.[28] Of all the children, she was the one most likely to speak up and challenge her father, especially when she was convinced that the eter-nal salvation of her beloved and unconverted siblings was at stake.

That she might fall ill when her outspokenness met with paternal dis-approval and censure is, again, far from unlikely. Mary was always consid-ered a particularly fragile child by her family, and, as we shall show in detail in the next chapters, her elder siblings George, Abigail, and Martha all tended to become ill when life proved troublesome. I therefore accept her story that she fell into a fever when she found she had crossed the line at which her father could look at her with indulgence. The association she makes between the moment her fever broke and turning to the Bible at her mother's suggestion also seems convincing to me. Mary Baker was changing from precocious petted child to young woman, and she had to learn the hard lesson that women might, like Abigail Baker, read their Bibles, but they might not speak in church or pray aloud. Faith was enjoined upon them, but theology was forbidden.

The fourth and final story-memory from Mary Baker Eddy's childhood, offers us brief but vital testimony on the relationship Mary had with her parents as a child, and on how she was beginning to frame her relationship to God within the parental context:

> Her mother had taught her to say, after she had been punished for any naughtiness, "I am sorry and will not do so again." One day, when sorely troubled by doubts, she asked her mother whether she thought that eternal punishment really was true.
>
> Her mother sighed deeply and answered, "Mary, I suppose it *is*."
>
> "What if we repent," said Mary, "and tell God 'we are sorry and will not do so again'—will God punish us? Then He is not as good as my mother and He will find me a hard case."[29]

2

Father
and Brothers

*I find the retrospect of departed years afford but little solid
satisfaction yet when I reflect and remember the days when our
Family Circle were compos'd of six children with tallents (pardon
me) and voices sufficient to raise a Mothers heart to Heaven I feel
to thank <u>God</u> for what he has done for them but O how have we
all perverted our tallents*

—ABIGAIL AMBROSE BAKER[1]

FARMING HIS OWN LAND HAD NO DOUBT BEEN A STEP UP FOR
the first Joseph Baker, but for his great-grandsons Samuel, Albert, and
George the five-hundred-acre Bow farm was a heritage that they no longer
prized.[2] Mary Baker Eddy's older brothers had no romantic attachment to
the family land and were indeed unalterably determined not to spend their
lives "diging on a farm . . . for a sustenance," as the young Abigail Baker put
it in a letter to her brother George in 1835. Even their father, Mark, was anxious to sell the beautiful but unrewarding acres in Bow as soon as he could.
Change was in the air in New Hampshire in the 1820s, and the talented, energetic, ambitious Baker children proved eager to trade in the familiar life of
hardscrabble farming for the dangerous opportunities of the rapidly indus-
trializing towns.[3] There was a legacy of independence and mobility in these
descendants of dissenting immigrants, and to follow in the footsteps of their

forefathers meant to refuse tradition and initiate a new way of life rather than to follow in the old. That we have so much detailed information about the Bakers in the 1830s and onward is, indeed, owing to the fact that in 1835 they cut off their ancestral roots in Bow and began to scatter all over New England. Separated by miles but still bound by affection, the Bakers engaged in a spate of letter writing.

So much has been made in earlier biographies of the exceptional piety of Mary Baker Eddy's family that I feel the need to stress that the Bakers were not boring cardboard saints or, worse, Pecksniffian bigots, but people of great natural vitality, eager for life, quick to explore, ready for fun and good company, trying to make their religion work in a rapidly changing world.[4] Questioning was, indeed, more characteristic of the Baker children than was conformity, and the youngest, Mary, inherited not only her mother's natural spirituality and her father's passionate interest in theology, but her brothers' rebelliousness. The letters which Albert and George wrote as young men give indications that there was a Baker style of talking and writing which Mary would later perfect—a salty mix of spirituality and practicality, of scriptural quotation and dry wit. One of the secrets of Mary Baker Eddy's extraordinary success was the Baker style of conversation, that, to the very end of her life, surprised and delighted her interlocutors.

In her memoir Mrs. Eddy noted that her father "kept his family in the tightest harness I have ever known."[5] This was no doubt true, and living with Mark Baker was certainly difficult. Nonetheless, the Baker papers make it clear that the relationships and the balance of power between the generations was much more complex in the Mark Baker household than earlier biographers have made it appear. It would be a mistake to think of Mark as one of those gloomy Protestant patriarchs immortalized in the fiction of Nathaniel Hawthorne, Charles Dickens, or Samuel Butler—tyrannizing his meek wife and quelling the spirit of his children.[6]

An able and energetic man, Mark Baker served his God and his country tirelessly as the counsel for Bow, as surveyor of roads (following in the tradition of his surveyor grandfather, Joseph Baker Sr.), as acting chaplain to the regiment of local militia, as school board member, town meeeting moderator, and selectman. All this work no doubt involved a lot of correspondence, and in one of the odd little autobiographical remarks she recorded about her childhood, Mary Baker Eddy told her son George Washington Glover II in a letter of December 21, 1896, that when her father had lost his finger, she served as his secretary. She declared proudly that she had mastered the official style of penmanship, and no one was able to distinguish her letters from those of a man.[7] The hours Mark Baker put in on behalf of his church and his community were of course in addition to his own work, which included farming his own acres and, with the active collaboration of his family, producing, over the years, wood, hay, oats, wool, potatoes, pumpkins, cabbages, cider, vinegar, butter, cheese, bundles of cornstalks, pork, veal, beef, skins, and soap, for home use and for barter. When he had time, Mark Baker also bartered his labor, helping out his neighbors by mending shoes, shingling, plowing, framing, hauling, planting, cutting and binding stalks, sowing, chopping wood, honing scythes, and breaking in roads.[8]

By any standards, Mark was a man of considerable talents, but his opportunities for self-realization had been limited, and it is not surprising that differences arose between him and his sons. These differences are candidly expressed in this letter from Albert Baker to his younger brother George Sullivan in December 15, 1835, when their father was just selling up in Bow and preparing for the move to Sanbornton Bridge.

> I came from Bow, last week, after a stay of several days, and left them all in their usual health. The girls told me they have written to you while I was there. Father is driving about like a thunder storm. Poor man I pity him. He thinks, because he can get away from Bow, he can get away from trouble, but I fear he will be disappointed. He can manage a farm pretty well, to keep clear of debt, and bring the year round even, but he is the least qualified to make money of any man that ever I saw of his natural abilities. He knows nothing of the world, and can be duped by the tricks of every knave, that will undertake to practice upon him. For his sake, I am glad he has sold, and purchased where he likes, and if he is contented, it is all I ask; the rest of us can take care of ourselves. . . . One thing is certain, if you have saved your money, you have done better the past year than to have stayed at home, for father has done all that both of you would have done, and you have your wages left. If you return home, I can tell you as I ever have, and with no fear but the event will prove what I say, that you will never do any thing, till you take upon yourself the management of the business, and manage it right. Father works like a slave, but he don't know how to manage.[9]

We see a huge generation gap opening up here. How coolly—and incorrectly, given George's disastrous later history—the son measures the father's abilities and achievements. How little the son seeks to emulate the father! The cold, rationalist eloquence of the educated Albert's pen is in strong contrast with Mark's dour, unpunctuated Calvinist scrawl. In this note written to George in 1850, after the Bakers had moved from the farm into a town house in Sanbornton and Mark's prudent investment had brought him a modest fortune, Mark was still saving and making do:

> I will send you fifty dollars more if that will do you speak of my labour I am obliged to labour I have Martha and children and Mary to maintain and a hired Gurl to give a dollar a week and so I must with might to keep from poverty right off.[10]

If Mark Baker's political conservatism and unwavering commitment to the Protestant work ethic made his three sons' lives difficult when they were young, he had to bear a good deal from them in turn when they became adults because none of the three cared to follow either his example or his advice. Mark Baker's financial fortunes improved notably over the course of his life, in good part owing to his own hard work and shrewd policies, but his fortunes within his family did not always fare as well as his investments, and all of his sons disappointed him.

The eldest son, Samuel, left home, probably in his late teens, to work as a building contractor in Boston.[11] Information about Samuel is in general scarce since there is no extant letter from or to him. All we know for sure about Samuel is that he was first married to Elizabeth Glover, had two children with her, also called Elizabeth and Samuel,[12] was widowed, and then married Mary Ann Cook. Until the latter years of his life, Samuel returned to New Hampshire only for short, infrequent visits. The extant letters from the early Sanbornton Bridge/Tilton period hint that the relations between the Bakers in Tilton and the Bakers in Boston were somewhat strained. Visits by the Baker parents and their other children to Samuel's family in Boston also seem to have been infrequent. Later letters indicate that Samuel may have had a drinking problem until his second marriage, and that early in his life he had strayed from the path of religious orthodoxy as his family understood it. Although he was the eldest son, Samuel does not seem to have been involved in the decisions about the family property that are constantly referred to in the Baker letters, and my guess is that his father had written him off. Of all the family members, Samuel probably played the least important part in the childhood of his sister Mary, thirteen years his junior, but he was to be instrumental in introducing her to two very important men in her life: George Washington Glover, Mary's first husband, was the brother of Samuel's first wife, and it was Samuel and his second wife, Mary Ann, who escorted Mary on her first visit to Phineas Parkhurst Quimby.[13]

Albert, the second son, may have had more difficulty than Samuel in making the break from the Bow farm, and he certainly returned more often to lend a hand when needed, as well as to recuperate from his frequent bouts of illness. Nonetheless, Albert also made a complete break from his father's way of life. When Albert wrote to George so disparagingly about their father's ability to "manage," he was only twenty-five but had been out in the world earning his own way since graduating from Pembroke Academy in 1829 at the age of eighteen, and he was at the time committed to making his way as a lawyer and a politician. Albert's decision to go in for the law probably sat well with his father since Mark Baker's own personal talents leaned more toward the church and law than toward agriculture. Nonetheless, Mark's taste for the law and his sympathy with his second son's ambitions did not extend to paying out hard cash for his son's legal training. Albert had to work with his brains as hard as ever his ancestors had worked with their brawn to earn the money to put himself through Dartmouth College and then to qualify for the New Hampshire and Massachusetts bars.

In her last years, Mary Baker Eddy described her brother Albert as a tall, commanding man with a massive head, high forehead, chestnut hair, clear brown eyes, and a glorious tenor voice. Still filled with sisterly love and admiration for this long-dead brother, she remarked that he was once mistaken in the legislature for Andrew Jackson, and that he had the manners of a Chesterfield (a reference to one of her favorite eighteenth-century authors from the Lindley Murray reader) and the tenderness of a woman.[14] The letters so lovingly kept by her brother George and now preserved at the Longyear Museum show Albert to be not only a tender man but one with great talent, ambition, and drive. Already in the Latin oration he wrote and delivered when graduating from Dartmouth College in 1834, a hint of originality emerges from the flowery and hackneyed rhetoric. In that speech Albert makes grudging acknowledgment of the presence of the trustees, whom he seems to criticize for taking no day-to-day interest in student life, and in his reference to his fellows as "*diu in aulis academicis seclusi*" (long secluded in academic halls) there is a suggestion of pent-up energy. A fellow student at Dartmouth later recalled that Albert held strong and individual opinions and would sometimes argue vigorously with the professors in the recitation rooms.[15]

In his private letters to his younger brother, Albert is the hardheaded man of the world, eschewing rhetoric and pious sentiment and offering advice of a generally cynical kind. Thus in a letter dated July 31, 1835, he takes up the canonical theme of friendship so often treated in student exercises and gives it a very different turn:

> I will tell you what it is, this world of ours, is no dumb-show, acted for the amusement or benefit of those that stand by as idle spectators. If we would make anything of the game, we must play it ourselves, and play it dexterously, not ever trusting another to look into our hand. Friendship! I am glad you have found out the meaning of that word, for, if there is any truth in God, that is a sound without signification. It has no archetype, no likeness, no not even a resemblance, on earth. I would not give a "whore's-tird" for the friendship of all the men that ever lived, any farther than it will subserve their own interest.

The letters to his sisters, which would have been read by all at home, are notably more circumspect and moralizing.

Not just the law, but politics constituted Albert's goal, and he knew that for a man of obscure origins such as himself, higher education was merely a necessary but insufficient first step toward the political life.[16] Patronage offered the next rung up the ladder, and recognizing this, Albert successfully endeared himself to the family of former New Hampshire Governor Benjamin Pierce. The Pierces were distantly related to the Bakers, and young Franklin Pierce, Albert's friend and contemporary, was clearly on the political fast track, even when he was a very young lawyer fresh out of Bowdoin. Albert moved in with the older Pierces, and for some years he served as Franklin Pierce's law partner and chief aide in Hillsborough, New Hampshire, when Pierce was in Washington. Albert was a surrogate son to the elder Pierces in their last years, and for a time he served as tutor to the son of their daughter, Mrs. Betsy McNeil, the wife of the famous General John McNeil.[17] In return, he lived for some time rent-free in the prosperous and agreeable Pierce home in Hillsborough, also gaining an entrée for himself and his sisters into the higher social circles in which the Pierces moved. More significantly, Albert also began to move slowly up the political trail Franklin had blazed. In 1837 the young Baker was elected to the New Hampshire assembly, where he rapidly became one of the most notable and controversial members.

In his student essays and the drafts of speeches he delivered in his last years, Albert emerges as a more original thinker and fiery orator than was his friend Franklin Pierce, the future president, who was already famous during Albert's lifetime for being the youngest U.S. senator ever elected. Like Pierce, Albert Baker was no friend to the growing abolitionist movement; in fact, perhaps the most lasting and least attractive part of Albert's political legacy to his family was his resistance to the movement to abolish slavery.[18] In other ways, however, Albert was more radical than Pierce. He was a leader of the New Democrats group in New Hampshire and an impassioned supporter of the rights of small farmers in opposition to the new railroad barons who were buying up the countryside.

Albert seemed destined for great things, but he had one enemy that could not be conquered—his own ill health. The poignancy of his life can be felt in the April 1837 letter he wrote to George from Sanbornton:

Dear Brother,
    You will be surprised at seeing the place from which my letter is dated. But so it is. I left the Hospital at Boston last Thursday, and what now, I cannot tell. . . . I had confined myself to the Office almost exclusively, through the fall and winter, and this occasioned a return of my old complaints, with increased severity. I scarcely survived. For several days I was almost entirely insensible, and think I must have died had they not carried me to the Hospital. I have now abandoned study forever, till my health is better. . . . I accomplished more while in Boston than ever before, and am now reaping the fruits of my labour. I have given up all thoughts of the West.[19] The rest of my life will probably be spent in <u>hoeing potatoes</u>. I think I shall stay in Sandbornton, and be

father's homestead.[20] Is not that worth spending eight years for?
Strange the vicissitudes of my fortune. Last fall I thought the old dame
within my grasp, but she has escaped me again, and I am the same cheer-
less wretch that I have always been. But I never yet have repined, and
never shall.

In 1841 Albert Baker won his party's nomination for the congressional
seat, a nomination that at that time guaranteed his eventual success at the
polls. Before the congressional election could take place, however, Albert
died on October 21, 1841, apparently of kidney failure. George's diary entry
notes that a postmortem examination revealed that Albert "had but one kidney and that swollen to an enormous size, weighing 2½ [pounds] and so
affected that an entire separation had taken place and collections of what is
term'd 'Pus' pervaded the whole organ."

Albert Baker was eulogized in obituaries in the New Hampshire papers
as one of the most promising lawyers and politicians of his generation. One
notice is all the more remarkable in that it was published in *Hill's Patriot,* a
weekly paper owned and largely written by Albert's bitter political enemy
Isaac Hill:

> Perhaps there was no young man in the State who filled a larger space
> in the public eye, and from whom his many friends had higher expec-
> tations, than Mr. Baker. His practice at the bar was scarcely second to
> any attorney of his county. As a legislator and a politician he was ardent
> and uncompromising, carrying his opinions of right to a point which
> led to the greatest success; as a student and a scholar, he was indefati-
> gable, leaving no abstruse and complicated subject until he had ana-
> lyzed and laid it bare.

Even after his death, Albert Baker remained a deeply controversial
political figure, and Isaac Hill in private was far less complimentary about
his former rival. Hill went so far as to claim that Albert had died impiously,
cursing fate, and ranting about politics to the end.[21] Hill charged that Albert
Baker even on his deathbed was still indiscriminately attacking the presiding
officer of the New Hampshire House "whose place he wanted," refusing to
accept that he was about to die, and of "a similar monomania to that which
has distinguished Joseph Mormon [*sic*] in his system."[22]

If, indeed, Albert Baker did find it hard to embrace death with pious
fortitude, I for one find it easy to forgive him. Bereft of religious zeal, he
seems, from the limited information available to us, to have lived yet like a
monk in his cell, deaf to the calls of the flesh. Then, when success seemed his
at last, death snatched all away. George Sullivan Baker, who was with Albert
in Hillsborough when he died and served as executor of his will, was filled
with anger and bitterness when Isaac Hill's attacks made his dead brother
the subject of barroom innuendo. George insisted in letters to several friends

and in a letter to the New Hampshire *Patriot and State Gazette* of March 31, 1842, that Albert had made a calm and Christian end. In his diary, which is at the Longyear Foundation, George noted: "Singular as it may seem, at his death no muscle mov'd—no nerve trembled but he slept in death, his last breath being like that of one in sweet sleep, nor did he gasp for more! So may his soul rest, until awaken'd to everlasting joy." The Baker family was devastated by Albert's death, and the continuing controversy surrounding him made bearing the loss more difficult. It is hard to overestimate the importance of making a good Christian death for New England society at this period, especially for a devout, respectable, and upwardly mobile family like the Bakers.[23]

Mary Baker Eddy often said that Albert was her favorite brother, and one cannot overestimate the effect on her of his early death at age thirty-one. Through her brother, Mary as an impressionable teenager had an insight into the world of law and politics, a glimpse of a world more educated, more cultured, more powerful, and larger in scope than her father's world. Politics, as a social practice and a way of life as well as a system of ideas, held much more fascination for Mary Baker Eddy than is usually supposed, and there is no doubt that her interest was sparked from childhood. Personally, Albert represented a masculine ideal to his little sister, an ideal that she would seek, largely in vain, to find again in her future husbands, colleagues, students, sons. His intellect, his personality, his achievements set a standard against which she would judge not only other men, but, more important, herself.[24]

Mary grieved for Albert, and in some deep, secret part of her she accepted the challenge of succeeding where Albert had failed. Like her brother, she was tall, handsome, chestnut haired and hazel eyed, brilliant of mind, engaging of manner, the kind of person people notice and remember. Though she would go on to experience as an old woman the agony of kidney pain that had tortured Albert in his last years, she would live long enough to find her way.

After Albert's death, Mary Baker turned with even greater affection and need to her third brother, the one closest to her age and known to her most intimately. The departure from home of his elder brothers had left George with a problem he was deeply unwilling to face. By forging new lives and new careers for themselves, Samuel and Albert had followed a pattern which some of their paternal uncles had already sketched out, and which their father to some extent at least understood and even approved. Their departure made sense given that division of the family acreage between too many sons would create nonviable economic units and lead to the kinds of disputes Mark Baker had had with his brother's son, Aaron. A house as small as the old Baker homestead could not readily accommodate the energies of too many large, self-willed, opinionated men.[25] But Mark was counting on one son to fulfill in the new generation the role he himself had played for the family—that is to say, staying at home, working the family estate, and eventually inheriting the privileges and responsibilities that went with it.

Unfortunately, George was as anxious as his brothers to get away from home, and his opportunity arrived when he became involved in a minor scandal.[26] This incident made such inroads in George's health that even though it was the hay season, Mark Baker grudgingly consented to let his son go off to a post at the Connecticut State Penitentiary in Wethersfield. It speaks volumes about George's distaste for farming, and about the seriousness of his illness, that he preferred to live and work in a prison rather than to stay at home and labor by his father's side—and that his siblings were all quite sure he had done the right thing.[27]

Where Albert Baker was ascetic, worldly, rational, and disillusioned, an eighteenth-century man, George Sullivan Baker was sensual, emotional, and susceptible, a romantic. George read Byron and Walter Scott, and in some letters and in his personal diary as a very young man he expresses ardent longings and deep melancholy that reflect his reading rather than his situation. Whereas Albert took to his bed only when he was at the end of his strength, George had a tendency to take refuge from life in illness, and to savor the symptoms of his own presumed decline. Thus George writes in his diary in 1837: "But my health, Ah! it is gone, I fear—I dread to fear, never to return! An almost unceasing cough preys upon my lungs, wearing away the pitiful remnant of a once generous constitution, now rent by disease!" In a letter of January 27, 1838, as recorded in his journal, George writes to his father of "having occupied the solitary hours for more [than] two years (and the best) of my life, until sight grew dim, the brain reel'd and sickening reason trembled upon her totering throne." The same letter ends thus:

> O could you realize, for one moment, the horrors of such an hour, would you call me a rash, passionate boy? Or, looking at the cause, would you accuse me of stubborn neglect, or careless indifference, whilst even now, I must weigh my abilities before commencing in application upon any subject? No! ever revered father! A parents heart could never thus condemn a child.

On the evidence of the extant letters, it seems clear that although Mark Baker did tend to call his son a rash, passionate boy, or worse, he never rejected him. I think, on some level, both he and George were aware of acting out some variation on the theme of the prodigal son, in which the father had much the more noble role.

Proof, if it be needed, that life for the young Bakers was not all church and toil can be gleaned from the diary George Baker kept of a precious vacation he took in March 1838, soon after leaving his post in Wethersfield, Connecticut. Footloose and fancy-free, armed with a little spending money, George headed first for New York City, determined to make the most of his eight-day stay. After getting in touch with several friends, including one of the Gault brothers from Bow, George visited museums, whose wonders he dutifully noted down, researched the commendable New York Mercantile Library Association, and attended service in a Catholic church where he was "delighted with the music" but "disgusted with the superstitious cere-monies"—a fairly predictable Protestant reaction for his day.

Less predictably for a son of such devout Congregationalist parentage, in the evening he attended the theater, was amused by the circus act that con-cluded the evening, and was even more interested in the prostitutes who fre-quented the area. George notes in his diary, "Plenty of those awful cretures present, call'd the ruin of mankind but I had little to do with them more than talk and listen to their answers for if I associate with vice I will go where it appears in a more comely form than it is exhibited at theatres. Return'd at half past twelve to boarding house in Cliff St." The next night, George and his friend returned to the theater and had somewhat more dealings with the "awful cretures." The diary continues in the manuscript,

> Play over—walked up Broadway and down to five points, called at No. 49 Orange St, at old Phebe Dota's publick house for convenience sake, got rather taken in with a whore so far that I could not back out and suffer'd her to undress me, but soon found occasion to accuse her, got mad, raised Hell with her and got clear without committing or expos-ing myself.

On this occasion, George and friend got home at four-thirty in the morning.

A day later young George started for home in Tilton via upper New York State and Vermont. Not surprisingly, perhaps, after all his experiences in New York City, he was feeling somewhat under the weather on Sunday: "Health poor, unable to attend meeting, pain in the head and limbs attended with considerable fever. After a light breakfast rode to Troy for the sake of exercise and fresh air, a distance of about ten miles . . . Return'd to Albany to dinner. Spent the afternoon walking the city, health improv'd." By the time he arrived in Brattleboro, Vermont, George had regained all his good humor, noting, "Brattleboro is a beautiful village lying in a valley containing about 3,000 inhabitants and O the gods what girls!—the handsomest I ever saw without exception. . . . Left Brattleboro at half past one morn. in the stage in company with <u>one Lady only</u>!"[28]

These words were written by George in a schoolboyish blue-ruled, leather-bound notebook, no more than one-third filled. They represent a very different side of him from the soulful angst we see in his letters to his father, the loving devotion of the tributes to mother love he collected, the dutiful and uninspired letters and poetry written for the young Martha Drew Rand, whom he would, eventually, take as his wife. Did his littlest sister Mary ever read these diary entries, did he confide his experiences to her in person, or were these the kinds of things an older brother did not discuss at home? One fascinating page in the diary indicates clearly that George felt free to confide even his religious irreverence to his young sister and that she could be counted on not to play the prudish miss. A piece of doggerel, headed "New York City 1848" and addressed to Mary includes the following stanza:

> I'm selling _rum_ for money
> (Though little do I drink)
> And wish myself at Sanbornton
> To get its Christians drunk,
>
> For I could do it, Mary,
> By charging _naught to pay_
> And send them reeking, reeling drunk
> Father's boasted "Judgement Day"![29]

By the 1840s George Baker had become an expert on machinery for the carding and spinning of wool, and for a time he was in partnership with his wealthy brother-in-law Alexander Tilton, serving as the firm's travelling representative.[30] George seemed to have settled down, becoming a colonel in the governor's militia, a leader of the church choir, and a member of the local school board. In the latter capacity he renewed his acquaintance with Miss Martha Drew Rand, a poor, rather sad, but respectable young woman who had attended school with his sisters, and, parentless, was seeking to make her way as a schoolteacher.[31]

Yet, despite the surface successes, all was not well with George Baker. A strange letter included among the Baker papers at the Longyear Museum indicates that George had not entirely renounced his lady-killer ways even when he became engaged to Miss Rand. Mary in an 1846 letter to George in New York enclosed and urged that he reply to a lengthy missive from a young milliner in Sanbornton Bridge who signed herself "HP," and who has been identified by researchers at Longyear as Hannah Page. Hannah is far from explicit, but the gist of her letter is that certain of the ladies in town have been spreading rumors about her conduct with George when he visited her during an illness. This letter shows again that Mary was a close confidante to her brother, and it is interesting that she implicitly sides with Miss Page. In 1846 Mary herself was once again a single woman following the tragic death of her young husband, George Glover. She too was a victim of the incessant rumormongering in the town.[32]

George Sullivan Baker's prospects in the mid-1840s were good. Not only were the Tilton mills thriving, making his partnership with Alexander Tilton a profitable one, but his father's financial position was improving steadily, and George stood to inherit his father's fortune. But if we are to believe the reminiscences of Tilton neighbor Addie Towns Arnold, George was far from an ideal citizen:

> Mother used to say that Martha's husband, George Sullivan Baker, neither looked nor acted like any other members of the family. He had red hair, was very coarse and uncouth, and no one liked him very well. Mother told me that when she worked in the Tilton Mill (possibly around 1850 before she was married) George Baker would come around the spinning frames and spit tobacco juice over the floor. As the girls were supposed to keep the floors clean around their spinning frames this used to annoy them very much. Mother said there was an old lady spinner working near her and she finally told George Baker that if he ever showed up around her spinning frame she would hit him on the head with a broomstick.[33]

George and Martha Rand were finally married in 1849, but soon thereafter the partnership with Alexander Tilton was severed; it is not known why. George sold out his shares in the company and went to New York, where he invested disastrously in "a Panorama-Voyage Around the World" at 406 Broadway. Subsequently, he held jobs as foreman or superintendent in various woolen mills across the United States, usually leaving his wife and child behind in Tilton.[34]

After Albert's death, George and Mary remained close for some years, but after the death of their mother in 1849, their relationship cooled, and misunderstanding took the place of the old free camaraderie. Both brother and sister would sink into a slough of economic worry and psychological depression from which only the sister would emerge. George, indeed, perverted his talents, to use his mother's expression, and I suspect that his exploits with women and his drinking and smoking became more than his sister could accept. When, in her later years, Mary Baker Eddy inveighed against the dangers of drink and tobacco and advocated chastity, it was not out of narrow prudery but from personal knowledge of what alcoholism and sexual license could do to promising young men like her brother. Thus although George kept Albert's letters, he was unable to follow Albert's example, failing notably to carry the family up the next social rung as his brother had promised to do. This task would fall to his little sisters, Abigail and Mary.

3

The
Baker Women
of Sanbornton
Bridge

O F MY MOTHER I CANNOT SPEAK AS I WOULD, FOR memory recalls qualities to which the pen can never do justice," wrote Mrs. Eddy in the swift, balanced epigrammatic style she falls into at moments of least self-consciousness and greatest focus. She also confided that she loved her mother more than anyone else in her family.[1] The extant letters of her children prove that Mrs. Abigail Baker won their lifetime love and respect, and the rare letters written in her own hand show her devotion, her resourcefulness, her sensitivity, her good humor, and her good sense. The love Mary Baker had known with her mother provided a crucial early model for her relationship with God, whom she conceived of not as a loud, stern, punitive figure but as a parent who could be counted on to listen, understand, correct, but also to forgive a daughter who was at times a "hard case." Mary Baker Eddy's work shows a steady insistence—radical for her day— on God as Father/Mother, male/female, he/she, and this insistence was not merely doctrinal or historical, but rooted in personal experience.

The world has been largely content to call Mrs. Abigail Baker a saint, but perhaps for this very reason the accounts we have of her are frustratingly generic. Good, as many great novelists have found, proved much harder to paint than bad, and by her very success in incarnating the nineteenth-century female domestic virtues and serving as what her obituary called "a living illustration of Christian faith" Mrs. Baker tends to fade into the family background.[2] No portrait or tintype has come down for us to analyze for psychological traits and family likenesses, though, questioned by a woman friend, Mary Baker Eddy did leave one brief description of her mother as short, stout, blue-eyed, and blonde—that is, very unlike herself.[3] During Mrs. Eddy's last years there were many reporters who were busy digging up uncomfortable information about her youth, but none of them found any witness to say a bad word about her mother, Abigail Baker. Unfortunately, few words were said at all, and even the best word portrait we have of her is more deductive than descriptive:

> Abigail Baker, the mother, seems to have been endowed with the best qualities of those outstanding pioneer women who could work eighteen hours a day in providing necessities for their families and still find time and spirit left to be a mother. Cooking, spinning, weaving, sewing, mending, scouring, doctoring, teaching, were all a part of her usual routine duties, yet she managed somehow to be more than a laboring automaton. Like so many others, Abigail Baker died early, worn out with the struggle; and her husband, like so many contemporary husbands, promptly married again.[4]

To get beyond stereotype we have to reach for the few little oral reminiscences about her mother that Mary Baker Eddy left. Mrs. Eddy used the following story about her mother to illustrate a particular moral about constructive criticism to a young male student. We, however, can see it as evidence that Mrs. Abigail Baker was no textbook saint but a real woman, beset with cares and overwork, who, as we all do, sometimes took her temper out on her children.[5]

> I remember when I was a very little girl that I troubled and teased my dear mother at one time until at last I drew from her unwillingly a quick and incisive retribution. She put one of my hands in the flies of the spinning wheel when in motion. After suffering from this a little I went to her with my tears, and putting my arms about her neck affectionately, I said, "I pity you, mamma." You see I soon recognized my delinquency and pitied Mother, because I had worked her up to the painful necessity of this sharp rebuke for my good, and thus her pathway was smoothed.[6]

The mother-daughter relationship between Abigail and Mary was fruitful and sustaining, but this did not mean that there were no problems or complexities, especially as Mary grew older. The way Abigail lived and died and her relationships to her husband and children were a legacy that Mary and her sisters both revered and rejected. Just as the Baker sons honored their father but wished above all to leave his house and live lives very different from his, so the Baker daughters honored their mother but were unable to live their lives as she had hers. As the Baker family left the farm, became more prosperous and urban, and rose in the social hierarchy, as the old homespun economy and way of life were left behind, the Baker sisters were given more education, more leisure, more fun—and more guilt. Spared much of the relentless domestic drudgery that had worn down their mother's generation, they also lost their roles as active, productive members of the community and thus acquired a load of confusion, depression, and self-doubt.[7] Mary's whole life was to be marked by her inability to live out her adored mother's legacy, by her invincible call to move beyond the domestic sphere, where her mother had reigned both supreme and unnoticed, and achieve in ways of which Abigail could at most dream.[8]

When in 1835 Mark Baker decided to move from the old Lovewell homestead in Bow to a new farm twenty-two miles away in the district of Sanbornton Bridge,[9] some eighteen miles north of Concord, he significantly promoted the prosperity and well-being of his family. Mrs. Baker was probably loath to leave her old friend and neighbor Sally Gault, and fourteen-year-old Mary had developed a youthful fondness for one of the Gault sons,[10] but the ties of Bow were stretched rather than broken, and any sadness felt in the Baker family about leaving seems to have been short-lived. The growing town of Sanbornton Bridge, which had almost three times the population of Bow, offered an admired academy that admitted both boys and girls, a Congregational church, a local newspaper, and far more social opportunities. The unpleasantness occasioned by George's escapade with Miss Putney, together with the continuing coolness between the various branches of the Baker clan, had made the already limited society of Bow even more constricting for a household with three girls to settle.[11]

Abigail and Martha, attractive young women of nineteen and sixteen, were unequivocally delighted to taste the social advantages of Sanbornton. Only one large cloud darkened their joy over the move—the fact that they seemed fated to arrive at their new home riding in their father's ox wagon! Never one to spend money on domestic luxuries when he could invest in land, Mark had steadfastly refused to exchange the useful wagon, which he could hire out with the span to neighbors, for a chaise, upon which he would have to pay a tax. The entreaties and sulking of his daughters at home had no more effect on Mark than the subtle hints from his sons (egged on by the girls) far away. The elder girls went so far as to declare that they would absent themselves from Sunday meeting if forced to ride to church in a wagon, but Mark remained obdurate.[12] Fortunately for Abigail and Martha, their mother entered fully into their feelings on the subject of the chaise and determined that her girls should not feel humiliated on their first day in their new dwelling place. Mrs. Baker worked a small miracle and secured the assistance of two charming young men who owned a chaise and who agreed to drive Abba and Martha into Sanbornton Bridge in the style to which both girls were determined to become accustomed.

Within weeks after the move, Abba or Abbie or Abi, as Abigail the younger variously referred to herself, was writing to her brother George in Wethersfield, on April 24, 1836, in a state of controlled, ladylike rapture, worthy of a Jane Austen heroine enjoying the social refinements of Bath.

> We go on finely here, almost as well as we could wish. The people are very kind and hospitable, we find society very agreeable and refined; but we associate with none but the <u>first</u> you may depend. We have been treated, since we came to this place, with every token of respect, by all classes of the people; but we have not <u>showed out much yet</u>, nor do not intend to at present, for we think a gradual rise in the esteem of people, more commendable, than a precipitate ascension. We have some fine young ladies here, brother; I think some of the most refined and accomplished that I ever met with; and they appear very solicitous to render us happy and contented in our new situation. The young gentlemen have not been slow in their attentions.

Abigail Barnard Baker's letters breathe the carefully educated young lady: they are written in a far more beautiful hand than her brothers' and with more respect for spelling and punctuation than either parent. But if her style is different from Albert's and George's, Abba's substance is very close to her brothers'. Like them, she is determined to get ahead and make what she can of herself and her talents, and for Abba, as for her brother Albert, this meant getting as much education as she could, although the female equivalent of Dartmouth did not yet exist.[13]

The state of New Hampshire was progressive for its time in that its fiercely religious local communities, though far from affluent, were often willing to build and maintain small schoolhouses and pay the modest wages of the schoolteachers. Education for girls was still highly controversial, but in some districts girls as well as boys were able to receive at least a basic education. The teachers in the local public schools were often college and seminary students in their late teens who needed to earn money to continue with their own education.[14] The terms for which the teachers contracted were fairly short, ten to twenty weeks, and depended on the local funds available. Parents had to pay small sums for their children, small sums they could not always command, and the students' attendance was spotty, at best. Boys usually attended during the winter months when their labor was not needed on the farm. Girls, on the other hand, went to school mainly in the summer, when the often lengthy walks to school were less difficult and dirty, and when the cold in the schoolroom was less extreme.[15] Conditions in these country schoolrooms were harsh at best. Students of all ages were herded into one room, often freezing in winter and airless in summer, and chaos all too often reigned as the inexperienced teacher tried to teach some rudiments to students ranging from tiny girls to hulking young men. Whipping and boxing ears were habitual ways to maintain order, but inexperienced and timid teachers were often intimidated by their students, and the little children were probably subject to much bullying.[16]

Once basic literacy was achieved in the village schools, some higher schooling was available in academies, which catered to those with the will to learn and the money to pay. These academies were usually boarding schools in the sense that the students came from their homes and boarded not in school dormitories but with local families. The students ranged widely in age: at the prestigious Litchfield Academy in Connecticut it was far from unusual for girls of twelve and twenty-two to be in the same class. The younger girls tended to come from prosperous, well-connected families who could afford to send their daughters away to school for years. The older girls, or young women, came from the tradesman and artisan classes and were often paying their own way with money they had earned themselves. Catharine Beecher, whose family lived in Litchfield, went to the local ladies academy when she was ten and graduated with great distinction at sixteen. When Clara Barton, on the other hand, attended the comparable Clinton Liberal Institute in New York, she concealed from schoolmates that she was already almost thirty years old, had barely enough money to pay for fees and lodging, and had been teaching school herself with great success since she was sixteen.[17]

The education of the Baker children exemplified this general pattern. By the time Mary was of school age, basic education was mandated by state law, and Mark Baker, who was active in local school matters, helped draw up the plans for School #3, which his children attended.[18] All six children attended sessions at the little local school at Bow, though they may well have learned to read at home. They studied at school from the books which they were able to bring from home and which were passed down from child to child.[19] In bad weather, the girls were escorted to and from school by a brother. The sisters were particularly happy to attend school in 1830—when Mary was nine—because their brother Albert taught a term in Bow before going off to Dartmouth.[20] The same year that Albert left Pembroke, Abba left home to attend the academy there and boarded with the Burnham family as her brother had done. Having taken some courses at Pembroke, Abba followed her family to Sanbornton Bridge, moving into the teaching role at the Bridge school. This school was located far enough away from her family's property that she could enjoy the freedom of boarding out with the Cate family, while being able to return home when anything interesting promised there.

After the family moved to Sanbornton Bridge, the educational opportunities for Martha and Mary, the remaining school-age children, improved notably. The local Woodman-Sanbornton Academy at Sanbornton Square was close to their home, and Martha and Mary were allowed to attend alternately—presumably their parents were not willing to lose the help of both girls at once. The academy was a stark, wooden building, without even a stove, but there were two rooms to hold the two divisions, male and female. The teaching was good, and the letters from the sisters prove how much they learned even from such a brief exposure to higher education. The Reverend Enoch Corser, the new well-educated and inspirational Congregational minister, taught some classes, and the female department was directed by Miss Sarah Bodwell, whose father, also a local Congregational minister, was a Harvard man who had given his daughter a fine education.[21] Money for school was in fact more of a problem for the last two Bakers than was having the opportunity to learn. It seems that Mark was unwilling to pay his daughters' school fees in any regular way, although he probably could have afforded to by this point in his life. A letter from Martha makes clear that brother George sent her the money to attend school, though she was determined to pay him back as soon as she began teaching in her turn. Mary, in a letter of April 17, 1837, notes that the writing master has come to encourage her and Martha to enroll but Martha is "not able and I have not wherewith."

Abigail had blazed the path for her sisters by seizing upon the educational opportunities available, doing well at school, and rising to become a teacher to others, as Albert had done. Teaching enabled her to leave home and meet new people—for a while she too boarded with the Pierces in Hillsborough—but ultimately the social and financial rewards of teaching were meager, particularly for women. The popular and ambitious Abigail Baker was an unlikely candidate for the career of schoolmistress, especially since that vocation entailed remaining single. The Baker girls were unable to leave home in search of fame and fortune as Samuel and Albert had done, and the professions of law, medicine, and the church were not open to even the ablest young women. Formal education was thus serving a different function for women of Abigail Baker's generation than for their brothers. Marriage was the career for which the Baker girls were fitting themselves, and at least a veneer of culture and artistic accomplishments had become essential for the upwardly mobile young lady seeking to make a good match in that period. Thus it is not surprising that, whereas the extant letters written by the Baker girls make occasional references to schooling, or the lack of it, and to making academic progress, much more space is given to describing parties, excursions, visits from eligible young men, and conveying news of who is engaged to whom or who has been jilted.

As we have seen, in her old age, Mary Baker Eddy would remember her father's "iron will" and "tight harness," but perhaps by the time his last two children, Martha and Mary, had reached their teens, even Mark had softened a little. Certainly the letters written by the Baker daughters at this time prove that they enjoyed considerable personal freedom and independence, if not very much spending money. Initially on his move to Sanbornton Bridge, Mark Baker had drawn the line at dances, refusing to allow his daughters to attend the local dancing academy. The girls were more chagrined than deterred by this stricture, however, and adopted a policy of silence and selective disobedience. Abigail confided to George on August 5, 1836, "Just between you and I, Martha attended a ball the 4. of July. A splendid one too. I suppose she would not have gone if she had asked consent; but she went without leave or license. I should have gone but had been sick and was afraid if I went I should not be able to finish my school."

That Abba herself determined to remain at home showed less filial obedience than prudent strategy on her part, as the early part of the same letter indicates. Alexander Hamilton Tilton, Sanbornton Bridge's most eligible bachelor, had already shown an unmistakable interest in Miss Baker, and Abigail was too intelligent to risk forfeiting her parents' indulgence for the sake of a mere party. This August 5 letter, written by Abigail to George only eleven months before her marriage to Alexander Tilton, deserves to be quoted in extenso as it offers a fascinating look into the social mores of young unmarried Americans at this period. It also develops the theme of socially useful ill health, which we have already seen announced in George's letters in the last chapter, and which had its own influence on the life of their youngest sister.

> When I wrote last, I had dismissed my school for a week on account of ill health, after a week's vacation I commenced again. My health is better now than formerly, though that is not saying much. The rest of the family are pretty well, and Mary has been able to attend school all summer. This is more than we could have expected once from her usual state of health.
>
> Since I wrote last, I have journeyed to the north. Do you begin to wonder where it could have been? "Be patient and I will tell you all." I have been to the White-Hills, and climbed the highest peak of Mt. Washington, a distance of about three miles over hedges and ditches, rocks and stumps. But to tell you the truth, this ride has been in contemplation for some time; but I knew nothing of it till the week before last. One, Mr. Tilton from our village (a Merchant you understand) called to Mr. Cafe's where I board, and requested the favour of my company to the White-Hills, a journey of about a week, and if I would consent to go, he would obtain the consent of the district that I might dismiss my school. I was at a loss what to say, for it was quite unexpected; but he obtained a permit from the Committee, and I complied with the invitation. We started on monday previous to the last in company with three other couple of the most respectable in town; were gone a week, and returned last sabbath eve.
>
> We had a delightful tour, and saw all there was to be seen; but I would not recommend for any young lady to ascend the mountain, for I think it altogether too fatigueing to warrant their return. There is not a house within ten miles of the summit, and we were obliged to ride seven miles on horseback, and then dismounted and ascended on foot

about three miles. This was hard enough, you may depend; but we wished to immortalize our names, and knew of no other means, and as we had gone so far we were determined to proceed. I blistered my feet in three places, and am so lame now that I can hardly step.[22]

Clearly, ill health meant something very different in Abba's life than it did in the life of her brother Albert. Capable of climbing a goodly sized mountain when out on a youthful jaunt with a group of young companions, Abba nonetheless understood that such energetic demonstrations were not quite the thing for a young woman with pretensions to "ton."[23] Whereas Abba's ancestress Hannah Lovewell Baker had carried her washing to the stream, and Abba's grandmothers and mother had spent most of their working days laboring in house, garden, and dairy, Abba herself aspired to a bourgeois feminine idleness, which her family and society in general were reasonably disposed to grant her.

We also notice from the quoted letter that even though Abigail had only just dismissed school for about a week on the grounds of her ill health, the local school committee was still happy to give the children another unexpected holiday so that their young teacher could go off mountain climbing with an eligible local worthy and three other couples. Delicate ill health, a frailty unsuited to labor, was coming to be considered attractive in the young lady of the 1830s and 1840s, and even in rural New Hampshire sharp young women like the Baker girls had enough access to the magazines and novels of their day to know the fashions, and enough determination to follow them.

Unmarried American women at this time enjoyed extraordinary freedom; in fact, their independence was the target of much comment and criticism, especially among European observers. The following article was reprinted in the Bakers' local newspaper, the New Hampshire *Hill's Patriot*, in 1841 and likely caught the attention of that devoted newspaper reader Mary Baker, then twenty years old and unmarried:

The independence of a Yankee girl . . . begins with the earliest stage of boarding school life. Early in the morning she walks out alone, sometimes for a distance of miles to her academy; who her tutors, who her companions, what her studies, what books she reads, what friendships and habits she contracts, her parents scarcely ever inquire; or, if asked, scarcely ever does she condescend to reply. In proportion as she grows, more complete and absolute does she acquire the mastery over her own actions. She chooses her dancing and music masters, her congregation, her minister.—She subscribes to cotillion parties, shines off at a fancy fair, or at a flower auction. She walks home late at night from a rout with her favorite partner, and takes a long tour by moonlight, to enjoy the coolness and sentimentalism of the night air. She introduces her male friends to her mother, and sends out invitations to tea without consulting the "old lady"; finally, she informs her parents that her lover has "popped the question," unless indeed she prefers the éclat and excitement of a runaway match. And yet this unbounded latitude is scarcely ever attended with mischievous results. . . . You never hear of a faux pas. . . . the Yankee girl—God bless her!—has a thorough knowledge of the world. She is up to every trick, secure against all dangers of amorous seduction. Else what were the good of the millions of novels she reads?[24]

The author of this piece is probably aiming for a certain caricatural exaggeration, but the kind of life he details here in sober fact closely resembles the life lived by the Baker sisters, as Abigail's excursion to the White Mountains proves.

To marry well was the goal set before every young woman of this period, and when she allied with the industrialist Tiltons, Abigail was succeeding as brilliantly in her female sphere as her brother Albert was in his. Abigail Baker was twenty-one, and Alexander Tilton thirty-two when they were married in July of 1837, and on Alexander's side it was clearly a love match, for Abigail had only beauty and talent to bring as her dowry. In any event, Alexander was to prove prudent as well as passionate in his choice of wife, and if the affluent Tiltons were probably not quite as pleased with the match as the frugal Bakers, neither side was to live to rue it.[25] As the change of the town's name from Sanbornton Bridge to Tilton indicates, the fortunes of various members of the Tilton family were to grow substantially over the next half century, becoming the cornerstone of the local economy, and Abigail Baker Tilton was to play no small part in this success. After the death of her husband in 1878, Abigail took over the direction of the business, as her son had died in 1870 and her daughter in 1876, and she was to prove a sound business woman.

In contrast to both her elder sister and her younger sister, Martha Smith Baker is a shadowy figure. Even in the letters written by Abigail and Martha Baker in their late teens and early twenties, it is hard to tell when Abigail leaves off and Martha begins. Both sisters emerge as lively, funny, mildly irreverent and unruly girls, whose handwriting is well schooled, and whose vocabulary, grammar, and spelling improved notably once they had managed to spend a few months at school. Martha was perhaps more literary than Abigail, and more of a gossip. In her letters she gave more details of what the sisters were doing when they were not going to church and school or paying visits and entertaining guests. For example, in 1837 Martha tells George that for three weeks they have been busy making seventy pounds of maple sugar as well as molasses. We also learn from Martha that at this point George's clothing was still being made at home, since in the letter she apologizes for having no time to make George a cravat, and she sends a message from their mother that he should send home his "feeting" for her to mend. Mary was to continue this service for her brother until his marriage.[26]

Martha continued to follow in her older sister's footsteps when, after attending and then teaching for a while at the local seminary, she married Luther Pilsbury in 1842.[27] He was the brother of Amos Pilsbury, the superintendent of the prison in Wethersfield, Connecticut, where George Baker had been engaged. The Baker papers suggest that the Pilsburys were better connected and more prosperous than the Bakers were. Nonetheless Luther, like his friend George, seems to have had difficulty earning a living, and after moving around from position to position in New England and New York, he decided he had to seek his fortune further afield. This ambition proved fatal, given that Luther died of cholera on a Mississippi steamer in 1850, and Martha was left to cope on a very small income with her small daughter Ellen and the newly born Mary. Martha never remarried, and in 1856 she was to endure further tragedy when the delightful and much loved little Mary succumbed after a long and painful illness. Amos Pilsbury and his wife Ellen seem to have helped by inviting Martha to stay and allowing her to earn her keep as a housekeeper. Both Mark Baker and Abigail Tilton offered Martha a home at different times and for different periods. (Martha in her turn did what she could to give financial support to her younger sister's second husband, with disastrous results for all, as we shall see.) The few extant letters written by Martha in later life contain none of the gossipy humor and mild rebelliousness of the teenage letters. They reveal a woman chastened by life, unable to react to events with the energy and initiative so conspicuous in both of her sisters.

While her elder sisters were moving out of the home as their brothers had done, taking up temporary teaching positions and finding themselves husbands, the youngest Baker child was moving quietly through childhood and adolescence into womanhood. In comparison with some of her famous contemporaries—the Beecher daughters, Margaret Fuller, Louisa May Alcott—Mary Baker Eddy was not well educated.[28] As we have seen, Mary's father, Mark Baker, was active in local school affairs and happy for his children, even his daughters, to get the education needed to read the Scriptures and get ahead in life. Mary's first cousin Ann True Ambrose later testified that the Baker home was considered in the neighborhood and by the family to be a highly intellectual one, possessing many books.[29] For all this, Mark Baker was not an enlightened advocate of higher education for women, and Mary may have received even less formal education than her older sisters because her father linked her frail health to her love of reading and sought to discourage her bookish tendencies. In the part of *Retrospection and Introspection* called "Early Studies," Mrs. Eddy remarks:

My father was taught to believe that my brain was too large for my body and so kept me much out of school, but I gained book-knowledge with

far less labor than is usually requisite. At ten years of age I was as familiar with Lindley Murray's Grammar as with the Westminster Cate-
chism; and the latter I had to repeat every Sunday. (*Ret.*, p. 10)

Already by the 1830s the old conviction that it was socially dangerous
for girls to be educated was being reinforced or replaced by the medical myth
that education endangered a girl's health and her sanity.[30] Mark Baker's fears
for Mary were not, of course, wholly unfounded. The schoolrooms were icy
in winter and steamy in summer, and getting girls, with their inadequate
clothing, to school in bad weather was always a problem.[31] School was a
rowdy and noisy place, and Mary was from childhood exceptionally sensitive to loud noise.

Piecing together all the available little scraps of testimony about Mary
Baker Eddy as a child, we arrive at the picture of a quaint and precocious little girl who liked sitting indoors and reading better than playing with the
other children. "When I was a little girl I could remember whatever I read,
never forgot anything, used to be the prompter for the entire family, my
father and all of them," Mrs. Eddy happily remarked to George Kinter in
1907.[32] Later in life she told Julia Bartlett that her father tried to hide her
books from her, and that she became almost preternaturally adept at finding
them. Miss Bartlett summarizes:

> When her father, who was a good man and deacon in the orthodox
> church, and for whom she had the greatest respect, saw these things and
> heard her express her views in a way he could not understand, he would
> rebuke her and tell her it was the work of the devil.[33]

From the Bow years we have the strange little story, passed down in the
family of Mary's cousin and near neighbor Clarinda Baker, that as a small
child Mary amused everyone by exclaiming, "I wish I could cut my thinker
off."[34] Then there is the other family story that as a tiny girl Mary was taken
to school by her sisters, and she amazed the other schoolchildren by declaring that when she was grown up she would write a book. Irving C. Tomlinson
in his reminiscences quotes a school incident from Mary's youth which she
confided in him toward the end of her life:

> One time some years later during a philosophy lesson, the teacher asked
> the class "If you were to take an orange, throw away the peel, squeeze
> out the juice, destroy the seeds and pulp, what would be left?" Many
> said they did not know. Some said that nothing would remain, while
> others kept silent. But when the question was put to Mary she replied,
> "There would be left the *thought* of the orange."[35]

For evidence of Mary's brilliance as a teenager, we have the testimony
of Bartlett Corser, the son of the Reverend Enoch Corser, Mary's clergyman
and teacher in Tilton, who recalled in a letter that his father had the highest

opinion of Mary's intelligence, that she was his favorite pupil, that he considered her superior to any other young woman in the region and always praised "her superior abilities and scholarship, her depth and independence of thought, and not least, her spiritual-mindedness."[36]

Mr. Corser's testimony, together with that of Miss Ambrose and other people who had known Mary Baker Eddy as a girl, was later actively solicited by the Church of Christ, Scientist to combat the attacks on Mrs. Eddy that began in the 1890s and reached a crescendo with the 1906–1908 *McClure's Magazine* series on her life. In those articles Burton Hendrick, writing under the name of Georgine Milmine, claimed to have found "scores of Mary Baker's contemporaries"[37] who would testify that the glowing picture of educational achievement and high religious culture in her family that Mrs. Eddy had painted in *Retrospection and Introspection* was quite false: Mary Baker, *McClure's* claimed, had in fact been born into a poor, uneducated rural family, which owned no books but the Bible. Furthermore, Mary almost never attended even grade school, and her hometown did not even boast an academy from which she could have graduated. As late as her late teens she could barely read and write and do sums, and she was wholly lacking in general culture.

For a reporter who boasted of his facts and objectivity, Hendrick had remarkably little evidence to support these claims. In the *McClure's* articles not one of the old friends and neighbors who supposedly contributed to the opening part of the series devoted to Mrs. Eddy's youth is actually identified or quoted verbatim. Perhaps spurred by criticism of the flimsy informational base of the magazine narrative of Mrs. Eddy's early years, the 1909 book, a somewhat revised version of the magazine series, did include a single lengthy quotation from one of these "scores" of contemporaries with excellent memories for events some seventy years earlier. This someone was identified by Milmine only as "one of her [Mary Baker Eddy's] classmates now living in Tilton."[38] The unnamed witness first recalls Mary's beauty and highly fashionable appearance at school then comments caustically that Mary was seated in the schoolhouse next to much younger girls—herself among them—and ends with the judgment that Mary was very backward and indolent.

> I was only nine, but I helped her with her arithmetic when she needed help. We studied Smith's Grammar and ciphered by ourselves in Adams's New Arithmetic, and when she left school in three or four weeks we had both reached long division. She left on account of sickness.[39]

Perhaps in the late 1990s it is necessary to stress the damaging force of this anonymous testimony. By a few apparently trivial and highly circumstantial details, Mary Baker Eddy's claims in *Retrospection and Introspection* to have been an excellent student are demolished. Furthermore, the unnamed testifier's comments on Mary Baker's appearance and attractiveness are not as innocuous as they seem. The Milmine biographers imply significance here, indications of future patterns. They will go on to portray the adult Mary as a scheming, scandalous woman, with too many husbands and male friends in her life to be respectable, much less revered as a religious leader. Each little piece of the "classmate's" testimony was in fact intended to be a nail in the coffin of Mary Baker Eddy's reputation.

Subsequent research by Sibyl Wilbur, a woman reporter who retraced Milmine's interview trail in New Hampshire, immediately established that Milmine's unnamed source was Mrs. Page Philbrook (i.e., Hannah Sanborn), a Tilton woman who had briefly attended school with Mary Baker Eddy and retained a lively dislike of her.[40] For some years before 1906 Hannah Philbrook had been writing to Mrs. Eddy herself and then to the press with scurrilous tidbits about her famous contemporary's youth. Wilbur talked to both Mrs. Philbrook and her friend Mrs. Noyes. Her report confirms the general outlines of the Milmine passage I quoted above, but Wilbur makes it plain that this is village gossip, from girls who were not particularly close to Mary Baker and her family, and who had envied and disliked a richer and more intelligent classmate.

> Mrs. Philbrook says of Mary Baker that she held herself superior to the children and would not join their games. That she was idle and backward in her lessons, and sat through the school hours scribbling. Mrs. Noyes, who was Priscilla Hannaford, says that Mary Baker used large words, affected extravagant manners. Both women said that she pretended to be ill when she was not. Hannah Sanborn was the daughter of the village blacksmith and Priscilla Hannaford's father was a butcher.[41]

Interestingly, Wilbur quotes Mrs. Noyes as saying that on one occasion Mary Baker succeeded in quieting a lunatic who had invaded the village schoolhouse and terrified the other children. This is the kind of story Mrs. Eddy's critics either omit or deride, but it is no more and no less trustworthy than any of the information provided, whether anonymously or by attribution, by Mesdames Philbrook and Noyes.

When Mrs. Eddy read what Georgine Milmine had published about her childhood she was both outraged and mortified, and she immediately wrote a vigorous rebuttal for publication in the *Christian Science Sentinel*.[42] We can all imagine how we would feel as worthy octogenarians to find that in researching our youth reporters were quoting only the girls who had hated us most at school! Ultimately, critics and biographers have considered the question of how intellectually able Mary Baker Eddy was as a child and teenager in terms of the value they placed on her mature work. If the founding of Christian Science can be accounted for in terms of dumb luck, low cunning, love of money, and shrewd exploitation of the talents of others, then Mary Baker Eddy, young or old, does not need to be smart. If, on the other hand, Mrs. Eddy's achievements in the public sphere seem to require ability, then one will expect to find evidence of that ability emerging in her child-hood, whatever the limitations placed on her by her sex, class, and era.

It is unfortunate that the Milmine book's claims to reportorial objectiv-ity and hard facts have been so readily believed and that the account of Mrs. Eddy's youth presented there has been carried down in the biographies to Dakin and Bates and Dittemore[43] and even to Martin Gardner in the 1990s. This is particularly true when we come to the other major claim Milmine made about Mrs. Eddy as a girl—that she used ill health as a weapon, manip-ulating her oversolicitous family through calculated displays of temper and illness that culminated in cataleptic fits. This story, too, can be traced back to a single source, Hannah Philbrook. Specifically, Hannah Sanborn Philbrook told the reporters of both the New York *World* and *McClure's Magazine* that Mary Baker left school after a few weeks because of ill health, and that this illness was often not of a simple and normal nature. In its open-ing pages, the Milmine biography states unequivocally that Mary Baker "was subject from infancy to convulsive attacks of a hysterical nature."[44] As she grew older, we are told, there were many occasions when she would fall into unconsciousness. Her father would send urgently for Dr. Ladd since "Mary is dying." By this behavior, Milmine claimed, Mary tyrannized over her poor, credulous family and earned lasting notoriety in the neighborhood. This story has proved even more tenacious and damaging than the one about her alleged educational weaknesses, and I therefore quote the critical passage in full from the original January 1907 *McClure's Magazine* text:

> She was extremely nervous and hysterical, and, as a child and woman, subject to certain violent seizures. Mary Baker's "fits," as outsiders rather crudely called them, are still a household word among her old friends. They frequently came on without the slightest warning. At times the attacks resembled a convulsion. Mary pitched headlong on the floor, and rolled and kicked, writhing and screaming in apparent agony. Again she dropped limp and lay motionless. At other times, like a cataleptic, she lay rigid, almost in a state of suspended animation. . . . These fits or hysterical attacks are important in the estimate of Mary Baker and her career. Mrs. Eddy was subject to them continuously for many years.[45]

That Mrs. Eddy was hysterical as a child is one of the facts routinely cited about her, by friends and foes. Pierre Janet, the famous French spe-cialist in the study and treatment of hysteria, read the Milmine book and declared, on its evidence, that Mary Baker Eddy was a classic hysteric. His book, in turn, has been cited as medical evidence, as if Janet had ever seen or treated Mrs. Eddy.[46] I was thus interested to discover in my research how slim the evidence for this diagnosis is. The hysteria issue is one instance where I think Robert Peel, Mrs. Eddy's most brilliant, informed, and judicious biographer, does her less than a service.

Peel begins as a skeptic by going on record as saying, quite accurately, that Milmine has no evidence for her statement that Mary Baker was hysterical as a child in Bow:

> There is no reliable evidence of the exact form Mary Baker's ill health took during the first fourteen years of her life. Whether it included the acute "spells" that occurred in the later years of her girlhood we do not know.[47]

Peel then goes on, however, to produce one new, hitherto unpublished piece of evidence which appears to establish that Mary Baker was hysterical in her late teens. Peel writes:

> Mary evidently could bear the ordinary sorts of pain stoically enough. But there were times when something more was involved, when, in her weakened condition the burden of the mortal state became too crushing to be borne. This was when life took on the look of nightmare, overburdened nerves gave way, and she would end in a state of unconsciousness that would sometimes last for hours and send the family in a panic. On such an occasion, Lyman Durgin, the Bakers' teen-age chore boy, who adored Mary, would be packed off on a horse for the village doctor; in later years he recalled that on cold winter nights he rode bareback so that the horse might help to keep him warm.[48]

Unlike Milmine or Janet, Peel puts a sympathetic and spiritual spin on the "fits," but nonetheless he accepts that they did occur, apparently on a regular basis ("she *would* end in a state of unconsciousness that *would* sometimes last for hours and. . . . Durgin . . . *would be packed off*" [my italics]). I personally find Peel's suppositions about young Mary's state of nerves rather far-fetched, but the details about Lyman Durgin and his horse are highly specific and command conviction—what you might call the Milmine effect. Furthermore, Durgin's testimony here is especially weighty since, unlike Hannah Philbrook, he actually lived with the Bakers and had a close and loving relationship with them, in particular with Mary.

Since the Lyman Durgin testimony was the only evidence of Mrs. Eddy's youthful hysteria that I was prepared to believe, I was anxious to examine it carefully, and fortunately this was one of the documents that I was allowed to see in the archives of The Mother Church in Boston. I established that the information Peel gives about Mary Baker's "spells" and the boy Lyman Durgin's night rides out for the doctor was obtained not from Lyman himself, but from an interview that Florence W. Saunders, assistant to the manager of the Committee on Publication, of the Church of Christ, Scientist, *conducted in 1936 with Lyman Durgin's son.* Walter W. Durgin was about to be seventy-nine when he talked to Mrs. Saunders about his father's association with the Baker family, and he told her that his father had died when he, Walter, was fifteen. According to the letter Mrs. Saunders wrote on September 15 to the Board of Directors of the Church of Christ, Scientist, Walter Durgin told her:

> The Durgin place was two miles from Sanbornton Bridge, as the town of Tilton was then called. As a lad Lyman worked for Mark Baker on his farm. . . . He was particularly fond of Mark Baker, and Mary Baker. He stated that the latter was very frail and frequently had attacks or spells at night. Then he, Lyman, would be sent for the doctor. He often told the story of going alone at such times and said that he generally rode bareback because if he was sent in the winter when it was very cold the horse helped to keep him warm.[49]

This testimony confirms that Mary Baker was often ill as a child, and that a doctor was often called in for emergency treatment, but this fact is already established much more directly in the Baker letters written in the 1830s and 1840s. What the Durgin testimony does not give is any name of a doctor or description of his treatment, or any detail at all about the nature of the "attacks" or "spells" which Mary Baker suffered. I find no reason to assume that these illnesses corresponded in any way to the dramatic hysteric crises described by Milmine.

The Baker family letters for the period when the fits are alleged to have occurred were discovered several years after both Milmine and Wilbur had published their work on Mary Baker Eddy. These letters strongly contradict the Milmine account in that they contain no hint that Mary was suffering from a severe hysterical disorder, or that her relation to her family differed from that of her siblings. In Lyman Powell's second book on Mrs. Eddy, he remarks that, for people of the younger Bakers' generation, "speaking of symptoms" was a kind of "indoor sport."[50] This seems to me to be right on the mark. Every one of the Baker letters makes some remark about some-one's ill health, and in many letters a catalogue of symptoms composes a major section of the narrrative. It is quite clear that Mary as a child and young woman was often sick, that she had a reputation for sickliness in her family, and perhaps her neighborhood, and that later in life she remembered herself as having been frequently sickly. Some of the symptoms reported in the early Baker letters—chronic indigestion, back pain, chest colds—may well indi-cate constitutional weaknesses, and these ills were probably exacerbated by the remedies Mary adopted to try to cure them.[51] Given this constant and deep preoccupation with health and symptoms, it is very unlikely that the Baker letters would contain no hint that young Mary was given to violent hysterical symptoms. Her sisters and brothers expressed their concern, apprehension, and a sympathy verging on admiration for her various, much-canvassed and catalogued complaints and symptoms, but they never registered shock, disapproval, or repulsion.

All three Baker girls competed with one another for the title of least healthy daughter. In the letters of 1835–1842, Mary and Martha took turns being seriously ill in their parental home, and, as we have already seen earlier in this chapter, even Abigail in her late teens did not care to appear too robust. The following sections from two letters written by Martha to George and now in the Longyear collection set the tone of this rather perverse rivalry:

> [April 17, 1837]
> My health has been feeble through the winter, and as spring approached it gradually declined, till ten weeks' since, I relinquished all business and took my room, and have kept it pretty snugly ever since. My sickness is not a very distressing one, but that which renders one comfortably ill, produced almost entirely, by a very severe cough.

> [August 6, 1837]
> My health improves so slowly, that I can hardly mark its progress. I am not able to perform any amount of labour, and if I had funds of my own sufficient, I think I should go to school this fall.

As we know, George himself was apt to fall ill at moments of emotional distress or social pressure, and he was very sympathetic to his sisters' situation and to the message they were sending, directly or indirectly, in their letters. He obligingly sent the money for Martha's school fees. Unfortunately on October 15, 1837, Martha was reporting to George that freezing temperatures at school had proved too much for her fragile health, and she had been obliged to stay at home for a few days to recover. Thus we see that, just as Mary Baker, according to Mrs. Hannah Philbrook's testimony, was at one point forced to leave school before the end of term because of ill health, this was a pattern that she shared with her sisters, and that was well accepted in the family and the neighborhood.

When we consider the serious illnesses and deaths of young family members which were to haunt all the Baker sisters later in life, it is poignant to see them in their teens taking a strange pleasure in detailing each other's symptoms and prophesying the worst for one another.[52] On the very same day that Martha was describing to George that she was comfortably holed up in her bedroom with a nasty cough, reading books, and hoping to be able to go to school, Mary was writing to George in dire terms about Martha's state of health:

> I have been studying evry leisure moment this winter I shal attend school this summer if I possibly can as my health is extremely poor occasioned by a cold I hope as almost every won is complaining of some disseas occasioned undoubtedly by our severe seasons. Martha has been

verry ill since our return from Concord. I should think her in a confirmed consumption if I would admit the idea, but it may not be so, at
least I hope not.⁵³

This letter has been much quoted by Christian Scientists as evidence of
Mary Baker's early understanding of disease as a mental phenomenon. My
feeling is that Mary's "if I would admit the idea," which she underlines for
special emphasis, means only "if I could entertain the thought" and is more
a reflection of the fashionable young lady's vocabulary of the period than a
statement of philosophy.

The consensus of the family was that Mary was the least robust of the
six children, and this frailty was more a subject of admiration and sympathy
than of shock or disrepute. In letters of 1837, which have been much summarized and quoted by biographers of all stripes, both of her sisters
described Mary's symptoms at some length and wondered sadly if she would
ever be able to lead a normal life. Martha wrote thus on July 18:

(Mary) was taken ill again soon after Cutchins⁵⁴ left, and her disease of
that nature, which for a time, gave no signs of her recovery. In addition
to her former diseases her stomach became most shockingly cankered,
and an ulcer collected on her lungs, causing the most severe distress you
can conceive of; the physician with the family thought her cure impossible, but she has a good deal recovered for two weeks past, and this
morning was carried out to ride; tis possible she may yet enjoy her usual
degree of health, but not without the utmost care, and exertion. My
health is gradually returning. I work a little, walk and ride considerable;
and find my strength increasing with exercise.

All this detailed medical diagnosis makes for excellent reading, but it
probably tells us more about Martha's rhetorical tastes than about Mary's
internal organs. Remember that in April of 1837 it was Mary who was fearing Martha was suffering from consumption, that is to say tuberculosis of the
lungs.

On October 13 sister Abigail took up the story of Mary's health in a letter that Robert David Thomas uses to support his analysis that Mary had
many near-death experiences in childhood and that these illnesses fatally
warped her personality. I would give a much less apocalyptic reading to this
letter, which I think it is important to quote extensively, rather than simply
use the section relating to Mary. Abigail writes to George:

When I was married I was obliged to neglect every thing that I could
possibly do without on account of the sickness in our family, and the
exertion of body and mind at that time was so great together with my
journey, succeeding my marriage, that I was fairly jaded out; and have
been sick most of the time since, untill now. . . . Mary spent the last
week with me and appears quite comfortable, but the poor girl can

never enjoy life as most of us can should she live any time, but this is altogether uncertain. It surely is with all of us and it seems to be more so with her, since she retains life only by dieting and brushing, and all such simple expedients.... Mother has been quite sick since you heard from us, but is much better now, able to be about. We heard from Albert not long since, and his health is remarkably good.

This letter does not give me the sense that Mary was the doomed weak-ling of the family, and the normalness of Mary Baker's youthful sicknesses was precisely the point made by Mrs. Eddy's first cousin Ann True Ambrose in 1907, in a statement offered to the Church of Christ, Scientist sponta-neously after Mrs. Ambrose had read the allegations about Mrs. Eddy's youth in *McClure's Magazine*:

> I cannot tell how many years since I saw Mrs. Eddy; her boy was about four years old when I saw her last. Never saw her husband, Mr. Glover. I stayed with her many weeks. Indigestion was her greatest trouble; she called a doctor occasionally. Never knew her going into trances. Nothing unusual about her; nothing different from anyone not in a very good state of health. She was a pleasant woman. I was always treated well. She had a good education.[55]

It is true, of course, that the Baker letters we have are a random collec-tion, covering only the periods 1836–1838 and 1841–1844 in any detail. It is possible that in the period 1838–1841, when Mary was in her late teens and all her sisters and brothers had left home, she became hysteric in the manner Milmine describes in such graphic detail. But why should we make presumptions of this kind on the basis of no evidence? As I shall show in later chapters, Mary's life changes after her disastrous marriage to Daniel Pattterson in 1853, when her health takes a very distinct turn for the worse and there is a small but trustworthy body of evidence on patterns of behav-ior, such as frothing at the mouth and lengthy periods of unconsciousness, which might be labelled hysteria. Some sense of development and chronol-ogy and etiology is important here, however, and there is no reason to assume that patterns of behavior documented in, say, 1859, or more certainly still in 1872, must already have been occurring in 1839, much less in 1829.

Hysteria is often confused with malingering. Much of the theory and therapy of hysteria developed by the nineteenth-century American medical profession was posited on the assumption that the modern woman lay on her sofa and developed symptoms because, unlike her hardworking pioneer ancestresses, she did not have anything better to do with her time. Obviously, it is often difficult and sometimes impossible to distinguish the deliberate malingerer, who invents physical complaints to avoid complying with the needs of her husband and children, from the unfortunate hysteric, who com-promises her present comfort and content through symptoms that express somatically the repressed memories and emotions which she cannot consciously formulate. My reading is that in their late teens and early twenties, George, Martha, and Mary Baker, and to some extent Abigail, were all inclined to use illness to avoid unpleasant tasks and situations.

There was an element of fashion here. The Baker children enjoyed Byron and other minor romantics, they revelled in Edward Young and his *Night Thoughts on Life, Death, and Immortality,* and a pale, wan countenance and a tendency to dwell on decline and death were not considered unattractive in either sex. Moreover, the very intensity of Mark Baker's espousal of the Puritan work ethic and his parsimonious sanctity may well have driven his children into illness as a form of mild rebellion. If being unwell was the only acceptable excuse for reading a book or taking a pleasure ride instead of doing a chore or attending the very protracted and chilly Sunday services, then illness was occasionally invoked. There is a marked pattern in the letters of all the young Bakers whereby mention of some minor complaint is followed by details of some enjoyable physical activity. George, as we saw in Chapter 2, on his brief holiday from the prison, wrote unself-consciously in his diary that he was too ill to attend meeting on Sunday morning but spent the time riding to Troy, New York. Abigail reported in her letter to George that illness had forced her to take what she referred to, again unself-consciously, as a week's "vacation" from teaching school, and then she went on immediately to narrate her strenuous climb of Mount Washington.

Tactical illness of this kind was all the more plausible at a time when aspirin, antibiotics, antihistamines, and safe laxatives were not available over the counter, and in a northern climate, where it was difficult to recover from even minor colds and flu. I don't want the reader to think that I am calling the young Bakers lazy. Each of them did his or her share of the work around the house and on the farm, and the documents show that, at different stages in their lives as adults, all had a notable capacity for hard work. The traditional labor of the small New England farmer was not to their taste, however, and they avoided it on occasion, while seeking to take advantage of opportunities for other kinds of work. However we interpret such behavior, it is surely not abnormal or hysterical.

Hysteria was undoubtedly common in the United States at the time of Mary Baker Eddy's youth, and it became increasingly so as she and the century grew older. The newly professionalized and masculinized but as yet unsuccessful medical profession joyfully pocketed the fees for treating hysteria, which they preferred to call neurasthenia. As Charlotte Perkins Gilman testified so eloquently in her story "The Yellow Wallpaper" and in her autobiography, hysterics got little affection and sympathy from their medical practitioners, even though they were in many ways ideal patients. Unlike those afflicted with cholera or Bright's disease or tuberculosis, hysterics rarely died, whatever "heroic" remedies were prescribed, and they came from families who could pay bills.[56] Doctors wrote reproving reports, documenting the course of what they termed an epidemic of hysteria among affluent American women. Too much leisure, too much education, too much dieting and too tight corseting, too many novels, too little work—all these factors were widely covered in popular magazines and learned medical treatises as causes of the malady. The medical establishment of the day was in fact making hidden connections between women's illness and their increasing social dissatisfaction. One of the best ways of dismissing an uppity woman was to label her a hysteric, and Mary Baker Eddy's unconventional life was prima facie evidence for men like Burton Hendrick and Pierre Janet that she must have some fundamental psychological disorder. Ergo, let us look for, and gratifyingly find, testimony to the fact that she was a violent hysteric from childhood!

The claim by Milmine that Mrs. Eddy was a hysteric *from childhood* is in fact immediately suspect because hysteria was not a disorder of children. Though America's nineteenth-century medical experts on hysteria did not like to discuss the matter, hysteria, or womb sickness, as its name implies, had always had strongly sexual connotations, and was still assumed by all the European experts, including Freud and Janet, to be a disease of virgins, widows, and frigid wives. Sexual congress with the male, followed by maternity, was the traditional cure, and although doctors could hardly prescribe sex for their young female patients, they could take advantage of the fact that many hysteric girls did indeed marry and get better, or at least move on to other, more acceptably organic complaints.

Furthermore, seizures and cataleptic fits such as Milmine describes Mary Baker as suffering from as a child and teenager are an advanced, relatively rare, and serious form of hysteria. Girls in the nineteenth century were increasingly admired for their tendency to swoon, but to throw oneself onto the floor convulsively and fall unconscious for hours is a very different matter. As historians of hysteria have noted, such behavior was routinely observed and reported not merely by medical men studying hysteria but by ecclesiastics in witch trials. Some of the symptoms of hysteria, including the globus hystericus, the opisthotonos, hyperesthesia, and catatonia, have been noted and recorded since the beginning of medicine in ancient Egypt, but it is also established that hysteria is largely a learned behavior, highly correlated with living in enclosed communities of women, and that epidemics of hysteria could be quelled by breaking up the community in some way. Mary Baker was not shut up in a madhouse, she was not part of an enclosed community, and there is no evidence of any epidemia of hysteria in Tilton, New Hampshire, between 1835 and 1842. I should have been much more prepared to accept that Mary Baker was a hysteric as a teenager if the symptoms she has been described as suffering were not those of classic epidemic hysteria, reported by doctors in medical treatises down the ages, but were instead the quirky, highly individualized and expressive symptoms reported by psychoanalysts like Freud and Lacan, or described in the works of actual patients like Charlotte Perkins Gilman.

My guess is that someone at *McClure's Magazine* had done some reading on the clinical work then recently reported on hysteria in French asylums, and that he or she then grafted those accounts onto the biographical details of Mrs. Eddy's early life. Pierre Janet could be especially confident in his diagnosis of Mary Baker Eddy's hysteria because the symptoms the Milmine account provided could have, and perhaps did, come out of one of his studies, or those of his notorious predecessor in research in female hysteria, Jean-Martin Charcot.

Before leaving the question of young Mary Baker's ill health, we need to take into account one more piece of evidence. In the first edition of *Science and Health* Mrs. Eddy follows closely her own strictures about personality and offers singularly little autobiographical information. But at one point, she does give a fascinating account of the digestive problems she had as a girl.

When quite a child we adopted the Graham system for dyspepsia, ate only bread and vegetables, and drank water, following this diet for years; we became more dyspeptic, however, and, of course, thought we must diet more rigidly; so we partook of but one meal in twenty-four hours, and this consisted of a thin slice of bread, about three inches square, without water; our physician not allowing us with this ample meal, to wet our parched lips for many hours thereafter; whenever we drank, it produced violent retchings. Thus we passed most of our early years, as many can attest, in hunger, pain, weakness, and starvation. At length we learned that while fasting increased the desire for food, it spared none of the sufferings occasioned by partaking of it, and what to do next, having already exhausted the medicine men, was a question. After years of suffering, when we made up our mind to die, our doctors kindly assuring us that this was our only alternative, our eyes were suddenly opened, and we learned suffering is self-imposed, a belief, and not Truth. . . . As a natural result, we took less thought about "What we should eat or what drink," and, fasting or feasting, consulted less our stomach and our food, arguing against their claims continually, and in this manner despoiled them of their power over us to give pleasure or pain, and recovered strength and flesh rapidly, enjoying health and harmony that we never before had done.[57]

Mrs. Eddy gives no dates here, but she is recalling with singular vividness a long and painful part of her life.[58] She seems to be describing what today we would probably term an eating disorder, beginning in early adolescence, ending in middle age, and severely aggravated along the way by adherence to the alternative medical theories of her time.

My guess is that a mild form of anorexia, not hysteria, was Mrs. Eddy's main health problem as a teenager and young woman, bringing in its wake a whole raft of related physical problems. Anorexia, so common in our own food-crazy culture, is predominantly the disorder of highly intelligent, sensitive, and overtly compliant young women, and it often becomes a weapon wielded against a powerful parent. Anorexia, under the guise of asceticism, is also common to many Catholic girls with strong religious tendencies— Catherine of Siena in the fourteenth century and Teresa of Lisieux in the nineteenth century are only two notable examples. Given what we know about Mrs. Eddy's family background, her relation to her father, and her early passion for religion, her account of her long struggle with anorexia, or something close to it, is very interesting. In the context of the progress of women in religion, it is noteworthy that this female founder of a successful religious movement rejects not just dieting as a special road to health but fasting as a special road to sanctity.

The precise nature of the link between the young Mary Baker's ill health and the religious movement she founded is, thus, more complicated and certainly less traditional than either Christian Science or its detractors have claimed. In Mary's own mind, as we saw in Chapter 1, her bodily sickness was linked directly to her religious strivings and the course that led her to discover Christian Science and write *Science and Health*. Just as her critics want to push the portrait of her as an impossibly difficult woman as far back as possible by pinning the label of child hysteric on her, so Mary herself sought to date her religious vocation as far back as possible and to link it to the whole issue of health and healing. Yet all the objective documentary evidence we have indicates that until her first widowhood Mary Baker Eddy was, at least on the surface, a very normal girl and young woman, neither the hysterical harridan, notorious in the neighborhood, as painted by the *McClure's* team, nor the youthful saint of devotional literature. I doubt that in her teens Mary Baker consciously aspired to become a religious leader like the late revered Mother Ann Lee of the local community of Shakers, though in later life this example was not to be lost on her.[59] Everything in Mary Baker's culture was, in fact, telling her that even if serving God was her mission, she could do this best by following the example of her mother and grandmother and becoming a wife and mother. Her extreme slenderness and apparent frailty would be no impediment to her progress to the altar, as many young beauties are still finding today.

4

First
Marriage

ALBERT BAKER'S DEATH IN 1841 CAST A DARK SHADOW over the whole Baker family. For Mary, Albert's loss was deeply felt since the relation between them, always close, had become more important to both of them when Mary became old enough to relate to her older brother as an adult. In a January 29, 1840, letter addressed to Mary, Albert described his relationship with his three sisters as "the <u>oasis</u> in the desert of life—the only spot upon which I rest with <u>entire</u> safety." On February 16, 1840, Albert wrote again to Mary, expressing concern over news of her latest attack of ill health:

> I hope your usual fortitude may not have deserted you; & that amidst the depth of your sufferings, you may receive the satisfaction, to feel, that however great may be your afflictions, it is for your good—that the chastisement is inflicted by that <u>Hand</u> which is never laid upon us but in mercy, though it may appear in anger.
>
> I hope you may yet enjoy health, but whatever may be your lot, I pray you to reflect upon it, with calmness and resignation. The ways of Providence are inscrutable, but however far above us, I rely with entire confidence in the justice of God; & whatever may happen to me, for good or for evil, I see the same hand in it all—and seeing it, I can say no less, than that God rules, let the earth submit.
>
> But don't give up your hope of recovery. I know a young lady whose sufferings have far exceeded yours, but is now in the prospect of health. Her complaints are almost entirely like yours.[1]

Albert's last letters were probably much read and wept over in later years, and his views on ill health as a divinely imposed test no doubt had some influence on the future author of *Science and Health*. The idea that God uses pain, both physical and mental, as a way of testing His chosen servants was an accepted Protestant idea which would come to Mary Baker Eddy from several different sources, and which she was to struggle with, refine, and reformulate in later life.[2]

Some of Mary Baker's early poems echo the sentiments Albert expressed in his letter, as in this simple stanza:

> *Weep lady weep*
> *There is a joy in weeping*
> *Christ hath all our tears*
> *Within His own kind keeping*
> *Those He loveth best*
> *He chastens till they love Him.*[3]

It would be rash, however, to read these poems as rhymed autobiography, or flat mirrors to Mary Baker's soul reflecting her as a deeply unhappy and pessimistic teenager. As A. S. Byatt remarks in *Possession*, young girls love to be sad, "it makes them feel strong," and aspiring writers of Mary Baker's era, nourished on pieces such as Young's *Night Thoughts*, wrote a dirge or elegy or lament as an essential poetic exercise, rather than as a form of self-expression.[4] Her adolescent poetry had a morbid depressed tone long before Albert's death, as we can see in "My Native Home," a poem which she later marked in her notebook as "among the first verses I ever wrote," and which dates probably from 1835, the year of her move to Sanbornton Bridge. It ends thus:

> *Full oft this retrospect begets*
> *A rising sigh, a sad regret*
> *That man was made to mourn*
> *But grief the instructor of the wise*
> *Seeks out the cause with apt surmise*
> *And sighs my native home.*[5]

Such sighs and regrets were largely conventional since, as far as I can gather, Albert's death was the first real shadow cast on Mary Baker's young life, and even it did not sap her joy in living. The surface at least of Mary's life in her late teens and early twenties was normal and contented. She was active in local groups in Tilton, enjoyed great popularity as a Sunday school teacher,[6] paid visits to family and friends, and enjoyed the company of her contemporaries. In November 1842, at age twenty-one, she completed her formal schooling, having done three full semesters at the Sanbornton Academy under Dyer Sanborn. At school she had made at least one strong friendship with Augusta Holmes, the daughter of one of the local mill owners,[7] but Augusta became Mrs. Samuel Swasey in November and moved away to Haverhill, New Hamphire. Only a month later Mary lost another invaluable friend when her sister Martha Baker married Luther Pilsbury on December 15. Both Martha and Mary, the two youngest Bakers, bemoan in their letters the increasing tightening of the family circle,[8] and when Martha moved away Mary felt bereft. The Baker home had for many years been bursting at the seams with young life, and now the days alone with mother and father, however much loved, no doubt had their stresses.

Abigail and Martha had moved away from home to teach school for a few semesters before marrying, but Mary did not follow this route. Mary Baker Eddy biographers of all persuasions traditionally attribute her failure to go into teaching at this time of her life, or later to persist in it, to her poor health, and Mary may indeed have hesitated to take on the noisy and physically demanding work of teaching a village school for this reason. But another plausible explanation is that as the last remaining child and youngest daughter Mary was expected to stay at home and take on some of her mother's domestic burden since her parents were by this time aging and more in need of the care their darling daughter could provide them than the wages she could earn by teaching.[9] For whatever reason, Mary turned to writing. As opposed to teaching, writing required little physical strength and could be done at home. Her family supported her literary aspirations, and her reputation as the local intellectual made those aspirations credible. Her first published writings were contributions to the *Belknap Gazette*, a local literary magazine that had been recently acquired by Colonel Charles Lane, the husband of Mary's former teacher Sarah Bodwell.

Since the eighteenth century, writing had been one area where it was possible, though difficult, for a woman to find a place and make a living, and the career of writer and journalist was certainly opening up to American women in the 1840s. Yet the idea of a woman having any kind of career was frowned upon by the culture in general, the figure of the woman writer was if anything even more anomalous in American society than in Europe, and an American woman usually required some clear-cut financial necessity to propel her into the literary marketplace. Nathaniel Hawthorne was extreme but not atypical when he wrote to his publisher James T. Fields that "*all* women as authors are feeble and tiresome. I wish they were forbidden to write on pain of having their faces deeply scarified by an oyster shell."[10] Given that Mary Baker was a very marriageable young woman from a family in increasingly easy circumstances and without literary tradition or connections, it is not surprising that her ambitions to be a writer were inchoate. From the letters she wrote around the time of her first marriage it seems that she expected to write for pleasure and social distinction and not for money, and the examples of Mrs. Lydia Sigourney and Mrs. Lydia Child seemed to indicate that in New England a married woman might do more as a writer than a single one.[11] Marriage was indeed the career that religion, society, family, personal taste, and ambition all dictated for the young Mary Baker, and the extant letters amply record her absorption in the marriage plot and her search for a suitable mate.

When we think of Mary Baker Eddy as a young woman, we would do well to forget the oft-published portraits of her as a stern middle-aged matron with corkscrew ringlets or as a serene old woman with neat rows of fluffy white hair. No portrait exists of her before her first marriage, but all the descriptions of her by contemporaries agree that she was exceptionally good-looking. The first unexpurgated version of the Milmine and Cather biography notes that all the Baker children had "striking good looks," and that "Mary Baker herself became the village beauty."[12] The account goes on to state that the following description is based on the testimony of "many witnesses among her neighbors and relatives":

> They remember Mary Baker as a most interesting and beautiful child. She was dainty, fragile, and precocious in development. Her baby manners, in an age which enforced the law that children should be seen and not heard, were considered a little "forward." She has kept her beauty all her life; apparently there was not even an awkward age for her. As a young woman she was slim, alert, and graceful. Of medium height, she had a well-formed figure which she has not lost even in her old age. Her feet and hands were exquisitely fashioned. Her features were regular and refined—a delicately aquiline nose, a rather long and pointed chin, a firm mouth, and a high, broad forehead. Her most striking feature was her big, gray eyes. Deep-set and overhung by dark lashes, they had the gift of emotional expression. "When she was angry," says an old neighbor, "they became fairly black." All her life, those eyes have had such an effect upon their beholders that they may justly be called an important factor in her career. Her skin was clear red and white, and her hair was wavy brown.[13]

The McClure's description continues by noting that Mary was extremely proud of her hair, that at fifteen or sixteen she introduced the "French twist" to Tilton, that her manners were fashionably languishing to the point of affectation, and that she always attracted attention, especially from men. "These baits lured the village boys; and at church festivals all the young farmers were at her feet," the article observes.[14]

Both the Baker letters and the reminiscences of her acquaintance are at one in testifying that Mary was not just beautiful but a witty, effervescent, interesting girl who was popular with her peers. In a letter he sent to Mary on May 17, 1848, after she was widowed, her brother-in-law Luther Pilsbury writes that he regrets to hear that she is "not so lighthearted, gay and frolicksome as formerly," and wishes she may keep up her "joyous spirits," and "naturally lightsome feelings." Men were undoubtedly attracted to her, and we may judge her reaction to them by the following poem, which may have been her first published work:

> *When I was a wee little slip of a girl,*
> *Too artless and young for a prude;*
> *The men as I passed would exclaim "pretty dear,"*
> *Which I must say I thought rather rude;*
> *Rather rude, so I did;*
> *Which, I must say, I thought rather rude.*
>
> *However, said I, when I'm once in my teens,*
> *They'll sure, cease to worry me then:*
> *But as I grew older, so they grew the bolder—*
> *Such impudent things are the men;*
> *Are the men, are the men,*
> *Such impudent things are the men.*
>
> *But of all the bold things I could ever suppose*
> *(Yet how could I take it amiss?)*
> *Was that of my impudent cousin last night,*
> *When he actually gave me a kiss;*
> *Ay, a kiss, so he did;*
> *When he actually gave me a kiss!*
>
> *I quickly reproved him, but ah, in such tones,*
> *That ere we were half through the glen,*
> *My anger to smother, he gave me another—*
> *Such strange, coaxing things are the men,*
> *Are the men, are the men,*
> *Such strange, coaxing things, are the men.*[15]

This poem has rarely been quoted in the literature on Mrs. Eddy, perhaps because neither her admirers nor her detractors are pleased to have her sounding more like Adelaide in Rodgers and Hammerstein's *Oklahoma* than a study in either hysteria or sainthood. Yet all the little fragments of information we have about Mary Baker at this period in her life indicate that she had many beaux, that she had a lively interest in parties and excursions with other young folk, and that, far from feeling that neurotic revulsion from sexual relations so often diagnosed in hysterical young women, she looked forward eagerly to marriage.[16]

A good sense of Mary's life at this period can be gained from the letter she wrote on February 24, 1843, to her friend Augusta Holmes Swasey. Evidently Augusta had written to chide Mary for forgetting and neglecting her, and Mary spends more than a page protesting undying friendship, as girls will, and explaining why she, as well as Augusta's mother, had been too busy to write. The main doings had been a five-week revival meeting, attended by many friends and acquaintances whose entertainment had proved absorbing. No sooner was the revival over than Mary had caught a "violent cold attended with such <u>extreme</u> pain in the side I have been unable to write until the present." The revival meetings themselves had been extremely interesting, and Mary names those of her close circle who had publicly attested their faith. These included Mary's sister Abigail and Mr. John Bartlett, a close friend and possible suitor. Mary expresses some skepticism about the conversion claimed by some who had "deceived <u>themselves</u>" but goes on, "methinks we have less to fear from fanaticism, than from stoicism; when a question is to be decided that involves our weal, or woe, for <u>time</u> and <u>eternity</u>." Here Mary is citing the orthodox redemption theology preached at the revival. Less orthodox is her mockery of another caller "the <u>marvelous</u> James Smith," who "professes to have religion, and so far succeeded in <u>exhausting</u> that interesting and exalted subject, I grew weary and retired." Obviously Mary and Augusta loved to make fun of especially earnest and rhetorical young men. Mary ends her letter with a postscript: "<u>Hymeneal</u> J. Tilton married—S. Bartlett is soon to be <u>married to Electa Curry</u> (second <u>choice</u>)."[17] This is the letter of a happy, popular, normal young woman, for whom religion was a crucial point of reference and constant part of everyday life but not a source of anguish and doubt.

Even for so handsome and popular a young lady, the list of suitors was not unlimited. Like Abigail, Martha, and her brothers, Mary Baker sought to move out of New Hampshire and looked for a mate outside the agricultural community of Tilton. This meant, in essence, that her principal candidates were the young men her brothers introduced into the Baker home. According to Robert Peel, Mary Baker had many suitors at this period, including her first cousin Hildreth Smith, who was later to write a glowing testimonial to her charm and intellect. Whether any of these gentlemen ever actually came up to scratch is not known.

The man she chose to marry was George Washington Glover. He came from a Concord, New Hampshire, family well known to the Bakers, and he had gone into the building trade at the same time as his friend and contemporary Samuel Baker. George Glover's sister Eliza was Samuel Baker's first wife. Like many women before and after her, Mary Baker probably accepted George Washington Glover not because she preferred him to all the other men of her acquaintance but because she found him attractive, and he actually proposed at a time when she was anxious to be married. It was 1843, and she was twenty-two. That George Glover was apparently the key to a larger and more interesting world beyond Sanbornton Bridge, where sister Abigail was poised to become queen of society, was probably another big point in his favor.

In the first edition of *Retrospection and Introspection* Mrs. Eddy tells of how she met her first husband for the first time at her eldest brother's wedding:

> The Colonel placed me on his knees, and said: "I shall wait for *you* to be *my* wife!" As I scrambled to get away from him he detained me, by showing me his gold watch,—a memorial now owned by our son. Years passed away before Colonel Glover again visited the North, and I was betrothed to him. He then returned to South Carolina, and every week for two years he wrote to me; when he once more came to the Granite State, and we were married,—the ceremony taking place under the paternal roof, in Tilton.[18]

After this youthful extravagance, the courtship of George Glover and the adult Mary Baker proceeded slowly and in sharp bursts since George had moved South by the late 1830s. He reportedly came north for the wedding of Abigail Baker to Alexander Tilton in 1837 and may have met Mary again on that occasion. Mrs. Eddy later remembered that when walking in the town one day while in her youth, she had seen a man whom she took to be her brother George Sullivan Baker. Walking up behind, she poked him familiarly on the back, exclaiming, "Oh, you're dressed up," and she was embarrassed to discover that it was instead George Glover.[19] Mrs. Eddy told Gilbert Carpenter around 1905 that George Glover began to court her seriously in 1841 when he again came to Tilton to visit. On the basis of marginal jottings in Mary Baker's youthful scrapbook, Jewel Spangler Smaus inclines to the opinion that far from meriting the epithet "impetuous wooer" bestowed on him first by Sybil Wilbur and then by Lyman Powell, George was cautious in his suit, hesitating to declare his love in September 1841. Perhaps his financial situation was not good enough to impress Mark Baker, who seems from the first to have been unenthusiastic about the match, and in 1841 Mary was only twenty, still young for a woman in her social group to marry.[20]

For a woman who adored her two older brothers, it was no doubt comforting that George Glover and George Baker looked alike. The two young people started a correspondence, of which nothing unfortunately has been retained, and when Mark took it upon himself to divert and destroy George Glover's letters, brother George Baker intervened, taking his sister with him on a business trip to the White Mountains. The trip not only revived Mary's spirits but permitted George Glover's letters to reach her. This romantic little plot was concocted with the assistance of Martha Rand, Mary's old school friend whom George Baker was already courting at this time.[21] We see here again how successfully the Baker children circumvented their father's "iron will" and escaped his "tight harness."

The brief diary Mary wrote narrating her adventures on this excursion to the White Mountains and the letter she wrote the same week to her brother George are invaluable sources of insight into Mary's mind at this period.[22] The diary chronicles Mary's rapid alternation of moods, with illness, exhaustion, depression, and romantic melancholy changing overnight to excitement, good health, exhilaration, and spirited social commentary. When on the first day of the trip the rain keeps her indoors, Mary is beset with gloom, seeing her sadness printed on the landscape as she thinks of home and an unnamed "thee"—presumably the absent George Glover. When the sun comes out, she waxes poetic about the Old Man of the Mountain, preparing for a later poem on the subject, and fills her lungs with mountain air.

High spirits are well in evidence in the report to George of her "<u>sky-rocket</u> adventure" in the coach and safe arrival in Haverhill, New Hampshire, to visit Augusta Swasey. Mary complains humorously that she is suffering from lack of sleep, since she and Augusta had talked the night away. Introduced to some of the notables in Haverhill, she notes acerbically in her diary that the local belle was quite lacking in feminine softness and dignity and that a New York lady was a consummate fool. She writes of long rides—whether in a carriage or on horseback is unclear—of playing nine pins, of visiting an Indian encampment, and of eating cake and confectionery with the new acquaintance she had met on the trip.

Despite Augusta's pleas and the many temptations of Haverhill, a shire town that included an academy, Mary unexpectedly informs George that she is returning home at once. Haverhill, she says, is just too noisy and tiring for her. Taken at face value, such an excuse seems once again to support the case that Mary Baker was already an invalid, unable to support any physical activity. But on my reading of the documents Mary's hasty return to Sanbornton Bridge had more to do with her freshly renewed contacts with George Glover than with her health. It seems likely that, with brother George acting as willing go-between, Mary and George Glover had at last come to an understanding, and Mary was anxious to return home to her parents to prepare the ground for her official engagement. Certainly, her unaccompanied return to Sanbornton Bridge by coach seems to have been impulsive and ill advised. The distraught final entry to the holiday diary hints that Mary underwent some disturbing experience on the night coach journey she made alone. She tells of locking herself securely into her room at the hotel way station after her arrival in the early morning, longing for the presence of her brother, and vowing never to ride again at night "without some associate."

The letter and diary of this brief time away from home have been cited by unfriendly critics as evidence of Mary Baker's early neurasthenia and chronic ill health, whereas the sympathetic Robert Peel uses them as proof of youthful metaphysical angst.[23] My guess is that on the last day she plunged into terror not because she was neurotic or inclined to mystic gloom but, quite mundanely, because some man had made unpleasant advances to her in the coach, and she was too naïve and inexperienced to cope. Mary was a highly impressionable girl who had read much more than she had travelled, and those few days away from her parents were a giddy seesaw of exciting events for her, all heightened by the ongoing romance with George Glover.

What was he like, this young man for whom Mary Baker was pining as she journeyed through the established tourist resorts of her native region? George Glover, a tall, handsome, virile man,[24] was both very familiar to his bride and virtually unknown. The best information she may have had of him was a phrenologist's reading of his character—"naturally cheerful and full of enterprise, yet too cautious to venture much himself, without he is sure of success!"—which she pasted into her scrapbook, with the penned comment "in proof thereof Sept. 5-1842."[25] Many years later Mrs. Eddy confided in a letter that she had married young the one she loved, and there seems no reason to doubt that there was a strong romantic attachment between Mary Baker and George Glover. Their courtship certainly obeyed the conventions of the romantic fiction beloved by young women of that time in that it was carried out largely by letters and against the will of her father. Mrs. Eddy told Irving Tomlinson that Glover asked her to correspond with him, "and in this way we got acquainted, for in writing to him I became very fond of him."[26]

"Emma Clinton," the romantic short story which Mrs. Eddy published in 1846 in the *The Covenant* may throw some light on the circumstances of her first marriage. In the story, Earl Clinton, Emma's father, is shown as being implacably opposed to her relationship with Colonel Beaumont, but this opposition does not prevent the young couple from getting married. At the wedding, Earl Clinton tells his daughter, as she is about to depart for her new home, that he never wants to see her again. The split between father and daughter is healed only when Colonel Beaumont dies of yellow fever, and Emma returns to her father's house to bear her son. I am tempted to see this plot as a highly romanticized version of Mary Baker's first marriage and of the tensions between her husband and her father. The impotence of Emma Clinton's autocratic father to prevent the match he so disapproves may strike us as strange, but this circumstance is explained by Ellen Rothman in her book *Hearts and Hands*, where she gives ample documentation on the limited role that New England parents played, and expected to play, in their children's choice of spouse. Society accepted that young people should follow their hearts in marriage, and gave them ample liberty to explore relationships and find a compatible mate, trusting them to choose wisely.[27]

It seems a little odd to me that Mary Baker's courtship correspondence with George Glover has not survived. Did she simply lose track of her letters in the upheaval following George's sudden death, or is it possible that she was ashamed of George's letters and destroyed them? As it is, George,

or "Wash" as he was known to friends, speaks to us directly only in two letters, which he scribbled to George Sullivan Baker in 1841, and which Mary
Baker probably never saw.[28] A variety of opinions about George Glover's
character have been based on this very slender evidence, to which I shall now
add my own.

Wash Glover wrote the two letters to his friend George Baker, Mary's
brother and his ally in the family, from Concord, New Hampshire, on April
20, 1841, and from Charleston, South Carolina, on May 19, 1841. He needed
to communicate with George by mail to explain why the pressure of business had prevented him from meeting George as the two had planned. In a
postscript to the second letter Wash told George to burn the letter as soon
as he has read it, and upon reading the letter one can well imagine why the
writer would not have wanted such frank, man-to-man prose shown to a sister or parent—or kept for posterity. George Glover writes with not a hint of
the literary and philosophical polish of Albert and George Baker, and his letters are fascinating just because we get the sense that he is speaking rather
than writing.[29]

Some scheme seems to have been hatched between the two for George
Baker to follow Glover down South, and the letters are designed to persuade
George Baker to take the step. Wash seeks to persuade his friend, and per-
haps himself, of all the advantages, economic, social, and sexual, that the
South could offer the enterprising and handsome young Northern male.
George Glover never mentions Mary's name, but he seems already to be
viewing George Baker as a future brother-in-law, since he makes much of the
success of his business in Charleston.

> [Letter of April 20]
> I left Charleston last Tuesday every thing appears to be in a prosperous
> condition there. I came north for stock and Triming for thirteen
> Dwelling Houses that I am now Building. I should visit you if I had time
> but I must be in Charleston on tuesday next as my Buiseness calls me
> there.

> [Letter of May 19]
> Buiseness appears to be Dull with all I beleve among 7 Builders I am
> Duing one half the Buiseness in the Citty, last Saturday Bills to my work-
> men was $1267.00.

Glover seeks repeatedly to be remembered to George's sisters—"Kiss
Martha for me—Ask Abba to name hir oldest son for me as I am a
Bachelder"—and recalls with great nostalgia the warm reception he had
received from the New Hampshire ladies on his last brief visit to the North.

> It is the sweet kiss from the Northern Ladey's that hold's my hart, I
> receved more solled cumfut while in NH in April those 3 Dayes than I
> have receved for the last 5 years before[.] before [sic] not a kiss[.] the

Southern Lady's [kiss no one]. It is wicked, but since I have returned I
<u>kiss them all thay like it</u> as well as I due thay say I am wild sence I
returned————[original long dash]

Putting this remark together with the poem about a stolen kiss attributed to Mary Baker, which I quoted earlier in this chapter, it is tempting to
conclude that the kiss that drove George Glover wild in New Hampshire was
one he stole from Mary Baker, and that she was the particular lady who held
his "hart."

The two letters indicate that life in Charleston was very different from
that in Concord. Even though he admits that the Southern ladies were far
less given to demonstrations of affection than their Northern sisters, Glover
would yet have Baker believe that he was being hotly pursued by a number
of rich and eligible Charleston women. Glover also intimates that slavery
added a whole new dimension to the sexual opportunities for young bache-
lors.

I find speculations can be made I was out at Mrs. McBurney's plantation last thursday she had sent 3 times to my office in my absance for
me to visit hir, she is a Prime Young Widow a Brick manufactory
Property to the amount of $14000.00 no children and I will be <u>Damd</u>
if I beleve She will ever have aney. I said she is Young She is about 65
but still talks of marriing Damit <u>Baker</u>. She will not live long and then—
————I said then, I mite say before you could————She has a grate
maney Prime young Yallow Girls well then————I told hir you
would visit me soon—however if you would rather receve a young lady
at 16 or 17 with one hundred or 100 thousan I will turn hir on your
hands 2 of this caind has ben offered to me sence I returned from the
North

Despite the incomplete sentences and phrases, it seems clear even today
that Glover is telling his friend that he could both make his fortune by marrying a Southern woman and have his pleasure on the side with the young
slave women, if his wife did not attract him.

The two letters we have show George Glover to be extremely aware of
the fact that the economic opportunities that he is exploiting in the South
are based on the labor of slaves. In his first letter he boastfully says that if
Abigail Tilton names her first son after him he will "give it a negro servant
worth one <u>thousand</u>." The value placed on a skilled slave craftsman was
accurate, though whether George Glover was in any position to make such
expensive gifts may be doubted. In a postscript to the same letter Glover
assures Baker, "Sir: Will you visit the South for a wife—if you do I will present you with a lady, plantation and ninety negroes." In the second letter
Glover paints a little vignette of himself, sitting at ease in his downtown office
building, smoking a cigar, and "see the poor Devels work God sais we air all

Born free and <u>equal</u>, if it is the case sum throwes thair freedom away, and chuse hard Labour rather than a more Gentlemanly way to gane subsistance pleasures and welth in this life we must trust to the next, what say <u>Baker</u>."

George's Puritan conscience seems to be dimly at work here. He does see that the American promise of "freedom and equality for all" is denied to the slave craftsmen he employs in his building projects, and that his own prospects of success and wealth are to be won at the expense of the "poor devels." The highly skilled urban slave craftsmen Glover employed were privileged in comparison to their plantation brethren, and he was not to live long enough to face the full moral dilemma of accommodating himself to the Southern slave economy.[30] Irving Tomlinson describes George Glover as "thoroughly impregnated with the Southern viewpoint," and he says that Mrs. Eddy told him that her antislavery views had "brought protests" from her husband, and opposition among his Charleston friends. It seems highly probable to me that George Glover in his letters to Mary would have avoided references to slavery, and that she only discovered this side of her husband's character and business life after she moved South with him.

Reading the two letters from George Glover, one can see why Mark Baker did not take to him as a son-in-law. Unsusceptible to the looks and charm that captivated the Baker women, unimpressed by the tales of financial derring-do down South,[31] Mark may have had real cause to worry about how his delicate and indulged youngest daughter might fare with such a man. In this case as in others, Mark seems to have grumbled and given way, capable of making his children uncomfortable but not able to change their course of action. Between July and Thanksgiving of 1843 all the impediments to the union were worked out, and Mary and George were married at the Baker farm in Tilton on December 10, 1843.

The marriage was a family celebration attended by all the brothers and sisters and their families. Sybil Wilbur says, without citing any evidence, that the new Mrs. Glover took "a considerable sum of money" with her on her journey South,[32] but the Baker family papers contain no information about any dowry for Mary or for her sisters, and dowries were not customary. We know from the Holmes correspondence that Abigail Holmes, a sister of Augusta Holmes Swasey, Mary's particular friend, was present both at the wedding in Sanbornton Bridge and at the subsequent celebration in Concord, where George's elderly parents lived. Abigail described the events to her sister Augusta in a letter of December 13, 1843. She says that "Mary looked sweetly in her drab riding dress and cape a plain collar and cravat— a neat blond cap—curls—a magnificent watch, chain etc." Abigail also notes, rather enviously, that, as well as her plain gold wedding ring, engraved with names and dates, Mary also wore "the finest cameo pin I ever saw, a diamond ring only 175. dollars."[33]

After the wedding, the young couple sledded out for a series of visits in

Concord. They stopped at the Gasses' house for dinner, attended a service at the South Church, then had a turkey supper at the home of George's parents, where the whole party spent the night. The next day the newlyweds paid a farewell visit to Mary's native village, Bow, and then travelled in the new train to Boston, where they seem to have shopped for carpeting and visited the Samuel Bakers.[34] On Christmas Day 1843 they took ship to their temporary new home in Wilmington, North Carolina.[35]

On their arrival in the South, George Glover sent immediate word to his friend George Baker that all was well, and, according to what Abigail Baker wrote in February, gave a reassuring account of his wife's health. Since Mary's family was most apprehensive about the dangers of the Southern climate, and since the distance between Wilmington and Sanbornton Bridge was seen as a grave disadvantage, it was thoughtful of Glover to seek to allay their fears. To her family's surprise, Mary herself did not write until January 25, and it seems that when she finally did write, she attributed her silence to the terrible effects of the sea voyage. Neither George's nor Mary's letter has survived; we have only the joint letter of response to them from Mark and Abigail and her sister Martha Pilsbury, who was visiting the elder Bakers during the last months of her first pregnancy. Mary had obviously written and described the terrors of the sea passage in vivid detail[36] since Martha replies with almost comical expressions of sorrow—new evidence that, as I argued earlier, at this stage in their lives both sisters were finding a certain relish in adversity and its attendant delicate health:

> I can only, dearest, sister, allude to your passage from N.Y. Vain indeed would be an attempt to express my grief, or measure the tears, the recital of your sufferings has caused me. My heart alone can be the true talisman, still let me assure you, that both have freely flowed in your behalf, and to the Father of mercies, shall my constant prayer ascend, that you may soon recover, and through the enjoyment of health, yet possess that happiness, for which a whole life has thus far been spent in vain pursuit.

A sea voyage in early January was almost bound to prove dangerous and uncomfortable,[37] and Mary no doubt felt very sick indeed, especially since, as would soon become clear, she had conceived immediately after her wedding. How seriously ill she was in February and how badly she was actually affected by the Southern climate is less certain. I get the feeling that the Bakers in New Hampshire—who were stuck at home on the farm in what they describe in their letters as one of the worst winters in memory, the ink freezing in the inkwell!—suffered and missed Mary more than she did them. Certainly the letters of Abigail and Martha mourn Mary's absence, complain of missing her "prattle" and "good cheer," remember how handily she had set up the home, and wish she was there to help with the new dress patterns.

The Baker letters include two more letters written to Mary on May 6 by her mother and Mahala Sanborn, an orphaned young woman who had been taken into the Baker home as domestic help and surrogate daughter. We shall be hearing more about Mahala when we come to discuss the youth of little George Glover, Mary's son. These letters tell much more about life in Sanbornton Bridge than about Mary's doings in Wilmington. Both Abigail and Mahala acknowledge the many "papers" Mary has sent to various members of the family, as well as gifts, and question Mary anxiously about her health—"and how is your back can you lie down and rise again without a groan? . . . have you an appetite? does your food distress you?" There appears to be some continuing ill feeling between George Glover and Mark Baker, since Mrs. Baker begs George to "let all these unpleasant things be buryed in oblivion for Mary's sake and mine"—but there is no indication that Mary has reported anything unfavorable about her new husband.

One point from the letters deserves emphasis. In Mary's social circle there seems to have been a common convention that friends could mentally communicate with one another at a distance, especially if they had agreed on a time. In her February 24, 1843, letter to Augusta Holmes Swasey, Mary writes, "Meet with me in spirit at our next anniversary, (town meeting) and I will magnetize a letter with 'sap sugar' and send you." Abigail writes on February 6, 1844, of wishing she had known that Mary was in peril at sea— "we should have watched with you though at such a distance." In a farewell poem written at the same period, Mary takes up her mother's theme: "Mother at eventide when lone/Commune with me afar." On May 6 Abigail writes, "don't never forget me—do you remember our Twilight meeting? it is a precious time to me for there I feel like meeting with you and sometimes I fear I worship Mary instead of the great Jehovah but I hope not." In her February letter, Mahala also requests that Martha remind Mary that she is with her in spirit every evening. Such notions were based on mesmeric theory and practice, then much in vogue in New England, and, as we shall see in subsequent chapters, mesmerism would achieve extraordinary prominence in Mrs. Eddy's life as she developed her concept of Malicious Animal Magnetism.[38]

———————

Between February and early June 1844, Mary Baker Glover enjoyed a happy, social, successful life.[39] Biographers such as Bates and Dittemore and Robert Peel were later to wonder at the disparity in character and intellect between Mary and George, but there is no evidence that he was not an affectionate and caring husband or that the two were anything but happy together. All the known facts of his brief life show that George had ambition, energy, and the willingness to take risks, and these were, I think, qualities Mary prized and longed to emulate. Furthermore, they made a handsome and complementary couple, his bluff physicality and good humor setting off her delicate beauty and witty mind, and they were eagerly greeted into the lively circle of recent immigrants from the North where her husband was already an established favorite.[40] In Charleston a new magazine for women had been started by Edwin Heriot, and Mrs. Glover at once became a listed contributor.[41] There were dinners, parties, excursions, daily horseback rides[42]—the Southerners found Mrs. Glover's enthusiasm for their landscape charming—and even visits to the theater. Mrs. Glover wrote an ecstatic review of *The Death of Rolla*. Above all, Mary was pregnant, and though this was a cause of justified apprehension to women of this period, it was also no doubt a source of pride to a young woman who had earned the label of delicate.

How far the happiness of this time was clouded by George's increasingly complicated and dangerous business ventures is unclear. All we know is that in the last week of June 1844, personal tragedy and financial disaster struck. George, it seems, had won the commission to build, or to supply the lumber for,[43] a new cathedral in Haiti, and he had invested all his capital in the venture. A poem Mary wrote and later published in 1845 suggests that George had planned to take his wife with him to Haiti, even though the island had been in violent revolt for some time, and its climate seemed even less likely than that of the Carolinas to suit her condition.[44] In fact, it was not the delicate Mary but the robust George who succumbed to infection while still in Wilmington,[45] and after a heroic struggle of twelve days, commended his soul to God and his wife to the care of his Masonic brethren, well aware that he was leaving her penniless.[46]

In the next month, the young widow was welcomed into the homes of various friends until a Masonic brother, Mr. Cook, was able to escort her north as far as New York, where her brother George was to meet her. All these expenses, as well as the cost of the funeral, seem to have been paid out of the Masonic charitable funds.[47] Mrs. Eddy in her last years confided to Irving Tomlinson how grateful she had been for the complete mourning wardrobe that the Masonic brothers and their wives had assembled for her in 1844. "Such wholehearted chivalry, such knightly courtesy," Tomlinson has Mrs. Eddy remarking, "seems indigenous to Southern soil and it blooms and flourishes there as it will some day the wide world over."[48]

Such expressions of gratitude for Southern kindness later came repeatedly to Mrs. Eddy's lips and pen as she recalled her brief sojourn in 1844, and it seems clear that Charleston-Wilmington offered a range of social and cultural events that she had never enjoyed in her native state. But in the early years of the twentieth century when Mrs. Eddy and her followers were intent on protecting her from the onslaughts of hostile biographers, Mrs. Eddy and her advisors felt it necessary to make it clear that her praise for Southern chivalry in no way implied a defense of slavery. In fact, Mrs. Eddy asserted that she had actively opposed slavery while living in the South as a young bride. Thus in the memories she confided to Tomlinson, Mrs. Eddy stated:

> Even while in the South I did all I could to teach and preach abolition, although it brought protests from my dear husband. I began the education of our servants. I spoke freely against slavery and wrote vigorous articles for the press in favor of freedom. This created such opposition that my husband came to me and said that, although he had many friends, he did not know that their friendship would save me, should it become known that I was the advocate of freeing slaves. I persevered, however, in my endeavors to benefit the bondsmen, although the antagonism became so intense that placards were posted destruction to the abolitionist.[49]

Christian Science biographies until Peel have told the story of how Mrs. Glover moved with her husband to Wilmington where he had urgent business because her outspoken abolitionism had made her too unpopular in Charleston. Furthermore, they claim that her extreme financial distress following Glover's death arose mainly because she had freed the slaves she had inherited, who constituted her main asset. In her 1902 Message to the Mother Church, Mrs. Eddy wrote: "My husband Colonel Glover, of Charleston, South Carolina, was considered wealthy, but much of his property was in slaves, and I declined to sell them at his decease in 1844, for I could never believe that a human being was my property."[50]

Informally, in chatting with members of her household at Pleasant View late in life, Mrs. Eddy embroidered on the pro-abolitionist version of her Southern sojourn in three vivid little stories. In February 1907, a secretary recorded that Mrs. Eddy told him that while living in Charleston, she had felt uncomfortable with the Episcopal Church, St. Phillip's, and begged her husband George to take her to the colored meeting house. George replied, "Why Mary, it is scarcely a fit place for you. They sometimes get the 'power' and become very boisterous. You are delicate and nervous and I don't want you to go." She insisted, however, and he drove her there, where they heard the old preacher give a new sermon about the sheep and the goats.[51]

The second anecdote involves a slave called Bill who had been locked up in anticipation of a whipping and whom Mrs. Eddy later claimed she let out on the night before she left for Wilmington. Bill was then forced into a life of crime, joining the kind of criminal band that was terrorizing the Charleston wharfs. After her husband's death, Mrs. Mary Baker Glover went with Mr. and Mrs. Cook and their daughter Lillie on a kind of camping trip out in the woods. At night, Mr. Cook was looking for a place to spend the night, and, seeing a light, made for a dwelling despite Mrs. Glover's pleas to keep away from the place. She and the Cooks found themselves in a very unpromising house, and, warned by one of the slaves, she determined to sit up fully dressed, discovering that the canopy over her head moved across, and that the wall behind the bed was only painted canvas. Bill, the negro slave she had helped to escape, burst in, armed with pistols, and contrived the escape of her and her friends from brigands who planned to murder them.[52]

The third, and mutually contradictory story, again involved the slave Bill—"a mulatto, a negro who stood six feet three inches in height; a very brave and powerful man"—whom Mrs Eddy inherited after her husband's death and whom she refused to take north with her "because her father was a strong abolitionist and would not keep a slave." Bill reportedly said to Mrs Glover: "Missus, I has always been a mean nigger and made Massa Glover lots of trouble. Now he is dead and I am sorry for it. I want to go with you Missus, and be your slave wherever you are."[53]

These are fascinating tales, rich in dialogue and local color, but their factual basis is shaky at best,[54] and opponents of Mrs. Eddy and Christian Science, from Georgine Milmine to Martin Gardner, have had a field day disproving Mrs. Eddy's claims that she was an active abolitionist in 1844. First, there is no evidence that George Glover owned any slaves—although he obviously hired them for his business and no doubt to take care of his home—that Mrs. Glover inherited any, or that she ever published any antislavery articles in the local press. In his authoritative three-volume biography, Robert Peel dryly comments in his endnotes: "An exhaustive search of the Charleston and Wilmington papers has not brought any such articles to light. Southern newspapers were definitely not publishing antislavery views in those days."[55] In a later note Peel writes,

> it was impossible to free slaves in South Carolina except by special action of the legislature. In North Carolina they could be freed legally but there is no record of any such action by Mrs. Glover. However, it was possible for her simply to let them go free, as owners did from time to time, although this sometimes led to later legal complications.[56]

Second, although the homeless and penniless Mrs. Glover did move around the area surrounding Wilmington in the month before her departure for the North, it seems highly unlikely that the Southern friends she visited would have exposed her to the kind of romantic overnight adventure she describes. Third, as I noted in Chapter 2, Mrs. Glover's family was certainly not abolitionist in the 1840s, or indeed later. Her brother Albert, the major intellectual influence on Mary, had been chairman of the New Hampshire Select Committee on Slavery "which adopted resolutions rebuking abolitionist propaganda and recommending that Congress should not interfere with the slave-trade between States. Without condoning slavery, Baker as a northern Democrat held in common with his party that the North had no right to intervene."[57] Her father retained these views throughout his life.[58]

Fourth, the various occasional political pieces that Mrs. Glover wrote in 1844—toasts, a song parody, and an acrostic—make undeniably clear that she was an enthusiastic Jacksonian Democrat. She supported Martin Van Buren for president, spurning not only the abolitionist candidate James Birney but even Henry Clay, and she backed Michael Hoke for governor of North Carolina over the moderate Whig John Morehead.[59]

Robert Peel, Mrs. Eddy's most intelligent defender in matters ideological, glosses her political position in 1844 thus:

> The Jacksonian Democrats detested the abolitionist agitation because it alienated the white South, whose support was vitally necessary to carry through the economic reforms to which they were dedicated. Intensely loyal to the political faith in which she had been brought up, Mrs. Glover found herself in contradictions—as, in fact, the whole country was.[60]

This statement is fair, and abolitionists certainly formed a small and very radical group at this time, even in New England, but the extant evidence still shows that, despite her later claims to the contrary, in 1844 Mrs. George Glover had not yet espoused an antislavery position.

Nonetheless, I do think that the six months she spent in a slave state made an intense impression on the young Mrs. Glover, and that what she saw and heard in Wilmington and Charleston compelled her to start rethinking her position on slavery and abolitionism. The emotional and ideological change she had undergone was not immediately apparent, since the problems she faced as a result of her husband's death gave her little time or energy for political thinking, and the Baker-Tilton family circle that reabsorbed her was still deeply opposed to abolitionism.[61]

Like many Americans in the North during the years leading up to the Civil War, like Abraham Lincoln himself, Mary Baker Glover moved slowly but surely to the position that slavery could no longer be tolerated, and during the war she would adopt an enthusiastically pro-Northern stance. Her experience during her first widowhood and second marriage may have had a further radicalizing effect. Whereas Abigail Tilton through marriage became a mainstay of the establishment of her hometown, the young Mrs. Glover would lose for many years not just her local roots but her caste position.[62] Brutally detached, after the Civil War, from the mill-owning establishment that kinship had provided her in Tilton, Mrs. Glover found herself in Lynn, Massachusetts, associating every day with wage-earning men and women from across the management-labor divide. Lynn had a stronger and more radical labor movement than Tilton did,[63] and the fortunes of the embryonic Christian Science movement were for a time tied in with those of the shoe trade. Though she was careful not to take political stands that would only exacerbate the controversies constantly whirling around her, she would express sympathy for women's suffrage, the temperance movement, and abolitionism.[64]

In conclusion, then, in my opinion the abolitionist sentiments which Mrs. Eddy attributed to her younger self were real and did make difficulties for her with her family, but they were almost certainly still tentative and theoretical at the time when, as a young pregnant widow, she journeyed sorrowfully back North to begin life again in her parents' home.

5

Single Mother

From Wilmington N.C. to Weldon in the Cars, thence to Portsmouth Va. through the dismal swamp; by rail Road from Portsmouth down the Elizabeth River and up the Chesapeak Bay and the Ptapsico River to Baltimore by steamboat abreast of Baltimore in the River changed steam Boats in which we proceeded down the Ptapsico up the Bay and Elk River to Frenchton from thence crossed the State of Delaware to New Castle where we embarked on Board the Ohio proceeding up the Delaware to Philadelphia there took the Boat passing up the Delaware to Bristol Pa. then took cars through Trenton N.J. Rokaway Elizabethtown Newark and other minor places to Jersey City crossing the Ferry to N. York took a Hack for the American Hotel remaining there until Monday night Then took passage in Boat on the North River for Boston landing at Stonington CT. Then took cars passing through Providence and other places till we arrived at Boston thence took cars for Concord N.H. Travelling in four days and Nights the distance of about 14 hundred miles—July 1844.[1]

THIS ENTRY FROM HER JOURNAL CAPTURES THE GRIM exhaustion of the widowed Mary Baker Glover's return to her parental home in New Hampshire in the seventh month of her pregnancy, and at the height of the summer heat. Mr. Cook, the Masonic friend from Wilmington who had been appointed by the lodge brothers to accompany the widow north, seems to have been in a great hurry to complete his assignment, and against the recommendations of his superiors, he allowed his charge only one night in a hotel.[2] Reading the scanty accounts of these weeks in Mrs. Glover's life, I am struck by the way she coped with bereavement, impoverishment, and advanced pregnancy with the help of only virtual strangers. One might have expected some male member of the Baker or Glover families to travel south to bring her home, but apparently she was determined to manage alone. As Mrs. Eddy later remembered, George Baker was eager to travel to Wilmington, but she refused.

> The disease [i.e., the yellow fever that had killed George Glover] spread so rapidly that Mrs. Glover (Mrs. Eddy) was afraid to have her brother George S. Baker, come to her after her husband's death, to take her back to the North. Although he desired to go to her assistance, she declined on this ground.[3]

Given the sorrow and stress she had endured during her pregnancy, it is not surprising that Mary Glover's confinement went badly. The baby was born safely on September 12, a large, healthy boy who received his father's name, George Washington Glover,[4] but Mary was laid low by the birth. We can now only hypothesize as to what exactly went wrong since there is no contemporary account of the birth, but we do know that she never had another child and that there is no evidence that she ever conceived again.[5] Infertility in a woman who was married for some twelve years between the ages of twenty-two and forty-four, who had conceived in the first weeks of her first marriage and bore a healthy child, points to the possibility that some serious gynecological problem arose in the course of the first and only delivery.[6]

Childbirth was often hazardous and usually painful at this time, and women approached the event with warranted trepidation. Every woman knew of a relative or friend who had died, suffered permanent injury, or at the least endured days of agony in childbirth. Change was in the air as the new medical specialty of obstetrics was inspiring in middle-class American women a dissatisfaction with the traditional practices of midwives. But medical school training was still very primitive, and the new obstetrical instruments, techniques, and anesthetics, which would ultimately revolutionize childbirth, were still being developed. Aggressive and invasive obstetric practices carried out by inexperienced doctors far from the leading teaching hospitals were in many cases less safe than the old midwifery since the risk of infection and internal injury was greatly increased.[7] As we shall see, Christian Science practitioners were to have some of their early and greatest successes in dealing with childbirth and the gynecological problems that resulted from botched deliveries. It seems probable to me that Mrs. Eddy was alerted to these issues in part by her own experience as a new mother.

In her old age, Mrs. Eddy told her close friend and companion Mrs. Clara Shannon that her baby had screamed uncontrollably from the time he was born, an unusual occurrence that indicates that the baby may have experienced trauma during the birth. Mary Baker Glover was in no state, physically or mentally, to cope with an active but deeply unhappy infant, and she was unable to nurse. Normal lactation does not start until some three or more days after a child is born, and whereas most babies are content to sleep peacefully, take what colostrum and comfort there is from the breast, and wait until the real food is ready, a very alert and energetic baby who wants to eat now, not later, can be an emotional problem in the best of circumstances and can easily inhibit nursing by crying. When the mother is inexperienced, sick, weary, and sad, as Mary Baker Glover was, the sound of the baby's inconsolable howling can induce a guilt and despair that is hard to understand if you have not felt it. The Bakers coped with the problem of the unhappy infant as well as they could, and physically young George did not suffer. Mrs. Morrison, the wife of a local locomotive builder, had lost one of her twins at birth, and she agreed to nurse George along with her infant daughter Asenath. But a pattern of maternal separation, illness, and incapacity was established, and relations between George and his mother were to be permanently shaped by the events of the first weeks of his life.[8]

When she had recovered from her long postpartum illness, Mary Baker Glover was faced with intractable financial and social problems as a widowed mother with no personal source of income. The dilemma of the single mother in our late twentieth-century culture, and the serious fall in economic status and social status suffered by the children of single mothers, are issues much in the public eye today, but such problems pale before those experienced by the single mother in the mid-nineteenth century. This was true even when, as in the case of Mary Baker Glover, the single mother was a member of an affectionate and well-to-do family. Responsible for her children's progress and well-being a widow might be, but if her husband had not left her the means to be self-supporting, she had very few options for earning the money she needed to carry out this responsibility. In comparison with the colonial era, mid-nineteenth-century American society had limited the legal rights and economic opportunities for married women and was implacably hostile to the idea of a woman with children working outside the home.

Left suddenly and unexpectedly penniless by her husband, Mary Glover was at first determined to earn enough money to make herself and little George independent of her family. As her later life would amply prove, Mary Baker Eddy was a woman of energy, discipline, and organization with a phenomenal capacity for focused work. As a widow of twenty-three, she also had youth, beauty, and charm on her side, and she probably thought that her chances of leading a happy and successful independent life were good. Her first attempts to make a way for herself in the public arena were apparently in journalism.

This was the most romantic, the most glamorous option, but it was not illogical. Mary had long been considered the intellectual of the Baker-Tilton clan, and friends and family no doubt encouraged her in her efforts to write for publication. There was at the time a wide array of publications, local and national, which were soliciting contributions, and she had had some little successes with her poetry and essays while living in the South.[9]

Of these one deserves attention, because its metaphysical theme and some of its images point toward *Science and Health*. Although the little piece was written before the death of George Glover could even be suspected, Mary Baker Glover was already seeing sorrow and difficulty as an essential experience whereby the mind is turned away from material pleasure and toward God and the eternal realities of the spirit.

> Life has its sunshine, but its shade is truly ours; when the bright hues of thoughts coloured o'er with fancy's rainbow tints in youth's fairy gay dream, lose their borrowed light—and the baseless fabric upon which the imagination builds her superstructure, returns to its primitive atoms. But not, as with an Empire's fall, is lost the wisdom of years! no, tis the medicine of the mind, calculated to chasten and subdue the erring passions and volcanic action of a mind, too sanguinary and fervid. Then it is, hope ever and anon turns aside, equally inured by moderation either state to bear; prosperous, or adverse—selects some new object, cherishes a more distant aim, which an ardent mind must seek forever, but seek in vain, to possess.[10]

Here already we have the two sides of Mary Baker Eddy as a writer, the two kinds of prose that Mark Twain was later to note and decide, categorically, could not have come from the same pen. Had Mary Baker Eddy known during the 1840s—or indeed at any point in her long life—someone capable of taking a piece like this and pointing out that the epigrammatic thrust of the first sentence is then weakened by the corny poeticisms of "fancy's rainbow tints" and "youth's fairy gay dream," or questioning the meaning of Latinate words such as *fervid*, many later problems would have been avoided. But the fact is that at this point in her life and later, she did not know any good writers personally, did not have access to a good library, and had few friends even to direct the course of her reading. When she sought out the company of the Reverend Richard Rust, a local clergyman of good education and some intelligence, but unfortunately married, his visits to her house were immediately the source of local gossip. She was always an avid reader of newspapers and magazines, deeply interested in what we would now call public affairs—law, politics, finance—but the New Hampshire publications that came her way were provincial in every sense, intellectually shallow, politically prejudiced, literarily affected, a tepid mixture of gossip column, community calendar, and manifesto.

Between 1845 and 1849 Mrs. Mary Glover wrote poems and essays for the newspapers and had quite a number of pieces accepted for publication, first in the *Covenant*, a national Odd Fellows publication, and then in the New Hampshire *Patriot and Gazette*. She even managed to get one piece accepted by the most successful ladies magazine of the time, *Godey's*, edited by that prosperous apostle of the cult of True Womanhood, Sarah Josepha Hale. I could not recommend any of this published work to a general reader today, and the poetry is dreadful, although it seemed to find a fairly ready market. The short story "Emma Clinton," though, as we have seen, of biographical interest because of the light it shines on the relationship between Mark Baker and George Glover, is unredeemably awful as fiction. Another short story called "The Test of Love," published in the *Covenant* of June 1847, is more interesting, not indeed as literature—it is lamentably full of phrases such as "a la moment," "but *n'importe*," "*in transitu*" and "his *nonpareil* mistress"—but for its focus on the financial plight of widows and the more general question about the value of charitable giving, an issue that was to plague Mrs. Eddy in her last years.

In "The Test of Love," Frank Cleaveland, a worthy young man with an income of $800 a year, is in love with the wealthy and beautiful Martha Graham. She has several suitors, all but Frank of considerable means, and, in a Victorian variant of an old fairy-tale tradition, she decides to put them to the test. She arranges for all the men to receive a letter from a worthy but impoverished widow begging for their assistance. The rich young men variously refuse to help, refer the widow to charitable groups, send a token donation of $5, or fail to reply at all. Frank, however, writes to the woman to explain that he has no large sums to give to charity, and in any case he never gives money unless he is thoroughly acquainted with the case. He offers to put the widow in touch with the Odd Fellows (the publishers of the *Covenant*, which ran the story) and continues to assist her until she finds herself set up in a small business:

> in a few weeks the widow found herself released from the withering hand of stern adversity; comfortably located, and engaged in a thriving little business, commenced by the recommendation, and carried on by the untiring aid of the noble-minded Frank. And all this was done in genuine Scripture style. There was no sounding of trumpets or vain heraldry, for the right hand knew not of the doings of the left.[11]

Seeing that Frank has helped a poor widow, Martha agrees to marry him, after he has "*popped* the *question*, 'to be or not to be' " [original italics], to quote the story's final sentence. It is fascinating to see how Mrs. Glover indulges her fantasy here by splitting herself into two worthy women, one rich, the other poor, both of whom find an answer to their prayers in the person of a young man called Frank. It was too bad that no Frank actually came calling on the widow Glover.

An essay called "The Immortality of the Soul," which Mary Baker Glover published in the *Covenant* of May 1847, though in many ways clumsy and trite, gives a hint of her future prospects as a writer and of her future ideas as a religious leader and theologian. She begins with the conventionally pious statement that everyone believes in immortality since life would just be too painful if we were not sure that something better awaits us after death. Then, as so often in her later writings, after a labored, uninspiring start, Mrs. Glover begins to focus and think. She gives a kind of Lutheran twist to the basic Platonic idea that reality is spiritual not material, and that souls may go through many cycles of purification. She argues that far from losing our spiritual heritage as we advance from birth to death, we are purified and enlightened by experience. Furthermore, this process will continue after our death; in other words, "immortality," or life after death, is not a static condition of perfection but a continuing process of moving toward enlightenment:

> The present order of nature seems fitted but to serve as an introduction to a higher and better state of existence. Decay and death are stamped on all terrestrial things, while our faculties partake not of the general mortality, except as connected with the body, but continue to improve, to increase in strength and activity to the last. These, then, will not perish, and how consoling the thought, how congenial with our aspirations!
>
> Who does not sometimes conjecture what will be his condition and employment in eternity? Will the mind be continually augmenting its stock of knowledge, and advancing toward complete perfection? It cannot be otherwise.

This is an adumbration of the unorthodox view of heaven and the life after death that Mary Baker Eddy would take in her mature theology, and it is important to note that she expresses it long before she met P. P. Quimby or any of the other gentlemen she is supposed to have plagiarized.

Mrs. Eddy then goes on to say that human words can never be adequate and that writers and philosophers and scientists like Newton are engaged in an ever imperfect but improving search toward ultimate truth. She envisages a time when communication will be conducted without words:

> Most authors have but dimly shadowed forth their own imaginings, and much of what they intended is involved in obscurity. This makes an approach to the regions of science and literature so extremely difficult; there this obstacle will be removed. No veil will hide from our observation the beauties, lovely, inimitable, of wisdom and philosophy; all their charms will there be displayed.

The imperfection of language will be no hindrance to the acquisition of ideas, as it will no longer be necessary as a medium of thought and communication. Intelligence, refined, etherealized, will converse directly with material objects, if, indeed, matter be existent. All will be accessible, permanent, eternal![12]

It is easy to point out that Mary Baker Glover is way out of her depth here, taking on issues without any of the necessary reading and training and guidance, making a bit of a fool of herself, and boring her target reader to boot. This will always be true of her—she will always bite off more than she can chew, and get whipped for her temerity and ambition—but the seeds of Mrs. Eddy's future greatness lie in the fact that even when plunged into penury and dependence she could still write, "if indeed matter be existent."

Mary Glover did not succeed in journalism. Her failure was partly a matter of ability and partly of circumstances. She did not live in a major urban center, she had no literary connections in New York or Boston, and contributions to local New Hampshire papers were poorly paid, if at all. Women writers tended to do best—or to earn the most money—with romantic fiction, sentimental poetry, and light, frothily cultured, occasional pieces. Mrs. Eddy had no talent for any of these, though she accurately identified her market and tried, all too hard, to satisfy it. Her private letters give hints that she had some native flair for parody or political satire, but these were not areas where provincial American women were likely to try their hand.[13]

In her later life, when she had had a highly successful career in journalism, having founded, edited, and written for two journals, Mrs. Eddy preferred as far as possible to pass in silence over her professional failures in the period of 1844 to 1866. When she looked back at that time, she consistently downplayed her own financial difficulties and overemphasized the talents and achievements of her first two husbands.[14] Her impulse was to cast her past self as one of the women of her early Frank Cleaveland story—either the rich girl who marries the man she respects, regardless of income, or the poor widow who is able, with some constructive help from friends at the beginning, to make her own, independent way. Mrs. Eddy always wanted to remember herself as an active, self-supporting, and independent citizen, and her tendency is to misrepresent the past rather than to try to solicit pity as the passive victim of circumstances. This independence and self-sufficiency was fiction, and an ultimately enabling fiction that would lead at last to the creation of Mary Baker G. Eddy, leader of Christian Science, but unfortunately Mary Glover was unable to make the fiction into fact in the Sanbornton Bridge of the 1840s.

Therefore in 1846 the widowed Mrs. Glover took another tack, opening a school for preschool children, using a building on the property of Alexander Tilton, which her sister Abigail helped her to furnish and equip.

Such schools were the dearest hope of distressed gentlewomen such as herself since a school offered the possibility of providing a modest income, an independent residence for woman and even for child, a socially valued role, and status in the community. Authorities would not hire widows to work in locally financed schools, but women could set up and run their own institutions, if they could find enough students and parents willing to pay. Sadly, independent schools rarely succeeded. Such notable and well-trained women educators as Catharine Beecher and Elizabeth Peabody consistently failed to achieve independence and income via this route, and even the extraordinarily driven and ambitious Clara Barton decided, after ten brilliantly successful years teaching schoolchildren, that education would break her heart and never fill her pocket.[15]

Mrs. Glover's school seems to have failed in a matter of months, for reasons that were probably more financial than pedagogic. Abbie Towns Arnold reported meeting a Miss Whittier whose siblings had attended the school and who told her that Mrs. Glover had charged only 25¢ tuition per pupil per week. Even in New Hampshire in 1846, 25¢ did not go far, and Mrs. Glover had described her hero Frank Cleaveland in "The Test of Love" as a poor man though he had $800 a year. Mrs. Arnold also said that Mrs. Eddy refused to use the ferule or whip to discipline the children, and this may have been a problem with some parents. Sarah Clement Kimball, who herself attended the school, confirmed this, saying that one day when she had been especially naughty, Mrs. Glover sent her out to choose her own switch, and when she returned with a tiny little twig, Mrs. Glover just smiled and sent her back to her desk.[16] This kind of pedagogy appears right and normal to us today, but the typical nineteenth-century parent was more inclined to believe that sparing the rod was spoiling the child, and that iron discipline was the only way to get children to learn.

Parents may not have appreciated Mary Baker Glover's methods in her kindergarten, but all the evidence we have is that her little pupils adored her. Throughout her life, Mary Baker Eddy would have a wonderful way with children, and small girls particularly would follow her around like shadows and seek her constant attention.[17] Sarah Clement Kimball was one of these special pets, and years later she still remembered the fascination she felt for her neighbor and teacher:

> I saw Mrs. Glover daily in those days of my childhood; the Tilton house was directly across the street from our house and Mrs. Eddy was a frequent visitor while I ran over to her house any time of the day, hanging about as children will, sometimes unobserved, but always observing. Mrs. Eddy was never too absorbed in what she was doing to be interested in my childish conversation. Tall, slender, and exceedingly graceful, she was, altogether, one of the most beautiful women I have ever seen. Her hair was wonderful, soft, silky, of a reddish-brown tint, and

very curly, the sort that is dark in the shadow, but has a gold or reddish tinge in the sunlight. Both she and Mrs. Tilton [Abigail Baker Tilton] wore it looped up in ringlets, parted in the middle of the forehead and drawn toward the back of the head where it formed a cascade of curls. . . . She had beautiful eyes, bluish-gray, I should say. As I remember, her features were rather small, her teeth even, white, and very lovely. . . . My uncle, who only died a few years ago, said that he would sit in church without thinking of the service, his thoughts busy contemplating Mrs. Glover's beauty. She was always neatly but simply dressed.[18]

The idea of having her own school continued to haunt Mrs. Glover in the coming years—she mentions it in an 1848 letter to Martha Rand—but such things were increasingly dreams, not practical possibilities. In an 1848 letter to her sister Martha Pilsbury, she wrote:

I feel as if I must begin something this summer, if my health is sufficient. I am weary working my way through life from the middle to the end. I want to learn to play on a piano so that I can go south and teach. Tis all I shall ever be able to do, and this once accomplished and I am independent. . . . O, how I wish I had a Father that had been ever willing to let me know something.[19]

There was no piano, no money for lessons, perhaps no teacher, and the whole idea of learning to play the piano from scratch at age twenty-six and making a living from music was idle daydreaming, driven by a kind of despair. Yet Mary Glover knew that giving lessons in art and music was one of the few ways middle-class ladies could earn a little money, and she was obviously wracking her brains for some escape from her father's house, to come up with some means of livelihood. The inertia, the sense of powerlessness, ate away at her. She thus became all the more susceptible to the physical illness that was to dominate her life increasingly in the next years.

Marriage was the obvious, conventional answer to Mary Glover's problem, and several potential suitors seem to have buzzed around Mrs. Glover in the years immediately following the death of her husband. Exploring a new relationship was notably difficult, however, in the fishbowl atmosphere of Sanbornton Bridge, where any lapse of propriety would immediately be noticed by the gentry and arouse the ribald commentary of the mill operators.[20] This awkwardness may explain the rather peculiar section of a letter Mary wrote to her brother George in 1848, telling him of an evening party at the Baker home attended by, among others, one of her putative suitors, Mr. Sleeper, and by George's fiancée, Miss Martha Rand. Mary tells George that Mr. Sleeper brought his own nuts and wine, that Mrs. Baker, whom all had expected to be in bed, appeared unwanted on the scene, and that she, Mary, had tried desperately to keep everyone happy and relaxed. She was obviously uneasy that the prim and silent Miss Rand had judged the whole scene most improper for a respectable widow.[21]

The two main contenders for the hand of Mary Baker Glover seem to have been John Bartlett and James Smith, two worthy local young men who had sought her hand a few years earlier.[22] We get a sense of these two from one of the rare things from this period in her life which she managed to keep hold of, and which was obviously very precious to her: an illustrated album which John Bartlett presented to her in March 1846, which contained contributions of this period signed by a number of male friends. Bartlett wrote a dedication on the opening pages, but he also contributed a poem, presumably of his own composition, which includes this stanza:

> *Oh! that my prayers had the power*
> *To gain from heaven a boon for thee.*
> *Thou shouldest dear Mary, from this hour*
> *The happiest of the happy be.*

James Smith wrote his piece into the album some years after Bartlett contributed his poem. Thus Smith certainly had the opportunity to read what Bartlett had said, and he very probably had also read Mary Glover's own piece in the *Covenant* on the role of suffering in bringing us toward the divine truth. Thus Smith, in a lengthy and very wordy prose offering, takes quite a different tack from Bartlett, asking not to be allowed to protect the beloved from harm, but actually wishing disaster to fall upon her.

> Would it be wrong to wish thee losses and crosses, trials and temptations, yea, even affliction and sorrow encompass thee, to the full extent and severity that Infinite Wisdom may see necessary to prepare thee, when thy "frail tenement of clay" shall be no longer able to imprison its immortal mind for higher and holier enjoyments and the more elevated devotions of heaven which I trust and pray is thy destined and eternal home?
>
> Yes, I would wish thee in the centre of this circle, thus hedged in on every side, with no light to guide thee, but the reflection from the throne on high, and no attraction that shall eclipse the dazzling charms of the eternal city.[23]

As we saw, the young Mary Baker had joked with her personal friend Augusta Holmes Swasey about the "<u>marvelous</u>" James Smith who "professes to have religion, and so far succeeded in <u>exhausting</u> that interesting and exalted subject, I grew weary and retired." In 1850 we can assume that Smith was still pressing his suit, and his religious views, with a continuing lack of success. Later, when she was married to Daniel Patterson, Mary was to write sadly in her album, beneath Smith's entry: "Died Aug. 22. 1859—A person of strong intellect and great moral strength. Perfect rectitude of principle characterized his life. He was one of the <u>best friends</u> I ever had. Mary M. Patterson."

Bartlett, unlike Smith, wore Mary Baker Glover down with his devotion. One of the stories Mrs. Eddy told in her old age may give us a clue as to why. She recalled John Bartlett successfully soothing the newly born, and inconsolable, George Glover II. This indicates that John Bartlett was not only intelligent and hardworking, but also a tender and loving man, willing to be a father to the boy. Sadly, he was also poor, a "Frank Cleaveland" without even $800 a year.

There is one extant letter from Bartlett to Mrs. Mary Glover, one which she kept safely until her death, along with the album. The letter was written in haste after Bartlett had torn himself reluctantly away from Sanbornton Bridge. The letter shows that Bartlett and Mary Glover were conducting a correspondence, and that he was still hoping to convince her to accept his proposal of marriage:

> Oh! Mary, is [it] not hard to be separated from our much beloved friends, such as we would ever rejoice to see, to cherish, to comfort and to enjoy their company. Yet some of us are so placed in this fleeting world that such is our portion—We meet, we are merry, we part, not knowing when, if ever, we shall meet again. Thus onward we move ignorant of what kind Providence has in store for us. . . . Shall I despair and repine because poverty gazes at me with eyes as big as full <u>moons</u>? Not <u>I</u>—truly riches are very <u>desirable</u> and should be sought <u>diligently</u>, and <u>fervently</u> for the comfort they afford. But do they always ensure happiness? Is it in them alone, that we find true enjoyment? Are we sure in their possession that our glory will never fade? If we look on the world, do we see, with the majority, joy and contentment hand in hand with opulence?[24]

It seems that Mary Glover was finally won over by Bartlett's love and eloquence. When he graduated from college in Cambridge, Massachusetts, she attended the ceremony, and, according to a notation in her notebooks, they were secretly engaged. But then, like her husband George Glover and her brother-in-law Luther Pilsbury, Bartlett felt the need to seek his fortune far from New Hampshire, moving West, as far as California. In the margin of the album John had given her and where he begged to be able to cherish and protect her, Mary wrote, "Died Dec. 11th, 1850."[25]

Despite suitors like Smith and Bartlett and admirers like Rust and Ladd, the central problems of Mary Glover's life continued to loom large—how to earn a living, how to find a loving and reliable father and guardian for little George. These were problems shared by many women of her generation and to which few had solutions. In order to support themselves, working-class widows went into service, did various kinds of needlework, or labored in factories and farms. None of these activities was guaranteed to earn a woman a living wage as women's earning habitually ran 30 to 50 percent lower than men's for comparable employment, and the work performed predominantly by women—notably needlework—was rarely paid at even subsistence levels.[26] Louisa May Alcott's unfinished fiction *Work* dramatically shows the paucity of options available even to the educated and able middle-class girl who needed to earn money. The widow's lot was even more difficult because employers preferred young single women, especially for the better paid factory work. If single and widowed working-class women failed to make ends meet, their situation was dire: they became destitute, fell into prostitution, and died in workhouses and public hospitals, and their children swelled the population of the orphanages. Middle-class women left penniless were cushioned against destitution by the affluence of their families and the tradition of family support, but their opportunities for actually earning money and becoming independent were if anything worse than those of working-class women. A very few talented, industrious, and lucky widows might make a living through journalism or other forms of writing, a meager living could be earned from private teaching, and there was some work for housekeepers and paid companions. To earn a living and have one's child near one was, however, almost impossible for poor widows of all classes.

The poor middle-class widow suffered in two special ways. Relative deprivation, the difference in affluence and social status between a widow and her married sister, added in many cases to the psychological burden in families of means. As we shall see, the difference in their postmarital fortunes was to have a corrosive effect on the relationships among the three Baker sisters, especially between Mary and Abigail. Furthermore, the middle-class woman's dependence on the charity of relatives tended to aggravate the weakness of a widow's legal position vis-à-vis her fatherless children. In a society where women were citizens and legal entities only in very limited ways and where children were in many respects the property of the husband, in the absence of a paternal will with guardianship provisions, the guardianship of fatherless children devolved not upon their mothers but upon their mothers' nearest male relative, if that person chose to exercise it.

Hence, after she failed to earn money by writing or by running a school, Mrs. Mary Glover's life in the late 1840s was marked by increasing poverty, desperation, and invalidism. Her dependence put a terrible strain on family relationships, and the widowed Mary paid a high price for her dead husband's high-rolling entrepreneurship. Basically, from July 1844 to June 1853, when she married Daniel Patterson, Mary Baker Glover was dependent on her relatives for her support and that of her child. Apart from brief periods away, she spent her time in Sanbornton Bridge—in her father's home until he remarried in December 1850, and thereafter in the home of her elder sister Abigail Tilton.

Mary Glover's health deteriorated steadily during her nine years of widowhood. Documentary evidence for this period is still very sparse, but it seems that she was by the late 1840s or early 1850s subject to some kind of chronic weakness or hysterical paralysis, and this condition would persist and even intensify for a further fifteen years. Mrs. Glover's condition was well known in the neighborhood and no doubt evoked some comment and criticism. This was still a period when it was the norm for American women to engage in constant activity all day; they were not really supposed to sit unoccupied in a chair for long, much less lie down. Addie Towns Arnold was told by her mother, a near neighbor of the Tiltons and the Bakers, that her father and other men in the neighborhood were at times called in by Mrs. Tilton to move Mrs. Glover from one place to another, as she could not walk. Yet Mrs. Arnold in the next sentence of her recorded reminiscences says her mother also remembered Mrs. Glover striding restlessly up and down the upper veranda of her father's house, "stepping briskly and then whirling on her heel as she retraced her steps." The pictures of the helpless invalid, carried around, and of the woman pacing like a caged beast are both probably true.[27]

When one of the Baker clan was sick, the others rallied round, whatever their own problems, and Mary's health problems were taken very seriously by her family, who gave her exemplary care. Again, basing its account on the sixty-year-old memories of unnamed Tilton residents, *McClure's* reports in its first issue on Mrs. Eddy's life that Mark Baker had bark and straw put down on the roads to muffle the sound of the carts passing when his youngest child was sick, and that he and Abigail would rock Mary to sleep in their arms. Milmine interprets this solicitude harshly, presenting it not as a family's loving response in a limited period of crisis but as a way of life pursued over an indefinite number of years. Milmine judges this care both strangely uncharacteristic of a family she has portrayed as flinty and impatient of weakness, and as further evidence of the exaggerated deference that Mary demanded from her entourage.

In fact, the practice of muffling cart wheels when someone was ill in the house was common at this period on both sides of the Atlantic—Dickens and Thackeray mention the practice routinely. No hints of special treatment or of despotic willfulness on Mary's part emerge from the contemporary letters written by members of the Baker family—discovered after the Milmine book was completed—which, written before Mary's marriage to Glover, give many details about Mary's ill health but contain no hints of hysterical frenzy. If, indeed, that stern old Congregationalist Mark Baker did rock his daughter to sleep in his arms, must we concur with Milmine that this was a sign of his weakness and her "pathological condition"?[28]

The most shocking thing the *McClure's* team seems to have uncovered about the period of Mary Baker Glover's first widowhood was that she loved to be rocked and swung, and that her family had constructed for her a bed on rockers and a swing which could be propelled to and fro by a rope.[29] That Mary Baker Eddy was fond of rocking and swinging is an interesting and undisputed fact. As we have seen, as a very small girl Mary Baker had a little rocker. Later, in the attic study of the first home she owned in Lynn, she certainly had a rocking chair,[30] and at Pleasant View she installed a swing chair on the back veranda, or piazza, as Calvin Frye referred to it in his diary. Her lifelong pleasure in carriage riding may also have been connected to her love of swinging. That this love of swinging should be cited as evidence of Mary Baker Eddy's "pathological condition" tells us more, I think, about the eagerness of Mrs. Eddy's critics to discredit her than it does about her psychology.

Again, if we are to believe Milmine and her unnamed firsthand witnesses to the events of Mrs. Mary Glover's time in Tilton, New Hampshire, when Mrs. Glover was not requiring men to carry her around in their arms, and young boys to rock her in her swing, she was in mesmeric trance or acting as a medium. Milmine states that the Baker family physician, Dr. Nathaniel Ladd, treated Mrs. Glover, diagnosed her as a hysteric, and used hypnosis to calm her fits, finding her an unusually susceptible subject. Milmine's source of this information may have been conversations with Dr. Ladd himself in the 1904–1905 period, but he is never quoted directly, and, unlike witnesses to later events in Mrs. Eddy's life cited in the Milmine biography, he never made any affidavit. In her 1862 letter to the *Portland Evening Courier* the then Mrs. Mary Baker Patterson herself states that she had earlier in her life been treated medically by hypnosis without receiving any lasting benefit, and this may or may not be a reference to her Tilton days and to Dr. Ladd. I shall have quite a lot to say about mesmerism when I come to discuss P. P. Quimby, but let me just say here that by 1907, when the *McClure's* series about Mrs. Eddy appeared, mesmerism was viewed as shabby music-hall trickery, or as a technique whereby unscrupulous men could control and seduce unwary maidens. By associating Mary Baker Eddy with mesmerism, the *McClure's* team was calculatedly ringing a chord of complex dissonance in the public's ear, and they did so on exceptionally slim evidence.

The Baker papers contain no mention of mesmeric sessions, and those members of the Tilton community who were interviewed in the early 1900s and willing to sign testimony deny that Mrs. Glover was involved in the kind of mesmeric experiments which Milmine describes.[31] By kinship, the Bakers and the Ladds were part of the same large clan, and in a lively and revealing letter to her brother George in 1848 Mary describes a phrenological lecture she had attended with Dr. Ladd, Mr. Sleeper, and "Ham," that is to say, her brother-in-law Alexander Hamilton Tilton. She recounts how the phrenologist had examined her head and determined that philosophy, truth combined with conscience, and affection were the three keys to her character, and she notes that Ladd had publicly attested to the accuracy of the phrenologist's judgment. Mary commented to George, "Only hear this Geo. from <u>him</u>. Oh, this <u>deceiving</u> world."[32] My reading of this letter leads me to categorize Nathaniel Ladd as perhaps an admirer and certainly a friend who may have been interested in the new fashionable subject of mesmerism, and he may have engaged Mary in some of his hypnotic experiments. Milmine's insinuation that Ladd somehow played Svengali to her Trilby is quite unfounded, and I could find no strong documentary evidence that he was even her attending physician.[33]

Whether or not she was treated mesmerically, in the late 1840s and early 1850s it is certain that Mrs. Mary Glover was very often ill, but, again, it is important to see her poor health in the context of a family in which all the women were more or less ill much of the time. In an earlier chapter I mentioned that the three Baker sisters competed for the status of most cherished invalid. By 1850 the competition was still continuing, but in grim earnest as each sister was encountering serious health problems of many different kinds that mirrored and complicated her marital and familial difficulties. In 1849 and 1850 a series of deaths, illnesses, and separations was to tear the Baker family apart, and to form the prelude to Mary Glover's sudden and disastrous decision in 1853 to accept Daniel Patterson's proposal of marriage.

By the later 1840s, symptoms of ill health were more than ever the dominant motif of the Baker letters. In July 1847 Mary was the focus of family concern as George reported to his fiancée Martha Rand on July 15, that he was escorting his sister Mary on another trip through the White Mountains, and she "appears to gain strength and her health to improve as we journey." In December 1848 Mrs. Baker reported to George that "Mary has not been able to make her bed since you left [?] though she is able to sit and work." In a letter written a month after her mother's, Mary told George more about the symptoms that had prevented her from bending down:

> You spoke of my lameness. Dr. Benton told me I should be well in a few days I am now of opinion that my old pains are centering in the right kidney and that it is in some way connected with the swelling I had in my right side last spring. I think it will event as it did with Albert. Tho' I am now better and can move around the house pretty comfortably, perhaps it will work off anyhow I shan't care much so long as I am free from the horrors of dyspepsia.[34]

On August 7, 1849, Mrs. Baker as usual gave her distant son George a rundown on the family's health:

> [O]ur health is pretty good, I have but one Cow and somewhat freed from drudgery; Mary has been absent seven weeks in Warner with Dr Whiden and its vicinity and we hope she may be reliev'd from her distresses the Dr sayes she could not live long as she was. . . . Abi has been confined pretty much of the time since last February with the Hip Complaint but is now better beginning to get about without her crutches.

Abigail Tilton, we may note, had more to concern her than a bad hip. Alexander Tilton, Abigail's husband, if too rich and important to be classified a drunkard, had a serious long-term drinking problem, which was well known in the town and at times interfered with his business activities. Hard liquor had always been frowned upon in Mark Baker's strict Congregationalist family, and it must have been difficult for Abi to deal with this problem. The pleasures of being rich and elegant and well dressed, the most important hostess in town, were not unalloyed.³⁵ The Alexander Tiltons' first son, Albert, born after almost eight years of marriage, was a weak and difficult child from birth, and a second son, Alfred, died soon after birth in 1846. Abigail was to wait until 1854 before bearing another child, the fragile Evelyn.

Things were far worse for the middle sister Martha Pilsbury who recalled the year of health disasters she herself had endured in 1850 in a letter of August 10, 1851, to her brother George and his wife:

> It is now, My dear Sister, just one year since I was lying on a sick bed, and receiving from you the kindest care that love and sympathy could bestow.
>
> Never—never can I forget your kindness, which I do believe, was an important means in saving my life, for you not only "<u>smoothed the pillow</u>," but also <u>soothed the mind</u>, oppressed by misfortune and foreboding fears, (which alas! were soon to be realized,) by your cheerful looks and still more cheering words. I trust, I may yet have many opportunities to prove my gratitude in other ways than words, though I would, by no means, invoke <u>typhoid fever</u>, as the medium through which, I might <u>act</u> the grateful part to you, but rather add in some way to the happiness you might be enjoying. After my recovery my health seemed improved, till the dreadful shock it received in the news of my dear Husband's death, and when again I began to recover, and feel the first pulse of returning energy, I met with an accident in being thrown from a sleigh which confined me four months, and I am not yet well. . . . We are all quite well now excepting dear Mary—her health is very feeble—much more so than last year, and we fear she will never be as well again.

Martha is in a difficult rhetorical position here. She has had an indisputably tragic year: she has had typhoid soon after a pregnancy and childbirth, lost her husband, and had a serious sleighing accident. Despite all this, she could surely have written at least a thank-you note to her brother and his wife, if only during those four long months in bed, especially since George and Martha Baker were themselves in need of family support and reassurance at this time. In any case, Martha's letter proves that the health crises undergone by Mary Glover in the period of her first widowhood were undoubtedly serious but far from unrivalled in her immediate family.

To return to 1847–1849, the Baker family letters make it clear that if all three sisters were having some degree of ill health, the most seriously ill person in the family was their mother. Mrs. Abigail Ambrose Baker complains to her son George in December 1847 of being continually taken up with household cares and of having received a "Tremendous Shock" after falling down the cellar stairs. In September 1848 Mrs. Baker is seriously depressed and listless: she can no longer bear without complaint or comment what she herself refers to as the drudgery of farm life. I shall quote the first part of the letter Mrs. Baker wrote to George in extenso because here Abigail Baker emerges from the pious obscurity that shrouded her character, writing of her weariness in a rare unguarded moment. Furthermore, this letter offers direct testimony to the drastic inadequacy of conventional medical treatment and of remedies such as morphine and calomel, a subject that was increasingly to preoccupy her youngest daughter.

> *Beloved Child*
> Again I take my pen to address you but I have nothing interesting to write and my spirits are so depress'd and exhausted that they will not bear the fatigue of invention I cannot spiritualize nor moralize but as I name'd to you when I got better I would write you I therefore have the happiness to releive your anxiety and say my health is partially restor'd though my mind seems to be stupid as if under the influence of morphine yet I hope as my strength increase's that will wear away I was taken with dysentary we were afraid of the Cholera as I had an attack last year sent for Woodbury he came and gave immediate releif but in dealing out his medicine he gave me some of the Chalk of Calomel without nameing what he gave at length my mouth became very sore I could neither eat nor speak much yet Woodbury was very loth to acknowledge it but at last was oblidge to from the smell but now my mouth is almost well and I think with care I may have my health again but Dear George I feel as though my glass was almost run yet I have Consolation and know—
>
> > *The God we worship now*
> > *Will keep us till we die*
> > *Will be our God whilst here below*
> > *And ours beyond the sky—*

By 1849 Mrs. Baker was so weak that she could not undertake the long-awaited move to the fine new house in the center of the town which her husband had had custom-built for them, next to the Alexander Tilton residence. She lived long enough to see her beloved George finally united to Martha Rand, but only two weeks after the couple married and left for Baltimore she died. Her last illness seems to have been a painful struggle, and Abigail Tilton is reported never to have forgiven Dr. Ladd for the treatment he gave her mother during her last weeks.[36] On November 22 Mary wrote to George:

My Dear Bro'——,

This morning looks on us bereft of a Mother! Yes, that angel on earth is now in Heaven! I have prayed for support to write this letter but I find it impossible to tell you particulars at this time. She failed rapidly from the time you saw her, but her last struggles were most severe, her Physician spoke of it as owing to so strong a constitution—

Oh! Geo, what is left of earth to <u>me</u>! But Oh my mother—she has <u>suffered long with me</u> Let me then be willing she should now <u>rejoice</u>, and I bear on till I follow her. I cannot write more my grief overpowers me—Write to me

> *Your affec. Sister*
> *Mary*

Died last night at half past seven o'clock will be buried next Saturday. I wish <u>you</u> could be here.[37]

Mrs. Baker's death was a terrible blow to her children. She had been the force that held the family together, and it is after 1849 that misunderstandings and hard feelings were to breed and quarrels break out in which there would be no mother to mediate. George Baker would roam across the United States in search of work, an increasingly sick, despairing, and, I fear, dissipated man; while his wife, with their only son, George Waldron Baker, born in 1853, would settle down to grass widowhood in Sanbornton Bridge. It seems the relationship between George and Martha Rand had always been a rocky one, but Martha grew closer to her sisters-in-law Martha and Abigail, even as George and Mary grew more estranged.

George, Abigail, Martha, and no doubt the distant and silent Samuel also, all mourned their mother, but for Mary, the death was particularly difficult. A deep affection for and reliance upon one's mother was not considered abnormal or undesirable in nineteenth-century America, and to lose such an elementary source of comfort and support was a terrible blow. Mary's mourning for Abigail Baker was made worse in December when news came that John Bartlett had died in Sacramento, California.[38]

Of all the Bakers, Mark Baker seems to have been the least affected by his wife's death. In the letter he wrote in January 1850 to George and Martha Rand Baker, some six weeks after Abigail's death, he devoted one page to tried and true expressions of sorrow at the death of "a dear friend a wife a mother" and to pious exhortations, but then, in apparent relief, he spent two pages on detailing his financial dealings with Alfred Tilton and the legal description of a lot which, with George's approval, he intended to sell to Gault, his old neighbor in Bow. Mark said that his hands were trembling as he wrote this letter, but his mind was still sharp, and in the next months he set about solving not only the latest financial issues but also the problem of his own domestic comfort.

In the first months of 1850 Mary Glover and her son, now five, were living alone in the new family home with her widowed father, a loving but very
crusty, opinionated, and economy-minded old man upon whose goodwill she
wholly depended. Mark had not cared for Mary's first husband, George
Glover, he did not take to little George, who resembled his father in looks
and temperament, and he had no wish to live for long with a sad, depressed,
and frequently ill daughter and her wild, fatherless son. When Luther
Pilsbury's death became known, and the household swelled to include the
widowed Martha and her two small children, the domestic situation in Tilton
grew even worse.

The Baker Thanksgiving feast of 1850 was a gloomy affair indeed,
attended by the widowed Mary and the even more recently widowed Martha
and their offspring, and haunted by the ghosts of the recent dead, but Mark
Baker had moved to solve his own problems, if not his daughters'. In a
Thanksgiving letter to her brother George, written in the terse, earthy style
typical of her when she was not seeking to be literary or philosophical, Mrs.
Mary Glover passed bitterly from a description of the mourning feast to the
plans for wedding festivities—not hers but her father's:

> Father is to be married to Mrs. Duncan of Candia N.H. next Thurs week;
> her best carpets and goods have arrived. Last year a little later than this
> I went into that cold damp house with Father, helped cleanse and set it
> in order and lived alone with a little girl and him all winter; in the Spring
> he told me if George was not sent away he would send him to the Poor
> House (after abusing him as he did through the winter) Now he comes
> to me to help arrange the things of his bride; but I will see them in the
> bottomless pit before doing it. Every thing of our departed Mother's has
> to give place to them and Father is as happy as a school boy. Perhaps tis
> needless for me to inform you this as you have a correspondence.[39]

This tart remark at the end of the letter signals the growing estrangement
between George and Mary.

Within a few days of her father's marriage, Mary Glover wrote to an old
school friend Priscilla Wheeler, who had also recently lost her mother. Would
it be possible for Mary to extend the visit she was planning to her cousins at
Boscawen and Fisherville with a visit to Priscilla? The tone of this letter
seems to me forced, and we do not know how Priscilla responded. What is
clear is that Mary Baker Glover could no longer count her father's house as
her home, that she had been ousted from the new house in Sanbornton
Bridge along with her mother's old furniture.[40]

I believe that her father's remarriage, even more than her mother's
death, marked an important stage in Mary Baker Eddy's life, a lesson that
made her a lonelier, more self-oriented person. Widowers in the Baker family's culture were expected to remarry, even when, as in the case of the elderly

Mark Baker, they had no young children to care for and were marrying for their own comfort alone. Affluent widowers also had a wide choice of marriage prospects, and Mark Baker was far from exceptional in quickly finding a woman willing to marry him who was both significantly younger than himself and possessed of means of her own. His bride, Elizabeth Patterson Duncan, was a well-connected woman who had already been widowed twice, and she had inherited a life share in half the property and income of her second husband.[41] Her furniture was no doubt much newer, more expensive, and more elegant than anything Abigail Ambrose had been able to bring with her as dowry when she married Mr. Baker, or that she acquired during the forty years she was married to a famously stingy husband. The new Mrs. Baker was to prove a good wife and loving mother and grandmother, but as a letter she wrote to George Baker in 1856 proves, she was poorly educated and had no pretentions to being clever. The first Mrs. Baker, with her elegant handwriting, her true piety, and her love of reading, was the intellectual and spiritual superior of her successor, and to her daughter Mary, at least, that mattered.

Comparing her own widowed condition with her father's, Mary was brought up hard against the fact that whereas the death of husbands of indifferent character could easily mean disaster for their wives and children, pattern-perfect wives and mothers such as Abigail Baker could easily be replaced with newer, improved models, with barely a trace of their existence left behind them. A daughter's sense of self-worth depends in large measure upon the value she sees accorded to her mother, and I think that the swiftness with which Mark Baker recovered from mourning his wife, together with his schoolboy glee at finding so excellent a new partner in life, taught Mary Baker Eddy something crucial about the power of the man in the marketplace and the real price society set on traditional female virtues and accomplishments. All this plunged her further into illness, depression, and self-doubt.

With the new Mrs. Mark Baker ensconced in the family home, Mary turned to relying on the charity of her wealthy sister, and the problem of little George now became overwhelming. Abigail Tilton was willing to offer a home to her sister, but not to her sister's child. George was from all accounts an unusually robust and energetic child, a great contrast to his fragile cousins Ellen Pilsbury and Albert Tilton, born within a year of him. Young George got on the nerves of his grandfather and his aunt Abigail, the very people upon whose goodwill his future depended.

While George was small, things were manageable since it seems that bachelor uncle George Baker had the energy and affection to play the role of surrogate father to the boy, and Grandmother Abigail could continue her habitual role of smoothing things over and preventing Mark from becoming too irritated. In four letters, one from Mary and three from her mother, there is mention of little Georgie speaking lovingly of his uncle George, gazing at his uncle's picture, and asking when he would be coming home.

One of the most famous "facts" reported about Mary Baker Eddy is that she was never a mother to her son. The *McClure's* series assert that from his birth, George was left to the care of servants, notably Mahala Sanborn. The *McClure's* articles further claim that when Mahala and her husband Russell Cheney removed the boy, first in May 1851 to North Groton, a community some thirty miles away from Sanbornton Bridge, and then in April 1856 to Winona County, Minnesota, they were simply making official and definitive a guardianship that had long been informal and partial. Milmine offers a devastating quote from Mark Baker: "Mary is like an old ewe that won't own its lamb. She won't have the boy near her."[42] How many readers would question hardheaded, folksy statements like this or note that Milmine in 1907 is quoting without attribute or reference something allegedly said by a man who died in 1865, in reference to a situation in the late 1840s? The Baker papers, and the research done by Jewel Spangler Smaus in the 1980s, both in New Hampshire and in Lead, South Dakota, where George Glover II later settled his family, sketch a very different picture of the development of the relations among Mary, her son, and the Cheneys.

Mahala Sanborn was the daughter of a blacksmith in Sanbornton Bridge, and in the early 1840s she served as superior domestic servant to the Bakers. There seems little doubt that she was devoted to the Bakers and that she adored Mary, who had the beauty and charm she herself lacked. There is an extant portrait of Mahala, and from this and written accounts and family reports uncovered by Jewel Spangler Smaus it seems that Mahala had some facial distortion and that she had a speech defect.[43] On the other hand, a letter written by Mahala Sanborn to Mary Baker Glover in Wilmington in May 1844 shows that Mahala had received some education—the handwriting is good, the spelling erratic but comprehensible—and that she was a softhearted, active, charitable woman. Mahala tells Mary how she has been called away to attend other families suffering sickness or misfortune, and, although at the time she was a poor, unmarried woman, she obviously played a valuable role in the community.

When Mary Glover had been brought to bed with a son in September 1844 and fell desperately ill, Mahala probably looked after her, and the love Mahala felt for Mary was ultimately transferred to the fatherless boy. But there is no evidence that Mahala cared for George as an infant. Immediately after his birth George was in the care of a local wet nurse, and court records which were unearthed by Jewel Spangler Smaus established that in 1845 Mahala, by that time in her late thirties, married Russell Cheney and went to live on his farm in North Groton, some twenty-five miles from Tilton. Thus she was not in charge of little George's care between 1845 and 1850, and accusations that Mrs. Mary Glover gave up all care of her son as an infant are unfounded.

Mahala's husband, Russell Cheney, was the eighth and least able of the Cheney brothers. Cheney family legend had it that Russell married Mahala because he needed a woman of proven work capacity. A poor farmer of poor land, Russell expected his wife to do all the household chores and help out on the farm to boot. Mahala, for her part, was to increase her labor and lose her liberty in exchange for the pleasure of being called Mrs. Cheney. Even after her move to North Groton, Mahala remained devoted to the Bakers, and her tyrannical husband must have seen that it was to their mutual advantage for her to keep up her contacts with a family of increasing wealth and social prominence.

The Baker letters prove indisputably that until his grandfather's remarriage in December 1850, George Glover II was resident in his grandparents' home and cared for mainly by his mother and grandmother, with the help of whatever domestics Mark then employed. Mrs. Abigail Baker's failing health, combined with Mary's recurrent bouts of debilitating illness, must have made caring for George increasingly difficult from 1847 on, but it was not until the end of 1849 that Georgie's fragile support system broke down when his uncle George married and left home for good, and his grandmother died.

In 1850, when neither Mark Baker nor Abigail Tilton would offer George a home with his mother, the solution the family settled upon was to send George, by that time six years old, to North Groton to live with the Cheneys. Mahala was a big, strong woman who could cope with such an energetic child, and, childless, she was prepared to love him. In accepting the boy, Russell Cheney for his part was not acting out of love and charity. George would eventually be of help on the farm, and in the meantime some sum of money no doubt also changed hands. It is a measure of how much the Baker-Tilton clan disliked the boy and disparaged his abilities that they were prepared to give him into the care of the mean-minded, unsuccessful, uneducated Cheney.

In the 1891 edition of *Retrospection and Introspection*, Mrs. Eddy wrote about saying good-bye to her son:

> A few months before my father's second marriage to Mrs. Elizabeth Patterson Duncan, sister of Lieutenant-Governor George W. Patterson, of New York—my little son, about four years of age, was sent away from me, and put under the care of our family nurse, who had married, and resided in the northern part of New Hampshire. I had no training for self-support, and my health was regarded as precarious [in later editions: "my home I regarded as very precious"]. The night before my child was taken from me, I knelt by his side throughout the dark hours, hoping for a vision of relief from this trial. The following lines are taken from my poem, "Mother's darling," written after this separation:

Thy smile through tears, as sunshine o'er the sea,
Awoke new beauty in the surge's roll!
Oh, life is dead, bereft of all, with thee,—
Star of my earthly hope, babe of my soul.
(Ret. [1891], pp. 26 – 27)

Hostile critics of Mrs. Eddy's have had a field day with this passage, challenging the facts and ridiculing the emotions, and it is too bad that Mrs. Eddy chose the loose and lacrimose rhetoric of the popular prose of her youth, opting for Mrs. Hemans not Mr. Wordsworth as her poetic model. But being a bad poet is not an infallible marker for being a bad mother, and when Mary Baker Eddy tells us that parting from her son was one of her darkest hours, and that she prayed all night, in vain, to be spared the separation, one has to have excellent reasons for doubting and disputing the truth of her feelings. Furthermore, all the documentary evidence now available indicates that her memory of the events leading up to little George's departure to the Cheneys was pretty accurate.[44]

That Mrs. Mary Glover was a normal mother, deeply attached to her child, is strongly indicated by the few extant letters which she wrote in the period when she and George lived together. In virtually all she makes some affectionate reference to her boy and, obviously defensive, praises his good qualities. In two letters to her brother George she apologizes for writing so poorly, but the boy was constantly at her elbow. Most poignant is the letter Mrs. Glover wrote to her brother-in-law Andrew Glover, to whom the unwelcome little lad had been sent on a visit in the hiatus between his grandfather's marriage and his move to the Cheneys in North Groton. This is the full text of the letter dated April 22, 1851:

> My dear Bro & Sis,
>   Mrs. Cheney came here last Thurs. and will return next week on Saturday.
>   You can send my dear child when you please, the latter part of the week, as she is very anxious to have him when she goes home. She is very fond of children and Georgy in particular, but her health is very poor, this I regret. She told me their school (which is about one quarter of a mile distant) will commence in a few weeks and I am anxious to have him attend. But Oh! how I miss him already! There seems nothing left me now to enjoy. I often stand by my window when the shades of evening close o'er me and gaze on yonder sacred spot where sleeps my peaceful Mother and invoke her blessing and counsel, while I almost envy her repose.
>   But I must not write on this subject for words are impotent things to utter the feelings of a Mother's heart.
>   Wont you send me a line by him or come yourselves? I want very much to know how you have succeeded with him and if he has been a

good boy (some naughty things of course). There is no child we expect mature in any respect, but take Georgy with the aggregate, is he not a pretty good and very dear boy? You can speak to the conductor to take care of him and his <u>little</u> baggage and Mr. Tilton is always at the depot so he will see to him there. Will dear little Sully be sorry to have him leave? How is Fath. and Moth's health? Give much love to them from me and accept the same yourselves. Kiss the little one for me and tell him aunty remembers those roguish eyes.

In much haste

Yours
Affectionately,
Mary[45]

Further but much less firm evidence for the essential truth of Mrs. Eddy's later account of her separation from George in *Retrospection and Introspection* was provided by the interviews Jewel Spangler Smaus conducted with George Washington Glover III, Mrs. Eddy's grandson, in the 1970s, but this testimony needs to be put carefully in context. The interviewer was clearly anxious to find evidence to support her beloved Mrs. Eddy, and she herself says that she was forced to prompt her subject by reading to him from her own published work on Mrs. Eddy's youth. George Glover III was at the time of the interview in his eighties, and it may be doubted how reliable his memories of what his father had told him years before could be. Nonetheless, this testimony should not be disregarded.

George Glover III told Mrs. Smaus that his father had spoken often to his family of how much he loved his mother, how much he had chafed against being separated from her. George Glover II told his son of the occasions when Mahala had brought him back from North Groton to see his mother in Sanbornton, or later in Franklin, of how she rejoiced to see him and gave him small treats, and how sad it was for both to say good-bye. George Glover II told his son George III how wild he had been when he was forced to leave his mother to move to Minnesota, how heartbroken he had been when he was told that she had died and that there was therefore no way for him to return to her side. Throughout the Civil War he carried a little daguerreotype of his mother next to his heart, as well as the Bible she had given him.

As we shall see in subsequent chapters, it proved to be a terrible mistake to entrust George Glover II to Mahala Sanborn Cheney. What was probably designed to be a temporary arrangement solidified with time, and Russell Cheney increasingly looked upon the boy as his indentured servant. New Hampshire law allowed for pauper children to be indentured even as infants, and the indenture lasted until the age of twenty-one for boys and eighteen for girls. Whereas Mary Baker Eddy's ancestors for several generations had been striving successfully to move up the social ladder by hard work, education, careful investment, prudent husbandry, and professional activities, her son was pushed back down to the level of illiterate, hardscrabble farmer and roving hired man. Mahala loved the boy, and he would love her too, but neither could prevail against the unlucky, improvident, mean-spirited, despotic Russell. Even if we grant that the then Mrs. Mary Glover loved her son and was loath to part with him, it is hard not to blame her for not saving him, not defending him more effectively against those who wished him ill and sold him short. Did she fail out of weakness, if not out of hard-heartedness?

Weakness was clearly at issue here: in the passage from the first edition of *Retrospection and Introspection* which I have quoted previously, Mrs. Eddy wrote that she regarded her health as precarious, but in a later edition she amended the text to reflect that she regarded her home as very precious, meaning, I assume, that faced with the choice of being cast off by her family if she would not give up the boy, she could not then find the strength to leave Sanbornton Bridge. Convinced in 1850 by bitter experience that she could not, by her own resources, earn enough to support herself and her child, Mrs. Mary Glover, unheroically but realistically, decided that it was in the best interests of herself and little George that they separate until such a time as she could find a way to get him back.[46] The loving Mahala, the school near her home, the relative proximity of North Groton to Sanborton Bridge in an age of increasingly effective public transportation, all these factors must have made the Cheney option seem a reasonable one to Mary Glover, and her family no doubt emphasized these points to her many times. At the time she could not know that she and her son were at the top of a steep slide and that their lives would go downhill henceforward.

As for the other members of the Baker clan, their hard-heartedness and distaste for little George can be understood if not forgiven. The child was making an already difficult situation worse. Mrs. Abigail Tilton had a busy life and problems of her own with young Albert. Martha Pilsbury was a widow in poor circumstances with two small children to care for. George Sullivan Baker was, by 1850, far away, plagued with domestic and professional problems. Mark Baker felt he deserved a peaceful and prosperous old age after so much labor, and he had his new wife to consider. Mark was legally and financially responsible for Mary's son, and Mary was in no position to flout her father's wishes or spurn his support. Mary was not able to discipline a boy whose naughtiness and inability to sit still and amuse himself disturbed the whole family's peace as well as their notions of infant virtue. Georgie was no Little Lord Fauntleroy, wise and moral in snowy lace collar and spotless velvet suit. In the short term, Mahala's offer to take the boy seemed like the answer to the family's prayers, and they looked no further ahead.

Mary Baker Eddy's relation to her son and her years as a wife and mother always constituted an area in which she felt herself peculiarly vulnerable.

Mark Baker, tintype, date unknown. In her later years, Mary Baker Eddy said that her father "kept his family in the tightest harness I have ever known." *Courtesy of the Longyear Museum, Brookline, Massachusetts.*

Mary Patterson, tintype given to Sarah Crosby around 1863. *Courtesy of Church History Department, The First Church of Christ, Scientist.*

Mary Patterson, tintype, Stoughton, circa 1867. While waiting to have her own portrait taken, Mrs. Patterson soothed a fractious baby. *Courtesy of Church History Department, The First Church of Christ, Scientist.*

Mary Patterson, tintype, Stoughton, circa 1867. *Courtesy of Church History Department, The First Church of Christ, Scientist.*

George Washington Glover, date unknown. Mary Baker Eddy's first husband who died after only six months of marriage. Miniature on ivory. *Courtesy of the Longyear Museum, Brookline, Massachusetts.*

George Washington Glover II, Mary Baker Eddy's only child, in his late teens.

Daniel Patterson, Mary Baker Eddy's philandering second husband, as a young man. She divorced him for desertion in 1873.

Asa Gilbert Eddy, Mary Baker Eddy's beloved third husband, as a young man. He died in 1882. Ambrotype that belonged to Mrs. Eddy. *Courtesy of Church History Department, The First Church of Christ, Scientist.*

Phineas Parkhurst Quimby, the Maine healer whose example deeply influenced Mary Baker Eddy, pictured in the last years of his life.

Emma Ware of Maine, a disciple of Quimby whose contribution to the development of mental healing has been slighted.

Some loyal Christian Science biographers have tended to explain away Mary Baker Eddy's unconventional career as wife and mother by casting the death of George Glover and much later of Asa Gilbert Eddy, the loss of little George, and the failure of Mary's marriage to Daniel Patterson as providential—the necessary, if unfortunate, preconditions for her emergence as a religious leader. The religious antecedents for this idea are impeccable. God tests the faith of Abraham by demanding he sacrifice his only son, of Job by killing his wife and children. According to Matthew 10, Christ bade his disciples to know neither parents nor child. The first thing Christian must do in *A Pilgrim's Progress* when he sets out on his pilgrimage to the Celestial City is to leave his wife and children behind. Thus the removal from the scene of spouses and children comes to be interpreted as part of some kind of divine plan. In her research paper on Mrs. Eddy's experiences in the South in 1844, Elizabeth Earl Jones offers her version of this common scenario:

> Had Mrs. Eddy's earthly experience flowed on in the usual channels of a happy marriage, beloved children, and the ordinary joys and cares connected therewith, she would have proved herself a devoted wife and mother, an exemplary Christian, friend, neighbor, and citizen, but she would never have discovered Christian Science. God had a greater task for her.[47]

Robert Peel offers a more sophisticated version of the same idea when he compares George being taken off to Minnesota by the Cheneys to Ishmael going into the wilderness so that the real son may emerge. The implication is that having lost her biological child, Mary Baker Eddy could give birth to her spiritual child, the Church of Christ, Scientist. Unfortunately, as even Mrs. Eddy's apologists are aware, in the nineteenth-century American context, interpreting the deaths of loved ones as part of the divine plan for a religious leader is much more problematic when that leader is a woman, and the ones who are sacrificed are male. Christiana, it may be remembered, when she undertakes her own pilgrimage in *A Pilgrim's Progress*, not only takes the children with her but finds a female friend to go along and help her with them.

As a mere biographer I am not obliged to offer a theory of divine providence, but I pause to note that the Christian Scientists are probably right on purely practical grounds in believing that it would have been impossible in Mrs. Eddy's generation for a married woman with children to found a new religion. Spending much of her adult life as a single woman without husband, children, or household to care for, Mary Baker Eddy, though poor, lonely, and a social pariah, yet had the freedom and the incentive to read, write, and think, and to develop a role in the public sphere.

At this time most women who had families found themselves so beset with domestic cares that they barely had the time and energy to write a personal letter or attend service on Sunday. The housekeeping and childcare extended over decades, as grandchildren replaced children, and little nieces and nephews and cousins from needy families were added to the household.[48] Abigail Baker was, in this respect as in others, typical, being rarely without a small child in the house from the first year of her marriage to the last. In many ways, Mrs. Harriet Beecher Stowe and Mrs. Elizabeth Cady Stanton, both of whom managed to continue a public role in their child-rearing years, were far more unusual than their fellow activist Angelina Grimké, who retired to the sidelines once she married Theodore Weld and started childbearing. With the help of her unmarried sister Sarah, Angelina was reduced to battling the forces of domestic chaos, leaving the cause of social reform to her husband.[49]

Yet if Mrs. Eddy's career as a healer and church organizer was in part made possible by her relative freedom from domestic duties, this freedom was won at enormous cost, paid in the currency not only of personal happiness and security but also of public notoriety. An irreproachable personal life was a first essential for those rare women who played a public role. Any hints of sexual adventures were usually fatal, of course, for single and married women alike—even the idolized Clara Barton was to suffer at times from reports of suspicious intimacy with male assistants. But whereas the morally impeccable Catharine Beecher and Elizabeth Peabody could be dismissed as fussy old spinsters, Mary Baker Eddy would come under double suspicion as a woman who had lost two husbands and divorced a third, and who had "lost" her only son in his boyhood.[50]

It was against the background of the grand Victorian theme of pure, self-sacrificing motherhood as the highest value to which a woman can aspire that Mary Baker Eddy and her son played out their own drama, and she was as aware as anyone that she was failing to play the heroine's role her culture had assigned her.[51] Like most of us, she had the qualities to make a good enough mother, given the right circumstances, but the circumstances in her case were not right. As we shall see in later chapters, the letters Mary wrote to George Glover after 1870, the efforts she made to make up to him as an adult for what he had lost as a child, all amply testify that she recognized her own failure as a mother and blamed herself for it.

6

Marriage to Dr. Patterson

MARY'S CHRONIC ILL HEALTH WAS ONE OF THE REA-
sons alleged for sending her unruly little son away from her, but after
Georgie had left for North Groton to join the Cheneys, Mary's health, far
from improving, took a sharp turn for the worse. Martha Baker Pilsbury
reported thus to her sister-in-law Martha Rand Baker on January 4, 1852:

> Was then sent for to take care of sister Mary, she having been taken much
> worse immediately after I left home. I left Ellen with her aunt Walker in
> order to give her my entire care—Mary Neal, (better known to you per-
> haps as Kitty) remaining with Mother [Elizabeth Patterson Baker].
> Found her very sick, from one of her most severe attacks of dispepsia,
> liver-complaint and nervous disease. It would be impossible to point out
> the changes, or trace the progress of disease down to the present time, or
> describe the hopes and fears, doubts and expectations that have affected
> us respecting the result, during this long period of continued suffering,
> having been all the time confined to the room and bed, except when pos-
> sibly able to be helped into a carriage to ride. And what can I say of her
> now? How tell you, that after so long and inconceivable suffering, though
> still living, and perhaps doomed to yet longer and greater affliction by an
> all-wise but inscrutable Providence, yet, that there is scarcely a ray of
> hope left us of her recovery. Her strength gradually fails, and all the pow-
> ers of life seems yielding to the force of disease.
>
> O Martha! it would move the sternest soul, and make mortality
> shrink, to witness the agony she often endures, while it pierces a sister's
> heart, with a pang that only affection <u>can</u> feel, or can endure.[1]

Nursed by her devoted family, Mary recovered from this illness as from others, but each struggle seemed to bring her a little lower and defined her, to herself as well as to others, as a confirmed invalid. As with so many women of her generation, sadness merged into depression, economic dependency and nonproductivity into frustration and a sense of valuelessness, and when these combined with those physical ailments which were the inevitable lot of human beings at this period, the result was a woman who could barely get up from her couch.

Mary Baker Glover's invalidism was both an individual problem and part of a national, or international, trend among women, and one which the medical and religious authorities of the day were largely powerless to understand, much less solve. In 1855 Catharine Beecher reported that having polled her extensive female acquaintance to establish the state of health prevailing among women, invalids outnumbered well women by about seven to one, and daughters almost never enjoyed the good health their mothers had taken for granted. Beecher concluded that there was a crisis of health among middle-class American women which was having serious consequences throughout society.[2]

In 1852 Mary's woes were complicated by severe dental problems, and, despite her growing disillusion with the medical profession in general, she consulted Dr. Daniel Patterson, a local dentist. She seems to have found Patterson by chance. According to the story she told later in life, she had embarked, suffering from intense toothache, for a visit to a dentist in another town, took the wrong car by mistake, and found herself in the town of Franklin, where she was forced to remain overnight with friends.[3] Overcome during the night with the pain from her tooth, she asked if there was a dentist practicing locally, and Patterson was recommended to her. He successfully treated the tooth, no doubt by pulling it.

Mary Glover lost several teeth, and in a letter of December 12, 1852, she wrote to Patterson: "I would like to retain as long as possible all I have left! feeling the chagrin of my present mouth, most essentially. Never knowing before the loss of teeth, I was ignorant of all the difficulties I find attend it."[4] Stoic about the pain, and attempting to make light of a problem that was certainly no joke to her, she wrote a little poem bemoaning the loss of her smile: "treacherous joy reveals the worthy crime / And gaping gums betray the tooth of time."[5] One of the most stupid "facts" set down in the Milmine biography of Mrs. Eddy was that "although she had excellent teeth, she had some of them replaced by false ones, 'made entirely of platinum,' as Mrs. Glover described them."[6] Confronted with such picturesquely staged untruths, one wonders whether the McClure's team of reporters was maliciously making things up or mindlessly collecting ridiculous but wounding local gossip.

Daniel Patterson, to whom Mrs. Glover's little poem was written, had a practice centered in the flourishing little town of Franklin, where the inhabitants of Sanbornton Bridge often went to do their shopping. Patterson was a man of the new school, anxious to fill teeth, pioneering in the use of anesthesia in extractions, and reputed to make good teeth. He carried his practice around to the local towns and villages, serving not only as dentist but as a specialist in homeopathy, the new medicine that was sweeping the country. In one of his letters to Mrs. Mary Glover he gives a humorous description of the ill-lit and ill-equipped room, eight by sixteen feet, which he leased in Wolfboro for $6.50 a week, its main advantage being that any patient taken faint during the treatment had little room to fall to the ground!

Patterson was a relation by marriage of Mary's stepmother, Elizabeth Patterson Duncan Baker. He came from a poor family in Saco, Maine, and was given the honorary title of doctor even though he had little formal education or medical training. A tall, well-built, handsome man with a long beard, Patterson always dressed carefully in top hat, frock coat, and kid gloves, and he was known to have a way with women. His correspondence with Mrs. Mary Glover seems to have begun in December 1852 with letters of a purely professional kind, but he rapidly determined to marry her and declared his love. Patterson's courtship is documented in seven letters which he and Mrs. Glover exchanged between January and May, when they became officially engaged.

A new husband formed the obvious, conventional answer to all of Mary Glover's problems, but from the outset there were serious doubts as to whether Patterson was husband material. In his letters to Mary, Patterson finds it necessary to defend himself vigorously against charges that he was first a Baptist and second a man of poor reputation. To be a Baptist was a serious flaw to a convinced Congregationalist such as Mark Baker; in fact, one of Mary's letters indicates that she initially rejected Patterson's marriage proposal on religious grounds. Patterson riposted that even if he was a Baptist, he was a loyal and God-fearing one, and he called to witness his own clergyman and members of his congregation, insisting that many a Congregationalist of his acquaintance would give him a good reputation. Certain dark rumors about Patterson's past had also reached the Baker clan, and these he again hotly denied, challenging Mark Baker to go out and talk to his friends and colleagues in other towns. The gentleman does seem to be protesting too much here, and given his later failure as a businessman and husband, we may now suspect that the slightly shady reputation Patterson had gained as early as 1852 was not undeserved. Mark Baker would have done well to investigate the dental doctor's record more thoroughly.

On a more personal level, Patterson admitted to Mary that he could not compete with her in learning, and he wished he could write her the kind of love letters which would win her heart and impress her friends:

It is proper that you should know me thoroughly, so that when we are married, and you leave me to visit your friends, you may not lack for either a Philosophic, or a Poetical letter from your husband and after reading my unsavory production, cry from very vexation and disappointment and say O! that I had only had sense enough to have married a man of genius, an intellectual, literary man, who could write to me something readable, that I would be proud to show my friends . . . but Alas! that power was not inherent . . . and I am determined that you shall not deceive yourself in this respect, as I have heard you often urge a lack of literary taste, as an objection to your late husband.

Daniel Patterson, in fact, compared favorably with the late George Glover in this literary respect. He certainly spelled better, was capable of exchanging verses, and manifested a properly romantic appreciation of mountain scenery. Daniel proclaims that he is no writer, a plain man who cannot make love in letters, but this confession is in itself an epistolary ploy, designed to win the reader over. In fact Patterson's letters smack of a sort of naïve yet canny sexual rhetoric and an instinctive understanding of romantic topoi.

There was one time in my ride in this place, when I said to myself— "how I <u>wish Mary</u> was with me"—it was on attaining the summit of a hill, the first view of the Lake burst on my vision with its smooth face scarified, and lacerated by numerous Islets, and points, and yet it was beautiful; <u>then I really wished you by my side</u>—

There is a manly self-assertiveness in the letters that shades, unexpectedly, into doubt, and into an almost Gothic suggestion of hidden secrets and Rochesterian depths that no doubt appealed to a lady who, as I have noted before, loved the Brontë novels:

I must confess I am not surprised that any lady should shrink from uniting themselves with me the only wonder is that you ever thought of such a strange thing—I know it must be love standing at the very threshold of Idolatry should induce such a woman I should want to marry me, and that is the <u>only</u> love that will satisfy <u>me</u>—no ordinary commonplace love will ever answer my purpose—it must be stronger than the love of life itself, and it would naturally be supposed that a woman would ask a guarantee of a suitable return which my caution must always prevent my giving—fearing I should raise hopes that would not be realised and I am resolved that my wife if I ever have one shall not have her hopes raised only to be dashed to the ground after marriage I have therefore persued the cours I have because I have no guarantee of my own better feelings after matrimony and my worst feelings may predominate.[7]

Later events proved that Patterson's doubts about his ability to offer his wife the adoration and fidelity he expected from her were all too well

founded. As Bates and Dittemore remark, Patterson was not even very successful in treating her dental problems to judge from another letter she wrote
after his return to Franklin in the spring:

> In this [letter] she complains that she has broken one of her false teeth,
> but consoles herself with the thought that "they never were disposed
> right in their constitution, always ugly!" She adds archly: "Shall <u>not</u> the
> clay say to the potter Why didst thou form me thus?" When she first
> had them, a friend said: "What hateful teeth, Mary," whereupon she
> *dropped* them, and the friend screamed. The letter ends: "Yours in
> Toothless Trouble, Mary."[8]

Mary Baker Eddy's biographers have wrestled with the question of what
brought Patterson and Mrs. Glover together and what they saw in one
another. Male biographers unsympathetic to their subject like Ernest Bates
have liked to take Patterson's side, casting him as a genial but unlucky rough
diamond, betrayed by the devious mind and calculated helplessness of a hysterical wife. Patterson's long, steep fall into destitution after his divorce from
Mary, the pauper's grave that would be his at last, are cited as proof that his
wife failed him as a helpmate.[9] Women critics sympathetic to Mary, such as
Jewel Spangler Smaus, have viewed Patterson as a traitor possessed of neither business acumen nor moral fiber, and they have marvelled that their
beloved Mary Baker Eddy could have been so deceived.

As I see it, Patterson was an ambitious man, in awe of the prosperous
middle class to which Mary's family belonged and into which Patterson's own
distant relative by marriage Elizabeth Duncan Patterson had married in
1850. All the information we have about Patterson's family indicates that
they were of very modest means and failed to ride the upward currents of
nineteenth-century American society. Mary Baker Glover represented for
him the way of life he aspired to, and he probably anticipated that the patronage of her family and their friends would be the passport to professional success which he had neither the stamina nor the ability to achieve alone. Mary
was also a very attractive woman, particularly to a dentist and homeopath for
whom the gaps in her mouth and her frail health represented a professional
opportunity rather than a blemish.

The attraction which Mary Baker Eddy exercised over many men
apart from Daniel Patterson, and which continued long after her girlhood,
can dimly be sensed from the earliest extant portrait of her, probably taken
during her stay in the house of her sister in Sanbornton Bridge Center.[10]
Thin, delicate, with long, shapely, ringed hands and huge haunting eyes,
dressed in a dark, tight, heavily ruched silk gown, she is an arresting figure. It is true that Mary was a confirmed invalid, but her very sickliness
was attractive in an age when the tubercular look was fashionable for
women,[11] and pale cheeks, a fragile frame, and delicate nerves were

considered by many to be characteristics of the well-bred woman of good family.

Desperation is the best reason I can find to account for Mrs. Mary Glover's decision to marry Daniel Patterson. Around 1847 she had still had the strength of mind, the common sense, perhaps the egotism, to refuse to marry good but poor men whom she did not really love, such as James Smith, just because they loved her and asked for her hand. She hesitated for a long time before accepting the attentions of John Bartlett, sending him away alone to make his fortune and hers in the legendary West, but prudence and restraint no doubt seemed poor guides to conduct when the news came of John Bartlett's death. By 1852 Mary Baker Glover was thirty-one years old and had known six months of marriage and eight years of widowhood. Her situation in Sanbornton Bridge, difficult from the outset, had become unbearable. With her mother dead and her father happily remarried, Mary Glover was living in the magnificent new house of her elder sister and brother-in-law. Abigail showed real affection and generosity in giving her impoverished sister a home, but she was a woman of ability and ambition, wielding increasing power and influence in the town, used to having her way, and not an easy person to live with. The Tilton mills, called the Corporation locally, was the biggest employer, and the Tilton clan in its various branches formed the aristocracy of the town. The Alexander Tiltons lived in a style and on a scale quite different from the one Mary Baker had grown up with, and smoking, drinking, and anti-abolitionist talk around the house were less and less to her taste.[12] Nineteenth-century novelists like Balzac, Dickens, and Thackeray saw enormous potential for tragedy and comedy in the life of the poor relative in the rich home, but no lover of fiction ever wanted to be such a character in real life. It does not take a doctorate in psychology to see that Mrs. Glover's increasing invalidism, her inability to walk, her retreat to her bedroom and to the porch swing were not just accidental organic problems but silent somatic protests against her life of dependency.

And then there was the practical, persistent, increasingly urgent question of young George, now nine years old, and growing wilder by the week. Mahala Cheney occasionally brought little George to see his mother at Sanbornton Bridge,[13] and Mary learned that the boy was spending more time at the forge and the mica mines in North Groton than in the overcrowded, unfriendly, chaotic little school. Mary now knew what kind of man Russell Cheney was, how he abused his wife and the boy, and perhaps she was already afraid that Russell Cheney was regarding the boy as his and treating him as an indentured servant, not a temporary guest. It may sound melodramatic, but I think that it is probable that Patterson's proposal of marriage came when Mary Glover felt that she must either escape or die. Thin, weak, paralyzed by pain and fear and anguish, she yet had a core of energy and hope that propelled her to seek change. She had not yet considered the possibility that she was rashly choosing the devil she did not know over the devil she did.

In the confidential chat she had with Janette Weller in 1884, Mrs. Eddy claimed that she had at first strongly resisted Patterson, but he had sought her out, courted her vigorously, and had finally prevailed upon her to marry him. She told Weller that after Patterson had helped cure her toothache, he came to visit her home, asking after her health, and was given a warm welcome by the Bakers and Tiltons. She herself loathed the man, tried to escape his attentions by going away on a visit, but she found him hot in pursuit of her. She then fell desperately ill, so ill, she told Weller, that her family and the doctors despaired of her life. Patterson consulted his books, came up with some remedy, which was administered, and which was credited with curing her. Mrs. Glover was now assured by her family that she owed Patterson her life, and therefore her gratitude, and she claimed that from that point onward "she learned to love him."[14]

Probably, in the end, Daniel Patterson prevailed in his suit for the simple reason that he was a single man who immediately declared himself in love and proposed marriage to her, and Mary Baker Glover desperately needed to have a husband to support her. Daniel seemed the kind of strong, kindly man who could be a second father to her boy, as the dead John Bartlett had promised to be, and he was a manly man, tall, strong enough to lean on— strong enough to carry her up and down stairs, as he reportedly did on their wedding day and on other occasions. Patterson was handsome and personally meticulous in his clothing and toilet, something always important to Mary, who had insisted upon cleanliness and order even as a child, unable to sleep, as she later told Adelaide Still, until she had put her shoes straight. He was also a man who had experience in conquering female reluctance, and with Mary he collaborated in a staging of female weakness and male strength whose erotic content their nineteenth-century contemporaries understood very well. I think she found him desirable, and that this attraction blinded her to his faults of character and situation, even to the lamentable job he made of her false teeth! As Henry James shows so exquisitely in *A Portrait of a Lady*, even intelligent, perceptive women have difficulty in divining the real nature of their male suitors. Like many a woman before and after her, Mary Baker Glover tended to choose a man on the basis of physical attraction, or perhaps to assume that a strong macho body must correlate with professional competence and social usefulness.

In *Retrospection and Introspection* Mrs. Eddy claims that she accepted Daniel Patterson because her son needed a father: "My dominant thought in marrying again was to get back my child, but after our marriage his stepfather was not willing he should have a home with me."[15]

Hostile critics, notably Milmine, Dakin, and Bates and Dittemore,[16] have treated such expressions of maternal concern with suspicion and even ridicule, but Jewel Spangler Smaus unearthed two important pieces of evidence that confirm the accuracy of Mrs. Eddy's statement. On the very day of her wedding she signed two legal documents designating Daniel Patterson as George Glover's guardian. By New Hampshire law, Patterson did not become George's guardian simply by becoming his stepfather, and Mary had obviously determined ahead of time that it was vital for her new husband to publicly and officially take responsibility for her child. In the first document—both of the documents are reproduced in facsimile in Mrs. Smaus's article[17]—Mary Glover acknowledges that she is the mother of George Glover, son of the deceased George Glover of Wilmington, North Carolina, herself declines guardianship of the boy, and recommends that Daniel Patterson be recognized as a fit person to be the boy's guardian. In the second document, Daniel Patterson, Mark Baker, and Dudley Ladd sign a bond of $400 binding Daniel Patterson as George Glover's guardian.

These documents are a strong indication that Patterson had promised Mrs. Glover that he would become her son's guardian, and that she married him confident that this promise would be kept. Unfortunately, whether moved by his own feelings toward George—whom he could have hardly known personally by the time of the marriage—or, more probably, influenced by the Baker family's negative judgment of the boy, Patterson from the outset refused even to try to be a father to Mary's son. The documents he signed on his wedding day were null unless Patterson made an appearance before the court, and this he never did. By failing to take the final legal step Patterson exempted himself from having any legal responsibilities for the boy, and all his efforts over the next years would in fact be aimed at separating his wife from her child.

After the wedding at the Baker home in Sanbornton Bridge, Dr. and Mrs. Patterson settled in Franklin, first in rather squalid lodgings and then on the first floor of a small house which Daniel bought and Mary furnished, largely with things she had inherited from her mother. Almost nothing is known of this time except that Mary had ceased to respond to her husband's homeopathic expertise, and that she retired even more resolutely into her bedroom, making very few contacts with the local community. One interesting piece of eyewitness testimony is on record. Miss Lucy Clark wrote to Mrs. Eddy in 1890, remembering how at age twelve she had come to Dr. Patterson for dental treatment and had been enthralled and inspired by the dentist's wife sitting close by in the window and reading the poetry of Ossian aloud to her. Later, as a student at Mount Holyoke, Miss Clark tried in vain to recapture her emotion by reading the poetry for herself, but she found it only when she came upon a copy of *Science and Health*. This girl, thrilling to the wild anguish of the quintessential romantic verse and forgetting the pain of the treatment, is an early testimony to the force of Mary Baker Eddy's presence.[18]

That money was tight for the Patterson ménage from the start and that the new Mrs. Patterson was making a solid attempt to keep down household expenses can be seen from the careful list of goods and services bought between December 1853 and March 1854, which Mrs. Patterson recorded in her copybook. There is a pathos in the smallness of the sums listed: a peck of potatoes—twelve cents; one beet and one turnip—four cents; one ball of soap—twelve cents; six and a half pounds of pie meat at eight cents—fifty-two cents. The Pattersons' diet at this period was apparently a balanced and traditional one, made up of various kinds of vegetables as well as the staple potatoes, some pork, mutton, and beef as well as fresh and salt fish, oysters, pickerel, halibut, and cod. Sugar, butter, eggs, raisins, lemon, ginger, cream of tartar, and "saleratus" (baking powder) were purchased for baking, and the principle flour they used was the popular Graham meal. Milk seems to have been an important item, since the Pattersons both kept a cow and regularly bought milk. Perhaps Mrs. Patterson ate mainly a vegetarian diet of porridges and baked goods but served her husband the more varied diet expected by an active male.

In 1855 the couple moved to North Groton, and it is at this point that things began to go really wrong with the Patterson ménage. Mary managed to persuade her sisters to stake her for one more attempt at both financial independence and reunion with her son, George. According to Elmira Smith Wilson, who worked as the Pattersons' maid for two years during this period, the main reason for the move was Mary's desire to be near her son. Mrs. Sarah C. Turner, a niece of the Cheneys, supported this view in her account taken in May 1907: "in making the effort to be with her boy by coming to Groton, Mrs. Patterson ultimately sacrificed her husband's profession for a time at least, there not being enough support for a dentist in that little place."[19] But it seems unlikely to me that Patterson could have been prevailed upon to leave Franklin if his practice there had been flourishing. More probably, having given up his horse in favor of a cow, he had let his itinerant dental business slip and was more than willing to contemplate moving to a new location and exploring other ways of making a living.

The North Groton property to which the Pattersons moved included a small house and a sawmill on four acres of land owned by the Tiltons and held under a mortgage to Martha Pilsbury. That it was the relatively impoverished Martha Baker Pilsbury who advanced the Pattersons this money, not the affluent Abigail Tilton, can probably be attributed to the fact that in 1855 the Tilton mill in Sanbornton burned down, and Abigail and her husband were marshalling all their capital to rebuild and start the business up again. At this point Martha Pilsbury had managed to move with her two young daughters out of her father's home and into a small house of her own, but her resources were slender, and the mortgage payments she collected from the North Groton property were an important source of income for her.

Daniel Patterson bought one hundred acres of forest up the mountain, and the timber from this parcel, plus the income from the sawmill, was meant to provide the couple financial stability. The Pattersons' new home was close to the main road and to other houses, and it was about a mile from the Cheney farm where little George was living.[20]

Today the Patterson house in North Groton is maintained by the Longyear Museum and is open to the general public. I set out to visit it on a fine summer day in 1993, and, after passing by signs for the tourist mecca of Lake Winnipesaukee, found an idyllic little New England home, backing steeply onto a stream and surrounded by trees in one of the more beautiful and unspoiled parts of New Hampshire. Such visits are an important part of a researcher's task but can also be profoundly misleading. The interior of the house is informative since it has been carefully restored to represent Mrs. Patterson's real living circumstances between 1855 and 1860. Yet as the nineteenth-century photographs contained in the house show, North Groton today and Mrs. Mary Patterson's North Groton are very different places. Far from being bucolic and devoted to tourists, North Groton in 1855 was an ugly, banal, but bustling little place of nearly a thousand inhabitants, with a good general store, a library, and several schools. The area had been deforested to produce lumber and to allow for the cultivation of corn, oats, potatoes, and buckwheat. The town also had important mineral deposits, and the mica mine, just up the hill from the Cheneys' property, was to flourish after the Civil War. Too hilly for the railroad, North Groton was still reached by horse or ox transport from the nearest depot at Rumney, six miles away.

The economy in North Groton was thriving in the 1850s, but this prosperity did not rub off on the Pattersons. In 1856 Patterson was failing to make his rent payments, and the household was in absolute want. Abigail Tilton came over bearing supplies and assurances to the Pattersons' invaluable maid that her wages would be met even if the doctor could not pay them, and Martha Pilsbury was already thinking of foreclosing on Patterson. We learn all this from the later testimony of the maid or that of her younger sister, from letters written by Martha to her brother George which are now at the Longyear Museum, and from the following letter, written to George Sullivan Baker by his stepmother, Elizabeth Baker, on June 6, 1856. Mrs. Baker notes that her nephew Samuel Baker Jr. has visited Sanbornton Bridge before departing on a voyage to South America, and that Ellen Pilsbury, Martha Baker Pilsbury's daughter, has remained with them while her mother paid a visit to Concord. Mrs. Baker continues:

> You spoke of Martha foreclosing her business with Docter Patterson Your father [i.e., Mark Baker] spoke to Col Kate about it he says the time is not up untill next spring that she can do it but he thinks she is safe haveing enough in her hands to secure her I feel sorry for her as it causes her much trouble We do not hear one word about Mary health

when he has written lately to anny one he says nothing about her they do not write to us she wrote to some one that she wanted me to go up and take care of her but I thought she needed some one who had some wit even one tallant but it was no use for me to go as in her opinion I did not possess even that We do not know what will become of them as it requires all his time to take care of her We pitty them. Mr Cheney Wife and little George was here about the time of Marys death they have moved to Minosoti they Arived in safety in six days much pleased with the place.

This letter demonstrates that in 1856 Mary was in very bad health and had ceased to correspond with her family, that Patterson was claiming that he spent all his time caring for her and was therefore unable to make his payments. It also shows that Mary, unlike her siblings, had not yet made her peace with her good-hearted, if, to judge by this single letter, ill-educated, stepmother, although the two would become friends in time. It also proves that the Baker-Tilton-Pilsbury family was fully informed about George Glover's move to Minnesota with the Cheneys, and that they were in correspondence with Russell—an important point, as we shall see later.

This letter is one of the very rare windows on Mrs. Mary Patterson's five years in North Groton. That she was deeply unhappy there is sure, that her invalidism was confirmed and intensified, equally so. Money, or lack of it, was a constant problem. Far from solving her financial and social problems by marrying Patterson, Mary had exacerbated them. The move to the hilly and somewhat isolated North Groton community was not conducive to establishing a flourishing dental practice, and it was doubtless harder for Patterson to move about the country looking for patients when he had a permanently sick wife at home.

It is impossible to know how far to accept Patterson's complaints to his in-laws that he was unable to work because he had to care for his ailing wife. My feeling is that the amiable Patterson was more of a dandy and a talker than a worker, that he expected his wife's rich relatives to support them both, and that Mary's health became an alibi for his inactivity and financial ineptitude. Had he been a better dentist or sawmill operator, he would have been able to afford to hire other people to look after his wife, and both of them would have been subject to much less social embarrassment. Donald Meyer has described the nineteenth century in America as a great age for men: "Men were in short supply everywhere. De Tocqueville's portrait was that of a society where every (white) male fancied his life in terms of his 'chances' and these were real. Once industry put down lasting roots and urban life began to spread, after 1830, practically every head and hand was found welcome."[21] Daniel Patterson was remarkable for failing to make enough money even to survive on, in an age of great opportunity and full employment.

For Mary, Patterson's incapacity as a breadwinner was another terrible blow. His increasing indebtedness brought them yet further down the social scale, poisoned their relations with other townspeople, and made the tensions with Mary's family much worse. In her later life as a famous public figure, Mrs. Eddy was to be accused of many things, but never of not understanding money. Once she started to make her own way financially, Mrs. Eddy proved a formidable worker, a thrifty manager of funds, and a shrewd investor. To the end of her days she abhorred debt with a Puritan passion inherited perhaps from her father. Thus during her marriage to Patterson his debts were undoubtedly a source of humiliation and shame to her, and she responded by withdrawing further from society.

There is good evidence that Mary Patterson was not appreciated by the adults of North Groton. As Mrs. Patterson grew older, as her social position sank, she failed to show the proper subservience, and this was held against her. Pride, reclusiveness, nervousness, eccentricity, emotional outbursts were not considered proper in a woman of her degraded station. The Milmine team found a neighbor who described graphically how, convinced that Mrs. Patterson was dying, he had fought his way through a blizzard to reach Dr. Patterson on his dental rounds and warn him to come home at once. Patterson received the news calmly, remarked, "I think she will live until I finish this job at least," and, indeed, when the two men reached the house in North Groton later that day, frozen and exhausted, they found Mary serene and cheerful, seated in her chair. Whether this was an isolated incident or part of a behavioral pattern, as Patterson's reaction suggests, is impossible to determine today.

The Milmine biography goes on to quote a letter from a North Groton correspondent published in the *Plymouth Record* on July 16, 1904:

> With the announcement of the dedication of the Christian Science Church at Concord, the gift of Mary Baker Glover Patterson Eddy, the thoughts of many of the older residents have turned back to the time when Mrs. Eddy, as the wife of Daniel Patterson, lived in this place. These people remember the woman at that time as one who carried herself above her fellows. With no stretch of the imagination they remember her ungovernable temper and hysterical ways, and particularly well do they remember the night ride of one of the citizens who went for her husband to calm her in one of her unreasonable moods. The Mrs. Eddy of to-day is not the Mrs. Patterson of then, for this is the sort of Mr. Hyde and Dr. Jekyll case, and the woman is now credited with many charitable and kindly acts.[22]

To list the names of all three of Mrs. Eddy's husbands is always a hint of actively hostile rhetoric in the Frederick Peabody tradition, and the phrase "who carried herself above her fellows" gives us a good clue to the prejudices of the unnamed writer. The phrase recalls a comment by Sarah Clement

Kimball: "Mrs. Eddy was so entirely unlike the run of New England country people that they could not understand her."[23] The North Groton correspondent might have considered the consecration of Mrs. Eddy's church in Concord as proof that Mrs. Patterson's assumption of superiority years before had not been entirely unmerited, but he or she prefers to interpret it as a case of female duplicity.

One other well-attested incident from the North Groton years shows clearly that Mrs. Patterson's invalidism was caused less by physical disease or disorder than by her state of mind. The *Nashua Gazette* of March 15, 1860, ran the following story, under the heading "Female Bravery":

> A North Groton (N.H.) correspondent of the Concord Patriot writes that on the 20th ult., Dr. Patterson, a dentist in that place, while employed in splitting wood before his door, was assaulted by two men, father and son, named Wheet. The elder Wheet rushed upon him with a shovel, which the Doctor knocked from his hands with his axe, at the same time losing hold of the axe.
>
> The elder assailant then attempted to get him by the throat, but the Doctor knocked him down, when young Wheet rushed upon the Doctor with the axe, and striking him upon the head, stunned and felled him to the ground. The father than seized him by the neck, and called upon his son to strike. The son was about to comply with the murderous request, when the wife of Dr. Patterson, almost helpless by long disease, rushed from her bed to the rescue of her husband, and throwing herself before their intended victim, seized, with unwonted strength, the son who held the axe and prevented him from dealing the intended blow. Help soon came, the assailants fled, and the feeble but brave wife was carried back to her bed.[24]

Men who are frustrated tend to get angry and vent their aggressions on the world, becoming either criminals or heroes, or both in the same life. Frustrated women tend to turn their feelings inward and assail themselves, not others, becoming madwomen or mystics or hysterics. The hysteric, who is almost always a woman, expresses frustration and impotence through somatic symptoms which, all too often, become in time the crippling or even lethal physical ailments the hysteric has mimed. Whereas I remain unconvinced by the evidence that as a girl Mary Baker was ever subject to attacks of "grande hystérie" in the manner of Charcot, I do believe that the adult Mrs. Mary Glover Patterson was a hysteric, that her main presenting symptoms—constant pain in the back and abdomen and an inability to sit up or stand—were not entirely or even largely a matter of diseased internal organs or of nerve damage.

What seems to me to be the first reliable report of Mrs. Eddy experiencing a hysterical fit comes from the North Groton period. It can be considered reliable because it comes from the pen of Sibyl Wilbur, who wrote unabashedly to defend Mrs. Eddy from attack, in a sympathetic narrative passage describing the results of Wilbur's own reportorial forays into New Hampshire.

> Of Mrs. Eddy's extreme invalidism at this time there is no doubt. "I had the honor to take care of Mrs. Eddy once," said a very old woman of Groton. "She was all alone in her home and I heard her bell ringing. I went in and found her lying rigid with foam on her lips. I brought her around with cold water. She motioned to her medicine chest, and I gave her what she wanted. Then I sat with her till she got better."[25]

Mrs. Patterson diagnosed her own ills accurately in a scrapbook entry of May 1857:

> I slept very little last night in consequence of memory and wounded feelings. My spine is so weak and inflammatory that the least mental emotion gives me suffering that language cannot depict. Then the debility which follows seems nearly as distressing. Oh! how long must I bear this burden life?[26]

It is fascinating that Mrs. Patterson underlines the word *memory* here—Freud was to become famous some forty years later by claiming that hysterics suffer from memories—and that she refers to "wounded feelings" and "the least mental emotion" as the triggers for her symptoms.

Diagnosis, however, is one thing, and cure is another. Cure for Mrs. Patterson's ills at this time was not to be found either in traditional medical remedies or in new fads such as the Graham diet or homeopathy. As the Wheet incident dramatically proved, when called upon by an external event, Mrs. Patterson could overcome her illness and take on the active physical role of savior or knight errant. Her problem was that she had been cast, apparently for life, in the role of the helpless princess chained to the rock, or couch, and was almost never called upon to show strength, initiative, or independence, much less bravery.

What did Mrs. Patterson do during those years of seclusion, especially during the long, cold, snowbound New Hampshire winters when her husband was away from home? The best answers to that question come from the testimony of her single live-in servant, Elmira (Myra) Smith (later Mrs. Wilson), a twenty-year-old blind girl whom Mrs. Patterson had taken in. Over a period of several years, The Mother Church in Boston collected statements from both Myra and her younger sister Mrs. Marcia Swett. The latter had often been in the Patterson home as a child and helped with the housework. Apart from Patterson himself, these girls were closest to Mrs. Mary Patterson at this period, and their evidence deserves close attention.

Both girls loved and admired Mrs. Patterson and felt a deep gratitude to her, although Myra Smith remembered Mrs. Patterson as a less than perfect employer. Myra recalled that sometimes her clumsy movements would violently irritate Mrs. Patterson, but immediately Mrs. Patterson would come and put her arms around the girl and apologize. When she said to the younger Smith girl that she wished to have a daughter like her, she probably spoke from the heart. Mrs. Patterson was usually confined to her bed, we learn from the sisters, and ate mainly Graham bread, rye pudding, and fruit. Whereas the North Groton adults disliked and gossiped about Mrs. Patterson, the children loved the poor sick lady who told them stories and read to them and to whom they brought berries and flowers. Forbidden to tutor her own son, Mary helped Daniel Kidder, her next-door neighbor's son, with his homework, as he was to remember with tears of gratitude in later life.[27] The Smith girls testify that they and the other children were afraid of Patterson, and that the doctor and his wife often quarrelled.

Mrs. Patterson spent much time poring over her husband's massive homeopathic manual, Jahr's *New Manual of Homeopathic Practice*, edited by A. Gerald Hull, popularly known as Hull's *Jahr*, and she had a kit of homeopathic remedies. Myra testified that "Mrs. Patterson practised homeopathy among the women and children, to get her sewing done." Once Myra dropped one of the bottles, and the pellets spilled all over the floor, but Mrs. Patterson told her not to mind—"they were no good anyway." This is important evidence that already in the late 1850s Mrs. Patterson was seeking for something that went beyond both the conventional and the alternative medicines of her time. In her later writings she consistently described herself as having practiced homeopathic medicine quite extensively, and she pointed to her experiments with homeopathy as being crucial to the development of her understanding of healing as something that occurs quite independently of "materia medica," whether full strength or in homeopathically attenuated solutions. Thus in the third edition of *Science and Health* (1881) Mrs. Eddy describes how she cured a woman of dropsy, first using homeopathic remedies in the prescribed attenuations but then successfully substituting unmedicated pellets. The incident she described may well have occurred in North Groton. Mrs. Eddy liked to compare the flash of insight as to the role of the mind in healing to Newton and the apple.[28]

Apart from the larger question of healing, which will increasingly take center stage as this biography continues, what interests me about this pill-spilling incident is the whole question of Mrs. Patterson as housekeeper. One of the niggling little charges later brought against Mrs. Eddy by the Milmine-Peabody faction and taken up by Lyman Powell in his first book on Christian Science, *Christian Science: The Faith and Its Founder*, was that she was an idle parasite who allowed others to wait on her while she sat in her room reading and writing, even when she was a penniless guest. Such charges were especially weighty in the nineteenth century when incessant domestic activity and efficiency in managing the home were still prime testimony to a wife's worth.[29] Thus it is interesting to consider the evidence of how Mary Patterson coped with housework when she was confined to bed and could afford to employ only a blind girl as maid of all work.

The testimony from North Groton eyewitnesses, though sparse, is undivided on one point: the Pattersons' little house was immaculate. Hysteric Mary Patterson may have been subject to violent fits and emotional scenes with her husband, spending much of her time on her couch or bed, a book in her hand, but none of her neighbors accused her of slovenliness. To me this is a bit remarkable. Since I am a rather reluctant housekeeper myself, I wonder whether it is better, in practical terms, to have a blind maid, or none. How could Myra move around the house, making porridge, carrying trays, washing up, and so forth?[30] Did Dr. Patterson do housework, did the little sighted girl do her older sister's work, or was Mary in fact much more active than she seemed, charitably taking in a blind girl whom no one else would house, and using her as a screen for doing work that no respectable middle-class woman was supposed to do for herself?[31]

If we turn from Mrs. Patterson's cleaning to the more important issue of her thinking and feeling at this time, the critical document is the scrapbook she kept during this period, containing pieces cut or copied from newspapers, with marginal annotations, and other entries. Both Bates and Dittemore and Robert Peel give accounts of the contents of the scrapbook and reprint some quotations from it. Both agree that unlike her compatriot Susan B. Anthony who was also in poor health in 1855 and who read widely while confined to a sanatorium, Mrs. Patterson was culturally isolated, with neither money nor opportunity to read the important new literature being published at the time in the United States and in Europe.

Bates and Dittemore give a fascinating account of the poems and stories Mrs. Patterson cut out from the local newspapers and put in her scrapbook. The authors comment on the degradation of her taste, on her failure to pursue any serious course of study, on her lack of intellectual curiosity. Where once she had copied out pieces by Wordsworth and Byron, now she chose examples of the most maudlin kind, literary dross long cast on the scrap heap of history. Derisively they quote three stanzas from the poem "Drunk in the Street," about a young wife and mother found in that condition, and five stanzas from "The Gambler's Wife," narrating the sad death from cold and hunger of a neglected wife and child. They summarize the contents of Mary Patterson's scrapbook thus:

> There was scarcely a poem in Mrs. Patterson's collection which did not introduce the subject of death. The mournful titles are sufficient to indicate the nature of these contributions to the literature of melancholia: "Funeral Song At the Grave of Eve," by the late Rev. Walter Colton; "Speak of the Dead," by Mary Annie E. Lease; "The Dying Poet," by Persa S. Lewis; "Angel Charlie," by Mrs. Emilie C. Judson; "On the

Statue of his Dead Child," by Richard Lane; "The Last Tear I Shed," and "Shall I See Them No More," by Robert Josselyn; "My Mother's Grave," by George D. Prentice; "The Dying Girl's Lament," by Mrs. C. Gore. Without further evidence one might be sure that the collector of this gallery was addicted to morbid brooding on disease and death."[32]

I have been unable myself to study the scrapbook, but based on samples of this vital document quoted by Bates and Dittemore and by the predictably more charitable Peel what strikes me is how Mrs. Patterson obsessively selected pieces about women in dire distress. Lamentable as these selections may have been in aesthetic terms, they spoke to her condition, expressed her feelings, and served some purpose in her life. Once she, too, had written poetry, of indifferent merit perhaps, but poetry that had served a therapeutic function, provided some outlet for feeling, some way to distance herself from events and display some public mastery. That now she mainly cut and pasted poetry instead of writing it is indeed a measure of her deepening depression, showing a form of melancholic brooding that we may accuse or excuse, castigate or empathize with, depending, perhaps, on our own experience of depression and our power of will to conquer it.

To add to the daily boredom, anxiety, and tension of Mrs. Patterson's life, there came family sorrows. Her niece and namesake little Mary Neal Pilsbury, only seven years old, and, we are told, a favorite with the elder Mary when she lived in Sanbornton Bridge, died in April 1856. Separated from the family, crushed under the guilt of the debt owed to Martha, whose precious income was going unpaid, unable to mourn with her relatives or to help alleviate her sister's grief as she would infallibly have done in the past, Mrs. Patterson could only sink further into depression and incapacity.

The second sorrow hit closer to home and had far greater impact. Mrs. Mary Patterson had not come any closer to gaining custody of her young son by moving so close to him in North Groton. Myra Smith Wilson in 1911 and George Glover III in the late 1970s testified that Daniel Patterson refused to allow his stepson into his house in North Groton, though occasionally the boy sneaked over to visit his mother when the doctor was away from home. George posed an increasingly painful problem for his mother and was a major reason for her hysteria and depression. It must surely have been salt on the wound for both mother and son to be so close and yet forbidden to see one another except in secret. We can imagine the sad drama of one occasion, which George much later described to his own son, when Patterson returned home unexpectedly, angrily discovered the boy there, and attacked him. In self-defense, George, who was a sturdy eleven-year-old by this time, threw a rock at Patterson, which glanced off him and shattered a window.[33] There was a consensus among all who knew him, except his mother, that George was an unconscionable young hooligan, beyond hope of reform or education.

In April 1856 the situation between George and his stepfather, between Mary's claims on the child and the Cheneys', was brutally and suddenly resolved when Russell and Mahala set off with George for Minnesota. The most probable hypothesis to explain how the eternally impoverished Russell at last found the money to buy farmland near his brother's property in Winona County, and to pay for his family to make the journey out West, is that Russell was furnished funds by the Baker family. Mark Baker or Abigail Tilton, in connivance with Daniel Patterson, financed the Cheneys' move in order to get rid of George Glover II. The Cheneys and George passed through Sanbornton Bridge on their way West, visited with the Baker family, and subsequently let them have news of their safe arrival in Winona.

There is also reportedly an extant letter from Daniel Patterson to Abigail Tilton, which I have been unable to track down, claiming that George had become unmanageable and was wrecking the domestic peace and his mother's health. Abigail visited the Pattersons in early 1856 to see for herself how bad things were with her sister in North Groton. Obviously Abigail must have decided that getting rid of little George was the only answer.

I see George Glover as a kind of Huck Finn who never found a treasure or a friend like Tom or Jim. Given the circumstances of George Glover II's life, it is not surprising that he had become wild by the age of eleven. Equally, we cannot be too hard on his aunt Abigail for so brutally casting him out of the family circle. In 1856 Abigail and her husband had suffered a major financial loss when the Tilton mills burned down, and her children were a constant source of worry to her. As the strongest and most affluent of the Baker children, she was having to cope not only with the problem of the doubly bereaved Martha Pilsbury but with a stream of bad news from her brothers. As far we know based on the scant evidence, Samuel Baker and his second wife Mary were currently spending time in Tilton, probably an indication that they were having financial problems, and it seems likely that the death of Samuel Jr. at sea occurred in 1857. George Sullivan Baker was unemployed and at odds with his wife, and his only son, George Waldron Baker, born in 1853, was seriously lame. Martha Pilsbury no doubt expressed the mood of the whole Baker clan when she wrote to Martha Rand Baker in June 1857:

> What dreadful news you gave me of Sam. O, Martha I sometimes feel that a fearful doom rests on our family—And yet tis so wicked to question the designs of Providence or seek there an excuse for our misfortunes.
>
> But why in every condition in life we must meet with disappointment and failure is to me a mystery. . . . Abi's visit to Mary has been constantly before my mind. I long to hear the particulars in a letter from her. I hope it will not make dear Abi worse, though such a picture of

suffering and misery is enough to break a sister's heart. But Mary! poor child—Alas what words can express her condition. Everything is nought compared to that. One year and a half confined to her bed, and perhaps now there is not even a hope that she will ever be able to rise again, though how long life may last, God alone knows.[34]

George's move to Minnesota with the Cheneys in 1856 was made against the boy's will and the will of his mother. George Glover III testified that his father told him that he was wild when he was forced to leave his mother, and that he quieted down and resigned himself only when assured by the Cheneys that she had died.[35] George Glover II seems to have understood that he could expect none of his relatives but his mother to miss him or care what happened to him. How much Mary Patterson was aware of the plan for the Cheneys to move to Minnesota has been much disputed. Here is what she herself wrote about the affair in her memoir:

> My dominant thought in marrying again was to get back my child, but after our marriage his stepfather was not willing he should have a home with me. A plot was consummated for keeping us apart. The family to whose care he was committed very soon removed to what was then regarded as the Far West, *thus depriving me of the opportunity of having my son classically educated.*
>
> After his removal a letter was read to my little son, informing him that his mother was dead and buried. Without my knowledge a guardian was appointed him, and I was then informed that my son was lost to me. Every means within my power was employed to find him, but without success.[36]

The Milmine biography does not accept this account, but a 1907 reminiscence of Elmira Smith Wilson confirmed that Mrs. Eddy was speaking the truth.

> Mrs. Patterson came there [North Groton] with the Dr, to be near her child, and so that she could teach him, but this she was not permitted to do as the Dr did not like children and would not allow him to come to the house. The boy was not liked by the other children at school and the Cheneys did not make him go. My Brother was working for Mr Cheney and while there he and the boy slept together. My Brother did not like him because he was rough and would not mind anyone. Mrs. Patterson grieved and worried, because she could not see her child and told the Dr that she had given up her folks and had come off up there with him and that she must see her boy and teach him, but Patterson would not let him come near, and without her knowing one day the Cheneys moved away, out west and took the boy with him [*sic*] and before they left my Father had a hard fight to get the money from him, that he owed to him for my Brothers years work.[37]

Young George Glover's lot in Minnesota, out of the sphere of his mother and deprived even of the negligent attention of his relations, was to be even harsher than in New Hampshire. Jewel Spangler Smaus's researches showed that by 1859 at age fifteen George had become so unhappy and dissatisfied with his life on Cheney's farm that he ran away and hired on with the neighboring farmer who at least paid him some money for his labors. This bit of money he later used to pay his way to the Northern army recruitment post. Not only had George worked for Cheney for nothing, but Cheney had actively prevented him from learning to read and forbidden him from going into town. According to what George II later told his son, he had also been unable to stomach the heavy farm labor which Russell forced Mahala to undertake, on top of all her duties as a pioneer wife.[38]

Russell's perennial and deepening financial difficulties were exacerbated by the loss of George's free labor, so he sought legal means to force George to return to him. He wrote to the New Hampshire courts, supposedly in George's name, requesting that he, Russell, be recognized officially as George's guardian, having been "given" the boy at the age of five. When the courts accepted the guardianship claim, Cheney sued Mark Baker and Daniel Patterson for $200, which he claimed they owed George, and which Mark Baker paid. The money was applied toward Cheney's debts. There is no evidence that the illiterate George Glover knew anything of this affair. The outbreak of the Civil War and his prompt enlistment in the Eighteenth Wisconsin Infantry took him out of Cheney's power.[39]

It is not at all impossible to understand that George Glover may have remembered his mother with deep affection and carried the few mementos of her with him as a kind of talisman, while at the same time bearing her an ineradicable grudge for having deserted him and left him to the mercy of the Cheneys. Whatever relation would later develop between George and his mother when contact was finally resumed between them, it could never be the ordinary relation of mother and son.

While George was moving from the tyranny of Russell Cheney's farm to the terrors and hardship of a soldier's life, back in North Groton the Pattersons' financial situation was going from bad to worse. The Wheets' physical assault on Daniel was just the most dramatic sign of the couple's bankrupt condition and of the hostility they had aroused in the town. In 1859 Martha Pilsbury finally carried through her threat to foreclose on the property, and even Mrs. Patterson's personal effects, such as her gold watch, were seized by creditors.[40] Mary and Daniel somehow managed to stay in their house for six months after the foreclosure, but on March 19, 1860, Abigail Tilton came in her carriage, together with Martha Pilsbury, to take Mary to Rumney. Elmira Smith Wilson remembered the journey out of North Groton thus:

Mrs. Tilton, her sister, and myself rode in the carriage with Mrs. Patterson. It was in the spring and the roads were very bad—in spots deep snow—other places mud. As we were leaving, the bell in the church was rung. It was said Joseph Wheat had his son Charles toll the bell. I walked the greater part of the way to Rumney and was very tired & Mrs. Tilton walking with me so that she would not hear the moans and grief of Mrs. Eddy.[41]

In her copybook on September 20, 1859, Mrs. Patterson wrote, "On this day my sister sells our homestead," and underneath, these lines of verse:

> *Father didst not thou the dark wave treading,*
> *Lift from despair the struggler with the sea?*
> *And seest Thou not the scalding tears I'm shedding,*
> *And Knowest Thou not my pain and agony? . . .*
> *For my sick soul is darkened unto death,*
> *With stygian shadows from this world of wo;*
> *The strong foundations of my early faith*
> *Shrink from beneath me, whither shall I flee?*
> *Hide me O rock of ages! hide in thee.*[42]

This double entry—the bald factual statement followed by the verse expression of spiritual despair—provides the crucial extra dimension to this narrative of Mrs. Mary Patterson's first six years of marriage to her second husband. The plunge into financial ruin and physical debility was accompanied by a spiritual crisis, a failure of faith. Using the ancient images of God as a safe stronghold, and of the sinner as a man at sea, helpless before the waves, Mrs. Patterson portrays herself as drowning in her own tears, foundering as the rock of her faith turns to shifting sand beneath her feet. In the past when misfortune had come she had trusted in God, found comfort in her faith, seen sorrow as a trial of the soul that would make her stronger. At this point in her life, isolated by misfortune from family and friends, even God seemed to hide his face.

Heading toward her fortieth birthday, already past the average life span for women of her generation, Mrs. Patterson had entered Dante's dark wood of the soul, and, pushed back by the leopard of desire, the lion of bad luck, and the she-wolf of ill health, had yet to find the straight way.[43] A Virgil was soon to enter her particular Inferno—in the somewhat peculiar shape of a mesmerist from Portland, Maine, Phineas Parkhurst Quimby.

PART TWO

DR. MARY B. GLOVER EDDY

1863 – 1882

INTRODUCTION

After 1862 Mary Baker Eddy began a period of transition. Slowly and painfully, falling and losing ground more than once, she gained control of her life and climbed a few rungs back up the social ladder. In Chapter 6 we left Mrs. Daniel Patterson the sad, disappointed, unappreciated wife of a feckless husband, a woman barely able to rise from her bed, but then she began a metamorphosis. By 1875, with her second husband and his name behind her, Dr. Mary Baker Glover had become active and independent. Still socially insecure and increasingly controversial, she was yet managing to earn enough to secure a mortgage on a modest home where she could live and teach students. She at last finished the book she had been working over for years and saw it in print, however imperfectly. Above all she had become defined, to herself and to a handful of others, as a woman with a mission. Such positive change in the life of a woman in middle age in nineteenth-century America was unusual, but it forms a mere prelude to the astonishing evolution in Mrs. Eddy's life that was to occur after 1875. It also lays out a pattern which thousands of women Christian Scientists would follow, to a lesser or greater degree, by the late 1880s.

Phineas Parkhurst Quimby, the mental healer of Portland, Maine, whom Mrs. Eddy first consulted in October 1862, was the catalyst for the chain of events that were to make Mary Baker Eddy arguably the most powerful woman in America by the turn of the century.[1] Yet the extent and nature of her debt to Quimby also became the single most controversial issue in her controversy-plagued life, beginning in the early 1880s when Mrs. Eddy was publicly accused of stealing Quimby's philosophy of healing, failing to acknowledge him as the spiritual father of Christian Science, and plagiarizing his unpublished work. Rivals and enemies of Christian Science found in the dead and long forgotten Quimby their most important weapon against the new and increasingly influential religious movement.

I am now firmly convinced, having weighed all the evidence I could find in published and archival sources, that Mrs. Eddy's most famous biographer-critics—Peabody, Milmine, Dakin, Bates and Dittemore, and Gardner—have flouted the evidence and shown willful bias in accusing Mrs. Eddy of owing her theory of healing to Quimby and of plagiarizing his unpublished work. I think, with important caveats, that the essence of the account she gave of the healer as a kind, lovable, but illiterate man, whose treatment was rooted in mesmeric practice and theory, was accurate and based on unrivalled experience. Anyone interested in the history of mental healing in nineteenth-century America, in the evolution of New Thought, and in the part played by P. P. Quimby would be well advised to look carefully at the testimony which Mary Baker Eddy left of the Portland healer. What she said and wrote about Quimby was certainly biased and shaped by polemic, but so was all the testimony of her New Thought critics, and their bias has been less obvious to historians outside of Christian Science, such as Charles Braden and Gail Thain Parker.

The questions of originality and influence are paramount in the Quimby controversy. Both P. P. Quimby and Mary Baker Eddy were to a large extent autodidacts who managed with great effort to carve out original careers for themselves largely through native intelligence, creative thinking, energy, and persistence. But the way the two have been treated in the historical record has been very different. Phineas Parkhurst Quimby's lack of education played a strangely important role in the legend that grew up around him after the early 1880s. Those who claimed that Quimby was the first practitioner and theorist of what came to be called New Thought presented him as that supremely American phenomenon—the backwoods philosopher, the untutored genius, the diamond in the rough, a man who owed his practical successes and theoretical insights to experience, not books. Even his greatest enthusiasts make no claim that Quimby read and learned from Plato, Berkeley, or Swedenborg, or that he was aware even of the work of his contemporary Ralph Waldo Emerson. In the course of the New Thought accounts of Quimby we learn that his only important area of study was mesmerism, but even here historians stress that he read books only to dismiss them for being less rich than the insights he gained from his long practice of mesmerizing. As Julius Dresser explained it in his *True History of Mental Science*, "True knowledge to him [Quimby] was *positive proof*, as in a problem of mathematics. Therefore he discarded books and sought phenomena, where his perceptive faculties made him master of his situation."[2]

According to this interpretation of the biographical facts, Quimby was original, and therefore great, because he owed nothing to any earlier or contemporary thinker. The delicate rhetorical task of Horatio Dresser when in 1921 he was finally able to publish the famous "Quimby manuscripts" was to establish at the same time that Quimby was obviously the origin of the theories since he was too lacking in literary culture to have read them elsewhere, and that he was quite literate enough to have written the material himself—though admittedly with the help of several acknowledged and faithful amanuenses!

This highly positive spin placed on the fact that the father of New Thought was, as Mrs. Eddy later claimed, barely literate, contrasts ironically with a criticism often voiced about Christian Science, namely that it was the work of a woman so uneducated and uncultured that she necessarily had to steal her ideas and plagiarize her manuscripts from someone else.[3] On the one hand, Dresser and his New Thought cohorts argued that the changes Mary Baker Eddy underwent in the course of twenty or more years were clear evidence of mingled stupidity and duplicity on her part, whereas Quimby's metamorphosis from stage mesmerist to metaphysical doctor, on the other hand, was the steady and thoughtful progression in understanding of a mind both practical and brilliant.

The New Thought rivals who attacked Mrs. Eddy and her church in the last thirty or so years of her life were a motley and quarrelsome bunch, deeply divided in their response to Christian Science. They agreed on one thing, however: Mrs. Eddy could not be given credit for her movement and her books. Somewhere there had to be a father for Christian Science, and, for all its manifest weaknesses and quirks, the Quimby paternity suit was the best they could come up with.

7

"A Devilish Smart Woman"

I N SADNESS AND IGNOMINY, MARY BAKER EDDY RODE
away from North Groton with her sisters in March 1860. The church bell
rang out to mark her departure, tolled by the triumphant Wheets who were
poised to take over the Pattersons' property. In Rumney, where the couple
settled, things improved a little. Mrs. Patterson first lived in Rumney town,
in the boardinghouse kept by Mr. and Mrs. John Herbert, and presumably
at Abigail Tilton's expense. The bankrupt Dr. Patterson reappeared and was
now in constant and gallant attention on his wife, as Sibyl Wilbur reports:

> As the frail, delicate woman had been criticized by the thoughtless
> mountaineers of Groton who in their rugged health believed the hand-
> some doctor to be a martyr to the whims of an exacting invalid, so in
> Rumney she was criticized by the gossiping ladies of the boarding-
> house. If Doctor Patterson, obedient to his better instincts of courtesy,
> picked up his wife's handkerchief or readjusted her shawl, they were
> jealously observant, or if in hearty buoyancy he displayed the tender-
> ness of strength toward weakness and lifted Mrs. Patterson in his arms
> to carry her up-stairs, they sat silently disapproving. For such misinter-
> pretation of her invalidism and lack of appreciation of her character she
> was misunderstood in that neighborhood for half a century.[1]

This passage offers us a rare clue to the Pattersons' marital patterns, and
I get the impression that it was more than convention and financial interest
that had so far held these two people together through the difficulties and
disasters of their marriage. No doubt, as Myra Smith reported, the Pattersons

often quarrelled, but the letters indicate that they also often got on well together. In 1856 Mary wrote of missing and longing for Daniel in a poem, "To My Absent Husband,"[2] and the few extant letters between Mary and Daniel express an easy affection and intimacy, a taste for family gossip, and a sense of shared interests. Certainly Daniel strikes an affectionate note in a long letter he wrote to his wife from Sanbornton Bridge in February of either 1857 or 1859:

> I have been out ransacking the village to try to find something for you and in the box you will find the plunder. I hope it will find your poor sick appetite and shake it hard till it wakes it up and sets it going in good earnest so that when I get home I may find you a good "Freemonter.". . .
>
> George's wife has been in just gone out she says she made arrangements last fall to go up and stay with you a while—but George S. did not go away as she expected and consequently she could not go to you seems very unhappy about her situation, says she will go to keeping house on her own hook soon if nothing new takes place—but I have written a murderously long letter and will close with a long embrace imaginary it is true but still I think I feel it with the warm kiss of unwavering love.[3]

The Pattersons soon moved out of the disapproving atmosphere of the boardinghouse into a small cottage in the more isolated part of Rumney called the village. Myra Smith continued to be their home help, at least for a short time, and she left a detailed account of the ritual daily airing of the house, during which all the windows were opened and Mrs. Patterson was wrapped in blankets and taken out onto the veranda, and then bathed, rubbed in alcohol, and returned to her newly made bed. Mary pursued a frugal diet of coarse grains, fruit, and water and shunned the slightest hint of butter. Myra Smith Wilson recounts playing a trick on her employer by putting a little butter into a cake she prepared. She was impressed that Mrs. Patterson immediately noticed the difference. Not surprisingly, perhaps, given such a diet, Mrs. Patterson was weak and thin.

Obviously, Mrs. Patterson was fully abreast of the latest health fashions and was attempting to follow in her home not only the diet recommended by Dr. Sylvester Graham but the stoic daily routines of cold water, fresh air, and slim living advocated by William Andrus Alcott. Equally obviously, just avoiding the dangers of "heroic" medicine and following the healthful regimes of the various spas and sanitoria of the day was doing nothing to allay her continuing pain and weakness in the spine and her chronic digestive problems. At this point in her life Mrs. Patterson was unable to find in the care of her husband, in homeopathy, in the health advice prodigally offered in the newspapers, in her own mind, or in her Bible the strength to rise up and walk.

The quiet but wasting existence in Rumney Village was changed by the outbreak of the Civil War, since under the stimulus of external events, Mrs. Patterson was somewhat revived, and she indulged her penchant for patriotic poems, four of which she was later to publish in the Portland *Daily Press*. Daniel Kidder, the neighboring lad whom Mary had tutored in Groton, was the fifth New Hampshire man to enlist,[4] and Mary's patriotic fervor was increased when in October 1861 she finally received a letter from her long-lost son, George. Cyrus Blood, a neighbor who happened to be present when Mrs. Patterson received the letter, noted in his diary that she wept with joy.[5] After this George and his mother were in fairly regular contact during the war, although none of their correspondence has survived.[6] It was a great shock to Mrs. Patterson to learn that some of her worst fears about the upbringing her son was getting with the Cheneys had been realized, and that he was incapable of writing himself, or of reading her letters.

Like every mother of a son in active service, Mrs. Patterson feared for her son's safety, as we see in a poem she published on December 31, 1863, in the Portland *Daily Press*. In this poem, entitled "Christmas Day," the writer, far from friends and family and without the seasonal gifts and good cheer associated with the holiday, reaches out, first to other mothers who cannot rejoice because they mourn for sons lost in the war, and then to the soldier sons themselves. The poem is very different from the labored expressions of Spartan resoluteness and patriotic tub-thumping of other verse Mary wrote and published during both the Mexican War and the Civil War, and it ends on a sad and personal note:

> Pale heart at the bier, or banquet,
> > Blank despair, or trembling joy,
> Fill our Northern Christmas chorus;-
> > What is thine, my soldier-boy?

> In the camp, or at the battle,
> > Weary on the march, or guard,
> Know, my brave boy, hearts are with thee,
> > Love and glory thy reward.

> How my sad eyes, dim with tear-drops
> > Long to look upon my son;
> Gazing back upon his childhood,
> > Wishing more I could have done.

> Merry Christmas! What's thy meaning,
> > Gifts to give, not as thou art?
> Robbed of joy, and dearer treasure,
> > Robbed of love,—replies the heart!

The poetic diction here is often conventional, the poet becomes both halting and convoluted as the standard rhetoric of jolly Christmas verse fails to match her actual experience, and there is perhaps too heavy a whiff of self-pity. Still, the main force of the poem is poignant, a heartfelt expression of regret, remorse, loss, and love for her distant son.

This poem marks perhaps the first but certainly not the last year when Mary felt especially alone and vulnerable on Christmas Day. The love of elaborate presents which she manifested in her old age, and which aroused such contempt and criticism, may possibly be traced back to this middle period in her life when gift giving and family celebrations at Christmas were becoming normal among American families, and she was excluded from the festivity. More important, however, this poem points to a crucial theme in Mary Baker Eddy's life—loneliness, which she would strive constantly to allay, conquer, theorize, accept, embrace. In 1862 the feeling is still a relatively simple homesickness, but later her loneliness was to be more complicated and more terrible.

Apart from revived patriotic zeal, and the welcome renewal of contact with George, the Civil War was to have another direct, unheroic, but I think motivating impact on Mrs. Patterson's life—it made her husband look a fool as well as a failure, and this moved her inexorably and reluctantly along the path toward independence. Daniel Patterson's most notorious failure came about when he was entrusted by the governor of New Hampshire with carrying to Washington certain funds that had been raised in New Hampshire to aid Northern sympathizers in the South. Patterson's mission was no doubt a source of pride and pleasure to him after all the ignominy of his bankruptcy, but he left his wife stranded and in serious financial difficulties. Moreover, in March 1862, soon after his arrival in the capital, Patterson foolishly went sight-seeing on the battlefield of Bull Run, wandered behind enemy lines, and was captured as a possible spy by Southern cavalry. He found himself first in Libby prison, and later he was transferred to Salisbury, North Carolina. In a letter breaking the news of his capture and imprisonment to his wife, a letter whose jolly insouciance is worthy of Mr. Micawber, Patterson professes to be mystified as to how he came to be captured, downplays the gravity of his situation, regrets he can send Mary no money, entrusts her to the care of the Lord, asks her to do what she can to get him released or exchanged, and begs her to inquire after some new boots he left behind in Washington. Fortunately for Patterson, the conditions in Salisbury prison were not as bad as they would become in the later years of the war, and after some months he was able to escape and find his way home, ragged and hungry but essentially unharmed.

His return caused something of a local sensation. An article in the New Hampshire *Patriot and State Gazette* of November 26, 1862, described Patterson's experience:

[In both prisons] they were all treated as only slave drivers know how to treat human beings. Dr. Patterson was on one occasion immured seven days in a "Black Hole" because he declined to pledge himself not to escape nor to allow any of his fellow-prisoners to do so without notification. On the 20th of September—a dark and rainy night—the Dr. with two associates effected their escape from a window, by means of a line made of bed clothes. Their first project was to descend the Yadkin river, but finding civilization not to be reached in that direction, they abandoned their boat, and put over land, levying on hen roosts, orchards, and flour mills for subsistence, and succeeded at last in reaching Gen. Milroy's headquarters in Western Virginia. A letter from the General, which the doctor has in his possession, secured him passage over the railroads to this city.

Characteristically, one of the first things Patterson did on returning north and finding his wife not in Sanbornton Bridge or Rumney, as expected, but in Portland, Maine, was to arrange for and publicize a lecture in Portland detailing his dramatic escape. At the admission price of fifteen cents per person, the lecture apparently did not find many takers.[7]

The news of her husband's capture proved a setback to Mrs. Patterson. She returned to her sick bed and once again had to rely on the direct care of her sisters in Sanbornton, since she had no means of support. Even as she wrote letters vainly seeking to interest officials in her husband's fate and to secure his release,[8] Mrs. Patterson was beginning more actively to seek relief from her own ill health. It was becoming increasingly clear that Patterson, however chivalrous and charming when in attendance, would bring her nothing but trouble, and returning to complete dependence on her family was a highly unpleasant option for all parties concerned. She must needs envisage a future without her husband and look again, with even more urgency, for some means to support herself. To get well was the first requisite for any scheme of independent living.

A newly urgent quest for Mary Patterson to find health had already begun in October of 1861 when Daniel Patterson read a circular sent round by the Portland healer Phineas Parkhurst Quimby.[9] Patterson was struck by Quimby's claims, and he wrote asking if Quimby really planned to visit Concord, New Hampshire, as advertised, and promising to "carry" his sick wife there for a consultation. Quimby replied that he had too much business in Portland to make a journey to Concord, but he would undertake to cure Mrs. Patterson if she would come to him. On May 29, 1862, Mrs. Patterson herself wrote to Quimby from Rumney, explaining that she had been "sick 6 years with spinal inflammation, and its train of suffering—gastric and bilious." "I want to see you above all others," she wrote. "I have entire confidence in your philosophy as read in the circular sent my husband Dr. Patterson. Can you, will you visit me at once?"[10]

As I see it, the letter to Quimby represented only one of the therapeutic options Mrs. Patterson was exploring at this time. Soon after writing to Quimby Mary Patterson set off, probably at the expense of her sister Abigail, to take the water cure at Dr. Vail's Hydropathic Institute at Hill, New Hampshire, where she boarded with Mr. and Mrs. Taylor, acquaintances of her husband.[11] This arrangement seems to have been in the air since the fall of 1861, and Mrs. Patterson confirmed to the Taylors that "My food is of the simplest sort. I take nothing for breakfast but Graham bread (Wheat meal bread) and a little thickened milk cold, in the shape of toast gravy. Eat but two meals a day no meat or butter."[12] This diet would have dovetailed well with the health regime advocated at Vail's, but diet was not the key to cure, as Mrs. Patterson had long known. Hydropathy, like other health systems and alternative medicines of the nineteenth century in America, had a strong spiritual flavor. The baths, the long draughts of pure water, the hours spent wrapped up in damp cloths like a mummy were designed not only to cleanse and invigorate the body but also to rouse the soul. Health was linked to salvation, sickness to sin.[13]

Perhaps it was this vague atmosphere of reproof, of blaming the patient, that made Vail counterproductive for Mary Patterson, or perhaps, as she later wrote, her dissatisfaction was caused by the crusading zeal of another visitor to Hill who claimed to have been cured by Dr. Quimby of Portland, and who was loud in his praises.[14] In any case, in August 1862 she wrote to Quimby again, saying that she was weaker by the day from the water cure: when she had come to the sanitorium, she had been able to walk half a mile; now she could barely sit up for a few minutes. She wrote that she was determined to use her last strength either to travel to Portland or to return home to die among her family and friends.[15]

Both Milmine and Wilbur claim that Mrs. Patterson transferred from Hill, New Hampshire, to Portland, Maine, against the wishes and without the financial support of her sister Abigail, but the extant correspondence of the period does not support this assertion.[16] Certainly, in her first letter to Quimby in May, Mary sought to use her family connections to persuade Quimby to come to her in Rumney, commenting, "Do you remember A. H. Tilton and Geo. S. Baker of Sanbornton Bridge? I am the youngest sister of the latter.—Mrs. Tilton is anxious you should see me." Baker family support for Mary's consulting Quimby is also suggested in that her brother Samuel and his second wife Mary Ann Cook Baker ultimately escorted her to Portland.

Let me interject here that the reappearance of Samuel Baker on the scene after all those years of exile in Boston needs a little explanation. His return to the bosom of his family and the prosperous ease of his sister Abigail's house in Tilton was probably owing to the reforming influence of his second wife, Mary Ann, a former missionary to the Indians, and to a sharp decline in the fortunes of the Samuel Bakers. In the affectionate and chatty letter he wrote from Sanbornton Bridge in either 1857 or 1859, which I have already quoted, Daniel Patterson had reported to Mary:

> your brother Samuel . . . is greatly changed in his appearance for the better, has left Mr. Parker's Meeting and attends regularly the Baptist Church on Park St. has resolved, to persue a new course of life—has left all of his profanity and other disagreable practices—and in fact has the appearance of a Christian . . . All the rough almost rudeness in his manners has given place to a sober gentlemanly turn which makes him the dignified brother which you and I so much admire and there is nothing in him apparent that we could wish changed unless it be the removal of a shade of melancholy.[17]

According to Mary Ann's later testimony, Mary was so weak as she set out on the journey to Maine that she had to be dressed one item at a time. George Quimby, the healer's younger son and chief assistant in the 1860s, said later that his sister Augusta watched Mrs. Patterson being carried up the stairs to his father's consulting rooms in the International Hotel in Portland. Milmine quotes an unnamed patient as describing the scene thus: "Mrs. Patterson was presented to Dr. Quimby as 'the authoress,' and her manner was extremely polite and ingratiating. She wore a poke bonnet and an old-fashioned dress, but my impression was that her costume was intended to be a little odd, as in keeping with her 'literary' character. She seemed very weak, and we thought she was a consumptive."[18] Mrs. Patterson's first move was to plead poverty and seek assistance in finding a cheap boardinghouse. Quimby personally managed to get her reduced rates in Chestnut Street.

Phineas Parkhurst Quimby,[19] the doctor whom Mrs. Patterson had come to consult, was a small, dynamic man of sixty, distinguished in person, according to his chief apologist, Horatio Dresser, chiefly by Quimby's ability to focus his piercing dark eyes on an object for long moments without blinking.[20] Born into a poor blacksmith's family in Belfast, Maine, Phineas had been a frail but bright and intelligent child who, as he himself would cheerfully admit, received only a few weeks of schooling. Initially successful as a watchmaker, and showing considerable ability as an inventor,[21] Phineas was forced by a brush with death in his early thirties to find some new and less taxing way to support himself and his family. Convinced that the traditional medicine of his day was valueless, Quimby became interested in mesmerism, and for a brief time he earned local fame as a mesmerist, travelling about New England doing exhibitions with the gifted subject he had happened upon, a young Belfast man named Lucius Burkmar.[22] When one day, as Quimby tells it in his autobiographical sketch, Burkmar turned his mesmeric glance upon Quimby himself, diagnosing and apparently curing the kidney problem that was once again threatening Quimby's life, Quimby came to his own, idiosyncratic conclusions.[23] In Quimby's view, Burkmar was a slow and limited youth, incapable of producing a cure by his own powers. What Burkmar had done, Quimby decided, was to read in Quimby's own mind the belief he held about his sickness—a belief nourished by medical opinions and general social consensus—and persuade Quimby to give up that error.

When the partnership with Burkmar broke up, Quimby took up the new and innovative profession of daguerreotyping and worked successfully in that field for some ten years. A playful advertisement in the Belfast *Republican* from the mid-1840s indicates that Quimby was maintaining his interest in mesmerism,[24] and he reportedly experimented in Belfast with healing using his new theory of illness as error. According to his son George Quimby, by 1855 Phineas had given up "picture-taking," I speculate because of the adverse effects of daguerreotyping on health, and was earning his living as a healer.[25] By 1859 his healing practice was lucrative enough for Phineas to make the move to the larger town of Portland, to advertise widely in New England publications, and to employ his youngest child George as his full-time assistant.

By the time he met Mrs. Patterson, Dr. Quimby of Portland, as old "Park" Quimby of Belfast now styled himself, was treating between three and five hundred patients a year.[26] According to his advertisements in the Portland press, he charged $2 for the first visit to his office, and 50¢—later raised to $1—for each subsequent visit. Treatments in the patient's home were more expensive, $2.50 for the initial visit and $1 thereafter. Most patients seem to have come to the office, and George Quimby, who served as his father's bookkeeper and secretary, later said that Phineas accepted as much or as little money as patients could pay, since few of his patients were well-to-do. Quimby's healing procedures were outlined in the printed circular which had reached Mr. and Mrs. Patterson in New Hampshire, and which was probably written by George Quimby around 1860:

> He [Quimby] gives no medicine and makes no outward applications, but simply sits down by the patients, tells them their feelings and what they think is their disease. If the patients admit that he tells them their feelings, &c., then his explanation is the cure; and, if he succeeds in correcting their error, he changes the fluids and the system and establishes the truth, or health. The Truth is the Cure.

Quimby made very strong claims for his methods. His son quotes him as saying: "People send for me and the undertaker; and the one who gets there first gets the case." Quimby alleged success with cases of "cancer, hip lameness, vertebral pain, consumption, heart disease, smallpox, fever, spiritual affection, cold, brain fever, lung fever, tumor, neuralgia, general debility of the nervous system, and diphtheria."[27] He backed up these claims with the firsthand testimonials of grateful former patients, and these testimonials

became an important feature of his advertising strategy, as well as of his consequent business success. This was a technique which Mrs. Eddy would
employ extensively when she later launched Christian Science.

Of these testimonials to Quimby's healing powers probably the most
famous and influential was that of Annetta Seabury Dresser, who, as the wife
of Julius Dresser and the mother of Horatio, could be termed the mother of
New Thought. Annetta's cure from what Freud or Janet might have diagnosed as hysteria was probably more typical of Quimby's successes than he
and his adherents cared to admit in public:

> In order to understand the great change which then came into my life,
> let the reader picture a young girl taken away from school, deprived of
> all the privileges enjoyed by her associates, shut up for six years in a sick-
> room, under many kinds of severe and experimental treatment in its
> worst forms, constantly growing worse, told by her minister that it was
> the will of God that she should suffer all this torture, seeing the effect
> of all this trying experience upon the dear ones connected with her,—
> simply struggling for an existence, and yet seeing no way to escape
> except through death,—and the reader will have some idea of the state
> I was in when taken before this strange physician.[28]

Annetta Dresser testified that Quimby so radiated confidence and
benevolence that his mere entrance into the room inspired hope. Even his
first visit to her produced a notable change for the better, and within a year
she was leading a normal life and had married Julius Dresser, a young
former seminarian from Maine whom Quimby had also cured of his long-
standing afflictions.

Annetta Dresser's picture of P. P. Quimby as a flood of light banishing
the shadows of sickness is the one which the Quimby family successfully promoted during Phineas's lifetime, and which the New Thought movement
repeated with philosophical embellishments between the 1870s and the
1920s. Unpublished documentary evidence from other contemporaries
shows that this picture was as much myth as reality. In her 1907 reminiscences of Quimby, Mrs. Georgiana Hodsdon is notably scathing about
Quimby as a man and as a healer. As a teenage girl Mrs. Hodsdon had lived
for a time with her aunt in Portland who boarded many of Quimby's patients,
and Mrs. Hodsdon thus had many opportunities to observe Quimby with his
patients. In her judgment Quimby was "no Christian gentleman," and she
saw no evidence that he benefited the majority of his patients. Hodsdon
relates the heartbreaking example of a small boy who tried desperately in the
months before his death to persuade himself that his sessions with Quimby
were doing him good. Even more interestingly, given the old connection
between mesmerism and immoral behavior, Hodsdon remembers that some
of the young mill girls who came to consult Quimby had told her that not
only had they received no benefit from Quimby's treatment, but Quimby had

behaved toward them in an improper manner. Hodsdon goes on to relate how a friend of her mother's, Mrs. S. Davis Gerry, emerged from Quimby's office screaming for assistance and confiding to her husband and relatives that Quimby had "grossly insulted her." Hodsdon's mother prevailed upon Mr. Gerry not to sue Quimby, as it would involve his wife in a public scandal. Hodsdon's testimony—as well as another account by the son of a former Maine patient as to P. P. Quimby's extraordinary vocabulary of swearwords—has never been made public or analyzed, in my view because it was in the interests of neither Christian Science nor New Thought to have any sexual shadows cast over Quimby's relations with his former female patients around 1860. When we come to discuss Richard Kennedy and the mysteriously violent breakup of his partnership with the then Mrs. Mary Glover in the early 1870s, the importance of this hidden side of the Quimby tradition will become apparent.[29]

Whether Phineas Parkhurst Quimby was not always or only the genial old philanthropist and miracle therapist he was portrayed to be in later accounts, there is no doubt that he succeeded even more brilliantly with his new authoress patient, Mary Patterson, than he had with Annetta Dresser. From the very first session, Mrs. Patterson reacted positively to Quimby's talking cure, as she herself explained in a jubilant letter published in the Portland *Evening Courier* of November 7, 1862, barely a month after her arrival in Maine:

> Three weeks' since, and I quitted my nurse and sick room en route for Portland. The belief of my recovery had died out of the hearts of those who were most anxious for it. With this mental and physical depression I first visited P. P. Quimby, and in less than one week from that time I ascended by a stairway of one hundred and eighty-two steps to the dome of the City Hall, and am improving ad infinitum.[30] To the most subtle reasoning, such a proof, coupled too as it is with numberless similar ones, demonstrates his power to heal.

Not content with being cured, Mrs. Patterson became an overnight convert to the Quimby method and enrolled herself at once among the proselytizers and publicists of his ideas, as we can see in this later section of the same public letter, where she intuits in Quimby an almost divine power:

> At present I am too much in error to elucidate the truth, and can touch only the key note for the master hand to wake the harmony. May it be in essays, instead of notes, say I. After all, this is a very spiritual doctrine—But the eternal years of God are with it and it must stand firm as the rock of ages. And to many a poor sufferer may it be found as by me, "the shadow of a great Rock in a weary land."[31]

The religious theme in Mrs. Pattterson's testimony letter to the *Evening Courier* was controversial, and it was roundly condemned in an anonymous letter published the next day in the pages of the rival Portland newspaper, the *Advertiser*. Not daunted by the response, Mrs. Patterson wrote again to the *Evening Courier*, making explicit her comparison of Quimby to Christ:

> P. P. Quimby stands upon the plane of wisdom with his truth. Christ healed the sick, but not by jugglery, or with drugs, as the former speaks as never man before spake, and heals as never man healed since Christ, is he not identified with truth, and is this not the Christ which is in him?[32]

Mrs. Patterson's admiration for and gratitude to P. P. Quimby was surely sincere, but the Quimby papers make it clear that she was writing here as a conscious publicist as well as a willing disciple. In her capacity as "authoress," Mary Patterson had been enrolled by the Quimby family and their allies Sarah and Emma Ware, Julius Dresser, and Annetta Seabury in an ongoing attempt not only to get Quimby some favorable press coverage, and thus bring in more clients, but to find a public forum for a discussion of his theories of healing.[33] Mrs. Patterson may even have received some remission on her treatment fees in return for writing her first adulatory letter to the press.[34] It was in part, I think, because she remembered the public relations context of these letters that more than twenty years later Mrs. Mary Baker Eddy would become so irritated when these letters were being used as evidence against her.

Mary Patterson's letters show, moreover, that even within weeks of her arrival in Portland she was not merely echoing the themes already established by Quimby and his acolytes but preparing new ground. She was carrying the defense of Quimby's work onto a new level by comparing him in print to Jesus Christ, and thus broaching in public an idea that Quimby had hitherto adumbrated only to a few privileged persons.[35] Neither Quimby himself nor his acolytes had made such claims in their communications with the newspapers. Indeed, in a March 1862 letter which Quimby wrote to defend himself against accusations that he was a mesmerist and a Spiritualist, he tried hard to dispel any idea that his healing methods had any religious overtones so as not to offend conventional Christians.[36]

There seems no doubt that the New Testament dimension of Quimby's work, his distinction between Jesus and the Christ, and his readiness to interpret the Bible and accept or reject Protestant religious orthodoxy had a special resonance for the deeply religious Mary Baker Patterson. Already in November 1862 she was focusing on the triangular relationship among patient, healer, and God as the key to cure, and this idea was not something she learned from Quimby but, if anything, something which she brought to him. Given the radical new interpretations which Mrs. Patterson was publicly voicing, we can see why Phineas Quimby proclaimed his newly healed patient "a devilish smart woman," and why Quimby's family and the other "disciples" soon began to harbor suspicions about her and would come to actively dislike her.

After her cure, Mrs. Patterson left Portland, but a letter she wrote to Quimby from Sanbornton Bridge/Tilton on January 12, 1863, shows her in high spirits and deeply committed to his system.[37] "I am to all who knew me a living wonder, and a living monument to your power." Five or six of her friends were planning to visit Portland, she informs Quimby, and her sister Abigail Tilton, though too busy with company from Boston to travel herself, means to send her son Albert. Mrs. Patterson reports that not only is she talking about Quimby and benefiting from his latest "angel visit," but she is also seeking to heal as he does. She apologizes that her handwriting is bad but explains that she has contracted a "felon finger" (that is, an infected wound on her finger) while treating a woman overcome with fits who gripped her hand with great force.

There were still health problems. She reports to Quimby that she suffers from sores, and these recurrent and quite visible "errors" have made more cynical folk doubt the efficacy of his cure. She herself is unperturbed. More seriously, the letter indicates that an "Esq. Colby," a patient of Quimby's, has unexpectedly died, and Mary repeats a joking remark made by a third patient that Quimby knew better than to heal such a rascal. At once she regrets any seeming lack of charity toward Colby, continuing, "but I always wish to tread softly on the ashes of the dead." In any case she insists that this death too has failed to shake her faith in the Quimby healing system: "I know the theory too well to even for a moment doubt." Summing up her situation, she writes: "I eat, drink, and am merry; have no laws to fetter my spirit now, though I am quite as much of an escaped prisoner as my dear husband was."

In another letter to Quimby from Sanbornton Bridge two weeks later, Mary seems much less well. The old spinal pain and digestive problems have returned as she eats the standard Tilton family diet—which probably consisted of immense servings of meat and starch, followed by pies rich in cream and butter. She sends a fee for the previous "angel visit" and requests another: "the habit is yet so strong upon me that I need your <u>occasional</u> aid. But if 'twere not for <u>visiting</u> I could manage myself; but not being at <u>home</u> I have no <u>tranquility</u> wherewith to aid myself." This longing for tranquility and a home of her own is a theme sounded over and again in Mary's correspondence and a practical problem she was unable to resolve for another twelve years. Mrs. Patterson ends her brief letter to Quimby with the news that Abigail is suffering from "an abdominal rupture" and will soon be visiting him in Portland, together with her son, Albert. "I am very anxious for her restoration. She is very useful to her family and community," Mary writes.

The next letter, still from Sanbornton Bridge, and dated March 10, 1863, gives details about Albert Tilton, upon whom Quimby had effected at best a partial cure. "He is beginning to smoke again, and they [presumably Albert's parents] so fear that if he indulges in this that the worst of all his habits, viz. drinking intoxicating liquor, may return." Mary herself had been seeking to heal Albert and had "taken on" his symptoms:

> Wont you laugh when I tell you since I have been trying to effect Albert, I am suffering from a constant desire to smoke!! Do pray rid me of this feeling. I should think it deplorable to feel long as Albert does. He says he constantly longs to smoke. But we think he has not drank improper beverages since his return; however, wont you include this in your cat-alogue when you send the subtle fluid of mind, or spirit, to govern matter.

These letters from Sanbornton Bridge indicate two aspects of Quimby's healing theories and techniques which Mrs. Patterson had fully accepted and which, in my view, were to have important and permanent ramifications for her development of Christian Science. The first of these refers to treatments at a distance—what Mrs. Patterson in her letter to Quimby calls "angel treat-ments." This was an idea and a practice which Quimby himself undoubtedly took from the animal magnetism model set up by Anton Mesmer. Perhaps at this point I should make it plain that the expression "animal magnetism" has nothing to do with animals but refers to that magnetism exerted by the mind, or anima.[38]

By Quimby's time, it was accepted in mesmeric theory that healing effects were or could be independent of the proximity of the mesmerist to the subject, and Phineas Quimby found important practical applications for this notion. Quimby firmly believed that he had clairvoyant powers and he could help others to recover their health, whether he was in the same room with them or separated by many miles. He went so far as to establish a spe-cial payment rate for those occasions when he would reach out, at a pre-specified time of day, to distant patients. In one incident detailed for our admiration in The Quimby Manuscripts, one gentleman wrote to Quimby begging the doctor's help in curing his long paralyzed wife. Quimby wrote that at a specific day and time he would administer an absent treatment, and the members of Quimby's entourage asserted that at the appointed time he got up and retired to another room alone to concentrate his thoughts on the absent woman. Also at or around the appointed time, the paralyzed woman began to feel tinglings and movements in her legs and was able to get up and walk that very evening, to her husband's deep gratitude.

Whatever the interpretation one places on such reports, there is no doubt that Quimby and his entourage saw in them signal proof of his heal-ing powers, and that he advertised and publicized his angel treatments. There is equally little doubt that Mrs. Patterson believed in angel treatments to the extent of imagining that she saw Quimby's apparition in her living room. This belief was to have an important influence on her practice as a healer, on her later doctrine as the founder and leader of a religious healing movement, and on her personal life.

A second important feature of Quimby's healing practice and his clairvoyance was his claim that he could "take on" his patient's pain. He said that as he established a rapport with the patient and became able to read the nature of his or her disease, he felt the symptoms of which the patient complained. Thus after a successful healing session he would have to take vigorous physical and mental exercise to rid himself of the phantom backaches and neuralgias he had just "cured." Again, this is an aspect of Quimby's understanding and development of mesmeric theory that influenced his patient and devotee Mrs. Mary Patterson, who, as we saw above, was convinced that in her attempts to cure her nephew Albert's addiction to tobacco, she herself took on the urge to smoke. More important, Mrs. Patterson was convinced by her experience with Quimby and her understanding of his personal life as well as his practice that healing involved a transfer of energy from healer to patient that could leave the healer severely debilitated and even, as we shall see in Quimby's case, lead to his untimely death.

Given all the various physical difficulties Mary reports to Quimby that she is having, it is a matter of judgment to decide whether he had "cured" her, as she so often claimed around 1863, or whether, as she was to claim in the 1880s, he had simply relieved her symptoms for a while. Certainly she returned to see Quimby in person in July 1863, was in and out of Portland for the next nine months, and paid her last visit in April 1865.[39] On these months which Mrs. Eddy spent, on and off, with Quimby in 1863 and 1864 we have disappointingly little firm information. It is not clear, for example, how she financed her time there, though we know that she had very little money. In the early part of 1863 she was at Sanbornton Bridge and in September in Saco, Maine, where Daniel's brothers lived. We do not know what Daniel was doing during this time, or whether he was able to support his wife, but it seems likely that the couple was moving apart.

While she was staying in Portland itself, her situation was far from comfortable either materially or socially. Mrs. Sarah Crosby was later to describe Mrs. Patterson at this period as having "no money, scarcely comfortable clothing,—most unhappy in her domestic relations."[40] We do not know how closely she associated with the Dressers and the Ware sisters, who, according to their own later claims, were in constant attendance on Quimby, or with the members of Quimby's family in Portland. According to biographers Bates and Dittemore, Horatio Dresser was told by his parents and by Mrs. Sarah Ware McKay that the Quimby entourage had no doubts about Mrs. Patterson's intelligence, but they were suspicious of her character: "Annetta Seabury suspected her of being too ambitious, George Quimby warned his father that she was unscrupulous and would steal his ideas, and Quimby himself admitted that she lacked 'identity' or integrity."[41]

In the Quimby file in the Boston University Library I found interesting new evidence about the impression Mrs. Patterson made on Quimby's family and friends in an unpublished and, I believe, hitherto unnoticed letter which Mrs. Phineas P. Quimby (a neglected lady whom nobody in New Thought or Christian Science talks about) wrote to Julius Dresser soon after her husband's death in January 1866. The letter makes plain that whereas Mrs. Quimby considered Julius and Annetta Dresser to be beloved friends of the family, she regarded Mrs. Patterson with suspicion and distrust. Mrs. Quimby begins by thanking Julius for writing to her and sending her a copy of the poem on P. P. Quimby's death which Mrs. Patterson had recently written and sent to him:

> I like to hear of her occasionally. her lines are truly lofty and a just [illegible] did I not know her, they would be beyond my comprehension and therefore unintelligible but I understand her and know her mode of praise. I think she might have sent me a copy but she does not like me, so would not gratify me enough to notice me by sending [illegible] I agree with your views of her exactly, she is ever aiming at her own popularity and endeavouring to build herself up at some others expense. She evidently thought when she so strongly endorsed the Dr [*sic*] theory at her first visit to him that he would put her forward to explain <u>for him his doctrine</u>, and she never fully abandoned the idea while he lived. She last summer visited B[elfast, Maine] (bringing a rich friend with her to bear expenses) and hung around and talked, at last, proposed (through her friend) giving a lecture but the Dr did not encourage it, and did not invite her to preach for him at all, so she did not stay long. I have thought she would [eventually?] go in for spiritualism heart and hand she said she did join them sometimes and would git quite excited and carried away while talking about them. Her case as she describes it is sad and had I never seen her or heard her talk I might have more sympathy or believe she was in the fearful condition she represents but she is so extravagant in her expressions and does not <u>always adhere closely to the truth</u> that I have less confidence than I ought.[42]

Mrs. Patterson was obviously not at all Mrs. Quimby's cup of tea. Perhaps the devoted wife's nose was out of joint because "Park" Quimby had liked Mrs. Patterson a little too much and had spent a little too much time closeted with her.

Snubbed by the Quimby, Ware, and Dresser ladies, Mrs. Patterson nonetheless managed to establish significant friendships with three Maine ladies in her boardinghouse in Portland—Mrs. Sarah Crosby and the Misses Mary Ann and Hannah Jarvis. Mrs. Crosby was a young woman who was consulting Quimby after suffering a series of debilitating pregnancies; she was also escaping the power of the tyrannous mother-in-law with whom she was forced to live. Mrs. Crosby is habitually referred to in the biographical literature as a widow, but her unpublished letters offer evidence that she was probably still married in 1863, and that her husband had separated from or deserted her. The difficulties both women were having with their husbands probably created a special bond between Mrs. Patterson and Mrs. Crosby.[43]

Mary Ann Jarvis of Warren, Maine, was in Portland mainly to accompany her consumptive sister Hannah on her visits to Quimby. The evidence of Mrs. Patterson's letters to Quimby as well as a poem she published in the Portland *Daily Press* on February 19, 1864, ("The Last But One—To Sister Hannah")[44] points to the fact that Hannah Jarvis died in Portland. In the most telling references to the Jarvis sisters, Mrs. Patterson writes to Quimby from Warren, Maine, "When I sit by her [Mary Ann] she seems frightened and nervous, I can not feel any physical suffering of hers as I did of Hannah"; and then again in a later letter, "I have changed the thoughts of some ignoramuses about Hannah's death, and your [i.e., Quimby's] practice." I conclude that Mrs. Patterson became much attached to Hannah Jarvis in Portland, that she allied herself with Quimby in an ineffective effort to save her, and thus she won Mary Ann's devotion and gratitude as a result. Such deaths were the dark side of the coin of Quimby's promise of miraculous cures of anything from cancer to consumption, and it is interesting that both New Thought and Christian Science historians prefer to avoid mentioning the fate of patients such as Hannah.

When she was in Portland, Mrs. Mary Patterson spent as much time as she could with Quimby, turning to him for "healing" of her continuing though much ameliorated problems, but she also talked to him at length about his theories of cure. From the limited evidence we have on this period, there seems little doubt that Mrs. Patterson's arrival in Portland spurred the little group gathered around Quimby to greater effort. She and Quimby had an interest in the theory of healing, as opposed to simply the healing business, that the men in the little group did not share. Given his later animosity toward Mary Baker Eddy, George Quimby's testimony on this point is particularly precious:

> she learned from him [Quimby], not as a student receiving a regular course . . . but by sitting in his room, talking with him, reading his Mss., copying some of them, writing some herself and reading them to him for criticism . . . I have heard him talk hours and hours, week in and week out, when she was present, listening and asking questions.[45]

Sarah Crosby also recalled that Mrs. Patterson used to spend the afternoons with Quimby in his rooms, after he had finished with patients, and that she would then return home to the boardinghouse and spend hours of the night writing. Some of this writing was certainly journalism, since Mrs.

Patterson was writing for the newspapers while in Portland, no doubt to supplement her income.[46] It is also very possible, however, that in her long nights of writing she was trying to commit to paper what she was discussing with Quimby.

All of this leads us to the much contested issue of Quimby's "manuscripts." How much or how little had he committed to paper by the time Mrs. Patterson was in Portland, how much of his work did she read, how much of it did she copy and carry off with her for later use? This issue came to the public's attention many years later in 1883 when Edward Arens, one of Mary Baker Eddy's former close associates, and his new ally Julius Dresser began claiming in the press, in public lectures, and in court of law not only that P. P. Quimby was the source of all the essential ideas of Christian Science but that in her published writings Mrs. Eddy had plagiarized Quimby's unpublished manuscripts. During Mrs. Eddy's lifetime and for decades afterward the Quimby controversy was always kept simmering on a back burner by her opponents. Sometimes it boiled over, for example, in 1904, when whole pages of the *New York Times* were devoted to a new discussion of the Wentworth documents which purportedly proved that Mrs. Eddy had incorporated into a pamphlet of her own whole sections of a document she had copied years earlier from Quimby's manuscripts.

The ghost of Quimby stalked Mrs. Eddy unrelentingly, and it stalks her biographer to this day. At the beginning of my research, having read the large body of published debate on the Quimby question, I hoped to be able to send the gentleman back across the Lethe in short order, but in fact I have been forced to give him room and entertainment in my text. Specifically, my research convinced me that all previous discussions of Quimby and his writings are not only shaped predominantly by politics and self-interest but are also both inaccurate and misleading since they fail to take all the documentary evidence into account. Specifically, they do not take into account the Quimby collection at the Mugar Memorial Library at Boston University, which contains the papers which Horatio Dresser had weeded out of the Quimby file given him to prepare for publication by Mrs. Pineo, Quimby's granddaughter. Baldly, in his official capacity as editor, Dresser was at liberty to eliminate certain documents which seemed not just irrelevant or repetitious but harmful to the New Thought legacy which he cherished and which he and his parents had traced back to P. P. Quimby. These documents were not excerpted, quoted, or referred to in Horatio Dresser's *The Quimby Manuscripts*, and they were not among the collection of Quimby papers given to the Library of Congress, which most scholars have assumed to be a complete collection of Quimby's writings.

A careful reading of the Boston University collection proves that Dresser had chosen not to publish not just those documents he considered unimportant but also those which weakened the claims for Quimby he and his parents had been making since the 1880s. Thus two little pencil-written letters by Mrs. Susannah Quimby were not offered to the nation: Horatio did not see how Mrs. Quimby mattered. Early handwritten letters from Quimby, especially one to his wife, were held back: they show all too clearly that P. P. Quimby was not just barely literate but incoherent, needing two sides of a sheet to inform his wife that he couldn't decide when he would come home, and that he missed her and the children. One copybook of the doctor's early writings, dated 1859–1860 (not, as far as I could see, in P. P. Quimby's handwriting) was withheld: it is barely legible for erasures and additions in several hands; it gives some hint of the editing that preceded the neatly penned, text-perfect "copies" of Quimby's "manuscripts" which Quimby's heirs first described to the world and later gave to the nation. The documents at Mugar offer important new evidence to help us answer some of the crucial questions in the Quimby-Eddy debate. How literate was P. P. Quimby? In which year did he begin to commit his theories of healing and illness to paper? What precisely was the role played in the writing process by Quimby's various acknowledged amanuenses, not only during his life but after his death? Are there any originals, that is, manuscripts clearly written in Quimby's own hand, corresponding to the copies of his works in various collections?

Everyone who has written about Quimby agrees that he published nothing in his lifetime but a few advertising circulars and letters to the editors of local papers, and that even these were heavily edited for publication by family members and friends. From the 1880s on, increasingly strong claims were made about the large body of unpublished theoretical writing Quimby had left behind, but there is only one clear reference to Quimby writing about his theories of healing that we can date indisputably to the period before Quimby's death. Ironically, this reference appears in the notorious and oft-quoted letter, extracted earlier in this chapter, which Mrs. Mary Patterson wrote to the Portland *Evening Courier*, a letter which the Dressers later circulated in an attempt to discredit Mrs. Eddy. The section runs: "At present I am too much in error to elucidate the truth, and can touch only the key note for the master hand to wake the harmony. *May it be in essays instead of notes, say I*" (my italics). I suggest that in this final sentence, we have clear and unique contemporary testimony that, at least as of the fall of 1862, there was no extended written exposition of Quimby's theories, or, if something along those lines existed, Mrs. Patterson had not seen it.

For some five or six years after P. P. Quimby's death in 1866, there was no public awareness of or reference to any unpublished manuscripts, and even the oral memory of him as a healer persisted in only two places—with the Quimby family and their friends the Wares, and with the small group of students of mental healing who began to coalesce around Quimby's former patient who by this point had changed her name back to Mary Baker Glover.

In the early 1870s, according to Christian Science historian Robert Peel, feelers were sent out from Lynn, Massachusetts, to Portland, Maine, by Mrs. Glover's disaffected students, anxious to learn more about P. P. Quimby.[47] It was at this point that word began to circulate about the existence of "manuscripts" which Quimby had left behind him, and of certain "copies" of those manuscripts which remained in the hands of certain former patients, among them notably Mrs. Mary Glover.[48] But if the existence of the Quimby manuscripts was discussed from the 1870s on, if many statements on their contents were issued, if their existence became an important polemical weapon wielded against Mrs. Eddy and Christian Science, the nature and content of these manuscripts were virtually unknown since only one or two extremely small sections of them were published before 1921, all from copies made by members of the Dresser family.

As far as I can piece it together, the history of the manuscripts was as follows. Immediately following Quimby's death, some effort was made—by Emma and Sarah Ware, by George Quimby and his mother, and by another ex-patient, a Miss Deering—to make fair copies of all the Quimby writings, which, based on the testimony of the participants themselves, already existed substantially as copies. The group also lovingly put together all the testimonials and press cuttings and advertisements and letters which Phineas had collected over the years. Interestingly, the Boston University collection includes an early attempt by someone, and I assume this was George Quimby, to present a section of the Quimby writings for publication. The pages he assembled have a handwritten mock-up of a cover page, together with admiring and quite fictitious reviews by national publications, and a dedication to Emma and Sarah Ware. For reasons unknown, nothing came of this attempt to publish Quimby's writings.

In the period immediately following Quimby's death, George and his manuscript assistants not only made fair copies of the existing copies; they also assigned dates to the various pieces, relying presumably upon communal memory and educated guesswork. It is a point of some importance to understand that the dates associated with Quimby's writings were probably assigned after his death, not at the time of composition. There is no independent proof that Quimby committed the major part of his work to writing between 1860 and mid-1862—that is, before Mrs. Patterson arrived in Portland, as George Quimby and the Dressers claimed twenty and more years later—and not after, as she herself claimed.[49]

In a draft of a letter to Julius Dresser contained in the Boston University collection, Emma Ware says that until 1882 she or her sister had physical possession of the notebooks into which P. P. Quimby's writings had been copied in various hands, but she then gave them to George Quimby, at his request. Then in 1883, at the time of the Arens plagiarism trial, George Quimby once again gave all his father's papers to Mrs. Sarah Ware Mckay to be taken to

Scotland, presumably to keep them safe from subpoena by an American court. In 1893 George Quimby decided that he wanted all the copies of his father's work in his own possession, and he requested that Julius and Annetta Dresser give up to him the precious copies of two short documents, "Questions and Answers" and "Volume 1," which they had made in the early 1860s. This was a heavy blow to the Dressers, who had based much of the authority of their attacks on Mrs. Eddy on the content of these copies. But by this time the materials the Dressers held had been recopied and made public, and Annetta would flout George's displeasure by republishing selections from Quimby's writings in her 1895 book. Nonetheless, George's persistent refusal to publish the materials he had in his possession and his efforts to make his father's papers inaccessible served if anything to enhance the Quimby myth.

George's lock on his father's papers lasted even after George's death, and only in 1921 was Horatio Dresser permitted to edit and publish what he polemically called *The Quimby Manuscripts: Showing the Discovery of Spiritual Healing and the Origin of Christian Science*. Faced with an unexpectedly large set of texts which no one outside the Quimby and Ware families had seen for perhaps fifty years, which no unprejudiced scholar had ever had access to, Dresser did not revise the positions he had already taken in his earlier books on New Thought and Christian Science. Instead he claimed triumphantly that he had at last provided the documentary proof to back up all the claims against Mrs. Eddy first his parents and then he himself had been making since 1883. It is now possible to see exactly how prejudiced and polemical Horatio Dresser's editorial labors were since, in 1988, for the first time, *The Complete Writings* of P. P. Quimby were published in a three-volume set, edited by Ervin Seale. It will be noted that in the title to his edition the judicious Seale has lowered the polemical ante by rejecting the word *manuscripts* in favor of *writings*. Seale explains that the unpublished documents upon which he based his work *are not manuscripts, in the sense of autographs penned by the declared author*, but handwritten copies made at various times by various members of the Quimby family, and by certain patients or students.

That P. P. Quimby is the author but not the writer of the work attributed to him has long been acknowledged. In his 1888 biographical essay on his father, George Quimby claims that his father became persuaded by his pupils around 1860 of the need to commit his healing philosophy to paper. The date of 1860 is crucial since Quimby set up practice in Portland in 1859, and Mrs. Patterson did not arrive until the fall of 1862. This is how George remembers the process of his father's ideas being committed to paper:

From that time he [Quimby] began to write out his ideas, which practice he continued until his death, the articles now being in the possession of the writer of this sketch. The original copy he would give to the Misses Ware, and it would be read to him by them; and, if he suggested any alteration, it would be made, after which it would be copied either by the Misses Ware or the writer of this article and then re-read to him, that he might see that all was just as he intended it. Not even the most trivial word or the construction of a sentence would be changed without consulting him.[50]

Horatio Dresser describes this same process in his 1921 edition of Quimby's work, and he adds the comment that the Misses Ware—inevitably referred to as an undifferentiated entity!—"who did most of the copying of the manuscripts and made changes in them according to [Quimby's] suggestions when he heard them read, were especially fitted to this service, since they brought forward no opinions of their own and were devoted to this part of the work."[51]

Further important testimony on the issue of originals and copies emerged in an interview Sibyl Wilbur conducted in Belfast, Maine, with George Quimby in 1906 while she was doing research on Mrs. Eddy's life for *Human Life* magazine. A visit to Portland to reexamine the Quimby affair had become more pressing than ever after the appearance of a long *New York Times* article in 1904, with its convincing presentation of parallel passages, purportedly from Mrs. Eddy's work and from a Quimby manuscript, apparently proving that Mrs. Eddy had plagiarized Quimby's writings. Shown first a copybook with dated entries in a neat hand, with no erasures or corrections, Wilbur asked if this was Quimby's handwriting. No, George replied, and then he produced from a big iron safe six or eight similar books, which Wilbur leafs through, noting that they are all similarly written. The conversation, which was later published in *Human Life* magazine, continues:

> "Are none of these in your father's handwriting?"
> "No, they are all copies. . . . These are the only manuscripts I have shown to any one and the only ones I will show."
> "But," I objected, "there have recently been printed facsimile reproductions of your father's manuscripts over the date 1863 in which appear the words 'Christian Science.' I particularly wished to see that manuscript."
> "I am showing you exactly what I showed others. That is the very page that was photographed."
> "And in whose hand is this?"
> "My mother's I believe, or possibly one of the Misses Ware; . . . they are copies of things my father wrote. He used to write at odd moments on scraps of paper whatever came into his mind."
> "And have you these papers now?"
> "Yes, I have."
> "Will you let me see a few pages of them?"
> "No, I will not. No one has ever seen them and no one shall. . . . I

tell you they have all been after them, Arens, Dresser, Minot J. Savage, Peabody, and these recent magazine and newspaper investigators. But I have never shown them. Dr. Savage wrote me that I owed it to the world to produce them."

"And did you not think so?"

"No, I have said I will never print them while that woman lives."

"Do you mean Mrs. Eddy?"

"That is just who I mean."[52]

The one dissenting voice in the post hoc discussion of how the Quimby documents came into existence is of course Mrs. Eddy's, and the assumption outside the Christian Science movement has been that her account was self-serving and revisionist, whereas George Quimby and the Dressers told the truth. Mrs. Eddy argued from the 1880s onward that Quimby had been quite incapable of committing his thoughts to paper; her detractors accused her of an unladylike lack of generosity and gratitude—even though the Quimby papers as we have them today amply support her assertions.[53] In 1896 Mrs. Eddy gave her most detailed and balanced account of what she remembered of Quimby and his writings:

> After treating his patients, Mr. Quimby would retire to an anteroom and write at his desk. I had a curiosity to know if he indited anything patho-logical relative to his patients, and asked to see his pennings on my case. He immediately presented them. I read the copy in his presence, and returned it to him. The composition was commonplace, mostly descrip-tive of the general appearance, height, and complexion of the individ-ual, and the nature of the case: it was not at all metaphysical or scientific; and from his remarks I inferred that his writings usually ran in the vein of thought represented by these. He was neither a scholar nor a meta-physician. I never heard him say that matter was not as real as Mind, or that electricity was not as potential or remedial, or allude to God as the divine Principle of all healing. He certainly had advanced views of his own, but they commingled error with truth, and were not Science. On his rare humanity and sympathy one could write a sonnet.[54]

If one compares all the various public accounts put forward about how Quimby produced his "manuscripts," it becomes clear that the Quimbyites advanced their claims on the basis of a very particular definition of copying. As semiotician Umberto Eco likes to remind us, to call some piece of text a "copy" is to imply that somewhere there exists an "original," and the defense of Quimby's intellectual legacy based on the notion of "copying" begins to founder once one confronts the fact that the Quimbyites have never been able to produce originals. Even Horatio Dresser in his book *The Quimby Manuscripts* could adduce from the large collection of Quimby papers only a few pages of a single, highly contentious, document that Dresser identifies as written in Quimby's own handwriting. The rest of the P. P. Quimby

autographs are personal letters or drafts that eloquently testify to his incapacity to spell simple words or write a simple, declarative sentence. Thus
there is no documentary proof that Quimby ever committed to paper the vast
majority of the texts ascribed to him, no proof that he produced any text that
someone else could, even in the loosest sense, "copy." What Quimby's family and friends did was to transcribe what Quimby dictated, or, more mundanely, take down what Quimby said. By their own testimony the so-called
copyists functioned at the very least as stenographers, copy editors, ghost
writers, and think-tank participants. These were no doubt disinterested and
even noble services, given freely to assist a man all loved and admired and
who was clearly incapable of writing for himself. But the claim that this activity was copying is very odd indeed, and, in my view, the claim is defined less
by truth than by polemic.

One small but significant result of the refusal throughout New Thought
history to allow that Quimby's "copyists" had any active intellectual part in
the creation of the writings has been the consistent misinterpretation and
devaluation of the role played in Quimby's career by Emma and Sarah Ware.
In the annals of New Thought, the "Misses Ware" go down as loyal disciples, self-sacrificing keepers of the Quimby flame. The documentary evidence at Boston University shows that, following his father's lead in his
judgment of the "Misses Ware," and anxious to give his parents prominence,
Horatio Dresser deliberately ignored and discarded those documents that
showed the women had been anything but "copyists"—to repeat Horatio's
words—"especially fitted to this service, since they brought forward no
opinions of their own and were devoted to this part of the work."

Among all the Boston University documents, perhaps the most destructive to the Quimbyite contingent is a small, handmade, blue-lined exercise
book, marked boldly by Horatio as "Not valuable not matter by PPQ," and
which turns out to be a patient's narrative of her first months under Quimby's
care. In the midst of all the memorabilia of Quimby, the admiring testimonies
to his talents and successes which the family had preserved for three generations, this document stands out like a sore thumb. The patient's initial
assessment of Quimby is not favorable, and although she does experience a
"cure" and expresses deep gratitude to Quimby for releasing her from the
depression and weakness and pain that had come to characterize her life, she
is never blinded to his faults and limitations. Horatio Dresser, guardian of
Quimby's legacy and champion of his reputation, had no incentive to publish what this woman wrote:

> The first impression a patient receives of Dr. Quimby is often of the bit-
> terest opposition to him. They feel ready to denounce him as an
> imposter & an infidel and should they give expression to their feelings
> they would spare not language in abusing him. . . . Some of his state-
> ments seem self-contradictory and certainly make him appear assuming

while the arguments by which he undertakes to prove them are absurd and nothing to the point. Pursue him with a few questions & he flies off into the realm of things incomprehensible by human understanding as fast as words can carry him: self-confidence gives him here a superiority over you & he silences but does not convince & only confuses you. . . . All this frequently creates an aversion too strong for language to describe for who creates all this disturbance?—an uneducated and unlettered man. This was my experience. . . . I first thought him an honest kind-hearted man of great simplicity of character. I felt no aversion to him more than to anyone else & I did not listen to him. . . . I thought he was a harmless theorist embracing a very small range of facts & of course very ignorant of the true nature of disease.[55]

This evaluation of Quimby is remarkably close to what Mary Baker Eddy said in her public statements on Quimby after 1883, and it becomes even more subversive if its author is identified as that loyal and supposedly uncritical and submissive "copyist" Emma Ware. I am no handwriting expert, but I have seen signed autographs by Emma in The Mother Church's collection, and I would judge that she was Quimby's critical patient. What is more, I note that on the cover of this document Horatio Dresser himself made, faintly in pencil, the identification "Some by EGW? Some by Q?"

On the basis of this document and other handwritten materials in the various Quimby collections which can be attributed to Emma Ware I have concluded that one of the critical turns taken in the history of mental healing was when the illiterate Quimby came into the orbit of the cultured Wares. Possibly, but far from certainly, Quimby had begun to try to codify and write up his ideas on healing before meeting them, but nothing in his life or education had prepared him for authorship. The unpublished and unheralded autobiographical fragment I ascribe to Emma Ware offers good evidence that in order to account for the healing which she and her sister had experienced with such wonder and which, by her account and that of so many other patients, Quimby was so lamentably unable to explain to her, Emma began to reach out for some larger conceptual framework. Emma had the intelligence, the educational background, and the literary skills needed for such a task. What she lacked was what both P. P. Quimby and Julius Dresser possessed—self-confidence, assurance, willpower, and drive.

I have devoted some space to reevaluating the role of Sarah and Emma Ware in the development of mental healing in the United States in the nineteenth century largely because I felt some tribute was owed them after all these years. Their lives shed important light on the difficulties able and intelligent women had at this period in taking a role in the public sphere, and thus on the nature and extent of Mrs. Eddy's achievement. Implicitly, "the Misses Ware" form the delicate, feminine, undifferentiated, and insubstantial double antithesis to that other former patient of Quimby's, the fiercely individual, ambitious, ultimately successful Mary B. G. Patterson Eddy.

To summarize, contrary to the report given by historians such as Charles Braden and Gail Parker, and repeated by critics such as Martin Gardner, the healing legacy left by P. P. Quimby did not pass by male succession from Phineas Quimby to Julius Dresser and from him to Horatio. For ten years or more after P. P. Quimby's death, only Emma and Sarah Ware and Mary Baker Glover, and possibly Annetta Seabury Dresser, continued to revere him and try to bring his message to a larger public. Painfully aware that by refusing to practice as a healer he had not fulfilled his father's fondest wish, George Quimby atoned as best he could for his filial impiety by fiercely defending his father's reputation and keeping his writings secret from all. The Dresser father and son duo, for their part, preferred not to remember the years they had left Quimby's name and his papers in the care of the despised Misses Ware, and not to admit that they began to exploit the legend of Quimby only after Mary Baker Eddy's new Christian Science had shown that mental healing was a paying proposition.

As I shall show in the course of this book, the evidence that Mary Baker Eddy's healing theology was based to any large extent on the Quimby manuscripts is not only weak but largely rigged. This does not mean that Quimby did not have a profound influence on her. What cannot be proved, one way or another, and what really matters, is what Quimby said to Mrs. Patterson and she to him during those long hours everyone agrees they spent together discussing healing. Mesmerist is the accusation that both Christian Scientists and Quimbyites were to hurl at one another from the 1880s onward, and which both camps sought vehemently to deny. Yet in some strange way, the mesmeric model developed in the nineteenth century—whereby one (stereotypically male) mind is assumed to dominate and control another (stereotypically female or at least weaker) mind against the weaker one's will—is at work here in the two competing versions of the relation between Mary Patterson and Phineas Parkhurst Quimby. Both define influence as a one-way street, a master-slave, father-child, tutor-student relation and therefore affirm or deny that influence existed. Had Mrs. Patterson been a forty-year-old man, a very different model would have come into play, and we would be thinking in terms of intergenerational influence, not of Svengali taking over Trilby's mind and body, or, as the Dresserites would have it, of a daughter of Eve betraying a cozy patriarchal Eden in Portland, Maine.

8

"Fired with the Prescience of a Great Mission"

WHAT WAS MRS. MARY PATTERSON DOING AND thinking and feeling in 1864, the year after her initial euphoric "cure"? Quimby had got her on her feet and inspired her to write and think as well as climb stairs, but he could not solve her persistent problems.[1] There was her son, George, a constant source of worry since he had been very seriously hurt in battle in the fall of 1862 and was trying in vain to make it back to New England. Above all there was her husband, Daniel, who was attempting without much success to take up his professional life and establish a home for them both in Lynn, Massachusetts. A letter she wrote from Portland to Daniel's brother James Patterson in Saco, Maine, in November 1863 indicates that Mrs. Patterson was sick, worried, and depressed but had not yet given up on her marriage: "When I get able to go I want to return at once to N.H. My son started by slow travelling a fortnight ago to come North this makes me very anxious to return, he may have reached Sanbornton. . . . I cannot live here as sick as I am. . . . I am homesick—almost. O! I want to see my Daniel so much. I cry half the time."

Daniel had no home to offer his wife, and it was no doubt with gratitude that in March 1864 Mrs. Patterson responded to a letter from Mary Ann Jarvis, her Portland acquaintance, who had suffered a relapse and begged her to come and stay with her in Warren, Maine. The few months of free board and lodging which Miss Jarvis was offering were much needed, but, like many guests, Mrs. Patterson was to discover that she would have to pay for her keep in the expensive coin of care and attention.

Based on the six letters Mrs. Patterson wrote to P. P. Quimby between March and May 1864, Mary Ann Jarvis emerges as a kind of Dickensian character, amusing to read about but not to live with. She was excessively anxious and dependent, suffered from coughs and breathlessness, and she was convinced that her health deteriorated every time the wind was in the east. She looked to Mrs. Patterson's greater strength and energy for relief from her ailments and relied on her visiting friend for company and affection. She immediately became worse at the slightest hint that Mrs. Patterson would be leaving and moving on, as promised, to visit their mutual friend from Portland, Mrs. Crosby.

Not surprisingly, Mrs. Patterson's own health began to suffer during this visit to Warren. She "took on" Miss Jarvis's pains, and in May she was reporting several nasty symptoms to Quimby. Not only had her old spinal and digestive problems returned, with insomnia and constipation, but she had developed the Jarvis sisters' problems, a chronically sore throat, asthmatic wheezing, and even spitting blood. She made special appeals to Quimby for spiritual "comforters," presumably both letters and angel visits, that would help both her and Mary. On April 10 Mrs. Patterson wrote Quimby that she had "seen" him in the parlor, that he was wearing a hat and dress coat, that she asked him how he did, and that he then smartly disappeared. Between them, Mrs. Patterson and the spectral Quimby managed to restore Miss Jarvis, since by April 24 she was feeling full of energy and cheer. "When I came here," Mrs. Patterson wrote to Quimby, "she could not do but a very little housework, had had a girl up to that time. In three weeks she did her washing! A thing she told me she had not thought of being able to do ever again, and had not done before for six months. She never knows which way the wind blows now, east or contrarywise."[2]

While in Warren, Mary continued actively to proselytize on Quimby's behalf, even daring to give two public lectures at the Town Hall. The second of these we know was entitled "P. P. Quimby's spiritual Science healing disease—as opposed to Deism or Rochester-Rapping Spiritualism."[3] These lectures were sparsely attended, but she reports,

> the precious few, were those whom a lady present (the manufacturer's wife) said were the uppertendom; only think of Yankee castes in all our country villages. I thoroughly wish we were understood as a people, the true American idea. But I felt pleased to know that there were men of intellect and comprehension present, such as Mr. Hodgeman, and Mr. Johnson of this place.

Though she was willing to talk in public about Quimby and to help Miss Jarvis maintain the improvement in health she had experienced in Portland with Quimby, Mrs. Patterson refused to contribute articles to the *Independent*, a well-known religious magazine, or, as she wrote to Quimby, to treat the woolen manufacturer's wife who had attended her lecture—"I returned a note that I was not done with my pupilage yet, and recommended her to visit you."

As in Sanbornton Bridge, Mrs. Patterson in Warren was meeting skeptics who challenged her upbeat message about Quimby's healing, reminding her that he was not always successful. A more pressing charge was that Quimby was a Spiritualist, associated with the movement begun in 1848 in Rochester by the Fox sisters. The label of Spiritualist was evidently not one Quimby appreciated since he had found it necessary to deny that he was a Spiritualist in a public letter to the Portland *Advertiser*. Mrs. Patterson's letters to Quimby also deny the charge of Spiritualism and mesmerism while showing considerable familiarity with both. Thus she begins her letter to Quimby about his spectral appearance in the parlor, "Some how I am 'impressed' to write you as the Spiritualists call it."

The letters that Mrs. Patterson wrote to Quimby in 1863 and 1864 afford far more insight into her life and thinking than her published works of the same period, and the biographer has to offer a prayer of gratitude that the Quimby family kept them and finally entrusted them to the nation. It is a tribute to Quimby that he was a man to whom a woman could address such frank letters. "My letters to you are for your private eye and ear no ones else" wrote Mary, after one particularly sharp reference to the bluestocking and aristocratic ladies who were making her life a misery. Ironically, these very private utterances were destined to become prime exhibits in the public trial of Mary Baker Eddy that began in the 1880s. I wonder whether Mrs. Quimby read these letters as they arrived, and what she thought of them.

From the Quimby letters, Mrs. Patterson emerges as a complicated, interesting, thoughtful woman, observing the society around her, quick to comment and critique, a loving friend and joyful companion, but always seeking to move beyond the surface of everyday matters and find a spiritually significant role for herself. The letters show that although Mary's life had much improved since her acquaintance with Quimby, she was still an unhappy woman. "Dear Dr.," she wrote on April 24, 1864, "I am a little bit lonesome, doing and suffering! Am wishing I was round the home-hearth with my child and husband amid the joys of liberty." The rest of this important letter makes quite clear that although she relies on Quimby and turns to him for help and comfort, Mrs. Patterson's greatest support is her Bible and her sense of God. The healing she looks for is spiritual, not merely physical, and, like many conventional Protestants of her generation, she turns to the Gospel story for parallels to her own experience:[4]

> Dr., I have a strange feeling of late that I ought to be <u>perfect</u> after the command of science, in order to know and do the right.[5] So much as I need to attain before that, makes the job look difficult, but I shall try. When men and above all women, revile me, to forgive and pity. When

I am misjudged because misunderstood, to feel; Wisdom forgive them for they know not what they do. . . . All things shall work together for good to them who love wisdom; i.e., if they have the courage to feel— these are not they whom my Father hath chosen. I can love only a good, honourable and brave career; no other can suit me. If I could use my pen as I long to do, and not sink under it; I would work after this <u>model</u> till it should appear a "thing of beauty which is a joy forever."

From Warren, Mrs. Patterson travelled south to Lynn and her husband, but she probably did not find anyplace she could call home there. Daniel Patterson was attempting to set himself up as a dentist again. He published the following advertisement in the *Lynn Weekly Reporter* of June 11, 1864:

DENTAL NOTICE
DR. D. PATTERSON

Would respectfully announce to the public that he has returned to Lynn and opened office in B. F. and G. N. Spinney's new building, on Union street between the Central Depot and Sagamore Hotel, where he will be happy to meet the friends and patrons secured last year while in the office of Drs. Davis and Trow, and now he hopes to secure the patronage of 'all the rest of mankind,' by the exhibition of that skill which close study and many years of first class and widely extended practice enable him to bring to bear to the aid of the suffering. He is aware that he has to compete with able practitioners, but yet offers his services fearlessly, knowing that competition is the real stimulus to success, and trusting in his ability to please all who need Teeth filled, extracted, and new sets. He was the first to introduce LAUGHING GAS in Lynn for Dental purposes and has had excellent success with it. Terms lower than anywhere else for the same quality of work.

Unsurprisingly perhaps, even the offer of cheap laughing gas did not attract a large clientele, Daniel's practice languished as it had earlier in the marriage, and it seems that at one point he was sued by his former partners.[6] Ineffectiveness as a provider was not the worst of his conjugal sins, however. Patterson's fondness for the fair sex had grown rather than diminished over the years, and, as his marriage itself proved, dentistry was a good way for him to meet women, especially when he carried his profession out of town.

The core problems between the Pattersons were exacerbated when in July Daniel had a very bad case of erysipelas. Mrs. Patterson writes to Quimby in obvious distress, because she has had no success at all in treating the condition and is afraid of "taking" the disease herself.[7] Abandoning her old trust in angel visits, she tells Quimby that she wishes fervently that he could come in person—"how easily you could save him." Given this variety of problems, new and old, the reunion of the two Pattersons was not very successful, and in the fall of 1864 Mary reverted to her earlier plan to pay a lengthy visit to another friend she had made in Portland, Mrs. Sarah G. Crosby of Albion, Maine. Mrs. Crosby, a younger, more intelligent and interesting companion than Miss Jarvis, lived on her mother-in-law's fine old farm with her five small children. Mrs. Patterson no doubt had high hopes of passing an enjoyable time.

The Quimby file contains no letters from Mrs. Patterson to Quimby during her stay in Albion, and the information we have about this time comes very largely from what Mrs. Crosby remembered some forty years later, under very different circumstances. In the opening to a conciliatory letter to Mrs. Eddy written in 1903, the purpose being to beg for money, Mrs. Crosby recalled the time she and her friend had spent together in 1864:

> [I]n fancy I often go back to the old farmhouse in Albion as it was forty years ago with grandma Crosby the presiding spirit, ruling as with a rod, the rather too yielding <u>nominal</u> mistress of the household, the brood of noisy children frolicing [*sic*] from cellar to garret, the "hired girls" and "hired men" forming a little colony by themselves.
>
> These form the background of a picture in which the central figures are two <u>lone women</u>. The <u>one</u>, fired with the prescience of a great mission, even in the depths of poverty, looking forth upon the world conscious of coming power;—the other, peering wistfully into a future that <u>seemed</u> full of shadows, yet with the aspirations of a young goddess.[8]

Mrs. Crosby also told Sibyl Wilbur that her little daughter Ada became so passionately attached to Mrs. Patterson that she followed her around like the nursery rhyme lamb. Unmollified by this nostalgic picture, Mary Baker Eddy sent a stiff letter of rebuke to her old friend and enclosed a check for fifty dollars—certainly not pocket change in 1903, but obviously not what Mrs. Crosby had envisaged or needed. By 1905, Mrs. Sarah Crosby had emerged as the first of Mrs. Eddy's old friends willing to sell very negative statements about her to the press.[9]

In her conversations with Georgine Milmine and Willa Cather for the *McClure's* series, Mrs. Crosby still conveyed some feeling of Mrs. Patterson's visit in 1864 as an idyllic interlude. *McClure's* reported:

> Mrs. Crosby admits that she was completely under Mrs. Patterson's spell, and says that even after years of estrangement and complete disillusionment, she still feels that Mrs. Patterson was the most stimulating and invigorating influence she has ever known. Like all of Mrs. Eddy's old intimates, she speaks of their days of companionship with a certain shade of regret—as if life in the society of this woman was more intense and keen than it ever was afterward.[10]

However, stimulating as Mrs. Patterson had been, Mrs. Crosby now insisted that she had not been the perfect guest because she refused to take part in the work of the farm and behaved as if she was a guest of honor rather than some homeless and destitute woman who was dependent on a friend's charity.

The accusation that Mrs. Patterson had eaten "bread that she had not earned and would not help to bake," in Lyman Powell's emotive phrase,[11] was a damaging one, but it paled in comparison with Mrs. Crosby's statement that Mrs. Patterson had conducted Spiritualist seances while staying in her home. According to the story Mrs. Crosby told Milmine, Mrs. Patterson had confided to her friend how much she (Mrs. Patterson) had loved and admired her dead brother Albert. Mrs. Patterson had then claimed that Albert was Mrs. Crosby's guardian spirit, for whom she, Mrs. Patterson, was the appointed medium. In the first communication from the other world, "Albert," speaking in a "sepulchral, mannish voice" from Mary's mouth, warned Mrs. Crosby to beware of placing her entire confidence in his sister:

> "He informed me," Mrs. Crosby continues, "through her own lips, that while his sister loved me as much as she was capable of loving any one, life had been a severe experiment with her, and she might use my sacred confidence to further any ambitious purposes of her own."[12]

Subsequently, Mrs. Patterson in trance informed Mrs. Crosby that letters from the dead Albert would be found under a certain cushion. Milmine includes the text of one of these letters, and a facsimile of the second page, which consists, rather anachronistically, of a glowing description of the healing practice of P. P. Quimby. Mrs. Crosby's later testimony that the then Mrs. Patterson had gone into trance and acted as a medium, together with the text of the spirit letters, was biographical dynamite, as the magazine staff understood. The Spiritualists of the nineteenth century were in some ways a socially and politically radical group, and by the time the Milmine series was published they had become associated in the public mind with such controversial and shocking issues as feminism and free love. Therefore, linking Christian Science to Spiritualism was not mere value-neutral reportage.

More specifically, Mrs. Crosby's testimony contradicted Mrs. Eddy's statement in the second edition of *Science and Health* that she had never been a Spiritualist and that the healings she and her movement effected were not done by the intercession of spirits. In a footnote to the seance incident in Albion, Milmine specifies that she is not accusing Mrs. Eddy of having been a professional medium, but she takes the opportunity to quote Mrs. Eddy's statement, denying Spiritualism:

> We are aware, that the "Spiritualists" claim whomsoever they would catch, and regard even Jesus as an elder brother! but we were never a Spiritualist: and never were, and never could be, and never admitted we were, a medium. We have explained to the class calling themselves Spiritualists, how their signs and wonders were wrought, and illustrated

by doing them; but at the same time have said, This is not the work of spirits, and I am not a medium; and they have passed from our presence and said, behold the proof that she is a medium![13]

The standard Christian Science rebuttal to Mrs. Crosby's Spiritualist anecdote was that Mrs. Crosby was a convinced believer in Spiritualism, and that while visiting her friend, the then Mrs. Mary Patterson had played a game with her, pretending to be a medium and speaking in Albert's voice, but really seeking to show Mrs. Crosby how easy it was to fake Spiritualism. As Sybil Wilbur explained, "It was simply an effort to disabuse a too confiding mind of its credulity, which failing, was turned into a harmless toleration of its limitations."[14] This "explanation" has been taken on faith by most of the Christian Scientist faithful but has aroused a chorus of ridicule elsewhere.[15]

If indeed Mrs. Patterson was pretending to be her long dead brother, this confirms for me that Albert, his high intelligence, his ambition, his great promise, continued to be much on Mrs. Patterson's mind, that he was a source of inspiration to her, and that she was speaking in his voice as she sought the strength and motivation to begin a new life of healing and teaching. The content of the first seance message to Mrs. Crosby from "Albert" is also interesting. Mrs. Patterson was seeking to warn Mrs. Crosby that their friendship, however close, could not determine the shape of their lives, and that each must go her own way. As she had with Miss Jarvis, though using a very different method, Mrs. Patterson was seeking to detach herself from a friend who was making too many demands, insisting that their relationship could not be exclusive. This pattern of intense involvement between Mary Baker Eddy and another person, male or female, then detachment by Mrs. Eddy, followed by resentment or even reprisals from the friend left behind, would characterize many of Mrs. Eddy's relationships in the next years. Mrs. Crosby would not be the last person who would find Mary Baker Eddy the most fascinating person she had ever met, and who would deeply resent the fact that Mrs. Eddy had not found her equally fascinating and remained her exclusive and devoted friend.

———————

The long visit to Mrs. Crosby ended when Daniel Patterson arrived in Albion to beg his wife to return with him to Lynn, Massachusetts. Mrs. Patterson complied, but, according to Mrs. Crosby's later testimony, the two women continued to correspond in a style of loving intimacy which Daniel Patterson declared was wasted between women. It seems to me significant that whereas Mrs. Crosby kept the letters Mrs. Patterson had written as "Albert" and many years later happily showed them to reporters investigating Mrs. Eddy's past, she claimed to have kept almost none of the voluminous correspondence which Mrs. Eddy had written to her under her own name.

Whether motivated by jealousy or passion for Mrs. Sarah Crosby, or some mixture of both, Daniel Patterson began writing letters of his own to Albion, Maine, seeking, it seems, to persuade Sarah to come and visit them in Lynn and engage in an affair with him.[16] When Sarah wrote to tell Mary all about this infamy of Daniel's, and to protest her own total innocence, the relationship between the two female friends cooled, and one more nail was driven into the coffin of the Patterson marriage.

For the time being, however, Mrs. Patterson ignored her husband's escapades and threw herself into her new life in Lynn. According to Robert Peel, during the remainder of 1864 and the first half of 1865, she wrote pot-boilers for the local newspapers to supplement the family income, came to the assistance of distressed patients from time to time in the dentist's office, and became an enthusiastic member of the local temperance group, the Linwood Lodge of Good Templars, rising to the position of Exalted Mistress of the Legion of Honor. She was remembered by one of the male lodge members as a woman who had the welfare of humanity at heart, who spoke sensibly and often at meetings, "an attractive woman in both looks and manner . . . bright and cheerful and very witty . . . a good woman, and I never knew her to do any wrong or to wrong any one."[17]

Mrs. Patterson's close involvement in the temperance movement at this time in her life has gone largely unremarked, but it is significant if only because it places her, at this point, within the accepted tradition of nineteenth-century female activism. Feminist historiography has connected women's political involvement with three main activist groups: abolitionism and the antislavery movement, the temperance movement, and, of course, the campaign for woman suffrage and other pro-women legislation. Mrs. Patterson's involvement with temperance was brief, not because she lost enthusiasm and commitment but because her separation, and later divorce, from Patterson and the accompanying loss of both income and social position made it essentially impossible for her to continue actively supporting the cause. Nevertheless, throughout her life Mary Baker Eddy would remain opposed to alcohol consumption and, in a move that once seemed old-fashioned but now comes to look avant-garde, she would classify alcoholism as a disease that needed to be healed. She supported not temperance but abstinence, as she made clear in an article she wrote in 1889:

> The cause of temperance receives a strong impulse from the cause of Christian Science: temperance and truth are allies, and their cause prospers in proportion to the spirit of Love that nerves the struggle. People will differ in their opinions as to means to promote the ends of temperance; that is, abstinence from intoxicating beverages. Whatever intoxicates a man, stultifies and causes him to degenerate physically and

morally. Strong drink is unquestionably an evil, and evil cannot be used temperately: its slightest use is abuse; hence the only temperance is total abstinence. Drunkenness is sensuality let loose, in whatever form it is made manifest. (*Mis.*, pp. 288–89)

Sadly, this period of relative tranquillity and renewed respectability in Lynn was short, through no fault of Mrs. Mary Patterson's. In July 1865 she learned that her son George Glover had been invalided out of the army with "consumption of the bowels" and had been unable to get further north to see her than Enterprise, Minnesota. In panic and despair she wrote with this news to Quimby—"the first thing I thought of doing was to go to you like the Mother of old." She said she planned to travel to her son though she was sick and knew nothing of the route, and she begged Quimby to save her son by an absent treatment. In fact, Mary Patterson did not set out on a journey to Minnesota; perhaps George was recovering, more probably she could not raise the money.

At the end of June, Patterson had announced in the *Lynn Weekly Reporter* that important business would take him out of town for a few weeks, and he then left, promising to send his wife $4 a week. This paltry sum stopped after four weeks.

On October 6, 1865, Mark Baker died at Sanbornton Bridge, and Mrs. Mary Patterson surely grieved for her father. Their relationship over the past ten years had been a rather cool one, but she had loved and revered her father as a child. His death marked the end of a chapter of her life and was a new source of sadness and depression. More practically, Mark's death caused a further rift in the family because he left behind him a characteristically eccentric will. As his father had done before him, Mark Baker showed great consideration for his widow, using his will to ensure her future ease and comfort and subordinating the interests of his children to hers.[18] Samuel Dow Baker, the eldest son, was willed the sum of $50, Martha received $1, Abigail $1 and "my mahogany <u>card</u> table." Mary inherited $1, "also my light-stand and I do hereby remit and forgive to her (said Marys) husband <u>all</u> and any claim I may have against him on account of my being his bondsman or on any other account, and I order my executor not to collect or to attempt to collect <u>any thing</u> whatever of her or her said husband on account of any claim I may have against either of them." The widow, Elizabeth Patterson Duncan Baker, was left with all the property and rights she had brought into the marriage with her, as well as the use and occupation of as well as the income from Mark's real and personal estate for the rest of her natural life. After her death, Mark's real estate would revert to George Sullivan Baker and to his heirs, "saving and excepting my [Mark Baker's] wood lot on the Gulf Brook so called and my lot in the cemetery," which would go to the other offspring.

We can see by studying the full provisions of the will that Mark Baker was not specifically manifesting his coldness and disapproval toward his youngest child by leaving her a dollar in his will, though Milmine makes such a claim. In fact, Mark discriminated against his eldest son and his three daughters in favor of his widow and his youngest son. What kind of debts Daniel Patterson may have incurred to his father-in-law has never been established, but it seems likely that Mark was showing some generosity toward Mary and her husband by wiping that particular slate clean. Obviously, even a fifty-dollar legacy would have made a difference to Mary at this stage in her life, but her sister Martha was also a widow of small means, and Mark Baker presumably believed that his family duty was to keep his estate intact for his grandson rather than to divide it up between all his children, needy or not, provident or not. Mark may have chosen his younger son George as his heir because George had a living son to carry on the Baker line.[19] Nonetheless, Mark's will did nothing to heal wounds or improve relations among his surviving children. Years later Mary Baker Eddy was to tell a friend that her sister-in-law, Martha Rand Baker, George's wife, had poisoned the minds of her father and sisters against Mary and influenced Mark to leave all his estate to George, and that this was something she (Mary) could never forget or forgive.[20]

Mark's apparently innocuous bequest of his cemetery lot to Samuel and the three Baker daughters was to prove astonishingly contentious. Most of the sparse existing correspondence between Mary Baker Eddy and her sisters after 1874 would focus on the problems arising from the joint ownership of the Baker funeral plot. First there is some dispute over who would pay the modest taxes on the lot, later over who had overall control of the lot, and therefore could decide which persons would be allowed to be buried there and the monuments permitted to be raised. Relations between Mary Baker Eddy and her sisters varied between cool and frosty until at least 1883, but by 1885 Abigail and Mary were blazingly at odds, and the touch paper to their final dispute may have been provided by a dispute over the control over that tiny plot of land left them by their father.[21]

In January 1866 Mary was living on the second floor of a house in Swampscott, a town close to Lynn, and was later described by George Newhall as spending hours in the garden alone reading and writing and gazing into the water of a little fountain.[22] Here Mary received the news that Dr. Quimby had died on the sixteenth of the month. He had been seriously ill from cancer for some time and had refused to take any medical advice but his own or to cut down on the long hours he devoted to seeing patients. His family was convinced that he was dying from overwork, and he himself felt that the energy he poured into healing other people so weakened him that he was no longer able to keep his own maladies at bay, as he had done in the past. Finally in the late summer of 1865, Quimby's strength gave way and he was forced to leave Portland for his old home in Belfast. To satisfy the demands of his family, who had never, it seems, been very confident about metaphysical healing, he consented to see a homeopathic doctor, but to no avail. His son, George, reported that just an hour before his father died he said:

> I am more than ever convinced of the truth of my theory. I am perfectly willing for the change myself, but I know you all will feel badly, and think I am dead; but *I* know that I shall be right here with you, just the same as I always have been. I do not dread the change any more than if I were going on a trip to Philadelphia.[23]

It may be remarked that Quimby's concept of death as "change" was much less in agreement with orthodox Protestant belief than it was with the mystic effusions of Emanuel Swedenborg and the mesmeric doctrines that Andrew Jackson Davis dictated in trance.[24]

Mrs. Mary Patterson responded to the news of Quimby's "change" with a poem which she wrote some six days after Quimby's death and which she published in the *Lynn Weekly Reporter* on February 14:

> *Did sackcloth clothe the sun, and day grow night,*
> > *All matter mourn the hour with dewy eyes,*
> *When Truth, receding from our mortal sight,*
> > *Had paid to Error her last sacrifice?*
>
> *Can we forget the Power that gives us life?*
> > *Shall we forget the wisdom of its way?*
> *Then ask me not amid this mortal strife,—*
> > *This keenest pang of animated clay,—*
>
> *To mourn him less! To mourn him more were just,*
> > *If to his memory 'twere a tribute given*
> *For every solemn, sacred, earnest trust*
> > *Delivered to us ere he rose to heaven.*
>
> *Heaven but the happiness of that calm soul,*
> > *Growing in stature to the throne of God;*
> *Rest should reward him who hath made us whole,*
> > *Seeking, though tremblers, where his footsteps trod.*

Mrs. Patterson sent copies of this poem to Mrs. Sarah Crosby and to Mr. Julius Dresser—though not, as we have seen, to Quimby's widow—and Dresser retained the accompanying letter she sent him, which runs as follows:

Lynn February 15, 1866

Mr. Dresser,

Sir: I enclose some lines of mine in memory of our much-loved friend, which perhaps <u>you</u> will not think over-wrought in meaning: others <u>must</u> of course.

I am constantly wishing that <u>you</u> would step forward into the place he has vacated. I believe you would do a vast amount of good and are more capable of occupying his place than any other I know of.

Two weeks ago I fell on the sidewalk and struck my back on the ice, and was taken up for dead, came to consciousness amid a storm of vapours from cologne, chloroform, ether, camphor etc., but to find myself the helpless cripple I was before I saw Dr. Quimby.

The physician attending said I had taken the last step I ever should but in two days I got out of my bed <u>alone</u>, and <u>will</u> walk; but yet I confess I am <u>frightened</u>, and out of that nervous heat my friends are forming, spite of me, the terrible spinal affection from which I have suffered so long and hopelessly. . . . Now can't <u>you</u> help me? I believe you can. I write this with this feeling: I think I could help another in my condition if they had not placed their intelligence in matter. This I have not done, and yet I am slowly failing.

Won't you write me if you will undertake for me if I can get to you?. . .

Respectfully
Mary M. Patterson[25]

The poem and the letter express Mrs. Patterson's love for Quimby, her admiration for his work, her commitment to Spirit, and her sense of personal abandonment now that Quimby was no longer alive to help her. From the letter we see that she was convinced that the work he did was important and should be continued after his death. She had managed to come through her recent accident, to resist the temptation to return to her old paralysis and dependence, but she was still unsure about whether she could maintain her health and her progress alone. She still hoped for someone to support and encourage her as Quimby had, and she turned, not unnaturally, to Quimby's most active male disciple in Portland. The diffidence and formality of the letter indicate that relations with Julius Dresser had not been very warm, that the letter was dashed off hurriedly and with little real optimism.

Julius Dresser replied three weeks later. He was by this time working as a newspaperman in Yarmouth, Maine, and he made it plain that his enthusiasm for the work of Dr. Quimby had waned and that he had no ambition at all to take over the doctor's work:

I am sorry to hear of your misfortune, and hope that with courage and patience neither the prediction of the Dr. nor your own fear will prove true. . . . As to turning Dr. myself, and undertaking to fill Dr. Q's place and carry on his work, it is not to be thought of for a minute. Can an infant do a strong man's work? Nor would I if I could. Dr. Q. gave himself away to his patients. To be sure he did a great work, but what will it avail fifty years from now, if his theory does not come out, and if he and his ideas pass among the things that were, to be forgotten? He did work some change in the minds of the people, which will grow with the development & progress of the world. He helped to make them progress. They will progress faster for his having lived and done his work. So with Jesus. He had an effect which was lasting & still exists. But his great aim was a failure. He did not succeed, nor has Dr. Q. succeeded in establishing the Science he aimed to do. The true way to establish it is, as I look at it, to lecture, & by [*sic*] a paper make that the means, rather more than the curing, to introduce the truth. To be sure, faith without works is dead, but Dr. Q's work killed him, whereas if he had spared himself from his curing, and given himself partly and considerately, to getting out his theory, he would then have, at least, come nearer success in his great aim than he did.

No, I wouldn't cure if I could, not to make a practice of it, as Dr. Q did. Yet, Mrs. Patterson, I would be glad to help you in your trouble. But I am not able to do it. My attention has not been given that way and my occupation . . . is of a nature such as to keep my mind from even the theory, much more the practice of it. I do not even help my wife out of her troubles, if she has serious ones, & of all in the world I could help her quickest & easiest, owing to the greater interchange of mind. My wife has lately given birth to a son . . . and I have a good opportunity to know whether I could easily become a Dr. or not. But I am not even Dr. for them. How then could I cure those to whose minds I have little or comparatively no access at all?[26]

The man who emerges in this letter is a practical, self-confident, and self-centered young man, with his way to make in the world, a wife and baby to support, and better things to think of than the theory and practice of mental healing. His appreciation of Quimby is markedly less fervent than Mrs. Patterson's, and in this letter he unequivocally calls the Portland doctor a failure, a man who worked himself to death to help other people but failed to make any lasting mark on the world, largely because he did not get his theory of healing down on paper. Dresser sees the healing power as a kind of clairvoyance, an ability to enter into the sick person's mind and read his or her thoughts; Dresser makes no suggestion that this type of healing involves tapping into a divine strength, as Mrs. Eddy would later claim for her Christian Science.

Dresser's letter completely lacks the religious intensity of Mrs. Patterson's letters of the same period, and I have to admit that I found that this former seminary student's casual dismissal of Jesus as another failure, just like

Quimby, came as rather a shock to me. Dresser's letter specifies that Quimby's failure was the result of his inability to disseminate his ideas among the greater public. Furthermore, Dresser gives no indication at all that he knew there to be a cache of Quimby manuscripts in Portland merely awaiting publication. That the writer of this letter was to emerge in the 1880s as a practitioner and lecturer on metaphysical healing, an apostle of the gospel according to Saint Quimby, and a founding father of New Thought is, to say the least, surprising. It is not surprising that in the Milmine biography's account of Mrs. Patterson's reaction to the death of P. P. Quimby, her letter to Dresser is quoted in full, but there is not even a sentence quoted from or a summary of Dresser's letter of reply.

This would be the last time that Mrs. Mary Patterson would reach out to Julius Dresser for help. Over the next nine years Mary would increasingly dedicate herself to continuing Quimby's healing work and, more important, to realizing the potential of the healing system by theorizing it and committing it to paper. Unlike Julius Dresser, she would for a time adopt Quimby's role, run the risks that Quimby had run, take on the arduous task of healing. But the meaning Dresser had drawn from Quimby's life was not lost on her. She would save enough strength for writing and teaching. She would have not manuscripts and handwritten copies hidden mysteriously away in a private vault, but books, articles, magazines, even a newspaper of her own, to spread the word.

9

The Fall
in Lynn

ON SATURDAY MORNING, FEBRUARY 3, 1866, READERS of the *Lynn Weekly Reporter* were met by the following news item:

> Mrs. Mary M. Patterson, of Swampscott, fell upon the ice near the corner of Market and Oxford streets, on Thursday evening, and was severely injured. She was taken up in an insensible condition and carried into the residence of S. M. Bubier, Esq., near by, where she was kindly cared for during the night. Dr. Cushing, who was called, found her injuries to be internal, and of a severe nature, inducing spasms and internal suffering. She was removed to her home in Swampscott yesterday afternoon, though in a very critical condition.

This was the first public account of an event which has attained almost mythic proportions among Christian Scientists, who celebrate it as the birth of their church, the point when Mrs. Eddy came to understand the nature of Christian healing. For her detractors this event has also proved a particularly favorable point at which to undermine Mrs. Eddy's good faith and the authority of the church she founded. Critics, led by Georgine Milmine, have taken particular pleasure in debunking what they call the "Fall in Lynn" as specious fiction.

Certain facts are agreed to by all parties. The then Mrs. Mary Patterson, in the company of some friends, was on her way to a meeting of the Linwood Lodge of the Good Templars when she slipped on the ice just outside the Bubier house in the center of Lynn, hit her head, and was knocked unconscious. She was sheltered for the night by Mr. and Mrs. Bubier who called in the busy, popular young homeopathic doctor and surgeon Alvin M. Cushing. The doctor paid her two visits that first night, which indicates that he considered the accident serious, and he returned to examine Mrs. Patterson again the next morning. At this point, even though she was complaining of terrible back pain and was clearly disoriented and in great distress, Mrs. Patterson insisted on being taken home, and Cushing arranged for two hired men to move her on a long sleigh, assuring her warmth with fur robes. Two neighborhood women, Mrs. Carrie Millett and Mrs. Mary Wheeler, took charge of caring for Mrs. Patterson at home since her husband was out of town. These women reported to the neighborhood that their charge had broken her back, and that she was paralyzed and perhaps close to death. Despite the bitterly cold weather, the minister was urgently called in.[1] On the Sunday, however, Mrs. Patterson asked for her Bible, sent everyone out of her room, and then amazed them all by getting out of her bed unaided.

Over the next thirty years or so, Mary Baker Eddy was to give various accounts of this self-healing and what it meant to her. Thus in 1871, in a letter to Mr. W. W. Wright, a prospective student, the then Mrs. Mary Glover wrote:

> I have demonstrated upon myself in an injury occasioned by a fall, that it did for me what surgeons could not do. Dr. Cushing of this city pronounced my injury incurable and that I could not survive three days because of it, when on the third day I rose from my bed and to the utter confusion of all I commenced my usual avocations and notwithstanding displacements, etc. I regained the natural position and functions of the body.[2]

As we can see, according to this letter the physician had made an even more serious diagnosis than what was evident in the earlier accounts, and Mrs. Glover was at this time casting the self-healing in New Testament terms. By the first edition of *Retrospection and Introspection* in 1891, Mary Baker Eddy was making her fall the beginning of Christian Science:

> It was in Massachusetts, in February, 1866, and after the death of the magnetic doctor, Mr. P. P. Quimby, whom Spiritualists would associate therewith, but who was in no wise connected with this event, that I discovered the Science of divine metaphysical healing which I afterwards named Christian Science. The discovery came to pass in this way. During twenty years prior to my discovery I had been trying to trace all physical effects to a mental cause; and in the latter part of 1866 I gained the scientific certainty that all causation was Mind, and every effect a mental phenomenon.
>
> My immediate recovery from the effects of an injury caused by an accident, an injury that neither medicine nor surgery could reach, was

the falling apple that led me to the discovery how to be well myself, and how to make others so.

Even to the homeopathic physician who attended me, and rejoiced in my recovery, I could not then explain the *modus* of my relief. I could only assure him that the divine Spirit had wrought the miracle—a miracle which later I found to be in perfect scientific accord with divine law. (*Ret.,* p. 24)[3]

It was the Milmine-*McClure's* team that first collected the accounts Mary Baker Eddy made of her fall in Lynn after 1870 and juxtaposed them with what she had written in 1866 and what other key eyewitnesses to the event remembered. The first key document which the Milmine biography printed was the letter the then Mrs. Mary Patterson wrote to Julius Dresser barely two weeks after her fall, and which I quoted in full at the end of Chapter 8. The letter is clear evidence that although Mrs. Patterson did indeed recover by her own efforts from the effects of what she perceived to be a life-threatening injury, she still lacked confidence in her power to remain well without the aid of a figure like Quimby. In her letter to Dresser Mrs. Patterson gave little indication that the fall and recovery she had just experienced constituted an enlightenment that, little by little, would fundamentally change her life and her worldview.

Two other documents unearthed around 1906 by the Milmine-*McClure's* team strongly indicated, first, that Mrs. Patterson's healing was far less complete than she later claimed, and, second, that the injuries she had sustained in her fall were quite minor. In a petition which she presented in late summer of 1866 to the city of Lynn Mrs. Patterson alleges that the city was responsible for the dangerous state of the streets, and seeks damages for "serious personal injuries from which she had little prospect of recovering." In the second document, a lengthy 1907 affidavit, which *McClure's* solicited, Dr. Alvin M. Cushing, at this point retired and delighted to be getting some visitors, denied that he had ever taken a serious view of Mrs. Patterson's condition or heard anything at the time about a miraculous cure. Dr. Cushing not only claimed to remember the case well but said he had retained his medical records for the period, which showed exactly when he had seen Mrs. Patterson and what remedies he had administered.

As Dr. Cushing recalled, Mrs. Patterson had indeed suffered some kind of concussion and was semihysterical, complaining of severe pain in her head and neck. But there had never been any suggestion on his part that her injury was so serious as to induce paralysis or death. Cushing was able to detail exactly what remedies he had prescribed for Mrs. Patterson, and he noted that she was an interesting case because she responded so strongly even to the highly attenuated doses—such as "the third decimal attenuation of arnica diluted in a glass of water"—that were dictated by his homeopathic theory. Thus when she demanded on Friday morning to be taken back to her own home, Cushing administered to her one eighth of a grain of morphine to kill the pain of the prospective sleigh ride over the snow to Swampscott. He was astonished to see that she then fell deeply unconscious for many hours. As Robert Peel and others have noted, Dr. Cushing's testimony, though clearly intended as an attack on Mrs. Eddy's veracity and reliability, serves at least, from the Christian Science point of view, to contradict the assertion—made first in the 1906 New York *World* articles and later developed in Edwin Dakin's 1929 biography—that Mrs. Eddy was addicted to morphine from her early twenties. Cushing's affidavit states:

> As I have stated, on the third and subsequent days of her said illness, resulting from her said fall on the ice, I attended Mrs. Patterson and gave her medicine; and on the 10th day of the following August, I was again called to see her, this time in the home of a Mrs. Clark, on Summer street, in said City of Lynn. I found Mrs. Patterson suffering from a bad cough and prescribed for her. I made three more professional calls upon Mrs. Patterson, and treated her for this cough in the said month of August, and with that ended my professional relations with her.[4]

Christian Scientists sought to counter the Cushing affidavit and the damaging conclusions as to Mrs. Eddy's truthfulness reached by Milmine in the *McClure's Magazine* series by diligently collecting their own affidavits. Various Lynn and Swampscott neighbors testified that everyone at the time had been convinced that Mrs. Patterson had done great damage to her spine, and those familiar with her injuries regarded her sudden ability to rise from bed and walk out of the sick room as next to miraculous. Sibyl Wilbur, Lyman P. Powell, and Alfred Farlow, who was the Church of Christ, Scientist's first manager of the Committee on Publication, went each in turn to visit old Dr. Cushing in his Springfield, Massachusetts, home and to consult his records. As Robert Peel reports, Farlow was able to blunt the force of Cushing's evidence somewhat, proving that he was not as dispassionate toward Mrs. Eddy and her church as he had claimed to be in the Milmine affidavit, and that the exactness of his memory of the case was somewhat suspect given the forty-year lapse of time and the large number of patients that he himself boasted of treating every day in the 1860s. Furthermore the written case records proved only that Cushing had visited the Patterson home in August, not which Patterson had been his patient.

There can be no doubt that Mary Baker Eddy revised her account of what happened after she fell on the sidewalk in Lynn in the winter of 1866, and that this revision moved consistently in the direction of presenting the incident as a moment of revelation. In her retelling of the event in *Retrospection and Introspection*, quoted earlier in this chapter, Mrs. Eddy herself uses a scientific analogy, likening her experience to the famous old story of Newton watching an apple fall, but more pertinent precedents perhaps are the personal conversion experiences narrated by Saint Paul in Acts of the Apostles, Chapter 9, by Saint Augustine in the *Confessions,* and by Paul Bunyan in *Grace Abounding to the Chief of Sinners.* It has been a strong tradition in the history of Christianity that the claim to religious leadership be based upon a man's experiencing one dramatic moment of clarity when he becomes so convinced of God's existence and of God's purpose that his whole life is changed. As Mary Baker Eddy moved out of powerlessness and destitution and despair, as she progressively defined herself as a metaphysical healer, a teacher of healing, and as the founder of a new Christian sect dedicated to healing, so also did her need grow for a moment of divine revelation that would give authority to her message. Her recasting in the 1870s and 1880s of the story of her fall in Lynn, like the stories she recounted in the last years of her life of the New Testament–like events surrounding her birth and childhood, form a part of her assumption of the identity of the religious leader.

To Mrs. Eddy's critics, this mythomaniac process is simply an exercise in deceit. Mrs. Eddy, according to Milmine or Dakin or Bates and Dittemore or Gardner, is a liar and a fraud, and not even a very clever one since she failed to anticipate that her lies would be revealed and her fraudulence made plain to the general public once the record was examined and material witnesses were questioned and had provided signed affidavits. Rather than seeking to exculpate or absolve Mrs. Eddy here, it seems to me important not only to acknowledge her tendency to engage in creative manipulations of the past but also to evaluate how far this practice served her as a religious leader.

Mrs. Eddy, like Joseph Smith, the prophet of the Church of the Latterday Saints, was a religious leader who faced special, modern issues when founding a new Christian sect. In nineteenth-century America, public recordkeeping was being standardized, newspapers, magazines, and books proliferated, the tradition of muckraking journalism was strengthening, and cynical secularism vied against religious credulity. In their manifold, doughty struggles to build the Christian church in earlier eras, at least Saint Paul and Saint Augustine did not have to worry about press coverage or publication of their early correspondence or affidavits from their defeated opponents. Given a general dearth of supporting documentary evidence for the early centuries of Christianity, history has been largely content to accept as truth the autobiographical narratives which the saints themselves created to buttress their religious authority. In a textual loop, we take their word about what happened to them because they are great saints, and at the same time we accept them to be great saints in some large measure because of what they have told us about themselves.

The accounts left by the great saints and divines of the fights they fought against the powers of unbelief did not prepare Mrs. Eddy very well for the onslaughts of Mark Twain, the New York *World*, and *McClure's Magazine*, or provide sufficient warning that her account of her own life would not be taken on faith or evaluated in terms of her greater accomplishments but rather in light of her petty, human weaknesses. Furthermore, as a nineteenth-century American woman, Mrs. Eddy could not adopt the model of virtue forged in the fires of vice that her great male religious predecessors had laid down. Nineteenth-century American culture had determined that woman was essentially purer, more spiritual, more virtuous, less susceptible to temptation and sin than man. Any fall from grace by a woman was therefore incommensurately censured and punished. Paul could admit that he had zealously persecuted the nascent Christian community, and he was allowed to atone. Augustine could confess that he had devoted his young manhood to exploring the pleasures of the flesh and the resources of classical pagan literature and Manichaean philosophy, and he was allowed to atone. Indeed, a male saint's religious worth was measured at least in part by the contrast between his past material depths and his later spiritual heights. Female sainthood, on the contrary, is traditionally defined by unblemished purity. Mary Magdalene, one of the Biblical Marys whom Mrs. Eddy identified with, was converted by Christ from her fallen state and was vouchsafed the first intimation of the Resurrection, but she did not become one of the apostles or a leader of the new Christian church.

In nineteenth-century Boston it was almost inconceivable that a woman could become a religious leader if any kind of scandal was attached to her name. As the vicious attacks on the Grimké sisters and Elizabeth Cady Stanton show, even women who led irreproachable lives would be publicly labelled as prostitutes or worse once they dared to enter the public sphere and challenge the status quo in any way. The vicissitudes of Mrs. Eddy's life left her far more vulnerable to attack than most of her suffragette sisters, and her best course of action was probably to conceal rather than confess. As the furor caused by the Milmine and Dakin biographies proves, Mrs. Eddy could not have become a religious leader in the 1880s if she had told all about her life from the outset.

Whether her policy of concealment was conscious deception or unconscious self-protection is impossible to establish, especially since there has not been free access to her personal notebooks and unpublished writings. Lacking documentation that would enable us to plumb her motivation, we can only observe how the course of action she took worked for and against her mission as a religious leader.

Whatever moral and religious interpretation one places upon it, the fall in Lynn clearly marked a turning point in Mrs. Mary Patterson's life, the moment when she began to take charge of her life and changed from victim to victor. She herself consistently, and with increasing fervor and conviction, attributed that change to a new understanding of God's relation to the world, and to a new sense of her own special divine mission. Whether we label this delusion or revelation, the fact remains that the woman was fundamentally empowered, and that there was no external, material change to account for that increase of power.

At the time that Mrs. Patterson fell down on the ice, she was particularly alone and vulnerable. Her marriage, never strong or successful, was finally collapsing; she knew that her forever absent and philandering husband was ready to leave for good. With her father and Quimby dead and Daniel gone, all her previous havens in Sanbornton Bridge, Portland, and Saco were lost to her. When she awoke in the Bubier home, surrounded by strangers, in terrible pain, she must have been remembering again with her whole body as well as with her mind the pains that had kept her bedridden for years, and she probably did assume that her end was at hand, that her life was over. She had long since lost any confidence that a homeopathic doctor such as the one who hovered over her, or indeed any other doctor, had the power to help.

Thus for Mary Patterson to get out of bed, get dressed, and walk downstairs to meet her amazed and incredulous friends, as all agree she did, was clearly to do something brave and decisive. What she called her healing was the first and necessary step on a road whose end she could not even conceive for some time. It was also, in my view, a new and conclusive reenactment of something that had happened to her before—in her childhood when she had fallen ill with a fever after arguing with her father over the doctrine of the Fall and the Redemption, and she had been brought back to health by her mother and her Bible. In 1866, when an even greater challenge came to her, her mother was long dead, there was no sister or husband or friend to fill the maternal role, but the Bible remained, and God, and it was enough.

The fact that Mrs. Eddy's chosen moment of illumination centers on an experience of healing from a physical injury is both obvious and crucial. Mrs. Eddy did not claim to have seen a blinding light or a vision of Christ or the Virgin. She claimed to have been faced with death and to have recovered her health and strength by reading an account in the New Testament of one of Christ's healings and by acting upon the firm conviction that such healings were not limited to a specific time and place and to the agency of one divine person. On subsequent reflection, she became convinced that healing such as she had herself known was a part of the very structure of the world as established by God. Healing could occur not by experiencing a miracle, an exception from the scientific laws governing human material existence, but by moving below the surface of matter and making contact with the spiritual divine science that was fundamental and eternal.

Mrs. Eddy's revelation is profoundly Protestant in that it came out of an unmediated reading of a Biblical text that the reader assumes to be the expression of the divine will and purpose. It is profoundly of the nineteenth century and perhaps of America in its assumption that good health and long life are man's heritage, that sickness and pain are not part of the divine plan, that physical suffering is not a prerequisite to virtue or a necessary test to be passed on the way to happiness after death. Furthermore, the healing depends on the individual's own receptivity and preparedness and resolution, not on the services of a doctor, a minister of religion, or a shaman. Alone with God and the Bible, the individual can find the resources not just for spiritual illumination but for physical well-being.

This is a very radical message. Why should it surprise us that it took Mary Baker Eddy months and years not just to conceive its general outlines but to learn to rely upon it for herself and to begin formulating it for others?

10

Homeless

Outwardly her life during these years was miserably sordid. She had no money aside from Patterson's irregular remittances. She underwent the indignity of expulsion from lodging after lodging, nearly always, one may be fairly certain, for the same reason. To be sure, our accounts of Mrs. Patterson at this time, derived from her exasperated landlords, emphasize the frailties of her character rather than the emptiness of her purse; but unpaid creditors are proverbially censorious. Thus large deductions must be made from the current stories of Mrs. Patterson's conduct during these lean years.

— BATES AND DITTEMORE, P. 118

IN MARCH OF 1866, THE PATTERSONS' LANDLORD, ARME-NIUS Newhall, decided to sell 23 Paradise Road,[1] and Daniel and his wife moved into an unfurnished room on the corner of Pearl and High Streets in Lynn. Their landlord was Mr. P. R. Russell, and he in turn rented half the house from his father, the Reverend Philemon R. Russell. At first Mrs. Patterson found a willing ear for her new ideas on healing in the younger Mrs. Russell, but unfortunately her unusual views, as well as her precarious social status and lack of money, were not at all to the taste of the Reverend Russell. He was a very conservative gentleman, well known in Lynn for his religious bigotry and fanatical opposition to abolitionism. When Daniel Patterson went off on one of his trips again, without leaving any funds, his wife was evicted by the Russells for failure to pay the rent of $1.50 a week. Patterson returned for a brief time in July, and the pair moved to the Clarks' boardinghouse on Summer Street, but their separation became permanent in late summer of that year.[2]

As Mrs. Eddy would later tell her student Janette Weller in 1884, one morning Daniel Patterson asked her to go out and buy him something for his breakfast, and she agreed, although this was an unusual request. Out in the street, she was rudely approached by a man who asked who she was and then informed her that he was on his way to her home with a warrant for her husband's arrest for committing adultery with his wife. When Mrs. Mary Patterson got home, she found her husband had indeed gone off with the wife of that wealthy local man.[3] The adulterous couple was soon found, and the woman was brought back to Lynn, where her husband kept her a virtual prisoner. Hearing of the wife's plight, Mrs. Patterson paid a visit to the husband and persuaded him to forgive his wife. "'And,' said Mrs. Eddy to me [Janette Weller], 'I have met them many times, riding happily in their carriage, while I was plodding my way on foot and alone.'"[4]

With or without his inamorata, Patterson set out north and paid a visit to his wife's relatives, presumably to explain his actions and enroll the sympathies of Abigail, the two Marthas, and their stepmother. Perhaps with their persuasion, he agreed to pay Mary $200 a year, and it seems that this money was paid in small installments for a few years. Even when the payments were made regularly, however, they were quite inadequate to cover expenses— even for a single person living in an unfurnished room in Lynn, Massachusetts. Peel reports that Patterson, who in the 1870s settled in Littleton, New Hampshire, made one further trip back to Lynn, presumably to attempt a reconciliation. His wife, who was then staying with the Phillips family, would have none of it, however. Mr. Phillips offered to throw Patterson out the door, but Mrs. Patterson refused. The Pattersons' separation was henceforward permanent.

The petition which Mary Patterson made to the city of Lynn for compensation for the injury incurred as a result of her fall on the ice was made during the last months Daniel Patterson spent with her; I suspect it was his idea, not hers. She may well have agreed to file out of desperation, realizing that her financial position would be dire once Daniel left her for good. This was a period when no state or federal safety net existed, and an abandoned wife who had no independent means or close family could turn for aid only to private charity. It is easy to see why, in later years, Mary Baker Eddy preferred to blot this part of her life out of her memory.[5]

In the fall of 1868 she decided to revert to the name Glover and explained this decision in emotional and somewhat cryptic terms to her best female friend of the period, Sarah Bagley, with whom we will be getting better acquainted later in this chapter. It seems that Miss Bagley had addressed her latest letter as usual to "Mrs. Patterson," and Mary in her response warned her friend not to do so again:

> I was sorry my dear one, that you superscribed my letter as you did for I am fixed upon my course, which is not to be changing names. I am not such a person, and now that the Demon of Amesbury Ferry [probably one of the Webster family] causes me to take my former name, I shall retain it until it is mine legally. Besides I can better explain my position before the world to be divorced for adultry from my husband, this in the sight of God and man is a sufficient cause for me to return to my widowhood, and not to occupy the anomalous position of a married woman without a husband. Also I cannot do business unless I do [i.e., change my name] while I have a husband I cannot collect a bill due me if it is refused![6]

Mrs. Mary Glover was writing swiftly and elliptically here. When she said that she was not changing her name, when obviously she was doing precisely that, I think she meant that the name Mrs. Patterson no longer corresponded to the person she felt herself to be. "Mrs. Patterson" was no more. The letter gives a vivid example ("while I have a husband I cannot collect a bill due me if it is refused") of the difficulties attending a married woman seeking to earn her own living in a society that would give her no independent legal status. The daughter and sister of excellent legal minds, Mrs. Glover both understood her predicament and, I think, decided that her best course was to act as if Patterson had never existed. Socially, a woman on her own, whether a widow or a divorcée, was perhaps in worse shape than a woman separated from her husband, but legally her position—and hence her earning potential—was clearer. Social standing was as important to Mary Baker Eddy as to most people, but survival was the issue she was facing at this time.

That said, however much Mary Baker Glover wanted to close the book on her life as Mrs. Patterson, the past was not so easily cleaned and put away on the shelf. To be a married lady without a husband was not simply an anomaly but a scandal, and vague, unsubstantiated rumors of immoral behavior were to dog Mrs. Glover's footsteps and make finding lodgings, for example, difficult for years to come.[7] She fought for respectability as best she could. All the material difficulties Mrs. Glover was experiencing at this time were compounded by her refusal to allow herself to be defined by her shabby clothes, empty purse, and anomalous situation. Circumstances were forcing her to live on intimate terms and in humiliating conditions with families much lower on the social scale than the Bakers and Tiltons—not just with the "overseers" of the world, to use a shorthand she uses herself in one letter, but with the "operatives"! Yet rather than expressing humble gratitude for the assistance and charity she was receiving, she always presented herself as a woman above her circumstances, acting as if she were doing her hosts a favor by living with them. In many ways, Mrs. Glover was a snob, but it was this snobbery in part that gave her the courage to resist being absorbed forever into the humble social strata where she found herself in midlife.

Her beleaguered sense of social superiority fused into her incipient sense of divine mission, and the resulting intensity and self-absorption did not make her an easy house guest. Several families with whom she lived during this period became polarized by her presence in their home, with some members of the family convinced that Mrs. Glover was a vain, lazy, parasitical fraud and others equally persuaded that she was a warm, wonderful, charismatic saint. Yet even those who hated her remembered her and admitted that in some strange fashion she had colored and enriched their lives. The testimony on this point by the *McClure's* biographical team is deserving of note, since they were responsible for digging up most of the colorfully disreputable stories from this period:

> Her being "different" did, after all, result in material benefits to Mrs. Glover. All these people with whom she once stayed, love to talk of her, and most of them are glad to have known her,—even those who now say that the experience was a costly one. . . . She was never dull, her old hosts say, and never commonplace. She never laid aside her regal air; never entered a room or left it like other people. There was something about her that continually excited and stimulated, and she gave people the feeling that a great deal was happening.[8]

Charisma, the effect one person's physical presence has on others, is a crucial element in human affairs and one that text can only attest to. Any account of the rise of Christian Science falls short of the mark if it fails to see and acknowledge that Mary Baker Eddy had charisma.

Between June 1866 and June 1870 Mrs. Glover moved at least nine times and lived for periods varying from a few weeks to two years at the Clark boardinghouse, the Newhalls, the Wheelers, the Ellises, the Crafts, the Websters, the Wentworths, and the Bagleys. Mr. George E. Clark, the young sailor son of the owners of the boardinghouse where Mrs. Glover took refuge several times, later offered a vivid picture of how she looked and acted.[9] Clark said that Mrs. Glover had an excellent relationship with his mother, Mrs. Brene Paine Clark, a progressive woman—"a come-outer, as you might say"— once Universalist but in 1866 very taken up with Spiritualism. Her husband, also called George, was an invalid. Presumably running a boardinghouse was

Mrs. Clark's way of making a living. Mrs. Clark and Mrs. Glover obviously had much in common, and one can see why they became good friends. Seances were often conducted at the Clark home, and Mrs. Glover participated in these, although she and her hostess would engage in long, vigorous but good-natured arguments about Spiritualism.

Forty years later, the younger George Clark was still able to recall the seating plan at his mother's table, and he placed Mrs. Glover at the head. He also remembered Mrs. Glover's appearance in surprising detail. He said that she was beautiful, with the complexion of a young girl, big, brilliant, deep blue eyes, and a shower of brown curls. She habitually dressed in black, with some accent of violet and pale rose, "and I remember well a dove-colored dress trimmed with black velvet that she wore in the summer." With surprising lyricism, he compared her to a lily and evoked her reserved but stately presence and brilliant conversation. Certain of her hand gestures were engraved upon his memory and would allow him to recognize her anywhere, he said.

Though charmed by Mrs. Glover the woman, George Clark was never converted to her doctrines of healing, and he stated flatly that, despite claims later made by her, or in her name, she did not cure either his father or John Clark, the crippled shoemaker who had set up shop in the basement of the Russell house. Just because of his jovial imperviousness to Christian Science, George Clark's final evaluation of Mrs. Glover at this nadir in her fortunes is peculiarly interesting: "I think she was hungry for hearts, if I may so express it, but she would draw them up to her level rather than go to theirs." Perhaps Mrs. Glover's ability to charm and impress "dashing sailor lads," as George Clark described himself, was one reason for the antipathy felt toward her by women like Julia Russell Walcott, her former landlord's sister.

While staying at the Clark boardinghouse, Mrs. Glover also spent time during the day with Thomas and Hannah Phillips, an affluent Quaker couple who lived on Buffum Street in Lynn, and with their married daughter Susan Oliver. Mrs. Oliver later converted to Christian Science, and she told biographer Sibyl Wilbur that Mrs. Glover had performed three healings around the late 1860s. Dorr Phillips, the teenage son of the house, was cured of a painful felon finger. A rich young man from Boston, visiting Lynn to learn the shoe trade and staying with the Phillipses, was cured of a life-threatening fever. Mrs. Charles Winslow of Ocean Street, a good friend of the Phillipses who had spent sixteen years in a wheelchair, recovered the use of her limbs. Wilbur accepts Mrs. Oliver's subsequent accounts of these healings as evidence of the strength of Mrs. Glover's newfound doctrine, but she also reports that none of the patients themselves gave Mrs. Glover credit for their recovery.

The Phillipses, though willing to admire Mrs. Glover as a wonderful and even inspiring friend, refused to accept her doctrine of healing, and, indeed, they strongly advised her to let it go. The young man from Boston was whisked quickly away from Lynn by his parents and put into the hands of conventional doctors. Of Mrs. Winslow, Wilbur writes, with some perspicacity: "Though a wonderful thing had been accomplished, the woman's pride kept her from acknowledging a cure.... To accept it was like convicting her of never having been ill. So she returned to her former beliefs."[10] Mrs. Glover found her visits to the Phillipses' home soothing and agreeable, and she became particularly close to the ninety-year-old matriarch, Mrs. Mary Phillips. The silent form of prayer which the Quaker family espoused was to have considerable influence on the form of service later adopted by Christian Science. Nonetheless, Mrs. Glover eventually realized that she would not make any immediate converts to her new ideas among the rich and settled Phillips-Winslow circle.[11]

When she had left the Clarks and was again without resources, Mrs. Glover was taken in for a few weeks by Mrs. Mary Ellis of Elm Cottage in Swampscott. Fred Ellis, Mary's schoolteacher son, remembered Mary Baker Glover with affection and admiration. He testified that during the weeks in the fall of 1866 that Mrs. Glover lived in his mother's house, she spent most of her time upstairs in her room, writing. At the end of each day, she would read the Ellises what she had written, inviting their criticism and debate. This is the first eyewitness account about the Genesis manuscript, a long unpublished work now in The Mother Church archives, which the leader of the church would keep with her to the end but never published and, indeed, did not show to many people during her lifetime.

In the late fall of 1866 Mrs. Glover was invited to move into the home in East Stoughton (now Avon, Massachusetts) of Hiram S. and Mary Holmes Crafts. Hiram was an expert heel-finisher who had come to do piecework in the Lynn shoe factories and had met Mrs. Glover at the Clark boardinghouse.[12] Quaintly, Hiram was known to friends for the excellence of his oyster stews, but he was an earnest and intelligent young man who, despite his humble background and education, had read enough to espouse the transcendentalist ideas of Channing, Parker, and Emerson. One reason he had probably chosen to stay in the Clark house was that he and his wife shared Mrs. Clark's interest in Spiritualism. It seems that Mrs. Glover's arguments against Spiritualism convinced Hiram at least that "her science was far superior to spirit teachings," and he soon became fascinated by the theories of healing which his fellow boarder was expounding over the dinner table.[13]

Hiram S. Crafts was Mrs. Glover's first student, and she soon began encouraging him to become a healer according to her system. As a teaching aid, she began to work on another manuscript which systematized the practice as well as the theory of teaching. This manuscript was certainly separate from her magnum opus of Bible exposition, but there is disagreement as to what it was.[14] When Mrs. Glover moved into the modest Crafts home in East Stoughton, the arrangement between the parties was, according to Hiram's 1902 affidavit, that he paid the board and lodging in return for receiving Mrs. Glover's instruction in the science of healing. He also said that she contributed the furniture for the parlor, though it is not clear which furniture he was referring to or where it had been stored during Mrs. Glover's recent enforced peripeteia. Mrs. Mary Crafts was assigned to play Martha to Mrs. Glover's Mary, as Mrs. Glover was to spend most of her day reading and writing, and her evenings talking to Hiram and other interested folk. For six or seven months everything seemed to be going well, and Hiram was so inspired by his teacher and so confident in his new powers that in April 1867 he gave up his shoe-making business to work full-time as a mental healer. The household moved to Taunton, Massachusetts, and a May advertisement in the Taunton papers claimed that Dr. H. S. Crafts guaranteed he could cure "Consumption, Catarrh, Scrofula, Dyspepsia and Rheumatism, with many other forms of disease and weakness." The advertisement included an endorsement from Mrs. Abigail Raymond of Taunton who attested to the cure she had experienced at his hands.[15]

By July 1867 the healing business in Taunton was going so well that Mrs. Glover felt able to pay a visit to her family in Sanbornton Bridge, in response to a cry of distress from her sister Martha Pilsbury. George Sullivan Baker had at last come home from his far-flung career as a highly competent but unlucky manager of woolen manufactures, but his return was of little comfort to his sisters, his estranged wife, and his son. George came back to his father's house a blind, sick, and deeply embittered man. He would be dead by the fall.[16] Even more poignantly, Martha Pilsbury's surviving child, Mrs. Glover's niece Ellen, had for weeks been lying in bed at the Baker family homestead, apparently at death's door.

Exactly what was wrong with Ellen Pilsbury is not clear, though her doctors diagnosed enteritis. Her aunt Martha Rand Baker testified that Ellen's bowels were so swollen and painful that she "could only be moved on a sheet from bed to bed," and she suffered pain at the slightest footfall in her room. What is certain is that within minutes of standing over her bed, Mrs. Glover had Ellen on her feet and stamping the ground, that the next day the girl came down to dinner for the first time in weeks and ate heartily, and that she departed with Mrs. Glover on the fifth day on "the cars" for the hundred-mile journey to Taunton.

The witnesses who have left testimony to this healing—Martha Rand Baker and George Baker's son, George Waldron Baker—may be trusted since they maintained a lifelong antipathy to Christian Science and a deep distrust of Mary's healing claims. On March 4, 1907, George reported in the *Lewiston* (Maine) *Evening Journal:*

The only actual case I ever saw of my aunt's power was, I think, in 1867, when she was called to Tilton to see a niece, who was supposed to be at the point of death. My aunt Mary came from Lynn, and stopped to get dinner, much to the disgust of the sick girl's mother. She went in to see the patient, and looked at her, sniffed, and said, 'You are going back to Lynn with me tomorrow on the 2 o'clock train.' And she did, walking apparently as well as ever.

The immediate reaction of the Sanbornton Bridge relatives to Ellen's recovery was intense relief: Martha Rand Baker told a friend many years later that "such a change came over the household. We all felt . . . 'the angel of the Lord appeared, and glory shone around.'"[17] However, the relief and pleasure were short-lived, and this "healing" occasioned a further deterioration in Mrs. Glover's relations with her sisters and sister-in-law and their families. Abigail Tilton had not been at home when Ellen recovered, but in a letter to her sister Martha she expressed deep exasperation with Mary's behavior and told of her fear that "no real good will result from all the stir she has made about Ellen."[18] Wilbur in her biography claims that in or around 1867 Abigail had written to Mary, offering to buy her a house in Sanbornton and to provide her with an income for life if she would only give up all her crazy theories about healing. Mary refused this offer, which although generous was imperious, and it seems probable that Abigail then washed her hands of Mary; she continued to love her sister but ceased to approve of or respect her.

Ellen Pilsbury, marched off to Taunton and subjected to the ministrations of Hiram Crafts, was rapidly horrified by the conditions in which her aunt was living. Based on a letter Mrs. Glover wrote to her sister Martha at the time of Ellen's visit, it is clear that Crafts had little idea of how to treat Miss Pilsbury, and the level of domestic comfort was probably very low since Mrs. Glover reported in a letter that she personally was emptying her niece's slops.[19] Ellen had come to Taunton for treatment, and when her aunt asked that the money be paid to her and not to Crafts, Ellen coldly refused. She then returned hotfoot to Sanbornton Bridge, reportedly to relate lurid tales to her aunts. In later years Ellen refused to allow any references to her 1867 illness, and although unwilling to make any public statements that could hurt her aunt, she was implacably opposed to Christian Science. According to one account, it was Ellen Pilsbury who, when the dying Abigail wished to send for Mary, convinced her aunt not to do so.[20] Martha Baker Pilsbury, as always, followed the line laid down by her stronger-minded older sister, and she was also influenced by the daughter with whom she was to spend the rest of her life. Although Mary visited Tilton a number of times over the next twenty years and called on Abigail at least once, the three Baker sisters were never together after the 1860s.

Not only was Ellen Pilsbury responsible for ruining her aunt's good name in the eyes of her mother and aunts; she also precipitated the end of Mrs. Glover's agreement with Hiram Crafts, which was being effected by Mrs. Mary Crafts, her brother Ira Holmes, and Ira's wife, Hiram's sister. Mrs. Crafts resented the considerable time her husband spent with their lodger and the food and services she was expected to provide, and she placed no great hopes on her husband earning fame and fortune as a healer. More fundamental was Hiram's lack of seed capital for the practice, a problem that would continue to bedevil Christian Science practitioners into the 1880s. The Craftses lived on the money Hiram earned and had small savings at best, and Mrs. Glover was so impoverished that she and Hiram fell out bitterly over the cost of a car ticket from Stoughton to Swampscott, which Hiram refused to pay as promised. In any case, Hiram proved unable to make that miracle cure of a key, affluent patient that might have generated interest in his practice throughout the community and brought in immediate income.

In August 1867 the healing experiment in Taunton was abandoned, and Hiram and his wife returned to their home in Stoughton, where he seems to have taken up his life as a shoemaker again. Hiram Crafts himself would have preferred to continue in the new work, but he was unable to resist domestic pressures. When Mrs. Glover wrote in 1868 asking if he was at all willing to take up healing again, he replied,

> I should be willing to do all you ask if I was in different circumstances. . . . But it would be impossible for me to come over there to help you at present. I should have no peace at home if I did. I have been through one hell and don't want to go through another. . . . Your letter was opened and read before I got it, if you send another have it delivered to me.[21]

Mrs. Crafts managed to separate her husband from Mrs. Glover, but not to destroy his strong admiration for her, and the ménage seems not to have prospered after the break. Many years later, in 1907, living as a widow in distressed circumstances with her brother, Ira Holmes, Mrs. Crafts addressed the following letter to Mrs. Eddy at Pleasant View:

> *Dear Mrs. Eddy:*
> Now Hiram has gone the people want me to tell them your history while you lived with us, the one that will pay me the most money if you will pay me the most I will still keep my mouth closed you can have your first choise I want you to be quick about it, not to delay for I don't want to be teased to death.
>
> > *With regards*
> > *Mary W. Crafts.*[22]

Mrs. Eddy and advisors did not respond to this blatant attempt at extortion, and soon afterward Mrs. Crafts's brother gave an interview and affidavit to the *McClure's* team, for which he presumably received payment. Though motivated by long-term resentment and short-term greed, Ira Holmes and Mary Crafts probably told the journalists the truth as they saw it. No doubt back when she was under their roof Mrs. Glover did complain about the way Mrs. Crafts ironed her cuffs, as Mrs. Crafts later told Sibyl Wilbur; no doubt Mrs. Glover did carry herself above folks; possibly she did, on some level, encourage Hiram to leave his nagging, illiterate wife and her no-good brother, but there is no evidence that Mary Glover acted with malice or self-ishness toward the Crafts, much less that she had designs on Hiram. Living with these people was her best option at a point in her life when options were few, but her situation as an attractive, single, middle-class woman with no means of support, living with an unhappily married working-class couple, was difficult if not impossible from the outset.[23] Certainly, for Hiram Crafts, expert heel-maker and would-be transcendentalist, Mrs. Glover was a brief ray of light in what he himself described as "this miserable life in darkness and error."[24]

When Mrs. Glover's living arrangement at the Crafts house was termi-nated, Hiram Crafts was left in henpecked misery, but at least he could earn a living. Mrs. Glover, on the other hand, for all her high and mighty ways, was now at the end of her resources. When Mrs. Ellis sent her $2 and invited her to visit again, Mrs. Glover was obliged to refuse because she had no money for the fare to Swampscott. Her Quaker friends the Winslows sent her to ask assistance and refuge from friends of theirs in Amesbury, and thus Mrs. Glover arrived destitute one night on the doorstep of Mrs. Mary Webster, claiming, Milmine tells us, to have been sent by the spirits. This was an introduction calculated to appeal to Mother Webster, who was both a "drawing" and a "rubbing" medium, known in the town for her intense interest in Spiritualism.[25] She was also an affluent, affectionate, charitable body whose husband was mostly away, and she happily took in forlorn Spiritualists and other people down on their luck. The Webster house was a large, comfortable dwelling close to the Merrimack River, and it included a "spiritual" room decorated in blue—the spirits' favorite shade, it seems—and featuring both a couch and a table for Mrs. Webster's seances and heal-ing sessions. Mrs. Glover was soon ensconced in a bedroom over the spiri-tual room, taking part in her hostess's activities, and meeting some other local people who were interested in Spiritualism and healing. Among them were an eighteen-year-old orphaned boy, Richard Kennedy, who was already mak-ing his way in the world in a small box company, and Miss Sarah Bagley, a genteel but impoverished single lady of good family who lived nearby.

There is no doubt that while living with the Websters Mrs. Glover was closely connected to the Spiritualist community and that the first advertise-ment she placed, listing her own name and offering instruction in meta-physical healing, appeared in the *Banner of Light,* the official Spiritualist organ. The issue of Spiritualism was a highly contentious one throughout

Mary Baker Eddy's lifetime, and her detractors consistently use the label "Spiritualist" to characterize Christian Science practice and implicitly thereby to denigrate her movement.[26] The Church of Christ, Scientist's response to this line of attack has often been muddled and intemperate, but, in essence, the Church is correct in asserting that whereas at some points in her life Mary Baker Eddy may have known many Spiritualists and taken part in some of their activities, she was never at any point a convinced believer. By 1866 she had become convinced that she had a system of healing and belief that was far superior to anything Spiritualism had to offer. Years later Mrs. Eddy herself would once tell Alfred Farlow that she had made many of her early converts and friends from among the Spiritualists "because they were liberal, kind-hearted people, and were quite ready to accept new ideas."[27] This seems an accurate description both of the individual Spiritualists that the then Mrs. Mary Glover met between 1866 and 1870 and of the Spiritualist community in general which was socially and politically liberal as well as theologically unconventional, with ties to such new radical movements as feminism, marxism, antiracism, and free love.[28]

In the first edition of *Science and Health* (1875) Mrs. Eddy presented a full and complex discussion of where exactly she and Spiritualism parted ways, and the current edition still includes a chapter called "Christian Science versus Spiritualism." More anecdotally, it is interesting to look at one of the little stories which she confided to Irving Tomlinson in the last years of her life, and which probably relates to the time when she was living in Amesbury with either Mrs. Webster or Miss Sarah Bagley:

> While I was engaged in uncovering and exposing the falsity of so-called spiritualism, I was present in a group which included Mr. Colby of the *Banner of Light,* Lucy Larcom, and the poet, John Greenleaf Whittier. When I entered the room, those present said, "Now she will have testimony that must convince her.". . .
>
> To show them their error, I consented and the young woman said, "I see a bright company of angels about her head." She then proceeded to give a minute and exact account of the following touching incident in my early career: Upon my father's estate in Tilton, New Hampshire, was a small cottage house which my father gave rent free to an invalid widow and her daughter. They were saintly people, members of our church, and my godly father was glad to help them. At the time of which I speak, the widow was very ill and mother and I called to sing and pray with them. . . .
>
> At the conclusion of the recital of this incident by the medium, there were tears in my eyes, so perfect was the representation of this memory of bygone years.
>
> Said Mr. Colby to the young woman, "Can you give me the name of the hymn which was sung?" She replied, "They sang 'Sweet Hour of Prayer.'" It was indeed the anthem we had sung.

The company was much moved and said, "Now, you must see that spiritualism is true." "No," I said, "I do not see it."

"Then," said Mr. Colby, "you shall have further proof." He said to the spiritualist, "Describe her mother." Instantly I pictured in thought the exact opposite of my mother. The medium described precisely what I held in thought and the company beamed with satisfaction. "There," said they, "you have your proof."

"Yes," I remarked, "I have proof that spiritualism is no way connected with the departed, but is simply mind-reading. My mother was the exact opposite of that which has been described. She was short, stout, blue-eyed, and fair-haired. I formed in my thought the exact opposite of my mother and she read my thought."[29]

Several things strike me as interesting about this story. First, there is the obvious respectability of those attending the seance, proving, if it needed proving, that attending a seance around 1868 was common in good New England society. Second, I'm annoyed that Irving Tomlinson did not have the intelligence or curiosity to ask Mrs. Eddy how she had found the poet Lucy Larcom, and whether they had had other meetings. Mary Baker Eddy and Lucy Larcom had so much in common, it would be fascinating to know how well they had been acquainted. Third, here we have proof that, until the end of her life, Mary Baker Eddy, like Phineas Quimby, believed in mind reading, believed that her mind could be read as she could read the minds of others. The implications of this belief are most important when we come to consider the whole issue of Malicious Animal Magnetism in Mrs. Eddy's life and doctrine.

Mrs. Glover stayed in the Webster home for some ten months, and, according to later accounts, she spent most of her time writing, rewriting, and tearing up sections of the commentary on the Bible which she had begun soon after her fall in Lynn. As Mrs. Webster later told her granddaughter, Mrs. Glover "would gather up all the pages she had filled with writing and tear them up, because she could not make them read as she wished."[30] In the evenings she would walk with her hostess along the river, and she had such a reputation for mystic power that two local girls would watch her to see if she would walk on water.

The relative peace and comfort of her stay with Mrs. Webster was rudely interrupted when William Ellis, Mrs. Webster's son-in-law, decided that he could not leave his two children in Amesbury for the summer with his dead wife's mother if she entertained such disreputable people in her home. Asked to leave, Mrs. Glover refused, and reportedly she was then put out on the street with her trunk, though it was late at night and raining very hard. She sat out on the stoop under the porch for a while, but at last she was rescued when two other Spiritualists, Mrs. Richardson and Mr. Kennedy, were also put outside. They conducted her to the nearby house of their mutual friend,

Miss Sarah Bagley, who took pity on them all. Young Kennedy carried Mrs. Glover's trunk.

Sarah Bagley lived in a simple but refined and ancient house at 277 Main Street, Amesbury. Her father, known locally as Squire Bagley, had been a local character who left an interesting diary but no fortune for his widow and daughters to sustain their station in life. Despite the goodwill of such neighbors as the poet John Greenleaf Whittier, after her father's death Sarah had to work hard teaching, sewing, and opening a little shop in order to keep a roof over her own head and that of her invalid mother, and, apparently, at least one sister. Sarah's interest in Mrs. Glover's theories of spiritual healing was clearly personal as well as intellectual, practical as well as theoretical. Nonconventional medicine paid little in comparison with the work performed by certified practitioners, but it paid much better than sewing![31]

As she had in the early 1860s with Mrs. Crosby, Mary Baker Glover at first developed with Miss Bagley a relationship of almost girlish intimacy. Each woman was starved for affection and fun, and one letter indicates that for a time they re-created as middle-aged women the playful, romping, caressing ways very common among conventional heterosexual American girls of the period.[32] But their relationship was soon threatened by Mrs. Glover's increasing absorption in Richard Kennedy. As Sarah's papers show, the obvious preference Mrs. Glover gave to Kennedy as a prospective disciple and healer made Sarah feel neglected and jealous.

In 1868 Sarah paid Mary $25 as an advance fee for instruction, and a verbal contract was made between them concerning future payments. Probably this payment arrangement was related in some way to their later written contract, which set out the interest to be paid to Mrs. Glover should Miss Bagley go into practice as a healer using Mrs. Glover's system. It seems that following her departure to Stoughton in early September of 1868 to live with the Wentworths, Mary appointed Richard as Sarah's instructor and gave him charge of her precious teaching manuscripts, and this offended Sarah so much that she ceased taking instruction. In a very stiff and unpleasant letter dated July 28, 1869, Mrs. Glover accused Miss Bagley of making illicit copies of "the Mss. of Dr. Quimby which belong exclusively to me and to such students as contract to receive their instructions," and, on the basis of vague legal threats, she attempted to levy $50 from Miss Bagley for holding on to the copies.[33]

Despite all the charges of bad faith and sharp business practice which the two women exchanged in 1868 and 1869, they did not quarrel irremediably at this stage. Mrs. Glover promised to undertake Miss Bagley's instruction personally once more, and in a letter dated January 25, 1870, she switches back from the stiff address to "Miss Bagley," to "Ever dear Sarah" and signs off not as "M. B. Glover," but "As ever your true & loving Mary." After Mary returned to Amesbury, bridges were once again built between them, and Sarah's faith in her friend's ideas grew so strong that she signed a written agreement on April 23, 1870, promising to pay Mary 25 percent of the receipts of her healing practice. This agreement remained in force at least until 1875, though, by mutual agreement, the percentage was reduced to 10 percent in 1872. After this date Mary "refused to receive any more percentage," according to Miss Bagley, and the two women ceased to correspond and had virtually no further contact.

That Sarah Bagley continued to love and regret Mrs. Glover is shown, I think, in her decision to keep all the letters she had received from her, some drafts of significant letters she either sent or contemplated sending to Mrs. Glover, as well as documents showing the business relationship between the two of them between 1868 and 1875. That Sarah Bagley later remained a true friend to Mary Baker Eddy, that she never during her lifetime sought to hurt or denigrate her friend to the public at large, is surely a credit to her generosity of character and to the strength of her Christian principles. Even as the controversy over Mrs. Eddy's past raged from 1883 onward, Miss Bagley kept to herself her personal knowledge of Mrs. Eddy and the extensive documentary evidence in her possession. Unlike Hannah Philbrook, Sarah Crosby, Ira Holmes, and Horace Wentworth, Sarah Bagley wrote no letters to the newspapers and offered no affidavits. It was only after her death in August of 1905 that news of her connection with Mrs. Eddy started to be made public, but even then the correspondence was not offered for reading to any interested parties, and the Milmine-*McClure's* magazine series and subsequent book have little to say about the boring Miss Bagley.[34]

In later years Mrs. Eddy's conduct toward her old friend and ally would prove considerably less generous and principled. After Miss Bagley's death, an article in the *Boston Herald* which appeared on August 24, 1905, asserted that she had been Mrs. Eddy's "first instructor." This provoked an angry reply from Alfred Farlow, head of the Church's Committee on Publication, which included the following statement by Mrs. Eddy:

> I taught my first student in 1867, in Lynn, Mass. I never saw Miss Bagley until about the year 1870, while I was stopping in Amesbury, Mass. Then she, Miss Bagley, applied to me for admission to a class in Christian Science that I was preparing to open, but I declined to accept her as a student. She was a spiritualist and a so-called medium when I knew her.

In protest against what he rightly perceived to be a slight to an old and worthy friend, the Reverend Samuel Beane of Lawrence, Massachusetts, wrote to Alfred Farlow and recounted what Miss Bagley had told him about her relations with the then Mrs. Glover. He pointed out that Miss Bagley had taken Mrs. Glover into her home when she had been denounced as a "disreputable and licentious woman" and had been shown the door summarily by her hosts, the Websters. He said that Miss Bagley had always spoken affectionately of Mrs. Glover but reproached her for vanity and an "apparently radical defect in the sense of truth."[35]

This letter written by Beane has never been published, and it is probable, from internal evidence in the letter, that the reverend gentleman had been contacted by newspapermen and had been influenced against Mrs. Eddy by all the sensational stories claiming she was a drug addict, nymphomaniac, and husband-killer which were then circulating. As I shall show in Part Four of this book, in 1905–1906 Mrs. Eddy, by then in her late eighties, was under extraordinary and increasing stress. Miss Bagley was a key that could open one part of her life she wished to keep closed, and she probably penned her rebuttal to the *Herald* article at a time when she was feeling especially hounded and vulnerable to attack. Nonetheless, Mrs. Eddy's letter, as quoted by Farlow, seems proof of the very lack of truthfulness which Beane alleged, and I find it hard to forgive Mrs. Eddy's callous and self-serving account of her relationship with her loyal old friend and ally, Sarah Bagley.[36]

After three months at Sarah Bagley's, Mrs. Glover left abruptly and soon took up an invitation to live with Alanson and Sally Wentworth at 133 Central Street, Stoughton. Several widely divergent accounts have been put on record of the months Mrs. Glover spent with the Wentworth family.[37] The Wentworths were friends and fellow citizens of the Crafts, respectable folk several steps down the social scale from Miss Bagley and finding it just as difficult to make ends meet. The household consisted of Mr. Wentworth, his second wife Sally Talbot Wentworth, and their three younger children: Celia, aged about twenty when Mrs. Glover moved in; Charles Orville, seventeen; and Lucy, thirteen. Alanson Wentworth seems to have been like Hiram Crafts—a man of more intelligence and intellectual curiosity than education, one who was more interested in books and religious discussions than in the work of farming the family's twelve acres and mending shoes. He suffered from long-term, very painful and debilitating sciatica and was often unable to get out of bed. Since her husband worked irregularly and her elder daughter was too sickly to work at all, Mrs. Wentworth was forced to try to support the family on her earnings as a nurse, masseuse, and Spiritualist healer. The eldest son, Horace Wentworth, was married to Susan Maria Tucker, a devout Methodist. The couple had one child and maintained a separate household close to his parents' property, and Horace not only followed his father's trade of shoemaker but showed even less capacity to earn a living than his father did.

It seems clear that whereas there was a general consensus of ideas among the Wentworths and Mrs. Glover, it was mainly on Mrs. Wentworth's initiative that Mrs. Glover was invited to come to Stoughton to live. Perhaps influenced by Hiram Crafts's early success in the healing trade, Mrs. Wentworth determined that she could learn from Mrs. Glover and thereby enhance her earnings as a nurse. She also seems to have been impressed by her visitor's own powers of healing and to have sought Mrs. Glover's help with her husband and daughter. The offer of free board and lodging for an unlimited period in exchange for instruction in spiritual healing seems generous, given the Wentworth family's limited resources, and it probably raised some dispute among family members from the beginning. If Peel is to be believed, Horace Wentworth did not mind living off his parents' earnings—as well as those of his wife—but he was all the more sensitive to anyone else's attempts to do the same, so he resented Mrs. Glover's coming from the first.

Dissension or no dissension, Mrs. Glover lived with the Wentworths for eighteen months, a lengthy stay for a nonpaying guest in a humble household. The available documentary evidence indicates that the contract between Mrs. Wentworth and Mrs. Glover worked in the interests of both.[38] Mrs. Glover gained a pleasant room to work in, good nourishing food, the use of a horse when she needed it, as well as full board. Mrs. Wentworth's income from healing rose to some fifty dollars per week, Celia's lung condition seemed to respond well to Mrs. Glover's treatments, and Alanson declared himself cured by her not only of his sciatica but of his old pleasure in drink and chewing tobacco.[39]

All the Wentworth testimony indicates that while she stayed with the family Mrs. Glover spent much of her time in her bedchamber writing, and that she had amassed a large pile of copy by the end of her stay, for which she was seeking a publisher. Catherine Isobel Clapp, the Wentworths' cousin, testified that she was paid $7 by Mrs. Glover to copy her manuscript. Horace Wentworth claimed that Mrs. Glover was quoted the sum of $600 to publish her work, and that the immediate cause of the rift that developed between their guest and his parents was Mrs. Glover's request that the family take out a mortgage on their property and lend her this sum.[40] What exactly the manuscript was that she was carrying about is less certain. Robert Peel, the most informed expert on Mrs. Eddy's written work and on her manuscripts, says the manuscript is not extant, and he gives as his opinion that it was a version of "The Science of Man," Mrs. Eddy's first copyrighted text, supplemented with some of the Biblical exegesis from her Genesis manuscript. "The Science of Man" was the precursor of the current chapter of *Science and Health* entitled "Recapitulation."

Mrs. Glover herself referred to the work in at least two letters of the period. To Mrs. Mulliken, a friend in Rumney, she wrote:

> I have just sent a work to the press for publication entitled—Science of Soul—I mean you shall read it sometime. I have written this and notes

on the entire book of Genesis within the last year and this, besides laboring for clothes and other expenses with teaching. I am worn almost out, I have lost my love of life completely and want to go where the weary have a rest and the heavy laden lay down their burdens.[41]

On June 10, 1869, Mrs. Glover wrote to Sarah Bagley: "My volume is finished, Sarah, and ready for the press and the outcry that will follow it; first the ridicule, then the argument, then the adoption by the public, but it may be long ere the public get it."[42] For all her weary pessimism, Mrs. Glover was unduly optimistic about her manuscript and its chances for publication. In fact, it would take her another five years of thought, painful drafting, and practical obstacles of all kinds before her life work, the book now known to us as *Science and Health,* would appear in print.

Mrs. Glover was apparently much pressed to undertake healings, and she is credited with one notable success around this time. Mr. John Scott was suffering from an acute and agonizing intestinal complaint; he called in Sally Wentworth, she declared the case beyond her powers and summoned Mrs. Glover, who promptly had the man out of bed, eating comfortably, and also swearing to be a better husband and father.[43]

Although she was herself frequently unwell during this period and suffering from depression and anguish, although she had no money and her marital situation still left her in a kind of social limbo, Mrs. Glover nonetheless showed more zest for living and capacity for fun than she had in North Groton ten years earlier. Young men and women in the neighborhood sought her company for talking and taking walks, for reading stories in *Saturday Night* and *Chimney Corner*—two magazines to which she subscribed, partly for the young people's sake—for playing backgammon, which she taught the Wentworth children, as well as euchre, a card game at which she excelled. William Scott later testified that he knew Mrs. Glover when he was sixteen and remembered her well as a wonderful woman whom he liked to visit two or three times a week. Lucy Wentworth recalled: "after she had worked for hours she always relaxed and threw off her seriousness. Then she would admit us, my brother Charles and me, and sometimes a school friend of Charles's. The boys would romp in her room sometimes rather boisterously, but she never seemed to mind it." Charles said that "her sojourn with us was one of the brightest spots in my life," and Lucy owned that she adored Mrs. Glover, followed her around like Mary's proverbial lamb, and felt very resentful when her older friend insisted she must work and shut the door of her room to visitors.[44]

Later in life Lucy gave this description of how Mrs. Glover looked and dressed at the end of her fifth decade:

She was a lonely woman past her prime who at the time had seen much of life. In appearance she was very straight of figure, a little above the average in height, with shoulders rather broad for her small waist, small hands and feet, dark brown hair and gray eyes with a faraway look in them, that were very expressive, and under excitement seemed darker than they really were. . . .

Her wardrobe at this time consisted of a black and white plaid, also a few morning dresses. Her one best black dress was of a very fine material, made after the fashion of that day and trimmed with narrow silk velvet ribbon. She kept her clothes very carefully. It made no difference what she wore, there always seemed to be a certain style about her.[45]

The most dramatic part of Horace Wentworth's affidavit as reproduced in the Milmine biography was his account of how Mrs. Glover at last became a tyrant in his parents' home, thumping over the head of his sick father to stop him from sleeping and so terrorizing his mother that she locked her bedroom door against her. According to Horace, finally, Mrs. Glover was told she must leave, and she went off while her hosts were absent, leaving her chamber door locked. When they broke into the room, the Wentworths found that the carpeting and bedding had been systematically shredded, and there was a pile of coals and newspaper in the closet, suggesting in Horace's mind Mrs. Glover's intention to set the empty house on fire. Clearly she was a dangerous, deranged woman!

In the affidavit he signed for Alfred Farlow, manager of the Committee on Publication, on March 27, 1909, Charles Wentworth absolutely denied that this event ever occurred. His testimony carries more weight than his brother's since, unlike Horace, he was living in his parents' house at the time that Mrs. Glover took her leave, and the destruction of property and threat of arson Horace described could not have occurred without his knowledge. Charles said that Mrs. Glover and his parents remained on good terms after she left, and he noted that he himself was personally responsible for maintaining the stoves in the household. He suggested that the story about the paper and coals in the closet was probably based on one occasion when the stove in Mrs. Glover's room got blocked with ashes and she correctly raked it out and placed the ashes on sheets of newspaper until he could remove them.[46]

After reading all the accounts, my conclusion is that the Wentworths had no dramatic separation from Mrs. Glover but were glad nonetheless when she decided to leave, since her presence was causing tension within the family. Lucy testified that her father was increasingly jealous of the attention and time his wife and daughters lavished on their guest. Furthermore, Mrs. Glover had suggested that Mrs. Wentworth go into full-time partnership with her and put up the money to pay for the publication of Mrs. Glover's manuscript, and the sum required was more than the hosts were prepared to give. When Mrs. Glover herself decided that it was in her best interests to move on, they were happy to drive her to the station, shake her hand, and wish her well. Richard Kennedy, who knew all the parties well, seems to me to give the best summary of Mrs. Glover's stay at the Wentworths' in Stoughton:

> The Wentworths were well enough in their way, as were the Crafts with whom Mrs. Eddy lived at an earlier period, and the Websters of Amesbury. It was an unfortunate fact that Mrs. Eddy with her small income was obliged to live with people very often at this time in her life who were without education and cultivation. It was never her custom to keep apart from the family. She invariably mingled with them and through them kept in touch with the world. She had a great work to do; she was possessed by her purpose and like Paul the apostle, and many another great teacher and leader, she reiterated to herself, "This one thing I do." Of course simple-minded people who take life as it comes from day to day find any one with so fixed an object in life a rebuke to the flow of their own animal spirits. Mrs. Wentworth was what old-fashioned New Englanders call "clever," that is to say, kind-hearted. She looked well after the creature comforts of those under her roof. Lucy was a spirituelle young girl, Charles was a sensible, lively boy, but Horace was something of a scoffer, without any leaning toward religious enquiry.[47]

Given the dramatically strained relations that were subsequently to develop between Mrs. Glover and Kennedy himself, the affection, understanding, and reverence which Kennedy shows here toward Mrs. Glover are interesting.

11

Rebellious Students

A FTER SAYING FAREWELL TO THE WENTWORTHS, MRS. Glover headed for Amesbury and the home of Miss Sarah Bagley, who was sufficiently mollified by her friend's new overtures to welcome her. Nonetheless, Sarah was probably aware that Mary was seeking to return to Amesbury above all to be closer to Miss Bagley's young friend, distant relative, and at that time her boarder, Richard Kennedy. He, too, had shown immense interest in Mrs. Glover's ideas and a willingness to try to put them into practice, and he had maintained contact with Mrs. Glover during the eighteen months she spent in Stoughton. The closer Mary grew to Richard, the more Sarah became anxious and jealous, fearing to lose both of these exciting friends, as they found each other.

The most important thing Mrs. Glover achieved in the first months of 1870 was to form a partnership with Richard Kennedy and concert with him how they might best set up in practice. From the world's point of view, establishing a partnership with Kennedy was a compromising act for a woman who had already earned a reputation for eccentricity or worse. Given that Mrs. Glover was separated from her husband and had no obvious means of support, any sort of arrangement she made with Kennedy could only harm her already anomalous position in society. Richard was twenty-one and Mary was forty-eight, but the disparity in age would not prevent the tongues wagging.[1] Interestingly, it is Sibyl Wilbur, the most canonical and protective of all the biographers, who shows the greatest awareness of how much Mrs. Glover risked in undertaking a partnership with Kennedy. She goes out of her way to stress that Kennedy was the initiator of the idea of moving to Lynn to set up the practice, and that his relationship with Mrs. Glover was one of mother and son. Wilbur gives the interesting suggestion that their choice of working-class Lynn—with its thirty thousand inhabitants a significantly larger and more prosperous place than Amesbury or Stoughton, but far less socially desirable—was itself prone to misunderstanding since the town had a reputation for immorality. Wilbur writes:

> Mrs. Glover was not so ready to enter into this agreement with her young student. He had an unblemished reputation, had honorably conducted himself toward her with the chivalrous devotion of a son to a mother; but he was untried in the ways of life, there had been no test put upon him such as she well knew lay before him if he took up the work with her. She knew the city of Lynn, its somewhat harsh industrialism, its free intermingling of the sexes in the factory life, and the nearby temptations of Boston—all very different from the village life of Amesbury.[2]

Mrs. Glover was far from careless of her reputation or unmindful of the power of gossip over a woman's life, but she nonetheless seized on the possibilities of partnership with Kennedy as the necessary next step in her life plan. Though she was still very far indeed from a complete understanding of the new movement she was beginning to envisage and her own role in it, one practical imperative had shaped her life ever since her fall in Lynn in February 1866. Whereas her new Science would center on the practice and experience of healing, she would not be primarily a healer but rather a teacher of healing and an instructor to healers, both in person and through writing. Quimby had had a successful healing practice, he had improved the quality of life for many individual patients, but he had worn himself out in his practice, and his power of healing had, it seemed in 1870, been passed on to only one student—Mary Baker Glover. Certainly she herself would heal when the need arose, but these healing acts would be important not so much for the immediate relief of the patients but as "demonstrations," as examples and motivators for her students.[3] The greater part of her own time and energy would be given to teaching and, more important yet, to writing, to communicating with those beyond her physical reach. Before the world would listen to her teaching and read her books, however, she needed to show that the ability to heal was not a personal power inherent in her, but a science that could be taught to and practiced by others. Thus she needed to find someone who was willing to call himself her student, someone who could establish a successful healing practice on the basis of her theory, while she herself concentrated her energies on proselytizing.

As she moved around from one family and one community to another between 1866 and 1869, she was always on the lookout for this student-collaborator, and her relationships with Hiram Crafts, Sarah Bagley, and Sally Wentworth, and no doubt with others we know less about, flourished and then faded as it became apparent that none was willing or able to take on Mrs. Glover as mentor and set up a partnership in healing with her. Crafts, though deeply under Mrs. Glover's spell and convinced of what she had to say, proved too weak to withstand the pressures of his wife and family and soon abandoned his practice as a healer. Sarah Bagley and Sally Wentworth, as women who needed to earn money in a marketplace fundamentally hostile to women's work, were receptive to the practical aspects of the healing science their friend expounded. Women like these two were ultimately to form the backbone of the Christian Science movement, but these two did not take the step their friend required of them. Sally was willing to call Mrs. Glover a saint, but she was too deeply embedded in her family and community to make any radical moves; besides, she had little understanding of the metaphysical levels on which Mrs. Glover was working. The educated and middle-class Sarah Bagley was more receptive to religion and metaphysics but also less willing to accept as a mentor and prophet a woman whom she had taken in, literally, off the streets, and whose errors and imperfections she knew too well.

Richard Kennedy was a more radical, yet more promising choice as a partner. He was indeed very young, but he was an intensely alive, interesting, sympathetic young man. I also get the feeling, from the very rare letters and statements we have from him, that Richard Kennedy had an excellent mind as well as a swift tongue, and that of all the people Mary Baker Eddy was close to in her Lynn and Boston years and who were receptive to Christian Science, Kennedy was by far the most intellectually able. He was also unmarried and orphaned, his own master, ready to take risks, and eager to make himself a name and a fortune. Two brief letters from Kennedy to Mrs. Glover of September 12, 1869, and March 1870, now in the archives of The Mother Church, are models of interest, deference, and affection. Mrs. Glover, like everyone else, was delighted by young Mr. Kennedy. She wrote to Miss Bagley: "Was ever there a more glorious nature, a more noble soul than Richard Kennedy possesses?"[4] Mrs. Glover's enthusiasm for Kennedy's beautiful nature did not, however, prevent her from making sure that the partnership agreement between them was put in writing. In February 1870 Kennedy signed the following contract with her: "In consideration of two years instruction in healing the sick I hereby agree to pay Mary M. B. Glover one thousand dollars in quarterly installments of fifty dollars commencing from this date."

To judge from two extant letters which Richard Kennedy wrote to Sarah Bagley from Lynn in early 1870, he had so far accepted the truth of Mrs. Glover's Science as to sound like her echo. Kennedy's style is so close to Mrs. Glover's in her metaphysical and Biblical mode that his letter reads uncannily like one from her. Even after his schism from Mrs. Glover in 1871 Kennedy continued at least for a few years to express views that were indistinguishable from hers. Thus, after telling Miss Bagley that he regretted they had so few opportunities to talk but felt it was better spiritually for them to remain apart—"I think we struggle more for not being together"—Kennedy noted: "At the end when the Principle is gained the mingling will be soul with soul and that basis will be correct." The capitalization, the vocabulary, is all Mrs. Mary Glover.[5] In another letter he also claims that very indifference to social pleasures which Mrs. Glover espoused in the teaching document she had been working on while with the Wentworths: "I do not go to the sea often you know I am not as fond of going about as the general class of people." This rings oddly from a very young man, generally considered handsome and charming, and already, based on the later accounts of contemporaries, being welcomed enthusiastically into the bosom of Lynn society.

The second letter to Sarah Bagley also makes quite plain that Kennedy had bought into the idea of absent treatment—an idea which, as we saw in Chapter 7, was devoutly espoused by Quimby, and which goes back to the early days of mesmerism. Kennedy wrote:

> It should not be necessary that we should be present in matter to be known and felt. I will try and call on you tonight at 9 o'clock tell me if you realize my presence when you write it is not necessary you should see me with your eyes.

This is an important point to note given the future charges of mesmerism that were to be bandied about by both Eddy and Kennedy supporters after the two partners had split up.

In May, Kennedy and Mrs. Glover moved back to Lynn, staying at first with Mrs. Glover's friends the Clarkson Olivers, while Kennedy scouted the town for a suitable place to rent. They sought rooms for consulting and teaching as well as separate living quarters, and they obviously wanted a respectable and pleasant address to encourage clients. Finally Kennedy was able to find rooms in an agreeable house set amidst lawns and trees on the corner of South Common Street and Shepard Street, within easy walking distance of the main thoroughfare.

The landlady was Miss Susie Magoun, soon to be Mrs. John M. Dame, and she used the first floor for her girls' school. She would later tell the *McClure's* group that when the very youthful Kennedy came around, she had been surprised to discover that he himself, not his father, was the doctor seeking apartments for his practice, and that he was also acting on behalf of an older lady who was writing a book. Miss Magoun hesitated a little before renting. Respectability was a key to the success of Magoun's school, and she feared the healing practice envisaged might involve disreputable Spiritualist seances. Kennedy had already been turned down by other landlords. His charm carried the day with Miss Magoun, however, and he and his mysterious older friend moved into rooms on the second floor. The third floor was occupied by Miss Magoun herself at first, and then, after her marriage, by the family of her sister-in-law Mrs. Carrie Colby. Fairly early in the course of the lease, Miss Magoun hired someone to prepare communal meals for herself and her tenants.[6]

Against all odds, the people of Lynn rapidly took the self-styled Dr. Kennedy to their hearts, and within weeks of arriving in the town and setting up the poor array of furniture and possessions he and Mrs. Glover commanded between them, young Kennedy was attracting lines of patients, achieving a solid percentage of cures, and making a comfortable living for himself and his partner. In July 1870 Mrs. Glover wrote to "Dear Student 'Sa'" (Sarah Bagley) to assure her that their rooms on South Common were not just agreeable but practical since the horse cars to Boston passed in front of the door. A week later she wrote again to let Miss Bagley know that as soon as it was known in Lynn that she had brought a student there, people had lined up for treatment, and that people were so grateful to be cured that they had made her a present of an expensive straw hat and sash, as well as some delicious cherries. She was also enjoying having company over to listen to a brass band concert on the common right outside her front door.[7]

As further evidence of her happiness and peacefulness during these months, Mrs. Glover wrote in a July letter to Mrs. Mary Ellis of Swampscott, "Never did the life that seems appear so small to me as this year, and never the life that is so vast, so glorious."[8] The sentence is important, not just as evidence of Mrs. Glover's frame of mind, but as a perfect little example of the metaphysical style she had been laboring over for so long, with its extreme concision, deceptively simple vocabulary, and neatly balanced syntax.

Miss Magoun adored her energetic and amusing male tenant. Kennedy was never behind with the rent and was ready to come down from his practice room and help out in the school, to play games with the children, and to help them on with their wraps and overshoes when it was cold. In return Miss Magoun allowed Kennedy to use her first floor parlor at times to seat the overflow of his patients, and she introduced him to her friends. Kennedy was soon a popular part of Lynn social life, and the townsfolk remembered him with affection when the reporters and investigators came around in the early 1900s asking about the years Mrs. Eddy had spent in Lynn.

The Kennedy-Glover healing duo did have one sad and perhaps chastening experience. They were asked to undertake the care of two Lynn residents, Jacob A. Allen and Ann E. Swan, who had been horribly burned in a disastrous rail crash on August 26, 1871. After a few days of agony, both died, and at the subsequent inquest into their deaths Richard Kennedy was called to testify. He reported that in association with Dr. Lodge he had washed and dressed Allen's wounds with oil, and given him laudanum, which "did not abate his suffering." It seems from the testimony given at the inquest that at that point the established medical attendants immediately despaired of the lives of the unfortunate Allen and Swan and walked away, whereas Mrs. Glover and Dr. Kennedy stayed at their bedside and did everything they could to alleviate their suffering. Mrs. Glover and Kennedy may have become involved with the accident victims because of their friendship with the Samuel Bancroft family, since the list of those killed includes two Bancrofts, one directly linked with the shoe firm of Bancroft and Purinton for which Samuel worked.[9]

Mrs. Glover, in contrast with Kennedy, had little to do with Miss Magoun and her young charges. She lived quietly, concentrating her efforts on her new group of students and on her writing. It is easy to imagine what a pleasure and relief it was for her simply to be settled at last, to have a room of her own and few domestic cares, to be at peace with the landlord, and to spend time alone or in company as she pleased. Kennedy reportedly was giving her not just the $50 per quarter stipulated in their contract but half of the proceeds of the growing practice. Mrs. Glover was thus relieved at last of the financial anxieties that had preyed on her, and she was able to give all her energies to her work. She put money away in the bank,[10] gained some weight, which became her, and was able to replenish her wardrobe—always tasteful, but threadbare when she arrived in Lynn. Milmine says that Mrs. Glover lost many of her "affectations and ingratiating mannerisms" and became "in every way a more commanding and formidable person."[11] Such a comment is valuable since Milmine and her team interviewed many people in Lynn and were never partial or sympathetic observers of Mrs. Glover.

The high point in the Glover-Kennedy partnership may well have come in December 1870, as Mrs. Glover herself recorded in a letter written to Sarah Bagley on Christmas Day. The day before, Richard and one of her students, Mr. Oliver, had arrived at her door out of the blue and presented her with a framed landscape of a New Hampshire scene, a silver pitcher—a gift from the whole class—and a silver casket containing an amethyst ring, the gift of someone whom, interestingly, she does not name.[12]

Mrs. Glover desperately needed this respite of cherries, straw hats, amethyst rings, and framed New Hampshire landscapes after the Stoughton/Wentworth period when she had drained all her mental and physical energies in order to write "The Science of Man." Unfortunately it was short-lived, since Mrs. Glover's early efforts as a teacher were very far from being as easy and successful as Kennedy's as a healer. In a letter to Sarah Bagley of April 10, 1871, Mrs. Glover rather reluctantly agreed to allow Sarah to come and join her class. She was obviously worried about what Sarah might hear—or say!—and warns her, with heavy underlining, that the students were not permitted to indulge

in backbiting, or malicious gossip, about each other or about their instructor.[13] Mischief, gossip, scandal, and injury were, as it turned out, to characterize the relations of these early students.

One source of dissent from the beginning centered on the fees Mrs.
Glover charged for her courses. For her very first class she seems to have
asked $100, though it is far from clear that any student paid the full amount.
For example, in his later court testimony, Charles Stanley said that he had
parted, reluctantly, with $25 or $50. By 1871 or 1872 the fee had risen to
$300, though again, each student's personal situation was taken into account,
and fees were lowered or waived for those who were unable to pay in full. It
is interesting to note, for example, that Dorcas Rawson, a single woman
working in the shoe industry, paid in full, whereas her affluent married sister Miranda Rice entered the class for free, because she was unable to persuade her husband to put up the money.

For the shoe operatives and housekeepers who formed the majority of
Mrs. Glover's target group, $300 was an astonishingly large sum. Robert Peel
estimates that $300 was about one third the average annual income for a shoe
worker. Later in *Retrospection and Introspection* Mrs. Eddy acknowledged
this fact:

> When God impelled me to set a price on my instruction in Christian
> Science Mind-healing, I could think of no financial equivalent for an
> impartation of a knowledge of that divine power which heals, but I was
> led to name three hundred dollars as the price for each pupil in one
> course of lessons at my College,—a startling sum for tuition lasting
> barely three weeks. This amount greatly troubled me. I shrank from ask-
> ing it, but was finally led, by a strange providence, to accept this fee.
> (*Ret.*, p. 50)

It is unclear to me whether it was Providence or some daringly accurate
estimate of what the market would bear that determined Mrs. Glover's fee
structure, but in the long run it was to serve her well. Freud famously asserted
that people value only the services they pay for, and the history of Christian
Science proves that, ultimately, all those who paid to take class with Mrs.
Glover got at the very least their money's worth, even if they soon rebelled
against their teacher and struck out on their own as mental healers. But in
the early days of Christian Science the high fees, as well as the contracts she
had her students sign, were bones of contention. Wallace W. Wright, as we
shall see later in the book, took his case to the newspapers when Mrs. Glover
refused his demands for a tuition refund plus compensation. She herself
threatened to pursue Sarah Bagley for copying her teaching manuscripts, and
later she unsuccessfully sued two students, Charles Stanley and George
Tuttle, for breaking their written contract and failing to pay her any percentage of their earnings as healers, as agreed.

Mary Baker Eddy's attitude toward money, and the financial aspects of the growth of Christian Science as a religious sect, have always been extremely controversial subjects. Her high fees, strict accounting practices, and general thriftiness, her prudent care for the bottom line, are matters of record that have elicited a variety of interpretive responses. Beginning with Mark Twain and Frederick Peabody, unsympathetic critics have built a detailed factual base for a portrait of Mrs. Eddy as a mercenary adventuress, interested above all in money and concealing her base urges under a cloak of religious metaphysics. Sympathetic critics, such as Sibyl Wilbur and Jewel Spangler Smaus, have downplayed Mrs. Eddy's financial dealings. They explain anxiously that she was motivated by the general work ethic of Protestantism, by Yankee traditions of thrift, by the Baker family tradition of never owing a cent, and by her personal experience of dependence and poverty as a widow and divorcée.

Lyman Powell, himself a rather unsuccessful former parish priest who was ineffective as a fund-raiser, takes a stronger line when he attributes Mrs. Eddy's success as a religious leader in large measure to the fact that she had the necessary practical skills, legal insight, and financial acumen. In his authorized 1930 biography, Powell praises her for understanding that religion has to forge some relation with money, and that a modern religious movement must use something more than the begging bowl if it is to get out its message, increase its membership, and achieve social acceptance. The issue of Mrs. Eddy and finance would continue to gain in prominence as her movement grew. But it was not the only or the most important reason for the dissent that racked the embryonic movement.

Among Mary Glover's first students in Lynn in her 1870 class were Charles S. Stanley and Mrs. Stanley's half-brother, George Tuttle. Charles was a hardheaded shoe factory worker and ardent Baptist; his brother-in-law was a bluff young seaman who had just returned from a journey to India.[14] Told that she was in the last stages of consumption, Mrs. Stanley had consulted Kennedy and received great benefits from his treatment. On Kennedy's recommendation she persuaded her husband and brother to sign up with Mrs. Glover for a twelve-week course of instruction. Stanley and Tuttle signed the following agreement:

Lynn, Aug. 15, 1870. We, the undersigned, do hereby agree in consideration of instruction and manuscripts received from Mrs. Mary Baker Glover, to pay one hundred dollars in advance and ten per cent annually on the income that we receive from practising or teaching the science. We also agree to pay her one thousand dollars in case we do not practise or teach the above-mentioned science that she has taught us.

Stanley and Tuttle proved to be disastrous students. Tuttle signed up only because his sister had asked him to, and he was more horrified than pleased

when he treated a case of dropsy with apparent success. Stanley, an orthodox Baptist, argued constantly with Mrs. Glover about her religious ideas,
so disrupting the class that she eventually asked him to withdraw.[15]

Other early students of Mrs. Glover in Lynn seemed at the outset to be
at least more tractable than were Tuttle and Stanley. Among the students in
these early classes, at different times and for different periods, were Mrs.
Mary Adeline (Addie) Spofford; her old school friend Samuel Putney
Bancroft, who was Addie's husband Daniel's foreman at the shoe factory of
Bancroft and Purinton; George W. Barry, a shoe factory foreman; Miss
Dorcas Rawson, a shoe factory worker; Miss Frances Spinney, "who had a
small specialty workshop for women's shoes"; George H. Allen, a worker in
his family's box factory; Mrs. Miranda Rice, sister of Dorcas Rawson; and
Wallace W. Wright. Of this group, only one, Bancroft, would remain a good
friend and a faithful believer of Mrs. Eddy's teaching in later years;[16] and
otherwise this particular early crop of students was to be the source of end-
less trouble to Mrs. Eddy. Over the next forty years, increasingly sensational
charges relating to money, sexual relationships, and drug addiction in the little Lynn community would be made, and all the parties concerned agreed
that this potent mix had some relation to mesmerism.[17]

Wallace W. Wright was the first of Mrs. Glover's students to publicly
criticize her and her teachings; many others would follow.[18] Wright came
from a prominent Lynn family; he was probably the most educated, articulate, and confident of Mrs. Glover's first students.[19] Both he and his father,
a Universalist clergyman, were interested in mental healing, and before joining her class in April 1871, Wright sent Mrs. Glover a letter with nine questions to which he requested written answers. It is in one of her responses to
Wright's question that Mrs. Glover gave the early account of her fall in
Lynn and subsequent self-healing which I quoted in Chapter 9. In another
question-and-answer sequence, Mrs. Glover gave Wright her evaluation of
P. P. Quimby and told of her debt to him.

> [Question by Wright]: Has this theory been advertised or practiced
> before you introduced it, or by any other individual?
>
> [Reply by Mrs. Glover]: Never <u>advertised</u> and practiced only by one
> individual who healed me, Dr. Quimby of Portland, Me., an old gen-
> tleman who made it a research for twenty-five years, starting from the
> stand-point of magnetism thence going forward and leaving that
> behind. I discovered the art in a <u>moment's time</u>, and he acknowledged
> it to me; he died shortly after and since then, eight years, I have been
> founding and demonstrating the science.[20]

This statement is important because of the spontaneous, benign tone
Mrs. Glover adopted: this was one of the last times she would discuss
Quimby outside the context of ongoing and bitter public debate. At the same

time Wright's question is an interesting indication that even in 1871 Mrs. Glover's debt to Quimby had begun to be an issue among her students, particularly her male students, and that his name was serving to crystallize debate and dissent.[21] Wright was more than satisfied with the answers given him, and with the quality of the instruction that Mrs. Glover then gave him, since he began to work as a healer.

Critics of the leader of Christian Science and her denomination have made something of a hero of Wright, celebrating him as the first man to take a principled stand on the sect and to warn the public of its dangers. However, archival documents at The Mother Church as well as the veiled story which Mrs. Eddy later told in the "Demonology" chapter at the beginning of the third edition of *Science and Health* (1881) complicate the conventional account of the Wright affair. I have come to the conclusion that Wallace W. Wright was not quite the apostle of reason and enlightenment heralded by the Milmine tradition of Eddyan biography, and that it is very likely that a much more murky drama unfolded behind the Wright letters, in which Kennedy was the chief villain.[22]

According to Wright's own published account, after doing some successful healing in Lynn, he was so enthusiastic about Mrs. Glover's Science that he decided to go down to Knoxville, Tennessee, in June 1871, to assist another of her students who was already established there. But after several months he ran into insuperable difficulties in the practice and then returned to Lynn in October to denounce to the public the ideas and techniques which Mrs. Glover had taught him. Mrs. Eddy was to tell a rather different story in "Demonology." The vital passage is both elliptical and very overwrought, but it indicates, without naming names, that the partner whom Wright went to join in Knoxville was his former classmate Mrs. Addie Spofford; that at the time marital relations between Addie and her husband Daniel were at best strained; and that Addie was having or had had an adulterous affair with Richard Kennedy. The relationship between Richard and Addie persisted in some form until at least 1875, when Daniel Spofford moved back North to Lynn to take class with Mrs. Glover. The Spoffords were later divorced. In essence Mrs. Eddy was claiming that Wright's stay in Knoxville had been motivated more by personal reasons than by a desire to heal Southerners, that he then found himself embroiled in a messy liaison-à-trois, as well as a healing practice of an unedifying nature. He then returned to the East and tried to browbeat his teacher—Mrs. Glover—into reimbursing him not only his tuition fees but also his expenses. When this effort failed, Wright determined to have revenge by denouncing Mrs. Glover to the press.[23]

Mrs. Eddy's later allegations about Wright, Kennedy, and Addie Spofford have generally been ignored or decried, but they make sense of some rather odd events, and there is external evidence to support them.

There is no doubt that Wright did go down to Knoxville to work with Mrs. Spofford, and the fact that Wright in his letter to the Lynn *Transcript* never mentioned the name of the student he went to work with indicates that either he or Addie did not want her name mentioned. I find it significant that the *McClure's* biography carefully omitted all mention of Addie Spofford, although Milmine certainly knew about her, and that Addie's name never appears in any of the subsequent accounts of the Wright affair until the Peel biography.

The public criticism of Mrs. Glover by her students was set off by Wallace Wright's letter to the editor of the Lynn *Transcript* on January 13, 1872, in which he claimed that his personal experience as a healer had led him to conclude that Mrs. Glover's moral science was merely mesmerism in disguise. He said that he was writing to the newspapers in order to put all potential students on their guard against her. He strongly implied that he had been mesmerized by her during the classes he had taken:

> Soon after settling in Knoxville I began to question the propriety of call-
> ing this treatment "Moral Science" instead of mesmerism. Away from
> the influence of argument which the teacher of this so-called science
> knows how to bring to bear upon students with such force as to out-
> weigh any attempts they make at the time to oppose it, I commenced to
> think more independently, and to argue with myself as to the truth of
> the positions we were called upon to take.

Mrs. Eddy, for her part, believed that in Knoxville, Addie had begun to go into trance, and Daniel Spofford, in a letter to Mrs. Eddy, asserted that Wright had failed with patients in Knoxville because he had used mes-merism.[24]

On January 20 Mrs. Glover fired back a letter to the *Transcript,* saying that Wright's letter was motivated by revenge because she had refused to accede to his financial demands. She went on to raise the issue of Wright's personal morality: "Also in his letter to me [she is referring to a July 9 letter Wright wrote to her from Knoxville] he never referred to mesmerism, but said (here I quote *verbatim*): 'While I do not question the right of it, it teaches a deprivation of social enjoyment if we would attain the *highest* round in the ladder of Science.'" It is undoubtedly true that in her teaching manuscripts of 1870—and indeed with increasing urgency throughout her career—Mary Baker Eddy made it abundantly clear that the key to spiritual healing is the healer's high spiritual and moral character. Smoking and drinking are specif-ically named as being incompatible with Christian Science, and sexual immorality is reproved in covert terms. For a young man of some means like Wright, such strictures would very probably have seemed harsh.

On January 27 Wright admitted to *Transcript* readers that Mrs. Glover's quotation from his letter was accurate, but he insisted that he had far from frivolous ideas (and certainly not Addie Spofford!) in mind when he referred to "social enjoyment." "To live as this so-called science teaches," he wrote to the *Transcript,* "would sever the affection between parents, and children, brothers and sisters, and forbid all mingling with society and friends." He then went on to quote another section of his August 24 Knoxville letter—of which he had providently kept a copy—which served to raise the issue of Mrs. Glover's mercenary instincts for the first time in public: "It would please me much to see this science in the hands of some one better fitted to represent and develop it, and if *perfection* is in it, to bring this out to the public, aside from selfish motives of gain." Thus, responding to Mrs. Glover's implication that he is a hedonist, Wright replied by accusing Mrs. Glover of caring too much about making money—another thing sternly reproved in her teachings.[25]

Mr. Wright's defense was clever, but he was also shifting his rhetorical ground here: is the doctrine taught by Mrs. Glover metaphysically worthless, a mere mask for mesmerism as he first claimed, or is it a search for a perfection, traduced by the mercenary personality of its proponent? Sensing the split in Wright's attack upon her, Mrs. Glover herself then made a profound and fascinating change of tack. In her next and final missive of February 3, instead of more quotes from letters and arguments about contract details and financial settlements, she wrote an admirably calm, concise, coherent, and nonpolemical statement of her essential beliefs: that God's creation "symbolizes nothing else but wisdom, love and truth," that he "made man in His 'image and likeness,'" good and perfect, that "Jesus demonstrated . . . moral control over matter and man, but this was not mesmerism," and "fearing to think we should follow this example of Jesus is an error of our education, for which theology and physiology are greatly responsible."

It is, of course, more than possible to counter the positions Mrs. Glover made in this short article, but to do so means moving onto metaphysical grounds, precisely where Wallace Wright, for all his statements about the perfection of Science, was unwilling and unprepared to maneuver. Here Mrs. Glover demonstrated to the no doubt surprised or merely inattentive readers of the Lynn *Transcript* that she was not, or was not simply, the scheming, ambitious money-grubber Wright had portrayed. Here she found for the first time a public, textual expression of the oral teaching that attracted students to her, that inspired them with a sense of high purpose and practical capacity, and that would finally lead to the foundation of a new religious sect.

If Mrs. Glover's letter of February 3, 1872, is heralded by apologists like Robert Peel as the first major public statement of her metaphysical and religious beliefs, Wallace W. Wright's reply of February 10 is seen as a landmark in the movement to expose the fundamental inanities, weaknesses, and dangers of Christian Science. Wright's brilliant polemic has a four-pronged attack: (1) He returns to his initial accusation that Mrs. Glover was teaching mesmerism under a fancy new name, and he asserts that although mesmerism had had its successes as a healing technique in certain types of cases (a probable bow in the direction of P. P. Quimby and his at times ally Richard Kennedy), its use must be acknowledged to the patient up front, since the subject submits to the control of the mesmerist.[26] (2) Wright points to certain medical conditions—bullet wounds, cancerous growths, ulcerating lungs, physical deformities, poisonings—which common sense tells us cannot respond to "rubbing," and which might have yielded to "recognized and tested therapies." "Someone might die under Christian Science care who might have lived under traditional medicine," writes Wright, expressing a criticism that would be repeated, with variations, in all critiques of Christian Science and other forms of mental healing. (3) If Mrs. Glover's manuscripts were, as she claimed, the product of revelation, why did they take so long to draft, and why did they change over time?

> The MS. from which Mrs. Glover taught this science two years ago differs from the present one almost as much as black does from white. So it seems she has been obliged to correct the dictates of inspiration, and remodel its work. She also stated, during the class to which I belonged, that she studied for hours on the fitness of a certain word to convey her meaning. Is inspiration as slow as that in its work?

(4) Mrs. Glover herself really cared not for religion and metaphysics but for money. Wright quotes her as having said to him, *"The world SHALL NOT have it* [her teaching manuscript] *unless they pay me for it."*

Wright's letter ended with a challenge which was to become famous in the annals of Christian Science:

> And now, in conclusion, I publicly challenge Mrs. Mary M. Baker Glover to demonstrate her science by any of the following methods, promising if she is successful, to retract *all* I have said, and humble myself by asking forgiveness publicly for the course I have taken. Her refusal to do this, by silence or otherwise, shall be considered a failure of her cause:—
>
> First. To restore the dead to life again, as she claims she can.
>
> Second. To walk upon the water, without the aid of artificial means, as she claims she can.
>
> Third. To live twenty-four hours without air, or twenty-four days without nourishment of any kind, without its having any effect upon her.
>
> Fourth. To restore sight when the optic nerve has been destroyed.
>
> Fifth. To set and heal a broken bone without the aid of artificial means.

Mrs. Glover made no public response to Wright's final challenge, but, rather surprisingly, to judge by her comments to Sarah Bagley, she was not depressed or disheartened by the exchange.[27] It seems probable that Mrs. Glover took the Wright problem so relatively lightly because she became pre-occupied with the far greater threat posed by Richard Kennedy. In fact, as she describes in considerable detail later in "Demonology," she gradually became convinced that Kennedy was the mastermind behind Wright's at-tacks, and that the two men plotted against her in concert.

She says that after the debacle of his partnership with Addie Spofford, Wright wrote to her demanding that she not only refund his $300 tuition but reinburse him $200 for expenses. When she refused to do this, Wright returned to Lynn, came to her house to renew his demands, and then threat-ened her with revenge. Rebuffed, Wright then made common cause with Kennedy, who he knew was planning to break with Mrs. Glover, and the two of them concocted the newspaper series in an attempt to discredit her. In "Demonology" Mrs. Eddy writes that she actually overheard Wright and Kennedy plotting against her, and she quotes an interview she had with Wright and a letter she received from him in late February of 1872 in which Wright offered to change sides once again and ally secretly with her against Kennedy. Wright told her he had a long-standing grudge against Kennedy, that the alliance with Kennedy had been based purely on immediate tactical and monetary considerations, and that his real interests and concerns lay with her camp. According to Mrs. Eddy, Wright made the following state-ments to her:

> Why should we [i.e., Wright and Mrs. Glover] be enemies, especially if we have one great object in common? Perhaps we can be united on this, and the result may be that this city will finally be rid of one of the great-est humbugs [i.e., Kennedy] that ever disgraced her fair face. All this can be accomplished; but, as I said before, it is necessary to be very cau-tious, and not let the fact of our communicating together be known, as a friend in the enemy's camp is an advantage not to be overlooked.[28]

Looking back on the events, Mrs. Eddy says that she spurned Wright's offers, pointing out that any help he might give her in the future could have little force against all the public attacks only recently made against her under his signature; she also refused his requests for money. She ends the section in "Demonology" by saying that excellent sources reported to her that after their final meeting, Wright had gone immediately to see Kennedy and suc-cessfully extorted the remainder of the money Kennedy had promised him, presumably as payment for the attacks in the Lynn *Transcript.*

Whether or not Wright had been conspiring with Kennedy, as Mrs. Glover believed, there is no doubt that by March 1872 Richard Kennedy had torn up his contract with her and refused to make any more payments. A clash in material interest and a difference in tastes were obviously involved in this split. According to the sources interviewed by Milmine and the

McClure's reporters, by the spring of 1872 Kennedy was well established in Lynn, earning a good living, and a firm favorite in the community. He no longer needed Mrs. Glover to lead him by the hand, was disinclined to give her half of the profit from a practice sustained by his efforts alone, and was probably weary of her society. Yet the essential source of dispute between Mrs. Glover and Kennedy, based on the testimony of both camps, was not money but Mrs. Glover's increasing insistence that Kennedy should cease "rubbing," that is, manipulating the head and solar plexus not only of the patients in his practice but of the students as a prelude to Mrs. Glover's classes.[29]

Mrs. Glover's prohibition of this practice was new. She had initially sanctioned its use by Sarah Bagley and others in 1867–1868 and was fully aware that, in his highly successful practice in Lynn, Richard was known as a "rubbing" doctor. On the other hand, she herself never practiced manipulation, and in her early teaching manuscripts she ruled that rubbing per se had no efficacy but could serve in certain cases to focus the patient's mind and offer some physical correlative to the metaphysical change that was taking place in the healing. By 1871 she had come to believe that all forms of manipulation were harmful, and she therefore put pressure on Kennedy to give them up. When he refused, the partnership was dissolved.

To understand why manipulation became such an issue, it is crucial in my view to remember that traditionally in mesmerism or hypnosis the head and abdomen were manipulated so that the subject would be prepared to enter into trance and so that the therapist could establish rapport with the subject. As P. P. Quimby himself discovered, problems sometimes arose in mesmeric healing since the rapport between male hypnotist and female patient tended to become eroticized.[30] Manipulation was the primary indication of and first step toward this eroticized relationship.

Mesmerism is a term which Mary Baker Eddy, over the rest of her life, was to develop as a code word for a wide variety of phenomena, mental and physical, and one which I shall have occasion to discuss in the rest of this biography. The extraordinary intensity of the relations between Mrs. Glover's new movement and Richard Kennedy over the next ten years can be understood only if this unacknowledged erotic dimension is restored to the mesmerism issue and we pick up on the small signs of unconventional sexual activity which occur in regard to him. Until at least the time of the death of Mrs. Eddy's third husband, Asa Gilbert Eddy, in June 1882, Kennedy was to have a crucial if indirect importance for the nascent Christian Science movement. Hence, for the researcher, it is frustrating and fascinating to discover that Kennedy's importance is in inverse ratio to the documentation we have on him after 1872. In Kennedy's case, it proves necessary to pore over every crumb of information and consider the possibility that we shall never know the real story of what happened between him and

Mrs. Glover because the interview testimony and the documentation have been deliberately limited.

To return to the weeks immediately after the split with Kennedy, however, Mrs. Glover's initial reactions were more or less what one might expect— disappointment, anger, social condescension, fear for the future. To Putney Bancroft, she wrote,

> Oh, how I have worked, pondered and constantly imparted my discoveries to this wicked boy that I shall not name and all for what! . . . I may as well jest over the absurd striplings that turn to rend me, to threaten me with disgrace and imprisonment for giving to them a discovery that money cannot pay for, but a little good breeding might at least have helped to reward the toil, and scorn, and obscurity, by which it was won for them.[31]

To her old friend Fred Ellis she wrote in August of 1872 that "Dr R K has called Wright to his rooms and has entered into conspiracy with him against me, and this is the meaning of that dreadful threat." She reports that Kennedy was spreading wicked rumors about her, "telling, no one can live near me without being defamed, quotes Dr Patterson as a Victim!" and asks for Ellis's help in defending her good name. To Sarah Bagley she is more paranoid and grandiose: "The great cause that I have established in the minds of thinkers in many places, and for which I have borne most of all the blows given to it, is now placed in the hands of <u>lust</u> and <u>lies</u>."[32] The underlined word *lust* here should, in my view, be given some importance.

So far it would seem that Mrs. Glover was reacting to the split with Kennedy with understandable emotions and normal intensity, but over the next years her view of Kennedy would darken. By the early 1880s he had become her nemesis, the principal personification of the malicious mesmerism which constantly threatened her world and brought down her most cherished schemes. According to Bates and Dittemore, in the seventies and early eighties, she had nightmares about Kennedy, nightmares that involved snakes jumping into her lap, her white garments being ripped and dirtied. She dreamed that Kennedy and his friends looked on laughing in their prosperity and health while she wasted away from consumption, that Kennedy took the form of an elephant or a great dog who chased her around the house and allowed her no exit. She dreamed on more than one occasion of Kennedy meeting her, being very agreeable, and then leading her into a house which proved to be a brothel and from which she could not escape. Without having the exact words of the dream texts that Mary Baker Eddy wrote down or dictated, it is impossible to do much meaningful analysis, but there is no escaping the sexual quality of the oneiric images, and the

way Mary Baker Eddy seems to associate Kennedy with brothels and defile-
ment.[33]

Three small and usually unnoticed pieces of information we have
about Kennedy in his Lynn years support the idea that Mrs. Glover may
have broken with him in part because of what she learned of his sexual
activities. First, Hugh Studdert Kennedy notes that Richard Kennedy's
extraordinarily successful Lynn practice was composed almost entirely of
female patients, and that the healer habitually used some form of "manipulation" with them. Studdert Kennedy describes the elaborate ceremony
engaged in at Richard Kennedy's practice, in which the women patients
would let down their hair before the treatment, and then dry and put up
their hair again afterward. Here the Freudian implications of "letting your
hair down" are exactly to the point, I think, and Studdert Kennedy is subtly suggesting that Kennedy's relations with patients had some undeter-
mined sexual component. Second, we know that Richard Kennedy was
involved in an adulterous relationship with one of his fellow students,
Addie Spofford. Third, the Church History Department has an unpublished and undated letter written by Mrs. Eddy to one of her students,
probably in the late 1870s, in which she refers to Kennedy as suffering from
"spermatorrhea or involuntary emissions." Spermatorrhea was, in essence,
a disease or disorder invented by the mid-nineteenth century medical profession to explain or control what was theorized to be the insidious weakening of a young man's strength by involuntary ejaculation. It may have
been what brought Kennedy to Mrs. Glover's theory of healing in the first
place.[34] Robert Peel was the first biographer to bring up this letter and the
spermatorrhea reference, though he buries it in an enigmatic note, without
documentation, and goes on to note, for no apparent reason, that Kennedy
spent his last days in a mental hospital. In my view, by putting these two
facts about Kennedy together, Peel is implying very delicately that there
might be some connection between Kennedy's early sexual history and his
later insanity.[35]

Charting the exact course of relations between Mrs. Glover and Richard
Kennedy before and after their split is difficult since both parties seem to
have taken care to erase the documentary record. During the time Mrs.
Glover spent with the Wentworths in Stoughton, she and Kennedy were certainly in correspondence, and they probably wrote to each other in Lynn,
especially when their partnership was foundering. Unfortunately no letters
survive from either party during these years. Kennedy left no private papers,
or none survived him. Mary Baker Eddy, who kept so much, did not keep
the Kennedy letters, except for the two brief and adoring notes dating from
the very early stage of their friendship, which I have referred to. The Bagley
papers, which I have used to illumine this period, might themselves have
been destroyed had they come into Richard Kennedy's possession while he

was still managing his own affairs, and had their existence not become too well known for his executors to suppress them.

One letter which has survived and which has received much attention is the letter Mrs. Eddy wrote to Kennedy on October 8, 1878, and which many analysts have quoted as proof of her crazy obsession with Malicious Animal Magnetism. Mrs. Eddy assures Kennedy in the first paragraph that she will "spare every blow in my power if only you will cease to commit in secret the sins you are committing." She repeats this theme later in the same letter:

> Now I come to you again with that spirit of forgiveness which you cannot understand, to ask you, if the world knows none of the error of your past, you will cease to commit the sin against the Holy Ghost by doing in secret what you would not have revealed, by trying to injure the helpless who know not that you are trying, and to stop the terrible malpractice you have fallen into.[36]

When I first read this letter, I assumed that the "secret sins" Mrs. Eddy was accusing Kennedy of were mesmerism and Malicious Animal Magnetism. Then I began to wonder if she was distinguishing the secret sins from the malpractice and referring very covertly to some other aspect of Kennedy's life that she found unacceptable.

Over the next eight years, Kennedy was to become Mary Baker Eddy's principal public enemy in the various disastrous and highly publicized lawsuits which she fought and which I shall be discussing in later chapters. By 1881, in the new "Demonology" chapter of the third edition of *Science and Health*, she was apocalyptic in her references to him:

> Some years ago, the history of one of our young students, as known to us and many others, diverged into a dark channel of its own, whereby the unwise young man reversed our metaphysical method of healing, and subverted his mental power apparently for the purposes of tyranny peculiar to the individual. A stolid moral sense, great want of spiritual sentiment, restless ambition, and envy, embedded in the soil of this student's nature, metaphysics brought to the surface, and he refused to give them up, choosing darkness rather than light. His motives moved in one groove, the desire to subjugate; a despotic will choked his humanity. Carefully veiling his character, through unsurpassed secretiveness, he wore the mask of innocence and youth. But he was young only in years; a marvellous plotter, dark and designing, he was constantly surprising us, and we half shut our eyes to avoid the pain of discovery, while we struggled with the gigantic evil of his character, but failed to destroy it. His nature is understood only as his acts behind the scenes are revealed. The second year of his practice, when we discovered he was malpractising, and told him so, he avowed his intention to do whatever he chose with his mental power, spurning a Christian life, and exulting in the

absence of moral restraint. The sick clung to him when he was doing them no good, and he made friends and followers with surprising rapidity, but retained them only so long as his mesmeric influence was kept up and his true character unseen. The habit of his misapplication of mental power grew on him until it became a secret passion of his to produce a state of mind destructive to health, happiness, or morals. His power to heal failed, because of his sins, and if he succeeded with the power of will to remove one disease, it was succeeded by a more malignant one. ("Demonology," *Science and Health,* 3e, pp. 1–2)

It is easy to see why such passages have been passed over in embarrassed silence by Christian Science apologists and cited by critics as evidence of Mrs. Eddy's deranged and vindictive nature. There is no doubt that by 1881 Kennedy not only cordially detested Mrs. Eddy herself but also saw her new Science as an important competitor and took any opportunities he could to damage her and her doctrines in the public eye.[37] Yet professional rivalry alone does not explain the passion and excess of Mrs. Eddy's denunciation of Kennedy in the third edition of *Science and Health* and her use of expressions such as "choosing darkness over light," "desire to subjugate," "despotic will," "gigantic evil," "unsurpassed secretiveness," and "marvellous plotter."

The hostility between Kennedy and Mrs. Eddy was a subject well covered among their contemporaries, and the relationship between the teacher and her erstwhile student has fascinated all of her biographers. Even those who met the man himself have little illumination to offer, however. Though interviewed around 1907–1908 by Milmine, Wilbur, and Powell, Kennedy was congenial but cagey, and he seems to have had neither the desire for publicity nor the financial incentive which led other old Eddy associates to "tell all." As we have seen, even his old friend and ally from the Amesbury-Lynn period, Sarah Bagley, never spoke to the press about Mrs. Eddy, and this may have been as much from respect for Kennedy's feelings as out of love for Mrs. Eddy. Robert Peel calls Richard Kennedy an enigma, going so far as to compare him to the mysterious and evil Stavrogin in Dostoyevsky's novel *The Devils.*

Georgine Milmine met Kennedy and earned his disregard by ignoring his direct, written request that she not name him as a source for the *McClure's* account of his partnership in Lynn with the then Mrs. Glover.[38] Lyman P. Powell also interviewed and corresponded with Kennedy, striking up a chummy, misogynistic, old clubman kind of relationship which resulted in a set of ten rare letters and cards written at the very time when the Milmine and Wilbur biographies were being issued in magazine form. This correspondence offers a tiny but unique window into Kennedy's mind in the years before he descended into madness. As might be expected, Kennedy had nothing but scorn for Wilbur's enthusiastic endorsement of Mrs. Eddy and

Christian Science, but it is interesting to find that he was hardly kinder about the Milmine series. Even though Milmine and Cather had given so glowing a portrait of him in *McClure's*, Kennedy's final comment on the way both Milmine and Wilbur had dealt with his association with Mrs. Eddy is interestingly sardonic and guarded:

> The two articles [i.e., Milmine's and Wilbur's] evidently seem contradictory to you [Powell]. In the main, they are not, nevertheless there are misrepresentations in both. The two women who prepared them have of very necessity been obliged to guess at a great deal as the material that has been concealed from them was so much more than has been disclosed that both articles are very incomplete and in many respects infantile.[39]

Sadly, if Lyman Powell did press Kennedy for more details about the nature of the "misrepresentations" and material which had been concealed from Wilbur and Milmine, he does not share any information he obtained from Kennedy in his personal papers or include it in either of his books on Mrs. Eddy and Christian Science.

My own surmise is that Richard Kennedy was actively exploring issues of sexual identity in the very years that he was closely associated with the then Mrs. Mary Glover, and that he may even have been bisexual.[40] Following the break between them, she became aware of his sexuality in some measure and rejected him and the closeness they had enjoyed with a peculiar kind of horror. Mary Baker Eddy was in many ways a wise and open-minded woman on sexual matters, but socially she was also the product of a conservative Christian tradition. My guess is that homosexuality would be something she could neither understand nor countenance.

Whatever it was about Richard Kennedy that aroused such deep emotions in her, there is no doubt that through him she began a long and torturous examination of what she variously called mesmerism, Malicious Animal Magnetism, or malicious malpractice. In 1872 Mrs. Eddy's conception of mesmerism was still embryonic, though some ideas were in place and would never change. Like P. P. Quimby before her, she believed that it was possible not only to read someone's mind but also to exert purely mental control over another's mind, without that person's consent or perhaps knowledge. As we have seen, Kennedy in the 1860s had also accepted the mesmeric theories about absent treatments and believed in clairvoyance and mind reading, and there is no evidence that he later changed his mind. This shared assumption should be kept in mind when we come to discuss Mrs. Eddy's later accusations that Kennedy and others were mentally working havoc on her movement to the point of killing her husband with mental arsenic.

As she evolved as a religious leader and a theologian, Mary Baker Eddy became convinced that one of her most vital tasks was to distinguish

Christian Science from hypnotism, to define Christian Science healing as the practical, on-the-spot invocation and demonstration of God's eternal perfection as manifest in man, His image—not the transient and imperfect influence of one human mind over another. Kennedy would not attempt to make the metaphysical move from mental healing to what his former healing partner would soon be calling Christian Science. As Mrs. Eddy saw it, Kennedy had not only deceived her and let her down; he had sought to subvert the very basis of her teaching by using his powerful mesmeric abilities to undo the good she was seeking to do for patients, to suborn the students she had converted, to hinder the great movement she was laboring to establish. Just as Freud's abandonment of the seduction hypothesis, though based, in the view of many, on faulty reasoning and inadequate self-knowledge, was essential to the evolution of psychoanalytic theory, so Mary Baker Eddy's rejection of mesmeric "manipulation" was a necessary stage in the evolution of her thought.

12

Science and Health
1875

SCIENCE AND HEALTH UNDOUBTEDLY HOLDS THE KEY
to understanding Mary Baker Eddy's religious philosophy. Its appearance in print in 1875 is an event of such importance to the history of Christian
Science that I shall be devoting this chapter to this famous work as the then
Mrs. Mary Glover first wrote and published it. I lay emphasis on "first"
because one of the most salient features of *Science and Health* as a foundational religious text is that from 1875 to 1907 Mary Baker Eddy was engaged
in a virtually daily revision of her book. Thus the text of 1875 and the text
of 1907, the one that Christian Scientists read today, are radically different.
Mrs. Eddy saw this work of revision as being a progressive clarification of a
divinely revealed message which was in essence unchanged but which she
needed to labor to understand for herself and find the words to express so
that others could understand it too. The central concept of Christian Science
is perhaps that reality, including the reality of human existence, is spiritual,
and hence eternal and unchanging. The truth of that reality is what Mary
Baker Eddy was inspired to express in *Science and Health,* and in her eyes
there was consonance, not contradiction, in the fact that her revelation was
achieved only—to use her own terms—by unceasing struggle against the
limits of materiality, and by constant struggle against error.

In this biography I shall not attempt to give a synopsis of *Science and
Health* as we know it today, nor will I even claim to offer the kind of informed
critique to be found in the many and various books on Christian Science.
Here I offer a personal reading, based on my own concerns and interests,

and, I hope, focusing on aspects of Mary Baker Eddy's most important work that have lain in shadow. In this chapter I am taking an approach that is the antithesis of Mrs. Eddy's, in that I will treat the 1875 edition as a kind of urtext, the one where the then Mrs. Mary Glover, alone and unaided, thinking and drafting in a kind of cultural vacuum, most clearly revealed her mind to us. Let me begin, pace Mrs. Eddy, by commenting on the material circumstances under which the first edition was written and published and then go on to exploring its technical qualities as a piece of published prose. Finally I shall examine some of the ideas which I consider of particular importance from the standpoint both of Mary Baker Eddy's life and of feminist theology. The latter is a subject of increasing interest in the late 1990s and to which I believe Mary Baker Eddy made a fascinating, original, and largely unappreciated contribution.

The BUSINESS RELATIONS heretofore existing between MRS. GLOVER and her student, RICHARD KENNEDY, are closed. Mary M. B. Glover.—Lynn *Semi-Weekly Reporter,* May 4, 1872.

Mary Baker Eddy's rise to success was an exceptionally long and bumpy road, but she prevailed because she was able to learn the lessons of failure and move on. Faced with the private disaster of her break with Kennedy, the public exposure incident upon the newspaper correspondence with Wright, and the increasingly raucous soap opera of her relations with her students, the then Mrs. Glover remained essentially undeterred in her commitment to her science. Loud at first in her lamentations and protestations and imprecations, she rapidly decided to save her breath to cool her porridge, as her beloved Scots might say, and made the next radical revision to the master plan that would lead her toward her goal. She determined that the imperative thing at this juncture was to have a full statement of her new religious philosophy of healing, so for the next two and a half years she dedicated as much of her time, energy, and financial resources as possible to writing, revising, and getting into print the text that we know today as *Science and Health.* Through writing, all the recent conflict would be explained and exorcized. The next years were to be ones of continuing strife and bickering with her students and friends, of petty financial worries, and constant, lonely labor, but in the end the book she had been trying to write since 1867 would see the light of day, and after that things, slowly, would be different.

Following the final severing of her partnership with Kennedy in 1872, Mrs. Glover retreated, as was her wont, for a month's summer vacation in northern New England. She stayed briefly in Tilton, where she found little solace with her sister Abigail and sister-in-law Martha Rand Baker, and then in Derry, where her good-hearted stepmother made her welcome.[1] In late

June she returned to Lynn to take up the struggle and continue with the sixty-page manuscript which she had started at the very beginning of the year.[2] Her remaining faithful students greeted her on her return with the gift of a Bible and Cruden's *Complete Concordance to the Holy Scriptures,* an invaluable reference book she would use for years. As a clear indication of how Mrs. Glover was spending the majority of her time, for Christmas the same students gave their teacher "fifteen quires of Congress letter paper, three boxes of initial notepaper and envelopes of assorted tints, two inkstands, a bottle of ink, two dozen postage stamps, two dozen pens."[3]

Unable to afford to keep up the rent on the large rooms in South Common Street which she had shared with Kennedy,[4] she moved after a few months to the Chadwell rooming house and later made brief stays in 1873, 1874, and the very beginning of 1875 at various boardinghouses, including the one that was still maintained by her old friend Mrs. Clark. It was from the Clarks' house, accompanied by the young George Clark, that she went to court in late 1873 and successfully finalized her divorce from Daniel Patterson on the grounds of his desertion and adultery.

The divorce was an important step toward normalizing her social and financial position, but Mrs. Glover still had to solve the immediate problem of making an independent living while devoting herself full-time to writing, since she would not resume teaching her classes until April 1875, and thus she had lost all tuition income. As it had been since George Glover died in 1844, money was a short-term headache and a long-term threat. But by this point in her career Mrs. Glover was showing the kind of practical resourcefulness and financial acumen which I admire in her but which the improvident Mark Twains and Frederick Peabodys of the world would find so unbecoming in a woman and so inconceivable in a woman religious leader.

She had saved some $6,000 from the Kennedy partnership money, and Sarah Bagley was faithfully paying her the agreed upon percentage of her income from her healing practice, although this amounted to fifty dollars a year at best. From the rather garbled transcripts of the suit brought against her by George Barry, I deduce that Mrs. Glover was generating more income by using her capital to buy up mortgages. According to the court notes for the Barry suit of 1878, the then Mrs. Eddy testified: "In 1872 took 2 mortgages and gave all the money I had 2000 apiece. Mr. Barry collected the interest for me." Barry, and perhaps Hitchings, were her agents in these mortgage dealings, collecting the interest for her and perhaps arranging the real estate transactions.[5] According to Bancroft, Mr. Edward H. Hitchings was one of Mrs. Glover's close acquaintances at this time. Being a real estate broker, Hitchings was charged with assisting her to find accommodation, and, if possible, a property to buy. When Mrs. Glover contemplated moving to Cambridge, Hitchings was supposed to find her something to rent there, but Bancroft says in his book that

Hitchings made no real efforts to find her a place there because he was anxious to marry her and keep her in Lynn.[6]

As far as can be deduced from the transcript of the Barry suit, in the winter of 1874 George Barry, Hitchings, and Mrs. Glover went into partnership in some property deal, but the three fell out over who should be named in the bond, who should take care of repairs, and who should hold the deed.[7] Under oath at the later trial Mrs. Eddy claimed that she had paid repair bills for work that Barry had neglected to perform, and that he had turned against her when she refused to give up to him the deed to the house. Barry had argued that he should have the deed for safekeeping since "anybody could trump up a bill against her [Mrs. Glover]," an interesting indication of how difficult it was for a single woman to conduct business in the Commonwealth of Massachusetts in the 1870s.

Boardinghouse living was expensive for a notably frugal woman who was mainly living on her savings;[8] therefore Mrs. Glover lived for various periods with her students Dorcas Rawson, Samuel Putnam Bancroft, and George Allen. There were small financial benefits for boarder and host in sharing accommodations, but Mrs. Glover also obviously craved some share in normal family life. Bancroft includes in his book an undated letter, poignant, naïve, confused, in which Mrs. Glover lamented the fact that she had not received any invitation to share Thanksgiving dinner,[9] and as I have already commented, the ache of loneliness was something she felt more or less acutely for most of her adult life. Moving in with a student's family probably seemed a good solution to a number of her problems, and she was to try to make it work several times over the years, but something always went wrong. It is clear that Mrs. Glover was a difficult tenant, demanding the rapt attention and loving solicitude of all at one moment, and needing absolute quiet and solitude at another. Barry was later supposed to have said that the months she lived with his family were the worst in his life, and even the loyal Bancroft did not fail to reveal in his account the stresses and strains of living with his beloved teacher at this period in her life. The attempts at shared living probably contributed to the tensions, irritations, and obsessions that characterized relations among the early Christian Scientists and their leader in Lynn.

The main source of our information on Mrs. Glover in this period is Samuel Putnam Bancroft, or "Putney," as Mrs. Glover liked to call him. Bancroft was a young shoe factory manager in his early twenties; he was second only to George Barry in the fervor of his affection for her.[10] When in the spring of 1871 Bancroft announced that he had become engaged to be married, he feared that his teacher would be less than pleased, because an important tenet of her teaching was the need to subordinate material and physical desires to spiritual goals. In fact, she received the news reasonably well, taking the opportunity when responding to his letter announcing the engagement to give her student a new lesson in Christian Science terminology and theology.

> You say "you are vainquished," but this is an error of statement; you are unchanging, this Mr. Bancroft is not.
>   You say "love has triumphed over wisdom." This cannot be, for love and wisdom are one, but you might have said, sense has overruled the soul for a brief time; ere long the case will be changed and you will wish this had not been the case. I fear you will inherit this truth through the discipline of affliction.[11]

Despite this rather frosty gloss on the joys of prospective matrimony, Mrs. Glover embraced Bancroft's fiancée, gave her free tuition in Christian Science doctrine,[12] and encouraged the young couple to take out a mortgage on a small house, engaging to live with them and pay them rent. Unfortunately, Mrs. Glover soon found her rooms in the house ill placed for her needs and too small and noisy—Mrs. Bancroft would keep playing the piano when Mrs. Glover was trying to work or talk to students!—so Mrs. Glover quickly moved out into a boardinghouse across the street, leaving the young couple to meet the house payments unassisted.

The trials of the young Bancrofts were far from over. In 1874 the firm of Bancroft and Purinton went bankrupt, and "Putney" found himself unemployed, with a mortgage to pay, and his wife expecting their first child.[13] Mrs. Glover had for some time been trying to generate interest in her Science in Boston—several references in her letters make it plain that convenient access to the cars into Boston was an important consideration for her in choosing lodgings—and she decided that this was the right moment to move out of the confines of Lynn and establish a new practice in a richer, more educated, and potentially more susceptible milieu. At this point Dorcas Rawson was the only one of Mrs. Glover's students who was actually seeing patients, but the very success of her practice in Lynn made it impracticable for Rawson to move. George Allen was unable to leave his family and his job in the box factory. George Barry worked full-time and was also very young and too useful to Mrs. Glover as a copyist and general assistant to be trusted with the task. Mrs. Miranda Rice was fully occupied with her husband and young family. Bancroft was the only possible choice, so Mrs. Glover persuaded him, although he mustered little enthusiasm or confidence, to undertake a three-month experiment with the new Science. He left Lynn, found rooms in an area then called Cambridgeport, a modest section of Cambridge close to what is now M.I.T., and put out his shingle: "S. P. Bancroft, Scientific Physician, Gives No Medicine."[14]

Through her letters, Mrs. Glover tried to encourage and advise him, and she promised to move to Cambridge as soon as she could find suitable accommodation. Bancroft returned to Lynn well before the scheduled three months were up, having failed to even cover his expenses. The letters she wrote to Bancroft at this time and which he printed in his later book indicate that Mrs. Glover understood that he had acted in good faith. Rather than taking him to task for a lack of talent or enterprise as a healer, she blamed the poor location he had chosen to establish himself in—too far from the hallowed halls of Harvard—but above all she blamed the machinations of Richard Kennedy, who, she had been assured, had taken to visiting Cambridge in order to seduce and turn away the prospective patients whose names she had supplied. Bancroft himself blamed neither Mrs. Glover nor Richard Kennedy for his failure in Cambridgeport, ascribing it to his own lack of preparation or inspiration. He seems to have been an extremely decent, modest young man, in the mold of Asa Gilbert Eddy and Calvin Frye, but because of his successful marriage, he was destined to play a lesser and less uncomfortable part in the history of Christian Science.

One little incident from this period has gained some prominence in the critical biographies of Mary Baker Eddy, beginning with Milmine, since it is evidence from an unimpeachable source that Mrs. Glover fell into some kind of coma or fit. The source of the anecdote is Samuel Putnam Bancroft, who later reproduced in his loyal defense of Mrs. Eddy this section from his diary, dated only "Jan. 11th," but probably referring to 1873 when Mrs. Glover was writing her book and still close to George Barry, Miranda Rice, and Mr. Hitchings:

> I received a letter today from George B[arry], giving me an account of a strange experience which my teacher passed through on Friday last, and which he was present to witness. It seems he called upon her with Mr. H[itchings], and, on rapping, heard a voice, hardly above a whisper, say "Come in." On entering, she arose to meet them, but fell back, lost consciousness, and, to their belief, was gathering herself on the other side. George went after Mrs. R[ice], who came, and immediately a change took place. George had called on her mentally to come back, but Mrs. R. called loudly, as for someone afar off, and the answer came, faintly at first, but stronger and stronger, till she was able to sit up and have the Bible and manuscripts read to her, and, finally, recovered.

Bancroft comments on this incident:

> Many times while writing her book Mrs. Eddy was obliged to call for assistance from the few students who had not deserted her. I have been present on such occasions. Mrs. Eddy, on her part, was always ready to respond to the call of these students, and was able to assist them.[15]

There is much to this incident that I find puzzling, for example what exactly Bancroft understood by the key phrase "gathering herself on the other side." I assume he meant some form of deathlike unconsciousness, catatonia, or coma. But on the basis of Bancroft's account, it would seem that not only was Mrs. Glover subject to falling into such states at this time in her life, but that her students were also, and that they established a technique for dealing with the condition that involved calling the sufferer back "to this side." Milmine, who makes much of similar but more lurid stories obtained from Miranda Rice, explains it in terms of medical pathology, but I feel it is more properly placed in the context of religious movements and compared with the exorcisms and Spiritualist trances that have been not uncommon to other small religious and mental healing sects.

In my opinion, these dramatic scenes from the 1870s when Mrs. Glover went catatonic before the excited and awed eyes of Mrs. Rice and her sister Miss Rawson were the origin of all the later tales of Mary Baker Eddy's hysterical fits as a child and young woman, first reported by Milmine in *McClure's* and since then accepted as true by virtually every biographer. Bates and Dittemore, for example, quote the Bancroft incident and then comment:

> Was this another of the cataleptic attacks to which she had been sub-ject in childhood? Or was it, more likely, the result of an overdose of morphine? Both Mrs. Miranda Rice, sister of Dorcas Rawson, and Mrs. Ellen Locke [sister of George Allen] asserted that she was addicted to the use of morphine during this period.[16]

As I have shown in earlier chapters, there is no solid evidence at all for Milmine's melodramatic description of the young Mary Baker repeatedly falling on the floor in hysterical catatonic fits. No family member, no close friend makes any mention of such fits, either when she was young or later. When questioned on the subject in the 1900s, those few remaining contem-poraries who had been familiar with the Baker family denied that Mary had shown any such abnormal behavior. In the 1870s things were quite different, however, and Mrs. Glover was experiencing "fits," whether hysterical or not. Miranda Rice and Dorcas Rawson were leaders of the group of students who split with Mrs. Eddy in the early 1880s, and who continued to practice in the mental healing field in direct competition with Christian Science. Mrs. Rice was to provide some of the most lurid anecdotes and accusations against Mrs. Eddy,[17] and, for some reason, there was a decision made at *McClure's* that the kind of incident that Mrs. Rice had indeed witnessed in 1872 or 1873 should be projected back into the 1820s and 1830s and represented, not as a peculiar and temporary behavioral pattern in a nascent religious healing group, but as a personal pathology of Mary Baker Eddy's, an early and determinative flaw in her psychic makeup.

If we are looking for traditional medical diagnoses, we might choose fainting fits caused by fatigue and stress, since there is no doubt that the three years Mrs. Glover spent completing and publishing the first edition of *Science and Health* stretched her to the limit of her physical strength. The split with the popular Kennedy had further alienated Mrs. Glover from general Lynn society, and Peel remarks, without documentation, that in 1875 "Numerous disquieting rumors about Mrs. Glover flew around Lynn in those days, and many a good citizen felt bitter hostility to what he supposed her to be."[18] Later in life Mrs. Eddy remarked in her interview with the journalist Arthur Brisbane that rocks were thrown at her windows while she lived in Lynn.[19] Even within the little group that had shown interest in her science of healing she lost many crucial friends and allies, such as the Olivers. In "Demonology" Mrs. Eddy wrote darkly of the patients who refused to see her and claimed she harmed their well-being, the friends who would no longer speak to her, and who spoke ill of her to others. Even if we wholly discount Mrs. Eddy's theory of malicious malpractice and refuse to see the evil mesmeric influence of Richard Kennedy behind tales of cold shoulders and slammed doors, her sense of betrayal and hostility were real.

It was in this atmosphere of tension within the movement and hostility from outside that Mary Baker Glover managed to complete a draft of the manuscript she had been dimly envisaging since 1866 and which would become *Science and Health*.

As she confided in 1893 to James Gilman:

> I moved nine times while writing the book and that chair was the only furniture and about all I possessed. My writing desk was simply a piece of book cover cardboard. There was no good reason for my moving except the antagonism that was felt to the ideas, and to me for voicing them.[20]

Bancroft confirms this:

> When convinced of the necessity of promulgating that which had been made known to her, in book form, Mrs. Eddy secluded herself for over three years for that purpose, depriving herself of all but the bare necessities of life as she wrote. I have known her when nearly crushed with sorrow, but she wrote on. I have known her when friend after friend deserted her, but she wrote on. I have seen student after student bring ridicule and reproach upon her, but still she wrote on.[21]

Sustaining her through all the hours of solitary labor and the external pressures was what we could call inspiration but what Mrs. Glover felt convinced was revelation. She later wrote of this period:

> I had no time to borrow from Authors. Such a flood tide of truth was lifted upon me at times that it was overwhelming and I have drawn quick breath as my pen flew on, feeling as it were submerged in the transfiguration of spiritual ideas.[22]

Such moments of exaltation gave her an irrepressible belief in a glorious future that everything in the present seemed to deny. "Do you see that church? I shall have a church of my own some day," she told George Clark, who probably thought she was quite mad.[23]

It is a truth universally acknowledged that the earliest editions of *Science and Health,* put out before Mary Baker Eddy could afford the editorial assistance of educated gentlemen such as the Reverend Wiggin, were little more than illiterate ramblings. In the 1900s, Mark Twain's merry satire and Frederick Peabody's fulminating wrath were at one in exposing the shortcomings of Mrs. Eddy's book. In the 1990s those indefatigable readers Martin Gardner and Harold Bloom similarly declared unreadable a text which, I suspect, they had not in fact read, though Bloom may have put one of his research assistants on to the job. The critical consensus is overwhelming that poor deluded Mrs. Eddy could, as the sayings go, neither rub two ideas together nor write her way out of a paper bag.[24] "Even after her eight years struggle with her copy," we read in the Milmine biography, "the book, as printed in 1875 is hardly more than a tangle of words and theories, faulty in grammar and construction, and singularly contradictory in its statements."[25] Even the Church of Christ, Scientist has shown little admiration for the actual text of the first edition of its great book, preferring instead to stress Mrs. Eddy's lifelong commitment to bringing the book to what they promote as its final and current perfection.[26] Even though I long ago in my research learned to take anything written about Mrs. Eddy with a tablespoon of salt, I was, I admit, influenced by all this negative press, and I put off reading the book rather longer than I decently could.

When, finally, I forced myself to sit down and read the 1875 edition of *Science and Health,* my central, and unexpected, conclusion was that both Christian Scientist loyalists and their opponents have attacked and avoided the book because it was too radical. The real issue is the author's audacity, her daring to think that a woman like her, with her resources, could write, not the expected textbook on mental healing techniques, not the comfortable compendium of healing anecdotes, but a book that takes on the great questions of God and man, good and evil, and that rejects orthodox verities.[27]

The 1875 text of *Science and Health* is one of the loneliest books ever written in modern times. From the point of view of her career as a writer, more important than the social ostracism which she suffered and which I commented upon earlier in this chapter was Mrs. Glover's cultural and intellectual isolation. The diligent help of one friend equipped with what she liked to call a "classical education" would have saved Mrs. Glover her "culture" mistakes, but she did not have such a friend. As we know, her acquaintance at this period in Lynn was limited to women with less education than herself and to grade-school educated male shoe factory workers and lower managers.[28] She did have, it is true, the devoted and youthful George Barry, who copied her manuscripts for her and may, if his court testimony is to be believed, have helped her with spelling and grammar, but this was hardly a great resource.

In view of this isolation, it is easy to understand why Mrs. Glover's text was—as so many critics have gleefully asserted—full of mistakes. The 1875 edition of *Science and Health* ends with a two-page list of errata, and there are certainly a lot more mistakes that do not appear on the list—errors of spacing, failure to close quotation marks, "toid" printed for "told," to name a few of the ones I picked up quite randomly. Apart from these errata, Mrs. Glover is also guilty of other mistakes that certainly reveal a lack of higher education. She spells *progenitor* with a *j*, for example, and *seige* for *siege*; she makes *strata* and *addenda* singular nouns, has no clear idea of the meaning of *antipodes*, and believes that "dernier resort" is a French expression.

In my opinion, such errata and mistakes are too rare to spoil the reading of any but the most persnickety, and, given the circumstances in which we know Mrs. Glover completed the 1875 edition, they are easily forgiven. Furthermore, as a letter she wrote to Daniel Spofford on April 7, 1876, shows, Mrs. Glover was more sensitive than anyone to the deficiencies of her text. No sooner had she seen her first edition in print than she started making corrections and preparing the second edition. She reported numerous crrata in the "errata" appended to the book—spelling the word *erata* in the letter to exemplify her problems!—and asked Spofford to correct only those things he was absolutely sure were not right, and to simply mark the rest of the problems so she could attend to them. She remarked wistfully that "our next printer should have a proof reader who is <u>responsible</u> for this."[29]

Organization was another huge problem that Mary Baker Eddy was to struggle with throughout her life, and the 1875 edition is often presented by critics as a chaotic mishmash, possessing no shape and following no clear line of argument. Critics note with glee that between 1875 and 1907 the composition of the book varies markedly from one revision to the next, that chapters appear and disappear at different points in the book, with "Prayer and Atonement," for example, appearing as Chapter 5 in 1875, being split into two chapters in 1891, and then getting promoted to Chapters 1 and 2 in the second 1902 version.[30]

Mary Baker Eddy is unquestionably nonlinear, but postmodernist and feminist critical theory has warned us that nonlinearity is not necessarily a failing. Those enemies of Mrs. Eddy who have accused her of using bastardized Hegelianisms were, perhaps, not entirely misguided, not in the sense that she read or plagiarized some potted version of Hegel, but that in her manner of thinking and arguing she is much closer to Hegel and Nietzsche than to Hume, Locke, and John Stuart Mill. The circular, oracular, repetitious, strongly metaphorical[31] progression of Mrs. Eddy's text, the demands it makes on the reader's active participation, its exploration of the semantics of typography, remind me of such Hegel- and Nietzsche-influenced modern thinkers as Lacan and Derrida and, above all, of Irigaray, the French philosopher, psychoanalyst, and feminist.[32] Like them, though for very different philosophical reasons, she believed that words are imperfect and opaque, twisted and oblique in their relation to "reality" and "truth," constantly needing to be put into question. Like them she sought to form a particular lexicon or idiolect, a code of words given a new range of meaning within a specified context. There are times when she is difficult to follow as, at crucial moments in her metaphysical argument, she makes an important transition in the middle of a paragraph, often after using a question that probes the positions that have been set forth so far and forces a movement onward in the argument.[33] Just as it is difficult to translate Derrida or Irigaray into English—and I speak here as Irigaray's chief English translator—so Mrs. Eddy's prose, like the poetry of her famous contemporary Edgar Allen Poe, could emerge into French with added luster.[34]

When they highlight the major organizational revisions that *Science and Health* underwent, critics are not only complaining about the chronic disorganization of the writer's ideas; they are also discrediting her claims that the book was the result of divine revelation. Revealed truth, according to the implied criteria of Mrs. Eddy's critics, must come swiftly and definitively, under exceptional, even mystic circumstances, not over forty years of unremitting labor, copious drafts, and constant erasures. The Book of Mormon, as revealed in golden tablets to Joseph Smith by the angel Moroni, obeys the conventional criteria for revealed text, as does the *Principles of Nature, Her Divine Revelations, and a Voice to Mankind*, dictated under hypnotic trance by Andrew Jackson Davis and published in 1847.[35] Frederick Peabody and those he influenced felt able to attack Mrs. Eddy for her failure to follow this model of revelation, while also levelling false charges that she had been active in the kind of professional Spiritualist seances by which Andrew Jackson Davis earned his living after he had achieved fame but not wealth as a hypnotic subject.[36]

What struck me about the organization of the 1875 edition is how uncompromising it is. Mary Baker Eddy offers almost no introduction to ease her reader into the book, almost no personal testimony to elicit sympathy and commitment, no summary of what is to come. The 456-page book consists of eight chapters with no explanation as to their order, and no transition between them. It is easy to understand why Daniel Spofford and Asa Gilbert Eddy found the book so hard to sell: no casual reader would have been likely to get past page 1.

She begins with what she considers the essentials of her Science, the metaphysics, the definitions of God and of man, and their relation, the reality of spirit, the illusion of matter. She then moves on to a highly critical discussion of "imposition"—as her chapter title refers to Spiritualism—which makes it crystal clear that she had had considerable personal experience with practitioners of the movement, had given much thought to it, and had long since rejected it as spurious, immoral, and potentially destructive humbug. Mary Baker Eddy's views on Spiritualism are interesting and unusual. She makes it clear that she accepts the phenomenon of clairvoyance and believes that thought can be transmitted, even at a distance. She says that possibly a person at the moment of death may have and impart some premonitory experience of what awaits him. She comments at some length on the eloquence of the medium, on those occasions when the medium transcends the limits of her (interestingly, she assumes mediums are female) education and personality and speaks with apparently preternatural brilliance and force. Such eloquence is real, says Mrs. Eddy, but it is not a matter of a spirit speaking through the medium's body, but of the medium tapping into the sublime resources of Spirit which are available to us all, and which have nothing to do with a person's normal intelligence or years in school.

Mary Baker Eddy's main objections to Spiritualism are as follows:

1. Spiritualism makes personal sense, that is, material individuality, even more important than does conventional religion, since it allows the person to continue essentially unchanged after death.

2. Spiritualism never explains why the dead person would wish to return and retain contact with this earth—why would the butterfly want to become a kind of caterpillar again, she remarks. "To admit the so-called dead and living commune together, is to decide the unfitness of both for their separate positions. . . . Any supposed midway between Life outside of matter, or in it, is a myth."[37] Elsewhere she notes that to believe that we can communicate with immortality is like a man who knows only English claiming to read Greek (*Science and Health*, 1e, p. 73).

3. Spiritualism comes close to eliminating all individual responsibility and thus morality: "We should not hang on the skirts of others, but in our own identity possess some merit of our own not borrowed from others; and is there any so blind as not to admit individual faults? But mediumship well nigh disavows all individual responsibility, and literally lays the charge of good or evil on the shoulders of the dead" (*Science and Health*, 1e, p. 88).

4. Most Spiritualist sessions are trickery and humbug and also immoral: "The majority of what is termed mediumship, is simply imposition, not even clairvoyance, or mind-reading, but catch-penny fraud" (*Science and Health*, 1e, p. 96). "[Spiritualism's] military drills on sabbath, the aboriginal vernacular of its oracles, its rites and cere-

monies that choose darkness rather than light, and above all its loose morals, do not entitle spiritualism to the standing it has gained in society" (*Science and Health*, 1e, p. 95).

Given that Mary Baker Eddy went to such lengths in her first published work to distinguish Spiritualist "imposition" from the "demonstration" she advocated to Christian Scientists, and to explain exactly what she found wanting in Spiritualism, it is easy to understand how irritated she became years later when Peabody and Milmine tried to sap her authority by asserting that she was a closet Spiritualist and had perhaps even worked as a professional medium.

After the apparent digression into Spiritualism of Chapter 2, Chapters 3 and 4, "Spirit and Matter" and "Creation," take up the explanation of what for Mrs. Glover constituted the "Christian" part of Christian Science. Here the reader is led into Biblical exegesis, notably a discussion of origins, the origin of the world and of man as narrated in Genesis 1 and 2, and the Virgin birth of Jesus Christ and the new conception of body and spirit that Jesus established by his death, resurrection, and ascension. Three brief chapters follow in which Mrs. Glover offers some pithy, rather fragmented and highly idiosyncratic ideas on "Prayer and Atonement," "Marriage," and "Physiology." The final chapter, "Healing the Sick," returns to the crucial theme elaborated in one form or another throughout the text, that modern medicine is both unnecessary and unproductive, that health is man's natural birthright, and that sickness and even death can be eliminated if we set out to follow the example of Jesus, who spent his life showing that Soul held ultimate authority over body, demonstrating by what are wrongly termed miracles that the forces of matter had no power over him. This is how Mary Baker Eddy summarizes this argument:

> Because Jesus understood God better than did the Rabbis, he arrived at the conclusion in advance of them that he was Spirit and not matter, and that these never blend; also, that there is but one Spirit, or Intelligence, therefore but one God, one Life, Love and Truth. All forms of belief deny this in the main, and contend that Intelligence is both God and man, that there are two separate entities or beings exercising antagonistic powers; also, that matter controls Spirit, that man is both matter and Spirit, and the supreme being is God and man; also, that a third person named devil, is another Intelligence and power, and that these three different personages, viz., God, man, and devil blend in one person. When we possess a true sense of our oneness with God, and learn we are Spirit alone, and not matter, we shall have no such opinions as these, but will triumph over all sickness, sin, and death, thus proving our God-being. That we are Spirit, and Spirit is God, is undeniably true, and judging by its fruits, (the rule our Master gave) we should say this is not only science, but Christianity; but the shocking

audacity that calls itself God, and yet demonstrates only erring mortality, surprises us! (*Science and Health*, 1e, pp. 155–56)

If we follow the example of Christ, Mary Baker Eddy says, we too will perform the "miracles" of the gospel. At the same time, it is folly to assume that we can yet do what he did. Equally it is folly to conclude that, because we cannot do something now, we shall never be able to do so:

> If man tarries in the storm until the body is frozen; or rushes into the flames and it be devoured; this is not obedience to the Wisdom that gave him "dominion over earth." . . . to do otherwise is the blunder a pupil in addition would make to attempt to solve a problem of Euclid, and because he has not reached this point in mathematics, to fail in his demonstration, and others perceiving this, to deny the Principle of the problem. (*Science and Health*, 1e, p. 51)

Radical and *revolutionary* are not words often associated with Mary Baker Eddy, yet they are two key attributes of the 1875 edition of *Science and Health*. Over the next twenty years Mrs. Eddy was to modify her radicalism as she was forced to acknowledge the blank incomprehension of the masses and the enraged opposition of the few when faced with her text. This is an important reason for reading what she had to say before she was subjected to the conventional wisdom and condescending collaboration of the Reverend Wigginses of the world. Writing alone and in a cultural vacuum, Mary Baker Eddy had defined for herself an ideal reader of some metaphysical sophistication and considerable willingness to question received wisdom, but she failed to find this reader in actuality. She would have to edulcorate her tone, veil her iconoclastic energy, reorganize her units, write longer and more factual prefaces, introduce subheadings and quotations from great writers of the past, and generally facilitate the reader's entry into her text before *Science and Health* could find an audience. In my view, the 1875 edition failed because of the ignorance and stupidity of its public, not of its author.

"The time for thinkers has come; and the time for revolutions, ecclesiastic and social, must come." This is a quotation not from *Beyond Good and Evil* or *Thus Spake Zarathustra*, but from the preface to the 1875 *Science and Health*, and Mary Baker Eddy continues on the same page to denounce "contentment with the past, or the cold conventionality of custom" (*Science and Health*, 1e, p. 3). Later in the book it is almost shocking to find Mrs. Eddy using the phrase "radicalism and free thought" with a positive force to describe her Science, that accelerating movement toward truth which, in her view, is producing an apocalyptic "aggravation of error," convulsing the world with "marvels, calamities, perils and sin," the necessary prelude to the final triumph of Truth (*Science and Health*, 1e, p. 173). Shortly after, she writes again:

Never soil your garments with *conservatism*, or let another's error dim the lustre of your own Truth; always separate yourself from evil. Right is radical.... If you have grown out of former things, hesitate not to put them away, and fear not, for conscience' sake, to overstep the boundaries and break the string chains of old opinions. (*Science and Health*, 1e, pp. 178–79)

It is clear from the preface that Mary Baker Eddy expected her book to be misunderstood, and the question of redundancy and obscurity was one she specifically sought to counter. Here I take the liberty of correcting Mrs. Eddy's—or her publisher's—punctuation, moving a semicolon to make the meaning clear:

Owing to our explanations constantly vibrating between the same points an irksome repetition of words must occur, also, the use of capital letters, genders and technicalities peculiar to the science; variety of language, or beauty of diction, must give place to close analysis, and unembellished thought. (*Science and Health*, 1e, p. 5)

Especially in those sections where she is discussing her idea of God and of His relation to man, notably the first chapter, "Natural Science," Mary Baker Eddy does repeat words and phrases with almost mantralike persistence. She sets up chains of binary pairs—God/devil, Truth/error, Reality/illusion, Spirit/matter, Harmony/discord, Soul/body, Immortal/mortal, Principle/person, Idea/belief, Spiritual Sense/personal sense, Wisdom/knowledge, understand/believe—and strings several capitalized nouns together into affirmations about the nature of God: "There is no physical science, the Principle of science is God, Intelligence, and not matter; therefore, science is spiritual, for God is Spirit and the Principle of the universe and man" (*Science and Health*, 1e, p. 10). Defining one's idea of God is not an especially easy task for the learned theologian any more than for the average citizen, and it is quite possible that a more gifted or experienced writer would have cut down on some of the redundancies. But repetition in *Science and Health* is also a deliberate propaedeutic technique, a way of imprinting upon the willing student's mind the idea the teacher considers most important.

Furthermore, it is fatal to adopt a speed-reading approach to Mrs. Eddy's prose and ignore that, while the same lexicon is used over and again, the metaphysical argument is *not* static, particularly in those passages where Mrs. Eddy seeks to define man. According to her radical concept, man is an immortal and different being, made by God and in God's image, coexisting with God, and necessary to God, but fundamentally not God, not containing or part of Him:

God is, was, and ever will be; and if this Intelligence exists, there is also the idea of it, named man, that cannot be separated for a single moment from this, its principle and Soul. We look on a corpse, or the body called man, but is it man? No! Is Soul in it? certainly not; has Soul escaped? No! where was the outside, infinite Spirit, if Spirit was in man? Can Soul be lost? impossible, for the immortal is without end; and Soul is Spirit, and Spirit, God. Is man lost? not if Soul be left! for Soul is Principle, and man its idea, and these forever inseparable; God would be lost, if man was blotted out, for entity signifies the particular nature of being; and God, without the idea, image, and likeness of Himself, would be a nonentity! Man is the complex idea of God, hence, they cannot be separated. (*Science and Health*, 1e, pp. 24–25)

It is perhaps in her consistent and frequent refusal of the idea that God is immanent in man that Mrs. Eddy separates herself most sharply from the New Thought people who see God in everyone and indeed everything and believe that by following one's natural bent, listening to one's inner deity, one can and will easily achieve health, happiness, goodness, and so forth. Mrs. Eddy returns constantly to the fact that the path to Christian Science is arduous and painful.

Even as Mary Baker Eddy envisages some essential ontological split in God, whereby He expresses Himself through His idea and image, man, so she sees man also split into an eternal soul and an eternal (nonmaterial) body, which are different from one another yet mutually determine or constitute each other's existence.

When we admit the immortality of the Soul, we have admitted the immortal body, also, for if Soul can be separated from man, Principle can be severed from its idea, which is fatal to a self-existent Intelligence, and equal to saying there may be a time when God is without a single expression of Himself. (*Science and Health*, 1e, p. 53)

Divest belief of substance in matter, and the movements and transitions possible to mind would be just as possible to the body; and then would Spirit identify being without the loss of body. (*Science and Health*, 1e, p. 77)

Mrs. Eddy further grapples with the question of why an all-powerful, all-knowing, immortal God created man when she advances a notion of essential transitivity, based on the assumption that one of the qualities of God is Love:

Love cannot be debarred a manifestation, and is joy and not sorrow, good and not evil, Life and not death; hence the perfect idea God gave of Himself in immortal man, the object of divine affections. (*Science and Health*, 1e, p. 33)

Without attempting to evaluate these passages on metaphysical or theological grounds, I would claim that they are complicated and thought-provoking, and I would challenge anyone to make the same points more directly and economically. Strict economy is as much a feature of Mrs. Eddy's natural prose style as is repetition, and it occurs especially when she is most metaphysically radical. Furthermore, though her metaphysics have aroused the derision of several biographers, notably Edwin Dakin, she was not the first religious thinker to come to the conclusion that reality is soul not matter. When I was preparing this chapter on *Science and Health*, I happened to be reading the *Confessions* of Saint Augustine and was struck by the resemblance between the great church father's theological ontology, notably his declaration that evil has no existence or substance, and the conclusions Mrs. Eddy came to on the same subject in the late nineteenth century. Let me quote two passages to illustrate this point:

> So we must conclude that if things are deprived of all good, they cease altogether to be; and this means that as long as they are, they are good. Therefore, whatever is, is good; and evil, the origin of which I was trying to find, is not a substance, because if it were a substance, it would be good. For either it would be an incorruptible substance of the supreme order of goodness, or it would be a corruptible substance which would not be corruptible unless it were good. So it becomes obvious to me that all you [i.e., God] made is good, and that there are no substances whatsoever that were not made by you. And because you did not make them all equal, each single thing is good and collectively they are very good, for our God made his whole creation *very good.*

> We will now consider more minutely the Principle, or Soul of man, named God; learn what it is, and how man is harmonious and immortal. The Scriptures inform us, "God is Love," "Truth and Life," and these certainly imply He is Principle, not person. Again Principle explains person, but person cannot explain Principle. God interprets man, but man cannot explain God, Spirit explains matter, but matter cannot define Spirit, Soul explains body, but body cannot interpret Soul. We must commence with God to explain immortal man, remembering God is Spirit, and Spirit the only substance, because it is Intelligence; holding the earth in equipoise, marking out the pathway of the stars, forming the minutia of identity, and comprehending the universe and man in the harmony of being. Spirit believes nothing, because it understands all, and is Life, not subject to death because it is exempt from matter.[38]

Augustine of Hippo was in his day acknowledged to be the greatest of intellects, and though his theology and philosophy have since been deeply contested from many viewpoints, he is still considered one of the most important thinkers of all time. I am very far from claiming for Mary Baker Eddy the intellectual stature of Saint Augustine. I am pointing out that the same idea developed by one man in the cultural isolation of a small fourth-century North African colony is considered brilliant, thought-provoking, fundamental to Western philosophy; whereas *Science and Health* is denounced by such small-time ecclesiastical hacks as Lyman Powell and James Wiggin as the inane, incoherent ravings of an illiterate female. That Mrs. Eddy as a religious thinker was never attacked for her plagiarism of Augustine—or the Gnostics, or John Calvin, or Jonathan Edwards—is, I believe, not because she was not known to have read any of these works, but because her critics had not read them.

To turn from the metaphysics of the 1875 *Science and Health* to its religious origins, one of the things that has most irked men such as H. A. L. Fisher or the young Lyman Powell was that Mrs. Eddy gave the epithet *Christian* to her Science. Mrs. Eddy departs from conventional Christian thinking on at least three major points: her idea of death and redemption, her attitude toward prayer, and her understanding of the Bible.

"Death," as we know it, is simply a change and a progression toward fulfilling the divine idea that is man, she tells us. No one is either elected to eternal bliss or damned, and Jesus Christ does not atone for us but offers a pattern of at-one-ment with God. His life as told in the Gospels exemplifies what each person must do for him or herself.

> If the change called death dispossessed man of the belief of pleasure and pain in the body, universal happiness were secure at the moment of dissolution; but this is not so: "they that are filthy shall be filthy still," every sin and error we possess at the moment of death, remains after it the same as before, and our only redemption is in God, the Principle of man that destroys the belief of intelligent bodies. When we gain the freedom of the Sons of God, we shall master sense with Soul. . . . The false views entertained of pardoned sin, or universal and immediate happiness in the midst of sin, or, that we are changed in a moment from sin to holiness, are grave mistakes. To suddenly drop our earthly character, and become partakers of eternal life, without the pangs of a new birth, is morally impossible. . . . as man goeth to sleep so shall he waken; when the belief of death closes our eyes on this phase of the dream of Life in matter, we shall waken, not to a final judgment or resurrection, not with a single change in character, but for the same judgment of Wisdom to go on in process of purification as before, until Truth finally destroys error. When the final triumph of Soul over sense is achieved, the last trump has sounded, and not until then. (*Science and Health*, 1e, pp. 35–37)

Prayer was an area where Mrs. Eddy's radical ideas put her immediately at risk. As we shall see in the next chapter, during the suit brought against Stanley and Tuttle, Richard Kennedy introduced some very damaging testimony that Mrs. Glover had thrown Stanley out of her class because of his Baptist habit of prayer. The accusation that she discouraged prayer was to haunt her for many years, and she rebutted it over and over again,[39] notably by choosing the heavily amended chapter on prayer as the opening to the final revision of *Science and Health*. Yet given the persistence of this accusation, it is important to clarify what she says on this subject in the inflammatory 1875 text.[40] Mrs. Eddy begins by taking a commonsense, Jonathan Edwards approach to prayer, noting that given our definitions of God as an all-knowing being, living across the dimensions of time and seeking only our good, it is irrational to consider prayer as an opportunity to inform God of what is happening to us or to ask him to give us what we desire. This is true even when we pray for good health: "Asking God to heal the sick has no effect to gain the ear of Love, beyond its ever-presence" (*Science and Health*, 1e, p. 290).

Mrs. Eddy becomes more revolutionary—or, quite arguably, more in the original spirit of the Gospels—when she notes critically how often prayer is used as a public display and substitute for action. "The danger of audible prayer is, that we fall into temptation through it, and become an involuntary hypocrite. First, by uttering what is not a real desire, and secondly, consoling ourself under sin with the recollection we have prayed over it. Hypocrisy is fatal to Christianity" (*Science and Health*, 1e, p. 284). Or again: "Prayer is impressive; it gives momentary solemnity and elevation to thought, but does a state of ecstasy produce lasting benefit?" (*Science and Health*, 1e, p. 285). Mrs. Eddy sees prayer as central and crucial to the Christian life, since when we are praying we are consciously and intently seeking to reach out to God and uncover our essential spirituality. But the test of the efficacy of our praying is its motive power: has praying changed our lives?

> Prayer is sometimes employed, like a catholic confession, to cancel sin, and this impedes Christianity. Sin is not forgiven; we cannot escape its penalty. Being sorry for its committal is but one step towards reform, and the very smallest one; the next step that Wisdom requires is, the test of our sincerity, namely, a reformation. (*Science and Health*, 1e, p. 284)

Jean Jacques Rousseau, the master manipulator of the confessional form, could have learned something from that last sentence, I feel!

Biblical exegesis occupies a smaller and less prominent position in the first edition of *Science and Health* than in later editions, which would contain a "key to the scripture." Nonetheless, the book does devote large sections to discussing the first two chapters of Genesis[41] and the meaning of Jesus Christ's life and death. Mrs. Eddy has no hesitation in attributing different values to different parts of the Bible. She flatly rejects the story of an angry God exiling Adam and Eve from the Garden of Eden: "A literal acceptation of this quotation [Gen. 3: 22, 23] implies malice, withholding from man the opportunity to reform, lest he should become better; but this is not our God, and so contrary to Love and Wisdom, we must accept it only as the pagan opinions of those re-writing the inspired word" (*Science and Health*,

1e, p. 251). She distinguishes sharply between Genesis 1 and 2, accepting the former as the word of God, and rejecting the latter as the revisionist work of timid scribes: "they spake from error, of error, and from the standpoint of matter attempted to define Spirit, which accounts for the contradistinctions in that glorious old record of creation" (*Science and Health*, 1e, pp. 252–53).

Mrs. Eddy reads Genesis 1 to say that gender is primary in man since God is both male and female:

> Male and female cannot be one in person, but are one in Principle, and if God is a person his gender would be both male and female, these being the likenesses of Him, as the Scripture informs us. . . . Gender is embraced in Spirit, else God could never have shadowed forth from out Himself, the idea of male and female; this idea comes from Soul and not body, from Principle and not person. (*Science and Health*, 1e, p. 236)

With even more daring she claims that woman is the higher of the two since she was the latter to be created: "We have not as much authority in science, for calling God masculine as feminine, the latter being the last, therefore the highest idea given of Him" (*Science and Health*, 1e, p. 238).

In accordance with this lofty idea of woman's place in the divine scheme of things, Mrs. Eddy gives a valiantly revisionist—if, in my view, not wholly convincing—account of the story of Adam and Eve, the apple, and the snake. In the passage which follows, while referring to God as "the voice of Truth," and not "the Lord," and thus rejecting the anthropomorphic image of God as the male owner and defender of his garden, she emphasizes Adam's weakness and cowardice by referring to him as "error," transforms Eve's speech about the serpent into a triumph of spiritual interpretation, and covertly refers to herself as continuing where Eve had led:

> This error, or belief, shrinks from the voice of Truth calling to man, "where, or what, art thou, Soul or personal sense? art thou Spirit or matter?" and belief replied, "I heard thy voice and was afraid." Fear was the first manifestation of the belief of Life in matter, for "the wicked flee when no man pursueth"; fear founded sickness and death. Error was naked, but it could not hide from the eye of Wisdom; and Truth replied, "who told thee thou art naked?" and error fell back on personality, saying, "She gave me of the fruit of knowledge," (a medical work perhaps). Woman, that was taken from my rib (as if man was less the origin of her fault because she was not back under that rib); told me I was in my body, and that Life and sensation are in matter. But when Truth questioned woman regarding the "knowledge" that said matter is intelligent, and personal sense is man, she replied, "The serpent beguiled me, and I did eat." Woman was the first to see the difficulty, owning this knowledge a serpent; as she is the first to lay down the belief that Life originates materially. (*Science and Health*, 1e, p. 249)[42]

Mrs. Eddy does her best to exculpate and exalt mother Eve, to ridicule the idea of creation out of Adam's rib, and, in a later section, to stress the incongruity of Cain knowing a woman and producing offspring when the Bible has mentioned the existence of only one woman so far, Cain's own mother. She ends with an almost Roman Catholic reverence for the Virgin Mary:

> Those who were taught by him [i.e., Jesus] the science of being reached the glorious perception that God is the only author of man. The virgin mother first conceived this idea of God and named it Jesus; the illumination of spiritual sense had put to silence personal sense with Mary, thus mastering material law and establishing through demonstration that God is the father of man. The science of being overshadowed the pure sense of the virgin mother with a full recognition that Spirit is the basis of being. The idea we call Substance, and Mary named Jesus, dwelt forever in the bosom of the Father, in the principle of man, and woman perceived it because of her more spiritual nature. (*Science and Health*, 1e, p. 303)[43]

The metaphysical and theological notions of woman's equality with, or even ontological superiority to, man which Mrs. Eddy elaborates in *Science and Health* are echoed on a much smaller scale in the very short and fragmentary chapter she devotes to marriage. Mrs. Eddy was no political activist and no worker in the vineyards of female suffrage. Her role, she believed, was to provide with her science a new theoretical and spiritual advocacy for the primary equality of the sexes, and the mother-fatherhood of God. But she does make clear that she supports her politically and socially active sisters:

> Law establishes a very unnatural difference between the rights of the two sexes; but science furnishes no precedent for such injustice, and civilization brings, in some measure, its mitigation, therefore it is a marvel that society should accord her less than either. Our laws are not impartial, to say the least, relative to the person, property, and parental claims of the two sexes;[44] and if the elective enfranchisement of woman would remedy this evil without incurring difficulties of greater magnitude, we hope it will be effected. A very tenable means at present, is to improve society in general, and achieve a nobler manhood to frame out laws. If a dissolute husband deserts his wife, it should not follow that the wronged and perchance impoverished woman cannot collect her own wages, or surely claim her own offspring free from his right of interference. (*Science and Health*, 1e, p. 321)

In her view of marriage Mrs. Eddy takes a traditional New Testament line.[45] Convinced that in due course, when Science has triumphed, men and women will be "like angels" and marriage as sexual union will cease, she nonetheless firmly insists on the need to marry in the present imperfect times, and to remain faithful even if the marriage proves imperfect. "Infidelity to the marriage covenant is the social scourge of all peoples" (*Science and Health*, 1e, p. 314). Ideally, she says, in our current circumstances, a married couple should be united in tastes, energies, spiritual goals, and mutual forbearance. Women should not be closeted up in their homes by the "narrowness and jealousy" of their husbands, and men should not spend their time in clubs. "Home is the dearest spot on earth, and should be the center, but not the boundary of the affections," she pointedly remarks. As a divorced woman herself, Mrs. Eddy urges women to exercise the utmost patience and affection when happiness does not at once come to them from marriage, but she recognizes that divorce exists and is necessary in some few, extreme cases. As she remarks ruefully in her final paragraph, "A husband is the best friend, or worst enemy of his wife" (*Science and Health*, 1e, p. 325). Pragmatism and idealism meet in Mrs. Eddy, and, as the development of Christian Science as a movement will show, they make an unusually potent mixture for the advancement of women in society.

A QUIMBYAN POSTSCRIPT
TO *SCIENCE AND HEALTH*

In this chapter, I have argued insistently upon the radical originality of Mrs. Eddy's work in *Science and Health*. Such a view swims against a strong anti–Christian Science current—running, roughly, from Dresser to Peabody to Milmine to Dakin to Bates and Dittemore to Braden to Gardner—which has claimed, and claimed to prove, that *Science and Health* is an unacknowledged recycling of Quimby's ideas, with some insignificant or unfortunate additions by Mrs. Eddy. The following statement from the Bates and Dittemore biography is in this respect typical:

> The chief question that arises in connection with *Science and Health* concerns its relation to Quimby. We may say at once that, as far as the thought is concerned, *Science and Health* is practically all Quimby. Mrs. Glover's one addition was the notion of "malicious malpractice"; every other important idea in the book can be traced to the Portland doctor. The conceptions of God as the sole reality, of the non-being of matter, of the soul as eternal and unchanging, of Christ as the revealer of divinity through mental healing, of disease as error—all these went back to Quimby. The technique of healing was his: the appeal to a higher truth to dispel the patient's error, the efficacy of absent treatment, the cure of children through influencing their parents' beliefs, the acceptance of "chemicalization" (that is, mental disturbances accompanying new ideas) as a phase of the process, the notion that the healer feels in his own person the pains of his patient. Quimby's, too, was the assertion that this system of thought forms a *science*, and his was the very name

which Mrs. Glover ultimately (though not in the first edition of her book) adopted for this science.[46]

As I have shown in Chapter 7, it is impossible to know from the current writings attributed to his name what exactly Quimby himself thought, and, more important, what he had set down in text before Mrs. Eddy came to Portland. In real terms, however, the debate over Mrs. Eddy's plagiarism concentrated solely on one short text, "Questions and Answers," the only text which escaped the custody of George Quimby and which, photostated and quoted at length first in the *New York Times* article of 1904 and then in the *McClure's* series, bore almost the whole brunt of evidence. The evidence turns out on careful scrutiny to be much shakier than first appears.

Horatio Dresser and Georgine Milmine were on firm ground when they claimed that a manuscript which Mrs. Glover gave Sally Wentworth to copy in 1867–1868 was composed in all essentials of the text called "Questions and Answers" ascribed to Phineas Parkhurst Quimby.[47] Mrs. Glover always referred to it as Dr. Quimby's manuscript, and this was the title written on it by Mrs. Wentworth, as illustrated by the Photostat that appears in the Milmine book. It is also accepted by all that by 1868 Mrs. Glover had appended to this text a signed preface of her own—again, a copy of which was partly reproduced by Milmine—and that in the next manifestation of the text, Mrs. Glover's preface had been integrated.

Unfortunately, it was not the project of Milmine and Dresser to show, simply, that, at one point in her development, Mrs. Glover had used and quoted and recommended Quimby's text to her students. They insisted that she had continued to use it, with minor alterations of her own, up to the mid-1870s, had by then given it a new name, or sequence of names "Science of Soul," "Science of Man"—taken it for her own work, used it as the essential basis of her book *Science and Health*, and, finally, incorporated it under the name "Recapitulation" in the third and all subsequent editions.

The problem with this line of argument is that it is untrue, and it is demonstrably untrue to anyone who holds a copy of Quimby's "Questions and Answers" in one hand and Mrs. Eddy's "Science of Man" in the other. Mrs. Eddy's work does use the question-and-answer format—one that Quimby himself, incidentally, used only once in all the 1,300 printed pages of his "writings" that are currently known—but her twenty-four questions and "Quimby's" fourteen are not the same.[48]

How, then, did the anonymous author of the 1904 *New York Times* article and the authors of the "Milmine" series manage to "prove" Mrs. Eddy's plagiarism in their famous double-column comparison? The answer is that out of either bad faith or bad scholarship, they added on to the end of what they labelled the original Quimby text a paragraph from the preface which Mrs. Eddy had written to her copy of Quimby's manuscript. She herself later incorporated this passage into her teaching manuscript, most notably in the copy she gave to Addie Spofford, which passed to her husband Daniel, and at last to Georgine Milmine. Thus Mrs. Eddy's own words were integrated into the Quimby text, compared against her own manuscript, found, not surprisingly, identical, and cited as a flagrant example of plagiarism.

Horatio Dresser was responsible for seeing that this sleight of hand remained unchallenged for another generation. No one was more familiar than Horatio Dresser with the details of the Eddy-Quimby debate, and when he finally received the Quimby papers and was faced with the text of "Questions and Answers," *minus* the notorious paragraph featured in the *New York Times* article and in the Milmine biography, he was on the horns of a dilemma. Should he print the text as it came to him in the Quimby papers, and thus invalidate all the claims made by his parents and himself and their allies over the years, or print the text as before, as if he had never seen the Quimby papers, and make the same claims? His decision was to fudge the issue, to print the text as it had been previously quoted in all the anti-Eddy works, but with a modest note to say that he had appended the final, the crucial, paragraph—from where, and why, he declines to specify.

It is only in the definitive three-volume edition of Quimby's writings edited by Ervin Seale and painstakingly compiled from all the various extant copies that "Questions and Answers" appears without Mrs. Eddy's coda— and dated simply 1862, leaving undecided the question of whether the manuscript was written before, during, or after Mary Baker Glover's first stay in Portland, and what part she may have played in its composition at that time.

Even if we admit the unlikely and the unproven—that P. P. Quimby had already by October 1862 committed to paper all the writings that are today attributed to him, that Mrs. Glover had full access to them and, although able to take a copy only of a small extract, now called "Questions and Answers," retained a virtually photographic memory of the whole—we can still strongly dispute the commonly held view that all the important and interesting parts of Mrs. Eddy's later work are stolen from Quimby. By putting all of Quimby's work before us, without editing, Ervin Seale has enabled us at last to assess for ourselves, without a many-layered screen of polemic and interpretation, the quality of Quimby's mind and his capacity for theoretical thinking. The Quimby writings are so illogical, scattershot, poorly expressed, and, in a word, boring that few readers with no previous interest in Christian Science and New Thought are likely to get past the first pages. I seriously doubt that anyone, confronted with these texts alone, would dub Phineas Parkhurst Quimby a great and original thinker. He was without any doubt an abominable writer, or dictater, despite all the correction and editing done by his numerous amanuenses.

Let me give one example, drawn from the famous "Questions and Answers" text, since it is the one which all the Quimbyites have chosen to stress and to praise. Here is one of the final, and shortest, sequences. I quote from the Seale text:

> Question 12: Do we receive impressions through the senses and do they, acting upon the mind, constitute knowledge?

> Ans. This question is answered by Paul to the Romans, although he did not use the same words. This belief means faith; the peace in the truth was through their belief. Hope is the anchor made fast to truth; belief is the knowledge that we shall attain this truth so that we glory in the tribulation or action of the mind, knowing that it brings patience and patience confidence and confidence experience that we shall obtain the truth. Knowledge is opinions, so when an impression is made on the mind, it produces a chemical change. This comes to the senses and opens a door of hope to the great truth. This hope is the world's knowledge or religion that is used like an anchor to the senses till we ride out the gale of investigation and land in the haven of God or truth.[49]

In comparison with the writings of P. P. Quimby, as revealed in the complete, definitive Seale edition, the 1875 edition of *Science and Health* is a model of English prose and informed reasoning—an odd, idiosyncratic, difficult text which cannot be read in a hurry, but one which carries an intelligent and willing reader along—the kind of book, in other words, that could start a new religion.

13

Spofford
and Eddy

WITH 1875 WE ENTER THE STRANGEST AND MOST dramatic period in Mary Baker Eddy's life, the years when a movement calling itself Christian Science began to attract attention in the Boston area, the years when she married for the third and final time, and when she became embroiled in a series of lawsuits that threatened to destroy everything she had so painfully built up. In this chapter we shall follow the progress of *Science and Health* and discuss the small group of Christian Scientists who gathered around the then Mrs. Glover in her final years in Lynn. Two men are of particular interest, Daniel Spofford and Asa Gilbert Eddy, but we shall also have a new arrival on the scene, Edward Arens, a brief reappearance by an old Maine acquaintance, Sarah Crosby, and we will feel the continuing presence behind the scenes of Richard Kennedy. The pace of activity in our story picks up noticeably as Mrs. Glover buys her first house, receives two marriage proposals, accepts the second, and achieves some local notoriety with press and public for her repeated recourse to the law.

Outwardly, little in Mrs. Glover's life had changed for the better by the end of 1874 when the main part of *Science and Health* was at the printer and she emerged from her self-imposed solitude. Fifty-three years old, divorced, impecunious, a social pariah to many, in constant conflict even with the few friends who remained to her, Mrs. Mary Glover was still poised on the brink of ruin. The changes in her life were inward and spiritual, but they were to prove decisive. She had a sense of purpose, a sense of moving forward, of being at the helm of her own vessel rather than drifting helplessly before the waves, and, even more important, she communicated this strength to other people. Milmine is the first biographer to acknowledge that contrary to all practical logic Mrs. Glover in the early 1870s increasingly emanated a sense of power, authority, and confidence. The idea that her science would be a religion, not just a healing method, seems already to have been present. Richard Kennedy told Milmine that in the days of their partnership, Mrs. Glover had often remarked to him that she would one day establish a great religion which would reverence her as its founder and source. "Richard," she would declare, "you will live to hear the church-bells ring out my birthday."[1] Almost imperceptibly the force that was to make Christian Science was at work, as Mary Baker Glover's inner assurance began to be realized in the outer world.

Samuel Bancroft says that he never knew Mrs. Glover as happy as she was in the later part of 1875, and, apart from the incalculable relief of having finished *Science and Health*, the main reason for this happiness was that she finally largely solved the domestic problems that had plagued her in one form or another since she lost her first husband in 1844. Continuing her peripeteia around the lodging houses of Lynn, in the winter of 1874–1875 Mrs. Glover had taken up lodging at 7 Broad Street, when she noticed that number 8 was up for sale. Long eager to own her own property, Mrs. Glover decided to try to buy the house across the road, and in March she at last moved into her own home, thus realizing a dream she had had for ten years. The house was modest, but its $5,650 purchase price stretched Mrs. Glover to the limit financially. I assume that in order to raise the $2,850 she needed to put down for the purchase of Broad Street, Mrs. Eddy sold the mortgages she owned as income-producing instruments, and she still needed to take out a $2,800 mortgage.

In order to pay the mortgage, Mrs. Glover was obliged to rent out most of the rooms in her new home, retaining for her own use only the front parlors of the first and second floors and the small attic on the third floor, which she made into her bedroom and study. Hot in summer and cold in winter, with natural light only from a skylight, the attic was nonetheless that room of her own that she had longed for and needed. There she installed her rocking chair and bed, and, propping up the manuscript on the cardboard sheet on her knees, there she put the finishing touches on *Science and Health*.

Probably the best portrait of Mrs. Glover at this time, as well as of the man soon to be her husband, Asa Gilbert Eddy, is given by Mary Godfrey Parker.[2] Mrs. Parker's mother, Christiana Godfrey, was a friend of Mary Baker Eddy until her death, and Mary Godfrey was one of the little girls who fell in love with Mrs. Glover and never forgot her. The Parker account is an important counterweight to the Milmine narrative, which relies almost wholly on the testimony of that disappointed suitor and unbalanced believer Daniel Spofford.

Mrs. Godfrey met Mrs. Glover in the dining room at 8 Broad Street, where Mrs. Godfrey's favorite nephew, William Nash, had rented the second floor for his family. Mrs. Nash had not recovered from the birth of her first child, and although William was able to pay for the services of a nurse for his wife and child, he still needed help with the household, so he begged his aunt to come. Mrs. Godfrey took over the family cooking and also provided board for the landlady, according to the Nashes' agreement.

According to Mary Godfrey Parker, although Mrs. Glover ate her meals with the Nashes and shared the second floor with them, she was careful not to intrude into their lives. In particular, she made no attempt to interfere with the medical arrangements of the Nashes, who were committed to conventional treatment. Indeed, when Mrs. Godfrey became concerned about the way the nurse was handling her baby grandniece, it was Mrs. Glover who calmed her down and recommended that she not intervene. But Mrs. Glover did remark upon Mrs. Godfrey's finger; the latter had accidentally plunged a needle into her finger, it had become horribly swollen and painful and was wrapped in tar poultices. According to Mary Godfrey Parker, the day after Mrs. Glover noticed and touched the finger, her mother awoke after her first painless night and found the swelling vastly reduced. Mrs. Glover acknowledged the improvement and begged Mrs. Godfrey to take off the tar poultices and do nothing else to correct the problem but have confidence in healing. In eight days, the finger had healed completely; eventually even the deformation of the nail was corrected.

All this Mrs. Godfrey attributed to Mrs. Glover's healing powers, and so strong was her faith in her new friend that she called upon her in a real family emergency. Little Mary Godfrey was an extremely precious child since both of her brothers had died in infancy. Always delicate and subject to attacks of membranous croup, Mary became terribly ill one winter's night, a few months after her return home to Chelsea from the stay with the Nashes. In despair, Mrs. Godfrey wrapped the sick child up in blankets and took the train to Lynn, despite the vigorous protests of the child's aunt who regarded Mrs. Glover at that time as a disreputable quack. Upon tumbling without warning through the back door of the Broad Street house, the Godfreys were greeted calmly and warmly by Mrs. Glover, and immediately little Mary began to play as if nothing was wrong.

The Godfrey parents were both eternally grateful to Mrs. Glover for her help, and in her turn Mrs. Glover deeply valued Mrs. Godfrey as a friend. Even though Mrs. Godfrey refused to become a Christian Science practitioner, she remained a loyal supporter and recommended and loaned copies of *Science and Health* to interested acquaintances. She was a close enough friend to declare what a barbarian she thought George Glover was when he appeared around Boston in 1887–1888, and even later to tell Mrs. Eddy in no uncertain terms around 1889 that she was making a huge mistake in adopting Ebenezer Foster.[3] One of the personal tragedies of Mary Baker Eddy's life was that her increasing fame and her narrowing focus on her movement lost her regular contact with loving, sensible women friends like Christiana Godfrey.

Mrs. Godfrey visited Mrs. Glover frequently, even after her move to Boston, often taking her daughter with her, but Mary Godfrey Parker's memories of the time in Lynn when she was a very small girl were particularly strong. She remembered adoring Mrs. Glover, being overjoyed when she was invited to sit outside with her mother's friend on the tiny flower-filled balcony at 8 Broad Street, and she was even permitted to enter the attic room where no one else was ever allowed to go. Like so many other children, Mary Godfrey Parker sought out Mrs. Glover's company, and Mrs. Glover for her part seems to have found it relaxing to have a child by her side or in her lap when she wasn't working at her desk or teaching. In later years Mrs. Eddy's lack of proper maternal feeling was to be one of the key accusations made against her by her opponents, but there seems to be every reason to accept that, whatever may have happened between her and her one biological child, she had a marvellous way with children, bringing to her interaction with them a mixture of physical strength and energy, mental firmness, and fun. For me, the testimony of those who as children knew Mrs. Eddy has a particular authority.

No doubt the major reason that Mrs. Glover was so happy in 1875 was that *Science and Health* was at last due to see the light of day, thanks to the financial generosity of her friends George Barry and Elizabeth Newhall who agreed to meet the costs of composing, making the plates, printing, and binding the thousand copies of the planned first edition.[4] Barry also engaged to act as courier and negotiator with the printer, W. F. Brown of Bromfield Street, a job that, even in liberal Boston and at a period when the city was rich in public transportation, was much easier for a man to undertake than for a woman. For her part, Mrs. Glover agreed to read proof and to take no royalty.

The long prepublication period was not without its own stresses, to say the least. W. F. Brown was a job printer, not a book printer, and the company had no expertise with long manuscripts that required careful proofreading. Of the principals involved in the contract with W. F. Brown, only the youthful George Barry had any commercial experience with contracts, production, and marketing, and none of them had any experience at all with the book trade. Not surprisingly, then, problems with their business plan for *Science and Health* were not slow in coming. The plates were made much too early in the book production process, before the composed text could be checked for errors, and the printer's proofs turned out to be a nightmare, for both the

publisher and the author. Not only did the proofs contain hundreds of printing errors, but the printer had taken it upon himself to make unsolicited corrections. He was reportedly a convinced Spiritualist, and the text offended
not only his ideas of conventional prose but also his faith, since the second
chapter of the book was a lengthy attack on Spiritualism.

This was the first, but far from the last, occasion when Mary Baker Eddy
was to encounter barriers on the road to publication, and she would diagnose them as the result of mesmerism, not just chance or inefficiency. For her
part, like many a neophyte writer, with her first edition Mrs. Glover could
not resist the urge to revise her own text. Because the plates had already been
made, each correction, to her distress, had to be made without a change in
the number of letters per line or the organization of paragraphs, if further
costs were to be avoided. On being informed by the publisher that the proofs
contained no more than the normal proportion of errata, Mrs. Glover was
obliged to go into Boston herself and show him that a single chapter had hundreds of mistakes.

Even after the difficulties with the proofs had been dealt with, if not truly
resolved, for some unknown reason in early 1875 the book was held up for several months.[5] Later Mrs. Eddy regarded this delay as providential since during the delay she wrote a new chapter, and she also discovered that there was
already a book in print under the title of *The Science of Life*. After casting
around for another title, she settled on *Science and Health*. The book finally
became available for sale in October of 1875, and in 1876 Mrs. Glover had the
first three copies off the presses bound in leather and inscribed with the names
of Elizabeth (Newhall), Daniel (Spofford), and Florence (Cheney Barry).[6]

Daniel Spofford's active involvement in the publication of *Science and
Health* heralded a new and, as it proved, turbulent era in Mrs. Glover's life.[7]
Spofford, then about thirty-three, was a tall, handsome man, born in Mrs.
Glover's native state and possessed of a winning combination of visionary
zeal and business energy. The younger of two brothers, Daniel had lost his
father, Asenas Spofford, when he was only ten months old, and during his
youth he had been forced to quit school early and work as a hired laborer to
put bread on the table for his mother Rachel and his older brother. At some
point Mrs. Spofford and her two young sons moved to Lynn, Massachusetts,
where she remarried, and Daniel went into the shoe business. At age nineteen he joined the Union army and served with courage and distinction, surviving many famous battles, until his unit was disbanded in 1864. Apparently
he limped all his life from a Civil War wound. Given the strong parallels
between the experiences of Daniel Spofford and Mary's son, George Glover,
it is perhaps not surprising that Mrs. Glover immediately took Daniel to her
heart and showed him unusual favor.

In 1867, Daniel married a young woman from Lynn, Mary Adeline
Nourse, usually called "Addie," an old schoolfriend of "Putney" Bancroft,

Daniel's foreman at the shoe company of Bancroft and Purinton. Addie was one of Mrs. Glover's first students. She was the one who gave her husband her copy of Mrs. Glover's teaching manuscript, and who introduced Bancroft to Mrs. Glover very shortly before the Spoffords decided to move to Knoxville, Tennessee, and she went into healing practice.

What precisely happened to Daniel and Addie between 1872 and 1875 is not known, but, as we have seen in Chapter 11, Mrs. Glover alleged that Addie had a long-term affair with Richard Kennedy and had also possibly been the object of the attentions of her sometime partner in practice Wallace Wright. By 1873, the Spoffords had split up—Daniel claimed in his later divorce suit that his wife had left him—and Daniel returned to Lynn, eager to work as a mental healer, a career which, rather against his wife's wishes, he had begun to dabble in in Tennessee. When Mrs. Glover moved into 8 Broad Street, she at once advertised classes again, and, as soon as the date of the first class was fixed, she wrote to Spofford to invite him to attend; she charged him no tuition. Daniel was an instant success, rapidly becoming Mrs. Glover's favorite student yet managing to maintain good relationships with the earlier students, notably George Barry. By April 26, Daniel was writing the kind of Biblically influenced prose Mrs. Glover was most susceptible to, and she was assuring him that he had missed nothing by "her"—that is, the unnamable Addie's—refusal to instruct him in Mrs. Glover's Science. "She" never had understood it, Mrs. Glover wrote, had refused to reply to Mrs. Glover's questions in class, and even refused to look at her.

Not content with words, Daniel—to whom Mrs. Glover, in a sign of high favor, had already assigned the pet name of Harry—was proving a man of action by organizing his fellow students to put up the money to rent a hall for Mrs. Glover to preach in, and to pay her $5 for her sermon.[8] In June eight students put up the modest total of $10 and resolved to constitute a society with a president, a secretary, and a treasurer in order to promote "the Science of Life," and taking the name of Christian Scientists.[9] The importance of this small event may be judged by the fact that it was at this point that Mary Baker Glover withdrew from membership at the Tilton Congregational Church.

Spofford had also been roped into helping in the final stages of the preparation of *Science and Health*. Although he had not made it through grammar school, he was later to claim in his own publications that he had been the editor of the first edition of Mrs. Eddy's work. It was to Spofford that Mrs. Eddy sounded one of the recurring themes of her publishing history—the complaint that a hostile mind was impeding the printing process:

> The blow I received before my dear students went out I could not quite conceal when I found my proofs were missing, for I had suffered from just such conduct before and from the same person. I knew Mr. Prescott had not kept them but I knew he had under the roof with him a <u>thief</u> that would not only rob God but steals from man (or woman rather)

Mr. Prescott called to-day and told me he had no knowledge of it and I knew the chapter on healing was with the proofs I let him read. But this <u>whole</u> chapter had been ferreted away and what should I do if there was no other copy? O Mr. Spofford you have not the faintest conception of the hidden evil that is in that wicked student. I had hoped nothing would bring him up before the class but you see the providence that compels me to speak of him <u>as he is</u> They ask me how he can heal, I answer, as Stanley and the other mesmerisers heal.[10]

Obviously Mrs. Eddy was unable to stop herself talking about mesmerism in her classes and was still obsessing about the hostile powers of Richard Kennedy.

By the spring of 1876, Spofford had moved in as one of Mrs. Glover's tenants at 8 Broad Street, had settled down to a flourishing practice bringing in some forty dollars a week, and was the leading light in the little Christian Scientist group. From the letters he wrote to Mrs. Glover at this time, and from her replies, it is clear that he was completely captivated by her doctrine and regarded her with a kind of adoration. The various printed and private documents that Spofford left behind at his death indicate that Spofford was in fact permanently imprinted by Mary Baker Eddy's ideas.[11] Milmine, after commenting on the extraordinary spiritual exaltation Mrs. Eddy induced in her students, reports specifically:

Mr. Spofford still says that no price could be put upon what Mrs. Glover gave her students, and that the mere manuscripts he had formerly studied were, compared to her expounding of them, as the printed page of a musical score compared to its interpretation by a master.[12]

The happy relationship between Daniel Spofford and Mrs. Glover lasted no more than a year, and it may have been imperilled before that time by his infatuation with her as a person as well as a teacher. Mrs. Glover was still a very attractive woman, looking far younger than her age, and it seems probable that despite the twenty-year disparity in their ages, Spofford for a time had more than a filial regard for his teacher,[13] and this attraction vastly complicated their relationship.

The biggest hitch in Spofford's matrimonial project was that he was still married to Addie, and Mrs. Glover knew this. Divorce in the United States was a relatively easy matter, however, and Daniel was confident he had good grounds for divorce and good witnesses, notably his mother, to help him establish them. Essex County Court documents prove that on October 21, 1876, Daniel Spofford libelled his wife, Mary Adeline Spofford (here referred to as Mary), as an adulteress and requested a divorce.

And your libellant shows that he has always conducted himself as a faithful and chaste husband to said Mary; but that said Mary, being wholly regardless of her duty in that regard, has upon divers days and times since the beginning of 1872, at Lynn aforesaid and in Boston . . . committed the crime of adultery with one John Eddy:—and especially since said month of July 1875, has repeatedly committed adultery with said Eddy, at said Boston.[14]

Spofford's attempt to obtain a divorce failed in 1876, even though Addie was successfully "served" with the summonses to appear and answer the libel charges, and, indeed, she had the gall to exploit the fact that married women had no independent standing at law by requesting that her husband pay her $50 so that she could prepare her defense against his libel of her. Daniel remained technically married to Addie until 1880, when she successfully filed an uncontested suit against him from Tennessee, on the grounds of desertion.

In "Demonology" Mrs. Eddy claims that Daniel Spofford's hopes of a quick divorce in 1876 were dramatically dashed when upon appearing in court his devoted mother altered her prepared testimony that supported his divorce petition. Mrs. Eddy blames mesmerism, and therefore Richard Kennedy, for this weird turn of events. I am inclined to speculate that Daniel's mother, however unenthusiastic she may have been about her errant daughter-in-law Addie, was unprepared to offer testimony about the purported adultery with the mysterious John Eddy, especially if this testimony would pave the way for her darling son to marry another dubious woman who was twice his age!

How did Mrs. Eddy react to Spofford's feelings for her? Most of her critics have implied, and assumed, that she actively encouraged her young suitor. Without actually accusing Mrs. Glover of nymphomania, as Frederick Peabody had done, and without, apparently, getting wind of Edward Hitchings—the man Bancroft says aspired to Mrs. Glover's hand around 1874—Milmine intimates that the founder of Christian Science had a distinct taste for men younger than herself. This allegation may well have been part of the local gossip the *McClure's* team picked up in Lynn, since hostility of quite a personal and palpable kind was her daily experience during her Lynn years according to Robert Peel:

> For a woman to preach, lecture, write for the newspapers, challenge the doctors and the clergy, claim a new religious revelation and a new scientific discovery—all this was in itself enough to make her an object of suspicion to cautious Yankees. But for a divorced woman to do these things—even though her husband had been the guilty party—put her clearly outside the pale of provincial acceptability. . . . Mrs. Glover was charged with rouging her cheeks and dyeing her hair, with teaching "free love" and practicing witchcraft, with being a loose woman, a despoiler of homes, a medium, a fraud, a termagant. The coming and going of men students at 8 Broad street was given the most sinister possible

significance; the respectable women in her circle were said to be held to her by a sort of hypnotic spell. It is small wonder that credulous parents hurried their children past her house as though it were a den of arcane iniquity.[15]

Milmine could hint at Mary Baker Eddy's sexual proclivities, but it was difficult to bolster raw gossip with precise fact, and this was where Spofford's eager cooperation with *McClure's* proved so useful. "Putney" Bancroft, George Barry, and George Allen were all at some time devoted to Mrs. Glover and were probably among those youths whose ready access to Mrs. Glover's apartments scandalized the neighbors. But any serious case of improper relations with these gentlemen was hard to make since they were family men, married to young women whom Mrs. Glover had approved or even chosen for them. In Spofford, however, *McClure's* found a handsome, virile man (the series included three pictures of him, in youth and old age, amply proving his good looks) willing to admit that he had nourished warm feelings toward Mrs. Glover at one period, and with epistolary evidence to indicate that she had nourished equally warm feelings toward him. As I have noted, the Milmine-*McClure's* account makes no mention at all of Addie and the Spoffords' interesting marital history.

The most important expression of Mrs. Glover's feelings for "Harry" is a much-quoted letter which she wrote to him on December 30, 1876. I shall quote from it again because it is a typical example of Mrs. Glover's over-wrought style at this period and shows her obsession with mesmerism:

Dr. Spofford won't you exercise <u>reason</u> and let me live or will you <u>kill me</u>? Your mind is just what has brought on my relapse and I shall never <u>recover</u> if you do not govern yourself and <u>turn your thoughts</u> wholly away from me. Do for God's sake and the work I have before me let me get out of this suffering I never was worse than last night and you say you wish to do me good and I do not doubt it. Then won't you <u>quit thinking</u> of me. I shall write no more to a male student and never more trust one to live with me. It is a <u>hidden</u> foe that is at work read Science and Health page 193, 1st par.

<u>No student</u> nor mortal has tried to have you leave me that I know of. Dr. Eddy has tried to have you stay you are in a <u>mistake</u>, it is <u>God</u> and not man that has separated us and for the reason I <u>begin</u> to learn. Do not think of returning to me again I shall never again trust a <u>man</u>. They know not what manner of temptations assail God produces the separation and I submit to it so must you. There is no cloud between us but the way you set me up for a Dagon is wrong and now I implore you to turn forever from this error of personality and go alone <u>to God</u> as I have taught you.

It is <u>mesmerism</u> that I feel and is killing me it is <u>mortal</u> mind that only can make me suffer. Now stop thinking of me or you will cut me off <u>soon</u> from the face of the earth.[16]

Milmine implies that this letter proves that Mrs. Glover was feverishly combating her attraction for Daniel Spofford, but I think this is a misreading. We know that Spofford wanted to marry her. Charles Dyer, Spofford's great-grandson, says that, according to a family story passed down to him, Daniel proposed to Mrs. Glover one day and drew out a pistol when she refused him. She kept her head, told him to put away the gun, and he obeyed. Daniel Spofford must have been the source of this incident, which is good evidence of his passionate feelings and her calm refusal. Spofford's advances were profoundly inconvenient, embarrassing, contrary to her doctrine, and harmful to the cause which was the focus of her life. Daniel's words may all have been of chaste devotion, but it was pretty clear that he was looking for a wife, not a spiritual mentor, and, more important, that he believed himself ordained as, at the least, coleader of the new Christian Science movement. As a divorced woman, Mrs. Glover had serious social and legal problems, but a liaison with Daniel Spofford was no solution to these. Perhaps she may have been flattered by the attentions of a young, attractive man, but more probably she felt a new fear that she would be unable to control his propensity for violence. The extreme agitation she expressed in her oft-quoted letter, begging Spofford to leave her in peace, is surely more easily explained in terms of fear than of sexual attraction.

From the point of view of Mrs. Glover's future development as a religious leader, even more crucial than her urgent refusal to compromise herself with a young married man was her insistence that Daniel give up "the error of personality" and cease to set her up "as a Dagon"—that is, as an idol of worship. Increasingly, for the rest of her life, Mary Baker Eddy would be faced with two diametrically opposite problems or challenges. The first, most apparent, and probably the most emotionally painful problem came from the attacks to which she was subjected by people outside her movement. The second challenge, weirdly counterbalancing the attacks from without, was the adoration she received from within her movement, and which she came to regard as spiritually a far more serious danger as it was in violation of the first commandment. She was to struggle against what she termed the error of personality for the rest of her life.

As Daniel Spofford's fortunes waned, those of Asa Gilbert Eddy grew, since Mary Baker Glover was to turn to this man as a solution to her personal and social problems. The defensive reference Mrs. Glover made to Dr. Eddy in the urgent communication to Spofford I quoted earlier is significant since this famous letter was written only hours before her wholly unexpected announcement of her coming marriage to Asa Gilbert Eddy. Daniel Spofford gave the *McClure's* group an entertaining but presumably not unbiased account of the extraordinary circumstances under which the Eddy marriage took place. He said that within hours of receiving the strangely passionate letter from Mrs. Glover which I quoted above, he received a visit from Asa Gilbert Eddy, asking him to go at once to the Unitarian minister and arrange the wedding for himself and Mrs. Glover on the following day. Questioned, Eddy admitted that he had not at all anticipated getting married, and Spofford said he was surprised to see that the marriage license showed the ages of both bride and groom as forty, since Mrs. Glover was at this time "in her fifty-sixth year." How Daniel Spofford knew Mrs. Glover's age at this stage we do not know, but the clear implication of the Spofford account as told to *McClure's* is that poor Asa Gilbert Eddy had been coerced into marriage by a woman who had even lied about her age. Eddy, incidentally, was about forty-five at the time, though his exact date of birth has never been established.

In any case, the marriage between Mrs. Glover and Mr. Eddy took place at 8 Broad Street on January 1, 1877, without any kind of celebration. On the thirty-first of that month a small surprise party with cake and lemonade and wedding gifts was held for the couple by their friends, but, despite the party, the little Lynn Christian Science group was both astounded and furious about their leader's marriage.

Asa Gilbert Eddy had joined the small band of Christian Scientists only in March of 1876, but by July, according to a letter Mrs. Glover wrote to her cousin Hattie Baker in Boston, he had already made a deep impression on her. She had had a "violent seizure"—presumably the same kind of fit that Bancroft reported in his diary in 1872—and Eddy, "calm, clear and strong, and so kind," had successfully brought her out of it. "Never before had I seen his <u>real</u> character, so tender and yet so controlling. Hattie, you would change your views of him if you were to read him spiritually," she wrote. It seems that Cousin Hattie had been one of those less than impressed upon first meeting "Gilbert," as Mrs. Glover was soon calling him.[17]

Spofford also claimed to have been the man who actually introduced Asa Gilbert Eddy to his future wife, but it seems more likely that in fact they met through the good offices of Mrs. Christiana Godfrey. According to Mary Godfrey Parker, Asa Gilbert Eddy had become a close friend of her family after he sold a Singer sewing machine to her mother. Mrs. Parker says in her reminiscences that as a small child she looked forward to Mr. Eddy's visits because he was so kind and such a good playmate. She describes Eddy's wonderful smile and disputes the Milmine claim that he dressed his hair in a high pompadour swept straight back off the brow, then called a roach, and ridiculously curled under at the back. The most frequently reproduced portrait of Asa Eddy features him with the roach, but one can also see the gentle eyes and sweet smile Mary Godfrey Parker remembered. Although adopting a silly hairdo might be thought a peccadillo too common in young men to justify comment,[18] this apparently minor detail about Eddy's appearance is important because the Milmine description of Asa Gilbert Eddy's hair is part of a consistent effort to portray him as effeminate, and thus to ridicule Mary Baker Eddy's third marriage.

According to Mrs. Mary Godfrey Parker, Asa Gilbert Eddy would listen avidly to the tales of life at sea told by her father and his friends who all came of old seagoing families from Maine. He may have been fascinated because the dangers and hardships met routinely by sailors were so far outside his own physical powers. "He was not strong," writes Mrs. Parker, "being subject to terrible attacks of illness, which I seem to remember hearing Mother speak of as heart trouble."[19] Everything we know points to the fact that Asa Gilbert Eddy had from early youth, or before, suffered from an incapacitating, life-threatening heart condition which he struggled with constantly and uncomplainingly. This was his personal tragedy, but it is an important key to his character, and it was an inconvenient matter for traditional medicine and alternative healing alike to deal with. Sneering at his physical frailty, as the Milmine book does, is, to say the least, unfair.

When Eddy was first introduced to Mrs. Glover, he was earning his living as a sewing-machine salesman, an unexalted profession which is easy to make fun of, but he had taken to this vocation only when the work of running a spinning jack in a woolen mill had proved too much for his strength. Born into a large rural New Hampshire family, poorly educated, forced from early childhood to fend for himself and turn his hand to every task, Asa Gilbert Eddy was also thrifty, industrious to a fault, and, in his own strange and quiet way, ambitious. I think that his poor health came as a terrible disappointment to his hopes of moving up in society, as well as being a personal burden of pain and anxiety.

To get back to 1875 and the dramatic healing of Christiana Godfrey's infected finger, Mrs. Godfrey returned to Chelsea from her visit to the Nashes full of talk of the wonderful Mrs. Glover, and she strongly advised her friend Asa Gilbert Eddy to go to Lynn to consult Mrs. Glover and perhaps become one of her students. Eddy followed the advice, professed to feeling remarkably better from the treatment, and became deeply interested in the new science. By the summer Eddy had given up sewing-machine sales and was challenging Barry and Spofford for the title of Mrs. Glover's most beloved student, to the deep chagrin of both. *Science and Health* was not selling well, and Mrs. Glover decided that a more vigorous campaign needed to be waged. She selected Daniel Spofford as the man for the job. Showing the extent of his devotion, Spofford agreed not only to take on the advertising and marketing of *Science and Health* as a full-time job, but also to give up his flourishing and lucrative healing practice to the newly minted Dr. Eddy.

Spofford may have accepted Mrs. Glover's fiat, but he was conspicuously unhappy with the way things were developing and jealous of Eddy. Mrs. Glover for her part was under extraordinary pressure. She was trying very hard to foster a new generation of students while keeping the old ones happy and successful in their practice, as well as to write new material and make the eternal corrections to her book. There was also quite a lot of house-work to be done, people like the Godfreys unexpectedly turning up with sick children to heal, and of course the mortgage payments to make. There was the constant pressure of people, practitioners like Miss Rawson and patients like Miss Lucretia Brown, wanting to tap her time and energy, to feel the magic of her presence, to take in the spell of her words. With all these pres-sures the rivalry between Eddy and Spofford was threatening to destroy the fragile balance that had been created since the break with Kennedy, and, not surprisingly, Mrs. Eddy felt physically and psychologically beset.[20]

She was suffering from what she herself hated to call illness and fatigue. In March 1877 George Barry had brought suit against her for $2,700 for ser-vices rendered, notably in copying *Science and Health*, but also for acting as her financial agent, buying her stamps and car tickets, carrying her coal, and putting down her carpets. This suit was to drag on until October 1879, when the judge awarded Barry a mere $395.40, but it was painful for Mrs. Glover to have the smallest details of her life discussed in court, and to have the man who had once called her mother and hung on her every word testifying against her, along with other former students and friends. From her letters of the period, notably those to Daniel Spofford, we might diagnose Mrs. Glover as a woman on the edge of a nervous breakdown. She diagnosed her-self as a victim of various kinds of mental attack—the continuing conscious attacks still directed by the evil Kennedy and his associates, but also the unconscious reaching out for help of her students and patients. She begged Spofford to tell people to *stop thinking about her* and give her the time and rest she needed to do the promised work on the book.

The most surprising, but also the most intelligent, thing Mrs. Glover did to try to address the difficulties of her life at this time was to marry Asa Gilbert Eddy. Whether Eddy had nurtured silent hopes of such a marriage or whether, as the Daniel Spofford account has it, he never thought about it until the night the proposal was made, is probably not important. All the evi-dence shows that Asa Gilbert Eddy adored his wife, that he and she had that union of tastes, interests, and characters which she had apostrophized as ideal in *Science and Health*, and that he never regretted the five years he spent married to Mary, even though the remarkable stresses occasioned by their union surely accelerated his death.

As they did with Mrs. Eddy's two earlier husbands, biographers have puzzled over why she married this particular man, though the marital imper-fections of Asa Gilbert Eddy were of a very different kind as compared with those of George Glover and Daniel Patterson. Whereas her two previous husbands were conspicuously tall, strong, sexually compelling men, Eddy was short and subject to ill health, and his financial position was barely more secure than Mrs. Glover's own at the time of their union. Milmine and those biographers who have followed her imply that poor little cloddish Asa Gilbert Eddy, or Gilbert as Mrs. Eddy called him, was pushed willy-nilly into proposing marriage to a demented and domineering woman who saw in him nothing but a useful and obedient man-of-all-work, and there is some truth in this. Gilbert did prove to be very useful: he was willing to work as hard as his wife, which was saying something, and he was never known to publicly go against her wishes or to contradict her even in her most extreme, exalted, and unreasonable moments. Nonetheless we would be wrong to dismiss theirs as a one-sided marriage of convenience.

Eddy had served a long apprenticeship for the exceptionally demanding role of consort to the founder of Christian Science. His father, also called Asa, had been an average hardscrabble farmer, but his mother, if we are to believe the colorful account given us in the Milmine biography, was a woman of such exceptional or eccentric stamp that she left an indelible impression on her neighbors. Mother to seven children, of whom Asa Gilbert was the sixth, it is said that she paid little attention to childcare or housework and left her brood to bring themselves up as best they might. I conjecture that Eddy's heart trouble may have been caused by rheumatic fever contracted during his neglected northern childhood. All the children, male and female, had little formal education but learned to turn their hand to almost any practical task. All in adulthood left the farming life to become skilled craftsmen. Gilbert learned to spin and weave at home on his mother's oft-neglected equipment. It is also said that he was a very slow learner, famous in school only for his penmanship. But he is said to have been an excellent shot. His sister-in-law, Mrs. Washington Eddy, told Milmine that whenever he visited her he always helped with the housework and "could do up a shirt as well as any woman."[21] His willingness to supplement all his many other tasks with a little cooking and cleaning aroused the derision of his wife's enemies, but these propensities might well endear him to a woman reader today.[22]

Milmine devotes more than a page to detailing the further peculiarities of Mr. Eddy's mother. The author tells us that as soon as she could get rid of her children, Betsey Eddy spent her days driving about the neighborhood:

> This drive usually lasted all day, and it was the one thing that was performed with promptness and regularity in the Eddy ménage. To protect herself from rough weather on these expeditions, Mrs. Eddy devised an ingenious costume. From the front of her large poke bonnet she hung a shawl, in which was inserted a 9 x 10 pane of window glass, so placed that when she donned the costume the glass was opposite her face. This handy contrivance kept out the wind or rain or snow, without obscuring her vision: and thus equipped Mrs. Eddy daily defied the vagaries of Vermont weather. The children of the village called her "the woman with the looking-glass."

This is colorful stuff, but I wish the reporters for *McClure's Magazine* had thought to ask for how many years this pattern of behavior persisted, where the neighborhood thought Mrs. Betsey Eddy was going, and what she did when she got there. The other important point Milmine makes about Mrs. Betsey Eddy was that she distrusted traditional medicine and relied on the healing skills of "Sleeping Lucy," a nearby clairvoyant of considerable local fame who went into trance in order to diagnose illness and prescribe remedies. Whatever may have been the true caliber of Mrs. Betsey Eddy as wife and mother, she was clearly not a conventional Victorian materfamilias.[23]

Asa Gilbert Eddy was not an articulate man—he neither spoke nor wrote much—but the few papers he left show that beneath the quiet, stolid exterior there was a mind of burning, evangelical zeal that thrilled to thoughts of apocalypse, of hell and damnation, of Revelation. The spiritual exaltation which characterized Mrs. Glover's oratory and to which, as all her students testify, she was capable of inspiring others acted perhaps more strongly and lastingly on Asa Gilbert Eddy than on anyone else. Gilbert Eddy had a fervent willingness to accept his wife on her own high estimation, to see her as the special instrument of God, as the appointed, destined leader of a new religion. Female spouses have not infrequently felt and manifested such devout admiration for their mates, and their devotion is usually perceived as admirable, even when, as was not the case with the Eddys, it proves undeserved.

One of the first persons to learn the surprising news of Mary Baker Glover's marriage to Mr. Eddy was Mrs. Sarah Crosby, with whom the former Mrs. Patterson had been so intimate in the Portland days and with whom she had renewed correspondence.[24] The then Mrs. Glover first reestablished contact with Mrs. Crosby in November 1876 in the hope that her friend would agree to become a selling agent in Maine for copies of *Science and Health*. Mrs. Crosby's response to the offer of a 33 percent commission for each copy sold has not survived, but it must have been positive since the newly minted Mrs. Eddy once again contacted her "Darling 'Sa'" on January 17, 1877, and asked her to come to Lynn and make a written record of the courses she was planning to give.[25] It has variously been asserted that this transcript was to be copied and distributed to the students, or else it was to serve as the basis for Asa Gilbert Eddy's proposed course. Mrs. Crosby was tickled to death at her old friend's new name—"Oh Mary, I am crazy to know about your husband, I am so glad you are married & I do hope & trust you have a noble husband"—but she was also very cautious about getting the financial arrangements for her proposed visit to Lynn clearly worked out in advance.

On January 20 Mrs. Eddy specified to Mrs. Crosby that her course would last three weeks, would entail classwork of some three hours a day for six or seven days, two to three hours on three days in the second week, and two days with the same hours on the third week. She offered Mrs. Crosby board and lodging at her home, agreed to pay her estimated travelling expenses, and stipulated that her friend not take away with her any copy of the transcript she was to prepare. In a postscript that turned out to have ominous implications, Mrs. Eddy noted that Mrs. Crosby would have the opportunity to listen for free to lessons for which the students were charged $200.[26] By return of post Mrs. Crosby agreed to undertake the work for $3 a day, plus board and expenses, and again by return Mrs. Eddy agreed to the terms and asked Mrs. Crosby to come to Lynn in the second week of February.

From the accounts Mrs. Crosby later gave to various people about her stay in Lynn it seems that dissension and suspicion marked the relation between the two former friends almost from the beginning of this arrangement. Mrs. Eddy was persuaded that she was giving Sarah an unrivalled opportunity to improve her financial position simply by attending the classes, and she refused to pay the agreed $3 per diem. Mrs. Crosby for her part claimed that she was terrified by her friend's hostility, that she had to barricade herself in her room at night because the door did not lock. She narrated that at one point Mrs. Eddy asked her to come to her bedroom and sit hidden behind a curtain to take down the conversation which she planned to have with Daniel Spofford. This scheme proved unnecessary since the wary Spofford did not appear as summoned. At the end of her visit, Mrs. Crosby threatened to sue the Eddys for the money due her, and she was setting out to interview lawyers when Mr. Eddy intervened and begged her not to leave the house without seeing his wife one more time. Mrs. Crosby travelled back to Maine with her fees, but not her travelling expenses. Mrs. Crosby is a notably unreliable source, and we have no corroboration for her account of the visit to Lynn in 1876. I doubt that any dramatic break occurred between her and Mrs. Eddy. That Mrs. Crosby conceived a grudge against her successful friend is clear, however, and was to have serious repercussions. As we saw in Chapter 8, Mrs. Crosby was to become the first named witness willing to publicly accuse Mrs. Eddy of being a Spiritualist and of having stolen her healing system from P. P. Quimby.

After Mrs. Crosby had gone off seething, Mrs. Eddy was faced with the ongoing problems of her book and her students, notably Daniel Spofford who was also the publisher and marketing agent for *Science and Health*. Back in April 1876 Spofford had bought out Barry's and Newhall's interest for $146, surely a bargain,[27] and negotiated a new contract with the then Mrs. Glover whereby he guaranteed sales of a thousand copies and agreed to provide her with monthly accountings of the sales and to give her a 10 percent royalty. She, for her part, committed herself to doing the corrections for a new edition as soon as possible, but within weeks the parties to the agreement were at war. Spofford complained that Mrs. Eddy was putting her time and energies into teaching, which brought immediate revenue, rather than editing and writing, and he was anxious to have a new, corrected edition which he felt would do better than the first. For her part, Mrs. Eddy demanded an accounting in vain from Spofford and received no royalty payments.

In April Mrs. Eddy felt so beset by the demands of her students and patients that she decided to go away for some five weeks with her husband to a place (in fact his brother's home in Fairfield, Connecticut) which no one knew and whither no one could, therefore, direct any thoughts. She wrote to Spofford on April 14:

> *Dear Student*
> This hour of my departure I pick up from the carpet a piece of paper & write you a line to say <u>I am</u> at length driven into the wilderness. Everything needs me in Science, my doors are thronged the book lies waiting but those who <u>call on me mentally</u> in suffering are in belief killing me! <u>Stopping my work</u> that none but I can do in their supreme selfishness. . . .
> Don't tell students they can call on me—if they do it deliberately it amounts to thrusting a dagger in my heart.[28]

The trip away did not help matters, and upon returning to a Boston hotel Mrs. Eddy continued to write pleadingly to Spofford that she was on her deathbed, saved only by the constant efforts of her husband, and that she was quite unable to do any work. On April 19, however, she wrote a long business letter to Spofford, detailing her plan for the second edition and asking him to sign a new agreement giving him a three-year interest in the book, but increasing her royalty to 25 percent.

In July Spofford sent to Mrs. Eddy a final accounting for the first edition of *Science and Health* and told her that he had forfeited the agreement he had with her to publish the next edition.[29] She and Spofford accused each other of financial misdemeanors and embarked on a campaign to discredit each other.[30] The Christian Scientist Association wrote formally in November to ask Spofford to return the funds he had collected to finance Mrs. Eddy's lectures, and in January 1878 he was expelled from the movement on the grounds of "immorality and as unworthy to be a member." Let me note that Daniel Spofford was almost certainly living with a young woman not yet his wife at this date, and thus the charge of "immorality" had some basis in fact. A notice to this effect was published in the Newburyport *Herald*, the local newspaper of the town where Spofford had set up practice. Mrs. Eddy also wrote to request that he return to her the gold pen she had ceremonially presented to him as the pen which had written *Science and Health*. Spofford disdainfully sent back the lecture funds, some twenty dollars, but he refused to return the pen, which is now in the Longyear Museum.[31]

All concerned in this dispute, the mild Mr. Eddy as well as his wife and her antagonist, viewed it, literally, in apocalyptic terms and quoted Revelation and Lamentations against one another in letters and notebooks. The flames of dispute were fanned by the arrival on the Christian Science scene of a new student, Edward J. Arens, who subscribed to the idea of Malicious Animal Magnetism even more enthusiastically than did Mrs. Eddy, and whose radical plans for counteracting it appealed to her more than anything Mr. Eddy could propose.

Stress was endemic to Mrs. Eddy's way of life at this time, but she probably hoped that she was at least on the road to resolving her financial woes, especially now that she was married. In fact, however, the marriage had brought on a financial crisis: Mr. Eddy was forced to withdraw from his practice to help Mrs. Eddy with her teaching, and thus the Eddys lost a good source of income; and the alienation of Spofford and Barry was creating a split in the embryonic movement that was costly in dollars as well as energy. By the beginning of 1878 the Eddys' financial situation had become dire. Money was needed to publish the new edition, George Barry's suit was threatening the title to the precious home on 8 Broad Street,[32] and then Mr. Eddy lost all his savings when his bank defaulted.

Mrs. Eddy's response to this dire situation was an unprecedented one—she went to court. She undertook a series of suits for breach of contract against students who had signed her standard agreement promising to pay her a proportion of their earnings yet had failed to do so. The targeted defendants were Richard Kennedy, Daniel Spofford, and Charles Stanley and George Tuttle. Mrs. Eddy later insisted that all these suits were undertaken on her behalf by Edward Arens who assured her that he would act for her, and that she need not appear or pay any expenses.[33] I must say I do not really understand why Mrs. Eddy decided at this point to entrust her interests to Arens. He was a rank newcomer to the movement, a man about whom nothing was known except that he had violent enthusiasms. He was a native German whose understanding of the American legal process was at best untested, and whose still imperfect command of the English language made him a dubious advocate. Relying on Arens proved to be one of Mrs. Eddy's worst lapses of judgment, and one for which she was to pay dearly.

The first suit, and perhaps the most emotionally charged, was heard in March of 1878. The defendant was Richard Kennedy. Mrs. Eddy produced an 1870 letter of agreement signed by herself and Kennedy, whereby in compensation for the two years of instruction in healing which she had given him since 1868, he contracted to pay her $1,000. It was conceded by both parties to the suit that Kennedy had paid $250, and Mrs. Eddy was seeking to recover the remaining $750, plus interest and costs. The letter of agreement cited in the suit was quite separate from the other one whereby Kennedy had contracted to pay the then Mrs. Glover 50 percent of the income he earned from healing during their Lynn partnership from 1870 to 1872, and which he had faithfully disbursed. Kennedy admitted that he had signed the letter brought in evidence by the plaintiff, but in his court testimony he said that he had signed the letter as a special favor to Mrs. Glover, who told him she would use it only as an advertising tool to prove the worth of her tuition to prospective students. He also testified that in 1870 Mrs. Glover was claiming that she still had a final secret of healing to impart to him, but that she had never revealed this information, and that he now doubted that any such secret existed. But the main grounds on which Kennedy contested Mrs. Eddy's suit were, first, that he had not received anything of value from her, and, second, that the contract was null under the statute of limitations.

The case of Eddy versus Kennedy was heard before a judge and resulted in a verdict for the plaintiff (Mrs. Eddy), who was awarded $768.63. Mrs. Eddy did not appear in court or testify. The judge decreed that the statute of limitations did not apply, and he noted that the defendant admitted signing the letter, and that by his earlier payment of $250 Kennedy showed that he felt himself bound by the agreement. The nature and content of Mrs. Eddy's teaching was not at issue, the judge noted. The fact that Kennedy had gone into partnership with Mrs. Eddy and had made a good living practicing something along the lines of what she had preached cast doubt on Kennedy's contention that her teaching was not of value.

Kennedy appealed the verdict. As he was to explain in a letter to Lyman Powell in 1907, he was deeply dissatisfied with the advice he had received from his lawyer, and he had never been confident that a hearing before a judge using the statute of limitations defense was his best tactic. He claimed that in the six years since their partnership had broken up, the relations between himself and Mrs. Eddy had become venomous, and he was particularly outraged to be sued for money when he felt he had acted more than generously toward her. He told Powell that not only had he split the income from his practice with her down the middle, but he had paid his and her common living expenses out of his half.

He was absolutely determined that his former partner should not prevail in this matter, and he requested a new Superior Court hearing before a jury in the hope of gaining not only a successful appeal but also public vindication. A measure of Kennedy's righteous indignation over this suit is perhaps demonstrated by the fact that the appeal was the only aspect of his relations with Mrs. Eddy which he discussed in detail when he was interviewed around 1907. It was also, of course, the only aspect of their relation which had a clear paper trail through the legal proceedings and the newspaper accounts.[34]

Kennedy's appeal was scheduled to be heard in November, but before that Edward Arens, acting for Mrs. Eddy, launched three other suits, two against Daniel Spofford and one against Mrs. Eddy's 1870 students Charles

Stanley and George Tuttle. In April a bill in equity was filed against Daniel Spofford for $3,000 in tuition and unpaid royalty on his practice. Spofford's property was attached, perhaps in retaliation for some maneuvering on the part of Spofford and George Barry to unravel or exploit the change-the-title-to-Broad-Street game Mrs. Eddy was playing.[35] This first suit against Spofford was dismissed in June "because of defects in the writ and insufficient service,"[36] which makes it seem likely that Arens, who had no legal training and, indeed, no education of a formal kind, had tried to do things himself without using the services of paid counsel and had failed right away on technicalities.

If the suit for breach of promissory note failed to bring Daniel Spofford low, or generate any income, the suit against Spofford brought to court in the name of Miss Lucretia L. S. Brown was more disastrous. Miss Brown, a woman of about fifty, lived with her mother and sister in Ipswich, and the three were famous in the community for their fanatical tidiness and cleanliness. After a fall in which she injured her spine as a teenager, Lucretia had become a chronic invalid, but she nonetheless managed to earn a modest living by giving out crochet piecework to local women.[37] That she was something of a classic hysteric is indicated by the story reported by Milmine that although at times claiming to be wholly confined to bed by illness, she would occasionally be caught at night creeping about to tidy up. Dorcas Rawson and Daniel Spofford had won this lady for Christian Science from the local Methodist church. Though "cured" so far as to be able to get up out of bed and walk around and even attempt to play healer to others in her turn, Miss Brown suffered relapses, or "chemicals" as the Christian Science world liked to term returning symptoms or resistance to its ideas. Since Miss Brown continued to need constant care and attention, Miss Rawson was not always able to cope and called in turn on Mrs. Eddy.

Thus Miss Brown had been a burden for Mrs. Eddy for some time, not because she rebelled against Mrs. Eddy's theories, but because she accepted them all, including the doctrine of malicious mesmerism, so completely. In several of her letters to Spofford before their final split, Mrs. Eddy had pleaded with him to undertake the case of Miss Brown—"Cure Miss Brown or I shall never finish my book." On April 19, 1877, Mrs. Eddy complained to Spofford that on the eve of the Eddys' departure for Connecticut, Miss Brown declared herself dying from the "convulsions from a chemical," and that she had herself almost died in the effort to save Miss Brown. The Spofford letters of 1876–1877 show clearly that at this point Mrs. Eddy believed not only that she was under attack from mesmerizers led by Kennedy, but also that her strength and health were being sapped by the mental calls made on her by students and patients.

This was the situation when, according to the account Spofford later gave to Milmine, he one day in the summer of 1877 had the charitable notion to call unexpectedly on Miss Brown to see how she was doing. During the visit Miss Brown, instructed by Miss Rawson and Mrs. Eddy to see Spofford as a demonic mesmerizer, became extremely agitated and red in the face. Spofford later claimed, picturesquely, that he attributed her flushed face to her being engaged with making jam. Whether he could really have been so unaware of what was going on in Miss Brown's mind may be doubted. As a result of this visit, according to the testimony later given to Milmine by Henry F. Dunnels, one of Mrs. Eddy's then students, Mrs. Eddy organized twelve selected students to meet at her house, and for two hours at a time they were to "take up" Daniel Spofford, that is to say, counter mentally the adverse mental influence he was seeking to bring to bear.[38]

This technique did not produce the required results since, if we are to believe the account Spofford gave Milmine thirty years later, the balance of power in the Newburyport area was tilting away from loyal Christian Scientists and toward the Spoffordites. Miss Brown, unsurprisingly perhaps, was making little progress as a mental healer; Spofford's practice was thriving. More dramatic measures seemed required, and Edward Arens was the man to come up with them. Prevailing upon the highly suggestible Miss Brown's fears of mesmeric illness, Arens filed the following complaint with the Supreme Judicial Court of Massachusetts:

> The plaintiff humbly complains that the said Daniel H. Spofford of Newburyport, is a mesmerist, and practices the art of mesmerism, and that by his power and influence he is capable of injuring the persons and property and social relations of others, and does by said means so injure them. That the said Daniel H. Spofford, has at diverse times and places since the year 1875, wrongfully, maliciously, and with intent to injure the plaintiff, caused the plaintiff, by means of his said power and art, great suffering of body, severe spinal pains and neuralgia, and temporary suspension of the mind; and still continues to cause the plaintiff the same. And the plaintiff has reason to fear and does fear that he will continue in the future to cause the same. And the plaintiff says that said injuries are great and of an irreparable nature, and that she is wholly unable to escape from the control and influence he so exercises upon her, and from the aforesaid effects of said control and influence.

This extraordinary suit was filed, above all places, in Salem, thus ensuring that everyone would make the connection between the crime Daniel Spofford was being accused of and witchcraft!

Not surprisingly, the Spofford suit in Salem caught the attention of the press, not just in Newburyport, Ipswich, and Lynn, but in Boston too. Christian Science was beginning to gain a reputation as a good story. The following report from the Newburyport *Herald* of May 16, 1878, captures the prevailing opinion well:

In the Supreme Judicial court at Salem, on Tuesday, a bill in equity was brought more befitting the new institution at Danvers [i.e., the nearby State Hospital for the insane] than the highest tribunal of the Commonwealth. The bill was nominally brought by Lucretia L. S. Brown, of Ipswich, to restrain Daniel H. Spofford, of Newburyport, from mesmeric influence over her, causing severe spinal pains and neuralgia; but we suspect the real complainant is Mary B. G. Eddy, of Lynn, who has a power of attorney to appear for the plaintiff in the case. Mrs. Eddy professes to cure disease miraculously, and to be able to impart her power, and Spofford was one of her pupils, with whom she has since quarreled. She tried, some time since, to induce us to publish an attack upon Spofford, which we declined to do, and we understand that similar requests were made to other newspapers of the county. At last the matter has come into court, and the bill in equity is a curiosity such as might have been looked for in the court records of two hundred years ago. The witchcraft delusion is not yet dead, even officially.

Mrs. Eddy's lawyer refused to plead the case, and Miss Brown herself refused to appear in court. Mrs. Eddy was given power of attorney, and Edward Arens was to argue the case before the judge. Mrs. Eddy is said not to have been in favor of Miss Brown bringing the suit. If this is true, it marks the beginning of some needed realism on her part. Yet since the bill in equity had been filed and scheduled, she was persuaded to give it her full support, and she attended the preliminary hearing with a crowd of twenty supporters, whom the *Boston Globe* reporter wittily dubbed a cloud of witnesses. What the witnesses would testify to was unclear, not least to the witnesses themselves, if Milmine's highly detailed and lively account is to be believed. The case was adjourned for three days, during which time Arens set out hotfoot to Newburyport to serve Spofford personally with a summons to appear, and the public waited eagerly for more. Milmine summarizes the outcome of the suit thus:

> On Friday morning the crowd which had assembled at the Salem Court House was disappointed. Mr. Spofford himself did not appear, but his attorney, Mr. Noyes, appeared for him and filed a demurrer, which Judge Gray sustained, declaring with a smile that it was not within the power of the Court to control Mr. Spofford's mind.[39]

The Brown suit against Spofford had thus been thrown out of court immediately, a disaster for Mrs. Eddy, to be followed immediately by another setback. On the very same day, in the same court, the third of the Arens-inspired suits had a preliminary hearing; it was filed on Mrs. Eddy's behalf against Charles Stanley and George H. Tuttle to recover royalties. Arens and Mrs. Eddy no doubt hoped that this suit would proceed along the same favorable lines as the March suit against Richard Kennedy had. In fact, however, the hearing on this matter was postponed by the court, giving Mrs.

Eddy some breathing space but also granting the defense more time to prepare its case and for the press to begin to influence public opinion and hence
prospective judges and jurors.[40]

Between mid-May and October Mrs. Eddy and her followers kept a relatively low profile as far as the local press was concerned. The suit George
Barry had filed against Mrs. Eddy demanding payment to the tune of $2,700
for the services he had rendered her still hung over the Christian Scientists.
The Kennedy appeal was scheduled for November, and, as Mrs. Eddy was
the first to admit, the very thought of Richard Kennedy—or any thought
from him, in her way of thinking—made her ill. Her husband, Gilbert, was
teaching a handful of students, and the couple was working to salvage what
they could of the new edition of *Science and Health*.

This edition, which Mrs. Eddy had labored over for so long and which
had been the immediate source of her split with Spofford, suffered even
more indignities at the hands of the printer than the first had, and its first
volume, which contained the mainly metaphysical sections, had to be
ditched. Volume 2 therefore appeared by itself on October 15 and contained
a diatribe against mesmerism updated to include a barely veiled anathema
against Daniel Spofford. As Robert Peel notes, "Generally known as the Ark
edition because of the Noah's ark stamped on the cover, it came close to sinking in a sea of misprints."[41] Far from being the powerful weapon to disseminate her new Science, the book seemed, if anything, well calculated to show
Mrs. Eddy at her worst. Apparently nothing had been learned from all the
publishing vicissitudes of the last three years, and Gilbert Eddy, far from
being a voice of moderation, if not reason, seemed to limit his role to
rubber-stamping his wife's ideas and facilitating her self-destructive
activities.

Despite the obvious shortcomings of the "Ark" edition, its appearance
in print brought a sense of relief to the beleaguered household at 8 Broad
Street, but this reprieve was short-lived. On October 29 Asa Gilbert Eddy
and Edward J. Arens were arrested and charged with conspiring to kill
Daniel H. Spofford.

14

The Conspiracy to Murder Daniel Spofford

THE JURORS for the COMMONWEALTH of MASSACHUSETTS, on their oath present that Edward J. Arens and Asa G. Eddy of Boston aforesaid, on the 28th day of July, in the year of our Lord one thousand eight hundred and seventy-eight, at Boston aforesaid, with Force and Arms, being persons of evil minds and dispositions, did then and there unlawfully conspire, combine and agree together feloniously, wilfully, and of their malice aforethought, to procure, hire, incite, and solicit one James L. Sargent for a certain sum of money, to wit, the sum of five hundred dollars, to be paid to him said Sargent by them, said Arens and Eddy, feloniously, wilfully, and of his, said Sargent's malice aforethought, in some way and manner by some means, instruments and weapons, to said jurors unknown, one Daniel H. Spofford to kill and murder; against the law, peace and dignity of said Commonwealth.[1]

THE MOST PUZZLING EVENT IN THE OFTEN PUZZLING history of early Christian Science is the arrest of Edward J. Arens and Asa Gilbert Eddy on the charge of conspiring with James L. Sargent to kill or injure Daniel H. Spofford. Spofford was, in point of fact, neither killed nor injured, and by the end of January of 1879 the charges against Arens and

Eddy had been withdrawn after a key witness admitted perjury. But back in October of 1878 both Spofford and the state police apparently believed that there was a plot against Spofford's life and that the Christian Scientists were somehow behind it. Spofford so feared for his life that he went underground for two weeks, leaving his family to fear the worst.

Several questions about this incident remain unanswered:

1. Was there a plot to kill Spofford, and if so why and how?
2. If no such plot existed, why did the police arrest, indict, and bring Arens and Eddy to trial over the course of almost three months?
3. Was there, on the contrary, a plot to pretend that Spofford's life was in danger, in order to injure Mrs. Eddy and her movement?
4. If there was such a plot, who put it in motion?

Over the years different biographers of Mrs. Eddy have provided different answers to these questions, none of them entirely satisfactory. In this chapter I will review the evidence and set out the various hypotheses. One thing is certain. No writer of fiction could have invented a more fitting conclusion to a period when people were fanatically preoccupied with Malicious Animal Magnetism than this event, solidly documented by court records and detailed reporters' accounts, or one more unlikely.

Let us take up the story in early October 1878 when Daniel Spofford received the first visit in his offices at the Hotel Tremont at 297 Tremont Street, in Boston, from a man called James L. Sargent.[2] Perhaps not incidentally, Richard Kennedy also rented space at the Hotel Tremont. Spofford was somewhat loath to admit Sargent, a very rough-looking man who said he kept a bar in Sudbury Street; Sargent was not the usual type to consult a metaphysical healer. Sargent had come to tell Spofford that two men, who had identified themselves as Miller and Libby, were out to kill him and had sought to hire Sargent's services to do the deed. Sargent urged Spofford to go to the nearby police station and speak to Detective Hollis Pinkham who would confirm the story, since Sargent had earlier gone to the police and asked Pinkham what he should do about Miller and Libby's business proposition. Spofford did talk with Pinkham, who reportedly confirmed Sargent's story but advised Spofford not to be too worried about the whole thing. But Spofford was extremely worried. He began to sleep in a curtained alcove between the chimney and a closet in his rooms, so that no one could get a clear shot at him from the door. He put a safety chain on the door, and he also installed some kind of hinged wooden plank over the doorjamb to serve as a barricade.[3]

Despite all these precautions, when Sargent reappeared to tell Spofford that Miller and Libby were pressuring him to get the job done, Spofford agreed to go into hiding and pretend to be dead. Sargent then drove Spofford to the house of his sister, Miss Laura Sargent, in Cambridgeport, by some reports before the eyes of Miller and Libby to convince them that the assassination plot was being executed. Let me interject here that Spofford's willing acquiescence to Sargent's suggestion at this point is surprising. Sargent was not a man to inspire confidence. If he told Spofford that one of the schemes discussed with Miller and Libby involved driving Spofford out into the country and doing away with him, would Spofford have happily assented to getting in a vehicle with Sargent and being driven away? And what would Spofford think of Sargent once Spofford learned that the house of Miss Sargent, where he was to lie low, was a house of prostitution? Presumably the continuing involvement of Detective Hollis Pinkham and his sidekick Chase Philbrick reassured Spofford. It is too bad that none of the people who later interviewed Spofford about the two weeks he spent in a whorehouse got him to say anything about his experiences for the record.

Spofford told no one where he was staying, perhaps not surprisingly, and his mother and older brother, alarmed by his sudden disappearance and probably aware that Spofford thought himself under threat of physical violence, went so far as to advertise in the newspapers for any news of him. Those who present Spofford as an innocent victim in this plot cite this as evidence, alleging that he was a devoted son and would never wittingly or willingly cause his mother such anxiety. In any case, at this juncture the press took up the question of what had befallen Daniel Spofford, and stories began to hint at foul play.[4]

Spofford's reappearance was coordinated with the police to occur soon after the arrest of "Miller and Libby," alias Arens and Eddy, for conspiracy to commit murder. The letter Gilbert Eddy wrote to his wife from jail, advising her of his arrest and of the charges and assuring her of his complete innocence, is a model of Christian piety in the face of adversity. Gilbert was as ready to quote the Bible as any man, and he casts himself, perhaps not wholly unpleasurably, in the role of Daniel in the lions' den or an early Christian facing the arena. He and Arens were held pending a preliminary hearing in the Charles Street jail, and a whopping bail of $3,000 each was set. Surety for such sums proved difficult to raise in the rather impoverished Christian Science community. It will be remembered that Mrs. Eddy had paid only $5,650 for her home, and that it was heavily mortgaged. Samuel Bancroft, whose fortunes were still precarious, tried in vain to stand surety for his friends, but his property qualifications were deemed inadequate. Finally it was Mrs. Miranda Rice, or more exactly one of her male relatives, James Rawson, who convinced the court to release Eddy. Whether Arens was released on bail is not known.

On November 7 the preliminary hearing was held in Boston Municipal Court. The press and the public had been primed, and there was an overwhelming presumption of guilt against the accused. Thus the *Boston Globe* of October 30 featured an article entitled "That Conspiracy" which began:

If there is any foundation in the accusations which led to the arrest of Asa G. Eddy and Edward J. Arnes [*sic*], by State detectives yesterday, the crime is one of the blackest that has come to light for some time, and its exact parallel has seldom, if ever, been seen. The officers engaged in the work have been very successful in cases of a like nature, and it is hardly possible that they have made a mistake in this instance; still the law holds every [word illegible] in doubt until proven guilty, and the following allegations may be without foundation. It appears that a woman in Lynn, known as Mrs. "Dr." Eddy, pretends to have a power from some divine source to heal the sick, and has imparted this knowledge to others, among them Dr. Daniel H. Spofford of this city. It is claimed that Spofford was more successful in his treatment than Mrs. Eddy, and that last spring, in order to get rid of a dangerous rival, the Eddy woman and her friends induced an Ipswich woman to file a petition in the Supreme Court praying that Spofford be enjoined from practising his art. The case is still pending. Finding that they could not dispose of their rival by any process of law, the Eddy combination next resorted to stronger measures, and thinking to find some one who, for money, would do their bidding, Dr. Eddy and one Edward J. Arnes visited Boston and bargained with a Portland street "bummer" to put Dr. Spofford out of the way, in other words, to

Murder Him in Cold Blood.

When the hearing for probable cause began on November 7, the reporter for the *Boston Herald* did a particularly good job of taking down the testimony. Since no other transcript was apparently made and no judge's or lawyer's notes have survived, the *Herald* accounts, supplemented by other newspaper articles, are the best source of information on what exactly was said at the hearing. Almost all of the evidence was given by James Sargent, who entered into great detail as to how he had come to know the men he identified in court as Eddy and Arens, and what had transpired among them.

According to the *Herald* account of November 8, Sargent said that he had seen Arens in his bar several times, and that Arens had told his fortune and the fortunes of other customers. One day Arens asked Sargent if he knew the whereabouts of a certain "Skip," as he had a job for him worth several hundred dollars. Sargent had lost track of "Skip," tried without success to interest another man he knew called Kelly in the affair, but later met again with Arens at Bowker Street and asked him what exactly the job was.

[H]e [Arens] asked me if I could be depended upon, and I told him yes; he then said he wanted a man licked, and he wanted him licked so that he wouldn't come to again; I told him I was just the man for him, and he then said there was between $300 and $400 in it, but that the old man [Eddy] would not pay out any more than was absolutely necessary to get the job done, as he had already been beaten out of $75, which he had paid to another party.

Sargent was, in point of fact, *not* just the man for Arens/Miller, and he had no taste for "licking." But he was tempted by the money being offered, while he remained, as he said in court, suspicious that the whole thing was some kind of put-up job directed against him. Therefore before his next meeting, which "Libby" was supposed to attend, he armed himself with a gun and asked a friend of his, George Collier, to hide in an old freight car in the deserted railway yard designated for the meeting and eavesdrop on the conversation. Sargent said that at this meeting he asked for $100 up front, Eddy offered him $75, which Sargent accepted, but then Eddy said he had only $35 on him. When a man was seen walking through the freight yard, Sargent hurriedly told the two others he would take the whole $75 when he and Arens next met. Within a day or so this money was duly paid over, and Arens identified Spofford as the proposed victim and provided Sargent with a newspaper advertisement giving Spofford's address and business hours in Boston, Haverhill, and Newburyport.

Sargent openly admitted in court that he was trying to extort money from Arens and Eddy on false pretenses, but he claimed that he never intended to make an attempt on Daniel Spofford's life, and that his "purpose in acquiescing in the scheme against Dr. Spofford was to give him up to the authorities after making what money I could out of it."[5] He further claimed that this course of action was recommended to him by the detective Pinkham, whom he consulted on the matter. The policeman and the criminal agreed to string "Miller" and "Libby" along until their real identity could be established, and the motivation for their plot to murder Spofford became clearer. That Sargent should enjoy some small profit for his involvement seemed only fair. In fact, over the next weeks he did nothing but spend the $75 and give Arens excuses for why he had not yet made an attempt on Spofford's life. Finally, having run out of temporizing excuses perhaps, or maybe having managed to track down his victim as he peregrinated around the Boston area, he met Spofford in Boston and gave him the warning described earlier in this chapter. Sargent continued to try to persuade Arens that he was trying to fulfill the contract, all the while hiding behind the fiction that he had subcontracted the job to the nonexistent Skip. But Arens eventually undertook some minor detective work of his own and told Sargent that he knew that Spofford was still going about his business because he had sent a boy down to Spofford's offices to check. The seclusion of Spofford in Cambridgeport was the scheme Sargent and Pinkham devised to persuade Arens that Spofford had indeed been "licked" and that the rest of the money was therefore due. Tiring in their efforts to extract the full price from the conspirators,[6] Sargent and Pinkham finally arranged for Arens and Eddy to be arrested and for Spofford to reappear.

Sargent's colorful and dramatic testimony carried the court through the morning of November 7 and into November 8. Sargent and Pinkham clearly presented themselves and were celebrated in the press accounts as men who had acted in the public interest to prevent the murder of an innocent man and to bring his would-be killers to justice. Cross-examined by Mrs. Eddy's lawyer Russell H. Conwell, a much reputed and expensive attorney, Sargent was forced to be more precise about the dates of the alleged meetings and the sums which had been paid him. The date of the critical meeting in the freight yard, which, according to the testimony of both Sargent and Collier, Arens and Eddy attended together so that they could discuss the conspiracy to kill Spofford, was determined to have been July 28. Collier was called to attest to what he had heard from the freight car, and the twenty-one-year-old James Kelly testified that Sargent had told him about the job. According to Milmine's account of the hearing, Laura Sargent and Sargent's barkeeper John Smith were also called to testify that they had seen Arens in Sargent's bar. But this testimony from such flawed witnesses was not referred to in the *Boston Herald* account, and, indeed, the presence of Miss Sargent and some of her associates in the courtroom was not reported, perhaps so that no cloud might be thrown over the social status and reputation of the witness, James Sargent.

Pinkham was called to corroborate what Sargent had told him, and to describe his own role in the affair, but he said nothing the *Boston Herald* reporter considered of interest. According to Milmine, Pinkham seemed to be thoroughly stupid, and the newspapermen may have had difficulty reconciling the real man with their image of the cunning and successful police detective, so they omitted his testimony. Another witness was the Eddys' former cook, Jessie MacDonald. She testified that she had heard Dr. Eddy say that Spofford was making his wife ill, and that he would be happy if Spofford were out of the way. She had also heard Mrs. Eddy read passages from the Bible that related to the destruction of sinners. Under cross-examination, Mrs. MacDonald admitted that she had recently left the Eddys over a dispute about wages.

Only the prosecution's case was presented at the preliminary hearing, and in fact this would be the whole of the court testimony. Spofford never testified in court about his experiences, nor did Eddy and Arens. Presumably Conwell, the lawyer Mrs. Eddy had engaged to defend her husband and Arens, judged, correctly, that the prosecution had a good enough case to justify the arraignment of the two men, and that it was better to reserve the defense for the higher court. Conwell also advised Mrs. Eddy to hire her own detectives, but no report of their findings seems to have survived. The arraignment took place in late November, bail for each man was again set at $3,000, and the trial was set for January.

On November 29 the *Boston Herald* launched another stirring indictment of the Christian Scientists:

PROCURING MURDER.

Grave Charges Against "Christian Scientists."
A Bar-Tender Hired to Remove a Rival Doctor.
He Works with the Police and Causes Arrests.

A murderous conspiracy, that at present has the blackest possible appearance, is now about to be investigated judicially, through the efforts of State Detectives Pinkham and Philbrick. The story of this crime, which is almost Borgian, implicates a number of people who have, during the past three or four years, figured in the Essex county courts with damaging frequency, as well as in some of the most absurd cases ever tried in modern times. The present story is not yet proven, and, it may be, is told simply to damage innocent people, but the probabilities seem to be that no unjust accusation has been made.

As nearly as the facts can be ascertained, it appears that some three months since a man named James L. Sargent, who keeps a saloon in Sudbury Street, called on Detective Pinkham and told him he had been approached by two men, whose names he gave, with

A PROPOSITION TO MURDER DR. DANIEL SPOFFORD,

a magnetic physician, or spiritual scientist, who had offices in Boston, Haverhill and Newburyport, and lived in the latter place. After making several appointments with one of them, he finally saw both in a deserted stable in Cambridge, where the older of the two agreed to pay him $350 for doing the murder and tendered all the money he had with him. This sum, which was $35, was declined by Sargent, who was afraid if he received anything he might be regarded as one of the criminals rather than a person seeking to prevent crime. His refusal to receive the money excited no suspicion in the minds of these procurers of murder, who left their supposed tool in full confidence that their villainous scheme would be carried out.

Sargent then went directly to Mr. Pinkham and told him the whole story, upon which Pinkham investigated the matter very carefully, but, finding no persons of the names given by the conspirators living in the towns in which they claimed to reside, he concluded that Sargent had been made the victim of a hoax.

I will not quote the whole of this article, but it will be apparent that the facts as summarized here differ from the testimony reported in the same newspaper some two weeks earlier, and that the motivation of Sargent and Pinkham has in the interim become more rational and civic-minded.

Unfortunately for the eager readers of the Boston-area press, the infamous conspiracy trial fizzled out. The much vilified Christian Science duo were released, if not exonerated, when the district attorney in January brought a motion of nolle prosequi which the judge accepted. The reason for this dramatic reversal was a letter which Mrs. Eddy received in late December from George Collier, the witness who had corroborated Sargent's statement about the critical meeting in the freight yard:

Taunton, Dec. 16, 1878.

To Drs. Asia [sic] G. Eddy and E. J. Arnes—feeling that you have been greatly ingered by faulse charges and knowing their is no truth in my statement that you attempted to hire James L. Sargent to kil Dr. Spofford and wishing to retract as far as poserble all things I have said in your ingury, I now say that thair is no truth whatever in the statement that I saw you meet James L. Sargent at East Cambridge or any outher place or offer to pay him money that I never hurd a conversation betwene you and Sargent as testifyed to by me whouther Spoford has anything to do with Sargent I do not know all I know is that the story I told on the stand is holy faulse and goton up by Sargent.

Geo. A. Collier.[7]

On the next day Collier made the same statement under oath. Mrs. Eddy, meanwhile, had secured several affidavits from Christian Science adherents who were willing to attest under oath that on the day named by Sargent for the freight yard meeting Asa Gilbert Eddy was teaching a class in Boston and then took a train to his home in Lynn, where he was greeted by his wife and one of her students. Thus he could not have had time for any meetings in Cambridge at 5:30 P.M. These affidavits, although given by people notable for their fierce loyalty to the Eddys, seemed reliable, and my judgment is that Asa Gilbert Eddy was indeed not present at any freight yard on July 28, but was teaching his class and then returning home to his wife, as attested. Arens also got a less detailed alibi together for the date and time specified in the indictment, but no efforts seem to have been made to check whether he could have been present at the many other meetings with Sargent, often in public places, which Sargent testified about in court.

Not only did Arens and Eddy get dismissed by the court under a nolle prosequi but their accusers were quickly discredited. The detective Pinkham was soon after removed from the police force, and Robert Peel reports that "an affidavit by a Lynn justice of the peace, David Austin, states that Pinkham confessed to him that 'the testimony of all parties in this case [including, presumably, Pinkham's] were perjuries.'"[8] Both Collier and Sargent were subsequently jailed on previous charges that included enticing young girls from their homes, and members of the press humbly admitted that they had been wrong in all that they had earlier reported about the "locally notorious Spiritual Scientists' Home at Lynn." On February 11 in the *Daily Evening Traveller* Asa

G. Eddy published a letter detailing for the public the recanting of Collier and offering his own account of his and his wife's relationship with Daniel Spofford. The *annus horribilis* of 1878 was finally over, and Mrs. Eddy would pass another twenty years before seeing another quite as black.

By now it will be apparent that the recorded facts in this case make very little sense. Who exactly was plotting against whom? Loyal Christian Science biographers, when they give any account of the conspiracy plot, take the position that Collier's confession of perjury and the later disgrace of Sargent, Collier, and Pinkham show that Eddy and Arens were completely innocent and that the whole thing was a plot to injure Mrs. Eddy. Mrs. Eddy and her followers were privately convinced that Richard Kennedy, the arch mesmerizer, was somehow behind the whole thing. Robert Peel not only defends the theory of malicious mesmerism and of Kennedy as mesmerizer but offers to the materialist and cynic some practical grounds as to why Kennedy, either in collusion with Spofford or not, indeed had reasons to launch a campaign against Mrs. Eddy.

It will be remembered that Kennedy had been successfully sued by Mrs. Eddy for $750 and had appealed the verdict entered against him in the lower court. This appeal was heard on November 8, the very day that the preliminary testimony in the Spofford case was continuing, and the result was a resounding victory for Kennedy. Mrs. Eddy's attorney at once filed exceptions, on the grounds that the judge had made a prejudicial charge to the jury, but the crucial document in the case, the promissory note which Kennedy had signed in 1870, disappeared from her lawyer's office, and finally her appeal was dropped.

Extensive court documentation on this appeal hearing and on the exceptions filed by Mrs. Eddy's lawyers makes it clear that Kennedy's triumph was a miscarriage of justice.[9] The judge was far from impartial in his summing up and accepted as truth everything to which Richard Kennedy testified, no doubt with his usual affable charm. As Mrs. Eddy's lawyer argued in the exceptions he filed after the verdict, there was no corroboration for Kennedy's testimony that Mrs. Eddy had asked him to sign the document as a come-on to other students, or that she had promised to reveal to him some further secret of healing but had failed to do so. It was up to the defense to prove these assertions, not for the prosecution to defend itself against them. The likely conclusion one can draw from all this legal evidence is that the extraordinarily bad press which Mrs. Eddy had received in 1878, and specifically the sensational news of the "Borgian" assassination conspiracy that broke during the hearing of the appeal, influenced judge and jury against Mrs. Eddy and in favor of Kennedy.

As I read the case Robert Peel mounts against Richard Kennedy, I am willing to accept that Kennedy benefited from the public humiliation of his former partner and savored it as a kind of revenge. What I find hard to entertain is the idea that Kennedy had the criminal savoir faire to put together a plan involving not only the participation of a Boston petty criminal like Sargent but the active collaboration of two state police detectives. Until, or unless, more is known about Kennedy's life, especially after he left Lynn for Boston in 1876, there is nothing to connect him to the criminal classes. It is also difficult to imagine Kennedy and Spofford concocting the plot together, though a cryptic little entry in Asa Gilbert Eddy's third notebook indicates that he thought that they had, and that Addie Spofford was also involved. Spofford and Kennedy were rivals rather than friends, though both shared the glory of being anathematized by Mrs. Eddy in print, and although both men had offices in the same building in Boston, there is no record that they had any dealings with one another. In the end, Spofford's story is consistent with all the reported facts, and the portrait he portrays of himself as a hapless victim is consistent and plausible.

The biographies that are hostile to Mrs. Eddy, while acknowledging the fact that Sargent, Collier, Miss Sargent, and Detective Pinkham were not model citizens, nonetheless quote enough of the evidence given at the preliminary hearing to make a strong case that, whatever Collier later said, Sargent had indeed been contacted in some scheme to do away with Daniel Spofford, and that Arens and Eddy were the awkward, uneasy, penny-pinching men behind the plot. According to this view of events, whatever their illegal activities before or after the alleged plot, Sargent and Pinkham had absolutely no motive to go after Arens and Eddy, unless they were paid to do so by someone else, and they seemed intellectually ill equipped to concoct such a complicated plot, depending on the collusion of so many witnesses.

What Milmine—and, following her, Bates and Dittemore, Dakin, and other hostile critics—really wanted to say is that Mrs. Eddy herself had incited her husband and her student to make an attempt on Spofford's life. At her behest, and perhaps with her knowledge, Arens and Eddy had enlisted the aid of Sargent, who unfortunately proved to be less crooked than they thought, because he went to the police. Pinkham and Sargent and perhaps Collier then concocted a plot to trap Arens and Eddy. But Milmine cannot convincingly argue that Mrs. Eddy was directly involved in this scenario for three main reasons. First, the putative heroes in the case, Sargent and Pinkham, are such unsavory individuals that they are much more likely as villains, and the Sargent plot would have included terrifying the innocent Spofford and his family; pocketing the money paid for the assassination; testifying selectively, if not falsely, at the hearing; and hiring a friend to give false corroborative testimony. Second, the active participation of Asa Gilbert Eddy in such a scheme was inherently unlikely.

The third and most important reason that Milmine could not directly point the finger of guilt at Mrs. Eddy was because there was no evidence of Mrs. Eddy's involvement. The only factual link between the Sargent group and Mrs. Eddy was the testimony of the disaffected cook, Jessie MacDonald, and any juryman back in 1878, or reader of detective fiction today, could see that there is a big difference between wishing someone dead and paying a thug to take him out. The only indications of conscious and deliberate plotting on Mrs. Eddy's part that Milmine can adduce are two very similar letters Mrs. Eddy sent on October 8 to Spofford and to Kennedy, and Milmine quotes these extensively. Milmine reads the opening sentence of the letter— "Won't you make up your mind before it is forever too late to stop sinning with your eyes open?"—as a veiled threat that Mrs. Eddy and her associates were about to take sterner measures against their enemies. This seems to me a highly dubious reading, and one which would never have stood up in court.

In my view, the letters to Kennedy and Spofford should be read more straightforwardly as further testimony to the way Mrs. Eddy's obsessive preoccupation with Malicious Animal Magnetism had been poisoning her life, and, more important, to her attempts to get beyond it and find some kind of serenity and control.

> Your silent arguments to do me harm have done me the greatest possible good; the wrath of man has praised Thee. In order to meet the emergency, Truth has lifted me above my former self, enabled me to know who is using this argument, when and what is being spoken,—and knowing this, what is said in secret is proclaimed on the house top, and affects me no more than for you to come and say it to me audibly, and tell me I have so and so; and to hate my husband; that I feel others; that arguments cannot do good; that Mrs. Rice cannot, that my husband cannot, etc, etc. I have now no need of human aid. God has shut the mouths of the lions. The scare disappears when you know another is saying it and that the error is not your own.[10]

This is a sad letter, but it accurately if incoherently charts the essential way Mrs. Eddy had determined to follow when she encountered Malicious Animal Magnetism. The letter is sad in that it shows that whenever Mrs. Eddy had doubts and feelings that she could not understand or accept, she tended to attribute them to the projected malicious influence, or "arguments," of others whom she believed to be her enemies. It also says that she is convinced that with God's help she has now learned definitively that she can rise above mental influence, and that thus Kennedy's alleged mesmerism, though painful, has served to strengthen and enlighten her.

This letter in my view is strong evidence against Mrs. Eddy's participation in a murder conspiracy. It makes plain that because Mrs. Eddy was so convinced that a mental argument was stronger than a physical one and that to convey a harmful suggestion mentally was more injurious than to actually say it aloud, she was the last person likely to engage in a criminal conspiracy.

On some level, she believed that an individual did not have to plunge a knife in, that the mind could do the same or more. Despite her apparent disarray, her deepest fear was not that Kennedy and Spofford's malicious powers would harm her, but that they would induce her to act as they did, forcing her to use her own mental powers to harm them—in other words to become, herself, a mesmerist. The letters are the confused, hastily written expression of that fundamental belief in her own divine mission, in her special relation to God, that Mrs. Eddy expressed more cogently and calmly in her teaching and writings, and it arose out of her profound commitment to Christian morality and the Decalogue. Mrs. Eddy's theology and morality were in certain ways idiosyncratic, but they precluded her absolutely from conspiring to injure, much less kill, another human being.

Having excluded Mrs. Eddy as a possible mastermind for the initial plot to kill Daniel Spofford, we have still to account for the Sargent testimony in court, much of which seems highly circumstantial and difficult to fabricate out of whole cloth. Some of the details which Sargent provided at the hearing indicate that he did indeed know the two men he had accused, or he had received a good deal of information about them. Notably, Sargent reported that when he told Arens that he had finally killed Spofford at 7:30 P.M., Arens said that he already knew this because of his special powers. This remark occasioned a laugh in the courtroom as it was exactly the kind of thing that Arens liked to say. Sargent also reported that Arens told him that Eddy was "a countryman, and green as h——l," which again caused a smile in the courtroom because it rang so true.

One strange aspect of Sargent's testimony is the reason he says Arens and Eddy gave him for wanting Spofford put away. Sargent is variously reported as saying he was told that Spofford, a married man, was courting Eddy's daughter, or because of "Spofford's unwillingness to allow his daughter to marry a man who had been divorced from his wife." One report has Arens actually weeping at the thought of the poor young girl who was being seduced. This detail seems to indicate that Sargent had some intimate knowledge of Spofford's affairs since, as I have noted, by October 1878 Spofford was probably cohabiting with a young woman who was not yet his wife.[11]

Because of these peculiarities in the testimony, I am led to advance the hypothesis that Edward Arens was in cahoots with James Sargent and did hatch some kind of plot with him. Asa G. Eddy, however, knew nothing about it and was never involved. Sargent, Collier, Miss Sargent, Kelly, and the two detectives, Pinkham and Philbrick, all testified that Arens had been to Sargent's bar and that they had seen Sargent and Arens together at various places. Sargent's testimony about Eddy's participation in the plottings is notably more limited and less circumstantially detailed and convincing than his testimony about Arens. The only occasion when Eddy's collaboration in the plot against Spofford is unequivocally detailed by Sargent is in his testimony about the crucial meeting in the freight yard, and it is precisely this incident which the Collier letter declared to be false. If the little we know about Edward Arens leads us to imagine he might conceivably have plotted against Daniel Spofford's life, the considerable data we have on Asa Gilbert Eddy make him one of the least likely conspirators to assassinate in American history. Even Mrs. Eddy's most hostile critics have difficulty pointing the finger at Asa Gilbert Eddy as a likely murderer precisely because they have chosen to paint such a vivid picture of him as an effeminate weakling.

Perhaps a more productive way of assessing this crazy scenario with its unlikely mix of characters is to establish what the actual results of the alleged conspiracy were, as opposed to the alleged objectives, and consider whether these ends might have been the goal from the outset. If we assume that Sargent's testimony held elements of the truth, that indeed he and Arens had several meetings at which money was exchanged, and Spofford was later told that he was to be the target of a criminal plot, what was the nature of that plot? Let us suppose that it involved not killing Daniel Spofford but terrifying him. As we have seen, one of the rare clean facts in this case is that not one hair on Spofford's head was ever actually harmed, and that Sargent, for all his alleged commitments to Arens and Eddy to do away with Spofford, approached his prey only to warn him. If Sargent was hired by Arens to kill or seriously injure Daniel Spofford, he showed from the very outset a singular lack of zeal as a hit man. If, on the other hand, Sargent was hired to scare Spofford and drive him out of the healing business, he did a good job, because Spofford certainly did get very scared. There would be good reason to scare Spofford, since he was having considerable success in his healing practice at the time of the alleged conspiracy and thus was a professional rival not only of Asa Gilbert Eddy but also of Edward Arens—who was to move from Lynn and establish himself successfully in Boston in 1879—and of Richard Kennedy.

What if Robert Peel was right about a Kennedy-Spofford plot? The plot would be aimed at discrediting Mrs. Eddy and her Christian Science movement, making it harder for her to win the various legal suits she was engaged in, and thus ruining the Eddys financially to such an extent that they would be removed from the metaphysical healing arena. What would it mean if this result had been the actual objective of the plot?

I wrestled with the enigma of the Spofford murder plot for some years and discussed it with a number of people. In the end, the hypothesis that best accounted for the facts was propounded by Judy Huenneke in the Church History Department. She suggested that the plot was actually two plots that became entangled together—an idea that will be familiar to all of you mystery readers! Edward Arens, whose efforts to get rid of the troublesome Daniel Spofford by legal action had already lamentably backfired, decided that brute force was his only option, so he hired James Sargent not to kill

Spofford but to threaten and terrify him. This was Arens's own idea: neither Mr. nor Mrs. Eddy had any part in it.[12] Spofford was duly terrified, and he confided his fears to Richard Kennedy, whom he had known for years and whom he saw regularly since they both rented rooms (perhaps even the same rooms) in the Hotel Tremont.

Kennedy then hatched the second plot. He saw an opportunity to deal the Eddys a death blow by implicating Asa Gilbert Eddy in Arens's scheme and getting both Arens and Eddy arrested. Sargent was charged with making it look as if Eddy and Arens had tried to have Spofford killed, and Sargent, on his own initiative, enrolled Pinkham, his sister, and Collier in the plot. Sargent would earn some money from Arens and appear to be a hero to the public at a time when he was under active investigation for various crimes and likely to go to jail. Pinkham would earn a much needed reputation as a smart, active detective at a time when he also was under investigation. Collier's timely letter and willing affidavit in December were always part of the plot, since the conspirators never intended for Arens and Eddy to be tried.

There was one problem which severely complicated matters for the plotters and has consequently made the plot more difficult to unravel. From Kennedy's point of view, it was crucial that the arrest and attendant attack on Mrs. Eddy's group be timed to coincide with his libel appeal. Thus Sargent had to lead Arens on for several weeks, and when Arens finally started to get suspicious and demand results Spofford had to go into hiding. According to this scenario, the fact that the whole murder plot fizzles out as soon as Kennedy has won his appeal is not incidental but the key to the whole affair.

In January of 1879 Kennedy and Spofford could retire from the fray well satisfied with their efforts and peacefully continue their practice in Boston and to the north of Boston. They had managed to defeat their most formidable rival, Mary Baker Eddy, in court, made her and her movement the subject of a devastating newspaper campaign, and caused her to incur crippling legal debts. Given that she was faced with the craziness and inefficiency of Edward Arens, her current ally so soon to become an enemy, and the active, conspiratorial enmity of Kennedy and Spofford, both of whom had once been such adoring disciples, is it any wonder that Mary Baker Eddy at this time was obsessed with demons and Malicious Animal Magnetism?

15

The Move to Boston
and the
Death of
Gilbert Eddy

W HEN ALL THE CHARGES AGAINST GILBERT WERE
dropped, the Eddys felt an immense relief, but they also found
themselves once again on the brink of insolvency. None of the suits they had
launched in 1878 had brought them anything but legal fees and court costs,
and their income from teaching and healing had declined as their expenditures soared. Defending Gilbert against the conspiracy to murder charge had
been particularly onerous since Mrs. Eddy had decided to spare no expense
to free her husband and reclaim his good name which had so recently become
her own. As we can see in his correspondence with the Eddys, their defense
attorney Russell H. Conwell was unambiguous about the hundreds of dollars he calculated would be necessary to pay his own fees and those of the
detectives he hired and the colleague with special criminal law expertise he
wanted to have by his side in court. He also made clear that he expected the
money to be paid up front.

A February 20 letter to the Eddys acknowledges that Conwell was paid
off in full, but discharging that bill was very difficult. At one point Mr. Eddy
contemplated declaring bankruptcy, and Mrs. Eddy was ready to pull up
stakes and move to Cincinnati. Somehow, however, by severe retrenchment
and unremitting hard work, they managed to crawl out of the financial hole.
Like many nineteenth-century Americans, the Eddys accepted sudden reversals of fortune stoically; they had looked poverty in the face before. They
were still the kind of people who assiduously noted in their pocketbooks the
expenditure of ten cents on a car ticket, and they knew how to work. Over

the next year or so there were times when students arrived at 8 Broad Street to find Mr. Eddy cooking the dinner and Mrs. Eddy scrubbing the stairs.[1] Mrs. Eddy was still reporting severe financial problems to Clara Choate in 1880, and it seems that one of the things exacerbating the situation between Mrs. Eddy and Arens was that she had loaned him $500 and he was refusing to repay more than a token amount. Mrs. Eddy comments with typical hyperbole: "Now you see they are not smoking us out, but starving us out. Insurances are to be paid on my houses, taxes, etc. And we can't go on so."[2]

Asa Gilbert Eddy was a pillar of strength at this difficult time of recuperation and regrouping, and his efforts were all the more important for being performed in the shadows. His pocketbooks for these years testify eloquently to the sheer volume of work, of many different kinds, this frail man got through every day. These jottings offer the clearest picture available of his life, his character, and his abilities. Eddy was constantly on the road, soliciting and teaching students, guiding those who had been recruited. At home, he was counsellor and healer to his wife, whose fragility in private often matched her strength in public. He was in charge of the couple's finances, he organized the rentals and ran the everyday life of the household, and he took care of much of the routine correspondence with the faithful. He was also once again seeing patients, no doubt the most taxing work of all.

The pocketbooks, some four in number, have entries of many different kinds, some written hastily in barely legible pencil, others penned in careful copperplate. There are glimpses of Asa Gilbert Eddy's religious fervor, as when he lists the names of seven conspirators in the Spofford murder affair and associates them with the seven "epochs of error" quoted in Revelation. Eddy notes his daily expenses, his fares and meals, as he moves around the Boston area, the household purchases he has made, the rents he has collected. Occasionally he uses the book to scribble a note to someone during a meeting or court hearing.[3] He writes the names and addresses of people he needs to see in the day. Not surprisingly, Eddy shows some practical preoccupation with the various court cases his wife was engaged in, reproducing, for example, the 1870 promissory note signed by George Tuttle and Charles Stanley, which was the basis for Mrs. Eddy's suit against the two. His informal notes also corroborate what Mrs. Eddy was to claim publicly in the next edition of *Science and Health*—that Richard Kennedy stole the affections of Daniel Spofford's wife, and that, in the hearing of several witnesses, Mrs. Eddy, then Mrs. Glover, had strongly advised Spofford not to separate from his wife.

A large proportion of the notebooks takes the form of vocabulary lists, organized both alphabetically and in categories. There are carefully copied definitions of words such as *language, discourse, sentence, orthography, etymology, syntax, prosody, versification*, together with notes on punctuation and the use of capital letters. There is a section of homonyms—*tail/tale, hair/hare, wait/weight, ought/aught*—and a sampling of words such as *stop/stoppage* where the final consonant is doubled. On one half-page, like a child in an old-fashioned grade school, Eddy writes the word *shall* twenty-five times. Quite a lot of the vocabulary being drilled is medical, as Eddy learns to write *neuralgia* instead of the *newraligy* or *nueralgia* of his hasty pencilled notes elsewhere in the notebook, *vaccination* not *vaxcination*, *diarrhea* not *diareah*, *womb* not *woomb*. Other words represent an effort to achieve a more literary vocabulary in writing and speech. Eddy notes that *Herculean* means strong and *Lilliputian*, very small; that Esculapius was the God of health; that Agassiz was a great naturalist; that Xantippe, pronounced *Zantippe*, was the wife of Socrates; that *satire* is pronounced *satur*; that the word *metastases* is stressed on the second syllable. He also notes that a *banana* is a fruit, and a *sandwich* is "a slice of meat between slices of bread."

These lists make it obvious why it was easy for people to despise Eddy for his ignorance and lack of culture and to ridicule Mrs. Eddy for marrying such a man. I myself found them poignant testimony to Asa Gilbert Eddy's ambition and social energy, and to the dramatic effect his marriage had had on his life. Here is a man in his mid-forties who has received little formal education but who is seeking in his few minutes of spare time every day to educate himself, to learn correct spelling, to acquire a more sophisticated vocabulary, to pronounce foreign words correctly. Deeply aware of his own limitations, in awe of his wife's gifts, he tries to learn. For her part, his wife sees the aspiration and the hard work and does what she can to help and encourage him. They were a team on many levels.

The most interesting and moving entries in Asa Gilbert Eddy's notebooks are the case histories. In these badly spelled scribblings which Eddy took down perhaps as the patient spoke, or in the car on the way home to Lynn, we get some sense of the medical situations that Christian Science healers were facing every day. I quote the longest of these entries:

Mrs H. O. Hall

Hereditary suffering at her monthly periods June [18]70 birth of a child ulceration of the womb and falling

Doctors expla[nation]

a fistular of the [cervix uteri] or neck of the womb and that had never healed

scarrified it and it then healed

but the ligaments of the womb were so weak that it fell then wore instruments until one yr since when riding created soreness rendering it impossible to wear them

two months since contraction of the nerves causing the mouth of the womb to become so small that the doctor dilated it by the use of insts and is now trying carbolic acid to the bend in the womb

ten days after her monthly period the D opens the neck of the womb with an instrument and applies carbolic acid

after monthly severe pain in the womb by being out of position

After that the pain is felt at the spine all the time caused by the neck of the womb being tender

Carbolic acid to heal the neck of the womb.[4]

This gruesome sketch of orthodox gynecological treatments of the time helps to explain how Christian Science appealed to so many patients with long-standing problems and how those who attributed their new health to Christian Science became converts.

Gilbert's private toil to keep domestic affairs above water and spread the Christian Science word to those in need was more than matched by Mary's undaunted efforts to find a new public for her message, a public which would be more receptive than the conspiracy-ridden little group in Lynn. Even in the darkest days of the Spofford conspiracy hearings, Mrs. Eddy held her head high and her voice clear and confident. From late November of 1878, dressed smartly in "a fur-trimmed velvet coat, a plumed black velvet hat, and gray kid gloves," a pair of gold spectacles occasionally perched on her nose but looking at least ten years younger than her fifty-seven years, she addressed a gradually growing number of people at the Tabernacle Baptist Church on Shawmut Avenue in Boston, and her fame as an orator began to grow. As she wrote on January 24, 1879, to Clara Choate, "I lectured in parlors 14 years. God calls me now to go before the people in a wider sense."[5] When others sought to pull her down, she moved, paradoxically, onto a higher plane of activity, and it was at this low ebb in her fortunes that she moved decisively to define her nascent movement not as merely an alternative healing group but as a Christian sect.

While her name was being dragged through the mud in the daily newspapers, she spoke inspirationally of the church she saw in vision, and she won her audience's sympathetic applause as she deftly answered the questions of the hostile and doubting. In April 1879 the Christian Scientist Association that Daniel Spofford had first organized decided, at Mrs. Eddy's prompting, to set up a church, the Church of Christ (Scientist), "designed to commemorate the word and works of our Master, which should reinstate primitive Christianity and its lost element of healing." In August 1879 the Christian Scientist Association, with twenty-six members, was incorporated and chartered by the state, with Mrs. Eddy as president, Edward A. Orne as clerk, Margaret J. Dunshee as treasurer, and Mrs. Eddy, Orne, Arthur Buswell, and James Ackland as directors.[6] As new, younger students were attracted into the movement from outside Lynn—such as Clara Choate in 1878, Buswell and Ackland in 1879, James Howard and Julia Bartlett in 1880, and Abbie Whiting and Calvin Frye in 1881—there was a sense of progress but also a feeling of change and uncertainty in the little Christian Science community.

Some relics of the past still had to be faced. A verdict was finally reached in the suit filed against Mrs. Eddy by her former devoted student George Barry, and whereas it was some relief that Barry was awarded only $395 of the $2,700 he sought, during the trial Mrs. Eddy had suffered the pain of seeing several former friends and adherents testifying in the witness box against her. The last of the Arens-inspired legal suits came up in June, again in Salem, and with the active support and advice of his friend Richard Kennedy Charles Stanley emerged triumphant. On this occasion Mrs. Eddy was forced to testify in court, and to defend her teachings against very hostile questioning from the defense attorney and the judge.[7] The spate of lawsuits had been disastrous, but it was at last over.

One major piece of old business that Mrs. Eddy confronted in 1879 was the arrival in Boston of her long-lost son, George Washington Glover II, for a prolonged visit. Wrenched apart when George was only twelve, separated by lies and misunderstandings as much as by distance and circumstances, mother and son had little in common when they finally met again. We have no description of what Mrs. Eddy felt when she first saw her thirty-five-year-old son, but George's striking physical resemblance to his father—who had died at almost the same age—must have been a shock. More shocking yet was the kind of man George had become. Tall, strong, handsome, with a full beard that only partly hid the big scar on his neck from the wound he had suffered at the battle of Corinth, dressed as the frontiersman he was, devoid of European culture, barely able to sign his own name, George was an exotic being on the Boston landscape.[8]

After returning home wounded and being invalided out of the army in 1864, George had moved out of Winona County, Minnesota, where there was no work, and staked a claim to what he describes in his letters as prime land in what would become Fargo, North Dakota. George showed considerable shrewdness in buying land in Fargo, since this was the place where the Northern Pacific Railroad was planning to cross the Red River from Minnesota to Dakota territory, and the area was thus prime for development. Unfortunately, following a lifelong pattern of impatience or overconfidence, George was unable to wait long enough to capitalize on this piece of intelligent market research. The life of a small farmer was even less pleasant to George Glover II than it had been to his father and uncles back in the 1830s, and he soon sold his land without realizing the small fortune which he had envisaged. Next he bought eight head of Percheron horses and for a short time went into freighting, but this too soon palled, and by August 1879

George had given up driving freight teams and moved to Deadwood, South Dakota. Here the financial prospects seemed more exciting because large deposits of gold and silver had been discovered.

By the time that George was reunited with his mother he was a married man with a growing family to support, so his financial needs had grown appreciably. In 1874 in Fargo he had married the barely sixteen-year-old Harriet Ellen (Nellie) Bessant, an English girl born in Southampton, England, to Samuel Bessant, a carpenter who brought his large young family to the United States after his wife died. "Nellie" was illiterate, and possibly, as the saying went, no better than she should be, two things which her mother-in-law discovered when they finally met in 1887 and which she never forgave. The couple's first child, Edward Gershom Glover, was born in March 1875 and was probably conceived out of wedlock.[9] Two more children arrived in close succession: Mary Baker Glover was born in October 1877, followed by Evelyn Tilton Glover in January 1880. The daughters' names are eloquent testimony that by this time the Dakota Glovers had reestablished contact with their New Hampshire relatives. Indeed, the correspondence of the period makes it plain that the Glovers were actively soliciting the Eddys to come and live with or near them and share in their new life.

We do not know what Mrs. Eddy was writing to George in 1879, but it seems likely that both mother and son were giving equally rosy and equally misleading pictures of their lives and financial circumstances. Certainly George's letters show that he is under the impression that his mother and stepfather had money to invest. Already in these letters George is stating a theme he would continue to develop throughout his correspondence with his mother over the next thirty years—his rare talents as a gold prospector and his certainty of making a fortune in mining if only he could get a little investment capital now. Thus in an August 12, 1879, letter to his mother and stepfather, George extols the superb housing site he has purchased in Lead; the wonderful economic prospects for the expanding urban area of Central City, Lead, and Deadwood; the beauty of the Dakota landscape; and the excellence of the climate.

> I have got up an attraction for gold by which I can not only locate gold leads beneath the surface of the ground, but can determine their width and richness. My attraction is purely a chemical one. On this principle I have been prospecting & opening mines all summer & now have six or seven very rich mines. None of them are yet developed sufficiently to sell, but in a month or so we expect to have one of them sufficiently opened up to sell at a pretty good figure, and by its sale develop the others & open new ones. If I had a little more money I could open a large number of very rich mines & make one thousand [dollars] bring a return of $10,000 or $100,000.[10]

A pathetic letter from Nellie to George in Boston, dated January 11, 1880, and begging her husband to return home from visiting his mother, paints a rather different picture of life in Lead from that habitually depicted by George. Nellie was at this time pregnant with her third child, and she reports feeling very unwell. What was worse, a recent fire had devastated the little wooden town, and the Glover home had barely escaped destruction. Nellie was unable to leave the cabin, had almost no domestic help, and had spent a miserable Christmas alone with the children, and there had been no presents for anyone. George's mining partner attached a postscript to Nellie's letter also begging George to return at once, saying that George's presence in Deadwood was essential for the success of various ventures that were afoot.

George's 1879 visit to Boston was clearly a major effort on the part of the impoverished Glovers to rekindle his mother's affection, or stimulate her guilt, and secure some backing for George's various mining ventures. It probably took George only a few days to establish that his mother and father-in-law were in no position to back him, but he was not a man to condemn another's economic problems or reprove anyone who exaggerated his or her financial prospects. While in Boston, George took a lively interest in his mother's affairs and embraced Christian Science. In a 1907 interview he gave to James Slaght of the New York *World*, George told one fascinating story about his experiences in 1879:

> Within a week of my arrival in Boston I learned many strange things. The strangest of these was that the rebellious students were employing black arts to harass and destroy my mother.
>
> The longer I remained with mother, the clearer this became. Pursued by the evil influence of the students, we moved from house to house, never at rest and always apprehensive. We would go to a new house and fellow lodgers would be all smiles and friendliness. Then, in an hour, the inevitable change would come; all friendliness would vanish under the spell of black magic, and we would be ordered to go. But mother made it all clear to me. . . .
>
> It was Kennedy that mother talked of most. He was a master hand at the black arts, as mother pictured him daily to me, until at last I made up my mind to cut him short in his evil work. But I kept my plan to myself. One morning I slipped my revolver into my overcoat pocket and left our boarding-house. . . .
>
> I had never seen this man, but I knew where he had offices, and I walked straight there. He was doing business as a healer, and his name, lettered on a brass plate, was on the door of his office.
>
> The girl who admitted me asked if I was a patient, and I answered "Yes.". . . The unsuspecting girl led me straight to Kennedy's office, on the second floor of the house, opened the door, bowed me into the room, and hurried away. Kennedy was before me, seated at his desk.

He looked up smilingly and asked, "Are you in need of treatment?"

Pulling out my revolver I walked up to him, pressed the cold muzzle of the weapon against his head, and said, "I have made up my mind that you are in need of treatment."

Then while he shook like a jellyfish in terror, I gave him his one chance to live. I told him that my mother knew of his black art tricks to ruin her and that I had made up my mind to stop him or to kill him.

"You needn't tell me that you are not working your game of hypnotism to rob us of friends and to drive mother into madness," said I. "My one word to you is this: if we have to move from one other boarding house I will search you out and shoot you like a mad dog."

I shall never forget how that man pleaded for his life at the end of my weapon and swore that the black art accusation was false and that my mother had deceived me.

But it did the business all right. We were not ordered out of another boarding house that winter.

Richard Kennedy denied that this dramatic interview, reported in the best traditions of yellow journalism, had ever taken place, and one may doubt the accuracy of Glover's memory of an event that had occurred almost thirty years earlier. Whether truth or fiction, however, the story tells us a lot about George Glover's personality and about his relation to his mother—his swift espousal of her interests after all their years of separation, his Western brand of chivalry, his physical courage and bravado, and also his willing embrace of his mother's religion and her ideas on mesmerism. Ironically, in 1907 at the very time that George was advertising the fact that he himself had not only accepted but acted upon the doctrine of Malicious Animal Magnetism, his lawyers were trying to build the case that Mrs. Eddy's obsession with M.A.M., as her enemies liked to call it, was the clearest sign of her insanity and inability to manage her own affairs. In fact, as we shall see, even if George's interview earned him some national notoriety and sold copies for the *World*, it did nothing to help him in his attempt to inherit his mother's fortune, as George's chief lawyer, William Chandler, no doubt realized.

George's first lengthy visit was probably a strain on the Eddys, but it did serve to reconnect the families. Certainly, after 1880 Mrs. Eddy was in regular, if not frequent, communication with the Glovers, and over the next twenty years she showed considerable financial generosity as well as affection for her son and his growing brood, if not for her daughter-in-law, whom she ignored. The letters Mrs. Eddy wrote to her son in the 1880s and 1890s amply testify to the love and concern she felt for him, but they also reveal her growing frustration as the money she sent him got swallowed up in the gaping hole of George's mining ventures and lawsuits. The Glover family was forever on the brink of not just financial ruin but actual starvation, and, particularly after the births of little Georgie in 1889 and of Andrew Jackson Glover in 1891, Mrs. Eddy tried to ensure the family's well-being without indulging her son's obsession with mining. I shall be taking up the dramatic story of Mrs. Eddy's relations with her son and his family later in Part Four.

Whether or not George Glover's threat to Richard Kennedy had anything to do with it, by the time George had left Boston in the first weeks of 1880, Mr. and Mrs. Eddy had managed to shake off the effects of mesmerism and to rent premises at 531 Shawmut Avenue, Boston. More precisely, George and Clara Choate, students who had become close friends of the Eddys, had leased the Shawmut Avenue house on the verbal agreement that the Eddys would share the expenses with them. In a repetition of what happened ten years earlier with the Bancrofts, a serious dispute broke out between the Eddys and the Choates when Mrs. Eddy decided to move back to Lynn, leaving the Choates to pay the whole rent on the Boston house. George Choate was extremely indignant over this and complained vigorously to both Eddys, but the storm blew over when the Choates were able to find other tenants, and the friendship between the two families grew even closer. The Eddys then spent a relatively calm year, moving between Lynn and Boston.

During the summer of 1880, as had become her wont, Mrs. Eddy sought to obtain some relief from writing, recruiting new students, and worrying about mesmerism by retreating north for a vacation. She spent at least some time in or near her old haunts in Tilton, New Hampshire, visited her sister Abigail, and seems to have been on good terms with her older sister at this time. Things were different with sister Martha and niece Ellen Pilsbury Philbrook, however—as Mrs. Eddy reported to George Glover in the kind of chatty, intimate, family-oriented letter he probably enjoyed. Martha and Ellen preferred to snub Mrs. Eddy by quitting the Tilton home two days before she came to call.

Possibly the Pilsbury-Philbrook connection was keeping aloof not only because they had not forgiven Mrs. Eddy's healing of Ellen in 1867, but because they feared some portion of the Tilton money might pass in the direction of the Glover family if Mary and Abigail became close again. The rich Mrs. Abigail Tilton was now childless as well as widowed, still mourning the 1876 death of her daughter Evelyn, and as her health declined concern about the provisions of her will no doubt grew among her relatives. Like characters in the George Eliot novels which they admired, Abigail, Martha, and Mary had, I imagine, all seethed when their brother George and his son George Waldron Baker had inherited all their father Mark Baker's estate. Mary and Martha, now Abigail's next of kin, were probably determined that at least some of the Tilton fortune should go to their children, if not to themselves. Certainly, in her letter to her son George that summer, Mrs. Eddy says that Mrs. Tilton's business associate had told her how much letters from George pleased his aunt, and Mrs. Eddy adjures George to write regularly, and always in the same hand—in other words to conceal the fact of his illiteracy from his Tilton relatives. Such shenanigans will strike chords in every woman's heart, and they remind us again that Mrs. Eddy was never as cut off from her New Hampshire kin as earlier critics have claimed.[11]

The visit to New Hampshire no doubt provided Mrs. Eddy with some much needed rest and relaxation and removed her from the intense web of rivalries and animosities and fears which continued to plague her movement from within and without and which she had by this time codified under the rubric of mesmerism. Even while on vacation, however, she worked on her next edition of *Science and Health* and pondered what path to take.

After the tiring and eventful winter spent in lodgings in mid-1880 the Eddys took possession of their Lynn home again. It is unclear how much their financial situation had eased by this time. On the one hand, according to Sibyl Wilbur, for the first time Mrs. Eddy was able to set up her own first-floor rooms as study and reception areas. Wilbur, probably quoting Mrs. Choate, gives an enthusiastic description of the new decor and furnishings which now greeted visitors to the Eddys' home.[12] On the other hand, the Eddys were still anxious to spare domestic expenses, and they exerted some pressure on James Howard, a new recruit to Christian Science who had started practicing with some success in Lynn, to move in with them and bring his young family.[13]

One might think that by now Mrs. Eddy would have realized that such domestic arrangements were doomed to failure, but her need to have normal, multigenerational family life around her was still stronger than her common sense. James Howard may have been willing to play son to his leader, and bring his children in as surrogate grandchildren, but Mrs. Howard was not a happy daughter-in-law. Like Mrs. Hiram Crafts and Mrs. George Barry before her, Mrs. James Howard feared Mrs. Eddy's influence over her husband and his career and did not enjoy doing Mrs. Eddy's domestic work and keeping her children quiet during the long daylight hours when Mrs. Eddy was working or meditating. Eventually the Howard children became ill—always an issue in a Christian Science household[14]—and the Howards moved out after only a few months. James Howard would later be one of the ringleaders of the rebellion against Mrs. Eddy's leadership in 1881.[15]

One major reason that Mrs. Eddy may have made extra demands for quiet upon her household was that she was still working on the third edition of *Science and Health*. This edition was notable in several ways, and it showed that the radicalism which characterized the first edition was far from dead in Mrs. Eddy's heart. Mrs. Eddy chose to open her second volume of that edition with "Demonology," the new chapter in which she publicly denounces the devastating Malicious Animal Magnetism campaigns waged against her and her loyal followers by certain evil former students, referred to only by a single initial.[16] Under the title "Recapitulation," the third edition also includes a revision of the sequence of questions and answers which had formed one of Mrs. Eddy's oldest and most important teaching documents, most often referred to as "The Science of Man."[17] Mrs. Eddy also revised her reading of Genesis, and throughout this edition—which continued, over twelve successive printings, to be the Christian Science textbook until 1886—she refers to Mind, Spirit, or God in the feminine gender as She and Her. Thus, rephrasing the verse which ends the first book of Genesis, "And God saw everything that he had made, and behold, it was very good. And the evening and the morning were the sixth day," Mrs. Eddy writes: "And Spirit comprehends every idea that She creates before it is evolved, and they are perfect even as their Principle is perfect. Nothing is new to Spirit. She rests from her labors, and the hush and stir of thought is the order of scientific evolution."[18]

The next important step in the development of the Christian Science movement occurred on January 21, 1881, when the Massachusetts Metaphysical College was chartered. Under the articles of agreement, the college was set up "to teach pathology, ontology, therapeutics, moral science, metaphysics, and their application to the treatment of disease."[19] The articles of agreement were signed by Mary B. G. Eddy, president; James C. Howard, treasurer; Charles J. Eastman, M.D.; Edgar F. Woodbury, James Wiley, William F. Walker, and Samuel P. Bancroft, directors. This list of names itself indicates that a new guard was assuming responsibility in Christian Science, since Samuel Bancroft was the only officer who had been one of the first recruits from Lynn.

The college was chartered under the provisions of an 1874 state law which set out certain minimal provisions by which diploma or degree-granting colleges could be established in the Commonwealth of Massachusetts. (These would prove unsuccessful and be repealed in 1883.) The opportunities provided under this act were probably brought to Mrs. Eddy's attention by Charles J. Eastman, whom Mrs. Eddy had known as a small child in Tilton, New Hampshire, and who had already founded his own Bellevue Medical School. For a few months Eastman's name, together with that of the Lynn doctor Rufus Noyes, was included in the advertisements for the new Massachusetts Metaphysical College, but it was soon dropped; Eastman probably gave at most one lecture. Far from lending Mrs. Eddy's establishment the expertise and authority of traditional medicine, in fact, Eastman, unlike his colleague Noyes who had received his medical training at Dartmouth College, probably had as little medical training as did the Eddys themselves. As a practitioner he was, indeed, himself the product of lax standards of medical accreditation. By 1883 Eastman's college had been closed down by the authorities, and he was being prosecuted, not for the last time, on charges of what Peel refers to as illegal operations, and what Bates and Dittemore claim were abortions.[20]

Eastman's association with Mrs. Eddy had ceased before these charges were made public, but, as we shall see below, he was an important figure in her household during and after the last illness of Gilbert Eddy, and she apparently liked and trusted him for a time. Milmine gives the most detailed account of Eastman, managing to make Mrs. Eddy look guilty by association. We may conclude that Mrs. Eddy cannot be held responsible in any way for Eastman's activities, which would have appalled her as much as they did her critics, but that does not change the fact that Eastman seems to be yet another example of the genial, smooth-talking male for whom Mrs. Eddy had an unfortunate susceptibility.

Despite its inauspicious origins, the Massachusetts Metaphysical College succeeded, and it was to become the cornerstone of Mrs. Eddy's movement from the last part of 1882 onward. By the time that she dissolved the college in 1889, about one thousand students had taken courses there,[21] paid between one and three hundred dollars in fees per course, and received diplomas which proclaimed them foundation members of the new and increasingly influential movement. The college's Boston address and the strong connection Americans outside New England made between Boston and higher education gave the diploma some extra cachet. Many people in Colorado or California or Kansas who wished to set up in Christian Science practice found it financially as well as spiritually worthwhile to spend their money to come to Boston and take instruction at the Massachusetts Metaphysical College. Virtually all the teaching at the college from beginning to end was done by Mrs. Eddy, and the college existed wherever she lived, starting out at 8 Broad Street, Lynn.

Mrs. Eddy's sense of personal calm and of firm progress for the movement was rudely overturned on October 26, 1881, when eight students in Lynn resigned from the association and explained their reasons in an extraordinary letter read in their absence at the Christian Scientist Association's general meeting:

> We, the undersigned, while we acknowledge and appreciate the understanding of Truth imparted to us by our teacher, Mrs. Mary B. G. Eddy, led by Divine Intelligence to perceive with sorrow that departure from the straight and narrow road (which alone leads to growth of Christ-like virtues) made manifest by frequent ebullitions of temper, love of money, and the appearance of hypocrisy, cannot longer submit to such Leadership; therefore, without aught of hatred, revenge or petty spite in our hearts, from a sense of duty alone, to her, the cause, and ourselves, do most respectfully withdraw our names from the Christian Science [sic] Association and Church of Christ (Scientist). (Signed: S. Louise Durant, Margaret J. Dunshee, Dorcas B. Rawson, Elizabeth G. Stuart, Jane L. Straw, Anna B. Newman, James C. Howard, Miranda R. Rice.)

This was apparently an unforeseen blow, not only to the embryonic movement but to Mrs. Eddy personally. Miranda Rice[22] and Dorcas Rawson had been among her very earliest students; they had supported her through the split with Kennedy and Wright, the feud with Spofford, the disastrous lawsuits, and the arrest of Mr. Eddy for plotting to kill Spofford. By their own testimony as well as that of others, Mrs. Rice had been particularly effective in "calling Mrs. Eddy back from the other side" when she went into one of her mysterious "fits."

Like Spofford and Wright before them, and repeating the same accusations that those gentlemen had raised in their time, the group of eight rebels may well have had sincere and well-founded reasons for rejecting the course which Christian Science was moving in under Mrs. Eddy's leadership. But some measure of "hatred, revenge, and petty spite" was also involved, and it was especially aimed at those newcomers like Clara Choate, Arthur Buswell, Edgar Woodbury, and Julia Bartlett who were capturing Mrs. Eddy's affection, admiration, and approval and moving Christian Science out of its Lynn matrix.

Mrs. Eddy's reaction to the public news of the defection is noteworthy, and it became part of her legend. Julia Bartlett's account of the event shows how, by sheer inspiration, Mrs. Eddy turned a practical disaster into a spiritual triumph. Bartlett had not been in Lynn for the fateful meeting when the rebels' letter was read out to the group of Christian Scientists, including Mary Baker Eddy herself. Hearing what had happened, Bartlett rushed to Lynn by the next train to offer comfort to her leader. She found Mrs. Eddy at home with her husband and two other students.

> I quietly took a seat near them as did Dr. Eddy also, and listened to Mrs. Eddy who was talking with a power such as I had never heard before. They were wonderful words she was speaking while we young students were receiving of the great spiritual illumination which had come through her glorious triumph over evil.
>
> Just before I had entered the room she was sitting with the others and the burden was still heavy upon her, when all at once she rose from her chair, stepped out in the room, her face radiant and with a far-away look as if she was beholding things the eye could not see. She began to talk and prophesy of the blessings which would reward the faithful while the transgressor cannot escape the punishment which evil brings on itself. Her language was somewhat in the style of the Scriptures. When she began, the three with her, seeing how it was, caught up their pencils and paper and took down what she said. When she was through speaking, she put down her hand and said, "Why I haven't any body," and as she came back to the thought of those about her, they were so moved by what they had seen and heard their eyes were filled with tears and one was kneeling by the couch sobbing. . . . Those three days were wonderful. It was as if God was talking to her and she would come to us and tell us the

wonderful revelations that came. We were on the Mount. We felt that we must take the shoes from off our feet, that we were standing on holy ground. What came to me at that time will never leave me.[23]

After the rebellion, Mary Baker Eddy was declared pastor of the church by the rump of the membership, and the rebels themselves were expelled from the Christian Scientist Association, rather than being permitted to withdraw. According to Sibyl Wilbur, this tactic enabled the association to continue under its original charter even after the departure of so many charter members. Mrs. Eddy's ties with Lynn had now been definitively broken, and she prepared to move into Boston and rent out the property at 8 Broad Street, Lynn, on a long-term basis. Before taking up residence and reopening her college in the new premises at 569 Columbus Avenue in Boston, however, Mrs. Eddy decided to leave the poisonous atmosphere of Massachusetts behind her for a while. As usual, acting apparently on the assumption that Malicious Animal Magnetism could be directed only to a known postal address, she kept her destination as secret as possible. This assumption is odd, to say the least, but it indicates, in my view, that for Mrs. Eddy mesmerism or Malicious Animal Magnetism was not just a theoretical construct but a code word for spying and sabotage activities by professional rivals, inside and outside the movement.

At the end of December 1881 the small group of remaining Christian Scientists met over the packing cases at Broad Street, and Julia Bartlett was made a member of the Church and put in charge of affairs in Boston while Mr. and Mrs. Eddy were away. In a letter to Miss Bartlett often quoted as evidence of Mrs. Eddy's messianic complex and her bad prose, Mrs. Eddy explained, "I will ask you to take this place not that you can unloose the sandals of my shoes, not that you can fill my place but rather that I think you rather more fit for it than any one I can leave."[24]

Washington was the Eddys' destination, and the eight weeks or so they spent in the capital were more successful than they had expected, as Mrs. Eddy reported in a series of excited letters to her chosen confidants back in Boston. The couple at first stayed right in the center of the city with a fine view of the Capitol. They then took an office on First Street, from which Mrs. Eddy issued copies of the following printed circular:[25]

Mrs. Eddy, President of the Mass. Metaphysical College,

Will interest all who may favor her with a call at her rooms,

13 FIRST STREET, N. E.,

With her Parlor Lectures on practical Metaphysics and the influence that mind holds over disease and longevity.

How to improve the moral and physical condition of man, to eradicate in children hereditary taints, to enlarge the intellect a hundred per

Richard Kennedy, aged about twenty, Mrs. Mary Glover's partner in Lynn, 1870–1872. She called him "a marvelous plotter, dark and designing."

Daniel Harrison Spofford, at the time he was Mrs. Glover's student in Lynn, 1875–1877. He demanded at gunpoint that she marry him.

Edward J. Arens, probably in the late 1870s. He led Mrs. Eddy into a series of disastrous legal battles and was arrested, with Asa Gilbert Eddy, for plotting to assassinate Daniel Spofford.

Mary Baker Eddy in about her sixty-first year. *Courtesy of Church History Department, The First Church of Christ, Scientist.*

Mary Baker Eddy, aged sixty-five, April 9, 1886. *Courtesy of Church History Department, The First Church of Christ, Scientist.*

Mary Baker Eddy between 1887 and 1889. *Courtesy of Church History Department, The First Church of Christ, Scientist.*

Ebenezer J. Foster Eddy, adopted son of Mary Baker Eddy, around 1891.

Josephine Curtis Woodbury, in a flattering portrait of unknown date. She claimed to have borne a son parthenogenetically.

Calvin A. Frye, probably in the early 1880s. Mrs. Eddy's most devoted and trusted associate from 1882 to 1910.

The original edifice of the Mother Church in Boston, shown soon after its dramatically swift completion in 1894. *Courtesy of Church History Department, The First Church of Christ, Scientist.*

cent., to restore and strengthen memory, to cure consumption, rheumatism, deafness, blindness and every ill the race is heir to.

We have a certificate from the most celebrated and skillful Obstetrician and Surgeon in Massachusetts, stating our qualification to teach Obstetrics. And what is better, our system prevents the suffering that has attended accouchment, and with the great auxillary of Mind, obviates the use of medicine.

CONSULTATIONS FREE

The claims made for Christian Science in this circular are easy to mock, and it is notable that here Mrs. Eddy, reverting to the commercial advertising style of ten years earlier, stresses healing in the manner of many mind-cure hucksters and makes no religious claims. Robert Peel and other loyal historians of Christian Science have ignored this flyer, but I have chosen to quote it because of its emphasis on obstetrics, painless childbirth, offspring without genetic "taints," and other "female" issues. Mrs. Eddy herself as a young woman had experienced some of the problems of pregnancy and childbirth, and Mr. Eddy, as we saw from his notebook, had experience with patients with gynecological problems.[26] Those who question how a Christian Scientist could possibly be of help in childbirth might recall that the practice of obstetrics was still in its infancy at this time, and that many women suffered more from the clumsy and infected hands of the obstetrician than from the vicissitudes of a normal labor, painless or not.

Success in obstetrical and gynecological cases was a key factor in the early spread of Christian Science across the United States. In all her advertisements in the *Christian Science Journal* of the mid-1880s, for example, Mrs. Eddy consistently identifies herself as "Professor of Obstetrics," and obstetrical and gynecological cases constitute the largest single category of personal testimonials to healings included in Mrs. Eddy's important collection *Miscellaneous Writings*. I shall quote just one of these accounts, which illustrates the excesses not only of Christian Science jargon— whereby a parturient woman has a "belief of birth"!—but the extent to which the American medical profession had convinced middle-class women, even those with a normal pregnancy, that pregnancy was an illness inevitably requiring professional intervention and ending in a lengthy and debilitating "confinement."

> I now write of the wonderful demonstration of Truth over the birth of my baby boy, two weeks ago. Sunday, September 23, we went for a long drive of three hours; at night I retired at the usual hour; toward morning I was given a little warning; when I awoke at seven o'clock, the birth took place. Not more than ten minutes after, I ate a hearty breakfast, and then had a refreshing sleep; at ten o'clock walked across the room while my bed was dressed; at twelve took a substantial dinner; most of the afternoon sat up in bed, without any support than Truth; at six

o'clock in the evening dressed myself and walked to the dining-room and remained up for two hours. Next morning I arose at the usual hour, and have kept it up ever since,—was not confined to my bed one whole day. The second day was out working in the yard and the third day went for a drive in the morning and received callers in the afternoon. If it had not been for the presence of my young hopeful, it would have been hard to believe that there had recently been a belief of a birth in the house, but then, I was sustained by Love, and had no belief in suffering to take my strength away. Before baby was two weeks old, I cooked, swept, ran the sewing machine, etc., assisting with the household generally. How grateful I am for the obstetrics of this grand Science![27]

The famous case of Christian Scientist practitioner Abby Corner in 1888, in which Mrs. Corner's own daughter and her newborn child both died under her care, was not just a personal tragedy for the Corner family and their friends and an oft heralded illustration of the dangers of Christian Science healing; it was also a setback for all who preferred to see childbirth as a natural event rather than a medical emergency. In the aftermath of this tragedy the associations of largely female healers, like Christian Scientists, were forced to yield the care of women in labor and childbirth to licensed medical practitioners, almost all of them male. The concept of "natural child-birth" would have to wait until the 1950s to burgeon, and then that movement came to strength largely in Europe.

To return to the Eddys' visit to the capital, while in Washington Mrs. Eddy worked as hard or harder than she had ever done, going to bed late, getting up early, lecturing for as much as three hours a day, engaging in lengthy correspondence with her students, and doing everything possible to spread the Christian Science doctrine. Despite all this work, or perhaps because it went so well, she had energy left for a social life and tourism. Her stay was particularly congenial since she encountered in Washington two figures from her New Hampshire past, Fanny McNeil Potter (Mrs. Judge Chandler Eastman Potter), who was the niece of the former President Franklin Pierce and also related to Mrs. Eddy's grandmother; and General Henry Moore Baker, one of her first cousins. These prominent citizens were eager to show Mrs. Eddy the sights of the town, which included, rather surprisingly, a trip to a prison to visit the recently convicted murderer of President Garfield.[28] After about a month in Washington, the Eddys moved on to Philadelphia for a less exciting but equally profitable stay. On their return to Boston, the couple was given a triumphant reception in the elegant town house of the Choates, where Mrs. Eddy moved, confident and gracious, among the guests, while privately expressing reservations about the worldliness of the reception.

Mrs. Eddy's triumphant return to Boston after her social and missionary successes further south and the failure of the revolt of the eight to seriously damage her movement all seemed to presage a new and smoother path, but tragedy was soon at hand. Even as his wife seemed poised to move on to a wider social scene, Asa Gilbert Eddy was drawing further into the shadows. His main purpose while in Washington was purportedly to make a serious study of copyrights. This task was useful not only because it served the immediate interests of the movement but also because it allowed Gilbert long hours of peace and seclusion.

The copyright research was directed against the threats posed by Edward Arens, who had been in open competition with Mrs. Eddy for several years already. Like other lapsed students of Mrs. Eddy, Arens found it advantageous to locate his professional premises as close to hers as possible, but he also encroached on her territory even more perversely in his publications.[29] In 1880 Arens published anonymously a pamphlet called *The Science of the Relation Between God and Man and the Distinction Between Spirit and Matter*, which alternated rather garbled rephrasings of Mrs. Eddy's ideas with verbatim transcriptions of pages from *Science and Health*. Arens later published and distributed to his students and prospective patients, also anonymously, a revised version of this pamphlet, but the Eddys were kept fully informed on his activities, as no doubt Arens was of theirs, and probably by the same sources.

For the third edition of *Science and Health*, Asa Gilbert Eddy, as publisher, wrote an indignant preface, fulminating against those who dared to plagiarize his wife's copyrighted work. At the time there was also much talk in Christian Science circles as to how best to counter the Arens threat. Unfortunately, by the time the Eddys returned to Boston and settled into their new home, it was clear to all that Mr. Eddy was not capable of taking an energetic measure against Arens or anyone else, although he continued to see patients into early May of that year. He was in fact dying, as quietly and inconspicuously as possible, all too aware that his death would pose notable practical and theoretical difficulties for his wife, whose Christian Science message seemed at last to be finding a public.

It is hard to know whether the small group of students and friends who clustered around Gilbert Eddy in his last weeks was really processing what was happening to him before their eyes. It is especially hard to understand what was going on with Mrs. Eddy, whose behavior before and after her husband's death was so unusual that critics have rightly focused upon it. On some level, everybody knew how to interpret his severe chest pain, breathlessness, insomnia, and lack of energy and appetite. In a public statement issued just after Eddy died, the students who had been attending him admitted that when, at an unspecified time in the past, he had consulted a medical examiner in order to get life insurance, the doctor had diagnosed "some unfavorable heart symptoms." Nonetheless, in a particularly egregious example of Christian Science doublethink, the students went on to insist after his death that Mr. Eddy had "never suffered from any heart difficulty before or since that time."[30]

Clara Choate was with Gilbert Eddy in his last days, and she gave Sibyl Wilbur an eyewitness account of that time:

> That Mr. Eddy suffered greatly, and that Mrs. Eddy suffered with him in her deep affection and sympathy is vouched for. . . . Mrs. Eddy had the work of her church to carry on; her room was littered with books and papers; there was no order there at this time, for she could give but snatches of attention to affairs while her husband was lying stricken in an adjoining room. He breathed with agony and with physical sobs. Sitting by him, Mrs. Eddy would lay her face close to his and murmur, "Gilbert, Gilbert, do not suffer so," and under her silent treatment he would be relieved for a time and sleep.
>
> But Mr. Eddy observed that he distracted his wife from her pressing business and heroically declared, "My sickness is nothing; I can handle this belief myself." He steadfastly declared he was coping with the attack and urged his wife to leave him. When she had reluctantly done so, he experienced a depression, but refused to have her called to relieve him. Just before his death he cried out, "only rid me of this suggestion of poison and I will recover." Mrs. Eddy had retired but was called; her husband expired, however, before she could reach him. This was before daybreak on Saturday morning, June 3, 1882.[31]

Immediately after her husband's death, Mrs. Eddy declared that he had been killed by mesmerism, directed upon him by her enemies, notably Edward Arens. She actually sent a messenger to summon Arens to come and view the corpse so that he could see the consequences of his actions.[32] By invoking mesmerism, she did not mean merely that Arens, Kennedy, Spofford, and others, by their professional rivalry, lawsuits, and general hostility had worried a seriously ill man to an early grave, although this was close to the truth. She meant, quite specifically, that they had mentally poisoned him, as she explained in an interview in the *Boston Globe* on June 4:

> Mr. Eddy, her husband, had died that morning, and she appeared much overcome at the event, and could scarcely control herself enough to make the following statement: Her husband, she said, had died with every symptom of arsenical poisoning. Both he and she knew it to be the result of a malicious mesmeric influence exerted upon his mind by certain parties here in Boston, who had sworn to injure them. She had formerly had the same symptoms of arsenical poison herself, and it was some time before she discovered it to be the mesmeric work of an enemy. Soon after her marriage her husband began to manifest the same symptoms and had since shown them from time to time; but was, with her help, always able to overcome them. A few weeks ago she observed that he did not look well, and when questioned he said that he was unable to get the idea of this arsenical poison out of his mind. He had

been steadily growing worse ever since, but still had hoped to overcome the trouble until the last. After the death the body had turned black.

Not content with summoning the *Globe* to take her statement, Mrs. Eddy demanded that Dr. Rufus Noyes and Dr. Charles Eastman conduct an autopsy. Eastman, who had received no formal medical training, issued a series of contradictory findings, stating variously that Eddy's heart and lungs had been diseased, that he had died from bronchial catarrh and emphysema, that there was full evidence of arsenical poisoning. Noyes, who was a competent traditionally trained physician, was for his part unequivocal. He found, according to the summary given by Bates and Dittemore, "the aortic valve completely destroyed and the surrounding tissues infiltrated with calcareous matter," and he reported on the death certificate that Asa Gilbert Eddy had died of heart disease.[33] In an extraordinary step, he sought to persuade Mrs. Eddy of the validity of his diagnosis once and for all by bringing out her husband's heart on a tray and pointing out to her the diseased parts. All in vain. The following day Mrs. Eddy again called a press interview and more fervently than ever pressed the claim that her husband had died of mesmeric poison.

The death of Asa Gilbert Eddy should not be melodramatized. He slipped into death in his chair in his own room, in his own home, in the company of affectionate and concerned friends. Had he not met and married Mrs. Eddy but remained a bachelor who needed to do active work to earn a living, given his medical condition, he could easily have died alone, indigent, and uncared for. It is perhaps true that Eddy did not take the strychnine and digitalis that Dr. Noyes had prescribed for him, but these medications would have been palliative at best. Medical science could diagnose Asa Gilbert Eddy's condition, it could prove the accuracy of its diagnosis by postmortem examination, but it held no possibility of cure. Perhaps the stresses involved in living with the founder of Christian Science took their toll. Perhaps Gilbert Eddy in his last six years worked too hard, worried too much about real practical problems, and suffered too much from the dread of Malicious Animal Magnetism. But it is as inaccurate to say that Christian Science killed Gilbert Eddy as it is to say that it could have healed him, given the right circumstances. Nonetheless, Mr. Eddy's death is too poignant and the subsequent accusations of mental arsenical poisoning are too bizarre to be passed over lightly. Our final judgment of Mrs. Eddy must, I think, be deeply colored by our understanding of this moment in her life.

First, what are we to make of her behavior toward him in the weeks before his death, when all acknowledge that she was not constantly in attendance at his bedside? How do we interpret Mrs. Eddy's claims of mental arsenical poisoning and the account she gave of her own treatment of the mental arsenic only two days after Gilbert's death in an interview with the Boston *Post?*

> Circumstances debarred me from taking hold of my husband's case. He declared himself perfectly capable of carrying himself through, and I was so entirely absorbed in business that I permitted him to try, and when I had awakened to the danger it was too late. I have cured worse cases before but I took hold of them in time.[34]

Here Mrs. Eddy casts herself in a very unfavorable light, since she implies that she could have saved her husband, as she had others, but she failed because she was too busy to appreciate the gravity of his case and too confident in his own ability to ward off the powers of Malicious Animal Magnetism without her help. This point was not to be lost on Mrs. Eddy's critics. Frederick Peabody's extraordinary antipathy for Mrs. Eddy is perhaps never better illustrated than in his sarcastic and cruel account of her husbands' deaths.

> Now even a woman Messiah could not be on the lookout all the time against these malicious thoughts directed at her third husband and, in a moment of inadvertence, one of them got by and killed Eddy, and killed him *dead.* . . . How sweet, how *charming*, is the wifely devotion, that, kissing the lips of death, speedily and forever loses track of the sacred ashes of the beloved *first* husband, rushes into the divorce court for freedom from the truant *second*, and, having twice restored the adored *third* to life, when a third time he thus eludes her refuses, positively and coldly refuses, to bring him back and looks with calm and critical eyes upon the formerly attached, but now, alas, detached heart![35]

In order to understand Mary Baker Eddy's responses to Gilbert's death, I think we need to focus on the peculiar status of death in Christian Science and, indeed, its status in all forms of mental cure and faith healing. From the earliest days of Christian Science, miracle cures of every ill known to man have been the fuel that propelled the movement, the essence of its propaganda, the heart of its weekly testimonial meetings. Yet every Christian Scientist knows that today, at least until some unpredictable moment in human evolution toward spiritual reality, at some mysterious point, the miracle must cease and the patient must die. The inevitability of death poses peculiarly difficult problems from within a Christian Science perspective, since death may involve not only the usual burden of sorrow and loss, but the additional onus of responsibility, failure, and guilt. The practitioner faithful to Mrs. Eddy's teaching, and more peculiarly Mrs. Eddy herself, is faced with the question, if I had worked more effectively as a healer, lived more purely as a Christian, reached out more strongly to the divine principle of eternal love and life, could I have saved the person who has just died?

As reported in graphic detail in the daily newspaper, Mrs. Eddy's claim that her husband was killed by mental arsenic probably struck many average citizens as almost comically crazy. In later years it would be cited by lawyers as prima facie evidence of her insanity, whereas for her followers it confirmed the strength of her commitment to the theory of Malicious Animal Magnetism. But the claim of mental arsenical poisoning was also a deeply personal response to loss. Forced to look at the heart which has just been cut out of the chest cavity of a loved one, most of us would be horrified, revulsed, traumatized, but we would have accepted the doctor's diagnosis based on the physical evidence, and we would have understood that the death was the result of natural causes, of anatomy and physiology, not of the healer's personal failure. The extraordinary passion with which Mrs. Eddy pursued the diagnosis of mental arsenic is, I think, due to the fact that she suffered not only the normal widow's grief, but the singular torment of the self-proclaimed healer of all maladies who has conspicuously failed to prevent the painful demise of the person she loved best.

By attributing such terrible powers of harm to the wretched Arens, Mrs. Eddy was seriously subverting her own higher metaphysics and infecting her embryonic movement with an obsessive dread of Malicious Animal Magnetism. These were problems she would later have to cope with, but in the short term the theory of arsenical poisoning allowed her to reconcile her Christian Science doctrine with the fact of Gilbert's death and retain her own confidence and efficacy even as she mourned. Theologically in the days to come, she would revert to an older position, accepting that God had determined that she should lose her husband, seeing his loss and her loneliness as another part of the price she would have to pay for the revelation given her. In practical terms, she knew she had to prevent Gilbert's death from immobilizing her. She could not bring her husband back, but she could accept his legacy of quiet, selfless work, build on their joint efforts, and marshall all her energies to ensure that Christian Science did not lose its new momentum.

PART THREE

THE
NEW
MRS. EDDY

1883–1905

INTRODUCTION

By 1882 Christian Science had moved out of Lynn and penetrated the Greater Boston area, but it was still raising barely a blip on the cultural radar of the nation as a whole. Numbering its adherents in the dozens rather than the hundreds, the movement had defined itself as a new kind of Christianity, not just an alternative healing system, but it was still more noted for controversy, sensation, and schism than for faith, hope, and charity. Its self-proclaimed leader and founder, Mary Baker Eddy, had perhaps managed to live down her reputation as the notorious divorced Dr./Mrs. Mary Glover (formerly Patterson), but she was still regarded by the press and the public as a quotable crackpot rather than a religious leader. Had Mrs. Eddy in 1882, like her husband, succumbed to physical illness or mental arsenic, she and Christian Science would have sunk into oblivion, meriting not so much as a footnote in the history of nineteenth-century American religious cults.

Yet a bare six years after Gilbert Eddy's death Christian Science had a membership numbering in the thousands and had moved through the Midwest and into California and Oregon, its startling progress signalled by the vigor with which it was being denounced by the clergy, the medical profession, and the press. By 1900 Christian Science churches had sprung up in most American cities, their size, elegance, and freedom from red ink proclaiming the promise of the new sect and the power of its leader. By 1905 Mrs. Eddy, whom respectable Lynn had once snubbed and thrown stones at, was regarded with reverence bordering on adoration by men and women all over the land and in several other countries and was widely hailed in the American press as the most powerful woman in the United States. *Science and Health*, of which Daniel Spofford had barely managed to sell one thousand copies by 1877, had become a best-seller, guaranteeing a nice income for its author, publisher, and printer. Ever since the death of her first husband, George Glover, in 1844, Mrs. Eddy had been, to use an image of her own, a lone swimmer in a dark, stormy sea, struggling to stay above water. Now, suddenly it seemed, she was a sturdy ark, breasting the flood and looking confidently for the sun to break out and the land to emerge out of the waters.

This triumph was all the more remarkable because it came so late in life, and to a woman without social connections or powerful friends. In materialistic terms, Mrs. Eddy was a self-made woman, but she did not come to fame in youth or middle age, when the powers of both men and women are commonly assumed to be at their height. She started, indeed, to make her mark at an age when most people, whether high achievers or ordinary Joes, are beginning to make room for a generation of children or even grandchildren.

The unusual trajectory of Mrs. Eddy's career, with its final steep upward curve, has also inverted the normal graph traced by biography. Whereas most lives peter out in a decline that biographers pass over as mercifully and briefly as they can, Mrs. Eddy's biographers of all stripes have agreed that she becomes interesting in the 1880s, and they typically devote a third or even half of their work to chronicling and examining the events of the last three decades of her life. Thus the story of her last years has been examined and analyzed exhaustively from a wide variety of points of view and is known in considerable detail.[1] Yet if the fact of Mrs. Eddy's meteoric rise is indisputable, the whys and hows of it are hotly debated. This debate centers on religion, on the importance of religious faith to Mrs. Eddy personally, and on the value of her religious theory and practice.

Given that Mrs. Eddy is famous because she founded a new religious sect, it is interesting that non–Christian Science commentators—the most celebrated of whom we shall soon be meeting in the second half of this book—though divided on many issues, are united in insisting that God played no part in the Eddy phenomenon. These critics disagree about the existence and nature of God and what management strategies He may pursue with His human creation, but all agree that it is impossible to account for Mrs. Eddy's career in her own terms—that is, to view her life as a special testimony to the eternal, unchanging, omnipresent power of God, as elucidated in *Science and Health*. The nonreligious refuse to see the hand of God in human affairs in general and in Christian Science in particular. The religious refuse specifically and indignantly to acknowledge even the possibility that God might have chosen Mary Baker Eddy as His instrument.

I confess that this religio-secular consensus on Mrs. Eddy had considerable appeal for me when I began this project. Like Edwin Dakin or Martin Gardner, I am generally loath to invoke the hand of God whenever something surprising occurs in my biographical subject's life. I confess to sympathizing with those who—like the eminent lawyer and United States Senator William Chandler whom we shall meet in Part Four—consider Mrs. Eddy to be deluded. I can raise a wry chuckle with those, like Mark Twain, who see her as a mercenary old humbug. But by the time I had researched and written my account of Mrs. Eddy's first sixty years, I had become convinced that the emphasis on purely nonreligious factors was self-defeating, and that Mrs. Eddy's critics were too blinded by their own prejudices to offer any useful or illuminating account of her. Not one of the nonreligious explanations in itself (she was crazy, she cared only for power and money, she was a shameless hustler and huckster, she was bad) begins to account for the phenomenon of Mrs. Eddy. When applied all at once, as they commonly are, they form not the links in a strong chain of logic but a number of disparate objects perilously kept in the air by second-rate jugglers.

According to our personal metaphysical systems, we may variously consider the visions and voices so consistently met with in religious history as messages from God, as delusions, or, indeed, as the manifestations of God through delusions, but we can agree that these "Tolle, Lege" experiences are dramatically effective motivators and instruments of change in human affairs. What matters, from both a historical and a biographical viewpoint, is whether the vision changes the person's life and activates him or her to achieve practical things which, on the scale of activity, would be placed between difficult and impossible. Let us, moreover, take into account that delusion is an essentially modern concept, and that modern technology has made knowledge of other people's lives far more expansive and detailed, and hagiography therefore more difficult. Fiction rather than reason makes it easier for us in general to credit the hand of God in a life lived in medieval Italy—or indeed in present-day Nepal—than in Concord, New Hampshire, in the late 1800s.

Whether faith is viewed as ultimate truth or as a cultural and psychological phenomenon, the best working hypothesis we can use in Mrs. Eddy's case is to assume that belief is the simple but essential factor in explaining the enigma of her worldly triumph. She believed that God had chosen her, and she acted on that belief, decisively, consistently, and with remarkable results in the world of fact. Following the philosophical guidance of William James in *The Varieties of Religious Experience*, we should give Mrs. Eddy the benefit of the doubt and assume that she was a religious leader as real and as genuine as others, and that diagnoses of religious delusion and psychopathology, of hucksterism, greed, or megalomania, explain her case as much, or as little, as they do the case of Joseph Smith, Martin Luther, Teresa of Ávila, Joan of Arc, Augustine of Hippo, or Mother Teresa.

Furthermore, it is important to understand that her gender is the major reason why Mrs. Eddy's claims as a religious leader have aroused such general hostility outside her movement and such ambivalent and countereffective protectiveness within it. Not only was Mary Baker Eddy a woman, but she was an unsettling mix of the ordinary and the extraordinary. On the one hand, she was a normal nineteenth-century American woman who married, became a mother, and lived to be old. On the other hand, she was the rare woman who sought power, accepted it, tried to learn how to use it, and lived with its implications. Moreover she was a woman who calculated the result of putting the female mind, body, and soul as factors into the equation of power, and then tried to *move on* from issues of male and female. Only when gender assumptions are made clear and set aside will it be possible to evaluate Mary Baker Eddy as she herself would have wanted—as a person of faith and a religious leader, not a freak.

In the remaining two parts of this biography I shall trace events which fed Mrs. Eddy's conviction that God was speaking and acting through her, and I shall analyze the practical ways in which she made her religious vision real. I shall show how confidence bred authority over others, and authority brought a wider social power. I shall tell how Mrs. Eddy toiled unremittingly not just to edit *Science and Health* so that it found new and better readers, but to develop de novo her roles as prophet and leader, and to establish the basis of Christian Science as an ecclesiastical polity and social presence. I shall also show how power, adulation, success, and wealth led her to experience a special kind of isolation and desperation, redoubling her need to throw herself upon God and define the expectation of love, happiness, and fulfillment in ways approaching mysticism.

While recognizing that, increasingly as her life went on, Mrs. Eddy's story is the story of Christian Science, I shall persist in focusing not on the movement per se, but on her—on the way her evolving sense of religious mission affected her physical condition, structured her psychological identity, altered her relationships with other people, laid out the patterns of time and space in her daily life, colored her dreams, drove her to despair, filled her with elation, kept her on the move, physically, intellectually, as well as spiritually, right into her ninetieth year.

We shall see how the private space Mrs. Eddy purposefully created about herself after her retreat into New Hampshire in 1889 led to her growing status as mythic presence, and this in turn led to her re-creation by the press as an early avatar of the twentieth-century media personality. This externally defined public presence loops back in turn to reshape her identity, invade her privacy, and trouble her peace. Thus the questions we shall be dealing with in these final two parts will be not so much what did Mrs. Eddy do, as, first, what was the nature of Mrs. Eddy's inner world; second, how was she perceived by others, close and far; and, third, how did the self she expressed in words and actions interact with the persona as perceived and created from outside?

16

The Massachusetts Metaphysical College

T HE PRESS INTERVIEWS, THE AUTOPSY, AND THE WHOLE controversy over "mental arsenical poisoning" kept Mrs. Eddy at fever pitch in the days immediately following her husband's death, but then emotion took its toll. She mourned her husband and deeply felt his loss. Asa Gilbert Eddy had certainly not been a match for his wife, but he had been what she perhaps needed more, a reliable partner and loving aide. Until his final illness he had filled important practical roles in her life, and up to the very end he had been unfailingly devoted, the one man whose loyalty and support she never had cause to doubt. During their short marriage, the Eddys were rarely out of one another's company for more than a few hours, and Mrs. Eddy, who had been forced for so many years to act independently and appear at all social events without an escort, enjoyed the simple pleasure of always having her husband by her side when she went out.[1] Perhaps one of the most intimate losses Mrs. Eddy suffered when Gilbert died was that she no longer had someone by her side at night, someone who could listen to her visions, calm her when she was troubled by nightmares, offer the elemental and inestimable comfort of warm, loving, physical presence. For twenty years before her third marriage, Mary Baker Eddy had mourned the loneliness of her life. Once again, at the age of sixty, she found herself alone, and she sought to understand and accept her widowed state in religious terms: "I could be happy with him [Gilbert Eddy] in a hut," she is reported to have said, "but God means I shall rely on Him alone."[2]

300

The day after the funeral service in Boston on June 5, 1882, George Choate accompanied Asa Gilbert Eddy's body to Tilton, New Hampshire, where it was laid in the Baker family lot, next to Mrs. Eddy's mother and father. As she had done since girlhood, Mrs. Eddy sought some relief from sorrow by writing a poem in which she imagined Asa Gilbert Eddy being greeted in the next life by her mother, and assuring Mrs. Baker that all was well with their loved one, who would soon join them.[3]

By the time all the formalities had been completed, it was clear that Mrs. Eddy desperately needed the support of friends and a little quiet space outside of Boston. The women students at the college—Julia Bartlett, Clara Choate, Abbie Whiting, Delia Manley, and Josephine Woodbury prominent among them—rallied round Mrs. Eddy,[4] but she seems to have felt an especial need for a man's arm to lean upon. In time of real misfortune, Mrs. Eddy still turned instinctively for comfort to her own kin, and she cabled to her son in Lead, South Dakota, to come to Boston at once. George did not come—he had many good reasons for not jumping on a train at a moment's notice and rushing to his mother's side, but Mrs. Eddy never forgot or forgave George's refusal to be with her when she so desperately needed help. The mother-son relationship was sabotaged once again.[5]

A surrogate son, in the shape of Arthur T. Buswell, did meet the summons. He left his work as superintendent of the Board of Associated Charities in Cincinnati, Ohio, to return to Boston and Mrs. Eddy as swiftly as he had gone to the Midwest in the first place. Buswell immediately proved his usefulness by arranging for Mrs. Eddy to spend some time at his family home in Barton, Vermont. He himself, together with the beautiful young singer Alice Sibley, long an enthusiastic friend of Mrs. Eddy, stayed with her there for the next six weeks or so.[6] In her reverent biographical sketch of Asa Gilbert Eddy, Mrs. Mary Longyear later set down what Buswell told her about Mrs. Eddy's stay with him:

> Although she had exhibited heroic qualities of energy and fortitude, neglecting nothing of direction and command before leaving Boston, she showed on the journey traces of nervous exhaustion and at times the hysteria of grief threatened to overwhelm her. . . . Mr. Buswell relates that her great struggle was known to his household, but that she carried it through alone, though they often watched outside her door. After a night of agony, she would emerge from her struggle with a radiant face and luminous eyes, and they would hesitate to speak to her for fear of disturbing the peace which enveloped her.[7]

Torment at night, visions, nightmares, physical agony, metaphysical travail form one of the most fascinating leitmotifs of Mrs. Eddy's life, particularly in her last thirty years.

In her letters to friends written at this period, Mrs. Eddy stressed how much she missed her husband and grieved for him. Thus she writes to Clara Choate on July 16:

> I am up among the towering heights of this verdant state, green with the leaves of earth and fresh with the fragrance of good will and human kindness. I never found a kindlier people. I am situated as pleasantly as I can be in the absence of the <u>one true heart</u> that has been so much to me. O darling, I never shall master this point of missing him all the time I do believe, but I can try, and am trying as I must—to sever all the chords [*sic*] that bind me to person or things material.[8]

Grief did not make her idle. As Willa Cather, writing as Georgine Milmine notes, "Mrs. Eddy . . . is never so commanding a figure as when she bestirs herself in the face of calamity."[9] During the long sunny summer days in Vermont, she set about finding practical solutions to the problems and fears that racked her at night. She was consciously gathering strength for the work ahead and considering carefully how to organize her affairs so that her energies could be devoted to what was most important.

For a woman of her age and experience who had spent much of her prime lying exhausted and pain wracked on her bed, Mrs. Eddy was now a miracle of dynamism and resilience. But even she had limits to what she could accomplish in a day, and she was more aware than many around her that she would need to ration her personal resources for the task ahead. One aging woman, even if inspired by God, could not get a new religious movement off the ground alone, and finding good lieutenants and aides had by this point become essential. Curious inquirers were clamoring at the door to see her, the mail was piling up, the classes at the college were filling with new students from all across the country, and her sermons and lectures, now held in the large Hawthorne Hall, were attracting more and more interest.

As leader of Christian Science, Mrs. Eddy needed someone to help her with correspondence, schedule her appointments, and screen the people who came to the door or wrote for interviews. As a private individual, she also needed someone she could trust to oversee her personal finances, since money from book sales, class fees, and property rentals was beginning to flow in more strongly. Even more mundanely, she needed someone to play the traditional woman's housekeeping role, to supervise the day-to-day chores of the college household on Columbus Avenue, get meals on the table, linen changed, rooms cleaned, and so forth. Mrs. Eddy enjoyed and excelled in doing such things, but it was clear to all that undertaking the management of these chores was not the best use of her time. She needed a combination of secretary, accountant, household manager, and social organizer.

Surprisingly, Mrs. Eddy actually found someone who could and would perform this wide range of functions, in the person of Calvin A. Frye, a thirty-seven-year-old widower and a recent student of Christian Science from

Lawrence, Massachusetts, then making his living as a machinist.[10] Frye is one of the most important figures in the history of Christian Science, and one of the most difficult to understand. A smallish, inconspicuous, silent man, inclined in his later years to embonpoint, Frye preferred to keep out of the limelight. In the 1880s, while Mrs. Eddy remained in Boston and was still obviously and actively in charge of things, Frye was seen at best as a workhorse, at worst as a cipher. Then, as Mrs. Eddy gained in power and prominence while simultaneously moving into seclusion, Frye was cast in the role of éminence grise or Madame de Maintenon. Mrs. Eddy was seen as a shadow puppet and Frye as the puppet master. The most rabid of Mrs. Eddy's enemies in her final years, Frederick Peabody chief among them, were, against all evidence, convinced that Frye's relation to Mrs. Eddy could be explained only if he was in fact her fourth husband.[11] On the other hand, just as critics have expressed their scorn for Gilbert Eddy by feminizing him, an even more overt, less subtle version of this exercise took place in the case of Frye. His celibacy, old-maidenly fussiness, and willingness to do anything Mrs. Eddy asked of him—from donning a demeaning footman's livery when he drove her out each day to taking down her dreams in shorthand—marked him for the subordinate, female role.

That a young and strong man like Frye was willing to drop everything and become Mrs. Eddy's lifelong factotum is indeed odd, and it is clear that his choice was not made for monetary reasons. Even in the final years at Chestnut Hill, as the most trusted employee of a wealthy woman, Frye made less than $2,000 and expenses a year. Although Mrs. Eddy made ample testamentary provision for him in the later 1890s, it was on the condition that he still be in her service at the time of her death. Had Frye one day been provoked beyond even his tolerance and walked away from her household, he would have had scant savings to fall back on.

Why, then, did he stay, and why did she keep him? Why did he serve, disliked, mocked, plotted against by the fellow members of the household, ignored, snubbed, and finally calumniated by the outside world? His relation with Mrs. Eddy was fraught with conflict. Frye was mulish, antisocial, taciturn, lacking in charm and grace, and Mrs. Eddy was constantly irritated by his limitations. She loved to declare her dislike of him, wildly berating him to his face and, while recognizing his virtues, she called him the most unpleasant man in the world in letters.[12] Conversely, if any man or woman was in the position of knowing Mrs. Eddy's faults, if anyone saw her at her worst, it was Frye, and the brutal intimacy of almost thirty years surely prevented him from feeling for her the simple adulation that Christian Scientists at a greater distance expressed.

The answer to the question of why they worked together for so many years lies, I feel, in the community of religious feelings they shared, in the neediness of the two persons involved, in the intensity of their relationship, and in the socially approved ways in which their emotions could find expression. In the days when people did not analyze their feelings much, or reach out for professional counselling, it was often the strains in the relationship which were overt and articulated, while the bonds remained silent and unseen. Both Mrs. Eddy and Calvin Frye came from closely knit New England families, tried in the crucible of Calvinist doctrine and economic hardship. Though unrelated by blood, they instinctively reproduced the often bitter, rivalrous intensity of a widowed mother–widower son duo, framed within a larger family and clan structure. In New England, as in the South Wales of my own childhood, it was much more normal to complain about one's loved ones, to express the negative, to carp, criticize, scream, argue. Thus, like a traditional mother, Mrs. Eddy was loud in her criticism of her son's weaknesses but swift to come to his defense if anyone else took up the cudgel against him. Testing his endurance with the flail of her tongue, she found him to be incorruptible, always striving to do his best, and, as the old sayings go, when push came to shove and the chips were down, she could be surer of him than of anyone else. She knew him, understood him, and relied upon him. He was indispensable. On his part, Frye found in Mrs. Eddy not just a woman but the mother he had never had as well as a faith that could fill the empty husk of his life.

Calvin Frye's life had been marked by tragedy and hobbled by limitations. His father, Enoch Frye, came from an old New England family and was a member of a very distinguished class at Harvard College, but any assumptions that rank and money would be his were destroyed when a long illness left him lame. Reduced to working as a schoolmaster and then as a small shopkeeper, Enoch Frye married Lydia Barnard and had four children by her, but he was to enjoy as little domestic happiness as he did financial prosperity. Lydia, while still a young woman, became insane and was to remain so for most of her long life. In a period of lucidity after being institutionalized for a second time, Lydia begged her family to allow her to remain at home, and they agreed. Calvin, the third child, grew up in the shadow of his mother's insanity, which the family coped with largely on its own by stoic withdrawal from society and reliance on their Congregational faith. Both Calvin and his sister Lydia married but endured early widowhood and had no children.[13] Into this affective wilderness burst the vivid figure of Clara Choate, who appeared to have some success in treating Mrs. Frye, and then Mrs. Eddy, with whom both Calvin and his sister Lydia Frye Roaf took classes and who subsequently converted them to Christian Science.

During the long years with Mrs. Eddy, Frye gave up the basic freedoms of the healthy male Anglo-Saxon artisan in America. In return, however, he lived at the center of activity and excitement, in an environment wholly different from his parents' desolate home. Mrs. Eddy was changing the landscape of American religion and medicine, and Calvin Frye was her right-hand man. Certainly, when, in August 1882, Mrs. Eddy invited Frye to come and live at her college and help her with her work, Frye had no idea of the life that lay ahead of him. He knew very well, however, the life that lay behind. Christian Science was dynamic, alive, changing, everything that life in the Frye house in Lawrence, Massachusetts, was not. Mrs. Eddy's summons was an opportunity for change in a life marked by tragic stasis, and I do not think Calvin Frye ever, fundamentally, regretted answering that call.[14]

Frye thus joined the household at 569 Columbus Avenue[15] and soon had his hands full since Mrs. Eddy had by 1883 embarked on an extraordinary number of important projects. In more and more demand as a preacher, lecturer, and teacher,[16] Mrs. Eddy engaged in a massive correspondence and was also absorbed in preparing the radically new sixth edition of her textbook, the first to be called *Science and Health with Key to the Scriptures*, which would appear in the fall. In addition to all of this, in April she broke new ground by starting her own periodical. The *Journal of Christian Science*, soon to be renamed the *Christian Science Journal*, was in its early days written and edited largely by Mrs. Eddy herself. Julia Bartlett was in awe before Mrs. Eddy's energy and capacity for hard work. She later recalled that there were times when she would be taking down letters in dictation from Mrs. Eddy and the pen would drop out of her hands she was so utterly weary, but Mrs. Eddy would plow on.

Some of the personal and professional problems Mrs. Eddy faced in these early days of the movement can be gauged from her correspondence with Clara Choate, who has a small but important place in the early history of Christian Science. When Mrs. Eddy first met her in 1878, Clara was an ambitious, energetic young woman with real talents for public speaking and healing. She was married to George Choate, a man of good Boston family who sadly had a taste for drink and showed little aptitude for business.[17] In a pattern not uncommon with young women, following the birth of her first child, Warren, Clara fell into a pit of depression and illness. From this Mrs. Eddy roused Clara, inspiring in the young woman a passionate and enduring gratitude. Both Clara and George became converts to Christian Science, as did Clara's mother, Mrs. Cynthia C. Childs. The Choates both took class with Mrs. Eddy and Mr. Eddy and set up as practitioners. But it was clear from the outset that Clara was the one who could bring people to Christian Science.[18] Her success in the field, joined with her frequently, fulsomely expressed adoration of her leader, endeared her to Mrs. Eddy and aroused envy in other students.

Clara seems to have been closer to her mother than to her wayward husband, and she reproduced that successful mother-daughter relationship with Mrs. Eddy, who was always on the lookout for surrogate children and grandchildren.[19] Mrs. Eddy could sympathize with Clara in her domestic problems,[20] she found Clara a congenial, reliable friend,[21] and she knew that her movement could grow only if it attracted dynamic people like Clara. She saw in Clara an example of the newly liberated feminine energy that was at that time changing the face of America. In March 1882, she wrote to Clara:

> It is glorious to see what the women <u>alone</u> are doing here for temperance, more than ever man has done. This is the period of <u>women</u>, <u>they</u> are to move and to carry all the great moral and Christian reforms, I know it. Now darling, let us work as the industrious Suffragists are at work who are getting a hearing all over the land. Let us work as they do in love, "preferring one another." Let us work shoulder to shoulder each bearing their own part of the burdens and helping one another and then the puny kicks of mesmerism will give up the ghost before such <u>union</u>.[22]

Unfortunately, Mrs. Eddy's dream of marching shoulder to shoulder with Clara Choate proved short-lived, and what she liked to call "the puny kicks of mesmerism" took their toll. Controversy swirled around Clara, who not only sang more solos and sold more copies of *Science and Health* than anyone else but also began to give lectures and sermons that aroused favorable attention and thus attracted to her students of her own. Other members of the Christian Scientist Association such as James Howard and Caroline Fifield complained that Clara was full of hubris, openly trumpeting her successes and her special closeness with Mrs. Eddy and spreading gossip which she claimed Mrs. Eddy had confided to her in private. For months Mrs. Eddy defended her friend in public and begged her in private to be more discreet and stop offending people gratuitously. In an attempt to both capitalize upon Clara's proselytizing skills and get her away from Boston, Mrs. Eddy alternately begged and ordered Clara to start afresh in Chicago, where there were signs of both promising growth of and harmful resistance to Christian Science. But Mrs. Choate, pleading her large circle of friends, her flourishing practice, the patients who relied upon her, her family's needs, even her lack of a suitable wardrobe, refused to go.[23]

By January 1884 the conflict between Mrs. Choate and the other students had gotten out of hand, and Mrs. Eddy wrote to Clara:

> This is my candid conclusion—that because the people are believing you the cause of pretty much all their disasters, you had better withdraw from the Church and Association, and not attend our defence. <u>Seven</u> years on this very question, and at the end of all this fidelity I hear of you accusing me publicly of working against you because I am envious of your popularity etc. etc.

In another letter written a few days later, Mrs. Eddy said,

> I can get a temporary suspension from the Association and a dismissal, instead of expulsion, from the Church and what has been found amiss buried so deep it shall never be spoken.[24]

What Mrs. Eddy was determined to "bury," and what would finally bring about Clara's ouster from Christian Science was a written complaint of what we would now call sexual harassment, filed by one of Clara Choate's former patients. This letter was placed in Mrs. Eddy's hands, I would guess, by another student, anxious to defeat a rival and establish himself as a replacement. The patient, Benjamin Ashley, claimed that during a healing session Clara had kissed and caressed him without his consent, and that she was seeking to control him mesmerically.[25] Mrs. Eddy sought to keep the precise nature of the accusations against Clara Choate secret, both to protect the good name of her protégée as much as possible and, even more pressingly, to protect the good name of her Science, but part of Ashley's letter was read out at an association meeting. Ever since 1872 and the split with Richard Kennedy, the use of "manipulation" in Christian Science practice had been absolutely prohibited (see Chapter 11). For me, it was very interesting that the first hard evidence I came upon that "manipulation" did indeed have strong sexual connotations referred to a woman practitioner touching a male patient inappropriately.[26]

Several times in her letters Mrs. Eddy referred to Clara's "sensuality," and, in my view, Mrs. Eddy was from the outset both fully aware and willing to overlook that her darling was a young woman, disappointed in her marriage, whose sexual energies could not always be sublimated into Christian Science. In a pattern she would repeat even more dramatically with Josephine Woodbury, Mrs. Eddy sought for years to give Clara a combination of public support, professional opportunity, private encouragement, and Christian rebuke which was designed to keep her on the path of conventional morality. It was not Mrs. Eddy's fault that she failed. Mrs. Eddy loved and enjoyed Clara Choate, Clara sincerely loved and revered Mrs. Eddy, and although their relationship ultimately foundered in the dangerous shoals of leader-follower power politics, it had a genuine core. It is one of the small tragedies of Mary Baker Eddy's life that as her movement grew larger and prospered, she would be forced to look to such slippery individuals as Ebenezer Foster for the fun and good fellowship which the sparkling, affectionate Clara had once provided from the heart.

The strong currents of rivalry, jealousy, and ill will that swirled around Mrs. Eddy, her students, and such rival mental practitioners as Arens, Dresser, and Kennedy were based squarely in the practical difficulties of making a living and a reputation in alternative healing, but these negative forces were theorized and referred to within the movement as mesmeric influence. In this respect, Mrs. Eddy's overwrought conviction that her husband had been mesmerically poisoned by Edward Arens was only an advanced symptom of a general condition. There is no doubt that Malicious Animal Magnetism or mesmerism was a constant subject of discussion not only formally in Mrs. Eddy's classes, but informally in the staircases and corridors of her college. But in my view too much has been written of the paranoiac atmosphere that reigned in the Columbus Avenue house follow-ing the death of Mr. Eddy. The obsession with mesmerism did not prevent students from enrolling in the classes in increasing numbers, nor did it pre-vent graduates from going out to their home communities to heal and spread the word. I would grant that life at the Massachusetts Metaphysical College probably was crazy, but more because the students were so busy, so stressed, and so competitive than because they were obsessed with fear over succumbing to unseen malice.[27] Four documents, written from dif-ferent points of view and at different times, allow us to get a sense of Christian Science life at this time, and they also form a collage portrait of Mary Baker Eddy at this period.

The Mother Church archives contain an odd fragment from a personal diary kept by Arthur Buswell which gives a clear sense of the rivalries and tensions of life at the college. This diary fragment apparently comes out of Mrs. Eddy's personal files, and it is fascinating to speculate on how it came to be there and why it was kept. Is it possible that one of the other college students tore out the pages?—for example, Calvin Frye, Buswell's roommate for a time, and his chief rival for Mrs. Eddy's attention? Part of the diary reads:

> April 14th 83 We have planned to receive another Miss B into our home myself and Dr. Frye to room together at $4.00 I making the change giv-ing up a single room to accommodate shortly after we are moved Mrs. E informs us that she must charge $5.00 each as she cannot make her expenses without considering her property (two houses in Lynn and real estate in N.H.) it seems strange indeed. But undoubtedly refers to the expenses of an injunction which is to be brought against one Arnes [*sic*]. This house is costing her (rent) 1000 per year she receives from rent $98.00 per month. Rooms bearing an equal expense Groceries hired help kitchen fuel etc.
>
> April Sunday Mrs. Eddy wishes me to occupy the desk in "Church of Christ"! how can she ask a liar and thief (as she recently in fearful rebuke called me) to take the stand as a Christian teacher is more than I can tell at present My duty I know is to be not only to do but to <u>speak</u> indeed speaking is part of doing after words
>
> Sunday April 29 P.M. I am again compeled to step forward But reluctantly because Mrs. E assertions before the ass'n and College res-idents recently of my character &c although I am a man the accusations are unjust not to say unladylike yet I hesitate to speak because of them how can a morally degraded person as I have been recently represented appear before an audience as a teacher of this high form of Christianity even if innocent? It appears the hight of hypocrisy some where and some how.[28]

The portrait we get here of life at the Massachusetts Metaphysical College is not a pleasant one, but money and Mrs. Eddy's quick temper and sharp tongue seem more the problem than Malicious Animal Magnetism.

Another view of life at the college in the 1880s comes from Julia Bartlett, who, unlike Buswell, was to become a lifelong pillar of Christian Science. Miss Bartlett's memories of Mrs. Eddy, written late in life, are deeply reverential and laudatory, but nonetheless she, too, in her naïve frankness, makes it clear how difficult the financial situation was in the early years, and how much the students had to put up with:

> As Treasurer of the Church I often found the subscriptions insufficient to meet the bills. This lack I supplied from time to time from my own purse, in order that the payments might be made promptly and that there be no debts. There were many uses for what we had and not a great abundance to draw from. The greater part of my time was given to work that brought no material remuneration. This I considered a privilege. I took a few patients, and had good success in healing, and this supplied me with necessary funds, until all at once not one came to be healed. I understood the cause of this and worked assiduously to overcome the error in realizing God's government and that He is the source of supply and in doing my part to start my practice again, yet with no apparent result.
>
> To be sure I had all I could do with work for the Cause, but my little practice which had met my daily expenses, was taken from me. To reduce expenses I then began to take my meals out and to reduce the supply as well, and for the first time I knew what it was to suffer from hunger day after day. I did not trouble Mrs. Eddy or anyone with the extreme conditions, so far as I could hide them. It was my problem to solve. I finally thought relief must come soon if I was to remain in the College, and taking my Bible for my guidance, I opened to these words: "Thou shalt remain in this house." It was no longer a question with me. I must and could work it out. Then one day the patients began to come. The attempt to take me away and deprive Mrs. Eddy of the help she needed had failed and I had no more trouble that way, and she said I never would.[29]

Writing at a time when Christian Scientists had learned to be reticent, Miss Bartlett does not say in so many words that her extreme financial plight was due to the Malicious Animal Magnetism of other practitioners, whether within or outside the fold.

It is interesting to compare the private Mrs. Eddy—vituperative and mercenary in the Buswell diary fragment, unseeing and preoccupied in the Bartlett memoir—with the public Mrs. Eddy of this period as remembered and described by two people who were quite independent of Christian Science. Around 1886 a young and rising clergyman, Thomas Van Ness, managed to have a personal interview with Mrs. Eddy, which he recorded in his 1926 book about influential New England divines of the previous generation. He remembered Mrs. Eddy as a woman "of one idea almost to wearisomeness," a woman who read little and had little logic, and he was deeply wary of her request that he come to Boston and investigate Christian Science. "She has abundant determination. She wants absolute obedience. . . . I would have to be her slave." Yet despite the reservations which he had about her, Van Ness was captivated and fascinated by Mrs. Eddy. He observed that "there is a sweetness about the woman, too, and she can make herself very agreeable as she did on the afternoon when she invited me to go out driving with her. I notice that she keeps an eye on things. She puzzles me by her double nature."

Mrs. Eddy failed to gain Thomas Van Ness as a convert to Christian Science, but he remained sufficiently impressed by her to give the following conclusion to his reminiscences of her forty years later:

> What if she was narrow, impetuous at times, even domineering; what if she brooked no opposition and insisted on developing an organization in accordance with her desires. All that counts for little now over against the fact that she gave practical expression to a great and helpful truth, and that she was able to state that truth in a way to have it understood by simple minds. We do not judge the Calvinistic system by what John Calvin was in his private life; nor the benefits of the Revolutionary War by what sort of a husband John Adams was. Christian Science, with all its faults, has saved the religion of New England from a hard, dry, mechanical sort of orthodox preaching on the one hand, and from a wishy-washy vague style of transcendentalism on the other hand.[30]

In July of 1885 the journalist Lilian Whiting had a scheduled interview with Mrs. Eddy, which she wrote up in an article for the Ohio *Leader*. By this time Mrs. Eddy had moved from 569 to 571 Columbus Avenue, and the early austerities of bare linoleum and functional furnishings had been upgraded at least on the ground floor where Mrs. Eddy and other practitioners shared a suite of consulting rooms. Miss Whiting appreciated the "daintily furnished reception-room, where pictures and bric-a-brac indicated refinement and taste." She was even more impressed by Mrs. Eddy herself, who emanated an "indefinable element of harmony and a peace that was not mere repose, but more like exaltation." Miss Whiting recalled that she had entered Mrs. Eddy's house feeling tired and depressed, but on leaving she skipped down the steps like a child and slept that night as if "I had been caught up into paradise."[31]

An even more reverential picture of Mrs. Eddy at this crucial period was given by William Lyman Johnson in his 1922 novel, *From Hawthorne Hall*. Johnson's father was an early and fervent convert to Christian Science, and the younger Johnson got to know Mrs. Eddy as a child and conceived a lifelong devotion to her. Johnson bases many of his characters on real Christian Scientists and has some historical basis for his plot. One of the virtues of the work is that it helps us see the social terrain that Christian Science was entering. Though a novel, the book is accurate in showing that Christian Science succeeded in part because Mrs. Eddy created a public persona that satisfied the tastes of both the rich financier and the aspiring artisan. Hawthorne Hall, the place Mrs. Eddy had chosen to preach in, was expensive and fashionable, and Johnson's Mrs. Eddy, when she appears to conduct the meetings—tall, slim, elegant, assured, dressed in a kind of Quakerly chic, sweeping up to the meeting in her carriage—blends with the surroundings and contrasts with the shabby dress and unfashionable ways of the congregation, most of whom have come on foot or by horsecar.

The novel also shows, in the character of Delia Barker, the way an encounter with Christian Science could revolutionize a woman's life. Another character, John Hamilton, muses thus about the revolution in the life of his cousin Delia, the character closely based on Julia Bartlett:

> "A few years ago she was without poise, she had no definite aim in life; she was anemic, fast going to seed, but pure gold in her heart, and filled with love for others, but so afraid to show it that she appeared cold and indifferent. Now everything is changed. She looks younger, although she is nearly forty, acts like a business woman, and by Jove she has decided poise and I *like* the way she talks."[32]

In *From Hawthorne Hall*, Mrs. Eddy herself is constantly evoked, her words quoted, her doings debated, and, through the combined influence of her writings and of the active participation of two of her followers, she is shown to be the source of the miraculous healings of the two protagonists, Mary Hamilton and Gerald Amory. Yet Mrs. Eddy appears in person, as it were, only late in the book when John Hamilton, Mary's father, attends a Christian Science service in Boston with his cousin. Johnson describes the charm and sensitivity with which Mrs. Eddy greets her followers and acknowledges newcomers, and he evokes the extraordinary effect of calm focus and indestructible confidence which her preaching has on those assembled. Johnson is writing here largely for the converted, and he is recalling events of forty years earlier, thus retouched by the blurring of memory and the enhancement of later triumphs. Nonetheless, the rise of Christian Science in the 1880s can be explained only in terms of the extraordinary effect which Mrs. Eddy was now having, the indefinable, but nonetheless real and decisive, effect of her physical presence and spoken words. That several people claimed to have been healed of physical woes during the services only increased the general reverence with which she was now regarded.[33]

In public, on scheduled occasions and in special interviews, Mrs. Eddy was the epitome of calm, sweetness, and grace, but she was under enormous pressure, not only from her students and followers, but also from her professional rivals, many of whom were former adherents. As Stephen Gottschalk has shown so brilliantly in his book on the emergence of Christian Science, Boston in the 1880s was seething with the activities of rival mental healing groups.[34] That Mrs. Eddy and her Christian Science were perceived as the leaders in the field can be gauged by the intensity of the attacks raised against her, and given how small and frail her movement still was in 1883, it is a sign of her great abilities that she continued to make such phenomenal headway. The most notable and long lasting of these professional controversies came up in early 1883, but troubles were destined to plague Mrs. Eddy for the rest of her life, and still occasionally her movement faces such troubles even today.

The extent of Mrs. Eddy's debt to Phineas Parkhurst Quimby was an old issue that had bubbled up at various times in the 1870s, but it would become a public matter in the 1880s as the result of an alliance between Edward Arens and Julius Dresser, two very different men who had known Mrs. Eddy in different capacities in her less confident and prosperous years and who found common cause in their hostility to her. Since 1880 Edward Arens had joined Richard Kennedy as a mesmerist and arch assassin in Mrs. Eddy's eyes, and, if one takes mental arsenical poisoning as a code term for malice, one could make a good case that Arens had done more than anyone else to hound the fragile Asa Gilbert Eddy into his grave. Julius Dresser's relation with Mrs. Eddy went back to the Portland days, but although each had looked then upon the other with cool suspicion, there had not yet been any overt hostility between them.

Following P. P. Quimby's death in 1866, Julius Dresser had given up all interest in mental healing. Employed in the 1860s as a journalist in Maine, he later moved to California, where he lived with his wife Annetta and only son Horatio until 1882 or 1883. At this point, word of the new successes being reported by Christian Science somehow reached the Dressers, and they dropped everything and came east, fired, according to later New Thought accounts, by the desire to defend the memory and record of P. P. Quimby, and, as far as I can see, by the intention to cash in on Mrs. Eddy's success. Julius Dresser took classes with Edward Arens. Dresser was in a position to offer Arens a theoretical justification for his practice of competing with Christian Science not only on its own turf but with its own texts. Specifically, Dresser told Arens that "the methods and ideas claimed as hers (Mrs. Eddy's) by right of 'revelation' were derived from Dr. Quimby."[35]

By the end of 1882 Dresser had apparently decided to take up the mental healing business in earnest, and he saw Mrs. Eddy and her movement as his most dangerous rival in the field. In February 1883, therefore, Julius Dresser for the first time went public with accusations that Mrs. Eddy owed everything to P. P. Quimby, airing his views in a letter to the Boston *Post*, signed only with the initials A. O. Mrs. Eddy's position vis-à-vis this first attack, both practically and theoretically, was strong. Chivalry was not Julius Dresser's forte, and his strategy of making an anonymous attack on a respectable and recently widowed woman could have gone against him. Furthermore, as many could testify, Mrs. Eddy, until at least the late 1870s, had been open and generous in acknowledging her debt to Quimby in both her teachings and her writings—more generous, in fact, than had been Warren Felt Evans, the Dressers' later ally in New Thought and the other Quimby patient who had gone into mental healing and had written books on the subject. Outside the Quimby family circle, the only other place where the name of P. P. Quimby had been remembered with reverence was in the then Mrs. Glover's small circle of students in Lynn.

Whereas in the Lynn period, as a woman without powerful allies, living on the margins of society, it had been expedient or even necessary for the then Mary Baker Glover to quote some male authority, by 1883 the situation was very different, and Mrs. Eddy's attitude toward Quimby had evolved. She was now an acknowledged leader. Aware of how far she had travelled intellectually and spiritually from the Quimby period, Mary Baker Eddy was no longer willing to play the part of disciple or acolyte. Still recovering from her husband's death, buried in work, and besieged by problems of many different kinds, she seems to have been taken off her guard by the Dresser accusations and lashed out against her attackers in a hasty letter of rebuttal, which she signed E. G.

Knowing Quimby as she did, knowing his limitations as a thinker and a writer, she found it both absurd and threatening that he should be identified as the real author of *Science and Health*, and in her amazement and fear she defended herself against the Dresser attack first rather vaguely but then with increased emotion, dismissing Quimby as an illiterate mesmerist. That Quimby was a mesmerist had been publicly stated by Warren Felt Evans in 1872,[36] and this charge would be repeated by Julius Dresser's wife and fellow Quimby patient, Annetta Dresser, in 1895. What Mrs. Eddy said about Quimby's limitations as a writer was also generally acknowledged by all who had known Quimby. Unfortunately, Mrs. Eddy's fierce indignation led her further, and she showed that tendency to trim the past to suit the needs of the present, which friends like Sarah Bagley and Miranda Rice had reproached her for in the past, and which her critics would later seize upon. Creating a kind of mirror image of the allegations made against her, she claimed that it was she who had influenced Quimby, that in her visits to Portland in 1863 and 1864 she had played an active role in shaping Quimby's ideas, in forming his vocabulary, and in drafting his manuscripts. Even worse, she downplayed the strength of her own relationship to Quimby as a doctor and the personal debt she owed him.

Ignoring Mrs. Eddy's correct statements that P. P. Quimby had been a mesmerist and was largely illiterate, Julius Dresser seized with glee upon her ill-conceived depreciation of Quimby and her new account of her relationship with him. These he had the means to disprove. Through the intermediary of Arens, who had been in correspondence with George Quimby, Dresser had acquired copies of the letters and poems which Mrs. Eddy had written to P. P. Quimby back in the 1860s, and which George Quimby had lovingly preserved in a scrapbook devoted to his father's professional life. Writing to the *Post* again, this time under his own name and identifying himself as Quimby's faithful student, Dresser published for all to read sections of the letters in which Mrs. Eddy loudly proclaimed how much she owed to Quimby—dithyrambs in dramatic counterpoint to the stringent critiques she had offered to the *Post* readers only days earlier.[37] In a magnificent rhetorical flourish, Julius Dresser concluded his second open letter to Mrs. Eddy in the Boston *Post*, dated February 24, 1883, thus:

> When Dr. Quimby's writing shall be given to the world in print, it will then be seen whether "E.G." has correctly called them "mere scribblings," or whether truly they are the master delineations of a science of truth and health that shall become the healing of the nations.

In later statements about her relation to Quimby, Mrs. Eddy would be both more circumspect and more truthful, but her failure to tell the whole or exact truth in the first instance would rouse ineradicable suspicion in the minds of many, and her own words would be quoted against her for the rest of her life. The two letters she wrote to the Boston *Post* rebutting Dresser were both mean-spirited and ineffective, a lethal combination. She appeared to be desecrating the memory of a New England man of genius—alas forgotten!—and thus the initial charges of plagiarism were reinforced with charges of ingratitude, a sin particularly egregious in a nineteenth-century woman.[38]

Mrs. Eddy was down for the count, but she was by no means out, and as always she learned from her mistakes. Given time to reflect, and given her real depth of knowledge of P. P. Quimby, she realized that in his final reference to the Quimby writings Dresser had let down his guard. Continuing to see attack as her best defense, Mrs. Eddy in April filed a bill of complaint against Edward Arens on the grounds that in his published pamphlets he flagrantly plagiarized long passages of her copyrighted and published works. In June in a counter complaint, Arens boldly argued that he was free to use the passages in question because Mrs. Eddy in turn had plagiarized them from unpublished manuscripts by P. P. Quimby which she had been allowed to copy and keep.

Mrs. Eddy had had all too many opportunities to observe how the law worked, and by bringing Arens, and in effect Dresser too, into the courts, she successfully changed the parameters of the debate. In the court of public opinion, the Dressers' personal testimony about Quimby and his work had considerable weight, especially among those who were ill disposed to Mrs. Eddy's newly founded church. With their letters to the Boston *Post* in the spring, the Dresser-Arens faction had managed, it seemed, to prove in print that Mrs. Eddy was an ungrateful student who demeaned her teacher. Now in the fall, however, they had to prove by legal standards not that Mrs. Eddy had known or been influenced by P. P. Quimby but *that she had plagiarized his writings*. Here unsupported anecdote was not enough. For Arens and Dresser to prevail, written proof of Quimby's theories was necessary, and, more specifically, the documents that Arens had claimed Mrs. Eddy copied would need to be produced so that comparisons could be made with her published work.

This was a problem that Arens, Dresser, and their legal team were not able to solve, mainly because the P. P. Quimby writings that they had taken to praising in such extreme terms existed largely in their imaginations. Julius Dresser did have his personal copies of the documents that would come to be known as "Questions and Answers" and "Volume 1," but the documents were short and clearly did not cover much of the theoretical ground covered in *Science and Health*. More important from Arens's point of view, they were not written in Quimby's own handwriting but in Dresser's own or his wife's, and thus they constituted a rather delicate piece of evidence in a trial or hearing. Despite all these manifest drawbacks, over the next fifty years or more these documents, particularly "Questions and Answers," were to bear the whole burden of the continuing charge of plagiarism against Mrs. Eddy.[39]

Acting on their own rosy memories of what Quimby had written, memories which were at least as retouched and unreliable as Mrs. Eddy's, the Dresser faction believed that Arens could win his case and thus win a major publicity victory if only they could gain access to the papers left behind in Portland after Quimby's death. Unfortunately, despite all the pleas from Julius Dresser and Edward Arens, neither Emma Ware nor George Quimby could be persuaded that the time had come to publish the Quimby papers or, indeed, to let anyone read them. As his letters and later published essay on his father show, George bore no initial grudge against Mary Baker Eddy, but, as the years passed, he was inevitably affected by the Dresserite portrait of her as a plagiarist and ingrate, and by her reactive moves to stress the ways she differed from P. P. Quimby. George's overriding concern, however, as he made clear from the first in his correspondence with Arens at the time of the libel suit of 1883, was not to attack Mrs. Eddy but to protect and promote his father's reputation. He considered this aim incompatible with making public his father's papers, and he grew cool toward the Dressers and their allies whenever they sought to advance their own interests, financial and legal as well as intellectual, by urging him to crush Mrs. Eddy and pursue a public vendetta against her.

Today, now that we have at last the complete and unexpurgated edition of the Quimby writings, it is obvious that there were only general similarities between them and Mrs. Eddy's published work, and that any charge of plagiarism, particularly of the blatant kind practiced upon Mrs. Eddy's writings by Edward Arens, could never be upheld. This was evidently the conclusion George Quimby had come to as of 1883, since far from complying with the requests to publish or produce the Quimby papers in court he took the extraordinary step of sending them out of the country to Scotland and into the possession of his father's old disciple Mrs. Sarah Ware McKay, presumably so that they would be safe even from subpoena.

One of Calvin Frye's early tasks as Mrs. Eddy's chief assistant was to superintend the collection of documentary evidence for the Arens case. From the transcript of the trial hearing, Frye emerges not only as the Christian Science movement's main tactician but as a witness whom no defense counsel badgering could deter from showing that pages and pages of the pamphlets which Arens published under his name and circulated in lectures and consultations to his students were taken unchanged from *Science and Health*. Frye's testimony is interesting because it shows him to be not only self-possessed and imperturbable in the witness box but also lucid and intelligent, understanding where the cross-examiner is trying to lead him, refusing to rise to the bait or to depart from the story he wished to tell.[40]

Since Arens was unable to present any proof of what P. P. Quimby had actually written, Mrs. Eddy won her suit, and Arens was forced to pay costs and destroy the offending pamphlets. After all the legal disasters into which Edward Arens had led Mrs. Eddy in the 1870s, it must have been very sweet to her to have found at last a disciple as capable as Frye and to see her cause so resoundingly seconded by the law.[41]

As a postscript, let me add that when, in 1887, the New Thought movement fired a new salvo in the shape of an article by the journalist A. J. Swarts which rehashed all the old Quimby plagiarism charges with no new proof, Mrs. Eddy was ready with a counterattack.[42] She fired back at Swarts with a public letter titled "Important Offer," which appeared in the Portland *Daily Press* of February 18, 1887. She denied categorically that she had "appropriated matter belonging to the aforesaid Quimby," and she offered to publish Quimby's manuscripts at her own expense, provided "that I am allowed to examine the said Manuscripts, and that I find that they were Mr. P. P. Quimby's own compositions, and not mine, that were left with him many years ago—or that they have not since his death in 1865, been stolen from my published works." She ended her public letter with the very shrewd point that Julius Dresser's excuse that Quimby's writings could not be published as "the times were not sufficiently enlightened" made no sense. Her own books were selling well, and if, indeed, everything she had published was to be found in Quimby, then his writings too would presumably find an eager public.[43] This important offer was never taken up, and the Dresserite faction was reduced to muttering, in effect, that of course the Quimby papers could not be shown to Mrs. Eddy, because she would destroy or change them to suit her own nefarious purposes. In fact it would be a century before it was possible for an honest edition of Quimby's writings to be issued, and thus, at last, before any people still interested would have the chance to read both Quimby and the 1875 *Science and Health* in parallel and decide for themselves how far Mrs. Eddy was indebted to her old friend.

17

Getting
Out
the Word

I F "DEMONSTRATION"—THE SPONTANEOUS, HERE-AND-now performance of healing—is the heart of Christian Science, writing is its brain. More than almost any other modern religion, Christian Science relies for its authority on text, and its ritual focuses narrowly on the reading of texts. In its Sunday services today the Church of Christ, Scientist replaces the spoken and often extempore words of the traditional Protestant sermon with paired, prescheduled readings from the Bible and *Science and Health with Key to the Scriptures* which many of those present have read and considered for themselves in advance. As she clarified her theology, Mrs. Eddy placed increasing stress on Christian Science not just as a healing praxis but as a lexis or exegesis of healing. Her Science claims not only to have restored to pride of place the healing practices recorded in the Gospels but to constitute a progress in that it offers an elucidation or statement of the divine truth which Jesus of Nazareth and his immediate disciples had "demonstrated."[1] By extension, Mary Baker Eddy conceived her own essential role as one of elucidator, offering a "Key to the Scriptures" and thus showing the way to the eternal truths which centuries of ecclesiastical dogma and institutionalism had hidden.

In the development of Christian Science, conversation, teaching, debate, lectures, and sermons were the first and indispensable avenues whereby the new teaching could be disseminated, and oral communication was an area in which Mrs. Eddy naturally excelled.[2] When she established the Massachusetts Metaphysical College, Mrs. Eddy finally managed to put into place the organizational structure which allowed her extraordinary class-room talents to flourish.[3] Both in Boston and elsewhere, a number of those who rebelled against Christian Science or were expelled from it set up institutes or colleges to copy and compete with Mrs. Eddy's college. None, however, had anything close to the same success, mainly because their principals could never inspire and motivate their students as Mrs. Eddy did.[4] Testimony to the power and effect of Mrs. Eddy's classes abounds in the reminiscences collected by The Mother Church, but I shall quote here two very different people who attended class with Mrs. Eddy at about the same time.

The first is from C. Lulu Blackman, a fervent and impressionable young woman who came from Nebraska in the fall of 1885 to take class, and who after considerable struggles, first to accept her own potential as a healer and then to understand the doctrine of Malicious Animal Magnetism, embraced Christian Science:

> When she entered the Class-room, I saw her for the first time. Intuitively, the members of the class rose at her entrance, and remained standing until she was seated. She made her way to a slightly raised platform, turned and faced us. She wore an imported black satin dress, heavily beaded with tiny black jet beads, black satin slippers, beaded, and had on her rarely beautiful diamonds. These she spoke of in one of the later sessions. She stood before us, seemingly slight, graceful of carriage and exquisitely beautiful even to critical eyes. Then, still standing, she faced her class as one who knew herself to be a teacher by divine right. She was every inch the Teacher. She turned to the student at the end of the first row of seats and took direct mental cognizance of this one, plainly knocked at the door of this individual consciousness. It was as if a question had been asked and answered and a benediction given. Then her eyes rested on the next in order and the same recognition was made. This continued until each member of the class had received the same mental cognizance. No audible word voiced the purely mental contact. Experience has been the lightning flash, that has revealed to me something of the mass mentality she confronted.[5]

A very different student was the Reverend James Henry Wiggin, a middle-aged, urbane, cynical, and theologically trained Bostonian who, exceptionally, was allowed to attend class with Mrs. Eddy as an auditor. Wiggin already knew Mrs. Eddy and her ideas very well when he began to sit in on her class, he had the education and training to be a good judge of her abilities, and, unlike Miss Blackman, he wrote up his impressions soon after the event. Even though Wiggin contributed these remarks to the *Christian Science Journal* and was no doubt paid for his contribution, he was never accused of looking at Christian Science through rose-colored spectacles.

> From hearing Mrs. Eddy preach, from reading her book (however carefully), from talking with her, you do not get an adequate idea of her

mental powers, unless you hear her also in her classes. Not only is she glowingly earnest in presenting her convictions, but her language and illustrations are remarkably well chosen. She is quick in repartee, and keenly turns a jest upon her questioner, but not offensively or unkindly. A brief exposition of the Book of Job, which one day entered incidentally into her statement of how God is to be found, would have done honor to any ecclesiastic. Critical listeners are often astonished at the strong hold she has upon her thought, and at the clearness of her statements, even when they cannot agree with her. While she is sharp to detect variations from her own view, and to expose the difference, she governs herself in the midst of discussion. In fact, Rev. M. B. G. Eddy is a natural class-leader, and three hours pass away in her lessons before you know it.[6]

Wiggin makes clear here that Mrs. Eddy's enormous success with her classes rested on her ability not only to give inspiring lectures, but also to interact deeply and personally with each student, to ask and answer questions, and to move confidently onto topics as they came up, rather than just sticking strictly to a format or schedule. Prepared by years of thinking and writing and debate, sure of her Truth, Mrs. Eddy could be pointed, argumentative, funny, informal, and spontaneous. Her potent combination of authority and charm influenced all who took class with her, at least for a time, and permanently inspired many.

Preaching and lecturing were obvious ways to extend Mrs. Eddy's influence beyond classrooms and living rooms into halls and churches, and her oratorical skills also proved considerable.[7] As we have seen, from the mid-1870s Mary Baker Eddy, despite the meager resources of her nascent movement, rented halls and also inserted advertisements announcing her coming addresses in the local Lynn and then the Boston papers. At first she spoke to tiny groups of the converted and risked the ridicule and hostility of hecklers. In late nineteenth-century America, a woman's place was assumed to be in the home, not on the platform, certainly not in the pulpit. Women who made public speeches still aroused deep suspicion and antagonism and were regarded by many middle-class people as actresses or mountebanks, or worse.[8]

Mrs. Eddy understood as well as anyone that the female orator had to present herself to the public as the epitome of respectability and to develop a rhetoric that inspired and captured the interest of an audience without contravening the prevailing conceptions of modest femininity. Impeccably groomed, tastefully dressed, graceful of movement, harmonious of voice, inspiring of tone, Mrs. Eddy was the match of any casual heckler. Once, when asked how, as the apostle of nonmateriality, she could appear for her addresses clad in purple velvet and diamonds, Mrs. Eddy managed to find a reply that both reinforced her femininity and carried her essential message of demonstration. Her dress, she said, was hardly expensive—the fabric being only velveteen, thirty-six inches wide, cost a dollar a yard, and surely many of the women in the audience had on something more costly. As for the diamond brooch and ring she wore, they had been given her as tokens of gratitude by patients she had healed.[9] With the small details of dressmaking, Mrs. Eddy established her place in the everyday female world, a world where, indeed, she had always been at home (remember how, back in 1844, Mary's mother had regretted that her daughter was not at home to help her with the dress patterns!). Through the outward signs of the diamond gifts, Mrs. Eddy reminded the world of her essential credential as a religious teacher—her proven ability to heal.

In one way or another, every sermon and address Mrs. Eddy gave was an ordeal, a test of strength, and her increasing success actually put further pressure on her to succeed since not only did her students expect so much, but the male clergy were increasingly alarmed. The hostility her preaching was arousing from the established Protestant clergy became public in 1885. For some years, Mrs. Eddy had been preaching on Sunday afternoons at Hawthorne Hall, a respectable yet modest venue only a few blocks away from the magnificent Tremont Temple where Joseph Cook held sway. The Reverend Cook preached regularly to thousands both at his Sunday services and at his even more popular Monday lectures, in which he undertook to examine the burning issues of the day from the enlightened view of modern religion. The people who gathered each week to hear Mrs. Eddy speak still numbered in the hundreds, but Christian Science was beginning to make converts from the established denominations, and the Reverend Cook and his colleagues started to feel some alarm.

In 1885 at one of his lectures Cook read aloud a letter written by a fellow divine, the Reverend A. J. Gordon, which condemned the new Christian Science as mere Spiritualism, pantheism, or theosophy, and its "lady apostle" for believing in "no personal Deity, no personal devil, no personal man, no forgiveness of sin, . . . no intercessionary prayer."[10] Any unbiased reader of *Science and Health* could have attested that the accusations of theosophy and Spiritualism were wide of the mark. Though highly respected members of the Protestant intelligentsia, Cook and Gordon had, it seems, not bothered to read anything Mrs. Eddy had written, and they preferred to make the accusations they thought most damaging, regardless of their lack of evidence. That Cook attacked from behind the shield of another man's words is, I think, an indication both of his intellectual contempt for and his anxiety about the new science's potential.

Mrs. Eddy promptly accepted the challenge posed by Cook's lecture. Not only did she reply in detail to his allegations in a piece she published in her own magazine[11] and in a Sunday sermon to her own faithful, but she demanded the opportunity to reply in public at the Monday lecture. Cook grudgingly offered her ten minutes, and she accepted. She knew full well that the briefness of the slot offered her was in itself an insult and that Cook was setting her up for failure. This estimation was confirmed when Cook was personally insulting to her when they finally met at the Temple on the appointed day. Gracious and elegant as always, Mrs. Eddy could only meet Cook's disrespect with quiet courtesy and steel herself to address nearly three thousand hostile faces.

The transcript of Mrs. Eddy's address, which was taken down in shorthand at the time, fills a mere three and a half pages in the current authorized edition of her writings, and the brevity of the address is in itself significant.[12] No one would be able to charge Mrs. Eddy with being some crazy, garrulous woman who was incapable of marshalling her thoughts and limiting her words. She spoke extempore, as was her wont, and within the limits set her by her male antagonist, and she managed to find a very female rhetoric— simple, personal, and unacademic, in tune with her small, low, but clear and carrying voice.

The address took the form of a series of questions and answers— "Am I a Spiritualist?" "Do I believe in a personal God?" "Do I believe in the atonement of Christ?" "How is the healing done in Christian Science?" "Is there a personal man?" Eschewing all rhetorical flourishes, avoiding any kind of easy appeal to the emotions, Mrs. Eddy managed to establish her own theological authority while employing a lexicon of everyday words and expressions and a few brief Biblical phrases. Her tone was modest, rational, and yet confessional, the dominant pronouns she used were *I* and *me*, and she moved from the personal into the abstract and general:

> Am I a spiritualist?
>
> I am not, and never was. I understand the impossibility of intercommunion between the so-called dead and living. There have always attended my life phenomena of an uncommon order, which spiritualists have mis-called mediumship; but I clearly understand that no human agencies were employed,—that the divine Mind reveals itself to humanity through spiritual law.

Having outlined her opposition to Spiritualism, Mrs. Eddy is equally emphatic in rejecting mesmerism or animal magnetism, insisting that Christian Science healing

> is not one mind acting upon another mind. . . . It is Christ come to destroy the power of the flesh; it is Truth over error; that understood, gives man ability to rise above the evidence of the senses, take hold of the eternal energies of Truth, and destroy mortal discord with immortal harmony,—the grand verities of being. It is not one mortal thought transmitted to another's thought from the human mind that holds within itself all evil.

Eschewing both the treacly sentiment so prevalent among her female contemporaries and the orotund bellowing common among the males, Mrs. Eddy managed to achieve an intensity of effect which was emotional as well as intellectual. Her rhetorical skill is particularly evident in her answer to the second question, "Do I believe in a personal God?" Here Mrs. Eddy combines a gospel-like plainness of vocabulary and the slightly archaic cadence of the Authorized Version. She challenges, in the most restrained way, those who claim to offer definitions of the omnipresent, omniscient Infinite. With due daughterly reverence, she both embraces the patriarchal Protestantism of her youth and quietly insists that our limited and necessarily anthropomorphic concept of God as Father must be stretched to include God as Mother:

> I believe in God as the Supreme Being. I know not what the person of omnipotence and omnipresence is, or what the infinite includes; therefore, I worship that of which I can conceive, first, as a loving Father and Mother; then, as thought ascends the scale of being to diviner consciousness, God becomes to me, as to the apostle who declared it, "God is Love," —divine Principle,—which I worship; and "after the manner of my father, so worship I God."

According to the account left for us by Julia Bartlett, who accompanied Mrs. Eddy to Tremont Temple, Mrs. Eddy returned home very silently and stayed in her room for the rest of the day. The insulting behavior of Joseph Cook had found its mark, and Mary Baker Eddy felt far from triumphant on that day; she felt, indeed, that she had failed to meet the challenge, had failed to find the right words. In retrospect, however, it seems clear that the precisely timed address was a success, that Joseph Cook's ill-researched hostility had misfired. The Tremont Temple address was a public measure of Mary Baker Eddy's intellect, rhetorical ability, and courage, and it gave Christian Scientists just cause for pride in their leader.[13] Her ultimate moment of triumph would come in 1899, when she addressed three thousand enthusiastic Christian Scientists, meeting in the same Tremont Temple for The Mother Church's Annual Meeting.

The Massachusetts Metaphysical College was an obvious success, and events like the Tremont Temple address proved her mettle to the public at large, yet Mary Baker Eddy placed only so much emphasis on oral proselytism. She understood clearly from a very early stage that only so much could be accomplished by word of mouth. As a woman, she had limited or contested access to most of the fora for public speaking, and in any case even the greatest orators of the day published their sermons and wrote for the general press. Men like Henry Ward Beecher strove to find a textual medium which would work as powerfully upon the general reader as their Sunday sermons did upon the gathered congregation. If the potential of the new movement was to be realized, Mary Baker Eddy would need to mobilize the

powers of the printed word successfully. In the critical years after the death
of P. P. Quimby and her fall in Lynn, Mary Baker Eddy became convinced
of the need to develop her ideas in writing and to produce a text that would
serve not just as a teaching aid to her students but as an exposition for the
general reader. By 1872 she clearly saw that this text would need to be a book,
not a manuscript, since only a published and copyrighted work could both
spread the author's word and establish her authority and property rights over
it. For a woman deprived of the institutional authority of pulpit or university, the intellectual authority conferred by a published work was of particular importance, both socially and psychologically. The problem was that if,
as teacher, preacher, debater, and conversationalist, Mrs. Eddy could hold
her own with the best, as a writer she had severe handicaps.

Most apparent was her lack as a child of what she herself liked to call a
"classical education," but she also had enjoyed few opportunities to explore
high culture as an adult woman. The discourse of the academy, elegant style,
classical allusions, literary quotations were things Mrs. Eddy appreciated,
revered, aspired to but never mastered, and, in fact, she never wholly got over
more basic problems with spelling, punctuation, and paragraphing. Certainly,
by the 1880s Mrs. Eddy had had some experience in publishing. From girlhood, she had written verse, much of which had found space in the columns
of local newspapers. During her first widowhood and her period of separation from Patterson she had also managed to get some small essays into print,
and during her Lynn period she had effectively used letters and cards and opinion columns to get across her Christian Science message. Yet none of this was
sufficient preparation for the book-length work of theological dissertation and
Biblical exegesis which she began to struggle with as early as 1866.

As we have seen, just putting together a manuscript, finding a publisher
willing to print it, and organizing some kind of marketing system for the work
was an enormous task for Mary Baker Eddy, but the publication of the first
edition of *Science and Health* turned out to be only the beginning. Never one
to rest on her laurels, no sooner had Mrs. Eddy seen her cherished text finally
roll off the presses in 1875 than she began work on the next edition, and this
work of editing, writing, and rewriting would take up more and more of her
time and energy as she grew older, and would end only with her death.
Between 1875 and 1910 *Science and Health* would appear in over 418 separate printings, many of them with minor changes in the order of chapters and
of text, and it would undergo six major revisions, in 1878, 1881, 1883, 1886,
1891, and 1902.

In 1883, as she recovered from the death of her husband and gave serious thought to the condition of her movement and to its possible development, Mary Baker Eddy was all too aware that her book was still selling in
ones and twos to the already converted, and that it had yet to make any
impact on the general public. Getting her message out was Mrs. Eddy's first

priority, and she decided that the best way to achieve this goal was to found her own periodical. This was a bold move, given the movement's still precarious financial situation, and Mrs. Eddy already had plenty to keep her busy; nonetheless, undaunted, she launched her journal in April of 1883, and initially took on the combined labors of publisher, editor, and writer, in addition to all her other work. Surprisingly, given the difficult circumstances under which it was launched and given its founder's limited journalistic experience, the *Christian Science Journal* was to achieve everything Mary Baker Eddy had hoped for, and it was to play a crucial role in spreading the new religion outside the boundaries of New England.[14] After the first three or four issues, the journal was already claiming a readership of some three thousand subscribers.

Most commentators have focused on analyzing the contents of the *Christian Science Journal* and the remarkable effect it had in getting out the word. Neglected has been the more prosaic question of how exactly Mrs. Eddy managed so quickly to get her journal in circulation not only in the Boston area but throughout the United States. The simple answer I have come up with is that techniques for starting, publishing, and circulating journals were well established in the United States by 1883, and that Mrs. Eddy was in this respect, as in so many others, a quick and effective learner. Each little group of Christian Scientists was strongly encouraged to give out copies of the new periodical in classes and meetings, and to persuade people to subscribe. The publisher advertised in every issue that anyone who supplied the names of three new subscribers would receive the journal free for one year. Anyone able to supply six names also got a copy of *Science and Health* for free.

Such standard marketing ploys can work only so far, and in the end people subscribed to the *Journal* because, from the outset, Mrs. Eddy had hit upon the kind of material that people liked to read. Perhaps the most effective of all the sections of the *Journal* was that devoted to firsthand testimonials from people who had been healed. Perhaps especially in the far reaches of the continent, where people did not have easy access to modern medical care, an enormous impact was made by the publishing of letters from average citizens, detailing how ill they had been and how well they now felt, thanks to Christian Science. As Penny Hansen has pointed out in her study, the *Journal* is a fascinating repository of information about sickness and health in the United States at the end of the nineteenth century, and it gives the medical profession a resounding vote of no-confidence.[15]

Whereas *Science and Health* had been targeted at the educated middle classes, with free copies dispatched to intellectual institutions and individuals at home and abroad, the *Christian Science Journal* was unabashedly addressed to people of modest means and limited education, and it offered them Mrs. Eddy's ideas in bite-size pieces. Personal testimonies to healing alternated with uplifting essays on points of theology, wise sayings, comic anecdotes, and letters to and from the editor. Every issue ended with a list of "cards"—the names, titles, addresses, and visiting hours of Christian Science practitioners whom Mrs. Eddy felt she could recommend. This steadily growing list of "cards" from a growing number of American cities has offered historians a standard measure of the progress of the movement, but in the 1880s and 1890s people read the "cards" carefully to get a sense of who was in and who was out with Mrs. Eddy.[16] Mrs. Eddy, interestingly, always advertised herself as "Professor of Obstetrics," but, as of February 7, 1885, she advises her readers:

> Prof. EDDY takes no patients at present, has no time for consultation on disease, and reads no letters containing inquiries in that department: all such should be addressed to those whose names appear below.

One idiosyncratic item in the *Journal* was the annual list, which lengthened over time, of the gifts Mrs. Eddy had received from her followers at Christmas. Cather and Milmine in their 1907 series gleefully included the 1889 list as an example of Mrs. Eddy's pretentiousness, greed, and mercenariness:

LIST OF INDIVIDUAL OFFERINGS

Eider-down pillow, white satin with gold embroidery. Eider-down pillow, blue silk, hand-painted and fringed with lace. Pastel painting of Minnehaha Falls, with silvered easel. Silver nut-pick sct. Painted Sèvres china tea-set. Book, Beautiful Story, 576 pages with steel engravings and lithographs. The Doré Bible Gallery, embellished. Brussels-lace tie. Silver sofa-scarf, inwrought with gold. Pansy bed, in water-colors, with bronze frame. Stand for lemonade-set. Silver combination-set. Silk and lace mat. Embroidered linen handkerchief, in silken sachet-holder. Chinese jar. Silk-embroidered plush table-scarf. Connected reclining pillows. Work of art, White and Franconia Mountains. Transparent painting of Jacqueminots. Satin and lace pin-cushion. Barometer. Cabinet photograph-holder. Perfumery. Large variety of books and poems. Face of the Madonna, framed in oak and ivory. Moon-mirror, with silver setting, and "the Man in the Moon." Hand-painted blotter. Embroidered linen handkerchiefs. Blue silk-embroidered shawl. Plush portemonnaie. Openwork linen handkerchief. Charm slumber-robe. Bible Pearls of Promise. Large white silk banner with silver fringe. Sachet bags. Two velvet table mats. Silver holder for stereoscopic views. Two fat Kentucky turkeys. Hosts of bouquets and Christmas cards.[17]

Obviously even at the time the editors of the *Journal* must have received some adverse criticism about these lists, because publisher William Nixon tried hard in 1890 to persuade Mrs. Eddy to refrain in future from listing her gifts. His effort was in vain. On this point Mrs. Eddy could not be moved, and I think her obduracy is easily explained by the decades of poverty and neglect she had known as an adult, and by her gratitude toward all who now thought and cared about her. Readers of this biography will recall how much Mary Baker Eddy enjoyed celebrating Christmas and Thanksgiving, how sad she had been to have no festive meal and no exchange of presents during her December stay in Portland in 1864, how delighted she had been by the gifts given her by her new students in Lynn in 1870. It is easy to laugh and criticize Mrs. Eddy's love of knickknacks, but it is also easy to understand what these tokens meant to her—respect, affection, communion. For my part, the sheer specificity of these lists delights me—they are so very postmodernist and so very Victorian all at once. I like to imagine Mrs. Eddy enjoying a rare holiday, surrounded by flowers and choice nature paintings, lying on her scented silk pillows, reading one of her new books, wearing her blue silk shawl over her charm slumber-robe—whatever that was!?—and looking forward to a fat Kentucky turkey for her Christmas lunch.

Many of the short essays and letters which Mrs. Eddy contributed to the *Journal* she later collected and edited as part of her published work, and they can now be read in *Miscellaneous Writings*.[18] In the periodical she could explain or reinterpret problems which had arisen from her correspondence and classroom experiences. It is in the *Journal* that Mrs. Eddy gave an important account of the fall in Lynn and what it meant to her. Elsewhere she explained how pain and suffering, though in no way part of some divine plan for us, could stimulate us better than pleasure to reach out to God and find for ourselves the eternal Truth, something the recent death of her husband, Gilbert Eddy, had underlined for her. She talked of the new spiritual pleasure she took in nature, asserting that "even the human conception of beauty, grandeur, and utility is something that defies a sneer" (*Mis.*, p. 86). She described her experiences with homeopathy and gave her opinion of marriage, free love, and celibacy. She declared her hatred of drunkenness and her conviction that an honest doctor was worth more than a crooked mental practitioner. She used the *Journal* to explain to those far away some of the divisive issues that had arisen in Boston, to advertise that time pressures were forcing her to limit the number of classes she would teach, and, finally, to explain why she had decided to close the college. She thundered against the disciples who misunderstood her and the rivals who stole her ideas:

> The educational system of Christian Science lacks the aid and protection of State laws. The Science is hampered by immature demonstrations, by the infancy of its discovery, by incorrect teaching; and especially by unprincipled claimants, whose mad ambition drives them to appropriate my ideas and discovery, without credit, appreciation, or a single original conception, while they quote from other authors and give them credit for every random thought in line with mine. (*Mis.*, pp. 263–64)

That Mrs. Eddy on several occasions remonstrated against those who plagiarized her work is interesting since, as I shall show at the end of this chapter, she has more commonly been presented as a perpetrator than a victim of plagiarism.

In some forthright pieces Mrs. Eddy responded to some of the "Unchristian Rumors" and "Malicious Reports" being spread about her. In "Falsehood," written and published in 1885, she details the charges made against her, and denies them:

> That I take opium; that I am an infidel, a mesmerist, a medium, a "pantheist;" or that my hourly life is prayerless, or not in strict obedience to the Mosaic Decalogue,—is not more true than that I am dead, as is oft reported. The *St. Louis Democrat* is alleged to have reported my demise, and to have said that I died of poison, and bequeathed my property to Susan Anthony.
>
> The opium falsehood has only this to it: Many years ago, my regular physician prescribed morphine, which I took, when he could do no more for me. Afterwards, the glorious revelations of Christian Science saved me from that necessity and made me well, since which time I have not taken drugs, with the following exception: When the mental malpractice of poisoning people was first undertaken by a mesmerist, to test that malpractice I experimented by taking some large doses of morphine, to see if Christian Science could not obviate its effect; and I say with tearful thanks, "The drug had no effect upon me whatever. . . ."[19]
>
> The false report that I have appropriated other people's manuscripts in my works, has been met and answered *legally*.[20] Both in private and public life, and especially through my teachings, it is well known that I am not a spiritualist, a pantheist, or prayerless. . . . None are permitted to remain in my College building whose morals are not unquestionable. I have neither purchased nor ordered a drug since my residence in Boston; and to my knowledge, not one has been sent to my house, unless it was something to remove stains or vermin. (*Mis.*, pp. 248–49)

It is fascinating to learn from the *Journal* that as early as 1885 rumors of Mrs. Eddy being dead were cropping up. In 1889 she wrote another *Journal* piece on the same topic, dryly insisting that, despite the ardent desires of her opponents, she was still alive and healthy, and that anyone could take up her invitation to "call at the Massachusetts Metaphysical College, in 1889, and judge yourself whether I can talk—and laugh too!"[21] Proving that she was alive was one of the strangest tasks Mrs. Eddy faced in her last twenty-five years of life, and one that would weigh upon her more and more heavily as she receded further and further from the public gaze.

One issue featured in the pages of the *Christian Science Journal* but not included by Mrs. Eddy in her *Miscellaneous Writings* was the tragedy of children who died under the care of Christian Science practitioners. The *Christian Science Journal* of March 1889 told of a young Christian Science mother in Pierre, North Dakota, whose two small sons died under her treatment. The conclusion drawn by the mother herself, by her husband who wrote the piece for the *Journal*, and by the editors was that the children died because of the malicious mesmerism directed upon her and them by members of her community who were fiercely combatting the recent conversions to Christian Science. In their biography of Mrs. Eddy, Milmine and Cather discuss this *Journal* piece at length and take a very different view. They attribute the children's deaths to their mother's obsession with Malicious Animal Magnetism and her consequent refusal to adopt standard medical procedures, and they conclude with this reasoned and moving statement which has been repeated in one form or another by many subsequent opponents of Christian Science:

> This case is chosen for illustration for the reason that the parents of these children were not ignorant or colourless people; they were not mystics or dreamers or in any way "different." They were young, ambitious, warm-hearted, and affectionate; they loved each other and their children, and their home was full of cordiality and kindliness. Their children were fine children; one, now grown, has become a young scholar of promise. The woman was not a religious fanatic, but a young mother. She could combat "the last temptation" over her dead baby simply because she believed with all her heart and soul that it lay with her, as a test of her faith, whether her child lived or died. Logically there was nothing extravagant about her conduct. The martyrdoms of a thousand years have proved what men and women can do and endure under the tyranny of an idea.[22]

In their conclusion, Milmine and Cather strikingly use the word *logically* to characterize the young mother praying over her dead child, yet their presentation of the case in Pierre is itself emotional, showing the logical problems inherent in all first-person testimony. What the Milmine presentation fails to deliver is any proof both that had the mother adopted other medical strategies her sons would have survived, and that their fatal illnesses were largely the result of her own fears about Malicious Animal Magnetism. In fact, as any memoir or biography of the period amply proves, in the 1880s children of intelligent, loving, and affluent parents, given the best available medical treatment still died in distressingly large numbers from common childhood illnesses such as measles, whooping cough, and diphtheria. It is true that better public sanitation and private hygiene were beginning to guard the population more effectively against infections, but there were no immunizations against infectious disease (except smallpox) and no antibiotics. By 1906 medical science had made great strides in preventing some types of infection and treating others, but, in focusing on this incident which took place in 1889, Cather and Milmine were making assumptions about the past that, factually and logically, were improper.[23]

The success of the *Christian Science Journal* correlates closely with the growing sales of *Science and Health* as new converts moved easily and even necessarily from first reading and then subscribing to the periodical and then buying and reading the book. Yet *Science and Health*'s advance to best-seller status, which few indeed would have predicted in 1875 or 1878, was not just a result of better marketing. The book itself changed significantly over time, and Mrs. Eddy never stopped looking for an arrangement of chapters, a choice of word, a line of argument that would better convey her essential message.

To recapitulate a little, technical problems had haunted *Science and Health* since 1874, and the second, so-called Ark edition of 1878 had been a disaster, consisting only of a "Vol. II" since the first volume had been so full of errors as to be unsalvageable. That the Eddys were even able to publish the second volume was thanks to the expert and disinterested help of John Wilson, head of the University Press in Cambridge.[24] Wilson was fervently committed to proofreading the books he brought out—and this attention to detail was exactly what Mrs. Eddy had so long needed and desired.

When she anticipated bringing out a new third edition, Mrs. Eddy was most anxious to find a reputable and conscientious printer who could solve the technical problems for her, and in April of 1880 Asa Gilbert Eddy contacted John Wilson about printing his wife's book, since he had been such a help with the earlier edition. Wilson replied in a businesslike manner, seeking more details on the length of the new edition, offering to give a more exact estimation of the costs to his firm, and requesting one half of those costs up front. The sum quoted was quite beyond the Eddys' resources, and Asa Eddy left matters there. Mrs. Eddy herself, however, did not give up easily, and in January 1881 she herself appeared at Wilson's office. Her famous charisma now came into play, and she so impressed Wilson with her ideas and her courage that, throwing his habitual Scottish caution to the wind, he agreed to print the book, and to await payment as the profits from sales came in—a highly unusual arrangement.[25]

The connection between Christian Science and the University Press was to continue for some seventy years, bringing a very considerable profit to both. *Science and Health* was to rise from its own ashes and become a best-seller. With her printer, Mrs. Eddy developed a system whereby small alterations could be incorporated into the text almost every year, without new plates becoming necessary.

Critics of Christian Science, such as Charles Braden, have made much of this constant reissuing of *Science and Health*, claiming that the Christian

Science faithful were severely enjoined to buy each new printing and to destroy their old one, and that this was how the church officials both made money and erased the potentially dangerous record of the past. Milmine and Cather, in their published work and in private letters, comment on the difficulty of finding copies of early editions of *Science and Health*; as of 1906 copies of, say, the 1875 edition or the Ark edition, were already collectors' items. This criticism has some basis in fact, but the truth of the matter seems to be that members were urged to buy each major revision of their textbook, not each printing. This was not unreasonable given the major differences in the text from edition to edition, which all commentators acknowledge.

There was one aspect of the constant reissuing of *Science and Health* which was probably unique to Christian Science—the preoccupation with Malicious Animal Magnetism that attended the editing and publishing process. In those years which saw a major new version, and the need to reset type from scratch, Mary Baker Eddy very probably became John Wilson's greatest headache. While insisting on her freedom to make changes long after deadline, and while agreeing to pay for them, she reacted with anxiety bordering on paranoia to any hitch in the publishing schedule that came up on the printer's side. Probably because Mary Baker Eddy placed herself under the greatest stress and anxiety when she was writing, some of the most famous and best-authenticated stories about Mrs. Eddy's fear of Malicious Animal Magnetism come out of the years when she was preparing a major edition of her book. She agonized that parts of her manuscript would be mislaid by editors, passed on to rivals, lost in the mail, or changed by printers or editors without her consent. To ward off these fears, she assigned to different members of her domestic staff the task of "treating"—that is, deflecting possible harmful mental influence from—all those upon whom she was forced to rely.[26]

Mr. Wilson and his successor at the University Press, William Orcutt, weathered the storms of the major editions and in their printed reminiscences cared to remember only the plusses of their relations with Mary Baker Eddy. Christian Science was probably the press's best customer, but financial interests were not the only reason for the long and successful partnership. Fundamentally, Mrs. Eddy understood publishing, she was a faithful and appreciative customer, and she paid her bills. She also forged a personal relationship with John Wilson based on a combination of warm affinity and cool business sense which both found to their taste. The charming, funny, practical, highly professional writer whom John Wilson describes in his reminiscences of Mrs. Eddy contrasts with the frantic, out-of-control harridan evoked by other accounts. Wilson was made in the Mark Baker mold, a Scottish gentleman of the old school who nonetheless did not mind taking his orders and his checks from a lady. It seems clear, furthermore, that Mr. Wilson was one of the rare people who did not require that Mary Baker Eddy always be wearing her "Founder and Discoverer of Christian Science" hat, who respected and deferred to her but did not display that complicated mixture of adoration and rebellion she found in her followers.

With her printing and proofreading problems solved by Wilson, Mrs. Eddy was able to move on to more substantive issues, and it was between 1881 and 1891 that Mrs. Eddy worked most intensively on the content, organization, and style of her book. Between 1885 and 1891 this process was conducted in part through a dialogue with an experienced editor whom Mrs. Eddy now had the professional contacts and financial resources to hire, the Reverend James Henry Wiggin.[27]

Wiggin was a gentleman of Mrs. Eddy's age, a fat, jolly married man, popular among his peers, who enjoyed the social and intellectual pleasures of Boston with its theaters, bookshops, and social clubs—and was notably different from most of the men who were attracted to Christian Science. A graduate of Tufts College and Meadville Theological School, he had been ordained a minister of the Unitarian Church in 1861 but had left his parish in 1875 and was making a meager but gentlemanly living as a writer and literary hack. Whether he had left the ministry for financial reasons or out of some crisis of faith is unclear,[28] but his expertise was still primarily in religious matters, and it was no doubt this background that made him particularly attractive as an editor to Mrs. Eddy. Wiggin was recommended to Mrs. Eddy by her printer John Wilson, who had employed him regularly as an indexer and proofreader, but Wiggin was also friendly with Mrs. Eddy's students the Woodburys, of whom I shall have much to say in Part Four. Over the next years, Wiggin became more and more closely involved in Mrs. Eddy's ventures, contributing to and editing the *Journal*. As we saw earlier in this chapter, in 1886 Wiggin was allowed to audit Mrs. Eddy's class.

Wiggin was closely involved in the preparation of the 1886 revision of *Science and Health*, and this edition, which differs in several important respects from the previous ones, bears his stamp. Wiggin was undoubtedly useful on the mechanics of writing since he was master of the problems with spelling and punctuation and grammar that had plagued Mrs. Eddy for many years. Well read in theological and philosophical literature, as well as in the literary classics, Wiggin could also be of help in smoothing out syntax and making paragraphs run more easily. Milmine and Bates and Dittemore are probably correct in claiming that *Science and Health* reads more fluently after 1886 and that Wiggin deserves credit for this. The more noticeable changes Wiggin made in *Science and Health* were of an ephemeral nature, notably his decision to preface each chapter with epigraphs from literary worthies past and present, and to introduce scraps of verse into the body of the text. At first Mrs. Eddy succumbed to the charm of such a display of erudition and culture, but she soon decided to take it all out because she considered it to be padding. Most specifically, in the next revision of 1891 she removed from her book all of the trendy references to Eastern religions which Wiggin had introduced.

Ernest Sutherland Bates—not incidentally in the biography he was writing with or for Mr. Dittemore!—referred to Wiggin as Mrs. Eddy's "ghostwriter" and admired Wiggin's—and therefore his own—line of work, commenting that Wiggin "found the career of a ghost writer more honest than that of a clergyman."[29] That Wiggin was in fact Mrs. Eddy's ghostwriter seems, however, a willful misrepresentation of the truth, based on the suspect testimony of a friend of Wiggin's.[30] The copious correspondence and textual evidence in The Mother Church archives make clear that Wiggin's work for Mrs. Eddy never went beyond that habitually done for established authors by copy editors in an era when copying was still difficult and expensive, and where expert publishing skills were needed to sort out the handwritten corrections and additions to the printed text. This note from Mrs. Eddy to Wiggin accurately conveys both the importance and the limitations of the help he gave her:

> I can see no end to its improvement, but I am so weary of the task I have not looked over all the pages or punctuated them. This I leave for you.
>
> If anything is a muddle and you so see it indicate it on a slip of paper page and par. or make it correct yourself, but never *change* my meaning, only *bring it out*.[31]

Wiggin was also useful to Mrs. Eddy in her other major publishing enterprise of the mid-1880s, the *Christian Science Journal*. An experienced journalist, Wiggin contributed essays and book reviews, often under the arch pseudonym "Phare Pleigh," and he edited the *Journal* from January to August 1886, and from January 1887 to January 1889. When Mrs. Eddy came under heavy attack from a California divine, he issued a pamphlet in her defense called *Christian Science and the Bible*. In his published comments on Mary Baker Eddy as a writer, Wiggin stresses the extraordinary care Mrs. Eddy gave to the perfecting of her message through making revisions to her book. In a passage which illustrates Wiggin's own fussy use of punctuation and pompous style, he marvels at the apparently unlimited time and money she was prepared to put in to get things right:

> Within a few months she had made sacrifices, from which most authors would have shrunk, to ensure the moral rightness of her book. . . . Day after day flew by, and the weeks lengthened into months; from every quarter came importunate missives of inquiry and mercantile reproach; hundreds of dollars were sunk in a bottomless sea of corrections; yet not till the authoress was satisfied that her duty was wholly done, would she allow printer and binder to send forth her book to the world.[32]

Wiggin worked in close touch with Mrs. Eddy, and he enjoyed a cordial relationship with her for some years. He brought out the witty, caustic, woman-of-the-world side of her personality, and although she wished earnestly to see him convert to Christian Science, she found in his company a welcome relief from the demands made on her by her followers and associates within the movement. With him she felt she could debate rather than quarrel, but that there was also simple affection in their relationship was demonstrated by the kindness she showed him when he was ill, plying him with fruit baskets and offers of carriage rides, as well as Christian Science maxims.

Wiggin never converted to Christian Science, and it seems probable that the tributes to Mrs. Eddy and the reasonably orthodox accounts of Christian Science doctrine he published in the *Journal* owed more to the demands of his pocketbook than to the dictates of his religious sensibility.[33] When work on the crucial fiftieth edition was in chaos, Wiggin was called back to sort matters out, but the correspondence shows that tempers were frayed on both sides, and after 1891 Mrs. Eddy ceased to use his services. It must have been galling for Wiggin to see that he had failed to influence Mrs. Eddy's ideas and that she firmly refused to see in him an intellectual advisor, rather than a copy editor. For a man of his personal and intellectual pretensions, and low actual achievement, it was embarrassing to be employed by a woman, especially a New Hampshire farmer's daughter, but to be let go was an insult. In the 1890s Wiggin was to find comfort and support with Mrs. Woodbury and the Dresser group, then headed by Horatio Dresser, whose Harvard degree and connections to William James were calculated to arouse Wiggin's respect.

As the following statements from an 1889 letter indicate, well before their professional relationship ended, Wiggin's private comments on Mrs. Eddy and her Science were in sharp disagreement with his public pronouncements:

> Christian Science, on its theological side, is an ignorant revival of one form of ancient gnosticism, that Jesus is to be distinguished from the Christ, and that his earthly appearance was phantasmal, not real and fleshly.
>
> On its moral side, it involves what must follow from the doctrine that reality is a dream, and that if a thing is right in thought, why right it is, and that sin is non-existent, because God can *behold* no evil. Not that Christian Science believers generally see this, or practise evil, but the virus is within.
>
> Religiously, Christian Science is a revolt from orthodoxy, but unphilosophically conducted, endeavouring to ride two horses.
>
> Physically, it leads people to trust all to nature, the great healer, and so does some good. Great virtue in imagination! . . . Where there is disease which time will not reach, Christian Science is useless.
>
> As for the High Priestess of it . . . she is—well I could *tell* you, but not write. An awfully (I use the word advisedly) smart woman, acute,

shrewd, but not well read, nor in any way learned. What she has, as documents clearly show, she got from P. P. Quimby of Portland, Maine, whom she eulogised after death as the great leader and her special teacher. . . .

As for the book, if you have any edition since December, 1885, it had my supervision. Though now she is getting out an entirely new edition, with which I had nothing to do, and occasionally she has made changes whereof I did not know. . . . As for clearness, many Christian Science people thought her early editions much better, because they sounded much more *like* Mrs. Eddy. The truth is, she does not care to have her paragraphs clear, and delights in so expressing herself that her words may have various readings and meanings. Really, that is one of the tricks of the trade. You know sibyls have always been thus oracular, to "keep the word of promise to the ear, and break it to the hope."

There is nothing really to understand in "Science and Health" except that *God is all* and yet there is no God in matter! What they fail to explain is, the origin of the *idea* of matter, or sin. They say it comes from *mortal mind*, and that mortal mind is not divinely created, in fact, has no existence; in fact, that nothing comes of nothing, and that matter and disease are like dreams, having no existence. Quimby had definite ideas, but Mrs. Eddy has not understood them.

When I first knew Christian Science, I wrote a defensive pamphlet called "Christian Science and the Bible" (though I did not believe the doctrine). . . . I found fair game in the assaults of orthodoxy upon Mrs. Eddy, and support in the supernaturalism of the Bible; but I did not pretend to give an exposition of Christian Science, and I did not know the old lady as well as I do now.

No, Swedenborg, and all such writers, are sealed books to her. She cannot understand such utterances, and never could, but dollars and cents she understands thoroughly.[34]

Wiggin's comments about Mrs. Eddy to his unidentified, but presumably male, friend deserve attention. A trained theologian, he deftly puts his finger on the most difficult and contested point in Christian Science—the genesis of evil-as-illusion—and as an intelligent man who had had the opportunity to see Christian Scientists in action, he argues that the healing succeeds by allowing nature and time to do their work unhindered. The comparisons of Mrs. Eddy with the sibyl and of her doctrine with gnosticism show some insight and could well be developed today with none of the negative assumptions Wiggin gives them.[35]

On the other hand, much of what Wiggin says smacks of sour grapes. Here speaks the disgruntled professional who sees his advice ignored by the client, and the client none the worse, who finds himself in the rather uncomfortable position of ridiculing in private a doctrine and a person whom he had once eulogized in public. Wiggin was enough of a gentleman to know that by willingly collaborating with Mrs. Eddy on her book and magazine, taking her money for so many years, and then later bad-mouthing her to friends he could be accused at the very least of inconsistency and ingratitude.

More seriously for Wiggin's reputation as a scholar, in his statements about Quimby Wiggin shows a willingness to allow prejudice and literary gossip to supersede his academic habits and keen mind. Obviously, the Dressers had allowed Wiggin to read Mrs. Eddy's letters to Quimby, and these letters had produced a strong negative impression on him. Yet even if the letters proved that Mrs. Eddy had become ungrateful toward her former benefactor—as she was increasingly ungrateful to Wiggin!—they did not prove that she had plagiarized Quimby's work. Furthermore, it is hard to imagine that as a trained philosopher and critic of style Wiggin could have found anything to admire in Quimby, and he may not even have had the chance to read the small extracts from Quimby's unpublished writings which the Dressers possessed. Moreover, if he never read anything by Quimby, Wiggin is being less than scholarly when he states so flatly that Mrs. Eddy owed everything to Quimby.

In private, especially in the comfortable male atmosphere of the club, Wiggin could be scathing about Mrs. Eddy, but in public he kept his tongue, and until Wiggin's death in 1900 he and Mrs. Eddy continued to correspond, cordially if infrequently. Unfortunately, one of Wiggin's friends, Livingston Wright, began around 1903 to circulate a very negative account of the relation between Wiggin and Mrs. Eddy. Wright claimed Wiggin had confided to him that *Science and Health* had been a mere mass of unreadable scraps before Mrs. Eddy employed him as her editor, that Wiggin had essentially authored the text now known as *Science and Health*, and that at least one section of the book was entirely Wiggin's own work, plagiarized by Mrs. Eddy. Wright's story found many willing listeners, notably Mark Twain, who wrote delightedly to thank Wright for confirming what Twain had already opined on textual evidence alone—that Mary Baker Eddy could not have been the author of *Science and Health*, or at least of those parts which Twain admired. Wright eventually published his story in the New York *World* in November 1906, at the time when that publication was running a campaign against Mrs. Eddy. Finally he issued a pamphlet under the inflammatory title *How Rev. Wiggin Rewrote Mrs. Eddy's Book*. By the time the Wright revelations had become headline news, Mrs. Eddy had had a long and sad apprenticeship in how to deal with defamation, and she responded with a simple and dignified statement: "I hold the late Mr. Wiggin in loving, grateful memory for his high-principled character and well-equipped scholarship."[36] Whatever the Reverend Wiggin's true opinion of Mrs. Eddy may have been, he probably would have been deeply upset about his private letters and personal confidences being published and used as part of a press campaign against her.[37]

Livingston Wright's articles and pamphlet were influential largely because they centered on the issue of plagiarism, an old issue which the Quimbyites had been harping on since 1883 and which Horatio Dresser's 1899 *Arena* article revived. By refusing to allow any access at all to his father's writings, George Quimby had stymied those opponents of Mrs. Eddy who sought to prove their allegations that Mrs. Eddy had published as her own work parts of his unpublished manuscripts. Casting the Reverend Wiggin as the writer of Mary Baker Eddy's main work and naming P. P. Quimby as the source of all her important ideas fitted the anti–Christian Science agenda.

Some minor charges of plagiarism by Mary Baker Eddy could be firmly tied down. There was considerable evidence that Wiggin had been instrumental in both thinking up and drafting a twenty-page section of *Science and Health* called "Wayside Hints," which appeared in the 1886 edition but was dropped from the 1891 edition. Later biographers Bates and Dittemore asserted that one of the articles Mrs. Eddy published under her own name in the *Journal* was an anonymous piece which she had cut out and pasted in her scrapbook years before.[38] None of these small sins of commission and omission provided the smoking gun of plagiarism that first P. P. Quimby and then J. H. Wiggin promised so tantalizingly.

Plagiarism was the charge brought most insistently against Mary Baker Eddy by her critics and rivals during the later part of her life, and the charge that would be pursued in attempts to weaken or discredit her church after her death. In a world where text and the print media still ruled, accusations of plagiarism, with their accompanying quotations, bi-column comparisons of parallel passages, and the citation of sources had a pleasantly solid feel of scholarly objectivity and high-minded intellectuality. It helped that most readers accepted an author's conclusion without seriously studying the evidence apparently laid out before them on the printed page, and that they were even less likely to study any later evidence put forth to disprove the initial accusation. For a movement so unusually devoted to a single, original, and newly printed work, it worked well to focus attack on the writer's authority and bona fides.

As a woman from a respectable but unillustrious family, as ill educated as most of her female contemporaries, bearing only the thinnest veneer of high culture, Mary Baker Eddy offered a peculiarly large, bright target for attacks based on plagiarism. Those who hated Christian Science and despised its ideas could, like Frederick Peabody, happily dismiss Mrs. Eddy's writings as the work of a limited, unenlightened, unstable mind yet claim that she plagiarized the ideas. Those, like Mark Twain, who, despite themselves, found things in Christian Science to admire and respect were convinced that Mrs. Eddy was not the author of the works she claimed copyright to, and they gratefully seized on any evidence that seemed to prove them right. Many critics varied inconsistently between two incompatible positions, claiming, like Wiggin, all in one breath that on the one hand, Mrs. Eddy's ideas were bunk, and on the other, that she owed everything to the brilliant Quimby; that she was too stupid to have read authors like Swedenborg and Plato and Hegel, and yet borrowed her ideas from them without attribution.

I have already argued in an earlier chapter that *Science and Health* is a flawed but fascinating and radical work. In its flaws and in its fascinations it bears the imprint of a single, unusual, unschooled but brilliant mind, Mary Baker Eddy's, and it should be judged by the same criteria as any other work of intelligence, for its intrinsic qualities and its historical importance. Mrs. Eddy was not an intellectual; she was not well read. In this she resembled many Americans of her generation, Mark Twain notable among them. Like many human beings, she was affected by people she met and things she read, especially in her youth, and the importance on her development of the Bible and of the great Protestant theological tradition is hard to overestimate, but by 1866 she had become increasingly the woman of a single idea. In her search to persuade the world of her great Truth, she was at times not always truthful, willing to take an idea from Wiggin, willing to recycle some of her old pre–Christian Science poems under new titles. But to equate such small inadequacies and minor deceits with plagiarism of major ideas is, I think, to miss the point about Mrs. Eddy.

I believe that the reason Mary Baker Eddy reacted with uncharacteristic ineptitude to the first accusations of plagiarism launched against her by the Dressers in 1883 was that she could not credit them. They left her breathless with amazement, impotent with rage—gobsmacked in the crude old Yorkshire expression. There was much in her life which she preferred to forget, large areas where she felt herself vulnerable to attack and as ready with defense, but in her authorship of *Science and Health* she felt herself on higher, holy ground. Remembering all too well the years of trouble her book had cost her, knowing how little help of any kind she had received while writing, feeling that through all the toil her hand had been guided by God, she was simply unprepared to be accused of plagiarism. None of the various defenses she prepared over the years could placate her critics. When, stung by the charge that she owed everything to Quimby, she gave an unflattering portrait of the old man she in fact revered, and she counterclaimed credit for some of his ideas and terminology, she was made to appear a liar and an ingrate. When she claimed that God had guided her hand as she wrote, that *Science and Health* was a work of divine revelation, she provoked outrage. In the end, she decided that the issue of the originality of her writings was one she could not win in the courts or the media or the academy, that it must be left up to God, who judges all hearts.[39]

18

More
Dissidents
and
New Rules

B Y THE LATE 1880S CHRISTIAN SCIENCE HAD ESTAB-
lished itself as a religious force to be reckoned with, not only in Boston
but in Chicago, Detroit, Denver, San Francisco, Cleveland, Minneapolis, and
smaller towns and villages throughout the continental United States. More
than one hundred healers advertised regularly in the *Christian Science
Journal*, which claimed ten thousand subscribers. By 1887, twenty-three,
admittedly small, Christian Science institutes had grown up, and a church
had been dedicated in Oconto, Wisconsin, the first building to bear the historic name of "First Church of Christ, Scientist." In February of 1889 Mrs.
Eddy welcomed sixty-five students to her Primary class at the Massachusetts
Metaphysical College, the largest class ever, and each month saw the list
growing of those anxious to take the Primary, the Normal, or the Obstetrics
course, or to pay the full $700 for the three courses combined. All this
progress was not occurring without a struggle—Mrs. Eddy was still being
hanged in effigy in her native state[1]—but the strength of the opposition was
itself a measure of the impact of the new denomination.

The success of her movement had also produced a sea change in Mrs.
Eddy's way of life and public persona. As the royalties from her publications
flooded in, she approached affluence for the first time in her life,[2] and she
showed this by buying a property in December of 1887 to house herself and
her immediate staff at 385 Commonwealth Avenue in the most fashionable
quarter of Boston. Whereas as recently as 1883 Mrs. Eddy's college at
Columbus Avenue had been furnished with a strict eye to economy, Mrs.

Eddy's new home was elegant enough to win both plaudits from some visiting journalists and critical comments from some members of her church who hewed to the antimaterialist line. The barely respectable Mrs. Patterson-Glover-Eddy of Lynn had been, it seemed, forgotten by the public, and within the movement Mrs. Eddy had become an object of reverence verging on adoration.[3]

As the Church of Christ, Scientist grew in numbers and influence, so did the challenge it met from those who had studied with Mrs. Eddy for at least a time, then challenged her authority, questioned her doctrine, and parted with her. Men such as Luther Marston, A. J. Swarts, and William Gill, and women such as Emma Hopkins, Mary Plunkett, and Ursula Gestefeld tasted Christian Science and Mrs. Eddy's leadership and, in most cases, found it too confining, both practically and theoretically. These people wanted to write their own pamphlets, develop their own healing methods and ideas, teach their own students, and set up practice where they wished. Mrs. Eddy's determination to control their activities enraged them, and, furthermore, they could not understand or accept the exclusively Christian cast of her thought. They found intellectual nourishment and spiritual inspiration in Eastern religions, and to them Mrs. Eddy appeared provincial and reactionary in her refusal to place the Upanishads or the Koran on the same plane as the Gospels.

Doctrinal dissents and personal resentments aside, however, all of the rebellious former students had a living to make in metaphysical healing and teaching, and they were fully aware that Mrs. Eddy's Christian Science had made a greater impression on the market than had any other group. In many ways they needed her far more than she needed them. They thus both opposed her and copied her. They set up institutes in imitation of her Massachusetts Metaphysical College, founded periodicals comparable to the *Christian Science Journal*, gave lecture courses modelled on her own, plagiarized shamelessly from her written work, and prominently featured *Science and Health* in their reading lists. The term *Christian Science* was used constantly by them. As Mary Plunkett remarked, "People have tried to get truth in various ways, but the world never knew how to get it until it came through 'Science and Health.'"[4] Mrs. Eddy's most faithful disciple could hardly have put it better.

This statement was made in 1887 when Luther Marston decided to organize a convention at which various mental healers would meet to discuss issues, make policy, and, no doubt, divide up turf. He convoked the meeting on Mrs. Eddy's own home territory, at the Parker Memorial Hall in Boston, in a gesture of defiance which also signalled a lack of confidence. Given that all those attending stressed the value of antidogmatism and eclecticism and preached breadth, tolerance, and fluidity; given that, beneath the façade of pseudo-Oriental benignity, they were all competing for the same limited pool of students-patients, there was only one thing that bound the conference participants together and defined them as a movement—their opposition to Mrs. Eddy.

According to Robert Peel, chief among those attending the October 1887 conference were Messieurs Marston, Gill, Swarts, and Dresser, and Mesdames Plunkett, Hopkins, Choate, and Stuart—colorful characters, most of them, worthy of a historical novel. Of the men present, the most important in the eye of history was Julius Dresser, no doubt seconded at the conference by his loyal spouse, Annetta, and perhaps also flanked by his twenty-one-year-old son, Horatio. All three Dressers were leaders in the establishment and theorization of New Thought, that amorphous movement that would challenge Christian Science most directly. Julius and Annetta provided the essential link to P. P. Quimby: they had been his students and close intimates; they had retained copies of a few extracts from the legendary writings; they had known Mrs. Eddy when she was sad, sick, impoverished, unhappy Mrs. Patterson; and they had access to the originals of the letters and poems she had written to Quimby in the early 1860s. In the 1880s Julius Dresser was the point man in the public opposition to Mrs. Eddy, and after his death Annetta took up the torch. One by one, men as different as Edward Arens, James Henry Wiggin, and William Gill, and women as different as Clara Choate, Emma Hopkins, and Josephine Woodbury would break with Mrs. Eddy and turn immediately to Julius Dresser and his heirs for the material that would sanction their rebellion and offer them ammunition for their assaults on Christian Science.

As my neatly balanced lists of names in the preceding paragraph indicate, the metaphysical healing subculture was somewhat atypical for its time in that women played an equal or even preeminent role. For some years the most interesting and talented women rivals to Mrs. Eddy were Emma Hopkins and Mary Plunkett.[5] Mrs. Hopkins was a serious, soulful, eloquent young woman with literary pretensions, who was at first accepted not only into Mrs. Eddy's class, but into her college as a resident, and into her journal as editor. Such swift ascension to favor with their leader and to prominence in the movement activated all the old animosities and hostilities among Mrs. Eddy's intimates, and Mrs. Hopkins confided to Julia Bartlett in 1885 that she had always felt that everything she did at the Massachusetts Metaphysical College, every word she said or wrote, was watched for evidence of unorthodoxy. In such circumstances, evidence is all too likely to appear, or be produced, and Emma Hopkins was well primed to heed the snake of apostasy when it turned up in the shape of a new student at the College, Mary Plunkett.

Robert Peel likens Mary Plunkett to Victoria Woodhull—the celebrated and, to many, notorious Spiritualist and advocate of feminism, socialism, and free love—and given the high moral tone Mrs. Eddy demanded of her students, and her unequivocal condemnation of free love and marital infidelity, it is unclear how Mrs. Plunkett managed to get accepted to the class. Mrs. Plunkett had two children and was ready to admit that neither was the child of Mr. Plunkett. It also seems that Mr. Plunkett was a cousin of Richard Kennedy, and that Mrs. Plunkett had earlier taken class with A. J. Swarts—two connections unlikely to endear her to Mrs. Eddy. Once she and Mrs. Eddy confronted each other in the classroom, they fell out in pretty short order, but by this time Mary Plunkett had probably gotten her money's worth, since in Boston she had met Emma Hopkins and rapidly struck up a bosom friendship with her. Mrs. Hopkins told Julia Bartlett in a letter of November 4, 1885, that she had carefully researched the whole question of P. P. Quimby's influence and had absolved Mrs. Eddy of guilt,[6] but she was obviously ripe for rebellion and willing to be convinced that her duty lay outside Mrs. Eddy's movement. Mary Plunkett, with her connections to Kennedy and Swarts, was in a position to stoke all the smoldering fires of rebellion in her new friend, and they soon decamped from Boston and made an alliance.

For three years or so, the Plunkett-Hopkins partnership was successful. Mary Plunkett cast her friend as a younger, more cultured, purer Mrs. Eddy, and Emma Hopkins accepted the role with increasing confidence. Mary took on the organization, marketing, and promotion side of things, smoothing the path for her inspired partner and providing the dynamism and chutzpah necessary for travelling evangelism. The two set up their own teaching institutes in Chicago, St. Paul, Louisville, Milwaukee, and New York, instituted their own journal, called *Truth: A Magazine of Christian Science* (later called *International Magazine of Christian Science*), and travelled indefatigably, spreading the word. In introducing her friend to new audiences, Mrs. Plunkett liked to describe how, with throbs and tears, Mrs. Hopkins "was finally induced to enter upon the work . . . this little woman, so modest in her personality yet so mighty in her powers to teach the great Truth that the rays of Divine Light seem to radiate directly through her."[7]

By 1888 Mrs. Plunkett had left Mrs. Hopkins in charge of the Chicago institute and magazine and had set herself up in New York, where she rapidly swallowed the operations run by her male competitors Luther Marston and Albert Dorman. Unfortunately, Mary Plunkett's commitment to what she still preferred to advertise as Christian Science did not fully satisfy her. She became enamored of a young man by the impressive name of A. Bently Worthington, whom she had employed as a clerk. In the rivalrous, gossip-ridden world she inhabited, such a relationship could not remain hidden for long, even had Mrs. Plunkett's bravura and rejection of convention made secrecy an option. Called to account, Mrs. Plunkett in her journal defended her choice of a new partner and her failure to seek a legal divorce on the loftiest of metaphysical grounds. Neglecting Mrs. Eddy's many published statements in favor of preserving the sanctity of marriage vows, Mrs. Plunkett tried to use a section of *Science and Health* which referred to some future, more perfect human state when marriage and sexuality would cease as a means of justifying her actions. She defended her relationship with Worthington as being one of higher spirituality. As we shall see, a few years later Mrs. Josephine Woodbury would try an even more blatant version of the same defense.

When Mrs. Eddy travelled to New York to give an address in February 1889, the buzzards were already gathering over Mary Plunkett's head. In a desperate move to gain Mrs. Eddy's support, Mrs. Plunkett came forward after the address and embraced Mrs. Eddy as her "dear teacher," causing something of a sensation. This demonstration served only to enrage Mrs. Eddy, who reportedly told Mrs. Plunkett that Mrs. Hopkins was so full of mesmerism that her eyes stuck out like a boiled codfish. By this time in her long career Mrs. Eddy had learned to avoid meddling in the marital and sexual affairs of her students, but obviously benign indifference would no longer work in the highly publicized Plunkett case. Far from being swayed by Mrs. Plunkett's declarations of loyalty and affection, Mrs. Eddy was outraged at Mrs. Plunkett's attempts to use the tenets of Christian Science in defense of free love, thus implicating the movement in her immorality. In both her published work and her private correspondence Mrs. Eddy made it clear that, indeed, she expected that one day Christian Scientists would live "like angels," but that in the meantime she rejoiced with those students who found happiness with a lawful and congenial mate.[8]

When Worthington turned out to be a bigamist and an embezzler, with wives in several states, even Mary Plunkett could no longer face down her enemies. As soon as the scandal broke, Emma Hopkins would no longer have anything to do with her former ally, whose business ventures collapsed. Refusing to give up the name Mary Bently Worthington which she had adopted with much publicity, Mary fled to New Zealand with Worthington and her two children. In Christchurch the Worthingtons established a religious healing movement first called the Students of Truth, and later the Temple of Truth, which had some initial success. A group of local clergymen, convinced that Bently Worthington was having a deleterious influence on public morals with his doctrines of free love, launched a campaign against the Temple of Truth and sought to have Worthington extradited back to the United States to answer charges of bigamy and embezzlement. In 1893 Worthington expelled his wife Mary from the movement, and she set up a rival group, at first under the name of Plunkett, and then as Sister Magdala. In early 1901 Mary Plunkett married a dentist called Atkinson and became seriously ill of "mental disease." In June she was found dead in a shallow ornamental fountain, her legs bound by "an elastic garter." The death was declared a suicide. Mary was only fifty-three years old.[9] Thus ended the life of one of the most unconventional and flamboyant women who featured in the early history of Christian Science.[10]

When judging many of the actions Mrs. Eddy took over the next decade or so to limit those who were permitted to teach Christian Science to those whom she had personally trained and who vowed loyalty to her, as well as to discourage her followers from attending addresses and reading pamphlets written by self-professed Christian Scientists, it is important to remember the intense, even unscrupulous, competition Mrs. Eddy's followers faced in the field. Unsurprisingly, Mrs. Eddy was by turns alarmed, confused, and enraged when people whom she had known as friends and followers became her opponents, one week seeking her love and cooperation and the next plagiarizing her work and spreading horrible rumors about her. Over the following years she demonstrated leadership, not paranoia, in guarding her copyrights, tightening her administrative control, and defining her message with increasing precision. If competition from the outside was an annoyance and a strain, by now Mrs. Eddy had enough experience to trust her abilities to win any contest. As she showed in her relations with the Dressers, once the opposition had defined itself and come out into the open, Mrs. Eddy would deal with it with increasing confidence and expertise.

The best example of this confidence in action can be seen in her greatest moment of public triumph—the address she gave in June 1888 at the Central Music Hall in Chicago. Mrs. Eddy had put out a special plea to members to attend this meeting of the National Christian Scientists Association, and she arrived there with a select group of trustworthy acolytes, which included William B. Johnson (the secretary of the Boston Association), Captain and Mrs. Joseph S. Eastaman, Calvin Frye, and Ebenezer J. Foster, a new convert and favorite about whom I shall have more to say in Chapter 20. She had agreed to come to the meeting only at the last moment, and she had clearly stipulated to the organizers that she would not address the delegates. But clearly the chairman of the convention and pastor of the Chicago church, George B. Day, had different ideas on the matter, and these may well have stemmed from his ongoing doubts about Mrs. Eddy and her teaching.[11] According to the canonic account of the event, as he and Mrs. Eddy were about to ascend the platform for the general session on the second day of the conference he informed her that he had publicized her as the main speaker of the morning. She thus had no choice but to gather her thoughts as quickly as she could during the opening remarks and to get up before the expectant audience and deliver an extempore address.[12]

It seems probable to me that the Reverend Day wanted to put Mrs. Eddy on the spot. The prominent position accorded Day on the podium in Chicago in a convention where women delegates outnumbered men by some seven to one was itself evidence of Mrs. Eddy's long-term efforts to attract men to her movement, especially educated men with leadership potential. But latent antagonism to her among her male disciples was more the rule than the exception, and the problem would only increase as Mrs. Eddy grew older. Beneath a surface deference, men like Day, or William Gill, or Luther Marston, or Joseph Adams all felt that they could lead Christian Science better than Mrs. Eddy could, and that the time had come for her to yield to their youth, energy, and experience.[13] In Chicago, as in Tremont Temple three years before, Mrs. Eddy was put to the test in public by a representative of the male clergy whom she was, implicitly, challenging. Had she failed to meet the expectations of those four thousand eager faces, the course of Christian Science might well have been different.

In fact, Mrs. Eddy succeeded beyond the wildest dreams of her supporters and the gravest fears of her opponents. The reporters from the three main Chicago dailies who attended were somewhat divided in their personal responses to what she said,[14] but all agreed that the audience reacted with a kind of mass rapture, so much so that it became necessary to rescue Mrs. Eddy from her followers.

> When the speaker concluded the audience arose en masse and made a rush for the platform. There were no steps provided for getting on the rostrum, but that did not deter those who wanted to shake hands with the idolized expounder of their creed. They mounted the reporters' table and vaulted to the rostrum like acrobats. They crowded about the little woman and hugged and kissed her until she was exhausted and a man had to come to her rescue and lead her away.[15]

Subsequently, at the Palmer House, Mrs. Eddy agreed to make an appearance in the parlors, which the hotel management had filled with flowers.[16] Once again she was mobbed by supporters, who trampled each other's feet and tore their own finery in an effort to shake her hand, look into her eyes, hear a personal word. Mrs. Eddy escaped after only a few minutes.

At the very time when Mary Baker Eddy was being mobbed by enthusiastic supporters in the Midwest, however, dissident elements in the Boston Church were taking advantage of her rare absence and staging a coup. This combination of triumph and treachery which took place in the course of a week was to make an indelible mark on her and determine much of the future course of Christian Science as an institution. Over its short history the Christian Science movement had again and again been rocked by the rebellion of Mrs. Eddy's most trusted and intimate associates. In 1881 Miranda Rice, James Howard, and Dorcas Rawson and others of the original Lynn circle had accused Mrs. Eddy of being a power-hungry, money-grubbing dictator, and only supreme inspirational leadership had kept Christian Science from foundering at that time. Mrs. Eddy had prevailed, but each successive rebellion demanded greater efforts on her part, made a deeper mark on her psyche, and left her increasingly mistrustful and suspicious. She must have wondered who, among those then closest to her, would prove to be the next Judas.

The immediate cause of the new insurgency in Boston was the Abby Corner case. Mrs. Corner was a Christian Science practitioner from West Medford, Massachusetts, whose parturient daughter and grandchild had died under her care in the spring of 1888. Mrs. Corner was consequently brought to trial for manslaughter. Claiming that she had always known Mrs. Corner would be declared innocent as charged, Mrs. Eddy distanced herself from her student, refused to allow Christian Scientist Association funds to be used for her legal defense, and went so far as to write to the press that Christian Science could not be implicated in the deaths of the child and its mother, since Mrs. Corner had never taken the Obstetrics course at the Massachusetts Metaphysical College, and therefore she was not qualified to attend a childbirth.[17] This letter sent shock waves through the Christian Science community.

Milmine, Dakin, Bates and Dittemore, and other writers opposed to Christian Science cite Mrs. Eddy's handling of the Corner case as an especially good example of her personal coldness and hypocrisy, as well as of the dangers of her theories of healing. These writers movingly describe Abby Corner and her family as the victims of an odious ideology, and they celebrate as heroes those in the Boston Association who saw in Mrs. Eddy's actions toward Mrs. Corner a reason for rebellion. There is no doubt that the Corner case is important and interesting not just in itself but because it was the first in a sequence of similar cases, and such cases still crop up from time to time in the present day. In many respects the way the press at the time and historians thereafter viewed the Corner case of 1888 would set a pattern for societal response to Christian Science.

When I first read about the case, my reaction was one of intense sympathy for Abby Corner, a woman who, it seems, saw her daughter hemorrhaging to death and could do nothing to help her or her newborn grandchild. This experience is something one would not wish on one's worst enemy, and, like Willa Cather, my instinct was simply to condemn any ideological system that would allow such a tragedy to occur, and to excoriate Mrs. Eddy for her apparent inability to see Abby Corner as other than a bad publicity problem. How could she be so heartless as to refuse to lend her loving support to a sister in such trouble? This emotional reaction has its own validity, but it was followed by other considerations as I asked myself what reasons Mrs. Eddy might have had—apart from her alleged natural nastiness— for acting as she did. It seems to me now that how one views the Corner case will in large part be determined by one's view of the history of obstetrics, and specifically of how, in the United States more than in any other country, childbirth became increasingly medicalized and clinicalized by the American medical profession.

While the coolness of her response cannot be denied, Mary Baker Eddy was essentially correct in her analysis of the case. Abby Corner was acquitted of manslaughter and needed no special defense since the prosecutors in her case could not prove that a "real" doctor could have done any better for the unfortunate patients. Whereas Mrs. Corner could win an acquittal in a court of law, Mrs. Eddy saw that if she involved the Church in the case Christian Science would fare less well in the court of public opinion, and that the positive experience many women had had with childbirth under Christian Science and which had brought women into the movement could now be lost.

Miranda Rice was the first woman, I believe, to testify to the public that thanks to Mrs. Eddy, who was in attendance at her delivery, she had experienced a painless childbirth,[18] and the pages of the *Christian Science Journal* were later to be filled with similar testimonials. As we have seen, in the first years of the organized movement, Mrs. Eddy advertised herself as "Professor of Obstetrics," and during her successful visit to Washington in 1882 she emphasized the healing of problems and conditions related to women, children, and reproduction, presumably because this was the area where she felt most confident of success. Her new course on obstetrics in 1888 probably contained more traditional anatomy and physiology than her critics have claimed.[19] But even as lived experience—what Mrs. Eddy was calling "demonstration"—was converting many to Christian Science obstetrics, the tide of professional opinion was running strongly in the other direction. Increasingly there were calls to equate a safe birth with a doctor-attended birth, to close down any institution that purported to offer nonconventional medical approaches to pregnancy and labor, and to get midwives and alternative healers out of the birthing process.

Mrs. Eddy was well aware of these trends and how they endangered lives, as well as her movement. I would surmise that perhaps the one critical piece of information she gave to students in the obstetrics courses she began running in the late 1880s was that at the first sign of any significant problem they should go immediately for the doctor. Mrs. Eddy knew that one tragic misfortune, such as the deaths of the Corner daughter and grandchild, counterbalanced hundreds of happy deliveries, provided much needed ammunition for opponents of the movement from all sides, and threatened one of the most effective and valuable services Christian Science was performing.

Mrs. Corner did more than create a public relations nightmare for Christian Science. She also engendered the split within the movement that occurred as Mrs. Eddy was speaking in Chicago with the Reverend Day. For some time there had been murmurings about the need for Christian Science to compromise, and to combine Christian Science training with standard allopathic or homeopathic medical education. About one third of the Christian Scientists in Boston wished to leave the approximately two hundred–strong membership of the Boston Association and practice their own particular mix of standard and alternative healing. Unfortunately the bylaws of the Christian Scientist Association explicitly decreed that members who sought to leave would be guilty of breaking their oath, and those who broke their oath would be expelled for immorality. By this time the success of Christian Science had made expulsion or charges of immorality a serious professional disadvantage to would-be healers, so the dissident group made a plan. In the absence in Chicago of William Johnson, the secretary of the association, one of the dissidents prevailed upon the unsuspecting Mrs. Johnson to give up all the records of the association. Upon her return from Chicago Mrs. Eddy learned that the books would be returned only if she agreed to allow thirty-six dissidents to secede on their own terms. When after a year had gone by and all attempts at negotiation had failed, Mrs. Eddy was forced to give in, and the thirty-six members were allowed to withdraw.

Even in 1888 the Church of Christ, Scientist still had such a small number of members that it could not help but suffer from the sudden loss of so many prominent people, but, as in the past, those who remained seemed confirmed rather than weakened in their allegiance, and recruitment efforts continued to find success, especially outside of New England. But the 1888 revolt had confirmed all Mrs. Eddy's worst fears about the inherent insubordination and instability of the Boston Church, and that event together with the complex experience she had had in Chicago provide the context for the astonishing decisions on institutional policy which she next made.

In the course of 1889, with shock approaching incredulity, Christian Scientists, past and present, watched Mary Baker Eddy dismantle one by one all of the structures and institutions which she had struggled to build up and, moreover, remove herself physically from the center of Church activities.[20] In May, from her vacation retreat in Barre, Vermont, she wrote to resign her pastorate of the Boston Church. In June she gave the *Christian Science Journal* to the National Christian Scientist Association and moved her residence to Concord, New Hampshire. In September she dissolved the Christian Scientist Association in Boston, in late October she dissolved the Massachusetts Metaphysical College,[21] and in December she dissolved the formal organization of the Church. In September 1890 she issued "Seven Fixed Rules" by which she intended to abide in the future:

1. I shall not be consulted verbally, or through letters, as to whose advertisement shall or shall not appear in the CHRISTIAN SCIENCE JOURNAL.
2. I shall not be consulted verbally, or through letters, as to the matter that should be published in the JOURNAL and C. S. SERIES.
3. I shall not be consulted verbally, or through letters, on marriage, divorce, or family affairs of any kind.

4. I shall not be consulted verbally, or through letters, on the choice of pastors for churches.

5. I shall not be consulted verbally, or through letters, on disaffections, if there should be any, between students of Christian Science.

6. I shall not be consulted verbally, or through letters, on who shall be admitted as members, or dropped from the membership of the Christian Science Churches or Associations.

7. I am not to be consulted verbally, or through letters, on disease and the treatment of the sick; but I shall love all mankind—and work for their welfare.[22]

The Milmine-Dittemore-Dakin school of biography has cast the events of 1889 as the first incontrovertible evidence of the aging leader's Machiavellian cunning, and her determination to keep the reins of power in her own hands, no matter the cost.[23] Wilbur and Powell, to the contrary, present the events as evidence of her inspired ability to lead the Church, perhaps despite itself, in the right direction. Peel and Gottschalk de-emphasize the radicalness of the institutional changes, seeing them as a part of a smooth and ongoing progression in Mrs. Eddy's vision of her movement, and they argue that Mrs. Eddy's move out of Boston was simply occasioned by exhaustion and a need for peace and quiet. In general, my purpose in this book is not to attempt a history of Christian Science, especially since the records of the Church are not yet open to scholars. But it is important to note that, weary or not, in and around 1889 Mrs. Eddy took a new organizational tack, making decisions which would put a unique stamp on her movement. Right or wrong, as I see it, she showed unusually strong leadership, and I think it less interesting to probe into her motivation than to recognize the style and the results of what one might call her executive decisions. Although she never received any formal education in management or business and acted out of natural acuteness, not textbook wisdom, Mrs. Eddy understood, as good CEOs do today, that past successes do not constitute future guarantees, and that precisely those policies which had worked so far might need to be abandoned if more progress was to be made. She possessed the crucial ability to look beyond the short term, decide what she wanted to occur in the future, and devise a plan to achieve her vision. She was able to do this in the teeth of received opinion and against the advice of her associates, and her vision proved to be more productive than anything the doubters and opponents could come up with.

Two facts are, after all, indisputable. First, Christian Science did not die or even falter as a result of Mrs. Eddy's unexpected actions, and none of the rival metaphysical or mental healing groups which sprang up in response to Christian Science, including New Thought, was to become nearly as influential. Thus experience would justify Mary Baker Eddy's claim to have superior judgment and to act in the interests of Christian Science. Second, there is no doubt that the accelerated progress of Christian Science is inseparable from the Church government which Mrs. Eddy conceived and set up, virtually single-handedly, and which vested the final authority on all matters in her. "God and Mrs. Eddy willing" was the covert motto of Christian Science, and the apparently all-powerful men who, over the final years of Mrs. Eddy's life, represented the movement to the world could only tremble and obey when Mrs. Eddy decided to intervene. Mrs. Eddy's reputation as divinely guided decision maker was the movement's single most important asset, and while she lived the concentration of power and authority she managed to secure for herself proved more of an advantage than a handicap to the movement she had founded. What happened after her death is a different story which others must tell.

Before leaving the public events of 1888–1889, let me note that one development is indisputable and of crucial importance: after this period Mary Baker Eddy essentially retired into private life and became increasingly inaccessible to anyone except members of her household and her selected Church officials. The public triumph in Chicago was, in fact, to be unique in the life of Mrs. Eddy and in the history of Christian Science. She was to give one other large public address, to a thousand people in New York in February 1889, but after that date she gave up all regular preaching or lecturing. From 1889 to her death the occasions when she gave a public address were so rare that they are always carefully listed and reverently described in Christian Science historiography. During those "years of authority," to use the title of Peel's third volume, as the number of Christian Scientists grew, fewer and fewer people would be able to claim to have heard Mrs. Eddy speak even briefly from a lectern or a balcony, much less at length in a parlor as she had done formerly in Stoughton or Lynn, or in a classroom, as she had done in the days of the Massachusetts Metaphysical College. Far from capitalizing on the fame she had achieved as an orator by 1889, and organizing speaking tours of the major American cities, or even simply preaching at regular scheduled intervals in Boston or in the church near her home in Concord, New Hampshire, in the final twenty years of her life Mrs. Eddy took to sending written sermons and messages to be read on her behalf. As we shall see in subsequent chapters, she would not attend the triumphant dedication of the Mother Church in Boston in January 1895, although she would visit during the following year, without any fanfare or forewarning, to address the congregation twice. She would never set foot in the great new Extension to the Mother Church, dedicated in June 1906, and her absence at the dedication services was to set off a series of questions, and rumors, and suspicions and attacks that would darken her last years.[24]

As far as I can chart her activities without having access to her complete correspondence, Mrs. Eddy began moving out of interaction with the larger public in the late 1880s, spacing out her speaking engagements and some-times even sending substitutes for occasions when she was scheduled to appear. One of Augusta Stetson's favorite stories was of the time (probably around 1886) that she had organized a large group of people in Reading, Massachusetts, to hear Mrs. Eddy, and she went down to the station to meet Mrs. Eddy's train. One train came in and another and another, but no Mrs. Eddy emerged, and finally Mrs. Stetson flew back to the assembled gather-ing and delivered a long and impassioned address, to great applause. When she saw Mrs. Eddy the next day, she reproached her for failing to appear, to which Mrs. Eddy replied, with sibylline effect, "I was there," adding, "But you stood, Augusta. You stood, you did not run." Mrs. Stetson was only one of many women who sincerely doubted their ability to stand up before a mixed audience and talk about Christian Science, and whom Mrs. Eddy con-vinced, cajoled, ordered, and obliged to conquer their fears and stand.[25]

The need to find and train new, younger people to carry the Christian Science message was obviously one important reason for Mrs. Eddy's move out of the spotlight and into the wings, but old age and fatigue were also key factors. Mrs. Eddy had so far prevailed in her ordeals by oratory, but she was less and less willing or able to marshall the energy necessary to captivate the attention of large audiences. For twenty years she had been impressing all her acquaintance with her beauty and glowing charm, her graceful and swift movements. She could still run up a flight of stairs like a girl and curl up in a chair, but it was getting more and more difficult at sixty-eight to look fifty, and sharp-eyed reporters, like the man from the Chicago *Times*, had begun to focus on the artifice of the dark curls, not on the glow of the great eyes.[26]

Her reactions to hysterical acclamation such as that which she had expe-rienced in Chicago also indicate to me that, unlike the Henry Ward Beechers of her day and the Billy Grahams of ours, Mary Baker Eddy did not thrive on mass adulation. To the contrary, I think she felt threatened by crowds, even of well-wishers, and for a variety of reasons her fear only grew over the years. On a simple level, she hated noise. Even as a child Mary Baker Eddy had relished calm and solitude and disliked loud voices. In the poverty of her midlife, she had demanded long hours every day of absolute quiet in her rental accommodation, much to the annoyance of her fellow tenants. As an old woman, she had even less tolerance for noise, and she could no longer bear the hubbub of conversation in a large room, the stress of several peo-ple all shouting at her at once.

I would also hypothesize that Mrs. Eddy was still influenced, despite herself, by Quimby's old mesmeric theories, and that she feared that her energy was drained away from her when she was with other people, with a resulting exhaustion and a loss of control. Mrs. Eddy continued to believe that absent treatments were possible, and she probably remembered how Quimby needed to lie down and rest or pace up and down outside in order to banish his own pain after seeing a patient, and that he attributed that pain to his "taking on" the patient's symptoms. Developing this basic concept, even as she extended the notion of healing to include psychological and social problems, Mrs. Eddy came to feel that she was being assaulted by the thoughts of the students and patients who were reaching out to her mentally for help and support.[27]

This belief was well in place in the Stoughton period,[28] continued strongly throughout the 1870s, and by the 1880s it was coming under the increasingly important rubric of mesmerism or malicious malpractice— more commonly referred to in non–Christian Science literature as Malicious Animal Magnetism. Thus she wrote to Daniel Spofford in December 1876, "Dr. Spofford won't you exercise reason and let me live or will you kill me? Your mind is just what has brought on my relapse and I shall never recover if you do not govern yourself and Turn Your Thoughts wholly away from me." Later, in 1877, she wrote, "Everything needs me in Science, my doors are thronged, the book lies waiting, but those who call on me mentally in suffering are in belief killing me! Stopping my work that none but me can do in their supreme selfishness . . . it would be no greater crime for them to come directly and thrust a dagger into my heart."[29] To a distant relative Hattie Baker, Mrs. Eddy wrote on May 1, 1876:

> unless the sick relieve me of so many minds calling on me alone for help I shall finish my work here soon. I rose from the grave as it were when I got up by means of my discovery, and never since have been able to keep myself in health under the pressure of the minds of the sick. It takes me down every time; hence *I chose the calling* that *I could follow and that was teaching* [italics added]. . . . If you knew what I suffer for the sick by this constant call on me that I have every hour through the mail and otherwise, you, I think, would pity me.[30]

One particular New Testament story has, in my view, important bearing on Mary Baker Eddy's fear of crowds. Mrs. Eddy's whole theology was based on the idea that the "miracles" recorded in the Gospels were literally true, and that once such events became recognized as part of divine science they could be routinely and commonly repeated. She thus took seriously all the reports of healings attributed to her and was convinced that merely by seeing her pass in her carriage, or by hearing her speak in a large auditorium, someone unknown could be relieved of his or her symptoms.[31] Exactly this scenario is enacted in the gospel accounts of the healing of the woman with the bloody flux. As we learn from the two accounts of this event in the gospels according to Saint Matthew and Saint Mark, the woman had hemorrhaged for twelve years and had lost all her fortune by consulting doctors without receiving any help. She was healed instantly by merely touching Jesus' robe as he passed her in a crowd. The crucial points of this story are that the unknown woman reached out to Jesus and was healed, and that, despite the lightness of the contact, Jesus was aware of strength going out of him.[32] This story had special resonance with Mrs. Eddy since women who suffered chronic bleeding in this way were notably responsive to Christian Science healing practice.[33] With slight modifications, the story in Saint Mark could have come straight out of the pages of the *Christian Science Journal*.[34]

Her ability to heal was central to Mrs. Eddy's authority, and she gloried in it, but it also made her anxious. Ultimately, she was convinced, Christian Science would lead people to the conquest of death, but, in the meantime, she recognized that, for her, aging was unavoidable and death not far off, and that she needed therefore to focus her energies and waste no time. Measures had long been in place in her household for coping with the problem of keeping unwanted thoughts at bay. Mrs. Eddy had long concealed her address while she was on vacation, used different mailboxes for important communications, and at the Massachusetts Metaphysical College small groups were organized to mentally counter the effect of Malicious Animal Magnetism. By 1889, however, I think it became apparent to her that these measures would no longer serve. Therefore she determined to so structure her life as to limit her interaction with the world even more drastically. In Chapter 21 I shall be dealing with the private way of life Mrs. Eddy developed especially after moving into Pleasant View in 1892. In the next chapter we shall see how her new institutional structures and policies took shape, quite literally, in the building of the Mother Church in Boston.

19

Building
The
Mother Church

IN 1886 MEMBERS OF THE BOSTON CHURCH OF CHRIST, Scientist used funds they had raised to buy some land on Falmouth Street in Boston upon which they planned to raise a church. The land was bought for $2,000 down from Nathan Matthews, a former mayor of Boston, but it was subject to a three-year mortgage of $8,763.50. The members set about clearing the mortgage in an organized way, paying off $3,000 in the first year, and in December 1887 they held a fair in Boston's Horticultural Hall which raised another $5,000. According to Bliss Knapp, whose father Ira Knapp was Mrs. Eddy's chief lieutenant in the affair of the church land, Mrs. Eddy had offered to buy the Falmouth Street land on behalf of the members, but they had refused. She was unenthusiastic about the standard religious fund-raising tactics which the members counted on, such as rummage sales, church sociables, and suppers. Nonetheless, she bided her time and gave the December 1887 fair her accolade by making a personal appearance, together with her son and his family who were then visiting Boston.

In what seemed a triumph for traditional fund-raising and a promise of traditional Congregational-style church organization, the fair raised almost all the money needed to clear the mortgage, but then disaster struck. The Church treasurer, William H. Bradford, absconded with all the funds. This egregious piece of embezzlement occurred several months before the so-called "medical group" led by Sarah Crosse and J. M. C. Murphy was, as we saw in the last chapter, holding the Boston Association's records hostage in order to secure their honorable dismissals from the Church. Having lost some thirty-six of its most prominent members and all its funds, the Boston Church was in turmoil, and it was at this point that Mrs. Eddy stepped in, determined to discipline the remaining members and prevent any further public dissent while at the same time pursuing the important long-term task of building a Christian Science church in the heart of Boston.

To effect these goals, she worked overtly and covertly. Even as she dealt body blows to the expectations and prestige of the Boston workers by closing the college which had become their base of operations and dissolving the Christian Scientist Association itself as a legal entity, she was also working behind the scenes to obtain ownership of the Falmouth Street site. In December 1888 her lawyer, Baxter E. Perry, obtained on her behalf an assignment on the remaining mortgage of some $5,000. When seven months later, the mortgage fell due, and the Boston Association members made no move to renew it or pay it off, she foreclosed on the property and subsequently, after publicly advertising the property for sale for three weeks, purchased it for $5,000. All these transactions were completed by Mrs. Eddy's lawyer or his son George so that her name never appeared. In December an even more complicated set of transactions was performed whereby the land was transferred from the lawyer Perry to one of Mrs. Eddy's chief lieutenants, Ira O. Knapp—who used a check supplied him by Mrs. Eddy herself.

Ira Knapp was perhaps Mrs. Eddy's most loyal student, ready to obey her to the letter, regardless of what anyone else said or did. Acting on Mrs. Eddy's instructions, Knapp prepared a deed of trust naming five men as directors of the Church—himself, Joseph S. Eastaman, Eugene H. Greene, David Anthony, and William B. Johnson—who were charged with maintaining regular church services. According to Bliss Knapp, the son of Ira, who provides an extremely detailed account of this whole sequence of actions in his book about the Church,

> The deed also provided for a board of three trustees, whose business it was to hold in trust the title to the church lot, but *only* for the purpose of erecting a church edifice thereon. They must begin building operations only after the sum of $20,000 had been collected for that purpose, and the treasurer was to give a bond to the Trustees of $5,000 to insure the faithful discharge of his duties in office.
>
> The deed further provided that none of the Trustees nor [any] of the Directors should bring to Mrs. Eddy any matter of business relating to the fund or to the building of the church, under penalty of forfeiting his position.[1]

From the beginning, the terms of this trust were contested. Mrs. Eddy's lawyer, Baxter Perry, refused to participate in the transaction or even to have his name on the deed. Knapp persisted in his course, however, and found a lawyer willing to prepare the trust document, and three trustees took title to the land—Alfred Lang, Marcellus Munroe, and William G. Nixon. These gentlemen set about raising the funds, and by December 1891 they had amassed the $20,000 specified in the trust document, but then they too began to get legal cold feet. After consulting lawyers and the Massachusetts Title Deed Insurance Company, William Nixon, who had taken the lead in the matter, argued to the directors that the trust deed was defective in four respects. The two most important defects were, first, that, according to the trust provisions as written, the land would revert to Knapp and his heirs should conditions not be met, and, second, that since the Church had been disestablished on December 2, 1889, "there was no avowed membership which could hold property, and therefore the trust might be termed a 'public charity,' under the supervision of the Supreme Court."[2]

Knapp came under extreme pressure from the trustees and some of his director colleagues to acknowledge the defects in the title and rectify them, specifically by reestablishing the church as titleholder to the land. Nixon seemed to have both the law and the support of most of the members on his side. What he did not have was the support of Mrs. Eddy, and this was really all that counted since, in all but name, she was the owner of the land.

Technically, Mrs. Eddy could not be consulted by either the directors or the trustees on the church building issue, but in fact Knapp and his associate Johnson had her ear and were following her strategy as it evolved. Nixon sought to gain Mrs. Eddy's favor by floating the idea that the proposed church should be made a memorial to her, but this was a terrible miscalculation since Mrs. Eddy said the idea smacked of the sin of "personality," and she rejected it out of hand. Things came to a head at a July 16, 1892, meeting at Pleasant View. Here it was admitted officially and in the presence of lawyers that the trustees had solicited money to pay for the erection on the site of a publishing house as well as a church, and, furthermore that the treasurer had failed to put up the $5,000 bond. Using these technical grounds, Mrs. Eddy declared the trust was broken. Knapp signed a quitclaim deed of the land to Mrs. Eddy, and for the first time she became the titleholder to the property. With much difficulty, all the money raised under the original trust was returned to the donors, and the Boston church seemed as far from realization as in 1889.

In July 1892 Mrs. Eddy reached out to the faithful throughout the United States and gave her own, rather extraordinary version of this whole process of buying the land and making the original trust. The message to the First Church of Christ, Scientist was published in the *Christian Science Journal*, and it is quoted here in part:

> On December 10, 1889, I gave a lot of land—in Boston, situated near the beautiful Back Bay Park, now valued at $20,000 and rising in value—for the purpose of having erected thereon a church edifice to be called The Church of Christ, Scientist.
>
> I had this desirable site transferred in a circuitous, novel way, the

wisdom whereof a few persons have since scrupled; but to my spiritual perception, like all true wisdom, this transaction will in future be regarded as greatly wise, and it will be found that this act was in advance of the erring mind's apprehension.

As with all former efforts in the interest of Christian Science, I took care that the provisions for the land and building were such as error could not control. I knew that to God's gift, foundation and superstructure, no one could hold a wholly material title. The land, and the church standing on it, must be conveyed through a type representing the true nature of the gift; a type morally and spiritually inalienable, but materially questionable—even after the manner that all spiritual good comes to Christian Scientists, to the end of taxing their faith in God, and their adherence to the superiority of the claims of the Spirit over matter or merely legal titles.

No one could buy, sell, or mortgage my gift as I had it conveyed. Thus the case rested, and I supposed the trustee-deed was legal; but this was God's business, not mine. Our church prospered by the right hand of His righteousness, and contributions to the Building Fund generously poured into the treasury. Unity prevailed,—till mortal man sought to know who owned God's temple, and adopted and urged only the material side of this question.

The lot of land which I donated I redeemed from under mortgage. The foundation on which our church was to be built had to be rescued from the grasp of legal power, and now it must be put back into the arms of Love, if we would not be found fighting against God. (*Mis.*, pp. 139–40)

The fact that even such carefully picked henchmen as Nixon had failed to obey the trust deed had confirmed for Mrs. Eddy all her fears and suspicions about the Boston membership. She was determined more than ever to put into place a structure which gave unhindered expression to the mandate of God, which she equated with her own. Now that the legal issues had been defined so carefully, she set her New Hampshire lawyers to do a legal search, and they managed at last to come up with an obscure Massachusetts statute which allowed donees to hold property in trust for a church, without requiring the Church to incorporate.

To quote the Knapp account once again, "on August 22, 1892, invitations were issued to twelve Christian Scientists, selected by Mrs. Eddy, to meet and incorporate a Church."[3] At a meeting held in Miss Julia Bartlett's rooms on Dartmouth Street in Boston, Mrs. Eddy, through her adopted son, Ebenezer Foster Eddy, announced that she had drawn up a new trust deed that gave the land title to four donees, Knapp, Johnson, Eastaman, and Stephen A. Chase. The members assembled then voted to declare the four donees the directors of the Church, and subsequently in September 1892 the trust was issued and the twelve selected members voted themselves First

Members of the First Church of Christ, Scientist. The twelve included five men—Ira O. Knapp, Willam B. Johnson, Joseph S. Eastaman, Stephen A. Chase, and Ebenezer J. Foster Eddy; and seven women—Julia S. Bartlett, Mary W. Munroe, Ellen R. Clark, Mary F. Eastaman, Janet T. Colman, Flavia S. Knapp, and Eldora O. Gragg.

As Bliss Knapp remarks, all of these twelve members except Foster Eddy were to remain pillars of Christian Science. In them Mary Baker Eddy finally found the unquestioning obedience to her wishes she had long sought in vain. Mrs. Eddy considered her handling of the Falmouth Street site issue a triumph for her new style of leadership and a key step in the formation of a new "spiritual" form of church governance. Her opponents and critics who see Mrs. Eddy as motivated exclusively by love of money and power point out that, materially, she had managed to take from her own church members a piece of land that had more than doubled in value, and she had given herself and her heirs complete title, should the four donees fail to put up the exact church edifice she specified. The projected Mother Church as envisaged by Mrs. Eddy would serve and belong to the whole membership of Christian Science. The Boston congregation which principally attended this church would have neither title to nor direction over Church matters since Mrs. Eddy had managed to finesse the whole issue of church institutionalization by putting in place a preselected and then self-perpetuating board.

It is a measure of Mrs. Eddy's leadership, of her vision of an international church, and of the effectiveness of her publishing arm that the new administrative structure for the Church which she had slipped into place was not merely accepted but welcomed by the membership at large. She had given the movement a new task, to build a Mother Church as soon as possible, and members set about their work with a zeal that aroused the admiration and envy of contemporaries and that still merits the descriptor *extraordinary*. Mrs. Eddy's radical new concept of fund-raising now went into effect, and the results amazed even the most sanguine. Once the church building was defined as a national, not a local institution, it became clear to those Christian Scientists who lived outside the Boston area, now in the majority, that their task was to provide the money for their Mother Church. More than $30,000 quickly poured into the building fund, and, although this was only a portion of the estimated total needed to bankroll the edifice, Mrs. Eddy decreed that it was enough for construction work to begin.

To begin construction of a large, complex, and expensive building before all the funds necessary to complete the work are in hand is contrary to sound business practice. And Mrs. Eddy compounded the risk and the difficulty of the enterprise by decreeing that the building should be completed and ready for service by the end of 1894. For the Boston directors, their wives and chosen associates, the task was Herculean—planning every aspect of the building from steel girders to hassocks and serving as general contractors for the whole enterprise, making the contracts, assuring payments, and coordinating the workforce at every stage, all to meet a timetable laid down from on high.

Throughout this crucial period in church history Mrs. Eddy maintained a brilliant strategy whose daring can only be appreciated once it is understood that most of the actual building work was completed in eight months. Remaining resolutely aloof at Pleasant View, she resisted all attempts to draw her into the day-to-day drama of the work site. She laid down the schedule, approved the architectural plans, eagerly worked on details of design, such as the scenes to be depicted in the stained glass windows, but she refused to hear about problems with workmen or fears that the building would remain incomplete for lack of funds. By placing her prestige on the line, by refusing even to contemplate failure, in fact by setting the stakes of success extraordinarily high, but at the same time giving her chosen lieutenants a large amount of discretion and keeping a close watch on them, Mrs. Eddy inspired her troops to victories they themselves thought impossible.

Only once did she personally intervene, and this was in the crucial area of financing. The year 1893 was a very bad one economically throughout the United States, and the Church of Christ, Scientist immediately felt the effects of the economic downturn. Money for the building fund slackened to a trickle, and it seemed that the building work would have to be halted before it had fairly begun. At this point Mrs. Eddy made a personal appeal to fifty-three members to donate an extra one thousand dollars apiece. For many of the people who were contacted, the sacrifice being asked was very considerable. These were not wealthy individuals for the most part; money they sent to Boston to pay for tiles and girders would not be available to feed the family or send a son to school. But all sent their contribution, and the financial crisis was resolved.

Two of the most interesting little booklets put out by the Christian Science Publishing Society are the accounts of the building of the Mother Church and the Extension written by Joseph Armstrong and Margaret Williamson.[4] Armstrong was the director given special charge of the original building project, and thus the man upon whom the greatest weight was laid; Williamson was an editorial writer for the *Christian Science Monitor.* It is perhaps only when one looks at the original Mother Church as it stands today and when one imagines raising the funds, planning, designing, and putting up the building for immediate regular use in the space of eighteen months that Armstrong's heroic achievement can be understood.

In 1893 the site on which the members planned to build was a corner wedge surrounded by three-story brownstone row houses such as can still be seen in Boston's Back Bay. As late as the summer of 1893 the directors were still considering alternative architectual models and revising their costs upward by more than one third to reflect the new city fireproofing code and a change from brick to stone. In order to get planning permission from the city to lay the foundations, plans for the whole construction and its cost had to be submitted. It was obvious that the $40,000 that had been raised thus far was quite inadequate to complete the building as planned, but nonetheless, acting on faith, the directors applied and were granted permission to begin. The Back Bay was formed by landfill and was still much subject to flooding, but when piles were driven down on the site, bedrock was found much sooner than expected, and the first stone was laid on Wednesday, November 8, 1893.

The directors next decided that they would begin to solicit contracts for building the walls, and they managed to find a New Hampshire company willing to supply the stone and the girders and do the whole job, and also to agree to stop building when and if funds ran out. It was at this point that Mrs. Eddy made the special request for funds totalling some $53,000 and thus assured that the stonework at least would be funded. All seemed to bode well, but March of 1894 came and then April, and no work had begun on the site. After some confusion, it came out that the stoneworkers had failed to ensure the manufacture and delivery of the requisite iron and steel beams.

A special hollow stone had been designed as a cornerstone, containing a Bible, all Mrs. Eddy's published works, various other Christian Science documents, and lists of the directors and those who had made special contributions to the building fund. The laying of this stone was scheduled for May 1, and then postponed until May 21, at which point Mrs. Eddy dug in her heels. The directors were forced to have a low course of stone built using the few ill-fitting steel girders into which the cornerstone could be laid, and this stone was filled with the commemorative box, consecrated, and cemented into the stone course late at night. From then until it found its place in the wall, the stone was guarded all day by the directors themselves, taking turns, and at night by two trusted young male students.

One director, William B. Johnson, went to Pennsylvania, to take personal charge of the girder problem. He discovered on his arrival at the beam manufacturer that nothing at all had been started, but he soon succeeded in convincing the company to devote all its efforts to completing the Boston order. On the journey back to Boston Johnson kept careful track of the freight car, ensuring swift delivery. Owing to communication problems between the stonemasons, the architects, and the floor-beam makers, the steel beams were made too long, occasioning further delay as the stone was chipped out to allow the beams more space. Further problems with ironwork manufacturers were encountered in June, when the columns to support the auditorium and galleries were first late and then condemned as substandard upon delivery. Another whole month was lost while this problem was resolved.

It was becoming all too obvious that no aspect of the job would proceed on schedule without daily, hands-on supervision. The directors were not simply fund-raisers, treasurers, and paymasters, though this was an essential part of their task. Much time and effort had to be expended on establishing a detailed payment schedule both for work in progress and for projected work. There was constant anxiety since the funds were coming in week by week, in fits and starts, and as of July the available funds were still insufficient to pay the whole estimated cost. All the multiple individual contracts with iron makers, masons, roofers, plasterers, and so forth, had to be negotiated, and the directors had to be on top of the whole building schedule and personally ensure that each set of workmen was on the job, working as many hours as possible, getting paid on time, and cooperating with all the other work crews. On one occasion an on-the-spot collection was taken up from Christian Science students who happened to be visiting the site, so that the directors could pay workmen who were threatening to lay down their tools because the contractor had failed to give them their weekly wage.

The building of the walls was so behind schedule that the roof had not even been started by mid-September, and in fact the roofer was far from ready to begin since a rail strike in Chicago had once again delayed delivery of the necessary iron beams. It was not until October 20 that the inscription on the pink granite tablet built into the circular tower wall was completed and unveiled for all to see. It read—and reads today:

THE FIRST CHURCH OF CHRIST SCIENTIST.

Erected Anno Domini, 1894.

A Testimonial to our beloved Teacher, the Reverend
Mary Baker Eddy;
Discoverer and Founder of Christian Science;
Author of its Text-book,
SCIENCE AND HEALTH with KEY TO THE SCRIPTURES;
President of the Massachusetts Metaphysical College,
and the first Pastor of this Denomination.

To have 1894 written in stone as the date of construction for a building still open to the elements must have struck the Christian Science community with panic. Armstrong in despair journeyed to Pleasant View at Mrs. Eddy's request, and he returned to Boston full of faith. He gave up all other work to devote himself full-time to the building, and he and the other directors put on their designer hats and began to work out the detailed plan of how the church would look inside. Should the floors be marble or wood, what color should the carpeting and cushions be, who should be commissioned to provide the stained glass windows, and what designs should be used for them? Anyone who has ever had a private home built, lived through the construction of a simple addition, or remodeled a kitchen, anyone who has worked with a church committee to commission so much as a rug for the vestibule or a new vestment for the pastor will be amazed to hear that Christian Scientists designed a whole church interior in the space of about two months.

October had at least been sunny and warm and ideal for building, but on November 6 an early snowfall filled the unroofed construction with snow, which had to be shoveled out. Problems with inadequate materials and balky contractors and defective plans for the roof duly cropped up, but Armstrong was by now a seasoned warrior in the daily combat with inertia, and by mid-November, the terra-cotta roofing was laid, canvas over the window openings was keeping the rain out, and work on fireproofing, heating, electricity, plumbing, and flooring could begin. Armstrong was now seconded by several reliable Christian Scientist subcontractors, notably Edward P. Bates, who came from Syracuse with his wife on November 12 and superintended all the heating and ventilation work. Armstrong's team of assistants was at this point living and sleeping in the leaky, bare shell of their church—they had six weeks before the building was due to be ready to hold services!

By this time, the exterior workmen understood that the Christian Scientists meant business when they made a schedule, and they were caught up in the spirit of the whole crazy enterprise. The ready roofing, the slate, the copper stripping, the pitch were put down speedily, although rain and cold made the work difficult and dangerous, and sometimes snow had to be shoveled off the roof. At this point, however, Armstrong and his crew were faced with a whole phalanx of new building trades, whose men were not accustomed to working alongside one another at all hours of the day and night. Plasterers laughed at the idea that they should begin work when the flooring and mosaic were still incomplete and water still sometimes leaked from the roof and the windows. Just getting the necessary quantity of plaster delivered from the wholesaler, late at night on a Saturday and in terrible weather, was a triumph of mind over matter.

December was a frenzy of activity, with two hundred workmen on the site all day and late into the night. Even getting permits to allow unloading on both Norway Street and Falmouth Street took time and effort, and Armstrong in his book gives the list of contracts and the date on which they were scheduled:

Decorations, December 5.
Vestry chairs, December 5.
Marble, December 6.
Pulpit, and the furniture for "Mother's Room," December 12.
Electric fixtures, December 8.

Marble for "Mother's Room," December 12.
Stereo-relief work, December 13.
Sidewalk, December 14.
Bronze torches and brackets, December 18.
Onyx mantel for "Mother's room," December 20.[5]

As this list indicates, one of the smaller yet most difficult aspects of the building project was the so-called "Mother's Room," a room in the tower of the church dedicated to Mrs. Eddy's personal use. Miss Maurine Campbell had made it her special mandate to organize children to collect money for this project, and eventually $5,000 was donated by the so-called "Busy Bees." Plans for designing and furnishing this apartment had been modest at the start, but, as the reality of the Mother Church took shape around them, women in the movement, in particular, became convinced that only the best was good enough for their leader. The entrance was redesigned to feature an archway of the finest Italian marble, and on December 11 a special letter from Mrs. Eddy requested that the word *Mother* be engraved on the marble floor of the entrance, and, on the arch above, the word *Love*. Mosaic on the floor, white and red marble throughout, gold-plated pipes, three stained glass windows inspired by Mrs. Eddy's poem "Christ and Christmas," an onyx mantelpiece specially ordered in Mexico—these structural features of the room were complemented by furnishings and ornaments donated by individual Scientists.

Armstrong's published account includes a rare photograph of the completed room, and this enumeration of its contents:

> Other remembrances [apart from the fireplace rug made from one hundred eider duck skins] were an elaborately carved imported chair, an onyx table, a large china lamp and shade, the desk lamp shade, an Assyrian bridal veil, jardinière and cloisonné clock, two water colors by an English artist, valuable vases, bookmarks and embroideries, a sofa pillow covered with white and gold tapestry, matching the other furniture, an Athenian hanging lamp two centuries old. Silvery green plush draperies and antique Persian rugs of similar tint harmonized with the delicate frescoing of the walls. A little onyx beehive contained the name of twenty-eight hundred Busy Bees. Everything was provided for the beloved mother's actual occupancy, as witness such tokens as a handkerchief, a tiny pincushion, dressing gown, slippers, and every needful toilet article.[6]

Mrs. Eddy herself contributed only one item to the decoration of her room. It was a large, six by five feet oil painting of the small black haircloth-covered rocking chair which had been the principal item contained in her little garret room at 8 Broad Street in Lynn. This painting came sometime after the rest of the room was completed and caused some difficulty because it was too large to fit comfortably on any wall. Finally the designers set it on the floor, put green draperies around it, and lit it with skillfully concealed electric lighting. The painting told a story, the story of Mrs. Eddy's struggle to reach the position of authority and reverence she now occupied, and which the church structure symbolized. But the awkward size and subject of the painting, the contrast it posed with the rest of the furnishings, also implicitly raised the issue of how far the newly successful denomination truly wished to embrace the embarrassingly mixed, confusing, origins of the woman they hailed as their leader and founder.

Mrs. Eddy had refused to allow Nixon to make the new Boston church a monument to her, and she was soon to regret allowing herself and the Church members to get carried away in the creation of the Mother's Room. Though filled with superficially useful, personal touches, the room was totally at odds with Mrs. Eddy's personal taste, which ran chiefly to the clean, neat, comfortable, and old-fashioned, and it served no real function.[7] Even after her removal to New Hampshire, Mrs. Eddy retained her large and comfortable house at 385 Commonwealth Avenue in Boston, and she could easily spend a night there when she came to Boston. In fact she visited the Mother Church only twice and used the Mother's Room only once, preferring in June 1899 to stay at 385 Commonwealth Avenue. After Mark Twain published a satirical account of Christian Scientists tiptoeing into the room in silent rapture while all the furnishings and their composition and cost were solemnly detailed by the lady guide, the room was closed, the contents stored and dispersed.

On December 30, 1894, however, such disagreeable problems lay well in the future, and Christian Scientists and Bostonians in general were gazing in amazement at the new building. As late as December 15 the tower was still incomplete, no marble had yet arrived, and the decorative work had not yet even begun. Caroline Bates was forced on two occasions to climb three twenty-foot ladders up to the bell tower to mediate a dispute over whether or not a large derrick could be rented for an additional day to hoist materials up to complete the work. Communication with the mosaic workers was difficult because they were Italian and spoke little or no English. When the wooden pews, ordered from Michigan and completed as a rush order under the personal supervision of Armstrong's delegate James A. Neal, arrived at the site on Friday evening December 21, the installer was outraged. The whole space was crowded with workers, scaffolding was everywhere, the floors were filthy and unfinished, and there was no place to store a carload of pews. The next day, when the Michigan man returned, he was amazed. All the staging was down, all the workmen but one (who was fitting the capitals on the pillars) had left, the floor was uncovered and clean. When, on December 29, the poured concrete for the sidewalk would not set because of the cold, the directors had a tent set up over the walk, had the tent attached to the building, opened the church doors, and set the heat on high. Inside the church, members were cleaning and dusting, and when the clock struck midnight the church was ready for service the next day, exactly according to Mrs. Eddy's instructions.

On January 6 the new church was dedicated, and the new service which Mrs. Eddy had decreed in her missive of December 19 was in effect:

> Hold your services in the Mother Church Dec. 30, 1894, and dedicate this church Jan. 6th. The Bible and "Science and Health with Key to the Scriptures" shall henceforth be the Pastor of the Mother Church. This will tend to spiritualize thought. Personal preaching has more or less of human views grafted into it. Whereas the pure Word contains only the living, health-giving Truth.[8]

Having put an end to all sermons and personal teaching, and instituted her own Word as Truth and her own text as Pastor, Mrs. Eddy did send the assembled followers at the four consecutive services a special dedicatory message. To the surprise of all and the dismay of some, Mrs. Eddy's words were read on her behalf by Henrietta Clark Bemis, a professional elocutionist hired for the occasion who was not a Christian Scientist. That Augusta Stetson, the head of the richest and most important of the branch churches, who had trained as a professional elocutionist and was famous in the movement as an orator, had not been asked to read Mrs. Eddy's message was seen as a message in itself.

But Mrs. Eddy's absence, her decision to remain in New Hampshire, sent the most important signal of all. It said that her discouragement of the cult of personality was sincere; it said that the new phase Christian Science was entering entailed more than stone walls and carved inscriptions and marble lintels. It said that even though the new Mother Church was the realization of an old dream, it also represented for Mrs. Eddy her old fear of Christian Science becoming institutionalized and thus materialized. By not attending the triumphant dedication services, by staying home, by continuing with the daily discipline she had set herself, by eschewing the praise and adulation she could expect, Mrs. Eddy was teaching by acts what she had long taught in words—that the material and public successes of Christian Science could be won only by a heart striving for good, that healing became possible only when the Christian Scientist was attuned to God and seeking actively every day to raise the level of his or her own thoughts and actions.

What Mrs. Eddy was beginning to formulate for herself was not just a politics of absence but also, and perhaps primarily, a metaphysics of absence. The politics would largely determine the evolution of her doctrine, the development of her church as an institution, and the public presence that Christian Science would have in the world. The metaphysics would be a personal, individual journey, with universal implications. All too often in her life Mrs. Eddy found herself accused of selling religion, of seeking money and success above all, of being a sham and a mountebank, and these accusations hit home. Mary Baker Eddy was above all a believing Christian and a daily reader of the Gospels. She knew that by her fruit she would be known, she believed that it would profit her nothing to gain the whole world if thereby she lost her own soul, and she was determined that her heart would be where her treasure was. The steep, hard, and dark path into the self and toward God was what Mary Baker Eddy now chose for herself. Prayer, meditation, an active thinking through of God's meaning, a passive openness to God's message would now take their place in her everyday life.

Such goals are the essential fabric of religious experiences across time and space. In Catholicism, in Buddhism, in Sufism, in Kabbalism, the kinds of aspirations Mrs. Eddy was increasingly voicing would have found unquestioning acceptance and swift understanding. Ashrams, monasteries, meditational communities have existed for many centuries to satisfy and clarify longings such as hers. Mrs. Eddy was building a new religion in a new country, however, and she had not only to find her own language of mysticism but to establish her own house of prayer. What form this religion might take remained unclear for several years after she left Boston for New Hampshire, but it took shape at last in a house called Pleasant View.

2 0

A
New Edition
of Science and Health
and a New Son

I N THE GREAT DISESTABLISHMENT OF 1889, MARY BAKER Eddy had signalled her determination to leave Boston, distance herself from the day-to-day workings of her church, and give herself more time for reflection. From this point she was freed from the burden of teaching and preaching, her staff was increasingly effective in helping her deal with the growing volume of correspondence, and by leaving the Boston area and setting up her household in Concord, New Hampshire, Mrs. Eddy was able to see only the people she wanted to see, and on her own terms. Leisure and relaxation were not, however, what Mrs. Eddy had moved north for, and, true to her stated purpose, she took up her pen and engaged in the most concentrated period of writing since the early 1870s. Much of 1889 and 1890 was devoted to a major revision of *Science and Health*, and the resulting fiftieth edition, published in January 1891, was to stand with only small corrections until the final revision of 1902. The 1891 edition constitutes a major step toward the text known to Christian Scientists today.

"Personality" was to be one of the most important issues for Mary Baker Eddy in the last period of her life, and one of the main aims of the new edition, as of so many of the other changes she was enacting, was to detach the textbook as far as possible from its writer. This was an extraordinary, even paradoxical task, since *Science and Health* was and is so essentially personal and individual, not in the sense of being autobiographical but in the sense of being the creation of a single mind, peculiarly detached from the influence of others. Furthermore, Mrs. Eddy's authorship of *Science and Health* was reinforced by her authority over its interpretation. From 1866 to 1875 she had read aloud and expounded to anyone who would listen the ideas that finally became *Science and Health.* Even after the book was published, it continued in most cases to serve as an auxiliary to Mrs. Eddy's personal teaching. It was accepted in Christian Science circles that those who had taken class with Mrs. Eddy herself had received a special message, and the Massachusetts Metaphysical College, with its faculty of one, succeeded for this reason.

To be the sole authority, the fons et origo of all knowledge, is a heady position to occupy, and Mrs. Eddy enjoyed it, all the more because achieving authority had been so long and difficult a task. Had she wished, she could have rested on her laurels and enjoyed her status as minor guru until her death. That she did not take the easy and pleasant way out is, in my view, a measure of her greatness as a leader and, more important, of the validity of her spiritual calling. As under her hands and before her eyes Christian Science took shape as a worldview, she knew she must seek to live its truth as well as teach it. Hence if the claims she had for Christian Science had validity, the movement must cease to be coextensive with her personal identity.

Her goal in 1889–1890 thus became to make *Science and Health* as far as possible self-interpreting to any reader of normal intelligence and goodwill and to eliminate from it all personal references. The book had always, and almost notoriously among its critics, been a text in constant flux, but whereas in the past Mrs. Eddy had changed the order of chapters, dropped one and added another, worked on individual paragraphs and expressions, at this juncture she attempted a root-and-branch reorganization and a major rewriting of her book. With the help, first, of an awed young assistant, Joshua Bailey, then of the acerbic yet still caring Wiggin, Mrs. Eddy worked to structure her book's argument more logically and smoothly and make the book as accessible and as impersonal as possible. Far from the fray in her newly rented house in Concord, New Hampshire, Mrs. Eddy felt able to achieve some psychological as well as physical distance, and thus in the new edition she relinquished the bitter recriminations and wild accusations against real-life enemies such as Kennedy, Spofford, and Arens that had found space in editions before 1883. Malicious Animal Magnetism was still a major player on her metaphysical stage, and a major character in the story of her everyday life, but Mrs. Eddy was refining and depersonalizing it, at least in her essential statement of doctrine, and this was a crucial step.

It is hard to exaggerate the spiritual, emotional, and intellectual investment Mary Baker Eddy had made in *Science and Health*; the radical revision undertaken for the fiftieth edition cost her enormous trouble and labor. Overwork, uncertainty, and stress were expressed in physical illnesses, in notable loss of weight, and in wracking nightmares.[1] The photographic record of Mrs. Eddy is limited in many ways, and making deductions from it is dangerous. Nonetheless, when one compares two well-known photographic studies of Mary Baker Eddy, the first of her seated in her study in 1883 and the second of her standing in outdoor clothing in 1891, the change in her appearance is almost shocking. Plump, dark haired, fashionably dressed, smiling, Mrs. Eddy in 1882 was, the picture tells us, still what men liked to call a fine figure of a woman. Some nine years later, she had become an old lady, thin, white-haired, her face gaunt.[2]

In early 1890 Mrs. Eddy wrote to the wife of her new publisher, William G. Nixon, that the edition was almost ready to go to press, but she then plunged again into doubt and reconsideration, tore her manuscript apart, and spent another nine months on more rethinking and rewriting. Many of the changes which had been made in the 1886 edition were abandoned, much to Wiggin's chagrin, and Mrs. Eddy added so much new material that Wiggin at one point counselled her to issue it as a separate text. If Mrs. Eddy had once worked in isolation and unassisted, now she was besieged by different readings and points of view. Bailey and Wiggin fought each other on editorial suggestions and innovations; printer Wilson and publisher Nixon inveighed about the financial costs of trying to publish a text that was in constant metamorphosis; and Frye and Foster Eddy, Mrs. Eddy's closest advisors, muddied the waters by issuing mandates, in person and by letter, which claimed to represent Mrs. Eddy's views. Combatting Malicious Animal Magnetism was again the watchword in Christian Science, as teams of mental workers were deputed to ward off "error" from publishers and editors and to ensure that the project proceeded on schedule.

When the new revision finally rolled off the presses, unlike its distant ancestor of 1875, it became an almost instant success. Competent professionals were in place to handle the marketing and distribution, and every Christian Scientist, of course, was ready to line up and pay $3 for his or her copy. From this point on the book's status was assured as a continuing best-seller and a growing source of income for all concerned. Although she would never stop tinkering with the text of *Science and Health*, Mrs. Eddy herself seems, after all her labors, to have looked on what she had done and found it good. As we saw in the last chapter, in 1894 at the dedication of the Mother Church building in Boston she took the unprecedented step of decreeing that henceforward *Science and Health* would be the Pastor for The Mother Church in Boston. In April 1895 she expanded this: all Christian Science church services would use this pastor and no longer include sermons by preachers. More and more convinced that the book was the product of revelation, that, in the final sense, it was God's work and not her own, she saw no contradiction in her increasing denunciation of "personality" and her institutionalized ban in Christian Science worship of any words but those she had penned. Others, not surprisingly, saw the declaration of *Science and Health* as pastor of the Church of Christ, Scientist as just the latest and most egregious sign of Mary Baker Eddy's growing egotism and will to power.

Revising *Science and Health* was not enough for Mrs. Eddy. She also attacked the issue of personality from another angle, issuing in late 1891 an extended version of a short personal memoir she had begun as a pamphlet in 1886. In this new publication, titled *Retrospection and Introspection*, she hoped to lay to rest the public's interest in her personal life, while at the same time insisting that autobiography had no place in Christian Science. These two aims were basically incompatible, and *Retrospection and Introspection* turned out to be an uneasy compromise which satisfied few. There were decades of her past life which Mary Baker Eddy simply wished to forget and which she therefore passed over in silence, and critics would soon seize on this gap as being suspicious, if not indicative of Mrs. Eddy's guilt. Riding her metaphysical hobbyhorse about the irrelevance of biographical minutiae, Mrs. Eddy made no attempt to check the information she did provide, and once again she gave her critics a perfect opportunity to call her a liar or worse. Autobiography was a nettle Mrs. Eddy refused to grasp firmly, and its sting would be with her for the rest of her life.[3]

While all this labor on the books and the planning for the new Mother Church were proceeding, Mrs. Eddy was also struggling to resolve the problem of her domestic situation. Spiritually and intellectually she was convinced that personality must yield as far as possible to Principle, and that physical needs and material concerns must be subordinated to metaphysical goals. But in the here and now, her body was real, her physical needs were increasingly difficult to neglect, and her individual position in the world was almost unique. On the one hand there were the growing power and authority she had as a leader of Christian Science, the veneration bordering on adulation she received as one with a special relation to God. On the other hand there were her loneliness, her pain, her anxiety, her boredom, her place in a material world as an aging woman with more money than friendship, and with enemies of many stripes.

Unlike the average woman of her age, Mary Baker Eddy was not living out her last years in the company of family members, people whose love and loyalties, even if strained, were known quantities and had been sanctified by time and familiarity. Instead she lived with strangers who were joined to her by an idea and a cause, and whose devotion, she feared from bitter experience, might turn at any moment to betrayal. Busy though she was, surrounded as she was by people forever proclaiming their devotion and clammering for her regard, she still longed for the loving care of the family life she had known in her girlhood, particularly from her mother and grandmother. Acting as swiftly and independently in this personal sphere as she did in the religious, Mrs. Eddy decided in 1888 that the best answer to her problems was to adopt a son.

Of course, Mary Baker Eddy already had a son, and indeed a daughter-in-law and a growing set of grandchildren, all living in Lead, South Dakota. George Glover was in many respects not a bad fellow. He had considerable personal charm, and he strongly resembled his dead father, of whom Mrs. Eddy retained fond memories. He not infrequently wrote to ask his mother to come and make her home with him in the Dakotas, and there had been times, particularly when Gilbert Eddy was still alive, when Mrs. Eddy had felt almost tempted to investigate these offers. But any lingering hopes she may have nurtured that her son would be the answer to her personal problems had been definitively dashed in late 1887 when George arrived with his wife and his three children to pay her a prolonged visit. If the long dead Abigail Baker epitomized for Mrs. Eddy the familial support she had had as a daughter when growing up, and missed, her son George Washington Glover II, very much alive and kicking, represented the problems Mrs. Eddy had faced as a wife and mother, and which she had never managed to resolve. George personified her failure as a woman, and she was forced to face these problems once again over the winter of 1887–1888.

The best that can be said about this visit is that it ended better than it began, and that it allowed all the parties to get to know each other better. When George wrote from Lead on October 23 of his intention to come east, Mrs. Eddy wrote peremptorily on October 31 to stop him. I quote this swiftly written, emotional and confiding letter in toto because it gives such a vivid impression of Mrs. Eddy as a private individual:

Dear George,

Yours rec'd. I am surprised that you think of coming to visit me when I live in a Schoolhouse and have no room that I can let even a boarder into.

I use the whole of my rooms and am at <u>work</u> in them more or less all the time.

Besides this I have all I can meet without receiving company. I must have quiet in my house, and it will not be pleasant for you in Boston the Choates are doing all they can by falsehood and public shame, such as advertising a College of her own within a few doors of mine, when she is a <u>disgraceful</u> woman and <u>known to be</u>.[4] I am going to give up my lease when this class is over, and <u>cannot pay your board</u> nor give you a single dollar <u>now</u>. I am alone and you never would come to me when I called for you, and now I cannot have you come. I want a quiet and a Christian life alone with God, when I can find intervals for a little rest. You are not what I had hoped to find you, and I am wholly changed. The world the flesh and evil I am at war with, and if any one comes to me it must be to help me and not hinder me in this warfare. If you will stay away from me until I get through with my public labors then I will send for you and hope to then have a home to take you to. As it now is, I have none and you will injure me by coming to Boston at this time more than I have room to state in a letter. I asked you to come to me when my husband <u>died</u>, and I so much needed some one to help me. You <u>refused</u> to <u>come</u> then, in my great need, and I then gave up ever thinking of you in that line. Now I have a clerk who is a pure minded Christian, and two girls to assist me in the College. These are all that I can have under the roof.

If you come after getting this letter, I shall feel you have no regard for my interest or feelings which I hope not to be obliged to feel.

<u>Boston</u> is the last place in the world for <u>you</u> or <u>your family</u>. When I retire from business and into private life then I can receive you if you are <u>reformed</u>, but not otherwise. I say this to <u>you</u> not to <u>any one else</u>. I would not injure <u>you</u> any more than myself.

As ever sincerely
M. B. G. Eddy[5]

This letter did not stop the Glovers. They arrived in town, bringing the letter with them, apparently unopened. Whether they read it then or later, they kept it, and it no doubt fueled the Glovers' sense of rejection and ill treatment. Wishing, now that they were virtually on her doorstep, to make the best of things and have peace not war, on November 17 Mrs. Eddy wrote a note begging them to return the letter to her unread. "I am worn into waiting for all things," wrote Mrs. Eddy, in obvious exhaustion. "Now please make your plans to come with your family and take Thanksgiving dinner next week on Thursday with your Mother. I shall then be through with my class and have a little more time to spend with you." She ends her note with special love to the dear grandchildren, Gershom, Mary, and Evelyn.

Resigning herself to the fact that her son would stay as long as he wanted to, and herself "<u>daft</u> with business," as she complained to one student at the time, Mrs. Eddy set the Glovers up in a house in Chelsea and deputed one of her faithful followers, the old seaman Joseph Eastaman, to look after them. Mrs. Eddy took the Glovers with her to the great fund-raising bazaar for the proposed new Mother Church, and she introduced the grandchildren publicly at one of the weekly Christian Science services. She tried to ensure that the children took daily lessons while in Boston, and she did her best to get her son into an overcoat of the right quality and cut, and her grandson into the right pair of gloves. In several notes, she begged George not to exchange her gifts for anything of lesser quality, and not to tell the tailor and draper that *she* was paying the bills.

The Glovers did not get to see a lot of their distinguished relative. Mrs. Eddy was an extraordinarily busy woman, and it would have been hard for her to give much time at this period even had she wished to. But with their loud voices, strange accents, outlandish clothes, and wild social conduct, the

Glovers were a deep embarrassment, and therefore they saw even less of Mrs. Eddy than they might have. Mrs. Eddy projected much of her discomfort and disapproval on her daughter-in-law, Nellie, whom she had not met before this visit and instantly disliked. An immigrant child born of the British urban proletariat, raised in a mining camp, illiterate and unrefined, Nellie Glover personified for her mother-in-law everything that was most to be regretted in George's life. I found that in the letters she was to write to the Glovers over the next fifteen years or so Mrs. Eddy almost never addressed, mentioned, or sent regards to her daughter-in-law, a conspicuous coldness given Mrs. Eddy's abiding respect for social etiquette.

If Mary Baker Eddy was guilty of some snobbish embarrassment, there seems no doubt that George for his part was much more interested in his mother's money than in his mother. He pursued his relationship with her mainly with an eye toward securing investment capital and, above all, ensuring his inheritance. In fact the correspondence between them makes clear that George's insatiable need for money sapped any possibility of a real relation developing with his mother. Though a loving and devoted family man, George was always prepared to plunge his wife and children into poverty and even bring them to the edge of starvation on the chance of at last locating the mother lode that would make them all rich. He was a gambler; his wife knew it, his mother knew it, and his children would grow to know it. Even though Mary Baker Eddy was a thrifty New Englander who never enjoyed parting with money, she would gladly have invested even large sums in her son's business interests had she not been forced early on to understand that any money she sent him would be poured, literally, into a hole in the ground. All too plainly, the reason the Glovers had insisted on coming to Boston in 1887 was not from any sudden rush of tenderness toward Mrs. Eddy but because George had heard that his mother was prospering, and the $10,000 legacy he had just received from his aunt Abigail had made the affluence of his long lost New England relatives very real to him. There was more money where that legacy had come from, and George and Nellie no doubt calculated that their children would help him win Mrs. Eddy over and persuade her to give him more money to invest.

In fact, Mrs. Eddy did make a big effort over the years to win the love and respect of her grandchildren. She had always loved children and easily formed strong relationships with them. Furthermore, as her letters over the years prove, although she was forced to accept that George could never be her strong right hand and inherit Christian Science from her, Mrs. Eddy had high hopes that her son's children at least, given the right education and advantages, could be a pride and, eventually, a help to her. These hopes too were doomed because as far as I can determine from the correspondence, Mrs. Eddy never managed to form any kind of real bond with her grandchildren. This was neither her fault nor theirs. George and Nellie, whatever their other problems, were good parents, and their children loved and revered them and not unnaturally took their side in the many and various disputes with Grandma, who was probably more myth than reality to them. The children were all too aware of their parents' financial difficulties. When in Boston in 1888 the elder children glimpsed Mrs. Eddy's growing affluence, they understood that if only Grandma could be persuaded to give them some of her money, things might go much more pleasantly in Lead. Then and in years to come, the Glover children would agree to play their part in their parents' schemes to win Mrs. Eddy's favor and therefore secure some of her fortune. They would write her occasional ill-spelled letters, acknowledge at least some of her small gifts, do some of the schooling she paid for. But they would not love her, and she knew it.

Illiteracy was, I think, the fundamental issue which divided Mrs. Eddy from the Glovers, and one which George and Nellie, and later all their children, proved incapable of understanding or addressing. The differences in clothing, accent, and social etiquette that made the Boston visit so difficult for all parties could have been worked on and solved. Fashion and well-bred behavior had currency in the Dakotas too, and the Glovers understood and respected the niceties. As the correspondence shows, even, or perhaps especially, the uncouth Nellie was anxious for her eldest boy, Gershom, to take music lessons and longed for her girls to gain the proper bourgeois female accomplishments. Furthermore, the Glovers were not really any more anxious to live in Boston than Mrs. Eddy was to have them settle there, and distance could have worked to ease relations between Lead and Boston. Absence could have made the heart grow fonder on both ends as Mrs. Eddy's money was used to buy the accoutrements of gentility which she possessed and which they desired. But in the nineteenth century, distance implied communication in writing, and the letters between Mrs. Eddy and this part of her family consistently destroyed the relationship the correspondents were seeking to build.

Illiterate themselves, George and Nellie Glover saw the immediate practical consequences of illiteracy and were anxious for their children to learn to read and write. Yet once one of the children was able to meet the family's basic correspondence needs, George and Nellie saw the issue as closed. Gershom, I deduce from the silence which surrounds his life, was probably as disinclined to book learning as were his parents, and he never moved into the slot of writing on behalf of his parents. The girls seemed much more promising when young, especially Evelyn, in whom Mrs. Eddy had thought to see something of herself, and of whom she was most fond.[6] But the girls' youthful promise proved largely illusory. Evelyn was too much an invalid to leave home and get schooling, and she died tragically when she was barely twenty-three. Mary, who became the family correspondent, had more energy and resilience but perhaps less intelligence than her sister, and her letters to her grandmother, whether composed or dictated, were increasingly to become a source of friction between Lead and Concord.

We can imagine that when little Mary was able to write a whole page to her grandma in Boston, her mother was thrilled and proud. But then Mrs. Eddy's reply would come, filled with plans for the children to leave home in order to get a decent education, with adjurations to make more effort to learn, and with lists of spelling mistakes which the child should recopy and commit to memory. With all the business she had to do, Mrs. Eddy no doubt felt she was showing real affection in taking the time to make these corrections, but Nellie and Mary were no doubt annoyed at the constant nagging and criticism which grew only more acerbic with the years. Spelling, punctuation, and vocabulary were not important in the world of George and Nellie Glover, and not surprisingly the children accepted their parents' views and rejected their grandmother's.

A letter Mrs. Eddy wrote to George while he was still in Boston in 1888 and which, presumably, Gershom managed to decipher for him, makes this point loud and clear. Mrs. Eddy has sent money for Gershom's schooling and is displeased to learn it is being used for music lessons.

> I want your children <u>educated</u>.
> No greater disgrace rests on my family name than the ignorance of the parents of these darling children.
> You could read in the Bible very well when you left your Mother long ago. It should be a shame to any one at any age not to be able to read. If I were 50 years old and could not read I would learn to do it then, even if I knew I should not live a year longer.[7]

In her next missives to the Glovers, immediately after they had regained Lead, Mrs. Eddy is much more affectionate and placatory, and over the next five years relations with the Glovers remained quite amicable on the surface. But something fundamental in the mother-son relationship had changed. The question of inheritance was never far from George's mind when he thought of his mother, and it weighed upon Mrs. Eddy increasingly as she grew older.

With the deaths of Martha Baker Pilsbury in 1884 and of Abigail Baker Tilton in 1886, Mary Baker Eddy saw herself as the last of her generation, and she was all too aware that none of her brothers and sisters had lived to see his or her seventieth birthday. Moreover, whereas just a few years before Mrs. Eddy was still collecting the fees from students personally[8] and putting linoleum not carpet on the floors of her college, by 1888 she had considerable assets, and it seemed likely that her earnings would increase rather than decline. The copyrights of her published work in particular were becoming increasingly valuable, and she saw these as central to the continuing growth and mission of her church. By 1890 Mrs. Eddy was beginning to make very discreet inquiries as to how to write a will which would leave all her property to her church and which her legal heirs, George Glover and his children, would be unable to contest.[9] She was also taking steps to give herself a legal heir who could be counted upon fully to share her aspirations for the church and ensure that her legal dispositions were respected.

Thus it must have been a bad day in Lead, South Dakota, when the Glovers heard in late 1888 that Ebenezer J. Foster had been legally adopted by Mrs. Eddy. Possibly they had the opportunity to meet Foster during their Boston visit, had perhaps noted the easy way he called Mrs. Eddy Mother, the pleasure she took in his company. The Glovers were illiterate, but they knew about property and wills and were all too aware that an important rival had appeared, one far better placed to benefit from Mrs. Eddy's wealth in the present, inherit a large slice of her estate later, and, potentially, have the administration of the rest.

The swiftness with which Ebenezer Foster moved into Mrs. Eddy's inner circle, the warmth of the partiality which she so soon showed for him, did not just dismay the Glovers out West. It sent shock waves throughout Christian Science in New England. It was hard even or especially for such old and proven associates as Calvin Frye, William Johnson, and Ira Knapp to understand what she saw in Foster. Women students such as Eldora Gragg were more sympathetic to her needs and perhaps similarly susceptible to Foster's charm, but at least one old and disinterested friend from outside Christian Science, Mrs. Christiana Godfrey, told Mrs. Eddy point-blank that Mrs. Eddy was dreadfully mistaken in showing Ebenezer Foster such favor.[10]

A small, plumpish, dapper, unctuous bachelor in his early forties, Ebenezer Foster had a taste for expensive clothes, modest skills as an amateur musician, and a blandly sunny disposition. Trained in homeopathic medicine at the Philadelphia Homeopathic College, Foster was a mildly successful practitioner in Waterbury, Vermont, when in 1887, through a friend's healing, he became interested in Christian Science. He applied to take class in Boston with Julia Bartlett, claiming in his letter that he had already been successful as a homeopathic healer but had devoted himself so much to poorer patients and missionary work that he was unable to pay the class fees. Pleas of poverty would form a leitmotif in all of Foster's correspondence, although he always seems to have lived in comfortable circumstances. Julia Bartlett wrote to inquire about Foster from his neighbor Mary Dillingham, who wrote back urging that Foster be accepted as a student and recommending him as a "perfectly moral upright man." Dillingham continued: "[Foster] seems in many respects to be like a woman. He is fond of music flowers and his greatest weakness to me appears love of personal flattery."

While in Boston, Foster managed to get in to see Mrs. Eddy and began a correspondence with her, of which the following letter of June 25, 1888, gives a flavor:

> When I look at you from the standpoint of mortal mind I wonder that you are able to stand against the "fiery darts of the wicked" and I would interpose my self between to receive them in your stead. Then I realize their nothingness and know that nothing [*sic*] harm my dear Mother. Something tells me that I shall not all ways be the child to be tenderly cared for by its mother but shall be a source of delight, joy and strength to dear Mother and may that time be hastened.[11]

Mary Baker Eddy proved greedy for this kind of homage. Within months of their first meeting, "Benny," as Mrs. Eddy soon took to calling him,[12] was being summoned back to Boston by some of Mrs. Eddy's famous telegrams, was accepted into one of her classes, and was living for free in her Boston home. He was already such a favorite in June 1888 that, as we saw in an earlier chapter, he was chosen to accompany Mrs. Eddy on her triumphant journey to the Christian Scientist Association meeting in Chicago.

If Asa Gilbert Eddy in December 1876 had been astonished to find himself suddenly engaged to marry Mary Glover, Ebenezer Foster was also probably surprised when Mrs. Eddy announced in October 1888 that she wished to legally adopt him as her son. He did not hesitate to accept, however, and soon settled into his position as chief favorite at home and selected emissary abroad. In her adoption petition of November Mrs. Eddy stated that "said Foster is now associated with your petitioner in business, home life, and life work, and she needs such interested care and relationship." One can imagine how this statement ate into the soul of Calvin Frye.

For some seven years, Foster Eddy played an important part in Mrs. Eddy's life, perhaps the most important to her as a private person.[13] Not only did Mrs. Eddy give her adopted son expensive presents, such as a large diamond and a fur coat, but she gave him responsibilities within the movement. Although she refused to give him the coveted position of First Reader of The Mother Church, by 1893 Foster Eddy had the important position of president of The Mother Church and publisher for *Science and Health*.[14] This last was a financial plum. It has been reliably reported—probably from Foster Eddy's own records—that *Science and Health* cost about 45 cents to produce and retailed at $3.[15] Under her agreement with Foster Eddy, Mrs. Eddy received $1 in royalty, leaving $1 to the publisher after production expenses. Given that advertising and distribution were mainly a function of the larger Christian Science organization, and that Mrs. Eddy herself or one of her household could always be relied on to undertake any disagreeable publishing task if the need arose, Foster Eddy's costs were not great, and he made an excellent profit.[16]

To contemporary observers it seemed that in adopting Ebenezer Foster as her son Mrs. Eddy had clasped to her heart a toad that she alone believed could one day become a prince.[17] Foster's educational and professional attainments, if perhaps still superior to those of many men drawn to Christian Science at the period, were average, his administrative talents were at best undeveloped, and even his friends in the movement saw little leadership potential in him. Those like Augusta Stetson who themselves aspired to succeed Mrs. Eddy as leader of Christian Science marked him as an enemy and determined to get rid of him. The members of Mrs. Eddy's household, Frye chief among them, tolerated him in her presence and bided their time.[18]

Foster's appeal to Mary Baker Eddy has also been a mystery to later commentators, and critics hostile to Mrs. Eddy have pointed to the obvious tawdriness of her pet "Benny" as proof of her own shallow and hypocritical character. Perhaps, however, his importance to her should be gauged not by his merits but by her need. He was a smooth enough screen upon which she could project her longing for family, for affection, and he was someone from whom she could expect that very limited amount of fun which she still allowed herself.

For Foster, it seems, could be amusing, and although she was a devoted friend to many women, and earned many women's devotion, Mrs. Eddy still found some extra piquancy in the company of men. Mary Baker Eddy in her youth had been a popular, fashionable belle, later she was an attractive, witty, satiric matron, and even as an impoverished, ill-dressed, gaunt, middle -aged divorcée she could still dominate the company at dinner at the boardinghouse and capture the attention of men, like George Clark, twenty years her junior. In her sixties she had managed to win respectability, authority, and wealth, and she was now increasingly receiving the reverence and obedience she demanded. All this was good, but there was still a part of her that wanted to be entertained as well as adored, to laugh over a joke, to eat a good dinner, and to savor some good conversation. Ebenezer Foster met these needs more easily than anyone she had recently encountered. The stalwarts who gathered around her—the Fryes, the Knapps, the Johnsons, the Bartletts, the Sargents—could be relied upon for devotion, but they were not fun; they had no sense of humor. They, as it were, played only hymns, and after a long day's work on her books and correspondence, Mrs. Eddy liked sometimes to hear another kind of tune, in a light baritone rather than an ethereal soprano or a deep bass. Children, particularly young adolescent girls, had often in the past offered Mrs. Eddy the opportunity to relax and laugh, and perhaps Foster's superficiality struck her as youthful lightness, his lazy complacence as like a child's good humor.

Foster was also notably unlike two other "sons" Mary Baker Eddy had had in her life. He had none of the dangerous fire, the energy and independence and male attractiveness of Richard Kennedy. He inspired scorn rather than fear in his enemies and was in no danger of being taken for a real-life

American version of Dostoyevsky's Stavrogin. Small and delicate of stature, educated, literate, fastidious in dress and manners, Foster also was quite unlike Mrs. Eddy's own son, George. In the Boston parlors and dining rooms where George Glover moved like a genial bull in a china shop, Benny was at his best, and his manner toward Mrs. Eddy herself was an effective and insidious mixture of intimacy and deference. That Foster came into Mrs. Eddy's life just at the time she was receiving a rather unwelcome visit from her son and his family is, I think, an important factor in explaining his swift rise to favor. And unlike George, Benny had no wife and children, no vulgar Nelly or sulky Gershom. Mrs. Eddy had by this time come to expect undivided attention and full-time devotion from all those she allowed into her circle of intimates, and Foster was free to devote himself to her. In a more worldly woman, Foster's bachelor life might have set off warning signals, but Mrs. Eddy was still in some ways a product of a sheltered Puritan upbringing, and she accepted that Foster was a pure and healthy single man who was as contented with the asexual life as was Calvin Frye.

Above all, Foster Eddy, like Daniel Patterson before him, had a gift for personal flattery and epistolary rhetoric. He had the words and the attentions to convince Mrs. Eddy not only that he accepted her Christian Science with all his heart, but also that he held her personally in deep, filial affection. Her need to believe him overcame all the learned suspicion and native astuteness that characterized her dealings with others. Foster Eddy's rhetoric is in full evidence in this letter of May 1, 1894, which I quote in full:

> *Dearest Sweetest Loveliest Mother of this World,*
>   Enclosed please find check for last month sales.
>   This is a beautiful morning and is May day. I woke early this morning, and my thought went out, as of old, to the flowers of Spring, but it did not stay with them long for at once I thought of a flower more beautiful and lovely than all the flowers of this earth—my Mama!! Blossoming all alone up among the granite hills of New Hampshire yet whose fragrance goes out to all the world to gladden and speak peace to the hearts of all men. God grant that we may be able to appreciate the value of this wondrous flower that He has planted in the wilderness of mortal mind, and may those around it care for it (her) so tenderly, so lovingly, that it will not wither either before the untimely coldness of hardened hearts and feel friendless, loveless and alone, a stranger among strangers. May she be fanned by the breath of tenderness, administered unto by deft fingers of love, fed by angels upon the nectar of heaven, protected by the Ever-presence of Good that her blessed influence may continue in the world to purify and redeem it. This is Benny's May day wish for Mama.[19]

This is sickening stuff, even by Benny's standards, and the excess in this 1894 letter, is in fact a mark of the weakening of his hold over Mrs. Eddy's affections. As the incongruous opening reference to the enclosed check indicates, by this time Benny's chronic inefficiency and constant demands for more money had finally begun to awaken Mary Baker Eddy's doubts and displeasure.

Foster Eddy's fall from grace was wholly his own doing, achieved with a combination of complacency and sloth, overconfidence in his dealings with Mrs. Eddy, and insolence in his dealings with others.[20] Through his analysis of the correspondence between mother and adopted son, Robert Peel shows that, far from dealing with Foster swiftly and capriciously, Mrs. Eddy showed remarkable forbearance, and that her general tendency was to overlook, forgive, and forget. Certainly, there were any number of people in the movement and some in her household who were anxious to bring to her attention things that Foster had said or done or failed to do, but the fact was that there was always a signal discrepancy between what he said and what he did, between what he promised and what he achieved. Even commentators like Dakin who portray Foster as a likable victim agree that he enjoyed his public prominence, exploited his growing influence, gave little time or attention to his official duties, and showed no talent for them.

The immediate cause of Foster Eddy's fall from grace was not, however, his gross idleness and inefficiency but his equivocal relationship with his private secretary, Mrs. Nellie Courtney. In his characteristically oblique fashion when discussing such matters, Peel describes this lady's career thus:

> Mrs. Nellie Courtney had studied with Mrs. Eddy in the late 1880s, but had gone her own way since then. Never very close to her teacher, she had maintained a questionable relationship with a maverick student, Frank Mason, who was teaching his own version of Christian Science and doing his best to discredit Mrs. Eddy.[21]

Dakin portrays this lady as a widow who was gamely working to support her orphaned children, claims that the relationship she had with Foster was wholly professional, and paints Mrs. Eddy as a hypocrite, hiding her own sexual passions for her "son" under the cloak of morality. In fact, Mr. Courtney was very much alive, as were the little Courtneys, and moral disapproval was much less of a factor in Mrs. Eddy's alienation from Foster than has been commonly assumed.

It is largely a male myth that sexual jealousy was what made Mary Baker Eddy finally, reluctantly, decide to cut Ebenezer Foster Eddy out of her life.[22] Far from being some kind of knee-jerk Puritan, in many ways Mrs. Eddy had an attitude toward sexual misconduct that was both nuanced and practical. Certainly, in her public utterances Mrs. Eddy was unequivocal in calling Christian Scientists to obey the strictest of Protestant moral codes and, apart from religious and ethical reasons, there were all kinds of good political reasons why this position was necessary. Christian Science was establishing itself as a movement when the anti-vice campaigns associated with Anthony Comstock were in full swing in Boston and New York, and, given the range of opposition her movement was attracting, Mrs. Eddy could not afford to open a new front by showing any leniency toward free love, any relaxations of the strict moral code.

Through her speeches and articles, Mrs. Eddy adjured her followers— most of whom were women, as we have seen—to lead pure lives and, if married, to take their marriage vows with the utmost seriousness. Divorce she accepted as sometimes necessary when a woman found herself linked to a partner whose irredeemable immorality threatened her life and that of her children, but mere disagreement or incompatibility was not sufficient grounds. In her private correspondence, on the other hand, Mrs. Eddy was flexible and understanding. Seeking above all to keep out of the private lives of her followers, and urging them to do the same in their dealings with each other, Mrs. Eddy was slow to condemn others even when proof of sexual irregularity was brought to her attention, and she was extremely sympathetic to women who were undergoing the stress of separation or divorce from their husbands.

Had Foster Eddy fallen in love with a woman and wanted to marry her, Mrs. Eddy would have been personally displeased. We can be fairly sure that she would have reproved his choice of marriage over celibacy, that she probably would have ceased to regard him as her heir-elect, but that she would have accepted his decision and his wife. This was how Mrs. Eddy reacted when Samuel Putnam Bancroft chose a wife in 1870 and how she reacted again with William McKenzie in 1901. Most of her followers were married, and, if Mrs. Eddy judged the state of matrimony as less than ideal, she viewed it as by far the best of the available options in the here and now, especially for men. When Foster Eddy brought Nellie Courtney back from the Midwest and made her his private secretary, he may or may not have been motivated by lust, but he was certainly being deceptive. Aware of Mrs. Courtney's past disagreements with Mrs. Eddy and of her ambiguous social situation, he was also implicitly challenging Mrs. Eddy's public policy. It was this deception, this covert challenge, which made Mrs. Eddy's disapproval of Foster's actions stronger than her love for him.

My reading of Ebenezer Foster Eddy is that he succeeded for so long in capturing Mary Baker Eddy's affection and trust because he was swift to understand the susceptibilities of people he wished to impress, and he had a gift for speaking the current language of spirituality so fluently as to deceive even, or especially, the truly spiritual. Mrs. Eddy saw in Foster Eddy not just a pleasant companion but a kindred soul, searching like hers to get closer to God. For example, in the following letter to Foster we see her expressing the apprehensions and anguish of her daily life:

I have nothing new to write. It is just struggle, work, pray, all the time. But Oh! how much we have to be thankful for midst this pain and suffering nameless . . . since God has told us that all this shall work together for good to them that love Good. This is my only comfort that I do know I love Good, and have done much to bring this great, this infinite blessing to others.

So let me be patient, trust the love that knoweth best, and hope that I can at last overcome the world, the flesh and all evil. But this is something to do, or seemeth so to those who try it. . . .

Dear me, how frail is our fortitude to annihilate the claims of personality! What a poor demonstrator of this am I. To resolve and re-resolve and then go on the same. Cannot Love better than the rod of Love wean us from all flesh and help us to love only the unseen, untouched, immaterialized person, the divine not human.[23]

Here Mrs. Eddy writes not as leader to follower, but as friend to friend, and in her Biblical rhetoric I read sincerity. Foster, I think, read weakness, and he exploited it. Flattered by her confidence and her favor, vain and encouraged in his vanity by her assumption, at least as expressed in her intimate letters to him, of equality between them, Foster Eddy had no scruples about playing the part Mrs. Eddy cast him in, talking the talk of mystic piety so successfully that for years she forgave him everything. Clinging to her vision of him as a man striving for the heights, if prone to stumble at times and fall back, for a long time she discounted the accumulating proofs of his inadequacy, his lack of zeal, his sexual misconduct, and, above all, his deception.[24] Foster Eddy was one of Mary Baker Eddy's most costly mistakes, and one for which she herself paid not just in money[25] but in renewed isolation, exacerbated loneliness.

21

Pleasant View

WHEN MRS. EDDY DECIDED IN THE SUMMER OF 1889 to leave Boston, one thing was clear to her, if not perhaps to her followers—that moving house in no way meant she was retiring. Though she was by this time in her late sixties, for her it was a given that the rest of her life would be devoted to the movement she had built almost single-handed. There were things only she could do—thinking about the meaning and purpose of the movement as it grew and changed, planning in the long term, writing. Her role would change, but her control would remain, or even strengthen through change. The new domestic setting would give her time and mental space and allow her to conserve her energy. There were others now who could do what she had been doing for twenty years—see patients, put out the *Journal*, run to and from the printers, pack and mail out the book orders, keep the accounts, work with the general press, and sort out the professional rivalries and marital disputes that constantly tended to create trouble within the new movement.

That Mary Baker Eddy should feel able to remain the head of Christian Science while moving away from her Boston center of operations is a mark of the technological changes America was experiencing at the turn of the century and of her own understanding of their implications. For a woman in her late sixties, Mrs. Eddy was remarkably well attuned to the communication revolution occurring around her, and she understood that distance from her movement's center of operations did not necessarily mean loss of control. Mrs. Eddy lived before computers made working at home and telecommuting possible, but in her day, unlike ours, public transport was excellent, the trains ran frequently and on time, reaching out to even small rural places, and the mail was delivered several times a day.

During the more than eighteen years Mrs. Eddy lived in New Hampshire, Church officials travelled daily between Boston and Concord, her household members often acted as couriers between Pleasant View and the Mother Church, visitors and new staff members, summoned by telegram, flowed in at a few days' notice from all over the country, and handling the mail became the work of several full-time secretaries. On many days Mrs. Eddy's factotum John Salchow could be seen pedalling his bicycle furiously across town to alert the courier that he must leave at once, and even flying down to the station to hold the train until the older man got there. Happy in her rural retreat, Mrs. Eddy created her own, highly efficient communications hub.[1]

The name of Mary Baker Eddy is now so closely associated with the city of Concord, New Hampshire, that her choice of a new home seems almost inevitable in hindsight, but in fact it took Mrs. Eddy several years to set up a permanent home there. Perhaps because she now had the luxury of choice, she had some difficulty in imagining what exactly her new domestic situation would be. There were still times when, as in the past, and in traditional American vein, she thought of going west—perhaps as far as Oconto, Wisconsin, home of two of her most beloved disciples, Laura and Victoria Sargent. In her more rational and conservative mood, she was drawn toward northern New England. New Hampshire spelled calm, beauty, freedom for Mrs. Eddy, and even in her poorest days she had retreated north for a few weeks during the heat of the summer.

The urge to establish a permanent residence in her native state probably intensified in the summer of 1888 when she spent five days on the farm in Lyman, New Hampshire, where Ira and Flavia Knapp were then living with four of their five children. Ira Knapp, with his long, flowing beard and flaming eyes, had an old-fashioned religious zeal, and he gave Mrs. Eddy an unconditional devotion which, after all her disappointments with earlier students, was peculiarly precious to her. When, on the first morning of her stay, Bliss, the youngest child, shyly came and laid first a baby chicken and then a small kitten in her lap, Mrs. Eddy was charmed. Bliss Knapp, for his part, would conceive a lifelong adoration. When Mrs. Eddy went into the Knapp kitchen and found there a motherly New Hampshire countrywoman with whom she delightedly exchanged memories of old times, she felt that she had come home again. In the Knapp family Mary Baker Eddy seemed to see a new version of the Mark Baker family, and all her longing for family life was rekindled.[2]

Unfortunately, even as the Knapps were welcoming Mrs. Eddy to their home and savoring her pleasure in it, they were planning to move away. For all the Knapps' zeal and hard work, Lyman, New Hampshire, had proved unresponsive or even hostile to Christian Science. Ira Knapp, a man who had inherited money and made more, was now committed to the life of a teacher and healing practitioner. His wife, Flavia, whose healing after a long life of invalidism had first brought the whole family to Christian Science, was more than willing for her husband to take up a new way of life in which she could share as an equal partner. Until her sudden death in 1898, Flavia Knapp rose higher and higher in the administration of Christian Science, and her prominence was only just exceeded by that of her husband. In Boston, the Knapps anticipated, correctly as it turned out, that they would find the collegial support and the patients that they lacked in New Hampshire. Therefore, within weeks of Mrs. Eddy's visit in the summer of 1888, the Knapps had given up their farm, and the great spreading butternut tree under which Ira had read Revelation and had visions, and they had moved to the Boston suburb of Roslindale.[3]

Mrs. Eddy's first stopover in her flight north was a rented house on North State Street in Concord, the capital of New Hampshire. This dwelling proved to be very noisy and in poor repair, and it was apparent to all that Mrs. Eddy needed something quieter and less central, with more land. One of the tasks which devolved upon the new son, Ebenezer Foster Eddy, was to act as Mrs. Eddy's intermediary with housing agents and property sellers, and his searches took him as far afield as Cincinnati. By the beginning of 1891 he thought he had come up with the right property, a large and luxurious house in Roslindale. Moving back to the Boston area represented an abrupt change of plan, but Mrs. Eddy agreed to make the move in May 1891. The beloved Benny painted the attractions of the new house in glowing colors. Mrs. Eddy would find herself only a short distance from the Knapps, and thus she would perhaps be able to recapture and make permanent the brief idyll of family life which she had lived three years earlier with the Knapp family in Lyman.

Perhaps inspired, in part, by the example of her stepmother, Elizabeth Patterson Baker, loved and revered in Tilton as "Mother" Baker, Mrs. Eddy still nourished some hope of a life that would include the joys of motherhood and grandmotherhood, and the visit of her son and his children some three years before had both revived and frustrated that deep aspiration.[4] She had made persistent attempts in the past to adopt a surrogate family—with the Crafts, the Howards, and the Choates—and despite all the bitterness and misunderstanding that those experiments in shared living had occasioned, she was still tempted to make a last try. The adoption of Foster had been the most important recent expression of her longing for family, but Mrs. Eddy wanted surrogate grandchildren as well as a surrogate son, and the Knapps seemed to be the perfect family. By this time she knew enough, and was rich enough, not to attempt a shared house and shared rents, but she could live near and be close enough to those dear children for frequent visits.

It took no time, of course, for Mrs. Eddy to realize that her need for quiet and space and privacy and distance was stronger than her need for the Knapps—whom after all she hardly knew—and to discover that Benny's taste in houses was not hers. "Dogs barked, children shouted, visitors called, the heat was oppressive," as Robert Peel reports, and within a month Mrs. Eddy had moved back to her State Street rental in Concord, telling her people that Roslindale would never suit. In a July letter she explained her moves to her friend Laura Sargent in Wisconsin:

> I have no desire to live in the place of beauty that the Roslindale home is—a beauty <u>unavailing</u> in <u>Christian Science</u>.
> There is no retirement, no solitude, no <u>quiet</u> in it.
> It is a hillside decked with flowers and ornamental shrubs and luxurious fruit and garden, but the walks are so steep that I cannot follow them, the arbor with call-bells from the house—tells of <u>lager</u>! The whole site is surrounded by streets . . . from every side you are saluted by noise.[5]

The failure of the Roslindale experiment was an annoyance for Mrs. Eddy's staff, who had spent time and effort locating and buying the house; no doubt they had hoped to convince Mrs. Eddy to remain close to Boston, which would be more pleasant and convenient for them. That she could maintain her house on Commonwealth Avenue, rent in Concord, and also afford to buy an expensive property in Roslindale, was, from the public affairs viewpoint, rather embarrassing proof of her new affluence, and enemies at this time and in the future would of course cite the house in Roslindale as an example of the leader's willfulness and indecisiveness. On the positive side, at least the brief exposure to Roslindale, as well as the lengthy stay in the center of Concord, had helped Mrs. Eddy gain some clarity on what exactly she was looking for in a house.

On one of her daily drives around Concord she found it. On Pleasant Street on the outskirts of the city was a modest, run-down farmhouse set on a knoll fronting some acres of sloping fields and meadows. It looked toward the Bow hills where Mary Baker Eddy had been born. This, at last, was what she had envisioned, and, after the years of uncomfortable indecision, Mrs. Eddy now moved with great speed and efficiency. As always, the prophet of spirituality was undaunted by merely material problems. Between locating the property in the fall of 1891 and moving in on June 20, 1892, Mrs. Eddy had the house extensively enlarged and remodelled. She acquired some neighboring land to increase her estate, provide space for building a carriage house for staff, and afford her more privacy. Areas of the property that had been boggy were drained and planted with rye so successfully as to provide in one harvest enough rye flour to satisfy all the household's needs for years to come. Loyal Christian Scientists paid for the diversion of waters into a fishpond to improve the prospect, and for a specially commissioned boat to provide some entertainment for the staff.[6]

From the beginning, Mrs. Eddy took an active daily interest in the property, and, to the frequent surprise of her staff, she demonstrated real expertise in choosing plants and animals and formidable talents for managing her estate. The Bow part of her life was once again made manifest. As Robert Peel puts it:

> [Mrs. Eddy] issued crisp directions for planting an orchard, trimming the shrubs round the fountain, moving the azaleas where the double buttercups had been, replacing the bittersweet on the front piazza with woodbine, caring for the lawns, bringing in the hay, painting the barn, buying an express wagon, and carrying out a thousand small improvements on the estate.[7]

The Pleasant View estate was a landscaped garden and a working farm: Mrs. Eddy successfully transplanted groups of elms onto her lawn, gave some thought to her ornamental shrubs, but also supervised the haying activities and the running of an, at times, inconveniently successful fruit and vegetable concern. Always a lover of horses, in the early days at the house Mrs. Eddy enjoyed visiting her stables and feeding her horses handfuls of her own hay almost as much as she enjoyed eating the peas, corn, cucumbers, and raspberries grown in her own plots. She was both the delight and the despair of her estate workers because she set such high standards and was so rarely wrong in her observations. Once when the buildings were being repainted, the conscientious and capable local painter hired to do the job was outraged when he learned that Mrs. Eddy was unhappy with his work. After comparing the paint shades, however, he discovered that, indeed, the paint he had begun to apply to the outbuildings was darker than that on the house. On another occasion Irving Tomlinson, informed by Mrs. Eddy that a bridge she passed regularly on her drive was unsafe, could at first see nothing wrong, but, on inserting a penknife into the supports, he discovered they were quite rotten.[8]

As far as she allowed herself to be defined by her physical environment, Mrs. Eddy was in her element at Pleasant View, and she was frank in acknowledging the pleasure and comfort the place gave her. The larger environment of Concord was also to her taste. Once the move had been accomplished, Mrs. Eddy sank gratefully into an urban but small-scale community where she could reclaim her cousinship with the small landholders, minor industrialists, tradesmen, and provincial professionals of her familial caste. That, at least when she moved in, Concord was largely unaffected by Christian Science was probably a point in its favor.[9] Given her deep desire to keep the thoughts of both needy well-wishers and enemies away from her, Mrs. Eddy was not averse to living among people who were indifferent to or ignorant of who she was. In Concord, at least for the first decade, Mrs. Eddy could lapse into relative anonymity and normality. Her household could be taken, by and large, at face value, and in her daily affairs she could escape the intense scrutiny, rivalry, and dissent that all too often characterized relations among Christian Scientists.

Concord was not perfect. Notably it lagged behind Massachusetts towns in paving its main streets, and Mrs. Eddy considered it a sad reflection on New Hampshire that even the very center of the state's capital should still have dirt streets. Over the years Mrs. Eddy was to wage a vigorous campaign with the town fathers, and offer to foot much of the improvement bill herself, before the roads in the center of the city were paved and the ways smoothed under her carriage wheels. Another disadvantage was that over the years not all of her Pleasant Street neighbors were thrilled to have the leader of Christian Science living next door. One lady nearby, Mrs. Foster-Piper, exercised a Miss Marple–like surveillance of the doings at Pleasant View, and another neighbor, John Kent, opposed Mrs. Eddy's street paving scheme with a persistence worthy of Dickens's Lawrence Boythorn.[10]

On the whole, however, Mrs. Eddy's personal exigencies became part of Concordian lore, and her need for privacy and quiet were respected, especially since she paid her bills so promptly, patronized local businesses whenever possible, and brought increasing prosperity to local stone quarries, souvenir makers, and printers. As the years wore on, Pleasant View became a source of local pride. During the apple season, when Mrs. Eddy's household had gathered as much fruit as they needed for winter storage, neighbors were welcome to come and pick the rest of the abundant harvest. Coming out to look at the tulip display at Pleasant View in spring became a weekend jaunt for hundreds of Concordian families, and in summer the rose garden, which Mrs. Eddy's staff tended with much love and labor, was an equal draw.

Mrs. Eddy called her new home Pleasant View, and the unpretentious statement of fact made by that name expressed well her vision for the property. The improvements to the house were designed to make the most of the scenery, with a veranda built on at the back—where Mrs. Eddy liked to take her exercise in inclement weather and placed her beloved swing-chair—a porte-cochère built onto the front so she could easily embark in her carriage every day, and a side tower built to house her own apartment from which she had a clear view in several directions. Living in a setting of natural beauty was an important thing for Mary Baker Eddy. Romantic poetry had taught her as a girl to see and admire the beauties of her native state, which was a tourist mecca in the nineteenth century. When living in the cramped, industrial town of Lynn she had sought nature in her long walks by the sea and in her yearly pilgrimages back north in summer. Having ample space around her and almost no uncontrollable ambient noise had also become vital requirements.

Pleasant View was certainly a spacious estate, and personal affluence allowed its owner to maintain the buildings and grounds in exemplary condition, but the property was not isolated, and it was not grand. In later years, when press reports, notably those of the New York *World*, described Pleasant View as a mansion and a luxurious estate, they were hyperbolizing, not reporting. For example, Mrs. Eddy's home was smaller, less grand, and far less expensive than the architect-designed residence which Mark Twain created for his family in Hartford. In her choice of home, Mrs. Eddy had emphatically not sought a wilderness or created a country house in the European manner. Pleasant View had no long, tree-lined, curving driveway, no high wall, no gatehouse to block the view of curious eyes and ensure privacy. For her dream house Mary Baker Eddy merely modified the topography of a substantial farm on the outskirts of a small New England town, where the vagaries of the weather made it sensible to locate the house right on the road to town. As photographs of the property show, Mrs. Eddy's front door was only yards from a main through road and in full view of anyone passing. A rather massive and ugly stone gateway shut no one out but served simply to proclaim the house's name and that of its owner.

There was a school just down the road, there were neighboring homes in sight, and during her tenure, and with her full consent, a state fairground was built on the boundary of her land. On two occasions the increasing affection between the town and Mrs. Eddy was made evident when she drove over in a rented landau to visit the fair and was given a kind of hero's welcome by the crowd. With the childlike enthusiasm which struck many people who met her, and which was one side of her complex personality, Mrs. Eddy watched raptly and clapped her hands in admiration when a man dived from a high platform into a small pool.[11] Mrs. Eddy was in fact fully integrated into the life of Concord, New Hampshire, as she had never been at 571 Columbus Avenue or 385 Commonwealth Avenue, or perhaps even at 8 Broad Street, Lynn.

Inside the house the furnishings and decor were chosen with considerable care and were always of good quality, but they were not luxurious by any measure, they were far from fashionable, and they were expected to last. Many pieces had been moved up from Mrs. Eddy's house in Boston and may already have done duty in Lynn. When Calvin Hill, a recent convert to Christian Science who worked with a carpeting company, came to Pleasant View in the spring of 1899 to assist in the renovations that had become necessary, he was forced to be diplomatic when Mrs. Eddy asked what he thought of the interior decoration:

> In your front parlor, Mrs. Eddy, you have very fine Brussels net curtains, beautifully upholstered chairs, and a couch with a delicate covering, but

in this rear parlor you have black walnut furniture with portieres and wallpaper which do not go together very well. A fine quality plain carpet, green or old rose, would look well in these double parlors. On the walls you should have the best paper that money can buy, and it would also be nice to have new window curtains.[12]

Hill's frankness turned out to be what Mrs. Eddy wanted. As she remarked to him, "You know I do not go shopping very often so that I do not know much about the styles," and she was happy to defer to his expertise, such as it was. In the next years Hill was the man she asked to solve her decorating problems, and he also helped with the hiring of staff since he understood her needs and her tastes so well. Ever since the last years in Lynn, Mrs. Eddy had wanted to convey in her public rooms a modest elegance which visitors could admire but which the household could still feel comfortable in, and this policy was continued in Concord. As a gesture toward luxury, in the parlors on the first floor of Pleasant View, where she herself spent relatively little time, Mrs. Eddy also kept some of the rarer and more costly gifts she had received, and, although she never made personal use of these, she loved to show them off. In 1901 the famous reporter Joseph I. C. Clarke came to Pleasant View to interview Mrs. Eddy for the New York *Herald* and was surprised and charmed by the personal tour he was given, and by Mrs. Eddy's unsophisticated show of delight in her collection.[13]

Mrs. Eddy's own rooms on the second floor were of very modest dimensions and expressed a taste for comfort, order, and familiarity. Space was something she savored looking out upon and having around her, light was important to her, but Mrs. Eddy liked her rooms to have the cluttered, haphazard, highly patterned tightness, full of knickknacks and whatnots and antimacassars, that we often associate with the Victorian era. Janette Weller, who paid a number of visits to Pleasant View, was greatly surprised one day when she was shown the elaborate white satin down quilts, covered with tassels and cords, and the oil paintings which Mrs. Eddy treasured in her collection of gifts, and she compared them with the "shabby-looking patchwork silk crazy quilt" which Mrs. Eddy actually used on her narrow bed.

On returning to Boston, Weller went looking for a practical down quilt and found something suitable, though rather ugly, since it was summer and stocks were low. Ugly or not, Mrs. Eddy was delighted with her new quilt and with Weller's thoughtfulness, and when she later moved to Chestnut Hill, she asked Weller to find another as like the old as possible. In a similar way, early on in his relationship with her, Calvin Hill endeared himself to Mrs. Eddy not just by advising her on the parlor carpets but also by secretly organizing the replacement of her beloved, much worn, gold plush armchair with an exact replica. Again, at the time of the move to Boston, Hill was commissioned to replace the replacement armchair with another exact replica.

The satin and marble and gold that visitors to the Mother's Room at the Mother Church were coming to gawk over in Boston had nothing to do with Mrs. Eddy's domestic taste.

If the Pleasant View land was run with careful balance between aesthetic beauty and economic efficiency, the household was a dream of organization—or a nightmare, depending on one's point of view.[14] Mrs. Eddy herself maintained an iron schedule, varied only by the season, and she expected her staff to do the same. She rose early every morning at six or seven and was served a breakfast of cornmeal mush and milk in her room by her maid, who brought up a pitcher of hot water[15] and set out the clothes Mrs. Eddy specified for the day. Mrs. Eddy had some elaborate black silk dresses which she wore on special occasions, but on most days she liked pale colors, lavender, pink, pale gray, and white.[16]

Women friends like Janette Weller were at first commissioned to seek out what Mrs. Eddy needed in the Boston stores, and Mrs. Stetson, in fashionable New York, also shopped and had things made up for Mrs. Eddy and sent on, at Mrs. Eddy's expense. Later Mrs. Eddy found a local dressmaker to make her dresses, and this lady, Miss M. Nellie Eveleth, was to become a full member of the resident household by the Chestnut Hill days. Being Mrs. Eddy's dressmaker was no sinecure, since Mrs. Eddy expected things to fit perfectly and correspond exactly to her expressed wishes, or, it seemed at times, to her unvoiced desires.

In the early mornings, while Mrs. Eddy completed her toilette and dressed herself, the maid would dust the rooms and be prepared to give a hand with the dressing if required. At the turn of the century, ladies' dresses were still secured, often in the back, with tiny buttons and clasps; hair was worn long and needed some care and skill in its arrangement; therefore women habitually called upon one another for help in dressing. It is clear, however, from the reminiscences of Minnie Adelaide Still, Mrs. Eddy's last personal maid, that Mrs. Eddy retained the modest habits of an old Protestant Yankee and used the maid not for basic bodily services but to maintain her personal affairs in immaculate condition and to assist her in always looking her best. For example, Still notes that Mrs. Eddy manicured her own nails, using a little penknife she kept in her pocket. Remarkably, until two days before her death at age eighty-nine Mrs. Eddy completed her own toilette and got dressed every day without fail and with a minimum of assistance. When she was well into her eighties she invited the maid's help only with finishing touches to her hair, the exact placement of jewelry, the securing behind the neck of her decorative collar or jabot, and the buttoning up of her shoes.

After eating breakfast and getting dressed, Mrs. Eddy would move into her study, open her Bible or *Science and Health* at random, and conduct a meeting of prayer and discussion, sometimes with the whole staff. She then came downstairs, inspected the parlors, talked with staff, and generally supervised the domestic work in fine detail. At twelve, on the dot, dinner, as Mrs. Eddy called it, was served, and woe betide any worker who arrived a minute late. In the first years, Mrs. Eddy joined her staff in the dining room, but when she was in her eighties she began to have all her meals served to her upstairs on a tray.

Mrs. Eddy enjoyed simple home-cooked foods and was very particular about the quality of what she ate. The cook liked to have an extra dinner on hand in case Mrs. Eddy found the soup too salty, the baked potatoes too hard, or the sponge cake too heavy. As the years went by, though never a pro-fessing vegetarian, Mrs. Eddy ate less and less meat, just a little liver or chicken occasionally, with perhaps fish hash for supper, or something light on toast. Bacon—or salt pork, as she called it—was her favorite meat, and pigs were kept on the estate to supply the household's needs. Mrs. Eddy took a cup of soup at dinner and supper, loving cream of tomato particularly, and she liked milk custards and above all ice cream. One of the rare noises hap-pily tolerated at Pleasant View was the daily sound of John Salchow coming in with the ice from the icehouse and beginning to turn the ice-cream churn. Of course there was no alcohol served at Pleasant View, and no tea or cof-fee, though Mrs. Eddy decreed that hot coffee should be provided for any local men working on the premises on cold winter days. It was details like this about Mrs. Eddy's everyday life and her personal habits and tastes that Christian Scientists hungered to know, and which Mrs. Eddy tried to keep, as far as possible, out of the press.

Every day after lunch Mrs. Eddy went out for a ride in one of the various carriages she kept or rented. So invariable was this habit that Concord-ians learned to set their watches by Mrs. Eddy's passage through town. Even on the day in 1903 when ten thousand Christian Scientists came to visit Pleasant View, Mrs. Eddy went out for her drive, and the precious lawns and beds had to be guarded against the careless feet of people scrambling to find a spot from which they could catch a glimpse of their leader as she drove in and out.

For the first six or seven years which she spent at Pleasant View this daily ride was one of her great pleasures, her chance to sit and relax, observe what was happening in her chosen world, say hello to acquaintances in the street, give little presents of candy to the children, and generally feel in touch. Mrs. Eddy was extremely fond of her horses, first the bays Duke and Prince and then the blacks Dolly and Princess, and she would talk to them sooth-ingly when they met any surprises along the route. In 1902 Mrs. Eddy pur-chased one of the first motorcars in Concord—not for riding in herself, but for use on and around the estate to accustom her carriage horses to the noise of motors. The two-cylinder monster responded only to the handling of John Salchow, who kept it in repair, drove it out on errands, and reports in his reminiscences that the sound of the automobile's motor, when it condescended to start up, could be heard all over Concord. The horses soon got used to the noise, but Mrs. Eddy was uncharmed by the noise and smell of the new vehicles and kept her horses and carriages to the end.

Going out for a ride through town meant getting dressed, and, with her immaculate white kid or silk gloves, her fur-lined coats or ermine cape, her tiny carriage parasol, Mrs. Eddy always looked, as Adelaide Still remarks, as if she had just stepped out of a bandbox. Like most nineteenth-century women, Mrs. Eddy always loved bonnets, and in her affluent old age she thoroughly enjoyed having a new bonnet each year for every season, as well as a special bonnet to wear when the weather was particularly wet. One of the hundreds of duties which devolved upon her personal maid was to put away the bonnets with the ribbons folded in the box just so.

As Mrs. Eddy swept down the stairs into the front hall to take her afternoon drive, her white kid gloves protected by an extra wool pair against the mere possibility of dust on the banister, Mrs. Eddy expected to see her carriage ready and waiting for her to climb in. Had the carriage swept up as she came out onto the porte-cochère, she might well have exclaimed like Louis XIV, "I *almost* had to wait!" Mrs. Eddy's maid, together with one of her female companions, would help Mrs. Eddy into the carriage and would be ready to greet her and help her out upon her return. To ensure that this routine was observed invariably, a member of the staff in later years was posted at a window to warn of the imminent return of the carriage.

On most days in Concord, Mrs. Eddy drove out alone, or more precisely with Calvin Frye, smart in uniform and top hat, seated not next to her but on the box next to the coachman. Milmine comments acerbically on the public humiliation Frye suffered in taking the role of liveried groom given that he came from such an old and honorable family, but I am not sure that Frye, or other Christian Scientists, saw things that way. Mrs. Eddy's drive started as a pleasant daily ritual and became over the years almost a religious rite, a sign that all continued well with Christian Science. Frye's sharing that ride with her every day was an expression of closeness and trust.

On returning from her drive Mrs. Eddy would attend to the day's correspondence with one of the secretaries, discuss organizational matters, and receive visitors. As she grew older, she would lie down for a rest on her study couch for a time each afternoon. At six she would have supper and then relax in the company of one or more of her associates, chatting, joining her staff round the piano for a sing-along, sitting in summer on the porch in her swing opposite Calvin Frye, watching the light fade. At nine-thirty she would retire for the night. By her bed, within easy reach, she kept a pad and paper, and frequently she would make notes during the night. When something really important was engaging her thoughts, she would summon someone, usually Frye, to take dictation. This had already become a well-established pattern in the Boston period, and Calvin Frye remembered the many chilly dawns he had spent back in the old Massachusetts Metaphysical College days wrapped up in a blanket while Mrs. Eddy dictated *Unity of Good*. These dictated texts were just the first stage in the long process of revision and reconsideration, but when inspiration came, Mrs. Eddy let nothing stand in its way, certainly not her helpers' need for a good night's rest.

The rigid domestic routine Mrs. Eddy instituted was a way of coping with the urgent, inconstant tide of Christian Science business which was forever threatening to drag her under. The gracious old lady living on Pleasant Street whom Concordians greeted each day on her leisurely drive was the leader of Christian Science—not a figurehead, not a constitutional monarch, but the final authority on all matters, doctrinal, legislative, and executive; the CEO of a growing corporation; an inspiration and visionary for the whole movement. To be able to pray and meditate and reflect, to find the time to write her articles, revise her textbook, plan the long-term strategy of her church, intervene in current operations when absolutely necessary, and keep her officials on their toes, Mrs. Eddy had to budget her time.

A good sense of the constant pressure under which Mrs. Eddy lived can be gained from this extract from a letter she wrote to her trusted friend and follower Caroline Bates in 1895:

> A long article for Encyclopedia . . . Another for the Press, another for my book that is to be pub. with Sermon etc. Also endless letters, and Mr. Johnson! Housekeeping etc. Old age!!! pounding into my ears but not brains, quarrels, gossip. In Concord, State law. Need of my articles in consideration etc.; proof reading and Mr. Frye! but he is at least honest. This is but a fractional part. . . . What is fame? Nothing. What is peace? Everything. When shall I find it, where? Not here.[17]

Some of the affairs which preoccupied her were difficult, complicated, but ultimately rewarding. Mrs. Eddy spent much of her time during her first two years at Pleasant View focused on the building of the Mother Church, which I have described in Chapter 19. Other problems she had to deal with were not as easy to solve as delays in the delivery of steel girders or the balkiness of workmen unused to synchronizing their tasks on the site. As we saw in the last chapter, both her real son and her adopted son were increasing headaches, and none of her efforts to make things work for and with them proved successful. Even more draining and traumatic were the problems with Mrs. Woodbury, which would grow increasingly serious during the late 1890s and destroy Mrs. Eddy's peace of mind and injure her health between 1899 and 1901 (and which I shall be discussing in Chapter 23).

One of Mrs. Eddy's reasons for moving to Concord had been to cut down on the number of people who visited her. Requests for interviews were screened, most people who just came to the door and asked to see Mrs. Eddy were politely turned away, and it was understood in the movement that Mrs.

Eddy did not appreciate it when people called on her without warning or even paused at the corner of a street to catch her eye as she passed on her ride. Despite these restrictions, Pleasant View was always filled with visitors, and local Concord people, in particular, were able to come and go much as they would in any large private home. Mrs. Eddy would have a chat with one of the gardeners she saw working in the beds under her window, summon the editor of a local newspaper for tea and a lively discussion of issues of mutual interest, welcome the surprise visit of some old acquaintance from her youth, or telegraph a friend, like Janette Weller, to come up from Boston and enjoy the raspberries and new peas her friend perhaps could not afford to buy for herself. In the first years at Pleasant View, when Mrs. Eddy still hoped for a seminormal life, she enjoyed asking students who had no close relatives to come to Concord and share Thanksgiving with her. There had been not a few years in her life when Mrs. Eddy herself had been what she called an "orphan," with nowhere special to go for the holidays, and she was glad to have the opportunity to invite other lonely people to a good feast.

Officials from the Mother Church were in and out of Pleasant View constantly, and as the household staff grew and filled every available cranny, the directors and trustees were forced at times to spend the night on cots in the parlor downstairs. Every Christian Scientist wanted to see Mrs. Eddy at least once, and those, like Julia Bartlett or Julia Field-King,[18] who had once seen her daily while she lived in Boston, longed to spend more time with her and feel again that resurgence of energy and commitment and confidence that Mrs. Eddy was able to impart. It was exactly this exchange of energy which Mrs. Eddy had come to dread for herself, and this reliance on her personal qualities that she had decided her movement must learn to do without. At Pleasant View Mrs. Eddy limited her visitors to those who happened by and whom she chose on impulse to entertain, those she needed to see on Christian Science business, and those she really wanted to see—people she trusted and valued, whose company she enjoyed and who were not involved in the complex power plays of movement politics.

The staff of Pleasant View was quite small at first but numbered in the teens as the years passed. At first, some local people were employed to do the rough housework and work outside on the estate, but it soon became established that all the work within the house itself, of however menial a nature, would be done by Christian Scientists. John Salchow, the simple, uneducated, tireless, and greathearted man whom Mrs. Eddy leaned upon more and more, literally and figuratively, as the years went by, made himself unpopular among local craftsmen as he took on the plumbing and the electrical work, on top of all the other chores that kept him busy from five in the morning to late at night.

The Christian Scientist staff was composed of people who had been asked to come and who chose to devote a year or, in later years, three years of their lives to serving Mrs. Eddy.[19] Mrs. Eddy herself urgently requested certain people to come and live with her—old friends like Laura Sargent and Clara Shannon, or the sons of loyal practitioners and former students, such as John Lathrop, Laura Lathrop's son. When it came to hiring people for less sensitive positions, Mrs. Eddy took advice from people in the field, and as Pleasant View took shape as a household and an institution within the movement a business committee, which notably included Calvin Hill and Daisette Stocking McKenzie, was formed to recruit or screen applicants and conduct the initial interviews. Mrs. Eddy after a few years ceased to interview every worker personally, but she kept a critical eye on all the workers in her house and was swift to intervene if things were not going as she wished.

The people who staffed Pleasant View often came at short notice, leaving families and work behind them. When in 1901 the young John Salchow, then living at his parental home in Junction City, Kansas, received a letter from his old friend Joseph Mann asking him to come to Pleasant View as groundsman and general handyman, he was aboard a train headed east within two hours. So abrupt was his departure, and so final, that Salchow left his personal affairs in disorder, and he subsequently lost property he could ill afford to lose. The Pleasant View workers earned very modest salaries. They were expected to be available twenty-four hours a day, seven days a week, and to observe the schedule set by Mrs. Eddy punctually and to the letter. Some of the women who came, who had been working as practitioners and healers in their own communities, able perhaps to afford some domestic help for themselves, were shocked that they were expected to work at Pleasant View as parlor or even scullery maids, and they soon departed.

The staff was divided into two main groups, although any Christian Scientist staff member might be summoned at any time for any task. These two groups can be rather roughly compared to the monks or nuns, on the one hand, and to lay brothers and sisters or conversi, on the other hand, in a monastic community, although obviously the divisions were not formalized nor the sexes separated. In the first group were the secretaries and watchers. The secretaries helped Mrs. Eddy with her correspondence and served as her agents in church business, and at first they regularly served for a year or six months. All the secretaries were men.

As we have seen, in the first years after he came into Mrs. Eddy's household Calvin Frye did most of her official correspondence and also ran the house and her personal affairs, but, to his regret, as Christian Science grew, some of his responsibilities devolved upon other employees. Frye's willingness and capacity for hard work were never doubted or equalled, as Mrs. Eddy acknowledged, but his typing was poor and his shorthand idiosyncratic.[20] At Pleasant View Frye still did much of the correspondence and still kept Mrs. Eddy's personal accounts, but he was seconded and to some extent outranked by Ebenezer Foster Eddy in the early days, and later by Rathvon,

Lathrop, Carpenter, Kinter, and others. The most difficult and controversial part of the secretaries' job was to sift the mail and decide which letters should be passed on to Mrs. Eddy to read and respond to herself. Inevitably, the secretaries would come in for criticism, both from those outside the house who cast suspicion on their motives and abilities and from the inside by their exacting employer. In a less extreme version of the lifestyle established by the press magnate Joseph Pulitzer after he lost his sight, Mary Baker Eddy both demanded that her quiet and privacy be defended at all costs and insisted that she be kept fully informed of anything important happening in her movement.

The "watchers," or spiritual staff, worked in shifts, under daily instructions from Mrs. Eddy, to "meet" the challenges of each day and to combat Malicious Animal Magnetism whether it manifested as a misplaced document, an unseasonal cold snap,[21] an infectious cold, or a hostile newspaper article. There were at least two hour-long "watch" meetings every day at Pleasant View, and watchers were also supposed to work on their assigned topic individually during the day. Some were considered to have special capabilities for specific topics. Mrs. Sargent, for example, was usually detailed to tackle the weather, and one day, to John Salchow's amusement, she took great satisfaction in having averted an alleged electrical storm, which Salchow knew had in fact been no storm at all but the sparks raised by the new trolley in town.

Mrs. Eddy got the term *watch* from the New Testament narrative of the night in the garden of Gethsemane, when Jesus chides his disciples for being unable to watch with him even a little while. By using the term *watching* I think Mrs. Eddy was giving a name to a particularly vigilant and active form of prayer, a set period of time when specific people would put their thoughts toward God, review questions and problems of the day, and seek spiritual understanding. She envisaged this prayer as an invisible wall of positive mental activity protecting her and her household. In a definition she may well have received directly from Mrs. Eddy, Adelaide Still says that the watchers were assigned to "work impersonally,"[22] and the adverb *impersonally* is key here. Mrs. Eddy was imperative in her instructions to the watch that there never be any attempt to reach out to specific individuals to influence their behavior. That would be mesmerism, the cardinal sin of Christian Science and the one against which Mary Baker Eddy inveighed constantly. Defending Mrs. Eddy's concept of Malicious Animal Magnetism was perhaps Gilbert Carpenter's most important aim in his reminiscences of Pleasant View, and he defines it as "anything that pulls thought down from its spiritual elevation."[23]

Carpenter insists that Mrs. Eddy was never in fear from outside hypnotic influence, as Milmine, Dakin, and Dittemore had claimed, but that like a housewife whose window panes were always clean, because she was always looking vigilantly for dirt, she was uniquely sensitive to Malicious Animal Magnetism and served as a kind of human divining rod or Geiger counter for its presence. In his attempt to define and explain, Carpenter makes it clear that his leader's preoccupation with mesmerism was not just a complicated theological issue for Christian Science but one of the most difficult aspects of life in her household. The image I use above of the housewife and the pane of glass is Carpenter's own, and it underlines the fact that at Pleasant View the presence of animal magnetism was most often apparent to Mrs. Eddy in domestic details—a pie that gave her indigestion, a bonnet string that was folded without due care, a haircut that was an inch too short at the back.

Among the second group of workers were, first, the housekeeper, cook, maids, all of them women, who were supervised in their work by Mrs. Eddy's chosen companions, usually Laura Sargent, Clara Shannon, and Pamelia Leonard. Then there were the men, two or three in number, the Mann brothers and John Salchow chief among them, who ran the buildings and grounds and contracted out for the work they were unable to do themselves. The workers in this last group—men who put in at least sixteen-hour days every day of the year and could certainly have found work elsewhere with shorter hours and better pay—remained in the estate's employ the longest and showed the most conspicuous loyalty to Mrs. Eddy. Joseph Mann, for example, the superintendent from 1898 to 1902, worked himself into a breakdown and was forced to give way to a younger man, or men, but he still came back to visit and lend a hand when he could.

The belief in Christian Science alone does not explain the extraordinary devotion of Mann and Salchow. As I see it, for these men, strangely enough, Mary Baker Eddy was not just their revered leader but the perfect employer. A connoisseur of good workmanship, she noticed everything they did and she expressed her appreciation as well as her criticism. Her demands pushed them to expand their range of skills and take on work for which they had no training but proved gratifyingly able to master. Salchow, who had received little or no education, and whom Mrs. Eddy's church officials considered a barely employable oaf, mastered the theory of the telephone and electrical system well enough to solve problems that defied the local electricians. He basked in Mrs. Eddy's approval of his new skills.[24] Mrs. Eddy treated him and other estate workers as valued professionals and trusted friends, while maintaining the authority and public presence expected from an employer, and she thereby earned their fierce loyalty, as well as the envy of their coworkers. It was the very extent of Mrs. Eddy's appreciation of the men who cut her ice and hay, hoed the beds, pruned the trees, and kept the whole estate in immaculate trim which aroused the jealousy of other workers, who, for their part, tried, with some success, to get the Mann brothers and Salchow dismissed.[25]

The workload at Pleasant View was severe and unrelenting.[26] Every room in the house was equipped with a bell, connected to Mrs. Eddy's room, and each staff member was expected to respond immediately to his or her special sequence of rings. The domestic workers, and especially the men on the estate, worked almost literally from dawn to dusk, seven days a week, but at least, except at times of real crisis, they were allowed to sleep through the night undisturbed. The secretaries and watchers had less physically strenuous work, but being responsible for something more complicated and intangible than the ice cream or the hay crop they were under much more stress, were subject to much more rebuke by their leader, and could be summoned at a moment's notice at any time of the day or night. One of the most important duties of the watchers was to be ready to help Mary Baker Eddy at night when she was unable to sleep or troubled by nightmares, and when she was ill and in pain. On these occasions, watchers would be called and then dismissed ignominiously if after they had tried to speak the words of healing for fifteen minutes she failed to feel any relief. Carpenter says that after failing to help on his first night on duty he discovered that Mrs. Eddy was suffering because she had lost "her consciousness of Truth," and that his role was to help her maintain "her consciousness of dominion, her realization of her ability to demonstrate good."[27] To the amazement of her exhausted staff, after a sleepless, angst-ridden night, Mary Baker Eddy would emerge in the morning, bright, cheerful, full of energy, confidence, and resolve.

Most of the workers summoned or attracted to Pleasant View contracted to work for a year, and during this year it was understood that they would have no days off and that the only time they would have to themselves in the course of the day was the time when Mrs. Eddy was not needing them. Woe betide someone if he was out taking a walk or picking some flowers and Mrs. Eddy's bell rang for him and went unheeded. On one occasion, when Mrs. Eddy had just moved to Chestnut Hill, it was found that the coachman, who had just arrived to take over the position, had died in his quarters, and his body had not been discovered in time by the other staff members. Death was thus about the only possible excuse for not appearing exactly on time to do one's allotted task. John Salchow found one diversion from his multiple chores on the estate—riding his bicycle up and down Pleasant Street for a half hour or so in the evenings. This was precious time indeed, and it gave him the opportunity to meet the young woman who would later become his wife. Laura Sargent, who served as Mrs. Eddy's chief companion for twenty years, was famed in the movement for not putting her foot onto a sidewalk for years on end, so closely did she keep to Mrs. Eddy's side during the final years.[28]

Occasionally even Sargent's health or energy was sapped, and she was allowed to go away for a holiday, but Calvin Frye was made of sterner stuff and spent only four nights away from Mrs. Eddy's house between August 1882 and her death in December 1910. At Pleasant View Calvin's room was next to Mrs. Eddy's suite, and his bed was against the wall of her bedroom. So closely was he attuned to her every movement that he barely needed to hear the bell sound. Two deep impressions in the thick carpet next to Frye's bed showed where he sat, his feet on the floor, ready and waiting for her summons.[29] On one banner day in 1910, Calvin Frye, who loved all things technical, was given special permission by Mrs. Eddy to go with some other members of the staff to see an air show nearby. He left as soon as his morning duties were complete and was back by five—a unique, three-hour vacation.[30]

Apart from their credentials as Christian Scientists, the most important criterion for selecting household members at Pleasant View was probably excellent health and fitness. No one with a previous history of serious illness was employed, and if, exceptionally, a staff member became seriously ill, he or she was asked to leave. While workers were in the house, no allowance was made for illness, and, on the contrary, any sign of sickness, any failure to complete one's allotted task because of feeling unwell, was considered by Mrs. Eddy to be evidence of susceptibility to Malicious Animal Magnetism.

Death might not be a sufficient excuse for not doing one's duty if you were as indispensable as Calvin Frye.[31] Several members of the household recount in their memoirs how on several different occasions Mrs. Eddy brought Frye back from the dead. George Kinter, a secretary, gives the most detailed and dramatic account of the healing he witnessed in 1905. One night Mrs. Eddy rang repeatedly for Frye, and, when other members of the staff came running to his room, they found Frye stiff, cold, and apparently lifeless in his chair:

> By this time Mrs. Eddy had rung for Laura Sargent, who arrived to find her already out of bed and advancing in her nightdress toward Calvin's room, regardless of the icy cold in the house. Paying no slightest attention to Kinter's and Mrs. Sargent's protests, Mrs. Eddy bent over the sitting figure and began at once to make "loud audible declarations" of truth.
>
> For more than an hour she continued to call upon Frye in one way or another to "wake up and be the man God made!" Mrs. Sargent meanwhile had rung for the maid, who brought a double blanket in which they wrapped Mrs. Eddy, while Kinter with an aching back supported her in the half-stooping position in which she bent over Frye's inert form, completely oblivious of what they were doing for her or of anything except the need to rouse him. At last he moved slightly and began to murmur. They could pick out broken phrases: "Don't call me back. . . . Let me go. . . . I am so tired." To which Mrs. Eddy replied that she would indeed continue to call him back from the dream-state in which he had been—that he loved life and its activities too well to fall asleep, that he was freed from the thralldom of hypnotism and alive to God, his Saviour from sin and death.[32]

The relationship between Mary Baker Eddy and Calvin Frye is strange and mysterious, but, when we seek to understand it, these scenes of healing must be given great weight. The extraordinary lapses into a deathlike state that Calvin Frye was reportedly susceptible to were clearly related to the unremitting stresses of his life with Mrs. Eddy,[33] and we may indeed wonder why on earth he put up with it all. On the other hand, for people who lived on such a pitch of religious intensity as Frye and Mrs. Eddy did, their occasional ability to enact two of the great gospel miracles—the raising of Lazarus and of Jairus's daughter—created a bond whose peculiar strength is hard to overestimate.

Even the most devoted of Mrs. Eddy's staff admitted freely and emotionally that what made their service to her hardest was her anger, the fury of her rebukes, the storm of criticism and reproach and invective that might fall upon their heads at any time, the unpredictability and suddenness of her determination that Malicious Animal Magnetism was ruling at Pleasant View. This issue had been a problem for those working closely with Mrs. Eddy from at least the early Massachusetts Metaphysical College period, as we saw in the diary entries of Arthur Buswell, but things got worse as Mrs. Eddy got older and became increasingly convinced that she alone saw the truth and that it was her religious duty to point out error, and therefore vulnerability to mesmerism, wherever it occurred. From her Pleasant View staff, Mary Baker Eddy demanded nothing short of perfection. Trying to do something was not enough; it had to be done exactly to her specification, or even her vision, on deadline or before.

Thus when her personal maid consistently turned down the bed the required two and a half inches, when John Salchow found exactly the right piece of iron to repair the footrest of Mrs. Eddy's carriage within the day, when Laura Sargent returned from her holiday earlier than planned, Mrs. Eddy was as pleased as a child, and full of loving praise. But if something went wrong or was late or was omitted, if a letter could not be found or bad weather kept her inside, mesmerism was evidently at work in the household, and then Mrs. Eddy's wrath was so terrible that Calvin Frye would stand frozen in silent angst, and Mrs. Sargent would burst into tears. These rages were well known to Mrs. Eddy's Boston officers, who commented among themselves on what William McKenzie would later call, in a letter to his future wife Daisette, "Sinaitic flashings" and "Elizabethan frankness against those who are serving her with their lives."[34]

For the staff at Pleasant View, the rebukes were a fact of everyday life and, to use an expression dear to them, a cross they had to bear. Even Calvin Frye once reached his limit. In his diary for 1897 he wrote:

On the evening of Aug. 29, Mrs. Eddy rebuked me severely but her accusation seemed so unjust that I told her it was not true and I would not remain in the house & hear such an accusation & she repeated it I left the house & went to the Hotel[;] afterward she sent a letter calling me back & I returned.

This evening she explained to me in what sense that accusation was true and then I saw the reasonableness of it and thanked her for her kindness. And I solemnly promised her & God that no matter what she should hereafter say to me I would not go and leave her because of it.[35]

When I read of the rigid routine; the priority given to punctuality, cleanliness, and unvarying order; the exact place each pin had to occupy on Mrs. Eddy's pincushion, my heart fills with gloom.

Even the different lengths of pins had their respective corners in her pincushion and she took out the pin she needed, without taking out and putting back the different lengths. No one would have thought of changing a pin in her pincushion.[36]

Had I been a Concord woman hired to do some especially menial job at Pleasant View I should certainly not have gotten through the day. It is hard not to wonder whether Mary Baker Eddy was not indeed a little mad in her daily denunciations of the workings of Malicious Animal Magnetism in her household and in her pursuit of domestic inerrancy. Was she prey to senile dementia, paranoia, or religious delusions as critics such as William Chandler would later argue? I believe it is possible to make sense of the domestic structure she and her staff evolved at Pleasant View and later carried over to Chestnut Hill.

Let us look at things first from Mrs. Eddy's own point of view. Neatness had always been a passion with her, and those critics who accuse her in her middle years of having been a slovenly housekeeper and a lazy houseguest, are, to my mind, way off the mark. To Irving Tomlinson, Mrs. Eddy recalled that as a child she would be unable to sleep if her shoes were not lined up perfectly, and she would weep if her busy mother ironed a false pleat into her dress. At Pleasant View Mrs. Eddy deliberately and untiringly set out to have a household so organized that false pleats did not occur.

Such a concept of domesticity was, of course, far from unique to Mrs. Eddy. Women of her generation and her class were often obsessively, almost psychotically, tidy. Favored by commerce and technology with a whole new range of appliances and products, treated by the press and publishers to streams of handy household hints and domestic how-to manuals, women were setting themselves new standards of cleanliness and tidiness, spending more and more time on less and less vital tasks in smaller and smaller houses. Affluent women with the old Puritan ethic and uncomfortably guilty memories of the domestic toil that had filled the lives of their mothers and grandmothers drove their servants hard, brooking no dust mote on the mantel, no tarnish on the spoons, no dimming of the door knocker's brass splendor. Mrs. Eddy's obsession with order and neatness and routine at Pleasant View was also related to her stage in life. Mrs. Eddy was a most remarkable old woman in many ways, but she too showed her age not just in her body but in her habits.

More deeply than a psychological need for routine, however, the idea of perfection in this life preoccupied Mrs. Eddy. The Christian Science she had founded and discovered taught that if one is truly in touch with the spiritual reality of life, all things become possible—not just healings, but raising people from the dead and defying the ravages of old age. Unlike some of her followers whom she had to adjure to keep their feet firmly on the ground, Mrs. Eddy accepted that what she called "demonstrations" of this kind could not be often expected now or even soon. But to reach them eventually necessitated strenuous spiritual exercise here and now, in small things and large. It involved putting one's faith to the test, and practicing to make perfect. If one could not manage with pincushions, how could one expect to heal?

To the non-Christian Scientist, perhaps the most difficult thing to understand about the system at Pleasant View is the taboo on illness. If Mrs. Eddy had the capacity for healing even the most advanced physical ailments which she and her followers claimed for her, why could she not simply heal the devout and devoted members of her staff? To my mind, some kind of doublethink is certainly going on here, and it is common to all kinds of alternative healing. Claims are routinely made about cures effected in certain individuals, but silence shrouds other cases that failed to respond to treatment. From at least 1866, Mrs. Eddy had understood this fundamental problem and had evolved a theology to account for it and a praxis for both herself and her movement to manage it. As she developed the idea conceptually, healing involved reaching out to God and moving into the fundamental spirituality of existence. It thus demanded the highest attention and the greatest integrity the healer could muster; it was deeply difficult, sometimes impossible, and always exhausting.

In Mrs. Eddy's view, metaphysical healing had always occurred in the world, across the boundaries of time and space, but it had remained largely unacknowledged. Even the testimony of Jesus' healings presented in the New Testament had not proved enough. One person could not heal the world, could in fact heal only a few, and the life of the healer was by its nature obscure and often short. This was where Christian Science represented a major breakthrough, since it posited healing as a constant, omnipresent, nonexceptional potential for all, not as the mysterious power of specific individuals, that is, in Christian Science vocabulary, it did not involve mesmerism. The goal Mary Baker Eddy had set herself from the beginning was to train healers, by her words and her writings, and to concentrate her energies and use her time to disseminate the message of healing as widely as possible. As she lived through her seventies and eighties, the need to focus and choose where to spend her time became paramount. Furthermore, there was in healing as a profession an element of showmanship, the constant risk that successful healing could become a source of personal pride and worldly ambition, and this pitfall Mary Baker Eddy had come to dread for her movement but above all for herself as she came closer to death.

Thus Mrs. Eddy decided, logically within her worldview, to spare herself the ordeal of healing. For the greater good, she had to be selfish and keep the physically and psychologically needy out of her domestic space. Many men, convinced that God has chosen them for a special mission, have made similarly ruthless choices. Many men have used their claim to a divine revelation to pursue goals and fulfill needs that had little to do with religion. Some men, like Jim Jones or David Koresh, have carried their Messianic convictions very far indeed, and in comparison with the events in Georgetown or Waco, the effects of Mrs. Eddy's self-absorption were small.

Whether we grant Mary Baker Eddy her revelation or not is a matter of individual judgment. That she had her own demons is clear; that at times she cloaked her own failings in doctrine is probable. But the struggle against imperfection is the stuff of saintliness, and even Edwin Dakin, whose portrait of Mrs. Eddy in her last years as a psychotic hypocrite has proved so influential, admits the evidence of struggle. Pleasant View begins to make much more sense if we see it as a religious community, a peculiar kind of ashram or monastery or lamascry, in which prayer and meditation are the main focus of activity, and to which the inhabitants commit themselves out of religious discipline and with the goal of reaching a higher spirituality.

For myself, I find that one of the people who understood what Mrs. Eddy was trying to achieve at Pleasant View and expressed it best was Adelaide Still, the young Englishwoman who served as Mrs. Eddy's personal maid for the last three years of her life. Miss Still was a tall, slim woman in her thirties who had recently emigrated from Great Britain. Her father, a God-fearing working-class Methodist, had fallen into illness when Ada was only thirteen, plunging the family into poverty. Ada, a highly intelligent girl who loved to learn and had no taste or talent for housework, was forced to leave school and go into service. Her apprenticeship in domesticity was very hard, and it was complicated by the increasing financial difficulties of her mother and younger siblings and her inability to understand "how God could allow it." In 1900 Still was working for a Christian Science family and read *Science and Health*. This was a revelation, healing her body and her mind, and in 1906 she managed to gain passage to the United States and entered Mrs. Eddy's household a year later.

For all her lack of education, Still had unusual intelligence, deep seriousness and sincerity in matters of faith, a sense of humility learned in the harsh school of poverty, and a prose style marvelously simple and eloquent and free from the grotesqueries of Christian Science-ese. Like several others who enjoyed a close personal relationship with Mrs. Eddy in her last years, Adelaide Still, though a young woman when Mrs. Eddy died, never became a major figure in Christian Science. To me it is one of the abiding mysteries of Christian Science that the memories of Adelaide Still remain unpublished and little read while the intellectually mediocre, obviously self-complacent and sentimental memoir by Irving Tomlinson was reissued in 1996 by the Publishing Society, in an expanded—though, I imagine, still heavily censored—form.

In the preface to her memories of Mrs. Eddy, Still explains that recent, renewed attacks on Mrs. Eddy have convinced her that the facts must be set down. Still defends Mrs. Eddy as worthy of our reverence and admiration because—not in spite of the fact that—she was a fallible human being whose life was not always sweet. Still has grasped what Mrs. Eddy herself so often tried to say, that to be granted a revelation from God is not to be given a guarantee of unceasing peace and contentment. Yes, one day, Mary Baker Eddy had found herself, suddenly, gloriously, inexplicably transported upon "a mount of revelation," but that moment of revelation was brief, and, upon finding herself back in the valley she had still to find the beginning of the way, climb laboriously each ever steeper step up, and also blaze the trail for others following after.

Mrs. Eddy took this task of perfectionism to heart in everything she did in her final years, both because this was her own, inescapable path to spiritual truth and because she had to set an example. When others failed in their daily challenge, this was of course to be expected, but, nonetheless, she was convinced, the error could not go unremarked and unchastised. As she constantly reiterated in person and in her many letters, her rebukes were not aimed at the person who erred but at the error, they were an expression of love, not hatred, and they hurt her more than they hurt others.

That this spiritual, even theological, interpretation of the intense discipline Mrs. Eddy required of her staff at times masked, or served as alibi for, some real defects in Mrs. Eddy's character cannot be denied. She could be bad tempered, irrational, capricious, inconsiderate, domineering, sanctimonious, unkind. In her own home, she was not, or not just, the towering voice of inspiration who roused feelings of awe and rapture in the select followers given the rare chance of talking to her. To her cook and her maid and her coachman she was not, or not just, the sweet, modest, soft-spoken, intelligent, well-informed old lady who charmed and disarmed and impressed every person from outside the movement, with the possible exception of William Chandler, from reporter to magistrate to alienist, who was granted an interview with her from 1892 to 1909.

The dark side of Mary Baker Eddy's personality was captured by James Gilman in his diary of the period around 1893 when he was completing the illustrations for Mrs. Eddy's poem "Christ and Christmas." An itinerant and perpetually indigent artist of limited talent, Gilman had become interested in Christian Science upon reading *Science and Health* some ten years earlier, and he had gotten to know Ebenezer Foster Eddy in Vermont. Gilman came to Concord initially in hopes of finding employment as a painter of Pleasant View.[37] An engaging fellow who had made a living by persuading people to offer him board and lodging in return for painting their homes, the forty-two-year-old Gilman presented himself as an ardent student, intent on enlightenment, and ready to adore the founder of Christian Science. He describes first seeing Mrs. Eddy from a distance, clad in black, her face deep in the shadow of a Quaker bonnet, pacing restlessly to and fro on her upper balcony, and he remarks on how impressed he was by her strange aura of sadness and mystery. For her part, Mrs. Eddy took a strong liking to Gilman and swiftly decided that he could help her realize her fancy of issuing an illustrated religious book in the manner of Phillips Brooks's immensely successful "Little Town of Bethlehem."

At first Gilman was warmly welcomed into the tight-knit society of Pleasant View—he was apparently rather an entertaining man, and in his diary he comments on how he and Mrs. Eddy and Mrs. Sargent and Calvin Frye would find themselves laughing together over some silly thing. Unfortunately relations between the two collaborators became tense after some months as Gilman found himself, willy-nilly, involved in intense rivalries for Mrs. Eddy's attention and affection, and as she discovered the limits of his artistic talent and the extent of his financial neediness. After some hesitation Mrs. Eddy refused to allow Gilman to make and reproduce her portrait, although she saw clearly that this would be a significant source of income to him, and she even reproved him harshly for his materialist motives: "Sunday evening, after a trifle of hesitation, she proceeded to her apparently painful task, I suspecting nothing, not realizing the glamour that had come over my thought, thinking of great pictures I was to make of a great subject with the *material* means that would be afforded to deliver me from the evil, &c. of poverty, and limitations as of old."[38] Unsurprisingly, Gilman was unhappy about this edict and resented Mrs. Eddy's power over him even as he declared his adoration of her.

Gilman was to remain a Christian Scientist until his death, his diary is written in the peculiar dialect of the sect, and he often proclaims the reverence and even awe his leader inspired in him.[39] For this very reason, the criticisms Gilman was moved to make of Mary Baker Eddy at points in his diary carry especial weight and have been much quoted:

> It was seeming to me as if she was the cause of most of the seeming magnetism by being so unreasonable and saying and doing just the things that would excite the antagonism that she often complains of. It seemed

to me that she was the one utterly lacking in the very Christian graces which she so loudly demanded of others.

It seemed then for a time as if Mrs. Eddy was seeking my complete subjection to that point that would make me her abject slave in which I should be compelled to listen to and accept whatever she might say to offend my proper sense of right, on pain of being denounced and rejected as disloyal to her.[40]

We do not have Mrs. Eddy's account of her relation with James Gilman, but it seems clear to me that her reactions to him, both her initial warm delight in his company and her later reproofs and denials, were strongly influenced by her deteriorating relationship with her adopted son, Ebenezer Foster Eddy. Gilman was another of those amiable and amusing son-substitutes who claimed to offer Mary Baker Eddy unconditional love but who always turned out to have a hidden agenda—usually involving money. The struggle to get beyond her own need for the affection and company of men like Gilman and Foster was one Mrs. Eddy had still to win in the early 1890s.

In the meantime, as she knew in her sunnier hours, she had many devoted people upon whom she could rely. Money, quite obviously, did not and cannot buy the devotion of a Calvin Frye, a John Salchow, or a Minnie Adelaide Still, and it is important to recognize that Mrs. Eddy found people not only willing to live with her and give her the care she required, but happy to express deep satisfaction about doing so. I have compared Pleasant View to a monastery, but the people who worked there were not bound by the kind of rules and traditions and physical barriers which monks and nuns experience even today. They could get up and leave when they wanted, and for the men at least there was no real dearth of jobs. The very prominence of Mrs. Eddy made her particularly vulnerable to the force of public opinion, and if some mistreated little maid had wanted to pour out her story of woe, she would surely have found a press representative, notebook in hand, eager to take it down and publish it. When Miss Still was being recruited in 1906, according to her reminiscences, Daisette Stocking McKenzie, after much silence and hesitation, told her: "Remember, half the world is condemning Mrs. Eddy and the other half is deifying her, and the workers stand there [i.e., at Pleasant View] between the two." This sense of being the bulwark protecting Mrs. Eddy against a variously hostile world steeled the efforts of the workers who were most important to her.

Little things Mrs. Eddy did and said made the day worthwhile for them, as we see in the matter of Minnie Adelaide Still's given name. One of the small but poignant themes sounded in the history and memoirs of domestic service in England is that maids frequently were given names by their employers, and that the loss of her own name was one of the small, unnecessary humiliations the servant girl had to bear. One day when Mrs. Eddy was wanting to give her maid a copy of one of her books, Mrs. Eddy asked how she should dedicate it. Still had always been called Minnie in her family, but at Pleasant View she had been given the name Ada by the housekeeper because the resident cook was called Minnie. When Mrs. Eddy learned that Still's name was not Ada, she asked what she wished henceforth to be called, and when Still decided on Adelaide, this choice was honored from then on in the household.

Still also is the one to note that Mrs. Eddy decreed that it should be the task of the male secretaries to bring up the heavy trays and the hods of fuel. This was menial work for middle-class young men, but in the course of her life, Mrs. Eddy had all too often had to make her own fire and carry up her own fuel, and she knew the problems of managing stairs in a full long skirt. Such moments of human understanding and considerateness endeared Mrs. Eddy to her staff, increasing the veneration they felt for her.

Perhaps it was the very changeableness of Mary Baker Eddy's character, the unpredictability of her response, the swift changes in her humor, that secured the devotion of those closest to her. Life was disciplined at Pleasant View, it was constant hard work, but it was not boring. Drama was possible at any moment, and the connection between the little domestic scene and the greater life of the movement was a thrilling one. Pressure, stress, fatigue, anxiety characterized life for the staff, but not boredom. Outside were the ongoing advances of Christian Science in the world, the extraordinary battle called the Woodbury trial or the Next Friends suit. Inside, at the heart of the house, was a woman waging a spiritual battle for perfection of action and vision. As she wrote in a letter to Calvin Hill:

> "When I first learned my Lord" I was so sure of Truth, my faith so strong in Christian Science as I then discovered it, I had no struggle to meet; but stood on the height of its glory a crowned monarch triumphant over sin and death. But behold me now washing that spiritual understanding with my tears! Learning little by little the allness of Omnipotent Mind; and the nothingness of matter, yea the absolute nothingness of nothing and the infinite somethingness of ALL. O bear with me, loved one, till I accomplish the height, the depth, the Horeb light of divine Life,—divine Love, divine health, holiness and immortality. The way seems not only very long but very strait and narrow.[41]

22

The Last Class

I N THE SPRING OF 1897, MARY BAKER EDDY PUBLISHED
her *Miscellaneous Writings*. Although this work was only an edited compendium of addresses, sermons, articles, and essays she had written between 1883 and 1896, Mrs. Eddy considered the appearance of the work so important, and its message so crucial, that she took the extraordinary step of banning all other forms of teaching within the Christian Science movement for a whole year. Mrs. Eddy saw this as a necessary measure to combat the increased outpouring of false or inadequate literature under the name of Christian Science, and she felt obliged to ask even her faithful followers to accept the financial losses and the fall in prestige that a moratorium on teaching would entail. For those who opposed Christian Science and loathed Mrs. Eddy, the ban was the most egregious example of the throttlehold she maintained over her movement and her megalomaniac style of leadership. But given what a fascinated public was to learn over the next ten years of the doctrinal and practical excesses of two prominent Christian Scientists, Josephine Woodbury and Augusta Stetson, Mary Baker Eddy's decision to trust no one except herself to make any statements for the movement would prove to be an astute one.

Once the year of moratorium was up, Mrs. Eddy moved quickly to put new institutional mechanisms in place that would curb and shape the growth of the movement. Thus early in 1898 she set up a Board of Lectureship. The members of this mainly male group were carefully selected and kept on a very tight doctrinal rein by Mrs. Eddy, but over the next years this body proved to be a powerful mechanism for gaining more public respect for Christian Science. It brought a number of new and eloquent voices to the movement, notably Edward Kimball. In 1898 Mrs. Eddy founded a new weekly journal, directed more specifically to intramovement concerns than the *Journal* was. The new journal was first called the *Christian Science Weekly*, and then a few months later it was renamed the *Christian Science Sentinel*, the name the publication still has today. Also in 1898 Mrs. Eddy set up a deed of trust for the Publishing Society, an increasingly vital sector of the general church structure as both propaganda machine and source of revenue, to whose operations she wished to give a legal framework. This trust document was to play an important role in later Christian Science history because it was to be the key document in dispute during the Great Litigation.[1]

As a further way of giving renewed impetus to the Church, Mrs. Eddy decided by November 1898 that she needed to get more closely and personally in touch with members of her movement, and that she would teach one more class. The doors of Massachusetts Metaphysical College had closed in the early summer of 1889, and there were by this point many people in Christian Science who had never heard Mrs. Eddy speak, even in public, and whose major chance even to glimpse her from afar had been in the summer of 1897 when 2,500 Christian Scientists had accepted Mrs. Eddy's invitation to come to Pleasant View. Nonetheless, for some years Mrs. Eddy had been increasingly stressing the dangers of personalization, and the decision to teach a class and thus use the power of her personal presence once more to put across her message was a not inconsiderable one. Perhaps she decided that the very best antidote to those who liked to deify her was to see her white hair and lined face up close and be reminded that she was a real woman, not an idea or an idol.

The way Mrs. Eddy chose to go about summoning students to the special new class was idiosyncratic, and it exemplifies why she was so often accused of being an autocrat. On Tuesday, November 15, seventy brief telegrams and letters, marked confidential, were dispatched from Pleasant View, inviting seventy individuals to meet Mrs. Eddy and receive a great blessing at 4 P.M. on the following Sunday at the Christian Science Hall in Concord, New Hampshire. No one else was to be informed of the event. The number of invitees was, apparently, in keeping with the Biblical verse "The Lord appointed other seventy also." Amazingly, of the seventy, only two or three failed to appear in Concord on time, although some received the missive late in the week and some came from far away.

George Wendell Adams, a young man who had decided while studying at the Massachusetts Institute of Technology to become a Christian Science practitioner, recalled his surprise at receiving his letter. Carefully saying nothing of his weekend plans, Adams asked a young fellow practitioner if he could borrow his suitcase, to which the other replied that he would be needing it himself. On Saturday morning both men met at North Station in Boston and boarded the same train to Concord. Sue Harper Mims received her letter on Wednesday but was unable to leave her home in Chattanooga until Friday morning. Mrs. Mims arrived in Boston at 9 P.M. on Saturday night, only to learn that the next passenger train left at 1 P.M. on Sunday. "Too impatient to wait until that time," Mrs. Mims took the 2 A.M. paper train, reaching Concord at five in the morning and then resting in her hotel room until she could attend the morning Christian Science service, presided over by First Reader Ezra M. Buswell. It was at this service that the invitees began to take stock of one another and realize that they were members of a group that had been carefully chosen to include not only such stalwarts of the Church as Edward and Kate Kimball, but young people just starting in the movement—Daisette Stocking, John Lathrop, Daphne Knapp, William McKenzie, James Neal, Irving Tomlinson, Carol Norton—all destined to play significant roles in the development of Christian Science in the twentieth century.[2]

Mrs. Mims in the lengthy account of this last class she gave to her own association of students on her return south remarks at length on the presence of an unexpectedly large contingent of well-educated young men under thirty. "The sweetest thing to me was to see those young men—just leaving all for Christ," she notes, and the forced sweetness of this remark may reflect Mrs. Mims's ambivalence about the composition of the class. Certainly, in choosing whom to invite to Concord Mrs. Eddy and her close advisors had tried to balance the numbers not only of young and old but of men and women. This in itself was a clear policy decision and may well have been a legitimate source of covert grumbling later on among the general membership, which was overwhelmingly female.

As this was the first time in years that many of the class members had seen Mrs. Eddy, and some had never seen her, it seems opportune to collect some of the members' descriptions of her in her seventy-seventh year. Mrs. Eddy's health was particularly bad in mid-1898, as the tensions grew over the Woodbury case, and rumors of problems at Pleasant View had certainly filtered out. Even as her followers were eager to see how physically and mentally fit she was, her personal staff members must have been anxious that she not have one of her bad days. One of the reasons that the invitations were sent out at such short notice, with such adjuring to secrecy, and fixing so near a date, was that in November Mrs. Eddy had recovered from her summer problems, but there was no assurance that she would not relapse.

In fact, she was in fine form on the appointed day. Much commented on were her swift step and general ease of movement, which gave an immediate and important impression of youthfulness and energy. Right up to the last years of her life she would surprise even her staff by her light step, which is often described as "floating." Erect carriage, graceful gestures, a small but clear and sweet voice, a face that beamed attention, pleasure, intelligence, and affection to all present, completed the external picture. Sue Harper Mims describes Mrs. Eddy as "the very picture of refined elegance," giving her students a detailed analysis of what Mrs. Eddy wore which is worthy of a fashion magazine:

> Around her neck was a little black and ermine cape. Her beautiful white hair was in loose waves or curls around her brow. She sat in a big red-cushioned chair, which made a beautiful background for her, and when she threw back her cape it revealed a very handsome black silk dress. The skirt was of black moiré, and the waist [i.e., bodice or top] was of white silk covered with net and heavily trimmed with jet. She wore a diamond cross given to her by one of her students, and an exquisite pin presented to her by the Daughters of the American Revolution. She wore white kid gloves.[3]

One can see from this description that the minute attention Mrs. Eddy devoted to choosing and maintaining her clothes was not just a personal obsession but an important factor in her public role. The middle-class and middle-aged women who composed perhaps the largest and most dedicated segment of the membership of the Church cared about appearance, and they would critique, almost automatically, what other women were wearing. During the 1880s, as we have seen, some followers had openly criticized Mrs. Eddy for her stylish clothes and the diamond ornaments she wore in public, but she would have been equally criticized had she appeared in public looking shabby. An acknowledged beauty in her youth and fully aware of her attractiveness, Mary Baker Eddy had never neglected her clothes even when she was forced by poverty to trim her own hats and turn her old gowns. Now in old age it still strongly behooved her to find the balance between ostentation and shabbiness, style and modesty.[4]

If Mrs. Eddy's queenly and healthful appearance reassured her followers, even more impressive was the quiet and unassuming sweetness of her manner. Soft charm, not stern correction, was the order of the day. Choosing for the two sessions of the class the question-and-answer format she had long favored, Mrs. Eddy had a clear and strong message to impart and was never afraid to correct her listeners. But the stinging rebukes so familiar to her household were absent here. Her aim was to inspire and invigorate, not to censure and condemn, and in this she succeeded. Mrs. Eddy's legendary strengths as a teacher were once again fully in evidence, and those present would go out to testify that although Mrs. Eddy had chosen to withdraw from the daily direction of Church affairs, she had indisputably acted from a position of strength, not weakness. It was noted by many that all of Mrs. Eddy's teaching focused on the positive, affirmative side of Christian Science and that she made almost no mention of Malicious Animal Magnetism. This positive focus represented, in the eyes of many, a major change not only in doctrine but in treatment practice. "Taking up" enemies, real or suspected, was now a thing of the past, if the message Mrs. Eddy delivered that day was accepted. This was undoubtedly important and controversial news, not perhaps so much to the students present, but to many leaders in the field, notably Mrs. Stetson and Mrs. Woodbury.

One point that Mrs. Eddy dealt with very emphatically was that students should be careful not to make her some kind of God. There was a difficult line to tread here because in many ways the class was designed to restore Mrs. Eddy's authority over the older members and instill it in the new ones. The class included a tribute by Judge Hanna, praising all that Mrs. Eddy had done in and for Christian Science. Hearing Hanna's words, Mrs. Eddy was moved to tears and heartfelt expressions of pleasure, but nonetheless she urgently instructed the class to detach Christian Science from her person and to avert any kind of worship or adoration of her. Judge Joseph Clarkson was to be the particular target for this lesson. He had been invited to the class because although he was a very new member of the Church he seemed to show exceptional leadership potential. But after hearing one of Clarkson's answers, filled with rapt adulation, Mrs. Eddy responded very solemnly. "I trust that no personal sense of me will ever stand between you and Christian Science," she said, discerning far more clearly than most of those present that, to use Robert Peel's excellent summation, "personal adoration . . . could just as easily turn to personal antipathy." Indeed, by 1900 Judge Clarkson was taking it upon himself to advise Mrs. Eddy that the good of the cause demanded that she give male administrators completely free rein, and within a few years after that he had left the movement, chagrined that his opinions had not carried the day.

Many critics have accused Christian Science of deifying its leader, and this issue will assume ever more importance as we move into the last years of Mrs. Eddy's life when her power and the opposition to her grew stronger. One of the strongest criticisms of her is that she promoted and codified her own apotheosis. There is overwhelming evidence that certain individuals and groups in the movement liked to give Mrs. Eddy an exalted religious role— Ira Knapp and his son Bliss, for example, identified her as the woman crowned with stars named in Revelation. The evidence is equally strong, however, that Mary Baker Eddy herself was quick to see and to censure any attempt to make her or any of her works into what she liked to call a Dagon, a false image. Thus in a private statement which she dictated to Foster Eddy in the early 1890s she tried to clarify exactly how she understood her relation to God:

> I am weary of waiting on the involuntary or voluntary motives of the
> infantile mind in Christian Science to become absolutely right on a

single point relating to me. To help settle this problem I will once for all silence my sensitiveness and give the definition of my present *genus homo*, so far as I understand it. . . .

1st. In belief, I am a human being and should be treated as such, and spoken of as such, until I find my place outside this state of being.

2nd. So far as I know myself, and history, I am the discoverer and founder of Christian Science. If my claim is unwarranted, show this fact by precedent or proof. Produce a single work before mine which contained *my statement* of Christian Science as in Science and Health, or show this statement incorrect demonstrably, and I will then say that my claim is invalid.

3rd. I believe in the Scriptural narrative and the evidence it affords that Jesus of Nazareth demonstrated and taught the divine Principle of Christian Science. But I have no written or verbal evidence that he taught the letter of this Science. . . .

In the flesh I am not what I desire to be; I am not what imagination would make me. I am not a heathen concept or idol. I am not a personality to which others look and are saved, and the world's present ignorance of the place I occupy should suspend its judgment. I am not the Door through which to enter, nor the Rock whereon to build, but what God has spoken to this age through me is the *way* and *sure foundation*, and no man entereth in any other way into Christian Science.[5]

This statement was never published, and it is far from perfect, but because it was quickly dictated, never edited, and left forgotten, it gives us a good sense of how Mrs. Eddy's mind was working, and of how her prose style would change and improve. The fragment starts off clumsily. As so often, Mrs. Eddy reaches for what she imagines to be the language of metaphysics and abstract reasoning, using abstract, polysyllabic words such as *sensitiveness* and *infantile*, using a convoluted sentence inversion, and abusing a Latin tag. As she moves on, however, Mrs. Eddy becomes confident, absorbed in her message, sure in her rhetoric. The prose becomes both Biblical and simple, the syntax balanced and precise until we get to the admirable concision of "In the flesh, I am not what I desire to be; I am not what imagination would make me."

Before leaving the discussion of Mrs. Eddy's last class, I would like to return to the issue of its balanced composition—balanced not only in terms of the ages of its participants but also their genders. The makeup of the class was far from reflective of the general membership since almost exactly half of those present were men, and from its inception Christian Science had been overwhelmingly a movement of women, and usually middle-aged women—

one of the demographic groups with the least power and prestige in the general culture. Healed by Christian Science of their own invalidism or having witnessed the dramatic healing of their loved ones, women converted to the new movement. As I have pointed out, much of the progress of Christian Science in the early years can be attributed to its success with obstetrical and gynecological cases. Once converted, women had psychological and financial incentives to try the difficult and risky life of practitioner, and it was in large measure their activism that drove the movement forward.

Mrs. Eddy was enough a product of the nineteenth-century American feminist movement to recognize, capitalize on, and encourage the flow of women into her movement. This was a group she understood and sympathized with, whose interests she actively sought to promote, and whose activities she passionately urged on, notably in her correspondence, which includes thousands of individual, handwritten letters to women followers. It was hard for any Christian Scientist woman to excuse herself to Mrs. Eddy for failing on the grounds that she was only a woman and that things were therefore weighted against her. For example, in 1899 Annie Knott had the unusual privilege of being summoned to Pleasant View for a special interview with Mrs. Eddy. Questioned as to her progress as one of the members of the new Board of Lecturers, Mrs. Knott replied that she had few requests to speak because most people, even friends, preferred to hear a man. This answer did not satisfy Mrs. Eddy, who energetically denied that a man had any more intellect than a woman, and urged Knott to "rise to the altitude of true womanhood, and then the whole world will want you as it wants Mother [i.e., Mrs. Eddy]." Inspired not only by Mrs. Eddy's words but also by her example, Knott set off from Concord determined to conquer her own fears and sense of inadequacy. Soon, she writes, the requests to give lectures began pouring in and "what is more, [I] felt the inspiration of Truth to accept these [calls to lecture] fearlessly and to prove that a woman can declare the truth and heal the sick as well as a man."[6]

By the 1890s, Christian Science, though still small, controversial to the general public, and often violently contested in certain communities, had achieved the status of a minor religious denomination. It was becoming respectable, practitioners were beginning to make a decent living, and with success came an influx of men to the movement, bringing with them inevitable changes in style and direction. One of the great concerns of both Mrs. Eddy herself and of her Mother Church officials at the time was to increase the participation of men in the Church overall, and to place the leadership in the hands of men. There were considerations of spiritual substance, of practical efficiency, of public image, and of private prejudice here.

Mrs. Eddy, like most people in American society at large, still regarded men as the natural leaders in public life, and in view of her own trials as a widow, divorcée, and single mother, she was sensitive to charges that

Christian Science women practitioners led irregular and roving lives and neglected their families. Practically speaking, however, attracting more men to the movement was not easy. American white middle-class males around this time—and Christian Science drew overwhelmingly from the white middle class—had many rich career options, and men tended to view the life of a practitioner and teacher as a sacrifice rather than as an opportunity. To balance this perception, as Christian Science became established and institutionalized, Mrs. Eddy adopted a policy of positive discrimination toward men, offering them rapid advancement to positions of authority, prominence, and affluence. The adoption and urgent promotion of Ebenezer Foster was only the most obvious sign of her efforts to find, convert, and give preference in her church organization to new male members, especially if they had a strong educational and/or professional background.

If Mrs. Eddy sought out men and gave them, in some cases, more authority and prominence than they deserved, this did not mean that she saw men as superior, or that she wished to see men take on all positions of authority in her church, as they did in other religious groups. The evidence is that what Mrs. Eddy sought was equality between the sexes on all levels of the Church, not male dominance. In fact, despite Mrs. Eddy's attempts to balance the gender composition of her church organization, Christian Science remained predominantly a women's religion at least until the first decade or so of the twentieth century. Mrs. Eddy's own leadership continued, essentially undiluted, at least until 1908, resting not only on her historical role but on the institutionalized supremacy she had ensured through the *Manual of The Mother Church*. Furthermore, in the field—that is to say, outside Boston or New England—women like Laura Lathrop, Augusta Stetson, Sue Harper Mims, Annie M. Knott, Hannah Larminie, and scores of others continued to form the majority not only of Church members but of leaders. It was only in The Mother Church that men predominated among the directors and trustees and readers, and even in Boston one or two women held major offices.[7]

A document that is key to understanding Mrs. Eddy's ideas on gender is a short essay called "Man and Woman," which she copyrighted around 1900 but did not publish. As a piece of close argument, the work is deeply flawed, and Mrs. Eddy was surely wise to keep it from the public. Mark Twain, had he received a copy, would have greeted "Man and Woman" as further proof that Mrs. Eddy could not have written *Science and Health*! Nonetheless, the essay offers us some fascinating insights into Mrs. Eddy's thinking at this important period of change and challenge in the movement.[8]

Mrs. Eddy's argument takes a zigzag course. She begins by taking up the cudgel against those who had criticized and even lampooned her movement as wholly female by defensively noting that the Board of Trustees of the Publishing Society, the Board of Directors, and the Publication Committees have only male members, the Board of Education has one woman and three men, and the Board of Lectureship has eleven men and two women. Having established the fact that she had "given the preponderance to the masculine element in [her] organizations for carrying out the functions of Christian Science," Mrs. Eddy then goes off on the other tack and argues an essentially feminist position on the gender issue. First she claims that to God there is no male, female, or neuter—all are one and equal—and then she goes on to note that the preponderance given to the masculine in all recorded religions is mere historical accident, not an eternal verity or a divine decree. The time has now come, she writes, for women to come to the fore and lead. Again moving off on an apparent tangent, Mrs. Eddy notes that, indeed, many women are petty and prone to gossip, but the male's violence in asserting his own rights, especially sexual rights, is at least as reprehensible. In conclusion, Mrs. Eddy writes a short, and perhaps conventionally Victorian, paean to women's selfless conduct, not only in the gospel story, where woman was last at the cross and first at the tomb, but in everyday life. Today, she writes, wives and mothers, daughters and sisters show a devotion to God and their fellow men which earns them an eternal reward.

As I read this strange rambling argument, I see Mrs. Eddy alternating, as feminists have done throughout the years, between a doctrine of difference and equality, of special identity and special merit for women, on the one hand, and of sexual undifferentiation before the eyes of God and of history, on the other. Intellectually, Mrs. Eddy's arguments will probably satisfy neither the militant feminist nor the ardent defender of traditional sex roles. But gender was not just an abstract issue for Mrs. Eddy but an urgent, daily, practical concern. As she once vigorously championed the cause of women's rights and women's strengths, Mrs. Eddy was now, in her last years, changing course to some extent by looking to the strength of men and casting them in a leading role in her overwhelmingly female movement.

She saw strengths and weaknesses in both sexes, sought a society and a theology of gender equality and even neutrality, and could not imagine a religious movement succeeding in the long run if it did not enroll, challenge, and exploit the energies and talents of both men and women. If women needed the opportunity to develop personal strength, social authority, and financial independence, men needed encouragement to affirm their spiritual heritage and develop their healing potential. As a theoretician Mary Baker Eddy can be pilloried, but, in my view, her praxis was interesting, effective, and far from unenlightened.[9]

23

Mrs. Woodbury
and Her
Lawyer

JOSEPHINE CURTIS WOODBURY IS ONE OF THE STRANG-
est and most famous characters in Christian Science history, and she not
only made Mrs. Eddy miserable but had an impact on Mrs. Eddy's religious
thinking. There is no doubt that the activities of Mrs. Woodbury were the
most painful and pressing reason—though far from the only or the greatest
reason—why, around 1900, Mrs. Eddy was placing more and more emphasis on love and purity of thought as the basis for effective healing, and looking to a new generation of young, educated men to assist her in leading the
Church into the twentieth century. The peculiarly gendered character of the
Woodbury case, involving as it does the flaunting of female sexual power,
adultery, and an illegitimate child, may have been influential in persuading
Mrs. Eddy that, as she told New York journalist Joseph Clarke, the future of
Christian Science leadership must lie with men. Before the fascinated eyes of
the nation, Mrs. Eddy and Mrs. Woodbury, personally and through their
supporters, publicly rehearsed the opposing roles of virgin and whore, Mary
and Eve, Babylonish woman and woman crowned with twelve stars, as
described in the Book of Revelation.

There has never been any disagreement that, in person, Mrs. Woodbury
could be an attractive, lively, intelligent, winning woman, an effective speaker
gifted with a fine sense of public relations. It was because of these qualities
that she rose to prominence in Christian Science and secured for a long time
Mrs. Eddy's friendship and protection. As I have remarked before, the effect
of someone's real physical presence is a part of history that is peculiarly dif-

ficult to understand or measure, but Josephine Woodbury seems to have been that rare person whose sex appeal translated effectively into text appeal.

Our first, most extensive, and least reliable source of information on Josephine Woodbury is her short memoir, *War in Heaven*, which recounts her "sixteen years of experience" in Christian Science. This book was published in 1897 after Mrs. Woodbury had been expelled from Christian Science. The book was carefully calculated, on the one hand, as an attempt to placate Mrs. Eddy one last time, and, on the other, as a preemptive move to secure public support in the battle Mrs. Woodbury was getting ready to wage against her leader. Mrs. Woodbury begins her memoir by telling us that she was born into an upper-middle-class family of high moral purpose. Her parents, Edwin and Josephine Curtis Battles, were dedicated abolitionists, and the event of her childhood which Mrs. Woodbury chooses to stress in the memoir is the year she spent in the Lexington academy headed by Theodore Weld and his wife Angelina Grimké Weld. On the staff of the school at different times, she informs us, were Theodore Tilton, Catharine Beecher, and Emma Lazarus,[1] and the pupils included "the Danas, the Sharps, Chases, Hills, Lincolns, Sewalls, Sargents, Tudors, two daughters of Nathaniel Hawthorne, and a niece of the poet Saxe."[2] Here Josephine Woodbury is implicitly staking what seems on reflection to be a rather tenuous claim to membership in the Boston liberal establishment, which had never embraced Mary Baker Eddy.

In 1874 Josephine Battles married Edward Franklin Woodbury, usually known as Frank, a gentleman she claimed could trace his ancestry back to English and French kings. He was now working as a mechanical engineer. It is not clear how successful either Edwin Battles or Frank Woodbury was in business, but I have the impression that Josephine was the moneymaker in the family from the 1880s on, and the rest of the clan stuck by her in part because her activities, however strange and nefarious, put a roof over their heads. One of the kinder ways to look at Mrs. Woodbury's career might be to see her as one of the many nineteenth-century women with little education, no professional training, and few respectable openings for their talents and energies who had to earn money to support not only their husbands and children but also their parents.[3]

The Woodburys had two children, Gwendoline and Curtis, and as a young mother, like so many women of her class and generation, Josephine fell into invalidism. She was converted to Christian Science by Clara Choate—who had, with Mrs. Eddy's help, suffered and recovered from similar problems with marriage and motherhood—when spiritual healing cured her child of his latest attack of membranous croup. Soon after, Mrs. Woodbury tells us, she herself fell ill and was told by her doctors that she was dying. Despite her suffering she refused to take morphine (this was a subtle dig at Mrs. Eddy that the initiated reader of *War in Heaven* would appreciate!) and healed herself through Christian Science. Then both she and Frank sought out Mrs. Eddy in Lynn and later took classes with her in 1884 at the Massachusetts Metaphysical College. In later years Mrs. Woodbury was to claim that she had been nursing Asa Gilbert Eddy at the time of his death, but this seems to have been a dramatic enhancement of her actual role.[4] Nonetheless, the fact that the Woodburys had stood with Mrs. Eddy in 1883 and supported her through the illness and death of her husband, the attendant press furor, and the libel suit against Arens may be one reason that Mrs. Eddy was later so extraordinarily patient and forgiving with Josephine Woodbury. Unlike so many others, the Woodburys had not deserted Mary Baker Eddy in her hour of trouble, and she showed them loyalty in return.

Throughout the 1880s Josephine Woodbury claimed successes as a healer, drew a number of devoted people into the movement, and was loud in her praise and adulation of her Leader. Based in Boston, where her extended family lived, where her husband had his engineering firm and patents business, and where he continued to act as an agent on behalf of The Mother Church,[5] Mrs. Woodbury, by her own account, made many gratifyingly close contacts with local clergymen and other worthies, and in 1886 she established her own Christian Science academy on Dartmouth Street in Boston. She wrote poems,[6] gave addresses, published her sermons and poems, but in Boston she had little success as a healer, and it was in healing that Christian Scientists could make money. As she herself tells the tale, Mrs. Woodbury began to make forays out of town to spread the new gospel, going first to Maine, and later journeying in the depth of the winter cold as far as Denver, Colorado.

The Milmine and Cather biography of Mrs. Eddy gives a spirited and detailed account of the Woodbury following, and I shall quote the section in full since it has been routinely adjudged both accurate and enlightening by all subsequent biographers who did not have access to the Mother Church archives:

> Mrs. Woodbury's group of students and followers were, on the whole, very different from the simple, rule-abiding Christian Scientists who had been taught directly under Mrs. Eddy's personal supervision. Mrs. Eddy's own people never got very far away from her hard-and-fast business principles, while Mrs. Woodbury's students were distinctly fanciful and sentimental, and strove to add all manner of ornamentation to Mrs. Eddy's stout homespun. There were two or three musicians among them, and a young illustrator and his handsome wife, and most of them wrote verses. Some of Mrs. Woodbury's students went abroad with her, and acquired the habit of interlarding the regular Christian Science phraseology with a little French. Mrs. Woodbury and her students lived in a kind of miracle-play of their own; had inspirations and revelations and premonitions; kept mental trysts; saw portents and mystic mean-

ings in everything; and spoke of God as coming and going, agreeing and disagreeing with them. Some of them affected cell-like sleeping-chambers with white walls, bare except for a picture of Christ. They longed for martyrdom, and made adventures out of the most commonplace occurrences. Mrs. Woodbury herself had this marvel-loving temperament. Her room was lined with pictures of the Madonna.[7]

This is lively stuff, and the group described reminds me a little of the Pre-Raphaelite brotherhood as parodied in Gilbert and Sullivan's *Patience*. It is the kind of passage where we feel the budding novelist Willa Cather revelling in the chance to portray an eccentric but likable and amusing woman character.[8]

A much darker and nastier view of Mrs. Woodbury's following emerges from the unpublished testimony the followers themselves gave to Mrs. Eddy's lawyers around 1899 after Mrs. Woodbury sued Mrs. Eddy for libel. Inhabitants of Boston, Montreal, and small towns like Augusta and Bath, Maine, they were in plain fact mostly naïve, ill-educated young spinsters, sad and dissatisfied young mothers married to modest businessmen, and such of the same women's male relatives who found themselves cajoled, fascinated, and entrapped into membership of Mrs. Woodbury's circle. These people were doubtless amazed and delighted in 1907 to find Milmine describing them as charming aesthetes and ascetics.

Mrs. Woodbury preached sexual abstinence, spiritual purity, and dedication to Christian Science, but she did not practice what she preached. Certainly, the extension of her healing and proselytizing mission to Montreal in the fall of 1889 was as much personal as it was professional. As far as I can determine the course of events based on unpublished testimony, by June of that year Mrs. Woodbury was already having a liaison with Henry L. Putnam of Montreal. The two had met in Boston, where Putnam seems to have come to study Christian Science in February or March of that year. By June, Mrs. Elizabeth Bangs, Mrs. Woodbury's chief disciple and friend, was having to literally place herself between Josephine and Henry to prevent them from making love. At one hotel near Niagara Falls, Mrs. Bangs went to her friend's room at 2:15 A.M., found Putnam there, as she had anticipated, and only prevailed upon him to leave by settling herself in there for the night. Many of those who saw Woodbury and Putnam together commented on their inability to control their passion for one another, and Mrs. Woodbury later confided to her friend Mrs. Burns that having known Putnam she lost "every particle" of her love for her husband. Putnam gave her "exquisite pleasure" and satisfied her completely. Learning of the relationship between Mrs. Woodbury and Mr. Putnam, Mrs. Eddy dismissed their claims that they were acting out roles scripted in the Book of Revelation, told them to separate once and for all, and sent Putnam back to his wife and family in Montreal.

It will be remembered that 1889 was the year that Mrs. Eddy left Boston for New Hampshire, announcing that personal problems among her followers would have to be resolved without consulting her.

Given the clear opposition to their liaison in Boston, it seems likely that Putnam was the reason that Mrs. Woodbury began to pay lengthy visits to Montreal in the fall of 1889, and that there they continued their liaison. Henry Putnam was soon spending hours locked up alone in his home with Mrs. Woodbury, to his wife's silent distress, and he was seen by several people kissing her and cuddling with her on the sofa. The eyewitness testimony by the Montreal Christian Scientists is circumspect, carefully limited by legal counsel to detailing exactly what was seen and heard, not what was rumored. Nonetheless, it is plain that everyone who was in the know assumed that Putnam and Mrs. Woodbury were lovers.

The Putnam liaison was not Mrs. Woodbury's only problem. Her way of dealing with patients and students had always been, to put it mildly, idiosyncratic, but once she was in Montreal and freed from Mrs. Eddy's presence and the censure of her Boston acquaintance, Mrs. Woodbury seems to have thrown caution to the wind. She may also have been particularly desperate for money at this time, since I would assume that neither her husband nor her father was happy about her passion for Putnam and ready to finance her trips to Montreal. According to the testimony of her students and followers in Montreal, Josephine Woodbury relied on two weapons in her proselytizing—the fear of mesmerism and her own sexual appeal. Women, in Montreal as elsewhere, were the ones first and predominantly attracted to Christian Science, and Mrs. Woodbury had some success in attaching to her person women who sought help in treating their own intractable complaints or the sudden, terrifying illnesses of their children. Her patients found Mrs. Woodbury unreliable, moody, and ineffective as a practitioner, but she caught the alarmed attention of some and the groveling obedience of a few by threatening to use her mental powers to cause illness and death and financial ruin in the family of anyone who opposed her. In the tiny group of Christian Scientists in Montreal, it was commonly believed that Mrs. Woodbury could, as she claimed in private conversation and in her class teaching, make a woman ill just by thinking about her or sending her a letter, bring a husband to bankruptcy, or cause loving families to split apart. Even one of Woodbury's closest associates, Mrs. Martha Burns, later claimed that Josephine had constantly threatened her and her family with ruin if Mrs. Burns did not obey Mrs. Woodbury in every way. "For years I was held by that fear," testified Mrs. Burns.

Peel believes that Mrs. Woodbury was an actual mesmerist, and he notes that she took lessons from the celebrated hypnotist Dr. Carpenter. It is possible that she actually did hypnotize certain people, and that, for example, the woman who, by her own testimony, on various occasions left her sick child and then her dying father to come to Mrs. Woodbury's classes did so under the power of hypnosis. On the other hand, the woman may also have been acting out unavowed resentments toward her family and using Mrs. Woodbury's supposed influence as an alibi for her uncharacteristic behavior. Moreover, people believed that Mrs. Woodbury's powers worked at a distance and could do such things as affect business accounts or start fires, and this type of mind control is hard to explain by any standard theory of hypnosis. In my view, what was happening in Montreal and elsewhere was a small example of the mass hysteria familiar to us now from the transcripts of witchcraft trials.

Success with women patients, though personally gratifying, at best secured Mrs. Woodbury free board and lodging, since women did not usually control the family purse strings. To solve her financial problems, Mrs. Woodbury made every attempt to have her women followers bring their menfolk to classes and meetings, since she was confident that she could charm any man she met. With the frankness that was characteristic of her relations with several slavishly devoted female intimates, Mrs. Woodbury admitted that she cared for women only as a means of getting close to men, that she was a very passionate woman, and that she could control any man through his sexual instincts, or desires, and get money out of him. To a group that included Mrs. Elizabeth McTeer of Augusta, Maine, she told the following anecdote about how she had got some publishing done in Boston:

> I wore a very pretty gown at the time. I saw the person whom I wished to publish what I had. He smoothed down the sleeve of my dress and said, "What a pretty gown you have! It is the prettiest I have seen in an age. I wish my wife would wear a gown like that." I got my publishing done.[9]

Unsurprisingly, after confidences of this kind, fear of Mrs. Woodbury's powers finally yielded to disapproval of her sexual mores, and the women students began to express public doubts about whether it was really Christian Science they were learning. Some of the men also reacted negatively to her sexual forwardness, finding her far less attractive than Mr. Putnam had done. Mr. McBean took such an instant dislike to Mrs. Woodbury that he would not even let her touch him, whereas Mr. Carr bet his wife that he could have Mrs. Woodbury if he wished. Faced with this double hostility, Mrs. Woodbury departed south back to Boston.

An additional and perhaps the preponderant reason for her departure from Montreal became clear in June 1890, when Mrs. Woodbury gave birth to her third child, a notably large and healthy boy. She devotes two short sections of her memoir, *War in Heaven,* to narrating this event:

WITH THE LEADER

In January of the new year I enjoyed a visit from my ever-beloved Teacher, who gave comfort in these words, though they were not at the moment received in their deeper import: "Go home and be happy. Commit thy ways unto the Lord. Trust Him, and He will bring it to pass."

RENEWED MOTHERHOOD

Here this narrative approaches a crucial point. On the morning of June 11, 1890, there was born to me a baby boy; though, till his sharp birth-cry saluted my ears, I had not realized that prospective maternity was the interpretation of preceding months of poignant physical discomfort, not unreasonably attributed to other physiological causes and changes,—growing out of my age, and former reliance upon medical opinion,—pointing in the direction of some fungoid formation.

Even the doctor, contemplating our unpreparedness, could not help an exclamation of surprise; though not the mother absorbed his attention, but the child, with its wholesome beauty and serene atmosphere.

An hour after the birth I rose and bathed. In the afternoon I was up and dressed, and at night dined with my family. The next day I went out of doors, and every day thereafter, the resumption of customary good health leading me into the open air. We named our boy Prince Woodbury, partly because he came into our family as a veritable harbinger of peace.[10]

One has to admire this brilliant and delicate piece of self-justificatory rhetoric from a woman who had made a career out of advocating celibacy and yet found herself giving birth to a child, and probably an illegitimate child at that. The whole passage is written in a kind of code. The general public would understand Mrs. Woodbury to be writing one of the encomiums to the efficacy of Christian Science obstetrics so common in the *Christian Science Journal*. On the surface, the authoress seems to be describing the painless birth of an unusually beautiful and healthy child, and her own immediate return to full vigor and activity, after a difficult pregnancy still shadowed by the unfortunate effects of previous conventional medical theories and practice. "We named our boy," she says, "Prince Woodbury," and she leaves us to assume that the father is her husband, Frank Woodbury.

The initiate reading the same sections, on the other hand, by yoking together the apparently unrelated events of Mrs. Woodbury's visit to Mrs. Eddy and the birth of her son, would understand that Mrs. Woodbury was insinuating that the "it" which Mrs. Eddy had prophesied would be brought to pass by the Lord was an actual male child, and that, according to the Woodbury scenario, Mrs. Eddy was playing some combination of the Holy

Ghost and the Angel Gabriel. Mrs. Woodbury's comments on the beauty and serenity of her son could be read as either normal maternal pride or as intimations of the child's higher spiritual nature and Christlike mission as the "Prince of Peace."

We learn from the unpublished pretrial testimony in Mrs. Woodbury's libel suit against Mrs. Eddy that the circumstances surrounding Prince's birth were much more peculiar than *War in Heaven* would have us believe. Toward the end of her final stay in Montreal, Mrs. Woodbury and Henry Putnam had fallen out. She had received a letter from him while in Boston which informed her that he had just visited a "house of assignation," and soon thereafter Mrs. Woodbury was loudly denouncing him for his immoral ways, and being threatened by him in return. In a statement to her students in 1893, Mrs. Woodbury referred to Putnam as the one "through whom she entered hell" and "learned the fulness of Satan's claims."[11]

The evidence strongly indicates that Mrs. Woodbury believed that Putnam was the father of her child, and that she kept her pregnancy hidden for as long as she possibly could because she feared the stigma of an illegitimate child. There is an unconfirmed statement by one witness that Mrs. Woodbury told her that Prince was in utero for eleven months. Such a long pregnancy is unusual but not unprecedented, and it would put Prince's conception back to July 1889, the summer when Josephine and Putnam were indulging in "immoral conduct" before the amazed eyes of Mr. and Mrs. Bangs. To Mrs. Burns, Mrs. Woodbury confessed in August of 1890 that "in February the baby tried to come out and she was in mortal fear that it would be born then because, she said, that would be sure proof to the world that Putnam was the father of it." Perhaps for a few months, Woodbury refused to admit even to herself that she was pregnant again at forty (although it seems hard to imagine that she actually thought she was suffering from a "fungoid formation"!)—and she may have hoped to miscarry. Even her two closest women friends in Boston, Miss Roach and Mrs. Bangs, were not told of the pregnancy until days before the birth, and Mrs. Woodbury assured them too that she had been wholly unaware of her condition until that time.

When at last she was forced to acknowledge that she would soon give birth to a real child, she was in a quandary. The simplest solution would have been to immediately name her husband as the father. This is what she would do by late 1899. Frank never showed any unwillingness to call the child his own probably because he was sure he was the father: according to one witness, George Lansil, there was a strong likeness between Woodbury and Prince. Possibly Mrs. Woodbury had been sleeping with both her husband and her lover around the time of Prince's conception, and she herself was unsure about who the father was. She may have hesitated at first to assert Frank's paternity because she had made it widely known in the movement that she and Frank had not had sexual intercourse for eleven months or more, and Prince would have been, at best, inconveniently public proof that she had lied.

The story of her pregnancy Mrs. Woodbury actually circulated at the time of her delivery was extraordinary, a fascinating mixture of bold-faced lies and cynical manipulation, on the one hand, and crazy self-delusion, on the other. Prince, she claimed, was a second Christ, immaculately conceived of the Holy Ghost in the specific nineteenth-century American guise of Mary Baker Eddy and the revelation vouchsafed to her in *Science and Health*. Once she had got her general theme, Josephine Woodbury showed some creativity and a complete lack of Christian scruples in embroidering her story with details taken from the New Testament account of Jesus' birth. She told followers that she had not been aware of her condition until she received signs of some great impending event. One of her friends, providentially called *Elizabeth* Bangs, had come to her house and prophesied a coming, just as Saint Elizabeth had for the Virgin Mary before the birth of Christ. Mrs. Woodbury herself received portents, even a vision of wandering the land with a wondrous child in her arms—and then there was her visit to Mrs. Eddy's home, when the leader had spoken so prophetically of something to come.

The exact doctrinal explanation for her immaculate conception,[12] which Mrs. Woodbury expounded to her followers, went as follows. Mrs. Eddy had written in *Science and Health*, and told many students in class, that when humankind had reached a higher level of Christian Science, men and women would live together as angels, there would be no more carnal inter-course, and children would be born in the spirit alone. She alone, Josephine Woodbury, in solitary and glorious emulation of the Virgin Mary—whose name her parents had unaccountably failed to give her[13]—had soared over her peers and engendered a child of pure spirit, who must be worshipped as Jesus had been. Spiritually, Mrs. Woodbury claimed that she was generations ahead of everyone else and, indeed, higher than the Virgin Mary since she had known and triumphed over sin and sex.

After the birth, Mrs. Woodbury's closest disciples were summoned, first to Boston, then to her summer retreat at Ocean Point, Maine, so that, like the shepherds and wise men, they might greet the child and bring him gifts. The naked baby was exposed to view in a basket so that visitors could kneel before him, and after she had given him a bath, his mother encouraged two of her female friends to wash their faces in the dirty bathwater, using it as a kind of healing balm. They kneeled down and obeyed. Later, in a baptismal ceremony on the Maine seashore, Mrs. Woodbury plunged her child into a deep rock pool and held him submerged for several minutes. This event is lyrically described in her book, *War in Heaven*:

> While there [in Ocean Point] occurred the thought of baptising little
> Prince in a singularly beautiful salt pool, whose rocky bottom was dry

at low tide and overflowing at high tide, but especially attractive at mid-tide, with its two feet of crystal water. A crowd of people had assembled on the neighbouring bluffs, when I brought him from our cottage not far away, and laid him three times prayerfully in the pool and when he was lifted therefrom, they joined in a spontaneously appropriate hymn of praise.[14]

Mrs. Woodbury's devoted student Miss Carolyn (Carrie) Roach remembered the baptism a little differently:

In August of '90 she sent for me and several others of her students and Christian Science friends to come to Ocean Point where she and her family were spending the summer. One morning she read to us from Science and Health an account of a father's teaching his son to remain under water for several minutes. She took her child to the water's edge and possibly thirteen of us followed, and she proceeded to lay him in a pool of water, entirely submerged. He choked and struggled and then lay perfectly quiet for possibly a moment. When she took him out he gasped and regained his breath. She blamed us all very much that he made any manifestation of discomfort, saying that our fear for his life was entirely the cause of the child's failure to remain under water naturally.[15]

In the weeks and months following Prince's birth, Mrs. Woodbury assiduously talked up Prince's extraordinary powers and preternaturally swift progress, and her favor was meted out in direct proportion to a follower's financial generosity toward the child. Later, women followers confessed, with some embarrassment, to the Mother Church investigators that they had sold possessions and deprived themselves of small comforts in order to be able to give $5 or $10 for Prince. Such sublimely female self-sacrifice was gratifying, but it obviously could not pay all the Woodbury tribe's bills, especially when they moved from Dartmouth Street to a smarter address at 144 Newbury Street, conveniently located not far from Mrs. Eddy's property on Commonwealth Avenue. Josephine upped the financial ante by demanding that followers buy shares in an air-engine scheme which her husband had floated.

It was at this point that things started to go wrong. Sinking substantial amounts of money into a hairbrained scheme proved too much even for the select Woodbury coterie, or at least for the men among them. Credulity and fanaticism finally proved to have their limits, and Mrs. Woodbury became the target of several suits. Fred C. Chamberlain began a suit for the alienation of his wife's affection; Evelyn I. Rowe applied for divorce on the grounds of nonsupport, claiming her husband gave all his earnings to support Prince; and George Macomber and H. E. Jones made public their dissatisfaction with Frank Woodbury's air-engine company. When the Boston

Traveler published accounts of all these interesting doings, Mrs. Woodbury sued the paper for criminal libel, but she lost the case.

Meanwhile, how were Mrs. Eddy and The Mother Church reacting to Mrs. Woodbury's activities? The correspondence shows that from as early as the mid-1880s Mrs. Eddy viewed Josephine Woodbury as a major headache, the center of constant dissent and intrigue within the movement. In her letters to Mrs. Woodbury, Mrs. Eddy reproaches her pupil for her excessive ambition, for promoting ill feelings among other Scientists, for unsound teaching, problematic relations with students, weaknesses of the flesh, and, above all, lying. Mrs. Woodbury, for her part, denied little or nothing in her letters or her occasional meetings with Mrs. Eddy.[16] Her line was abject confession, fervent prostration before the superior spirituality of her Leader, desperate pleas for forgiveness, and passionate resolutions to henceforth sin no more. She also asserted that she was the unhappy object of mesmerism—an assertion she may well have actually believed. As we have seen, she had for some years been assuring her students that she herself could mentally cause illness and death and bring ruin down upon any individual or family who dared to leave her or oppose her, and she probably feared reciprocity of mental malpractice.

Mrs. Eddy has been condemned for her purple passages and flat-footed rhetoric, but she was a piker in comparison with her most notorious pupil. In fact, as far as I can determine from the letters I have seen, by the 1890s Mrs. Eddy in her private correspondence had become a terse, straightforward, and hardhitting prose stylist whom Mark Twain might have enjoyed reading. An extract from the Woodbury-Eddy correspondence may give some of the flavor of both writers:

> [Josephine C. Woodbury to Mary Baker Eddy, March 3, 1895] Do you know,—way off in that pure realm where you dwell, that the sharpest sting I feel,—is the awful sense of what your disappointment in me is? You say there is a promise of joy ahead if I will trust the dear Mother to guide me, and if I try to do right steadily, but can that Love prevent me from bearing this anguish of regret even to the end? . . . Even now when you know I ought to bear every pang and without complaint, you come with your soft wing and bear me up lest I fail utterly. You know I could not have borne rebuke better than this letting out of your love upon me.

> [Mary Baker Eddy to Josephine C. Woodbury, April 8, 1895] Now dear student try one year not to tell a single falsehood, or to practise one cheat, or to break the decalogue, and if you do this to the best of your ability at the end of the year God will give you a place in our church as sure as you are fit for it.[17]

Mrs. Woodbury pursued this line of dramatic confession and emotional self-condemnation in an interview she specially requested with Mrs. Eddy's faithful, and straitlaced, disciple Julia Bartlett, which Bartlett later remembered thus:

> She [Woodbury] said no one knew the terrible sins she had committed and that it seemed as though she were nothing but evil and that she sometimes said that she believed there was a personal devil and that she was that devil. She also said, at that time, that I had no idea of the number of people she had been the means of putting out of the cause of Christian Science. . . . She then said I did not know what a wicked woman she was and when she realized the enormity of her sins her agony was almost unbearable but fortunately these times did not last long. She repeatedly spoke of Mrs. Eddy's great love and how she had borne with her for so long. As she was going out the door she said she did not think one would make such a confession, as she had made to me, for the fun of it.[18]

Successful hypocrites, on some level, believe the fictions they are spinning, and for many years Josephine Woodbury probably did love and revere Mrs. Eddy and aspire to be like her. Mrs. Woodbury's fascination with Malicious Animal Magnetism also ran deep, in my view, and she may have truly feared Mrs. Eddy as the supreme magnetist—as it were casting Mrs. Eddy in the role of Richard Kennedy's teacher and most brilliantly successful rival. (Kennedy, it will be remembered, was both a legend in Christian Science as the epitome of mesmerism, and a real alternative therapist, practicing successfully on Tremont Street, several blocks from Mrs. Woodbury on Dartmouth Street, and from Mrs. Eddy's own house on Commonwealth Avenue, which by 1895 had become the home of the Reader of The Mother Church!) The theme of insanity runs through the lives of many early Christian Science adherents, and Mrs. Woodbury strikes me as more than a little mad at times, as evidenced by her interview with Julia Bartlett.

Critics of Mrs. Eddy from Milmine on have assumed that Mrs. Woodbury was the victim of Mrs. Eddy's envious and domineering nature, and that she was driven out of Christian Science by her leader, but the evidence points in quite the opposite direction. Although Mrs. Eddy was never as close to Mrs. Woodbury as the latter claimed, it is true that for more than ten years Mrs. Eddy closed her eyes to Josephine's faults wherever possible, and when forced to see unpleasant truths she was happy to have the sinner put on her rhetorical hair shirt and beg pardon. When Prince was born and some account of Mrs. Woodbury's doings in Maine reached Pleasant View, Mrs. Eddy was outraged, but, having secured the sinner's confession of fault and fervent promise to reform, she went against all her church's public policies on sexual morality and forgave even this. As I have noted on several earlier occasions, Mrs. Eddy was far from the Victorian prude critics have made her out to be, and sins of the flesh were something she had to condemn in public but readily forgave in private. This policy of forgiveness went against the advice of all her friends and advisors, and thus it is in fact Mrs. Eddy's forbearance that needs to be explained, not her alleged malice. Peel theorizes that Mrs. Woodbury's hypnotic powers were of the very highest—or lowest—kind, affecting even Mrs. Eddy, and it seems that Mrs. Eddy herself, at some particularly troubled moments, believed something of the kind. When, years later, the Woodbury crisis was at its height, Mrs. Eddy would at times severely chastise her watchers at Pleasant View for their inability to preserve her against the mental attacks of her enemy.

Other Christian Scientists, unsurprisingly, were far less lenient and far less subject to Mrs. Woodbury's charm than was their leader. Mrs. Woodbury was in trouble with the Mother Church authorities almost continuously from 1890 onward. In 1895 her application to become a member of the newly reconstituted church body was refused or tabled, on two occasions she was placed on probation, and then she conspicuously failed to comply with the terms. Nonetheless, she continued to attend church services and meetings, and, amazingly, it was not until the lawsuit revelations published in the Boston *Traveler* that the authorities of The Mother Church excommunicated Josephine Woodbury for good.

If it is astonishing how long Mrs. Eddy tolerated and supported Mrs. Woodbury, it is also odd, at first glance, that Mrs. Woodbury should have tried so hard to cement her association with a church association which she publicly disregarded, and which was so anxious to see her gone. My guess is that money was the real issue. Christian Science practice was starting to pay, and the movement's followers now had a long enough group memory for it to be plain that those who rebelled against Mrs. Eddy and tried to start up on their own did not prosper. Mrs. Woodbury certainly knew the sad story of Mrs. Plunkett, another woman who once had been a successful practitioner but had been brought low by an unfortunate love affair, and I see in Mrs. Woodbury's extraordinary rhetoric of self-abasement before Mrs. Eddy a clear indication that she feared that without Mrs. Eddy's favor she would be expelled and fall into oblivion and ruin.

Nonetheless, once it became absolutely clear that her expulsion from Christian Science was definitive and that she could no longer count on Mrs. Eddy rescuing her, Mrs. Woodbury moved energetically onto the offense. Richard Kennedy was a name she had long been quoting as the very devil incarnate, and now that the Church had officially pronounced her a devil, she knew where to find allies. She dug up all the old scandals from the Lynn years, reached out to the Christian Science rebels who were scattered over much of the country, and in Boston she made common cause with the Quimby faction, now under the leadership of Horatio W. Dresser.

When Kennedy and Wallace Wright had broken with Mrs. Eddy in the early 1870s their most effective weapons had been the double accusations that Mrs. Eddy used Malicious Animal Magnetism and that she owed all her main ideas and much of her actual text to P. P. Quimby. Josephine Woodbury now used both charges with a new efficacy. In 1899 Mrs. Woodbury co-authored with Horatio Dresser a two-part diatribe against Mrs. Eddy and Christian Science, published by *Arena*, a Boston magazine temporarily associated with New Thought. The article announcing " 'Eddyism' Exposed" sent shock waves through all of Christian Science.[19] While Dresser's essay, rehashing the so-called facts of Mrs. Eddy's unacknowledged debt to Quimby, was useful in keeping an old polemic alive, the real sensation was the second part by Mrs. Woodbury, in which she capitalized on her long experience within the movement.

Whereas she had as late as 1897 been fulsome in her published words of praise, and shrill in her protestations of loyalty, Mrs. Woodbury now denounced her former idol Mrs. Eddy as a mercenary, hypocritical tyrant, and Christian Scientists as a cowed, craven, and cretinous group, wholly under the sway of their Leader, incapable of independent thought or moral conduct. Seeing the need to explain why she had so long believed and striven so actively to promulgate this supposedly pernicious doctrine, Woodbury in her article has recourse to our old friend the doctrine of Malicious Animal Magnetism, of which she has much to say:

Faith in a leader being absolutely implicit, whether the leader be Joseph Smith, John Noyes, El Mahdi,[20] or Mary Eddy, any departure from the dictator's demands engenders a contagious fear, difficult to analyze. Reason loses its hold on the mind, logic and common sense go to flinders; and their prerogatives are usurped by a semi-hypnotic sub-consciousness easily influenced by an evil hint, which stultifies the intellect, and leads into baleful subservience. Mary Eddy has no use for people who think. Each grim suggestion in her interest, must infect her crowd of believers, among whom it spreads like wildfire. Those who differ from their teacher, through greater light as to her motives and history, are pronounced devil-possessed, and capable of producing contagious horrors, till the very thought terrifies the devout, and they think restraint, or even injury, to such a one, is service to God; especially if the error can be dealt with mentally, although the treatment involve gross bodily injury.

Here Mrs. Woodbury denounces exactly the kind of hold which she herself had wielded for some years over her small group of followers in Maine and in Montreal. Interestingly, as the last sentences of the quotation show, even as she denounces the horrors of mesmerism as practiced and theorized by Mrs. Eddy, Mrs. Woodbury shows that she still believes that "gross

bodily injury" can be caused mentally, and that a Christian Scientist, persuaded by his or her Leader that a certain person is "devil-possessed," can
harm an innocent person, *merely by thinking harm.*

Mrs. Woodbury concludes her article with a passage that has been much
quoted as a definitive indictment of Mary Baker Eddy:

> What [Mrs. Eddy] has really "discovered" are ways and means of per-
> verting and prostituting the science of healing to her own ecclesiastical
> aggrandizement, and to the moral and physical depravity of her dupes.
> As she received this science from Dr. Quimby, it meant simply the heal-
> ing of bodily ills through a lively reliance on the wholeness and order
> of the Infinite Mind as clearly perceived and practically demonstrated
> by a simple and modest love of one's kind. What she has "founded" is
> a commercial system monumental in its proportions, but already tot-
> tering to its fall.[21]

This vivid and expertly aimed diatribe shows that Josephine Woodbury
had some real talent for polemic, and one can imagine how effective she
might have been as a speaker. But it is not her style and oratory that have
impressed most commentators, but her status as victim. As one looks over
all the documents in the Woodbury affair, it is striking how kindly this fascinating but hardly admirable woman has been treated by the press, critics,
and historians. Since Mrs. Woodbury dared to attack Mrs. Eddy, and since
she supplied priceless ammunition for future attacks, critics from Milmine
onward have looked on her benevolently and even swallowed the story of her
immaculate conception. Cynics like Frederick Peabody, Edwin Dakin, and
Ernest Sullivan Bates skirt delicately around the issue of Prince's paternity.
They repeat all that Woodbury herself alleged about Mrs. Eddy's teaching
on possible virgin births, and about the effect of such teaching on vulnerable female minds such as her own. They refuse to acknowledge publicly what
in private they surely understood—namely, that Mrs. Woodbury must have
had sex with some man or other to produce Prince, that she believed the
child to be illegitimate, that, whatever the doctrinal beliefs of Christian
Science, she was certainly a liar and a hypocrite and an adulterer, and that to
blame Mrs. Eddy for what happened to her is, to say the least, a stretch!

In his book on Mrs. Eddy and Christian Science, Frederick Peabody
actually has the gall to assert Mrs. Woodbury's chastity:

> I make no defense of Mrs. Woodbury's absurdities when she was a
> Christian Scientist. She went the limit. Nothing could have exceeded
> her confidence in Mrs. Eddy's teachings and her zeal for the cause; but
> I am absolutely certain that there was nothing in the slightest degree jus-
> tifying the reflections upon her chastity.[22]

Dakin, wisely, does not claim that Mrs. Eddy and her followers were
wrong to accuse Mrs. Woodbury of adultery and bearing an illegitimate

child, but he still manages to make Mrs. Eddy out to be a villain by claiming that she was furious when Prince was born, since

> obviously, if anybody was going to achieve a virginal conception in this modern day and age, such a distinction should not come to a mere follower instead of the founder of the system by which such miraculous results could be achieved.

Ernest Bates must have found this sally much to his taste, because he reprises it in 1932:

> Mrs. Eddy failed to see the beauty of the virginal birth, the baptism, or the attendant publicity. It seemed to her most unfitting that a mere disciple should be vouchsafed a miracle that had never been granted to the Discoverer and Founder.[23]

After stressing Mrs. Eddy's three marriages, pointing accusingly at other relationships she had with men like Calvin Frye, insinuating not very subtly that even as a septuagenarian she greatly enjoyed the company of young men like Ebenezer Foster, all the biographers in the Milmine line are silent on Mrs. Woodbury's sexual proclivities and activities. That Mrs. Eddy accused Mrs. Woodbury in private letters of having an illegitimate child and then making up some absurd and blasphemous story to cover up her problem is presented as an expression of Mrs. Eddy's indelicacy, unkindness, and envy. That Mrs. Woodbury actually admitted to Mrs. Eddy that Prince was "incarnated with the devil" is ignored. Paranoia has been endemic in Christian Science since its inception, but given the "standard," "unbiased," "factual" accounts of Mrs. Woodbury which we owe to the largely mythical Georgine Milmine and her secret ghostwriter, Willa Cather, one can see why Christian Scientists have thought that people were out to get them.

Within two weeks of the appearance of his wife's *Arena* article, Frank Woodbury died, and all the parties to the now highly publicized falling out between Mrs. Eddy and Mrs. Woodbury interpreted the death as some kind of judgment, related in one way or another to Malicious Animal Magnetism. By this point, Mrs. Eddy had come to regard her former student not just with displeasure but with a peculiar horror and loathing. Stories were by this time reaching Pleasant View of how Mrs. Woodbury explicitly and repeatedly, for her own gain, had presented her son as a new and higher Christ and reenacted the gospel stories of the birth of Jesus. Some of the young unmarried women who had been close to Mrs. Woodbury were probably already telling shocked friends in the movement what they later told Mrs. Eddy's lawyers—namely that on at least one occasion, when discussing Sodom and Gomorrah, Mrs. Woodbury had graphically explained sodomy for their unwilling edification. In 1890s New England such things were not discussed among respectable women. On another occasion, Mrs. Woodbury had advised Miss Carrie Roach that if she would only let a man roll over her a few times, he would be her slave for life. The news would be out that Mrs. Woodbury had claimed to use Malicious Animal Magnetism to ruin the McTeer family, induce Mrs. Mary Roach to neglect her sick child and flee her dying father, and cause the madness and death of Miss Nash. Finally Mrs. Eddy accepted that she had been fooled—magnetized, as she saw it—and that Mrs. Woodbury was indeed diabolical.

I think that the best measure of Mrs. Eddy's revulsion and condemnation of what had been happening in her own movement, in her own name, was that she found it necessary to express it in the most public way available to her—in her Communion Message, which had by now become an annual event in the movement. Moved by uncontrollable emotion, just as she had been when she wrote the "Demonology" chapter of the third edition of *Science and Health,* in which she had denounced Kennedy, Wright, and Spofford, Mrs. Eddy allowed herself the luxury of declaring her outrage and condemnation of Mrs. Woodbury in public. The Message of June 1899 was read four times in the Mother Church, to packed and rapt audiences. It was an act Mrs. Eddy was to rue, and I imagine that her Church officials sat listening in their pews in silent dismay, anticipating trouble ahead.

As many another Christian preacher has done, Mrs. Eddy turned for her inspiration, and her rhetoric, to the Book of Revelation, and with apocalyptic fervor she denounced moral corruption in the name of "the Babylonish woman."

> This woman, "drunken with the blood of the saints, and with the blood of the martyrs of Jesus," "drunk with the wine of her fornication," would enter even the church,—the body of Christ, Truth; and, retaining the heart of the harlot and the purpose of the destroying angel, would pour wormwood into the waters—the disturbed human mind— to drown the strong swimmer struggling for the shore,—aiming for Truth,—and if possible, to poison such as drink of the living water. But the recording angel, standing with "right foot upon the sea, and his left foot on the earth," has in his hand a book open (ready to be read), which uncovers and kills this mystery of iniquity and interprets the mystery of godliness,—how the first is finished and the second is no longer a mystery or a miracle, but a marvel, casting out evil and healing the sick. And a voice was heard, saying "Come out of her my people" (Hearken not to her lies), "that ye receive not of her plagues. For her sins have reached unto heaven, and God hath remembered her iniquities . . . double unto her double according to her works: in the cup which she hath filled fill to her double . . . for she saith in her heart, I . . . am no widow. . . . Therefore shall her plagues come in one day, death, and mourning, and famine; . . . for strong is the Lord God who judgeth her." That which

the Revelator saw in spiritual vision will be accomplished. The Baby-lonish woman is fallen, and who should mourn over the widowhood of lust, of her that "is become the habitation of devils, and the hold of every foul spirit, and a cage of every unclean . . . bird"?[24]

Perhaps already regretting her words, and conscious that she had put weapons in the hand of the enemy, in the weeks following the reading of her annual message, Mrs. Eddy was unusually active in the public arena. For the first time since her retreat to New Hampshire she came to Boston for the Annual Meeting of the Church membership, held at the Tremont Temple, because by this time the Mother Church building was too small to hold all who wished to attend. On this occasion, Mrs. Eddy gave a calm and loving address, and the *Boston Globe* described her thus:

> She looked as she sat there the ideal of the gentle, kindly old lady, who had led an uneventful life and who was enjoying the peace and quiet of a conscience-clear old age. The lines of her face were soft, and there was nothing about her in repose to indicate the force of character and genius which she is credited with possessing.[25]

There are times in a woman's life, though not many, when looking old can be an advantage. Few will see a respectable-looking grandmother as either demon or genius or angel of the Apocalypse.

The Christian Science press campaign to counter Mrs. Woodbury's efforts to influence public opinion took other forms. After an article appeared in the Chicago *Inter Ocean* stating that Mary Baker Eddy was actually dead, a young *Boston Journal* reporter came to Pleasant View late in the evening, on the off chance that he would be able to get some crumb of information. Quite against his expectations, he was asked in and told that Mrs. Eddy was not in bed and would be happy to talk to him. Then Mrs. Eddy tripped down the stairs and smilingly invited him to decide on behalf of his readers whether or not she was dead. Forceful, focused, witty, she went on to describe in careful detail her daily routine of work and all the correspondence she had dealt with that day. It was another media tour de force by a seventy-seven-year-old woman known to her closest friends and associates to be under severe stress. But it was a very short-lived success.[26]

After she was stalemated in the press, and with the fiery rhetoric of her *Arena* article more than matched by Mrs. Eddy's Communion Message, Josephine Woodbury's next line of attack was in the courts, where on July 31, 1899, she brought a libel suit against Mary Baker Eddy and many of her senior officials. Mrs. Woodbury now had an attorney, Frederick Peabody, who sought to make up in daring, persistence, and flamboyance what he lacked in forensic skill and legal insight. From the beginning, Frederick Peabody seems to have nurtured a visceral dislike of Mary Baker Eddy that would only increase over time. A debt-plagued lawyer whose marriage had failed, Peabody saw in the Woodbury case an opportunity not only to redeem his fortunes by a lucrative win in court but to score a public relations victory over Christian Science. Over the next year and a half the Woodbury-Peabody duo were to be a thorn in Mrs. Eddy's flesh, and the most pressing issue faced by her church administration. The October 4, 1899, edition of the Boston *Post* reported that "one of the most extraordinary legal papers ever filed in a lawsuit has just been filed in the clerk's office of the Superior Court of this city." Mrs. Woodbury's declaration, as scripted by her lawyer, was fifteen thousand words long and contained thirty-seven counts. The Boston *Post* needed almost a whole page, three and a half full columns in tiny print, to quote the greater part of it.

Over the next twenty-five years Frederick Peabody was to have an immense influence on Mrs. Eddy's life and reputation, and to understand his actions, a little background is necessary.[27] From 1899 to the late 1920s, Peabody managed in one way or another to keep his name before the Boston newspapers, and later the national press, and thus press clippings in particular offer a fascinating set of isolated highlights in the life of a man who apparently thrived on sensation and controversy.

Born in Brooklyn, New York, in 1862, Frederick Peabody was not related to the famous Peabody sisters and hence unconnected by birth to the world of the Boston literati. He attended the New York Polytechnic Institute and then Columbia University, taking his degree in law in 1888, was admitted to the New York bar, but then, for reasons unknown, moved to Boston. There "he was generally believed to be a man of considerable means and was a member of several Boston clubs."[28] In 1894 Frederick married Anna G. May, the daughter of a prominent New England family. Louisa May Alcott, whose mother was born a May, had given Anna's maiden name some fame. At least one of Anna's uncles was a judge, and her sister married an Eliot.[29] In later Boston press accounts, Mrs. Anna May Peabody is described as a feminist or even "the prominent suffragist." The word *feminist* apparently had some of the negative connotations it has today, since in 1912 someone close to Mrs. Peabody felt the need to defend her reputation by writing to the editor of the Boston *Post* to protest an article that had appeared in the *Post* describing Mrs. Peabody as a feminist.[30]

Anna May was one of the many women who have married for love and lived to regret it (I detect a touch of the Isabel Archer in her). Frederick, too, may have been in love when they married, but it seems clear that Anna's small personal fortune and good social connections were at least as important to him as were her personal charms, and that the two were radically unsuited for one another. From the beginning, the marriage was fraught with problems, and, according to subsequent court testimony, Frederick Peabody deceived his fiancée and her family as to his financial circumstances. To quote of Judge Almy's decision in a 1912 libel case brought by Peabody against his divorced wife:

> Before they were married he borrowed a considerable sum from her to pay his debts and did not pay them at all; he borrowed from her money given to her as a wedding present to pay the cost of the wedding journey; he made an assignment to his wife as a security for a loan of his interest in her father's estate and after the separation collected his share himself, claiming the assignment to be invalid legally, which I [Judge Almy] do not find to be the case, and that her refusal to live in his house relieved him from any moral liability.

Not content with deceiving his new wife and stealing her money, Peabody also verbally abused her. Again to quote from Judge Almy's decision in favor of Mrs. Peabody in 1912:

> During this marriage the libellant [Frederick Peabody] was critical of the dress, appearance and housekeeping of his wife, to herself and to others in her presence; of a temper easily aroused, but which delayed expression until fully developed, when it found vent in unkind and brutal words to his wife and to others concerning her.[31]

The Peabodys had two daughters, Mary and Helen, born in 1896 and 1898, but by 1901 Mrs. Peabody had left her husband and taken the children with her, unable to bear the humiliation of living in debt.[32] According to later court testimony, although Anna always paid the living expenses for herself and the children, and although her father constantly lent Frederick small sums to cover his office rental and expenses, Peabody continued to live in a style he could not afford and to contract debts that threatened the family's good name and security. Again to quote Judge Almy's decision: "The libellant [Frederick Peabody] is a man who cares much for externals, of very loose financial habits, borrowing when he had no reasonable prospects of repaying, spending money which he ought to save or apply to his debts and to his family."[33]

Peabody was outraged when his wife left him, and when she proved able to support the children and herself on her own earnings and family resources. Between 1901 and 1908 Peabody three times took his wife to court and personally cross-examined her in the witness box, in what was then classed as a libel suit, claiming that he should be given a divorce on the grounds of her having deserted him. The first two suits seem to have been aimed at getting his wife back, rather than legalizing their separation, and they were obviously a source of deep embarrassment and worry to a woman whose social and financial position was delicate. Twice Peabody managed to prevail upon his wife to move back in with him, telling her and the court that he was now in a position to support them, had rented a house, hired a housekeeper, and so forth, but he was never able to make good on his promises. In 1905 Peabody was arrested for larceny, and the amount of bail was $2,500. He begged his wife to stand bail for him, which she did, but after he was acquitted of the charge and she wrote to congratulate him on his freedom, he replied only with bitter reproaches.

In 1908 he finally gained a decree nisi and was granted liberal visiting rights to his children. Ever successful in persuading other men that he was fundamentally a very good fellow, Peabody got a remarkably favorable report on his divorce published in the Boston *Post* on January 31, 1908. Here there is no mention of Peabody's debts or his inability to support his family, only of Peabody's unbroken adoration of his wife—and of her suffragist persuasions:

> To love a woman and wish to forsake her; to seek legal separation from a wife and still esteem her above all other women—that is the romantic and remarkable situation of Frederick W. Peabody, the Boston attorney whose years-long fight with Mrs. Mary Baker G. Eddy and Christian Science has made him famous.

> After three times bringing suit for absolute divorce from Anna May Peabody, the prominent woman suffragist, and a Radcliffe graduate, and twice dropping proceedings because their mutual love has brought them together again, Mr. Peabody has been awarded a decree nisi.

> Each time the attorney conducted his own case, even to cross-examining his wife when on the witness stand. And yesterday the proceedings being finished and he a free man once more, Mr. Peabody said to a Post reporter: "There is no woman in the world whom I love and respect more than the woman from whom I have been divorced. As the mother of my children I esteem her above all other women."

Despite such assertions, by 1912 Peabody had remarried and become the father of two small boys. But in the same year that his second son was born, Peabody applied to the court for increased visiting rights to the children of his first marriage. Anna resisted the petition, apparently unwilling to allow her daughters, now fifteen and thirteen, to spend the night at their father's home. Judge Almy, who heard the case, gave a crushing indictment of Peabody's faults (cited earlier in the chapter), summarizing the evidence given in the previous divorce applications, as well as testimony from current witnesses, and disallowed Peabody's request.

Perhaps this final failure in court and unequivocal public indictment of his behavior as husband and father broke not Peabody's morale, which was armor plated, but his credit. In September the Boston *Post* was reporting that Frederick Peabody, his charming young second wife, their small son and newborn baby, had packed up their belongings in a van and moved away in the night, perhaps toward the West, without informing their landlord, or, presumably, paying their bills.[34]

With these facts in mind, let us return to 1899 and the declaration of libel that Peabody filed on behalf of Mrs. Josephine Woodbury. The heart of the declaration was the accusation that the "Babylonish woman" section of Mrs. Eddy's June 1899 Communion Message referred directly to Mrs. Woodbury and constituted gross libel, for which the plaintiff requested damages of $150,000. Peabody's swift legal action, his decision to file six separate suits in both New Hampshire and Massachusetts and to name not only Mrs. Eddy personally but also the Board of Directors and the Trustees of the Publishing Society and three other Church officials struck fear into many hearts at The Mother Church as well as at Pleasant View. At first glance, Mrs. Woodbury seemed to have a good case. The dispute between herself and Mrs. Eddy had been widely publicized in the press since 1897, and it was well known what ripples had spread through the whole mental healing and alternative medicine community as a result of Mrs. Woodbury's *Arena* article. Mrs. Woodbury was not alone in interpreting Mrs. Eddy's Communion Message as the latest salvo in the Eddy-Woodbury struggle, and, although texts inspired by the Book of Revelation are proverbially hard to interpret, some of the things Mrs. Eddy had written, notably the reference to the "widow," seemed, indeed, to indicate that she had the recently bereaved Mrs. Woodbury in mind.

Peabody had two aims in the Woodbury suit—to earn money and to win a resounding success in the public arena—aims which probably coincided with his client's immediate desire for revenge but proved not to be in her ultimate interests. Both Peabody and Woodbury were forever in need of money, and by 1899, as we have seen, Peabody had spent all his wife's fortune and exhausted his father-in-law's goodwill, and the debts were still piling up. To defeat Mrs. Eddy in court would bring him a large fee and help him win new clients, but in his defense of Mrs. Woodbury's good name Peabody seems to have been moved as much by ideology as by financial difficulties. He aimed to bring Mrs. Eddy down and fatally sabotage her movement. He therefore decided that the suit should be argued on the broadest possible grounds, offering not just charges of a specific case of libel, but a sweeping indictment of Christian Science and of Mrs. Eddy's whole career as a religious leader. As a lawyer, Peabody's mandate was plain—to prove that Mrs. Eddy had said certain things, that they related to his client and were generally understood to do so, and that what Mrs. Eddy had said was both false and detrimental to his client. As a defender of virtue and reason and public health, he wanted Mrs. Eddy flayed in the eyes of the world.

The first count of the 1899 legal declaration Peabody filed in Boston states that his client Mrs. Woodbury "says that she is and always has been a person of chaste life and conversation."[35] As a lawyer, of course, Peabody had to presume his client innocent, but I doubt that he actually believed that she was chaste.[36] Certainly, Mrs. Woodbury was a very charming and persuasive lady, and by the time Peabody came on the scene, she had renounced her claims to have achieved the stage in spiritual development when parthenogenesis was possible, preferring the story that she had been mesmerized by Mrs. Eddy's doctrines and that Prince was the fruit of her legal union with her husband. But Peabody was a Boston clubman who prided himself on being a man of the world, and it is hard to imagine that he did not know exactly what kind of woman he was dealing with.[37]

Following on his analysis that the weight of his case could be understood only by indicting Christian Science as a whole, Peabody, in the libel declaration he wrote for his client, does not get to the events of June 4, 1899, until the fifteenth count. Only in the sixteenth does he finally state that on that day Mrs. Eddy intended and strove, "revengefully and cruelly" "to injure . . . and to bring the plaintiff into public contempt, infamy, and disgrace, to forever ruin her . . . good name and reputation, and to utterly destroy the plaintiff's influence with all good people and to cause the plaintiff to become a social outcast." Clauses 2–14 of the document consist of a lengthy indictment of Christian Science and Mrs. Eddy. Following are some representative sections, as reported by the Boston *Post* on October 4, 1899, which provided the most detailed coverage of the Woodbury affair and seems most hostile to Mrs. Eddy:

> II. And the plaintiff further says that the defendant, Mary Baker G. Eddy, claims to be the discoverer of an alleged science, or religion, which she has named Christian Science, and that the alleged discovery of said alleged science, or religion, was due to her selection by God as the medium, or instrument, through which God should reveal himself and his nature, and man's relation to him . . .
>
> III. That the defendant further claims that in her person and life she is the fulfilment, or realization, of the biblical prophecy, or vision, contained in the Holy Bible in the twelfth chapter of the Book of Revelations [lengthy quote] . . .
>
> VI. That the defendant further claims and teaches in her said book . . . that she . . . is the equal of Jesus Christ; that she is possessed of all the powers said to have been possessed by Jesus Christ, and in her own person and to this age is, and ought to be considered, what Jesus Christ was to his age; that she is the feminine manifestation of the qualities, attributes and powers of divinity, just as Jesus Christ was the masculine manifestation of the qualities, attributes and powers of the divinity, that she has completed the alleged incomplete mission and work of Jesus Christ

by discovering his principle for healing and treating disease . . . and that she has had and has now the power to heal the sick, raise the dead, cleanse the leper and cast out devils; and that defendant . . . teaches . . . that masculinity, as such, is not an essential factor to the process of human reproduction, which may or will occur through and be caused by mental effort—that is to say, that human generation is independent of sex and may, and ultimately will, be caused by mind alone and that defendant claims to be possessed of the power by mental effort alone to cause and to destroy human conception.

VII. [Further] that the defendant also claims that sickness, suffering and death of another human being [may be caused] by mental effort.

X. [Further that] many thousands of good people within this Commonwealth and within the United States . . . believe implicitly in each and all of the aforesaid extraordinary claims of the defendant . . . [and so believe] . . . the defendant to be a most extraordinary and most exceptional and most superior being; that opposition to defendant . . . is opposition to Almighty God, and that death and destruction will and should overtake all who oppose . . . her . . . and all of this greatly to the increase of the defendant's power to injure the plaintiff as hereinafter set forth and to the enhancement of the plaintiff's damages.

Moving at last in Clause 15 to June 4 when, allegedly, the plaintiff was injured by the defendant, Peabody notes that until 1896 his client had been a loyal member of Mrs. Eddy's church, but that she was then excommunicated, without any reason or any hearing, simply as a result of Mrs. Eddy's jealousy and ill will. The declaration continues that, following her excommunication, the plaintiff came to her senses, rejected Christian Science, and then, "calmly and without malice," denounced her former error and her leader's faults in an article published in the *Arena* magazine. About three weeks after the sudden death of the plaintiff's husband, Frank Woodbury— who is described movingly in the declaration as Josephine's friend, counselor, and protector for twenty-five years—the defendant, Mrs. Eddy, caused to have read in the hearing of thousands a message which defamed her former disciple. Building on her own alleged identification with the woman crowned with twelve stars of Revelation, Mrs. Eddy libeled and condemned the plaintiff as the "Babylonish woman," "drunken with the blood of saints," "with the heart of the harlot," and so forth (lengthy quotations from Revelation).

As one reads the declaration, one can feel Peabody's pleasure in his own eloquence as well as the intensity of his animus toward the founder of Christian Science. Sections 6 and 10 of Peabody's declaration in particular indicate how specifically his hatred and contempt for Christian Science was based on the fact that the movement was founded and led by a woman. It is simply aberrant, in Peabody's view, that a woman should set up a church

institution which empowered her at will to promote or demote her male officers. Here Peabody's male hormones are speaking, not his brain. Worse, Mrs.
Eddy teaches that "masculinity, as such, is not an essential factor to the
process of human reproduction" and she prophesies the time when "human
generation is independent of sex." Despite his insistence that men must
always play a part in conception, Peabody simultaneously accepts as fact
Mrs. Woodbury's absurd and self-serving claims that "Prince" was quite literally the child of Mrs. Eddy's doctrine—her mental offspring—and never
stops to question whether Mrs. Eddy ever actually taught what Mrs. Woodbury says she taught.

Peabody was supremely confident that he would win his case, and it was
his certainty of not only being clever but being right that brought him down.
As all his subsequent polemics prove, Frederick Peabody was a deeply ideological man who opposed everything Christian Science stood for, but in the
very force of his convictions lay his failure. As I see it, Peabody assumed that
against so ignoble an enemy as Mary Baker Eddy, a man could afford to be
intellectually lazy and was obliged to fight dirty. Then to his amazement, he
found that the enemy could win the fight he had engaged by using the
weapons of evidence, logic, and due process of law which he himself had laid
down as useless. In my discussion of the Next Friends suit of 1907–1908 in
Part Four I shall show that this is a pattern that was to be repeated over and
over again by many of the talented and well-educated men, most notably
William Chandler, whose deep and principled commitment to Enlightenment values led them to oppose Christian Science.

Confronted by the amazing document Peabody had prepared, the judge
appointed to hear the case may well have been fascinated, even convinced
by Peabody's rhetoric, but as a lawyer he was unimpressed. Even if everything Peabody alleged in counts 2–14 were true, none of it was *illegal*. People
in the United States of America had the freedom to think and believe as they
chose, as long as they obeyed the law. To attack a religious group for its doctrines or a religious leader for his or her teachings was deeply unpopular in
American society and deeply reproved in American jurisprudence. By arguing his case on so wide a basis, Peabody fatally weakened it, and he also gave
his opponents a tactical edge which they were well positioned to exploit.

By this point in her career, Mary Baker Eddy was no longer having to
sweep her own stairs to pay her legal bills or use crazy amateurs with poor
English skills like Edward Arens to argue her case in court. The lawyers she
now engaged to act for her—Samuel Elder and William Morse[38] in Massachusetts and Frank Streeter in New Hampshire—were the best in the field,
and they were quickly able to persuade the court that the first sixteen parts
of Peabody's document should be struck out. When Peabody went ahead
and had the text of his declaration published in the Boston *Post* anyway,
when he and his client gave interviews on the case to other newspapers,

notably the New York *World*, Mrs. Eddy's lawyers moved successfully to have Mrs. Woodbury found guilty of contempt of court and fined $50. As the slow wheels of justice worked on motions and demurrers and counter-motions, members of Mrs. Eddy's counsel were working furiously behind the scenes to prepare their defense.

Mrs. Eddy's defense would consist of two parts. First, her lawyers gathered a mass of affidavits and written statements from followers of Mrs. Woodbury to counter Mrs. Woodbury's leading assertion that she was "a person of chaste life and conversation." There were more than twenty people who had known Mrs. Woodbury intimately over many years and who would testify to the untruth of this statement. Despite the overwhelming evidence they prepared on Mrs. Woodbury's amoral behavior, the Eddy counsel hoped fervently that it would never need to be heard in a court of law. The inevitable press sensation and resulting public outrage about Mrs. Woodbury's dalliance with her fellow student Putnam, her illegitimate child, and, above all, her blasphemous performance as the Virgin Mary would bring down Josephine Woodbury, but it would also drag Mrs. Eddy and the whole of Christian Science into the mud.

The second, more promising but also less principled line followed by the defense was to make it hard for the Woodbury side to prove that Mrs. Eddy was referring to Mrs. Woodbury in her Communion Message.[39] Here time was on their side. Mrs. Woodbury's name had never been uttered in Mrs. Eddy's message, and, as the months went on and news of Mrs. Woodbury's doings leaked out, support for Mrs. Eddy grew ever stronger. It became increasingly difficult for Peabody to find anyone who had heard Mrs. Eddy's message read out who would admit that he or she had identified Mrs. Woodbury as the Babylonish woman.

As it turned out, Mrs. Eddy's legal team triumphed easily in court; the judge dismissed the suit at the end of the first week without hearing any of Mrs. Eddy's witnesses. Edward Kimball, who had been precipitated to the top of the Christian Science hierarchy during the time leading up to the Woodbury suit, wrote to Mrs. Eddy:

> Only one like myself who is on the inside of the whole history can understand how thoroughly Peabody was beaten yesterday on the generalship of the case. All of his hopes and threats to the effect that they would expose Christian Science and reveal its unfavorable workings, were utterly shattered yesterday because the court ruled over and over again that all of those outside matters had no relation to the issue in hand at all. Peabody was in a state of almost complete discomfiture.[40]

In the end, Peabody could find only two witnesses to support his contention that it was generally understood by those present at the Communion service that Mrs. Eddy in her message was referring to Mrs. Woodbury when she talked of the Babylonish woman. One of these two, William Nixon, was a less than creditable witness because he had left The Mother Church in a storm of controversy and under a financial cloud, and he was known to be one of Mrs. Eddy's most violent opponents. Mrs. Clara Choate, the second witness, was also well known to have fallen out with Mrs. Eddy, and her own personal reputation for spotless virtue was less than established. Under oath she weakened her evidence by telling the court that what she had remarked on June 4, when leaving The Mother Church, was not that Mrs. Eddy had been referring to Mrs. Woodbury, but that, *if* indeed it was Mrs. Woodbury to whom Mrs. Eddy had been referring, she felt sorry for her.

In retrospect, it seems obvious that Elder, Morse, and Streeter had shown superior understanding of the law and pursued an excellent strategy. But in the long months that preceded the 1901 hearing, there was no certainty of victory in the Eddy camp. Dissension and confusion racked the Christian Science defendants and threatened a new split in the movement. Mrs. Eddy was at the heart of the whole long struggle, both as the person most directly targeted in the suit and as the leader of the team by reason of her authority in the church. Mrs. Eddy saw Woodbury as a threat to all she had achieved, as an indictment of her leadership, as the epitome of all she feared and combatted. For years Mrs. Eddy had been striving in her everyday life as much as in her teaching to lessen her movement's preoccupation with Malicious Animal Magnetism, to define it as a nonreality which has power only insofar as one believed in it. Now mesmerism rose again in its old avatar of personal mental attack. At night Mrs. Eddy felt the fear of Mrs. Woodbury's hatred in her body, and she and her advisors feared she might even die from the strain.

Joined to this personal agon were the public problems of defending her authority as leader and finding the correct strategy to defeat Woodbury and Peabody unequivocally in a court of law and in the eyes of the world. According to Robert Peel, Mrs. Eddy had to fight constantly with her own advisors and her lawyers and even order them point-blank to do things her way. Judge Septimus Hanna, one of Mrs. Eddy's most loyal and trusted associates, was at first put in charge of the defense, and he became the target of Mrs. Eddy's wrath when things seemed to be going badly. While Hanna was laid low in mind and body by the torrent of Mrs. Eddy's criticisms, the other men looked on, horrified that their leader should act more like a virago than an angel, and that she should seem so quick to forget all the services her officials had loyally rendered her in the past.

Both Mary Baker Eddy herself and her male associates were aware that in acting the harridan she was exemplifying one of the main charges levied against her by Peabody in his declaration. Crazy with sleeplessness and pain, the victim of paroxysms of fear for herself and her movement, lashing out constantly with what often seemed and sometimes were irrational accusations of disloyalty and condemnations of incompetence, Mary Baker Eddy appeared to her advisors the personification of female illogic. Their fear was personal and financial as well as ideological. They feared not only that she would lose the case, but that her loss would inevitably entail their loss in the parallel suits Peabody had brought against them. Under Mrs. Eddy's By-Laws as laid out in the *Manual of The Mother Church*, the directors and trustees could be held personally responsible for damages brought against them. Many of them thought she had mishandled the Woodbury affair from the beginning, that her Communion speech was feminine spite, not church strategy, and they seriously considered resigning. Mrs. Eddy gave some sense of her feelings in a letter to Judge Ewing:

> O that you had been here. I felt so alone. Judge H [Hanna], Mr. A [Armstrong] and Mr. J [William B. Johnson] sat with the lawyers in my room hours—the latter cutting my heart out, the former <u>speechless</u>. I felt as if I were in the presence of headsmen waiting to take me to the scaffold. Why O why are the declining years of a life like mine so haunted hounded soulless unpitied. God only knows![41]

Yet, in the end, the conclusion of the Woodbury suit was a public triumph and a private affirmation for Mrs. Eddy. If Peel is to be believed, time and again Mrs. Eddy proved to be in the right in her analysis of the case and of what step should be taken next, and her lawyers were forced to acknowledge as much and tip their hats to her. From that mixture of native wit, long experience with the issues, and deep understanding of the people opposing her which is too often dismissed as mere "woman's intuition," her sense of the case proved to be sound, and the strategy she insisted upon proved to be the right one.[42] But the fight had been long and hard, the hardest so far in the life of one accustomed to difficulty, and it left Mrs. Eddy exhausted and longing above all for peace. Mrs. Woodbury, for her part, left Boston with her family, then moved to England, and ended her life in France.[43]

Frederick Peabody was left on the scene. The end of the trial found him howling in impotent rage and protest, but he quickly channelled his bitterness into activity, turning all the inside knowledge of Christian Science which he had acquired into a meal ticket. Over the next ten years, he became the most violent, the most determined, the most quotable opponent of Christian Science and Mrs. Eddy, lecturing to large groups of doctors and lawyers and clergymen all over the country, and following up his speeches with his pamphlet, *Complete Exposure of Eddyism or Christian Science: The Plain Truth in Plain Terms Regarding Mary Baker G. Eddy*. This twenty-five-cent pamphlet was first issued soon after Peabody gave a highly successful address at the Tremont Temple on August 1, 1901; it was enlarged and reissued in 1904 and then reissued again in 1906. Peabody's most famous work, *The Religio-Medical Masquerade: A Complete Exposure of Christian Science*, a further enlargement and revision of his pamphlet, was first published in 1910 and reissued in 1915. In his final salvo against the church, in 1925 Peabody collaborated with psychology professor Woodbridge Riley and Professor of Surgery Charles E. Humiston on *The Faith, the Falsity and the Failure of Christian Science*. In this volume most of Peabody's old accusations against Mrs. Eddy were gratifyingly taken up and given intellectual authority by his academic collaborators, and Peabody himself was able to publish new material he had gained from ex-director of the Church John Dittemore, on the sins and failings of the current members of the Board of Directors, most especially Adam Dickey.[44]

From the press clippings I have seen, it is clear that at least for a few years Peabody had a lot of success on the lecture circuit, and audiences of several thousand people listened with appreciation to his denunciations of Mrs. Eddy and her Science. Although he had signally failed to make his case in a court of law, Peabody based his authority as a lecturer on his expertise as a trained lawyer and upon the privileged knowledge he had gained as Mrs. Woodbury's attorney. He claimed "to tell the plain truth in the plainest of terms" and to have based his work on ten years of research and sound legal principles, and for a long time his assertions were accepted as statements of fact by even discerning audiences and readers. Reviewing his book, the *New York Times* critic said what many felt at the time: "Either Mr. Peabody is the most shameless of calumniators or Mrs. Eddy is the basest of charlatans."[45]

It is interesting to read all of Peabody's work in chronological order and to see how his mind worked. From the beginning he is on exceptionally shaky factual ground when discussing Mrs. Eddy's first fifty years, since none of his early informants had known her during that time. Peabody works hard to show that everything Mrs. Eddy wrote about herself in her little memoir *Retrospection and Introspection* was untrue or misleading, but, ironically, almost every fact about her childhood and youth which he gives the reader is wrong. Mary Baker was not brought up in poverty; she was given a reasonably good education for her sex and generation, and she in fact studied at a highly reputed lady's academy in Tilton. Neither her husband nor her eldest brother was a mere "bricklayer"; her first husband was not laid in the Potter's Field; her second husband Patterson was not a Harvard graduate and did not enlist in the Union army; she did not divorce him while he was a prisoner of war. She did not work in Boston for many years as a Spiritualist, and so forth and so on.

As Peabody continued his lecturing and writing, however, as he became known as a focus of opposition to Christian Science, information began to flow his way, and people from Mrs. Eddy's past began to contact him with their stories. Peabody tells us in the introduction to *The Religio-Medical*

Masquerade that after the Woodbury trial the Reverend Minot J. Savage, an ally of Horatio Dresser and the Quimbyites, hired him to investigate Mrs. Eddy and take signed affidavits. Through Mrs. Woodbury, Peabody had learned about the Dressers, Arens, Kennedy, Clara Choate, William Nixon, and Ebenezer Foster Eddy. It is also possible that Peabody knew James Henry Wiggin from his club connections, and that it was Wiggin who introduced Peabody to Mrs. Woodbury in the first place, rather than the reverse.[46] Later other people from Mrs. Eddy's past began to surface, people with an old score to settle like Hannah Sanborn Philbrook, Sarah Crosby, Miranda Rice, Daniel Spofford, and Horace Wentworth.

With the interviews, affidavits, and the documentary evidence provided by these people, Peabody was able to mount a persuasive indictment of Mrs. Eddy which I would put under nine main counts: (1) From childhood she was a hysteric, prone to the kinds of fits described in the annals of medicine, and using her condition to manipulate those around her. (2) From childhood she had taken morphine for her various mental and physical ills, and she had become an addict by her middle years. (3) She had received almost no formal education, came from a poor, uncultured background, and was barely literate. (4) She was a Spiritualist and had even earned her living as a medium. (5) She had taken all her essential ideas from Dr. P. P. Quimby, the man who had healed her, and important sections of her early written work were copied directly from sections of Quimby's unpublished work. (6) She had an abnormal interest in sex, which she sought to conceal under a hypocritical emphasis on chastity. (7) She had no genuine religious feeling and sought only money and power. (8) She was devoid of all maternal feeling, having abandoned her only child, George Glover. (9) Under her pernicious doctrine, thousands of innocent children died in agony every year, before the very eyes of their deluded mothers.

To give some sense of Peabody's style, following are quotations of a few odd sections from what could be called his masterpiece or final statement— *The Religio-Medical Masquerade*:

> [From the introduction] The founder of this pretended religion, this bogus healing system, audaciously and irreligiously professing equality of character and power with Jesus, has, throughout her whole long life, been in every particular precisely antithetical to Christ. Sordid, mercenary, unprincipled, the consuming passion of her life has been the accumulation of money.

> I am going to hold up for the inspection of mankind the soul of a woman, of a woman eighty-eight years of age, and I am going to do it without regard to the fact that she is feminine and aged. There is no other way to present Christian Science in its true aspect. It rests exclu-

sively upon Mrs. Eddy's representations and Mrs. Eddy's character. . . . It is, notwithstanding, distasteful to a man, if he be half a man, publicly to assail the character of a woman. . . .

Mrs. Eddy has succeeded, not because of her greatness, but because of the avidity with which unreasoning people swallow the most monstrous absurdities. . . .

Mrs. Eddy does not believe in marriage—for others. . . . But in so far as she herself was concerned, it cannot be denied that she seems to have had a distinct fancy for marriage, and I may go so far as to say something approaching fondness for variety in the marriage state.

How sweet, how *charming*, is the wifely devotion, that, kissing the lips of death, speedily and forever loses track of the sacred ashes of the beloved *first* husband, rushes into the divorce court for freedom from the truant *second*, and, having twice restored the adored *third* to life, when a third time he thus eludes her refuses, positively and coldly refuses, to bring him back and looks with calm and critical eyes upon the formerly attached, but, now, alas, detached heart!

My purpose in showing Dr. Quimby's authorship of Mrs. Eddy's Christian Science is to establish the falsity of her claim that God revealed it to her. The thing itself, as Dr. Quimby's, is of no greater weight and of no more consequence than as Mrs. Eddy's. Dr. Quimby and Mrs. Eddy were evidently upon the same intellectual plane, both uneducated and crude. He was a good and sincere and unselfish and trustful man, and she appropriated his ideas.

It would seem like a waste of time to contend that God is not the author of "Science and Health;" . . . that of all the personalities who have lived on this earth since the time of Jesus, the one selected by God to lead the world unto Him should be this uncultivated and vulgar woman, whose variegated career has been somewhat presented.[47]

By 1907 Peabody's lectures and pamphlets lambasting Christian Science were no longer in demand, but with the launching of the Next Friends suit by Senator William Chandler there came a new and glorious chance for Peabody to make some money, use his legal and investigative talents, and get his revenge on Mary Baker Eddy. But the Next Friends suit failed, leading to a strong public reaction in favor of Mrs. Eddy, and Peabody's brand of ad feminam attack came to seem in bad taste. Although Peabody had certainly been able to make money by attacking Christian Science, he was never able to make a fortune, or even a successful career as a lawyer, and he faded from the picture from this point.[48]

Of far greater importance than his own actual work was the influence Peabody had on other writers and publications. From 1899 to at least 1909

Peabody was the chief conduit of information, or misinformation, about Mrs. Eddy. Having discovered the Wentworth manuscript and interviewed Mrs. Crosby, in 1904 he successfully recycled the accusation that Mrs. Eddy had plagiarized Quimby, managing to persuade the *New York Times* to publish his material, allegedly comparing two texts by Quimby and Mrs. Eddy—but without mentioning his name.[49] After James Henry Wiggin died, Peabody helped spread the report that Wiggin was the man who had actually written *Science and Health*, again acting as an anonymous conduit between Wiggin's friend Livingston Wright and the New York *World*. Around 1906–1907 Peabody was especially busy corresponding with Lyman Powell, Georgine Milmine, and then Willa Cather, who for a time rented rooms literally around the corner from Peabody's office. Powell's book came out in 1907 and was heavily critical of Mrs. Eddy and Christian Science, regurgitating many of Peabody's "facts" and making most of the points Peabody had made in his pamphlets, although in somewhat more measured terms. When the *McClure's* biography of Mrs. Eddy appeared, many of the most obvious factual inaccuracies had been weeded out by the magazine's investigative team, but nonetheless Peabody's basic analyses and responses were repeated. Most gratifyingly of all, Samuel Clemens, alias Mark Twain, corresponded with Peabody, read his pamphlets, and was supplied with documentation that was damaging to Mrs. Eddy. Peabody could not dictate to his world-famous new correspondent, but he could influence him, if only because the two men had had problems with wives and daughters and had suffered financial reversals. The result of the Peabody-Clemens correspondence was the most famous collection of essays on Mary Baker Eddy and her religion that has ever been written.

24

Mark Twain
Fails to Come
Calling

MARY BAKER EDDY CELEBRATED HER SEVENTY-FIRST
birthday soon after moving to Pleasant View, and she was to live
there for fifteen and one half years. During those years, the Church saw
extraordinary growth, spreading not only throughout the United States but
to Canada, Great Britain, and Germany. In the early days in Lynn the then
Mrs. Mary Glover had dared to hope that one day she would found a religious movement of her own, and that the bells would peal out from the spire
of her own church, but reality had long since outpaced her hopes and
dreams. Mary Baker Eddy the religious leader had won for herself success
and fame perhaps unparallelled for a woman, but by character and experience she was not one to sit back and enjoy the fruits of her labors. She had
devoted half her life to Christian Science, it absorbed her more and more as
she grew older, and its rapid progress was a source of untold gratification to
her. Nonetheless, the price she paid for success had always been a heavy one,
psychologically and socially, and calm content was not to be hers in her final
years.

The placid joys of old age have probably been much exaggerated, and
Mrs. Eddy was far from unusual in feeling increasingly beset by feelings of
loneliness, isolation, abandonment, anxiety, and a sense of betrayal. Such
feelings grew despite the fact that the money she had managed to earn and
save, as well as the cocoon she had created for herself at Pleasant View,
gave her a security that few people in their mid-eighties enjoy. What made
Mary Baker Eddy so sharply different from most women of her age and

generation, and gave her last years their special poignancy, was that she continued to play an important and controversial role in the public arena. The problems she faced right to the very last days of her life were mainly generated outside her home and family, involved large-scale interests, and were not amenable to simple, personal solutions. Who would succeed Mary Baker Eddy as leader of Christian Science? How could she protect her movement from the ad feminam press attacks on her which redoubled in vigor as she herself grew weaker? Was there any way to prevent her estate, and especially her copyrights and all the publishing and real estate interests relating to the Church, from passing to her blood relatives when she died? However deeply Mary Baker Eddy retreated into the privacy of her second-floor apartment at Pleasant View, however zealously her staff guarded the door against unwanted intruders, however carefully she shunned publicity and skirted controversy, these issues were always waiting at Mrs. Eddy's elbow, fueling her anxieties, shattering her peace. And death, the common enemy, had also to be faced, and the next accounting with God.

Perhaps the best expression of the imbalance Mary Baker Eddy felt between public renown and private unhappiness in her final years can be seen in a letter she wrote to her son George Glover on April 27, 1898. Mrs. Eddy appears to be responding to a letter from George expressing alarm at recent reports that she was dead or dying, and concern about the state of her financial affairs.[1]

Dear Son:

Yours of latest date came duly. That which you cannot write I understand and will say, I am reported as dying, wholly decriped [*sic*] and useless, etc. Now one of these reports is just as true as the others are. My life is as pure as that of the angels. God has lifted me up to my work and if it was not pure it would not bring forth good fruits. The Bible says the tree is known by its fruit.

But I need not say this to a Christian Scientist, who knows it. I thank you for any interest you may feel in your Mother. I am <u>alone</u> in the world, more lone than a solitary star. Although it is duly estimated by business characters and learned scholars that I lead and am obeyed by <u>300,000</u> people at this date! The most distinguished newspapers ask me to write on the most important subjects. Lords and Ladies, Earls, Princes, and Marquis and Marchioness from abroad write to me in the most complimentary manner. Hoke Smith declares "I am the most illustrious woman on the continent"—those are his exact words. Our Senators and Members of Congress call on me for counsel! But what of all this? I am not made the least proud by it or a particle happier for it. I am working for a higher purpose.

Now what of my circumstances?

I name first my home which of all places on earth is the one in which to find peace and enjoyment. But my home is simply a house and a beautiful landscape. There is not one in it that I love only as I love everybody. I have no congeniality with my help inside of my house, they are no companions and scarcely fit to be <u>my</u> help.

I adopted a son hoping he would take Frye's place as my book-keeper, and man of all work that belongs to man. But my trial of him has proved another disappointment. His books could not be audited they were so incorrect etc. etc. Mr. Frye is the most disagreeable man that can be found, but this he is, namely (if there is one on earth) an <u>honest man</u> as all will tell you who deal with him. At first mesmerism swayed him but he learned through my forebearance to govern himself. He is a man that would not steal, commit adultery, or fornication, or break one of the ten Commandments—I have now done, but I could write a volume on what I have touched upon.

One thing is the severest wound of all, namely, the want of education among those nearest to me in kin. I would gladly give every dollar I possess to have one or two or three that are nearest to me on earth possess a thorough education. If you had been educated as I intended to have you, today you could, would, be made President of the U.S. Mary's letters to me are so misspelled that I blush to read them.

You pronounce your words so wrongly and then she spells them accordingly. I am even yet too proud to have you come among my society and alas! mispronounce your words as you do; but for this thing I should be honored by your good manners and I love you.

With love to all
Mary Baker Eddy

I am especially struck here by the scorn Mrs. Eddy expresses for her domestic staff. I have had frequent occasion in this biography to comment on Mrs. Eddy's peculiar intellectual and social isolation and her hunger for family life. The withdrawal to Pleasant View had worked for Mrs. Eddy on many levels, but it must have exacerbated her need for the company of equals, and if possible beloved equals, the need which led her to reach out hungrily to professional associates such as James Henry Wiggin and John Wilson and made her vulnerable to plausible scoundrels like Ebenezer Foster and Josephine Woodbury. That her son George should resemble her so little, should be so much a Glover and so little a Baker, was something Mrs. Eddy could never stop regretting, and the policy of disinheriting her kin in favor of her church which she would follow in her last years went against some of her deepest instincts.

As we saw in the last chapter, the endemic sadness and gloom which Mrs. Eddy expressed in her 1898 letter to her son George had deepened to panic and despair during the subsequent long struggle with Mrs. Woodbury. Even after the libel suit of 1901 ended so successfully, Mrs. Eddy had little time to rejoice and relax because she was next faced by an escalation of public attacks triggered in many cases by the indefatigable hostility of Frederick Peabody and taken up with increasing energy by the New York *World*. On July 10, 1904, Peabody's attacks were given new credibility in an anonymous article almost certainly drafted in large part by Peabody himself which appeared in no less a publication than the *New York Times*. Stretching over more than two full pages of newspaper, the article claimed to offer conclusive new evidence in support of the old allegations that Mrs. Eddy had not only received her essential ideas on healing from P. P. Quimby but had plagiarized sections of his unpublished manuscripts in her own published work, and offering as proof an alleged comparison between her work and Quimby's. Plagiarism was again alleged in a 1906 New York *World* article in which Livingston Wright claimed that his old friend James Henry Wiggin, now deceased, had told him that he, Wiggin, was the real author of *Science and Health*. Out of the massive heap of incoherent textual fragments Mrs. Eddy had handed him, Wright claimed, Wiggin had fashioned the coherent text which had made Christian Science a force in the nation.

Mrs. Eddy was peculiarly sensitive to the accusation of plagiarism since her book, *Science and Health*, was of such importance to her religious message and she had wept and toiled over the text for so many years. Nonetheless, the ghost of Phineas Parkhurst Quimby had been haunting her for so long that she had grown in a manner used to it, and Christian Science had grown strong in the teeth of the opposition from New Thought. As for the claims made on behalf of James Henry Wiggin, they could so little stand the test of written evidence that they were best ignored. Humbled by controversy, educated by dispute, when Mrs. Eddy responded publicly to the articles in the New York press, she was restrained and dignified.[2] Increasingly, she left the task of rebuttal and defense of herself and her movement to the newly formed Committee on Publication, the arm of the Church organization charged with correcting misstatements in the press, a body led at this time by Alfred Farlow.[3]

More hurtful because unexpected and more insightful was the ambivalent and wounding series of magazine pieces written by Mark Twain between 1899 and 1903, and published in a much revised form in 1907 as a book called *Christian Science*.[4] By this time the writer's greatest work was behind him, but he nonetheless enjoyed vast fame and could command an international audience. Twain had various and conflicting reasons for devoting his pen to a study of Christian Science. First, and most important, he had considerable experience and great respect for mental healing in general and Christian Science in particular. Second, Christian Science was such a topical subject that publishing success seemed assured, and Twain still needed to earn money and keep his name before the public. Third, if what Mark Twain wrote in a letter to Frederick Peabody is true, like many men of his time, the author heartily disliked Mary Baker Eddy and savored the idea of exposing her faults to the public. "I am not combating Xn Science," Mark Twain wrote, "I haven't a thing in the world against it. Making fun of that shameless old swindler, Mother Eddy, is the only thing I take any interest in."[5]

In his first piece on Christian Science, published in 1899 in the October issue of *Cosmopolitan*, Mark Twain, then forced by his bankruptcy and continuing financial problems to retrench by taking up residence in Vienna, gives a hilarious and wholly fictional account of his falling down a mountain in the Austrian Alps, thereby breaking a preposterous number of bones. He—or his narrative alter ego—is attended first by an American Christian Science matron who happens to be vacationing in the neighborhood, and second by the local vet. Rather surprisingly, Twain ends his story back on his feet, with his multiple fractures and massive contusions healed almost overnight. This lighthearted romp seems well designed to appeal to the readers who liked their Mark Twain droll and fantastic, and I can imagine Mary Baker Eddy laughing with the best of them. There was one misrepresentation in the piece: Mark Twain humorously describes his horse doctor charging a mere thirty kreuzers for the "drench of turpentine and axle grease" he had prescribed, and compares this with the long itemized bill submitted by the lady Scientist. She not only charged $1 for each of the 234 "imaginary" fractures she had healed; she also sued the patient for "substantial dollars" to boot when he presented her with an imaginary check to cover the imaginary healings. The comic implication that Christian Scientist practitioners charged unusually high rates was untrue—one of their appeals for less advantaged patients was that they charged so little per visit in comparison with allopaths, homeopaths, osteopaths, and so forth. This small injustice was a hint of things to come since Mark Twain would go on in later articles to charge that Mrs. Eddy and the "Trust" of handpicked men who ruled under her cared for nothing but the bottom line.

In 1902 Mark Twain again turned his attention to Christian Science. By this point his finances had been taken in hand by the Standard Oil mogul Henry Huttleston Rogers, and he was able again to hold his head high and return to his native America. Once back home, Mark Twain was fêted as a new kind of American hero—the self-made man who had made a great fortune and then lost it, declared bankruptcy but then earned the money to pay his creditors one hundred cents on every dollar owed. Public acclaim meant a great deal to Samuel Langhorne Clemens, but the personal debt in money as well as gratitude which he owed to Rogers was a bitter pill to swallow for a man who had long, in public and private, inveighed against the excesses of Big Capitalism and "the Gilded Age." Furthermore, his personal life was darkened by the rapidly worsening health of his beloved wife, Olivia, who became so frail that her husband was forbidden access to her room and ordered to communicate with her by notes. Olivia

Langdon Clemens was to die of hyperthyroidism and heart disease in Florence in 1904. It is this darkness which pervades the writings of Mark Twain's last years, many of those works suppressed until after his death, and which so changes the tone of his new and greatly extended treatment of Christian Science in 1902–1903.

He now takes Christian Science very seriously indeed. As the husband of a woman who had spent two years of her late adolescence in thrall to apparently hysterical paralysis and whose health was always poor,[6] and the father of a sickly son who died in his second year and of three fragile girls, of whom only one would survive him, Mark Twain had as much acquaintance as any American of his time with illness of every kind, and with death, sudden or long and drawn out.[7] Given this background, it is a signal mark of the inefficacy of conventional medical treatment in the second half of the nineteenth century that Mark Twain strongly endorses the claims of mind cure in general and Christian Science in particular:

> Remember its principal great offer: to *rid the Race of pain and disease.* Can it do so? In large measure, yes. How much of the pain and disease in the world is created by the imaginations of the sufferers, and then kept alive by those same imaginations? Four-fifths? Not anything short of that, I should think. Can Christian Science banish that four-fifths? I think so. Can any other (organized) force do it? None that I know of. Would this be a new world when that was accomplished? And a pleasanter one—for us well people, as well as for those fussy and fretting sick ones? Would it seem as if there was not as much gloomy weather as there used to be? I think so.[8]

Mark Twain, in fact, saw mind healing in terms virtually identical to those presented by Mrs. Eddy—as a power of the spirit to heal the body that humans of all cultures had always known, a power given new but still limited force by the healing mission of Jesus of Nazareth and his first disciples, and which has more potential to improve the quality of human life than any other factor.

> For the thing back of it is wholly gracious and beautiful: the power, through loving mercifulness and compassion, to heal fleshly ills and pains and griefs—*all*—with a word, with a touch of the hand! This power was given by the Saviour to the Disciples, and to *all* the converted. All—every one. It was *exercised* for generations afterwards. Any Christian who was in earnest and not a make-believe, not a policy-Christian, not a Christian for revenue only, had that healing power, and could cure with it *any disease or any hurt or damage possible to human flesh and bone.* These things are true, or they are not. If they were true seventeen and eighteen and nineteen centuries ago it would be difficult to satisfactorily explain why or how or by what argument that power should be non-existent in Christians now.[9]

Not only was Mark Twain able, in passages like the one just quoted, to give voice to the spiritual poetry of Christian Science in a way Mrs. Eddy had long awaited in vain from her devotees, but he also gave notably short shrift to two of the most serious accusations made against Christian Science. The first of these accusations was that its founder owed everything important to P. P. Quimby. Mark Twain was unimpressed by the figure of Quimby. He had seen many men of the kind before—one of them, in a single session, had cured his own wife of her teenage paralysis—and he appreciated their usefulness, but he saw a fundamental difference between the multiple Quimbys of the world and the singular Mary Baker Eddy.

> Her enemies charge that she surreptitiously took from Quimby a peculiar system of healing which was mind-cure with a Biblical basis. She and her friends deny that she took anything from him. This is a matter we can discuss by-and-by. Whether she took it or invented it, it was—materially—a sawdust mine when she got it, and she has turned it into a Klondike.[10]

Even more summarily Mark Twain dismisses the Quimbyites' charges that Mrs. Eddy plagiarized Quimby's unpublished manuscripts, noting that only when and if some of these manuscripts were produced could anything to the point be said about them.

The second, and more serious accusation against Christian Science which Twain takes on is that its practitioners were responsible for many unnecessary deaths, in particular those of children. In the book edition of his writings on Mrs. Eddy, Mark Twain dismisses this issue, first breezily in his main text, reprinted from 1902, then with bitter sarcasm in a note. After reviewing with more sympathy and admiration than cynicism some reports of healings featured in the *Christian Science Journal*, Mark Twain goes on:

> Does the Science kill a patient here and there and now and then? We must concede it. Does it compensate for this? I am persuaded that it can make a plausible showing in that direction. For instance: when it lays its hand upon a soldier who has suffered thirty years of helpless torture and makes him whole in body and mind, what is the actual sum of that achievement? This, I think: that it has restored to life a subject who had essentially died ten deaths a year for thirty years, and each of them a long and painful one.

> NOTE.—I have received several letters (two from educated and ostensibly intelligent persons), which contained, in substance, this protest: "I don't object to men and women chancing their lives with these people, but it is a burning shame that the laws should allow them to trust their helpless little children in their deadly hands." Isn't it touching? Isn't it deep? Isn't it modest? It is as if the person said: "I know that to a parent his child is the core of his heart, the apple of his eye, a possession

so dear, so precious that he will trust its life in no hands but those which he believes with all his soul, to be the very best and the very safest, but it is a burning shame that the law does not require him to come to *me* to ask what kind of healer I will allow him to call." The public is merely a multiplied "me."—M.T.[11]

Mark Twain here takes the position that neither the state nor some smaller group of citizens has the right to dictate to parents how they should have their children's illnesses treated. Today this position is still hotly debated in the United States, but no one has, I believe, much improved on Mark Twain's statement of one side of the debate.[12] What is more, as a parent who had had two children die while under the care of the best available physicians—the one as a chronically sick infant from diphtheria, the other as a healthy adult from meningitis—and who had in vain consulted all brands of doctors for help in dealing with his last child's epilepsy, Samuel Clemens had the moral authority and the practical experience to take the stand he does.

Mark Twain believed in the power of the mind to heal, and he was thus willing to celebrate Christian Science for giving that power greater currency. On the other hand, as a social critic and satirist he hated the movement's tendencies toward institutionalization and commercialization, and he believed Mrs. Eddy herself was fatally compromised by her pursuit of the "almighty Dollar." Mark Twain was unwilling to take on institutions like Standard Oil, as Ida Tarbell had done. Christian Science, however, as a public entity and Mary Baker Eddy as a public figure were easy targets for the satiric missiles which he feared to let loose on groups with real power to hurt him in his prestige and his finances.

It is this larger context of not irrational fears for the future of the nation and of complicated personal emotions which accounts for the futuristic nightmare which is usually known as the "Eddypus" manuscript, parts of which were published in a section of the third installment of the *North American Review* series. In this text Mark Twain imagines what might become of the newly centralized Christian Science, with its iconic Leader, its holy texts, its zealous propaganda machine, and its superb financial talents. Letting loose his personal demons, Mark Twain imagines a twentieth century in which the whole world is governed mind and body by Pope Mary Baker G. Eddy IV—a man, although always referred to as "she"—who stands at the head of a small self-electing Trust. A chronicler, some time in the future, writes "The Secret History of Eddypus," in which he describes the exponential growth in the new century of organized Christian Science, which has learned to combine religion and capitalism and thereby achieve the

> destruction of the Republic, the erection of the absolute Monarchy, the swallowing up of the civil Monarchy in the colossal religious Autocracy

of the World-Empire of Eddypus, the exalting of the Founder of Divine Science to the Second Place in the Holy Family, the extinction of the world's civilizations, and the closing down of the Black Night through whose sombre and melancholy shadows the human race has now been groping, hopeless and forlorn, these eight hundred years.[13]

Fortunately for his reputation among his contemporaries, in other chapters of the book he eventually published on Christian Science Mark Twain got down off his apocalyptic high horse and showed his old skills as a devastatingly witty commentator of contemporary mores. When he poked fun at the Christian Science Publishing Society's prices and retail practices, when he described the pilgrimages to the Mother's Room, where burned an eternal flame, when he discussed the notorious "The" of "The Mother Church," when he exposed the absurdities of Mrs. Eddy's dictatorial edicts in the *Manual of the Mother Church*, Mark Twain tickled his audience and at the same time found attentive ears at Falmouth Street in Boston and especially at Pleasant View.[14]

Stung by Twain's observations, Mrs. Eddy officially forbade her followers to address her as Mother, insisting on the title Leader, and she had the Mother's Room in the 1894 Mother Church in Boston shut down permanently. Henceforward, thanks to Mark Twain's satire, the editors of the *Christian Science Journal* would think twice before printing claims of animal healings or celebrating the adorable cuteness of infant Christian Scientists as they bonded with *Science and Health*. More subtly, but more fundamentally, Church officials and members had seen their own tendencies to adore and even apotheosize Mary Baker Eddy reflected in the distorted glass of Mark Twain's prose, and this helped to stem, or at least to drive underground, the more flagrant references to her as the Woman of Revelation and of Prophecy.

If one read only those parts of Mark Twain's *North American Review* Series which I have quoted from so far, one would find a rather astonishing congruence between the writer's understanding of the movement, its power, its potential, its flaws—and Mrs. Eddy's own. As she herself remarked, in many ways Mark Twain was saying in a new voice and a new medium what she herself had been repeating, largely unheeded, for years in her *Journal* articles, in *Science and Health*, and in her other theological writings. In focusing on the dangers of institutionalization and of the cult of personality he clarified and reinforced what she had been feeling for years, and his negative pressure gave her the energy to make certain reforms which she had long envisaged. According to her own oft expressed doctrine that it is through pain and correction, not through pleasure and praise, that we make spiritual progress, Mary Baker Eddy could accept Mark Twain as one more necessary goad to push her onward.

But Mark Twain's portrait of Mary Baker Eddy the woman was calculated to wound, and his forebodings about the future progress of Christian Science and what it might portend for American society were based on his largely hostile reaction to Mrs. Eddy herself. Mary Baker Eddy did not correspond to Mark Twain's ideas of femininity and the place of woman in society. Whereas Livy Langdon Clemens had inherited money from her industrialist father and given it to her husband as a marriage portion to gamble away, Mary Baker Eddy had earned her own money and managed to keep it, through good financial cycles and bad. Her publishing company, her journals had prospered, whereas Sam Clemens's had all been lost. From what Mark Twain knew of her, Mary Baker seemed to have little in common with Livy, that frail, sensitive, affectionate creature with whose portrait he had first fallen in love, whom he had courted and finally married.[15] The thrice-married Mrs. Eddy did not have the kind of virginal womanhood to which Clemens insisted his daughters aspire—locking them in the modern-day tower of a luxury hotel suite, where they were safe from the depredations of decadent old European roués, like Henry James's fictional Gilbert Osmond, or ambitious young blackguards like the very real Samuel Langhorne Clemens, but not, sadly, safe from sickness and death. Most immediately, perhaps, the formidable Mary Baker Eddy ruling her movement from her New Hampshire stronghold seemed to Clemens to have nothing in common with his aging wife who lay dying in a room nearby, too vulnerable to take one more puff of his cigar smoke, one more whiff of the whiskey on his breath, one more nihilistic broadside from his tongue.[16]

Like everyone interested in writing about Christian Science in Mrs. Eddy's last years, Mark Twain inevitably began a correspondence with Frederick Peabody. It seems clear from the letters that Peabody fanned the writer's patriarchal insecurities and persuaded him that Mrs. Eddy was indeed a monster who broke down all the stereotypical gender roles and upset the balance of power between the sexes, in the home and in the public arena. Peabody sent Mark Twain copies of his own pamphlets, provided him with Christian Science literature, and even persuaded him to meet Mrs. Woodbury in a New York hotel and hear what she had to say.[17]

Mark Twain recognized Peabody's deep personal animus against Mrs. Eddy, criticized his bilious rhetoric, and sensed that he himself was being manipulated, but Twain was always a lover of "facts," and Peabody seemed to have a lot of them. For much of the time at least, Twain believed that Peabody's portrait of Mrs. Eddy as a monster of monomania and concupiscence was exaggerated or inaccurate in details but correct in essence. Peabody's influence on Mark Twain can be felt directly in the following passage from *Christian Science* in which Twain describes Mrs. Eddy as

> grasping, sordid, penurious, famishing for everything she sees— money, power, glory—vain, untruthful, jealous, despotic, arrogant,

insolent, pitiless where thinkers and hypnotists are concerned, illiterate, shallow, incapable of reasoning outside of commercial lines, immeasurably selfish.[18]

Perhaps the most important additions Mark Twain made for the book version of his work on Christian Science were his detailed, witty, and devastating analyses of passages from Mrs. Eddy's writings, notably her juvenile verse and the original first preface to *Science and Health*. These he describes as "virgin" in the sense that they had not been revised or redrafted by someone else, and he lists their characteristics:

Desert vacancy, as regards thought.
Self-complacency.
Puerility.
Sentimentality.
Affectations of scholarly learning.
Lust after eloquent and flowery expression.
Repetition of pet poetic picturesqueness.
Confused and wandering statement.
Metaphor gone insane.
Meaningless words, used because they are pretty, showy, or unusual.
Sorrowful attempts at the epigrammatic.
Destitution of originality.[19]

Mark Twain's critique of selected sections of Mrs. Eddy's published prose style is devastatingly accurate. Where he went wrong was in comparing these bad passages with the body of the text of *Science and Health* which, over the years, he had come to admire despite himself, and in decreeing, unequivocally, that Mrs. Eddy could not possibly have written the book.[20] It is odd that Mark Twain, himself so protean in character, so strange a mixture of craft and art, raw ambition and lofty sentiment, at one moment a Grub Street hack, the next the inspired scribe of a nation's soul, could not imagine the complexity of Mary Baker Eddy, could not conceive in her a radical duality which made it possible for the same hand to write at one moment like a simpering schoolgirl and at another like an Old Testament prophet.

Mark Twain was a modern master of invective, and much of his portrait of Mary Baker Eddy aims to hurt and destroy. But it is quite inaccurate to state or imply, as many critics have done, that his definitive word on Mrs. Eddy was vituperative. In some passages in his book, Mark Twain places her high on the list of human achievers, not indeed as a Protestant Joan of Arc, but as a female Cromwell or Napoleon. In one of his more reflective moments, Twain admits that Mrs. Eddy's character remains "crooked" or elusive to many people, including himself, but he goes on:

> No matter, she is interesting enough without an amicable agreement. In several ways she is the most interesting woman that ever lived, and the most extraordinary. . . . She started from nothing. . . . When we do not know a person—and also when we do—we have to judge his size by the size and nature of his achievements, as compared with the achievements of others in his special line of business—there is no other way. Measured by this standard, it is thirteen hundred years since the world has produced any one who could reach up to Mrs. Eddy's waistbelt.[21]

Later in the book, Mark Twain traces Mrs. Eddy's rise to prominence and attributes it to the following qualities:

> A clear head for business, and a phenomenally long one;
>
> Clear understanding of business situations;
>
> Accuracy in estimating the opportunities they offer;
>
> Intelligence in planning a business move;
>
> Firmness in sticking to it after it has been decided upon;
>
> Extraordinary daring;
>
> Indestructible persistency;
>
> Devouring ambition;
>
> Limitless selfishness;
>
> A knowledge of the weaknesses and poverties and docilities of human nature and how to turn them to account which has never been surpassed, if ever equalled;
>
> And—necessarily—the foundation-stone of Mrs. Eddy's character is a never-wavering confidence in herself.[22]

The ambivalence of Mark Twain's estimation of Mary Baker Eddy becomes apparent in this passage, which might be the description of one of the great nineteenth-century American capitalists, all of them men. On some fundamental level, Mark Twain is alienated by finding in a woman who could be his big sister or young aunt some of the quintessentially American *male* qualities which he had espoused and praised and satirized—and also failed, in certain important ways, to manifest.

If I myself were to cite one passage which reflects Mark Twain's final judgment of Mary Baker Eddy it would be the following one, full of ambivalence and doubt, but going beyond stereotype and prejudice. Here, for a moment at least, the writer attempts to put himself in Mrs. Eddy's shoes and allows the possibility that she, like himself, was as much the victim of circumstance as the master of her fate and was ending her long and full life a very different being from the one she had been at the start:

Chapter 10

In the beginning, Mrs. Eddy was probably interested merely in the mental-healing detail. And perhaps mainly interested in it pecuniarily, for she was poor.

She would succeed in anything she undertook. She would attract pupils, and her commerce would grow. She would inspire in patient and pupil confidence in her earnestness; her history is evidence that she would not fail of that.

There probably came a time, in due course, when her students began to think there was something deeper in her teachings than they had been suspecting—a mystery beyond mental-healing, and higher. It is conceivable that by consequence their manner towards her changed little by little, and from respectful became reverent. It is conceivable that this would have an influence upon her; that it would incline her to wonder if their secret thought—that she was inspired—might not be a well-grounded guess. It is conceivable that as time went on the thought in their minds and its reflection in hers might solidify into conviction. . . .

It is conceivable that the persuasive influences around her and within her would give a new and powerful impulse to her philosophizings, and that from this, in time, would result that great birth, the healing of body and mind by the inpouring of the Spirit of God—the central and dominant idea of Christian Science—and that when this idea came she would not doubt that it was an inspiration direct from Heaven.

Chapter 11

I must rest a little, now. To sit here and painstakingly spin out a scheme which imagines Mrs. Eddy, of all people, working her mind on a plane above commercialism; imagines her thinking, philosophizing, discovering majestic things; and even imagines her dealing in sincerities—to be frank, I find it a large contract. But I have begun it. and I will go through with it.[23]

Mary Baker Eddy and Mark Twain never met. In the period when he was researching Christian Science, Mark Twain rarely went far from his wife, and Mrs. Eddy never left her Concord home. But if Mark Twain had received a telegram, asking if he could possibly find time, at his earliest convenience, to come to Pleasant View and meet Mrs. Eddy, I think he might well have taken the next morning's train to Concord. Such a meeting with the famously temperamental writer would have been a huge gamble for Mary Baker Eddy, but one which, as would be shown later by her successful interviews with journalists and medical experts at the time of the Next Friends suit, could well have paid off.

Given a chance to talk, the two of them would have been able to find out how much they had in common. Both were of humble and provincial origin and had felt the need to embroider upon their familial pasts. Both had brothers they deeply loved but could not keep from self-destruction. Both took years to work out for themselves positions on race and gender that were singularly more enlightened than those of their immediate family members. Both knew the anxiety of want and the cruelties of good society. Both rose high in society by their own efforts and talents and made money in ways they were not particularly anxious to discuss in affluent old age. Both had an abiding belief in the power of one mind over another and felt that they had especially strong mental powers. Both had dreams and visions which they recorded for the world, unself-consciously opening a window into their unconscious. Both had an innate sense of costume, great personal vanity, a passion for neatness and order. Both were beloved tyrants in their own homes. Both understood, exploited, and suffered from the power of the press.[24]

Like so many of the men who arrived at the door of Pleasant View full of hostility and prejudice, Mark Twain would have been surprised by Mrs. Eddy's social grace and natural femininity, enjoyed her wit, and found in her a wonderful listener—not, after all, so very unlike his wife. Even the nightmare ideas which increasingly assailed Twain in his last years, and which made his wife recoil, would have struck a chord in Mrs. Eddy, who had her own dark visions. For her part, Mary Baker Eddy was famished for good company, for minds as sharp and eager as her own, for someone witty who could make jokes and talk about the world, for someone anxious to open up the big questions, however dark. To have Mark Twain in her study for an hour or so of conversation would have been a treat. And inevitably, at some point in their conversation, Mary Baker Eddy would have begun to talk about Christian Science, and Mark Twain, like so many others, would have seen the transformation that came over her face and her language. Already predisposed to believe with her, he might, I think, have begun to believe her, perhaps even believe in her. But Mark Twain never made the journey to Pleasant View.

M A R Y
B A K E R
E D D Y
F I G H T S   O N

1 9 0 6 – 1 9 1 0

INTRODUCTION

The Mother Church, built in Boston's Back Bay with such dizzying speed and dedicated so triumphantly on January 6, 1895, was within months too small to accommodate all those who wished to attend meetings. By April 1896 the church was holding two Sunday services, and by October 1905, three. Still all of the thousand seats were filled, and people sat on the window ledges and stairs and stood at the back. In 1899, as we saw, the Church's Annual Meeting, which, exceptionally, Mrs. Eddy attended, had to be held at the Tremont Temple to accommodate all who wished to attend. As time went on and the pressure of numbers increased, various plans were put forward by the Boston officials to rent other halls or extend the current Mother Church edifice, but Mrs. Eddy counselled delay. By June 15, 1902, however, she had decided that the time had come to build something larger. In her Message to the Church she referred to "making another united effort to purchase more land and enlarge our church edifice so as to seat the large number who annually favor us with their presence on Communion Sunday" (*Miscellany*, p. 7), and this simple remark was enough to galvanize the church organization.

Three days later, at the Annual Meeting, Edward A. Kimball, probably Christian Science's most respected lecturer and teacher, rose and made the following motion to the assembly: "Recognizing the necessity for providing an auditorium for The Mother Church that will seat four or five thousand persons, and acting in behalf of ourselves and the Christian Scientists of the world, we agree to contribute any portion of two million dollars that may be necessary for this purpose" (*Miscellany*, p. 7). With virtually no debate, the motion was passed. As the *Boston Journal* of June 19, 1902, noted: "Learning that a big church was required, the money to provide it was pledged with the readiness and despatch of an ordinary mortal passing out a nickel for car-fare."[1]

Handsome new First Churches of Christ, Scientist had by this time sprung up in cities all over America—Detroit, Atlanta, Toronto, Los Angeles, Pittsburgh, Cleveland, St. Louis, San Jose, Wilmington, Duluth, two in New York, two in Chicago—and they still grace the center of cities from Portland, Oregon, to Concord, New Hampshire.[2] Crowning all this building activity, the proposed new church building in Boston aroused national interest, and press and public watched with growing astonishment as the new Extension, one of the largest houses of worship in the United States, took shape on the Boston skyline and on the nation's religious land-scape. As in other communities, but on a larger scale, the building of the new church building meant money for the city, and the respectability of the church nationwide expanded exponentially as its officials became known as excellent men of business who used local materials, hired local contractors, liked to be on the technical cutting edge, and paid their bills on time.

Both the construction and the design of the building commanded respect. The foundation consisted of thousands of thickly clustered piles driven down through the notoriously shifting landfill of the Back Bay. What was worse, the site was a very difficult one. Not only were the architects pre-sented with a small and irregular triangle of land that made most traditional church floor plans impossible, but they also had to incorporate into the total design the existing Mother Church building, which Mrs. Eddy flatly refused to have razed. It is true that the timetable the Board of Directors set for them-selves was not quite as daunting as the one which had been set in 1894, and those involved in the Extension work had some hard experience as contrac-tors behind them. Nonetheless, in erecting their church extension in just two years, the Christian Science managers and their chosen architects and con-tractors once again showed that it was possible to get workmen to do three-shift days, to achieve overlapping transitions from one phase of construction to another, with a minimum of intertrade conflict, and, by organizational hard work and ability, to push toward deadlines without compromising either the safety of the workers or the quality of the work.[3]

The funding of the new Extension sounded a wake-up call at the head-quarters of every other religious denomination. At their Annual Meeting, Christian Scientists were given a target figure of $2 million, and they not only accepted the figure and trusted the honesty of those handling the building fund but began sending in their contributions at once. Later Church mem-bers responded with more and larger checks as the project neared comple-tion and the big bills came due. Funds were raised through individual contributions, solicited by a general appeal, and involved no public acknowledgment. Each member was asked to decide what he or she would contribute, and to send it in to the treasurer. It is noteworthy that the organ was not named after contributor X, the bells were not named after the children of contributor Y, and no window was given in memory of contributor Z's wife. Even before dedication day, the Extension was paid for, and the treasurer officially requested that members send in no more money to the fund. No money had been given or asked for from anyone outside the Church community, and no fund-raising events of any kind had been arranged. All of this was quite extraordinary. Many Americans doubted Mrs. Eddy's talents as a theologian, but her genius for fund-raising was now written in walls of granite and limestone and marble, tolled by the bells atop the 224-feet dome, pealed out by the great organ,[4] enumerated in the Santo Domingo mahogany pews.

Thirty thousand Christian Scientists poured into Boston to attend the dedication on June 10, 1906. Horticultural Hall was turned into a giant convention center, with full modern telephone and telegraph facilities, where visitors were welcomed by local volunteers and helped to find accommodation. Hotels and boardinghouses were filled to overflowing, and every taxi driver and bellhop in downtown Boston was busy. On the designated Sunday, six consecutive dedication services were held, with overflow crowds lining up each time to gain entrance. The 12:30 service was reserved for children, who with their parents filled all the pews—an excellent piece of public relations. Reporters noted the good humor of those attending the dedication, the speed with which they were ushered in and out of the building, the orderly and civil way they fanned back out into the city. On Wednesday evening, the testimonial meeting drew so many visitors that even the great Extension could not hold everyone, and overflow meetings were held in the original Mother Church and in four public halls. Boston was, of course, particularly impressed by this display of concerted enthusiasm and commitment, but the event was covered by newspapermen from all over America and from abroad since many of the participants had come from far away. Not just nationally but internationally, the dedication of the Extension served notice that Christian Science was a movement to be reckoned with.

Amid all the rejoicing within the membership and the media attention outside it, one thing was noticed by all. Mary Baker Eddy did not come to join in the celebrations. She had made it quite plain early on that she would not be present, and the implicit statement made by her absence from the festivities was intended to be even stronger than the actual words of her Message which was read out during the six consecutive services. As I read this strange, uncompromising four-page Message, I wonder what people made of it at the time.[5] Mary Baker Eddy speaks again in that radical, quirky, unedited voice first heard in the 1875 text of *Science and Health*. The

Message is entitled "Choose Ye," and, although rambling and incoherent in many ways, its intent is plain—to challenge her listeners to think beyond bricks and mortar, beyond Sunday finery and trips to Boston's Public Garden, beyond complacency and self-congratulation. The message is the old one, the hard one—that Christian Science is a never-ending search "to reveal man as God's image, His idea, coexistent with Him—God giving all and man having all that God gives."[6] Mrs. Eddy enjoins her followers to act on their faith, to show the power of God in their lives, to obey the Golden Rule of loving their neighbors as themselves, and, above all, to put God first.

It is not until her final paragraph that Mrs. Eddy makes any reference to the Extension and its dedication, remarking briefly that she is "greatly impressed and encouraged" by the "magnificent temple" her followers have "dexterously and wisely provided." This is modified rapture indeed, and Mrs. Eddy makes things worse by going on to recall the old Mother Church, the "modest edifice" with its Mother's Room, which, after causing untold headaches for architects and contractors, now clung inconveniently to the side of its "Extension." As a woman, Mrs. Eddy enjoyed to her memories of *her* Mother Church, which she had played so important a role in realizing. As the leader of a growing movement, she was gladdened by the size and splendor of the new building, by the evidence it offered of success, and by the glowing reports it had elicited from the press and general public. As a spiritual guide, however, Mrs. Eddy worried, I think, that prosperity might prove more dangerous for her movement than adversity.

As in so many of her writings of this period of rapid growth, Mary Baker Eddy's tone is more admonitory than celebratory.[7] She continues stern and somber to the end of her 1906 Message to her church, using her concluding paragraph to insist that her followers should see the church building not as a material triumph, not even just as a demonstration of the power of spirit over matter, but as a symbol—

> a mental monument, a superstructure high above the work of men's hands, even the outcome of their hearts, giving to the material a spiritual significance—the speed, beauty and achievements of goodness. Methinks this church is the one edifice on earth which most prefigures self-abnegation, hope, faith; love catching a glimpse of glory. (*Miscellany*, p. 6)

25

The Next
Friends
Suit

THE ASTONISHING PROGRESS BEING MADE BY CHRIST-
ian Science was national news in America, and Joseph Pulitzer, owner
of the sensationalist New York *World*, had as good a nose for a story as anyone.[1] Stricken with blindness in his prime and afflicted by a strange condition that made noise, unexpected physical shocks, and the company of any
but handpicked associates increasingly intolerable, Pulitzer had by 1906 constructed around himself a kind of luxury carapace that enabled him to deal
with the world only on his own terms. From the early 1890s the daily management of his publishing empire devolved upon various associates, but
unless wholly incapacitated, Joseph Pulitzer still dictated policy for the newspaper from his yacht and various international retreats, and exercised tyrannical control over his highly paid but never wholly trusted subordinates. The
emergence of Christian Science and the various rumors about Mrs. Eddy's
life at Pleasant View would not have escaped Pulitzer, whose interest in and
memory for the minutiae of contemporary American life were if anything
sharpened by his neurological problems.

Since late 1904 word had been out in Christian Science circles and in
the New York press world that *McClure's Magazine* was preparing a long and
critical biography of Mrs. Eddy, and by fall 1906 the series was poised to
appear. That Sam McClure should both get the scoop on Christian Science
and receive credit for stemming the tide of fake healing and religious mumbo
jumbo was not a circumstance designed to please Joseph Pulitzer, any more
than the fact that his greatest publishing rival William Randolph Hearst was

supporting Christian Science.[2] When the spotlight of the world press was turned in 1906 on the new Extension to the Mother Church, Pulitzer, like many others, probably noticed that Mary Baker Eddy had failed to attend the dedication ceremonies. Perhaps projecting his own fears as a wealthy, powerful, and much hated man, he decided that there could be only one explanation for her absence on such a triumphant occasion—she was either dead, or terminally ill, or mentally incompetent, or a prisoner of her own entourage, or some complicated mixture of all of the above. Personal prejudice, public principle, and professional rivalry inclined Pulitzer to take on Christian Science, and, despite Mrs. Eddy's age and sex, he had no reservations about subjecting her to public scrutiny. Unlike Mark Twain, Joseph Pulitzer put no stock in mental healing, or indeed in the emerging theories of neurosis, which might in fact have been more help to him than all the multitude of eye doctors and neurologists he consulted. Anyone who preached the unreality of disease and claimed to effect spiritual cures of all physical ills was fair game for Pulitzer, and he therefore dispatched two of his crack reporters from the New York *World* up to Concord, New Hampshire, to get the story on Mary Baker Eddy.

The experienced *World* team of Slaght and Lithchild was busy in Concord for much of the summer of 1906, reading local financial records, vigorously trolling the town gossip, and exchanging information with the *McClure's Magazine* team which was also active in the area. It was perhaps during this period that John Slaght discovered that opposition to Mrs. Eddy in Concord was headed by former Senator William Chandler, and he and Chandler may even have met and begun discussions. On the afternoon of Sunday, October 14, Slaght and Lithchild arrived at Pleasant View and demanded to see Calvin Frye. They told Frye that they had interviewed several people who had once known Mrs. Eddy, including Richard Kennedy, Daniel Spofford, and Miranda Rice. They had heard that Mrs. Eddy was dead or incapacitated, and in order to disprove these rumors once and for all, they needed to see Mrs. Eddy for themselves. What was more, they said, they intended to bring with them to the interview John Kent, who knew Mrs. Eddy and could therefore identify her. One of Mrs. Eddy's near neighbors on Pleasant Street, the so-called Professor Kent, a former principal of the Concord High School, was well known in Concord as Mrs. Eddy's most persistent and vocal opponent. He was thus one of the people least welcome in her home.

Confronted with this ultimatum and barely veiled threat, Frye agreed to try to persuade Mrs. Eddy to see the three men the next day, but the agreement went very much against the grain. Frye was correctly known in Christian Science circles as Mrs. Eddy's faithful attack dog who guarded her night and day. Thus it was not until the next day, when she had returned from her drive, that Frye told Mrs. Eddy that he had felt obliged to accept the reporters' proposition. She immediately sent for the *World* reporters and for Kent and prepared herself to receive them.

The meeting with Mrs. Eddy lasted only a few minutes. Members of Mrs. Eddy's staff who were present at the interview, notably her secretary Lewis Strang, later wrote that she stood resolutely to receive the three men, held out her hand to Kent, remarked that she hoped he would soon regain his position at the school (thus proving that she knew who he was and remembered his recent professional setbacks), and stood alone by the window with her back turned as the men left. According to Strang's later statement, the *World* reporters even remarked to the staff upon their departure that Mrs. Eddy was a remarkably well preserved woman for her age. For his part, in a letter to Frederick Peabody, Kent stated that he was sure that the woman they had seen was Mrs. Eddy, appearing much older and—perhaps unsurprisingly!—with a look of anxiety on her face he had never seen before, but definitely not an imposter.[3]

Strang and Lithchild did not leave Concord; if anything, they redoubled their efforts. One day they followed Mrs. Eddy on her daily ride and boldly jumped up, one on each side of her carriage, to oblige her to show her face to one of them. At the end of two weeks, the *World* team sent back to the paper's editors a long and apparently circumstantial story which gratifyingly confirmed all their publisher's suspicions and which was trumpeted on page 1 of the Sunday, October 28, edition:

MRS. MARY BAKER G. EDDY DYING
FOOTMAN AND "DUMMY" CONTROL HER

Founder of X Science Suffering from Cancer and Nearing Her End, Is Immured at Pleasant View. While Another Woman Impersonates Her in the Streets of Concord.

Drives Out Daily in Closed Carriage with Calvin A. Frye, Secretary
Footman, Who is the Supreme Power at the Eddy Home—Founder
Estimated to Have Accumulated a Fortune of $15,000,000, and to Have an
Income of $1,000,000 a Year, but Members of Her Coterie Say She Has Spent
It All in Charity, Though No Records of Large Gifts Can Be Found.[4]

The reporters went on to assert that Mary Baker Eddy was dying of cancer and receiving regular secret visits from a physician. Further, they claimed that she was so weak and ill that the "coterie" led by Frye had installed at Pleasant View a lady from Brooklyn called Pamelia Leonard who regularly impersonated Mrs. Eddy for visitors. It was Mrs. Leonard who sat up in the carriage during the daily drive, a ploy designed to prove to all that Mrs. Eddy was still alive and well. The *World* team claimed that they had brought from

New York a gentleman who knew Mrs. Leonard and had identified her as being the occupant of the carriage on a specified day, despite the large hat and carriage parasol that the carriage's occupant habitually carried to shield her face.[5]

Having seen Mrs. Eddy with their own eyes, and having had her identified by a witness of their own choice, even the *World* reporters could not now tell the American public that Mary Baker Eddy was actually dead. Undismayed, they claimed instead to have seen for themselves that Mrs. Eddy was so weak she could hardly stand, so senile she could hardly speak, much less make any sense, and that she was undeniably the pathetic tool of her entourage. They gave a lurid account of the few minutes they had spent in Mary Baker Eddy's presence when Kent was verifying her identity:

> Mrs. Eddy looked more dead than alive. She was a skeleton, her hollow cheeks thick with red paint, and the fleshless, hairless bones above the sunken eyes penciled a jet black. The features were thick with powder. Above them was a big white wig. . . .
>
> Her weakness was pathetic. She reeled as she stood clinging to the table. Her sunken, faded eyes gazed helplessly, almost pleadingly, at her visitors. The air of the room reeked with the odors of powerful stimulants. In a corner, as though hastily pushed aside, stood a galvanic battery with its surgical basin full of water and a sponge wet from use.
>
> To every eye it was clear that this unfortunate old woman had been doped and galvanized for the ordeal of identification. But it was equally clear that the utmost stimulation could not keep the tortured woman upon her feet much longer.
>
> Strang glided to her side and held an outstretched arm behind her in readiness for the threatened collapse. But old Mrs. Eddy was nerved to supreme effort.
>
> Her listless eyes were fastened upon Prof. Kent as he stepped toward her. As he bowed formally she released her hold upon the table, swayed toward him, clutched him with her shrivelled fingers, and held on with desperate strength. Had Prof. Kent withdrawn his support she would have fallen.
>
> "My-dear-dear pro-professor!" she cried in the high crackling voice of extreme age. "H-h-how glad I am to see you. Let me co-congratulate you on getting back-your position. I-I am so glad that you are at the head of your sc-school again. . . ."
>
> As the visitors were hurried from the room, Mrs. Eddy, surrounded by attendants, was sinking helpless into a pillowed chair.[6]

The New York *World* was read for sensation, not accuracy, but even by the paper's own standards the claims made in this article on Mary Baker Eddy were extreme. To understand why they were believed, and in particular by people who did not usually get their facts from yellow journalism, one has to understand the peculiarity of Mrs. Eddy's situation. She was increasingly famous, her movement was increasingly influential, but she had retreated to New Hampshire in 1889, and since the late 1890s fewer and fewer people could claim to have spoken to her or had a handwritten letter from her.

Rumors that Mary Baker Eddy was really dead and that someone was impersonating her had been alive in the Christian Science movement since at least 1899 and had found their way into press reports which may well have reached the *World* newsdesk and influenced its subsequent reporting.[7] After the stresses she had endured as a result of the Woodbury suit, Mrs. Eddy had grown more famous and more reclusive, and her staff were increasingly high-handed in their rebuffs of anyone who asked to see her in person or corre-spond with her by mail. The rules she had made as early as 1889, refusing to read any personal mail sent to her, were now in full force, and the flood of handwritten communications which had once poured from her pen had eased. Secretaries now did much of the voluminous correspondence, send-ing out typewritten missives on Mrs. Eddy's behalf, under their own names or with her signature at the bottom, and the authenticity even of the signa-tures was coming into doubt. The sight of her script was becoming almost as rare as the sound of her voice, and Mary Baker Eddy had come as close to anyone to personifying that cliché, "the living legend."

Some of Mrs. Eddy's relatives felt her refusal to communicate very per-sonally. Her sister-in-law Martha Rand Baker and nephew George Waldron Baker tried on various occasions to get in to see Mrs. Eddy, but they had failed even before 1889 when Mrs. Eddy was still in Boston. Finding them-selves in recent years in a state of penury which contrasted strongly with the affluence of Pleasant View, George Baker had in 1906 only with great diffi-culty prevailed upon Gilbert Carpenter, then the assistant secretary, to pur-chase a watch that had once belonged to Albert Baker, Mrs. Eddy's long dead brother, and present it to her, and then as Carpenter's personal gift. Both the $50 price Carpenter bargained him down to for the watch and the subse-quent refusal by Pleasant View even to acknowledge George and his mother's pleas for financial assistance chafed at the Bakers. Remembering the good times when Mary had been a beloved and admired friend, Mrs. Martha Rand Baker and her son preferred to believe that Mrs. Eddy was being willfully separated from her family, and they were not entirely wrong. However, it is also probable that out of past rancor or present fatigue, Mrs. Eddy simply had no wish to see or hear from them.[8]

Many of Mrs. Eddy's devoted flock also felt both aggrieved and puzzled by her reclusiveness. By 1906 Mrs. Eddy rarely came downstairs except to go out for her daily ride, and she never walked in her grounds. More partic-ularly, she had become less and less able to bear what Robert Peel calls the "mental drain" of being gazed upon and waved at by members of her own movement. Christian Scientists were now specifically enjoined in a By-Law of the *Manual* not to come to Concord.[9] In an essay called "Personal Contagion" which she contributed to the *Sentinel*, Mrs. Eddy once again adjured her followers not to cling to the personality of their leader if they wished the denomination to thrive in the future.

> This state of mind is sickly; it is a contagion—a mental malady, which must be met and overcome. Why? Because it would dethrone the First Commandment, Thou shalt have one God. . . . I left Boston in the height of prosperity to *retreat* from the *world*, and to seek the one divine Person, whereby and wherein to show others the footsteps from sense to Soul. To give me this opportunity is all that I ask of mankind. (*Miscellany*, pp. 116–17)

In this attempt to dampen a cult of personality among her following and to retreat into a more reflective way of life, Mrs. Eddy contrasts most favorably with those gurus and cult leaders who seek to bask in ever greater personal glory. But Mrs. Eddy's increasingly fierce indictments of "personality" and the day-to-day implications of the theory of mesmerism meant that details of her domestic life and routine were kept as secret as possible.[10] The issue of who had access to Mrs. Eddy personally and who did not became a highly charged one, and some Christian Scientists nurtured the conspiracy theory that the Boston men or some cabal at Pleasant View itself had control of Mrs. Eddy's person and therefore unchallenged authority over the whole Church and access to its financial resources.

That a cabal had successfully plotted to imprison Mrs. Eddy at Pleasant View was a rumor, not a fact. There seems to be no doubt that Mary Baker Eddy herself set up what might be called the policy of reclusion for herself, that she believed in it, insisted upon it, and theorized it. Mrs. Eddy had always needed large areas of silence around her, and in the 1880s the clammering, insistent "noise" of reports from friends and followers and rivals and critics and nosey parkers had threatened to deafen her. Some of her efforts to withdraw, to curtail personal correspondence and social calls, and to seek protection from intrusive admirers can be seen as the perfectly sensible efforts of an octogenarian woman to conserve energy. Nonetheless, as I read the various accounts of the last four years of her life, I wonder how far she came to regret her isolation and by the first few years of the 1900s to feel obscurely disturbed by the silence and the narrowing space she had set up around herself. The cell can serve prisoner and madman as well as monk, and sometimes Mrs. Eddy must have felt not powerful but vulnerable.

As I read Mary Baker Eddy's personal situation in her final years, chronic insecurity, well-grounded suspicion, and a not irrational fear of betrayal explain, in part at least, why Mary Baker Eddy so often railed at her

Mary Baker Eddy in 1891, pictured around the time of the publication of the important fiftieth edition of *Science and Health. Courtesy of Church History Department, The First Church of Christ, Scientist.*

Senator William Eaton Chandler, at about the time he was engaged by the New York *World* to lead the Next Friends suit which charged that Mary Baker Eddy was senile, legally incompetent, and ruled by a clique of advisors.

Frederick W. Peabody, date unknown. After his disastrous failure in the Woodbury libel suit, Boston lawyer Peabody fought for over twenty years to blacken Mary Baker Eddy's name and destroy Christian Science.

General Frank S. Streeter of Concord, New Hampshire, probably in the early 1890s. Mary Baker Eddy's trusted lawyer and advisor who helped her win the Woodbury libel suit and the Next Friends suit.

Augusta E. Stetson, the leader of the First Church of Christ, Scientist in New York City and Mary Baker Eddy's most successful and most controversial student. Pictured probably in the early 1880s. She was expelled from the Church in 1909.

George Washington Glover II, Mary Baker Eddy's son, at the time of his involvement in the Next Friends suit, 1907.

The entrance to Pleasant View, Mary Baker Eddy's beloved home in Concord, New Hampshire, around 1907, with members of her household standing by the roadside. *Courtesy of Church History Department, The First Church of Christ, Scientist.*

Mary Baker Eddy, photographed by Calvin Frye in about 1903, seated in her gold plush chair in her study at Pleasant View, with (l. to r.) Lida Fitzpatrick, Pamelia Leonard, and John Lathrop. *Courtesy of Church History Department, The First Church of Christ, Scientist.*

Mary Baker Eddy in her study at Pleasant View on February 22, 1903. Calvin Frye photograph. *Courtesy of Church History Department, The First Church of Christ, Scientist.*

The Christian Science Center, Boston, aerial view, circa 1987. *Courtesy of Church History Department, The First Church of Christ, Scientist.*

domestic staff and sometimes talked so wildly of mesmerism. The institution of Christian Science, with its Mother Church, its Board of Directors, its Trustees of the Publishing Society, its Committee on Publication, and so forth, stood to protect her against the world, and, as the combined attacks in 1906–1907 of Mark Twain, the *World*, and *McClure's Magazine* amply proved, she needed that protection. But throughout her life, the attacks on her from without had always been less dangerous than the attacks from within, and the movement's extraordinary recent successes had not changed this fact. Mrs. Eddy was old and she was tired, but she was not stupid, and she knew that her personal interests and those of Christian Science were no longer perceived by all within the movement as indistinguishable. All would doubtless mourn but some would not regret her passing on. As we come to look at the people who lined up on one side and the other of the Next Friends suit, it is, in my opinion, crucial to understand that some of the people on the "Nexters" side, a few of the men who supported the petition brought against her chosen associates, a few of the men who opposed her chosen lawyers in court, a few of the men who gave advice and support to the men Mrs. Eddy considered her enemies felt real affection and respect for her and acted in what they perceived to be her best interests.[11]

To return, however, to the situation in Concord at the end of October 1906, what neither the members of the press corps who crowded into the town nor the Christian Scientists in Chicago or New York understood was that Mrs. Eddy had never ceased to be accessible to a number of citizens of Concord—to odd-job gardeners and painters, or to local editors and bank managers—*especially if they had no connection with Christian Science.* Two of these men—Fred Ladd and Henry Baker—were not only notable citizens with no affiliation with Christian Science or fealty to The Mother Church in Boston; they were Mrs. Eddy's cousins and could thus be considered to be solicitous of her interests as a private citizen. To these people, the idea that someone was impersonating Mrs. Eddy and that she was a helpless, dying pawn was not merely ludicrous but offensive. The citizens of Concord, therefore—with some notable exceptions, as we shall see—prepared to go to Mrs. Eddy's defense and combat the press attacks she was facing, not just from the New York *World* and its more careful but no less hostile colleague, the *New York Times*, but from *McClure's Magazine*, which was to print the first part of its long-awaited series on Mrs. Eddy in the December 1906 edition.

Mary Baker Eddy was widely respected in Concord, she was New Hampshire's most famous resident, and she and her church had brought a good deal of money into the state. (Later, after Mrs. Eddy suddenly left Concord in January 1908 for her new home in Chestnut Hill, a group of local businessmen made a rough estimate of what sums Mrs. Eddy had brought into Concord, and they came up with a total of $1,570,000.[12]) As George Moses, the editor of the *Concord Monitor*, wrote in the conclusion to the statement he quickly made for publication, denying the truth of the October 28, 1906, *World* report:

> While it would be futile to assert that Mrs. Eddy is wholly without critics or opponents in Concord, it is entirely within the bounds of accuracy to say that by the vast majority of all our people, and most emphatically by those who by their position in the community are most entitled to represent that intangible spirit which we call public opinion, she is regarded as our foremost citizen. Her numerous good works, her constant and consistent charities here, her keen interest in all that makes for the betterment of the community, and her blameless, laborious, and useful life among us, all contribute to make her beloved and respected by the people of Concord, and we all hope that she may live long in her present full possession of physical, mental, and spiritual power to continue her good work among us.[13]

Even before the *World* article appeared in 1906, Michael Meehan, the Roman Catholic editor of the *Concord Patriot* who had had various professional dealings with Mrs. Eddy over the years (and who would go on to write his own book about the Next Friends suit) got wind of what the *World* reporters were preparing to print. He wrote to Joseph Pulitzer at Bar Harbor, Maine, to warn him that if he accepted his reporters' claims that Mrs. Eddy was dead or incapacitated he would be making a great mistake and committing an equally great injustice. Pulitzer, personally and publicly, ignored Meehan's letter and also a subsequent interview given to the Associated Press by the mayor of Concord, Charles R. Corning, and General Frank Streeter, Mrs. Eddy's lawyer. The two men described a meeting which they had had with Mrs. Eddy on October 28, and they stressed that the agility of both mind and body she had then displayed was astonishing in one so old. Corning, who had never before met Mrs. Eddy and could thus be seen as an impartial witness, gave a longer interview to the *Boston Herald*, in which he stated:

> I had gone expecting to find a tottering old woman, perhaps incoherent, almost senile. Instead, when she rose to greet me, her carriage was almost erect, her walk that of a woman of forty. I have seen many old ladies, but never one with the vigorous personality of Mrs. Mary Baker G. Eddy. . . .
>
> She remembered local incidents and happenings of recent date, talked family matters with General Streeter, and to try her mind he asked her concerning the date of her donation of one thousand dollars annually to the State fair. She remembered within a few days when the agreement was drawn up two years ago. To say that she is mentally vigorous is

inside the mark. She is wonderful for an octogenarian. Her face is not full, her figure is slight, but she looks commanding, her eyes are bright, her handclasp is firm. We talked with her for half an hour, and at the end of that time, when she rose to bid us good-by, Mrs. Eddy showed no sign of fatigue.[14]

The *World* was not swayed from its opinions by this kind of interview, its reporters preferring to believe that there was a conspiracy in Concord to conceal the truth at Pleasant View, and that the businessmen of the town had been bought off with some of Mrs. Eddy's supposedly fabulous fortune.[15] Concord was swarming with reporters, and the demand was now made that Mrs. Eddy again subject herself to an interview, this time with a larger group of newsmen, answer some questions, and, once again, prove to the unbelieving that she was quick of mind and body. The meeting was agreed to and set up in great detail for Tuesday, October 30. Representatives of (depending on the report!) fourteen, eleven, or nine leading newspapers and press associations were invited to gather at 12:50 P.M. in the main parlor at Pleasant View. On her way out to her carriage, Mrs. Eddy would come in, answer four presubmitted questions, and then leave the house under the eyes of the press. The reporter whom Pleasant View chose to ask the questions was Sibyl Wilbur O'Brien who had done a previous, highly laudatory piece on Mrs. Eddy, based on personal interviews. The Christian Scientists were aware at the time, as the other reporters were not, that Wilbur was writing a "positive" biographical series on Mrs. Eddy that would within weeks be competing head-to-head with the "negative" Milmine series.[16] The reporters from the New York *World* were barred from attending the scheduled interview.

Despite efforts to put on a good face and keep busy, Mary Baker Eddy not surprisingly anticipated the proposed press interview on October 30 with dread. Disproving the charge that one is incapacitated, time after time, is grim work at any age, and Mrs. Eddy was now a very old lady whose strength had been tested in January by a severe attack of her old kidney stone problem. She had always seen her home as her refuge, and now she had to suffer its invasion. She was used to bad press, but the Sunday article in the *World* had hit a new low, proving just how unfair and inaccurate journalists can be, even when one has attempted to cooperate with them. All in all, she felt acutely under attack from the forces which she called mesmerism, and which on this occasion were very real and camped out in force on her front lawn, composing lies for the mass market. Thus when she opened the door to her parlor and stood facing the expectant press members on October 30, Mrs. Eddy quailed, and her hands shook. She gave brief answers to the first three questions, but then she turned on her heel and left the house for her carriage ride before the fourth question could even be asked.

The interview was a disastrous failure, too short to prove or disprove any specific fact, leaving the journalists to fall back on their preconceptions and write down what they had expected to see—with the rhetorical flourishes needed to make the front page. In a passage which Robert Peel says is famous in Christian Science biography, Fleta Campbell Springer summarized the different reports:

[Mrs. Eddy] "bowed low and with ceremonial precision, reminding one of the entrance of a great diva before an audience made up of fashion and wealth"; "shaking and trembling, she tottered forward, clutching the curtains with palsied hands and paused swaying in the door"; "her eyes, large, dark and lustrous, sought out Mrs. O'Brien, whom she greeted with a smile"; "her faded, lusterless eyes roamed vacantly in space above the heads of the crowd"; "her feebleness seemed only consistent with her great age"; "she stood before them shaking with palsy, a physical wreck, tottering, pallid like a vision from beyond the grave"; "she stood before them erect and upright, nerved for the ordeal"; she wore a black cloak; she wore a cape of white ermine.[17]

As far as I can deduce from the published accounts by pressmen and the internal memos of the Pleasant View staff, one reason that the whole event failed in its purpose was because it had been so carefully orchestrated and staged by the Christian Scientists that it aroused suspicion. The four questions were stupid,[18] the questioner Sibyl Wilbur O'Brien turned out to be a stooge, and the answers were obviously rehearsed. Dressed in furs and feathers and diamonds, but drained of color and energy, Mrs. Eddy looked to many eyes like a grotesque puppet. The reporters were prevented by the closed doors of the parlor from seeing Mrs. Eddy walking down the stairs— which she did every day—so reports of her falling and being supported or even carried could not be contradicted even by a journalist who was willing to form a new opinion. On the very next day, alerted to their error, the Pleasant View staff arranged for two worthy men to stand unseen and unannounced and watch Mrs. Eddy walk downstairs and get into her carriage— an event which, in itself, illustrates the unavowed combination of external and internal espionage Mrs. Eddy had to face and which doubled the stress she was under.[19] Above all, feeling a stranger in her own front parlor, Mrs. Eddy was unable to look the reporters in the eye and command respect. The staff's obvious efforts to support and protect her, though grossly exaggerated in press reports, gave credence to the story that there existed a plot to rule Christian Science with Mrs. Eddy as a figurehead.

Given society's ready assumptions about women's mental infirmity, especially in old age, it was hard for strangers even to conjecture that the reverse was true—that without the firm authority of their leader the Pleasant View secretaries and even the Boston public relations staff led by Alfred Farlow were running around like chickens before the fox. Only those fully conversant with Christian Science history knew that it was Mary Baker Eddy herself who had always held things together when disaster struck, and that it was the combination of a relentless barrage of hostile press coverage from several quarters with a real but temporary ebb in her own vitality that had produced the recent media debacle. Thus, far from ending all the controversy once and for all, as Mrs. Eddy's household had hoped, the encounter with the massed forces of the press only fueled the fire.

Nothing that Joseph Pulitzer heard about this crucial interview from his own representatives or read in other publications was calculated to convince him that he was wrong in his analysis of the situation at Pleasant View. To the contrary, he felt encouraged to continue his crusade. Judging from his actions in the next months and the written statements of his chosen agents and representatives, I surmise that Pulitzer's thinking went as follows. Mary Baker Eddy had founded a religious movement whose influence must be arrested. She was now a poor, pathetic old ghost with far too much money for her own good. Chivalry as well as public spirit demanded that something extraordinary be done to break up the cabal led by Calvin Frye, to reveal its machinations to the world, and to free Mrs. Eddy. Even the power of the press was not adequate to this task, especially given that the Christian Science movement had long experience with newspapers and had developed its own active propaganda unit, the Committee on Publication. Force of law was needed here; hence Joseph Pulitzer decided to take an extraordinary step. He would hire legal counsel and instigate a suit which would bring the men controlling Mrs. Eddy's affairs into court and expose their wrongdoing, thus proving the essential truth (if not the precise factual accuracy!) of his paper's recent assertions. Unfortunately for Pulitzer, he himself did not have the legal standing to bring such an action, but there was one man who certainly did—Mary Baker Eddy's son, George Washington Glover II. This son, and perhaps some other relatives who could be hunted up, would have the legal status and moral authority as Mrs. Eddy's next of kin to instigate an inquiry into the state of her affairs. But before approaching Glover—who was known from the press record to have accepted Christian Science and to be loyal to his mother—Pulitzer needed the right lawyer to prepare the brief and to direct strategy.

I conjecture that one of the reasons that Pulitzer was so swift to take a legal tack was that he or his agents had already located a chief counsel ready, willing, and qualified to proceed against the Christian Science movement. This person was the former U.S. Senator from New Hampshire William Eaton Chandler.[20] In 1906 Chandler was living in Washington and presiding over the Spanish Treaty Claims Commission, but he was one of New Hampshire's most famous native sons, he considered Concord his home, and he and his eldest son owned the Concord *Monitor*. Born in Concord in 1835 and a graduate of the Harvard Law School, Chandler had already had a long and prestigious career, not so much in the practice of law as in Republican Party politics at the state and national level. A party activist and lobbyist as well as a political office holder and federal and state appointee, now the grand old man of the New Hampshire Republican Party, Chandler was nevertheless not rich by the standards of his caste. Thus, blessed with excellent health and boundless energy, he had not notably slowed down the rate of his professional activities as he entered his seventies.

Known for his intellectual brilliance and capacity for hard work as well as for his probity and commitment to public service, Chandler also had a reputation as a firebrand, swift to pick quarrels and relishing a fight. One of the people with whom he had publicly taken issue in recent years was his Concord neighbor Mary Baker Eddy. Philosophically a positivist who probably put as much trust in reason and science as in the Protestantism of his upbringing, Chandler was averse to what he had learned of Christian Science, with its claims to spiritual healings and its preoccupation with hypnotic influence. Furthermore, as practical politicians and men of business, Chandler and his Republican friends were at odds with the Concord group which Mrs. Eddy had entrusted with her affairs on returning to her native state—notably with Congressman Henry Baker, Mrs. Eddy's cousin and confidant; Josiah Fernald, her local banker; and General Frank Streeter, her main legal advisor. Professional rivalry, financial competition, intellectual hostility all combined to make Chandler eager to direct a new legal challenge at Christian Science.

Chandler never seems to have worked full-time on what would become known as the Next Friends suit, and he was still spending most of his time in Washington up to the point when the suit was heard in Concord in the late summer of 1907; hence he needed to communicate with his legal associates and local contacts in Concord by mail and telegram. Over the nine months of the suit, Chandler became more and more embroiled in it, and we can follow his day-to-day activities as chief counsel to the Next Friends through the meticulous records which he maintained and preserved. After his death, these records, along with a large collection of his personal papers, were donated by his heirs to the New Hampshire Historical Society, and they are required reading for anyone interested in Mary Baker Eddy in her final years, as well as American society's reactions to Christian Science in the first decade of the twentieth century. I spent some of my most absorbed hours as a researcher reading in the Chandler papers, and the following account of the Next Friends suit mainly adopts the fine but slightly distorted lens which the papers offer.[21]

It seems probable that Chandler had been contacted by the Pulitzer people at the time the *World* team was preparing its bombshell article for publication on October 28. Certainly, the documents show that by November 22, 1906, Chandler was in close communication with John Slaght, was negotiating financial terms with the *World* editors, and was taking on lawyer John W. Kelley of Concord to run affairs for him in New Hampshire. Kelley was chosen in part because he, too, had tangled in the past with Streeter and Baker. Chandler was fully aware that his client, the New York *World*, had no legal standing in the suit which was being considered, and in an early letter to his new associate, Chandler explained how he saw the situation:

> [A]ny proceedings must not be merely sensational or cover up an attempt at blackmail. It is necessary to be sure that there are genuine relatives of Mrs. Eddy who sincerely desire and have a right to take suitable steps. If there is reason to believe that she is practically imbecile and not having made a will while she was competent to do so, any property she may possess or may leave belongs to her existing heirs, and unless she comes back to her senses and capacity she cannot make a will to give it to any one else.[22]

Acting on this analysis, Chandler decided that Pulitzer's point man in the Eddy matter, John W. Slaght, should be dispatched to Lead, South Dakota, to inform Mrs. Eddy's son of what was happening in Concord, and to bear to Glover a letter addressed to Slaght and written by Chandler himself, outlining the situation in Concord, as he understood it, and his own and Pulitzer's intentions. Slaght handed this letter to George Glover, who had been prevailed upon by his wife Nellie to receive the journalist and hear what he had to say. The Glovers had not only read the *World* article; they had also received a letter from Hermann S. Hering of the First Church of Christ, Scientist in Concord, denying the *World*'s account. Also enclosed were the rebuttals written by local worthies which had been printed the following day in the Concord *Monitor*. But Slaght, visiting the Glovers in person, was the ideal man to give them a graphic eyewitness description of poor Mrs. Eddy's state, and of the control exercised over her by her villainous entourage.

The request that, in essence, he urgently join in a legal suit against the officials of his mother's church placed George in a dilemma. George was an affectionate man with a strong sense of family who wished his mother well, was proud of her reputation, and sought to protect her. The hostile press coverage which she had been receiving in recent years angered him, and, although he no doubt was awed by receiving a visit in his isolated home from the personal representative of a New York press magnate, he was not favorably disposed toward the *World*. George had also long subscribed to his mother's teachings, and he believed fervently in her powers as a healer, attributing his survival after being wounded in the Civil War to her absent treatments.[23]

On the other hand, the very sincerity of George's conversion to Christian Science had caused serious problems between him and his mother.

In 1889, when Evelyn Glover had seemed at the point of death, George had written in despair, begging his mother to take her granddaughter's case personally and perform an absent treatment, but she wrote firmly but affectionately to say that this was impossible.[24] In 1893 George took the step of bringing his sick wife unannounced to Concord, so that Mrs. Eddy could heal her. Not only did Mrs. Eddy refuse to intervene personally in Nellie's case; she would not even see her son for six weeks and then accorded him only a brief twenty-five-minute interview.[25] Although Nellie soon mended and was, indeed, to live into the 1940s, the ever sickly Evelyn died at the age of twenty-three, less than two years after her wedding to Warren Schell in 1902. There is no evidence that George understood the theological reasons for his mother's adamant refusal to treat members of his family and, although Mrs. Eddy in fact sincerely mourned her favorite grandchild, Evelyn's untimely death was another scar on the relationship between mother and son.[26]

Eternally complicating the relations between George and his mother was the question of money. To summarize the recent history of relations between George Glover and Mary Baker Eddy, in 1894 or 1895, alerted to the Glover family's needy situation, Mrs. Eddy had invested some $12,000 in mortgages on landholdings in Wichita, Kansas, through her agents in the West. She then transferred the properties to her son, as a way of assuring that he receive a regular income but not get his hands on a lump sum he could divert from living expenses into gold prospecting.[27] This proved a bad investment for all concerned, exacerbating relations between mother and son, since George was infuriated by his mother's lack of confidence in his financial acumen. According to what George wrote to his mother on August 7, 1895, the Wichita real estate was worth only a fraction of what she had paid for it, and, far from getting income from it, he was forced to sell, at bargain-basement prices, a portion of the land in order to make tax payments on the rest. When apprised by her son of what had occurred, Mrs. Eddy wrote that she not only believed his story but was glad to hear that he had acted responsibly in selling the plot of land, and she wearily sent a check for $1,000.[28]

In earlier letters she had taken another tack, and remembering her own early difficulties as the marriageable daughter of a notably thrifty man, Mrs. Eddy made a number of offers to pay for the two girls to be educated at a school in St. Joseph, Missouri.[29] She wanted Evelyn and Mary to attend a boarding school where they could "learn a thousand times faster and more practically books, manners, language, orthography and music."[30] None of her efforts in this respect succeeded. The amounts of money Mrs. Eddy's agents sent west always seemed very miserly to George and Nellie, who in any case resented having to send their daughters away from home. They also disliked Charles Howe, the Christian Scientist Mrs. Eddy had appointed to superintend the girls' education in St. Joseph, and when Howe proposed marriage to Evelyn, both Evelyn and Mary were brought home by their not unreasonably indignant parents and received no further education.

The Glovers' exceptionally meager living accommodation was another thing which upset Mrs. Eddy, and which she felt she could reasonably do something about.[31] Thus after years of encouraging her son to buy a nice home for his growing family, to no avail, in 1899 Mrs. Eddy arranged for a splendid house to be built in Lead for the Glovers as a Christmas gift. Unwilling, as usual, to trust George with money, Mrs. Eddy employed a Christian Scientist to supervise the building of the home. Sadly the house proved to be badly constructed, poorly suited to the Glover family's needs, and was far too expensive for them to maintain.[32] The Glover house in Lead has been portrayed by loyal Christian Science biographers as an example of Mrs. Eddy's generosity, and by her detractors as an expression of her taste-less grandiosity. My feeling is that it above all symbolizes the strains that were again threatening to snap the fragile bond between Mrs. Eddy and her son. Camping out in their fine new mansion with its leaky walls and unpaid taxes, George Glover must have seen the gift as a tantalizing taste of the wealth and social position to which he had ceaselessly and vainly aspired, which his mother enjoyed, and which she seemed determined to withhold from him.[33]

By 1903 George was in such desperate straits that he journeyed to Concord to make a personal appeal to his mother for money. By this time he was aware that his letters might not get past her secretaries. Overwhelmed as always by the physical presence of her son, and by her real affection for him, Mrs. Eddy listened to George's pleas for capital, and on the spot she wrote a check for $5,000 to cover his debts. She was also agreeing to give him $30,000 for a quartz mill when Calvin Frye walked into the room to take her out for her daily carriage ride. Glover went out and quickly cashed the check, and his haste was justified when subsequently his mother wrote to retract her promise to finance the mill, claiming that Calvin Frye would not let her dispose of her money as she liked. It seems clear that, on the one hand, Frye was just Mrs. Eddy's convenient excuse for going back on an impulsive offer that she swiftly regretted. Had she given her son $30,000 in 1903, he probably would not have been any richer by 1906, when by the account of his own lawyer he was again $6,000 in debt. Nonetheless, this final interview served to convince George that his mother was financially well able to give him all the money he needed or desired, and also that Frye and the other Christian Science men surround-ing Mrs. Eddy would never allow her to do so. Once again, as in his childhood, there was a plot to keep him and his mother apart.[34]

As Slaght was privately reporting back to Chandler on December 5, 1906, the Glover family had been living on credit for three years, had received no help from Mrs. Eddy since 1903, and were at this point living "in abject poverty."[35] This was hardly Mrs. Eddy's fault since for almost thirty years she had tried in various rather innovative ways to make the family self-supporting. George's blithe conviction that he had discovered a mysterious "attraction" to "locate gold leads beneath the surface of the ground [and] determine their width and richness," as well as an expensive taste for litigation he developed in later years would defeat even her.[36] The family's urgent money problems predisposed Nellie and her children, if not George himself, to view Slaght and Chandler as the cavalry coming in the nick of time to save them.

Given the complex financial and psychological relationship between Mrs. Eddy and her son, what Chandler wrote in the letter addressed to Slaght and delivered to Glover proved exceptionally astute. The unedited version we find in the Chandler papers reads as follows:

Washington D.C. Nov. 22, 1906

My Dear Mr. Slaght: I consent to act as counsel concerning certain questions which arise in connection with Mrs. Mary Baker G. Eddy. It seems clear that there are doubts about several points.

I.

Mrs. Eddy MAY BE detained in the custody of strangers against her will.

II.

She MAY BE so nearly worn out in body and mind as a confirmed invalid that she is incapable of deciding any questions whatever, according to any will or pleasure of her own—and necessarily therefore incapable of managing her business and property affairs.

III.

Being thus restrained or incapable and without relatives near her she MAY BE surrounded by designing men who either have already sought or MAY hereafter seek to wrongfully possess themselves of her large property, or induce her to make a disposition of it contrary to what would be her sane and deliberate intentions if she were in perfect possession of her liberty and mental faculties.

These doubts have arisen in connection with investigations recently made by you and having come to Mr. Pulitzer's knowledge, they pass beyond the domain of newspaper enterprise and impose the steps which you and Mr. Pulitzer and others are contemplating to solve the doubts, to correct the wrong, if it exists, and to establish the right in every respect.

This work should be done, if possible, in cooperation with Mrs. Eddy's son, or any other relative who may be impressed with his duties in this respect: and if the relatives do not move, it should be done by such right-minded citizens as are in sympathy with the commendable movement.

Yours truly,
William E. Chandler[37]

While couching his fears about Mrs. Eddy's health and safety in a good lawyer's carefully hypothetical terms, Chandler appealed not to George's pocketbook but to his sense of duty and male chivalry. The good-hearted George could respond readily to the plea that he join with other public-minded citizens in saving his beloved mother from the vile schemes of her treacherous associates. All the same, the subtext of the letter and of Slaght's visit—that the great Eastern lawyer who was offering his services might be the way to ensure that George inherited his mother's millions—was also calculated not to displease. If, as Slaght maintained, Mrs. Eddy had in fact been in the control of a wicked "crowd of controllers," led by Frye, since her retreat to Pleasant View, or even earlier, this would provide an agreeable explanation of the many disagreeable things she had done to George and his family, and her recent silence. Finally, by responding to Chandler's plea, George could both adore the wonderful woman his mother had once been, and at the same time rush east to save the helpless puppet she had become. Furthermore, he would prevent the family fortunes from falling, against her wishes, into unworthy hands.

Glover therefore responded to Chandler in a letter of November 30, saying that he wished above all to assess his mother's condition in person, and that he would welcome the help of any friend willing to give him the financial means to make the necessary trip east, together with his daughter Mary. Initially this request that Mary too come east was resisted as an unnecessary expense; it took a while for Slaght and Chandler to grasp that George and Nellie could neither read nor write and that each of them would therefore need someone at hand at all times to process written communications. Glover also agreed in this letter that he would give to Slaght and the *World* an exclusive account of his intended meeting with his mother.

Slaght reported by letter to Chandler that Glover was willing to "do anything you advise," but noted, "his [Glover's] real fear is that if by chance his mother should be fairly sound in mind and not incompetent, as he firmly believes her to be, any action by him would lead to his certain disinheritance." This comment shows that George Glover was by no means stupid. While attracted to the dazzling prospects laid before him by Chandler and Pulitzer, George in fact knew his mother and understood her situation better than either of them, and he had doubts that she was quite as far gone as they had represented her to be. He was aware that he had much to risk in cooperating with them, and that he was placing his family's future in the hands of strangers who had interests and priorities very different from his own. But George Glover had always been a gambler, and he was a true Baker in his taste for litigation.

As George Glover and his daughter and amanuensis Mary delightedly prepared to travel to Washington to meet Chandler at the end of December, all expenses paid, Chandler himself was putting together his legal team and

working out the complex legal situation he found himself in, vis-à-vis the
New York *World*, his client. At the newspaper's headquarters there was still
enthusiasm about the dramatic news Slaght was telegraphing back about his
experiences in South Dakota, which would appear as part of a two-page
spread in the paper's March 2, 1907, edition. But Joseph Pulitzer's son Ralph,
who was officially in control at the paper, and the financial manager Bradford
Merrill and the legal counsel John M. Bowers were alarmed at the legal crusade their leader had embarked upon. These men at the *World* saw themselves not only writing a blank check for legal and personal expenses and
becoming party to a notably thorny suit in which they had no direct interest,
but also, and perhaps most important, risking the loss of readers at the same
time.

Thus when Senator Chandler's chosen junior counsel, John Kelley, travelled to New York and met with Bowers and Merrill on December 4, he was
disagreeably surprised by his reception at the newspaper, as he hastened to
report back to Chandler. Bowers told Kelley, in the presence of Merrill, that
he himself had consistently refused to conduct "litigation of a public nature"
on behalf of the New York *World*, implying that Joseph Pulitzer had tried to
embark on lost causes in the past but had been pulled back in time by his
advisors. Worse still, Bowers, according to Kelley, "plainly expressed contempt for any evidence or reports adduced by *World* reporters" and said flat
out that he did not think Chandler and Kelley "had any facts to go on."[38]

Amazingly, William Chandler took no notice of this brotherly warning
from the distinguished counsel in New York not to take as truth anything
that appeared in the pages of the New York *World*! He was undeterred even
after receiving a response from Merrill in the form of a letter written on
December 12, which offered vague reassurances and a $500 check to pay the
expenses for George Glover to travel east and to begin the preparations for
a bill in equity. The letter ended with some important news: Joseph Pulitzer's
"state of . . . health has compelled him to leave New York for the winter. He
is now at Mentone, and is receiving no business communications whatever,
and therefore cannot be consulted."[39]

Had Chandler reacted with his usual intelligence to what Bowers and
Merrill were telling him, had he believed Bowers instead of Slaght, had he
understood that the famous Joseph Pulitzer no longer called all the shots at
the *World*, and that younger men might view the Eddy affair very differently,
he would have saved himself a great deal of trouble. Instead, he went on
researching the law, planning his course of action, finding out as much as
possible about Christian Science and Mrs. Eddy's financial affairs, and reassuring his official and insolvent client George Glover that he had nothing to
fear. If Mary Baker Eddy is out of her mind today, to paraphrase what he
wrote to George on December 10, she cannot make a will, so we have lost
nothing by our suit. If she has already made a will, as seems most probable,

it is unlikely you will inherit much if anything, given the poor state of relations between both of you. If the will were to be successfully challenged in court, you stand to get all or much more of your mother's estate. But in any case, he urges George, sounding the chivalry theme again, it is your filial duty to protect your mother and her interests.

In January 1907 a new figure entered the scene, in the person of our old friend Frederick Peabody. After his return east, Slaght was still acting as Chandler's investigator, presumably on the *World*'s payroll, and he had moved to Boston to find out everything he could about Christian Science— who its officers were, what properties Mrs. Eddy owned, whether she received any revenue from the healers in her church, what had happened at the Massachusetts Metaphysical College. Inevitably Slaght's researches brought him to Peabody's offices on Tremont Street,[40] and to the latter's intense joy, Peabody was hired as another junior counsel in the suit. Peabody then began to funnel to Chandler and his New Hampshire team all the "facts" about Mrs. Eddy and her Science, which he had amassed, first for his client Josephine Woodbury, then for his client Minot J. Savage, and most recently for Georgine Milmine and Willa Cather of *McClure's Magazine*. Like Mark Twain, William Chandler did not particularly care for Peabody as a man; he must have recognized that Peabody's eagerly avowed hatred for Mrs. Eddy was extreme and could pose a potential liability in the suit. Also like Twain, however, Chandler himself nourished a largely unconscious antipathy toward Mary Baker Eddy which clouded his judgment and predisposed him to accept as truth all the "facts" which Peabody related to him, backed as they were by so much apparently objective evidence—affidavits, interviews, old documents, letters, and so forth.[41]

Once Chandler began working with Peabody, the course of the Next Friends suit became inextricably entwined with the Milmine biographical series which was appearing in *McClure's* at precisely the same time as Chandler was building his case. Chandler accepted as true the vivid picture *McClure's* painted of Mrs. Eddy as a youthful hysteric who in her late forties had been afflicted with religious delusions heavily tinged with paranoia, and was now, in old age, a victim of senile dementia and paralysis agitans (i.e., Parkinson's disease).[42] The working assumption of the team of men working on the Next Friends suit under Chandler's leadership was that *McClure's* was presenting the facts, and that all other accounts of Mrs. Eddy were false, prejudiced, and designed to mislead. That factual errors in the Milmine account began to show up immediately—the picture of Mrs. Eddy featured at the head of the December edition with her signature superimposed over it proved, in fact, to be a picture of Mrs. Sarah C. Chevaillier!—did not disturb Chandler's fatal presumption of the accuracy of the *McClure's* series.

On January 2 George Glover and his daughter Mary arrived at Pleasant View to see Mrs. Eddy, and later that day Mary and a stenographer recorded a memorandum of their visit.[43] According to the later account given to the *World*, the Glover party was kept waiting for fifteen minutes, and Mary fancied she had heard the whir of the famous and almost certainly mythical galvanic battery Slaght had described in October. As they entered the room, Mrs. Eddy appeared not to notice her son and granddaughter for several minutes, but then she embraced them affectionately and with tears. She complained that the press was maligning her first husband, George's father. This remark the Glovers no doubt believed justified, since the most recent issue of *McClure's* had, indeed, reported that George Glover Sr. had been a "bricklayer" and had been buried in an unmarked pauper's grave. Thinking someone was listening at the door, George went to close it. (I imagine he may well have been right!) Mrs. Eddy asked the Glovers what had brought them to Concord, and she seemed to accept George's vague reply about business interests. As on so many occasions in the past, he assured his mother that, although he was rather in debt just at present and engaged in a few lawsuits, he owned several fine mining properties and needed only the capital to develop them. When also, as she had many times before, Mrs. Eddy remarked that he would never make any money in mining, he begged to differ. Mrs. Eddy asked her relatives if they had seen the new Extension in Boston. She told them that she had given the land for the small old church, and when they wanted to build the new big one she had refused to allow the small one to be torn down.

The Glovers came away from Pleasant View convinced that Mary Baker Eddy was, indeed, wandering in her wits, as well as distinctly paranoiac. They adduced several points to support their conclusion. Under questioning, Mrs. Eddy had shown no knowledge of what had happened in San Francisco (1906 was the year of the terrific earthquake and great fire) or of the doings of President Roosevelt: she said she no longer had a chance to read the newspapers. Mrs. Eddy claimed that two men from Lead had stolen her will, forcing her to make another, which she had now put away safely; she was unable to name her lawyer. She claimed that an expensive pair of horses had been given her by a Southern man who wanted to kill her. When the young Mary made some ill-advised remark about Christian Science doctrine, Mrs. Eddy was stung into noting that she should know better since she had taken class with "Mrs. McMann." When Mary denied this, Mrs. Eddy claimed she had a letter to prove it, called for her secretaries to find the letter, and, when they failed and denied knowledge of any such letter, she searched feverishly and vainly for it through her own drawers.

Over the next months Chandler and the Glovers would work diligently to find out the facts about the will, the horses, and "Mrs. McMann," and as a result of their researches some conclusions can be made about Mrs. Eddy's mistakes. It is certain that her 1901 will was lost and a new one had to be enacted in 1903; the loss of so important a document is peculiar and must have caused a sensation in a household perpetually preoccupied with signs of mesmerism. There is, however, no evidence that I know of that any men from Lead stole the will. As for the horses, an adoring admirer of Mrs. Eddy's did send, unsolicited, a gift of two very handsome and very spirited horses, called Tattersall and Exersall, who proved unsuitable for her use and probably did give her a great scare on their single excursion. Mrs. Eddy was obviously very worried about having an accident while out on her drive, and in her sadder moments she may well have believed the strange horses represented a plot to kill her.[44] As for the reference to "Mrs. McMann," Mary herself subsequently remembered that she had been in touch with a Christian Scientist lady called Mrs. Frances Mann, née Mack, who had gone west. This lady had maintained some correspondence with Mrs. Eddy, who thus had not been far off the mark on the subject which interested her most—Christian Science.

From all the evidence, it seems that on January 2, whether from emotion at seeing her son and granddaughter after so many years or from justified fears that it was not simply love and concern that brought them to Concord, Mrs. Eddy was not at her best. On the other hand, the mistakes she made, her general vagueness, were hardly unusual in a woman of eighty-five who was being subjected to personal and private scrutiny and was hence under stress. If paranoia was her problem, she had been markedly more paranoiac when George had visited her back in 1879 and learned about the mesmeric machinations of Richard Kennedy. It may be remembered that George's reaction then had not been to have his mother committed, but to embrace Christian Science and to threaten Richard Kennedy with death if he did not cease his mesmerist activities.[45] In 1879, of course, Mrs. Eddy was an attractive and dynamic woman in her fifties with a husband by her side and all her supposed millions still to make.

Following their visit to Concord, the Glovers went to stay in Washington for several months. There they had meetings with Chandler and fell under the spell of his brilliant mind, and, in Mary's case, of his old-world charm and courtesy.[46]

Meanwhile, from the Christian Science side, things were also moving. Irving Tomlinson was sent out to Lead, South Dakota, to try to persuade Nellie Glover to give up the letters which Mrs. Eddy had written to her family over the years. Tomlinson bore a personal letter from Mrs. Eddy, dated February 8, 1907, addressed not to Nellie herself, but to her widower son-in-law Warren Schell. By ignoring Nellie and so obviously marking the fact that she could not read, Mrs. Eddy or her advisors were again pouring salt in the Glovers' wounds and did not ingratiate themselves with the inhabitants of 11 North Main Street, Lead. In the letter Mrs. Eddy told Schell that she had received a letter from James P. Wilson, George Glover's former business partner, warning her that Glover was planning something underhanded and advising her to reclaim the letters. Telegrams flew between Washington and Lead, with George and his lawyers advising Nellie to conceal not only that the letters were now in Chandler's possession, but that George Glover was not intending to give them up.[47]

Glover had by this time found it necessary and possible to hire himself a rather distinguished legal counsel in Deadwood City, Judge Granville G. Bennett, who basically served as Chandler's point man in the Dakotas. In his several lengthy communications with Judge Bennett over the next months, Chandler wastes no ink on chivalrous concern for Mrs. Eddy's safety and the public interest; he concentrates on Glover's financial expectations as Mrs. Eddy's heir. With Bennett's help Chandler defines the property and inheritance issues as carefully as possible, keeps tabs on events in Lead, and seeks to prevent the Glovers from getting too restive and acting independently. It is Bennett who tells Chandler that he has been drafting for Glover an indignant response to a recent interview published on March 13 in the Denver *Post* by James P. Wilson, the same man who had written to Mrs. Eddy recommending she get her letters back from George. Wilson had for a time handled his former business partner's correspondence, and he claimed—not inaccurately!—that George Glover was in deep financial distress as a result of bad mining ventures, that for years he had relied on his mother to bail him out but that she had finally balked, and that he was now trying to prove her senile in order to get his hands on her large estate. Glover was sensitive to public criticism of this kind—especially from former friends with first-class information—and Chandler and Bennett feared that things like the Wilson interview might make George Glover regret his cooperation with them and push him instead into the arms of The Mother Church.

On his return to Lead in early March, George would face more than one piece of disturbing news. Still uncertain about whether the Glovers would choose to cooperate in the suit, Chandler's colleague Kelley in New Hampshire had located another relative willing to expose the cabal at Pleasant View and eager to secure the release of Mrs. Eddy from captivity—her nephew George Waldron Baker. Although the amount of his indebtedness was smaller, George Baker was as impecunious as his first cousin in South Dakota, and he too had dependent relatives, in the persons of an aged mother and an epileptic wife. As he explained at length to Kelley, he had once been extremely fond of his aunt Mary, and she of him. In the 1880s he had made several unsuccessful attempts to get in to see her, and in recent years she had not even responded to his letters. He was now convinced that she had never, in fact, received them.

Provided that he was sent all his expenses in advance, George Baker was more than willing to be party to the proposed suit, and to make statements and offer written substantiation. He had providently kept copies of all the letters he had sent to Mrs. Eddy, as well as the replies from the staff secretaries. Kelley and Chandler saw George Baker as potentially a better party to the suit than George Glover. Chandler was especially moved by the fact that in his most recent letters to Carpenter the impoverished Baker had enclosed a two-cent stamp and had still received no reply. Here at least, Chandler felt, was an obviously honest man who loved his aunt and feared for her safety, and who could not be accused of being after her money, since he was not her direct heir. For as long as possible, Chandler concealed from George Glover the fact that George Baker was also to be party to the suit.[48]

Worse news for George Glover in his capacity as heir to the putative Eddy millions came after Frederick Peabody thought to remind Chandler of the existence of Ebenezer Foster Eddy, Mrs. Eddy's estranged adopted son. If the adoption had been completed properly, Peabody noted in one of his letters, Foster Eddy was presumably entitled to half of the estate, so he should be contacted to see if he was interested in becoming party to the suit. In fact, Foster Eddy himself, reading each new issue of *McClure's Magazine* as well as the press reports about possible legal action by Mrs. Eddy's heirs, perhaps also getting some private news about the situation at Pleasant View from old friends in Christian Science, had decided for himself that the time had come to remind his darling Mother of his existence. Familiar with how things worked at Pleasant View, Foster addressed his letter not to Mrs. Eddy, who he feared would never get it, but to her friend and companion Mrs. Laura Sargent. Unlike the male secretaries, Laura could be expected not only to read the letter herself but to disclose its contents to Mrs. Eddy.

The letter was a prime example of the Tartuffe–Uriah Heep school of rhetoric:

March 4, Waterbury Center, Vt.

Dear Sister:—I want the Dear little Mother, and the older members of "the household," to know that I am not at all in sympathy with these diabolical actions against her.

I believe her perfect demonstration will be of more value to the world than all the money in it. My constant prayer has been that none of you should have anything to meet through me for I am not a channel for error to any one. All channels are filled with God.

I send you this because of what I saw in the paper yesterday.

With a whole lot of love to our dearest Mother, and kindest regards to you all, I am, as ever,

E. J. Foster Eddy.[49]

In this small masterpiece of doublespeak, by "perfect demonstration" Foster Eddy was, as I read him, referring in code to the belief held by certain of the most devout Christian Scientists that Mrs. Eddy would actually conquer death and live forever. In saying "I am not a channel for error" he was claiming that he was not directing malicious thoughts at Pleasant View, which, with further decoding, meant that he was not undertaking any action to harm Mrs. Eddy. He was also, and not incidentally, "as ever" Mrs. Eddy's legally adopted son and therefore her heir.

Pleasant View presumably did not respond adequately to this olive branch, so within a week of writing to Mrs. Sargent, Foster Eddy was in Boston negotiating terms with Chandler at the Parker House. Unlike the other "next friends," Foster Eddy drove a shrewd bargain, agreeing to become party to the suit provided that the lawyers work entirely on a contingency basis and that he be liable for no costs or expenses of any kind. His general tone was of righteous indignation and public-spiritedness, as in this March 8 letter to Slaght:

> My Dear Sir: Did my enemies have any mercy on me or spare me in any measure? No! that is no reason why I should act in any way but as a straightforward, honest, upright Christian gentleman. I would not tolerate a spirit of revenge or vindictiveness nor act in any way in this matter that I did not believe to be right and result in good to the world at large and especially to our beloved America.

After striking this patriotic note, Foster Eddy ends his letter by asking Slaght to reclaim from Mrs. Eddy's house on Commonwealth Avenue (on his behalf but not at his expense!) a certain rolltop black desk he (Foster Eddy) had left there. A secret drawer in the desk contained a large cache of letters to Foster Eddy from Mrs. Eddy.[50]

Gathering all these various clients who were related to Mrs. Eddy was a crucial part of the legal strategy that Chandler had adumbrated as early as November 1906, and which he worked out in detail in Washington during the first months of 1907. Chandler had decided to file in Concord a friendly suit in which, in the name of Mary Baker Eddy herself, certain named "next friends" of hers called certain named officials and staff members of hers to account for their alleged misuse of her property and abuse of her person. The first petition of the "Next Friends" was filed by John Kelley in Concord Court on March 1, beginning as follows:

> The petition of Mary Baker Glover Eddy who sues by her next friends George W. Glover, Mary Baker Glover and George W. Baker *against* Calvin A. Frye, Alfred Farlow, Irving C. Tomlinson, Ira O. Knapp, William B. Johnson, Stephen A. Chase, Joseph Armstrong, Edward A. Kimball, Hermann S. Hering, and Lewis C. Strang.[51]

On March 11 the names of Ebenezer J. Foster Eddy and Fred W. Baker were added to the list of Next Friends.[52] Section 3 of the petition states that Mary Baker Eddy lives "in the custody" of Strang and Frye, "carefully surrounded and secluded by themselves and by household servants of their selection, and that very few persons are allowed to see her, and no one is allowed to see her except for a few minutes at one time." Sections 4 and 5 summarize the unsuccessful efforts made by the Next Friends to see or contact Mrs. Eddy by letter. Section 6 claims that Mrs. Eddy has extensive and valuable property in New Hampshire and Massachusetts which is being administered "either in her name by others or by her while unfitted for the transaction thereof." Section 8, the longest, goes into some detail about Mrs. Eddy's publications, copyrights, and estimated royalties, her estimated earnings from the Massachusetts Metaphysical College and from The Mother Church, and her real estate holdings. The petition ends by requiring the defendants to account for all the transactions they have made on behalf of Mrs. Eddy and to restore any property they have wrongfully disposed of, enjoins them to take no further official or financial action while the suit is pending, and asks for a receiver to be appointed to take over Mrs. Eddy's property until the court comes to a decision.

Chandler's files show that in the months of January and February he maintained a pace of activity that would have exhausted a much younger man. This activity was all the more surprising since, on February 6, Ralph Pulitzer sent a handwritten note saying that a council, composed of himself and two members of the *World* staff, had decided that they could not accept Chandler's plan of legal procedures. When Chandler protested, Pulitzer wrote again on February 18, this time on official letterhead paper, a typed missive stating that the *World* was definitively withdrawing from the suit and sending $5,000 to pay for all expenses incurred to date. Personal pleas from Chandler to Joseph Pulitzer met with no answer, and henceforward Chandler, Kelley, Peabody, and the legal firm of Martin and Howe of Concord who had joined the team, were representing three bankrupt male clients—George Glover, George W. Baker, and Fred Baker—the penniless Mary Glover, and the financially unforthcoming Ebenezer Foster Eddy.

Once it became clear that the *World* was withdrawing its financial support, Chandler acted honorably. Clearly informing the others of his decision, he used the Pulitzer money to pay all his legal colleagues' fees to date, as well as the expenses of his impoverished clients. He calculated his own fees and expenses to date but said that he would take no reimbursement until the suit was won. Left with some $1,500, he told Kelley et al. that he would use this money to prosecute the suit and, in effect, took responsibility for paying the rest of the costs out of his own pocket.

To understand why Chandler decided, apparently without hesitation, to continue the suit, literally at whatever the cost, after the *World* withdrew, I think we must look at his sense of responsibility toward his clients, whose neediness deeply affected him, and his stubborn confidence in himself, in the justice of the cause he had espoused, and in the strength of the suit he was preparing. Just as Frederick Peabody had been sure that he would win the suit for libel he had brought on behalf of Mrs. Woodbury, so Chandler thought he would win the Next Friends suit and that his clients would amply reward his efforts, once they were in control of Mrs. Eddy's estate. Information about Christian Science and Mrs. Eddy's dubious past and peculiar present was flooding in from all sides. All of Chandler's suspicions and preconceptions were being confirmed. Virtually no news was coming from the offices of General Streeter, Mrs. Eddy's lawyer,[53] and the gang at Pleasant View seemed paralyzed with fear. Chandler was sure that he could win more gloriously alone, without Joseph Pulitzer's money. A legal David, he would slay the Goliath of Christian Science.

26

Mrs. Eddy
Wins
in Court

AT 5:30 P.M. ON MARCH 1, 1907, WILLIAM E. CHAND-ler's associate in Concord, John Kelley, personally informed Mrs. Eddy's New Hampshire lawyer, General Frank S. Streeter, that he had filed a bill in equity petitioning, among other things, that "a receiver or receivers be appointed to take possession of all the property" of Mrs. Eddy. Streeter became extremely agitated at this news, as Kelley at once reported by letter to Chandler in Washington. Streeter said that the timing of the suit was peculiarly unfortunate for all parties. Just half an hour earlier he had himself dispatched a messenger to Washington, where he assumed George Washington Glover to be, with a letter from Mrs. Eddy informing Glover that on February 25 she had set up a trust fund of over $125,000 for the benefit of his family. Streeter asked Kelley if it was possible to speak at once with Chandler on the phone to try to sort things out without going to court, but the arrival of the press—alerted by Kelley to the filing of the suit—made this call impossible, and Streeter sent at once to recall his messenger and thus cancel the trust.[1] Nevertheless, news of this trust fund made ripples in New Hampshire and in South Dakota, especially since Streeter ignored Kelley's written request for a copy of the trust deed.

Not until June 19 would Streeter inform the Glovers in Lead of the precise terms of the trust.[2] Mrs. Eddy had established a trust of $125,000, to be administered by Streeter himself, Archibald McLellan, and Irving Tomlinson, which would pay out to the Glover parents $1,500 a year during their lifetimes, and also pay the taxes, insurance, and repair bills on their house in Lead. The trustees were also specifically enjoined to pay any exceptional expenses that might occur over the years, and thus ensure the Glovers' comfort and well-being. Mary and Gershom Glover would each receive $500 a year for the term of the trust. George Glover III would have all his expenses paid at a liberal arts college, and Andrew Glover would have all his educational expenses paid up to, but not including, college. After the death of both parents, the trust would be wound up, and the remaining funds would be disbursed in equal parts to the Glover children. For their work on the trust, the three trustees were to be given 5 percent of the interest on the trust per year, plus all expenses incurred in performing their duties. The trust was made with one provision, that the beneficiaries under it would lose all benefits if they "directly or indirectly made any contest or opposition to my [i.e., Mrs. Eddy's] last will or to the disposition of other property by me."

Even without knowing the details, the report of some $100,000 that might have come their way was definitely enough to attract the interest of the destitute Glovers.[3] With the suit filed and the offer of the trust revoked, it was too late. When Streeter's letter finally arrived at the Glovers' house, George would tell Chandler that he was humiliated at the mere idea of having Tomlinson, McLellan, and Streeter doling money out to him at their discretion. The gross discrimination between the education offered to George and that planned for the younger brother Andrew was also infuriating.

Showing a certain paranoia of his own, and happy to find a convenient scapegoat to take the blame for his own lifelong failure to make money, Glover, through the intermediary of Bennett, told Chandler in a letter of March 21 that he believed that the

> the main object of the clique is to humble me and crush all prospects of
> my developing any mining property or doing any other business that
> they are not at the head of. I am satisfied that it was through that clique
> that I have been held back in my business.

Chandler and Bennett both sought to reassure Glover and each other that the rumors of the trust merely confirmed how much money was at stake, and that they had their opponents at Pleasant View and in Boston running scared.[4] A letter he wrote on March 4 to Bennett proves that Chandler was considering how it might be possible for his clients to have their cake and eat it too—that is, settle with the Church, agree to all the terms, and accept Mrs. Eddy's trust money, knowing the agreement not to contest the will could not be enforced. This was the casuistical policy that Chandler would later advise his client to take in 1909 and then again in 1911.

During the month of March both camps involved in the suit worked furiously to develop their legal case and to keep their plans from the opposition. After sessions in New Hampshire and in Boston[5] conferring with his various clients and colleagues, Chandler returned to his Washington head-quarters in April and methodically set about answering all the mail that had piled up in his absence. As we might expect, Chandler fielded letters from his Glover and Baker clients as well as from Ebenezer Foster Eddy, and from his colleagues, John Kelley and Dewitt Howe. But he also heard from other, less predictable sources since the *World*'s publication of the complete text of the petition of the Next Friends, as well as its carefully edited account of how the suit came to be filed, had caught the attention of people who had a passionate interest in Christian Science and Mary Baker Eddy. Five of these people—Henry Robinson of Concord; Robert and Emily Hannon of East Windsor Hill, Connecticut; A. J. Park, alias Philo Junius, of Boston; and Henry Reed Hopkins of Buffalo, New York—wrote a series of letters, to which Chandler replied. All of the five, in very different respects, influenced Chandler, shaped the course of the legal suit he was directing. All tell us something interesting about the various perceptions of Christian Science at the turn of the twentieth century.

Henry Robinson, the postmaster and former mayor of Concord, was important to Chandler since he was one of the rare people Chandler was in touch with who had actually met Mary Baker Eddy. Robinson had been at Pleasant View on a number of occasions, had corresponded with Mrs. Eddy, and had written an admiring monograph on her, using material he had gained from a long interview in around 1895. Robinson had a good sense of how Mrs. Eddy was viewed in the community, and he accepted the role of answering Chandler's inquiries on subjects of local interest. Thus on March 20 Robinson was able to inform Chandler that the pair of horses Mrs. Eddy had mentioned in her January interview with George and Mary Glover, claiming, they said, that the horses had been meant to kill her, had been given to her in September 1906 by L. L. Temple of Texarkana, Arkansas. The horses were valued between six and twelve thousand dollars. In a later letter, around March 23, again replying to some request by Chandler for information about Mrs. Eddy's mental state, Robinson says that in none of the letters Mary Baker Eddy had written to him does she mention Malicious Animal Magnetism, that all her letters to him were clear and lucid, and that he has no doubt that she had written, or at least dictated, the letters herself.

In his letter of March 28 Robinson offers a lucid analysis of the household at Pleasant View, noting that "Frye and Co are arbitrary, unpolitic, undiplomatic. Mrs. Eddy herself is very gracious," but many a reporter, such as Miss Milmine, has gone away "aggrieved and nonplussed." "You can only get in to see Mary Baker Eddy if you understand the domestic set up and can get past Frye," he explains. "Mrs. Eddy would sometimes see Concord people, not in Science, when her devout followers, contributors and church leaders have been held aloof. . . . There was a shrewd policy in it." This observation was pretty close to the mark.

Robinson conspicuously refuses to provide Chandler with the negative information about Mrs. Eddy he sought. A comment he makes about Mrs. Eddy's campaign to get the roads near her home paved is the closest Robinson comes to criticizing Mrs. Eddy or seeing her behavior as aberrant. It is clear from all his letters that the reason Robinson is willing to serve as Chandler's local informant is that he feels respect and even affection for her. He is genuinely concerned for the old lady, unimpressed by the caliber of her entourage, and worried by what he sees as her increasing isolation at Pleasant View. He sees Chandler as a solution to what he considers to be Mrs. Eddy's problems, as in fact representing her *next friends*—those who should be looking after her personal interests and ensuring that all is well with her.

Robert C. Hannon and his wife Emily were also concerned for Mrs. Eddy, but their reasons were very different. The Hannons were or had been Christian Scientists, and they deluged William Chandler with lengthy scrawls in which they described the nefarious plots woven by Augusta Stetson and her supporters. In one particularly strange letter dated April 17 Emily Hannon explained that Mrs. Lida Fitzpatrick lived at Pleasant View and was Augusta Stetson's agent. According to Hannon, Fitzpatrick planned to assure Stetson's accession when Mary Baker Eddy died, and even to alter the text of *Science and Health*. Stetson and her forces had a secret which had terrified Mrs. Eddy into submission and insanity, and Mrs. Hannon offered to tell Chandler or Ebenezer Foster Eddy this secret—but only if one of them came to East Windsor to hear it in person.

When I was reading the Chandler files, I became rapidly convinced that the Hannons were, in a phrase, off their rockers, as well as enormous bores, and I assumed that Chandler had simply dismissed them. But a letter which Chandler wrote on March 6 for publication in the New York *World* indicates that he took the Hannons' analysis of the situation at Pleasant View very seriously and saw them, even if delusional, as representative Christian Scientists. Here is part of that letter:

> On the one side jailor Wilson [H. Cornell Wilson] with his female assistants are persecuting the feeble and helpless Mrs. Eddy with demands that she shall not issue a decree making Augusta E. Stetson her successor as the mother of the Church C. S. On the other side jailor Calvin A. Frye and his female allies are worrying Mrs. Eddy with demands that she shall accept the Stetson argument and proclaim the new headship of the Church C. S. This picture alone is sad enough; and is sending the aged and infirm prisoner surely even if slowly toward earthly dissolution. But what shall we think of her woeful case, without a relative near her, not only beset by persecutors present in the body but also tormented by double headed hags of religious healers, "workers" so-called, giving her "absent treatment," of whose efforts she has been told and in the reality of whose power she has all

her life believed. Can she long survive the pressure on her enfeebled brain of such a superstition now at work to utilize the authority in the church which she still retains? The days of witchcraft had no fiercer horrors; suicide has no greater inducement than Mrs. Eddy's sad situation presents.[6]

Chandler is heightening his rhetoric in this letter, but I think that he believed that he was describing the situation at Pleasant View accurately.

The three anonymous letters from "Philo Junius" in Chicago of March 2, 4, and 5, two sent to Chandler himself and one to George Glover in Lead, also wax eloquent on the rotten condition of Christian Science, but these missives have more of a financial focus than those of the Hannons. Junius, whose handwriting Chandler recognized and identified in a reply as that of A. J. Park of Boston, says that for a brief time he had been a part of Christian Science but had left the movement when he discovered that it was being run by a "clique of scoundrels" who cared only to line their own pockets. The anonymous writer assures George Glover that he (Glover) is being denounced as a "liar, scoundrel, and blackmailer," and goes on:

> You of course must be aware that there is an <u>unscrupulous clique of grafters</u> who have <u>controlled</u>, and <u>now control</u> Mrs. Eddy's business, income and investments. During the construction of the Temple, the <u>appeals</u> for <u>financial assistance</u> brought from the West, drafts, currency and checks, over $25,000 weekly. Her income from her books, prints & church has averaged $375,000 per annum. There are scores of <u>suckers, grafters</u>, and <u>officious scamps</u> who have gotten rich by robbing Mrs. Eddy.

> There is one piece of property in Boston, worth $3,000,000 which the sharpers have got <u>irrevocably, beyond recall</u> or <u>redemption</u> from <u>Mrs. Eddy</u>. I live in Boston, and am out here [Junius writes from a Chicago hotel] on business. I know of my own personal knowledge that ten years ago, several men, who were out of business, broke and impecunious, are <u>now rich,</u> and have thousands of dollars to invest, several, who lived in flats, have bought fine residences, furnished elegantly, and have <u>invested large amounts in gas and water bonds</u> and now have an income from their securities. Of course, any man, who has grown rich by working with the "<u>syndicate managers</u>," will <u>swear that Eddy is just as clear mentally</u>, and as <u>strong physically</u> as she was 25 years ago, she is seriously & constantly kept <u>under observation, a prisoner</u>, she has been for several years failing physically & mentally. When these conditions <u>first appeared</u> or began to <u>manifest their presence, there was a meeting of the Syndicate in Boston</u>—and <u>at that meeting</u> it <u>was decided</u> that she <u>must be under</u> the <u>constant watch, care,</u> and <u>guard</u> of one of the <u>trusted syndicate, who must swear and assert, vehemently,</u> that <u>Eddy is all right</u>; because if she was <u>declared</u> & <u>found otherwise</u>, the business of the Syndicate would be ruined.

These facts are known to a few of the keen observers in Boston, and those who are posted—The <u>Syndicate would not stop</u>, or <u>hesitate for a minute</u> to put a <u>traitor to death</u>, who would disclose the truth, and unmask the inner methods of the fleecing process—Junius.[7]

Junius's claim of purveying unprejudiced "insider" information was highly influential on William Chandler's conduct of the suit. None of the documentation Streeter would supply the court, none of the testimonials by auditors and local worthies about the money Mrs. Eddy had earned over the years from royalties and bonds and about the careful and honest management of her funds by Frye and others would ever convince Chandler that financial malpractice of some kind was not going on in Christian Science, and that it would be revealed once an honest man like himself gained access to the books. It was, I think, because the high-minded and relatively impecunious Chandler was sure that the Mother Church officials were not just religious zealots but crooks that he felt he need have no scruples about pursuing them to the full extent of the law.

Of all Chandler's informants, the most interesting, and the most fatal to his cause, was Dr. Henry Reed Hopkins, a medical man who apparently specialized in mental illness. If the extant files are to be believed, Hopkins was almost as assiduous and influential a correspondent as was Frederick Peabody. If Peabody believed Mrs. Eddy was evil, Hopkins thought her clinically insane, and he went about finding more and more ingenious and less rational diagnoses of her mental condition. Hopkins first wrote on March 15, recommending that Chandler hire a medical expert on paranoia, and that he investigate the publication of *Christ and Christmas*. Chandler replied on March 20, saying he agreed that Christian Science was a dangerous fraud, but that its exposure must await the conclusion of the lawsuit. Hopkins should contact his medical colleagues as well as members of the clergy and start his own crusade against Christian Science.[8]

On April 6 Hopkins wrote to Chandler again. He had been reading the *McClure's* material, and Milmine's accounts of Mrs. Eddy's hysterical fits in youth and her catatonic fits and paranoia later in life had not fallen on deaf ears in the case of clinician Hopkins:

Dear Senator Chandler:

The heredity of an insane person is always an important factor in the case—where the insanity comes early in life or is grafted upon some distinct nervous condition like hysteria in the case of Mrs. Eddy the heredity is still more important.

You should secure if you have not already done so the facts of the ages and causes of death of Mrs. Eddy's brothers and sisters, fathers and mothers uncles and aunts for as many generations as possible.

Remembering that females transmit disease propensities more often than men, be very careful to look into the stories of the women.

Certain facts are more important than others—in cases of insanity, of epilepsy, of palsy, of eccentricity, of cancer, of consumption, of drunkenness or of harlotry these are to be especially noted.

It was too bad for Chandler and his expert witness Hopkins that Mrs. Eddy's ancestors were so singularly long-lived, productive, moral, and sane!

By April 9 Hopkins was sure, again on the basis of what he had read in the latest installment of *McClure's*, that Mary Baker Eddy had suffered since 1888 from paralysis agitans or shaking palsy. Somehow Hopkins had got hold of two recent samples of Mrs. Eddy's handwriting and found in them signs of Parkinsonian deterioration of motor coordination. He adduced as further proofs for this diagnosis (a) that she withdrew to New Hampshire in 1889, and (b) that she is "always covered in a black velvet coat." Where Hopkins got the second "fact" or how he interpreted it is unclear.

By April 17 the eager Hopkins was in personal contact with Georgine Milmine, who gratifyingly assured him that Mary Baker Eddy had had paralysis agitans for over twenty-five years. "Of course, I have no means of knowing what Miss Milmine's evidence is," Hopkins wrote immediately to Chandler, "but I believe that you can depend upon the accuracy of the judgment." Neither Hopkins nor Chandler seems to have paused to note that accepting the assertions of others without evidence and passing them on as accepted fact is not in the highest tradition of either law or medicine. By April 21 Hopkins had extended his correspondence to Frederick Peabody, to whom he writes:

> I don't believe you can make a case of incompetence from wickedness or dementia senile or otherwise. It seems to me that the only chance you have is to lay the foundation of abnormal brain, nerves, standards and conduct in youth, to build upon this foundation a case of insanity with hallucinations, delusions, exalted notions, falsifications of memory, peculiar moral standards in fact the whole curse of religious paranoia.[9]

On April 24 Hopkins begged Chandler's pardon for writing again, but he could not get Mary Baker Eddy off his mind. He was convinced that the gang at Pleasant View would never allow a competent physician to examine Mrs. Eddy, and that they would kill her first. Chandler, for his part, was so impressed with the quality of the analyses Hopkins had been sending him that he asked Hopkins, in a letter dated July 9, if he would come to Concord as an expert witness and take part in the projected interviews to ascertain Mrs. Eddy's sanity.

> It does not seem to me that we ought to lose your services because you have made such a study of Mrs. Eddy's life and writings that you have ready-made ideas that will serve you whenever you undertake to reach a formal opinion concerning her fitness to do business and take care of her property.

Although Chandler was unable to offer even to pay expenses, much less a fee for Hopkins's professional services, it seems that Hopkins did, indeed, come to Concord, but I can find no evidence that he managed to see Mrs. Eddy. During his stay in New Hampshire, Hopkins caused a small sensation by taking early-morning runs in somewhat unconventional costume. Concordians were unaccustomed to the notion of elderly joggers, and, ironically, the local Concord *Patriot* reported that some people had taken the alienist (a medical doctor specializing in insanity) Hopkins for an escapee from the local asylum.[10]

Dr. Henry Reed Hopkins and his long-distance, literary diagnosis of Mrs. Eddy's hereditary insanity, female instability, youthful hysteria, middle-age paranoia and religious mania, old-age Parkinson's, and senile dementia (check one or all alternatives) so defy parody that one risks losing sight of the fact that the man was a respected clinician and that he, in combination with Milmine and Peabody, heavily influenced the course of Chandler's strategy for the Next Friends suit. As the spring waned and summer came on, Chandler became increasingly convinced that the core of the case was Mrs. Eddy's long-standing, perhaps congenital, insanity. More precisely, Chandler became so sure in his own mind that Mrs. Eddy was, had long been, had perhaps always been clinically insane, that he concentrated his efforts on proving her insanity.

This represented something of a change of focus in the case. In his petition of March 1 on behalf of Mrs. Eddy's Next Friends, Chandler had alleged that a group of men had taken charge of Mrs. Eddy's large estate and were misusing it. One could call this the Philo Junius line of attack, and Chandler never wholly dropped it. Unfortunately for him, despite all his diligent research and requests for information, Chandler was unable to come up with any evidence that Mrs. Eddy's affairs had in fact been mishandled or diverted. This problem became even more difficult, as we shall see, once Mrs. Eddy's affairs were taken over by three trustees, and all her financial and legal records were carefully examined by men whose authority and credentials were hard to challenge.[11] Since even Chandler had to admit that Mrs. Eddy was, at the moment, alive, the question of the legality of her will and the eventual disposition of her estate could not yet be raised. Thus he made the decision to concentrate his financial firepower on the legality of the complicated sequence of transfers of real estate and copyrights which Mrs. Eddy had made to different bodies and individuals in the 1890s and on the question of whether, at the time those transfers were made, she was of sound mind and thus legally competent to act.[12]

These transfers had been Mrs. Eddy's answer to the problem of how to give the Boston real estate, notably the land beneath The Mother Church building, and the copyrights to her published works to the Church in such a way that her natural heirs could not contest the gift, despite the fact that the

Church's status as a legal entity was subject to dispute. Acting on behalf of his clients Glover and Foster Eddy, who would have stood to inherit the land interests and the copyrights at the time of Mrs. Eddy's death had these properties not been transferred to the Church during her lifetime, Chandler sought to argue that, notably in 1898, when the most important of these transfers had been made, Mrs. Eddy had been insane and thus incapable of conducting legal business. Chandler outlined his strategy for the suit in a letter to Foster Eddy dated April 14, 1907. Chandler takes up what Foster Eddy had told him about Mrs. Eddy's preoccupation with Malicious Animal Magnetism and urges the adopted son to document the events of that time as closely as possible.

> It is these delusions of hers that made every conveyance of hers away from Glover and away from you null and void, and also any will she executed. . . . We cannot in this proceeding test the validity of any will. But we can secure the annulment of any conveyance or agreement which she made; certainly those for which she received no value; certainly all her donations which are so situated that they can be recovered from their present possessors. . . . Of course we are not going to attack the religion or attack her as in any way insincere. But we must recognize her delusions and the effect of them upon her business contracts. To me she appears to be a person who from infancy has been in a state bordering on lunacy.

In order to make the charge of insanity stronger, Chandler set out to find evidence that Mrs. Eddy had been mad not only in 1898, or 1890, but in 1866, when she had the fall in Lynn, or, indeed, in the 1830s, as a schoolgirl. Increasingly, as he confided in one of his private memos, Chandler, like Peabody before him, became convinced that Mary Baker Eddy was legally incapable because she believed herself to be the messenger of God. In other words, she was mad *because she had founded Christian Science*—even though it was only through founding Christian Science that she acquired the properties which she had transferred in 1898 and which Chandler hoped to see his clients gain through inheritance. As he wrote in "Desultory 6," which was circulated to his legal colleagues,

> Just think of it. Christ supposedly healed the sick, so did the apostles for 300m years. Then the art died away and remained dead till 1866 when Mary Baker Glover Patterson discovered it. God, Christ, Mrs. Eddy! It is all a delusion as the facts show. She thought she succeeded the Savior and discovered metaphysical Healing.

Pursuing this line, William Chandler retraced the steps back into Mrs. Eddy's past, finding in the evidence brought before him by Milmine and Peabody more and more gratifying proof of Mrs. Eddy's craziness. Following in the now well-worn tracks made by Peabody, Milmine, the *McClure's* team,

Minot J. Savage, Wilbur, Powell, and others less well known, Chandler contacted George Quimby about the Quimby plagiarism, Dr. Cushing about the 1866 fall in Lynn, Luther Marston about Malicious Animal Magnetism at the Massachusetts Metaphysical College in the 1880s, and William Nixon and Ebenezer Foster Eddy about the growth of the Christian Science movement in the 1880s.

As far as one can judge by the extant correspondence, Chandler turned up nothing but problems from all this research. George Quimby refused, as always, to have anything to do with legal cases involving Mrs. Eddy, and he would not let his father's papers out of his hands for even a moment. Cushing's son was increasingly unhappy about his elderly father's name appearing in the popular press, and he was counselling him to make no more affidavits. Men like Marston were hardly ideal witnesses because they were openly willing to say pretty much anything for money. All of this was discouraging, but having made the decision to move forward on the basis of insanity, and therefore of incapacity to make legal transactions such as the major copyright and real estate transfers of 1898, Chandler had no choice but to continue in the direction chosen.

In fact, he was still confident of winning because, thanks to Peabody, he was sure he had turned up the key document that would win the case for his clients. It was a letter which Mrs. Eddy had written in 1890 to William Nixon, at that time the head of the Publishing Society and a close and trusted advisor, telling him that she had that morning realized that "the enemy" would seek to break her will. Therefore she instructed her "Dear Student":

> Enquire of the best copyright Lawyer out of Boston you can find, if I can assign my copyright of *Science and Health* and Unity of Good to some one who would hold it if my will was broken and never name this party in my will or name him to whom it is assigned, whichever would make it legal.[13]

Mary Baker Eddy began her letter by saying that her son George Glover was controlled by mesmerism, that he had often resorted to the law in the past and would surely contest her will. Chandler and Peabody both jubilantly agreed that this letter was the smoking gun they needed, since it was proof that George Glover had been deprived of valuable parts of his mother's estate because of her insane belief in mesmerism. Other letters provided by Foster Eddy would similarly show that it was because she believed he was the tool of mesmerism that Mrs. Eddy later also disinherited her adopted son.

The jubilation Chandler and Peabody felt over these letters was tempered by their awareness that they depended for their proofs on two problem individuals. Chandler never warmed to Foster Eddy as he did to his Glover and Baker clients,[14] and Nixon was a man whose venality, pretentiousness, and violent delusions would become painfully apparent to the counsellors of the Next Friends as the suit progressed. Nixon, like most of those who had broken with Mrs. Eddy, was always hard up, and his current need for money was more acute because he had recently become engaged to be married.[15] As soon as he realized that his letter was important in the suit, he made it clear that he would not give it away; he would require money even to allow its text to be copied. Nixon believed, incorrectly, that Peabody was receiving fat fees from Chandler, so he demanded as much or more. Peabody and Nixon quarrelled over the issue of the letter, and on April 2 Nixon wrote a very rude letter directly to Chandler, insisting that he be cut in on the final settlement, since his letter provided the key to the case. Nixon wrote he wanted $1,000 but would settle for $300 in addition to the $100 Peabody had passed on to him already. At the same time, as Chandler came to know, Nixon was also negotiating terms with Burton Hendrick at *McClure's*. On March 25, S. S. McClure himself wrote to Nixon offering him $250 for the originals of the letters, on the assurance that no one else would get copies, and that he could keep them until the November magazine issue came out. Also at the same time, Peabody, one of Chandler's chosen junior counsel, was privately asking Chandler for more money, as well as finding interested members of the press to take down his colorful views on Mrs. Eddy and her Science, and thus prejudicing the suit.[16]

Increasingly anxious about how to finance the suit, finding himself surrounded by impoverished crazies of one kind or another, not surprisingly Chandler began showing signs of strain. On April 5 he wrote to Kelley:

I need much thoughtful help in this business—and you must give it. I am growing old like Mrs. Eddy.

The amendment needs careful consideration. There are objections to filing it. There are troubles ahead if we do not file it. If we confine ourselves to the last three years, she is now in responsible hands.

If we go back into the delusions of the past 40 years it will be said we are <u>attacking the religion</u>. If we do not go back we are unlikely to get the evidence that will destroy her will and codicils. Glover probably does not get $50,000, Foster doubtless nothing, and both are our clients.

Do not rely too much on me. This is a big case.

Back at Pleasant View, the Streeter group was seeking to establish its own strategy for answering the petition of the Next Friends. There is no precise equivalent to the Chandler papers for following the day-to-day moves of those opposing the Next Friends suit, but we do have two very valuable sources, in Peel's biography and in Michael Meehan's unfortunately rare book *Mrs. Eddy and the Late Suit in Equity*.[17] Meehan reproduces most of the public documentation, as well as press reports and court transcripts, and thus gives us a great deal of information. Peel, for his part, had unrivalled access to The Mother Church records and can take us behind the scenes at Pleasant View.

Those opposing the Next Friends had many signal advantages, the first of them being money. Mrs. Eddy had often been criticized for her parsimony, and she still took little pleasure in spending for spending's sake. This trait notwithstanding, one of her strengths was her ability to adapt to new circumstances, and since the 1870s her motto in regard to legal expenses had become "Money is no object." Thus in 1907, when she saw her own freedom and the future of her movement at risk, Mary Baker Eddy assembled some of the most prestigious and expensive legal talent in New England in her defense. Apart from General Frank Streeter, a brilliant and experienced lawyer, and his partner, Allen Hollis, there was Samuel Elder dealing with the Massachusetts side of things, a man acknowledged within the profession for his technical expertise in all matters of legal procedure. In view of the eventual court hearing, Streeter had also enlisted the help of the attorney general of New Hampshire, Edwin J. Eastman.[18]

Chandler, Peabody, Bennett, Kelley, and Howe were intensely aware that they and their impoverished clients had taken on an adversary with very deep pockets, and they complained constantly to the court of the grave financial disadvantages under which they labored. They went so far as to petition the court in late spring to have their expenses paid by Mrs. Eddy, whose interests they claimed to represent, but this petition was denied. Mrs. Eddy's lawyers were not just expensive; they were also very good. Personally, in education and ability, William Chandler considered himself and probably was the equal of any one of the notable gentlemen opposing him, but he had no associates of his own caliber, with the possible exception of Bennett in South Dakota. There was no one on his team who was able or willing to contradict him or keep him focused on law—and not allow him to get carried away with rhetoric or hypothesis or myth.

Even more important than the money available for fees, and the quality of the lawyers, however, was the quality of the clients the two sides represented, and the quality of the relationship between client and lawyer. Chandler represented a motley group of people, united only by their need or greed for money, offering their names and little else to the suit, passively reliant on the expertise of the lawyers who had sought them out. Streeter, on the other hand, represented a single client who was not only passionately involved in the suit, but peculiarly competent to further her own interests. As she had always done, Mary Baker Eddy planned her own strategy, and she did not expect the able men she had chosen to assist her to carry the ball on their own. The Woodbury trial, when they had first been retained by Mrs. Eddy, had given Streeter, Hollis, and Elder experience in dealing with her, and they were now much more prepared to trust that however unconventional and even illogical her approach to the legal problem at hand might at first seem it might prove right in the long term, especially given the blatant illogicality of the opposition.

Paradoxically, because the Next Friends suit was so much more of a direct and personal threat to Mrs. Eddy, it was a simpler problem to deal with than the Woodbury suit had been. Streeter and his colleagues, like Chandler and his, realized that the key issue was Mrs. Eddy's competence, and that if she could be proved in a court of law to be able to manage her own affairs, the Next Friends would have no case. Chandler complained to the court that he and his colleagues had no access to Mrs. Eddy herself, but his assumption in these requests for free admittance to Pleasant View was that once the doors to her rooms were opened to her relatives the fact of her insanity and incompetence would be revealed. Chandler, Kelley, Howe, and Bennett had never met Mary Baker Eddy, and since they so cordially disliked her and all she stood for, they did not see this as a problem. By contrast, Streeter had the incalculable advantage of knowing Mrs. Eddy, knowing that she was not mad or senile, knowing that she was in control of her life. He and his colleagues had the advantage of not basing their case on a delusion.

The matter of Mrs. Eddy's trust illustrates very clearly both how Mrs. Eddy directed the course of things and how the fact of her direction, and the nature of her strategy, were misunderstood by William Chandler. In February, in the very weeks in which the first petition by the Next Friends was secretly being hatched, Mrs. Eddy decided that the time had come for her to give up control of her personal fortune. As was habitual with her, the decision came in Biblical terms—render unto Caesar the things that are Caesar's, and unto God the things that are God's. All her critics—Mark Twain, the New York *World*, *McClure's*—were accusing her of caring more about money than religion. Well, perhaps there was something in that criticism: making money had been important to her, she was good at financial matters, and she had found pleasure in the steady mounting of her personal worth, at the acumen she displayed in choosing her bonds and directing her expenditures. So now the time had come to give up all that, to let other people worry about money, and to concentrate exclusively on what she claimed was important—demonstrating Christian Science as an individual soul and as a leader. Therefore, Mrs. Eddy summoned her lawyer, and on March 6 in the presence of her major personal and church advisors she signed a deed of trust that placed all her personal property in the hands of three trustees: Henry Baker, her cousin; Archibald McLellan, a member of the Board of Directors of The Mother Church; and Josiah Fernald, head of the National State Capital Bank in Concord.[19]

As I analyzed the case, it became clear to me that initially the signing of this trust deed seemed to present an enormous new organizational and technical problem for Mrs. Eddy's legal team. The Next Friends petition had charged that Mrs. Eddy was incompetent and that she was ruled by others, and the new trust she established seemed to confirm this. In the face of her decision to make the new trust, Streeter had to devise a procedure that would make it impossible to challenge the fact that Mrs. Eddy was acting of her own free will and was fully competent to make the decision. Hence the signing of the trust deed was elaborately staged, with Mrs. Eddy reading aloud, without the use of glasses, the clauses of the deed, commenting on each, and expressing her approval and understanding. The men present—the trustees as well as Streeter, Fred Ladd, (another of Mrs. Eddy's numerous cousins), Calvin Frye, and perhaps others—then made signed statements as to what had occurred which could and would be made public. The trustees then carried off all of Mrs. Eddy's financial records and documents, and at the bank they carefully and in full view of witnesses, checked and verified everything that had been transferred.

Streeter kept Chandler in the dark about the trust until April 2. Then he petitioned the court to allow the three trustees under the deed of March 6 to be substituted for the Next Friends and charged with ascertaining the state of Mrs. Eddy's affairs, and her personal situation. As I see the case, Streeter hesitated to make the trust deed known because he was afraid of offering his opponents an advantage. Certainly, this was Chandler's conclusion. As their correspondence shows, Chandler in Washington, Bennett in Deadwood, and Peabody in Boston were all jubilant when they heard about the trust—because they were convinced that Streeter had made a fatal error, and that by setting up the trust the opposition had as good as admitted that Mrs. Eddy was incapable of managing her own affairs. On May 23 Chandler opposed Streeter's motion asking for the substitution of the trustees for the Next Friends, derisively referring to Mrs. Eddy as "this aged palsied woman," and claiming that the men around her would inflict any torture on her to make her do their will. "The poor woman is crazy," Chandler told the court, and Baker, McLellan, and Fernald were "the three most capable trustees to take care of a lunatic that ever were."[20]

Chandler's jubilation was short-lived, however, because the decision Mrs. Eddy had made from conscience proved to have excellent legal consequences. By the time the case was due to come to a hearing, Streeter had organized his legal strategy in terms of the trust deed, and he in fact had found that it facilitated his presentation before Judge Chamberlin, and then before the court-appointed master, Judge Aldrich. Whereas Chandler argued long-term insanity, and hence legal incompetence, and sought to persuade the court to allow him to take depositions—at Mrs. Eddy's expense—about events in 1890, or possibly earlier, Streeter and Eastman asked the court to make a simple determination. Was Mary Baker Eddy sane on March 6, when she had signed the trust document? If she was sane then, she was free to do as she wished, and the legality of any previous decisions need concern no one. Let the court, or its chosen representatives, interview Mary Baker Eddy and establish her mental state, once and for all, for themselves.

In preparation for presenting these arguments before the court, Mrs. Eddy and her advisors organized a brilliant series of public relations moves designed not only to prove her competence but to enlist the public's sympathy on her behalf, and thus potentially bring pressure to bear on the court. Chandler's initial petition had accused Frye et al. of mishandling Mrs. Eddy's financial affairs and profiting personally from her money. Therefore a reputable firm of accountants was brought in to audit Mrs. Eddy's books for the fourteen years previous to March 6, 1907. They found, first, that she was worth not millions as reported in the *World* but somewhere more than $900,000, and, second, that her bookkeeper, Calvin Frye, had made "all kinds and classes of clerical errors," but all of these amounted to $677.41 against himself. As she had so often remarked, Mrs. Eddy could easily have found herself a more competent bookkeeper, but never one more honest or devoted to her interests.[21]

Mrs. Eddy had helped her own cause by replying in writing to the first editions of the *McClure's* series, in a letter which was first published in the January 5 edition of the *Christian Science Sentinel*, was republished with minor corrections on January 12, and now appears in *Miscellany* (pages 308–16). In this letter she strongly defends those of her family whom she says Milmine has calumniated. She admits having made two unwitting errors in *Retrospection and Introspection*: she had not, as she had claimed, become a member of her local church when she was twelve; and she had mistakenly accepted her cousin Fanny McNeil Potter's assurance that she could use the McNeil crest as her own. She insists, with more loyalty than accuracy perhaps, that her first two husbands were excellent men of high professional capacity, and she resolutely glosses over the economic hardships she underwent when widowed by Glover and, later, when she was forced first to separate from Patterson and then later to divorce him on the grounds of his desertion of her. Critics have often pointed to Mrs. Eddy's lapses of memory as self-serving, but more interesting to me is the fact that, while giving God all the credit for her achievements in life, Mary Baker Eddy notably refuses, even when under attack, to present herself as the helpless victim of circumstances. One of the secrets of Mary Baker Eddy's astonishing life was, I believe, her tendency to react intensely to misfortunes and express a great deal of emotion in words and actions, but then to let go of the past. As the events receded, she could look toward the future, with her energies unchecked by past failures.

Mrs. Eddy also helped her cause with the impressive letter she wrote to Judge Chamberlin on May 16. The letter was written in her own hand—an important point since there were all sorts of rumors going around about her "palsied" hands and changes in her writing that proved her mental collapse—and it managed to convey both dignity and pathos. "Respected Sir:" wrote Mrs. Eddy,

> It is over forty years that I have attended personally to my secular affairs, to my income, investments, deposits, expenditures and to any employees. I have personally selected all my investments except in one or two instances and have paid for the same.
>
> The increasing demands upon my time labors and thought and yearning for more peace and to have my property and affairs carefully taken care of for the persons and purposes I have designated by my last will influenced me to select a board of trustees to take charge of my property namely Hon. Henry M. Baker, Mr. Archibald McLellan, Mr. Josiah E. Fernald.
>
> I had contemplated doing this before the present proceedings were brought or I knew aught about them and I had consulted lawyer Streeter about the method.
>
> I selected said trustees because I had implicit confidence in each one of them as to honesty and business capacity.
>
> No person influenced me to make this selection. I find myself able to select the trustees I need without the help of others. I gave them my property to take care of because I wanted it protected and myself relieved of the burden of doing this.
>
> They have agreed with me to take care of my property and I consider this agreement a great benefit to me already.
>
> This suit was brought without my knowledge and is being carried on contrary to my wishes. I feel that it is not for my benefit in any way but for my injury and I know it was not needed to protect my person or property.
>
> The present proceedings test my trust in divine Love. My personal expectation is assailed and some of my students and trusted personal friends are cruelly unjustly and wrongly accused.
>
> Mr. Calvin A. Frye and other students often ask me to receive persons whom I desire to see but decline to receive solely because I find that I cannot "serve two masters"—I cannot be a Christian Scientist except I leave all for Christ. Trusting that I have not exceeded the bounds of propriety in the statements herein made by me
>
> *I remain Most Respectfully Yours*
>
> *Mary Baker G. Eddy*[22]

Continuing the campaign to win public support, Mrs. Eddy's staff also set up personal interviews for her with three of the most famous and reputable journalists of the period—Arthur Brisbane of the *New York Evening Journal*, Edwin J. Park of the *Boston Globe*, and William E. Curtis of the *Chicago Record-Herald*. After their visits to Pleasant View all three gentlemen pronounced themselves charmed and delighted by Mrs. Eddy, amazed at the acuity of her mind and her physical dynamism, and horrified that she was being sued in court and publicly described as a lunatic. Asked by Arthur Brisbane why she believed the lawsuit had been started, Mrs. Eddy replied,

> Greed of gold, young man. They are not interested in me, I am sorry to say, but in my money, and in the desire to control that. They say they want to help me. They never tried to help me when I was working hard years ago and when help would have been so welcome.[23]

Two other famous comments Mrs. Eddy made at this time show that the old sharpness and radicalism were not dead in her. Again to Arthur Brisbane she remarked: "Young man, I made my money with my pen, just as you do, and I have a right to it." To a member of household, she said: "If I were a man, they would not treat me so."[24]

The final part of the campaign to convince the public that the Next Friends had no basis for their legal request to intervene in Mrs. Eddy's affairs and act on her behalf took the form of interviews she gave two noted "alienists." The first of these interviews, on July 10, was conducted by Dr. Edward French, superintendent of the Massachusetts Hospital for the Insane at Medfield, who, at the request of Mrs. Eddy's counsel, promptly issued a report. Dr. French wrote that he was fully persuaded "that there was not the least evidence of mental weakness and incompetency," and that he was "impressed with her intelligence and business ability."[25] Even more telling, however, was the interview Mrs. Eddy gave on August 12 to Dr. Allan McLane Hamilton. Indisputably one of America's leading experts on mental disease at the time, Hamilton was a Fellow of the Royal Society of Edinburgh and also, according to Meehan, a man of some social prominence, being the grandson of both Alexander Hamilton and Louis McLane, minister to England and secretary of the treasury under Martin Van Buren and Andrew Jackson.

In his long and prestigious career, Allan Hamilton had given expert testimony on many famous cases, for both the prosecution and the defense, and he had as much experience of court proceedings and of the law as relating to insanity as any alienist in the United States. Most specifically, from the point of view of Christian Science, Hamilton had given testimony against Augusta Stetson and her First Church of Christ, Scientist in New York City in the 1901 Brush Will case. Mrs. Stetson and her forces had emerged triumphant in the case, with the court ruling that "the truth or falsity of a religious belief is beyond the scope of a judicial inquiry," although it was rumored within the movement, and perhaps without, that in their court testimony the Stetsonites had committed perjury.[26] A man of unimpugnable integrity, Hamilton provided professional assessments which carried real weight with his peers and with the public, and he was not suspected by anyone of feeling any sympathy for Christian Science. It is a tribute to Frank Streeter's sagacity and his confidence in his client that Hamilton was the man he asked to take on the task of assessing Mrs. Eddy's mental condition.

Hamilton wrote up his findings in two persuasive reports: the first was issued to the general press; the second took the form of a special interview with a reporter for the *New York Times*, which Hamilton gave in his own home, and which appeared in print on August 25, 1907.[27] Before meeting Mrs. Eddy, Hamilton read the original bill filed by the Next Friends and the affidavits presented to the court; some one hundred of Mrs. Eddy's personal letters, written to Alfred Farlow, Frank Streeter, Archibald McLellan, and others; as well as the drafts of and instructions relating to the two trust deeds of 1907. It will be remembered that Dr. Henry Hopkins had managed to get his hands on a couple of letters, on the basis of which he diagnosed that, as Georgine Milmine had claimed in her biographical series for *McClure's*, Mary Baker Eddy suffered from paralysis agitans. Dr. Hamilton's opinion was quite different. Noting the logical and connected way Mrs. Eddy constructed her argument and the way she amended her autograph texts to clarify her meaning, Hamilton saw in the hundred letters given him for analysis "inherent evidences of mental vigor," the letters being "the products of an unusually intelligent mind." In his opinion, the handwriting was "remarkably firm for a person of her age," and the slight tremor sometimes apparent was evidence perhaps of old age but also perhaps of a mind that "travels faster than her pen."[28]

Hamilton confessed to the *New York Times* that when he came to Pleasant View for his two o'clock appointment he was in "a decidedly prejudiced state of mind," and that he was sharply on the lookout for those symptoms of mental weakness which had been reported in the press. But the half hour he spent with Mary Baker Eddy produced in him a "complete revulsion of feeling," convincing him not only that she was sane, competent, and in charge of her affairs, but that she was "sincere in all she says and does . . . unselfishly spend[ing] her money for the perpetuation of a church which, in her estimation, is destined to play an important part in the betterment of humanity."[29]

Hamilton reports diligently on the questions of fact which he posed to Mrs. Eddy, principally relating to matters of investment, and on her clear, informed, and rational answers. He notes that she was simply but carefully dressed, showed detailed knowledge of her household, and had total command over the staff whom she summoned by a complex sequence of bells. Mrs. Eddy's hand did not shake, Hamilton notes, and in her easy and pleasant manner of communication she manifested no delusions or signs of paranoia. Far from being the weak and easily coercible personality presented in the Next Friends suit, Mrs. Eddy appeared to Hamilton to "take the initiative upon all occasions." Her personality was an extremely strong one, "and she has succeeded in impressing it on all around her." "The idea that this strong-minded woman is ever a victim of coercion is manifestly absurd," he observed. Challenged by the *New York Times* reporter to explain why he had failed to see in Mrs. Eddy the physical weakness and mental incapacity described so vividly by some of the journalists who had been present at the famous interview of October 30, 1906,

> "One journalistic inquisitor," he replied, with a suggestive twinkle of the eye, "is frequently enough to perturb an ordinarily sane person. What can you expect, therefore, when an army of them is suddenly let loose upon you? The placidity of the Buddha yonder might be ruffled by such an invasion—and I am not at all surprised that a lady of eighty-six years old was agitated, to say the least, by the ordeal![30]

Hamilton's analysis seems to me right on the mark. The evidence of the interviews of 1906–1907 indicates that, like most of us, Mrs. Eddy shone in a sympathetic, calm situation but became vague and flustered in a hostile, invasive one.

Hamilton's written report directly addressed two highly controversial topics—Mrs. Eddy's alleged obsession with Malicious Animal Magnetism and her alleged belief that she would never die, and his conclusions here are interesting.

> The allegations concerning Mrs. Eddy's belief in "malicious animal magnetism" are ridiculous. I am convinced that the words are only used synonymously with "malign influence," "malignant," or "mendacious animal magnetism" and is therefore a *façon parler* [*sic*], as the French say. She certainly has been subject to sufficient annoyance to entertain the fear that she is to be subjected to further disturbance. False reports that she was dead are among those, and her home has been broken into and valuable documents have disappeared. That she has delusions regarding her son is an absurdity, for only a few days before he brought the suit to have her declared incompetent, she had without suggestion made the trust deed to have him and his family provided for. Mrs. Eddy has no insane delusions, and in print and elsewhere simply enunciates the conventional part of her creed which she and eight hundred thousand believe in.

> In the matter of her longevity some Christian Scientists have gone so far as to assert that she will never die. She herself, however, does not hold to any such ridiculous belief, but refers frequently to the life after death as a state of existence to which she is liable. I fancy that the belief among some of her followers involving the indefinite continuance of her earthly life arises purely from the visible evidence of Mrs. Eddy's great vitality and the absence of any of the usual tokens of mental breakdown natural to one of her great age.[31]

All these detailed comments by Hamilton are interesting, and they are well articulated. But the deciding factor in the two reports seems to be that from the moment Hamilton took Mrs. Eddy's hand he knew that she was not mad, and also that he instinctively liked her. He appreciated her intelligence, her grace, her dignity, her cordiality, her calm, her wit. Like so many interviewers, Hamilton reports being struck by the "extraordinary intelligence" of Mrs. Eddy's eyes, which he describes as "large, dark and at times almost luminous," quite unlike those of most people of her age. Hamilton concluded that, for a woman of her age, Mrs. Eddy "is physically and mentally phenomenal."[32]

Hamilton met with Mary Baker Eddy only the day before the masters hearing was scheduled to begin, and the *Times* article did not appear for another two weeks. By this time Mrs. Eddy and her lawyers had already triumphed, and the publishing of Hamilton's report served mainly to confirm and summarize the court's findings. While Mrs. Eddy's superbly conducted public relations campaign was proceeding throughout the summer, Streeter and his associates had been wearing Chandler down in the courtroom, filing a sequence of motions and counter-motions, which the lawyers for the Next Friends could barely process much less counter. In preliminary hearings, which Chandler's New Hampshire associates had to cope with, Streeter, a large, commanding man of considerable oratorical skills, accused the counsel for the Next Friends of being hired mercenaries, of having instigated the suit at the behest of a great newspaper—the name of which he did not mention—whose only interest was to sell more copies at the expense of a venerable and defenseless old lady. To the relatively impecunious Chandler, working pro bono and paying most expenses out of his own pocket, such accusations bit deep.

Chandler complained constantly to his associates and through them to Judge Chamberlin that he needed more time:

[Chandler to Kelley, June 7] I am not going to be rushed around the country by Streeter and argue questions when I am not ready. I cannot stand it and feel inclined to give up in despair.

A fundamental principle is never to let a Judge be crowded when he is inclined to be with you. To stand back and let the Judge fight it out with a persistent bully and trickster like Streeter is folly and cowardice.

[Chandler to Martin and Howe, July 9] Say to court that we cannot in justice to the great interests involved meet and argue on no time or on short time the many solecistic and complicated motions of Mr. Streeter; that I earnestly object to any consideration and decision concerning mode of trial until pleadings are finished and issues joined; and that we want a jury trial and if it is resisted ample time to prepare for and argue in its favor.

The various counsels for the Next Friends began disagreeing over court strategy, and, in a series of events which Mrs. Eddy would have found most significant, Chandler even started losing important documents and accusing Kelley of having mislaid them. When it became evident that the crucial test would be an interview with Mrs. Eddy, Peabody wrote angrily to Chandler on July 24, insisting that he be part of the interviewing team.

I do not see how I can forego the satisfaction of being present at the first meeting of the masters and counsel so you may expect me on Friday morning.

The subjects for examination of Mrs. Eddy are so numerous as to make selection difficult and may I suggest if the masters are to personally examine her, it be upon the express understanding that exhaustive cross-examination be allowed? And may I further say that your personal consideration for Mrs. Eddy's feelings appears to me to be excessive? You seem to me to be too kind and if I believed in the power of mind to influence your attitude, I should be inclined to think the concentrated so-called mind of Christian Sciencedom had unduly influenced your heart.

Clearly, when Frederick Peabody began accusing William Chandler of yielding to the powers of Malicious Animal Magnetism, all was going ill for the Next Friends and their suit, but it seems that nonetheless Chandler and his forces entered the court in Concord on Tuesday, August 13 with a strong presumption that they would prevail. It was true that Judge Robert Chamberlin had refused a jury trial, had narrowed the scope of the inquiry to the issue of whether Mrs. Eddy had been competent to make the trust deed of March 6, had appointed masters to settle the question of her legal competency, and had allowed Streeter to accelerate matters out of courtesy to Mrs. Eddy. But the choice of the masters themselves had aroused jubilation among the "Nexters," as Mrs. Eddy referred to them. The senior master appointed on June 27, Judge Edgar Aldrich, was a popular local man who had had a long and distinguished career in the law and was known as a reasonable and able jurist. More agreeable to Chandler and his men was the appointment as comasters of two alienists, Drs. George F. Jelly and G. Alden Blumer. Even when Blumer refused to serve and was replaced by New Hampshire attorney Hosea W. Parker, the Chandler camp was convinced that Dr. Jelly was a man who could be absolutely counted on to see things their way and to recognize that Mrs. Eddy was mad and/or senile, and therefore incompetent, as they claimed. Peabody, on hearing of Jelly's appointment, was so sure of his alienist that he began at once to name new trustees for Mrs. Eddy's estate, make plans to pay everyone's fees, and administer Mrs. Eddy's magnificent assets.

It had been agreed by Judge Chamberlin that the counsel for the Next

Friends should both open and close the hearings, and Chandler spent the majority of the first day explaining in detail the various restraints and handicaps under which he and his associates had been forced to prepare their case. He also spent some time listing and describing the various "delusions" under which Mrs. Eddy had suffered for many years, and which in his view constituted prima facie evidence of her insanity. These delusions included the belief that matter did not exist, that "she was miraculously and supernaturally selected by Almighty God to receive divine revelations," that Christian Science could cure disease, and the belief that all manner of evils could be produced by Malicious Animal Magnetism. In general, Chandler concluded, Mrs. Eddy suffered from both "the delusion of grandeur and the delusion of persecution."[33]

On the second day, August 14, Streeter limited his reply to noting that, as he understood it, the issue before the masters was strictly a financial one—could Mrs. Eddy manage her affairs or not? If she could, then the Next Friends had no suit. He suggested that the masters should on the next day at 2 P.M. repair to Pleasant View and meet with Mary Baker Eddy, and, despite Chandler's protests, the court accepted this suggestion. On the following morning Chandler presented the court with various requests which would, in effect, have made the interviewing of Mrs. Eddy a much longer process. Chandler asked that not just the masters but a large group of persons including his clients George and Mary Glover—who were present in the court—should be allowed to meet with Mrs. Eddy over a series of days, arriving without notice, and that no member of the Pleasant View staff be present at the meeting. Chandler insisted again that "this bill is a bill for an accounting to find out things we do not know," and that if the court admitted a lengthy inquiry, going back many years, it would be possible to prove that Mrs. Eddy's delusions unfitted her for doing any kind of business.[34]

In notable contrast to Chandler's emotive rhetoric and wide claims, Attorney General Eastman made a careful and pragmatic reply, countering that Mrs. Eddy's religious views were no concern of the court. The current proceeding was not aimed at a general accounting but sought to answer a very specific question:

> The question now is as to the rights of these parties to appear as "next friends." If Mrs. Eddy is competent to manage her business affairs, then they have no standing in court. Now, that is the question which we are to pass upon, not the matter of the accounts; that is, is or was Mrs. Eddy on the first day of March competent to manage her business affairs? That is the question. If she was, why, then, there is no occasion for the interposition of "next friends," or anybody else. She is competent and has a right to manage her affairs the same as every other citizen of this country.[35]

Answering the remarks made by counsel of both parties, Judge Aldrich noted that, indeed, it was the question of financial competency which concerned the court, and that the question of religious belief or delusion could be examined only if grounds were established that that belief or delusion had influenced Mrs. Eddy's financial judgment and thereby adversely affected the legal rights of her heirs. Aldrich then determined that in view of Mrs. Eddy's great age the examination should be undertaken by himself and his comasters, with no intervention by the counsel of either side.

The interview at Pleasant View which immediately followed was virtually an anticlimax. Aldrich, Jelly, Parker, Chandler, and Streeter were ushered into Mrs. Eddy's second-floor study, were greeted by a slim, frail, slightly deaf old lady, charming, polite, authoritative, who answered their questions of fact, insisted, despite their demurrals, upon giving a brief and lucid history of Christian Science and its doctrine, and begged them to take the time to listen to her marvelous new gramophone before they left the house. Some of Mrs. Eddy's answers showed touches of inaccuracy, but who does not make mistakes in such stressful situations, especially when in one's eighties? Aldrich was reminded of his mother, and even the redoubtable Jelly was both convinced and abashed.[36] As he left, commenting bitterly within earshot of the Pleasant View staff that Mrs. Eddy had a mind like a steel trap, did even William Chandler realize at last that although Mary Baker Eddy might be many things he did not care for, she was not mad, and she was not incompetent?

Within the space of a week, the Next Friends suit was over; Mrs. Eddy had won. After the interview with Mrs. Eddy the court was clearly sympathetic to her, steadfastly defining the issue as one of Mrs. Eddy's competence in her business dealings, and refusing to see the relevance of the events of 1866, or even 1898. Dewitt Howe failed lamentably to persuade Judge Aldrich that Christian Science was not a religion but an insane belief and thus not protected by the Constitution and the law. Only a handful of the depositions and letters and witnesses which Chandler and his colleagues had so carefully collected, and of which they expected so much, were allowed as evidence, to the chagrin of the assembled press corps. On August 21, 1907, the sixth day of the hearing, William Chandler informed the masters that the counsel for the Next Friends had filed a motion to dismiss the pending suit, and "that they hereby withdraw their appearance before the Masters without asking from them any finding upon the questions submitted to them by Judge Chamberlin."[37] In a powerful speech, General Streeter took exception to the dismissal, requesting that the masters determine the issue of Mrs. Eddy's financial competency which had been put to them so that she and the ten men named in the suit could be completely cleared of all the charges brought against them.

Judge Aldrich refused to consider the issue of Mrs. Eddy's competence ex parte but said he would report the evidence he and his comasters had received to Judge Chamberlin. On September 30 Judge Chamberlin refused a number of motions filed by Senator Chandler, including one which sought to make Mrs. Eddy liable for all the costs incurred in the suit, and another which would allow the counsel for the Next Friends to file a brief detailing all their objections to the rulings of the masters. General Streeter at once objected that the motion was merely intended to give the press the chance to publish the impounded depositions which Chandler had taken and which had never been accepted in evidence. Streeter said that he would consider paying the costs of the masters if Chandler accepted that the three trustees would act on behalf of Mrs. Eddy. Judge Chamberlin allowed the suit to be dismissed and decreed that Chandler's brief could not be filed. It was agreed by all parties that Mrs. Eddy's trustees would be brought into the court to consider the question of costs, and in this way Chandler and his associates and clients tacitly accepted the legality of Mrs. Eddy's March 6 trust deed and hence her competence on that day to do business. On November 12 by consent the trustees were made responsible for the costs of the masters. But to offset this expense the trustees were given a judgment against the Next Friends for all the defendants' costs and all the regular court costs.

For the plaintiffs in the Next Friends suit this was a stunning defeat, and it was heralded across the nation as a victory for justice.[38] George Glover and George Baker had gained nothing by their suit but more debt, a heavy weight of public opprobrium, and worsened prospects. William Eaton Chandler retired to lick his wounds, dry his powder, and reassure his stunned clients that they would live to fight another day. Mary Baker Eddy could not live forever.

27

Chestnut Hill

FTER THE TAXING WINTER OF 1905–1906, WHEN HER old renal problem had flared up again, Mary Baker Eddy had fought her way back to physical health and mental resilience and had successfully mapped a defense and directed, starred, and triumphed in the lengthy drama of the Next Friends suit. By the fall of 1907 the New Hampshire court system had finally come down on her side, but the win had cost her a lot, not so much in money as in stress. Mrs. Eddy's private anxieties about the future were far from allayed by her public triumph. Although the exact terms of Mrs. Eddy's will were, of course, known to only a handful of people, it was assumed by all parties that she intended to leave the bulk of her estate to her church. Given the difficulty of disinheriting family members in favor of an institution, Mrs. Eddy had excellent reasons for assuming that her will would be contested and could possibly be broken. William Chandler was known to be determined to press his clients' case further in the courts, and George Glover, always a gambling man, was likely to agree to any course of action, however desperate, since his financial situation had only deteriorated as a result of the recent fruitless legal action. Mary Baker Eddy correctly anticipated that a legal battle over her will might damage her young church, or at least impede its progress.

These fears for the future of her movement were exacerbated by anxiety over her own situation in the present. As her next of kin, George Glover had considerable legal rights, especially if he ever gained physical access to her residence and could claim to speak on her behalf. Senator Chandler had stated this right clearly in his public letter to the New York *World*:

To be sure, her lawful relatives and her only heirs, who are her son George Glover and her adopted son Dr. E.J. Foster-Eddy, have the lawful right to go to Pleasant View and enter and take custody and care of their mother. But the resistance that would be made by Wilson and Frye and their backers would so disturb Mrs. Eddy that she would not survive; and the sons would be blamed for the fatal result.[1]

Mrs. Eddy seriously entertained the possibility that her son might manage to get into her house, expel all the members of her household staff, and, in essence, kidnap her and hold her for ransom. At some point during the Next Friends suit she specifically outlined such a scenario in a letter to one of her attorneys:

> If you let this case remain as it now is could the "next friends" take possession of my person? If they could not then is it not better to let this suit stand *as it is?* I fear if you press it they will get Judge . . . to decide it against me and give my person to my enemies (called "next friends") and they will take me away from my real friends, students, and thus *get rid* of me by such means, then fight over my last will.[2]

After the trial, in view of all these dangers, and seeking a positive solution, Mrs. Eddy sent messages of reconciliation to her son and to Foster Eddy. She was even ready to summon William Chandler for a personal interview, hoping to win him over as she had so many others, but she was dissuaded by General Streeter from requesting such a meeting. He assured her that Chandler was not only implacable in his hostility toward her but a trickster who would only use her efforts at making peace for his own ends.

Given the Glovers' financial neediness and Mrs. Eddy's longing for reconciliation, as well as her anxieties about her own safety, there seemed a good possibility that some kind of settlement could be worked out between Mrs. Eddy and her son. For some weeks in late 1907 Chandler tried to negotiate a deed of settlement with Streeter whereby the Glovers would renounce all attempts to challenge Mrs. Eddy's will and her earlier transfers of property, in exchange for a lump sum payment of $140,000. The desperate Glovers were ready to apply their signatures, and were even preparing to travel east for a reunion at Pleasant View on Christmas Day, but when they continued to haggle over money and failed to meet one of Mrs. Eddy's famous deadlines, she became sickened by the whole process and abruptly told her trustee McLellan to withdraw her offer. This abrupt move was probably dictated more by emotion than by strategy, and Mrs. Eddy lived to regret it. Both Streeter and Chandler saw the refusal to sign the negotiated settlement as a new example of Mrs. Eddy's capriciousness. Her decision was also rued by her church advisors. Nonetheless, I feel for Mrs. Eddy's predicament. She loved her son and was willing to help him and let bygones be bygones, but she did not feel she owed him anything. On this occasion, as on many others, however much money she offered him, he still wanted more. At the end of 1907 Mary Baker Eddy was still strong from her victory in the Next Friends suit, and she balked at what she saw as an attempt at blackmail by her nearest relatives.[3]

The fear that her son might try to force his way into her house heightened Mrs. Eddy's growing sense of insecurity and lack of privacy at Pleasant View. For some years the staff had had to cope with the disadvantages of looking after a national celebrity who had chosen to live in a modest house situated on the outskirts of town yet very close to the street. It was absurdly easy for a really determined or unscrupulous person to walk into Mrs. Eddy's parlor and, unlike the old days in Lynn or at the Massachusetts Metaphysical College, she was no longer willing to have people drop in and take her as they found her. By 1905 Mary Baker Eddy had ceased to go out into her gardens, or even spend time on the first floor of her home. Her staff, as we have seen, guarded her from visitors with a zeal that earned them little praise. There were many complex reasons for this pattern of living, but safety as well as privacy counted. On two occasions a deranged woman had managed to get into the house, although she did not make it up to Mrs. Eddy's rooms; another time a lunatic had perched in the trees near her window until he was persuaded to come down by the local authorities. A thief entered the ground floor and stole some items from Mrs. Eddy's collection of expensive gifts, and although efforts were made to conceal this event from her, she probably understood something was wrong when at last it was decided that a night watchman had to be hired. There were often reporters waiting and watching at the front gate, which made every exit into the street a trial, and the occasion when the two *World* reporters had jumped up on each side of her carriage had heightened Mrs. Eddy's fears about driving out.

All of these small and unsettling events added fuel to the Pleasant View household's persistent fears of Malicious Animal Magnetism, for which the activities in the Concord court and the increasingly onerous presence of the press served as potent symbols. It had also become apparent even to Mrs. Eddy that Pleasant View had become far too small to serve as the pivot point of a growing organization, and she envisaged extending the Concord house in some way. Rooms for the live-in staff were notably small and inconvenient, there were only two bathrooms, and the directors and trustees had to sleep on cots in the living room when they came up to visit and were obliged to spend a night in Concord, which probably was no pleasure for anyone.

Thus it was sound logic rather than irrational fear, as her critics have charged, which caused Mary Baker Eddy to decide that she must leave her beloved Concord retreat and move closer to The Mother Church in Boston and the practical and psychological support it offered. The decision to leave Pleasant View was made even before the successful conclusion of the Next Friends suit. According to John Salchow, Mrs. Eddy's faithful man-of-all-work, in June 1907 she took him aside and told him that she had decided it was best to move her household back to Boston, if he would agree to move with her.

Instructed at all costs to protect the identity of the potential buyer, the Church directors in Boston cast around for a new home for their leader, and their task was not an easy one. The property needed to be large. Mrs. Eddy's new home and headquarters needed to be convenient to the Mother Church complex and to offer the gardens, views, and smooth carriage trails which Mrs. Eddy required for the daily drives which by now had become such a famous part of her daily routine. Some Christian Scientists, such as Gilbert Carpenter, were also anxious to see their Leader in a dwelling that was more elegant than Pleasant View, although here their views and Mrs. Eddy's were at odds. Luxury was emphatically not what she liked, and she rejected one property the directors proposed to her because a show of "arrogant wealth" was abhorrent to her, as "one who works as well as preaches for and of the nothingness of matter."[4] All of this made house hunting difficult, but if a buyer has a large enough purse, the real estate industry exists to solve such problems as Mrs. Eddy's. By early October Archibald McLellan, who was both a director and one of the three trustees of Mrs. Eddy's estate, purchased on her behalf for about $100,000 a twenty-five-room gray stone house on a twelve-acre estate in the rich and leafy Boston suburb of Chestnut Hill.[5] The house had to be extensively modified, and all the work was done at the accelerated pace by now traditional in Christian Science, with workers on the job twenty-four hours a day.

In Concord, meanwhile, the Pleasant View household was in a state of discreet upheaval. Apparently the rule of secrecy was extended even to many Pleasant View residents, and everyone, from Mrs. Eddy down, was in a heightened state of nervousness. It was planned that only the essential belongings were to be moved in the first instance, and to avoid arousing suspicion all the packing was done at the nearby Aiken house, which Mrs. Eddy had by that point rented to prevent its being used by people who wanted to snoop on her. When any official came to visit from Boston, he would return to town with an extra trunk. It was not an easy time for anyone, and several of the men who came to serve as secretaries, including John Lathrop, moved into Pleasant View and out again very quickly.

On the afternoon of Sunday, January 26, 1908, Mrs. Eddy left Pleasant View as if she were taking her usual daily drive. In fact, she drove directly to the Concord railway station where a special train was waiting to take her and her immediate staff to Boston. According to the various accounts left by Christian Scientists who were present, McLellan and Tomlinson, as well as John Lathrop and Calvin Frye, were at the station to attend her departure, but, as Salchow later reported proudly, she told them, "I don't want you, I want my John." Mrs. Eddy walked briskly across the platform on John

Salchow's arm and then climbed into the carriage before any of the men present had thought to move to give her the customary hand up. Along the track south, another locomotive went on ahead to ensure that there were no problems, and Mrs. Eddy's train was allowed to make a special detour to the Chestnut Hill station so that Mrs. Eddy would not have to alight in downtown Boston and travel across town to her new home. During the short journey to Boston, Mrs. Eddy was alone in her compartment with her personal maid Adelaide Still. She apparently felt a little cool, and Miss Still used her own winter coat to put over Mrs. Eddy's feet as they had neglected to bring a robe. In the other carriage travelled Mrs. Eddy's staff, which on this occasion included her relative Dr. A.B. Morrill, but, although messages were relayed between the carriages, none of the men in attendance was summoned.

So far the great move had gone according to plan, and Mrs. Eddy was cheerful and alert, enjoying the view from the train, no doubt feeling stimulated by the rare break in her daily routine. At the station, the transfer to a carriage for the final lap to the house went without a hitch[6] but the view was less cheery as Mary Baker Eddy approached her new home on Beacon Street. A large group of reporters was massed around the door. Having been alerted to Mrs. Eddy's arrival by a telephone call from the railroad station in Concord, they were waiting for her carriage to pull up and for her to alight. John Salchow was riding in the last of the hacks that followed Mrs. Eddy's conveyance, and, as soon as he saw the situation, he leaped out and ran to her. She looked down at him from the carriage window and, unwilling to run this gauntlet of photographers and reporters, she said, "John, can you get me into the house?" His reply was to pick her up bodily and carry her swiftly past the reporters and into the house, where he deposited her, roaring with laughter, in an armchair.[7]

Quickly, however, her laughter turned to sadness as she looked about her at her new home. Pleasant View had been lit by gas; it was kept rather cool, especially at night, as the furnace setting was tended by the ever frugal Calvin Frye. Even the first-floor "company" rooms had been modest in size. In Chestnut Hill the new electric lighting blazed, the house was very warm, and the large reception rooms on the first floor were elegantly appointed in the modern style and filled with hothouse flowers. None of this was much to Mrs. Eddy's taste, but the real shock came when she took stock of her own second-floor apartment. The directives she had given for her rooms had been quite specific. The rooms which she had occupied at Pleasant View were to be reproduced exactly. Asked if the size of the rooms could be expanded slightly, she had agreed without enthusiasm. Her new rooms were, in fact, almost double the old in size, and the new dark wallpaper was smart but not what she liked. At first roused to anger, she then sank into silence, murmuring, "Oh splendid misery, splendid misery." Comforted somewhat by the familiar meal which the cook had brought with her from Concord, and by the sight of all her belongings arranged in exactly their right place in her bedroom bureau by the thoughtful Adelaide, Mrs. Eddy went to bed. But the next day, on entering her study, she was again upset at the sight of her familiar furniture, exactly duplicated but now standing like islands in a sea of new, aggressive rose-patterned carpeting. Even worse, when she sat in her chair, the window was too high to permit her to look out on the driveway and street, as she liked to do. She had written to Alfred Farlow from Concord when the move was planned: "I want a window in my room like the one here. It relieves my lonely hours."⁸ It was clear that the Boston officials to whom Mary Baker Eddy had committed herself might offer her more security, but they did not yet understand her personal needs and tastes.

This new "great barn of a place," as she called it, would not do, and Mrs. Eddy moved immediately up to her dressmaker's rooms on the third floor, where she found the view excellent and the space cozy. Rapidly after that time, work began on remodelling Mrs. Eddy's living space to her liking. In three weeks' time the rooms of her second-floor apartment were converted to Pleasant View dimensions, the window frames were lowered, a small elevator was installed, the slope of the driveway was changed to afford more privacy when Mrs. Eddy came out, and a large tree was cut down to allow her to look out on nearby homes. As so often happened in Christian Science, the architect who was called in to superintend the project swore that there was no way an elevator could be fitted where Mrs. Eddy wanted it, but Mrs. Eddy said that there was, and an elevator was duly installed. Mrs. Eddy had her old gaslight fixture installed at the head of her bed, as she found the electric light glaring, and she used her old washstand set. The space that was cut off from the bedroom and living room was converted into a pleasant little sitting room for Calvin Frye.

When in late February the new bedroom was ready, Mrs. Eddy departed for her daily drive, which by this time tended to last only forty minutes, and in that time every staff member cooperated in moving all her furniture and possessions back into their precisely ordained places. This would be the final move of her life, and it was a particularly intense enactment of a regular drama observed by Mrs. Eddy's domestic staff. Noise, disturbance, and dust were equally abhorrent to her. Therefore, each day, to ensure that she would never be upset, all the cleaning of Mrs. Eddy's rooms was done during her drive. The maids, armed with dusters and pails of the damp, shredded newspaper which was used to clean the carpets, would be ready to whisk in as soon as the elevator moved their leader downstairs. As the length of the drives shortened, to assist the cleaners in their work, a system of brass nails was instituted, without Mrs. Eddy's knowledge, to mark the exact place of everything. According to Adelaide Still, the wet paper rigamarole ended when Mrs. Eddy happily invested in that new domestic marvel, a vacuum cleaner.

Ever the activist and the authoritarian, Mrs. Eddy had not simply moped when her new setting proved not to be to her liking. She had it remade exactly to her specifications. But the view from the lowered windows could not be of the Bow hills, and the attempt to re-create Pleasant View in Chestnut Hill was inevitably doomed; thus the move from Concord cost her a lot emotionally. "There is no doubt that a belief of homesickness tried to tempt Mrs. Eddy during the first months after she left Pleasant View," writes Adelaide Still carefully, noting that Mrs. Eddy took no interest at all in the general running of the house and barely looked at the fine rooms on the ground floor. John Salchow more forthrightly says that she was never at home at Chestnut Hill and once confided to him: "This is not my home. Pleasant View will always be my home." She also told a friend at this time that "the strongest tie I've ever had, apart from love of God, has been my love of home," and there is no doubt that the move from Concord took an enormous toll on her.[9]

At this time of trial and transition, Mrs. Eddy's personal staff drew closer round her in protection, and her dependence on them increased. As she herself remarked to Calvin Frye:

> There is a great gulf between old age and middle age, a second childhood. When a member of my family is absent now, I watch and am anxious for his return, the same as I did when I was a child.[10]

Adelaide Still, Mrs. Eddy's maid, says in her reminiscences that in her last years Mrs. Eddy was never alone during the day, that either Still herself or Laura Sargent or both were required always to be in the room, even, much to some officials' displeasure, when Mrs. Eddy was discussing important Church business. Still and Sargent seem to have viewed each other as fellows, cooperating in the task of attending their beloved but exhausting leader, but Calvin Frye's position was embittered by the fact that he felt himself once again in competition for Mrs. Eddy's favor with younger men. Irving Tomlinson was still on the scene, and now there was also William Rathvon, who had the assistance of his wife Ella, whose frequent presence Mrs. Eddy not only tolerated but enjoyed. The important new favorite was, however, Adam Dickey, whom John V. Dittemore, another of Dickey's rivals, describes as "a bull-necked Canadian with the face of a prize-fighter," and an "athletic tiger-cat."[11]

As far as I can make out from the Church's wooden minibiographies and from Frederick Peabody's vitriolic portrait,[12] Dickey was a pragmatic, nuts-and-bolts kind of man whom many in the movement found coarse and lacking in intellect, but whose combination of steady faith, practical skills, and unflappable obedience suited Mrs. Eddy. To take one example, when, unexpectedly, the coachman was found dead, and Mrs. Eddy was all ready to go out for her drive, Dickey climbed up next to Calvin Frye and took the reins. For all his limitations, Dickey was a strong and loyal man who stood by Mary Baker Eddy's side in the difficult days ahead, and for this he was rewarded. One of Mrs. Eddy's last official acts was to name Adam Dickey a member of the Board of Directors of the Church, and he was thus to be in the forefront of the battles waged after her death.[13]

The devolution of authority and organizational activity which Mrs. Eddy had begun to engineer in 1889 was greatly accelerated after the move to Boston, as Mrs. Eddy engaged less and less in the daily course of Church affairs. Reading between the lines of the various accounts of Mrs. Eddy's last years, I surmise that there was some tension and even animosity between the old guard, who had been in the movement since the 1880s, and the new-comers, who had not been taught by Mrs. Eddy personally. The members of the inner circle increasingly felt it was their responsibility to buffer her not just from the general world but from the Christian Science bureaucracy. For their part, as Mrs. Eddy grew frailer and more detached, as the end came nearer, and the questions of the succession in particular became more acute, the Church officials suspected and feared the influence of the inner circle on her.

The clearest evidence I have of this friction is John Salchow's account of a journey he was forced to make to attend to urgent family business. Salchow, it will be remembered, was the untutored and rustic man-of-all-work at Pleasant View who felt a mission to serve Mrs. Eddy and give her unquestioning obedience, and upon whom she relied implicitly. This jour-ney out of state was the first time Salchow had left Mrs. Eddy's side in over eight years, and he promised he would return on a given day. But on the journey home Salchow was plagued by delays and difficulties. He wrote therefore to Mrs. Eddy herself to explain his problems and warn that he might be delayed, and he sent the same information to another member of the household. Mysteriously, the letter to Mrs. Eddy never reached her hands, and when she inquired anxiously about "my John," she was told that nothing had been heard from him, and that he was probably not com-ing back at all. By superhuman effort, Salchow managed to arrive home on his appointed day, just in time to assist Mrs. Eddy as usual as she departed for her drive, thus, he believed, gladdening the heart of his adored leader and confounding the plots of his enemies, whoever they might be. There was no doubt a streak of paranoia in both Frye and Salchow, but there were also people who really would have been happy to see them leave Mrs. Eddy's side.

Mrs. Eddy had left Pleasant View to achieve more privacy, but there were problems which moving could not solve. The press, though now forced to keep a greater distance, was always on the watch for any slight flicker of activity at 384 Beacon, and the public still showed an inordinate interest in Mrs. Eddy's doings. One young woman in the new neighborhood was shamed out of her persistent snooping only by being sent an extravagantly beautiful gift of fruit, accompanied by a personal note from Mrs. Eddy.[14] The drive around the Chestnut Hill Reservoir was now widely identified as the barometer for the state of affairs in Mrs. Eddy's carefully guarded household; if Mrs. Eddy failed to drive out, this was considered a reliable portent of her death or imminent demise. Once again on May 15, 1908, she found it necessary to write to the New York *Herald* and deny to the general public a report of her decease. The same message was repeated in even stronger terms for her followers on the next day, when this notice appeared in the *Christian Science Sentinel*:

> Since Mrs. Eddy is watched, as one watches a criminal or a sick person, she begs to say, in her own behalf, that she is neither; therefore to be criticized or judged by either a daily drive or a dignified stay at home, is superfluous. When accumulating work requires it, or because of a preference to remain indoors she omits her drive, do not strain at gnats or swallow camels over it, but try to be composed and resigned to the shocking fact that she is minding her own business, and recommends this surprising privilege to all her dear friends and enemies.[15]

The heavy sarcasm here may have come as a surprise to some of her newer followers, but it probably reassured others that the real Mary Baker Eddy was not just alive but was keeping her wits about her and her hand on the helm.

Being constantly forced to deny that one is dead or senile or mad necessarily takes its toll, and by the summer Mrs. Eddy was forced to interrupt her drives. That she herself was aware of weakening is indicated in a poignant confession she made to Calvin Frye which he recorded in his diary on July 2, 1908:

> *Beloved*: if you knew with what I am beset continually arguments of dementia; incompetence, old age etc. it would explain why I am so changed.

These chronic fears of succumbing to old age became critical only weeks later when Mrs. Eddy was beset by a new attack of renal calculi. The brief entries of Calvin Frye's diary are eloquent:

Tuesday, July 14, 1908. Mrs. Eddy had sudden attacks of intense pain through umbilical region and was confined to her bed today with little help from mental work but would not consent to send for an M.D. Did not drive out today.

Tuesday, July 28, 1908. At about 12 o'clock last night an editor of Boston Herald called Mr. Dickey by telephone and asked at what hour Mrs. Eddy died! He said the rumor on the streets is that she is dead. She had been having a series of attacks for over a week which kept her in bed and on the lounge almost the entire time and last night she despaired of living until the morning, but when this telephone was recd it revealed cause of attacks & gained much relief.

Aug. 5, 1908. Mrs. Eddy had a sudden attack last night at 11.30 help-lessness & respiration stopped for a time & she called me & asked for help; soon she called for Laura and afterwards for I.C.T. [i.e., Irving Tomlinson] We all worked for and talked to her for about ¾ hour when she recovered. She afterwards told me to handle paralysis of spinal nerves.

Sunday, Aug. 23, 1908. Mrs. Eddy woke with severe pain this morning and called for W. H. B. [William Bertram, a student of Mrs. Eddy's who left Christian Science and became a physician in the 1880s] at 12.45. He arrived at 2.45 a.m. but she did not require his services the pain having been relieved by the students at home.

Monday, Aug. 3, 1909. Intense pain last night—she requested an M.D. to administer a hypodermic; called W. H. B.

Mother heard an audible voice from God saying: Leave alone succes-sor contention before it is meddled with.[16]

In their very different accounts of Mrs. Eddy's last years, both John Dittemore and Robert Peel are agreed that life at Chestnut Hill was dark and difficult when Mrs. Eddy was passing kidney stones or suffering from what was probably pneumonia or bronchitis—conditions, incidentally, which are readily treated today by conventional medicine, but for which medical sci-ence had little to offer in the first decade of the twentieth century. There were brief times when the pain was too great for her to cope with, even with the most loving and devoted help of her group of attendants. At this point, and only then, she would resort to the standard painkiller, morphine, but the relief she and therefore the staff felt as a result of the drug was always tem-pered by the feeling of failure peculiar to those involved in the spiritual heal-ing movements. It was at this point that the theory of Malicious Animal Magnetism came to their aid. As the above Frye diary entries indicate, once Mrs. Eddy had managed to identify some immediate source of what we would usually label hostility or opposition, and which she coded as mes-merism, this explanation would allow her to move beyond the pain and begin to cope.

For the summer of 1908, as the quoted diary entries have shown, Frye identified two sources of mesmerism, one external to the movement and the other internal—the continual press siege Mrs. Eddy was forced to live under, and the problem of how the movement would be governed if Mrs. Eddy failed to name a successor. Yet the underlying force of all the different sources of mesmerism which Mrs. Eddy detected centered, of course, on her death. The press wanted her dead because then the newspapers would have one last good story and could finally publish their obituary on the founder of Christian Science and close their file of press clippings on her. At least some part of Augusta Stetson wanted Mrs. Eddy dead so that she could at last take over the leadership of the Christian Science movement. Even some of the men in the Mother Church bureaucracy, in their heart of hearts, chafed under Mrs. Eddy's leadership, felt that she had done her work, and longed to be fully in control at last.

On the other hand, others in the movement, or perhaps the same men for different reasons, wanted her to live forever. One of the most sensational and controversial charges levelled against Christian Science has been that it promoted or at least tolerated the belief among its followers that Mary Baker Eddy, the movement's leader and founder, would offer the final demonstration—that is, she would achieve immortality.[17] Calvin Frye's diary offers evidence that, at least as of the late 1890s, Mary Baker Eddy herself believed that she could "demonstrate" over death and old age.

> [*October 8*] *1894.* She requested me yesterday that if she should seem to die, not to bury her body for 3½ days, and to keep perfectly quiet about it during that time.

> *January 24, 1896.* This morning Mother said St. Paul comes nearer to my thought than any other writer in the Bible. He said David fell on sleep [See Acts 13:36].

> 1. David saw corruption. The body was buried & decayed.

> 2. Jesus died in belief but the body did <u>not</u> see corruption but was raised again.

> 3. The demonstration for me is that it shall not be death, even, but a body transformed "by the renewing of Mind" spiritualization.

> [*November 28*] *1898.* Mother gave me a cutting rebuke this eve, for what I did about circulating article from Monitor, about 2 hours afterwards in talking pleasantly with me again, she said to me "This will go on for a little while and then I will be young and won't be with you any more (or I won't need you anymore)" I'm not sure which of these two she said.

But if one part of Mrs. Eddy believed fiercely in her potential to grow spiritually and therefore to live on or even regain her youthful strength, another part recognized and feared the forces of what she called mesmerism—those mental forces in the world which were actively, persistently, wishing her gone. This was the mental challenge against which her watchers were charged to protect her, and which she constantly chided them for failing to check.[18]

By the summer of 1908, the time of her eighty-seventh birthday, Mrs. Eddy was clear in her own mind that the final demonstration was not possible for her. As she saw it, the force of Malicious Animal Magnetism was literally impelling her into the grave, and although she continued to fight, she now began to denounce what she saw as the reason for her impending death. Thus on August 25 she told Dickey,

> If I should ever leave here, will you promise me that you will write a history of what has transpired in your experiences with me, and say that I was mentally murdered?[19]

An entry from Calvin Frye's diary, which was written after Mrs. Eddy's death, perhaps in 1912, elaborates on this theme:

> Some week or more before our beloved Leader passed from us, she called me to her and asked me to promise her that I would tell her students it was malicious animal magnetism that was overcoming her and not a natural result from the beliefs incident to old age and its claims of limitation. She had hoped to demonstrate the way over old age but the malice and hate which poured in upon her thought left through the next friends suit in the New Hampshire courts, I believe was largely burden which seemed to undermine her vitality.

Yet even as she fought with the pain in her chest and her back, and with the growing fears of death, Mary Baker Eddy was not wholly controlled by the weakness of her body. Although she had given up the day-to-day management of Church affairs, at least until the beginning of 1910 she continued to work regular, if shorter, hours, to read and correct *Science and Health*, write letters, comment on the various Christian Science publications, think about the movement in the long term, and make high-level policy decisions. The most public of these was the founding of the *Christian Science Monitor*, which I have referred to in my preface as one of Mrs. Eddy's most celebrated, influential, and farsighted accomplishments.

The treatment she had received from the New York *World* and from *McClure's Magazine* had taught Mary Baker Eddy a peculiarly painful lesson about the press's quest for sensationalism and disregard for truth. She felt herself to be in a position to do something about this, not just because her movement had—barely, perhaps!—the material resources, but because she felt empowered by God to make changes in the world. And so on July 28 Mrs. Eddy wrote a letter to the directors, and on August 8 a short note to the Trustees of the Publishing Society, instructing them to begin publishing a daily newspaper. The subsequent success of the *Monitor* has masked quite how ambitious Mrs. Eddy's directive was, and how much faith and obedience her officials had to muster as they put her wishes into action. It is true that Mrs. Eddy had always had a profound understanding of the role of what we now call the media in modern society, and that her founding of the *Christian Science Journal* and the *Christian Science Sentinel*, and her close guidance of the early stages of both publications had been very important in spreading the word of her new movement. It is true that the Christian Science movement had an active and efficient Publishing Society, and that it had some twenty years of experience in magazine publishing. Nonetheless, the leap from establishing a religious house organ to publishing a daily newspaper designed for not only national but international circulation was big indeed, and the risk of failure was high. It took an experienced risktaker like Mary Baker Eddy to put the prestige and the financial resources of her movement on the line for a concept and a principle.

The directors and trustees certainly saw the venture as difficult and risky. Archibald McLellan tried to explain to Mrs. Eddy just how difficult the job she had ordered would be—that correspondents from all over the world would have to be hired, that the Publishing House buildings would have to be enlarged, and so forth. Mrs. Eddy asked him how long the process would take, and when McLellan said three months, she agreed and held him to the deadline. Adelaide Still, Mrs. Eddy's personal maid, remembered what an interest Mrs. Eddy showed in every detail relating to the new newspaper, how samples of paper and type were brought to her, and a sample issue was made up for her inspection. It was Mrs. Eddy herself who demanded a better quality of paper and who chose the motto "First the blade, then the ear, then the full grain in the ear" and told the people at the newspaper where it should appear. When they told her that the name she had chosen for her paper, the *Christian Science Monitor*, would mean swift failure, she refused to back down, and they were forced to obey. On November 25 the first issue rolled off the presses, to Mrs. Eddy's intense pleasure.[20]

Founding the *Monitor* was an act of affirmation, and its success itself affirmed Mrs. Eddy's instruction that the way to live is always to strive for the best, meet challenges head-on, and refuse to envisage defeat. Mrs. Eddy had by her own labors built an organization which made something like founding a daily newspaper possible, and this accomplishment was a source of deep satisfaction for her. Moreover, as a private individual, and a lifelong newspaper junkie, Mrs. Eddy loved getting the *Monitor* every day and discussing the editorials or exchanging interesting tidbits with her staff. Such small sources of pleasure and relaxation were becoming rarer and thus more important as her health declined. For even as the *Monitor* emerged on schedule and began to thrive, two other issues claimed Mrs. Eddy's attention and promised no pleasure. The first involved Mrs. Eddy's most famous and difficult lieutenant, Augusta Stetson of First Church of Christ, Scientist, in New York City, and the whole issue of succession. The second concerned her son, the continuing economic plight of his family, and the probability that he would mount a legal challenge to his mother's will.

All of Mrs. Eddy's biographers from Dakin to Peel to Thomas have devoted a large section to Augusta Stetson, her life and career, and the complicated sequence of events by which Mrs. Stetson was finally expelled from the Church. I confess that I am loath at this late stage in my story to spend too much time on Mrs. Stetson since the more I read of and about her, the less I like her. I get the impression that even Dittemore and Dakin really thought Gussie Stetson was a dreadful woman—yet they depicted her as the last prey of that jealous, vindictive, and vacillating paranoiac Mary Baker Eddy, of course![21] Whether we like it or not, however, the Stetson case has to be given due consideration since it raises crucial doctrinal and ethical issues in Christian Science and catalyzes the crucial question of Mrs. Eddy's succession.

To recapitulate briefly, Augusta Emma Stetson started her long and successful career as a Christian Science healer and teacher in 1884 when she was about forty (she consistently refused to reveal her actual date of birth).[22] Capturing Frederick Stetson, the scion of a prosperous Maine family, had been a marital coup for the voluptuous and talented young Gussie Simmons, but he suffered rheumatic fever as a prisoner during the Civil War, and within a few years he was a permanent invalid, unable to earn a living. Although the couple never had any children, Augusta, Frederick, and her parents were forced in 1873 to move to Somerville, Massachusetts, in an attempt to find new sources of income, and the 1880s brought the whole family to a nadir in their fortunes. Augusta was just beginning to work as an elocutionist when she heard Mrs. Eddy speak, experienced a moment of ecstatic release from all her problems, and was persuaded to look into Christian Science. Stetson quickly recorded some dramatic successes, and her stock in the embryonic Boston movement soared, as did the animosity felt toward her by her fellow—or rival—practitioners. In 1886 Mrs. Stetson was asked by Mrs. Eddy to move to New York City and begin work there.[23] Augusta was reluctant to make the move, because her family was settled in New England, and she had no connections in New York, where Mrs. Laura Lathrop was just becoming established. But unlike Clara Choate, who had refused to move to the Midwest at Mrs. Eddy's request and had soon fallen away from the Church and into low fortunes, Augusta did as she was told and eventually succeeded beyond her own dreams and her leader's expectations.

By the fall of 1908 Stetson was indisputably the leader of the largest, richest, and most celebrated branch church of Christian Science. This success came after Stetson had endured some very lean times, and it was largely her own personal achievement. Even when she was poor and unsuccessful, Mrs. Stetson managed to project the image of a stylish, cultured woman that appealed to New York's nouveau riche population. As success came her way, Mrs. Stetson saw no contradiction between her Christian Science doctrine of spirit as the only reality and the money that flowed in to her church's coffers and, not incidentally, into her own pockets, and this attitude fitted well with New York's Gilded Agers. The healings that were recorded, the recruits who started coming into her congregation after 1886, and the reverence she inspired in them were largely based on her ability as a healer, her inspirational rhetoric, and her private charisma. She bound her students to her by a powerful mixture of attraction and fear, and there were many, even or especially among her devotees, who credited Augusta Stetson with the old mesmeric ability to compel people to do things against their will and their interest, and mentally to wreak even mortal damage if she chose. Like Josephine Woodbury before her, Augusta Stetson tended to read the New Testament as a blueprint for her personal career, and she thrilled her followers by the increasingly exalted terms which she used to refer to the leader of Christian Science, and to describe her own role in the movement. Some of this rhetoric filtered into Mrs. Stetson's letters to Mrs. Eddy, and it may have flattered the older woman at times, but accusations that in this respect Mrs. Stetson was accurately reflecting Mrs. Eddy's views and carrying out her wishes are false. The full correspondence[24] shows that Mary Baker Eddy consistently, and with increasing seriousness and rigor, chastised her student for personalizing the religion, for forgetting the first commandment to worship only God, and for suggesting that she, Mrs. Eddy, stood on the same level as Jesus Christ.[25]

In terms of sheer numbers, no single church group outnumbered Augusta Stetson's First Church of Christ, Scientist in New York City, and the personal power she wielded over her flock greatly exceeded that of any individual at The Mother Church, or, indeed, of the Board of Directors as a whole. Thus it is not surprising that Mrs. Stetson felt she was the person most fitted to take over the leadership of Christian Science when Mrs. Eddy passed on. Among Stetson's New York students it was virtually a matter of faith that Stetson would play the role of Paul to Mrs. Eddy's Jesus Christ, and that the center of Christian Science would soon pass to New York. Of course, the whole question of succession was a very delicate matter, since Mrs. Eddy did not intend to step down, and therefore a succession could occur only after her death, an event whose prospect aroused all kinds of strange and special responses within the movement. Everyone had understood since the 1890s that no one could expect to succeed Mrs. Eddy who was known to aspire to the position. Therefore in public, in correspondence to Mrs. Eddy herself or to any of the Boston officials, Mrs. Stetson never said she wished, or thought herself qualified to become, Mrs. Eddy's successor.[26]

Nonetheless, Mrs. Eddy and everyone else who was prominent in the movement knew of Augusta Stetson's position as heiress presumptive, and they were preoccupied with the question of whether Mrs. Eddy would be persuaded during her lifetime to anoint Augusta officially, or whether, after Mrs. Eddy's death, Mrs. Stetson would attempt some kind of coup. As we have seen from the memos in the Chandler papers, some Christian Scientists like the Hannons believed that the Pleasant View household had been infiltrated by Stetsonite fighters such as Lida Fitzpatrick, who were either keeping the leader hostage or were preparing some kind of coup. The famous memo from Hermann Hering to Mrs. Eddy's secretary H. Cornell Wilson which was reportedly picked up off the street, but more probably stolen, and found its way onto the pages of the New York *World* established that the watchers at Pleasant View were detailed to combat the Stetsonite error, and that Calvin Frye, of all people, had been identified as the conduit by which the error was entering.

For her part, Mrs. Eddy was fully aware of Augusta's ambitions, and she took what opportunities she could to make it clear in public that she would not appoint Augusta Stetson her successor and that she did not see Mrs. Stetson as a *prima inter pares*. On the occasion of the dedication of the Mother Church, the scheduled performance by Augusta Stetson's choir was cancelled at the last moment,[27] and Mrs. Eddy pointedly paid a professional woman elocutionist, not a Christian Scientist, to read her Message to the Church. In her policies of preferment within the growing Church bureaucracy, Mrs. Eddy showed, as I have commented earlier in this book, an increasing preference for young, educated males, and Augusta Stetson was not made a member of the Board of Directors, or even appointed to the Board of Lectureship. More important, a number of the By-Laws in the *Manual of the Mother Church* were written specifically to curb what were perceived to be the excesses at the First Church in New York. In obedience to the *Manual*, Mrs. Stetson was forced first to give up her position as First Reader, although there was no real transference of power, and later she and all her practitioners were obliged to give up the luxurious offices which they had installed in the church building, and move next door. All of these snubs and reproofs from Boston no doubt galled Augusta Stetson, but she preferred to see them not as evidence of Mrs. Eddy's will but of the directors' hostility and envy. She bowed her knee in humility and obedience, swallowed her resentment in public at least, and bided her time.

Augusta Stetson was constantly at war with other Christian Science leaders, and her turf quarrels with Mrs. Laura Lathrop in particular were widely known in the movement.[28] That she had emerged victorious from many of these disputes was almost certainly owing to the strength of her personal relationship with Mary Baker Eddy. Long after she had officially given up all mediations among different factions and individuals, Mrs. Eddy had continued to intervene to negotiate terms, insist on peace accords, and keep the Stetsonites both in check and within the movement. The nature of the relationship between Mrs. Stetson and Mrs. Eddy has been the subject of much discussion, and male critics have seen rivalry, jealousy, and deception as the dominant emotions, quoting nasty remarks each woman made about the other when speaking off the record. Dakin and Bates and Dittemore assert that Mrs. Eddy took so long to expel Mrs. Stetson because she was afraid that Mrs. Stetson would kill her with Malicious Animal Magnetism.

As I see it, the Stetson-Eddy rivalry was perfectly real, but more real was their collaboration for twenty-five years, the sense both had that one would be weaker without the other, that working messily through difficulties was better than making a clean break. Mary Baker Eddy understood Augusta thoroughly, and she knew both her strengths and her failings. There were also parts of Mrs. Eddy's nature and aspects of her past life and her climb to prominence which Augusta Stetson understood better than any of the newer young men. Both women had been close to their mothers and enjoyed acting out the mother-daughter relationship. Both were attractive women who had worked out as they aged how to construct a public persona on the basis of personal charm. The intractability of heart disease to mental cure was an issue which darkened the lives of both and which neither cared to discuss. Both Asa Gilbert Eddy and Frederick Stetson were for many years invalids whose disease proved sadly and inconveniently resistant to the powers of their celebrated healer wives. Both Mary Baker Eddy and Augusta Stetson understood the importance of public relations, propaganda, and fund-raising in a modern religious movement, and they excelled in these fields of activity. Both women had seen dramatic changes in fortune, had come close to falling off the edge of polite society, and had been forced to take on the task of supporting themselves and other family members in a society structured to discourage economic independence for women. Both had earned affluence and felt they deserved it. Both were survivors who preferred a compromised success to a pure failure and intended to live long enough to atone.

Understanding, sympathy, and affection, as well as shared interests, held Mrs. Eddy and Mrs. Stetson together, and Mrs. Eddy was deeply grateful to Augusta for her help and support during both the Woodbury trial and the Next Friends suit. Yet once Mrs. Eddy moved to Chestnut Hill and came as it were under the aegis of the Board of Directors of The Mother Church, her long relationship with Mrs. Stetson began to unravel. By 1908 Mrs. Eddy was bone weary of conflict and no longer unwilling for someone finally to rid her of this troublesome healer. The directors, for their part, were weary of the unending New York disputes and intent on getting the succession issue resolved once and for all in their favor. They saw their opportunity in the last month of 1908.

On November 30 the *New York American* informed the public that the First Church in New York City planned to build a branch church on Riverside Drive which would exceed in size and splendor the Mother Church Extension. This proposal was a double challenge to the status of The Mother Church, and an editorial in the December 5 *Sentinel* fulminated that, as laid down clearly in the *Manual*, only The Mother Church could have branches. Perhaps Mrs. Stetson for her part had tired of eating humble pie and playing the waiting game; perhaps she was afraid that Mrs. Eddy really was dead, as the papers had reported so many times, or at least that she had been deposed in all but name, and that the time had come to make a formal challenge to the Boston establishment.

Rallying her energies, perceiving that her student Augusta was on the brink of making an irremediable mistake, and seeking, I think, to pull her friend back one last time, on December 7 Mrs. Eddy invited Stetson to come to Boston at her convenience and take a turn with her around the Chestnut Hill Reservoir. This was an extraordinary request since for many years Mrs. Eddy had allowed very few of her followers to come to see her for social visits. Mrs. Stetson therefore dropped everything and took the night train. Later she would leave a detailed account of this final meeting. According to Mrs. Stetson, during the drive Mrs. Eddy was all affection and solicitude, sharing her lamb's-wool lap rug in the carriage and listening most earnestly, and with a perhaps unusual lack of comment, to everything her student had to say. Shortly after their return to the house, Mrs. Eddy summoned Mrs. Stetson to her study, blessed her kneeling and sobbing disciple, and embraced her like a daughter. Dittemore alleges that Mrs. Eddy was being deliberately deceptive throughout all her conversations with Stetson, that all the while she was intending to throw Mrs. Stetson to the directorial wolves. I think, on the contrary, that both she and Augusta left each other convinced that the personal meeting had worked, that they had once again managed to solve the issues which had come between them, and that they could move on to the future in friendship and understanding. The emotion which Mrs. Stetson documents in her record of all their conversations was, in my view, real and overwhelming for both, but it was to prove short-lived.[29]

Sure that she was once again firmly installed in Mrs. Eddy's favor, Mrs. Stetson was ready to compromise, especially since she had now seen for herself how frail her leader had become. On her return to New York, she announced that there had been a great misunderstanding; there was never any question of building a branch church, and the First Church was merely seeking to aid with the construction of the Seventh Church.[30] Confident of Mrs. Eddy's weakness and affection for her, and no doubt feeling that she had waved the olive branch long enough, in January 1909 Augusta Stetson haughtily refused, on grounds of principle, to contribute to the appeal fund launched by Alfred Farlow to pay off some unpaid debts incurred by one of the contractors involved in building the First Church in Concord, New Hampshire. The existence of this problem had been concealed from Mary Baker Eddy, who was well known to be unalterably opposed to debt, and Stetson probably thought she would gain some points with Mrs. Eddy by refusing to make any contribution. In fact Mrs. Eddy was not amused. She did not care to see her church officials publicly embarrassed, whatever thunderbolts she might hurl at their heads in private. The directors of the Church themselves were, of course, furious and more convinced than ever that Mrs. Stetson was a rank weed which had to be pulled out of the field of Christian Science ministry. Their opportunity came at last in July.[31]

On July 9, 1909, in anticipation of the semiannual Communion service, the practitioners at First Church in New York presented Mrs. Stetson with a gift of gold and a composite letter which included statements such as

> The voice of the Father-Mother God is ever speaking through you.

> And you, our blessed teacher, as the manifestation of truth . . . Our hearts are filled with gratitude and awe as we see, in you, Christianity demonstrated. . . .

> May a purified life attest the endless gratitude I feel for the manifestation of Christ you have given us, while with Mary of old, I cry, Rabboni—Teacher.

> Your unselfish life, fast approaching the perfect idea of Love is to my hungry sense for Truth, "the bread of heaven and the water of Life." Eating this bread and drinking this water is to me eating the body of Christ and drinking his blood.

Mrs. Stetson promptly dispatched both the gold and the letter to Mrs. Eddy, with an accompanying missive of her own, which I think she felt was finely calculated to build on the affection and spiritual exaltation both had experienced at their recent meeting:

> I feel they belong to you, dearest, and are your fruit; for without your divine instruction and Christly guidance I should not have had them, so I send this copy of the dear letters to you, with the type of the gold of human character which is fast melting into spiritual understanding in each of these students. . . . These are thine, Holy One; I trust they are all strong in Christ. . . . May none fall away! They desire to honor you, our great forever Leader, they have come up out of great tribulation, and have washed their robes. . . . Precious Leader, my love for you is inexpressible. God grant my constant prayer that I may be worthy to be called Your faithful, obedient, loving child.[32]

Mary Baker Eddy may have been old and sad and tired, but she could still recognize heresy when she saw it. The meeting with Augusta had been a last surge of the old desire for earthly affection and an attempt to wield the power of personality—the very power she had been inveighing against for many years. Once again, events would serve to humble and chastise Mrs. Eddy. But at this point at least her way was plain, if painful.[33] There was no way to change or reform Augusta Stetson; she must be purged from the body of Christian Science. Mrs. Eddy sent the gift and letter she had received from

Mrs. Stetson to the board with the terse directive: "Act, and act quickly. Handle the letters according to *Science and Health*, and the Mother Church *Manual*."[34] To Augusta herself, Mrs. Eddy replied via a letter, a copy of which she sent for publication to the *Sentinel*, aware, no doubt, that often in the past Stetson had used highly selected passages from Mrs. Eddy's letters to prove her privileged relationship with her leader.

> I have just finished your interesting letter. I thank you for acknowledging me as your Leader, and I know that every true follower of Christian Science abides by the definite rules which demonstrate the true following of their Leader; therefore, if you are sincere in your protestations, and are doing as you say you are, you will be blessed in your obedience. . . .
>
> You have been duly informed by me that, however much that I desire to read all that you send me, I have not the time to do so. . . . Mr. Adam Dickey is my secretary, through whom all my business is transacted. (*Miscellany*, pp. 357–58)

On July 24 Mrs. Eddy authorized the Board of Directors to summon Mrs. Stetson to appear before them and answer charges that she and her students were influenced by mesmerism to deify human personality. Despite the testimony given by a former student, Mrs. Maude Babcock, that she and her husband, after breaking with Mrs. Stetson, had been overcome by icy blasts of Malicious Animal Magnetism, Mrs. Stetson emerged from this first inquiry apparently unscathed.[35] Then a more circumstantial witness came forward, in the person of Virgil O. Strickler, a former Omaha lawyer who had been healed, joined First Church in New York City in about 1906, and had become privy to Mrs. Stetson's private meetings. Strickler kept a diary, and of special interest was the entry detailing the meeting which was held on the day after the first board of inquiry in Boston.

> Mrs. Stetson . . . returned from Boston at 7 o'clock this morning. . . . At 12.30 [she] went to the practitioners' meeting. [Mrs. Stetson] took her accustomed seat and began to talk. . . . She said that she had an idea she would be called upon in Boston to furnish statements from her practitioners showing how she had taught them. I asked her what points they wanted her to cover and she said, First, as to the question of her malpracticing on people, second, as to her taking personal control, and, third, as to her teaching of Christian Science. I asked her if these statements were to be put in the form of affidavits, and she said they could be sworn to later. I then said that in order to get at what she wanted I would repeat some of the things that she had said to us from time to [time] and see if we understood what we were asked to write. I then said, "We have repeatedly heard you say, 'You are the bond woman and your son is the son of the bond woman and I am the free woman, and

the bond woman and her son must go out before the free woman.' Now what must we say to this?" She said that she did not know, that God must show us what to say. I said, "Mrs. Stetson, if we tell them this, they will expel you instantly from the Mother Church." She said, "I know it, what shall we do?"... After a while she said, "We must deny that I ever said any of those things. I deny that I ever said them." I said, "Mrs. Stetson, but you did say them and you habitually took people up by name and treated them [i.e., deliberately sought to affect individual persons mentally, without their consent]." She replied that it was not her who took them up; that it was the human that said those things and that the human was not her real self, and that she could say that she never said them, and do it with the mental reservation that her real self had never said them. . . .

I then repeated several of the things that she had said by way of treatment of McLellan and others and asked her what her attitude would be at this time with respect to them, and she said that she would deny that she had said them; that she was now in the "absolute," and that those things were not said by her real self; therefore she could with perfect propriety deny that she had said them. . . .

[Mary Pinney, one of the practitioners] then broke in to say that she testified in this way in the "Brush Will Case" [1901] and that it was perfectly proper to deny something you had done if you only did it with the mental reservation that while the human self may have done the thing it was the real self that denied having done it.[36]

In mid-November final charges were drawn up against Mrs. Stetson, and she endured twenty-six hours of cross-examination before being at last dropped from the Church membership. Such had been the turmoil caused by the case, and so shocking had been the evidence against Mrs. Stetson, that all but a few of her closest associates accepted the banishment with more relief than protest. John Dittemore has rarely been accused of being soft on Mrs. Eddy, and since he knew Mrs. Stetson very well and was closely involved in her case, his final analysis of her deserves to be quoted:

No one can well say that the Directors were unjustified. By their act they placed the stamp of the Church's disapproval on a fungoid growth that threatened to smother the central stem of Christian Science. All their charges against Mrs. Stetson were true. Malpractice, perverted sex teaching, self-deification, deliberately misleading use of language—she was proved guilty of them all. And every one of them she derived directly from Mrs. Eddy, parent alike of the tree and the fungus. It might plausibly be said that Mrs. Stetson was condemned for following Mrs. Eddy's teachings, not wisely, but too well. Yet this would hardly be true. The doctrines which Gussie particularly emphasized were the very ones that Mrs. Eddy outgrew. Although it can hardly be denied that in the early eighties she at least approached "malpractice," nevertheless, in her later years, she became increasingly rigorous in denouncing any "treatment" of individual persons. The doctrine of spiritual conception was disavowed after the Woodbury incident. The attempts of her students to deify her were more and more frowned upon. . . . [Mrs. Eddy] at least endeavored, however unsuccessfully, to keep her standards clear, and, however surrounded by rotting pulp, there was a core of spirituality in her teaching. Gussie lacked this core, and she lacked her leader's capacity for growth.[37]

With the expulsion of Augusta Stetson, there was no longer any individual with clear claims or ambitions to take over Mrs. Eddy's position. As they saw the certainty of her death approaching, the directors put increasing pressure on Mrs. Eddy to make some formal, legal statement that her functions as laid down in the *Manual* were to be filled after her death by the board.[38]

According to Robert Peel, there was some movement, perhaps led by Rathvon, to form an advisory council that would take over her authority should she become incapacitated. This weak attempt at a palace revolution was opposed by Adam Dickey and faded away, particularly after Henry Baker, Mrs. Eddy's cousin and trustee, reassured the directors about their legal standing:

It is a matter of common law in a case of this kind, where it is physically impossible to carry out specified conditions by the one named, that the next in authority assume that jurisdiction. And in this case the next in authority is the Board of Directors of The Mother Church. Any competent court in the land will uphold the Manual just as Mrs. Eddy intends it to function whether her signature is forthcoming or not.[39]

News of Christian Science's sensational struggle with Augusta Stetson inevitably reached the ears of William Chandler, and he took advantage of this new burden on Mrs. Eddy to approach General Streeter once again about the possibility of arranging a settlement for his clients.[40] Chandler's timing was good because Mrs. Eddy was obviously failing, and it was becoming of paramount importance to her advisors that the question of the will be resolved.[41] Thus on October 28, 1909, Chandler signed on behalf of his Glover clients a settlement agreement which was extremely close to the one which Mrs. Eddy had withdrawn at the last moment in December 1907.[42] In essence, George Glover and his heirs and assigns agreed that they had been given an inventory of Mrs. Eddy's estate and had been apprised of and understood the various transfers of real estate holdings and copyrights which she had made during her lifetime. On the basis of what was agreed to be full disclosure, the Glovers covenanted to yield all present and prospective rights and interests in her estate in exchange for $120,000 in hand and a further $125,000 in trust. George Glover also agreed to return to Mrs. Eddy "all letters written by my mother to me or to any member of my family, and all documents dictated by her, in my possession or control or which have been placed in the hands of my counsel." On November 1, George Glover himself signed the October 28 deed, and on November 10 a confirmatory deed was finalized "evidencing the terms of a family settlement between George W. Glover of Lead, South Dakota, and his mother, Mary Baker Glover Eddy of Concord, New Hampshire."

The two documents of October 28 and November 10 are interesting to compare because they show how strenuously General Streeter and his legal team worked, right up to the last moment, to produce a document which would make it impossible for any Glover ever to contest Mrs. Eddy's will. The November text is even more specific and repetitious than the October one, as is clear in these excerpts:

[*October*]

I do hereby, for myself, my heirs, executors, administrators and assigns, covenant with her and her executors, administrators, devisees, legatees and assigns that neither I nor any of my children, nor any person claiming by, through or under me or them, shall ever, upon any ground, contest or retard the probate of any will which my mother may leave at her decease or attempt to set aside any gift, deed, contract or other disposition of property which she has heretofore made or may hereafter make, or make any claim either during or after her decease to any portion of her property or estate. . . .

[*November*]

Now therefore, know all men by these presents

1. that I, the said George W. Glover, in consideration of [$120,000 in hand, and $125,000 trust fund] do hereby assign, release and forever quitclaim unto my said mother, Mary Baker Glover Eddy, and her executors, administrators, devisees, legatees and assigns all interest or claim which I, as her heir at law, and which my heirs and legal representatives may, now or at any time hereafter or at her decease, have in and to any portion of her property or estate, either as heir at law or as legatee under any will now or heretofore made by said Mary Baker Glover Eddy; and I, the said George W. Glover, for myself, my heirs, executors, administrators and assigns do hereby accept said sum of one hundred and twenty thousand dollars as a present advancement in lieu of and in full settlement and satisfaction of all my present and prospective rights or expectant interests of myself and my heirs in my mother's estate, upon her decease, as her heir or heirs at law, and under any will or testamentary disposition now or heretofore made by her; and I do hereby, for myself, my heirs, executors, administrators and assigns, covenant with her and her executors, administrators, devisees, legatees

and assigns that neither I nor any of my children, nor any person claiming by, through or under me of them, shall ever, upon any ground, contest or retard the probate of any will which my mother may leave at her decease or attempt to set aside any gift, deed, contract or other disposition of property which she has heretofore made during her lifetime or after her decease to any portion of her property or estate; the third sum of one hundred and twenty thousand dollars and the establishment of the trust fund of one hundred and twenty-five thousand dollars heretofore described being hereby accepted in full settlement and discharge of any and all such possible claims.

2. I, the said George W. Glover, further covenant and agree that I have been advised by my counsel and fully understand the scope, terms and binding character of this settlement and release, and understand that the same forever precludes me and my heirs and legal representatives, both in my mother's lifetime and after her decease, from making any further claim upon her property and estate or questioning any disposition of the same she may see fit to make; and that in making this settlement and executing this release I am acting upon the advice of my counsel, and in accordance with the deliberate judgment of myself and my counsel.[43]

For years, Mary Baker Eddy had, literally, lived with the nightmare that her son George would break her will. Frank Streeter and Henry Baker no doubt came to Chestnut Hill with the final text of the family agreement, happy to be able to reassure their client that she could now rest easy, that they, one of the finest legal teams of the day, had solved her most important remaining legal problem. Perhaps she believed them, perhaps not, for she was a very savvy old bird, not given to taking anything for granted or underestimating the forces of human resentment. She knew that her son George Glover was in such desperate financial straits and so blinded by the prospects of her millions that he would do anything to inherit the estate he believed was his by blood right and in atonement for past wrongs. She also knew that Chandler felt he had lost a battle but not the war, that he had scars that would not heal, that he would do anything to settle old scores with her, her lawyers, and her church. But the business of the will would have to be left to her successors. She now had to face an opponent more daunting than William Chandler.

In the course of 1909 it was obvious to all that Mrs. Eddy's strength and energy were declining steeply. There were still days when she would light up with the old fire and amaze her staff and directors with her incisive intelligence, swift wit, and command of doctrine.[44] There were days when she would still challenge her staff, as in an incident recalled by Adam Dickey, when she put them all on the spot by asking them point-blank whether a Christian Scientist could control the weather. At this time, one of the more picturesque and taxing of the daily charges laid upon the watchers was to protect Mrs. Eddy from bad weather, especially now; Mrs. Laura Sargent had for some years been detailed to concentrate on the weather. Hence the staff members were both confident and unanimous in replying to Mrs. Eddy's question that, indeed, a Christian Scientist could control the weather. To this, Mrs. Eddy remarked with scorn that only God governs the weather, and no other influence can be brought to bear on it.[45] On another occasion she astonished Irving Tomlinson by suddenly quoting from memory the famous speech when Macbeth asks the doctor who is tending his deranged wife,

> *Canst thou not minister to a mind diseas'd,*
> *Pluck from the memory a rooted sorrow,*
> *Raze out the written troubles of the brain,*
> *And with some sweet oblivious antidote*
> *Cleanse the stuff'd bosom of that perilous stuff*
> *Which weighs upon the heart?* (Macbeth 5.3.40–45)

Tomlinson thought to ask the other staff members whether Mrs. Eddy had ever recited this before—they said she had not—but he apparently did not try to find out why the speech had suddenly come to her mind. Was there something in particular she wished to pluck from her own memory?[46]

During these last months, Calvin Frye described Mrs. Eddy's decline day by day in his diary.

[*June 2*] *1909*. Mrs. Eddy called her students to her this morning & said, "Yesterday I suffered a great deal during the entire day & I said to Mrs. Sargent 'the cause of this is nothing but a lack of love.' I went to bed in that same condition; my warning not having been heeded.

"After my watcher came and spoke to me in love without any special argument & it relieved me immediately."

Tuesday, Aug. 11, 1909. Monday at about 10 oclk Mrs. Eddy awake in a severe belief and called for help but all seemed so dazed they were unsuccessful. She was surprised & declared we wanted her to die & did not love. When I told her I love her more than any other person on earth, she said, "You lie!"

Monday May 9, 1910. Mr. Adam H. Dickey last night told Mrs. Eddy that she shall not have any more morphine! She had for several days been suffering from renal calculi and had voided stones in the urine; but yesterday the water seemed normal and so having hypodermic injections twice within a few days, he believed she did not need it, but that it was the old morphine habit reasserting itself and would not allow her to have it.

If there is a smoking gun on the topic of Mrs. Eddy's possible morphine addiction in the sections of Calvin Frye's diaries that Dittemore chose to extract and publish, it is in this last entry. As we have seen, the reports that Mrs. Eddy was a morphine addict date back at least to the 1880s, but this one phrase from Calvin Frye's diary ("it was the old morphine habit reasserting itself") is the only hard evidence supporting the accusation. It encouraged Dakin and Bates and Dittemore to recirculate in the 1930s all the old Peabody rumors, and to sensationalize their portrait of Mrs. Eddy for a new generation. Many loyal Christian Scientists have wished that this notorious diary entry was a forgery, but there is apparently no doubt that the passage is authentic. Researchers at the Church History Department tell me that they have checked the section from the Photostat which Dittemore made of the original handwritten diary entries.[47] Authentic or not, the diary entry is deeply puzzling. Dickey had known Mrs. Eddy for only a couple of years, and, as Mrs. Eddy's maid Adelaide Still later noted, it is odd that Dickey should be the one to refer to an old habit, and almost unbelievable that Mrs. Eddy would allow him, or, indeed, anyone else, to dictate to her in this way. Of all the people who were close to Mrs. Eddy in August 1910, only one, Calvin Frye, had known her since the 1880s, and the handful of other references to Mrs. Eddy taking morphine in Frye's diary make it clear that she was using the drug only at moments of unbearable pain.

Experts in pain control have often pointed out that there is an important difference between morphine addicts and those people who are given occasional morphine medications for pain. This is especially true in a historical period, as in Mrs. Eddy's lifetime, when the prescription of such medications was standard practice. If Calvin Frye devoted other diary entries to an old morphine habit, John Dittemore did not find them, and it seems clear that he was looking. Although I cannot account for the remark Frye attributes to Dickey, I remain convinced that Mary Baker Eddy was never addicted to morphine.

If the years 1908 and 1909 had often been troubled with pain and dark with conflict, after January 1910 life at the Chestnut Hill house became suddenly easier. Mrs. Eddy now ate very little, barely enough to "support a kitten,"[48] but she slept more, and more peacefully, lengthened the time of her drives, and for hours she would sit silent and still, gazing out her window. At least one of the women companions was always with her, but the other workers were able to read the paper for an hour or so after breakfast and go out on a few jaunts in the new motor car that had been acquired. Once Irving Tomlinson and George Kinter were able to get in a round of golf. Properly rested for the first time in years, Calvin Frye became positively chipper, to the amazement of his fellow workers, and he even took a unique three-hour vacation to attend an air show.

In late July Mrs. Eddy's health took a turn for the worse. The daily drives out were now becoming less a pleasure than an ordeal and a point of pride. Just getting her white gloves on to go out was becoming exhausting, and Mrs. Eddy had every day to conquer her fear that the horses would shy at the electric cars and she would die in an accident. Despite all this, perhaps sensing that she had no time now to lose, on Friday, July 29, 1910, Mrs. Eddy demanded to go and look at the Extension to the Mother Church, which she had once seen but never entered. She drove to her house at 385 Commonwealth Avenue and then on to the Fenway, where she could see the great building from afar. Then, however, according to Frye's diary, "she had such a sense of exhaustion from the long ride over rough roads that she hardly realized where she was."

On September 26 Mrs. Eddy rallied enough to call Frye, the Rathvons, Dickey, Tomlinson, and Mrs. Sargent, her most devoted and trusted helpers, into her room. The entry in Frye's diary is poignant:

Monday, Sept. 26, 1910. Mrs. Eddy called I.C.T. [Tomlinson] A.H.D. [Dickey] W.R.R. [Rathvon] E.S.Rathvon [Mrs. Rathvon] L.E. Sargent & C.A.F. and demanded of us to heal her for she was tired of going on in this way confined to her bunk &c &c. she added that she would give any one of us $1,000 to heal her. A.H.D. said he would give $1000 to be able to heal her &c so said the others in substance. I did not reply for some time, for I felt quite confused and discouraged, but finally said, "Well, all we can do is to keep up our courage and work up to our highest understanding." She replied: "Has it come to this!"

She afterwards said If you all feel like that turn your minds away from me & know that I am well.

In the last week in November Mary Baker Eddy caught cold. By the beginning of December she was racked with coughing and spent most of the day on a daybed, but she insisted on dressing every morning and going out briefly in the afternoon. Now Laura Sargent sat next to her in the carriage, and, of course, Frye and Salchow were always at hand. On December 1 she had to be carried back into the house, and John Salchow says that she "seemed to be contending with some strong belief." It looked for a while as if she would not survive the day, but she rallied and asked, as so often before, for her pad of paper. She wrote, in clear if labored script and choosing the triumphant present tense, the four-word sentence which can serve as her epitaph:

God is my life.

On December 2 Mary Baker Eddy did not have the strength to leave her bed, although she continued to talk rationally with her staff members as they took turns looking after her. On the night of December 3, watched over by Laura Sargent and Adam Dickey, she fell into a sleep and died at about 10:45 P.M.

Epilogue

AROUND 3 A.M. ON SUNDAY, DECEMBER 4, ALFRED Farlow and Archibald McLellan arrived at Chestnut Hill and took council with the stricken staff there as to how to deal with the new situation. To avoid any implication that the fact of Mrs. Eddy's death had been concealed even for a short time, or that there was anything untoward about her death, the local medical examiner was ushered in by 8 A.M. to examine the body and issue the death certificate. Dr. George West determined that Mary Baker Eddy had died of natural causes, probably pneumonia. At the end of the regular 11 A.M. service at the Mother Church, Judge Smith, the First Reader, read a section from a kind of farewell letter Mrs. Eddy had written in 1891 to the students at the Massachusetts Metaphysical College, which ended with the sentence: "You can well afford to give me up, since you have in my last revised edition of Science and Health your teacher and guide." According to Peel's account, Smith then paused before announcing:

> Although these lines were written years ago, they are true to-day, and will continue to be true. But it has now become my duty to announce that Mrs. Eddy passed from our sight last night at 10.45 o'clock, at her home in Chestnut Hill.[1]

The nation's press had been preparing for some years to tell the world that Mrs. Eddy was dead, and reporters were thus doubtless gratified to find that Dr. West was also prepared with a highly publishable description of the dead woman's face.

The entire countenance bore a placid, serene expression, which could not have been sweeter had the woman fallen away in sleep in the midst of pleasant thoughts. I do not recall ever seeing in death before a face which bore such a beautifully tranquil expression.[2]

Less lyrical, but offering interestingly precise details of a professional nature, was the subsequent description of the body by the undertakers, Frank S. Waterman, George A. Pierce, and Katharine M. Foote:

To Whom It may Concern:

We were called to the residence of Mrs. Mary Baker Eddy in Chestnut Hill, Mass., at 8.15 a.m., Sunday December 4, 1910, to care for her body. We found it in an excellent state of preservation when first called, and also fifty eight hours after death. No preserving compounds were used until that time. The tissues were remarkably normal; the skin was well preserved, soft, pliable, smooth and healthy. I do not remember having found the body of a person of such advanced age in so good a physical condition. The walls of the arteries were unusually firm and in as healthy a state as might be expected in the body of a young person. The usual accompaniments of age were lacking, and no outward appearance of any disease, lesion or other conditions common to one having died at such an advanced age were noticeable.

In the process of embalming we found the body at sixty hours after death, in as good a condition as we always find at twelve to twenty-four hours after death.

This is our voluntary statement made without solicitation or influence of any kind.[3]

The *McClure's* series had noted that Mary Baker Eddy had kept her beauty all her life, never knowing even an awkward age, and it seems that this beauty was retained even in death.

Mrs. Eddy had made no provision for a form of Christian Science burial, but because the funeral was delayed until December 8 to allow the Glover family to attend there was time to think of an appropriate ceremony of remembrance.[4] Some one hundred and twenty men and women were invited to assemble at eleven o'clock on the first floor of the Chestnut Hill house where Mary Baker Eddy was lying, perhaps for the first time. I wonder if she had instinctively understood that the large elegant rooms would be perfect for her funeral, and therefore she ignored them for as long as she could. When all were assembled, Judge Clifford P. Smith, the First Reader at the Mother Church, read the Ninety-first Psalm and passages from the Gospel according to Saint John. Mrs. Carol Hoyt Powers, Second Reader, read Mrs. Eddy's poem "The Mother's Evening Prayer," and the Lord's Prayer was recited in unison. Finally all filed past the open bronze casket where the embalmed figure lay, dressed in a white silk dress, with a filmy white lace shawl draped from throat to feet. The casket was then carried out "on the shoulders of affection," as Powell nicely puts it.

A concern with plots and cemeteries was a characteristic of the Baker family, and Mrs. Eddy had discussed the question of her own burial spot with her Board of Directors. One option which accorded with an old and strong part of Mary Baker Eddy's nature would be for her to lie next to her family. A share in the family burial plot in the Park Cemetery in Tilton was the only lasting thing Mrs. Eddy had inherited from her father, and she and her sisters had struggled over payment and control of the lot. When Asa Gilbert Eddy died, his widow had transferred his body to Tilton for burial in the Baker family plot, next to her parents and her beloved brother Albert. In her will Mrs. Eddy had been careful to reaffirm the $500 deed of trust she had set up in 1895 as a contribution to the general upkeep of the cemetery plot in Tilton. In the end, however, Mrs. Eddy and her advisors decided on the Mount Auburn Cemetery in Cambridge, thinking, I suppose, that the place for the monument to the leader and founder of Christian Science belonged in a spot already associated with New England's most distinguished citizens. Nonetheless, as I gaze at the magnificence of the Mount Auburn monument today, I can't help wondering what Mrs. Eddy herself would have made of it.[5]

Certainly, the story, or the myth, of the monument is one of the small pieces of trivia that the public still retains about Christian Science. Let me quote the account given by Bates and Dittemore, who were happy to sensationalize Christian Science to the bitter end:

> And then at last the disappointed world was gratified with sensational news. The coffin, taken to the general receiving vault at Mount Auburn to await the hurried construction of a special tomb, was being watched night and day by armed guards, electric flood-lights had been installed and a special telephone wire. What could all this mean? Gussie Stetson in New York hinted that the Directors feared Mrs. Eddy's resurrection and that the guards were placed there to force her back into the coffin when she should attempt to arise. Others equally accepted the resurrection hypothesis, but held that the guards were there to welcome her.

In the face of all this unseemly publicity, Alfred Farlow, the head of the Committee on Publication, was obliged to make an official statement that whereas Christian Scientists were confident that, ultimately, death would be conquered, they knew that the time for this achievement was still far in the future and believed that the resurrection begins in this life and continues here or hereafter until perfection is attained. This is the belief that they entertain concerning Mrs. Eddy. They do not look for her return to this world.[6]

———————

After the funeral, as readers of British detective fiction know, comes the will, but Mary Baker Eddy's will, though in the quirky tradition of the Bakers, held no big surprises. The original will had been made on September 13, 1901, and then, as we have seen, this document mysteriously disappeared. It was reexecuted on November 7, 1903, together with a codicil. A second codicil was made on May 14, 1904.[7]

The main terms of the will were as follows: Small legacies of between $1,000 and $5,000 dollars were left to a few individual nonfamily members, but no one inside or outside the Church was made wealthy under Mrs. Eddy's will, and therefore none could be accused of having influenced her unduly out of self-interest. Mrs. Stetson inherited the diamond crown breastpin, famous in Christian Science iconography, but since she had originally given Mrs. Eddy the brooch as a present, the meaning of the legacy was unclear. This marvelous ambiguity was underlined for the cognoscenti by the fact that Mrs. Stetson's great rival in New York City, Laura Lathrop, inherited Mrs. Eddy's equally celebrated diamond cross. Henry M. Baker of Bow, Mrs. Eddy's cousin, one of her three trustees, and the sole executor of her will, inherited her portrait set in diamonds.

The strangely cantankerous yet needy quality of Mrs. Eddy's relationship with Calvin Frye was apparent in her various legacies to him. Frye was to inherit first $10,000 and then $20,000—the largest of the individual legacies—"provided he continues in my service to the date of my decease." Frye, who had remained a poor man through his service to Mrs. Eddy, was also allowed to choose personal mementos from Mrs. Eddy's possessions, but to a value specified not to exceed $500. In the second codicil Frye was also bequeathed the right to exclusive, expense-free occupancy of two furnished rooms in Mrs. Eddy's house at 385 Commonwealth Avenue in Boston for the rest of his life. By contrast, Laura Sargent, Mrs. Eddy's other most faithful and constant companion in the last years, inherited only $5,000, increased from the original $3,000, but Mrs. Eddy removed the condition that Laura still be in her service at the time of her death.[8] Irving Tomlinson inherited the note, for an unspecified sum, which Mrs. Eddy had signed for him, relieving him of his debt to her.

Moving on from small bequests to individuals, Mrs. Eddy left a $100,000 trust fund for teaching and assisting indigent Christian Scientists to establish themselves. She left up to $175,000 to pay off the mortgage on the Second Church of Christ, Scientist, in New York. She ratified all the trust arrangements and declarations, notably those she had made in 1892 and 1898 in relation to the land beneath the Mother Church, the property housing the Christian Science Publishing Society, and the house on Commonwealth Avenue. And finally, the "rest, residue, and remainder" of Mrs. Eddy's estimated $3 million estate was bequeathed to The Mother Church, the First Church of Christ, Scientist, in Boston, "for the purpose of more effectually promoting and extending the religion of Christian Science as taught by me."

George Glover was perhaps sincere in his desire to pay his mother his last respects, but the journey east for the funeral also allowed him to be present when the will was made public and to consult with William Chandler. George himself and each of his five children received $10,000. The will noted that these sums were in addition to four mortgage deeds for property in the state of Kansas and the house and lot in Lead, South Dakota, which George had received earlier, together with other monies at various times. Nellie Glover was not mentioned in the will, and neither she nor her living daughter Mary received any personal memento. Since even the final codicil to the will was executed in 1904, there was no mention of the 1909 family settlement whereby George Glover had accepted $245,000 in exchange for renouncing all claims by his family to Mrs. Eddy's estate.

Within months of Mrs. Eddy's death, William Chandler went into the New Hampshire courts to contest the terms of Mary Baker Eddy's will on behalf of his client, George Washington Glover II.[9] Although he now accepted that Mary Baker Eddy had been legally able and mentally capable of making the will which her executor had filed for probate, Chandler yet sought to persuade the court that the residuary legatee under the will, the First Church of Christ, Scientist, in Boston, was a church and thus specifically precluded by the laws of New Hampshire from taking "property (beyond parsonage funds) the income of which would be more than $2,000 a year."[10] Chandler's ingenious argument did not prevail, and George, Gershom, and Mary Glover spent in fruitless legal fees part of the inheritance which the executor Henry Baker had speedily released to them.

Chandler did succeed in tying Mrs. Eddy's money up in a trust in New Hampshire, thus bequeathing to the Board of Directors of the Church in Boston a persistent legal problem, but Chandler himself emerged from his second encounter with Frank Streeter with his reputation even more battered. Streeter, during the taking of Chandler's deposition, successfully planted the idea that Chandler in 1911 as in 1906–1907 was a publicity hound, bleeding his poor clients while seeking above all to attack Christian Science. Venality was a charge Chandler could withstand with honor, but he was forced to defend in public his early connection with the *World* newspaper, whose former assistant editor, John Slaght, sat in court, identified as Chandler's personal assistant. Streeter really drew blood, however, in his claim that Chandler had always intended to contest Mrs. Eddy's will, and that he had negotiated the family settlement in bad faith in 1907 and 1909. Streeter charged that Chandler had secretly represented the settlement to his clients as something they could benefit from in the short term while assuring them that a loophole existed which would enable them to contest the will once Mrs. Eddy had died.

A surprising amount of the text of the 1901 will and the 1903 and 1904 codicils was concerned with the future of Pleasant View—where Mrs. Eddy was still living at the time the will was drawn up, in which she had invested enormous care and affection, and which she had then no plans to leave. Mrs. Eddy often said that when it came to purely personal matters she had great difficulty making up her mind what to do, and the legal fate of Pleasant View offers a case in point. In 1901 the will decrees that the house and grounds should be maintained in "a perpetual state of repair and cultivation" at the expense of the residuary legatee, and that her faithful helpers Joseph Mann and Calvin Frye should occupy and take care of the house for their natural lives. In a rather poignant flight of testamentary imagination, she envisages her grandson living in the house while on vacation from Dartmouth, and her granddaughters also staying there if they liked, while finishing their eastern education.

By 1903 Mrs. Eddy had severed relations with the Glovers, and Joseph Mann had left her service. She therefore left the right of life occupancy of Pleasant View to Irving and Mary Tomlinson. But by May of 1904 Mrs. Eddy had had a major change of mind: perhaps the Tomlinsons had proved a disappointment in some way; perhaps she had decided that to keep Pleasant View as a kind of living monument would smack of the cult of personality and encourage all kinds of inappropriate behavior by her followers. For whatever reason, in the first clause of the May 14 codicil she specifically revokes all the previous clauses that related to Pleasant View. She now directs that her executor put the house and homestead at Pleasant View up for sale after her death and give the proceeds over to the Board of Directors of The Mother Church, which would also inherit all the contents of the property, to dispose of at will. But then, showing a deep ambivalence, Mrs. Eddy half changes her mind again, unable, perhaps, to accept the idea of Pleasant View being sold to strangers. The first paragraph thus ends:

> Nothing contained in my will or codicils thereto shall be considered inconsistent with said Church [i.e., The Mother Church] purchasing said real estate [i.e., Pleasant View], if the Directors may consider it desirable so to do.

We know that Mrs. Eddy could have changed her will again in her last five years of life, and that she did not, that she could have sold Pleasant View, and that she did not. Hence it must be assumed that the ambiguity of the 1904 codicil expresses her inability to decide the fate of the house, and thus her ineradicable love for it.

After Mrs. Eddy's death, the directors did nothing about Pleasant View. As we have seen, Mrs. Eddy's will was contested, and when that legal battle was over the directors had more urgent issues to deal with. The house sank into disrepair, taxes went unpaid, and by 1917 Henry Baker was in court protesting the amount of taxes being levied on the property.[11] Mary Beecher Longyear was by this time embarking on her campaign to preserve physical traces of Mrs. Eddy's life, and to purchase the houses she had lived in with the intent of restoring them and making them available to the public. Unenthusiastic about Mrs. Longyear or her passion for material relics of the past, the Board of Directors at last acted decisively. In May 1917 Mary Baker Eddy's home at Pleasant View was razed and burned, and a Christian Science rest home was erected on the site in 1927.[12] In 1975 the property finally passed out of the Church's ownership.[13]

And so today no veranda is left to creak under Mrs. Eddy's rocker or echo in thought with her ready laughter, but the view back to the Bow hills still pleases the eye and stirs the memory.

R E S E A R C H N O T E

As a preface to the extensive notes to this volume I think it is important to be specific about my relationship with The Mother Church and the conditions under which the research for this book was done. Let me say at once that I am not and have never been a Christian Scientist, and that until 1990 I would have been hard put to write a single sentence about Christian Science.

Luck more than anything accounts for my engaging in this biography. Around 1990 I was looking for some new biographical subject and had for some time been in touch with Merloyd Lawrence, who, as the editor of the Radcliffe Biography Series, has as good an acquaintance as anyone with the field. One day when we were chatting on the phone and had gone through some possible names Merloyd mentioned Mary Baker Eddy as a famous woman whose life had not attracted the attention of feminist scholars. I knew nothing of Mrs. Eddy and Christian Science, but something led me down to my local library to take out the first volume of what Merloyd had told me was the standard biography by Robert Peel. The first twenty pages were enough to catch my interest and set me on the research trail. I felt that this was a woman I could say something interesting about, and that feeling has sustained me through almost seven years of work.

One of the loudest messages I picked up when I began serious reading on Mrs. Eddy was that the Church of Christ, Scientist had sought since 1900 or even earlier to control public access to sources of information on her life, and that it was almost impossible to get permission to read in the Mother Church archives. Acting on this information, I submitted a proposal to Merloyd and her Radcliffe Biography Series based on the assumption that the Christian Science authorities would swiftly and absolutely deny any requests from me to read in their collections. The book I proposed would be an exhaustive survey and newly focused examination of the *published* information on Mrs. Eddy. As things have turned out, the proposal the trade division of Addison Wesley (now Perseus Books) accepted from me in late 1992 had little in common with the present book, which has not turned out to be the safe little literary biography that I had envisaged.

My proposal accepted, I turned my attention to the Longyear Museum, which contains probably the most important collection of unpublished documents on Mrs. Eddy outside the Church History Department of The Mother Church. At Longyear I experienced a sudden conversion to primary sources. Historians will groan in disbelief to hear that I had waited so long to undergo a conversion, but it is probably because historians believe in primary documentation and believed that the Christian Science archive was inaccessible that feminist historians in particular have ignored Mary Baker Eddy and her movement. Sometimes enterprise is the result of ignorance.

In any case, seized by a fierce desire to get my hands on more of the papers, in the spring of 1993 I wrote to the Church History Department requesting access to its collection. Some weeks went by, and I finally found the courage to call the head of the Church History Department, Yvonne Caché von Fettweis, confidently expecting her to give me a firm but polite no. Instead she expressed surprise that I had not yet received her reply to my letter (which arrived more than a week after our conversation), and great pleasure at the prospect of our getting together very soon. Then the telephone conversation took an unexpected turn. Before we met, "they" would want me to send in a list of the documents I wished to consult. In some puzzlement I said that this would be difficult since I did not know what the collection contained, and I had assumed that one of my first tasks, if allowed access, would be to consult a catalogue of some kind. Would the head of the Church History Department tell me what they had? "We have everything," was the reply, and I was tempted to say in turn that I wanted to see everything, and thus risk stopping negotiations dead. Something kept me talking, however, and I agreed, verbally on the phone and subsequently in writing, to send in before our meeting some list of documents I wished to read, with the proviso that it would be recognized as preliminary, noncomprehensive, and nonbinding.

Compiling even such a preliminary list in a week loomed before me as a barely possible task, but fortunately Tom Proctor, who was then the curator of the Longyear Museum and a precious source of information and insight, supplied me with the solution to my problem. What I needed to do was exhaustively go through Peel's three-volume biography of Mrs. Eddy, and most especially his capacious notes, and list every document he mentioned or quoted, and ask to see it in its entirety. This solution now seems glaringly obvious, but I had not come up with it on my own, and, in the face of the Church's refusal to grant me access to listings or catalogues, it has largely shaped the course of my research on Mrs. Eddy.

I should note here in passing that some of the most important keys I used to unlock the doors of Christian Science history were people, not documents. One of the first and least expected aspects of my work on Mrs. Eddy has been the importance of word-of-mouth information. Perhaps just because information is such a closely guarded commodity in Christian Science, word gets out with astonishing rapidity. Once I had contacted one or two people, once I had passed some unspoken test of acceptability, once my goals were determined to be congruent with some unwritten agenda, people started to contact me, offering names, willing to talk, lending works that printed sources stated were no longer available. I learned who was out and who was in, how to refer to X and Y, to whom I could acknowledge that I knew X and Y, in what places it was safe to meet X and Y.

The Mother Church itself displayed an astonishing knowledge of my doings. I shall always remember one day in 1994 when I had been invited to give an informal dinner talk on a subject of my choosing at an exclusive, private Boston club. The meeting was open to members only and was advertised only in the club's newsletter. The title I chose for my talk made no mention of Mrs. Eddy. While speaking I was vaguely aware of the presence of two ladies sitting outside the main group at the big table and vigorously taking notes. I was astonished when, after I had finished speaking, the club's facilitator announced stiffly to those present that two uninvited nonmembers were in the room and, when challenged, had identified themselves as members of the Legal Department of The Mother Church. At this time I was in the midst of protracted and difficult negotiations with The Mother Church, negotiations being carried out by my lawyer and theirs, so the uninvited and unheralded presence of these women at my talk was a breach both of club etiquette and, as I was later informed, of legal practice. I was impressed by the lengths the Church apparently considered it necessary to go to find out more about me and my view of Mrs. Eddy.

Let me return, however, to the spring of 1993 and my first meeting with officials of The Mother Church. For the first time I walked into the lonely, imposing vestibule of the administration tower, had my presence announced by the charming woman at the desk, was given an identity tag, and was permitted to ride one of the bank of elevators up to the twenty-second floor. There I learned that the members of the Church History Department had been doing research on me. Not only had they got hold of copies of my book on Agatha Christie; they had dug up from the files of their defunct television station an interview on Christie I had done in 1990. While waiting for one member of the Church's interview group to arrive, I was given the strange experience of watching the video of that old television interview, which I had never seen, and wondering if the liveliness of my remarks could compensate for what I now saw clearly was an ugly pink suit and a frizzy hairdo. In fact, I was soon reassured that the avowedly embattled Church of Christ, Scientist was inclined to favor me as a potential new spokesperson on Mrs. Eddy. As the gentleman from the Committee on Publication rather candidly pointed out, the Church was accustomed to getting 80 or 90 percent unfavorable press coverage, and therefore any writer who could potentially improve their rating to even fifty-fifty would be viewed positively.

I was elated as I left the Christian Science Center on the day of that first meeting. I had been greeted with such enthusiasm, flattered so delicately, treated with an exquisite politeness and cordiality that I have since found to be characteristic of Christian Scientist officials. They professed themselves delighted by my proposal, eager for me to read their documents, and ready to cooperate in any way possible with me during the course of my project. They made it clear that as part of the process of getting materials to me, they would be offering me the services of a knowledgeable and competent research assistant, as well as additional access to a complete library of published sources on Christian Science. For an independent scholar with no institutional support or funding, such offers were dazzling. Yet before I could come in and really start working with them, I needed to sign their release form.

I was by this time panting with desire to sink my teeth into the documentary riches I had seen shelved all around me, but I refrained from signing anything on the spot. I carried the document out with me, and when at last I read it, over coffee and croissant nearby, my elation turned to dismay. I learned that the Church would entertain my lists and provide me with documents, but I would be unable to quote, paraphrase, or comment on anything they showed me without their express permission. Furthermore, the document detailing terms for access which they had given me that day referred in turn to a copyright document which had not been included in the package, and whose terms I was therefore being asked to agree to sight unseen. As it turned out, this copyright document did not yet exist, and it would take many months to extract drafts from the Church Legal Department. Worst of all, if I read under the Church's aegis a document already wholly or substantially quoted in the published literature, of whatever date and under whatever

copyright provisions, I would have to ask permission from the Church to quote, paraphrase, or comment on that document.

At this point I decided in my coffee shop that I was in way over my head here, and
I subsequently hired to negotiate for me a very lively, energetic, well-informed young
woman partner at the kind of Boston law firm I thought the Church might respect. In
1994 my lawyer and theirs seemed at last to have developed drafts of both a document
defining terms for gaining access to unpublished material, and a copyright document
detailing the process for securing permission to quote in the eventual published book.
Then suddenly negotiations were torpedoed by a letter, attached nonchalantly to what my
lawyer and I had thought would be the final draft. This letter defined "unpublished material" as material, published or not, over which the Church "claimed copyright" and
included a list of works to which the definition applied. Most of these works were small
but vital parts of the Eddy bibliography, published before 1915, and by groups independent, at least in name, from The Mother Church. The letter also sought to establish the
Church's claim of copyright to documents which are in the possession of other research
foundations. Furthermore, while reiterating its verbal assurances that it was interested
solely in ensuring that my references and quotations were accurate, not in censoring my
comments on the material, the Church's lawyers insisted that I submit the complete manuscript of my book and give the Church History Department unlimited time to complete
its "editorial" labors.

By this time I had run up an uncomfortably high legal bill, my initial deadline for
the book was already past, and my patience was exhausted. I called my lawyer, and she
agreed that in almost two years we had got precisely nowhere. I then wrote to the General
Counsel of the Church that I was suspending all negotiations and had decided, regretfully, to revert to my original plan. I would write a book using the resources in the public domain and in other private collections, as well as all the documentation circulating
informally, with which I was now familiar.

I sent a copy of this letter to the chairman of the Board of Directors, Mrs. Virginia
Harris. Another month of complete silence passed, and then I got a telephone call. Mrs.
Harris had been out of the country for some weeks, and she apologized for not acknowledging my communication earlier. She wished to talk to me. She talked, and she was extraordinarily charming and funny and informed. She told me things would be worked out, and
they were. A few months later a document setting terms for access to the collections was
signed by myself and Olga Chaffee, the Clerk of the Church, and a draft copyright document was agreed upon. Essentially, the access agreement established that I could come at
will to the Church History Department, that my requests for documents would be considered and probably met, that I would have the right to quote from their documents, and that
they would have the right to read those typescript pages which included quotations, so that
any necessary corrections to the text could be made. Once corrections had been duly made,
within a specified time period the agreed upon form of copyright acknowledgment would
be signed. Authorities at The Mother Church would not see the complete manuscript, and
hence there would be no question of their censoring my work.

Following the signing of this agreement, in the late fall of 1995 I began to go in to
the Church History Department once or twice a week for a day's concentrated reading.
The love affair with unpublished materials which I had begun at the Longyear Museum
became a passion. But even though I had finally managed to get the tap turned on, I was
still not in control of the flow; indeed, my initial fears of being flooded with thousands of
letters and diaries and reminiscences proved quite unfounded.

The access procedure went as follows. By passing a fine-tooth comb through all the
published biographical accounts of Mrs. Eddy, I would produce a list of documents which

were established to be in The Mother Church's collection. I then submitted this list, in person or by phone, to Judy Huenneke, the wonderful young researcher the Church detailed to look after me. She would then try to find the documents on my list. Even this initial search at times met with failure, as she would explain to me that things not written by Mrs. Eddy or immediately related to her were catalogued rather haphazardly and had been moved around so often in some cases that a document quoted in, say, 1930, could be unfindable in 1996. The initial list I had prepared served, however, as the basis for a free-flowing discussion of issues related to Mrs. Eddy which was extremely important to me, and this process led, not infrequently, to the archives volunteering documents which I had not known existed.

When Judy Huenneke had located the document, she would show it to her immediate supervisor, who, fortunately, was almost always at his desk. If he felt unable to give permission himself, the document was submitted to the head of department, who was usually not in the building, and often away on business. When the head of the department's approval was inadequate, as was the case in anything unpublished written by Mrs. Eddy herself or anything determined to be of unusual sensitivity, Mrs. Huenneke had to prepare a typed transcript, if the document was handwritten, copy the material in sextuplicate, submit it to her department head, Mrs. von Fettweis, and then send it up for approval by the Board of Directors of the Church of Christ, Scientist. This body usually met once a week, and, not surprisingly given the volume of business in its charge, often did not find time to consider "my" documents.

Thus however considerate and helpful the staff in the Church History Department, at least a week, and often a month or more, would elapse between my request for a document and its actual appearance. But delay was not the most important barrier to research progress. It worked out that much of the crucial unpublished documentation was to all intents and purposes unavailable to me even as photocopies of the original handwritten items because the materials were too long or too delicate to photocopy. This was particularly true of the famous numbered and bound volumes of Mrs. Eddy's autograph "Letters" and "Articles," which are the heart of the collection, and which were described in great detail and with much admiration by Powell in 1930. (See Appendix.) I was told that all of this material had been transcribed with the greatest care, and, more recently, it had been entered onto computer disk, but the very elaborateness of the format in which the writings had been preserved precluded the autographs from being photocopied. There was never any question of my using the originals as research tools. To summarize, then, I was able to see transcriptions of selected pieces of Mrs. Eddy's unpublished correspondence, but I was not allowed to see the autographs or to read extensively through the whole collection and decide for myself what I wanted to focus on.

An even greater problem I encountered was with the so-called Eddy-Frye notebooks, written by Mrs. Eddy herself or dictated to Frye, which Robert Peel, Lyman Powell, and John Dittemore cite briefly and tantalizingly. I requested on at least two occasions to see these, because personal notebooks can be, like Rousseau's famous laundry lists, a reliable and informative guide to a subject's everyday life. Unfortunately, here again I drew a blank. I was told that no effort had been made to transcribe these books, and since there were so many of them—a new fact in itself—and they were in such a difficult format, there was no way to photocopy them in sextuplicate for board approval.

In May 1997 I had completed the manuscript of the biography, and it was accepted for publication. In late fall I sent to the Church History Department 145 manuscript pages which included all the quotations from unpublished materials which I had used, with two pages of the manuscript on each side of a quotation they were checking as set out in my agreement with The Mother Church. This material was accepted readily, and the terms of the copyright agreement, covering not only the unpublished materials but quotations from works published by the Christian Science Publishing Society and a large number of photographs, were amicably negotiated and speedily signed.

The Board of Directors then suggested that Judy Huenneke, the researcher who had been my main contact with the collection for over two years, should be detailed to fact-check the whole manuscript, working in complete independence from the other members of the staff, but able to call upon the unparallelled resources of the Church History Department. I accepted this offer with gratitude. With the copyright agreement signed, there appeared to be no way that The Mother Church could attempt to exercise censorship over my work and thus delay or hinder its publication, as I had once feared. I was all too aware that I needed a fact checker, since the biography had been more than six years in the writing, I had had almost no research assistance, I had often been forced to write on the basis of handwritten notes, and I knew that even quotations in published sources were not necessarily accurate. Above all, I was eager to accept the board's offer since I knew Judy Huenneke and had come to value the quality of her work. As the corrected chapters came back into my hands, with every reference checked, every quotation corrected, against the autograph original wherever possible, I saw that, indeed, in Mrs. Huenneke I had found perhaps the most perceptive and certainly the most assiduous reader I could have envisaged.

A P P E N D I X

The Essential
Published Source Books

The following bibliographical essay is my contribution to the persistent and lively debate over documentation and sources that has characterized the history of Christian Science. The peculiar difficulties of the fact-finding process have made such technical affairs as footnotes, indexes, and bibliographies a highly politicized and rhetorical part of any biography of Mrs. Eddy. Even today, the work of early biographers has peculiar importance, and questions of how Milmine and Cather or Dakin or Powell acquired the information they retail in their works and whether their sources can be accessed today become paramount. In this appendix, I trace the publishing history and offer my critical review of those biographies which are the preliminary crucial working texts for anyone interested in studying Mrs. Eddy and Christian Science.[1] Each biography has a tale of its own, and each is shaped by specific circumstances which radically affect the nature and amount of information the work affords. None, not even the three-volume work by Robert Peel, can be read innocently, without awareness of the publishing history and the political context.

GEORGINE MILMINE WELLES

The first and still most influential biography of Mrs. Eddy was first published in fourteen parts in *McClure's Magazine* between January 1907 and June 1908, and then in revised form as a book in 1909. The title of the book was *The Life of Mary Baker Eddy and the History of Christian Science*; it was credited to Georgine Milmine, and hers is the name by which the book is usually known. The history of the writing of the Milmine biography is one of the small, fascinating, and paradoxical stories of Christian Science. It involves not only Georgine Milmine but two other women writers of considerably more repute, Ida Tarbell and Willa Cather.

The Church of Christ, Scientist's efforts to prevent and then to suppress first the magazine series and then the book have long been part of the legend of Milmine's work. Getting wind of the Milmine work, Church officials, notably John Dittemore, at that time the head of the New York Committee on Publication, tried in vain to negotiate with S. S. McClure to prevent publication or at least to influence the content, but the magazine owner was having none of this. Thereafter the Church was obliged to try different tactics. In the highly polemical bibliography to his own biography of Mrs. Eddy, Edwin Dakin wrote around 1929, with typical inaccuracy.

> The copyright [to the Milmine book] was eventually purchased by a friend of Christian Science, and the plates from which the book was printed were destroyed, according to information which appears to be authentic and accurate. The author has been informed that the original manuscript was also acquired.[2]

In recent years, however, it has been established, largely on the basis of unpublished documentary evidence, that Georgine Milmine did not actually "write" the book which is her one claim to fame. Furthermore, the book's claims to be reliable, objective, truthful reporting are at best an effective rhetorical strategy, and at worst a deliberate falsification.

Apart from the fact that she is listed as author on the cover of a biography of Mary Baker Eddy, remarkably little is known about Georgine Milmine. She was, according to early reports from other biographers who knew her, a minor journalist, perhaps originally from Canada, working in New York State. When she started to work on Mrs. Eddy, she was in fact not Miss Milmine, but Mrs. Welles, married to Benjamin Welles, a newspaper editor. Later again, according to one source, she became Mrs. Arthur E. Adams of Auburn, New York.[3] Unlike her rival in Eddy biography, Sibyl Wilbur O'Brien—who also preferred to write under her maiden name—Georgine Milmine never managed to make any name for herself nationally, and nothing is known about her political opinions, her professional interests, or her journalistic assignments before or after her work on Mrs. Eddy. Whereas there are several photos of Miss Wilbur at various stages in her life culled from press clippings, I have never been able to turn up a picture of Miss Milmine, which is rather surprising.

According to Henry Robinson and Frederic Remington, two gentlemen who met her in the teens and twenties, in 1903 Georgine Milmine planned to write a series of twelve monthly articles on eminent American women and wanted to include Mrs. Eddy. But when Miss Milmine arrived at Pleasant View and asked to interview Mrs. Eddy for her series, she was, by her own account, refused and rebuffed by Mrs. Eddy's staff.[4] Convinced that Mrs. Eddy's refusal of an interview must mean that she had something to hide, Milmine next contacted Mrs. Josephine Woodbury—one of Mrs. Eddy's most famous opponents—and Woodbury passed Milmine on to her lawyer, Mrs. Eddy's relentless adversary, Frederick Peabody (see Chapter 23).

If, indeed, Mrs. Eddy's household did dismiss Mrs. Welles, it proved to be an exceptionally costly mistake, since the reporter now appears to have devoted much of her time to following up the many leads provided her by Frederick Peabody, and to uncovering all the areas of Mrs. Eddy's life that had been omitted from *Retrospection and Introspection*. Beginning around 1903, Milmine located a number of people who had known Mrs. Eddy in New Hampshire and Massachusetts, most of them former friends and colleagues who had fallen out with Mrs. Eddy before Christian Science became a national movement. How Milmine financed her research efforts is an unanswered question, but by this time Christian Science had roused considerable public interest and had many enemies.

In December 1906 *McClure's Magazine* announced a forthcoming series of articles on Mrs. Eddy, claiming that the author, Georgine Milmine, had "spent more than two years of close research" on the project. *McClure's*, a popular periodical founded and edited by the colorful S. S. McClure, specialized in investigative reporting. In the "Editorial Announcement" to the series, *McClure's* identifies Georgine Milmine as "the author," while acknowledging that five unnamed staff members "have confirmed facts or helped correlate the data." The Editorial Announcement presents this team work as a signal advantage: "many minds, each looking on things from a different angle, have been turned upon these events; and the result is probably as near absolute accuracy as history ever gets."[5]

Other background documents offer a significantly different picture of the vaunted teamwork at *McClure's* and cast doubt on Georgine Milmine's research and her authorship. In late 1904 Milmine came to New York and submitted the research materials she had collected on Mrs. Eddy to Ida Tarbell. A single woman with a strong commitment to feminism, Tarbell had achieved a national reputation at *McClure's* and greatly boosted the magazine's circulation with her articles on Napoleon Bonaparte, Madame Roland, and Abraham Lincoln. In 1902, after two years of intensive research, Tarbell hit the headlines with a series of highly critical articles on the oil industry. Her subsequent book, *The History of the Standard Oil Company* (1904), caused a sensation and is the work by which she is still best remembered. Tarbell was part of an important movement in American journalism to expose corruption in the life of the nation—a movement labelled "muckraking" by Theodore Roosevelt. She was a notable radical and thus both philosophically disposed to think the worst of Christian Science and professionally appreciative of the commercial possibilities of publishing a series on perhaps the most famous and mysterious woman in America at the time.

The *McClure's* staff apparently decided from the beginning that Milmine did not have the skills to turn her research into a full-blown biography. The available documentation indicates that Milmine's role in the subsequent hit series was to keep in touch with those witnesses with whom she had established a good working relationship, and to channel money to them from the magazine. In the months between Milmine's initial contact and the first issue of the series, Peabody was hired to collect new affidavits, tailored to the paper's suggestions, and five of the *McClure's* staff were deputed to do research and to write Milmine's material up for serial publication. These five initially included Ida Tarbell, Burton J. Hendrick, Will Irwin, Mark Sullivan, and the thirty-two-year-old Willa Cather, newly brought to New York by S. S. McClure in 1906. But after a dispute at *McClure's* in 1906, Tarbell left the magazine and thus had little or nothing to do with the actual manuscript. According to Cather, Hendrick wrote the first installment of the Eddy series, but he was so deeply antagonistic to Mrs. Eddy and her church that, to his chagrin, he was taken off the project and replaced by Cather, whom Mr. McClure considered more religious and therefore likely to be fairer.

McClure's decided to run the series solely under Milmine's name, and this was probably not just a gesture of editorial goodwill toward a young, up-and-coming colleague. As I see it, the shrewd New Yorkers realized that it would be better for an attack on a famous woman to come from an unknown young independent female reporter rather than from their own staff, who had something of a reputation for putting sensationalism ahead of accuracy. Certainly, the fiction of Georgine Milmine's authorship remained important for those critical of Mrs. Eddy and her church. Twenty years after the Milmine material was first published, Edward Dakin was still asserting that Milmine was a reporter to be relied on for absolute accuracy, although he offered some qualifiers about her "authorship." In his main text Dakin is almost apocalyptic in his enthusiasm about the Milmine book:

Until the close of 1906 the world at large had really known nothing whatever about her [i.e., Mrs. Eddy] except that information she herself had chosen to supply. Suddenly, however, the temple veils were rent. Whole rivers of unexplained facts started to flow. Georgine Milmine, after months of patient investigation, inquiry and interviews in the New England communities where Mrs. Eddy had spent her life, was publishing in *McClure's Magazine* a biography so detailed and annotated that it was nothing short of a monumental piece of work. Miss Milmine was not content to give mere facts, she presented them in the form of sworn affidavits from the persons who vouched for them. Presented in this form, without sympathetic interpretation or explanation, much of the material seemed damning.

A footnote on the same page is slightly more nuanced. The note reads:

A great many of these affidavits were collected by Frederick W. Peabody, Boston lawyer, who had prosecuted Mrs. Woodbury's libel suit, and who thereafter made it his life's work to "expose" Mrs. Eddy. Of Miss Milmine he (Peabody) said, "She assured me she had searched the whole of Mrs. Eddy's life for a kindly, a generous, a fine womanly deed, and would have been only too glad to have recorded it, but had not found one." (Vd. Peabody, *The Religio-Medical Masquerade*, p. 73). The *McClure's* biography was in many ways— although Miss Milmine did the greater part of the work—essentially a group effort of a staff of investigators and reporters who combed New England for facts for over two years.[6]

The virulently ad feminam animus of this note betrays the influence of Frederick Peabody, and it is enlightening to see how Milmine's work is both praised and subtly explained away: she worked only for months, although the team worked for two years; the affidavits were Peabody's initiative, not hers; and Dakin never actually says that Milmine *wrote* anything. Miss Milmine does "the greater part of the work," yet the project is "essentially a group effort."

As I see it, Georgine Milmine is here being recast in the image of the real-life Ida Tarbell and other famous pioneer women reporters. By the early twentieth century, the American public had grown to appreciate the story of the plucky girl reporter who hits pay dirt after much digging and writes a crackerjack book. This story was so much more romantic and appealing than the life of the real Mrs. Welles, who, as far as can now be determined, was fed a lot of material by interested parties, proved smart enough to take it to New York, but did not have the ability to write it up herself. Behind the unknown and subtly mythical Georgine Milmine we find the well-known staff of *McClure's*, and behind the magazine loom the ghostly figures of the strongly implicated Woodbury and the avowedly prejudiced Peabody. How ironic it is that plagiarism is one of the most damning accusations Georgine Milmine laid against Mrs. Eddy, yet Milmine herself wrote little if any of the book which bears her name.

Milmine's claim to authorship was finally challenged in print when in 1993 the University of Nebraska Press issued a facsimile version of the 1909 Doubleday edition and hailed it as an early yet significant and unknown work by Willa Cather, whose literary stock had risen greatly in the 1970s and 1980s. With this new, updated edition and new author, the Milmine biography achieved a new lease on life and greater authenticity. The Nebraska editors based their attribution of the work to Cather on a recently discovered letter from Cather to Edwin Anderson dated November 24, 1922, which confirmed what had been hinted in other Cather letters; namely that, whereas Milmine had provided extensive preliminary documentation on Mrs. Eddy, it was Cather who actually wrote parts 2–14 of the series and also directed much of the later fieldwork.

According to the terms of Cather's will, her letter cannot be quoted, and therefore I can only paraphrase it. Cather tells what she knows about Milmine herself—which was not much—and asserts unequivocally that the material she wrote up herself was as close to the truth as she could get it. She says that Milmine admitted up front that she did not have the skills to write a biography, and after several editors competed to write the Eddy series, Mr. McClure gave the job to Cather because she had no axe to grind. Cather mourns the disappearance of the Milmine file after McClure sold the magazine, since much of the material it contained—old newspaper cuttings, court reports, early editions of *Science and Health*—had become virtually unfindable at the time she was writing. (Let me note here that at least some of the Milmine files were bought by The Mother Church.) Cather says that Mr. Doubleday no doubt had good reasons for not reissuing the book, that she herself had no interest in pushing for its reissue, and that Mrs. Wells (as she spelled the name) was doubtless in an awkward position since she did not write the book attributed to her. Cather also notes that she had no part in writing the first installment in the series, and she comments that much of that installment was based on the testimony of a few envious people and jealous relatives and was largely legend.

This letter to Anderson is taken by David Stouck, editor of the Nebraska edition, to be Cather's definitive and truthful account of her part in writing the Eddy biography. I would accept this view since the letter is so detailed and circumstantial. Yet as Stouck also acknowledges, in a later letter to Genevieve Richmond on December 8, 1933, Cather firmly denies that she did anything but standard copyediting on the Milmine manuscript. She begs Richmond to deny the rumors being spread by some of Cather's friends that she had written the Milmine book. One thing is clear from all the letters—Cather did not wish to be publicly associated with the Eddy biography, and she would not have been pleased to see her name at the head of the Nebraska edition.

The main motivation of the Nebraska editors in reissuing the biography was to pub-lish what they regarded as an early and unknown work by a famous local author. They saw the book essentially as a literary exercise, an early development of some of Cather's themes and characters. The exposure of Georgine Milmine as a sham was not important to them, and neither was the accuracy or inaccuracy of the biography's portrait of Mrs. Eddy. The University of Nebraska staff was content to accept Cather's affirmation that the major part of the portrait she had painted of Mrs. Eddy was accurate and based on careful documentation. That the book was written in 1907–1908, two years before Mrs. Eddy died, and that much important research has been done since that date was not a concern for them.

The Milmine biography has fundamentally influenced succeeding work, and thanks to the University of Nebraska edition it is still influential. Milmine and the *McClure's* group claimed to have interviewed hundreds of witnesses who knew Mrs. Eddy, and this reported testimony has achieved extraordinary significance. In any publication not writ-ten by a faithful Christian Scientist, Milmine is quoted as the single trustworthy source of information, especially on the first half of Mrs. Eddy's life. The work also strongly influ-enced three subsequent biographies of Mrs. Eddy: Lyman P. Powell's 1907 *Christian Science: The Faith and Its Founder*, Edwin Franden Dakin's 1929 *Mrs. Eddy: The Biography of a Virginal Mind*, and Ernest Sutherland Bates and John V. Dittemore's 1932 *Mary Baker Eddy: The Truth and the Tradition*. Whereas Mrs. Eddy's own memories of her life and firsthand testimony about her by friends and loyal students have tended to be ignored or else attacked as blindly partisan, the firsthand testimony collected by those unassociated or disenchanted with Christian Science has been accepted uncritically as objective and unbiased. As Martin Gardner notes in his 1993 work on Christian Science, the Milmine book "was the first major attack on Mrs. Eddy, and the primary source for all later unauthorized biographies, including these chapters."[7] In her 1996 *New York Review of Books* review of the Nebraska reissue of the Milmine book and of the 1994 Thomas biography, Caroline Fraser offers a potted biography of Mrs. Eddy which grudgingly respects much of the recent biographical work done on Mrs. Eddy, notably that by Robert Peel and Thomas himself, but she still feels bound to insist that Milmine is basically reliable.

There is no doubt that the Milmine biography is one of the most important sources of information on Mrs. Eddy. All the interviewing and dredging up of legal papers and newspaper files, all the collection of primary documents done by Peabody, Milmine, and the *McClure's* team of reporters not only amassed an invaluable data bank, it also stimulated the Church of Christ, Scientist to do its own research and its own collecting. The Milmine biography is a work of considerable style and great intellectual passion, it has a message and a mission, and, perhaps for that reason, it is still very readable. I have used it extensively in this book. Yet as I hope I have shown just as extensively, the Milmine book is as much a work of polemic as a piece of reporting. When it vows, as it were, hand on heart, to speak the truth, the whole truth, and nothing but the truth, when it claims not rhetoric but reportage, not passion but objectivity, it lies and compromises the very truth of the standards it claims to espouse.

SYBIL WILBUR O'BRIEN

Sybil Wilbur was Georgine Milmine's rival in the biographical stakes, coming out for Mrs. Eddy as vehemently as Milmine came out against her. Wilbur had a strong sense of personal identification with Mary Baker Eddy, and, like many women who met Mrs. Eddy, she experienced a virtual conversion experience after talking to her. Her interest in Mrs. Eddy was sparked after she spent some weeks working on a story about the workers in Lynn.

> There is a little room in Lynn, Mass., up under the eaves in a shabby house not far from the sea. This is the room where Mrs. Eddy wrote "Science and Health." I once occupied a room almost identical to this in a street not far away while studying the lives of the workwomen in the shoe factories. The room was not comfortable; it was very cold, for I was there in the depth of winter. It would have been intolerably hot in summer. I had a window exactly like the one in Mrs. Eddy's room, a trap casement that lifted from the roof. I could stand on a chair at this attic window and look out at the lights of Lynn, the city all beneath me in a panorama of struggle and strife. . . .
>
> There is a mass of brown granite off an unfrequented bit of Lynn Beach, not unlike Norman's Woe outside Gloucester. These rocks are now popularly called the Eddy rocks, for it was there Mrs. Eddy used to sit alone in meditation. On these same rocks, without knowing their name or history, I sat many hours during the sojourn in Lynn.[8]

Unlike Milmine, Wilbur was an experienced, enterprising, and fairly well-known journalist of strong feminist and even radical tendencies.[9] After doing a personal interview with Mrs. Eddy in 1905, Wilbur wrote some positive accounts of Mrs. Eddy for *Human Life* and the *Boston Herald*. Satisfied that Miss Wilbur was the reporter most likely to take a favorable view of Mrs. Eddy's life, the Christian Science authorities, with the rather grudging assent of Mrs. Eddy herself, commissioned Wilbur to write a biographical series that would challenge the material scheduled to appear in *McClure's*. Wilbur was encouraged to go over Milmine's ground and reinterview the same witnesses, but this time to elicit testimony favorable to Mrs. Eddy. The *Human Life* series followed breathlessly one month behind the *McClure's* series, and in each of her articles Wilbur scurried to correct inaccuracies and present Mrs. Eddy's side of events, supported by a rival set of documents and affidavits. All of Milmine's main witnesses—George Quimby, Daniel Spofford, Richard Kennedy, Sarah Crosby, the members of the Wentworth family, the Crafts, Alvin Cushing, Miranda Rice—were reinterviewed by Wilbur.

With regard to both the Milmine and the Wilbur biographies, I strongly recommend that any scholar interested in Mrs. Eddy consult the original magazine series. These stay closer to the documentary and interview data than the succeeding books do. Quite apart from the text, the photographs both magazines gave are invaluable, offering fascinating evidence of how apparently innocent illustrations can become rhetorical weapons. For example, rival pictures in the two series of Mrs. Eddy's Bow birthplace and of her Sanbornton Bridge school implicitly offer the reader radically different impressions of the social status of Mrs. Eddy's family background and of the quality of her education.

Wilbur was not a writer of great talents, and she had no Willa Cather to "edit" her work, but after reading the *Human Life* series carefully and comparing it directly with the *McClure's* I found the reporting much more solid than I had expected. Although Wilbur does not use affidavits, she at times names names and clarifies sources more carefully than "Milmine" does, and I have come to trust many of the long interview statements she quotes verbatim. Those who had collaborated enthusiastically with Milmine complained that they were tricked into talking to Wilbur or spoke to her only from politeness and later accused her of misrepresenting them, but I think this is, in its turn, a form of rhetoric and misrepresentation. What they mean, I think, is that Wilbur asked them different questions, came in with a different agenda, and elicited different responses. Almost everyone who gave hostile affidavits about Mrs. Eddy to the *McClure's* investigators had, at one time, deeply admired, even adored, her and could recall her with pleasure, as well as opprobrium, if prompted to do so.

Wilbur also claims that, unlike the *McClure's* team, she did not offer any money to the persons she asked to interview, and that therefore the testimony she offers is not tainted by the financial self-interest of the witnesses. This claim is both true and misleading. Literally, Wilbur herself did not pay anyone, and she was not the conduit for payments, whereas there is incontrovertible evidence in the Church's unpublished materials that at least four of Milmine's most important witnesses—Sarah Crosby, Daniel Spofford, Horace Wentworth, and Catherine Clapp—were paid for their testimony by *McClure's*. As the notes to this book show, I have been able to verify that under prodding by journalists several witnesses gave significantly more negative and more selective testimony as the process of corresponding and giving statements and publication continued. They learned to remember what the press wanted them to remember.

On the other hand, Wilbur's research work was financed by the Church, and she was negotiating terms for an eventual book with John Dittemore. Furthermore, Mrs. Eddy and/or representatives of her church also gave selective financial assistance to some of those who gave positive testimony. I found proof in the Alfred Farlow files at The Mother Church that one Stoughton family that was prepared to go on record about an early healing performed by Mrs. Eddy was given help with household expenses. Mrs. Eddy also gave considerable financial support to Mary Ann Cook Baker, the widow of her brother Samuel, while turning a deaf ear to the requests of her nephew George Waldron Baker on behalf of his mother, Martha Rand Baker. Unsurprisingly given this financial pattern, Mary Ann was the family source quoted by Wilbur; whereas Martha and George Baker were, I deduce, the unacknowledged sources of some of the unflattering information Milmine gives about Mrs. Eddy's childhood. The issue of financial motivation for testimony is, thus, a knotty one, but it is one which the Milmine biography, for all its claims to complete disclosure and lack of bias, totally skirts and which Wilbur at least raises.

Still operating in close but inverse relation to one another, the two series of articles were reissued in book form within a year or so of one another, and just as Milmine's book deleted much of the information given in the magazine which might be considered favorable to Mrs. Eddy, so in her book Wilbur abandoned her reportorial style in favor of invented dialogue and dithyrambic hagiography. Wilbur's book is much longer than the earlier magazine series, and it is written in a style so sycophantic that later biographers and critics refer to it only for details that could be interpreted as being unfavorable to Mrs. Eddy. The changes made between the magazine series and the book may have been an attempt to placate Mrs. Eddy. Wilbur seems to have had an agreement with Dittemore that her series would appear as a book, and Dittemore and a partner of his had acquired the rights to the book and planned to market and publish it as an independent business venture.[10] But this plan hit an unforeseen and serious snag when Mrs. Eddy opposed publication. She seems to have been far from sure that she wanted anyone to write her biography, and in any case she had several better candidates for the job than Wilbur. Yet when Mrs. Eddy tried to prohibit the selling of Wilbur's book to the non–Christian Science public, Wilbur dug her heels in, applying legal pressure which the Church was in a poor position to withstand. The book at last was published by the obscure Concord Publishing Company in 1908, headed by an equivocal imprimatur from Mrs. Eddy,[11] and it received little positive attention at the time. Like the Milmine book, the Wilbur book is currently in print again. The Christian Science Publishing Society has issued what seems at first sight to be a facsimile reproduction of the 1908 edition, but which in fact contains many corrections and editorial changes. The reader is alerted to these differences by a change in the typeface.

By far the best piece of writing Sybil Wilbur did on Mrs. Eddy is one of the earliest ones—written, I would judge, before she started trying to please the Committee on Publication. I quote at length from Wilbur's January 1907 article in *Human Life* because it gives a good idea of the reporter's style of journalism; it mounts an informed, insightful, and rational analysis of the apparently objective and reportorial slant of the press coverage lavished on Mrs. Eddy in her final years; and, finally, it places Mary Baker Eddy in the ancient and revered tradition of women mystics.

> A human life looked at objectively performs a certain set of functions very similar to any other life. A certain amount of nourishment, a certain amount of exercise, a certain amount of repose and the twenty-four hours of the day are completed. It is not by laying a net to catch all these acts and by examining them minutely that we shall snare greatness. From another aspect, a human life shows forth its moods, passions, temper, vanities and renunciations, antipathies and loves. Herein we think we have the man, but we are again mistaken. You may love tranquility and yet be taken in the act of disputing a tradesman or upbraiding the cook; you may be a philanthropist and yet pass a beggar on the street corner; you may be a staunch advocate of justice in all human relations, and still cherish an unaccountable aversion to Chinamen.
>
> It is not in separate acts, sudden gusts of temper, negligence on particular occasions to perform a proper deed;—but it is in the prevailing action of a human being upon the circumstances that surround him that he must be judged. I do

not believe that Theodore Roosevelt could stand the searchlight on his every act, or the microscopic investigation of his years, months, days, and hours better than John D. Rockefeller. I do not believe that Julia Ward Howe or Clara Barton could come off blameless of whims, moods, tempers, and vanities, if the associates of a lifetime were interviewed for gossip. And yet I think these are great lives. Let every man apply the microscope to himself and consider.

Mary Baker Eddy it appears is to be investigated by the microscopic method. Eighty years are to be scanned of evidence for and against her character. From the gossip of old men and women in rural districts, persons who in years of dotage have prattled without any special attention being paid to them, are now dignified into witnesses before the court of public opinion. A garment is to be pieced together from patches; a human being is to be created by the method of a Frankenstein. What monstrosity will result. . . .

Having lived for a brief time in this environment practically alone with my thoughts, I can go back in imagination very vividly to that year when a shabbily gowned little woman toiled up her garret stairs, or strolled alone along the sea coast. I do not believe that under these mighty influences she was vain, egotistical, dreaming of power, and formulating worldly ambitions. I believe that she was lifted out of herself, that the physical discomforts of her existence were swept away by an inrush of God's truth. I believe she stood erect spiritually while her body crouched on those rocks; that the ego slipped away from her in some supreme moment and she made the plunge of the true religious, the mystic, who cries: "My soul swims in the Being of God"; or "I have become one with God, I have seen God in my own soul." St. Theresa, the Beguine Mechthild, Madame Guyon, all have so recorded the transcendental mood. Mary Baker Eddy wrought her experiences into a religious creed and proceeded to live it and give it to the world.[12]

In my view, the oft-reviled Sybil Wilbur here shows herself not only a feminist but an early contributor to women's studies.

LYMAN PIERSON POWELL

The second, as it were, authorized biography of Mrs. Eddy, which like Wilbur's is still in print with the Christian Science Publishing Society, was by Lyman P. Powell. His 1930 book was clearly a public relations attempt by the Mother Church directors to present an alternative account of Mrs. Eddy to that given by Edwin Franden Dakin in his 1929 book, and to queer the pitch for the book by Bates and Dittemore which the Church knew to be forthcoming. It was no accident that at the very time when it was known that large sections of hitherto unknown documents were about to be published by Bates and Dittemore and Dakin, Powell was offered, by his own account, complete financial and editorial freedom as well as access to all the documents in the Church's possession. He was also, according to some reports, offered a salary while he worked on the project.

Lyman P. Powell was a friendly, optimistic, industrious, and well-meaning clergyman of no great intellectual distinction, in my opinion, who possessed a thirst for information and a fascination with the modern world. At different times Powell was the pastor of parishes near Philadelphia and in Northampton, Massachusetts. He then left the ministry, became a professor of business ethics at New York University, and then went on to serve for a brief and controversial period as president of Hobart College. After the end of World War I Powell launched a new career as a freelance lecturer and educator, and then he became minister to a church in the Bronx. Thus when in the preface to his 1930 book on Mrs. Eddy, Powell refers to himself, in the third person, as "The Rector of St. John's Episcopal Church in Northampton, Massachusetts," he is being autobiographically selective, and thus somewhat deceptive.

Powell had no private income and supplemented his earnings as an Episcopalian priest through journalism and editing. As a graduate student, he was employed to edit or ghostwrite a work by the Canadian protopsychiatrist William Osler which would achieve considerable success, and to the end of his life he retained a lively interest in the mental aspects of healing. Thus while living in Northampton he was active in the Emmanuel movement, which sought to incorporate selected elements of spiritual healing into Episcopalianism. Powell continued to do editorial work, notably for the Putnam publishing house, but he also wrote a large number of works under his own name, the most famous of which is his 1930 book on Mrs. Eddy. Powell wrote extensive autobiographical works, mainly concerned with the famous men and women whom he knew, and notable for their sustained cheeriness. For a less rosy view of his life and the kind of difficulties and reverses he suffered, one needs to read his wife's brief account of their life together, which is included in the MacFarland biography of Powell.[13]

In 1907 Lyman Powell wrote a book, *Christian Science: The Faith and Its Founder*, which was highly critical of the movement and claimed to substantiate the charges that had been laid against Mrs. Eddy by Woodbury, Peabody, Dresser, and Milmine. In this 1907 book the whole issue of the Quimby manuscripts is explored, and Powell concludes unambiguously that Mrs. Eddy stole the essential principle of healing from Quimby, that for many years she used a manuscript by Quimby as the basis for her teaching, and that she was being less than truthful and principled in her denials of these facts in the late 1880s. Because Powell was a clergyman who had written widely on the contemporary religious scene and was well versed in the issues of spiritual healing, his account of Christian Science was well calculated to succeed. In fact, the 1907 book enjoyed some considerable commercial success and was much cited by opponents of the Church of Christ, Scientist.

When preparing his first book on Christian Science, like everyone else writing about Mrs. Eddy, Powell was in close touch with Milmine and the *McClure's* team, and therefore with Peabody. He seems to have had access to much of their material before it was published, and he all but quotes sections of the Milmine material in his book. Rather coyly, in his acknowledgments to the 1907 book, Powell lists "Mrs. Benjamin Welles," aka Georgine Milmine. The collaboration moved in both directions. Researchers at the Church History Department are convinced that it was Powell who wrote the doctrinal chapter on *Science and Health* that now forms Chapter 11 of the Milmine biography. Conversely, the influence of the Peabody-Woodbury rhetoric is clearly discernible in the first Powell volume as in so much other early work on Mrs. Eddy. In the preface to the 1907 volume, Powell wrote:

> In considering Mrs. Eddy's personal history, I have made free use of Georgine Milmine's articles in *McClure's*. I have taken the pains, however, in each instance to verify her statements by correspondence or by interviews with those concerned. For this purpose alone I have travelled more than twenty-five hundred miles and am glad to be able to testify to the singular accuracy of the articles and the thoroughness with which they have been prepared.[14]

Given his track record as one of Christian Science's most reputed and vocal opponents, how did it come about that by 1929 Lyman Powell had become a persona so very grata with The Mother Church that he was charged with doing a new authoritative biography using the full resources of the Church's archives? Even though a man may surely change his mind, it is still startling to read all the various accounts Powell gave of Christian Science and establish how he revised his views on such central issues as the influence on Mrs. Eddy of P. P. Quimby. To illustrate this change, let me juxtapose just two examples of Powell's analysis, one from his early period and one from his transition.

> For many years Mrs. Eddy seemed to be the winner in the so-called Quimby controversy. But in this year she is losing, and at the age of eighty-six, when visions that charm and bless alone should visit her, Mrs. Eddy has to face the ghost of her ungenerosity which had enlarged her fame as the founder of the Christian Science Church at the expense of her reputation as a woman. Even from the standpoint of mere policy, it has been a mistake not to acknowledge in these later years as she did in the earlier ones, the efficient source of the idea on which she has erected a structure Quimby could never have claimed as his, but which could not have been built at all except on the foundations laid by Quimby in the receptive mind of Mrs. Eddy.

> Christian Science as it is today is really its founder's creation. Where she got this idea, or where that, little matters. As a whole the system described in *Science and Health* is hers, and nothing that can ever happen will make it less than hers.[15]

By 1930 Powell had veered a hundred and eighty degrees not only in his views of Mrs. Eddy but in his judgment of the accuracy of the Milmine biography. In the prologue to his second biography of Mrs. Eddy, Powell quotes a letter from "a critic" of the Milmine book who confides to him that "much of that testimony was one-sided," given by witnesses anxious to emerge into "a nation-wide notoriety" and not at all "the kind of sources we would have chosen."[16] I was told by Judy Huenneke at the Church History Department that there is evidence that "the critic" was Milmine herself. Lyman Powell certainly knew a great deal more about Milmine and the way her book came into being than he ever confessed in writing, and his second book would have been much more interesting to us today had he been more explicit on this subject, as on a number of others.

I am prepared to believe Powell when he says that his change of mind about the Church and Mrs. Eddy was a gradual and a principled one. As I see it, as a practical man above all, one who lectured on business ethics, consulted with educational foundations on fund-raising tactics, and loved to collect statistics on things like Church memberships and endowments, Powell was sincerely impressed with what he saw as the directors' efficient management of the Church since Mrs. Eddy's "passing." The number and size of Christian Scientist congregations was growing apace at the time that Powell was writing his book,[17] and he knew all too well from his experiences in his Bronx church how difficult it was to fill a church on Sunday or pay for repairs and pastoral salaries. Powell's new enthusiasm for Mary Baker Eddy nonetheless struck many readers as odd, and, according to his biographer MacFarland, there were some veiled accusations in the press reviews of the 1930 biography that Powell had been bought by the Church of Christ, Scientist, accusations that wounded Powell deeply. In my judgment, although Powell did make money on his 1930 book, which went into several editions, and although he also needed that money, he was not in any normal sense venal.

On the Board of Directors' part, the choice of Powell was similarly practical. Powell could be counted on to do a swift and workmanlike job—he prided himself on meeting deadlines—and as an Episcopalian, his work would appear to be more objective. A public confession by Powell that he had been wrong about Mrs. Eddy, that indeed he had not, in 1907, held all the facts necessary to make a balanced judgment but was now fully informed would soothe the faithful and might even convince some of the cynics. In the long term, however, it may be doubted whether the Church authorities made a very good bargain when they opened their arms to Powell. Having found themselves a reliable ecclesiastical hack, they got only hack work. Powell completed his 1930 biography in six months, and he seems to have been careful not to look in the archives for anything controversial. Powell's newly sympathetic and adulatory view of Mrs. Eddy was greeted with some cynicism in the religious press, and this second book failed in its purpose of countering the explosive revelations of the Dakin and Bates and Dittemore books. It is of limited interest today.

Perhaps the most interesting section in Powell's 1930 book occurs in the prologue, when he describes in great detail the archive which he consulted so very desultorily. This description is important since, as I have indicated in my "Research Note," it is not clear that in the years since anyone but the archivists and Robert Peel has seen and handled the volumes described.

> Her original letters, amounting to more than eight thousand, a large proportion of them written with her own hand and many of special value only recently added, are mounted in fifty-seven large volumes having a general index, cross references, and a subject index in concordance style. Bound in fine leather, specially imported from England, the volumes are approximately fifteen inches by twelve inches in size. They are kept in a moisture-proof vault, specially fitted for them. . . . The preserving of the letters is done by a special process. Before its mounting, each letter is placed in a bowl of water and thoroughly soaked. Then it is stretched out even on a zinc board and covered with a coating of paste. Next it is set in a large sheet of special grade paper cut out to form a frame. Then it is hung up on a line like clothes to dry.
>
> After drying, the letters are put under a heavy press with wax paper between the sheets to keep them from adhering to each other, and large paste boards beneath them for protection. . . . Upon removal silk sheets are placed on either side. . . . Afterwards [the pages] are assembled in signature, sewn to make volumes of about one-hundred pages, and are ready for the binder, who comes to the church offices to do his work.
>
> The leather for the binding is of the best blue-black levant, and the volumes are hand-tooled.
>
> Looking back with reverent appreciation of this rare privilege of studying the life of a notable religious leader, as reflected in this mass of unusual detail over which he has pored night and day, the author vividly realizes how necessary such sources are in any writing on this theme.[18]

How frustrating that despite all the reverent efforts at preservation the keepers of Mrs. Eddy's autographs should decide that they are too valuable and too fragile for anyone ever to examine!

Edwin Franden Dakin, John V. Dittemore, and Hugh A. Studdert Kennedy

In the days between my early reading of the published sources and my later gleanings in the Mother Church archival holdings, I was surprised and pleased to discover that the concerted, institutional efforts by the Board of Directors of The Mother Church to collect and lock away all the documents relating to Mrs. Eddy had long been met by a balancing effort by a few determined individuals within the Christian Science fold to keep copies of the most essential documents and make them available on a private, very limited basis. In Christian Science, merely to have copies of certain documents has been considered heretical, and the history of the small but persistent dissident movement has been linked to the possession and dissemination of materials contained in the Church History Department and to which The Mother Church has, at different times, claimed copyright. The battle between the copyrighters and the copiers is one of the important leitmotifs of the recorded institutional history of Christian Science.

Two names and three men are especially important here: John Valentine Dittemore and the two Gilbert Carpenters—the latter a father-son duo who shared the same name and the same mission. Dittemore, in early life an Indiana businessman, was appointed during the last years of Mrs. Eddy's life to direct the Committee on Publication, the propaganda arm of the Church, and he was then the last director Mrs. Eddy named to the Board of Directors. John Dittemore seems to have met Mrs. Eddy only once. She had no memory of their meeting, and perhaps she failed to exercise her famous charm over him. Certainly when Dittemore broke with his fellow directors just before the Great Litigation began in 1919, he expressed his resentment toward The Mother Church by making public some of the Church's most cherished secrets.

Dittemore's chief responsibility and care for ten or more years before his break with the Church was to react to the various attacks on Mrs. Eddy in the press and to collect for The Mother Church all the documents and interview testimonials about Mrs. Eddy he could. Perhaps fearing that he might have future difficulties with his Christian Science colleagues, and understanding as well as anyone the importance of Mrs. Eddy's biography in the Church's institutional politics, Dittemore made copies of all of the most sensitive documents he collected and kept the copies for his personal files. In the 1932 book he cowrote with Ernest Sutherland Bates, Dittemore details the hitherto unpublished documentary material used in the book:

> The substance of this unpublished material constitutes largely the new sources on which the present volume is based. These include about fifteen hundred letters of Mrs. Eddy; letters of her brother Albert Baker; letters of her first and second husbands, George Washington Glover and Daniel Patterson; about five hundred letters of her students; two photostated manuscript books of poems; photostated copies of her scrap-books; her elaborate unpublished commentaries on the Scriptures; Mrs. Julia Field King's unpublished book entitled "The Genealogy of Mary Baker Eddy"; reminiscences, many pages in length, by Sarah Clement Kimball, Clara Choate, Julia S. Bartlett, Caroline Dorr Noyes; all the important part of the diary of Calvin Frye and the complete diary of James F. Gilman. Much use has also been made of the suppressed and very rare *Mrs. Eddy As I Knew her In 1870* by Samuel Putnam Bancroft, and of the suppressed *Mrs Eddy and the Late Suit in Equity*, by Michael Meehan.[19]

I was told at The Mother Church that when Dittemore broke with the Board of Directors, he, in fact, took away not just copies of documents but originals which he had acquired at the Church's behest and with its funds. Dittemore also gained access to Calvin Frye's rooms at the Puritan Motel in the hours following Frye's death on April 14, 1917 and excised chosen sections from Frye's diaries, which he had transcribed and photographed. Later the diary pages were burned. The trunks of documents were first housed in the attic of Mrs. Longyear, and some of the original documents allegedly passed through Dittemore into the Longyear collection. The trunks were later removed when Dittemore and Mrs. Longyear ceased to see eye to eye. According to Keith McNeil Dittemore always insisted he bought his originals from his friend, the dealer Allan A. Beauchamp. Toward the end of his life, Dittemore sold his collection to the Church for $5,000 after letting the Carpenters photostat it for $500.

Dittemore had failed conspicuously to be charmed by Mrs. Eddy, but for Gilbert Carpenter Sr. things went very differently. He was summoned to spend a year serving in Mrs. Eddy's household at Pleasant View, and she seems to have made an indelible impression on him. For Carpenter, Mrs. Eddy was Christlike, infallible, and he and his son were determined that nothing about her and nothing by her should be lost—or hidden from the faithful in the Mother Church archives. Instead of exposing Mrs. Eddy to the public as Dittemore had done, the Carpenters put out the documents they had collected in very limited private editions. These documents include unpublished texts by Mrs. Eddy, collections of her published texts, notes on Mrs. Eddy's classes taken by disciples who attended them, and a long interpretive narrative of her later life.

The first person who tapped into the resources of the unofficial archive was Edwin Dakin, a New York advertising executive, only in his late twenties at the time his biography of Mrs. Eddy was published, a man whose only important work is his biography on Mrs. Eddy. Fascinated by Dakin's book and unable easily to account for its being written, I made an effort while in the Church History Department to pull together all the information on Dakin which the Church had. This did not yield very much, but the little I found was both confusing and interesting. According to the *New York Times* files, Edwin Dakin was born in 1898, in Hannibal, Missouri, took a liberal arts degree at Washington University in St. Louis in 1921, and then went into advertising and public relations. A report submitted to the Boston Committee on Publication says that Dakin was the eldest of three children of Horace and Alice Dakin, that his mother left his affluent father when Edwin was still quite young, in order "to be free of family ties and burdens," and that in the late 1920s she worked as a buyer in a New York department store. Later on, Dakin and his mother must have continued or renewed their relationship since when his book on Mrs. Eddy appeared Dakin dedicated the book to his mother: "In grateful acknowledgement to My Mother Elmore [*sic*] James Dakin, who by devoting many weeks to research and transcription, poring laboriously over yellowed files, and exploring with painstaking care the obscure haunts of data, made possible through her enthusiastic collaboration the writing of this book."

Questioned by the press as to why he had decided to write about Christian Science, Dakin said that he had served in the medical corps for two years during World War I, that his experiences in the war had made him question the value of human life, and that on his return to civil life he had begun a systematic inquiry into religions, from Christ, to Mohammed, to Madame Blavatsky, and finally to Mary Baker Eddy. In an introduction to the 1970 Scribner reedition of his biography, Dakin fleshes out this early story of the genesis of his biography. He says that, unable to find out much about Mrs. Eddy's life, he had a kind of epiphany when he happened upon a rare copy of Georgine Milmine's book. He was told by the bookseller that all the copies of the book were being methodically bought up by Christian Scientists and destroyed. Dakin discovered Milmine's address and wrote asking for information, but he never received a reply. Dakin then began talking to people in New York City who had known Mrs. Eddy, notably Augusta Stetson and John Dittemore. Excited by the possibility of taking up Mrs. Eddy's story where Milmine had left off, Dakin began to write the book after his regular work day, assisted by his mother. In the 1970 introduction, Dakin claims that he did not write his book for money since he had always been a highly paid executive, and his royalties never amounted to a single year's salary. Between 1930 and 1967 little is known about Dakin except that he published a translation of Spengler's *Decline of the West*, that he married and had one daughter, later Mrs. Robert K. Scott, and one grandchild, and that he died in Covington, Louisiana, in 1976.

There has long been a rumor circulating in Christian Science circles that Dakin's book was an act of revenge since Dakin's mother had been employed briefly at Pleasant View in some minor capacity and had been wrongfully discharged. I am now pretty sure that this rumor is false. According to The Mother Church, there is no record of a Mrs. Dakin working at Pleasant View, and the scholar who has devoted the most work to researching Dakin's life, Keith H. McNeil, dismisses the revenge hypothesis. There is evidence, however, that Dakin's mother had a much more important role in writing the book than the one of research assistant which he acknowledged. Lyman Powell reports that his son accidentally met Edwin Dakin, who remarked that much of his, Dakin's, book had been written by his mother, and that someone like Powell should write a more accurate biography. A fascinating little press cutting from the *Pharos-Tribune* of Logansport, Indiana, which I turned up in the Committee on Publication file on Dakin, presents Mrs. Dakin as "Lady Elmore, American psychoanalyst." She seems from the brief article to have been on a lecture tour advocating a kind of Summerhill school—a psychoanalytically based education for children that would involve no coercion or compulsory activities. The article says that Lady Elmore is writing a book on children brought up under her method, and it ends by describing her as the author of *Mrs. Eddy: The Biography of a Virginal Mind*, which she wrote in collaboration with her son, Edwin Dakin. I assume that the journalist contributing this article is merely reporting what "Lady Elmore" told him. The more I find out about Edwin Dakin, the more I wish I had been able to interview him myself and ask him about his childhood, his relationship with his unconventional mother, and how it may have affected his reading of Mrs. Eddy's character.

Dakin's book was a considerable commercial success, going through three printings in as many weeks, receiving favorable reviews from most of the major news outlets, and being chosen by the *New York Times* and the American Library Association as one of the forty notable books of 1929. Of the Dakin book, Julius Silberger notes: "An immediate attempt at suppression by Christian Science was met with equal and insistent resistance by Dakin's publisher, Scribner's, and a second edition was issued in which Dittemore allowed Dakin to publish an appendix of excerpts from Frye's diaries."[20] The alleged campaign by the Church's Committee on Publication to destroy Dakin's book was, in fact, as several contemporary reviewers of the book pointed out, probably the single most important factor in assuring its long-term success. For the second edition, Scribner's was able to issue a preface denouncing the efforts taken by an "organized Minority" to suppress the book and fervently espousing freedom of speech. Once the free speech issue had been raised, the book got further free publicity, which engendered superb advertising copy and a succession of different editions at different prices. Dakin may, as he later claimed, have made more money at his regular job, but if the publishers were accurate in claiming that thirty-three thousand copies of the book had been sold by April 16, 1930, he did not lose by his biographical labors. I only hope his mother got a share of the royalties!

The Dakin biography is perhaps the most compulsively readable of all. The author appears to have the literary and philosophic culture that is lacking in many Christian Science publications, and he creates a clear and seductive picture of Mrs. Eddy. Dakin's foreword is a masterpiece of rhetoric, subtly arguing that although no author can ever claim to be objective, he can at least proclaim his bias and strive for accuracy as far as possible. Dakin takes a resolutely areligious, anti-authoritarian stance, with strong Nietzschean resonances. He decries those who seek to mold Mrs. Eddy into their stereotypic image of piety:

> Now it is because Mrs. Eddy was a woman with an impassioned urge for life and self-expression throbbing in her veins, and not a passive figurine, that she has any possible human significance. It is because of this that hers was a gorgeous adventure—gorgeous no matter what the beginning and what the end. What if she was indeed a soul obsessed? Few who have become instruments for great ideas were ever less. What if she was indeed ignorant, distraught, fearful—lustful of power and glory—tortured by self and the universe—eager for wealth and grandeur? What if she made a mad mystery out of ignorance, inspiration out of dread?
>
> The streets of the whole world are thronged by those who are her kin.
>
> In these pages, then, will be found no fumbling apologia for Mary Baker Eddy, and no effort to fit her into the image of a saint on calloused knees. Any attempt to understand reality must at least be a braver human tribute than any feeble effort to extenuate. When she said that her course was "impelled by a power not one's own," it would not matter if she erred. For at least she was impelled, this is enough. The force in her of that great inner Will which in every being creates its own fulfillment—compensate how it must—needs no justification. It is beyond the little human labels of "good" and "evil." Such a force in all things, in all men, is that which is.[21]

Unfortunately, after this rousing hymn to the force of Will, Mr. Dakin wrote a biography notable for its lyrical inventiveness and factual inexactitude. Despite his fascinating character analyses, I would warn any reader of this book to check any statement of "fact" offered by Dakin, especially if it appears in the apparently corroborative footnotes.[22]

Dakin is particularly strong and detailed in his coverage of the Pleasant View years, concentrating more than half of his 550-page book on the last twenty-five years of Mrs. Eddy's life, and 150 pages on the last three. Dakin is convinced that Mrs. Eddy was a heroin addict from the 1840s to the time of her death, and he neglects no opportunity to describe, or imagine, the dramatic scenes in which the leader of Christian Science revealed her true self to her chosen domestic circle of, mainly, young men. Even if we agree with Dakin's point in the foreword of the book that it wrongs Mrs. Eddy to represent her as a cardboard figurine of a saint, it is equally wrong to picture her as he does—as a drugged, hysterical, nymphomaniac, paranoiac old harridan. Even more important, having portrayed the young Mary Baker Eddy as a rather stupid, uneducated, vain creature, Dakin is forced to account for her undoubted success and the adoration she won from thousands in terms of luck, the usefulness of suggestion in healing, and the power of publicity, and to manage some especially lame transitions: "Suddenly released from the necessity of turning her gaze away from a bitter and ugly world into her own dream life, she grew overnight into an able and dominant personality."[23] When one is faced by passages such as this, it is sobering to consider that many critics of Christian Science have confidently declared that the greatest biography of Mary Baker Eddy was written by Edwin Dakin and that it is tragic that, thanks to the Church's efforts, few people have had the chance to read it!

Perhaps inspired by the critical and commercial success that Dakin's book had enjoyed, perhaps embarrassed by its wealth of factual errors, John Dittemore, the expelled director of the Church, determined to write his own biography of Mrs. Eddy. Dittemore was a better businessman than he was a writer, and he therefore secured the services of Dr. Ernest Sutherland Bates, an experienced biographer. In an interesting overt repetition of the covert relationship between Milmine and Cather, and then between Dakin and "Lady Elmore," Dittemore provided the documentation, and Ernest Sutherland Bates did the "actual literary labor," and the book appeared under both of their names.

Like Dakin, Bates and Dittemore were satisfied with the Milmine book's slant on Mrs. Eddy's life before 1880 or so, and they repeat that story, although with some corrections and additions, mainly included in the footnotes. They ignored the work published after 1907 by biographers loyal to Mrs. Eddy. Furthermore, Bates and Dittemore hewed to *McClure's* claims to reportorial objectivity and plain facts as established by first-hand testimony and direct quotations—a rhetorical model that seems peculiarly well designed to convince the American public. The Bates and Dittemore biography improves upon all earlier works and becomes invaluable source material for later biographers in its accounts of the last five or so years of Mrs. Eddy's life, and its insider view of the development of the Church and of the relationship between Mrs. Eddy and her appointed officials. Furthermore, like Cather, Bates has a lively, interesting style, and he takes a strong position on Mrs. Eddy, acknowledging her achievements and talents, but above all stressing her faults and weaknesses. Of the Bates and Dittemore book Charles S. Braden writes: "So seriously did the Directors [i.e., of the Christian Science Mother Church] regard the Bates-Dittemore book that they finally bought its copyright and plates from the publisher, Alfred A. Knopf, thus suppressing a valuable source book."[24] The book has never been reissued.

Hugh A. Studdert Kennedy's 1947 *Mrs. Eddy: Her Life, Her Work, and Her Place in History* was the third biography based on Dittemore's papers, and although its declared mission was directly opposed to theirs it was to suffer the same fate as the Bates and Dittemore book. Studdert Kennedy was an English Christian Scientist and journalist who was recruited in 1914 to come to America and serve as the foreign editor for the *Monitor*. He withdrew from the Church following the publication of his book *Christian Science and Organized Religion* in 1930, but he remained devoted to Mrs. Eddy and her ideas and was convinced that there was an urgent need for a new biography of her that would combine sympathy and veneration with factual accuracy.

At first Studdert Kennedy fought hard to get access to the Mother Church archives, and it seemed for a long while that the Church authorities not only would collaborate with him but would undertake the publication of the book. Ultimately, however, all this encouragement and promise of cooperation turned sour. Persuaded at last that his projected work would never receive Church approval, Studdert Kennedy decided to make use of the Dittemore materials, whose authenticity he had had officially, although privately, attested to by Clifford Smith, the head of the Mother Church's Bureau of History and Records. The biography he wrote is full of new insights, gracefully written, and informed by a liberal, cultured, and inquiring mind—exactly the kind of mind which had been so painfully lacking in Christian Science historiography. The main problems with the book, from the point of view of the reader today, is not with the author's religious views, which are honestly and openly explained, but with factual inaccuracies which Studdert Kennedy shared with Dakin and with Bates and Dittemore.

Hugh Studdert Kennedy might have anticipated Peel by twenty years if he had been given free rein in the Church's archives. Instead, according to historian Charles Braden, he was exposed to a campaign of censure and censorship by the Mother Church authorities. Not only was his manuscript turned down by the Publishing Society, after many time-consuming readings by officials; the Church also successfully dissuaded another commercial publisher from undertaking the book. It was only in 1947, after Mr. Studdert Kennedy had died, that his widow and her second husband, a notable movement dissident, brought the book out in a small edition printed by the renegade California Christian Science publishing company, the Farallon Press. Even then, reportedly, Christian Scientists were enjoined not to read the book, and, indeed, they were actively encouraged to hinder its sale in book stores. As a result, few people have ever had the chance to read Studdert Kennedy's humane and elegant book. In 1991 there was public discussion of a new edition of the biography, as part of the Christian Science Publishing Society's Twentieth-Century Biography Series and a balance to the Bliss Knapp biography, but this reissuing has never materialized. Contrary to legend, Studdert Kennedy, not Georgine Milmine and Edwin Dakin, may well have been the real victim of the Church's censoring impulses.[25]

JEWEL SPANGLER SMAUS

Following the publication of the competing Powell and Bates and Dittemore biographies of 1930 and 1932, no important new information about Mrs. Eddy's life was available until Jewel Spangler Smaus did her work in the 1950s and 1960s. A loyal Christian Scientist who was neither a trained scholar nor a writer of natural elegance, Mrs. Smaus differed sharply from the tired hagiographers who had long presided over the Church's biographical accounts, because she believed in the power of physical evidence and the possibility of acquiring new facts even in the mid-twentieth century. Smaus yielded to none in her admiration of Mrs. Eddy, but she was an indefatigable researcher, using her own family resources to track down historical records in New Hampshire, uncover mossy tombstones in Minnesota, and interview living relatives, notably Mrs. Eddy's grandson, for oral history and family records.

Smaus at first received some collaboration from The Mother Church, and she was able to read in the archives in preparation for her book on Mrs. Eddy's youth, *Mary Baker Eddy: The Golden Years*. The Christian Science Publishing Society brought out the book in 1966, and it is still available in local reading rooms. Subsequently, Mrs. Smaus's work proved less to the taste of The Mother Church, and her book has never been reissued. Thereafter, Smaus did much of her work under the auspices of the Longyear Museum, which published, notably, her important research on Mrs. Eddy's descendants and the family's memories of her. Despite her long and happy collaboration with Longyear, Smaus did not leave the museum her collection of documents and taped interviews, because, it seems, she feared that in the end the Longyear collection would come under the jurisdiction of The Mother Church, and her materials would be swallowed up in the Church archives. Smaus's papers, including the tapes of her interviews with George Washington Glover III, are lodged with the Daystar Foundation in Oklahoma City.[26]

Smaus's work is little read and suffers perhaps, like Hugh Studdert Kennedy's, from the double disadvantage of being too factual for Christian Science tastes, and too adulatory of Mrs. Eddy for the general public. Published in large part in the Longyear *Quarterly News*, which has very limited circulation, her work serves mainly as a footnote for some of the early chapters in Robert Peel's biography. Yet I believe it is important to acknowledge Smaus's contribution as a local historian and to see her as part of an established Christian Science feminist tradition.

ROBERT PEEL

No biographer in the history of Christian Science has known the archival materials at The Mother Church as well as Robert Peel did, and no one has read them more closely or more astutely. At one time counsellor with the Committee on Publication and a close associate of the longtime archivist Lee Z. Johnson, Peel was probably the best mind Christian Science has attracted, and the biography he wrote is at least one order of magnitude better than any other. One of the many Englishmen who have come into Christian Science, providing some of the Church's most distinguished servants and most notable heretics, Peel was devoted to Christian Science and Mrs. Eddy. Throughout the biography his love, sympathy, and reverence for his subject shine through. But Peel was also dedicated to historical truth and serious scholarship, and his text is supplemented by references, quotations, and copious notes which form a treasure trove for scholars.

Peel's massive three-volume work—*Mary Baker Eddy: Years of Discovery* (1966), *Years of Trial* (1971), and *Years of Authority* (1977)—was first published by Holt, Rinehart and Winston and later by the Christian Science Publishing Society. In his biography Peel looks closely at all the things in Mrs. Eddy's life that apologists gloss over as challenges and critics assert were faults and mistakes, and he tries to understand them. Certainly he takes Mrs. Eddy's part, but unlike most of Mrs. Eddy's biographers he does present the evidence, and readers have an ample opportunity to make up their own minds.[27] Thus for anyone honestly concerned to estimate the truth of the accusations made by the Dressers or Mrs. Woodbury and her associate Peabody, it is important to compare Peel's account with that of Milmine, Dakin, or, more recently, Gardner. Peel's presentation of the Quimby controversy, probably the most deeply controversial and harmful episode in Mrs. Eddy's life, the root of virtually all the later attacks on her, is especially detailed, scholarly, and convincing. It is not Peel's fault that this episode is so knotty, so dependent on complicated dating and sophisticated textual commentary as to defy simple summary for or against the basic accusation that Mrs. Eddy stole her ideas and documents from Quimby.

Complexity, detail, and scholarly apparatus are unfortunately the last things desired by many people involved in the ongoing controversies over Mrs. Eddy's life, and Peel has suffered critiques from both sides. To those with no love of Christian Science, Peel's open acknowledgment of his membership in the Church, his admiration for Mrs. Eddy, and the years he spent as a paid official in the Church hierarchy make everything he writes suspect, even derisory. This attitude is comparable to rejecting out of hand any contributions to the historiography of Marxism or Freudianism by those who revere Marx and Freud and devote their lives to research on the master. Within the Church, each new volume of the biography seems to have increased the hostility felt toward Peel and his assistants and supporters. Although always remaining a loyal Christian Scientist, Robert Peel became estranged from The Mother Church, and I am told that his last years were darkened by the attacks and snubs he suffered from fellow Christian Scientists.

A decidedly cool note was even struck in the 1991 announcement from the Christian Science Publishing Society introducing the new Twentieth-Century Biography Series. This text made it clear that the Peel volumes would remain in print as a complement to the series, and remarked on the "close to one thousand pages of text and another 250 pages of footnotes." Apart from commenting on its length, however, the writers of the introduction apparently found little to admire in the Peel work. Their potted biography of the author lists none of the official positions Mr. Peel held within the Christian Science hierarchy, and it chooses to single out for praise only his knowledge of Mrs. Eddy's "setting," which is odd given that Peel was not a native New Englander. The Christian Science Publishing Society evaluation of Peel concludes thus:

> His three-volume biography . . . will suffice for years to come for most scholars as their surrogate search of the new Archives and will remain in print as a complement to the new series. Mr. Peel's work goes into even more detail than did the Studdert Kennedy in exploring the challenges which Mrs. Eddy had to face along her way, as well as the lessons learned from each of them. By the time the last of the Peel books had been published, a consensus had developed among Christian Scientists that it helped in their growth as students of Christian Science to have a fuller picture of the trials Mrs. Eddy faced.[28]

This is faint praise indeed, and the reference to Studdert Kennedy has very bad resonances to anyone familiar with Church history. I am forced to conclude that Peel's work became an embarrassment within at least some sectors of the Church. He opened up boxes long shut and quoted and supplied archival numbers for documents not known to exist. He did not write the Christian Science style, and he sought to defend his faith on new and uncomfortable grounds. I do not share Robert Peel's beliefs, and I have taken issue with him on a number of points. But without his monumental study, none of the recent work, including my own, would have been possible, and his achievement deserves to be better acknowledged.

N O T E S

Short Titles for the Works of Mary Baker Eddy as Cited in the Notes

Science and Health   *Science and Health with Key to the Scriptures;* current edition
unless otherwise cited.

Prose Works   Compendium volume including *Miscellaneous Writings; Retro-
spection and Introspection; Unity of Good; Pulpit and Press;
Rudimental Divine Science; No and Yes; Christian Science versus
Pantheism; Message to The Mother Church, 1900; Message to The
Mother Church, 1901; Message to The Mother Church, 1902; The
First Church of Christ, Scientist, and Miscellany*

Ret.   *Retrospection and Introspection;* current edition unless otherwise
cited

Manual   *Manual of The Mother Church*

Mis.   *Miscellaneous Writings 1883 – 1896*

Miscellany   *The First Church of Christ, Scientist, and Miscellany*

These works, together with *Christ and Christmas, Poems, What Christmas Means to Me,*
and *A Complete Concordance to Science and Health with Key to the Scriptures* are published by The First Church of Christ, Scientist, in Boston, Massachusetts.

Short Titles for Key Works about Mary Baker Eddy Cited in the Notes

Bates and Dittemore   Ernest Sutherland Bates and John V. Dittemore. *Mary Baker Eddy:
The Truth and the Tradition.* New York: Knopf, 1932.

Dakin   Edwin Franden Dakin. *Mrs. Eddy: The Biography of a Virginal
Mind.* New York: Charles Scribner's Sons, 1929.

Milmine and Cather	Georgine Milmine. *The Life of Mary Baker G. Eddy and the History of Christian Science.* New York: Doubleday, Page and Co., 1909.
Peel	Robert Peel. *Mary Baker Eddy,* 3 vols. New York: Holt, Rinehart and Winston.
Discovery	*The Years of Discovery,* 1966.
Trial	*The Years of Trial,* 1971.
Authority	*The Years of Authority,* 1977.
Powell	Lyman P. Powell. *Mary Baker Eddy: A Life Size Portrait.* New York: Macmillan, 1930.
Smaus	Jewel Spangler Smaus. *The Golden Days.* Boston: The Christian Science Publishing Society, 1966.
Studdert Kennedy	Hugh A. Studdert Kennedy. *Mrs. Eddy: Her Life, Her Work, and Her Place in History.* San Francisco: The Farallon Press, 1947.
Thomas	Robert David Thomas. *"With Bleeding Footsteps": Mary Baker Eddy's Path to Religious Leadership.* New York: Knopf, 1994.
Tomlinson	Reverend Irving C. Tomlinson, M.A. C.S.B. *Twelve Years with Mary Baker Eddy: Recollections and Experiences.* Boston: The Christian Science Publishing Society, 1996.
Wilbur	Sibyl Wilbur. *The Life of Mary Baker Eddy.* New York: Concord Publishing Co., 1908.

Full reference to all the works relating to Mary Baker Eddy which are used and cited in the text of this biography are given in the Notes. The Appendix is a critical review of the most important published sources on Mrs. Eddy's life.

The Church History Department numbers all unpublished documents written by Mary Baker Eddy, whether or not The Mother Church has physical possession. During my own research I was not able to make use of these numbers to access documents in The Mother Church collection, but in order to facilitate the work of future researchers, these numbers have been appended where appropriate. Hence the reference to, for example, "F00035" for a letter by Mrs. Eddy held in the Longyear Museum.

Chapter 1: Early Influences, Later Memories

1.   The site of Mary Baker Eddy's birthplace is owned and maintained by the Church of Christ, Scientist, although the house itself was moved from its site by her cousin Aaron Baker and used for storage after he bought up the family property. It burned down in 1910 shortly before Mrs. Eddy died. The site now sits right next to the main highway and close to some unprepossessing industrial plants, but enough of the land has been retained to give some idea of the rounded hills and pastures which Mrs. Eddy remembered with pleasure from her childhood. One of the rare facts uncovered by Martin Gardner in his highly critical book about Mrs. Eddy is that a forty-ton granite pyramid was mounted on the site in 1918 and then dynamited into fragments in 1962 (*The Healing Revelations of Mary Baker Eddy* [New York: Prometheus Books, 1993], 14–15; hereafter referred to as Gardner). Gardner finds this fact significant for reasons that are unclear.

2.   In her brief autobiography *Retrospection and Introspection* (first published in 1891; the current, revised edition was published in 1892; hereafter this work is referred to as *Ret.*), Mrs. Eddy quotes the eulogy for her mother written by the Reverend Richard S. Rust, an old family friend, praising Abigail as "a living illustration of Christian faith" (*Ret.* p. 6). Whatever their ideological slant, all Mrs. Eddy's biographers, except Robert Thomas, are agreed that Mrs. Abigail Ambrose Baker was a singularly lovable, accomplished, and valuable woman who had a deeply positive influence on her famous daughter's life. **All of Mrs. Eddy's works are now published by the First Church of Christ, Scientist, in Boston.**

3.   On family composition in early nineteenth-century New England, Gerda Lerner notes:

In 17th- and 18th-century America the average married couple lived alone for only a year or two before their first child was born. After that, a woman lived in a household, in which there were young children, until the time her husband died. The median length of time a woman spent between marriage and the end of the child-bearing stage of life was 17.4 years. Eighteenth-century women were of a median age of 60.2 when their last child married and left home; they spent 39.7 years in child-rearing. Due to high mortality, the median duration of marriage was 30.4 years; thus most marriages were cut short by death of one of the spouses nine years before the last child left home. While the basic family unit consisted of husband, wife, and their children, relatives frequently lived within walking distance. Single female relatives often lived within the household, so that household chores were accomplished in a social setting. (*The Majority Finds Its Past* [New York: Oxford University Press, 1979], 131)

Mrs. Baker's life fitted this statistical pattern since she died less than a month after the wedding of her son George, the last of the children to marry.

4.   This pattern was to change in the next generation of Bakers when Mrs. Eddy's New York and Canadian cousins, for example, preferred to name their daughters Georgianna, Almira, Lucinda, Malina, Cornelia, and so forth. See *Family Statistics of the Bakers,* a pamphlet prepared in 1850 by Joseph Baker, son of Mrs. Eddy's uncle Jesse.

5.   Identifying women of this period is somewhat complicated by the fact that family names were frequently used for middle names at birth, but this middle name tended to be replaced by her maiden name when the woman married. Thus Mary Morse Baker became Mary Baker Glover when she married George Glover. When a woman married more than once, the situation was more complex, and personal choice came into play. At the end of her life Mrs. Eddy signed herself Mary Baker G. Eddy, the *G* referring to her marriage to George Glover. She preferred not to use an initial *P* to make any reference to her second, divorced, husband, Daniel Patterson. Mrs. Eddy commented on the changes in her signature in the preface she wrote to *Miscellaneous Writings,* a compilation of her prose works which she first published in 1897: "My signature has been slightly changed from my Christian name, Mary Morse Baker. Timidity in early years caused me, as an author, to assume various noms de plume. After my first marriage to Colonel Glover of Charleston, South Carolina, I dropped the name of Morse to retain my maiden name— thinking that otherwise the name would be too long" (p. x; hereafter cited in the text as *Mis.*).

6.   The first words and first footnote of the Milmine and Cather biography of Mrs. Eddy offer the information that the founder of Christian Science was named Mary Ann Morse Baker, after her paternal grandmother Mary Ann (or Maryann or Marian) Moore Baker, and that she signed her name "Mary A. Morse Baker." (*Mary Baker G. Eddy: The Life of Mary Baker G. Eddy and the History of Christian Science* [1909; reprint, Lincoln: University of Nebraska Press, 1993]; hereafter cited in the text as Milmine and Cather.) Unfortunately, this first "fact," with its corroborating evidence, is not correct. The records of the Bow church establish that at baptism Mary was not given the name Mary Ann, but Mary Morse (see the photo reproduction of the church document in Jewel Spangler Smaus, *Mary Baker Eddy: The Golden Days* [Boston: The Christian Science Publishing Society, 1966], facing page 16; hereafter cited in the text as Smaus). The surviving letters from the period before Mary Baker's marriage to George Glover, for which I have consulted the original autographs, are signed Mary M. Baker. It is true that in the records of the Tilton Congregational Church which show when Mary Baker was accepted as a member of the church by profession, she is referred to as Miss Mary A. M. Baker—this record is reproduced in facsimile on p. 232 of the January 1907 issue of the magazine series on which Milmine and Cather is based ("Mary Baker G. Eddy: The Story of Her Life and the History of Christian Science," *McClure's Magazine,* fourteen-part series, December 1906–June 1908). One of Mary Baker's aunts was also called Mary Ann Baker, so the *McClure's* investigators may have seen documents signed by or referring to another

person. Such small errors are, however, always interesting, especially when they occur on line 1 of Chapter 1 of a work that begins by loudly proclaiming its dedication to objective reporting and fact checking. On some level, it was important to Georgine Milmine— or to Burton J. Hendrick, who wrote up these first chapters for the *McClure's* series (see Appendix)—to establish that Mary Baker Eddy's name was Mary Ann, or Marian, not Mary.

7. Mary Baker Eddy's only child, George Washington Glover, raised five children, three boys and two girls, whose many descendants have lived and thrived in the Lead, South Dakota, area and elsewhere. Samuel, George, Abigail, and Martha Baker had eight children among them, six of whom died in childhood or early adulthood, and none of whom had children.

8. According to Gerda Lerner, women had better legal rights to property in the Colonial era than after the American War of Independence: "Colonial authorites were more lenient toward the wife's property rights by protecting her dower rights in her husband's property, granting her personal clothing and upholding pre-nuptial contracts between husband and wife" (*The Majority Finds Its Past,* "The Lady and the Mill Girl," p. 17).

9. The first chapter of Hugh A. Studdert Kennedy's biography of Mrs. Eddy perhaps offers the most detailed account of Mrs. Eddy's ancestry, though there are some inaccuracies. (*Mrs. Eddy: Her Life, Her Work and Her Place in History* [San Francisco: The Farallon Press, 1947]; hereafter referred to as Studdert Kennedy.)

10. N. F. Carter, *History of Pembroke, N.H. 1730–1895,* vol. 1, (Concord, N.H.: Republican Press Association, 1895), 59–60.

11. Chandler Eastman Potter, *History of Manchester, N.H.* (Manchester, N.H.: C. E. Potter, 1856), 185–87. This was recorded by Alfred Farlow in his unpublished manuscript on Mrs. Eddy's life ("Historical Incidents," pp. 2–3. Original in Church History Department, The First Church of Christ, Scientist, Boston). The story may well have been told to Mrs. Eddy as a little girl by her father or her grandmother.

12. See Smaus, p. 23, for the reference to Mary Baker Eddy's little rocking chair.

13. Milmine and Cather state that the Baker household contained only one book, the Bible. This apparent objective reportage was quite unfounded as the Baker letters prove, and as was testified to by Baker relatives who wrote in indignation to the Christian Science authorities to protest the portrait of the Baker family given in the Milmine series.

14. After the publication of Mrs. Eddy's autobiographical essay, *Retrospection and Introspection,* considerable publicity was given to the fact that Mrs. Eddy falsely claimed a kinship with Sir John McNeill, the former British ambassador to Persia, and that she made unwarranted use of the McNeill coat of arms and motto, *"Vincere aut mori"* as her personal letterhead and in the decor of her home at Pleasant View in Concord, New Hampshire. She was criticized for lying about her undistinguished roots and satirized for claiming noble British ancestry in the appendix of the Milmine and Cather biography, which details how a letter from Mrs. Florence Macalister of Edinburgh to the London magazine *Truth* disproved Mrs. Eddy's claim, published not only in *Retrospection and Introspection* but in the November 1903 edition of the *Ladies Home Journal,* that she was descended from Sir John McNeill. Robert Peel, discussing the McNeil story, says that Mrs. Eddy's cousin Fanny McNeil Potter had visited Sir James McNeill some years earlier and had told Mrs. Eddy that they were all related. Fanny McNeil was the niece of President Franklin Pierce and filled in as his hostess at the White House on some of the many occasions when Mrs. Pierce was absent or indisposed. Given the social prominence of this cousin, one can see how Mrs. Eddy might have been inclined to accept her word on this matter. I would add in defense of Mrs. Eddy that she was writing *Retrospection and Introspection* when she was in her late sixties, and recounting stories which were part of the family legend and which she had probably been told by persons she trusted. I find it unsurprising that she would fail to seek substantiation for them.

Furthermore, the discovery or invention of distinguished ancestors is hardly uncommon in the lives of the upwardly mobile. Such family myths, though perhaps rooted in snobbery, may give an ambitious young person of humble background that impetus to succeed which bare reality cannot. One example of this empowering mechanism in the lives of poor but ambitious women can be found in Ina Taylor's biography of the Macdonald sisters, *Victorian Sisters: The Remarkable MacDonald Sisters and the Great Men They Inspired* (Bethesda, Md.: Adler and Adler, 1987). These impoverished English women were inspired by the romantic history of the noble and famous—but quite unrelated—Scottish MacDonalds, such as Flora, and used their beauty and talent to marry so far up the British social system that their delusions of grandeur were changed into sober reality.

Finally, it seems to me that other famous contemporaries of Mrs. Eddy's who published memoirs of their family and their youth have been held to a notably less strict standard of truth, both in their lifetimes and since. Mark Twain's various accounts of his family's relations to their slaves during his childhood, and of how he came to escape serving in the army during the Civil War are far more self-serving than anything Mrs. Eddy wrote, and these stories have been treated with amusement by his biographers.

15. **Unless otherwise noted, quotations in the next section of this chapter are from the unpublished archival material relating to the Baker family, which is preserved in the Longyear Museum of Brookline, Massachusetts.** The heart of the Longyear collection is a set of letters, diaries, and legal documents retained by Mrs. Eddy's youngest brother, George Sullivan Baker, and including the papers of their brother Albert Baker who died in 1841. The documents were discovered in a trunk after the death of Mrs. Martha Rand Baker, George's widow, and were hailed as providing new and unimpeachable evidence about Mrs. Eddy's youth. (See the first publication of Mrs. Eddy's own letters in *Munsey's Magazine* [April 1911] with a commentary by Isaac Marcosson.) The first letter in the collection (written by Joseph Baker to his cousin George) dates from 1832, and the mass of data relates to the period 1835 to 1851. The Longyear papers are the essential source of reliable information about Mrs. Eddy's childhood and teenage years, and even they chiefly illuminate the period after her thirteenth year.

16. For careful documentation of this problem for elderly widows, see Laura Thatcher Ulrich's *A Midwife's Tale: The Life of Martha Ballard, Based on Her Diary, 1785–1812* (New York: Vintage Books, 1990). After a life of great social usefulness and incessant labor inside the home and without, Martha Ballard faced dependence and economic penury in her widowhood.

17. A document in the Longyear collection dated January 29, 1801, has James Baker, Joseph's second son, leasing to his "honoured Father Joseph Baker of Bow & to Mary Ann my Hon'd Mother" certain lands from the Lovell or Lovewell estates, "Excepting my house standing on the above mentioned Hundred acre lot in Consideration of Divers favors received." In March 1807 Mark Baker leased to Joseph Baker, his father, for his natural life five tracts of land in Bow as laid out to the heirs of Capt. John Lovewell. Joseph Baker died in 1815.

18. Mark sold his property to Josiah Rogers for $6000. See Robert Peel, *Mary Baker Eddy: The Years of Discovery* (New York: Holt, Rinehart and Winston, 1966), 315; hereafter referred to as *Discovery*.

19. Mark Baker fell out with his nephew Aaron over theological matters, as well as financial ones. Aaron became a Universalist, and Mrs. Eddy remembered being kept awake by the theological disputes between Mark and Aaron. See Peel, *Discovery*, p. 5.

20. To take just one contrasting example, much more is known about Clara Barton's childhood, though Barton was almost an exact contemporary of Mrs. Eddy's, lived for a comparable period, and was only ten or so years younger when she came to prominence. Elizabeth Brown-Pryor's *Clara Barton: Professional Angel* (Philadelphia: University of

Pennsylvania Press, 1987) is full of testimony to Barton's young years from relatives and friends and former pupils—all laudatory.

21.   The first account I read of this claim was in Adam Dickey's memoirs (*Memoirs of Mary Baker Eddy* [Brookline, Mass.: Lillian S. Dickey, 1927], 131–32). Dickey was part of Mrs. Eddy's household only after January 1908, when she moved to Chestnut Hill. His memoirs were completed from his notes only shortly before his own death and thus constitute a less than reliable source. Much more trustworthy, in my view, are the unpublished reminiscences of Mrs. Eddy left by Mrs. Janette E. Weller, a Christian Scientist of great faith but little prominence. Mrs. Weller seems to have been that rare thing in Mrs. Eddy's late life, a friend of real affection and understanding, not allied with any of the power factions and with no political agenda. Weller says that Mrs. Eddy confided in her in 1884 a lengthy account of her personal life, beginning with how, as a small child deemed too young to understand, she had overheard her mother tell a very religious friend that she had prayed God to forgive her for the feeling she had had when pregnant with Mary that she was carrying "some holy thing" (Reminiscences of Janette Weller, pp. 11–12. Original in Church History Department). Weller also reported that on the same occasion Mrs. Eddy told her of being called aloud by God as a child and being told by her mother to respond with the words of the child Samuel. As Mrs. Weller noted, this story would only be told to the public in 1891 in the first edition of *Retrospection and Introspection*.

22.   Irving C. Tomlinson recounts all these stories, which he says Mrs. Eddy confided to him in the last years of her life, in his book *Twelve Years with Mary Baker Eddy* (Boston: The Christian Science Publishing Society, 1945). I have used the newly reissued, extended volume (The Christian Science Publishing Society, 1996; hereafter referred to as Tomlinson).

23.   Lyman P. Powell, *Mary Baker Eddy: A Life Size Portrait* (New York: Macmillan, 1930), p. 284; hereafter referred to as Powell.

24.   Mrs. Eddy herself here made the comparison with the prophet Samuel, but Lyman Powell in his second, authorized and reverential book on Mrs. Eddy (see Appendix), also points to the obvious parallel beween Mrs. Eddy's voices and Joan of Arc's.

25.   Jewel Spangler Smaus did the most thorough research on this issue. See Smaus, Chapter 10.

26.   Tomlinson, p. 7.

27.   The experience of Catharine Beecher and her sister Harriet Beecher Stowe is highly relevant here since, like Mary Baker Eddy, they were subjected to intense familial pressure to accept predestination. Like her, they reacted at first by falling ill, using illness unconsciously to both express their resistance and gain some respite, and then by firmly and publicly rejecting the doctrine. Catharine and Harriet were two of the devoted daughters of Lyman Beecher, a dynamic and charismatic Congregationalist preacher who devoted a long life to combatting the Universalist Unitarian heresies and maintaining the old doctrines. When Catharine, the eldest Beecher child, became engaged to be married, her father waged an unremitting campaign to secure her conversion. Catharine, who adored her father and was deeply committed to religion, nonetheless resisted him, and succumbed to illness under her father's pressure. Thus Lyman Beecher wrote to his son Edward, who had already followed his father's teaching by being converted and even entering the ministry: "Catharine has been sick these three days. The first in acute distress. I had been addressing her conscience not twenty minutes before. She was seized with most agonizing pain. I hope it will be sanctified." Catharine was stiffened in her resistance when her fiancé, the brilliant scientist and mathematician Alexander Fisher, was drowned off the coast of Ireland. Since Fisher had never given any public testimony of conversion, Lyman Beecher regretfully but firmly concluded that, despite the young man's manifest piety and virtue, he was doomed to eternal punishment. Catharine's sorrow was greatly sharpened by her father's attitude, but she refused to accept that Alexander was in hell. Much later on, Harriet

Beecher Stowe went through a similar period of sorrow intensified by religious questioning when her most beloved son, Henry, a student at Dartmouth, was drowned in a pond. Harriet dramatized her agony of mind and weakness of body, as well as her refusal of traditional Calvinist doctrine, in her 1857 novel *The Minister's Wooing,* whose female protagonist is based on her sister. The quote from the Beecher letters is on p. 33 of Katharine Kish Sklar's *Catharine Beecher: A Study in American Domesticity* (New Haven: Yale University Press, 1973). See also Ann Douglas's important study, *The Feminization of American Culture* (New York: Knopf, 1977).

28. In *Retrospection and Introspection* Mrs. Eddy wrote: "From my very childhood I was impelled, by a hunger and thirst after divine things,—a desire for something higher and better than matter, and apart from it,—to seek diligently for the knowledge of God as the one great and ever-present relief from human woe" (p. 31). I see no reason to doubt the truth of this statement.

29. Peel, *Discovery,* pp. 20–21, paraphrasing archival document A&M4-101 34.

Chapter 2: Father and Brothers

1. This quotation is from the letter which Mrs. Abigail Baker, Mary Baker Eddy's mother, wrote to her third son, George Sullivan Baker, on August 7, 1849, three months before her death. **Unless otherwise noted, the quotations in this chapter are again taken from the Baker papers in the Longyear Museum.**

2. Alexis de Tocqueville comments on the social results of the law of partible inheritance. He notes that whereas primogeniture passes estates on in the family intact, and the family becomes inextricably identified with a specific piece of land, in the United States, properties were split after each generation, and the sons, even if as rich as their fathers, did not hold the same land. There was a tendency to sell since "floating capital produces higher interest than real property and is more readily available to gratify the passions of the moment. . . . Thus not only does the law of partible inheritance render it difficult for families to preserve their ancestral domain entire, it deprives them of the inclination to attempt it" (*Democracy in America* [New York: Penguin Books, 1956], p. 52).

3. They were part of a major trend. For an account of the changes in agricultural communities in New England at this period, see Christopher Clark, *The Roots of Rural Capitalism: Western Massachusetts 1780–1860* (Ithaca: Cornell University Press, 1990).

4. Irving C. Tomlinson is typical in opening his account of Mrs. Eddy's life with a discussion of the religious affiliations of both Bakers and Ambroses and commenting on the "atmosphere highly conducive to spiritual unfoldment and devout living" into which Mary Baker Eddy was born (Tomlinson, p. 2).

5. See *Ret.,* p. 5; and Tomlinson, p. 8.

6. Mark's grandson George Waldron Baker, who had lived with him in his childhood, tried in an interview to counteract the vivid portrait of Mark Baker as a boorish, repressive, humorless ogre that Georgine Milmine had offered the public in the pages of *McClure's:* "Although he was set as the hills on politics and religion he was as kindhearted a man as ever lived. He never turned anyone from his door hungry. If there was nothing ready in the house he would give money to procure something at the tavern. The needy had always a welcome at the house of Mark Baker. The clergymen came and went as they pleased" (*Lewiston* [Maine] *Evening Journal,* March 4, 1907, p. 3). Many people in New Hampshire who had known Mark Baker were infuriated by Milmine's portrait of him, and they wrote in with corrections of fact and contrasting reminiscences which gave examples of Mark's humanity, kindness, and intellectual ability.

7. N00146. New Hampshire Historical Society. This is a copy of L02123, an original letter at The First Church of Christ, Scientist, Church History Department. Mark Baker probably lost his finger when Mary was in her late teens.

8. I have compiled this list of Mark Baker's activities from his account book, part of the Longyear collection. Mark detailed what various local men owed him for services and products in the period 1830–1855. Everything was minutely priced, but payment was probably in other products and services rather than in cash. In the whole of this account book, as far as I have been able to decipher it, there is only one record of Mark Baker bartering his agricultural services for a luxury item: in 1849 he exchanged with his prosperous son-in-law Alexander Tilton, the mill owner, "cloth and trimming for a tippet to balance the haying."

9. Young Abigail Baker took the same attitude toward her father's farming as George and Albert but seems not to have been privy, in the ways her brothers were, to the financial maneuvers that were taking place. In August 1835 she wrote to George from Hillsborough, New Hampshire, where she and Albert were living with the Pierces and she was attending school: "And they tell me Father has sold his place? Well I am glad of that if he does not get a worse one. But I fear not much from this for he cannot well get a worse one." As the presumptive heirs, the sons had a right to know what their father was doing with his property, as well as the duty to manage it with him. As Abigail well knew, her duty was to find a good husband and cease to be a charge on the family estate.

10. Mark's disgruntlement about the "hired Gurl" needs to be put in context. As Christopher Clark makes clear in *The Roots of Rural Capitalism,* New Englanders of Mark Baker's generation were not accustomed to hiring labor for work on the farm or in the home. Farmers and their sons and daughters worked on an exchange basis for their neighbors when they did not have their hands full at home.

11. Milmine and Cather, following Peabody, refer to Samuel as a bricklayer, just as they call brother George "a worker in a Tilton woolen mill." This is all part of the *McClure's* strategy to push Mary Baker Eddy's family down the social scale, and to present her youth as having been impoverished and deprived of education and culture.

12. Both of these offspring died as young adults, Samuel probably at sea in 1857, and Eliza, aged twenty-five, in November 1860.

13. Mrs. Mary Ann Cook Baker, Samuel's widow, who died in 1902, was always a good friend of Mrs. Eddy's. Mrs. Eddy generously supported her sister-in-law in her last years.

14. Tomlinson, pp. 9, 18.

15. Clifford P. Smith, *Historical Sketches* (Boston: The Christian Science Publishing Society, 1941), p.18.

16. See de Tocqueville's comment, "As the lawyers [in the United States] form the only enlightened class whom the people do not mistrust, they are naturally called upon to occupy most of the public stations. Furthermore, as most public men are lawyers, and all citizens have access to and knowledge of law as jurors, the language and thought processes of the law affect all political and public discourse" (*Democracy in America,* p. 126).

17. A mysterious, passionately confessional letter in the Longyear collection from Albert to Mrs. McNeil seems to suggest that there was a closer relation between the two. General McNeil was a second cousin to Mary Ann Moore Baker, Albert's paternal grandmother (Peel, *Discovery,* p. 19) and was famous for leading the bayonet charge in the battle of Chippewa in the War of 1812 (Smaus, p. 24).

18. Albert's father and sister Abigail were to maintain their hatred of President Lincoln for decades to come. I shall be discussing the evolution of Mary Baker Eddy's views on abolitionism in Chapter 4.

19. Albert, like so many young men of his generation, seriously considered going west to make his fortune, notably when things were going badly for him professionally in New Hampshire. His good friend from Dartmouth College James W. Grimes moved to Burlington, Iowa, and tried to persuade Albert to follow him. Grimes later became both governor and then United States senator for the new state of Iowa (Smith, *Historical Sketches,* p. 22).

20. The Bakers habitually spelled the town's name *Sandbornton.* By "homestead," Albert means that he would become a settler on his father's land.

21. Hill's attack of June 6 is reprinted in an article defending the dead Baker written by John Atwood in the New Hampshire *Patriot and State Gazette* of June 23, 1842.

22. The Longyear papers show that Albert was still the subject of attack by Isaac Hill and his supporters in 1842, months after his death, during the election campaign of Henry Hubbard, so fiery was the debate over the railway rights issue.

23. A number of the letters and poems in the Longyear collection are occasioned by the death of a relative or close friend, and the pattern of response is unvarying: personal grief is acknowledged and expressed, but must always yield to the Christian belief in God's infinite mercy and wisdom and to the assurance that all will be reunited in the next life.

24. Angelina Grimké and Elizabeth Cady Stanton were two other nineteenth-century American women who seem to have been propelled into achievement in the public sphere after the death of a very promising and much loved elder brother.

25. In a reminiscence about her childhood, Mrs. Eddy recalled acting as the peacemaker between her older brothers, who were given to fighting. This is one of the rare indications that life in the crowded little house in Bow had its ups and downs. See Smaus, p. 39.

26. The Longyear papers allow us to trace this affair in some detail. Highly susceptible to female charm, in 1835 the twenty-three-year-old George incautiously wrote to Miss Putney some passionate letters which contained warm criticism of a local rival, Mr. White. Sadly Miss Putney preferred Mr. White and showed the letters to him. The indignant Mr. White made them public, causing much delightful gossip in sleepy, agricultural, unrefined Bow, and sending George to bed in an agony of embarrassment and disappointed passion.

27. Captain Amos Pilsbury was superintendant of the Wethersfield facility, aided by his younger brother Luther, a good friend of George's, and later to be George's brother-in-law. Amos Pilsbury was destined to win national renown as a prison reformer, and it seemed that the worthy Pilsbury family might advance the career of young George as the Pierces did Albert's.

28. Brattleboro was the site of a famous hydropathic spa, founded by Dr. Robert Wessellhoeft, who would become the physician of the Peabody sisters, of the Hawthorne children, and of Margaret Fuller. Henry Wadsworth Longfellow, Harriet Beecher Stowe, James Russell Lowell, Richard H. Dana, and William Dean Howells all visited Brattleboro, and Catharine Beecher went there regularly. Brattleboro was a center for women and for female culture. See Sklar, *Catharine Beecher.* Also Penny Hansen, "Women's Hour: Feminist Implications of Mary Baker Eddy's Christian Science Movement 1885–1910," (Ph.D. diss., University of California at Irvine, 1981).

29. The Longyear collection contains a brief, hastily written letter from Mrs. Abigail Baker to her son George in New York City: "My Dear George This may be the last Caution I Ever give you, and be not Angry with me if I say Touch not Taste not neither use a Profane word; for you are Bought with a price and Precious & my Love abideth with you Ever—your Affectionate Mother." This letter is undated, but I would date it at the end of 1846 as I deduce from Mrs. Baker's swift and anguished response that she had got wind of George's poem and the news that he was selling liquor and blaspheming his religion.

30. Testimony of Martha Rand Baker, George's widow, to Sibyl Wilbur in 1906. (*The Life of Mary Baker Eddy* [New York: Concord Publishing Company, 1908]; I have used the 1945 edition published by The Christian Science Publishing Society in Boston; this work is hereafter referred to as Wilbur.) The book was based on a series of articles Mrs. Wilbur wrote on Mrs. Eddy for *Human Life,* which consisted of twelve articles published between January and December of 1907.

31. The *Human Life* magazine series reproduces two pictures of Martha in middle age

and in old age, and she does not look in any way a beauty, though Addie Towns Arnold, who knew Martha well, says she had beautiful hair and fine teeth. Reminiscences of Addie Towns Arnold, p. 10. Original in the Church History Department.

32.   Most commentators have assumed that Mary Baker and Martha Rand were close friends as young women, and it is true that they attended school together. Yet in their letters neither Mary nor her mother shows any particular affection for Martha Rand during the long engagement. Abigail Baker complained to George in August 1849 that her pressing invitations to Miss Rand to visit them at the farm had been ignored. Mary Baker's early letters to Martha alternate between punctilious expressions of concern and empty local gossip: there is no sense of intimacy. If Mrs. Baker and Mary feared that the prim Miss Rand was not the right spouse for George, they were prescient.

33.   Reminiscences of Addie Towns Arnold, p. 9. Original in the Church History Department. The Towns family lived directly across the road from the Baker house, both parents at different times worked in the "Corporation," as the Tilton Mill was known locally, and Addie as a child was a pupil of a little school run by Mary Baker Eddy's niece Ellen Pilsbury. After being healed by Christian Science, she discovered that Mrs. Eddy was the former Miss Mary Baker of Tilton, and she found out all she could from her mother and friends about Mrs. Eddy's family. It is possible that alcoholism was at the root of George Baker's coarse behavior, and that he was not the only man in the family with such a problem. Mrs. Arnold commented that Alexander Tilton, George's partner and brother-in-law, was a very heavy drinker, sometimes incapacitated by liquor when he came to the mill, and he was suspected of actually owning a local saloon.

34.   When he finally returned to Tilton in 1864 to live with his wife and son, George Sullivan Baker was a sick, blind, embittered man, and he died in 1867, leaving to his heirs—either his widow or his son—the interests in the Tilton property he had inherited from Mark Baker in 1865. The son, George Waldron Baker, had a sickly childhood, mainly as a result of a hip problem that left him permanently lame. He had an even more unprosperous career than his father, working later mostly in printing. He married a woman whose health was even worse than his own, and he had no children. When his mother died, he sold off the Baker papers she was discovered to have retained in her home. Many of these were purchased by Mrs. Mary Longyear from the dealer Allan Beauchamp, probably with the connivance of John Dittemore, who as a Church officer had been charged with purchasing the letters for The Mother Church.

Chapter 3: The Baker Women of Sanbornton Bridge

1.   *Ret.,* pp. 5, 6. "My second brother Albert Baker was, *next to my mother,* [my italics] the very dearest of my kindred."

2.   Mrs. Eddy quotes from the eulogy delivered for her mother by the Reverend Richard S. Rust on pp. 5–6 of *Ret.*

3.   "Short and stout; she had golden hair, and beautiful blue eyes; she was a blonde." Recollections of Clara M. S. Shannon, quoting what Mrs. Eddy told her (Powell, p. 283, n. 2). There is no tintype of Abigail to match that of Mark Baker, and I surmise that Mark's portrait was taken after his first wife's death, though it is not a companion to the extant tintype portrait of his second wife, Elizabeth Patterson Duncan Baker.

4.   Edwin Franden Dakin, *Mrs. Eddy: The Biography of a Virginal Mind* (New York: Scribners, 1929), p. 4; henceforward referred to as Dakin. Jewel Spangler Smaus draws on her research into domestic life of the period in this description of Mrs. Baker's activities: "Abigail went about the unending tasks of the New England housewife—cooking in the great open fireplace, washing, cleaning, spinning, weaving, sewing, making gallons of soap and dozens of candles, churning butter, and pressing cheese. In the fall she added to her work the preserving of food for the winter. She dried apples, herbs, and berries" (Smaus, p. 19). It is interesting that both Dakin and Smaus, biographers of very different

views, endow Mrs. Abigail Baker with "faculty," the ability to achieve perfect and apparently effortless household management which Harriet Beecher Stowe lovingly evokes for her character Kate Scudder in *The Minister's Wooing.*

5. The only revisionary account of Mrs. Baker is to be found in the 1994 biography of Mrs. Eddy by Robert David Thomas (*"With Bleeding Footsteps": Mary Baker Eddy's Path to Religious Leadership* [New York: Knopf, 1994]; hereafter referred to as Thomas). Guided by his training as a psychoanalyst, Thomas views Mrs. Baker as a repressive and overprotective mother, and in the course of his book, he gives an increasingly sinister interpretation to some of the small incidents that Mrs. Eddy recounted about her childhood. Thomas focuses on the spinning wheel story as proof of a pattern of maternal repression, and as the origin of the psychic divisions and traumas he diagnoses in Mrs. Eddy throughout her life. I tend to see the incident more matter-of-factly as evidence of childrearing methods in early nineteenth-century America which differ from our own but which were not necessarily deleterious. Unlike Thomas, I see Abigail Baker as, at the very least, one of D. W. Winnicott's "good-enough mothers," and very probably as an extraordinarily good mother who, in her daughter's first ten years at least, gave her the freedom and encouragement necessary to develop a strong sense of self. Both my reading and my personal experience lead me to believe that when she sees in her mother someone whom she can both love and respect, a young daughter is able to establish a belief in her own powers which paves the way for future achievement as an adult. The French philosopher and psychoanalyst Luce Irigaray has over the years adopted an increasingly sophisticated and nuanced theory of both the difficulties and the essential importance of the mother-daughter relationship, not just for women but for the whole of the human race. The Demeter-Persephone relationship has become perhaps the central myth of her psychoanalytic, ecological feminism. To the mother-daughter bond, American feminists have devoted a body of work—political, theoretical, fictional, and poetic—too large for a footnote. In my 1990 biography of Agatha Christie, I carefully examined the complicated relationship of Christie and her mother, almost certainly the most important in Christie's life.

6. Reminiscences of James Franklin Gilman, diary entry for August 15, 1895. Original in Church History Department.

7. For example, Catharine and Harriet Beecher were extremely divided in their interpretation of the legacy left them by their mother, Roxana Foote Beecher, who died apparently of consumption after a very brief illness when Catharine, her eldest child, was only sixteen. Roxana Beecher had worn herself out in devoted, obedient service to her demanding husband, Lyman, and her eight children. Soon after Roxana died, Lyman remarried and produced another five children. After his second wife died, Lyman married for the third time. Catharine and Harriet were able to remember their mother as a lay saint but, unsurprisingly, were deeply anxious, in their different ways, not to repeat her life.

8. In the introduction to *The Oven Birds* (Garden City, N.Y.: Anchor, 1972), her collection of writings by late nineteenth-century women, Gail Thain Parker claims that women of the post–Civil War generation were all afflicted by a debilitating, and, in her view, justified sense of their inferiority to their mothers and grandmothers, the pioneers of the reform movements. Judging by Mary Baker Eddy and other women born before 1825, such a sense of inferiority was already common among the pioneers vis-à-vis their own saintly "homespun" mothers. Ann Douglas seems closer to the truth than Parker when, in *The Feminization of American Culture,* she shows that the increasing industrialization of society essentially made it impossible for mid-nineteenth-century middle-class American women to live the same lives as their mothers and grandmothers.

9. Sanbornton Bridge, New Hampshire, was renamed Tilton in 1869, in honor of Charles Tilton, the nephew of Abigail's husband, who acquired a very large fortune in banking and commerce in the West. Charles built a palatial estate, complete with triumphal arch and mausoleum, on the outskirts of his native city and endowed Tilton with a town hall, street lamps, and a bandstand.

10. One of Mary's earliest poems is said to mark her feelings at parting from Andrew Gault. See Powell, p. 65.

11. The 1835 and 1836 letters of Abigail, Martha, and Mary testify to a continuing feud between their family and Aaron Baker and Isaac White. **Quotations from the Baker letters in this chapter are once again taken from the collection at the Longyear Museum.**

12. See Martha's hasty footnote to Abba's letter to George of April 24, 1836: "I want you to use your influence in removing one particular source of embarrassment and chagrin; this is prominading the streets in a waggon I know Father can get a chaise if he will & if does not I will not go to meeting a time this summer & I shall tease him this way about it. Should you write don't pray implicate us."

13. Lyman Powell notes that in 1830, when Mary Baker was nine, Emma Willard was only embarking on her first fact-finding trip to Europe, and that Mary Lyon was to found the Mount Holyoke Seminary only in 1836. The seminary became a college fifty years later. See Powell, p. 60.

14. This system was still operational in North America much later in the century. Canadian author L. M. Montgomery has her heroine Anne Shirley teach school after she had finished high school in order to earn money for college.

15. The Litchfield Academy for girls in Connecticut flourished in the early two decades of the nineteenth century, and its extensive documentation has been carefully studied by historians of late. A conference and exhibition, entitled " 'To Ornament Their Minds': Sarah Pierce's Litchfield Female Academy," held in Litchfield in April 1993, celebrated the school and the recent research on it.

16. The decision finally made by idealistic young schoolmarms to use the whip to control the excesses, particularly of young schoolboys, is a theme in novels and autobiographies of the period. Both the fictional Anne Shirley and the real Clara Barton learned from experience that judicious use of physical punishment was necessary for some boys.

17. In her biography of Clara Barton, Elizabeth Brown Pryor details Clara's successful but unsatisfying career as a local schoolmarm in her late teens and twenties, and the misogyny which she encountered. Catharine Beecher spent much of her life campaigning to extend and improve women's careers as teachers.

18. "School #3 was only twenty-two feet square, with a low ceiling and small-paned windows. The walls were whitewashed plaster, without any sort of decoration or color. The main concerns of the school committee were the continual repair of broken windowpanes and the never-ending problem of obtaining wood for the fireplace. Mark Baker often supplied the wood and mended the windows" (Smaus, p. 33).

19. Many of the Baker family books were kept by Martha Rand Baker until her death and are now part of the Longyear collection.

20. Albert Baker taught school several times. In his first position as a teacher at school #18 in the Iron Works District adjoining Bow, Albert, at age sixteen and still a student at the Pembroke Academy, earned $3.35 a month for teaching thirty-two students. See Smaus, p. 30. Later, Albert helped finance his law studies by serving as the principal of the Hillsborough Academy.

21. Martha and Mary Baker may also have attended classes at the more distant Sanbornton Academy, but the records of this school have been lost. The famous American educator Dyer Sanborn was associated with both academies. In one of many lapses from truth, Milmine and Cather not only accused Mrs. Eddy of lying when she claimed to have graduated from "Dyer H. Sanborn's Academy in Tilton" but asserted that there was no academy in Sanbornton. This claim aroused the ire of Sanbornton/Tilton inhabitants, quite apart from Christian Scientists, and much research effort was devoted to proving the history of academies in the town, Dyer Sanborn's long collaboration with them, and the connection of the Baker girls to them.

22.   Winslow Homer left several depictions of fashionable young women ascending peaks in the White Mountains on horseback at almost precisely the period when Abigail Baker was going to the top of Mount Washington. The women ride sidesaddle, an athletic feat in itself. For those who do not live in New England, it may be necessary to note that Mount Washington is the highest mountain in New Hampshire's Presidential Range, and that it can pose a challenge even today when hikers are not encumbered with long skirts and are wearing modern boots.

23.   *Ton* (in the sense of aristocratic style) is one of the French expressions that Mary Baker introduced as literary flourishes into youthful fictions she wrote such as "Emma Clinton." Her French never amounted to more than a set of random words and phrases, often misunderstood or misapplied.

24.   Extract from *Foreign Quarterly Review,* comparing the different upbringing of young ladies in Italy, England, and the United States, reprinted in the Concord, New Hampshire, publication *Hill's Patriot* in November 1841.

25.   Albert reported to George on August 23, 1836, that Abigail would probably marry Alexander Tilton, and that "Father is as happy as a clam and I don't think he will ever want to die, though he were sure of going to Heaven."

26.   This service from his unmarried sisters continued until George married at thirty-seven. In a letter of January 1846, Mary wrote: "Your shirts are ready. Oh! it was a luxury for me to fix the bosoms for you the first I ever did for any one I do hope they will set good" (F00035, original at Longyear Museum). Like most American girls of her generation, Mary Baker was a very competent needlewoman, dressmaker, and milliner, and these skills continued to be important in her thirties, forties, and fifties when money was scarce and every garment and hat had to be turned and retrimmed and repaired.

27.   The New Hampshire *Patriot and State Gazette* reported on September 16, 1841, that Mr. Sanborn had opened a new high school, that despite the recent attacks on his character, he had already enrolled almost seventy students, and that "he has an able and efficient Female assistant, Miss Martha S. Baker." In December the same newspaper reported that Miss Baker had been promoted from assistant to preceptress.

28.   The lives of Catharine Beecher, Margaret Fuller, Rebecca Harding Davis, and Louisa May Alcott are testimony, sadly, to the fact that education was no recipe for happiness for women, since society offered so little opportunity for them to exercise their talents or use their qualifications. Moreover, their male contemporaries, Hawthorne and Emerson notable among them, reacted defensively, with coldness, scorn, and even malice, when they encountered a woman who was their intellectual equal. It is possible that Mary Baker Eddy may have gained more than she lost by not being born into the New England intelligentsia.

29.   From a letter written by a first cousin, Ann True Ambrose, to Farlow, in support of Mrs. Eddy and in protest at the presentation of the Baker family in the Milmine and Cather series. (Alfred Farlow, "Historical Facts Concerning Mary Baker Eddy and Christian Science." Original in Church History Department.)

30.   Moliere's plays *Les Précieuses ridicules, L'Ecole des femmes,* and *Les Femmes savantes* are some of the best expressions of traditional uncertainties about the social consequences of educating women. By the late nineteenth century, opponents of higher education for women were bolstering their case by referring to medical "evidence" that the rigors of education made women susceptible to infertility and more inclined to mental illness. See Elaine Showalter, *The Female Malady: Women, Madness, and English Culture, 1830–1980* (New York: Penguin Books, 1987), pp. 124–27. Jewel Spangler Smaus quotes Clifton Johnson's 1904 *Old Time Schools and Schoolbooks*: "One father was startled to hear his daughter was studying mathematics. The father is said to have remarked to the girl's mother about the 'unnatural' tendency: 'Peg, we must put a stop to this or we shall have Mary in a straight-jacket one of these days' " (Smaus, p. 175, n. 1).

31.   The Litchfield Academy's records show that even at this academically elite school, the girls were readily excused from school when the walking became too muddy. It was considered hazardous to one's health to sit in wet clothing, and, since even affluent young ladies at the time had only very limited wardrobes, the wear and tear on clothing occasioned by walking in mud outweighed the potential educational gains of attending school. Mrs. Eddy told Tomlinson that she was sometimes carried home from school on the shoulders of her brother George.

32.   Powell, p. 285.

33.   Reminiscences of Julia S. Bartlett, p. 34. Original at the Longyear Museum.

34.   Mary Ladd to Mrs. Eddy, about 1899: "I have been thinking of a remark you once made to my dear Mother. You had been troubled in your mind and once said you 'wished your thinker was cut off.' " Original in the Church History Department.

35.   Tomlinson, pp. 10–11.

36.   Wilbur first published the full text of this August 1902 letter from Bartlett Corser in the February 1907 edition of the biographical series she did for *Human Life.* Corser knew Mary Baker when she studied with his father, and he remembered with admiration the "deep" conversations the two had, which he was unable to follow. Reportedly, Bartlett Corser was so deeply in love with Abigail Baker that he never married.

37.   *McClure's Magazine,* January 1907, p. 235. Also Milmine and Cather, p. 15. In the competing magazine series for *Human Life,* Sibyl Wilbur states in her introduction that the elderly New Hampshire people whom Milmine and the *McClure's* people had contacted for firsthand testimony about Mrs. Eddy's childhood constituted not "scores" but "a small, a very small group" (*Human Life,* February 1907, p. 11). Given that Mrs. Eddy and her contemporaries were in their eighties in 1907, Wilbur's "very small group" seems inherently more likely than Milmine's "scores." Furthermore, since the Baker family did not move to Tilton until Mary was about fifteen, the Tilton witnesses had no direct knowledge of her childhood years in Bow. Wilbur also says that the testimony of the Tilton witnesses was fragmentary and often contradictory, and, more sensationally, she claims that they "betrayed evidence of having been tampered with by suggestion, the imagination having been incited by vanity or cupidity" (Wilbur, p. xv). To put it more bluntly, Wilbur accuses the *McClure's* team of bribing their witnesses and shaping their testimony to fit a preconceived agenda. For more on these two biographies, see the Appendix.

38.   Milmine and Cather, p. 16. See Appendix for Cather's own negative evaluation of this opening section of the book, which was completed before she was appointed to draft and edit Milmine's research.

39.   Milmine and Cather, p. 17.

40.   The town of Tilton was generally outraged by the portrait of the Baker family given in the *McClure's* series, and I imagine that Mrs. Hannah Philbrook was not anxious for her neighbors to know for certain that she was Milmine's main source, and that she stipulated that, in the book edition, she could be quoted directly, but not named. When in the revised edition, Milmine actually quotes Philbrook's evidence, and has her say that Mrs. Eddy was backward in "sums," a tiny hole actually opens in the text, through which suspicion of the speaker's truthfulness might come. One thing Mrs. Eddy's critics never accused her of was having no head for figures!

41.   *Human Life,* February 1907, p. 13. Both Milmine and Wilbur later published revised versions of their series of magazine articles as books, but whereas "Milmine" edited mainly by adding detail to the text to make it appear more circumstantial, Wilbur moved in the opposite direction by eliminating interview testimony. Thus it is crucial, when judging what Wilbur did as a reporter (as opposed to a dithyrambic apologist) to read the original, and, unfortunately, rare and never republished *Human Life* articles.

42.   "Mrs. Eddy's Reply to the January McClure Article," *Christian Science Sentinel,* January 5, 1907, pp. 311–12. This piece, now titled "Reply to McClure's Magazine," is

included in *The First Church of Christ, Scientist, and Miscellany* in *Prose Works,* pp. 308–16; hereafter cited as *Miscellany.*

43.   Ernest Sutherland Bates and John V. Dittemore, *Mary Baker Eddy: The Truth and the Tradition* (New York: Knopf, 1932); hereafter cited as Bates and Dittemore.

44.   Milmine and Cather, p. 12.

45.   *McClure's Magazine,* 28, no. 3, January 1907, p. 236.

46.   Janet spent much of his professional life dealing with working-class patients in institutions, and he was convinced that hysterics, of whom he saw many, almost all women, were of inferior intelligence and defective willpower. Freud, Janet's contemporary, whose hysteric patients, also women, came from the upper-middle classes, was convinced to the contrary that hysterics were unusually gifted and intelligent. Thus the label *hysteric* meant radically different things even to the greatest medical specialists of the day. See Henri Ellenberger, *The Discovery of the Unconscious: The History and Evolution of Dynamic Psychiatry* (New York: Basic Books, 1970); also Joseph Breuer and Sigmund Freud, *Studies on Hysteria,* 1895.

47.   Peel, *Discovery,* p. 13. This seems accurate, since the testimony Milmine cites, as far as it is identified at all, relates to the Tilton period of Mary Baker's life, that is, after she was fourteen. Peel establishes that Hannah Sanborn did not know the Bakers in Bow, and that Milmine's apparently corroborative reference to Dr. Ladd is a definite error since the Bakers did not know Nathaniel Ladd until they moved to Sanbornton Bridge.

48.   Ibid., p. 45. He also states that in Tilton Mrs. Eddy's "regular physician was Dr. Nathaniel Ladd," and he says that Ladd diagnosed "that the dyspepsia which constituted her chief suffering was caused by a disease of the spinal nerves, there being 'a connection between stomach and spine' " (*Discovery,* p. 95). As confirmation of this statement, Peel has a cryptic note referring to an entry in one of the notebooks of Asa Gilbert Eddy (*Discovery,* p. 328, n. 75). I have looked at these notebooks with some care, and the "entry" Peel refers to is an isolated sentence scribbled on the back cover of one notebook, with no reference or explanation. The entry indicates that Mr. and Mrs. Eddy may have discussed Ladd, and that Mr. Eddy found it worthwhile to note down something his wife presumably told him about her past ill health. Otherwise the entry tells us nothing about the then Mary Baker's relationship with Ladd, or his treatment of her.

49.   Original in Church History Department. Florence Saunders's communication to the directors focused on the issue of whether the Church wished to acquire the little Bible which Walter Durgin had inherited from his father, and which has "Mary" and "Mary Baker" written in it several times, probably in Mrs. Eddy's handwriting. Presumably Mary had given this Bible to Lyman.

50.   Powell, p. 12.

51.   Louisa May Alcott's childhood journal offers testimony to the discomforts of regimens like the Graham diet, which was followed at the Fruitlands communal farm, and consisted in large part of bread, apples, and cold water. She also suffered after the age of thirty from disastrous effects of treatment for dysentery by calomel, a mercury compound and remedy of traditional medicine, used as an emetic and highly poisonous. See Martha Saxton, *Louisa May: A Modern Biography of Louisa May Alcott* (Boston: Houghton Mifflin, 1977). This book, let me add, is considered heretic and not offered for sale at the Alcott sanctuaries in Concord, Massachusetts, because it presents such a negative picture of Alcott family life, in particular of the relation of Bronson Alcott to Louisa.

52.   The New Hampshire communities in which Mary Baker lived while single were very healthy for the period. There is no mention of outbreaks of cholera or typhoid, and tuberculosis does not seem to have been endemic, though there are suggestions that Bright's disease was not uncommon. Albert, in his letters to George and other friends, always mentions potential health hazards when he is discussing the possibility of moving south or

west to improve his financial position, and it is not just chance that both Martha and Mary Baker were to lose their husbands to infectious disease in Southern states.

For the Baker family, greater wealth also seems to have brought worse health. Three of Mary's grandparents lived into old age, as did her parents. Mark is the only one of the family whose health was never mentioned in the letters, and he never talked of it on his own, and he seems to have led an active life well into his seventies. Abigail Baker, as we shall see in more detail in the next chapter, was in failing health for some five years before her death in 1849, but her death at age sixty-five can be considered premature mainly in contrast with her mother-in-law, who was over ninety when she died. As far as we know, Albert, who died at the age of thirty-one, was the first of Mark Baker's children to die. The next generation would be much less healthy than their parents, grandparents, and great-grandparents before them. As I have already noted, only Mary produced a child who would have children and grandchildren of his own, and that child lived outside New England from the age of almost twelve.

The few letters we have from Martha and Abigail in the period after 1850 record their experience of serious illness, such as Martha's bout with typhoid and a sleigh accident in 1850, and Abigail's hernia and hip problems around 1860, but their own health concerns pale in comparison with those of their husbands and children.

53. F00028, April 17, 1837. Original at Longyear Museum.

54. "Cutchins" was a lively young friend of George's who paid a number of visits to the Baker farm, and whom both Martha and Mary seem to have taken a liking to. When Mr. Cutchins, inexplicably, stopped coming to Tilton, both girls expressed their chagrin with medical symptoms.

55. Alfred Farlow papers, in the Church History Department. (He was the first manager of the Committee on Publication of The Mother Church for most of the period from 1899 to 1914 and thus was in charge of dealing with the press during the difficult last years of Mrs. Eddy's life.) At another point in his account of Mrs. Eddy's life, Farlow has Mrs. Eddy mentioning, quite incidentally, that as a girl she had been subject to intense headaches. Headaches are a problem that runs in my own family, and I know that there are times when lying absolutely still and quiet is the only way to cope. Perhaps all the tales of Mrs. Eddy's hysterical comas as a girl might stem from something as simple as this.

56. Working-class hysterics, whose families tended more often to commit them to institutions, did not, of course, fare as well as their more wealthy sisters. The extraordinary plight of women committed to the hysteria ward of Salpêtrière hospital in Paris is superbly documented by records and photographs. It is now clear that the "grande hystérie" reported, theorized, and publicly put on display by the famous Charcot and his team was a complex and imaginative cooperative creation of the ambitious doctors and their powerless patients. See Georges Didi-Huberman's *L'Invention de l'hystérie: Charcot et l'iconographie photographique de la Salpêtrière* (Paris: Macula, 1982).

57. *Science and Health,* 1st ed. (Boston, 1875), pp. 189–90. A revised version of this account is found in the current edition of *Science and Health with Key to the Scriptures* on pp. 221–22. *Science and Health* henceforth cited as *Science and Health* 1e for the first edition, or *Science and Health* for the current edition.

58. Odd phrases in the letters from Mary Baker's siblings confirm her memory of extreme dieting and food fads.

59. In the letter to her brother George of April 17, 1837, Mary relates that she was invited to join an excursion to the local Shakers colony, but her father would not let her go as it was on the sabbath. (F00028. Original at the Longyear Museum.) Many commentators have noted the probability that Mary was acquainted as a girl with some of the ideas and habits of the Shakers and may have been influenced by the example of Mother Ann Lee and her theology.

Chapter 4: First Marriage

1. Original letter in the Longyear Museum. **Quotations in this chapter from the Baker family papers are once again taken from the Longyear Museum unless otherwise indicated.** The reader will note how different is Albert's tone in this letter to Mary from the cynical, worldly one he adopted in the earlier letters to George which I quoted in Chapter 2.

2. See for example *Science and Health,* 574: 27–30: "The very circumstance, which your suffering sense deems wrathful and afflictive, Love can make an angel entertained unawares." Or *Mis.* 276: 19–23: "Out of the gloom comes the glory of our Lord, and His divine Love is found in affliction. When a false sense suffers, the true sense comes out, and the bridegroom appears. We are then wedded to a purer, higher affection and ideal."

3. A10020. Original in Church History Department. The poem in full is published in Peel, *Discovery,* pp. 43–44.

4. Christina Rossetti, a British near contemporary of Mrs. Eddy and an incomparably better poet, is a good example of someone whose work is best not read as biographical outpouring. According to standard biographical accounts, Christina was a bright, energetic teenager, but she wrote poems of extreme melancholy, obsessed with death, loneliness, and suffering. Rather than reflecting or expressing her current experience, these juvenilia could be said to lay down the patterns Christina was to live out, a tragic case of life reflecting art. The recent attempt to read backward from the teenage poems and allege that Christina was sexually abused seems to me misguided and dangerous.

5. Copybook 2, p. 73. Original in Church History Department.

6. Lyman Durgin, who came into the Baker home at age eleven as a hired boy, expressed his lifelong gratitude and affection for Mary Baker Eddy in a letter written late in his life. Lyman remembered that as a lad he had difficulty reading and thus refused to attend Sunday school. When Mary volunteered to tutor him, however, he was able to conquer his difficulties, and subsequently he went on to a successful career as a railroad mechanic (Smaus, pp. 89–90). One of Mary's other students in Tilton recalled how much the children appreciated their Sunday school teacher for "her daintiness, her high-bred manners, her way of smiling at us, and her sweet musical voice" (Wilbur, p. 34).

7. One of the small documentary problems for this period in Mary Baker Eddy's life is that certain letters written to Augusta Holmes and signed simply "Mary" were incorrectly attributed to Mary Baker Eddy. Since the materials on the early years are so slim, these letters have been given some importance, notably in the biographies by Bates and Dittemore and by Hugh Studdert Kennedy. Augusta Holmes was born in Meredith (now Laconia), New Hampshire, in 1820. Her father, Nathaniel Holmes, who died in 1840, built the first mill in Sanbornton Bridge. This mill and the Holmes house were purchased by Alexander Tilton, Mary Baker's brother-in-law, in 1849. Augusta attended the Plymouth Academy for four sessions in 1837 and perhaps two in 1838 and corresponded with her Sanbornton Bridge friends Lydia Ann Swasey, Sarah C. Gates, and Alice C. Clough. In none of the letters between these young women is there a mention of any Miss Baker. At the Plymouth Academy, Augusta became friendly with Mary Bean and Betsey Richert. Playfully, among the three girls, Mary was referred to as mother, Augusta as father, and Betsey as daughter. In January 1839, Mary Bean wrote to Augusta Holmes: "Oh, agony, (as you say) to lose the blessed privilege of being called your 'little spouse,' would be more than I could well endure. You do not call me by those 'endearing epithets,' as you were wont to do, in times past. And why not? Have I done any thing my dear husband to merit this?" (L02679. Original in Church History Department.) As feminist historians have shown, such an intimate and emotional style was common among young women of this period. See Nancy Cott, *The Bonds of Womanhood* (New Haven: Yale University Press, 1977); Lillian Faderman, *Surpassing the Love of Men: Romantic Friendship and Love between Women from the Renaissance to the Present* (New York: William Morrow, 1981); and Carol Smith-Rosenberg, "The Female World of Love and Ritual," collected in various anthologies including *A Heritage of Her Own,* ed. Nancy Cott

and Elizabeth Pleck (New York: Simon and Schuster, 1979). Read in the post-Freudian light of the twentieth century, the letters appear to have lesbian connotations, and thus Mary Bean's letters have become one more stick with which to beat Mrs. Eddy. The correspondence between the various members of the Baker family show conclusively that Mary Baker did not attend Plymouth Academy in 1837, and it seems that her friendship with Miss Holmes began after 1840 and intensified when both enrolled at the Woodman Academy. Elsie Evans, senior researcher at the archives of The Mother Church, did the research that established which of the letters written to Miss Holmes were written by Mary Baker, and identified Miss Bean as the probable author of six others.

8.   One new member had been added. Mary's nephew, Samuel Baker Jr., was at this point living in Sanbornton Bridge with his grandparents in order to attend the Sanbornton Academy.

9.   Such an expectation is standard in many cultures, even today. The successful novel and movie *Like Water for Chocolate* dramatize the plight of the daughter who is designated by the family to remain unmarried and take care of the parents in their old age.

10.   Quoted in Martha Saxton's *Louisa May,* p. 263.

11.   The life and work of Lydia Huntley Sigourney and of Lydia Maria Child were well known to the young Mary Baker and influenced her and other women of her generation. Mrs. Sigourney, born in 1791, married an older widower in 1819, published anonymously for some years after her marriage and gave the proceeds to charity, at the request of her husband. When his business failed, however, the family came to depend on her earnings, and the Sigourneys moved sharply up the social scale. Mrs Child, born in 1802, had published two popular novels and started a school by the time she was twenty-three. The rhyme "Mary Had a Little Lamb" is based upon an incident in her school. She continued a successful career as editor, journalist, and social commentator after her marriage in 1828.

12.   *McClure's,* January 1907, p. 233. The version of the Milmine and Cather biography which appeared in book form and which is now once again available in the University of Nebraska edition (1993), was considerably revised. Thus this early description of Mary Baker is notably different in the second, revised, version, with the negative aspects of the description expanded upon and the positive ones cut. A close comparison of the texts of the two editions shows that any favorable testimony about Mary Baker and her family was systematically weeded out, or at least drastically toned down in the book version.

13.   Ibid., p. 235. The *McClure's* account, in all its versions, devotes considerable space to the subject of mesmerism and asserts that at various points in her life Mary Baker engaged in mesmerism and in seances. This description of her hypnotically beautiful eyes prepares the ground for this line of argument.

14.   Ibid.

15.   This poem was published anonymously in *Hill's Patriot,* December 23, 1840, and was first attributed to Mrs. Eddy by Gilbert C. Carpenter Jr. in his collection *Early Verse* (n.p.: privately printed, 1933).

16.   In *Hearts and Hands: A History of Courtship in America* (New York: Basic Books, 1984), a study of letters and journals from New England couples, Ellen Rothman shows that when Mrs. Eddy was young, kisses and other warm expressions of affection were considered quite normal behavior among young people, and that parents and society at large were far from "puritanical" in the attitude they took to courtship (see p. 122 ff.).

17.   L02682. Original in Church History Department. Both John Bartlett and James Smith reappear in Mary's life as potential suitors after her widowhood. Both seem to have been very worthy young men, and it is interesting that she was not tempted by them as an unmarried girl. Mrs. Eddy was, according to Robert Peel, a devoted reader of Charlotte Brontë, and she may have seen Bartlett and Smith as too much like St. John Rivers; she may have been determined to wait for her Rochester.

18. "Marriage and Parentage," *Ret.,* 1st ed., p. 24. This section was omitted from subsequent editions of *Retrospection and Introspection.*

19. This story is narrated in Powell and in Smaus, taken from the privately published reminiscences of Gilbert Carpenter Sr., one of Mrs. Eddy's secretaries at Pleasant View.

20. Bates and Dittemore wrongly state that Mary was twenty-five when she first married and was therefore considered an old maid. Mary was in fact twenty-two and, according to Jewel Spangler Smaus, it was not customary in her community for either men or women to marry young. Smaus randomly sampled seventy-five men and women listed in the *History of Pembroke* for the period 1780–1860, and "all except nine were over twenty at the age of marriage" (Smaus, p. 173, n. 4). Rothman's book *Hearts and Hands* confirms this pattern in couples of Mrs. Eddy's period, region, and social group.

21. Tomlinson (p. 13), quoting what Mrs. Eddy told him.

22. The letter can be consulted at the Longyear Museum; the diary is in the Church History Department.

23. "On the other side of the world about this time, Søren Kierkegaard was ... exploring the immeasurable solitude and subjectivity of human existence. A young girl full of lively hopes but alone and terrified in a stagecoach clattering through the unknown night might serve as the very symbol of the individual predicament as Kierkegaard saw it" (Peel, *Discovery,* p. 65). This is an interesting but unsubstantiated reading, in my view.

24. Bates and Dittemore characterize George Glover as a "swaggering blade, proud of his business success, full of a cocky kindliness" (Bates and Dittemore, p. 28); and Hugh Studdert Kennedy agrees with this assessment. Bates and Dittemore go on: "What had the delicate Mary Baker to do with this loud-voiced young man? There is no evidence she was violently in love with him. He never inspired even such youthfully amorous verses as those to Andrew Gault. Mary's muse did not find him a sufficiently impressive theme until after his death. He obviously had no share in her literary aspirations" (Bates and Dittemore, p. 29). The only extant image of George Glover, a tiny framed portrait painted on ivory of a handsome young man with thick, wavy fair hair (see photo insert), is now part of the Longyear collection. The resemblance between this portrait of George Washington Glover and photographs of his namesake son and grandson is very striking.

25. Keith McNeil Collection. Quoted in Smaus, p. 103. Smaus makes no comment on George Glover's character and does not quote at all from "Wash's" letters to George Baker. I have the feeling that Mrs. Smaus did not approve of Mrs. Eddy's first husband.

26. Tomlinson, p. 13. I note that Mrs. Eddy does not say that Glover's letters to her made her love him, but that she grew to love him by writing to him. This implies that, like many correspondents, she fashioned an ideal image of George and fell in love with it— but it is dangerous to put too much stress on expressions which may be Tomlinson's rather than Mrs. Eddy's.

27. "Emma Clinton, or A Tale of the Frontiers," by Mrs. Mary M. Glover, (International Order of Odd Fellows) *The Covenant,* August 1846.

28. These two letters formed part of George Baker's papers, and the earlier of them was first published by Ernest Bates and John Dittemore in 1932 in their highly critical biography of Mrs. Eddy. They now form part of the Longyear collection. Bates and Dittemore wrongly assume that the two letters, addressed to "Brother Baker," were written to Samuel. Edwin Franden Dakin is even further off the mark, since he claims that the Dittemore papers included passionate love letters from Mrs. Eddy's first husband. Would that this were so!

29. It is interesting to compare the spelling, punctuation, and grammar of the various correspondents represented in the current Longyear collection. It is clear that George Glover's achievement as a writer ranked below those of two far from literary female contemporaries—the Bakers' "hired gurl" Mahala Sanborn and the milliner Hannah Philbrook. The letters of the Baker children all show, in turn, a notably higher educational

level than Glover's, Mahala's, or Hannah's. It is possible that we have no letter from Samuel Baker because he was even less proficient in writing than was his builder friend Wash.

30.   Some scholars at the Longyear Museum are of the opinion that the two letters from George Glover to George Baker are jokes, in which George Glover parodies for his friend the language, spelling, and views of Southern men.

31.   In her research notes for her 1949 manuscript, "Mary Baker Eddy in Wilmington, North Carolina," (Church History Department), Elizabeth Earl Jones discovered that 145 acres of central Charleston had burned down in 1838, and she speculates that George Glover had gone South to take advantage of the movement to rebuild the city.

32.   Wilbur, p. 40.

33.   According to the Longyear *Quarterly News* (Fall/Winter 1989–1990) the wedding ring (diamond ring) is still in the possession of the Glover family. The article doesn't mention the cameo, however. The original letter from Abigail to Augusta is in the Church History Department.

34.   Mrs. Abigail Baker in her letter to Mary of February 6, comments eliptically, "I am glad to learn your stop at Boston was so pleasant (so much for Family friendship astonishing)." The implication seems to be that the Samuel Bakers had once again failed to come up to family expectations.

35.   The Glovers spent about a month in Charleston, where George was part-owner of a house on fashionable Hasell (or Hassell) Street, but their ultimate destination seems always to have been Wilmington. Hugh Studdert Kennedy gives a characteristically lively and detailed description of the cultured aristocratic plantation society of Charleston, but, though George is known to have been a member of the socially prominent St. Andrews Lodge, there is no evidence that his wife was able even to nibble at these elegant pleasures.

36.   Bates and Dittemore describe this journey in some detail, apparently basing their account on the memories Mrs. Eddy later recounted to members of her staff at Pleasant View ("as Mrs. Eddy remembered"). They say that the ship was battered by a storm, the captain feared for the worst, the Glovers prayed, and their prayers were answered. Powell tells the same story, stating that "Mrs. Eddy related to Miss Shannon, Mr. McKenzie, and Mr. Tomlinson this almost tragic experience. . . . A penciled note in Mrs. Eddy's handwriting on the margin of her old scrapbook records that she 'was hopelessly seasick' " (Powell, 76). Mrs. Eddy also recalled that her mother Abigail Baker had entrusted a sealed package to George Glover when he and Mary left Sanbornton, and when he opened it after the storm was over he found a poem by Mrs. Sigourney, in which a mother commends a beloved daughter to her new husband's care. George wept copiously at this.

37.   In his journal, George Baker gives a detailed account of the horrendous sea voyage he made to Alexandria, Virginia, via Baltimore in 1849, and this helps give some concrete idea of the travails the newly married Mrs. Glover went through on her journeys to and from the South. Original at the Longyear Museum.

38.   "Malicious Animal Magnetism" is an important concept in Christian Science which bears many and contested meanings. Some Christian Science scholars argue that "Malicious Animal Magnetism" or "M.A.M." is a term used by Mary Baker Eddy's detractors, and that she herself, as her doctrine evolved, preferred the term "malicious malpractice." I have been assured by other scholars who have had access to Mrs. Eddy's correspondence that she herself used "malicious animal magnetism," "mesmerism," and "malicious malpractice" interchangeably. The Church History Department believes that the expression should not be capitalized, but on its own computerized transcripts the term appears as "Malicious Animal Magnetism," and it is this form I have chosen to use.

39.   Not surprisingly, documentation on this short but important period in Mrs. Glover's life is slight and often controversial. There are a few contemporary letters, odd entries in

Mrs. Glover's copybook, and such public records as the minutes of the St. John's Lodge in Wilmington and records of George's business dealings and real estate transactions in Charleston and Wilmington. In the speeches and pamphlets he wrote between 1895 and 1910, Frederick Peabody made a series of scurrilous and erroneous statements about Mary Baker Eddy's first marriage. He referred to George Glover as a "bricklayer," asserted that he had no claim to a military title, charged that he was given a pauper's burial and that, despite the widow's affluence in later life and her protestations of undying affection, no stone marked his grave. (We will learn more about Mr. Peabody and his grudge against Mary Baker Eddy in Parts Three and Four.) In the last decade of Mrs. Eddy's life, successful efforts were made by the Church to establish the truth about the Glovers and their life in the South. Loyal Scientists dug up Masonic records, George's obituary, newspaper accounts of his funeral, and so forth, and interviewed anyone who could remember meeting the young couple in 1844. The memories they elicited were of pleasant social functions where the young Glovers appeared as a happy, handsome, popular couple. About 1900, Mrs. W. J. Callis recalled meeting the Glovers at a private dinner party given in their honor, and in an interview she described Mrs. Glover in 1844 as "brilliant, beautiful, cultured, witty and charming, and always sincerely interested in those around her. She said that Mrs. Glover dressed daintily and beautifully, and was in every sense a superior being." This interview material was re-collected from newspaper and other sources by Elizabeth Earl Jones of North Carolina ("Mary Baker Eddy in Wilmington, N. Carolina"). Miss Jones's research was done at the time when a highway marker commemorating Mrs. Eddy was being set up in North Carolina. She hoped that a suitable article on Mrs. Eddy's life in the South might be produced for the local Wilmington paper, but her work did not meet the approval of The Mother Church. The most authentic and most controversial source of information on her six months of married life to George Glover was, of course, Mary Baker Eddy herself, and in later life at Pleasant View she confided a number of reminiscences that were recorded by her faithful staff. These stories are retold or ignored by subsequent biographers, depending on their personal reactions to the material.

40. George was, in the words of Mrs. William Huntingdon, formerly Harriet S. Brown, "a man of fine character, and he was highly regarded as a man of integrity. He had an industrious spirit. . . . Possessed of an ambitious character, he felt and believed that his opportunities for advancement in his home village were altogether too limited" (Elizabeth Earl Jones, "Mary Baker Eddy in Wilmington, N. Carolina," reporting the work of R. W. Sears, 1901 and 1906.

41. In the May 1844 edition of *The Floral Wreath and Ladies' Monthly Magazine* just below a contribution signed "Mrs. G. W. Glover" appeared "Female Talent," an essay by "Mrs. John Sanford." The piece may well have caught the young Mrs. Glover's eye as it points to exactly the problems and dilemmas posed by conventional womanhood which she herself was beginning to face. I quote the piece in full.

> Censorship is always severe on female talent, and not unfrequently is a woman prejudged a slattern because reputed a genius. Slovenly attire, an ill-conducted household, and an ill-arranged table, are, in the the minds of many, identified with female accomplishment. Yet lighter accomplishments may be the more likely cause of such disorder; and she who has spent her life at her harp, or at her frame, will be less disposed to active duties than one to whom exertion is habitual. If the woman of mind bears with equanimity petty vexations, if she had lends a reluctant ear to family tales, if she is not always expatiating on her economy, nor entertaining by a discussion of domestic annoyances; she is not the less capable of controlling her household, or of maintaining order in its several departments. Rather will she occupy her station with more dignity, and fulfil its duties with greater ease.
>
> At the same time she should ever bear in mind, that knowledge is not to elevate her above her station, or to excuse her from the discharge of its most

trifling duties. It is to correct vanity and repress pretension. It is to teach her to know her place and her functions; to make her content with the one, and willing to fulfil the other. It is to render her more useful, more humble, and more happy.

The principal ambition of a twenty-two-year-old middle-class woman in 1843 was to marry the man she loved and safely bear and rear his children. Mary Baker was never an average woman, but she surely nursed this ambition and thought for six months she had achieved it through her union with George Washington Glover. But Mrs. John Sanford poignantly indicates how restricting and repressive marriage tended to be for able women of her generation and Mrs. Eddy's.

42.   Georgine Milmine (Milmine and Cather, p. 28) reported that the widowed Mrs. Glover would later boast to the local sewing circle in Sanbornton of her daily rides out on horseback while in Wilmington. Bates and Dittemore take up this report, which Milmine and her crew had presumably culled from the Tilton locals, as one more example of Mrs. Eddy's lifelong proclivity for embroidering the truth: "For one with her weak back actual horseback rides had of course always been out of the question" (Bates and Dittemore, p. 42). I am inclined both to accept Milmine's report and to believe Mrs. Glover did indeed enjoy going riding in Wilmington. Horseback riding was extremely popular with young women of this period, and such notable contemporaries as Catharine Beecher and Clara Barton, both redoubtable horsewomen who were also subject to regular periods of nervous prostration, testified to how liberating and therapeutic they found the exercise. That many fashionable specialists in neurasthenia put a sinisterly sexual connotation on their female patients' love of riding is only one small example of conventional nineteenth-century medicine's often perverse view of the female body and the healthy life for a woman.

43.   The source for this story is a signed memorandum of August 1904 by the Pleasant View secretary George H. Kinter, attesting that Mrs. Eddy confided that "Maj. Glover's business there [presumably Wilmington] was to purchase and ship the lumber and other materials for a large cathedral which he was to build in Haiti. The lumber was stolen off the docks, and she never realized a dollar from it, as she should."

44.   In the poem Mrs. Glover wrote in 1844 and published in the Odd Fellows publication *The Covenant* in 1845, she anticipates leaving her native land and sailing away to Haiti. Elizabeth Earl Jones ("Mary Baker Eddy in Wilmington, N. Carolina") found in the Charleston newspapers a report that a large band of thieves was operating there and in Wilmington. Robert Peel reports an article in the *Wilmington Chronicle* for April 1844 on a fire at the wharf that destroyed lumber and building materials (Peel, *Discovery,* p. 322, n. 137).

45.   Biographies and memoirs of women of this period show how remarkably customary it was for them to take long and arduous journeys even in the last months of pregnancy. To take an example from the Longyear papers, Martha Baker Pilsbury was unexceptional in leaving her mother's house to rejoin her husband in his new position in Wethersfield Connecticut, only weeks before her delivery on April 21, 1844, of a "little fat beautiful daughter," her first child.

46.   He suffered from "bilious fever," probably yellow fever, although officially no outbreak of this dreaded disease was reported in Wilmington. See Peel, *Discovery,* pp. 322–23, n. 138.

47.   The Reverend Albert Case wrote an edifying summary of Glover's death for the *Masonic Magazine.* See Bates and Dittemore, p. 36. Jewel Spangler Smaus managed to discover the will which George Glover wrote just before his death, as well as the inventory of his possessions, dated October 8, 1844, in which he asks to be interred with all Masonic honors and requests that his body be taken to his home in the North, if this is at all possible. He then goes on to throw himself on the charity of his Masonic brethren since he has no money on hand to pay for either his funeral or for the return of his wife to her relatives in the North. Glover appointed Isaac North, L. H. Marsteller, and William Cook

[*sic*] as his executors and charges them with taking over the papers in his trunk, settling his debts, which he says are few, and collecting the money owed him. See "Family — The Carolina Glovers, Part VI" Longyear *Quarterly News* (Winter/Spring 1990–1991). Minutes of St. John's Lodge, June 25, 1844: "Bro. G. W. Glover being represented as very sick and in indigent circumstances, his case was referred to the committee of charities."

48.   Tomlinson, p. 21.

49.   Ibid., p. 19.

50.   Message to the First Church of Christ, Scientist, or The Mother Church, Boston, June 15, 1902 (*Prose Works,* '02, *Miscellany,* p. 15). At this period, civilian American men commonly used military titles, and George Glover could rightly use the title of Major, though not Colonel, through his position on the staff of the South Carolina militia. George Sullivan Baker rose to the rank of colonel in the New Hampshire militia and used the title. See also Carpenter Ms. in McNeil Collection

51.   The first story is found in Elizabeth Earl Jones's 1949 manuscript "Mary Baker Eddy in Wilmington, N. Carolina," and the other two are in Alfred Farlow's files.

52.   Tomlinson records another of the Bill Glover stories, quoting Mrs. Eddy as saying: "My father read in the *New York Tribune* that Bill Glover, a fine carpenter, had been arrested because it was claimed by a company of Southerners that Colonel Glover had sold him to them. He had been my husband's foreman in his building operations. I wrote a letter which freed Bill from the prison and by the underground railroad he reached Canada and safety" (Tomlinson, pp. 30–31).

53.   Peel (*Discovery*) gives a circumspect summary of the first of these stories in his main text but omits all reference to the other two. In his unpublished biographical account of Mrs. Eddy, Alfred Farlow notes that accounts of a Bill Glover's experiences as an escaped slave had been published in a New York daily paper. This would have occurred around 1900. Farlow states that Glover was one of Mrs. Eddy's first husband's slaves to whom she gave freedom, but I think it more likely that either she and/or her associates applied to her own experiences of 1844 the "stirring accounts" they had read in the newspaper.

54.   The Board of Directors of The Mother Church may have been prudent in its refusal to reply to Miss Elizabeth Earl Jones's requests in 1949 to recirculate these stories, discreetly hidden in unpublished or privately printed memoirs from the Pleasant View years.

55.   Peel, *Discovery,* p. 322, n. 135.

56.   Peel, *Discovery,* p. 323, n. 2. I think it is this kind of careful, documented correction of the record that has made Robert Peel's biography so unpopular among certain groups of Christian Scientists. Researchers at the Church History Department argue plausibly that Mrs. Eddy, unfamiliar with the complex economic patterns of the South, did not understand that the slaves working for her husband were "self-hired," and that she believed she was freeing them when she let them go in 1844.

57.   Bates and Dittemore, p. 23.

58.   The *McClure's* biography reported that Mark Baker expressed joy on hearing the news of Lincoln's death. In 1907 this was a point deeply detrimental to Mrs. Eddy. George Waldron Baker, Mrs. Eddy's nephew, sought to palliate the Milmine account of his grandfather as a fervent anti-abolitionist but told the *Lewiston Evening Journal* (March 4, 1907) that he well remembered the day when old Mark "drove the peddlers out of the house, who offered him Lincoln's picture. He did not like Lincoln, but was honest in his views as were hundreds more in those days."

59.   See Peel, *Discovery,* p. 71.

60.   Ibid. Bates and Dittemore (pp. 33–35) were the first critics of Mrs. Eddy to challenge her assertions that she held antislavery views in 1844.

61.   On her return to New Hampshire, Mrs. Glover wrote one interesting little piece for

the Odd Fellows publication *The Covenant*, called "Erin, the Smile and the Tear in Thine Eyes," which expresses compassion for the Irish and support for famine relief being sent to them, a mildly radical position to take at the time.

62.   Addie Towns Arnold's father worked as a wool sorter in the Tilton Mills which were known locally, she says, as "the Corporation." The Towns family lived on the same street opposite both the Mark Bakers and, until the richer family moved to their magnificent new home further down the same street, the Alexander Hamilton Tiltons. Mrs. Arnold recalls how her mother would engage in a flurry of cooking and cleaning when Grandmother Baker came once a year to tea with her and comments thus on the social scene in Tilton: "In New England mill towns such as this the sense of caste was sometimes very deeply imbedded, and this was specially true of Tilton where the line was definitely drawn between the working people and the wealthier classes" (Arnold reminiscence, pp. 1–2). This was the line Mrs. Mary Patterson was later forced to cross when she lived as a separated then divorced woman, earning her own living, in Lynn, Massachusetts. Martha Baker Pilsbury, who was also widowed and impoverished while still a young mother, never had to cross this line since, with the help of relatives on both sides, and later of her married daughter, she was able to acquire a small house in Tilton and eke out a penurious but decent living on the fringe of her sister Abigail's affluence.

63.   For information on the labor movement in Lynn, see Alan Dawley, *Class and Community: The Industrial Revolution in Lynn* (Cambridge, Mass.: Harvard University Press, 1976); and Mary Blewitt, *Men, Women, and Work: Class, Gender and Protest in the New England Shoe Industry,* (Urbana: University of Illinois Press, 1988).

64.   Today, and perhaps at the time when she lived there, a portrait of President Lincoln occupies a prominent place in Mrs. Eddy's parlor at 12 Broad Street, Lynn. Mrs. Eddy's address was 8 Broad Street. The street addresses were later renumbered.

Chapter 5: Single Mother

1.   Mrs. Eddy's journal is in the Church History Department. This account has been published in "Family: The Carolina Glovers, Part VI," Longyear *Quarterly News* (Winter/Spring 1990–1991), p. 421.

2.   The letter George Baker subsequently wrote to the *Wilmington Chronicle,* expressing the family's thanks to everyone who had helped his sister, indicates that there was some mix-up in New York and that Cook was obliged to escort Mrs. Glover further north than planned before George was able to meet up with them.

3.   "Major Glover's Record as a Mason," *Miscellany,* p. 336.

4.   In her December 26, 1847, letter to her son George Sullivan Baker, Mrs. Abigail Baker notes that "Mary has had her Child baptized called his name George Sullivan agreable to her own desire." Exactly why his grandmother thought little Georgie had been named for his maternal uncle not his father is unclear. **Unless otherwise noted, all quotations from the Baker family letters are from the Longyear Museum.**

5.   It is, of course, possible that at some point Mary Patterson had learned some reliable method of birth control. In his essay "Family Limitation, Sexual Control, and Domestic Feminism in Victorian America," Daniel Scott Smith notes the radical decline in nineteenth-century marital fertility in America, and argues that this was owing to women's ability to control fertility not by birth control devices but by persuading their husbands to agree to practice coitus interruptus and abstinence. (In Cott and Pleck, eds., *A Heritage of Her Own,* pp. 226–27.) Ellen Rothman notes that Frederick Hollick's *The Marriage Guide: or, Natural History of Generation,* first published in 1850 and fairly well distributed, offered birth control advice to Americans, and that there were other sources of information (*Hearts and Hands,* pp. 140–41). Other historians of women have suggested that female invalidism was in many cases itself a means of ensuring sexual abstinence and hence preventing unwanted pregnancies. All of these factors may

have played a part in Mrs. Mary Patterson's marital relations with her second husband, Daniel Patterson.

6.   Lyman P. Powell was the first to suggest that the persistent back pain that Mrs. Eddy suffered from after 1845 was the result of some damage done during childbirth (Powell, 87). Medical opinion on such problems in Mrs. Glover's time was, at best, confused. Thus Mrs. R. B. Gleason, who ministered to hundreds of women in the Elmira Water-Cure establishment founded by herself and her husband, wrote in 1855: "a displacement of the uterus will cause a sense of weight, dragging, and throbbing, accompanied by pain in the back and in front of the hips. But inflammation, ulceration, and induration of this organ will produce precisely the same results; and sometimes mere nervous debility in these parts will induce these symptoms" (Cott, ed., *Root of Bitterness* [Boston: Northeastern University Press, 1972], p. 271).

7.   See Judith Walzer Leavitt, *Brought to Bed: Childbearing in America 1750–1950:*

> Middle-class women in the integrationist category, who utilized the wide variety of general practitioners, put themselves into the most unpredictable and risky situations. Their physicians exhibited a range of skills from poor to excellent, and were among those most often accused of practicing "meddlesome midwifery." These doctors may have put their parturient patients in greater jeopardy for infection and iatrogenic complications than they might have been with traditional midwife attendants. ([New York: Oxford University Press, 1986], pp. 82–83)

8.   Wilbur, p. 40. The work of Swiss infant psychoanalyst Bernard Cramer has shown the profound effect the early months or even weeks of a child's life can have on the development of the crucial relation with the mother, and thus on the child's development and self-identification. See Cramer, *The Importance of Being Baby,* trans. Gillian C. Gill (Reading, Mass.: Addison-Wesley, 1992).

9.   On the spread of public education in the United States in the early nineteenth century, the new mass readership, and the consequent burgeoning of print media of every kind, see Lawrence Buell, *New England Literary Culture from Revolution to Renaissance* (New York: Cambridge University Press, 1986); and *The Profession of Authorship in America, 1800–1870,* ed. Matthew J. Bruccoli (Columbus: Ohio State University Press, 1968).

10.   "A Fragment," *The Floral Wreath and Ladies' Monthly Magazine* (May 1844), p. 8.

11.   "The Test of Love," *The Covenant* (June 1847), p. 246.

12.   "The Immortality of the Soul," *The Covenant* (May 1847), pp. 193–94.

13.   In Chapter 3, when I was discussing Mrs. Eddy's literary efforts and aspirations before her first marriage, I commented that writing as a career was opening up to American women of her generation, and this is true. But the absolute number of women who were successful, whether by aesthetic standards or financial ones, was still very small, in comparison with that of men. In Britain and America, a few gifted and capable women such as Louisa May Alcott, Frances Trollope, and Margaret Oliphant, at the cost of enormous effort, did manage to support their families with their publishing income. But the spur of financial need did not lead to the production of great literature even for these gifted few, and it may well have inhibited it. Even Margaret Fuller, a superbly educated woman with strong connections to the literary elite of her day, someone who was acknowledged by many to have had one of the finest minds of her generation, had difficulty earning a living by her pen and never wrote the literary masterpiece she aspired to.

In *Victorian Wives* (New York: Saint Martin's Press, 1974) Katharine Moore describes how the widowed Margaret Oliphant was burdened with supporting not only her own three children, but, subsequently, her feckless brother and his four children:

Of course I had to face a prospect considerably changed by this great addition of the family. . . . I remember making a kind of pretence to myself that I had to think it over, to give up hopes I had of doing now my very best, and to set myself steadily to make as much money as I could. . . . but it had to be done and that was enough. One cannot be two things and serve two masters. Which was God and which was Mammon in that individual case it would be hard to say, perhaps, for once in a way, Mammon, which meant the money which fed my flock, was in a kind of poor way God. (Moore, p. 77)

Katharine Moore sees New England women as enjoying much greater freedom and opportunity for independence and achievement than did British women of the same period.

14.   Thus she told *Boston Globe* reporter Edwin J. Park in June 1907, "When my son was eight years old I determined to leave my father's house to pursue my literary work. . . . I was then able to earn $50 a week by my writings, and I had been offered $3000 a year to write for 'The Odd Fellows Covenant,' as it was called in those days." (This interview was published in the June 16, 1907, issue of the *Globe* and can also be found in Michael Meehan's book, *Mrs. Eddy and the Late Suit in Equity* [Concord, N.H.: Michael Meehan, 1908], p. 254.) This statement is an example of Mrs. Eddy's wishful thinking, a failure of memory, or a lie, depending on one's viewpoint.

15.   "Schoolteaching, a slight possibility for wives, was a likelier one for widows whose children had reached school age. One widow's 'cares,' as described by her sister in 1841, were 'enough to occupy all her time and thoughts almost. . . . [She] is teaching from 16 to 20 sholars [*sic*] boarding a young lady, and doing the housework, taking care of her children, &c' " (Cott, *The Bonds of Womanhood*, p. 45). For the fascinating story of Elizabeth Peabody's five years of unpaid work as teacher and amanuensis in Bronson Alcott's revolutionary school, see Louise Hall Tharp, *The Peabody Sisters of Salem* (Boston: Little, Brown, 1950).

16.   Mrs. Kimball's recollection is published in Peel, *Discovery,* p. 82. One of Mrs. Glover's charges in the short-lived Tilton school was Charles J. Eastman. He reappeared in 1881, when he advised Mrs. Eddy about chartering her own college and became a signer of the articles of agreement of the Massachusetts Metaphysical College.

17.   Four other examples of such young girls I shall be mentioning in the course of this book are the daughters of Sarah Crosby, Lucy Wentworth, Nadia Swartz Williams, and Mary Godfrey Parker.

18.   Reminiscences of Sarah Clement, later Mrs. Kimball, the niece of Mrs. Eddy's friend Augusta Holmes Swasey, whose family was close neighbors and friends of the Bakers and Tiltons in Sanbornton Bridge. Original in Church History Department. Sarah's father was, reputedly, Mark Baker's best financial advisor. Mrs. Kimball remembers attending Mrs. Glover's school for several years, but this does not seem to be possible.

19.   L11150. Original in Church History Department. Quoted in Peel, *Discovery,* pp. 82–83.

20.   See Peel (*Discovery,* pp. 91–92), for an incident from the Sarah Clement Kimball reminiscences. Original in the Church History Department.

21.   F00035. Original at Longyear Museum. This is the only point I have found in the Baker correspondence where Mrs. Glover expresses any disagreement with her mother or seems to chafe against the maternal authority. I can find no documentary evidence from this early period to support David Thomas's contention that Mary Baker Eddy's development was severely distorted by dependence on a clinging, overprotective mother. Obviously, many daughters do suffer from this problem, and modern psychoanalytic theory has much of interest to say about it, but I need more proof than Thomas offers in his book that this was Mary Baker Eddy's problem.

22.   James Smith wrote a very proper and high-flown letter to Mary on the occasion of her mother's death, signing himself "Semaj" (Longyear Museum).

23.   The album is now in the Church History Department. The tissue-paper-covered plates are undistinguished, but one of them, called "Virgin Bower," showing a young dark-haired woman at a window, is marked in Mrs. Eddy's handwriting: "This book was given me by J.H.B. because of the fancied resemblance this picture had to me years ago."

24.   Original in Church History Department.

25.   In fact, Bartlett died in 1849, as we shall see.

26.   See Gerda Lerner, "The Lady and the Mill Girl," in Cott and Pleck, *A Heritage of Her Own,* pp. 182–96; also Carroll Smith-Rosenberg, *Disorderly Conduct,* especially "Bourgeois Discourse and the Age of Jackson: An Introduction" ([New York: Oxford University Press, 1985], pp. 79–89).

27.   Mrs. Eddy moved in with the Tiltons in 1850, so these recorded reminiscences would refer to the years 1850–1853.

28.   In her "Reply to McClure's Magazine," Mrs. Eddy wrote:

> The various stories told by *McClure's Magazine* about my father spreading the road in front of his house with tan-bark and straw, and about persons being hired to rock me, I am ignorant of. Nor do I remember any such stuff as Dr. Patterson driving into Franklin, N.H., with a couch or cradle for me in his wagon. I only knew that my father and mother did everything they could think of to help me when I was ill. (*Prose Works, Miscellany,* p. 313)

29.   Addie Towns Arnold confirms that Mrs. Glover did have a porch swing, and that neighborhood boys were employed to swing her. Much of the Milmine account of the swinging seems incorrect or overblown, however. For example, if, as Milmine reports, Mary's nephew Albert Tilton was the boy chiefly employed to "rock Mrs. Glover" in her "cradle," then the cradling must have occurred between December 1850 and June 1853 when Mary was living with the Tiltons. However, this seems unlikely given that Albert was only six when his aunt moved in, and he was a weak, pampered child.

30.   This chair is now on exhibit in the Broad Street house in Lynn. Another rocking chair is on exhibit in the Longyear Museum collection. Mrs. Eddy donated a large painting of her Lynn rocker to the Mother's Room at the Mother Church. See Chapter 19.

31.   The charge of mesmerism in Tilton is denied specifically in the reminiscences of the Bakers' and Tiltons' neighbor, Addie Towns Arnold.

32.   F00035. Original at Longyear Museum.

33.   In his biography, Robert David Thomas seizes upon Dr. Ladd and his assumed long and close professional relationship with Mrs. Mary Baker Glover as a lead-in to a long section on the doctor-patient relationship and its psychoanalytic implications (Thomas, pp. 55–58). I think this is an example of Thomas allowing his interpretation to get ahead of his evidence. In the list of Mrs. Eddy's expenses between 1848 and 1850, owned by the Longyear Museum, there are notes of payments to Dr. Woodbury, to his associate Kelley, and to their boy for various visits and medications, but there is no record of a payment to Ladd. Mark Baker's account book indicates that he did a number of jobs for Nathaniel Ladd, and that his bill was settled in cash, not by the usual barter system. In the admittedly few letters from the period, mention is made of Drs. Benton and Whidden.

34.   F00035. Original letter at the Longyear Museum.

35.   Sarah Clement Kimball remembered Abigail around 1848 as being beautiful and dressed for effect: "She would wear white when no one else thought of doing so" (Sarah Clement Kimball reminiscences, Church History Department).

36.   See Peel, *Discovery,* p. 111, quoting Sarah Clement Kimball.

37.   F00031. Original at Longyear Museum.

38.   The entry mentioned earlier about John Bartlett's death was recorded by Mrs. Glover in her notebook directly after the entry for her mother. The double entry is in

smudged, blotted, hasty black ink characters: "Died at Sanbornton Bridge Nov. 21st 1849/ My precious Mother. Abigail A. Baker/65 years and six months/ Died at Sacramento City California/ Dec 11 1849 John H. Bartlett Esq. 27 years." Original in Church History Department.

39.   F00036. Original in Longyear Museum. The letter begins with Mary seeking to mend a quarrel, apparently sparked by some remark George had made about little Georgie to his mother, and which had given rise to an angry letter of protest from Mary. She says of herself, "My temper is hasty but not sullen," and though obviously continuing to think herself the wronged party, she wants bygones to be bygones.

40.   Mrs. Glover held on for a time to at least one small piece of her mother's furniture, a small drop-leaf table, but she later lost possession of it during the last years of her unfortunate marriage to Daniel Patterson. The piece, which has been a part of the Longyear permanent exhibit, came into the collection through a niece of Dr. Patterson's. See Longyear *Quarterly News* (Spring 1979).

41.   The will of Mrs. Elizabeth Baker's second husband is part of the Longyear collection, and it is clear that she was given a very advantageous settlement. Mr. Duncan seems to have chosen Elizabeth's son by her first marriage as his principal heir over his own son.

42.   Milmine and Cather, pp. 26–27.

43.   Mahala later married Russell Cheney. *McClure's* published companion portraits of the two Cheneys (January 1907, p. 232).

44.   There are two obvious inaccuracies in the account Mrs. Eddy provided in *Ret.* George was six not four when he was separated from his mother, and he left after not before his grandfather's remarriage. Given that Mrs. Eddy is summarizing in 1891 the events of 1850, both these inaccuracies can be seen as normal slips of memory, and both work against her not for her.

45.   F00030. Original at the Longyear Museum.

46.   Addie Towns Arnold says that she often discussed with her mother why Mrs. Glover had allowed her child to live with the Cheneys, and her mother was of the opinion that, having seen how small-town life had corrupted her brothers and their contemporaries, Mary wanted her boy out of Tilton. The Towns family were strong Methodists and perhaps were shocked by what they perceived as the alcoholism of the Tiltons and their friends.

47.   Elizabeth Earl Jones, "Mary Baker Eddy in Wilmington, N. Carolina."

48.   The mother of Henry James Sr., the novelist's grandmother, is a perfect and tragic example of a woman who devoted herself uncomplainingly and unstintingly to her husband, her children, their children, and her siblings' children, and who died largely unappreciated. After the death of her husband, Mrs. James had even to contest his will since this sought despotically and illegally to deprive her of the established rights of a surviving spouse. See Alfred Habegger, *The Father—A Life of Henry James, Sr.* (New York: Farrar, Straus, and Giroux, 1994), Chapter 1.

49.   See Gerda Lerner, *The Grimké Sisters from South Carolina* (Boston: Houghton Mifflin, 1967).

50.   Charles Dickens's portrayal of Mrs. Jellyby in *Bleak House* was both symptomatic and formative of mid-nineteenth-century social attitudes. Mrs. Jellyby—like many real-life middle-class women of the time—is absorbed in religious and reform movements, being especially dedicated to the mission to Borrioboula-Gha. While their mother writes tracts and attends meetings, the many little Jellybys run wild like savages, ill nourished and barely dressed. The eldest Miss Jellyby is sadly aware of her mother's domestic shortcomings and the trials of her younger siblings, but, deprived by her mother of all domestic training and forced to spend most of her time serving as her mother's amanuensis, she can offer only verbal comfort to her father, who wanders like a ragged ghost through his own home. Many of today's British women writers with deep roots in the nineteenth-century novel—such as Penelope Lively, Sue Townsend, Jeanette Winterson, and

Margaret Drabble—seem devoted in their fiction to disproving Dickens's thesis that women with children should leave politics and social activism alone and concentrate on child rearing. They present women protagonists who leave the home not to earn money but to promote the causes in which they believe, and whose neglect of their children's comfort is matched by a fierce love for them and a confident assumption that working for nuclear disarmament, racial justice, or religious conversion is ultimately in the children's interest, as well as their own. The real-life example of Nobel Peace Laureate and left-wing activist Alva Myrdal indicates that a daughter, as an adult, may be more able than is a son to accept the preference a mother has shown for large social issues over small familial duties. Whereas Myrdal's daughter Sissela Bok has written a loving but realistic book celebrating her mother's life, the eldest child and only son Jan Myrdal in his autobiography presents Alva as the Ice Queen, wholly self-centered and uncaring of her child's interests. From childhood on, Jan quarrelled loudly and violently with his father, but his hatred of his mother and determination to drag her down in public estimation is something deeper and nastier. See Sissela Bok, *Alva Myrdal* (Reading, Mass.: Addison Wesley, 1991); Jan Myrdal, *Childhood,* trans. Christine Swanson (Chicago: Lakeview Press, 1991).

51. To give one notable literary example of how this theme was worked out, the widowed mother in Frances Hodgson Burnett's *Little Lord Fauntleroy* sacrifices herself wholly to bringing up her son and never considers remarriage even when the child is taken from her by her dead husband's father. The book shows that a lengthy period of uncomplaining poverty, loneliness, and self-renunciation is necessary before the eponymous hero's mother, an American woman of modest but respectable background, can be seen as worthy to live with her child in his ancestral grandeur. Cedric, Lord Fauntleroy, himself emerges in the novel as a paragon who combines the religious morality of his American mother's family with the wealth and refinement of his English father. Written in 1886, *Little Lord Fauntleroy* was Frances Hodgson Burnett's first successful publication and launched her career as a writer. The book caused, in the words of a 1918 *Good Housekeeping* article, "a public delirium of joy . . . Young and old laughed and thrilled and wept over it together." Mrs. Burnett was born twenty-eight years after Mrs. Eddy, but her book, written for children, embodies peculiarly well the Victorian ideal of the widow's life, and her role in giving her son the moral vision that the male world lacks. In one of the odd little turns of fate that occur during one's research, it was only sometime after I reread *Little Lord Fauntleroy* and made the above parallel between it and Mrs. Eddy's situation as a widow that I discovered that, at the time she wrote her famous story, Frances Hodgson Burnett had become deeply interested in Christian Science.

Chapter 6: Marriage to Dr. Patterson

1. Baker papers, Longyear Museum. **Unless otherwise noted, all quotations from the Baker family letters are from the Longyear Museum.** Martha's testimony about Mary's health is invaluable, and it is important to make the connection between Mary's severe illness in late 1851 and young George's departure in May of that year. Nonetheless, Martha has a habitually emotive, highly charged style, and one always needs to take what she writes with a grain of salt, especially when she is discussing illness. Martha's recent loss of her husband and her own terrible ill health in the year 1850, which I discussed in detail in Chapter 5, had made her more likely than before to fear the worst and to use the rhetoric of disaster.

2. *Letters to the People on Health and Happiness* (New York: Harper, 1855). Sections of this work are quoted in Cott, ed., *Root of Bitterness,* and in Parker, ed., *Oven Birds.* The accuracy of Catharine Beecher's descriptions and statistics—if not of her explanations and remedies—is amply confirmed by biographies of women of this period. Invalidism, associated with somatic problems but from which a woman could be roused to normal activity by external circumstances, characterized lengthy periods of the life of almost every notable woman of the period—Clara Barton, Catharine Beecher, Harriet Beecher Stowe, Sophia Peabody, Alice James, Florence Nightingale, Elizabeth Barrett Browning,

Jane Carlyle, to name but a few. Michel Foucault is surely right when, in his *History of Sexuality,* he lists the hysterization of women as one of the four major elements in the sexualization of society in the nineteenth century. Perhaps the most eloquent and insightful firsthand accounts of nervous debilitation of this kind are given by Charlotte Perkins Gilman, both in her famous story "The Yellow Wallpaper" and in her autobiography.

3.   Janette Weller reminiscences, Church History Department. Weller says that Mrs. Eddy told her this story in confidence in 1884 after Weller made some chance reference to a Patterson she had known in her hometown of Littleton, New Hampshire.

4.   L08902. Original in the Church History Department. The letters between Mary Glover and Daniel Patterson were collected by John Dittemore, and Patterson's letters were published in full in Bates and Dittemore. The original courtship correspondence between the two is now in the Church History Department.

5.   Copybook 1, p. 28. Church History Department.

6.   Milmine and Cather, p. 31.

7.   Quotations from Patterson's letters are from Bates and Dittemore, pp. 60 and 63. Peel quotes extensively from the courtship letters in the first volume of his biography.

8.   Bates and Dittemore, p. 65.

9.   The most notoriously inaccurate biography of Daniel Patterson is to be found in the October 30, 1906, New York *World* front-page article on Mrs. Eddy, published without any author's byline but almost certainly issuing from the pen of Frederick Peabody. (See Parts Three and Four.) Patterson is introduced as a magnificent man, six feet, eight inches tall, a Harvard graduate, skilled in his profession, and with a lucrative practice. This is all complete fiction. Neglecting even elementary chronology, the article then goes on to assert that Patterson's wife deserted him when he enrolled in the army and was taken prisoner of the Southern forces in 1861, and that he was forced to give up his practice in Lynn and move to North Groton because of her involvement with Spiritualism. Again, apart from the imprisonment by Southern forces, all of this is wrong. The section on Patterson concludes elegiacally,

> There is no mystery connected with the last days of this good man. In despair he sought his old home Saco, Maine where he was born and where his father, also Daniel, and his mother, lived. He was then forty-four, still a splendid specimen of a man and in full possession of his faculties. He wandered back to the scenes of his childhood, but did not resume relations with those with whom he had been intimate in his youth. His small fortune was dissipated and he was almost penniless. Finally a time came when the weight of years and the encroachment of disease rendered him unfit to live an outdoor life, and he was forced to throw himself on the charity of the county. He entered the poorhouse and died there August 14, 1896, in his seventy-eighth year and was buried in the Potters Field.

The author of the article may have obtained some of these "facts" from Patterson's relatives in Saco, Maine, but he also invented some of them from whole cloth. By 1908 the team of fact checkers at *McClure's Magazine* knew enough to erase from their biographical series the obvious untruths about Harvard, the lucrative practice, and the enrollment in the army, but they still gave the general impression that Patterson was a good man who had been destroyed by his beloved wife's eccentric behavior and cruel desertion.

10.   This portrait, reproduced on the cover and frontispiece of this volume, was first discovered by Lyman Powell in the research for his 1930 book (*A Lifesize Portrait*). It was in the possession of the daughter of Mrs. Abigail Tilton's trusted friend and business partner, Selwyn Peabody.

11.   For the attraction of the tubercular look in women in the nineteenth century, see

René Dubos, *The White Plague* (Boston: Little, Brown, 1952); and Susan Sontag, *Illness as Metaphor* (New York: Farrar, Straus and Giroux, 1978).

12. In her book on Mrs. Eddy, Sibyl Wilbur offers a spirited dialogue between Mary and Abigail that was meant to have occurred at a gathering at the Tilton house. Hugh Studdert Kennedy also uses the incident. The slavery issue came up, and Abigail publicly asked what Mary's views were on the subject. Mary declared her belief that "not only the North but the South suffered from the continuance of slavery and its spread to other states; that the election of Franklin Pierce would tend to inflame the situation, and she did not think his election would benefit the country as a whole. Abigail Tilton was aghast, but when she asked Mary how she dared to make such a statement in her house, Mary replied quite firmly that she dared say what she believed in any house" (Studdert Kennedy, p. 84). Wilbur, the source of this incident, names no sources, merely stating that the scene "is still remembered in that community," that is Sanbornton Bridge/Tilton (Wilbur, p. 50). Robert Peel, on the other hand, pours cold water on the idea that Mrs. Glover was openly taking an abolitionist position in 1852, noting that Mrs. Glover campaigned hard for Franklin Pierce, an anti-abolitionist candidate for president in 1852, and citing two poems she published in July and October of that year (*Discovery,* pp. 88 and 326, n. 50). Robert David Thomas seems to me to have found the right balance, summarizing Mrs. Eddy's letters of 1852–1853 to prove that she shows a keen interest in various reform movements (Thomas, p. 66). My conclusion is that Mrs. Glover had moved far more toward the abolitionist position than her sister Abigail and father, and she may well have been sufficiently provoked by Abigail on one occasion actually to express her still inchoate views. Her public support of Pierce for president does not disprove her new opposition to slavery, since the Pierce family was closely allied with the Bakers, and pride at the prospect of seeing a personal friend in the White House often prevails over political principle. Love of her dead brother Albert, if nothing else, could have led Mrs. Glover to support his close friend and law partner.

13. Testimony of George Washington Glover III, as recorded by Jewel Spangler Smaus, "Family — From New England to the Black Hills, Part II," Longyear *Quarterly News* (Winter 1982–1983): 302.

14. Weller reminiscences, Church History Department. I believe the main line of the account Mrs. Eddy gave to Janette Weller, but I am not sure that she found Daniel Patterson personally repugnant. Mrs. Weller had known Patterson during his last years in her hometown of Littleton, New Hampshire, and she knew him to be a strange, puzzling man, with a particularly bad reputation with women. Weller had been shocked and horrified to learn by chance that her adored Mrs. Eddy had once been Mrs. Patterson, and Mrs. Eddy may have felt obliged to echo her new friend's distaste. Her feelings for Patterson in 1853 were much more complicated, and I think she was at least as attracted as repelled by his courtship at that time.

15. *Ret.,* p. 20. Mrs. Eddy made the same point in an unpublished statement which her secretary Lewis Strang recorded in 1906, and which Strang subsequently passed on to Alfred Farlow in January 1907 when the latter was marshalling Mrs. Eddy's rebuttal of the *McClure's* series: "When my father married the second time, he refused to have George in the house any longer. . . . I married the second time, Dr. Patterson, for the express purpose of having the boy with me, but my husband thought that I cared more for George than I did for him, and again I had to send my son away. The last time I saw George he was about ten years old." Farlow Papers, Church History Department.

16. Dakin is particularly eloquent on Mrs. Eddy's lack of proper maternal feeling. For Dakin's relationship with his own unconventional mother, see the Appendix.

17. "Family — From New England to the Black Hills, Longyear *Quarterly News* 20, no. 3 (Autumn 1983): 315.

18. Peel, *Discovery,* p. 116. Lucy Clark Barker wrote Mrs. Eddy in 1890 about this experience. Original in Church History Department. There are other later indications

from the Lynn period that Mrs. Patterson would come in to offer assistance to patients overcome by the dental treatment.

19. Peel, *Discovery,* p. 117.

20. See Richard C. Molloy, "North Groton—Then and Now," Longyear *Quarterly News* (Spring 1980).

21. Meyer, *The Positive Thinkers* (Garden City, N.Y.: Doubleday, 1965), p. 47.

22. Milmine and Cather, pp. 35–36.

23. Mrs. Kimball's recollection is published in Peel, *Discovery,* p. 329, n. 109.

24. Bates and Dittemore, p. 73; also Peel, *Discovery,* pp. 140–41. Peel says that while the dispute between Patterson and the Wheets could have been ascribed to Patterson's trifling with the affections of the elder Wheet's wife, Myra Smith testified that the men quarrelled over a load of wood, purchased by Patterson but not paid for.

25. Wilbur, pp. 59–60.

26. Peel, *Discovery,* p. 119.

27. Unpublished reminiscences by Elias F. Bailey—who testified that Mrs. Eddy was "a lover of children and in return all children loved her"—and others who knew her during this period are referred to in Peel, *Discovery,* pp. 122–23, and notes. Sybil Wilbur notes that Mrs. Kidder was a confirmed Spiritualist who tried hard to convert Mrs. Eddy to that belief (Wilbur, p. 62).

28. See Studdert Kennedy, p. 93. This incident is found on p. 156 of the current edition of *Science and Health.* Stephen Gottschalk has argued strongly that homeopathy was at least as important to the then Mrs. Patterson as Quimby's doctrine would become, and in terms of her intellectual development, this is probably correct. As a biographer, I have chosen to focus much more on Quimbyism since Mrs. Eddy's supposedly unacknowledged debt to Quimby has been considered to be her Achilles' heel and therefore the designated point to attack, for all her opponents. Equally, she never had to defend herself against accusations of having been a homeopathist as she did for having, allegedly, been a Spiritualist. Quimbyism is discussed in detail in Chapters 7 and 8.

29. Powell, *Christian Science: The Faith and Its Founder* (New York: G. P. Putnam's Sons, 1930). One characteristic plot element in nineteenth-century fiction and biography is the able young man who falls madly in love with a silly, helpless, but charming damsel, marries her, and then finds his life ruined by her chronic inability to keep house. The marriage of David and Dora Copperfield is perhaps the most famous fictional example of this problem, and Dickens resolves it by making Dora die young, thus releasing David to marry the highly efficient and intelligent Agnes Wickfield. In real life neither Dickens nor his contemporary Thackeray could find such neat solutions to the housekeeping problem.

30. In Sibyl Wilbur's *Human Life* series there are two pictures of Myra Smith Wilson, taken around 1854 and around 1906, and in both there is clearly something abnormal about her eyes.

31. In her "Reply to McClure's Magazine," Mrs. Eddy wrote that when they first came to North Groton she and Dr. Patterson employed a housekeeper of very strong opinions. After Mrs. Patterson took in Myra Smith, the housekeeper told her that she must choose between Myra and herself. Mary Patterson unhesitatingly chose Myra, and the housekeeper left (*Miscellany,* p. 311).

32. Bates and Dittemore, p. 72.

33. See Jewel Spangler Smaus, "Family—From New England to the Black Hills, Part II," p. 302.

34. Peel, *Discovery,* p. 120. It seems likely that when in June 1857 Martha Pilsbury wrote to Martha Rand Baker "what dreadful news you give me of Sam," she is referring not to her brother but to the death of her nephew Samuel, who died at sea around this period. The deaths of nieces and nephews were to continue. In 1860 Eliza Baker, Samuel's daugh-

ter, died in Sanbornton Bridge at her aunt Abigail's house at the age of twenty-five. In what must have been a reenactment of horror, Abigail's own daughter Evelyn would die sixteen years later, at the age of twenty-two.

35.   George Glover III also said that his father never forgave Cheney for refusing to allow him to take to Minnesota his precious collection of minerals. George's fascination with the mica mine in North Groton and his lost collection of mineral samples were to lead to a lifelong fascination with prospecting and mines.

36.   *Ret.,* pp. 20–21. The section in italics was published in the 1891 edition and later omitted.

37.   Peel, *Discovery,* pp. 117–18.

38.   That George had great affection for Mahala is indicated by the fact that he returned to the Cheney farm in 1865 when he was invalided out of the army, and he remained there until Mahala died on Christmas Eve, 1866.

39.   Smaus, "Family—From New England to the Black Hills, Part IV," Longyear *Quarterly News* (Autumn 1983), pp. 314–16. Despite help from his kin, who had prospered in the area, Russell Cheney finally went bankrupt and lost his property in 1870.

40.   Elmira Smith Wilson testified: "Dr. Patterson . . . had bought a piece of land without consulting his wife and of which she did not approve, but in her loyalty to him, . . . she consented to his mortgaging a part of her own household goods, six upholstered chairs, one large mirror, a large dictionary, also her gold watch chain, the mortgage was afterwards foreclosed owing to the doctor's inability to pay the price, and she lost these things." Elmira Smith Wilson reminiscences, the Church History Department. Mrs. Eddy managed to hold on to her first husband's watch, which in several later photographs she is shown wearing on a long chain round her neck. This watch was given to her son and passed on in the Glover family until it was acquired for the Longyear collection.

41.   Powell, p. 292, n. 37.

42.   Church History Department. Although the "homestead" was apparently sold in September, the Pattersons' move took place the following March.

43.   Mrs. Eddy's spiritual state during this long trial is obviously crucial, but there is very little documentation on it since she herself wrote so little, and that little has remained largely unpublished. The most informed and insightful conjectures as to the development of Mrs. Patterson's thought in the Groton years are those of Robert Peel who devotes some of his most beautiful and moving pages to what he calls the "wilderness" years. Every reader interested in Christian Science and Mrs. Eddy should go back to sections 3–5 of Chapter 4 of Peel's first volume, *Mary Baker Eddy: The Years of Discovery.*

Part Two: Dr. Mary B. Glover Eddy: 1863–1882

1.   Measures of fame and influence are difficult to establish, but to mention just a few, in 1932 the *Ladies' Home Journal,* at the request of the National Council of Women, conducted a poll to establish the most important women leaders of the last hundred years. Mrs. Eddy came in number one. In its Series Announcement of February 1907, *Human Life* referred to Mrs. Eddy as "the most famous, interesting and powerful woman in America, if not in the world, today." *McClure's Magazine* in its editorial announcement for the Eddy biography called Mrs. Eddy "one of the richest women in the United States. She is more than that—she is the most powerful American woman." In 1995 Mrs. Eddy was finally admitted to the National Women's Hall of Fame.

2.   Julius Dresser, *The True History of Mental Science* (Boston: A. Mudge, 1887); quoted by Horatio Dresser in *A History of the New Thought Movement* (New York: Thomas Y. Crowell, 1919), p. 24.

3.   Mark Twain gives no doubt the most spirited version of this argument, but it is taken up in different tones by Frederick Peabody and Milmine and Cather, in Lyman

Powell's first work on Mrs. Eddy, in Dakin, Bates and Dittemore, and in H. A. L. Fisher (*Our New Religion: An Examination of Christian Science* [New York: Jonathan Cape and Harrison Smith, 1930]). When Livingston Wright published in the New York *World* in 1906 the assertion that his friend the Reverend Wiggin had ghostwritten the later editions of *Science and Health,* Twain/Clemens wrote to the author thanking him for providing proof of what Twain had earlier asserted in his *Cosmopolitan* series, merely on the basis of his long experience as a writer and on his literary flair—that Mrs. Eddy was incapable of writing those sections of *Science and Health* that Twain found compelling. See Chapter 24.

Chapter 7: "A Devilish Smart Woman"

1. Wilbur, p. 65. Wilbur seems to be summarizing testimony given not only by Myra Smith but by Sarah C. Turner, a niece of Russell Cheney, and Sarah Clement Kimball about the public reaction to Mrs. Patterson in Tilton, Franklin, and Groton in the 1850s. They report that Mary was always impeccably dressed in black silk when she went out, and she carried herself with such an air that people whispered that "she walked on her uppers."

2. Bates and Dittemore note that this poem, lightly revised, is retained in Mrs. Eddy's poetic works, under the title "Constancy."

3. Peel, *Discovery,* p. 121. This is also partially quoted in Bates and Dittemore, p. 69. The original letter is in the Church History Department.

4. Smaus, "Family—From New England to the Black Hills, Part III," Longyear *Quarterly News* (Spring 1983): p. 306.

5. Peel, *Discovery,* p. 144.

6. David Hall of Iowa, a soldier who wrote and read many letters for illiterate comrades in arms, later claimed to have done Glover's correspondence to his mother.

7. One of the most egregious lies which Frederick Peabody later spread about Mrs. Eddy in his lecture and pamphlets was that she had divorced her second husband while he was a soldier captured by the Southern forces. Faced with the uncomfortably hard evidence that Dr. Patterson had not been a soldier and that he and his wife separated and then divorced well after the Civil War was over, Peabody in his final book on Mrs. Eddy merely repeats his former allegations as possible facts.

8. In 1899 John Patterson of Saco, Maine, Daniel Patterson's brother, wrote to Mrs. Eddy reminding her that she had borrowed $30 from him in 1861 to expedite Daniel's release, and asking that she now return the money with interest, which he calculated at a further $64. Mrs. Eddy duly authorized a check for $94.

9. Studdert Kennedy (pp. 101–102) suggests a rather different scenario to explain how Mrs. Patterson became interested in travelling to Portland. He cites a long and highly favorable article on Quimby published in the Lebanon, New Hampshire, *Free Press* in December 1860 which was reprinted in other newspapers and was likely to have reached the attention of that avid newspaper reader Mrs. Mary Patterson. At his wife's instigation, then, Daniel Patterson wrote to Dr. Quimby about his possible visit to Concord, and Quimby replied and included his circular with the letter.

10. V03341. The original letter is in the Library of Congress, Washington, D.C. This excerpt is published in Peel, *Discovery,* p. 146.

11. According to Studdert Kennedy, Mrs. Patterson was accompanied to Hill by a trained nurse-companion, Miss Susan Ward, all at the expense of her sister Abigail (Studdert Kennedy, p. 106).

12. L14349. Original in the Church History Department. This is published in Peel, *Discovery,* p. 145.

13.   Peel and Thomas give good summaries of hydropathy, but the best account I have found is Penny Hansen's in her unpublished thesis, "Women's Hour: Feminist Implications of Mary Baker Eddy's Christian Science Movement, 1885–1910" (Ph.D. diss., University of California at Irvine, 1981).

14.   This is the account Mrs. Eddy gave of how she came to find herself in Portland in "Inklings Historical," *Mis.,* p. 378.

15.   The original letters Mrs. Mary Patterson wrote to the Quimby family are deposited in the Library of Congress. The letters were first published in full in the first edition of Horatio Dresser's *The Quimby Manuscripts: Showing the Discovery of Spiritual Healing and the Origin of Christian Science* (New York: Thomas Y. Crowell, 1921). Dresser's book was reissued in 1976 (Secaucus, N.J.: Citadel Press), but I have used the 1921 edition. **Unless otherwise noted, all quotations from Mrs. Patterson's correspondence with the Quimbys are from this source.**

16.   In one of his many garbled and slipshod summaries, Martin Gardner writes: "Her sister Abigail, who often helped Mrs. Eddy out financially, considered Quimby a fraud. It led to a rift between the two sisters that was never healed. Mrs. Eddy's other sister, Martha, and a brother, Albert, also had no use for Quimby or for Christian Science" (Gardner, p. 39). Whether or not Abigail Tilton thought at any point that Quimby was a fraud, she certainly travelled to Portland after her sister returned, and she sought Quimby's help in treating her own physical problems and her son Albert Tilton's alcoholism and smoking habit. Mary and Abigail quarrelled over many things, but Quimby did not cause a permanent rift between them. As for Mary's brother Albert, he might well have dismissed Quimby as a fraud had he not died some twenty years earlier!

17.   Peel, *Discovery,* pp. 120–21.

18.   Milmine and Cather, p. 56. I suspect the author is quoting Mrs. Annetta Dresser here, but no name is given—perhaps because the Dresser name was too well established as the enemy of Christian Science, and Milmine wants the testimony to appear quite free from bias.

19.   Quimby left behind him a mass of documentation which is now divided between three library collections: the Library of Congress contains the most important holding, including the letters Mary Patterson and her husband exchanged with the Quimby family. The rest is divided between the Special Collections section of the Mugar Memorial Library at Boston University, and the Houghton Library at Harvard University. I have found the B.U. collection most interesting because it contains documents, including three Quimby autograph letters, which Horatio Dresser decided, for various reasons, not to include or refer to in his edition of the Quimby papers. The most important published work on Quimby is Ervin Seale's three-volume edition of his works, *Phineas Parkhurst Quimby: The Complete Writings* (Marina del Rey, Calif.: Devorss and Co., 1988); hereafter cited in the text as Seale. Still invaluable because of its status in the history of the Quimby–Christian Science controversy is Horatio Dresser's *The Quimby Manuscripts.* Horatio Dresser's introductory chapters to *The Quimby Manuscripts* reprised much of the material he had already published, notably in his 1919 book *A History of the New Thought Movement,* also published by Thomas Y. Crowell. Both books relied heavily on the works of Horatio's parents: his father Julius A. Dresser's *The True History of Mental Science,* the text of his 1887 lecture first published in Boston by A. Mudge and Son, edited by Horatio, and reissued in 1899; and his mother, Annetta Seabury Dresser's *The Philosophy of P. P. Quimby* (Boston: Geo. H. Ellis, 1895). The most valuable analyses of Quimby and his work are to be found in Charles S. Braden's *Spirits in Rebellion: The Rise and Development of New Thought* (Dallas: Southern Methodist University Press, 1963); and Catherine L. Albanese, *Nature Religion in America: From the Algonkian Indians to the New Age* (Chicago: University of Chicago Press, 1990). Information on Quimby's life, particularly on the years before he set up his practice in Portland, is sketchy. The most important and most interesting sources are the autobiographical sections of the Quimby papers. George

Quimby, Phineas's son, also contributed a biographical essay on his father to the *New England Magazine* in March 1888, but this, although obviously valuable, was too much framed by the ongoing controversy, too much an *apologia pro vita eius,* to be taken at face value. The Church History Department at the Mother Church in Boston has an interesting collection of reminiscences about Quimby by fellow townsfolk in Belfast and Portland and by former patients. Basic research, notably in newspaper archives and town records, is still needed to illuminate many dark years in Quimby's life that his apologists have chosen not to discuss.

20.   This is the information given in a description of P. P. Quimby by Horatio Dresser in *The Quimby Manuscripts,* p. 30. Dresser seems singularly unaware that, even as he argues that Quimby had long ceased to be a mesmerist when he took up healing, the physical description he gives of Quimby has strong mesmeric connotations.

21.   Between 1834 and 1850, Quimby patented at least three inventions: a version of the chainsaw, a special lock for fastening chests and doors, and a steering apparatus for boats. For the design drawings, patents, and business letters relating to these inventions, see the Boston University collection.

22.   A section of Burkmar's diary is reproduced in Seale, and it indicates to me that he was a young man with much more intelligence and acumen than his partner Quimby gave him credit for. Particularly interesting, given Burkmar's famed talent while in trance for describing distant and unknown places, are the detailed descriptions of buildings Burkmar gets to see on his travels. My reading in mesmeric literature has led me to doubt the whole nineteenth-century assumption, which P. P. Quimby fully endorsed, that the mesmerist is the strong and gifted mind and the subject the weak one. Given that mesmerists were usually older men and subjects were either women, young boys like Burkmar or Puységur's Jean, or non-Europeans such as the Haitians studied by the younger Puységur brother, or the Indians studied by James Esdaile, this assumption has sexist, racist, and colonialist implications which deserve more study. In my discussions on mesmerism throughout this book, I have relied on the following works: Stefan Zweig, *Mental Healers: Franz Anton Mesmer, Mary Baker Eddy, Sigmund Freud,* trans, Eden and Cedar Paul (Garden City, N.Y.: Garden City Publishing, 1932); H. B. Gibson, *Hypnosis: Its Nature and Therapeutic Uses* (New York: Taplinger, 1977); Slater Brown, *The Heyday of Spiritualism* (New York: Hawthorn Books, 1970); Howard Kerr, *Mediums, and Spirit-Rappers, and Roaring Radicals: Spiritualism in American Literature, 1850–1900* (Urbana: University of Illinois Press, 1972); Johanna Johnston *Mrs. Satan: The Incredible Saga of Victoria C. Woodhull* (New York: Putnam, 1967); Ruth Brandon, *The Spiritualists: The Passion for the Occult* (New York: Knopf, 1983); Ann Braude, *Radical Spirits: Spiritualism and Women's Rights in Nineteenth-Century America* (Boston: Beacon, 1989); and Adam Crabtree, *From Mesmer to Freud: Magnetic Sleep and the Roots of Psychological Healing* (New Haven: Yale University Press, 1993). Henri Ellenberger's magisterial work *The Discovery of the Unconscious* (New York: Basic Books, 1970) was also as usual invaluable.

23.   Seale, vol. 3, "My Conversion," pp. 176–77. Quimby's autobiographical sketch was first published in Julius Dresser's book *The True History of Mental Science.*

24.   "P. P. Quimby is prepared to execute Daguerreotypes . . . perhaps Mr. Quimby can throw you into a magnetic state and then change your features to what you were in younger days." Newspaper files in the Church History Department.

25.   See the biographical sketch of his father, which George Quimby published in *New England Magazine,* March 1888. In the earliest period at least, daguerreotyping involved holding plates over vaporized mercury, an extremely toxic process.

26.   Charles S. Braden says that Quimby claimed to have treated some twelve thousand individual patients in the Portland period, 1859–1865 (*Spirits in Rebellion,* p. 63). This seems an impossibly high number.

27.   Ibid., p. 61.

28.   Annetta Seabury Dresser, *The Philosophy of P. P. Quimby,* p. 44.

29.   The wife of a prominent Maine stove manufacturer and state senator, Mrs. Hodsdon never became a Christian Scientist and regarded all alternative healers with a skepticism bordering on contempt. The Hodsdon reminiscences are in the Church History Department.

30.   An entry in Julius Dresser's diary also comments on this remarkable recovery:

> The most peculiar person I have seen of late is Mrs. Patterson, the authoress, who came last Friday, a week ago today, from Vail's Water-cure in Hill, N.H., where Melville, Fanny Bass, and I were; & is now under Dr. Quimby, & boarding also, at Mrs. Hunter's. She was only able to get here, & no one else thought she could live to travel so far, but today she, with Mrs. Hunter & sister, Nettie [i.e., Annetta Seabury] & I went up into the dome of the 'New City Building' up seven flights of stairs, or 182 steps. So much for Dr. Quimby's doings. (Original in Church History Department; quoted in Bates and Dittemore, p. 88)

31.   The full text of both of these letters is quoted in Milmine and Cather, pp. 59–60, and extensive sections appear in Dakin, Bates and Dittemore, Peel, and so forth.

32.   Portland *Evening Courier,* probably November 9 or 10.

33.   For a fuller discussion of this little press campaign, most specifically of the detailed description of Quimby's theory of healing published in the Portland *Advertiser* of March 22, 1862, and signed simply "D," see the first volume of Peel's biography (*Discovery*), especially Appendix B. Peel argues persuasively that "D" was Julius Dresser, not Emma Ware, as Annetta Seabury Dresser later alleged in her 1895 book on Quimby.

34.   In his unpublished manuscript on the Quimby controversy (see the Longyear Museum) Frederick Remington makes this point, and I found in the Church History Department a little pencilled memorandum indicating that Mrs. Patterson's sister-in-law Martha Rand Baker was also under the impression that she had subsidized her stay in Portland by writing letters praising Quimby.

35.   Despite what Peel argues, based on the evidence of Christian Scientists who had been former patients, Quimby did "talk Bible" with at least some of his religiously minded patients, and he did compare his healing work to that of Jesus Christ. This is the testimony of the Emily Pierce letters of 1860 (see note 55, following) unimpeachable because never published. Mrs. Pierce wrote: "You know he cares nothing about your sickness and does not even ask you where you have pain. His most interesting and most usual conversation is from the Bible and if I get no physical benefit from him I shall value greatly the ideas wh [*sic*] imparts—He reads the whole Scripture spiritually and makes many passages wh have always been almost absurd and wh one always wished out of the Bible full of truth." Original letter in the Church History Department.

36.   This letter has a certain importance as it is one of the rare pages of Quimby's "writings" that exist in autograph.

37.   All the letters Mrs. Eddy wrote to Phineas and to George Quimby were circulated, quoted from, and copied during her lifetime, and they were finally published by Horatio Dresser in *The Quimby Manuscripts.* First published in 1921, this book was quickly recalled when the Church of Christ, Scientist threatened to take Dresser and the publishers to court for publishing without permission a set of letters written by Mrs. Eddy that were in the possession of the Quimby family. The book was reissued including extensive paraphrasings of the letters instead of the verbatim texts. The action taken by the Church was, however, a Pyrrhic victory, becoming a famous example of Christian Science's efforts to stifle all criticism and thus serving to confirm Dresser's assertion that Quimby was the movement's originator. Large sections of the letters are to be found in Milmine and Cather and the biographies derived from Milmine.

38.   Mesmer in his "Twenty Seven Propositions on Animal Magnetism" had pointed the way to the theory of absent treatments: "13. Experiments show the passage of a substance whose rarified nature enables it to penetrate all bodies without appreciable loss of activ-

ity. 14. Its action is exerted at a distance, without the aid of an intermediate body" (James Wyckoff, *Franz Anton Mesmer: Between God and Devil,* [Englewood Cliffs, N.J.: Prentice-Hall, 1975], p. 76). Mesmer attempted to produce his effects on patients through an intervening wall, and the other early pioneer of hypnosis, or mesmerism, the Marquis de Puységur, pushed these experiments much further.

39.   See Richard A. Nenneman, *Persistent Pilgrim: The Life of Mary Baker Eddy* (Etna, N.H.: Nebbadoon Press, 1997), p. 75.

40.   From a letter Mrs. Crosby wrote to Allan A. Beauchamp in 1909. See Powell, p. 110.

41.   Bates and Dittemore, p. 95.

42.   Original letter in the Quimby collection, Mugar Memorial Library, Boston University.

43.   The Crosby letters are in the Church History Department. Milmine and Cather, and the subsequent biographers who have accepted their account, paint Mrs. Crosby as a blameless and respectable lady who fell on difficult times in the late 1860s but made her way by hard work and enterprise. Mrs. Crosby was a much more interesting character and a much less reliable witness than Milmine made her out to be, and as we shall see in later chapters, she had very strong motives of financial gain and personal animus to make sensational claims about Mrs. Eddy.

44.   This was a revised version of the 1849 poem "To My Mother in Heaven."

45.   H. Dresser, ed., *The Quimby Manuscripts,* p. 438.

46.   In 1863 she published some heavy-handed tributes to the tourist wonders of the town, some even more leaden "Wayside Thoughts" on contemporary issues such as slavery, and some five poems, new or recycled.

47.   In *Mary Baker Eddy: The Years of Trial* (New York: Holt, Rinehart and Winston, 1971; hereafter cited as *Trial*) Robert Peel quotes two important and hitherto unknown archival documents which prove that on two occasions former students of Mary Baker Eddy's wrote to Portland to inquire if P. P. Quimby had left any manuscripts. The first letter, written in 1872 by Peter Sim, but, according to Peel, at the instigation of Richard Kennedy, met with no answer. The second, written by Daniel Spofford in 1878, was answered by George Quimby, who said that his father had left manuscripts but had never published anything. A few months later, George remembered Mrs. Eddy as "very intelligent and smart," and a woman who had taken a great interest in his father's ideas, and he asked Spofford to send him a copy of her recently published *Science and Health*. In a later letter to Spofford, George Quimby noted that there were parts of Mrs. Eddy's book that he believed were grounded in his father's thinking, and other parts that were quite different from it. He doubted that the book was practical enough to find many readers. In his letters to Spofford, George Quimby shows a lack of animosity toward Mrs. Eddy, which is surprising given the deep dislike and distaste he was later to express for her. (See Peel, *Trial,* pp. 126–28.) It seems clear to me that it was the Dressers who really poisoned George's mind and convinced him that Mrs. Eddy was his father's enemy and not to be trusted. If the evidence of the Boston University documents is correct, it was some years after corresponding with Spofford and reading *Science and Health* that George reclaimed his father's papers from the Wares.

48.   In an unpublished letter in 1904 to Minot J. Savage, a wealthy clergyman dedicated to combatting Christian Science and perennially anxious to get hold of the Quimby writings, George Quimby stated that his father had allowed dozens of his students or patients to make copies of his writings. This seems a great exaggeration. The importance of the Quimby writings became much publicized in the last two decades of the nineteenth century, and only six sets of copies of parts of the alleged manuscript holdings are known to have existed in the period before Quimby's death in 1866—those of Mrs. Eddy, the Dresser parents, of Sarah and Emma Ware, of Mrs. Sarah Crosby, and Miss S. M. Deering,

later Mrs. Sabine. Only Mrs. Eddy's and the Dressers' copies remained outside the control of the Quimby family.

49.   In February 1899 Mrs. Eddy wrote in the *Christian Science Sentinel*: "Quotations—published, purporting to be Dr. Quimby's own words — were written while I was his patient in Portland and holding long conversations with him on my views of mental therapeutics." An angry George Quimby denied categorically that Mrs. Eddy made any contribution to his father's writings, and none has been found among the Quimby papers. Unfortunately, given that George Quimby had exclusive possession of those papers for many decades, and that he made no secret that he loathed and distrusted Mrs. Eddy, we have only his word as an honest man that he or an associate did not tamper with the evidence. In his unpublished manuscript on the Quimby controversy, Frederick Remington notes that several of Horatio Dresser's efforts to assign Quimby's work to the period, as it were, BE—before Mrs. Eddy!—are inaccurate. Essays in which reference is made to Lincoln's assassination are dated 1863—i.e., two years before the event!—and to one crucial piece, "Aristocracy and Democracy," cited by the Dressers to prove Quimby's use of a key Christian Science term, Horatio gives the date of 1863, forgetting, it seems, that by then Mrs. Patterson had already paid her first visit to Portland, and thus actually supporting Mrs. Eddy's account of her influence on Quimby.

50.   George Quimby, "Phineas Parkhurst Quimby," *New England Magazine* (March 1888), p. 274.

51.   H. Dresser, ed., *The Quimby Manuscripts,* p. 5.

52.   Wilbur, *Human Life,* April 1907, 98. Wilbur has often been accused of bias and misrepresentation, but her report of what George Quimby said rings true, since he said much the same in private letters to Mrs. Eddy's opponents. Even the Dressers never claimed to have been allowed to see the scraps of writing from which the famous copies had been made. Indeed, when A. J. Swarts, one of Mrs. Eddy's alternative healing rivals, came to Portland in 1888 to interview George Quimby and consult the Quimby papers for an article on Quimby and Mrs. Eddy for his Chicago *Mental Science Magazine,* he got to see even less than Sibyl Wilbur or Willa Cather saw. According to the account of Swarts's visit given by Horatio Dresser in *The Quimby Manuscripts,* George read aloud extracts from his father's work and then allowed the Chicagoan to read "excerpts from the press concerning Quimby's work" (p. 16). On the basis of this interview, Swarts felt able to write a piece confidently asserting that he had been given proof that P. P. Quimby was the real father of Christian Science and the author of *Science and Health.* Horatio Dresser, for his part, seemed even in 1921 quite unaware of the shortcomings of this kind of "proof."

53.   To give some sense of Quimby's style, the following spellings appear in two letters to patients which Quimby drafted in his own hand on May 10, 1861, and April 27, 1862—shortly, it will be noticed, before Mrs. Eddy came to Portland: *seames/seems; coman/common; shur/sure; sistom/system; youses/uses; nuse/news; promes/promise; coff/cough; right/write; incorrage/encourage.* It is illuminating to compare these efforts to the smooth, well-penned, grammatical missives sent out under Quimby's signature in his final years, presumably by his son George (Boston University Collection).

54.   *Mis.,* Chapter 10, "Inklings Historic," p. 379, written in 1896. Mrs. Eddy had written two poems in praise of Quimby, one while she was in Portland, one after his death.

55.   Mugar Memorial Library, Boston University. Quimby's failings as a therapist and theorist of cure are dramatically confirmed by two unpublished letters now in the Church History Department written by Mrs. Emily Pierce to her sister Nelly Ware, wife of Joseph Ware, the brother of Sarah and Emma Ware. Emily Pierce came to Portland in the spring of 1860 to see if P. P. Quimby could do anything to ease her increasingly serious health problems. Mrs. Pierce died in 1866, and the letters she wrote to Nelly on February 28 and March 6, 1860, and which remained in her husband Lewis Pierce's papers until his death many years later, are very poignant, revealing an unusually intelligent, educated, percep-

tive, amusing, and lovable woman. The account she gives her sister of what exactly passed between her and Quimby and her evaluation of his theories and his treatment, are small jewels which deserve to be quoted at length. Mrs. Pierce was an unusual patient in that she wished to be cured by Quimby, strove to cooperate with him as exactly as possible yet divined that, apart from a reassuring presence, some picturesque if derivative opinions, and an ability to engender an odd sensation of heat on the part of her body on which he placed his hand, his treatment consisted of repeating back to her with authority what he had heard her say about her own health. Refusing to allow herself to supply the wanted clues or to influence the healer, Mrs. Pierce received no benefit except diversion from Quimby's intervention, and comments: "We hear of some wonderful cures but like a mad dog story it comes through a good many hands. Ask the patients themselves and it is singular how different the affair looks." Mrs. Pierce notes that her friends the Ware sisters "swallow him [i.e., Quimby] whole. He is their religion and their love and yet Sarah is far from well." It was Mrs. Pierce's daughter, also called Emily, who, having become a Christian Scientist, recognized the significance of her mother's letters. In her own letters to the officials at The Mother Church enclosing the old letters from her mother and the Wares, Emily Willis Pierce narrates what she herself remembers of Emma and Sarah. She says that, despite their supposed "cure" by Quimby in 1859 or 1860, and the deep devotion to the doctor which this engendered, both sisters continued to suffer from very poor health, and Mrs. Sarah Ware MacKay, together with her small daughter, died a tragically early death, "seemingly of starvation." When Miss Pierce told Emma Ware of her own discovery of health and subsequent conversion to Christian Science, Emma said: "My dear, I scarcely know whether to be glad or sorry for you, you have gained health, but it will lead you into the deepest, darkest valley of the shadow you have ever imagined." These sad events and private comments to family members are in stark contrast to the enthusiasm and gratitude Emma and Sarah expressed about Quimby when writing to, for example, Edward Arens, when he applied to them for information about Quimby that would help him in the libel suit brought against him by Mrs. Eddy.

Chapter 8: "Fired with the Prescience of a Great Mission"

1.   **Unless otherwise noted, the passages from Mrs. Patterson's letters quoted in this chapter are taken from the Quimby Papers in the Library of Congress.** Extensive sections of these letters have been published in earlier biographies, notably Milmine and Cather, and Bates and Dittemore.

2.   It emerges from letters and diaries of this period that doing the household wash was widely considered by women to be one of the biggest tests of their health and resolution.

3.   Testimony from Martha Hinds, wife of a Quimby patient, also indicates that Mrs. Patterson gave a few successful lectures while in Portland.

4.   This tendency to see gospel stories as patterns for events in one's own life and to use New Testament language became stronger and stronger as Mary Baker Eddy evolved as a religious leader, and it has been sharply attacked by twentieth-century critics as a form of blasphemous self-aggrandizement.

5.   It is interesting to find Mrs. Eddy raising this issue of possible perfection for humans in this life as early as 1864. It was to cause some disssent within the small group of followers in Lynn in the late 1870s, and even so loyal a follower as Bancroft did not understand that when Mrs. Eddy insisted that she was perfect now, she meant that, within her as within every human being, there was the perfect being created by God in God's image, and which no material fault or failing could affect. The belief that it was possible to achieve perfection while still on earth was one of the theological currents in America at this period. See Robert Thomas, *The Man Who Would Be Perfect: John Humphrey Noyes and the Utopian Impulse* (Philadelphia: University of Pennsylvania Press, 1977).

6.   In the *Lynn Weekly Reporter* of November 4, 1865, J. M. Trow wrote to advise citizens that "an individual calling himself Daniel Patterson" has been accosting patients

and demanding payments for dental services performed when Patterson was in partnership with Trow." Trow reproduces a stamped document in his possession from January 21, 1864, in which Patterson acknowledges receipt of $28. 23 in full settlement of all acounts and promises not to try to collect from patients. On November 11, in the same newspaper, Patterson makes an amazingly lengthy and eccentric answer to Trow in which he says that he regrets that he had no time to respond fully to Trow's "scurrilous attack" having been busy in his practice, following a lengthy stay in the country, and he ends with a long and strange anecdote about an Irishman and a skunk.

7.   The Merck manual describes erysipelas as "an acute streptococcal infection of the skin, sharply demarcated, red, swollen area, with accompanying fever and malaise." It is contagious but dangerous only to puerperal women and responds readily to penicillin or erythromycin. No doubt Daniel Patterson was extremely uncomfortable, bad-tempered, and unresponsive to talk of Quimby during the acute stage of the disease, and the wife who was nursing him ran some risk of catching it.

8.   Original letter in the Church History Department.

9.   That Mrs. Crosby was asked to give her testimony in the form of a legal affidavit may be an indication that the more reasoned and professional journalistic approach of Willa Cather was beginning to take hold of the Milmine biography at *McClure's,* or it may point to Mrs. Crosby's special eagerness to go on record and get back at her old friend.

10.   Milmine and Cather, p. 65.

11.   Lyman P. Powell, *Christian Science: The Faith and Its Founder,* p. 58. One of the lines of attack on Mrs. Eddy which Frederick Peabody established and Lyman Powell adopted in his early work on Christian Science was that Mrs. Eddy was a parasite on her friends and was never willing to take on a woman's normal domestic load.

12.   Milmine and Cather, p. 66.

13.   *Science and Health,* 2d ed. (1878), p. 161. Quoted in Milmine and Cather, p. 66, n. 4.

14.   Wilbur, p. 111.

15.   When a version of this explanation was published by Christian Scientist Caleb Cushing in the Waterville, Maine, *Morning Star* on February 14, 1907, Mrs. Crosby fired back an angry rebuttal, insisting that in 1864 she had never even heard of Spiritualism and that, for all her faults, Mrs. Eddy would never have been guilty of so egregious a deception as feigning a trance (see Bates and Dittemore, p. 101). In fact, Mrs. Crosby's December 14, 1864, letter to Mrs. Patterson is full of Spiritualist allusions and concepts.

16.   Bates and Dittemore refer coyly to Patterson's letter as being "quite unprintable," and they refuse even to identify Mrs. Crosby as the close friend of Mary's whom Daniel sought to seduce. Probably they did not wish to give the reader even the slightest suspicion that their important witness, Mrs. Sarah Crosby, was anything but an irreproachable young widow. Peel is the first biographer to identify Mrs. Crosby as the target of Patterson's amorous advances. Patterson's letter has not survived, but I have seen in the Church History Department Mrs. Crosby's letter to Mrs. Patterson, informing her of Daniel's treachery and stating unequivocally that he had proposed that she sleep with him.

17.   Edwin J. Thompson reminiscences, quoted in Peel, *Discovery,* p. 188. Thompson, a dentist and the head of the Linwood Lodge in 1864, wrote his recollections as a protest against what he saw as the grossly unfair portrait of Mrs. Eddy presented in the 1907 Milmine and Cather biography.

18.   Mark Baker's will is at the Longyear Museum.

19.   On October 11, 1861, Mark Baker signed a quitclaim deed in which he traces his ancestry back to the original immigrants to Roxbury, Massachusetts, and then declares "George S. Baker of Northfield N.H. is my son and was born in said Bow Aug. 7 1812 to whom I have quitclaimed all my rights and interests in any state in New England."

20. In 1904 the destitute and very sick Mrs. Martha Rand Baker became acquainted with Christian Science practitioner Miss Nemi Robertson. Through Miss Robertson Mrs. Baker appealed to Mrs. Eddy for assistance and was sent twenty-five dollars. In a letter to Robertson now in the Mother Church's collection, Calvin Frye relates that Mrs. Eddy had told him that Mrs. Martha Rand Baker had lied about her [Mrs. Eddy] to Abigail and to Mark Baker, had persuaded Mark to leave his considerable fortune to George, her husband, and had later left her blind husband alone in Sanbornton Bridge to die.

21. Only a very few, and mainly brief letters from the Tilton relatives to Mrs. Eddy exist. The fact that so much of these communications relate to the cemetery plot may have nothing to do with the core disagreement with the Baker-Tilton clan, but it was certainly the issue which forced them to contact one another and therefore the point where conflict could be generated. One measure of Mrs. Eddy's growing respectability and authority in the community was her ability first to pay her cemetery taxes, then to bury her dead husband Asa Gilbert Eddy across the avenue from her brother Albert and raise monuments to her parents, and in the 1890s to create a $500 trust fund to maintain the plot and contribute to general cemetery maintenance. In this apparently minor matter, she was contesting her sister Abigail's dominance on her home turf. In the context of all this conflict over cemetery plots, I was interested to note that in her will of 1886, Abigail Tilton left nothing to her surviving sister and next of kin, Mary Baker Eddy. To her brother George's impoverished widow, Martha Rand Baker, she left "the note I hold against her," and to her other sister-in-law, Mary Ann Cook Baker, also destitute, "her heirs and assigns forever," Abigail left "all my Cemetery property unoccupied at my decease." (Original document in the Church History Department.)

22. Clifford P. Smith, *Historical Sketches,* p. 55.

23. George Quimby, "Phineas Parkhurst Quimby," *New England Magazine* (March 1888), p. 276.

24. For an account of Swedenborg and of Jackson's vastly popular 1847 *The Principles of Nature, Her Divine Revelations, and a Voice to Mankind,* see Slater Brown, *The Heyday of Spiritualism.*

25. LO7796. Original in the Church History Department. This letter is given in full in various biographies, beginning with Milmine and Cather who say that in 1866 Julius Dresser was editing the Webster, Massachusetts, *Times.*

26. Original letter in the Church History Department. This is partially published in Peel, *Discovery,* p. 199 and was first published in the May 1907 issue of Wilbur's *Human Life* series.

Chapter 9: The Fall in Lynn

1. Testimony of George Newhall, the milkman at Paradise Road, Swampscott. See Peel, *Discovery,* p. 196; and Clifford Smith, *Historical Sketches,* pp. 55–56.

2. V03416. Original in the New York Public Library. This letter is partially published in Milmine and Cather, p. 83. Mary Baker Patterson reverted to the name Glover in 1868.

3. Mrs. Eddy's critics have delighted in noting that she did not consistently identify the passage from the New Testament that had given her the crucial revelation. As Robert Peel says, "In several editions of S&H she wrote of turning to Mark 3 but in her Article 'One Cause and Effect' (*Mis.,* p. 24) she tells of opening up Matthew 9:2, and this is the passage which stands as her final recollection of the incident" (Peel, *Discovery,* p. 346, n. 17).

4. Milmine and Cather, pp. 85–86.

Chapter 10: Homeless

1. Mrs. Eddy wrote an awkwardly dithyrambic ad for the property, presumably to help her landlords find a buyer and to palliate her own deficiencies as a tenant.

2.   George Clark later described the visit Dr. Patterson and his wife made to his mother to secure the lodging. Patterson was still a very impressive man, it seems, as was his wife. Testimony in the Church History Department files on Clark.

3.   Janette Weller reminiscences, Church History Department. Before he left the house, Patterson "secured"—in Mrs. Weller's word—all his wife's personal valuables, including the watch given her as a marriage present by her first husband, George Glover. I am unclear whether by "secure" Mrs. Weller meant that Patterson took the valuables away with him, leaving his wife destitute, or whether—which seems unlikely—he had put them somewhere safe, or whether he had used them as securities for loans. In her interview with Mrs. Weller, Mrs. Eddy showed her the man's watch she always carried on a long chain and tucked into her waistband, so if Patterson did abscond with it in 1866, she must have managed to recover it.

4.   There is no corroboration for this story of Patterson's exodus from Lynn, and, with the exception of Wilbur and Peel, biographers have tended to pooh-pooh it. I certainly accept that this was the story Mrs. Eddy told Janette Weller in 1884, since Weller seems a very reliable reporter to me, and there seems no good reason why Mrs. Eddy would have invented the story out of whole cloth on this particular occasion. Moreover, as I look at the Patterson marriage, and the many squalls it had weathered, I feel that something new and important must have happened in 1866 to explain why at last Daniel went off for good. The various little notices he placed in the *Lynn Weekly Reporter* establish that Patterson was often out of a town and away from his patients, and no other explanation for these absences has ever been offered, except that given by his wife—that he was engaged in one or more adulterous liaisons.

5.   On December 26, 1866, Mrs. Patterson was granted leave by the city of Lynn to withdraw her suit. Peel, *Discovery,* p. 201.

6.   L07800. Original in the Church History Department.

7.   The Farlow papers contain two undated documents stating that in the early 1870s Mrs. Glover came to a lodging house in Lynn where she had been promised a room by the landlord. She healed the landlord's child from a serious illness but was nonetheless refused the promised room by the landlord's wife, the child's mother. Furthermore, Farlow collected a large number of letters from various people Mrs. Glover had known in the 1860s and 1870s—many of them, such as Daniel Spofford and Clara Choate, Mrs. Glover's opponents and professional competitors—who testified that she led a morally blameless life and had never been guilty to their knowledge of any improper behavior. To me, this indicates once again that all members of the mental healing movement, whatever their disagreements among themselves, were sensitive to and anxious to rebut charges that mental healers lived immoral lives.

8.   Milmine and Cather, pp. 122–23.

9.   It is not entirely clear to which exact year George Clark's vivid description of Mrs. Eddy's looks and dress belong since she seems to have spent two brief periods in 1866 at the Clark boardinghouse, the first with her husband, the second alone. She returned to the house in 1872 after her split with Richard Kennedy. Young George Clark was called as a witness when the Pattersons' divorce proceedings were heard in 1873. Clark, who died in the Old Soldiers' Home in Chelsea in 1914, was interviewed by Milmine and Wilbur and also wrote out his reminiscences of Mrs. Eddy for the Church in 1888. Clark's recollections as reported here and in the next two paragraphs are from the Clark reminiscences, the Church History Department.

10.   Wilbur, p. 144.

11.   Peel quotes a 1913 affidavit from Charles Allen Taber, Mrs. Winslow's nephew, who describes the tremendous attraction Mrs. Glover exerted over them all at this period, and their bewildered fascination with the Bible exegesis which she was working on and would read extracts from to the assembled company. Taber writes: "I said to Mrs. Winslow that Mrs. Glover suggested Lucretia Mott whom we had met and held in high esteem. Mrs.

Glover seemed to fill the room with her presence and the ideas she expressed compelled attention" (Peel, *Discovery,* p. 209).

12.   The Crafts, husband and wife, are featured in George Clark's diagram of the seating at table at his mother's boardinghouse. Wilbur, *Human Life,* July 1907.

13.   Crafts's correspondence is at the Church History Department.

14.   Milmine, and all the critics that follow her work, claimed that the teaching manuscript was based at least in whole or in part on the copy of P. P. Quimby's "Questions and Answers" which Mrs. Glover had brought with her from Portland. Ira Holmes, Hiram Crafts's brother-in-law, and also the husband of his sister, later testified to the *McClure's* team, "I have heard her (Mrs. Eddy) say these words: 'I learned this science from Dr. Quimby, and I can only impart it to but one person.' She always said this in a slow, impressive manner, pronouncing the word 'person' as if it were spelled 'pairson' " (Milmine and Cather, p. 113). Milmine further stated that in 1902 Mrs. Eddy summoned Crafts to her house in Concord and persuaded him to give her back the manuscript he had retained. Milmine claims that the Crafts manuscript, if produced to the public, would prove the influence of Quimby, and that Mrs. Eddy was calling in all documents that could prove embarrassing to her. This claim, accepted as fact by subsequent non–Christian Science biographies, is both incorrect and biased. The correspondence between the Church and Hiram Crafts, and a Photostat of the copy of the manuscript which Crafts sent to Mrs. Eddy at her request, shows that the manuscript lovingly retained by Crafts consisted of a verse-by-verse exegesis in Mrs. Eddy's handwriting of Matthew, chapters 14–17. In February 1902 when, at Mrs. Eddy's request and expense, he had the manuscript photostated and swore out an affidavit, Hiram testified: "She never taught me to hurt others, but only to heal the sick and reform the sinner. She taught me from the scriptures and from manuscripts that she wrote as she taught me." Elsewhere he said, "We used nothing outside of the New Testament, and had no manuscripts of any kind until after I had been studying six months." Crafts's teaching document and other correspondence are part of the Church History Department. Mrs. Eddy paid Crafts the $4.50 he incurred in legal and postal expenses. See Peel, *Discovery,* pp. 211–18, plus notes.

15.   Church History Department.

16.   Since Elizabeth Patterson Baker, Mark Baker's widow, would not die until June 1875, the house and property in Sanbornton Bridge had not yet passed to George Baker and would in fact fall to his heir, his widow Martha Rand Baker. The Longyear Museum has a file of letters of application by and recommendations for George Sullivan Baker which testifies to his wanderings, his financial difficulties, his professional misfortunes, and his personal competence.

17.   Peel, *Discovery,* p. 215. This is from the reminiscences of Addie Towns Arnold.

18.   Abigail Tilton to Martha Pilsbury, August 4, 1867. Original letter at the Longyear Museum.

19.   L11154. Original in the Church History Department. There is no exact date for this letter.

20.   Statement by the widow of Albert Tilton, Abbie G. Durgin. Longyear Museum.

21.   Peel, *Discovery,* p. 217.

22.   Ibid., p. 218.

23.   Charles Wentworth, who lived close to the Holmeses and Craftses, later testified that Ira Holmes was well known in Stoughton as a bad lot, and that had there been any hint of Mrs. Glover trying to get Hiram to ask for a divorce, the whole community would have known about it. Farlow papers, the Church History Department.

24.   Letter of November 27, 1868. Original in the Church History Department.

25.   To simplify a not uncomplex matter, "rubbing mediums" were alternative healers who manipulated the head and abdomen of their patients in order to induce trance.

"Drawing mediums" produced drawings and writings while in trance and supposedly under the influence of spirits.

26.   Frederick Peabody, especially in his early 1901 speeches and pamphlet, represented Mrs. Eddy's connection to Spiritualism as an important chink in her armor, and he claimed that Mrs. Eddy had worked and earned money as a professional medium in Boston in the late 1860s. The Mother Church's Committee on Publication had no difficulty in disproving Peabody's claims, showing that those who had testified to having known Mrs. Eddy as a medium were either lying, misremembering, or simply confusing her with another woman, since ample documentation showed that the then Mrs. Glover had been far away from Boston at the time that Peabody was speaking about.

27.   Farlow papers, the Church History Department.

28.   The Woodhull sisters exemplify all these trends, but they were on the cutting edge— or lunatic fringe—of a large and influential Spiritualist community.

29.   Tomlinson, pp. 75–76.

30.   Hugh Studdert Kennedy, p. 152, quoting an article by Mrs. Mary Ellis Bartlett in *McClure's Magazine*; this also appears in Milmine and Cather, p. 116.

31.   Miss Bagley was blind for the last three years of her life and died in August of 1905. Her estate passed by will to her companion Hattie Gunnison, and upon the latter's death to Richard Kennedy. Gunnison died within months of Kennedy, but whereas the Bagley house and artifacts were acquired by Mrs. Longyear, the Bagley papers came to The Mother Church, and have remained unpublished. I was given permission to read the Bagley file in the Church History Department. The file contains, among other things, a fairly large correspondence between Miss Bagley and Mrs. Eddy between 1868 and 1875 and thus offers some of the most important information on this period.

32.   Mary Baker Glover to Sarah Bagley, November 8, 1868: "Could I just breathe in an undertone 'Sarah,' and out of the dream land call you to my bed, do you not think we would chat busily for a little? Yes, & live again a thunder-storm tete a tete! Was not I lover-like then to 'embrace' you, i.e. to call you up in night gown to keep your eyes staring wide while I nestled to your side in 'tremula tremendo?' " L08307. Original in the Church History Department.

33.   L07799. Original letter in the Church History Department.

34.   Sarah Bagley did allow Richard Kennedy to use her correspondence with Mrs. Eddy in the lawsuit with Mrs. Eddy in which he ultimately prevailed.

35.   Farlow papers, the Church History Department.

36.   Robert Peel, the first, it would seem, to read the Bagley papers that had lain in the archives of the Church of Christ, Scientist for some fifty years, made extremely partial use of them, casting Sarah as a worthy but intellectually limited healer, a silly old maid. I see Sarah Bagley differently because she seems a real-life American version of Miss Bates in *Emma* or the spinster sisters of *Cranford,* and Austen and Gaskell have taught me as well as her heroine that it is crucial to see the value as well as the absurdity of such women.

37.   In the 1906–1907 period, when the rival Milmine and Wilbur biographies were in preparation, the Wentworth episode in Mrs. Eddy's life achieved considerable importance, offering fuel to both fires. Each camp scurried to interview and secure the allegiance and affidavits of as many Stoughton residents as possible, in what was probably a minor bonanza for the small rural community. The Wentworth parents and most citizens of Mrs. Eddy's own generation were, of course, dead or senile by this time, so the interview testimony had to come from their children. These people were happy to describe how they as teenagers and young adults had interacted with Mrs. Eddy and what they remembered their parents telling them about her. The elder Wentworth sister Celia, like her parents, was long since dead, having succumbed to consumption soon after Mrs. Eddy's departure. Her name and existence were omitted by the Milmine account and

played down in the Wilbur and Powell accounts, no doubt because all the Wentworths, whether or not they remembered Mrs. Eddy with favor, had an investment in the alternative healing their mother had practiced for so long, and they found Celia's resistance to cure inconvenient. Horace Wentworth, his wife Susan, and his cousin Mrs. Catherine Clapp became keystones in the Milmine account of Mrs. Eddy as a parasite who preyed upon good, charitable people and as a plagiarist passing off as her own the work of her noble mentor and healer P. P. Quimby.

Charles Wentworth, after much hesitation, contradicted Horace's account, presenting Mrs. Eddy as a brilliant, lovable, fascinating woman who had brought light and color into their lives. There can be no doubt that Horace Wentworth had strongly disliked and distrusted Mrs. Eddy from 1868 onward and needed little encouragement in 1907 to make his feelings of animosity public. It also seems very likely that Horace was paid for his testimony, which was shaped and in part dictated so that it became more sensational and damning. The best evidence for this shaping of testimony is provided by a letter Burton J. Hendrick, one of the *McClure's* editors assigned to the Eddy biography and the one known to be most bitterly opposed to Christian Science, wrote to Frederick Peabody. The letter makes clear that Frederick Peabody not only had been responsible for obtaining the original affidavits from the Wentworths, Dr. Cushing, and Sarah Crosby but also had been employed by the magazine to get the affidavits resworn and tailored to *McClure's* concept. Hendrick writes: "I have added to Mr. Horace Wentworth's statement a paragraph containing his story of Mrs. Glover's room after she left it in 1870. I suppose he will have no objection to including it: it is certainly an essential detail. I have also added to Mrs. Clapp's affidavit a few lines concerning Mrs. Glover's room. I saw her myself some months ago and understand her to say that she was willing to stand for this. I regard these affidavits as among the most important documents in the Eddy history, they surely once and for all dispose of Mrs. Eddy's claim to divine inspiration. I think that you are to be heartily congratulated for obtaining them" (Letter of January 17, 1907, Chandler File 48/2, original in the New Hampshire Historical Society).

On the other side, the Farlow files, which record the dealings between Charles Wentworth and the Mother Church authorities, document how Charles, though he initially collaborated with the Milmine group, was not up for sale like his brother; he was deeply resistant to cooperating with either faction. After extensive wooing by Alfred Farlow, Charles first contributed some brief and specific replies to questions of fact and eventually agreed to make a detailed statement about Mrs. Eddy's relations with his family which was generally very affectionate and laudatory and which specifically denied the truth of most of his brother's testimony. Lucy Wentworth Holmes was the person living in 1907 who had known Mrs. Eddy best during the Stoughton period, but her testimony was less quoted than that of her brothers. In my opinion, as far as the Milmine faction was concerned, Lucy loved Mrs. Eddy too well; but the Wilburites felt that Lucy blamed Mrs. Eddy too strongly for leaving the family and never returning or writing.

38.   The Farlow papers contain a written contract signed by Sally Wentworth agreeing to give Mrs. Glover free board for as long as she cares to stay, and to pay her $2 a week when Mrs. Glover is absent from the Wentworth home, in return for instruction in healing the sick and teaching the "science whereby I have learned to heal."

39.   Affidavit by Alanson Wentworth in 1868, and in the Farlow collection at the Church History Department, presumably made at Mrs. Eddy's request and collected by her as she strove to build up her healing practice.

40.   According to Stoughton town records, the whole Wentworth property rose in value from $825 in 1851 to $1725 in 1871. See Kenneth Hufford, *Mary Baker Eddy and the Stoughton Years* (Brookline, Mass.: Longyear Foundation, 1963).

41.   Undated letter, probably written in 1869. Quoted by Peel, *Discovery,* pp. 229–30. Mrs. Mulliken seems to have been a close friend of the Pattersons and someone who kept in touch with Daniel, since in the same letter Mrs. Glover asks for news of her separated

spouse: "Is Dr. Patterson in your vicinity now and how does he <u>support</u> himself? Has he much business there? Does he ever call on you, and who does he board with?"

42.   L07798. Original letter in the Church History Department.

43.   There is considerable published and unpublished documentation on this healing, which caused some local stir and promoted Mrs. Glover's reputation. In 1900 Alfred Farlow published an article in the Boston *Traveler* detailing Mrs. Eddy's cure of John Scott. Based on the Farlow files, it appears that the Scott family had willingly cooperated with the Church, which had helped to give the care necessary to John Scott's very elderly and infirm widow.

44.   Peel, *Discovery,* p. 227.

45.   Ibid., pp. 225–26. Note: Mrs. Eddy is shown in this plaid dress in one of the rare photos of the period. The expression of the thin face, framed in straggly ringlets, is extremely sad and winning, the eyes huge. The "best black dress" Lucy refers to is undoubtedly the one Mrs. Eddy wore for the photo (see photo insert) session where she was pictured holding the baby.

46.   The Farlow papers suggest that this same story of the coals in the closet and the threat of arson was being spread by Mrs. Hiram Crafts. To me this suggests, in turn, that the story was being planted on various witnesses, probably by Peabody, who was going round interviewing and collecting affidavits.

47.   Wilbur, p. 178. It is somewhat surprising that Kennedy, one of Mrs. Eddy's oldest and bitterest enemies, even agreed to be interviewed by Sibyl Wilbur, whose reports were designed to counter the hostile biographical information appearing in *McClure's* in 1907.

Chapter 11: Rebellious Students

1.   Indirect proof of this can be found in the efforts Alfred Farlow, the head of the Committee on Publication, made in the early 1900s to secure signed statements on her respectability and moral conduct from people who had known Mrs. Eddy in her less prosperous days, such as her early students Clara Choate and Daniel Spofford. Thus Mrs. Carrie Colby, who had lived upstairs from the then Mrs. Glover when she and Kennedy were sharing accommodations in Lynn notes: "She lived as far as I know a good life. There could not possibly be anything wrong there; there was not room enough. Dr. Kennedy had his apartment and Mrs. Eddy had hers. I never saw anything that indicated anything wrong" (Farlow papers, the Church History Department).

2.   Wilbur, p. 186. See Appendix on Wilbur's own experience of living in Lynn when working on a story about women in the shoe industry.

3.   One of the most important publishing projects of the Church History Department in the 1990s was the exhaustive cataloguing and description of Mrs. Eddy's personal healings. This was first published as a series in the *Christian Science Journal* and is now available as the book *Mary Baker Eddy: Christian Healer* by Yvonne Caché von Fettweis and Robert Townsend Warneck (Boston: Christian Science Publishing Society, 1998). This series is an attempt to show how wrong are those many critics, from Milmine on, who have snidely commented that Mrs. Eddy herself never healed anyone. In this book I discuss only those healings for which there is good third-party documentary evidence and which play a particularly important part in her life, such as the healing of her niece Ellen.

4.   Peel, *Discovery,* p. 238. L08304. Original in the Church History Department. The letter probably dates from 1868.

5.   The Longyear Museum owns six letters from Richard Kennedy to Sarah Bagley. The last four are clearly dated—September 9, 1872; September 18, 1872; April 17, 1873; and October 8, 1878. The original Kennedy letters quoted here are from the Longyear Museum. The first two letters, headed simply "Lynn," obviously refer to the early months or perhaps weeks after Mrs. Eddy and Kennedy moved from Amesbury to Lynn. The collection clearly traces the rapid and dramatic change in the relations between Mrs. Eddy

and Kennedy during this period. The Church History Department also possesses a few short letters from Kennedy to Mrs. Eddy, dating from the first years of their relationship, in which Kennedy expresses nothing but admiration and obedience for his teacher, in words that might have been her own. It is doubtful how much of the real Richard Kennedy can be gauged from any of these pious letters written to women thirty years his senior. How different our view of him might be if we had even one letter to, say, Wallace Wright, or Charles Stanley, or Addie Spofford!

6.   Milmine and Cather, pp. 135–38.

7.   L03918, L03919. Originals in the Church History Department.

8.   Peel, *Discovery,* p. 255.

9.   I was led to make inquiries about this rail crash incident by a brief remark made by Mrs. Colby, Mrs. Eddy's upstairs neighbor at this time, who said in testimony she gave Alfred Farlow that Mrs. Glover never left the side of the burn victims, even at night. I thank the Lynn Historical Society for supplying me with copies of the article on the Revere Beach and Lynn rail tragedy published in the *Lynn Transcript* of September 2, 1871, p. 2.

10.   Hugh Studdert Kennedy says that in the notebook Mrs. Eddy kept to record her receipts and expenses in this period, between June 1870 and May 1871, she received $1,742, after all the partnership's expenses, rent, and living costs had been met. When the partnership with Kennedy was finally wound up in the spring of 1872, Mrs. Eddy's share of the profits amounted to $6,000.

11.   Milmine and Cather, p. 138.

12.   On December 31, 1870, Mrs. Glover sent in a note to the local Lynn newspaper thanking her students for their Christmas gifts, which she describes in almost the same dithyrambic detail as in the letter to Sarah Bagley. Peel notes that at about this time Mrs. Eddy received a visit from her nephew, George Waldron Baker, who had just completed his studies at the New Hampshire Conference Seminary—another indication that Mrs. Eddy's connections with her family in Tilton never really broke. See Peel, *Discovery*, p. 253. A short piece by Mrs. Eddy that was published in the Lynn *Semi-Weekly Reporter* on August 12, 1871, records another pleasant party, when she and a group of friends were rowed out to visit Egg Rock off Nahant for a picnic and a visit to the lighthouse.

13.   L03921. Original in the Church History Department.

14.   Also in this first class, according to Peel, were probably Clarkson and Susan Oliver, Mrs. J. R. Eastman, and Addie Spofford.

15.   The document is quoted from Milmine and Cather, pp. 140–41; it does not appear to be extant. After their time with Mrs. Eddy, Tuttle returned to the sea, but Stanley went on to become a successful homeopath in Amesbury. (See John F. Kellett's biographical piece on Sarah Bagley, "Sarah Osgood Bagley, Magnetic Healer, 1820–1905, Mary Baker Eddy's First Amesbury Student.") In 1879, Edward Arens, on Mrs. Eddy's behalf, took Stanley and Tuttle to court for failure to pay her the monies stipulated in their contract of 1870. The Milmine team managed to dig up the judge's notes on the case, which Mrs. Eddy lost largely because of the court testimony on behalf of the defendants by Richard Kennedy which indicated Mrs. Eddy had no proper regard for the Christian religion. This trial was one of the few occasions when Mrs. Eddy was obliged to testify in court, and she gave an early account of her theology of healing which did not sway Judge Choate but which is of some interest given her later career:

> I can argue to myself that striking my hand upon the table will not produce pain—I don't think I could produce the effect that the knife would not produce a wound, but that I could argue myself out of the pain. I have not claimed to have gone so far as that. I have said that belongs to a future time. I can alleviate—I cannot prevent a broken bone. I would send for a surgeon and set the bone—and after that I would alleviate the pain and inflammation. Can't do more in my present development. (Milmine and Cather, p. 145)

16. One of the most important documents of the period 1870–1875 is Bancroft's *Mrs. Eddy As I Knew Her,* published privately in 1923 by the Longyear Foundation. In this book Bancroft reproduces the teaching document which he received when in class with Mrs. Glover in 1871 to prove that it was not a copy of Quimby's "Questions and Answers," as alleged by Horatio Dresser in his 1921 edition of the Quimby papers.

17. I deal with the eventual apostasies of these early students in this and the next chapters. In the early 1900s Miranda Rice became an important source of allegations that Mrs. Eddy was a hysteric, a morphine addict, and (in more guarded terms) a nymphomaniac.

18. My sources for the Wallace Wright controversy are the full text of the *Transcript* debate, supplied by the Church History Department, various accounts given of Wright in the published biographies, the letters to Sarah Bagley, the letters and statements of Daniel Spofford, the unpublished biography of Spofford by his great-grandson Charles Dyer, and the veiled remarks Mrs. Eddy makes about the Wright affair in the "Demonology" chapter of the third edition of *Science and Health* (1881, vol. 2, pp. 1– 46). The "Healing the Sick" chapter which ends the first edition of *Science and Health* also deals with the Wright and Kennedy affairs, but in even more veiled and much more measured terms.

19. According to Milmine, Wallace Wright became a prominent businessman in Lynn after his brush with mental healing. "He was drowned in the wreck of the City of Columbus, off Gayhead Light, January 18, 1884" (Milmine and Cather, p. 148).

20. Wright's letter and Mrs. Glover's reply (V03416) are both in the New York Public Library.

21. Richard Kennedy was also becoming interested in Quimby at this time. We know from a letter the then Mrs. Glover wrote to a friend in 1871 that she had considered making a possible visit to Portland and staying in a boardinghouse she knew since, she says, Richard had taken a fancy to spend some time in a hotel there. Mrs. Eddy, in fact, took her habitual summer vacation in New Hampshire, not Maine, but Robert Peel argues that Kennedy went to Portland without her and made contact with the Quimby family or the Ware sisters. Peel thinks that Kennedy was seeking to quote the authority of Quimby in his arguments with his partner over the use of manipulation, and his argument is supported by a section of the 1875 edition of *Science and Health* in which Mrs. Eddy specifically notes that Quimby's example was being used as a justification for manipulation:

> In defence of mesmerism is urged, that Dr. Quimby manipulated the sick. He never studied this science, but reached his own high standpoint and grew to it through his own, and not another's progress. He was a good man, a law to himself; when we knew him he was growing out of mesmerism; contrasted with a student [Kennedy] that falls into it by forsaking the good rules of science for a mal-practice that has the power and opportunity to do evil. Dr. Quimby had passed away years before ever there was a student of this science, and never, to our knowledge, informed any one of his method of healing. (*Science and Health,* pp. 373–74).

This is the only place in the book where Mrs. Eddy refers to Quimby, and it seems to me a balanced and fair assessment, by one presumed to know.

22. "Demonology" was included in the third edition (1881) against the advice of the publisher, Asa G. Eddy, who seems, rightly, to have felt that his wife could not profit from washing the dirty linen of Science in public in so dramatic and intemperate a way. Withdrawn in subsequent revisions of the book, "Demonology" has achieved notoriety in the history of Christian Science, and few commentators, either for or against Christian Science, have read it carefully or taken it seriously. In my view, given the extreme paucity of any contemporary documentation on this important period in Mrs. Eddy's life, we cannot afford to ignore her own contemporary account of Wright and Kennedy.

23. Here is the relevant passage in "Demonology":

A married lady [Addie Spofford], and member of the Methodist Church, became his [Kennedy's] patient, and afterwards went to the South with her husband [Daniel Spofford], whom we had never seen but once before they left the city where we resided. In 1871, after she revisited this city, we had a letter from his wife, in which she wrote, 'I do not regret my journey North, you did me so much good with your teachings of virtue and Truth. I gain much spiritually from you.' [This letter from Addie Spofford to Mrs. Eddy is extant.] After three years her husband returned to our city, and it was rumored that he had left his wife. In their absence we had a letter but once from the husband, to ask permission to join our class in metaphysics, but requesting that his wife should not be informed of this application. To this we replied in a letter addressed to his wife. The aforesaid mesmerist [Kennedy] had gained such control over his wife [Addie] that after her husband [Daniel] had studied and entered into practice she kept away from her relatives where he was located until this fellow [Kennedy], who had an office in that city, sent for her. We were told by her husband that her only terms for peace with him were that he should vindicate this villain. He refused to do that, and they again separated. He finally sued for a divorce. (*Science and Health,* 3e, [1881], p. 7)

I shall have more to say about Addie and Daniel in Chapter 12.

24.   Letter of January 20, 1872. Original in the Church History Department.

25.   To quote from Mrs. Glover's early teaching manuscript "Questions and Answers in Moral Science,"

You cannot destroy error, by error: if you are profane swearers, if you are adulterers, if you are thieves, if you are murderers, you would not hesitate to say, these errors must be given up if you would heal with truth. . . . you will not love money beyond the appreciation of it as a means for usefulness; you will not lie or deceive, you will be just and merciful, and if you hold any habit that places pleasure in sense you must be rid of this or how can you destroy it in others?

26.   This charge that mesmerists could control their subjects and make them do things against their wills and moral convictions was made from the very beginning of the mesmeric movement, but it achieved new urgency in the mid- and late nineteenth century when mesmerism merged with Spiritualism and reached much further down the social ladder. Bram Stoker's *Dracula* played with this idea, but most influential was the play *The Bells,* first produced in London in 1871 with Henry Irving in his first starring role, and later brought to the United States.

27.   Five of her students, George W. Barry, George H. Allen, Amos Ingalls, Dorcas Rawson, and Miranda Rice wrote a protest to the Lynn *Transcript,* February 17, 1872, ignoring Mr. Wright's challenge, but defending their teacher and her science, and declaring that his charges against both were untrue. In her letters to Sarah Bagley, Mrs. Glover insists that Wright's motivation was wholly one of revenge, after she refused to meet his financial demands, and that he had announced this to her and to Richard, whom she presumably had yet to suspect of being in collusion with Wright. She was surprisingly undeterred by the debate in the *Transcript.*

28.   "Demonology," *Science and Health,* 3e, p. 12, Mrs. Eddy quoting Wright's letter to her. Let me note that neither Wright nor Kennedy ever publicly denied Mrs. Eddy's account of events in "Demonology," and that I have seen most of the correspondence she quotes. Wallace Wright's August 24, 1871, letter to Mrs. Eddy suggests that rumors were afoot that his relationship with Addie had been more than professional—hence his grudge against Kennedy, a successful rival in love as well as healing.

29.   "Before studying we were treated by Dr. Kennedy, in order to render us receptive and to acquaint us with the physical methods used, after which Mrs. Patterson was to teach us the spiritual methods" (Bancroft, *Mrs. Eddy As I Knew Her,* pp. 2–3). Kennedy

himself never denied that he used manipulation and advised others to do so. He testified to this in court when Mrs. Eddy unsuccessfully sued his friend Charles Stanley in 1879.

30.   In his book *From Mesmer to Freud: Magnetic Sleep and the Roots of Psychological Healing*, Adam Crabtree devotes his sixth chapter to "Love, Sexuality, and Magnetic Rapport." Crabtree notes: "From the earliest years, concern that the magnetizer might sexually misuse the mesmeric relation was expressed by both practitioners and opponents of mesmerism" (p. 92). The report on mesmerism for the French Academy by the commission headed by Benjamin Franklin contained a secret section, warning King Louis XVIII of the libidinous aspects of mesmeric practice. "Ordinarily the magnetizer has the knees of the woman gripped between his own, the knees and all the parts below are therefore in contact. The hand is applied to the diaphragm area and sometimes lower, over the ovaries," the report noted. Interestingly, the only extant picture of Quimby and his most successful subject, Lucius Burkmar (reproduced in the Seale edition of Quimby's complete works), show the two men seated facing one another with their knees interlocked in the classic mesmeric position.

In 1800 an anonymous letter to the Marquis de Puységur, the second famous European pioneer of mesmeric or hypnotic theory, accused Puységur of immorality in the treatment of a young girl. The letter read in part: "Will not a young man who takes a young woman of nervous disposition into his arms, rubbing the vertebrae, the diaphragm, the stomach, the nipples of the breast, the navel area, cause a revolution . . . in the subject he is massaging? Surely he will. If imagination is struck by fear and hope, or by a sensual delirium that no word can express, then the subject is experiencing a dangerous abandon, and the physician will be able with guilty daring . . . I have to stop here! . . . This sect is embraced among voluptuous and credulous women—surely it is an evil" (quoted by Crabtree, p. 95). J. F. P. Deleuze, in his 1810 practical handbook on how to hypnotize, described the lengthy session of passes over the head, arms, and whole torso of the subject that would ensure mesmeric sleep, and he acknowledged the possible sexual uses and abuses of such practices. Deleuze cautioned young women that they should never allow themselves to be hypnotized by gentlemen except in the presence of a chaperone. Crabtree notes that the 1829 English translation of Deleuze's book was extremely popular in the United States, and I assume that it was one of the works consulted by P. P. Quimby.

As the nineteenth century progressed, doctors in the United States and in Europe demonstrated the usefulness of hypnosis during surgical procedures. In 1843, for example, P. P. Quimby was called in to mesmerize a woman who had to undergo an extremely painful operation to her throat. As the surgeon, Albert T. Wheelock M.D., reported in the *Boston Medical and Surgical Journal,* the hypnotized woman went through the operation with no sign of pain. (See Jerome Eden, *Animal Magnetism and the Life Energy* [Hicksville, N.Y.: Exposition Press], p. 65.) One reason why the potential application of hypnosis as an alternative to anesthesia was largely abandoned in the nineteenth century was because the erotic dimension of the rapport had been so well publicized and doctors were afraid that their women patients might appear to be sexually aroused when under hypnosis. Thus the highly respectable dentist Dr. Peabody of Salem experimented by taking on a young mesmerist, Dr. Fiske, as a partner in his dental practice, and his younger daughter Sophia consulted Fiske in search of relief from her headaches and general ill health. Sophia ceased to submit to Fiske's hypnotic therapy when she became engaged and her fiancé Nathaniel Hawthorne expressed his disapproval. He warned Sophia that by submitting to mesmerism, she surrendered her immortal soul to another and became, in some manner, less chaste. (See Louise Hall Tharp, *The Peabody Sisters of Salem* [1950; reprint, Boston and Toronto: Little, Brown, 1988], pp. 103 and 121.)

31.   Peel, *Discovery,* p. 267, quoting Bancroft's reminiscences.

32.   The original Ellis and Bagley letters are in the Church History Department.

33.   These visions are summarized in Bates and Dittemore, pp. 231–32. Bates and Dittemore give no dates for these visions, which they attribute to the Calvin Frye diaries, and the way that Dittemore came into possession of the material was far too criminal for

him to offer much precision. (See Appendix.) Church History Department sources told me that these visions are noted down not only in the diaries but in notebooks written by Mary Baker Eddy herself or dictated by her to Asa Gilbert Eddy, Frye, or a secretary, as well as in miscellaneous fragments in the collections. Unfortunately, I was not allowed to see any of this material for myself.

34.   Peel, *Discovery,* p. 326, n. 47. This note in Peel puzzled me greatly, and it was only after repeated inquiries that Judith Huenneke at the Church History Department finally managed to locate the letter in which Mrs. Eddy refers to Kennedy's complaint. Frantic to prevent the arousal that their doctors told them would lead to weakness, paralysis, and dementia, educated middle-class American men resorted, variously, to mercury and heavy-metal medications, straps, toothed rings, electric-shock devices, and rectal eggs, with predictably poor results. (See John S. Haller, "Bachelor's Disease: Etiology, Pathology, and Treatment of Spermatorrhea in the Nineteenth Century," *New York State Journal of Medicine,* [August 15, 1973]: 2076–82.) Marriage, with regular but limited sexual intercourse, was the sovereign remedy for spermatorrhea, but not one of which Richard Kennedy availed himself.

35.   The heavy-metal treatments customarily prescribed for venereal diseases and sexual problems in the nineteenth century often led to neurological problems and were also destructive of the alimentary tract. Tertiary syphilis also leads to madness, but it seems unlikely that Kennedy would have developed tertiary syphilis in his late sixties. The exact nature of the insanity that led to his being confined to the Retreat, a Vermont asylum, is in fact unknown: he could simply have become senile. According to his death certificate, of which the Church History Department has a copy, Kennedy died in the asylum in March 1921 "as a result of an intestinal operation."

36.   Peel, *Trial,* p. 49, and n. 50. Peel quotes a copy of the letter made by Asa Gilbert Eddy, found in Mrs. Eddy's papers.

37.   His friendship with Charles Stanley is our best example of this, since Kennedy is on record for taking credit for Stanley's successful defense against Mrs. Eddy's suit, seeing the case as "my opportunity in a public way to say I did not value her teachings" (Letter from Kennedy to Lyman P. Powell, Church History Department). In one of his letters to Miss Bagley, soon after his split with the then Mrs. Glover, Kennedy refers to her in deeply vituperative terms, and twenty-five years later, in his letters to Powell, Kennedy is still ready to express his hatred for Mrs. Eddy.

38.   Kennedy to Milmine: "I improve this opportunity to remind you how distasteful it would be to me to have my name interjected with any of this reading material [i.e., the *McClure's* series]. I shall rely upon your sense of honor to see it [K's name] is not inserted." Original in the Church History Department.

39.   Kennedy to Powell, June 8, 1908. Original letter in the Church History Department.

40.   The Church History Department has an exceptionally slim file on Richard Kennedy, and even the meager information I was able to glean there was scattered through the collection and very hard to find. Of Kennedy after 1880 all I could learn was that he never married, that he lived and practiced as a physician or masseur out of respectable hotel rooms on Tremont Street in Boston, that he had no obvious financial problems, and that he became a pillar of the local Episcopal church in Boston. When, in his late sixties, Kennedy was committed to the Retreat, a Brattleboro, Vermont, asylum for the insane, a wealthy friend called Wadleigh took charge of his affairs until his death, including the Bagley bequest. This, I presume, was the same Wadleigh who in 1878, with another gentleman, went surety for Kennedy when his goods were attached by Mrs. Eddy's lawyer. Kennedy was buried in Boston and survived by a niece.

Chapter 12: Science and Health *1875*

1.   Peel, *Discovery,* p. 274.

2.   Information Mrs. Eddy gave in her testimony during the hearing of the George Barry suit in 1877.

3.   Mrs. Eddy detailed the items of this gift in a card she submitted for publication in the Lynn *Semi-Weekly Reporter,* January 8, 1873.

4.   There is a strange story in testimony given at the Barry trial of Barry discovering Kennedy in the process of picking the lock of Mrs. Eddy's rooms. It is unclear if Barry was influenced by Mrs. Eddy's obsessive suspicion of Kennedy, but if, indeed, she suspected Kennedy of having illicit access to her rooms and papers, perhaps through his friendship with the Dames, she may have had an extra reason for moving out.

5.   Barry trial records in the Church History Department. Mrs. Eddy kept account books throughout this period, and, indeed, her secretaries continued to keep them until her death. These books exist, more than thirty in number, but I was not able to consult them for reasons I explain in my Research Note.

6.   "Mr. Hitchings, the real estate man, had made no progress in his efforts to find a house in Cambridge for Mrs. Eddy. I do not think he tried. . . . In fact, he did not wish Mrs. Eddy (or Mrs. Glover, which was the name she bore at the time) to leave Lynn. He wished to marry her. He was a fine-looking man, about her age, and if he had not been a confirmed Spiritualist, I think she would have accepted him" (Bancroft, *Mrs. Eddy As I Knew Her,* pp. 26–27). This passage is quoted in the Bates and Dittemore biography with one interesting error: they transcribe, "He [Hitchings] was a fine-looking man, about my [i.e., Bancroft's] age." This may be an innocent slip, but the change of the possessive adjective appears to offer subtle, and apparently unimpeachable, evidence from a devoted student who had "known Mrs. Eddy in 1870" that she encouraged the courtship of men young enough to be her sons.

7.   It is not known what the property was that Hitchings, Barry, and Mrs. Glover were involved with, or how the ownership was structured. Mr. Hitchings disappears from the scene at this point, although he was called to testify at the Barry trial. I myself would doubt that Mrs. Eddy seriously considered marrying this man.

8.   Boardinghouses were also difficult places for a writer to work in. A woman who had been one of Mrs. Glover's boarders described her as a crank since she required such perfect quiet in the house (Peel, *Trial,* p. 13).

9.   Bancroft, *Mrs. Eddy As I Knew Her,* pp. 16 – 17.

10.   One indication of Bancroft's close relation to Mrs. Glover, and of her trust in him, is that he was the one called in to assist her on one occasion when she fell down the stairs and was carried up to her rooms by Kennedy, unconscious and bleeding. This story was narrated to Alfred Farlow by Mrs. Carrie Colby, sister-in-law to Miss Susie Magoun, who lived on the floor above Mrs. Glover and Richard Kennedy at South Common Street. The fall probably occurred in 1871, since both Bancroft and Kennedy were present, and it is interesting that Kennedy did not himself take on the treatment immediately. Peel comments, following Mrs. Colby's testimony, "In a few hours she [Mrs. Eddy] was up and dressed, came down to supper as usual, and went on with her work without fuss or complaint" (Peel, *Discovery,* p. 255).

11.   Letter of April 28, 1871. Bancroft, *Mrs. Eddy As I Knew Her,* p. 6.

12.   Mrs. Eddy followed this same pattern with Florence Cheney, who became Mrs. George Barry, and she went so far as to have one of the three first copies of *Science and Health* inscribed with the name "Florence" rather than "George." At the time of the hearing in Barry's suit against Mrs. Eddy, Mrs. Florence Barry testified for her husband.

13.   The stock market crash of 1873 plunged Lynn into five years of hardship. See Peel, *Discovery,* p. 277. Peel indicates that Mrs. Eddy was blamed by her critics for her apparent insensibility to the economic difficulties of her fellow townspeople.

14.   One of the tiny little issues that comes up in Christian Science research is this one of the signs, cards, and advertisements used by different persons at different times. In one of his letters to Lyman Powell, Richard Kennedy protests vigorously against the account given by Sibyl Wilbur of his taking down his sign at the time of Mrs. Eddy's suit against him. He says that the same sign had been affixed for thirty years, and that it read "R. Kennedy." If this is indeed all the sign said, it is interesting in its failure to define a professional activity as is customary among gentlemen signalling their place of business to the public. Thus we do not know how Kennedy himself defined what he did for a living at the Hotel Tremont. By contrast, there are many business cards and advertisements for Daniel Spofford, clearly indicating the nature of the services he offered.

15.   Bancroft, *Mrs. Eddy As I Knew Her*, p. 10.

16.   Bates and Dittemore, p. 151. Their source is the testimony given in the New York *World*, October 30, 1906.

17.   Notably in the famous, or notorious, 1906 accounts of Mrs. Eddy published in the New York *World,* which were both sensational and inaccurate in almost every respect.

18.   Peel, *Discovery*, p. 290.

19.   *What Mrs. Eddy Said to Arthur Brisbane* (New York: M. E. Paige, 1930), p. 57. This book is a reprint of an interview originally published in *Cosmopolitan*, August 1907.

20.   *Painting a Poem, Mary Baker Eddy and James Gilman Illustrate "Christ and Christmas"* (Boston: Christian Science Publishing Society, 1998), p. 132.

21.   Bancroft, *Mrs. Eddy As I Knew Her,* p. 127.

22.   Peel, *Discovery,* p. 284, quoting an unpublished document in the Church History Department.

23.   Wilbur, p. 203.

24.   The only contemporary of any eminence who read the 1875 *Science and Health* with pleasure and admiration, and wrote to tell its author so, was Bronson Alcott. Mrs. Eddy met and corresponded with Alcott in 1876 and 1877, and, more briefly, with his daughter Louisa, in 1876 and 1877. The course of the brief relationship is detailed sardonically in Chapter 17 of Bates and Dittemore and is given a more sympathetic treatment in Robert Peel's *Christian Science: Its Encounter with American Culture* (New York: Holt, 1958).

25.   Milmine and Cather, p. 178. Milmine gives a whole thirty-four-page chapter to analysis of *Science and Health*. Every section of Mrs. Eddy's book is given careful discussion, with lengthy, though unnumbered, quotes. Even though scathing in its criticisms and negative in its tone, the essay is still required reading for anyone seriously interested in Christian Science doctrine. One interesting omission in the Milmine discussion is the second chapter of *Science and Health,* "Imposition and Demonstration," which attacks Spiritualism. No one who reads this chapter could come away thinking that Mrs. Eddy, whatever her other faults might be, was a Spiritualist or had any positive feelings toward Spiritualism. Since the Milmine biography has gone out of its way to paint Mrs. Eddy as, at some periods, an active and always secretly unrepentant Spiritualist, discussion of "Imposition and Demonstration" would have been embarrassing.

26.   One of the points made in most of the important critiques of Mrs. Eddy and Christian Science, notably, Milmine, Dakin, and Braden, is that the Church worked zealously to produce new editions of *Science and Health* and to destroy old ones. This is presented as both a fund-raising mechanism for the movement and a deliberate effacement of the historical record so that the Church leadership could not be held accountable either to its members or to the general public for past mistakes or even simple changes of policy. The Church hotly denies this accusation has any validity.

27.   I find remarkable and even admirable, in fact, exactly what a Swedenborgian clergyman critic objected to, in a rare contemporary review: "Its style [i.e., that of *Science and Health*] is the oracular, the author does not give opinions nor elaborate theories, but announces laws and principles. This saves the reader a great deal of trouble though it

imposes a severe tax upon his faith." The reviewer concedes that the author may be "a great and good healing medium," but there are "healing mediums in Boston to be reckoned by the score." He suggests that she devote her remaining years to healing the sick, and leave the writing of books upon philosophy and religion to others." See Peel, *Trial,* pp. 8–9.

28.   It seems that Mrs. Eddy even lost the friendship of the Olivers after her split with Kennedy, and the Olivers and the Phillipses were her main links to the more affluent and educated parts of local society. Susie Oliver later converted to Christian Science and reestablished her friendship with Mrs. Eddy.

29.   L07808. Original in the Church History Department. From the autograph Spofford letters that I have seen in photocopy, Mrs. Eddy was right not to trust his abilities as a corrector of punctuation and grammar.

30.   Bates and Dittemore are typical here: "[Mrs. Glover] was aware of the desirability of coherent development in her book and labored all her life to attain it. This was the initial reason for her continual re-editing of *Science and Health,* although financial considerations later entered in. In the successive editions she strove pathetically to supply the lack of an internal and organic principle in her book by merely rearranging its chapters" (Bates and Dittemore, p. 153).

31.   Mrs. Eddy's use of metaphor and analogy deserves to be studied in detail, especially in the 1875 edition where her imagination runs free of correction or suggestion from others.

32.   A side to Luce Irigaray's thought that has received relatively little attention is her interest in religion, and her understanding of a concept of God in relation to both ecological and gender politics. There are interesting correlations to be made, on the level of feminist theology, between Mary Baker Eddy and Irigaray. See, in this regard, Irigaray's essay on mysticism in *Speculum of the Other Woman* (trans. Gillian C. Gill [Ithaca: Cornell University Press, 1985]); the section called "When the Gods Are Born" in *Marine Lover of Friedrich Nietzsche* (trans. Gillian C. Gill [New York: Columbia University Press, 1991]); "Belief Itself," "Divine Women," and "Women, the Sacred and Money," in *Sexes and Genealogies,* (trans. Gillian C. Gill [New York: Columbia University Press, 1993]); and the reading of Spinoza's "Of God" in *An Ethics of Sexual Difference* (trans. Carolyn Burke and Gillian C. Gill [Ithaca: Cornell University Press, 1993]).

33.   Good examples of this occur on pages 33 and 37 of the first edition of *Science and Health.*

34.   "Unreadable" is, of course, only one of the negative adjectives increasingly used to describe deconstructionist prose, and defending Mrs. Eddy's book in terms of its likeness to Derrida or Irigaray may be counterproductive. But it is important to gloss the old criticism of "unreadability" in new ways, and the manner in which the organization and style of the philosophical work of Nietzsche and Heidegger are habitually explained and praised can, I believe, unexpectedly, be applied to Mrs. Eddy.

35.   Appendix B of the Milmine biography attempts to establish the debt of Mrs. Eddy to the works of Andrew Jackson Davis who was born five years after Mrs Eddy but became a nationally famous author and sage in his very early twenties. The appendix ends with the information that Davis, after publishing his trance works, became a Spiritualist. The Milmine account of Davis is, to put it mildly, partial. There is no mention of his fall into disgrace and poverty after a scandalous affair with the wealthy married woman twenty years his senior who paid for his work to be published and also supplied him with a home in Waltham, Massachusetts. The Milmine account also fails to point out that Davis not only carefully chose his hypnotist, Mr. Lyon, but his amanuensis, a thirty-five-year-old Universalist minister. The Reverend Fishbough, who supposedly took down the mystic and learned revelations spoken by the uneducated youth, was an experienced and fluent writer whose later works show considerable knowledge of religion, philosophy, and mysticism. I am willing to consider Davis to have had some kind of genius, but, as Lyon's

and Fishbough's own testimonies make clear, he was incapable of writing a correctly spelled and punctuated sentence—one of the criticisms levelled against Mrs. Eddy by Milmine. A further example of double standards in Milmine's book is the author's attempts to make Mrs. Eddy guilty of appropriating Davis's ideas, but to whitewash P. P. Quimby of the same thing, even though Quimby and Davis were active in mesmeric circles at precisely the same time, and Quimby had every opportunity to read Davis's books. Robert Peel is surely right to argue that Quimby owed a huge, and wholly unacknowledged debt (Quimby acknowledges no debts!) to "the Seer of Poughkeepsie," as Davis was known in his heyday. (See Chapter 7 of Slater Brown, *The Heyday of Spiritualism.*)

36.   All profits from Davis's most famous and popular book went to Lyon and Fishbough, who asserted that, while under trance and before witnesses, the young mystic had renounced all claim to copyright and proceeds from the sale of the book.

37.   *Science and Health,* 1e, p. 66. **Unless otherwise noted, all quotations in this chapter are from the 1875 edition of *Science and Health.*** Those familiar with the edition of *Science and Health* now in use will recognize most of the passages I have chosen to quote, but I have not attempted to provide cross references between first and last editions, or to print the definitive version.

38.   The quotation from Saint Augustine is taken from the R. S. Pine-Coffin translation of Augustine of Hippo's *Confessions* (Harmondsworth, England: Penguin Books, 1961), book 7, chapter 12, p. 148. The quotation from Mrs. Eddy is from *Science and Health,* 1e, p. 17. There is no evidence that Mrs. Eddy read Saint Augustine's work, and his understanding of God, of good and evil, of the nature of man, and so forth came down to her only as part of the general theological tradition she was exposed to in youth. Probably she associated Augustine's name above all with the doctrine of original sin and the redemption of the elect which, by her own testimony, she rejected almost from childhood.

39.   For example, in the ten-minute speech Mrs. Eddy was allowed to give in defense of herself at the Tremont Temple in Boston in 1885, she is careful to declare her belief in prayer, and her constant recourse to prayer in daily life.

40.   In this section, I have found very valuable the unpublished doctoral dissertation by Thomas C. Johnsen, "Christian Science and the Puritan Tradition" (Ph.D. diss., Johns Hopkins University, 1983). This is available from University Microfilms.

41.   As I have noted in earlier chapters, in the mid-1860s Mrs. Eddy was intent on writing a long work of exegesis which she never published and which is now usually referred to as the Genesis manuscript.

42.   This page is particularly full of errata, mainly failings of punctuation, some of which I have modified for clarity's sake. These errata are perhaps a measure of the difficulty Mrs. Eddy was having with this interpretation.

43.   Mrs. Eddy's doctrinal stress on the Virgin Mary and Virgin birth was to be viciously distorted when Mrs. Woodbury claimed to have borne a parthenogenetic son and named him Prince of Peace. See Chapter 23.

44.   It is very significant that Mrs. Eddy should specify "parental claims" in this short list of the injustices society inflicts on women. This is a tiny confirmation for my argument that, far from being an indifferent or cruel mother, Mrs. Eddy was never able to accept or forgive herself for her legal and financial powerlessness to keep her son and promote his well-being.

45.   See Luke 20: 34–36: "And Jesus answering said unto them, The children of this world marry, and are given in marriage: But they which shall be accounted worthy to obtain that world, and the resurrection from the dead, neither marry, nor are given in marriage: Neither can they die any more: for they are equal unto the angels; and are the children of God, being the children of the resurrection."

46.   Bates and Dittemore, pp. 156–57.

47.   Peel says that there are in fact at least five manuscripts of "Extracts of Doctor P. P. Quimby's Writings" in Mrs. Wentworth's handwriting, each a little different, and only two with Mrs. Glover's preface. It seems unlikely that Mrs. Wentworth needed five copies for her own use, and likely that she made copies for her own patients, and probably charged for them. Mrs. Eddy herself asked $50 from Sarah Bagley for such a copy, but Miss Bagley did not find the piece valuable enough to buy.

48.   Showing some of the inability to follow a logical argument that they reproach in Mrs. Eddy, Bates and Dittemore, who had access to most of the key documents and perhaps to the unpublished research on the Quimby question by Frederick Remington, acknowledge that "Questions and Answers" and "Science of Man" are not at all the same but continue throughout their book to harp on Mrs. Eddy's debt to Quimby. This point was noted in 1931 in the *New York Saturday Review* of the Bates and Dittemore biography, by Woodbridge Riley, a professor of psychology who in 1925 had collaborated with Frederick Peabody and Charles E. Humiston in a particularly excoriating attack called *The Faith, the Falsity and the Failure of Christian Science* (New York and Chicago: Fleming H. Revell, 1925). Riley accuses Bates and Dittemore of muddying the waters of the debate by admitting in a trade publication for the first time that Quimby's "Questions and Answers" and Mrs. Eddy's "Science of Man" had almost no questions and answers in common.

49.   Erwin Seale, ed., *Phineas Parkhurst Quimby: The Complete Writings* (3 vols.), vol. 3 (Marina Del Rey, Calif.: Devorss and Company, 1988), p. 274.

Chapter 13: Spofford and Eddy

1.   Milmine and Cather, p. 138.

2.   Milmine gives by far the longest and most detailed account of Asa Gilbert Eddy's early life and background. Unfortunately, Milmine names none of her sources, but she seems to have gone to Eddy's hometown and interviewed friends and neighbors of his family. Eddy himself was, of course, long since dead when the *McClure's* series was prepared, but some of the detail given sounds as if it might have come from a near relative, probably his sister-in-law, Mrs. Washington Eddy. Mary Godfrey Parker's reminiscences of Mrs. Eddy (which were written in 1932) form part of the series called *We Knew Mary Baker Eddy,* republished in one volume in 1979 by the Christian Science Publishing Society.

3.   Mrs. Eddy and Mrs. Godfrey corresponded for many years, and it is one of the tragedies of Eddy historiography that the large cache of letters from Mrs. Eddy that Mary Parker saw in her mother's drawer was destroyed uncopied in the 1908 Chelsea fire.

4.   Edward Hitchings may also have contributed some money toward the publication of *Science and Health*. Mrs. Eddy tried to find a publisher earlier. In 1873 she went into Boston with George Clark, who had a manuscript of his own, but whereas Clark found someone interested in issuing his tales of the sea, Mrs. Eddy met only refusal.

5.   See *Ret.,* p. 38:

> After months had passed, I yielded to a constant conviction that I must insert in my last chapter a partial history of what I had already observed of mental malpractice. Accordingly, I set to work, contrary to my inclination, to fufil this painful task, and finished my copy for the book. As it afterwards appeared, although I had not thought of such a result, my printer resumed his work at the same time, finished printing the copy he had on hand, and then started for Lynn to see me. The afternoon that he left Boston for Lynn, I started for Boston with my finished copy. We met at the Eastern depot in Lynn, and were both surprised,—I to learn that he had printed all the copy on hand, and had come to tell me he wanted more,—he to find me *en route* for Boston, to give him the closing chapter of my first edition of Science and Health. Not a word had passed between us, audibly or mentally, while this went on. I had grown disgusted with

my printer, and become silent. He had come to a standstill through motives and circumstances unknown to me.

6.   Charles Dyer, in his unpublished biography of his great-grandfather Daniel Spofford, says that Daniel's bound copy, which would have been the most valuable item of Eddy memorabilia he possessed, was somehow lost, and that only the "Florence" copy survives, in the Longyear collection.

7.   The sources I have used in this chapter are as follows. I was given access to the Church's files on Spofford, including the full text of Mrs. Eddy's letters to him; the unpublished biographical essay on Spofford by Charles Dyer; and some research notes on the assassination plot. At Longyear I saw the Spofford letters to Mrs. Longyear, other letters to various people, Spofford's account books and personal memorandum book, his second wife's copy of the 1870 manuscript, and various pamphlets he wrote.

8.   Six students put up a total of ten dollars a week to rent the Good Templars Hall in Lynn. Mrs. Eddy spoke five times but was heckled so severely by Spiritualists that she stopped. As usual, after she had so unpromising a beginning, one wonders where she found the strength of mind to go on.

9.   Note that the formal constitution of the newly named Christian Scientist Association did not take place until July 4, 1876. Peel, *Trial,* p. 11.

10.   L07807. Original in the Church History Department. I am assuming that the unnamed wicked student whom Mrs. Eddy accuses of stealing her proofs from Mr. Prescott was Kennedy, especially since Kennedy was a friend of Stanley's, whom Mrs. Eddy does name in the letter. Peel says that Kennedy was lodging with Prescott, a merchant on Broad Street.

11.   Spofford and his second wife seem to have continued to practice a version of Christian Science since, presumably for their own use, his wife Ellen made a new hand-written copy of Addie's copy of Mrs. Eddy's 1870 teaching manuscript which is signed by herself and Daniel and dated February 25, 1893. Original at Longyear Museum. Spofford also says in his 1921 letter to Mrs. Longyear: "These Mss. after reading a few times I declared to be that for which the Christian Church had been looking for lo these eighteen centuries." Spofford authored at least two pamphlets of Biblical exegesis and became obsessed by the significance of his name and by the fact that his parents, who were first cousins, were both descended from David. Spofford wrote to communicate this insight to Mrs. Eddy in a letter of October 18, 1901, ending, "Conceived of the Holy Spirit, and born of Mary without sin, through a conception of the immaculate. Rev. XII, 5." This, of course, was not the kind of information that Willa Cather and the *McClure's* team wanted to convey about one of their star witnesses. It is not entirely clear how Spofford made his living after 1878, but it seems that he may have abandoned mental healing sometime after 1882, since on his death certificate his daughter Marion lists his occupation as shoemaker. Spofford and his second wife and their four children lived for many years in a specially built home on the Amesbury road in Haverhill, opposite the old Whittier homestead. This places Spofford suggestively close to Amesbury, home to Sarah Bagley (and her visitor and collaborator Richard Kennedy) as well as to Charles Stanley, another successful practitioner of alternative medicine.

12.   Milmine and Cather, p. 158.

13.   "'She was a very attractive woman,' wrote a young man whose cousin occupied part of the house at Broad Street a little later, 'with a lovely face and a very good figure.' The cousin herself described Mrs. Glover as always beautifully dressed, often with flowers pinned to her gown, and added that she never seemed to be without flowers in her sitting room" (Peel, *Trial,* p. 12).

14.   If Mary Adeline Nourse Spofford is largely erased from Christian Science history, John Eddy is even more of a mystery. No one seems to have any idea who he was, though

all authorities I consulted say he had no connection to Asa Gilbert Eddy. Mrs. Mary Longyear researched and published a genealogy of Asa Gilbert Eddy, going back to the 1600s, but she probably did not have the court documents from 1876, and thus she had no illumination to offer about John Eddy. I was told that efforts by members of the Church History Department to track down the identity of this John Eddy have failed. As a literary critic, and one who has spent a lot of years working on both psychoanalysis and detective fiction, I am fascinated by the appearance of this unknown Eddy at the same time that the known Eddy was emerging as Spofford's main rival in Christian Science, and by the fact that the adulterous lover more usually associated with Addie Spofford was called Kenn-edy. In one of the more mysterious passages in "Demonology" on the Kennedy–Addie Spofford–Daniel Spofford triangle, Mrs. Eddy wrote: "We were told by her husband that her only terms for peace with him were that he should vindicate this villain [Kennedy]" (*Science and Health,* 3e, p. 9). Could this "vindication" have extended to an agreement that, in his divorce libel suit, Daniel Spofford would conceal the name of his wife's lover, Richard Kennedy, and invent a fictional "John Eddy"? I presume that the relationship between Addie and Richard broke down in the 1870s and that she returned to Knoxville, where she filed her successful divorce suit against Daniel, on the grounds that he deserted her. Why the Spoffords chose Knoxville has never been explained.

15.   Peel, *Trial,* p. 14.

16.   L07811. Original in the Church History Department. This letter is quoted in extenso by Milmine and by Peel.

17.   Letter of July 14, 1876. L09897. Original in the Church History Department.

18.   The standard picture of Samuel Bancroft at about the same age also features him with an off-center roach.

19.   *We Knew Mary Baker Eddy,* pp. 2–3.

20.   It was also during the period of the late 1870s that, according to the later testimony of Miranda Rice and Dorcas Rawson, two of Mrs. Eddy's most trusted students and close friends at that time, she was taking opium or morphine. In 1885 she herself said in an article in the *Christian Science Journal* that at one time she experimented with opium products in order successfully to prove to herself that they could not affect her.

21.   Milmine and Cather, pp. 171–72.

22.   Asa Gilbert Eddy was perhaps closer to his parents than his siblings were, as he seems to have cared for them in their last years, and it was he who inherited the family farm in South Londonderry. When Gilbert died, his widow inherited this property, along with all the rest of his estate, and she sold it to a neighbor for $1500. This was not a very large sum, but perhaps it was because this inheritance had gone out of the family that some of Gilbert's remaining relatives were willing to talk to Milmine about him and provide so many details about his upbringing and appearance. In an 1881 letter to her son George Glover, Mrs. Eddy tries in vain to persuade him to move with his family to New Hampshire to take on the Eddy farm and forget all about gold mining.

23.   Milmine and Cather, p. 169.

24.   I was allowed to see Sarah Crosby materials at the Mother Church archives, which include her correspondence with Mrs. Eddy from 1876 to 1903, with Georgine Milmine and Lyman Powell in 1907, and with the New York rare book dealer Beauchamp in 1909, as well as some Crosby family letters and interview materials. Quotations and references to the contents of correspondence between Sarah Crosby and Mary Baker Eddy are from the Church History Department. The correspondence makes clear Mrs. Crosby's various disputes with her old friend Mrs. Eddy, the desertion by her husband which led her family into bankruptcy, her deepening financial problems in the 1870s, her pleas to Mrs. Eddy at Pleasant View for financial assistance, the small checks and acerbic letters Mrs. Eddy sent in reply, Mrs. Crosby's active cooperation with those look-

ing for ways to attack Christian Science, and her shrewd sale to the highest bidder of her testimony, affidavits, and memorabilia relating to her relationship with Mrs. Eddy. There is little doubt in my mind that had Mrs. Eddy responded to the implied threat of blackmail by sending her old Maine friend a series of big checks signed with love and kisses in the late 1890s, the Peabody-Milmine school of biographers would have lost one of their star witnesses, and Mrs. Crosby's testimony about Quimby and Spiritualism would have been very different.

25. L02015. Original in the Church History Department.

26. L02016. Original in the Church History Department.

27. This amount, $146, is the one noted by Spofford in his private account books which came into the Longyear collection after Spofford's death. The accounts for 1870–1877 are meticulous, detailing for example, not only how many copies were sold but to whom, and by what agent. Thus between November 1875 and May 1876, 235 copies were sold, averaging 39 per month. Between May 1, 1876, and January 1, 1877, 413 more were sold, with total gross profits of $550.10, and expenses of $327.80.

28. L07814. Original in the Church History Department.

29. In their account of Spofford's break with Mrs. Eddy, Bates and Dittemore portray Spofford as an honorable man who worked hard to sell copies of an unsalable work and showed integrity by returning the meager $600 profit not to the author, despite her demands, but to the investors who had lost their capital. By this account, Spofford worked for free and even covered marketing expenses out of pocket. Spofford's own account book tells a different story. When he resigned as Mrs. Eddy's agent on July 3, all the first edition had been sold—1,000 copies in nine months—albeit at the discounted price of $1. When Spofford wrote to Mrs. Eddy castigating her for failing to complete the manuscript corrections she had promised, Spofford himself claimed that there was a market for a new edition, so the book had been far from a failure. The sales figures Spofford recorded for himself show a profit of $724, out of which he deducted $304 in expenses for himself. What happened to the remaining $419 is unclear, but it was not paid in a lump sum to Newhall and Barry, to whom Spofford recorded paying $42.46 and $23.16, respectively, in November 1877. In late 1877 Spofford recorded contracting for $750 in repairs on a house at 55 State Street in Newburyport, on behalf of Ellen Carter. By January 1878 Spofford was paying rent to Miss Carter, whom he would marry in 1880. By the fall of 1877 Barry and Spofford were in alliance against Mrs. Eddy, but the financial records we have indicate that Mrs. Eddy had reason to question Spofford's activities since he was the only one who made some small profit on the sale of the first edition of *Science and Health*. I am indebted to Judy Huenneke of the Church History Department for advising me to look carefully at Spofford's accounts.

30. Barry and Newhall published a public letter defending Spofford against malicious accusations being circulated against him. They state that he had loyally performed everything he had contracted to with them, in regard to *Science and Health*. Miranda Rice, who at this point was still in the Eddy camp, in turn published a letter asking Barry to be specific about the accountings with Spofford and Mrs. Eddy and accusing him in turn of spreading malicious accusations about Mrs. Eddy. See Bates and Dittemore, pp. 185–87.

31. This pen may be the one mentioned in the transcript of the Barry trial as one that George Barry had given Mrs. Glover.

32. Apparently fearful of losing Mrs. Eddy's home to liens, Mr. and Mrs. Eddy evolved a strategy of passing title to the house from one disciple or friend to another. Bates and Dittemore, p. 203, detail the extraordinary sequence of title for the Broad Street property between June 10, 1875, and November 10, 1883. The title passed between Dorcas Rawson and Mrs. Glover twice, then between Warren Livermore and A. G. Eddy twice, then between Henry Dunnels and George Prescott, back to Dorcas Rawson, over to Abbie Whiting, and finally back to Mrs. Eddy herself. Given the constant defections by Mrs. Eddy's students, it must have been a problem to know whom to trust with title to

the house. This strategy has some importance since Mrs. Eddy would adopt the same principle in the 1880s and 1890s for her real estate holdings and copyrights.

33. In the third edition of *Science and Health* Mrs. Eddy herself claimed that she had been led astray by Arens, and her account is upheld, rather surprisingly, by Bates and Dittemore who assert that she was not litigious by nature and that all the suits were a complete departure from her normal procedure (Bates and Dittemore, p. 188).

34. Barry trial records in the Church History Department. In all that he said about the case, Kennedy gave the impression that he was a man of means. Whereas Mrs. Eddy had so few financial resources after leaving their partnership that she was driven by such desperate and abject expedients as filing suit against him, he for his part did not need to care about sums like $768.63 and was appealing her suit purely on principle. One wonders how exactly Kennedy's new practice in Boston was leaving him so affluent since he himself told Powell that he had made only a $300 profit from the Lynn partnership, after settling accounts with Mrs. Eddy.

35. This is how I interpret a somewhat mysterious letter from George Barry to Daniel Spofford of January 25, 1878. Original at Longyear Museum.

36. Milmine and Cather, p. 239.

37. The Milmine account of Miss Brown is the most detailed we have, and a good example of Willa Cather's talent for characterization. Milmine and Cather, pp. 234–36.

38. In an attempt to limit the damage of Dunnels's affidavit about the two-hour vigils, Sibyl Wilbur says that the students may, indeed, have met to "take up" Spofford in the way described, but that this was against Mrs. Eddy's wishes. However, Dunnels's testimony is confirmed by a letter from Mrs. Eddy included by Samuel Bancroft in his book, in which she urges him to take up Spofford at four in the morning and at four and nine at night, since these were supposedly the times when Spofford was wielding his deadly influence. Bancroft, *Mrs. Eddy As I Knew Her,* pp. 42–43.

39. Milmine and Cather, p. 242. The reporter for the Newburyport *Herald* concluded his account of the allegations against Spofford's mesmeric influence by questioning what jurisdiction a court of law could have "inasmuch as prison walls could not restrain such power, and since death would be unable to terminate it." If we are to believe Mrs. Eddy's chief defender, Robert Peel, this was not the conclusion she herself drew. To judge from a July letter she sent the Peabody *Weekly Reporter,* her feeling was that, since mentally inflicted wounds were as real or, indeed, indistinguishable from physically inflicted ones, the courts should be moving to extend their domain to include them. An edited form of these remarks can be found in the current edition of *Science and Health,* pp. 104–105.

40. The case was heard finally in June 1879, and the decision was filed on October 14.

41. The edition "contained only . . . 'Imposition and Demonstration' [a critique of spiritualism], 'Physiology,' 'Mesmerism,' 'Metaphysics,' and 'Reply to a Clergyman'—chapters weighted on the negative side, since most of those setting forth the positive teachings of Christian Science were in the disabled 'Vol. I' " (Peel, *Trial,* p. 46).

Chapter 14: *The Conspiracy to Murder Daniel Spofford*

1. The first count of the indictments made by the grand jury on December 3, 1878. The second count accused Eddy and Arens of conspiring to "beat, bruise, wound and evil treat" Spofford.

2. Spofford gave part of this story to the police and press when he reappeared on the afternoon of October 29. Arens and Eddy had been arrested the same morning. Around 1907 he gave a more detailed version of the same story for the Milmine book. Spofford was not asked to give evidence at the preliminary hearing against Eddy and Arens, and he was never publicly cross-examined.

3. These details are from the special dispatch to the *Boston Herald* of October 29, 1878, from the correspondent who was covering the Spofford disappearance case.

4. According to one account, there was a newspaper report of his body having been taken to the morgue, but no actual reference has been found.

5. Sargent's testimony under cross-examination as reported by the *Boston Herald,* November 8, 1878.

6. From various newspaper accounts of testimony given at the trial and perhaps interviews with Sargent and Pinkham, it seems that Sargent claimed Arens had given him $75, $15, and $20, at different points in the alleged plot, or perhaps $150 in all.

7. Milmine and Cather, p. 260.

8. Peel, *Trial,* p. 55.

9. The documentation was gathered by the Legal Department of The Mother Church, and I consulted it at the Church History Department.

10. Excerpt from L13376. Original in the Church History Department.

11. The quote about what Sargent said he was told about Spofford comes from the Newburyport *Herald,* November 9, 1878. Milmine gives the most information about Arens before he joined Christian Science: "He was a Prussian who as a young man had come to Lynn, where he worked as a carpenter until he was able to open a cabinet-making shop. He was a good workman but was not particularly successful in his business and was frequently involved in litigation. Although his educational opportunities had been limited, he had an active mind. He read a great deal, was restless, eager and ambitious" (Milmine and Cather, pp. 249–50). Peel reports that around 1880 Arens married Miss Adelma (Dell) Atkinson, the daughter of Mr. and Mrs. Benjamin Atkinson, Christian Scientists in Newburyport, who broke with Mrs. Eddy in the same year.

12. Robert Peel interprets a remark made later by Mrs. Eddy to mean that by 1882 the Eddys "had begun to suspect that Arens' hands were not entirely clean in the 1878 conspiracy-to-murder case" and that they had spent hundreds of dollars exculpating a guilty man. Peel, *Trial,* p. 112 and n. 85.

Chapter 15: The Move to Boston and the Death of Gilbert Eddy

1. The Eddys' correspondence with their lawyer Russell H. Conwell is in the Church History Department. Perhaps I should stress that at this period even quite modest New England families were able to afford to hire someone to do the cooking and the major household cleaning, and that Mrs. Eddy herself had been accustomed to having her board provided for her ever since she and Patterson separated in the late 1860s. Lyman P. Powell makes the most interesting use of Mrs. Eddy's notebooks, which I was not able to consult, and he includes in his notes an entry from September 26, 1874, indicating how carefully the Eddys kept their accounts— "Postage 18cts. Expressage 15cts" (Powell, p. 298).

2. L04084. Original in the Church History Department.

3. For example, there is this pencil note, probably passed to Spofford in court: "S.— Kenedy has ruined in every respect and is making you sick and it is not Mrs. E or students you can't make Dr hate her and not heed her advice" (Asa Gilbert Eddy, notebook 1, p. 25. Original in the Church History Department).

4. Asa Gilbert Eddy, notebook 4, pp. 46–51. Original in the Church History Department.

5. Peel, *Trial,* p. 63.

6. Wilbur, p. 257.

7. Robert Peel gives a fascinating extract from Mrs. Eddy's notebook about this cross-questioning, and correctly labels the style Dickensian (*Trial,* p. 67). It is too bad that Mrs. Eddy felt obliged to keep this kind of prose unpublished, as it shows a side of her char-

acter that would endear her to many in the general public. For more on the Stanley and Tuttle suit, see Chapter 11.

8.   In her reminiscences, Mary Godfrey Parker recalls the amazement she felt at meeting Mrs. Eddy's son in a Chelsea grocery store at the time of his 1887–1888 visit to Boston:

> I did not know who he was then, but I recall very vividly how surprised I was to see a man of such peculiar appearance. He stood there calling out his orders in a loud voice, and his manner was so boisterous and his costume so unusual that I could not help telling my mother about it when I returned home. I do not recollect the details of his clothes now, except that his legs were encased in great high boots such as I had never seen before, and his trousers were tucked into these boots. I remember his hair was long and he wore a beard. He seemed entirely out of keeping with the surroundings there. (*We Knew Mary Baker Eddy,* pp. 14–15)

9.   Some vague cloud seems to hover over Gershom's head, and I wonder if the sixteen-year-old Nellie conceived him before her marriage to George Glover. Certainly, it was the fourth child and the Glovers' second son, born in January 1889, who received the name George Washington Glover III, and to whom Mrs. Eddy sent one of her most treasured possessions, the watch that had belonged to her first husband. In an irate letter to his Concord, New Hampshire, lawyer, William Chandler, in 1907, George Glover II makes a puzzling reference to the fact that the trust document sent him by Mrs. Eddy's lawyers declares Gershom "wrong" and therefore not covered by the trust.

10.   Original in the Church History Department.

11.   I was surprised to discover that this strategy of Mrs. Eddy's successfully endeared her son to his aunt. Even though Mrs. Tilton left nothing to either her sisters or her sisters-in-law, she left a handsome $10,000 in her will to the prodigal George Glover in Lead, South Dakota, and only $3000 to George Waldron Baker, her other nephew who lived in Maine.

12.   Wilbur writes:

> The walls of the reception-room were finished in plain gray paper with gold cornices. The windows were hung with white lace draperies, looped back over high gilt arms. A crimson carpet covered the floor and the furniture was of black walnut. The tables always held vases of flowers, for Mrs. Eddy was devoted to the cultivation of plants in summer and winter, and her success with them was an evidence of her continual love of the beautiful. (Wilbur, p. 253)

The Broad Street house is today maintained by The Mother Church as a shrine and is regularly open to visitors, but it is hard to recapture Wilbur's enthusiasm for Mrs. Eddy's furnishings, which seem comfortable and hard-wearing rather than elegant.

13.   Apart from his work in the Christian Science movement, James Howard also served as the Eddys' business agent in Lynn when they were away from home, collecting rents, pressuring tenants to pay, and so forth. Asa Gilbert Eddy had reason to correspond with Howard in both capacities, and The Mother Church allowed me to see a small collection of these communications. Mr. Eddy's letters are notable for their careful script, extremely Biblical style, religious fervor, and guarded content. Eddy was obviously very reluctant to say anything in black-and-white, probably wisely given the speed with which gossip and calumny spread among the students. On August 21, 1880, he remarks to Howard that they can discuss things in person when they get together, and thus avoid the possibility of someone reading their letters.

14.   One of the accusations launched against Mrs. Eddy in 1906 by her former student Mrs. Miranda Rice was that Mrs. Eddy drove the Howard children into convulsions.

15.   James Howard also became one of the main informants on Malicious Animal

Magnetism used in the Milmine biography, the New York *World* series on Mrs. Eddy, and by the lawyers representing the "Next Friends." Howard claimed that Mrs. Eddy had inspired such terror in the Lynn household with her preoccupation with mesmerism that his little son went into convulsions, and the whole family had to flee the house. As so often was the case in the testimony of those cited by press or hostile parties as evidence of Mrs. Eddy's preoccupation with Malicious Animal Magnetism, Howard's anecdotes show how far he himself actually still accepted a version of the same doctrine, but with Mrs. Eddy herself converted into the diabolic mesmerizer.

16.   I have already considered "Demonology" in some detail in my discussion of Wallace Wright and Richard Kennedy in Chapter 11.

17.   *The Science of Man* was published by Mrs. Eddy as a pamphlet in 1876. As I have explained in some detail in other chapters, the debate over whether Mrs. Eddy had plagiarized from P. P. Quimby's writings centered almost exclusively on this piece.

18.   Quoted in Robert Peel, *Trial,* pp. 92–93.

19.   Milmine and Cather, p. 281.

20.   According to Milmine and Cather (p. 289), in 1893 one of Eastman's patients died, and he was prosecuted, found guilty, and imprisoned for five years.

21.   Mrs. Eddy sometimes claimed that four thousand students had gone through the college between 1881 and 1889, but Calvin Frye insisted on the lower number. See Peel, *The Years of Authority* (New York: Holt Rinehart Winston, 1977), p. 483, n. 104; hereafter referred to as *Authority*.

22.   In February 1882 Miranda Rice was enjoying the delights of tourism and spreading the Christian Science gospel in Havana, Cuba, and wrote to her fellow rebel James Howard asking for news of his young family and assuring him that "Mrs. E" had no way of hurting them (Original in the Church History Department). Mrs. Rice's sister had sent her the glad news that the Eddys had left Lynn, apparently for good since the sign was down on their house. Peel gives the information that two years after her break with Mrs. Eddy, for reasons that are unclear, Mrs. Rice moved to San Francisco and began to preach Christian Science as her own creation. Her practice did not prosper, and in 1887 she took class with another apostate, Emma Hopkins, but she was then forced to spend some time in a mental asylum before returning to Lynn. Although she remained a kind of Christian Scientist, her hostility toward Mrs. Eddy never abated, and she would be one of the main sources of information on Mrs. Eddy's life in Lynn quoted by Peabody and Milmine.

23.   The full text of Julia Bartlett's memoirs is at the Longyear Museum. A somewhat shortened and amended version was published in the book *We Knew Mary Baker Eddy.* The section I have quoted is also given in full in the Powell biography and noted by Peel as an important turning point in Christian Science: "Here was the evidence of one of those moments in religious history when a movement, emerging from its earliest formative stage, begins to view as a prophet chosen of God a leader whose guidance has hitherto been accepted in limited charismatic terms" (Peel, *Trial,* pp. 99–100).

24.   Bates and Dittemore quote this passage, whereas Peel prefers to summarize it, replacing Mrs. Eddy's hasty reference to the Biblical text with the correct "not . . . that any of the students were ready to unloose the latchets of her shoes" (Peel, *Trial,* p. 101).

25.   I have tried to reproduce here the typography of the text as recorded in Bates and Dittemore, p. 217.

26.   Miranda Rice, one of Mrs. Eddy's earliest students, had experienced childbirth without pain under Mrs. Eddy's care, probably in 1873, the year after she took class.

27.   Testimony of Mrs. Dora Hossick, Carrolton, Missouri, *Mis.,* pp. 413–14.

28.   Mrs. Eddy recounts this visit in *Mis.,* p. 112.

29.   "Edward J. Arens had moved to Boston immediately after the conspiracy case and had opened an office at No. 32 Upton Street, where he obtained an uncertain practice

among the market men and hucksters who thronged the neighborhood of Faneuil Hall" (Bates and Dittemore, p. 207).

30.   This quote is from a statement made in 1882 about the circumstances of Asa Gilbert Eddy's death, signed by George and Clara Choate, Ellen P. Davis, Arthur T. Buswell, Abbie K. Whiting, Julia S. Bartlett, and Hanover P. Smith. Eddy had apparently wanted to join a temperance organization, as this was his "favorite cause," but in order to do so he needed to have life insurance, so he consulted a medical examiner. The statement does not say whether Eddy was actually able to buy the life insurance. This story makes me wonder if the devoted and practical Gilbert, feeling himself near death from whatever cause, had tried to insure his life and thus provide better for his wife's future. Robert Peel says that Mr. Eddy had consulted Dr. Noyes who diagnosed "organic heart disease, dangerously advanced" (Peel, *Trial,* p. 113).

31.   Wilbur, p. 269.

32.   Arens did not come, and according to what his son said in 1929, he protested that he had liked Asa Gilbert Eddy and wished him only good. If he could have killed anyone, Arens said, it would have been Mrs. Eddy. Hermann Arendtz told this to Lucia Warren when he was trying to sell to The Mother Church a receipt written by Mrs. Eddy to his mother, Mrs. Dell Atkinson Arens, acknowledging payment of $150. One of the many grievances Mrs. Eddy held against Arens was that he failed to repay most of the $500 he once borrowed from her. Church History Department.

33.   Bates and Dittemore, p. 220.

34.   Mary Baker Eddy, interview, Boston *Post,* June 5, 1882.

35.   Frederick W. Peabody, *The Religio-Medical Masquerade: A Complete Exposure of Christian Science* (New York: Revell, 1910), pp. 43–44.

Part Three: The New Mrs. Eddy: 1883–1905

1.   The comprehensive detail with which Mrs. Eddy's last years are known is due to the exponential growth in her correspondence, to her increasing use of professional secretarial assistance in dealing with that correspondence, and the multiplication of people around Mrs. Eddy whose duty and pleasure it was not only to take down what she said, formally or informally, but to record her daily doings. The great mass of documentation on Mrs. Eddy relates to her last thirty years, and virtually all of it is held in the Church History Department.

Chapter 16: The Massachusetts Metaphysical College

1.   In her reminiscences of the Eddys, Clara Choate, who had known them more intimately than perhaps anyone else, noted that Mrs. Eddy was accompanied everywhere by Mr. Eddy, and that they competed with each other in expressing affectionate concern, each urging the partner to eat better, get more rest, and so forth.

2.   Powell, p. 165. Milmine, Dakin, and Bates and Dittemore interpret the vigor and speed of Mrs. Eddy's recovery after her husband's death as evidence that she had no real affection for him, and that she was, if anything, glad to have lost a spouse who had been useful for a while but whose humble background, failing energies, and limited intellect had become a handicap to her as she and Christian Science began at last to achieve some success. There can be no doubt that Mrs. Eddy's work accelerated forward after Gilbert Eddy's death, and that he probably would have been of little practical or public help to her in the next stage of her career. However, in my view, it is a mistake or an oversimplification to assume that Mrs. Eddy after 1882 was nothing but the leader of Christian Science, that she did not have very real emotional needs which a loving husband could satisfy better than anyone. She was able to do without this normal source of support, but to claim that she neither missed nor wanted it is, quite unnecessarily, to make her a mon-

ster. I would also note that Leo Tolstoy and Mohandas Gandhi became similarly persuaded that married life and religious mission were incompatible and that it was necessary that they give up the love and comfort of marriage if they were to move closer to God. Given the way critics have reacted to Mrs. Eddy's failure to retire or lose momentum after her husband's death, it would be interesting to imagine how the same critics would have reacted had she, like Tolstoy and Gandhi, deliberately left a living and loving spouse behind in order to pursue her religious mission.

3.   This poem was published in the December 1, 1883, issue of the *Journal of Christian Science* and is the second included in *Miscellaneous Writings*. Bates and Dittemore point out that this poem was a revision, with an extra stanza, of the one Mrs. Eddy had composed some thirty years earlier when her fiancé John Bartlett and her mother had both died in the same year (Bates and Dittemore, p. 251).

4.   In her reminiscences Mrs. Manley remembers standing alone in the hallway at the Massachusetts Metaphysical College at the time of Asa Gilbert Eddy's death, and Mrs. Eddy coming downstairs and laying her head on her shoulder and weeping. " 'I feel that there is something in your heart,' she confided, 'that will understand what is in mine.' " Mrs. Manley says that most of the students expected their leader to meet sorrow and disaster without flinching (see Peel, *Trial,* p. 116). Mrs. Woodbury later claimed to have been present at Asa Gilbert Eddy's death, but this seems to be an aggrandizement of her role in the household at this point.

5.   As far as I have been able to consult it, the correspondence between George Glover and his mother lapses between 1882 and 1886, and this gap may reflect the breakdown in the relationship following Asa Gilbert Eddy's death. In October of 1887 when Mrs. Eddy wrote to her son in an effort to try to deter him from coming with his family to pay her a long visit in Boston, she is still harking back to this incident: "I am alone and you never would come to me when I called and now I cannot have you come. You are not what I had hoped to find you, and I am wholly changed." L02085. Original in the Church History Department.

6.   On Mrs. Eddy's friendship with Alice Sibley, see Peel, *Trial,* pp. 101–4.

7.   Mary Beecher Longyear, *The Genealogy and Life of Asa Gilbert Eddy* (Boston: Press of Geo. H. Ellis Company, 1922), p. 77. Buswell, it should be remarked, was by at least 1906 deeply engaged in selling off his reminiscences of Christian Science to the highest bidder and tailoring his memories to suit the paying client or allowing clients to edit as they wished. Thus what Buswell remembered about Mrs. Eddy for Mrs. Longyear differs notably from what he remembered for Georgine Milmine.

8.   L04089. Original in the Church History Department.

9.   Milmine and Cather, p. 292.

10.   The Milmine and Cather biography gives the most detailed biographical material about Calvin Frye. As evidence of what she sees as Frye's excessive fealty to Mrs. Eddy, Milmine notes that Frye took no vacations or even weekends from his duties, that in 1886 Frye hurried quickly away from the funeral of his father, and that in 1890 he neither attended his sister Lydia's funeral nor responded to letters asking him to assist in defraying the burial expenses. This picture of Frye as an unloving family member is belied by a group of Lydia's letters to her brother in the Church History Department. They all date from 1886 and are warm and affectionate in tone. But the letters also indicate that Lydia's relations with her brother Oscar and his wife, with whom she then lived, were strained at best and openly hostile at worst. It is unknown who Milmine's source was.

11.   Frederick Peabody returns obsessively to this phantom marriage in his public addresses and pamphlets as well as in private letters. He claims that he was told that Frye and Mrs. Eddy were married by William Nixon, and he insists that Nixon was in a position to know the truth.

12.   Thus Mrs. Eddy wrote to her son, who in 1898 had already begun to question the

role Frye played in her household: "Mr. Frye is the most disagreeable man that can be found, but this he is, namely (if there is one on earth) an <u>honest man</u> as all will tell you who deal with him. At first mesmerism swayed him but he learned through my forbearance to govern himself. He is a man that would not steal, commit adultery, or fornication, or break one of the ten Commandments" (L02127. Original in the Church History Department).

13.   Willa Cather gives a memorable portrait of the industrious, long-lived, antisocial Frye family, commenting that "their solitary manner of life seemed to come from a general lack of interest in people and affairs, and they stayed at home not so much because of an absorbing family life as because they felt no impulse to stir about the world" (Milmine and Cather, p. 296). This seems to me somewhat uncharitable, ignoring the effect on any family of, first, social decline, and, second, of living for decades with a madwoman. Mrs. Frye, Milmine says, lived to be very old and had only brief periods of lucidity. After losing her husband, Lydia Roaf served as her mother's chief attendant.

14.   His sister seems to have fared much less well in Christian Science, although I have not been able to find out anything new about her. Bates and Dittemore write: "She followed her brother to Boston and became a kind of housemaid to Mrs. Eddy, but her health broke down and she returned to Lawrence, where she underwent a severe operation. After her father's death, in 1886, she fell into meager circumstances, and died in 1890 at the home of a relative" (Bates and Dittemore, p. 228 n. 4).

15.   Mrs. Eddy and her college moved in March 1884 to the house next door, 571 Columbus Avenue. The Columbus Avenue neighborhood was, it seems, a comfortable and respectable one at the time, but far from chic. When in December 1887 Mrs. Eddy bought herself a house at 385 Commonwealth Avenue, she was moving considerably up the social scale and showing her new affluence.

16.   Peel reports that in a letter to a student of October 1882 Mrs. Eddy jubilantly remarked that she was teaching her largest group of students ever, and she estimated that fifty students would graduate in the spring. "The ship of science is again walking the wave, rising above the billows, bidding defiance to the flood-gates of error, for God is at the helm" (Peel, *Trial,* p. 121).

17.   In view of my interest in P. P. Quimby, Emma and Sarah Ware, and Richard Kennedy, I was interested to discover that George Choate either went or was sent by Mrs. Eddy to practice in Portland, Maine, and there he kept an eye on the doings of the newly coalescing Quimby faction. Thus on March 3, 1880, Mrs. Eddy wrote to George Choate: "One thing please bear in mind, to add one more noble deed to the one you have already done, and get her that was EW (now in Scotland) word to look out for K's mesmeric control that he will try on her to make her yield to his wishes; and another measure that he will take, and that is to get it through a third party into his hands" (Letter of March 3, 1880. L0480. Original in the Church History Department). Peel hypothesizes, I am sure correctly, that "EW" is Emma Ware, "K" is Kennedy, and that the mysterious "it" refers to the Quimby texts. George Quimby in 1883 did in fact spirit his father's "manuscripts" out of the country to Scotland and the safekeeping of Sarah Ware McKay.

18.   In June 1880 Mrs Eddy had a dream about George Choate which indicates her idea of his character and her fears about allowing him to practice Christian Science: "She saw Mr. Choate take a beautiful white dress that she had made and cut it in two . . . then put one half of the dress on to his child then from her jewels he scraped all the gold and put into a tiny bottle to wash his jewels with. NB The part that he put on the child was the skirt which looked very awkward as he put it on and he left all the waist and trimmings and that which was beautiful" (A10822. Church History Department). By February 1882 Mrs. Eddy is referring to Choate's continuing alcoholism and failure with patients in a letter to James Ackland.

19.   Little Warren Choate became a great favorite with Mrs. Eddy and has a special place in Christian Science history as the child for whom Mrs. Eddy conceived the plan to form

a Sunday school. In her reminiscences, Clara Choate relates, with rather cloying detail, the story of Mrs. Eddy coaching Warren for his platform appearance for the announcement of the new Sunday School.

20.   In March 1882 Mrs. Eddy wrote to Clara: "Still when I see the great advantage or disadvantage a partner is, it seems hard, hard, that some women who are formed to love must be so awfully situated always" (L02500. Original in the Church History Department). Given Mrs. Eddy's experience with Daniel Patterson, she speaks here from the heart, I think.

21.   One small indication of the mother-daughter relationship between Mrs. Eddy and Clara is that Mrs. Eddy asks Clara to go to 551 Shawmut Avenue "and put my curls, that once was on my head and I prize them very much, my muff and tippet into a paper and send them to me" (Letter of October 26, 1880. L04085. Original in the Church History Department).

22.   Letter of March 15, 1882. L04088. Original in the Church History Department.

23.   Mrs. Eddy's policy of sending students here or there across America or even the globe was much criticized, but, at least in some famous instances, it was extremely successful in spreading the movement. Some measure of what seemed arbitrary despotism was perhaps essential since one inspired and inspiring teacher really could make Christian Science a vital player in the life of a large city or a state. Arthur Buswell went to Cincinnati for several years after receiving such a mandate from the leader, and he managed to both make a living and spread Christian Science. Mrs. Augusta Stetson was as reluctant as Clara Choate to leave Boston, but when Mrs. Eddy requested that she move and begin practicing in New York, she obeyed and, as we shall see in Part Four, succeeded better than anyone could have expected. Things worked out much less well when Mrs. Eddy summoned people from other parts of the United States to come and work in Boston. The case of Mrs. Julia Field-King, chronicled by Milmine, was particularly sad.

24.   Quotations are from the letters of January 5 (L02527) and January 8 (L02528). Originals in the Church History Department.

25.   Arthur Buswell was a friend of Ashley and gave Mrs. Eddy the letter. The two-page, pencil-written statement by Benjamin T. Ashley of December 17, 1883, reads:

> I have seen things that I consider immoral in a married woman. She worked upon me two hours and a half mesmerically. I went in for treatment one evening she seemed to feel that she was losing her influence over me; she drew her chair parallel with mine, arm to arm, so that she could lean upon my chest. And after going through a certain amount of caressing she ventured, finally, to kiss me, without my returning it, this operation she repeated many times at that sitting and finally I returned the kiss once. She seemed to have accomplished all she desired and dismissed me. I knew finally that she was trying to get control of me in a mesmeric sense. I felt that I was in her power although at first I thought it was merely a friendly greeting. At last when she dismissed my case she appeared very angry. I considered that I had risen above her influence and she realized it also. (Church History Department)

26.   In one of her letters in January 1884 Clara herself claims to be ignorant of the grounds for her expulsion from the Christian Scientist Association, but Clara is such a master of emotional rhetoric that it is hard to tell how sincere she is. Certainly, she chose to withdraw soon afterward, so she may have learned that Mrs. Eddy had received written proof of the incident with Ashley, and she realized that this was one issue Mrs. Eddy could never overlook or condone. On my reading of the letters between Clara and Mrs. Eddy, quite apart from a congruence of interest, there was a real affection between them which was never quite lost even as circumstances drove the two apart. For all her faults, Clara Choate was not Josephine Woodbury. Clara Choate left Christian Science very unwillingly, and she continued to operate on the edges of the movement, literally around

the corner from the Massachusetts Metaphysical College, and sought constantly for some way to be reconciled with her former leader. Julia Bartlett was perhaps the most important and famous convert that Clara Choate brought to Christian Science, and a good indication of Clara's difficult situation after her expulsion from Christian Science is that Julia, in her highly orthodox memoirs, never mentions Mrs. Choate's name or says who her first teacher and healer had been. Clara Choate's reconciliation with Mrs. Eddy and the Church began when she refused to support Mrs. Woodbury in her suit against Mrs. Eddy and then later refused to supply any titillating information about Malicious Animal Magnetism or any sensitive documents to the reporters from *McClure's* or the New York *World*.

27. The main sources of information about Mrs. Eddy and Malicious Animal Magnetism were Luther Marston and Arthur Buswell, who had been close to Mrs. Eddy and her college in the 1880s and then left the movement. There is no doubt that both men had eyewitness testimony to give, but anyone reading their reminiscences should keep in mind that they are writing more than twenty years after the events, and that they were inspired less from ideological zeal than from a desire to cash in on the popular press's interest in Mrs. Eddy. Thus in March 1907 Buswell wrote to the managing editor of *McClure's Magazine* claiming detailed knowledge of the period in Mrs. Eddy's life which the series was about to embark upon:

> There are strange and unholy methods of secret practice entirely unknown to the great body of her followers, which she has established in her household— methods the exact opposite of the teaching and evident practice of the healer. These questionable practices are engaged in only by the trusted few, the purpose being to inflict, through a concentrated bombardment, as it were, the real and imaginary enemy. This secret practice forms, in the leader's opinion the most important part of her system. I returned from the west and took up the work at a most discouraging period in the history of the movement, remaining in the home of Mrs. Eddy and seeing her several times daily for a period of nearly three years; during which time I often filled her place in the pulpit when she was indisposed, lectured, taught, healed (I was very successful in healing the sick), acted as her private secretary, press-agent, etc. etc. I thought possibly you would like certain information I possess, and which I am certain cannot be had from any other source. (Church History Department)

Buswell did Primary class with Mrs. Eddy in the summer of 1879 and became a charter member of the Church of Christ (Scientist). In the fall of 1879 he was dispatched by Mrs. Eddy to Cincinnati, where he remained, as superintendent of the Board of Associated Charities and as a Christian Scientist practitioner until he was recalled to Boston in June 1882. In December of 1882 he was elected to be one of the directors of the Church, and he lived in the college for about fourteen months and served as clerk and treasurer. He continued to be active in the movement until late in 1885, but he was expelled from the association of Christian Scientists in December and expelled from membership of the college in January 1886.

Buswell was clearly happy to tell *McClure's* what it wanted to know, but his assertion that the movement was obsessed with Malicious Animal Magnetism is confirmed by a letter, also contained in The Mother Church's file on Buswell, which Hanover P. Smith wrote to Buswell in Cincinnati in October 1881, describing the recent rebellion of Howard, Rice, and others. Smith calls the rebels "malpractioners" [*sic*] and remarks: "They had thirty five mesmerists employed to kill her [Mrs. Eddy] beside Howard who was in the house living on her charity to report to them and aid in this awful crime" (Church History Department). For his part, Marston said that two thirds of Mrs. Eddy's classes were devoted to Malicious Animal Magnetism—a fact which is contradicted by more closely contemporary testimony—that she asked her students to "take up" Kennedy and Arens, and that, as recorded in Bates and Dittemore, "her students were taught that the mesmerists had secret-service men and women who watched every movement of Mrs. Eddy and her followers so that the latter could not leave the house without being shadowed. The United States Post Office was believed to be so mesmerized that it was necessary for the Christian Scientists to mail their letters secretly" (Bates and Dittemore, p. 229).

It seems clear to me that one of the things referred to under the code term of Malicious Animal Magnetism was domestic espionage, and Mrs. Eddy's concern with it was practical as well as theoretical. She had more than enough reason to be aware that with students and associates moving constantly in and out of the small centers of alternative healing, all aggressively competing for patients and disciples, everything she did and said was indeed noted and passed on. During the 1880s and 1890s, Richard Kennedy, Edward Arens, Clara Choate, and Josephine Woodbury, to name only the most celebrated, were all established within blocks of Mrs. Eddy.

28.   Church History Department.

29.   Julia Bartlett reminiscences. Original at Longyear Museum.

30.   The Van Ness quotes are from *The Religion of New England* (Boston: Beacon Press, 1926), pp. 168, 173. Van Ness's book is a little odd in that it praises the innovatory influence not only of Mrs. Eddy but also of two of her most energetic clerical enemies, Joseph Cook and Minot J. Savage.

31.   Lillian Whiting's interview was published in the *Cleveland (Ohio) Leader* on July 5, 1885.

32.   From *Hawthorne Hall: An Historical Story, 1885* (Boston: The Homewood Press, 1922), p. 211. (This rare and interesting work is available from the Bookmark in California.) Julia Bartlett came from an upper-middle-class family in Connecticut, but at the age of sixteen she lost her parents and found herself responsible for her five younger siblings. Although Miss Bartlett is extremely discreet in referring to this period in her life, the young Bartletts seem to have faced some mistreatment at the hands of their relatives, and while still a young woman Julia fell into illness and confirmed invalidism. She was roused from this condition by Asa Gilbert Eddy, and soon after she came to Lynn to study with Mrs. Eddy in 1880 she became one of the most trusted of her students.

33.   It is an accepted part of Christian Science lore that a number of people were healed by listening to Mrs. Eddy preach, reading her books, or even seeing her pass by.

34.   See Stephen Gottschalk, *The Emergence of Christian Science in American Religious Life* (Berkeley: University of California Press, 1978), especially Chapter 3, "The Tares and the Wheat."

35.   H. Dresser, ed., *The Quimby Manuscripts,* p. 433.

36.   As Gail Thain Parker has noted (*Mind Cure in New England,* p. 5), none of the New Thought gurus, until the Dressers, bothered to acknowledge their debt to Quimby. The earliest significant reference in print to P. P. Quimby's work which the New Thought historians could come up with appears in an 1872 book by Warren Felt Evans:

> The late Dr. Quimby, of Portland, one of the most successful healers of this or any age, embraced this view of disease, and by a long succession of most remarkable cures, effected by psychopathic remedies, at the same time proved the truth of the theory and the efficiency of that mode of treatment. Had he lived in a remote age or country, the wonderful facts which occurred in his practice would have been deemed either mythical or miraculous. He seemed to reproduce the wonders of the Gospel history. But all this was only an exhibition of the force of suggestion, or the action of the law of faith, over the patient in the impressible condition. (*Mental Medicine* [Boston: William White and Company, 1872], p. 210)

Evans was a patient of Quimby's in 1863. He had already appeared in print before going to Portland with books of a Swedenborgian cast, and he was to write a series of books after 1872 showing increasing interest in Eastern mysticism. Evans himself later had a clinic and was a moderately successful healer. The quotation I have given is the only place in all his published works where Evans acknowledges Quimby: most significantly, his 1869 work, *The Mental Cure,* makes no mention at all of Quimby, although, as Robert Peel has shown, the book is full of ideas which Quimby espoused and put into practice, even if he did not originate them.

In the face of this massive neglect of Quimby and this complete absence of references to any writings or manuscripts by him, it is significant that in her first 1875 edition of *Science and Health* Mrs. Eddy gives a short appraisal of Quimby's work, at least as admiring as that of Evans. But whereas Mrs. Eddy was consistently from 1883 on reviled as an ungrateful plagiarist, Warren Felt Evans was hailed as an early hero of New Thought whose relation to Quimby is seen as wholly unproblematic. As Peel correctly notes, the assessment Evans makes of Quimby also directly contradicts that of the Dressers and confirms that of Mrs. Eddy, since it clearly adjudges that Quimby used the powers of suggestion on suitable subjects, that is, he used mesmerism. Evans's understanding of Quimby is a far cry from the high metaphysics which New Thought historians liked to attribute to Quimby as the founder of the movement. See Peel, *Trial,* pp. 126 and 210.

37.   The Mother Church owns Arens's notebook which contains his copies of the letters which he had made from the originals lent him by George Quimby to aid in the preparation of the Arens defense against Mrs. Eddy.

38.   Bates and Dittemore sum up this reaction of condemnation with typical hyperbole: "In disowning Quimby she disowned herself. Though she would live to be almost ninety, she would never find again the woman of generous enthusiasm whom she slew" (Bates and Dittemore, p. 236).

39.   At the time of the Arens trial, Mrs. Eddy wrote to her old Portland acquaintance Mrs. Sarah Crosby, asking her to give an affidavit that "Dr. Quimby and I were friends, and that I used to take his scribblings and fix them over for him and give him my thoughts and language which as I understood it, were far in advance of his." Mrs. Crosby did not reply to this letter at the time, but in 1907 she supplied Milmine with an affidavit in which she swore that she had not supplied Mrs. Eddy with the statement she requested because it would not have been true (Milmine and Cather, pp. 100–101). Milmine and Bates and Dittemore quote Mrs. Eddy's letter as proof of her failed attempt to suborn a witness. To the contrary, I see Mrs. Eddy's approach to Mrs. Crosby as evidence that she counted on Mrs. Crosby to support what she said about Quimby in the Boston *Post* letters, and that Mrs. Crosby later greatly exaggerated their disagreement in 1877. I read Mrs. Crosby's silence in 1883 as evidence that, indeed, she did remember the Quimby matter much as Mrs. Eddy did, but she refused to do her former friend any favors.

40.   This document is part of the Mother Church file on Arens. The defense counsel tried to make something of the fact, admitted by Frye, that he had sent a boy to Arens's house on the express purpose of asking to be sold a copy of the offending pamphlet.

41.   One can sense Mrs. Eddy's pleasure in this judgment from the section she devotes to the plagiarism action in "Inklings Historic," a section in her book *Miscellaneous Writings.* She narrates how a bill in equity was filed in U.S. Circuit Court in Boston prohibiting Arens from circulating the pamphlets and his countering allegation that her works were not original to her "but had been copied by her, or by her direction, from manuscripts originally composed by Dr. P. P. Quimby." After Arens had refused to testify and his counsel had admitted to the court that no supporting evidence would be produced, a decree in favor of Mrs. Eddy was drawn up whereby she recovered all her costs, Arens was enjoined from disposing in any way of the enjoined pamphlet, on penalty of ten thousand dollars, and thirty-eight hundred or so of the infringing publications "were put under the edge of the knife, and their lawful existence destroyed" (*Mis.,* p. 381).

42.   Swarts had briefly taken class with Mrs. Eddy in Chicago, and he repeated the Dresser accusations of 1883 in an article on Quimby and Mrs. Eddy for his *Mental Science Magazine* and then in an 1887 pamphlet called *The True History of Mental Science.* For more on Swarts and his visit to Portland and George Quimby, see Chapter 7.

43.   George Quimby indignantly refused Mrs. Eddy's offer, and he later explained his refusal in a letter to Dr. Minot J. Savage in August 1904: "Just think of it! My letting her or anyone else, have Mss I knew were father's because I saw him write them, and copied many of them myself, to see if she didn't write them and leave them with him" (Dresser, ed., *The Quimby Manuscripts,* p. 438).

Chapter 17: Getting Out the Word

1.   "It is a question to-day, whether the ancient inspired healers understood the Science of Christian healing, or whether they caught its sweet tones, as the natural musician catches the tones of harmony, without being able to explain them" (*Science and Health,* pp. 144–45). For an excellent discussion of this point, see Gottschalk, *The Emergence of Christian Science*, pp. 23–25.

2.   As far as I can determine, Mrs. Eddy did not write her sermons out in full but preferred to speak extempore, with the help of brief notes. Her voice was clear, low, but not large, and she had certain characteristic and eloquent hand movements. From 1880 on her reputation as an orator grew, and by 1885 the opportunity to hear Mrs. Eddy preach was regarded by her followers as a signal privilege. Nonetheless, the quality of her sermons was probably rather uneven, as there were days when, even by her own account, she was more inspired and energized than others. Since she did not in any systematic way write her sermons, efforts were made to take down her words in shorthand, and such often unauthorized texts became prized and contested parts of the Christian Science legacy. It was said of Mrs. Eddy, as of so many great orators, that a transcription of what she had said, however accurate, gave little indication of the effect of her spoken words.

3.   Mrs. Eddy did almost all her teaching in Boston, at her college, but she did make one trip to Chicago in 1884, where she gave one very influential class in the spring.

4.   In Boston, Edward Arens, Clara Choate, and Josephine Woodbury enjoyed decreasing success with their institutes as their ties with Mrs. Eddy and Christian Science faded, and even Emma Hopkins, who was centered mainly in Chicago and ranged far afield in the Midwest and West in areas well removed from Mrs. Eddy's orbit, was a pale reflection of the founder of Christian Science, especially after the debacle of her relationship with Mary Plunkett. See Chapter 18. Only Augusta Stetson rivaled Mrs. Eddy as a preacher and as a fund-raiser. Yet by remaining within Christian Science until shortly before Mrs. Eddy's death, she not only contributed to but benefited from the Church teaching and organization which Mrs. Eddy had put in place. It is not certain that Mrs. Stetson would have fared any better than Mrs. Choate, Mrs. Woodbury, or Mrs. Hopkins had she been forced like them to operate independently.

5.   C. Lulu Blackman reminiscences, as quoted by Powell, p. 154. Her full reminiscences appear in *We Knew Mary Baker Eddy,* pp. 53–62. Powell also notes the extraordinary concentration which Mrs. Eddy required of her students. The sessions were not usually long, but during them no fidgeting or even coughing was permitted. Miss Blackman reported that at the class she attended Mrs. Eddy absolutely forbade taking notes, and that, after three repetitions of this rule, all students complied.

6.   *Christian Science Journal,* May 1886, p. 39; quoted by Peel, *Trial,* p. 191.

7.   In her master's thesis, "Mary Baker Eddy at the Podium: The Rhetoric of the Founder of the Christian Science Church," Jean A. McDonald gives a useful list of the public speeches Mrs. Eddy is known to have made and some of the descriptions of her style as an orator (University of Minnesota, 1969).

8.   In *The Bostonians,* Henry James offers a vivid picture of the complex responses of the public to women speakers during this period, and to the radical new roles and issues they were associated with.

9.   Powell, p. 152. He is quoting from the reminiscences of Mrs. Mary Harris Curtis.

10. Quoted in the *Christian Science Journal,* March 11, 1885, p. 1. See Peel, *Trial,* pp. 155–56.

11. "Defense of Christian Science," *Christian Science Journal* (March 7, 1885), pp. 1– 4. This piece was subsequently expanded and republished in 1887 under the title *Christian Science: No and Yes* and then under the title *No and Yes* and appeared in *Prose Works.*

12. The following quotations from her address are from "Addresses: Christian Science in Tremont Temple," *Miscellaneous Writings,* Chapter 4, pp. 95–98.

13. Stephen Gottschalk gives a long and brilliant analysis of the theological and professional issues underlying Cook's attack in the introduction to his book, *The Emergence of Christian Science.*

14. The magazine was in fact first called the *Journal of Christian Science,* and the name was changed in April 1885.

15. See the introduction to Hansen, "Women's Hour."

16. For example, Mr. and Mrs. Choate and Mrs. Choate's mother, Mrs. Cynthia Childs, feature in the small list in the first editions, but Clara's and Cynthia's names disappear in April 1884, and George—who, incidentally, was then practicing in Providence, Rhode Island, not in Boston with his wife—disappears in the next issue (the publication was bimonthly, not monthly at this point).

17. Milmine and Cather, p. 316.

18. In the summer of 1906 Mrs. Eddy began working on a book that would contain her published writings from 1897 on, as well as materials relating to the June 1906 dedication of the Extension of the Mother Church. This compilation was laid aside in 1909 and not touched again until after Mrs. Eddy's death. *The First Church of Christ, Scientist, and Miscellany* is, then, a kind of combination *Pulpit and Press* and *Miscellaneous Writings.* In 1913 the trustees under the Will of Mary Baker Eddy began to prepare the book for publication, making some changes in the process. It was published late that year, using the title that Mrs. Eddy had originally selected for the work in 1906.

19. I think Mrs. Eddy refers here to the period of her life when she split with Richard Kennedy. Who precisely was spreading rumors of her being addicted to opium at that period is unclear to me, though Miranda Rice was the witness most frequently cited in later years. I confess I find it rather hard to swallow Mrs. Eddy's claim in the *Christian Science Journal* that she took large doses of morphine to prove her immunity to the drug's effects, but I don't find Miranda Rice a credible witness either. The hard evidence on this subject is, as I have already indicated, sparse, and since opium medications of many types were still legal, freely available, and commonly prescribed in the 1870s in Massachusetts, the whole question of addiction was posed quite differently. If long-term morphine addicts such as Thomas de Quincey and Elizabeth Barrett Browning were transplanted into our 1990s American culture and tried to acquire the drugs their doctors had happily supplied them with by prescription, they would very probably be in jail. The accusations of opium addiction would continue to float around Mrs. Eddy, and in Part Four we shall see how she and her household dealt with the issue when in her last years she occasionally resorted to morphine injections when she could not bear the pain from kidney stones.

20. Here Mrs. Eddy refers to her successful prosecution of Edward Arens for plagiarizing her work. (See Chapter 16.)

21. "Mrs. Eddy Sick," *Mis.,* p. 239.

22. Milmine and Cather, pp. 326–27. The mother of the children gives no medical diagnosis, and from the symptoms she describes it is impossible to establish what caused the deaths of the little boys, or whether, indeed, they both died from the same cause. Cather and Milmine do not give the names of the bereaved parents as Mr. and Mrs. William Nixon, although the parents clearly identify themselves as such in the March 1889 *Journal*

article. I assume this is because William Nixon, who rose high in the Church administration and in Mrs. Eddy's favor, until he quarrelled with her over the legal status of the The Mother Church (see Chapter 19), is one of the Milmine biography's most important sources of negative information on Mrs. Eddy in the 1880s and 1890s. Nixon also has a small part to play in the Next Friends suit (see Chapters 25 and 26). Nixon's status as eyewitness to Mrs. Eddy's evil and crazy ways would obviously have been suspect had he been identified as the father of the two dead little boys in Pierre and the author of the essay claiming they had been killed by Malicious Animal Magnetism.

23.   In contrast, in a similar case which occurred a hundred years or so later a jury could convict the Twitchell parents for the manslaughter of their child on the basis of clear evidence of the child's medical condition, and of the existence of tried and true, standard medical procedures for treating that condition. See Preface.

24.   See William Dana Orcutt, *Mary Baker Eddy and Her Books* (Boston: Christian Science Publishing Society, 1950), p. 13.

25.   Orcutt gives probably the most authoritative account of this scene, which he says was recounted to him by Wilson himself.

26.   Milmine, Bates and Dittemore, and Dakin make much of the craziness surrounding this Malicious Animal Magnetism in publication issue. Robert Peel tries both to defend Mrs. Eddy's concept of Malicious Animal Magnetism on philosophical grounds and to show how Mrs. Eddy increasingly downplayed its importance as time went on:

> The incredible confusion which attended the printing of the fiftieth edition [1891] seemed to her to call for protective mental work to be done for John Wilson and the printers at the University Press. Foster Eddy was put in charge of the work for Wilson himself; several other trusted students were detailed to pray for the printers. But eventually Mrs. Eddy called them off. The typographical mistakes were actually getting worse, the delays were multiplying, and the students were clearly incapable of handling the situation (Peel, *Trial,* pp. 285–86).

27.   I introduced the Reverend Wiggin at the beginning of this chapter as an admiring auditor in Mrs. Eddy's classes. As Peel makes clear, several gentlemen who were more philosophically attuned to Christian Science than Wiggin offered to help Mrs. Eddy with her manuscript problems, but their efforts were counterproductive, or even disastrous in 1890.   All the men, however deferential initially, were convinced that they knew much better than Mary Baker Eddy herself what she wanted to say, and how she should say it. This was not exclusively a male-female problem, as Mrs. Ursula Gestefeld also tried to "explain" to Mrs. Eddy, with as little success.

28.   Wiggin attended one set of Mrs. Eddy's classes on the agreement that she would not ask him any questions and he would not ask any of her. One day, however, Wiggin could not contain himself and burst out with the question, "How do you know that there ever was such a man as Christ Jesus?" (*Miscellany,* p. 318). This indicates to me that Wiggin may have moved through the New Biblical Criticism to a position of extreme religious skepticism. Bates and Dittemore, who give the most detailed information on Wiggin, call him "a cultured sybarite," and say "he was quite devoid of deep religious convictions" (Bates and Dittemore, p. 266).

29.   Bates and Dittemore, p. 267.

30.   An interesting discrepancy occurs in the Bates and Dittemore account of Wiggin's "ghostwriting" for Mrs. Eddy. On the one hand, the account stresses Wiggin's radical editorial revisions of Mrs. Eddy's manuscript. On the other hand, the account concludes that "The redeeming features of the original *Science and Health*—its glimpses of religious ecstasy, its hints of poetry, its sincere, if willful, passion—were all lost in Mr. Wiggin's eminently prosaic version. . . . The peculiar drabness and uniformity of the present *Science and Health* are due to Mr. Wiggin, not to Mrs. Eddy" (Bates and Dittemore, p. 268). This

may be a section where Mr. Bates and Mr. Dittemore did not see things in entirely the same way, or perhaps Mr. Bates had some reluctant admiration for Mrs. Eddy and her work which he allowed to leak through at times despite himself. They nevertheless manage to end this section on their expected note of criticism by pointing to Mrs. Eddy's lack of integrity as an author: "No one whose style was fundamentally sincere could have brooked such high-handed methods as those of Mr. Wiggin" (Bates and Dittemore, pp. 268–69). One of the incidental pleasures of Eddy bibliography is seeing how the secret collaborators (Willa Cather and Georgine Milmine) and the avowed collaborators (Ernest Bates and John Dittemore) condemn Mrs. Eddy for using ghostwriters!

31. Quoted in Peel, *Trial,* p. 187.

32. Peel, *Trial,* pp. 188–89.

33. Bates and Dittemore comment on Wiggin that Mrs. Eddy's "steady payment of his salary had lifted him out of the uncertainties incident to his profession" (Bates and Dittemore, p. 271).

34. This letter is quoted at even greater length in Milmine and Cather and praised as "the most trenchant and suggestive sketch of Mrs. Eddy that will ever be written [by] an unprejudiced and tempered mind" (Milmine and Cather, pp. 336–38). Milmine does not state to whom the letter was written, identifying the recipient as "an old college friend."

35. Two notable women writers and religious historians have taken on gnosticism and the sibyl, respectively Elaine Pagels in *The Gnostic Gospels* (New York: Random House, 1979); and Marina Warner in *From the Beast to the Blonde* (New York: Farrar, Straus and Giroux, 1995).

36. Quoted in Peel, *Trial,* p. 284; *Miscellany,* p. 319. This was first published in the *Christian Science Sentinel* in December 1906 in response to the Wright allegations.

37. Sibyl Wilbur indicates that if Wiggin did indeed say what Wright claims he said, he was both a cad and a hypocrite. This seems a fair comment to me.

38. This piece, "Taking Offense," is now found on pp. 223–24 of *Miscellaneous Writings.* Judy Huenneke of the Church History Department is convinced that Mrs. Eddy herself wrote and published the piece anonymously during the 1850s or 1860s.

39. Perhaps the most egregious example of the strength of the plagiarism charge against Mrs. Eddy can be seen in the case of the so-called Lieber-Hegel manuscript, the text of which first appeared in a book-pamphlet published in 1936 and was reissued by its supposed editor and actual author Walter M. Haushalter in different forms over the next twenty years. In the pamphlet, Haushalter, a minister first with the Disciples of Christ and later with the Episcopalians, claimed that Mrs. Eddy had stolen her essential metaphysics from an eleven-page manuscript entitled "The Metaphysical Religion of Hegel" which Francis Lieber, a respected German-American political scientist, had written in 1866 under the pseudonym Christian Herrmann. The pamphlet included letters which allegedly proved that the manuscript had been sent to Mrs. Eddy's early disciple Hiram Crafts, who in turn passed it on to her. Haushalter finally claimed to have combed New England library and manuscript collections before finally, fortunately, coming upon the lost documents. Haushalter finally published the text after he had made repeated efforts to sell the supposed manuscript to the Church of Christ, Scientist for $150,000. He managed to find four eminent professors from Johns Hopkins University to endorse the authenticity of the manuscript which they later claimed they had in fact not examined. The Lieber-Hegel document was enthusiastically received by those anxious to find evidence for their assumption that Mary Baker Eddy had been, in the words of one correspondent, "enslaved to some brilliant mind to whom she was indebted for both thought and terms." The *Times Literary Supplement* declared the Haushalter charge of plagiarism "possibly the most important ever brought against Mrs. Eddy's personal and doctrinal integrity." It took the work of two American academics, Conrad H. Moehlman and Frank Freidel, to show on internal evidence that the document could not have been written by Francis Lieber. Faced with this evidence, the four professors recanted. Finally the archival

research of Christian Science scholar Thomas C. Johnsen told the tale of how Haushalter got the idea of concocting the text from sources he found in the Harvard library. I am indebted for this information, and specifically for the quotations given in this note, to the definitive account of the Lieber-Hegel document scam given by Thomas C. Johnsen, "Historical Consensus and Christian Science: The Career of a Manuscript Controversy," *New England Quarterly* (March 1980).

It is symptomatic of the force the plagiarism issue has carried as a means of attacking Christian Science that Haushalter's allegations were accepted for so long, even by scholars as distinguished as Charles Braden. In this instance, the Committee on Publication of The Mother Church had overwhelming documentary evidence to disprove the charges being made against Mary Baker Eddy, but such was its reputation for censorship, media manipulation, and cover-up that it could not get its message across. It was not until the more enlightened tenure of archivist Lee Z. Johnson in the 1960s and 1970s that a new breed of Christian Science scholars, like Thomas C. Johnsen and his associates at the archives, notably Robert Peel and Stephen Gottschalk, did serious archival research and challenged some of the taboos. Two of the minor tragedies of Christian Science intellectual history are that Gottschalk's book was never reissued and is now hard to come by, and that Johnsen's superb doctoral dissertation, "Christian Science and the Puritan Tradition," never found a publisher.

Chapter 18: More Dissidents and New Rules

1. Bliss Knapp relates: "Only a short while before, some of the leading citizens [of Lyman, New Hampshire, home of the Knapps in 1888] had hanged an effigy of Mrs. Eddy in the town square; and in the 'horrible procession' on the previous Fourth of July, Mrs. Eddy had been caricatured as an insane woman in a cage, to whom a man, representing a local Scientist, was feeding medicine through the bars of the cage. These demonstrations showed how much the community was aroused against Christian Science because of the healings that had been accomplished there" (Knapp, *The Destiny of the Mother Church* [Boston: Christian Science Publishing Society, 1991], p. 24).

2. Bates and Dittemore estimate that Mrs. Eddy taught 626 students between 1883 and mid-1889, earning some $100,000 even with the reductions in fees she frequently allowed (Bates and Dittemore, pp. 274–75).

3. According to Milmine and Peel, the new editor of the *Christian Science Journal,* Joshua Bailey, had taken virtually to apotheosizing her in his editorials.

4. Quoted by Peel, *Trial,* p. 228.

5. Another capable woman joined forces with the Dresser-Swarts-Hopkins group, Mrs. Ursula N. Gestefeld of Chicago, who had taken class with Mrs. Eddy in 1884 and enthusiastically espoused Christian Science. In 1888 Mrs. Gestefeld published a book which purported to explicate *Science and Health,* and when this work failed to find favor with Mrs. Eddy, Mrs. Gestefeld published a pamphlet, *Jesuitism in Christian Science,* which vigorously attacked Mrs. Eddy and her followers for their inability to "separate person from principle." According to Gottschalk (*The Emergence of Christian Science,* pp. 103–4), Ursula Gestefeld continued to write, published her own magazine, and became a much respected leader of New Thought.

6. "I saw all the letters said to be written by Mrs. E. to Dresser and Quimby and not one of them could be held as an argument against her supreme originality. I was always ferreting out things to their basis in fact back of the statements made—I do not care who by, and I know this, that with my critical, cynical gaze I found her true to her own original marvellous inspiration" (Mrs. Hopkins to Miss Bartlett, quoted in Peel, *Trial,* pp. 179–80). Peel also notes that Mrs. Plunkett suggested that she and Mrs. Eddy divide up the territory, offering to take everything west of the Mississippi herself. Mrs. Eddy indignantly rejected this proposal, probably made around 1887.

7. Gottschalk, *The Emergence of Christian Science,* p. 102.

8. See Peel, *Trial,* pp. 262–63 for quotations from Mrs. Eddy's letters on this issue.

9. Information on the death of Mary Plunkett is taken from an unidentified contemporary press account in a New Zealand newspaper which was sent to the Committee on Publication of The Mother Church.

Arthur Bently Worthington (born Oakley Crawford, 1847–1917) left Christchurch and a pile of debts in December 1895, settling with his most recent wife Evelyn first in Hobart, Tasmania, then in Melbourne, Australia. There in 1902 he was jailed for defrauding a wealthy widow by claiming to be the reincarnated god Osiris. After his release, he and his wife Evelyn and their four children sailed back to the United States, surviving a shipwreck en route. Worthington became a Presbyterian pastor in the Poughkeepsie, New York, area but was arrested again in January, and while in custody died on December 13, 1917, of a heart attack "after being confronted by one of his latest female victims" (August 1993 edition of *Southern Skies,* the in-flight magazine of Ansett Airlines, New Zealand). Materials on Mary Plunkett and Bently Worthington were found in the Church History Department.

10. After the ruin of Mrs. Plunkett, Mrs. Hopkins continued to prosper, and she became one of the most important New Thought teachers. See Gottschalk, *The Emergence of the Christian Science,* p. 103.

11. The Reverend Day would waver between Christian Science and other branches of the metaphysical healing movement for some years, but he left the movement definitively in 1890.

12. This is the account given by Peel (*Trial,* pp. 241–43). The Bates and Dittemore account is rather less dramatic but little different in essence.

13. Peel in his second volume (*The Years of Trial*) goes into considerable detail about the various challenges to Mrs. Eddy's leadership at this time, particularly by men such as William I. Gill and Joseph Adams.

14. The Chicago *Times* gave the least admiring account, making much of Mrs. Eddy's alleged mesmeric rolling of eyes, and of the prosy appearance of all the women in the audience. It satirically remarked that their belief in spirit did not protect them from the intense heat of the closed, tightly packed room. At the other extreme, Christian Science historians report that several healings occurred during Mrs. Eddy's speech.

15. Chicago *Times* report, quoted by Peel, *Trial,* p. 242.

16. This may have been an act of atonement since on her previous stay in Chicago Mrs. Eddy had been unable to get a room at the Palmer House until a Chicago friend intervened with the management on her behalf. In 1884 she stayed in a private home.

17. Following is what Mrs. Eddy wrote to the Boston newspaper:

> To the Editor of the [Boston] Herald: The lamentable case reported from West Medford of the death of a mother and her infant at childbirth should forever put a stop to quackery. There has been but one side of this case presented by the newspapers. We wait to hear from the other side, trusting that attenuating circumstances will be brought to light. Mrs. Abby H. Corner never entered the obstetrics class at the Massachusetts Metaphysical College. She was not fitted at this institute for an accoucheur, had attended but one term, and four terms, including three years of successful practice by the student, are required to complete the college course. (quoted in Milmine and Cather, pp. 355–56)

18. See Peel, *Discovery,* p. 256.

19. In the final Obstetrics course she gave she asked her new protégé, Ebenezer J. Foster, trained in a college of homeopathic medicine, to give an introduction to the physiology of child bearing.

20. Peel quotes the reaction of Mrs. Eddy's close associate Frank Mason to the announcement that she was closing the college: "To say that I was surprised when I

heard . . . is a mild statement. I was simply astounded. I supposed the College like the gate to Heaven would always be ajar. The West and in fact the whole country is dazed at the apparent sudden termination of the original source of Christian Science teaching" (letter of late August 1889 from Mason to Mrs. Eddy, quoted in Peel, *Trial,* p. 252).

21.   The closing of the Massachusetts Metaphysical College was the most radical and dangerous expression of this new policy of personal withdrawal, and it showed the extraordinary confidence in herself and the future of the movement which now possessed Mary Baker Eddy. The college had not only trained the leaders who were spreading the gospel of *Science and Health* throughout the country; it had also given the movement a firm base and helped Mrs. Eddy become financially secure. There was no lack of candidates eager and willing to take over the college for Mrs. Eddy, but, after some initial uncertainty and yielding to intense pressure, she decreed that God had commanded her to close the college. Mrs. Eddy seems for a time to have envisaged passing the direction of the college to her new protégé Ebenezer Foster, and he co-taught some of the final classes with her. In the end, for whatever reason, Mrs. Eddy decided against this course of action, and it is fortunate that she did so, for everything we know about Foster makes it clear that he could not have stepped into her shoes. In response to the initial howls of outrage and despair at the news of her closing the college, Mrs. Eddy called upon a much more capable and reasonable man than Foster to replace her—General Erastus N. Bates of Cleveland. This reportedly charming and distinguished man came when she summoned him, taught one successful course, and then was sent back to Cleveland. Mrs. Eddy was now clear that God had ordered her to close the college.

22.   These were published in the *Journal* and can also be found in Bates and Dittemore, p. 296. The different measures taken in 1889 to deinstitutionalize Christian Science were the first in a complex campaign whereby, over the next ten or so years, Mary Baker Eddy would put in place a radically new form of church government. In this new and constantly evolving structure, the day-to-day management of church affairs was delegated in 1892 to a small handpicked group of loyal followers: the four-man Board of Directors and the twelve First Members. This latter group grew in number to over one hundred, and in 1901 Mrs. Eddy disbanded them, on the grounds that the group had become too unwieldy and too disputatious; she transferred their responsibilities to the Christian Science Board of Directors. The First Members remained until 1908, with the sole function that only First Members were eligible for election as Readers or as President of the Mother Church. In 1903 she expanded the board to five members. Mrs. Eddy herself retained her position as leader of the movement, continued to do some of the long-term planning, kept a vigilant eye especially on the teaching, and gave herself ultimate veto over every level of organizational activity. All the activities of the Church were regulated by the By-Laws which Mrs. Eddy began creating after 1889 and which were codified in 1895 as the *Manual of The Mother Church.* This document was modified constantly, almost to the time of her death, either directly at her dictation or in consultation with her, and she identified it as the Church's most important text after *Science and Health.* The extraordinarily detailed and historically determined nature of some By-Laws, and the frequent, and unaltered, invocation of Mary Baker Eddy as supreme authority on all questions, has laid the *Manual* open to parody and censure, notably by Mark Twain. The final section of the final article of the *Manual,* Article 35, reads: "No new Tenet or By-Law shall be adopted, nor any Tenet or By-Law amended or annulled, without the written consent of Mary Baker Eddy, the author of our textbook, SCIENCE AND HEALTH."

23.   To give only one minor example, Bates and Dittemore point out that the *Christian Science Journal* was heavily in debt and that Mary Baker Eddy's "gift" of it to the National Christian Scientist Association was more self-serving than generous. One could equally argue that Mary Baker Eddy was, correctly, assuming that the journal she had founded, like all her publishing enterprises, would sooner or later make a profit and that the Association was the fitting group to publish, edit, and reap the potential future profits from the movement's main publicity and information organ.

24.   Mrs. Eddy addressed The Mother Church on May 26, 1895, and on January 5, 1896. In July 1897 she talked with and greeted many of the twenty-five hundred Christian Scientists who had accepted her invitation to come to Pleasant View. In November of 1898 she gave her last class in Concord. In June 1899 she addressed three thousand supporters at the Annual Meeting of the Church in Tremont Temple. On July 1, 1903, she briefly addressed ten thousand faithful supporters from her balcony at Pleasant View, her final public speech.

25.   Augusta Stetson recounts this story in her *Reminiscences, Sermons, and Correspondence* (New York: G. P. Putnam's Sons, 1914), pp. 15–16.

26.   Peel's comments on this issue show the deep ambiguity in Christian Science about descriptions of Mrs. Eddy's appearance and health:

> Some of Mrs. Eddy's students had been concerned for a year or two that she was working too hard and pleaded with her to take more time for herself. They noted with anxiety every sign of age or strain in her appearance and rejoiced in the continued and frequently astonishing evidences of her resilience. While the disaffected students complained that she was getting 'too old' to head the Christian Science movement, the new students who were flocking to the college seemed almost uniformly struck by her vitality, the erectness of her figure, the freshness of her complexion—and, above all, by her eyes, which they described variously as blue, gray, violet, deep gentian, black, even brown, and as flashing, sparkling, kindling, clouding, looking right into one, changing with every mood. (Peel, *Trial,* p. 249)

Mrs. Eddy's appearance changed radically around 1891, when she lost some fifty pounds in weight, and her hair went white.

27.   Mrs. Eddy believed and taught that a person with mesmeric power, either from malevolence or carelessness, could steal into another's consciousness, like a thief into a house, and steal or do damage. To perpetrate such a mental crime was a cardinal sin in Mary Baker Eddy's book.

28.   See Richard A. Nenneman, *Persistent Pilgrim,* p. 106.

29.   See Chapter 11 for a fuller discussion of Mrs. Eddy and Daniel Spofford. These letters to Spofford are quoted at length in Milmine and Cather and again in Dakin. The originals are in the Church History Department. L07811 and L07814

30.   Nenneman, *Persistent Pilgrim,* p. 131.

31.   Yvonne Caché von Fettweis and Robert Townsend Warneck describe a number of such healings in their book *Mary Baker Eddy: Christian Healer.*

32.   The longest version of this story is given in the gospel according to St. Mark:

> And a great crowd followed him and thronged about him. And there was a woman who had had a flow of blood for twelve years, and who had suffered much under many physicians, and had spent all that she had, and was no better but rather grew worse. She had heard the reports about Jesus, and came up behind him in the crowd and touched his garment. For she said, "If I touch even his garments, I shall be made well." And immediately the hemorrhage ceased; and she felt in her body that she was healed of her disease. And Jesus, perceiving in himself that power had gone forth from him, immediately turned about in the crowd, and said, "Who touched my garments?" And his disciples said to him, "You see the crowd pressing around you, and yet you say 'Who touched me?' " And he looked around to see who had done it. But the woman, knowing what had been done to her, came in fear and trembling and fell down before him, and told him the whole truth. And he said to her, "Daughter, your faith has made you well; go in peace, and be healed of your disease." (Mark 5: 24–34, Revised Standard Version)

33. I would note that such women were also notably responsive to psychoanalysis and, diagnosed as hysterics, were the most important body of patients treated by the young Sigmund Freud. As further confirmation, in her autobiographical novel, *Les Mots pour le dire,* written in the 1970s, Marie Cardinal tells how she herself suffered from uncontrollable vaginal bleeding for some years, and after consulting the best doctors and surgeons to no avail she was finally cured by a course of classic psychoanalysis.

34. Variations on the expression "touch the hem of the garment" occur frequently in Mrs. Eddy's writings, as well as those of such followers as Augusta Stetson. See, for example, *Science and Health,* where Mrs. Eddy refers to the New Testament healing not as an example of physical contact bringing healing, but as an example of Jesus' "quick apprehension of [a] mental call" (p. 86).

Chapter 19: Building the Mother Church

1. Bliss Knapp, *The Destiny of the Mother Church,* p. 61.

2. Ibid., p. 71.

3. Ibid., p. 89.

4. These are now united in one volume, Joseph Armstrong and Margaret Williamson, *The Building of the Mother Church* (Boston: Christian Science Publishing Society, 1990). See also Margaret Pinkham, "This 'Miracle in Stone': The Building of the Mother Church, the First Church of Christ, Scientist, Boston, Massachusetts" (Master's thesis, Boston University, 1994).

5. Armstrong and Williamson, *Building of The Mother Church,* p. 39.

6. Ibid., p. 69.

7. It is interesting to compare pictures of the Mother's Room at the Mother Church, all fussy grandeur, with pictures of the small, homey apartment Mrs. Eddy set up for herself in Pleasant View, and which she insisted on reproducing, virtually foot for foot, and piece for piece, in the mansion at Chestnut Hill.

8. L02748. The original letter is in the Church History Department and has been published in Armstrong and Williamson, *The Building of the Mother Church,* pp. 70–72.

Chapter 20: A New Edition of Science and Health and a New Son

1. Robert Peel offers an interesting section on the writing of the fiftieth edition, and its aims and effects, in Chapter 10 of his second volume, *Years of Trial.*

2. Both these portraits are reproduced in the photo inserts of this volume.

3. I discuss a number of these inaccuracies in Chapter 1. Judy Huenneke of the Church History Department has pointed out to me that it is much easier to understand the structure and goals of *Retrospection and Introspection* if you compare it not to memoirs or journalistic auto-narratives but to spiritual autobiographies, combining personal information and pious reflection, which constituted a well-established genre and with which Mary Baker Eddy was surely familiar.

4. George had presumably gotten to know Clara Choate and her family on his earlier visit to Boston in 1879–1880.

5. L02085. Original in the Church History Department. All of the existing original letters Mrs. Eddy wrote to her son George Glover are in the Church History Department. Copies of a number of letters from Mrs. Eddy to her son can be found in the Chandler papers at the New Hampshire Historical Society in Concord, New Hampshire.

6. Evelyn's portrait was kept on the whatnot in Mrs. Eddy's room to the end of her life.

7. L02089. Original in the Church History Department.

8. Janette Weller notes that in the class she took in 1884 Mrs. Eddy was still taking students' money, entering the sums paid in a ledger, and giving receipts.

9. I shall say more on this question in Part Four when I deal with the Next Friends suit.

10. See the memoir left by Mary Godfrey Parker, Christiana's daughter, in *We Knew Mary Baker Eddy,* p. 15.

11. Foster's letter and Mrs. Dillingham's letter are in the Church History Department.

12. As I have already noted, Mary Baker Eddy liked to give special men in her life special names. Thus Richard Kennedy was "Dick," Daniel Harrison Spofford was "Harry," Samuel Putnam Bancroft was "Putney," and Asa Gilbert Eddy, "Gilbert."

13. Thus in a letter of May 29, 1889, Mrs. Eddy wrote to Foster Eddy in Boston from Barre, Vermont: "I feel too far away from you up here. I miss you more than pen can tell. . . . Write me dear one at once, will arrange our money matters in full when I see you, at present all is right. You are doing grandly I have no doubt but mamma wants to be herself and to be with you. Love love love 'oooooooo' Ever Thine own." N00027. Original at the New Hampshire Historical Society.

14. The position became vacant after William Nixon resigned over Mrs. Eddy's plans for the Mother Church. Nixon had done well financially as Mrs. Eddy's publisher, although, according to William Dana Orcutt, he was an ineffective and unreliable executive, and his financial position declined rapidly after his departure. The disgruntled, hard-up Nixon would play a small but key role in the Next Friends suit.

    The Milmine biography is inaccurate in the breakdown it gives of the publishing costs of *Science and Health.* The book cost about 75 cents to produce—not 45 cents. Mrs. Eddy received a royalty of $1.00 per copy, Nixon received $1.00, and Foster Eddy, who was already getting 25 cents a copy under the Nixon regime, received $1.25 per copy when he was appointed publisher. These are the figures given in the records of The Mother Church. Milmine probably received the information that Mrs. Eddy short-changed her adopted son when she made him publisher from Foster Eddy himself and/or William Nixon. William Dana Orcutt is by far the most reliable and sober source of information on these publishing issues after 1890. It appears from the Foster Eddy correspondence that Foster Eddy also got 65 cents on each copy sold of *Christ and Christmas.*

15. The retail price of *Science and Health* was one of the things that aroused the ire and the envy of Mark Twain, who had about as much experience with all aspects of the publishing business as any American of his time and could appreciate the success of the Christian Science Publishing Company. Mark Twain himself made huge sums of money as a publisher, notably through his publication of Grant's memoirs, but he lost it all through personal extravagance and unwise investment.

16. Dakin notes that Foster Eddy made enough money during his years with Mrs. Eddy, mainly through his position as publisher, to support himself without working for the rest of his life. This is largely accurate, although Dakin makes no mention of the generous $15,000 settlement Mrs. Eddy made on Foster Eddy when they finally parted ways. Dakin says that Mrs. Eddy herself made $11,692 in royalties in 1893, $14,834 in 1894, and $18,481 in 1895.

17. Even Edwin Dakin, whose account of the relationship between Foster Eddy and Mrs. Eddy is heavily weighted in Foster Eddy's favor and largely based on Foster Eddy's own selective, even fanciful, testimony, portrays Foster at the time of his adoption as a very unattractive man. "Dr. Foster was then about 41 years old, a rather baldish man with small nostrils, large ears, dainty hands, and a certain sleekness about his well-rounded cheeks. Like almost all the men whom Mrs. Eddy had around her, he was rather negative in personality, and without dynamic force of character" (Dakin, p. 248). Dakin's whole book shows an obsession with sex, and the suggestion he gives in his portrait that Foster was some kind of eunuch fits in with the sexual schema.

18.   Calvin Frye's hostility and fear is evident in his April 1896 diary entries describing Foster Eddy's fall from favor.

19.   Church History Department.

20.   William Dana Orcutt reports the amazement at the University Press when Foster Eddy, as the new publisher, arrived in a cab, which he had wait for him—a luxury neither Mrs. Eddy herself nor her other Boston officials had ever permitted themselves.

> [Foster Eddy] was immaculately dressed, the climax being his magnificent fur-lined coat, fur cap, and the stunning diamond in his shirtfront. We found in him an agreeable personality, with a gratifying willingness to accept suggestions and make promises to cooperate; but there it stopped. Over and over again we had to refer details direct to Mrs. Eddy because Dr. Foster-Eddy was not at his office and could not be located for days at a time. (*Mary Baker Eddy and Her Books,* p. 47)

21.   Peel, *Authority,* p. 81.

22.   Milmine presents Mrs. Eddy as an elderly prude imposing the rules of her own rigid chastity on the young and virile Foster Eddy, but Dakin, much more sensationally, portrays Mrs. Eddy as a sexual virago, a version of Potiphar's wife, an older woman whose efforts to seduce a younger man fail, and who then vents her scorn on him with vile accusations and casts him into the equivalent of a dungeon. To portray the founder of Christian Science as an elderly nymphomaniac is a seductive scenario, and it was with claims of this kind that Dakin's book became a best-seller in 1930 (see Appendix). Peel in his account of Foster Eddy conclusively proves that most of the Dakin account of the fall of Ebenezer Foster Eddy is inaccurate or even created out of whole cloth.

23.   L01831. Original in the Church History Department.

24.   To give just one more taste of Ebenezer J. Foster Eddy, let me quote from a letter which he wrote in September 1891 to Augusta Stetson: "We all love you just the same as ever. . . . [we] know you can have no other desire than to be a dear good girl—no matter how much Satan wants you he can't have you for you belong to us. Very kindly, your little brother" (Sarah Gardner Cunningham, "A New Order: Augusta Emma Simmons Stetson and the Origins of Christian Science in New York City, 1886–1910" [Ph.D. diss., Union Theological Seminary, 1994], p. 63). This sounds like a parody of Mrs. Stetson, herself a parody of Mrs. Eddy, and one cannot imagine that this sickly and fulsome missive commended itself to the redoubtable Gussie, or persuaded her to regard her "little brother" as anything other than enemy number one in the Boston–Pleasant View camp. We shall have the opportunity to examine more of Foster Eddy's style and his unctuous hypocrisy when we come to look in detail at the Next Friends suit, in which he played a small but important part.

25.   Adoptions cannot be undone, and in breaking with Foster, Mrs. Eddy sought first to give him a last opportunity to make good in the movement, but outside New England, and then she paid him a substantial sum to get out of her life. As we shall see, by 1907 Ebenezer Foster was living in comfort in Vermont on the proceeds of his relationship with Mrs. Eddy and would reap another $45,000 as a result of his part in the Next Friends suit.

Chapter 21: Pleasant View

1.   In a rare rejection of technology, Mrs. Eddy herself refused to use the telephone, and even resisted having an outside line in her home installed until her move to Chestnut Hill in 1908, but her church organization was quick to exploit every communication innovation that came along.

2.   See the account of Mrs. Eddy's visit given by Bliss Knapp in *The Destiny of the Mother Church,* Chapter 2.

3.   The Knapps, father and son, were exponents of that brand of Christian Science that

sees Mary Baker Eddy as the woman of Prophesy, the woman of Revelation, a figure to be ranked with Jesus of Nazareth. The Knappite persuasion has usually been regarded as unorthodox or even heretical in the movement, but, as I explain in the Preface, the Board of Directors did authorize the Christian Science Publishing Society to reissue Bliss Knapp's 1947 book *The Destiny of the Mother Church* in 1991.

4.   Addie Towns Arnold lived as a child in the house opposite that of Mark and Elizabeth Baker and remembered the times when her mother would feel happy and honored to entertain Mrs. Baker to tea. I gather that the widowed Mrs. Mark Baker was a simple, affectionate, neighborly woman of some affluence but few pretensions, who ended her days as a valued member of her community and a beloved part of an extended family.

5.   Peel, *Trial*, p. 300.

6.   Mrs. Eddy thanked the contributors in a piece called "Pond and Purpose" published in the August 1892 *Christian Science Journal* and reproduced in *Mis.*, pp. 203–7.   Until 1996 the boat was on display at the Longyear Museum, along with other pieces saved from Pleasant View.

7.   Peel *Authority*, p. 11.

8.   Tomlinson, *Twelve Years with Mary Baker Eddy*, p. 254.

9.   Of course, rapidly during Mrs. Eddy's time there Concord became a lively and successful center for Christian Science, and Mrs. Eddy both encouraged and contributed generously toward, first, the renovation of a big house as a hall for services, and then the building of the large and imposing stone structure still to be seen in the center of the city.

10.   In *Bleak House* Boythorn dedicates his life to combatting the pretensions of the local landowner Sir Lester Deadlock to close off an ancient public right of way across his estate.

11.   John Lathrop, one of Mrs. Eddy's secretaries, recalls this high dive in his memoir: "She looked upon the exhibition as an example of overcoming fear, and she wanted to see it. . . . When the man in red disappeared, Mrs. Eddy turned to Judge and Mrs. Hanna and said, 'I beheld Satan as lightning fall from heaven' " (*We Knew Mary Baker Eddy*, p. 116).

12.   Calvin Hill reminiscences, *We Knew Mary Baker Eddy*, p. 156.

13.   His report of his interview with Mrs. Eddy at Pleasant View was first published in 1901 in the New York *Herald* and reprinted in the 1925 book *My Life and Memories* (New York: Dodd, Mead, & Co.). Clarke describes Pleasant View as an "ample, richly furnished house," pleasantly warm on a chilly, damp spring day. Mr. Hill had obviously had a major influence for change, since Clarke says the large parlor was carpeted in white and overlaid with expensive rugs, including one made of ostrich feathers, "a perfect delight of creamy fluffiness." Clarke comments: "Mrs. Eddy was charmingly simple about all this, her delight in it spontaneous, almost girlish" (*My Life and Memories*, p. 334).

14.   There is more firsthand testimony and documentation about Mary Baker Eddy after she moved to Pleasant View than for any previous part for her life, and it is in the Pleasant View years that the legend of Mrs. Eddy begins to emerge. This legendary aspect is well exemplified by Irving Tomlinson's book *Twelve Years with Mary Baker Eddy*, which the Christian Science Publishing Society issued under the heading "authorized literature" in 1945, again in 1966, and in an expanded form in 1996. Tomlinson makes it clear that his book deals with "Mary Baker Eddy," Religious Leader, not with "Mary," the human being who happened to be born in Bow in 1821, and he quotes Mrs. Eddy herself to support and authorize his emphasis. Tomlinson's published texts, and the notes from which those texts were taken, are the most important source of the claims made for Mrs. Eddy as a healer which have recently been exhaustively detailed by von Fettweis and Warneck in *Mary Baker Eddy: Christian Healer*. Given the aura of "authority" and "authorization" that surrounds Tomlinson, I was interested to find in the available extracts from Calvin Frye's diary an entry where Frye gleefully quotes Mrs. Eddy as telling him that Tomlinson was not broad enough to write her history. To my mind, Mrs. Eddy was right on the mark here, because to anyone

outside Christian Science Tomlinson's book is unreadable. His prose is dreary, most of the information he gives is hearsay, and he never gives the impression of having had a real relationship with his subject. I have chosen to base the account of Pleasant View I give in this chapter on the unpublished reminiscences of M. Adelaide Still and John Salchow, and on the privately published but rare book by Gilbert Carpenter, *Mary Baker Eddy: Her Spiritual Footsteps* (privately printed, 1934). Carpenter was a secretary, and I discuss him in the Appendix. Salchow and Still served Mrs. Eddy in humble capacities, never achieved any prominence in the movement, and spoke as eyewitnesses, their bias up front and overt. The other major source is, of course, the Calvin Frye diaries, or, more precisely, those sections of the diaries which John Dittemore cut out of the diaries in the hours following Frye's death. Dittemore burned the original handwritten pages but retained photographic copies, and Gilbert Carpenter Sr. transcribed the text since Frye had used abbreviations and in places an outdated form of shorthand which made his written work very hard to decipher. After he was forced out of the directorate and after his long and unsuccessful legal battle with the Church, Dittemore first leaked the Frye pages to Edwin Dakin, to sensational effect, and then used them again in his own hostile biography of Mrs. Eddy. The original diaries passed to Frye's heir, his nephew Oscar Frye, who later sold them to the Church, which also acquired from Dittemore the Photostats of the cut pages. The Frye diaries are one of the most precious and secret documents in Christian Science history, and Robert Peel is one of the rare people to have had access to them. When I requested to see them, the head of the Church History Department, Mrs. Yvonne von Fettweis, told me that they were currently being transcribed in full so that the directors could finally read the whole text and decide when or if the text could be released to Church members. She told me that the sensitivity of the diary resides in what it reveals of Mrs. Eddy's methods of healing. I think it is important to note that when he took scissors to Calvin Frye's diaries, John Dittemore was looking to remove those sections which were most likely to be damaging to Mrs. Eddy's reputation, and he was peculiarly well qualified to decide what these might be. Therefore, when Peel claims that the unpublished and unknown majority of Frye's diary entries chronicle small routine matters and are entirely uncontroversial, he may be correct—but how nice it would be to use the diaries to piece together a much more detailed picture of everyday life at Pleasant View! The Dittemore pages and the Carpenter book are available from Ann Beals of the Bookmark in Santa Clarita, California, and Guilford, Surrey, in Great Britain.

15.   Pleasant View had only one full bathroom, plus an extra lavatory, and staff members still washed in their rooms, bringing up water to fill their china basins.

16.   One of the many odd points in which Mary Baker Eddy and Mark Twain were alike.

17.   Peel, *Authority,* p. 85.

18.   Mrs. Julia Field-King is one of the colorful minor figures in the history of Christian Science and has been strongly represented by Milmine and Cather and Bates and Dittemore as an innocent and lovable victim of Mrs. Eddy's autocratic ways. Peel, on the other hand, sees Julia as a deeply unstable and very irritating follower who bombarded Mrs. Eddy with correspondence, lauded her to the heights at one moment, and suggested darkly at others that she was a ready prey for the mesmerists. It was Mrs. Field-King who spent time in Great Britain and had presumably caught the genealogical bug, who persuaded Mrs. Eddy that it would be possible to trace her ancestry back to the kings of England, and perhaps to Christ. She was one of the people Mrs. Eddy refused to see at Pleasant View, writing in reply to the latest request for an interview: "I have found it does no good where my students have my works and read them for them to talk with me. It only is a soothing syrup and the error returns sometimes more severely[;] it must be cured by yourself not me" (Peel, *Authority,* p. 84).

19.   Article 22, Section 11 of the *Manual of The Mother Church*:

At the written request of the Pastor Emeritus, Mrs. Eddy, the Board of Directors shall immediately notify a person who has been a member of this

Church at least three years to go in ten days to her, and it shall be the duty of the member thus notified to remain with Mrs. Eddy three years consecutively. A member who leaves in less time without the Directors' consent or who declines to obey this call to duty, upon Mrs. Eddy's complaint thereof shall be excommunicated from The Mother Church. Members thus serving the Leader shall be paid at the rate of one thousand dollars in addition to rent and board. Those members whom she teaches the course in Divinity, and who remain with her three consecutive years, receive the degree of the Massachusetts Metaphysical College.

In a whiff of the Mrs. Eddy of old lawsuits and high student fees, Section 14 stipulates that those who leave Mrs. Eddy without permission before the stipulated time is up "shall pay to Mrs. Eddy whatsoever she may charge him or her during the time of such service."

20. In 1897, when Mrs. Eddy was getting together the volume that would finally be called *Miscellaneous Writings,* she wrote in exasperation to Directors Joseph Armstrong and Edward Bates: "I have tried two weeks to have Mr. Frye type the Contents of my book and each time he did it wrong. He is trying again this morning." According to Peel, even when Frye had got the typing right, he managed to cause legal complications by having the book copyrighted from Concord instead of Boston (*Authority,* p. 103).

21. When I first read in Milmine about Mrs. Eddy's belief that she and her staff could affect the weather, I assumed that this was a unique case. But more recently I have learned from Garry Wills that claims to be able to affect the weather are standard in certain evangelical groups. Pat Robertson, it seems, works on weather issues regularly in his television program, and he claimed, most notably, to have changed the course of a tropical storm to spare his denomination's home base. Gilbert Carpenter devotes a chapter to the subject of the watch against the weather at Pleasant View, arguing that Mrs. Eddy never believed that by prayer or by willpower one could change the direction of a storm or stop the snow falling. This would be magnetism. What she claimed was that harmony is the divine reality, that weather, like all material manifestations, is an illusion or error, and that with effort and practice one can regain contact with divine harmony and restore the meteorological balance. See Carpenter, *Her Spiritual Footsteps,* Chapter 62.

22. M. Adelaide Still Memoirs, Chapter 2. Original in the Church History Department.

23. Carpenter, *Her Spiritual Footsteps,* p. 132. He defines animal magnetism again on p. 150 as all "that did not emanate from God, operating in a subtle way to shut God out."

24. In similar fashion, Laura Sargent was aghast when Mrs. Eddy first asked her to keep the household books, explaining that it was quite beyond her powers. Mrs. Eddy insisted, and soon Sargent was delighted to find that bookkeeping was in fact within her competence.

25. Salchow was an extraordinarily self-effacing and tolerant man—he says that he was known in his family as a kind of doormat—and he wrote his reminiscences of his life with Mrs. Eddy more than twenty years after her death for, and in collaboration with, the Mother Church archival staff. Despite all the editing which his memories have undergone, despite Salchow's unfailing commitment to Christian Science, he makes it clear that jealousy and rivalry were daily problems among the staff at Pleasant View, and that anyone who enjoyed an especially close relationship with Mrs. Eddy or was perceived to have won her approval could expect sabotage attempts from coworkers. At the very beginning of his time at Pleasant View, Mr. and Mrs. Alfred Baker, important members of the Concord community, lobbied strongly to have Salchow sent away, considering him to be too uncouth to represent Christian Science to the public, even in so humble a capacity as groundsman. At another point, someone reported, falsely, to Mrs. Eddy that Salchow had had tuberculosis in his youth—a condition that would have made him ineligible for service at Pleasant View. Fortunately another staff member tipped him off to this misinformation and he was able to reassure Mrs. Eddy.

26.   Salchow's memoir offers perhaps the most extreme example of this. When Pleasant View had been broken into and some items stolen, Salchow volunteered to do all his normal work as well as stay up all night as watchman. With the help of a patented device that jolted him awake when his head started to nod, he managed to make do on about three hours' sleep for three months, after which time Mrs. Eddy hired a regular night watchman. Salchow says that Mrs. Eddy herself was never told about the initial break-in, nor about his assumption of double duty. This seems possible to me since by this time Mrs. Eddy never walked outside in her grounds, she came downstairs only at scheduled times, and she would have no notion of where Salchow was spending his nights. But her secretarial staff certainly knew, and it is possible, in my view, that someone at Pleasant View would not have been unhappy to see John Salchow finally reach his physical limit and be forced to leave, as Joseph Mann had done.

27.   Carpenter, *Her Spiritual Footsteps,* p. 183.

28.   It is the rareness of leisure at Pleasant View that makes the little snapshots reproduced in some works on Mrs. Eddy showing staff members with bicycles or rowing on the little lake so poignant. William R. Rathvon wrote of Laura Sargent in his diary:

> March 28, 1909: LS is the one member of the household who for 25 years has stood closest to our Leader and is today more indispensable than ever in the past. Rarely does a day pass that she gets over twenty minutes to meals and her sleep is shortened proportionately, six hours one night with eight the next is the present allowance which is much more liberal than has been in times past. The rest of the day is spent in personal service, rarely out of sight, always within hearing. She is a Scientist of many years' standing, a teacher, one who holds her friends permanently and wins them easily so that she would find much to her liking in the world; but never a nun in her cloister was more voluntarily or completely cut off or isolated, nor was ever a devotee more sincere in offering her all at the shrine of her religion without a pang of regret. The world may some day know of the debt it owes this woman, but it never can repay her. (Rathvon reminiscences, Church History Department)

29.   There were nights when even Calvin Frye was too exhausted to attend his Leader at night. In 1905 he recorded in his diary: "When Mrs. Ed asked me to talk with her when she had just retired I believed I could not & left her without a comforting word which nearly [killed?] her, but I gave the alarm & called others to her rescue. They watched with her the rest of the night & I was allowed to go to my room and . . . sleep for the rest of the night" (quoted in Peel, *Authority,* p. 245).

30.   Small details of this kind, with careful references, have been recirculated in the Publishing Society pamphlet *They Answered the Call,* which contains small portraits of, among others, three members of Mrs. Eddy's personal staff, M. Adelaide Still, Calvin Frye, and Laura Sargent.

31.   Both during Mrs. Eddy's lifetime and since, the Church has claimed that Mrs. Eddy's healings included several instances when she raised people from the dead. The chapter Tomlinson devotes to Mrs. Eddy's healings details some of these. The emblem that appears on many Christian Science authorized publications shows a cross embraced by a crown, the whole surrounded by the words "Heal the Sick · Raise the Dead · Cleanse the Lepers · Cast Out Demons."

32.   Peel summarizing a section from the unpublished reminiscences of George Kinter (*Authority,* pp. 245–46). Tomlinson in his published reminiscences and Ada Still in her unpublished reminiscences give accounts of Mrs. Eddy calling Frye back from the dead. I find the case of Calvin Frye's various resurrections fascinating but am somewhat at a loss as to how to interpret them. There were a number of eyewitnesses to all of the healings, and there is no reason to doubt their bona fides, but, of course, no one present had any medical training, and their collective judgment that Frye was dead is unsubstantiable.

Frye may have had some form of epilepsy, or, more probably, some kind of hysterical cata-tonia. As I have pointed out, for many years Mrs. Eddy had been refusing to see patients, and her Pleasant View household was carefully constructed to eliminate anyone with a chronic physical disorder. The healings of Calvin Frye thus take on an extraordinary sig-nificance because of the stage in Mrs. Eddy's life at which they occurred, and because they were witnessed and later attested to by so many people. In the view of Christian Scientists, they prove conclusively that, at the height of her powers, Mrs. Eddy could raise a person from the dead.

33. Some hereditary component in Frye's ailment may also be suspected. Frye's mother, it will be remembered, went mad as a young woman.

34. See Peel, *Authority,* p. 169.

35. Ibid., pp. 87–88.

36. Memories recorded by Martha W. Wilcox, a member of Mrs. Eddy's household at Chestnut Hill, which appear in *We Knew Mary Baker Eddy,* p. 201. The pins in the pin-cushion were not for sewing, but were hair- and hatpins. One of Adam Dickey's great innovations at Chestnut Hill was to drive in sets of brass nails into the carpet which were meant to indicate the exact position of each piece of furniture in Mrs. Eddy's room. The maids cleaned the whole room punctiliously every week, moving each piece of the furni-ture to get the dirt from beneath it, and Mrs. Eddy would notice and complain about the slightest change in position. In his book Carpenter insists that Dickey's nails were directly in contravention of Christian Science, since they removed one of the little ways Mrs. Eddy had developed for detecting magnetism. This kind of critique of one of the directors of the Church was, I surmise, one reason why Carpenter became such a persona non grata and why his book was outlawed.

37. The way in which Gilman came to make Mrs. Eddy's acquaintance is explained in *Painting a Poem: Mary Baker Eddy and James F. Gilman Illustrate Christ and Christmas* (Boston: The Christian Science Publishing Society, 1998). This work reproduces much of the work Gilman did for the Eddy poem, and this work is in the Church's collection. In her book *James Franklin Gilman: 19th-Century Painter* (Canaan, N.H.: Phoenix Publishing, 1975) Adele Godchaux Dawson gives the standard biography of Gilman and reproduces some of Gilman's pre–Christian Science landscapes.

38. *Recollections of Mary Baker Eddy, as Preserved in the Diary Records of James F. Gilman Written During the Making of the Illustrations for Mrs. Eddy's Poem, Christ and Christmas, in 1893. With an Introductory Critique by Gilbert C. Carpenter, C.S.B., Sometime Assistant Secretary to Mrs. Eddy and Gilbert C. Carpenter, Jr., C.S.B.* (np, nd), p. 12. Also *Painting a Poem,* p. 45.

39. How the Gilman document came to public notice is unclear, but since Dittemore was the first to cite it I deduce that in his official quest to collect all available materials on Mrs. Eddy for the Mother Church collection, Dittemore ran across Gilman—who was sup-ported by the Church in his last years—discovered the diary, perhaps commissioning the preface, kept a copy of this document, as of so many others, and later exploited it as valu-able ammunition in his long fight against the Church. Those commentators who have seen Gilman as a key source of insight and information on Mrs. Eddy's hidden life have failed to note the political and rhetorical context in which the diary appeared, and they have also taken at face value everything Gilman says. Thus Gilman's reports of how little Mrs. Eddy paid him for his labors are taken as evidence of her meanness of pocket and spirit, but other sources indicate that the sums he received from Mrs. Eddy were more than he had been paid by others, and that he did receive other commissions from the Church as a result of his illustrations of *Christ and Christmas.* Dawson says Gilman was never paid more than a few dollars for his paintings, and from the reproductions Dawson gives in her book and from the original Gilman works owned by The Mother Church, which I was able to see, I would say that his talent was for landscape, not figure drawing and illustration. In general, I am far less ready than other critics to always take Gilman on his own estimation—i.e., as

a naïve and unmaterialistic man, with no axe to grind. Gilman in 1893 was a middle-aged man who had still to make his way in the world, and who saw in Mary Baker Eddy his best chance to make his life easy and independent. When this goal was frustrated, when Mrs. Eddy told him he was mesmerized—i.e., motivated by a materialism he refused to acknowledge and could thus never conquer—he was angry, and he expressed that anger in his diary. Gilman's confused sense that he was betraying the leader he claimed to revere is evident in the preface he wrote in 1917 to accompany his 1893 diary entries:

> Thus much appears in these diary records, which in the writing were ever intended to be impartially yet lovingly accurate, might be misunderstood if not spiritually interpreted as above explained. Mrs. Eddy's true and abiding glory, however, cannot be dimmed to the spiritually discerning mind, and this result follows true reading of honest records, of loving, healing deeds which ever characterized Mrs. Eddy's real life to the writer. (p. 119)

The fact is that many readers of the diary refused to "interpret it spiritually" and argued that many entries served indeed to dim Mrs. Eddy's glory.

40.   Gilman's diary is a fascinating and important document, deserving of careful analysis. I first read the typed transcription of the diary which was given to the Longyear Museum by Mrs. Edith Dittemore in 1924. This contains a number of sections that do not appear, as far as I can determine, in either the Carpenter edition or in the 1998 edited account of the illustrating of the poem put out by the Christian Science Publishing Society. It is also notable because in the transcription the pronouns that relate to Mrs. Eddy are capitalized. The two passages I quote, one in note 39 and the other in the text, are taken from the Dittemore transcription of the Gilman diary entries, pp. 119 and 122. The original manuscript is in the Church History Department, and unfortunately I became aware of the fact that there were different versions of the diary only when it was too late to request to see the original and make a careful comparison.

41.   *We Knew Mary Baker Eddy,* p. 174. In his diary of the months spent on Mrs. Eddy's staff at Chestnut Hill, 1908–1910, William R. Rathvon specifically comments that those most convinced of Mrs. Eddy's divine mission were those who knew her best: "Never was there another like her. An outstanding evidence of it all is that those who have been longest with her and closest to her, and who have endured the most and been rewarded no more, save by close and continued companionship, than others less favored: these, I say, are the ones who pronounce with least hesitation the conviction that she was God-sent and God-governed" (his reminiscences are in the Church History Department).

Chapter 22: The Last Class

1.   In the Great Litigation of 1917–1921, the Board of Directors of the Mother Church were pitted in court against the Trustees of the Publishing Society over the issue of whether Mrs. Eddy's trust deed of 1898 gave the Publishing Society an authority and an identity independent of the directors' control. Although the trustees' legal arguments carried by far the greater weight in the eyes of the judiciary, the vast majority of Christian Scientists were vigorously, even violently, in favor of the Board of Directors, and the final decision on appeal was that although the legal provisions made by Mrs. Eddy in the trust document and in the *Manual* seemed to set up a double and balancing power structure, the practical situation in the Church demanded that the directors be allowed to have their way. In *Christian Science and Organized Religion,* a pamphlet privately published by the rebellious Farallon Press in California and now available from the Bookmark group, Hugh Studdert Kennedy reviews the case in detail and makes an impassioned defense of the trustees' position as representing Mary Baker Eddy's original and revolutionary concept of noninstitutionalized religious governance. An almost equally detailed but pro-directors account of the Great Litigation is given in Norman Beasley's *The Continuing Spirit* (New York: Duell Sloan and Pierce, 1956).

2.   Powell includes a full list of those who attended the last class in the notes to his 1930 book on Mrs. Eddy. George Wendell Adams, "The Call to Concord," pp. 107–110; Sue Harper Mims, "An Intimate Picture of Our Leader's Final Class," pp. 127–38. Both the Adams and Mims reminiscences are reprinted in *We Knew Mary Baker Eddy* (Boston: The Christian Science Publishing Society, 1979).

3.   *We Knew Mary Baker Eddy,* p. 130.

4.   Mrs. Eddy's appearance was of interest not just to Christian Scientists. In his interview for the New York *Herald* in 1901 (which he later reprinted in his book *My Life and Memories),* Joseph Clarke devotes almost a whole page to describing the leader of Christian Science. It is clear that Mary Baker Eddy still knew how to make an entrance, and that from her first appearance Clarke was surprised and somewhat disarmed.

> She entered with a gracious smile, walking with that short step of courtesy, that gentle lowering of the head in token of recognition, and that frank extension of the hand which have somehow passed out of parlor greetings—not to their betterment. It was not, however, this grace of the old school grande dame, but the gentle air of conscious motherhood that made the meeting most agreeable. Her white hair was parted in wavy puffs. The strong nose and rounded temples, the mobile mouth, the bright eyes were all as they had been in her younger days. Signs of time were in the fine lining of the face, a general thinning of the flesh— a sense of frailty rather than weakness. As her thin lips parted in a pleasant smile they disclosed two sets of very white, even teeth. On her cheeks was a faint flush of color. Her hands were soft and white, and neither large nor small. She had walked erect and now sat with ease.
>
> It was clear that Mrs. Eddy had graced the occasion with a toilette of special brilliance. Matching the whiteness of her hair, a collarette of fine point lace that covered the shoulders and bosom was caught at the throat by a breastpin in the likeness of a golden crown, and a little below the latter by a cross of large diamonds set in gold. Her gown, with high embroidered neck and long cuffed sleeves in the prevailing fashion, was of purple satin—royal purple. It fitted her slim figure closely. At her waist hung a chatelaine of gold net in which reposed a dainty lace handkerchief. She wore on her left bosom some badges of orders in gold and enamel. Altogether it was an appealing ladylike figure, at ease in her home and receiving a formal call, that faced me. (*My Life and Memories,* p. 333)

5.   Quoted in Peel, *Authority,* pp. 431–32, from unpublished archival material (A10281) in the Church History Department. No precise date given.

6.   See *We Knew Mary Baker Eddy,* pp. 82–83.

7.   Mrs. Eddy was especially concerned that men serve on the Committees on Publication because she was convinced that men could more easily move in the world of journalism and find a public voice.

8.   A101428. Church History Department.

9.   Mrs. Eddy's position on gender was clarified and made public in the 1901 New York *Herald* interview which she granted to Joseph I. C. Clarke, a famously hard-hitting Irish journalist. Clarke had written a piece highly critical of Mrs. Eddy and of Christian Science as a new Papism, and he came to Pleasant View determined to ask her the tough questions. Thus he tells us that he began by asking Mrs. Eddy point-blank about the accusation that she enjoyed unlimited personal power and about her plans for her succession. She replied that, although she had been called a Pope, she had never sought such a distinction, and then she added that "no present change is contemplated in rulership." She went on to state that her successor would be a man, not a woman, but she declined to name the man. When Clarke again pressed her to comment on the great preponderance of women in her church's ranks, Mrs. Eddy replied: "Woman has the finer spiritual

nature. She more readily takes the impress of Christian Science. If, as you say (I leave all statistics to the publication department), there are 13,000 women against 5,000 men out of a book total of 18,000, it shows that their minds are more receptive; their enthusiasm is greater at the beginning of a struggle, but in the strength of men lies the power of carrying on" (Clarke, *Life and Memories,* p. 337).

Chapter 23: Mrs. Woodbury and Her Lawyer

1. The American Jewish Historical Society has no evidence that Lazarus ever taught in Weld's school, or indeed in any school. Lazarus was only one year older than Woodbury.

2. Josephine Curtis Woodbury, *War in Heaven: Sixteen Years in Christian Science Mind-Healing* (Boston: Press of Samuel Usher, 1897), pp. 7–8.

3. Unfortunately, this hypothesis about Mrs. Woodbury's financial dilemma is hard to prove because neither her critics nor her supporters cared to discuss for publication how much money could be earned in alternative healing practice, and all use the term *mercenary* as a stick with which to beat the opposition. The interviews later given by her students show indisputably, however, that Mrs. Woodbury was constantly seeking to get money out of them, and extant letters to her lieutenants talk about little else but fees, and who is entitled to demand payment from which patients and students.

4. One of the oddments tucked into the Dittemore pages of the Calvin Frye diaries (see Chapter 21, n. 14 of the present volume) is a list of all the students who had been involved with nursing Asa Gilbert Eddy in his last days. Mrs. Woodbury's name does not figure, and possibly Frye's entry indicates a need to assemble evidence to counter one small piece of the Woodbury propaganda machine at the time of the libel suit.

5. According to his wife, Frank Woodbury was instrumental in negotiating the purchase of the land between Norway, Falmouth, and Saint Paul Streets on which the Mother Church was built. Frank Woodbury was apparently not related to Edgar S. Woodbury, one of the original trustees of the Massachusetts Metaphysical College.

6. James Wiggin, whom we have already met as Mrs. Eddy's editor, wrote an introduction to one of Mrs. Woodbury's books, and he may have helped in the writing. It was only after I had tried to read the work of Josephine Woodbury and discovered how bad it was that I realized how low Wiggin had sunk by lending this woman the support of his name and reputation. Wiggin does seem to have been mesmerized by Woodbury, whatever meaning one places on that verb, and the dislike and discredit he began to express toward Mrs. Eddy in his last years are very probably in part a result of Woodbury's influence.

7. Milmine and Cather, p. 429. To do him justice, Martin Gardner does not accept the Milmine account without question, and he reports in a footnote what Robert Peel discovered about the actual nature of Mrs. Woodbury's following. Gardner is rational enough to make no claims about Mrs. Woodbury's purity and chaste life, and to assume that her son Prince was the maculate result of an illegitimate affair.

8. After long study of the Milmine and Cather book, I have learned, as a fellow biographer, to pay some attention to lively and persuasive passages for which, as here, there are no references, no named sources, and no quotation marks. The *McClure's* team that worked on the Eddy story were enthusiastic members of the objective-factual-reportorial school of American journalism, with its emphasis on affidavits, signed statements, direct quotation from eyewitnesses, and so forth, and I strongly suspect that when they fail to name names, Milmine and Cather are quoting the interview testimony of a single, well-informed witness who does not care to be identified. That witness could well have been Josephine Woodbury herself—not just through her writings, which Milmine and Cather certainly had copies of, but in person.

9. Josephine Woodbury files, Church History Department.

10. *War in Heaven*, pp. 50–51.

11.   The pretrial testimony gathered in preparation for the Woodbury libel suit is in the Church History Department. Peel, *Authority,* p. 422, n. 6.

12.   Several commentators have commented that someone, presumably Mrs. Eddy, used the term "immaculate conception" for "Virgin birth," since she misunderstood the Catholic dogma of the Immaculate Conception of the Virgin Mary. I think either Mrs. Woodbury or Mrs. Eddy was quite capable of making this error—although the dogma had been promulgated quite recently by Pius IX—but would note that even Mrs. Woodbury, as the mother of two large, healthy, and visible children, could not have claimed to have been a virgin when she bore Prince.

13.   One witness remembered Woodbury urging her mother in vain to admit that she had planned to give her daughter the name Mary, and on another occasion reproving her mother for referring to Prince as her third grandchild.

14.   Quoted in Milmine and Cather, pp. 430–31.

15.   Josephine Woodbury papers, Church History Department.

16.   Robert David Thomas gives the most detailed summary of the Woodbury-Eddy letters in his chapter "Strange Children." He is interested in a dysfunctional mother-daughter pattern of relationship which he sees played out between Mrs. Eddy and, first, Mrs. Choate, then Mrs. Hopkins, then Mrs. Woodbury, and finally Mrs. Stetson. Without denying that some relational pattern pertains here, and that it has some connection to the mother-daughter relation, I would argue that the differences among the four cases are at least as striking, and much more interesting, than the similarities. I think Thomas, like almost all male critics of Mrs. Eddy, is far too easy on Josephine Woodbury.

17.   Woodbury's letter is found in Peel, *Authority,* p. 145; the original is in the Church History Department. Mrs. Eddy's letter, L02644, is partially published in Milmine and Cather, p. 434. The original of the letter is no longer extant, and the copy in the Church History Department is an attested copy by Calvin Frye.

18.   Peel, *Authority,* 147. Original statement is from the Josephine Woodbury papers, Church History Department.

19.   The May issue of the *Arena,* heralded as "Eddyism Exposed" and entitled "Christian Science and Its Prophetess," consisted of Part 1, "The Facts in the Case," by Horatio W. Dresser; and Part 2, "The Book and the Woman," by Josephine Curtis Woodbury. An expanded form of Mrs. Woodbury's piece which simply incorporated the Dresser material (without attribution and perhaps without Dresser's permission) was later published under her name with the title *Quimbyism, or the Paternity of Christian Science* (Letchworth: Garden City Press, 1909).

20.   This was the Islamic leader who had recently led an anticolonialist revolt in the Sudan, notably encircling the British general Kitchener in Khartoum.

21.   These two quotations are from Woodbury, "Christian Science and Its Prophetess," Part 2, "The Book and the Woman," pp. 568, 570.

22.   Preface to Peabody's *The Religio-Medical Masquerade,* p. 11.

23.   Dakin, p. 309; Bates and Dittemore, p. 366.

24.   Peel, *Authority,* pp. 153–54. The entire address is published in Mrs. Eddy's compilation *Miscellany,* pp. 124–31.

25.   Peel, *Authority,* p. 155.

26.   Ibid., p. 155, referring to the *Boston Journal* article of June 21, 1899.

27.   My sources for this account are Peabody's published works, a number of his letters, notably those to William Chandler and Willa Cather, in the Church History Department, The Mother Church's press file on him, and the Radcliffe College Alumnae Office.

28.   Boston *Post,* April 13, 1912.

29.   Anna Greenough May Peabody, 1865–1939, was the daughter of Frederick W. G. May and Martha Rand Morse May. She was a second cousin of Louisa May Alcott. According to a short memorial biography contributed to the Radcliffe Alumnae files in 1943 by Mary May Hotson, one of her two daughters—both of whom graduated from Radcliffe—soon after her marriage to Peabody, Anna enrolled as a special student at Radcliffe and took two Harvard courses in philosophy taught by William James and Josiah Royce which greatly influenced her. According to her daughter, Mrs. Peabody was an ardent worker in the causes of feminism and pacifism and a devoted member of the Unitarian Church. "She was always looking eagerly out and ahead for finer things, while at the same time keeping close, loving touch with the lives around her." Mrs. Hotson implies that her mother never remarried and gives no information at all about her father, Frederick Peabody.

30.   Letter to the editor in the Boston *Post,* September 17, 1912. The writer states that Mrs. Peabody had always been a loyal Unitarian and had never been a Christian Scientist, and that she had left her husband because "he failed to support his family, and being an honorable and conscientious woman, she could not endure to live in debt without her household bills being paid." The writer cautiously says he has never heard Mrs. Peabody "speak of [suffrage], and she has taken no active part in the movement."

31.   Boston *Post,* April 13, 1912. This portion of the trial transcript as well as subsequent quotes from the trial were published in the Boston *Post.*

32.   In one letter quoted in court, in which Frederick wrote asking his father-in-law to pay some of his bills, he says that the dishonor is killing Anna.

33.   Boston *Post,* January 31, 1908.

34.   Boston *Post,* September 6, 1912. Again the Boston *Post* reporter contrived to put the best possible spin on Peabody's flight. Rather than finding out whether Peabody was up-to-date on his rent payments, the reporter quotes a friend who remarks that Frederick "was one to whom I could go at any time and borrow $5 or $10 and never feel that it was incumbent on me to liquidate the obligation before I called for another loan if at all." In a caption beneath the headline the reporter summarizes Peabody as "Impulsively Liberal" and comments: "His friends said yesterday that his life told the old story of a quick, bright, disputatious mind, willing to champion any cause that appealed to him without considering whether the venture was worth his effort from an economic point of view." Like his former friend and client Josephine Woodbury, Frederick Peabody had an excellent way with the press corps, who usually gave him the benefit of the doubt.

35.   Peabody's legal declaration was published in the Boston *Post* of October 4, 1899.

36.   In all his public statements, in 1899 and later, Peabody is uniformly chivalrous in his defense of Mrs. Woodbury as a chaste and respectable woman, but he says very little about her and is generally evasive.

37.   No reporter seems to have inquired as to how Mrs. Woodbury came to select Peabody as her legal counsel or what financial terms the two had agreed upon. As we have seen, Mrs. Woodbury was not averse to paying for professional services with personal favors, and it would not surprise me if she and Peabody had been lovers.

38.   Peel tells an interesting little anecdote about William Morse, who apparently had a serious drinking problem. Late one evening he appeared at Pleasant View to discuss the Woodbury case in a state of obvious inebriation. Christian Science condemns the use of alcoholic beverages, and the members of Mrs. Eddy's staff who greeted Morse were so shocked by his condition that they sent him away. Mrs. Eddy saw him weaving down the street, sent someone after him, and ordered that he be lovingly taken care of and given a safe bed for the night. This treatment made a great impression on Morse and secured his loyalty to Mrs. Eddy. (See Peel, *Authority,* p. 430, n. 73.) As I have noted, Mrs. Eddy was fiercely opposed to alcoholic drinks not because she was a narrow prude but because she had seen the terrible effect of alcoholism on several people in her own family, notably her brother George Baker and her nephew Albert Tilton.

39.   According to Bates and Dittemore, (p. 370), Mrs. Eddy wrote to a number of her students, immediately after her 1899 Message had been read, explaining to them that in speaking of the "Babylonish woman" she had been referring not to an individual but to a type. As Stephen Gottschalk has explained to me, Mrs. Eddy is using *type* in reference to a variety of Biblical criticism common in her day, according to which characters and events in the Bible were seen as patterns for general human experience. Thus a person could be, typologically, a John the Baptist or experience a temptation in the garden. Peel quotes several interesting sections from Mrs. Eddy's unpublished writings from this period in which she tries to make clear how she used Biblical passages as types and symbols.

40.   Peel, *Authority,* p. 170.

41.   Ibid., p. 160. Letter of January 5, 1901. L08531. Original in the Church History Department.

42.   As far as I can judge from the material quoted by Peel, Mrs. Eddy's chief concern was secrecy, that no hint of what her legal counsel were planning should reach the opposition, and that Peabody and Woodbury should be given all the rope they needed to hang themselves. At one point Frank Streeter wished to file interrogatories which Mrs. Woodbury would be obliged to reply to. Mrs. Eddy refused to allow him to do this and alleged, to Streeter's amazement and outrage, that the thought of the interrogatories had been placed in his mind by Malicious Animal Magnetism. Although Streeter never accepted the doctrine of mesmerism, he did come to acknowledge that Mrs. Eddy's order had been tactically correct, that the idea of filing the interrogatories was a poor one since they would have tipped off Peabody about how he should prepare his court case.

43.   In England she had some initial success in persuading people of Mrs. Eddy's villainy, but then she found it necessary to move onto the Continent where, like Thackeray's Becky Sharpe, whom she somewhat resembles, she faded from sight. She died in 1930 at the age of eighty. Her older son is known to have sued her at one point for possession of a house. Little is known of the life of Prince of Peace Woodbury, who died in England in the 1960s, although a very amusing little piece by Alexander Woollcott in the *New Yorker* of February 19, 1932, pleads for information about him.

44.   Frederick Peabody, *The Religio-Medical Masquerade: A Complete Exposure of Christian Science*; and Frederick Peabody, Woodbridge Riley, and Charles E. Humiston, *The Faith, the Falsity and the Failure of Christian Science.*

45.   This quotation, attributed to the *New York Times,* appears as part of the promotional material attached to the 1904 expanded version of Peabody's pamphlet "Complete Exposure of Eddyism or Christian Science: The Plain Truth in Plain Terms Regarding Mary Baker G. Eddy."

46.   In the introduction to his book, Peabody says that he first became involved with Christian Science when he was hired by the *Arena* magazine to defend it in some legal challenge filed by the Christian Science people against Mrs. Woodbury's article. But the legal department at The Mother Church has no record of any suit being filed against the *Arena*. The Wiggin files at The Mother Church show that Wiggin was in his last years closely associated with Mrs. Woodbury, and that he was trying unsuccessfully to get some of his own work on Christian Science published in *Arena,* which was edited at least for a time by Horatio Dresser. Minot J. Savage was a Unitarian clergyman of some means who was deeply opposed to Christian Science and hoped to destroy it by uncovering unpleasant information about its founder.

47.   Peabody, *The Religio-Medical Masquerade,* pp. 5–6, 21–22, 24, 40–41, 44, 98, 100.

48.   In 1912 Peabody closed his law practice, and in the 1920s he was living in Ashburnham, Massachusetts, keeping cows and living in very reduced circumstances. In 1926 he again reached a national audience by writing a letter to President Coolidge, pleading for total cancellation of the World War I obligations of the Allies to the United States. This letter set off a heated public debate, and Peabody organized the American Association Favoring Reconsideration of the War Debts. He died in 1938.

49.   Sections of the long July 10, 1904, *New York Times* article ("True Origin of Christian Science: Documentary Evidence Refuting Mrs. Eddy's Claims That Her System Was Revealed by God") claiming to prove Mrs. Eddy had plagiarized a text of P. P. Quimby are virtual quotations from Peabody's own writings. For more on the Wentworth manuscripts, see Chapter 10.

Chapter 24: Mark Twain Fails to Come Calling

1.   L02127. Original letter in the Church History Department. I quote everything but the postscript, where Mrs. Eddy assures George that Calvin Frye is absolutely to be trusted as her accountant since a recent audit had found only a small error, and that had not been in his favor. Milmine and Bates and Dittemore, who also quote and refer to this letter, comment that Mrs. Eddy exaggerates her own importance since, in fact, only some very minor members of the British nobility had become Christian Scientists. There is some truth to this—the Earl and Countess Dunmore, who had visited Mrs. Eddy at Pleasant View in 1898 and 1901, were far from feudal nobility—but many of us tend to exaggerate a bit in our family letters. The substance of what Mrs. Eddy says is true, and Governor Hoke Smith, the son of her cousin and former admirer Hildreth Smith, had reason to call her the most illustrious woman in the United States. Mrs. Eddy's comment about her son becoming president had he been properly educated seems extreme until one remembers George Glover's uncle Albert Baker, who by sheer ability and hard work had launched a brilliant political career and seemed all set to follow his good friend and law partner Franklin Pierce to the U.S. Senate, or even the White House.

2.   "I hold the late Mr. Wiggin in loving, grateful memory for his high-principled character and well-equipped scholarship," concluded Mrs. Eddy in her response to Wright (*Miscellany,* p. 319).

3.   The activities of the Committees on Publication have attracted a large body of adverse comment, and the central committee was on the nation's list of Public Enemies at the time of the Dakin biography, which it was supposed to have gone to extraordinary lengths to suppress. I have read the extensive press coverage of the Dakin book, and, as I discuss in the Appendix, it seems clear that, if it sought to keep Dakin's work from the public, the Committee on Publication failed spectacularly since the book rode onto the best-seller list on the strength of its author and publisher's well-publicized espousal of freedom of the press. My gut feeling is that by setting up its own propaganda machine and entrusting its public relations to a group of devoted but intellectually unimpressive men, the Church of Christ, Scientist won a reputation as an opponent of truth and, paradoxically, could henceforth never gain a fair hearing, even when, as in the case of the Lieber-Hegel document, it was in the right.

4.   The complicated history of Mark Twain's book *Christian Science* is well explained in the most recent edition of the work for *The Oxford Mark Twain* series (edited by Shelley Fisher Fishkin, with an introduction by Garry Wills and an afterword by Hamlin Hill [New York and Oxford: Oxford University Press, 1996]). In 1898–1899, while he was living in Vienna, Mark Twain wrote a "burlesque tale followed by philosophical musings on the tale" (Introduction, p. 22). He got the tale published by *Cosmopolitan* in October 1899. The musings went deeper, and apparently scared Twain's American publishers, Harper and Brothers. In the next volume of his collected stories, the tale and musings (the first eight chapters of *Christian Science* as we have it) were included in the German and British editions but excluded from the American. The musings (Chapters 5–8) eventually appeared in the *North American Review* for December 1902, by which time responses to his tale had prompted Twain to plan a book on Mrs. Eddy and her Science. What became Chapter 9 of the book ran in the *North American Review* in February 1903, and "Mrs. Eddy in Error" ran in the April issue (Introduction, p. 33). In 1903 Twain submitted the book manuscript to Harper's, who set it in type but then decided not to publish it. Harper's finally brought the book out in 1907, when Christian Science was under

a battery of attack and was a subject of great public interest. According to Hamlin Hill, Twain believed that Harper's reluctance to publish was due to pressure from Christian Scientists (Afterword, p. 5), but it seems equally possible, given the adverse reactions to the magazine pieces which are reported by Wills and Hamlin, that Harper's was simply persuaded that the book would rouse bitter attacks and hurt the author's reputation. *The Oxford Mark Twain* volume reproduces in a facsimile the 1907 edition of *Christian Science*. Twain excluded from the book a futuristic fancy called "Later Still," which had appeared in the February issue of the *North American Review* and would have formed Chapter 10 of Book 1. The most disturbing and extreme of Mark Twain's writings on Christian Science, an expansion of "Later Still" called "The Secret History of Eddypus, the World-Empire," was not published until 1972. For more exact information on the period in which *Christian Science* in its various forms came into being, see William R. Macnaughton, *Mark Twain's Last Years as a Writer* (Columbia: University of Missouri Press, 1979). From the specific point of view of the relations between Mark Twain and Christian Science, the best single account is still probably the fifth chapter of Thomas C. Johnsen's 1983 doctoral dissertation, "Christian Science and the Puritan Tradition." This in turn builds on the strong archival and analytic work done by Robert Peel in the third volume of his biography of Mrs. Eddy. I am indebted to both these accounts.

5. Letter of December 5, 1902. As Peel points out, Peabody wrote to Mark Twain that he intended to publish this letter, or this remark, and use it in his campaign against Christian Science. Mark Twain objected vigorously and warned Peabody he had no right to publish private correspondence without the writer's permission. After Mark Twain's death, Peabody did include quotes from the letter in his book *The Religio-Medical Masquerade*. Peel, *Authority*, p. 446, n. 84.

6. Laura Skandera-Trombley gives the most detailed account of the ill health that plagued Olivia Langdon Clemens through most of her life, and challenges Mark Twain's account of his wife's "cure" in her late teens after she had spent two years as a helpless invalid. See "Mark Twain's Fictionalizing of Dr. Newton's Miraculous Cure," *American Literary Realism* 26 (Winter 1994): 82–92.

7. According to Isabel Lyon, Mark Twain's secretary in his last ten years, the author believed that his eldest daughter, Susy, might have lived, had some Hartford friends not introduced her to Christian Science. Susy was "so interested in this new religion that in the early stages of her tragic illness she refused to see a doctor, & then it was too late" (quoted in Hamlin Hill, Afterword, p. 1). The Isabel Lyon anecdote is confusing. Nothing Mark Twain wrote between 1898 and 1903 about Christian Science *as a healing method* indicates that he saw a connection between the death of his adored daughter and Christian Science, or that he was seeking any kind of revenge or vindication for her death. Susy died in 1895 from spinal meningitis, a condition which can occur for several reasons and can still prove fatal. As I have pointed out, Twain was convinced that conventional medicine held few answers to the problems of disease, and it is unclear how much a doctor could have done for Susy Clemens without the diagnostic techniques and powerful antibiotics available today.

8. *Christian Science,* Book 1, Chapter 6, p. 53.

9. *Christian Science,* Book 2, Chapter 15, p. 284. It was passages from *Christian Science* like this which led Frederick Peabody privately to excoriate Mark Twain, accusing him of having converted to Eddyism and becoming an apostle of the Christian Science faith. To Twain himself, Peabody expressed more diplomatically his disappointment with certain sections of the *North American Review* articles. See Peel, *Authority,* for the most complete discussion of Peabody and Twain's relationship.

10. *Christian Science,* Book 2, Chapter 1, p. 102.

11. *Christian Science,* Book 1, Chapter 6, pp. 65–66.

12. I hesitate to interject my personal beliefs, but I do not want to be misunderstood on this extraordinarily emotional issue. Let me note, therefore, that I am made uneasy by

Mark Twain's reference to children as the parent's *possession*—cherished or not—and I do believe that in certain extreme cases the state has a duty to intervene in family life to ensure for children their rights to life, liberty, and the pursuit of happiness. On the other hand, the Christian Scientists I have met in the course of my research seem to have their children given routine injections, follow careful and sensible preventative health-care strategies, take their children to traditional doctors in critical situations, and resort only in extreme emergencies to surgical procedures and medications such as painkillers and antibiotics. This seems to me a stoic but not unenlightened policy which many traditional physicians would endorse.

13.   *North American Review* (February 1903): p. 181. Let me note that in the same essay in which he foresees Christian Science taking over the whole world, body and soul, Mark Twain also cavalierly dismisses the potential influence of Mormonism in the United States and of Islam in the world, thus showing singularly little talent for prophecy.

14.   Mary Baker Eddy's "Reply to Mark Twain" can be found in *Miscellany,* pp. 302–3.

15.   Following Peter Stonely, Hamlin Hill in his Afterword to *The Oxford Mark Twain* edition of *Christian Science,* notes that the most obvious parallel between Olivia Langdon Clemens and Mary Baker Eddy was that they both were injured after slipping and falling on an icy pavement, and were then "miraculously cured" (Afterword, pp. 7–8. See also Stonely, *Mark Twain and the Feminine Aesthetic* [Cambridge: Cambridge University Press, 1992], pp. 92, and 121–22). It seems to me that the different ages of the two women, their different circumstances when the accident occurred, the medical treatment each received, and, above all, the way in which they became cured makes this parallelism an exercise in contrast rather than comparison. Livy's "cure" by Dr. Newton—as narrated by Twain in his *Autobiography*—comes very close to Mary Baker Eddy's experience with Quimby when she first went to Portland, or, even more exactly, to that of Annetta Seabury Dresser. Mrs. Eddy's experience after the fall on the ice in Lynn was of a qualitatively different kind since, as I have shown, it led slowly but directly to her "discovery" of Christian Science and her founding of a new religious sect.

16.   The relationships among Samuel Clemens and his wife and three daughters have been the subject of much scholarly debate and critical dissension. Fortunately, there is a wealth of documentary evidence in publication—the Samuel-Olivia courtship letters, the biographical memoirs of their father by Susy and Clara, the memoirs of Kate Leary, to name only a few—which allow those interested to make up their own minds. It does seem likely that the daughters, especially as young adults, found it difficult to bear the weight of their adoring and adored father's demands on them, and that being the children of such a famous and famously temperamental man had an impact on their health. After Susy's death from meningitis, the lives of Clara and Jean were further darkened by their parents' deep and abiding grief. By her own published memoir, Clara Clemens Gabrilowitsch found lasting help in Christian Science. (See *Awake to a Perfect Day: My Experience with Christian Science* [New York: Citadel Press, 1956].)

17.   Robert Peel argues that Mrs. Woodbury actually hypnotized Twain on this occasion and mesmerically caused him to write deeply insulting letters to William D. McCrackan, a Christian Scientist who was also corresponding with him about Mrs. Eddy. Twain soon repented sending the letters and was very grateful when McCrackan at once returned them to him for destruction. Peel cites evidence of Twain himself describing how he felt overwhelmed by some mental force and doing and saying unnatural things. Though I doubt very much that Mrs. Woodbury actually had such powers, it does seem possible that she might think she had, and that Twain himself, who firmly believed in hypnotism, should have come up with this explanation for his behavior. Even Peabody the arch rationalist was beginning to explain events in terms of mesmerism by the time of the Next Friends suit.

18.   *Christian Science,* Book 2, Chapter 15, p. 285.

19.   Ibid., Book 2, Chapter 3, pp. 130–31.

20.   In his first references to *Science and Health,* Mark Twain dismisses it as unreasonable. Three years later he had found large sections of the work to admire, and cannot reconcile these passages with other parts of the same work, and other works by Mrs. Eddy, especially her juvenile poems. Mark Twain's solution to this dilemma is to declare that someone else wrote the good bits of *Science and Health.* According to Robert Peel, in 1899, after the first essay ran in *Cosmopolitan,* James Wiggin wrote to Mark Twain congratulating him on his satire of Christian Science and saying that he had had a hand in polishing Mrs. Eddy's work. Wiggin also told Mark Twain, however, that in money matters Mrs. Eddy was both honorable and generous. Mark Twain seems to have ignored or forgotten what Wiggin had written, and after Livingston Wright had written his *New York Times* article claiming Wiggin had actually written *Science and Health,* Clemens wrote to Wright thanking him for confirming his own gut instincts and authorial experience that there was another writer involved. (See Peel, *Authority,* pp. 452–53, n. 6.)

21.   *Christian Science,* Book 2, Chapter 1, pp. 102–3.

22.   Ibid., Book 2, Chapter 12, pp. 275–76.

23.   Ibid., Book 2, Chapters 10 and 11, pp. 270–71, 272. Critics of Christian Science, such as Caroline Fraser, have claimed that what Mark Twain writes in praise of Christian Science and Mrs. Eddy has to be taken as ironic, that is, that the writer is saying one thing but meaning the opposite. Certainly, in the passage I quote I can feel that Mark Twain is writing tongue in cheek, with strong comic intent. Nonetheless, overall, I believe Twain's work on Christian Science is best characterized as ambivalent rather than ironic, that the ambivalence is often expressed as irony and parody, but that to select only the positive or only the negative parts of the writer's argument is to impoverish and misunderstand it.

24.   As I read the standard accounts of Mark Twain by Justin Kaplan and others, I was struck by how easily his commentators gloss over the writer's tendencies to exaggerate, misrepresent, basically lie about important moments in his past (notably his running away to safety in the West at the very opening of the Civil War) and accept his early racism and late paternalism. Kaplan casually notes, without elaboration, that even the famous anecdote whereby Mark Twain, the intrepid investor, refuses to take some hundreds of shares in the telephone company, at bargain basement prices, is probably an invention. It is interesting and infuriating to note the contrast between the lack of a reaction to Twain's problems with the truth and the harsh critical reactions to Mrs. Eddy's mistakes and fibs in *Retrospection and Introspection.*

Part Four: Mary Baker Eddy Fights On: 1906–1910

1.   *Miscellany* p. 65. Part 1 of *Miscellany* in the volume of Mrs. Eddy's *Prose Works Other Than Science and Health* is devoted to the Extension, and it includes not only the official correspondence, messages, addresses, and so forth but also a large selection of press reports dealing with the event, from all over the United States.

2.   A *Boston Globe* reporter noted: "One thing is certain: for a religion which has been organized only thirty years, and which erected its first church only twelve years ago, Christian Science has more fine church edifices to its credit in the same time than any other denomination in the world, and they are all paid for" (*Miscellany,* p. 70).

3.   In *The Building of the Mother Church,* Margaret Williamson comments that the schedule for completion appeared quite impossible to meet at the late stages of the project, but it was in fact met, to the amazement and joy of all.

4.   The Boston *Post* noted in awe:

> [T]here is nothing more wonderful than the organ which has been installed. Nowhere in the world is there a more beautiful, more musical, or more capable instrument. In reality it is a combination of six organs, with four manuals, seventy-two stops, nineteen couplers, nineteen adjustable combination pistons, three balanced swells, a grand crescendo pedal, seven combination pedals, and

forty-five hundred and thirty eight pipes, the largest of which is thirty-two feet long. Attached to the organ is a set of cathedral chimes, stationed in one of the towers, and some of the most intricate discoveries of organ builders enable the organist to produce the most beautiful effects by means of the bells. (*Miscellany,* pp. 70–71)

In 1952 the organ was replaced by a new and even larger and more beautiful one, and renewal work has been ongoing since 1988. In the fall of 1996 I was lucky enough to be at the Church complex when a short lunchtime concert had been announced, and I was thus able to get a taste of the full glories of this remarkable instrument.

5.   This Message constitutes the first chapter of *Miscellany.*

6.   *Miscellany,* p. 5. As I noted in my chapter on the first edition of *Science and Health,* Mrs. Eddy's mind works in leaps and bounds, and she will often break off a paragraph with an inconvenient yet pressing question. Immediately after the section on man as God's coexistent idea, she writes "Whence, then, came the creation of matter, sin, and death, mortal pride and power, prestige or privilege?" This is, I think, the key question which every Judeo-Christian thinker has asked and to which no very good answers have been given. Mrs. Eddy attempts no direct answer here—she simply moves on to the first commandment, confessing her bedrock belief in God and, implicitly, relying on him for the ultimate answer to the problem of evil. In another short paragraph she shows a disregard for conventional Biblical scholarship which today's feminist theologians might find radical, referring to the second account of creation in Genesis as "the Adam dream, according to the Scriptural allegory, in which man is supposed to start from dust and woman to be the outcome of man's rib,—marriage synonymous with legalized lust, and the offspring of sense the murderers of their brothers!" That on such a day of triumph, both personal and institutional, she should not hesitate to include such difficult and controversial material, is, to my mind, a strange tribute to her unfailing need to ask the great questions and to put them, however unwelcome, insistently before others.

7.   For another example of this same tone, see the Message which Mrs. Eddy wrote on the occasion of the dedication of the First Church of Christ, Scientist in Concord, New Hampshire. The building of this church was a project very close to her heart, and she contributed $100,000 of her own money, but she still sternly warned the congregation to concentrate on spiritual values and on demonstrating faith, notably by healing, rather than spend their energies on material projects.

Chapter 25: The Next Friends Suit

1.   The best accounts of Pulitzer I have found are George Juergens, *Joseph Pulitzer and the New York World* (Princeton, N.J.: Princeton University Press, 1966); and W. A. Swanberg, *Pulitzer* (New York: Scribner, 1967), but neither book is useful on the Mary Baker Eddy campaign.

2.   Hearst's enthusiasm for Christian Science strengthened in 1908 when his infant son and heir, who had failed to respond to standard treatment for a blocked pyloric sphincter, recovered under Christian Science treatment.

3.   Kent's letter to Peabody is in the Chandler Papers at the New Hampshire Historical Society. See note 21. Peel reports that Kent, who was an honest man, later stated publicly that he felt he had been used by the New York *World* and regretted that he had been instrumental in hurting Mrs. Eddy. See Peel, *Authority,* pp. 482–83, n. 99.

4.   One of the obvious errors or exaggerations in the *World* article was its estimate of Mrs. Eddy's personal fortune. As we shall see, external auditors in 1907 put her estate at $900,000, and at her death she was reportedly worth $3 million. However, these figures do not include the real estate and copyrights covered under her 1898 trusts, which increased markedly in value in the last years of her life.

5.   Immediately after the article appeared Mrs. Leonard issued a public statement not

reported in the *World* in which she said that she had never even been inside Mrs. Eddy's carriage and had never ridden out in her place. Anyone who actually knew Mrs. Leonard would know that she was too young and too plump to stand in for Mrs. Eddy even at a distance. According to Robert Peel, the *World* reporters also tried to bribe Ernest Gosselin, an Amesbury, Massachusetts, chauffeur to testify for the record that he had driven a certain doctor to Mrs. Eddy's home on a specific occasion, by a roundabout route and under great secrecy. The driver refused; instead he made a public statement describing the proffered bribe and stating that he had never undertaken the fare described.

6. See Peel, *Authority,* p. 263–66. As far as Mrs. Eddy's physical appearance goes at this time, it is certain that she was very thin, that she had false teeth, and that, like many women at the time, she used a hairpiece at the back to supplement her bun. Joseph Clarke, who interviewed Mrs. Eddy in 1901, also comments rather more subtly on Mrs. Eddy's pearly white teeth and glowing cheeks. All the details about the galvanic battery still carelessly in view and the heavy drug odors seem made up out of whole cloth, especially given Mrs. Eddy's fanatic neatness.

7. On June 26, 1899, George W. Glover wrote to the editor in chief of the *InterOcean* in Chicago, requesting that he officially contradict the false statement recently made in his newspaper that "Mary Baker Eddy had long been dead and that an imposter trained to represent her was living in conspicuous seclusion in Concord, New Hampshire." Glover went on to say that he had seen his mother on August 16, 1898.

8. As I have noted earlier, Calvin Frye told Nemi Richardson, a practitioner dispatched to attend Mrs. Martha Rand Baker, that Mrs. Eddy believed her sister-in-law had turned her father and elder sisters against her, had secured for her (Martha's) son, George Waldron Baker, the fortune of Mark Baker, and had failed to care for her (Martha's) husband, George S. Baker, during his last illness.

9. Peel makes it clear that Mrs. Eddy's increasing reclusiveness was less a reaction to the attentions of her opponents and hostile reporters than to the pressures she felt from adoring Christian Scientists who came to Concord and hung around street corners hoping to catch her eye. Mrs. Eddy felt such attentions as "a mental drain," and in 1904 she drafted a new By-Law: "A member of The Mother Church shall not haunt Mrs. Eddy's drive when she goes out, continually stroll by her house, or make a summer resort near her for such a purpose" (*Manual of The Mother Church*, Section 27, p. 48).

10. To buttress what I have already written about the strange ramifications of the Malicious Animal Magnetism doctrine, let me quote a 1907 letter sent to Frederick Peabody by Luther Marston, who had been a Christian Scientist and lived at the Massachusetts Metaphysical College in the early 1880s. Long a declared opponent of Mrs. Eddy's movement, Marston in Los Angeles had heard that Peabody was collecting information about Malicious Animal Magnetism which would prove Mrs. Eddy's insanity, and he wanted to cash in as William Nixon was reportedly doing. In a picturesque paragraph Marston writes:

> I was taught that the Postal Clerks were so mesmerized that letters to and from the College would never reach their destination unless certain conditions were complied with, also that the Telegraph operators were so under this malicious influence that a message sent by telegraph would not reach the person to whom it was sent unless certain precautions were taken; I was once sent from her house to West Newton, to forward a telegraph message to Chicago, so that it would be sent by way of Worcester, instead of Boston." (Chandler Papers, New Hampshire Historical Society)

11. To give some flavor of this feeling among some Concord citizens that Mrs. Eddy was a prisoner in her own house, let me cite a March 9 letter which Mrs. L. Howe Huff of Ticonderoga, New York, wrote to Martin and Howe, the Concord legal firm assisting Chandler in the Next Friends suit. Mrs. Howe Huff had shared life in a Concord boardinghouse with Mr. and Mrs. Fred Ladd and Mr. and Mrs. H. Sargent. Ladd and Sargent

were much occupied with Mrs. Eddy's business and talked over the table about the extent of her financial interests and income. Mrs. Sargent told Mrs. Howe Huff of a time when she went to visit Mrs. Eddy at Pleasant View and was shown by her all the gifts and collections. According to Mrs. Howe Huff, Mrs. Sargent had felt creepily aware all the time of being watched and that someone was eavesdropping on her conversation with Mrs. Eddy. Along the same lines, Edward C. Corbin, an attorney in Concord, wrote to tell William Chandler that his client Mrs. Foster Piper, Mrs. Eddy's nearest neighbor, could see the whole premises at Pleasant View and look directly on the carriage house, and she was willing to testify that Mrs. Eddy was a prisoner in her own home. It is hard to know how much credence to give to such unsubstantiated local gossip, but I found Mrs. Howe Huff's testimony very suggestive, as no doubt did Chandler. Original documents in the New Hampshire Historical Society.

12.   According to Lyman Powell, the men of the Wonolancet club estimated, and later published in the Manchester *Mirror* of February 3, 1908, the following figures:

> The Christian Science Church—Mrs. Eddy's gift—$225,000; charitable donations, $25,000; For good roads, $25,000; Miscellaneous gifts and contributions, $25,000; Pleasant View Estate, $40,000; Household expenditures, $100,000; Income from special privileges granted to Concord manufacturers and businessmen, $40,000; Granite contracts for Christian Science churches obtained because of Mrs. Eddy's residence and through her influence, $1,000,000; Other known expenditures, $90,000." (Powell, p. 218)

After Mrs. Eddy had moved to Chestnut Hill, the Concord City Council passed a resolution regretting her departure and thanking her for all she had contributed to Concord.

13.   This statement is quoted in one of the key source works on the Next Friends suit, *Mrs. Eddy and the Late Suit in Equity* by Michael Meehan (Concord, N.H.: privately printed, 1908), p. 20. To anyone with a regard for truth, Moses's statement was particularly telling since it was so disinterested. Moses knew all too well that the foremost critic of Mrs. Eddy in Concord was probably William Chandler, former owner of the *Monitor*, and that the Chandlers, father and son, who still controlled the newspaper, would not relish their associate Moses taking such an independent line.

14.   Peel, *Authority*, p. 267. Frank Streeter, Mrs. Eddy's lawyer in Concord; Calvin Frye, her chief secretary; Lewis Strang, her assistant secretary; and Pamelia Leonard all made public statements denying everything printed in the *World* article of October 28. In his book, *Mrs. Eddy and the Late Suit in Equity,* Michael Meehan lists all of those who made statements, and he quotes many of them.

15.   Over the next month the newspaper continued to report disquieting news about the Church of Christ, Scientist. In a two-part series on November 4 and 5, *World* readers learned from Livingston Wright "How Rev. Wiggin rewrote Mrs. Eddy's book," and on November 11 there was a piece on "Mark Twain's Suppressed Book on Mother Eddy" which tried hard to make the author and his publisher, Harper's, admit that the book on Christian Science had been suppressed as a result of pressure from The Mother Church.

16.   In *Human Life* of January 1907 (vol. 4, no. 4) Sibyl Wilbur introduced the series, "The Story of the Real Mrs. Eddy," which would run from February through December, 1907. The *McClures* series in fourteen parts ran from January 1907 to June 1908.

17.   Fleta Campbell Springer, *According to the Flesh* ([New York: Coward-McCann, 1930], pp. 413–14). The passage is quoted in full by both Peel and Bates and Dittemore. In one of the most bravura sections in his book, Edwin Dakin not only describes the scene in the Pleasant View parlor in vivid detail and narrates exactly what occurred; he also expatiates on Mrs. Eddy's actions and thoughts as she drove away:

> It was a remarkable and heroic piece of acting. As poor Mrs. Eddy leaned back wearily in her carriage, it would not have been strange if hot tears of relief had suddenly rolled down her hollowed cheeks to make little furrows in the rouge.

The coachman clicked to the horses. Frye on his perch gazed vacantly at the sky, and the great carriage rolled ponderously through the Concord streets. Mary Baker Eddy sat huddled inside with the curtains half drawn, utterly alone. She had been alone all her life. She had hungered alone, fought alone, suffered alone. There had never been anyone near her to help her. There were many to render her homage. There had never been one to give her understanding. And yet. . . .

After all she was Mary Baker Eddy, anointed of God. Alone, yes. But to be unique is to be alone always. Only ordinary men gain understanding. Only puerile souls find comradeship. God is Himself alone for all eternity.

The white plumes nodded vigorously as she shook with constant tremor. But she continued to gaze steadily, unseeingly, straight ahead, as the carriage rolled ceaselessly on through the quiet streets that the plump horses knew so well. (Dakin, p. 411)

Need I say that Edwin Dakin, who was born in 1899, was not among the reporters in Concord in 1906. It is the mix of high specificity, actual inaccuracy, emotive rhetoric, and hints of psychological insight in passages like this that makes Dakin so infuriating.

18.   The questions were (1) Are you in perfect bodily health? (2) Have you any other physician than God? (3) Do you take a daily drive? (4) Does anyone besides yourself administer your property or attend to your business affairs? The Pleasant View people may have felt able to choose the positively prejudiced Wilbur to ask the questions since the *World* reporters had earlier chosen the negatively prejudiced Kent to do the identification.

19.   It is small things like this that make it unremarkable to me that Mrs. Eddy was increasingly reclusive, suspicious, and difficult as she drew toward death—she really could not trust anyone always to tell her the truth, except Frye, some of the men on the estate like Salchow, her last personal maid Adelaide Still, and her companions Laura Sargent and Pamelia Leonard. Even they, as dedicated Christian Scientists, were susceptible, on certain unforeseeable occasions, to outside influence—that is, to what Christian Scientists would have interpreted as Malicious Animal Magnetism or malicious malpractice.

20.   There is a standard biography, *William E. Chandler: Republican*, by Leon Burr Richardson (New York: Dodd, Mead and Company, 1940). The New Hampshire Historical Society also gave me a very useful eight-page inventory of the main holdings in its William E. Chandler manuscript collection, as well as a thumbnail sketch of the senator, who died in 1917 at the age of eighty-two.

21.   The Mary Baker Eddy Litigation section of the William E. Chandler papers consists of eleven standard file boxes. These boxes contain all the general correspondence, internal memoranda, telegrams, notes, and so forth, of Chandler and his office staff, arranged chronologically. Though obviously one-sided, these files give an amazingly detailed picture of exactly what was happening, day by day, in the Next Friends suit, and specifically evidence as to what Chandler and his associates believed and planned. Once Chandler had filed the suit, he received letters from many people who had an interest in Christian Science, and these are fascinating in themselves. The most valuable box of materials contains letters written by Mrs. Eddy, and this is the material which is best known in the bibliography of Christian Science. I had been given to understand that the Chandler papers contained the autographs of Mrs. Eddy's letters to her son, George Glover, and that New Hampshire therefore possessed one of the rare caches of her correspondence outside the Christian Science Mother Church archives and thus open to the general reader. Some handwritten letters by Mrs. Eddy are in the collection—notably many letters to George Moses and some to Ebenezer Foster Eddy—but the Glover correspondence is not in autograph. In fact, what the New Hampshire Historical Society has is the typed copies of the Glover letters which, I deduce, were made in the Chandler office during the pro-

longed legal conflict, and which Chandler retained for his own purposes. As early as November 1906 Mrs. Eddy's advisors had sought to regain possession of her letters, and one of the things Chandler first did in December 1906 was to persuade George Glover to bring the letters with him to Washington and give them to him for safekeeping. One clause of the final 1909 settlement between Mrs. Eddy and her son stated that George should return to his mother all the letters she had written to him, and it seems that he did so. The letters then became part of the famous bound volumes of correspondence held in the vault of the Mother Church collection, which I describe in the Appendix, and they are generally available to scholars only in transcript. **Unless otherwise noted, the correspondence between Mrs. Eddy and her son George Glover quoted in this chapter was read in the Chandler transcripts at the New Hampshire Historical Society, and the originals reside in the Church History Department.**

22.   William E. Chandler to John W. Kelley, November 20, 1906, New Hampshire Historical Society.

23.   George said this in an interview with the Detroit *Free Press* published in March 1907. Further interesting evidence of the Glover family's commitment to Christian Science is the letter George sent to his mother on February 19, 1900, in which he proudly reported that the youngest child, Andrew, was out of school since he (George) had refused to have his children vaccinated, and he had taken the Board of Education to court over his rights to refuse. Mrs. Eddy's response was tactful and probably puzzled George and Nellie sorely: "But if it were my child I should let them vaccinate him and then with Christian Science I would prevent its harming the health of my child."

24.   George wrote to his mother on June 12, 1889:

> Dear Mother, I do not know any thing that I have done that you should not write to me. I received a letter from you a long time ago and I answered it. Evelyn received one wich she is unable to answer it. I wrote for her. I am afraid she will never be able to write you another. She was first taken down sick with the yellow [illegible] from that she has a touch of St Vitice dance her lungs are badly afected in belief her left lung is the worst. She doesn't talk any unless spoken to she answers yes or no by the nod of the head she eats but very little. She always sits up to the table for the last 4 days and I feed her with a spoon or fork some times she tryes to feed her self with a spoon but throughs her food all around her plate trying to get it on her spoon it is all most impossible for her to get it up to her mouth. I had her out walking in the garding and up the stable yesterday and to day and I thought she was a little better but tonight she seems worse again. (Original in the Church History Department)

25.   In a letter to Lead on June 21, 1893, soon after the Glovers' visit, Mrs. Eddy wrote:

> You speak of not seeing me again before you left. You know how much your mother has always doted on seeing you, and how many years she lived in the hope of sometime having you with her. But it is past.
>
> When you do not let me know you are coming, if any member of your family comes East to be doctored never expect that I shall feel obligated to see them. Such is not my practice with my students. If you had written me the circumstances and named your wife's sickness—I should have advised you to call Dr. Buswell of Nebraska [to] your aid; and if you had decided not to take my counsel I should decide not to see the patient. I am deeply interested as I always were in your health, happiness and prosperity. I have no kindred to care for me, but God has so far been most merciful and I can trust Him. (L02108. Original in the Church History Department)

26.   Mary Baker Eddy consistently interpreted Evelyn's ill health as being the result of mesmerism. Thus on August 16, 1893, she wrote to George: "It is nothing but mesmerism that has caused this state in her health. When she was in Boston she was regarded as

somewhat like me, and that she would be a scholar, etc. This was enough for the result before named" (L02109. Original in the Church History Department). As in the case of Asa Gilbert Eddy, the doctrine of Malicious Animal Magnetism offered Mrs. Eddy some complicated comfort when she was forced to deal with the serious illness of a person she loved and longed in vain to see well.

27.   This is the transaction which, in her August 1907 interview with the masters appointed in the Next Friends suit, Mrs. Eddy referred to as her only bad investment, and the only one in which, acting against her better judgment and on the advice of others, she had not followed her conservative but successful policy of investing only in bonds. (See Meehan, *Mrs. Eddy and the Late Suit in Equity,* p. 158.)

28.   It is sad to see, as one reads the letters, how much both George and his mother wanted to be in peace and harmony with one another, and how quickly relations between them became poisoned. On this occasion, in gratitude at the unexpected check, George wrote on September 11: "Really, mother, I did not expect so great kindness and I will try and use the money in a useful manner. I have been wondering what I can do for you to repay this kindness but you are surrounded with so many luxuries and are the recipient of so many favors, the best I can do at present is to wish you well and hope that our love for each other may never grow less and that I shall be able before long to make you a good visit" (original letter in the Church History Department). Mrs. Eddy replied to this seemingly heartfelt letter of conciliation and affection with a brief and perfunctory note. She seems above all to respond to the implication that she is surrounded with luxury. September 16, 1895: "The seasons as you say have been very lovely, both Summer and Autumn. But I am so busy they pass almost without recognition. Time affords me only the opportunity to find <u>luxury</u> in helping others" (L02116. Original in the Church History Department). I think it is important to stress once again that George Glover always needed the help of another person when he wanted to write a letter, and that the writer—neighbor, business partner, lawyer, child, or whoever—probably had some hand in shaping the tenor of the letter as well as taking George's dictation. The extent of George Glover's illiteracy can be judged by a remark in his mother's letter of January 13, 1900: "Practice writing your name properly as in this copy and not run the last part of George off the line" (L02129. Original in Church History Department).

29.   Mrs. Eddy writes quaintly on July 18, 1892, "But dear child, when will you have a house for your family in a pleasant location and such an one as young ladies would feel pleasantly over inviting into it the highest toned society?" (L0299. Original in the Church History Department). St. Joseph's is a long way from Lead, and I can only assume that the town was chosen because it was the nearest Christian Science center that also had a decent school for girls.

30.   Letter of August 12, 1892. L02104. Church History Department.

31.   A photograph I saw at the Longyear Museum in its exhibit on the Glovers in Lead showed the family posed outside a very rudimentary log cabin.

32.   "The house was so badly built that it was hardly finished before large cracks opened in the plaster, the windows sagged, and the fireplace fell in." The house cost $20,000, and the man employed to supervise construction was Charles M. Howe, First Reader of St. Joseph, Missouri (Bates and Dittemore, p. 388). When George Glover asked his mother for a further $1,100 for repairs, she refused for some time, again causing needless resentment to build up on both sides.

33.   The Glovers also sent presents to Mrs. Eddy which she acknowledged with great praise and affection. These gifts included a gold ring in 1892, unfortunately much too large for her finger as she had recently lost fifty pounds; also in 1892 a heart filled with gold dust; and some crystals and minerals; in 1893 a gold brick; in 1895 a gold chain. In 1895–1896 Mrs. Eddy requested that George supply her with two watch chains which she wished to present to Foster Eddy and to Henry M. Baker. She is rather appalled by the cost of the chains, sends one back for extensive alterations in the design and the length,

but sends $200 in payment and profuse thanks and compliments on "the prettiest gen-tlemen's watchchains I ever saw."

34.   Relations between Mrs. Eddy and her son seem to have been cut when he wrote an angry letter accusing Frye of abusing his position as her accountant and financial advisor, and she wrote back furiously defending Frye's honesty and comparing Frye's loyalty and disinterested service with George's own behavior toward her.

> [He] does not own a cent of my property, real estate or personal. . . . I have given you a far better house than I occupy myself. I have given you money when you asked for it—thousands of dollars. What have you ever done for your mother? And now you have disgraced yourself by what you said so falsely of her home, your <u>mother's home</u>! where you should naturally be with her in her declining years. I have always tried to make my people respect you, and is this your return for it? (Quoted in Peel, *Authority,* p. 276)

Swift to chastise and find fault with those she loved, Mary Baker Eddy would never stand for them to be criticized by anyone else.

35.   Given their inflated notions of Mrs. Eddy's personal wealth, Slaght and Chandler no doubt blamed her for allowing her son and his family to starve, but George was sixty-two years old by this time, surely old enough to be held responsible, and his elder two children, Gershom and Mary, were adults and quite able to contribute income.

36.   Quote from the letter George wrote to his mother on August 12, 1879.

37.   Three versions of this letter are included in the Chandler files. The version quoted by Michael Meehan in his book *Mrs. Eddy and the Late Suit in Equity* does not include any reference to "Mr. Pulitzer."

38.   Quotation from Kelley's letter to Chandler of December 4, 1906. New Hampshire Historical Society.

39.   On December 17, 1906, Kelley wrote to Merrill telling him that his legal fees would be $25 a day for in-office legal work, $35 a day plus expenses for work outside the office, and $100 for court days. Kelley planned to spend two or three days a week on the case, mainly taking depositions. This letter is at the New Hampshire Historical Society.

40.   Tremont Street is a fairly long one by Boston standards, but it nonetheless strikes me, as I type in all these names and addresses, that Peabody and Richard Kennedy both had offices on Tremont Street.

41.   One particular bee which Peabody tried to plant in Chandler's bonnet was the assur-ance that Mary Baker Eddy was secretly married to Calvin Frye. Peabody himself may have come by this idea via William Nixon. Certainly Slaght told Chandler that Nixon had been present at the supposed marriage, but Nixon makes no mention of this in any of the correspondence I have seen. Chandler makes no comment one way or another about the supposed marriage, but he was lawyer enough to see that if Peabody was right, the Next Friends suit was completely baseless. As Mrs. Eddy's husband, Frye would be her "next friend," could use or misuse her property like any other husband under the law, and had a strong claim at least to part of her estate. As in earlier periods in her life, Mary Baker Eddy was legally vulnerable because she had no husband.

42.   As Chandler wrote to Foster Eddy in April of 1907:

> In childhood she believed voices were calling her; prior to 1866 she was con-tinually seeking occult influence to help her. In 1866 she believed that she cured herself of a severe injury and sickness by re-discovering Christ's art of healing. Dr. Cushing's testimony proves her delusion. Going on she came almost to believe she was a second Christ, and Christian Science healing has been her life's occupation. Whatever charity may be extended towards her and her beliefs and the beliefs of others, she has all her life been in a condition where the validity of her business acts could be successfully disputed. Her heirs at law are not to

be deprived of their rights by any deed or will made while under all the various delusions that have possessed her mind for forty years. (New Hampshire Historical Society)

Apparently, as William Chandler saw it, crazy women could be allowed to make millions out of the stuff of their delusions, but they should not be allowed to will those undelusional millions away from their heirs.

43. The account of this meeting was to form one section of the lengthy article for the *World* which Slaght sent in after the Next Friends suit was filed on March 1.

44. In his reminiscences John Salchow gives a detailed and quite humorous account of these horses and the groom who brought them to Concord and was forced to take them back. Gilbert Carpenter also gives a detailed account of the horses in his memoir.

45. As I noted in Chapter 15, George Glover gave an interview in 1907 in which he claimed to have marched into Kennedy's office and threatened him with a gun to his head.

46. In the correspondence between Chandler and Mary in the New Hampshire Historical Society, there is a vague flirtatiousness which is weird given the huge disparity in their ages, and which she seems to initiate. April 1, 1907 William E. Chandler writes to Mary Baker Glover assuring her that the pictures of her that have appeared in the press are flatttering. "Have you had any offers of marriage on account of the publicity?" he writes. Chandler also sends Mary a copy of Longfellow's poems. Mary Glover is not a woman one can easily warm to, seeming from her letters to have been silly, vain, pretentious, and pushy. She married Harry Eugene Billings in 1913 and had two children.

47. While Tomlinson was trying to make progress in Lead, Farlow was endeavoring to persuade George in Washington to formally endorse the version of his separation from his mother and her healing of him during the Civil War which the Church was planning to make public. George also stonewalled, claiming that he could make no statements about what had happened in his youth without having access to his records in Lead.

48. There seems to be no doubt based on the correspondence that until he returned to South Dakota, George Glover was kept in ignorance of the fact that his cousin George Baker had also been contacted by the Chandler group and had joined in the suit. A letter George Baker wrote to Mary Glover in 1909 indicates that Baker felt he was carefully prevented from seeing the Dakotans while they were in New Hampshire or contacting them when they were in Washington. George Glover and Ebenezer Foster Eddy both received cash payments in 1909 in return for agreeing never to contest Mrs. Eddy's will, and Baker was probably wondering why, as one of the first parties to the initial suit of March 1, 1907, he had received nothing. In a second letter George Baker wrote to Mary: "I don't <u>care</u>, Mary; I have no <u>claim</u> on Aunt Mary's <u>property</u> at all; but I was a party to that first suit, and it was at first represented to me that I was the <u>only</u> one to bring the suit, and upon that basis I 'put in' because I believed, <u>as I do now</u>, that Frye was the backbone of the lies" (see Peel, *Authority,* pp. 481–82, n. 98; original in the Church History Department).

49. Original in the Church History Department.

50. Foster Eddy letters in the New Hampshire Historical Society. As far as I can determine from inquiries at The Mother Church, Slaght's representatives did manage to get the desk out of Mrs. Eddy's house. Certainly Foster Eddy began from this point to summarize and quote from letters to him from Mrs. Eddy.

51. As Peel notes, this was a rather motley group of defendants, scattered, furthermore, across the country, thus making legal action difficult and expensive. Four of them were resident in New Hampshire (Frye, Tomlinson, Hering, and Strang), five of them in Boston (Farlow, Knapp, Johnson, Chase, and Armstrong), and one in Chicago (Kimball). "The Petition of 'Next Friends' " is reprinted in full by Michael Meehan in *Mrs. Eddy and the Late Suit in Equity.*

52. Even in comparison to his relatives George Glover and George Baker, Fred Baker

was a pitiful case, a chronic alcoholic with a wife and daughter, and at his wits' end for money. He, too, had tried to contact Mrs. Eddy and had been refused entrance at Pleasant View. Aware of his client's condition, Chandler did as much as he could to get Baker treated at a hospital and to encourage him personally and in letters to give up drinking. When Fred Baker left the hospital and fell off the wagon disastrously again, he asked the court for permission to drop out of the suit. He reported to Chandler that he had then received calls from pressmen wanting to know if he had been bribed to withdraw. In his dealings with both George and Fred Baker, Chandler emerges as an honorable and caring person who was not too busy to try to help those less fortunate than himself and a lawyer who felt a real responsibility to his clients, paying or not.

53.   The most important exception to this point is, of course, the news of the $125,000 trust which Mrs. Eddy had set up on February 25 in favor of her son and grandchildren, which Streeter told Kelley about on the day the petition for the Next Friends was filed with the court. I shall be discussing this trust in the next chapter.

Chapter 26: Mrs. Eddy Wins in Court

1.   Information given in a letter from Streeter to George Glover of June 19, 1907. **Unless otherwise noted, quotations from letters concerning the Next Friends suit are taken from the William E. Chandler papers at the New Hampshire Historical Society.**

2.   The decision to delay sending details of the trust demonstrates the excellence of Streeter's strategic thinking. The Glovers learned the exact terms of the trust when the public reaction to the Next Friends suit was already beginning to turn in favor of Mrs. Eddy, and when George Glover's unresolved financial problems were again becoming onerous. Furthermore, the letter from Streeter arrived in Lead at a time when Judge Bennett, the Glovers' local counsel, was away at a meeting. Streeter had carefully refrained from sending the text of the trust deed to any of Glover's lawyers, so Chandler had to deal with the Glovers' untutored accounts of what the document said. One measure of the inexactitude with which the Glovers read the trust deed is that it took some time for the illiterate Glover to be assured that the trustees would receive not 50 percent of the annual income on the capital, as he first believed, but 5 percent. In the suave letter he wrote to George Glover about the trust, Streeter concentrated on expressing the trustees' anxiety to cooperate fully with the Glover parents in ensuring the well-being of their family, especially in regards to the education of their two youngest children.

3.   In February of 1907 there had already been a poorly calculated effort to buy off the Glovers. Josiah Fernald, Mrs. Eddy's Concord banker, wrote to George saying that a fund had been sent to the First National Bank of Lead which would pay out $125 a month for the Glovers' household expenses and taxes. George on February 15 actually accepted this offer, but then, probably at Chandler's prompting, he wrote to refuse it on the next day.

4.   "New York March 4, 1907. My Dear Mr. Glover: Show the bill in equity in the World to Judge Bennett. Where there is $1200 and $100,000 there is much more. Keep quiet and trust your counsel. Yours truly, Wm. E. Chandler."

5.   It was while Chandler was staying at the Parker House in Boston and meeting with various colleagues and clients that Miss Mary Tomlinson, the sister of one of Mrs. Eddy's closest associates, threw herself to her death from one of the hotel windows. It appears that Chandler's room was one floor above Miss Tomlinson's, and that he heard her two brothers shouting at the door which she had locked as they tried in vain to get to her before she jumped. Both Tomlinson brothers were rumored to bear responsibility for their sister's death, and, according to Peabody's published account, Vincent Tomlinson blamed both his brother Irving and Mrs. Eddy for so preying on Mary's mind with their fears and strategies about Malicious Animal Magnetism that she lost her mind (*Religio-Medical Masquerade,* pp. 191 ff). There is also in the Chandler papers an April 22 letter in which Peabody gives his senior counsel a less dramatic account of the event. Whatever the exact circumstances, Mary Tomlinson's death surely reinforced Chandler's low opin-

ion of Christian Science as a therapeutic system, and as an organization in which men like Irving Tomlinson could prosper.

6.   The source for this quotation is the typewritten draft of the letter. Chandler continues in the same vein for more than another foolscap page, decrying the witchcraft at Pleasant View and the quarrel between Frye's "diabolism" and Stetson-Wilson's Malicious Animal Magnetism.

7.   I have found no substantiation for Junius's claim that huge sums of money sent in from the field disappeared into the pockets of officials of The Mother Church. Even the most severe and informed critics of Christian Science—Georgine Milmine, Frederick Peabody, and John V. Dittemore—who consistently accuse Mrs. Eddy and her assistants of a preoccupation with money do not accuse them of fraud and theft. The Mother Church has no information on any A. J. Park, and I found no information on how Chandler might have known him.

8.   Chandler did try to follow up on Hopkins's tip about "Christ and Christmas," but his investigation seems to have reached a stalemate after he received a very stiff letter from Edward N. Pearson, the secretary of state for New Hampshire. Pearson ends by saying:

> I hope you will not find it necessary to drag the Rumford Printing Company [which was initially charged with the printing of *Christ and Christmas*] into the controversy over Mrs. Eddy's affairs. She has been a generous customer of the Company and its predecessor during her entire residence in Concord, and certainly an officer and stockholder in the Company ought not to be the person to use business transactions of hers with the Company to her disadvantage. (Letter of March 27, 1907, New Hampshire Historical Society)

9.   I hypothesize that Hopkins may have begun writing to Peabody as reassurance, because the latter had warned Chandler that Hopkins was probably a Christian Science spy, planted to give the Next Friends misinformation. Paranoia was certainly not restricted to the Christian Science camp.

10.   Peel, *Authority,* p. 487, n. 118. A family friend of Hopkins told Peel in the late 1950s that Hopkins had become profoundly convinced of Mrs. Eddy's greatness, but Peel does not explain how Hopkins might have been converted.

11.   Chandler tried to establish that Mrs. Eddy had not paid her local taxes, and that Henry Baker, the chairman of her trustees under the March 6 trust deed, was living beyond his means, on the brink of insolvency, but these avenues of inquiry came to nothing.

12.   The first letter which Frederick Peabody sent to William Chandler after he was taken on as junior counsel dealt largely with legal transactions of 1898 (letter dated January 3, 1907). Peabody told Chandler, inaccurately, that in 1898 Mary Baker Eddy had transferred to the Board of Directors of The Mother Church or the Trustees of the Publishing Society the ownership or tenancy of 385 Commonwealth Avenue and the $200,000 property abutting it, eight or ten lots of land in West Roxbury, which Mrs. Eddy had acquired in 1891, the Falmouth and Caledonia Streets lot upon which the Mother Church building stood, and two further lots on Falmouth Street.

13.   Chandler Papers, New Hampshire Historical Society. L02256. Original in the Church History Department.

14.   Chandler wrote a notably stiff letter to Foster Eddy on April 4, saying that records showed that the copyright of Mrs. Eddy's published pamphlet *Unity of Good* did not belong to Foster Eddy as the latter had claimed, but the copyright had been reconveyed to her in 1893. Chandler also notes that although Foster Eddy had told him (Chandler) that he (Foster Eddy) had never signed a release of his rights as an adopted son, Foster Eddy had told Slaght that he had received $15,000 in return for the release, which was the truth. Chandler ends the letter by replying to a question from Foster Eddy, confirming that under Massachusetts law natural and adopted sons enjoyed equal rights of inheritance.

15.   Peel had access to the Nixon correspondence, including Nixon's letters to his "fiancée," Mrs. Fulmer. Peel, *Authority,* p. 483, nn. 105–6. In fact, in 1906 William Nixon was still married to, although separated from, Helen Andrews Nixon, a Christian Scientist who was loyal to Mrs. Eddy and who never divorced him. Peabody was Nixon's lawyer and thus well aware of his marital problems, although he did not inform Chandler of them. In 1908 Mrs. Fulmer donated Nixon's letters to her to The Mother Church after she discovered he had lied to her.

16.   On June 13 Peabody insisted in a typed letter to Chandler's New Hampshire colleagues Martin and Howe that he had never, as Streeter claimed in court, boasted he would "drag [Mrs. Eddy] down from her pedestal," had never planned to publish the affidavits he had collected in the press before the trial, and, indeed, had forsworn all commerce with journalists since being hired as junior counsel.

17.   Michael Meehan, the editor of the *Concord Patriot,* was Mrs. Eddy's most vigorous champion in the city; he knew many of the participants, followed the press reports, and covered the various court proceedings with care. Soon after the Next Friends suit ended he produced a privately published book intended "to lay before the reader a fairly complete and accurate report of the court trial known to the public as 'Mrs. Eddy and the Late Suit in Equity.' " Five thousand copies of the expensive work came off the presses, and the first was sent to Mrs. Eddy who sat up far into the night reading it. The next day she wrote asking the author to withhold the book from sale, and he dutifully agreed. Mrs. Eddy's motives reportedly were that she feared the book would ruin her son's reputation, and she had no wish to "keep alive a memory of bitterness and discord." Financially Meehan did not lose by withdrawing the book from the market. Mrs. Eddy wrote to him: "You will render me a statement of all expenses to which you have been put. Make liberal allowance for those who have aided you in the work. Put a value upon your own time and service while engaged in it, and when you have done this, double the value you have placed on your own work, and double it again, and then send me the bill" (this account and the quotations are from Powell, p. 214). Mrs. Eddy seems remarkably fair and clearheaded in her dealings with Meehan. Yet taking Meehan's book out of circulation was probably an error, as an uninformed reader might well assume, quite incorrectly, that Mrs. Eddy had bought out a book which contained damaging information. I found Meehan's transcriptions of the courtroom proceedings particularly fascinating because they give a flavor of the verbal jousting between Chandler and Streeter, and of the strong line taken by Judge Aldrich. The account of the court proceedings and the quotes from trial motions and responses as well as excerpts from alienists who wrote reports for the case appear in Meehan's book *Mrs. Eddy and the Late Suit in Equity.*

18.   Meehan gives useful professional minibiographies of the participants in the suit at the end of his book, and he also includes portraits. Mrs. Eddy used the firm of Streeter and Hollis for her personal counsel. Eastman, Scammon, and Gardner were retained for the remaining New Hampshire defendants in the suit (Frye, Hering, Tomlinson, and Strang). The Massachusetts defendants (and Edward Kimball) retained William A. Morse and the firm of Elder and Whitman.

19.   For a full description of the procedure for signing this trust, and its terms, see Meehan, "Mrs. Eddy Creates Trusteeship," *Mrs. Eddy and the Late Suit in Equity*, pp. 35–39.

20.   Peel, *Authority,* p. 283, quoting the *Boston Journal* of May 25, 1907.

21.   Meehan, "Annual Audit of Mrs. Eddy's Accounts," *Mrs. Eddy and the Late Suit in Equity*, pp. 79–84.

22.   I have transcribed this letter from the photocopied handwritten letter which Meehan reproduces in his book, as do Bates and Dittemore, but the text appears in *Miscellany,* p. 137.

23.   Meehan reproduces all or large extracts from all these articles. Arthur Brisbane's especially detailed and laudatory interview first appeared in the August 1907 edition of

Cosmopolitan, one of the Hearst publications, and was reprinted several times.

24.   This remark was probably made to Hermann Hering, quoted in Powell, p. 213.

25.   Dr. French's second report of mid-July is published in Meehan, *Mrs. Eddy and the Late Suit in Equity,* p. 247.

26.   A rich New York Christian Scientist, Miss Helen Brush willed some sixty thousand dollars to her church, which was led by Augusta Stetson. When Miss Brush died of consumption, her sister, Mrs. Southard, although also a Christian Scientist, contested the will on the grounds that her sister had been mentally incompetent. Essentially Mrs. Southard's lawyers argued that belief in Christian Science was in itself evidence of insanity, and that the doctrine of Malicious Animal Magnetism had so terrified Miss Brush that she had changed her will. Mrs. Stetson testified for a whole day and proved a brilliant witness. Those of her followers who were called to the witness stand backed her up loyally—so loyally, in fact, that they "testified in the absolute," or, in more prosaic terms, knowingly made false statements of fact. Mrs. Stetson triumphed, but the triumph was short-lived, as we shall see in the next chapter.

27.   Meehan reproduces both of Hamilton's reports in *Mrs. Eddy and the Late Suit in Equity:* "Dr. Allen McLane Hamilton's Report," pp. 233–40; and "Additional Report by Dr. Hamilton," pp. 241–46.

28.   Meehan, "Dr. Allen McLane Hamilton's Report," p. 235.

29.   Meehan, "Additional Report by Dr. Hamilton," pp. 241, 244.

30.   Ibid., pp. 245, 242.

31.   Ibid., p. 245.

32.   Ibid., pp. 242, 245. Even at the age of eighty-five Mary Baker Eddy could surprise and delight men with her beauty. In the report of his interview with her, Arthur Brisbane gave a detailed description: "Her thick hair, snow-white, curls about her forehead and temples. She is of medium height and very slender. She probably weighs less than one hundred pounds. But her figure is straight as she rises and walks foward. The grasp of her thin hand is firm; the hand does not tremble" (Ibid., p. 265). "Women will want to know what Mrs. Eddy wore. The writer regrets that he cannot tell. With some women you see the dress; with Mrs. Eddy you see only the face, the very earnest eyes, and the beautiful quiet expression that only age and thought can give to a human face. She wore a white lace collar, no jewelry of any kind, and a very simple dress" (Ibid., p. 266).

33.   Quoted in Peel, *Authority,* p. 284. "As to the delusion of persecution from which Mrs. Eddy was said to suffer, a good many sympathizers at the time asked how it was possible that a man of Chandler's intelligence could labor under the fixed delusion that she was *not* being persecuted" (*Authority,* p. 285).

34.   Meehan, "Second Day of the Hearing," *Mrs. Eddy and the Late Suit in Equity,* p. 143.

35.   Ibid., p. 145.

36.   [Judge Aldrich] I want to say before going that my mother is still living and she is eighty-seven years of age.
    [Mrs. Eddy] Give my love to her.
    [Dr. Jelly] Good afternoon, Mrs. Eddy.
    [Mrs. Eddy] Excuse my sitting; come and see me again. (Meehan, *Mrs. Eddy and the Late Suit in Equity,* p. 164)

37.   Meehan, *Mrs. Eddy and the Late Suit in Equity,* p. 215.

38.   Michael Meehan devotes the fifth section of his book to "Editorials from Many Newspapers" (Meehan, *Mrs. Eddy and the Late Suit in Equity,* pp. 280–324).

Chapter 27: Chestnut Hill

1. New York *World,* May 8, 1907. Draft in the Chandler papers, New Hampshire Historical Society.

2. L02632. Original in the Church History Department. Quoted by Powell, p. 213.

3. William Chandler gave an account of this first attempt at a monetary settlement with Glover and Foster in his deposition at the time of the contesting of the will in 1911. Dakin gives a typically colorful, inaccurate, and unfair account of this aborted settlement, pp. 457–58.

4. Letter from Mrs. Eddy to Alfred Farlow, quoted in Peel, *Authority,* p. 297.

5. Dakin says the house at 384 (now 400) Beacon Street had thirty-four rooms, and he calls it a baronial mansion, which is a typical exaggeration. Today this house is maintained by The Mother Church as a museum to Mrs. Eddy and is regularly open to the public. The neighborhood is still exceptionally gracious, but although the house is maintained unchanged, much of the acreage surrounding it has been sold off and subdivided for other housing, so one gets much less of that sense of isolation of which Mrs. Eddy complained. Much of the information on the move to Boston and Mrs. Eddy's life in her Chestnut Hill house has been taken from the reminiscences of her maid, Adelaide Still, and her man of all work, John Salchow, which are in the Church History Department.

6. As with so many other apparently trivial events in Mrs. Eddy's life, there are several differing accounts of this journey by train to Boston. I have relied on the accounts left by John Salchow and Adelaide Still, who were certainly close by Mrs. Eddy's side. I puzzled for some time over the fact that all the accounts of this journey mention the presence of Dr. Morrill with Mrs. Eddy's party. I deduce that critics of Mrs. Eddy were suggesting that she was so ill/drug addicted/senile that she needed the constant assistance of a medical gentleman. The Christian Science chroniclers, on the other hand, stress that Dr. Morrill was Mrs. Eddy's cousin, escorting her from her native state to her new home, and that he never needed to assist her in a professional capacity, remaining in the next carriage throughout the journey.

7. Powell, pp. 220–21. This was the only point during her journey when non–Christian Science observers were able to see Mrs. Eddy, and I believe that subsequent press reports that she had had to be carried to and from the train were based on this event.

8. Peel, *Authority,* p. 297.

9. Still and Salchow reminiscences. Church History Department.

10. The Dittemore pages of the Calvin Frye diary, entry for September 26, 1909.

11. Bates and Dittemore, p. 420.

12. Using new material given him by the recently severed director, John V. Dittemore, Peabody offers information about all five members of the Board of Directors in his section of the 1925 book *The Faith, the Falsity and the Failure of Christian Science* ([New York and Chicago: Fleming H. Revell Company, 1925], pp. 189–201). He is especially scathing about Adam Dickey, then chairman of the board, whom he calls Mrs. Eddy's flunky and accuses of sexual obscenity and of pocketing Church funds.

13. Mrs. Eddy offered the position to Frye, but he refused it.

14. Powell, p. 239.

15. Bates and Dittemore, p. 423; also in *Miscellany,* p. 276.

16. The quotations in this chapter from the Dittemore pages of the Calvin Frye diaries are taken again from the Bookmark edition, which has no proper pagination but has been checked against the Church History copy. (See Chapter 21, n. 14.)

17. Mary Baker Eddy's most complete statement on this subject is probably *Unity of Good,* which she first published in 1888 as a small book or pamphlet but revised in 1891 and again in 1908. This work contains a chapter entitled "Is There No Death?" in which

she writes: "To say that you and I, as mortals, will not enter this dark shadow of material sense, called *death,* is to assert what we have not proved" (p. 40). And she also writes: "This generation seems too material for any strong demonstration over death. . . . I have by no means spoken of myself, I *cannot* speak of myself as 'sufficient for these things' " (p. 43). *Unity of Good* is now included in the compendium volume *Prose Works Other Than Science and Health.*

18. Let me give one example of the charges Mrs. Eddy gave to her staff each day, as reported by Calvin Frye in his diary entry for October 10, 1893:

> Mrs. Eddy's charge to Mrs. Monroe and myself.
> The first thing in the morning call on God to deliver you from temptation & help you to be awake. Then do your chores, not as a dreary hashish eater but with a clear sense of what to do and just how to do it.
> Then sit down and first get yourself into a consciousness of your power with God & then take up the outside watch. Sit until this is clear if 2 hours.

19. Quoted in Bates and Dittemore, pp. 424–25. Mrs. Eddy made essentially the same request of Calvin Frye.

20. One of the meaner stories put out by Mrs. Eddy's critics has been that she deserves little credit for starting the *Monitor* because the idea was given to her in a March 1908 letter from John L. Wright, First Reader of First Church of Christ, Scientist in Chelsea, and a *Boston Globe* reporter. Certainly Wright's letter was important; it perhaps served to crystallize Mrs. Eddy's thinking, and his contribution has deservedly been acknowledged by Christian Science historians like Peel (see *Authority,* p. 309) and also in Erwin D. Canham (*Commitment to Freedom* [Boston: Houghton Mifflin, 1958]). But Wright mostly articulated, at the right moment to the right person, certain ideas which were common at that time as they still are today, inside and outside Christian Science—that the press cares only for profit and is increasingly purveying vicious and sensational gossip in lieu of news, and that a sincere need exists nationally for a newspaper that, according to what Wright wrote, "gives more attention especially to the positive side of life, to the activities that work for the good of man and to the things really worth knowing."

21. Mrs. Stetson was, among other things, an excellent publicist, and a great deal of information about her is available because after Mrs. Eddy's death she published several books and articles offering a detailed account of her life in Christian Science and of her relations with her former leader: *Reminiscences Sermons and Correspondence* (1914); *Vital Issues in Christian Science, with Facsimile Letters of Mary Baker Eddy* (1914); *Sermons and Other Writings* (1924, 1277pp.!) all published by G. P. Putnam's Sons in New York. Also "The Demonstration of Mary Baker Eddy," *The Independent,* January 26, 1911; "Mrs. Eddy and Mrs. Stetson," *The Independent,* October 9, 1913. Unfortunately, like Josephine Woodbury, Augusta Stetson was an incurable mythomaniac, by which I mean that almost nothing she says, especially about herself, can be taken at face value, and she can be relied upon to cut the cloth of truth to suit her own interests. For example, as Sarah Cunningham notes, Mrs. Stetson actually cut and reassembled sections of Photostats of some handwritten letters she had received from Mrs. Eddy and subsequently reproduced them in apparent facsimile in her self-exculpatory book. (See Sarah Gardner Cunningham, "A New Order: Augusta Emma Simmons Stetson and the Origins of Christian Science in New York City, 1886–1910," [Ph.D. diss., Union Theological Seminary, New York City, 1994].) Since she was also one of Edwin Dakin's main sources in the later 1920s, Mrs. Stetson's influence on Eddyan biography has been not inconsiderable, and largely negative. Dakin describes his first meeting with Mrs. Stetson in her magnificent New York apartment in his introduction to the 1970 edition of his book (p. xvi).

As a resident of New York, Dakin must have been aware of the extraordinary radio station which Mrs. Stetson and her followers ran following her split with Christian Science, but he makes no mention of it. I was told by a researcher at The Mother Church that this station broadcast an extraordinary mixture of protofascist propaganda and classical music. Most of Augusta Stetson's papers are housed in the Huntington Library in San Marino, California.

22.   Dakin has a great deal to say about Augusta Stetson, who emerges from his pages as a lovely and likable, if addlepated, victim of Mrs. Eddy's jealousy. Dakin offers this visual portrait of Mrs. Stetson in 1884, the year she met Mrs. Eddy: "medium in height; well formed, with the large bust so esteemed in fashion plates of the period; eyes widely set in a rather mobile face; small nostrils above a generous, determined mouth" (p. 178). Dakin, of course, was not even born in 1884, and I surmise that most of these details are taken from the heavily retouched photograph of Mrs. Stetson in one of her books.

23.   In her dissertation, Sarah Cunningham quotes the draft of a letter dated December 13, 1895, from Mrs. Eddy which gives one notably frank version of this event:

> Your letter astounds me with its contortions of history. My chief motive in sending you to New York was to locate you and lessen the influence on you of the Boston mental mob, instead of being as you wrote. You had no fixed practice, . . . and did publicly what mortified me by imitating a Negro playing on a banjo and went to the stage in a low-necked dress. . . . You were not always at home before you entered my college but travelled and gave readings. Your husband was as you informed me demented through an accident. I wanted you to heal him but you did not; if you had I should not have sent you to New York. ("A New Order," p. 79. L09587. Original in the Church History Department)

Calvin Frye noted that Mrs. Eddy never sent this letter to Mrs. Stetson. I have commented several times in this book on Mrs. Eddy's love of fashion and sense of style, but I should point out that there is no record of her ever having worn a dress without a high neckline and long sleeves. That Mrs. Stetson and her female students wore low-necked dresses even in the daytime was considered by many New England women to be scandalous.

24.   Between 1886 and 1909 Mrs. Eddy and Mrs. Stetson corresponded regularly, and selected passages from the letters from Mrs. Eddy in particular, which Mrs. Stetson edited and published, have been much studied. As noted earlier, most of the Stetson papers, including the letters from Mrs. Eddy, are at the Huntington Library; and the letters Mrs. Eddy received from Mrs. Stetson are in the Church History Department. Although Mrs. Eddy tends to express censure and reprobation, often sugar-coated in affection, Mrs. Stetson is all overflowing adoration and consistent resolutions (never to be fulfilled) to sin no more. It is all, I confess, very irritating to read, especially since over the years the writing ceases to be a private exchange of news and views and becomes a public relations event or propaganda campaign. Robert David Thomas gives an extremely close and valuable analysis of the Stetson-Eddy correspondence in Chapter 12 of his biography of Mrs. Eddy, which I shall not attempt to repeat, but he comes to rather different conclusions from my own about the relationship between the two women.

25.   In general, one of Robert Peel's chief doctrinal purposes is to show evidence that Mary Baker Eddy did not seek to apotheosize herself and that she resisted the attempts by some of her followers to do this. He offers a number of passages from letters and published works in which Mrs. Eddy defines her own religious position and her mission. In relation to Stetson and her personalizing of religious leadership, he cites at length from one particular letter in which Mrs. Eddy warns Stetson to give up the idea that she is spiritualistically guided by Mrs. Eddy and would look to such guidance even after death. The letter ends: "I am trying to get away from personality, and you are trying to fasten yourself to personality. Opposites cannot affiliate. You are taking yourself away from my teaching by this course." See Peel, *Authority,* pp. 333–34.

26.   Dakin explains Mrs. Stetson's situation well, and his account has authority, since he had not only read her books but had had the opportunity to question her personally:

And there can be small doubt that Mrs. Stetson expected to succeed Mrs. Eddy to the leadership of the Christian Science Church. Mrs. Stetson in later years always denied this, by inference, asserting time and again that neither she nor any one else could ever take Mrs. Eddy's place. The truth was, of course, that Mrs. Stetson did not expect to take Mrs. Eddy's place as the "discoverer and founder" of Christian Science, but she undoubtedly had expected to inherit the mantle of directorship over the church organization, and so informed some of her associates. As she pondered over this probability, she decided that after Mrs. Eddy's death she would move the headquarters of the church from Boston to New York; she intimated as much to several of her confidants of the moment. Revelations of this nature were also published in the New York papers in 1907. (Dakin, pp. 468–69)

27.   Augusta Stetson was a trained and probably a gifted musician, who had earned praise in her teenage years as a singer and as an organist, and there seems to be no doubt that one of the reasons the First Church in New York succeeded was because of the aesthetic beauty which she managed to impart to Christian Science services and meetings.

28.   Thomas has done the most detailed work on this rivalry between Lathrop and Stetson, as well as the strenuous efforts Mrs. Eddy was forced to make to keep some balance between the two congregations. Mainly this involved weighing in on the Lathrop side, since Laura was conspicuously less robust a fighter than was Augusta. As we have seen, Mrs. Eddy took John Lathrop, Laura's son, into her household as secretary, and she seems to have shown him much favor. Even more personally hurtful to Stetson was the treatment Mrs. Eddy gave to Carol Norton. This young man was for some time Mrs. Stetson's most beloved protégé, and when Norton and Stetson quarreled, Mrs. Eddy called Norton to Boston and put him on the Board of Lecturers. Soon after that time Norton was killed in a bizarre accident, and I was told by a reliable source that many Christian Scientists believed that Mrs. Stetson had killed him by Malicious Animal Magnetism, causing him to suffer in his body the emotional heartbreak he had caused her when he broke away.

29.   Stetson wrote down what she remembered of her last meeting, but there is no account from Mrs. Eddy's side. This makes it all the more curious that Edwin Dakin is able to give so detailed and lively an account not only of Mrs. Eddy's words and acts, but of her thoughts and feelings.

30.   Issues of building had inflamed relations in the New York City Christian Science community several years earlier, when Mrs. Eddy had been forced, against all her wishes and directives, to intervene directly to prevent Mrs. Stetson from building a new church only two blocks away from the one projected to be built by her greatest rival, Mrs. Laura Lathrop.

31.   My account of the complicated and astonishing sequence of events that led to Stetson's expulsion is based mainly on the detailed narratives given by Dittemore, Peel, and Cunningham. Dittemore is a particularly important source here since he was himself one of the members of the Board of Directors who had to cope with the Stetson affair.

32.   Both quotes are from Bates and Dittemore, p. 432.

33.   In his detailed account of the expulsion of Mrs. Stetson, Dittemore notes that throughout July Mrs. Eddy vacillated between angry demands for punishment and pleas to the directors of the Church to have mercy on Stetson and avoid a split with her. Dittemore, and even more strongly Dakin, attribute this indecision to Mrs. Eddy's terror that Mrs. Stetson would manage to kill her through Malicious Animal Magnetism. As usual in these cases, the analysis of the reason for Mrs. Eddy's delays depends upon what one thinks Mrs. Eddy understood by Malicious Animal Magnetism.

34.   Bates and Dittemore, 432.

35.   The Babcocks later regaled the New York *Evening Mail* of November 10 with a chilling account of this experience.

36.   Strickler diary, July 31, 1909. Original in the Church History Department. Blaise Pascal would have appreciated Mrs. Stetson! I am reminded of his brilliant satire on the Jesuits and their doctrine of mental reservation in the *Lettres provinciales.*

37.   Bates and Dittemore, pp. 441–42.

38.   According to one account of Mrs. Eddy's last months, Septimus J. Hanna is said to have told Mrs. Eddy of a particularly cruel plot against her:

> At that time, the question of the choice of her successor was foremost among the leading workers in the Cause. It came to light that three of her students were conspiring to take control of the Church before her passing. William Rathvon, her Assistant Secretary, Clifford Smith, First Reader, and Archibald McLellen [*sic*], Chairman of the Board, asked Judge Hanna to deliver an ultimatum to Mrs. Eddy that they were prepared to have her declared senile and put away if she did not give them the authority to take charge of the organization.
>
> Judge Hanna refused to deliver this ultimatum, but he did warn her of the conspiracy. When she learned of it, she finished her work on earth and passed on December 3, 1910.   In doing so, she made it impossible for anyone to set aside the Manual and legally take over the church. (*The Bookmark Review*, undated but received by me in 1996, p. 58)

This account is almost certainly apocryphal.

39.   Peel, *Authority,* p. 347.

40.   Chandler kept in touch with the Glovers, and apparently in 1910 the two youngest boys, George and Andrew, came to stay on Chandler's property over the summer and were sent to pay a visit to their grandmother at Chestnut Hill. They were very reluctant guests and stayed only a few minutes, saying almost nothing, but she was touched and delighted and treasured the picture of the two boys that was taken by press photographers outside the house. Apparently, while he was in New England, Andrew managed to get a girl pregnant, which must have done nothing to improve Chandler's temper.

41.   Chandler stirred up the press to pressure Mrs. Eddy to settle, and he made her deeply anxious. Frye's diary:

> Friday, Sept. 25, 1909. W.E. Chandler published in the newspapers today that the "Next Friends" suit is to be revived again &c&c. By Mrs. Sargent's advice, Mr. Dickey told Mrs. Eddy about it, and it has nearly upset her. This evening I heard her pray Mr. Dickey to prevent it. He replied, There will be no suit. All the next friends want is money—to compromise Mrs. Eddy told him to get a settlement with them.

Then: "Mrs. Eddy called to her room L.E. Sargent, Mrs. Rathvon, Mr. Rathvon, I.C. Tomlinson, A.H. Dickey and myself and requested each to hold up his right hand and promise that we would not leave her but would stand by her till this 'next friend' threat was met—the threat to revive the next friends suit."

42.   Parallel settlements, for smaller sums of money, were also carried out on behalf of Ebenezer Foster Eddy.

43.   Copies of both documents furnished by the Church History Department.

44.   See Peel, quoting William R. Rathvon's diary for April, 9, 1910: "As all hands . . . were assembling in the Pink Room, AMcL[ellan] arrived and joined us. Then for forty minutes our Leader held forth in most remarkable fashion at her very best. She took the high ground and held it; she thrust and parried and had everybody on the run, yet it was all straight Science" (Peel, *Authority,* p. 349).

45.   Section from Dickey's *Memoirs of Mary Baker Eddy,* quoted in Powell, p. 223.

46.   Tomlinson, p. 17.

47. The reader will remember that, for reasons of his own, Dittemore burned the actual handwritten entries which he cut from Frye's diaries, preserving a Photostat and a transcription of the text by Gilbert Carpenter.

48. Rathvon's diary quoted in Peel, *Authority,* p. 353.

Epilogue

1. Peel, *Authority,* p. 361.

2. Ibid., p. 360.

3. Powell, pp. 319–20, n. 63; and partially quoted in Peel, *Authority,* p. 513, n. 114.

4. Mrs. Eddy's most thoughtful biographer, Robert Peel, follows his leader in this as in so many things, reserving for an endnote his very abbreviated account of the final ceremony. Since John Dittemore, as one of the five directors of the Church, was certainly in attendance, I have also relied on the account of the funeral given in the Bates and Dittemore biography. In an article for the *Boston Globe,* Edwin Parks listed the names of seventy-three attendees, and noted that the only people in tears were George Baker, Mary Baker, and Ebenezer Foster, the Next Friends!!!

5. For a complete account of the burial and the monument erected at the Mount Auburn Cemetery, see Michael R. Davis, "The Mary Baker Eddy Memorial," *Sweet Auburn* (Winter 1997/1998).

6. Peel, *Authority,* p. 514, n. 116. Let me note that the question most frequently put to me as Mrs. Eddy's biographer has been "Is it true that they put a telephone in her tomb in case she woke up?"

7. Copies of the wills of Mary Baker Eddy were made available to me by the Church History Department.

8. Peel says that Laura Sargent lived for some years after Mrs. Eddy's death in the Chestnut Hill mansion, together with Adelaide Still.

9. A parallel suit was filed on behalf of George Washington Glover III, who claimed he had been a minor at the time of the 1909 family settlement and that his father had had no right to sign away his rights to his grandmother's estate. At the time of the 1909 settlement, there had been some effort made to determine whether George Glover II could act on behalf of his heirs. Mary was living with her parents and was a party to the settlement. But Gershom, the eldest child, had left South Dakota and could not be contacted by the lawyers, and the two younger boys were both minors.

10. Deposition of William Chandler, taken in the Eddy Will Litigation at Concord, New Hampshire, between September 7, 1911, and January 1, 1912, p. 117, section 527. Church History Department.

11. My thanks to the Longyear Museum staff for supplying me with press clippings related to the end of Pleasant View.

12. In 1975 the Church sold the rest home property, upon which, I am informed by scholars at Longyear, the cottage which housed some of the staff and some of the outbuildings from Mrs. Eddy's day still stand. At this point Longyear was able to acquire the front gate, the fountain, and two gazebos from the garden at Pleasant View and incorporated them into its grounds. On the history of Mary Beecher Longyear and her inspiration to establish an institution devoted to Mrs. Eddy, see the Longyear *Quarterly News* 31, no. 4 (1994). A plaque commemorates the fact that Mary Baker Eddy lived at the site.

13. See, for example, the article in the Concord *Monitor* of August 17, 1975.

Appendix

1. In this Appendix, I give no account of Mrs. Eddy's two most recent biographers. Robert David Thomas's psychobiography *"With Bleeding Footsteps": Mary Baker Eddy's*

Path to Religious Leadership, was published in late 1994 by Knopf. As Professor Thomas explains in his preface, he spent almost ten summers working in the Mother Church archives, and he probably had freer and more generous access to the unpublished materials than I did. But before the book was ready to go to print, the head of the archives, Lee Z. Johnson, was forced to leave, and Dr. Thomas was faced with a new regime at The Mother Church. As a result, the Thomas biography, while showing expert knowledge of the materials and offering archival document numbers in the notes, was unable to include any quotations that had not before appeared in print, and even the paraphrasing is less detailed than one might wish. Thus Thomas's work does not bring new material into print, and, while interpretatively rich, it is not archivally as valuable as he no doubt had hoped and expected.

At the outset of my own research into Mrs. Eddy's life, I became aware, first, that a new biography by Thomas was in the works at Knopf, and then that the announced work was held up because the author was having problems with permissions. In the acknowledgments and preface to his book, Thomas makes no mention of difficulties he had with The Mother Church, but he does discuss these in a letter he wrote to the *New York Review of Books* in 1996 in protest when the reviewer of his biography suggested that he had edited his work to suit the tastes of The Mother Church.

Richard A. Nenneman's book, *Persistent Pilgrim: The Life of Mary Baker Eddy,* came out in late 1997 with the Nebbadoon Press in Etna, New Hampshire. Nenneman was editor in chief of the *Christian Science Monitor* from 1988 to 1992, and he has been a Christian Scientist since his undergraduate days at Harvard. His new one-volume biography was announced for publication by the Publishing Society in 1991, and he was given free access to the collection for a period. In the end, however, the Christian Science Publishing Society decided not to go ahead with the book. Nenneman has interesting things to say about the early years of Christian Science and was able to quote new sections of Mrs. Eddy's correspondence which will suggest research leads for future scholars. Unfortunately I received this information only after my own research was complete and my manuscript was in press. Some reports reached me at the beginning of my work on Mrs. Eddy about the difficulties Thomas and Nenneman were having with issues of archival access and permission to quote from unpublished materials, and these influenced the way I myself negotiated with the Mother Church authorities.

2.   Dakin, p. 529. Church History owns a Milmine Ms. but the book's copyright was extended in 1937 by "Georgine Milmine Adams." Mrs. Longyear bought the plates about 1916.

3.   Remington Manuscript, Chapter 7, note 1, Longyear Museum.

4.   Frederick Remington was chiefly known in Christian Science history as an active agent for the sale of Eddy memorabilia, but he also wrote an interesting unpublished essay on Mrs. Eddy's debt to Quimby. It includes an account of the Milmine biography's handling of the Quimby debate. Remington gives no supporting reference for the story, but since he claims to have had some correspondence with Milmine, it is reasonable to assume that he is relating what she told him in person or in writing. I could at first find no confirmation for Remington's story, but then I found it repeated with more detail in a letter written at the time of the Next Friends suit to William Chandler by his friend and ally Henry Robinson, a Concord newsman and public official who regularly reported local gossip about Mrs. Eddy to Chandler in Washington (letter of March 28, 1907, William E. Chandler Papers, New Hampshire Historical Society). The Church History Department told me that there is no record that Georgine Milmine ever wrote to ask for an interview with Mrs. Eddy or presented herself at Pleasant View, and the household records are, reportedly, meticulous on such matters. In 1903 Mrs. Eddy was living in carefully protected seclusion, her relations with the press were, at best, guarded, and it is possible that Milmine simply appeared at the front door and was turned away — any such casual caller with no personal acquaintance with Mrs. Eddy would have been treated thus. I have found no record that Milmine ever wrote or published any other essays on famous American women.

5. *McClure's Magazine,* December 1906, p. 212.

6. Dakin, p. 418 and n. 2.

7. Gardner, *The Healing Revelations of Mary Baker Eddy*, p. 41.

8. Wilbur, "Glimpses of a Great Personality: The Four Meetings with Mrs. Eddy Face to Face; My Impression of Her as She Is Today; Her Home, and How She Lives and Works," *Human Life,* January 1907, p. 4.

9. The Mother Church owns an interesting file of press clippings on Wilbur's career. She, rather surprisingly, seems in many ways a minor Ida Tarbell.

10. The Wilbur file in the Church History Department, which I was permitted to read, contains a lengthy correspondence between Dittemore and Wilbur on the subject of her book.

11. All this is detailed in Peel, *Authority,* p. 322 and ff.

12. Wilbur, *Human Life* (January 1907), pp. 3–4.

13. See *Lyman Pierson Powell*, by Charles S. MacFarland (New York: Philosophical Library, 1947).

14. Powell, *Christian Science: The Faith and Its Founder*, p. v.

15. The first quote is from Powell, pp. 65–66; and the second is quoted by MacFarland, p. 221, from Powell's entry on Christian Science in *The Cambridge History of American Literature* (Cambridge, England: Cambridge University Press, 1922).

16. Powell, pp. 6–7.

17. The Twentieth-Century Biography Series published by the Christian Science Publishing Society includes a reissuing of the 1930 book by Powell. The introduction to this series comments that the Powell biography is of special interest because it presents the Church at a period "close to the highpoint of church membership during the twentieth century" (p. 14).

18. Powell, pp. 23–24.

19. Bates and Dittemore, p. iv.

20. Julius Silberger, Jr., *Mary Baker Eddy: An Interpretive Biography of the Founder of Christian Science* (Boston and Toronto: Little, Brown, 1980), p. 10. Silberger was never allowed to read in the Church History Department and was given only limited access to the Longyear collection, so he was forced to write an elegant rehash of the Milmine-Dakin-Dittemore-Peel materials. I met Dr. Silberger early in my research and was grateful for his warm encouragement and practical advice on the Church administration.

21. Dakin, pp. viii–ix.

22. Dakin remained astonishingly proud of his footnotes and corroborative details to the end of his life, stating in his introduction to the 1970 edition: "Scribner's required me to verify my every statement with exact reference notes and with a bibliography that would make the text impregnable" (Dakin, p. xix). In the course of my book I have pointed out various errors that Dakin made.

23. Dakin, p. 212.

24. Charles S. Braden, *Christian Science Today: Power, Policy, Practice* (Dallas: Southern Methodist University Press, 1958), pp. 384–85.

25. For a detailed narrative of the trials and tribulations this book endured both before and after publication at the hands of the Board of Directors and the Committee on Publication, see Braden's *Christian Science Today: Power, Policy, Practice,* Chapter 6.

26. I contacted the Daystar Foundation, asking for permission to hear the Glover tapes for myself, either in Oklahoma City or at Longyear, which has a copy, but my request swiftly met the kind of road block I had initially encountered at The Mother Church, and

I decided regretfully that I could not prolong my work by starting on a fresh round of negotiations on issues of access and copyright.

27. It is hard to overestimate the debt I owe Robert Peel in my own research and understanding of Mrs. Eddy. This is especially true of the first two volumes, which cover Mrs. Eddy's life up to 1892. The third volume, although the longest of the three, and the one dealing with the movement correspondence and official documentation which I myself had least access to, is also the least satisfying, the most guarded. I found myself consulting Peel *Authority* in vain for information I knew the author must have had, and it seemed to me that Peel was increasingly being obliged to toe some invisible party line.

28. Announcement circulated by the Christian Science Publishing Society in 1991, introducing its proposed Twentieth-Century Biography Series.

INDEX

ABOUT THE AUTHOR

Gillian Gill, Ph.D., received her doctorate from Cambridge University. She has taught at Wellesley, Yale, and Harvard, has translated six important French works in the fields of psychoanalysis and philosophy, and is author of *Agatha Christie: The Woman and Her Mysteries.* She is a board member of the National Coalition of Independent Scholars.